Lecture Notes in Computer Science 12626

More information about this subseries at http://www.springer.com/series/7412

Hiroshi Ishikawa · Cheng-Lin Liu ·
Tomas Pajdla · Jianbo Shi (Eds.)

Computer Vision – ACCV 2020

15th Asian Conference on Computer Vision
Kyoto, Japan, November 30 – December 4, 2020
Revised Selected Papers, Part V

 Springer

Editors
Hiroshi Ishikawa
Waseda University
Tokyo, Japan

Tomas Pajdla
Czech Technical University in Prague
Prague, Czech Republic

Cheng-Lin Liu
Institute of Automation of Chinese Academy
of Sciences
Beijing, China

Jianbo Shi
University of Pennsylvania
Philadelphia, PA, USA

ISSN 0302-9743   ISSN 1611-3349   (electronic)
Lecture Notes in Computer Science
ISBN 978-3-030-69540-8   ISBN 978-3-030-69541-5   (eBook)
https://doi.org/10.1007/978-3-030-69541-5

LNCS Sublibrary: SL6 – Image Processing, Computer Vision, Pattern Recognition, and Graphics

This Springer imprint is published by the registered company Springer Nature Switzerland AG
The registered company address is: Gewerbestrasse 11, 6330 Cham, Switzerland

Preface

The Asian Conference on Computer Vision (ACCV) 2020, originally planned to take place in Kyoto, Japan, was held online during November 30 – December 4, 2020. The conference featured novel research contributions from almost all sub-areas of computer vision.

We received 836 main-conference submissions. After removing the desk rejects, 768 valid, complete manuscripts were submitted for review. A pool of 48 area chairs and 738 reviewers was recruited to conduct paper reviews. As in previous editions of ACCV, we adopted a double-blind review process to determine which of these papers to accept. Identities of authors were not visible to reviewers and area chairs; nor were the identities of the assigned reviewers and area chairs known to authors. The program chairs did not submit papers to the conference.

Each paper was reviewed by at least three reviewers. Authors were permitted to respond to the initial reviews during a rebuttal period. After this, the area chairs led discussions among reviewers. Finally, an interactive area chair meeting was held, during which panels of three area chairs deliberated to decide on acceptance decisions for each paper, and then four larger panels were convened to make final decisions. At the end of this process, 254 papers were accepted for publication in the ACCV 2020 conference proceedings.

In addition to the main conference, ACCV 2020 featured four workshops and two tutorials. This is also the first ACCV for which the proceedings are open access at the Computer Vision Foundation website, by courtesy of Springer.

We would like to thank all the organizers, sponsors, area chairs, reviewers, and authors. We acknowledge the support of Microsoft's Conference Management Toolkit (CMT) team for providing the software used to manage the review process.

We greatly appreciate the efforts of all those who contributed to making the conference a success, despite the difficult and fluid situation.

December 2020

Hiroshi Ishikawa
Cheng-Lin Liu
Tomas Pajdla
Jianbo Shi

Organization

General Chairs

Ko Nishino   Kyoto University, Japan
Akihiro Sugimoto   National Institute of Informatics, Japan
Hiromi Tanaka   Ritsumeikan University, Japan

Program Chairs

Hiroshi Ishikawa   Waseda University, Japan
Cheng-Lin Liu   Institute of Automation of Chinese Academy
    of Sciences, China
Tomas Pajdla   Czech Technical University, Czech Republic
Jianbo Shi   University of Pennsylvania, USA

Publication Chairs

Ichiro Ide   Nagoya University, Japan
Wei-Ta Chu   National Chung Cheng University, Taiwan
Marc A. Kastner   National Institute of Informatics, Japan

Local Arrangements Chairs

Shohei Nobuhara   Kyoto University, Japan
Yasushi Makihara   Osaka University, Japan

Web Chairs

Ikuhisa Mitsugami   Hiroshima City University, Japan
Chika Inoshita   Canon Inc., Japan

AC Meeting Chair

Yusuke Sugano   University of Tokyo, Japan

Area Chairs

Mathieu Aubry   École des Ponts ParisTech, France
Xiang Bai   Huazhong University of Science and Technology,
    China
Alex Berg   Facebook, USA
Michael S. Brown   York University, Canada

Tat-Jun Chin	University of Adelaide, Australia
Yung-Yu Chuang	National Taiwan University, Taiwan
Yuchao Dai	Northwestern Polytechnical University, China
Yasutaka Furukawa	Simon Fraser University, Canada
Junwei Han	Northwestern Polytechnical University, China
Tatsuya Harada	University of Tokyo/RIKEN, Japan
Gang Hua	Wormpex AI Research, China
C. V. Jawahar	IIIT Hyderabad, India
Frédéric Jurie	Université de Caen Normandie, France
Angjoo Kanazawa	UC Berkeley, USA
Rei Kawakami	Tokyo Institute of Technology, Japan
Tae-Kyun Kim	Imperial College London, UK
Zuzana Kukelova	Czech Technical University in Prague, Czech Republic
Shang-Hong Lai	Microsoft AI R&D Center, Taiwan
Ivan Laptev	Inria Paris, France
Laura Leal-Taixe	TU Munich, Germany
Yong Jae Lee	UC Davis, USA
Vincent Lepetit	Université de Bordeaux, France
Hongdong Li	Australian National University, Australia
Guangcan Liu	NUIST, China
Li Liu	National University of Defense Technology, China
Risheng Liu	Dalian University of Technology, China
Si Liu	Beihang University, China
Yasuyuki Matsushita	Osaka University, Japan
Hajime Nagahara	Osaka University, Japan
Takayuki Okatani	Tohoku University/RIKEN, Japan
Carl Olsson	Lund University, Sweden
Hyun Soo Park	University of Minnesota, USA
Shmuel Peleg	Hebrew University of Jerusalem, Israel
Shin'ichi Satoh	National Institute of Informatics, Japan
Torsten Sattler	Chalmers University of Technology, Sweden
Palaiahnakote Shivakumara	University of Malaya, Malaysia
Hao Su	UC San Diego, USA
Siyu Tang	ETH Zurich, Switzerland
Radu Timofte	ETH Zurich, Switzerland
Yoshitaka Ushiku	OMRON SINIC X, Japan
Gul Varol	University of Oxford, UK
Kota Yamaguchi	Cyberagent, Inc., Japan
Ming-Hsuan Yang	UC Merced, USA
Stella X. Yu	UC Berkeley/ICSI, USA
Zhaoxiang Zhang	Chinese Academy of Sciences, China
Wei-Shi Zheng	Sun Yat-sen University, China
Yinqiang Zheng	National Institute of Informatics, Japan
Xiaowei Zhou	Zhejiang University, China

Additional Reviewers

Sathyanarayanan
  N. Aakur
Mahmoud Afifi
Amit Aides
Noam Aigerman
Kenan Emir Ak
Mohammad
  Sadegh Aliakbarian
Keivan Alizadeh-Vahid
Dario Allegra
Alexander Andreopoulos
Nikita Araslanov
Anil Armagan
Alexey Artemov
Aditya Arun
Yuki M. Asano
Hossein Azizpour
Seung-Hwan Baek
Seungryul Baek
Max Bain
Abhishek Bajpayee
Sandipan Banerjee
Wenbo Bao
Daniel Barath
Chaim Baskin
Anil S. Baslamisli
Ardhendu Behera
Jens Behley
Florian Bernard
Bharat Lal Bhatnagar
Uttaran Bhattacharya
Binod Bhattarai
Ayan Kumar Bhunia
Jia-Wang Bian
Simion-Vlad Bogolin
Amine Bourki
Biagio Brattoli
Anders G. Buch
Evgeny Burnaev
Benjamin Busam
Holger Caesar
Jianrui Cai
Jinzheng Cai

Fanta Camara
Necati Cihan Camgöz
Shaun Canavan
Jiajiong Cao
Jiale Cao
Hakan Çevikalp
Ayan Chakrabarti
Tat-Jen Cham
Lyndon Chan
Hyung Jin Chang
Xiaobin Chang
Rama Chellappa
Chang Chen
Chen Chen
Ding-Jie Chen
Jianhui Chen
Jun-Cheng Chen
Long Chen
Songcan Chen
Tianshui Chen
Weifeng Chen
Weikai Chen
Xiaohan Chen
Xinlei Chen
Yanbei Chen
Yingcong Chen
Yiran Chen
Yi-Ting Chen
Yun Chen
Yun-Chun Chen
Yunlu Chen
Zhixiang Chen
Ziliang Chen
Guangliang Cheng
Li Cheng
Qiang Cheng
Zhongwei Cheng
Anoop Cherian
Ngai-Man Cheung
Wei-Chen Chiu
Shin-Fang Ch'ng
Nam Ik Cho
Junsuk Choe

Chiho Choi
Jaehoon Choi
Jinsoo Choi
Yukyung Choi
Anustup Choudhury
Hang Chu
Peng Chu
Wei-Ta Chu
Sanghyuk Chun
Ronald Clark
Maxwell D. Collins
Ciprian Corneanu
Luca Cosmo
Ioana Croitoru
Steve Cruz
Naresh Cuntoor
Zachary A. Daniels
Mohamed Daoudi
François Darmon
Adrian K. Davison
Rodrigo de Bem
Shalini De Mello
Lucas Deecke
Bailin Deng
Jiankang Deng
Zhongying Deng
Somdip Dey
Ferran Diego
Mingyu Ding
Dzung Anh Doan
Xingping Dong
Xuanyi Dong
Hazel Doughty
Dawei Du
Chi Nhan Duong
Aritra Dutta
Marc C. Eder
Ismail Elezi
Mohamed Elgharib
Sergio Escalera
Deng-Ping Fan
Shaojing Fan
Sean Fanello

Moshiur R. Farazi
Azade Farshad
István Fehérvári
Junyi Feng
Wei Feng
Yang Feng
Zeyu Feng
Robert B. Fisher
Alexander Fix
Corneliu O. Florea
Wolfgang Förstner
Jun Fu
Xueyang Fu
Yanwei Fu
Hiroshi Fukui
Antonino Furnari
Ryo Furukawa
Raghudeep Gadde
Vandit J. Gajjar
Chuang Gan
Bin-Bin Gao
Boyan Gao
Chen Gao
Junbin Gao
Junyu Gao
Lin Gao
Mingfei Gao
Peng Gao
Ruohan Gao
Nuno C. Garcia
Georgios Georgakis
Ke Gong
Jiayuan Gu
Jie Gui
Manuel Günther
Kaiwen Guo
Minghao Guo
Ping Guo
Sheng Guo
Yulan Guo
Saurabh Gupta
Jung-Woo Ha
Emanuela Haller
Cusuh Ham
Kai Han
Liang Han

Tengda Han
Ronny Hänsch
Josh Harguess
Atsushi Hashimoto
Monica Haurilet
Jamie Hayes
Fengxiang He
Pan He
Xiangyu He
Xinwei He
Yang He
Paul Henderson
Chih-Hui Ho
Tuan N.A. Hoang
Sascha A. Hornauer
Yedid Hoshen
Kuang-Jui Hsu
Di Hu
Ping Hu
Ronghang Hu
Tao Hu
Yang Hua
Bingyao Huang
Haibin Huang
Huaibo Huang
Rui Huang
Sheng Huang
Xiaohua Huang
Yifei Huang
Zeng Huang
Zilong Huang
Jing Huo
Junhwa Hur
Wonjun Hwang
José Pedro Iglesias
Atul N. Ingle
Yani A. Ioannou
Go Irie
Daisuke Iwai
Krishna Murthy
    Jatavallabhula
Seong-Gyun Jeong
Koteswar Rao Jerripothula
Jingwei Ji
Haiyang Jiang
Huajie Jiang

Wei Jiang
Xiaoyi Jiang
Jianbo Jiao
Licheng Jiao
Kyong Hwan Jin
Xin Jin
Shantanu Joshi
Frédéric Jurie
Abhishek Kadian
Olaf Kaehler
Meina Kan
Dimosthenis Karatzas
Isay Katsman
Muhammad Haris Khan
Vijeta Khare
Rawal Khirodkar
Hadi Kiapour
Changick Kim
Dong-Jin Kim
Gunhee Kim
Heewon Kim
Hyunwoo J. Kim
Junsik Kim
Junyeong Kim
Yonghyun Kim
Akisato Kimura
A. Sophia Koepke
Dimitrios Kollias
Nikos Kolotouros
Yoshinori Konishi
Adam Kortylewski
Dmitry Kravchenko
Sven Kreiss
Gurunandan Krishnan
Andrey Kuehlkamp
Jason Kuen
Arjan Kuijper
Shiro Kumano
Avinash Kumar
B. V. K. Vijaya Kumar
Ratnesh Kumar
Vijay Kumar
Yusuke Kurose
Alina Kuznetsova
Junseok Kwon
Loic Landrieu

Dong Lao
Viktor Larsson
Yasir Latif
Hei Law
Hieu Le
Hoang-An Le
Huu Minh Le
Gim Hee Lee
Hyungtae Lee
Jae-Han Lee
Jangho Lee
Jungbeom Lee
Kibok Lee
Kuan-Hui Lee
Seokju Lee
Sungho Lee
Sungmin Lee
Bin Li
Jie Li
Ruilong Li
Ruoteng Li
Site Li
Xianzhi Li
Xiaomeng Li
Xiaoming Li
Xin Li
Xiu Li
Xueting Li
Yawei Li
Yijun Li
Yimeng Li
Yin Li
Yong Li
Yu-Jhe Li
Zekun Li
Dongze Lian
Zhouhui Lian
Haoyi Liang
Yue Liao
Jun Hao Liew
Chia-Wen Lin
Guangfeng Lin
Kevin Lin
Xudong Lin
Xue Lin
Chang Liu

Feng Liu
Hao Liu
Hong Liu
Jing Liu
Jingtuo Liu
Jun Liu
Miaomiao Liu
Ming Liu
Ping Liu
Siqi Liu
Wentao Liu
Wu Liu
Xing Liu
Xingyu Liu
Yongcheng Liu
Yu Liu
Yu-Lun Liu
Yun Liu
Zhihua Liu
Zichuan Liu
Chengjiang Long
Manuel López Antequera
Hao Lu
Hongtao Lu
Le Lu
Shijian Lu
Weixin Lu
Yao Lu
Yongxi Lu
Chenxu Luo
Weixin Luo
Wenhan Luo
Diogo C. Luvizon
Jiancheng Lyu
Chao Ma
Long Ma
Shugao Ma
Xiaojian Ma
Yongrui Ma
Ludovic Magerand
Behrooz Mahasseni
Mohammed Mahmoud
Utkarsh Mall
Massimiliano Mancini
Xudong Mao
Alina E. Marcu

Niki Martinel
Jonathan Masci
Tetsu Matsukawa
Bruce A. Maxwell
Amir Mazaheri
Prakhar Mehrotra
Heydi Méndez-Vázquez
Zibo Meng
Kourosh Meshgi
Shun Miao
Zhongqi Miao
Micael Carvalho
Pedro Miraldo
Ashish Mishra
Ikuhisa Mitsugami
Daisuke Miyazaki
Kaichun Mo
Liliane Momeni
Gyeongsik Moon
Alexandre Morgand
Yasuhiro Mukaigawa
Anirban Mukhopadhyay
Erickson R. Nascimento
Lakshmanan Nataraj
K. L. Navaneet
Lukáš Neumann
Shohei Nobuhara
Nicoletta Noceti
Mehdi Noroozi
Michael Oechsle
Ferda Ofli
Seoung Wug Oh
Takeshi Oishi
Takahiro Okabe
Fumio Okura
Kyle B. Olszewski
José Oramas
Tribhuvanesh Orekondy
Martin R. Oswald
Mayu Otani
Umapada Pal
Yingwei Pan
Rameswar Panda
Rohit Pandey
Jiangmiao Pang
João P. Papa

Toufiq Parag
Jinsun Park
Min-Gyu Park
Despoina Paschalidou
Nikolaos Passalis
Yash Patel
Georgios Pavlakos
Baoyun Peng
Houwen Peng
Wen-Hsiao Peng
Roland Perko
Vitali Petsiuk
Quang-Hieu Pham
Yongri Piao
Marco Piccirilli
Matteo Poggi
Mantini Pranav
Dilip K. Prasad
Véronique Prinet
Victor Adrian Prisacariu
Thomas Probst
Jan Prokaj
Qi Qian
Xuelin Qian
Xiaotian Qiao
Yvain Queau
Mohammad Saeed Rad
Filip Radenovic
Petia Radeva
Bogdan Raducanu
François Rameau
Aakanksha Rana
Yongming Rao
Sathya Ravi
Edoardo Remelli
Dongwei Ren
Wenqi Ren
Md Alimoor Reza
Farzaneh Rezaianaran
Andrés Romero
Kaushik Roy
Soumava Kumar Roy
Nataniel Ruiz
Javier Ruiz-del-Solar
Jongbin Ryu
Mohammad Sabokrou

Ryusuke Sagawa
Pritish Sahu
Hideo Saito
Kuniaki Saito
Shunsuke Saito
Ken Sakurada
Joaquin Salas
Enrique Sánchez-Lozano
Aswin Sankaranarayanan
Hiroaki Santo
Soubhik Sanyal
Vishwanath Saragadam1
Yoichi Sato
William R. Schwartz
Jesse Scott
Siniša Šegvić
Lorenzo Seidenari
Keshav T. Seshadri
Francesco Setti
Meet Shah
Shital Shah
Ming Shao
Yash Sharma
Dongyu She
Falong Shen
Jie Shen
Xi Shen
Yuming Shen
Hailin Shi
Yichun Shi
Yifei Shi
Yujiao Shi
Zenglin Shi
Atsushi Shimada
Daeyun Shin
Young Min Shin
Kirill Sidorov
Krishna Kumar Singh
Maneesh K. Singh
Gregory Slabaugh
Chunfeng Song
Dongjin Song
Ran Song
Xibin Song
Ramprakash Srinivasan
Erik Stenborg

Stefan Stojanov
Yu-Chuan Su
Zhuo Su
Yusuke Sugano
Masanori Suganuma
Yumin Suh
Yao Sui
Jiaming Sun
Jin Sun
Xingyuan Sun
Zhun Sun
Minhyuk Sung
Keita Takahashi
Kosuke Takahashi
Jun Takamatsu
Robby T. Tan
Kenichiro Tanaka
Masayuki Tanaka
Chang Tang
Peng Tang
Wei Tang
Xu Tang
Makarand Tapaswi
Amara Tariq
Mohammad Tavakolian
Antonio Tejero-de-Pablos
Ilias Theodorakopoulos
Thomas E. Bishop
Diego Thomas
Kai Tian
Xinmei Tian
Yapeng Tian
Chetan J. Tonde
Lei Tong
Alessio Tonioni
Carlos Torres
Anh T. Tran
Subarna Tripathi
Emanuele Trucco
Hung-Yu Tseng
Tony Tung
Radim Tylecek
Seiichi Uchida
Md. Zasim Uddin
Norimichi Ukita
Ernest Valveny

Nanne van Noord
Subeesh Vasu
Javier Vazquez-Corral
Andreas Velten
Constantin Vertan
Rosaura G. VidalMata
Valentin Vielzeuf
Sirion Vittayakorn
Konstantinos Vougioukas
Fang Wan
Guowei Wan
Renjie Wan
Bo Wang
Chien-Yi Wang
Di Wang
Dong Wang
Guangrun Wang
Hao Wang
Hongxing Wang
Hua Wang
Jialiang Wang
Jiayun Wang
Jingbo Wang
Jinjun Wang
Lizhi Wang
Pichao Wang
Qian Wang
Qiaosong Wang
Qilong Wang
Qingzhong Wang
Shangfei Wang
Shengjin Wang
Tiancai Wang
Wenguan Wang
Wenhai Wang
Xiang Wang
Xiao Wang
Xiaoyang Wang
Xinchao Wang
Xinggang Wang
Yang Wang
Yaxing Wang
Yisen Wang
Yu-Chiang Frank Wang
Zheng Wang
Scott Wehrwein

Wei Wei
Xing Wei
Xiu-Shen Wei
Yi Wei
Martin Weinmann
Michael Weinmann
Jun Wen
Xinshuo Weng
Thomas Whelan
Kimberly Wilber
Williem Williem
Kwan-Yee K. Wong
Yongkang Wong
Sanghyun Woo
Michael Wray
Chenyun Wu
Chongruo Wu
Jialian Wu
Xiaohe Wu
Xiaoping Wu
Yihong Wu
Zhenyao Wu
Changqun Xia
Xide Xia
Yin Xia
Lei Xiang
Di Xie
Guo-Sen Xie
Jin Xie
Yifan Xing
Yuwen Xiong
Jingwei Xu
Jun Xu
Ke Xu
Mingze Xu
Yanyu Xu
Yi Xu
Yichao Xu
Yongchao Xu
Yuanlu Xu
Jia Xue
Nan Xue
Yasushi Yagi
Toshihiko Yamasaki
Zhaoyi Yan
Zike Yan

Keiji Yanai
Dong Yang
Fan Yang
Hao Yang
Jiancheng Yang
Linlin Yang
Mingkun Yang
Ren Yang
Sibei Yang
Wenhan Yang
Ze Yang
Zhaohui Yang
Zhengyuan Yang
Anbang Yao
Angela Yao
Rajeev Yasarla
Jinwei Ye
Qi Ye
Xinchen Ye
Zili Yi
Ming Yin
Zhichao Yin
Ryo Yonetani
Ju Hong Yoon
Haichao Yu
Jiahui Yu
Lequan Yu
Lu Yu
Qian Yu
Ruichi Yu
Li Yuan
Sangdoo Yun
Sergey Zakharov
Huayi Zeng
Jiabei Zeng
Yu Zeng
Fangneng Zhan
Kun Zhan
Bowen Zhang
Hongguang Zhang
Jason Y. Zhang
Jiawei Zhang
Jie Zhang
Jing Zhang
Kaihao Zhang
Kaipeng Zhang

Lei Zhang
Mingda Zhang
Pingping Zhang
Qian Zhang
Qilin Zhang
Qing Zhang
Runze Zhang
Shanshan Zhang
Shu Zhang
Wayne Zhang
Xiaolin Zhang
Xiaoyun Zhang
Xucong Zhang
Yan Zhang
Zhao Zhang
Zhishuai Zhang
Feng Zhao
Jian Zhao
Liang Zhao
Qian Zhao
Qibin Zhao

Ruiqi Zhao
Sicheng Zhao
Tianyi Zhao
Xiangyun Zhao
Xin Zhao
Yifan Zhao
Yinan Zhao
Shuai Zheng
Yalin Zheng
Bineng Zhong
Fangwei Zhong
Guangyu Zhong
Yaoyao Zhong
Yiran Zhong
Jun Zhou
Mo Zhou
Pan Zhou
Ruofan Zhou
S. Kevin Zhou
Yao Zhou
Yipin Zhou

Yu Zhou
Yuqian Zhou
Yuyin Zhou
Guangming Zhu
Ligeng Zhu
Linchao Zhu
Rui Zhu
Xinge Zhu
Yizhe Zhu
Zhe Zhu
Zhen Zhu
Zheng Zhu
Bingbing Zhuang
Jiacheng Zhuo
Mohammadreza
    Zolfaghari
Chuhang Zou
Yuliang Zou
Zhengxia Zou

Contents – Part V

Video Analysis and Event Recognition

Biomedical Image Analysis

Face, Pose, Action, and Gesture

Video-Based Crowd Counting Using a Multi-scale Optical Flow Pyramid Network

Mohammad Asiful Hossain[1(✉)], Kevin Cannons[1], Daesik Jang[1], Fabio Cuzzolin[2], and Zhan Xu[1]

[1] Huawei Technologies Canada Co., Ltd., Burnaby, Canada
{mohammad.asiful.hossain,kevin.cannons,daesik.jang,zhan.xu}@huawei.com
[2] Oxford Brookes University, Oxford, UK
fabio.cuzzolin@brookes.ac.uk

Abstract. This paper presents a novel approach to the task of video-based crowd counting, which can be formalized as the regression problem of learning a mapping from an input image to an output crowd density map. Convolutional neural networks (CNNs) have demonstrated striking accuracy gains in a range of computer vision tasks, including crowd counting. However, the dominant focus within the crowd counting literature has been on the single-frame case or applying CNNs to videos in a frame-by-frame fashion without leveraging motion information. This paper proposes a novel architecture that exploits the spatiotemporal information captured in a video stream by combining an optical flow pyramid with an appearance-based CNN. Extensive empirical evaluation on five public datasets comparing against numerous state-of-the-art approaches demonstrates the efficacy of the proposed architecture, with our methods reporting best results on all datasets.

1 Introduction

Crowd counting is a well-studied area in computer vision, with several real-world applications including urban planning, traffic monitoring, and emergency response preparation [1]. Despite these strong, application-driven motivations, crowd counting remains an unsolved problem. Critical challenges that remain in this area include severe occlusion, diverse crowd densities, perspective effects, and differing illumination conditions.

The task of crowd counting is well understood: Given an arbitrary image of a scene without any prior knowledge (i.e., unknown camera position, camera parameters, scene layout, and crowd density), estimate the number of people in the image. In general, there are two methodologies for estimating the person count in an image: detection-based (e.g., [2–4]) and regression-based (e.g.,

Electronic supplementary material The online version of this chapter (https://doi.org/10.1007/978-3-030-69541-5_1) contains supplementary material, which is available to authorized users.

© Springer Nature Switzerland AG 2021
H. Ishikawa et al. (Eds.): ACCV 2020, LNCS 12626, pp. 3–20, 2021.
https://doi.org/10.1007/978-3-030-69541-5_1

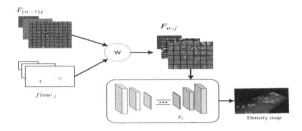

Fig. 1. Overview of the proposed approach to video-based crowd counting. Motion information is incorporated via a pyramid of optical flow that is computed from consecutive frames of the input video. The flow field is applied to multi-scale feature maps extracted from the previous frame via an image warp, W, and injected as an additional source of information into the decoder portion of the baseline network, which is described in Sect. 3.1.

[5–11]). Detection-based approaches leverage the rapid advancements of convolutional neural network (CNN) object detectors, applying them to the specialized task of identifying human bodies/heads. Although significant progress has been made recently with detection-based approaches, they still perform better at lower crowd densities, with accuracies degrading on challenging images with very high densities, low resolution faces, and significant occlusions. In contrast, regression-based approaches typically employ a CNN to produce a density map, representing the estimated locations of persons within the image. With regression-based methods, the overall person count can be attained by integrating over the entire density map. Thus, with regression-based approaches, the detection challenge is bypassed completely and the problem is transformed to that of training a CNN to learn the correspondence between an input image and a crowd-density map.

Although most prior work on crowd counting has focused on determining the number of people in a static image (e.g., [6,8,12–15]), in most real-world settings, a video-stream is available. In such settings, it is natural to consider what techniques can leverage this additional temporal information and improve count accuracies. Intuitively, motion information can effectively remove false positives and negatives by combining information from neighboring frames, thus producing more temporally-coherent density maps. Moreover, temporal information can benefit occlusion scenarios where people are blocked from view in a specific frame, but are visible in surrounding frames.

One of the most well-studied representations of motion information in computer vision is optical flow, which can be computed using traditional (e.g., [16]) or deep learning (e.g., [17]) techniques. The fundamental idea explored in this paper is to improve crowd counting estimates in video by utilizing the motion information provided by explicitly-computed optical flow.

Figure 1 shows a conceptual overview of the proposed approach. The foundation of the method is a baseline CNN that receives a single image as input and produces a crowd density map as the output. In this work, a novel CNN is used that consists of two sub-sections: a feature extractor and a decoder. As shown in

Fig. 1, motion information is incorporated into the full system by computing a pyramid of optical flow from consecutive video frames. The multi-scale pyramid of flow is used to warp the previous frame's feature maps (i.e., feature embeddings) from the decoder sub-network toward the current frame. These warped feature maps are concatenated with the corresponding maps from the current frame. By complementing the decoder sub-network with motion information, the overall system is able to produce more temporally coherent density maps and achieve state-of-the-art accuracies.

There are four contributions of this paper:

– A novel video-based crowd counting system that incorporates motion information via a multi-scale embedding warp based on optical flow. To the best of our knowledge, integrating optical flow with a deep neural network has not been attempted previously for region of interest (ROI) crowd counting.
– An extensive evaluation on three video-based crowd counting datasets (UCSD [18], Mall [19] and Fudan-ShanghaiTech [9]) showing the proposed model outperforms all state-of-the-art algorithms.
– An illustration of the transfer learning abilities of the proposed approach, whereby knowledge learned in a source domain is shown to effectively transfer over to a target domain, using a small amount of training data. Here, the source and target domains correspond to two different scenes/environments observed in video datasets.
– Although not the primary focus, a secondary contribution is a new coarse-to-fine baseline CNN architecture for image-based crowd counting. This customized network is an extension of CSRNet [7], with a novel decoder sub-network. In an extensive evaluation on two challenging image datasets (UCF_CC_50 [20] and UCF-QNRF [20]), as well as the abovementioned three video datasets, this enhanced network meets or exceeds alternative state-of-the-art methods.

2   Related Work

2.1   Counting in Static Images

In recent years, most crowd counting systems are based on convolutional neural networks (CNNs). An early example of such an approach was that by Zhang et al. [12], which introduced a cross-scene crowd counting method by fine-tuning a CNN model to the target scene.

One of the major research directions within crowd counting is addressing the challenge of scale variation (e.g., [6,8,13,15,21,22]). Specifically, a crowd counting system should produce accurate results regardless of the size of the people within the image. One such work that addresses this challenge proposed a multi-column architecture (MCNN) [8]. Other approaches have taken a different tack whereby coarse-to-fine architectures are used to produce high-resolution density maps (e.g., [6,15]).

One work on image-based crowd counting by Li et al. [7] proposed a novel architecture called CSRNet that provides accurate estimates in crowded environments. CSRNet shares a similar network architecture to the baseline proposed here; however, their decoder sub-network uses dilated convolution to produce density maps that are $1/8^{th}$ of the input image size. In contrast, the proposed decoder has a deeper network structure and employs transposed convolution to attain density maps at the full image resolution.

Recently, PGCNet proposed a single column architecture to resolve intra-scene scale variation with the help of an autoencoder-based perspective estimation branch [23]. S-DCNet [22], which is another recent algorithm, operates in a divide-and-conquer fashion where feature maps are split until the person count within any one division is no greater than a set value. The system then classifies person counts into a set of intervals to determine the best count for each division. In contrast to S-DCNet, our baseline does not require any classification stages and is independent of assumptions regarding person counts within a division, such as interval ranges.

2.2   Video-Based Counting Methods

Most previous works in crowd counting focus on the single image setting; there are much fewer examples of video-based crowd counting in the literature. Within the video domain, two sub-problems have emerged for crowd counting: region of interest (ROI) [9–11] and line of interest (LOI) [24–26]. For ROI counting, the number of people within a certain image region (or, the entire image) is estimated; whereas, for LOI counting, a virtual line in the image is specified and the task is to determine the number of individuals that cross this line.

Several LOI works extract temporal slices from the line of interest to detect the transient crossing events [26–28]. Challenges for these approaches include foreground blob detection and processing, as well as disentangling confounding variables (e.g., blob widths are affected by number of people as well as velocity). More recent LOI counting work has considered using deep neural networks, including one system that included an ROI counting sub-module [24]. Although ROI and LOI counting share common challenges (e.g., perspective distortion, scale variation, occlusions), the specialized problem definition tends to drive different technical approaches, which are not typically directly transferable. The methods proposed in the current work focus on ROI counting, which will be referred to simply as crowd counting in the remainder of the paper.

For video-based crowd counting, a significant open problem is how to best leverage temporal information to improve count estimates. In one such work, ConvLSTMs were used to integrate image features from the current frame with those from previous frames for improved temporal coherency [11]. Further, Zhang et al. [10] proposed the use of LSTMs for vehicle counting in videos. Most of the LSTM-based approaches suffer from the drawback that they require a predefined number of frames to use as 'history' and, depending on dataset, some of these frames may provide irrelevant or contradictory information. Fang et al. [9] updated their model parameters using information based on dependencies among neighbouring frames, rather than via an LSTM. However, in their approach, a density regression module was first used in a frame-by-frame fashion to produce regression maps, upon which a spatial transformer was applied to post-process and improve the estimates. Although focusing on LOI counting, Zhao et al. used a convolutional neural network that processed pairs of video frames to jointly estimate crowd density and velocity maps [24]. The sole work that we are aware of that has incorporated optical flow for ROI crowd counting is a classical approach using traditional computer vision techniques (e.g., background subtraction and clustering the flow vectors) [29]. Their proposed system includes numerous hand-tuned parameters and employed the assumption that the only moving objects in the scene are pedestrians, which is not realistic in most scenarios. Differing from the above, our proposed approach integrates optical flow-based motion information directly, by warping deep neural network feature maps from the previous frame to the next.

2.3   Optical Flow Pyramid

Many recent works applying CNNs to video data have demonstrated the benefit of including optical flow. Two-stream and multi-stream networks have already shown effectiveness for action recognition [30,31] and action detection [32–35]. These approaches mostly use optical flow as an additional, parallel source of information which is fused prior to prediction. Other work has utilized optical flow to warp intermediate network features to achieve performance speed-ups for video-based semantic segmentation [36,37] and object detection [36].

Most similar to the current work is an approach to semantic segmentation in video that introduces a "NetWarp" module [38]. This module utilizes optical flow, modified by a learned transformation, to warp feature maps between consecutive frames and subsequently combine them with maps from the current frame, resulting in more stable and consistent segmentation results. In contrast, our proposed solution adopts an optical flow pyramid to capture motion at multiple scales and applies the unmodified flow to the feature maps directly for the task of crowd counting. To the best of our knowledge, no prior work has made use of optical flow-based feature map warping for video-based crowd counting, as proposed here.

3   Technical Approach

3.1   Crowd Counting Baseline Network

The baseline network serves as a single-frame crowd density estimator and contains two sub-modules: a feature extractor and a decoder. Although it is not the primary technical contribution of this work, the baseline network extends CSR-Net [7], yielding a significantly more accurate density estimator. These extensions will be highlighted in the following.

Feature Extractor: A customized VGG-16 network [39], initialized with ImageNet [40] weights was selected as the feature extractor in order to perform

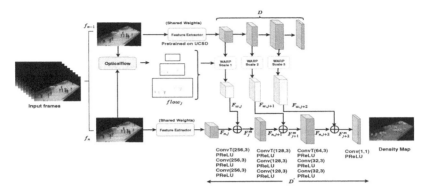

Fig. 2. System diagram for MOPN. The input image is passed through the feature extractor and optical flow is computed between the previous and current frame. Multi-scale feature maps from the previous frame are warped via the computed optical flow and concatenated with the corresponding feature maps in the current frame. This step combines complementary scale-aware motion based features with traditional, appearance-derived features in the proposed network. The crowd count can be obtained by summing over the entries in the predicted density map provided by the 1×1 convolution layer.

fair comparison with other methods [6,7] using the same backbone network. To avoid feature maps with small spatial extent, three maxpool layers were used, which results in feature maps of $1/8^{th}$ of the input image size at the bottleneck. Differing from [7], ReLU activation functions were replaced with PReLU [41] for each layer to avoid the 'dying ReLU' problem.

Decoder Network: The decoder of CSRNet consists of six dilated convolution layers followed by a 1×1 convolution, resulting in an output density map that is $1/8^{th}$ the size of the input image. In contrast, the proposed decoder is comprised of nine convolutional layers, three transposed convolution layers, followed by a final 1×1 convolution layer. This modified decoder design results in coarse-to-fine feature maps and a high-resolution (i.e., same as input size) density map as the final output. The ReLU activation functions in CSRNet were also replaced with PReLU throughout the decoder.

The main motivation for these architectural changes was three-fold: i) The proposed coarse-to-fine design eases the integration with the optical flow pyramid in the full, proposed model. ii) By using transposed convolution, the decoder output is full-resolution, making it more practical to resolve small humans within the image. iii) The additional learnable parameters introduced by the extra convolutional layers and PReLU activation functions empirically leads to significantly improved accuracies. In Sect. 4.2 and Sect. 4.3, the performance of the proposed baseline network is compared against state-of-the-art methods.

3.2   Multi-scale Optical Flow Pyramid Network (MOPN)

The general philosophy of the proposed full model is to leverage complementary appearance and motion information to improve counting accuracies.

One challenge with optical flow is effectively capturing large object displacements while simultaneously maintaining accuracies for small movements. Video camera configurations for crowd density estimation are varied: Some cameras are high resolution and have frame rates of 30 fps (e.g., FDST Dataset [9]), while others may be low resolution with frame rates of 2 fps or lower (e.g., Mall Dataset [19]). For a 30 fps video, the inter-frame motion of objects tends to be small, but for cameras running at 2 fps, scene objects can move significantly between consecutive frames.

To accommodate the range of inter-frame motion that may be encountered in crowd counting scenarios, an image pyramid is utilized when computing optical flow. With this method, large pixel displacements will be captured by the coarse scales, which are subsequently refined to have higher precision at the finer scales. This pyramid of multi-resolution optical flow maps is then applied to the corresponding feature maps from the decoder network. With this approach, both large and small displacements are modeled and addressed.

In detail, let f_n and f_{n-1} represent the current and previous input video frames, respectively. The proposed approach computes optical flow between f_n and f_{n-1} at three scales in an image pyramid, using a pixel subsampling factor of two between pyramid layers. As shown in Fig. 2, Scale 1 (S_1) captures large inter-frame displacements found in the video, while Scale 3 (S_3) effectively captures small motions that would typically be found in 30 fps video. The middle scale, S_2, describes mid-range optical flow bounded by S_1 and S_3. FlowNet 2.0 [17] is employed for computing the flow in the current work, although the overall approach is agnostic to the specific optical flow algorithm adopted.

As shown in Fig. 2, once the multi-scale pyramid of optical flow is computed, each flow map is applied as a warping transformation to the feature maps at the corresponding pixel resolution from the previous frame. The warped feature map is then concatenated with the corresponding embedding computed for the current frame. By including the motion information via the previous frame's warped feature maps, MOPN achieves improved temporal consistency and robustness when appearance information is unreliable (e.g., partial occlusions, objects with human-like appearances).

3.3   Training Details

The training method for the proposed MOPN system consists of two steps: baseline network training and full model training. Baseline network training proceeds by initializing the network with ImageNet weights, from which it is subsequently updated. During this stage, a dataset is selected (e.g., UCSD [18]) and the network is trained using samples from that dataset. Based on the validation samples, the best model is selected and evaluated on the test samples. All images and corresponding ground truth are resized to 952×632. In Fig. 2, the upper portion of the network depicts the baseline network.

For the full MOPN model, the parameters of the feature extractor portion of the network, θ_z, are initialized with the corresponding baseline pretrained weights, θ_P, and frozen. To incorporate motion information into MOPN, the baseline decoder, D, is replaced with a trainable, motion-based decoder, D'. For every frame, the image is first downsampled to create a three-level image pyramid from which optical flow is calculated to yield $flow_j$, where j is the pyramid level.

For each epoch, i, training of the MOPN motion-based decoder proceeds as follows. The feature maps for the previous frame, $n-1$, and current frame, n, are computed using, $F_{(n-1)j} = \mathcal{Z}'_j(f_{n-1}, \theta_{D'_{n-1}})$ and $F_{nj} = \mathcal{Z}'_j(f_n, \theta_{D'_{n-1}})$, respectively. The term $\mathcal{Z}'_j$ denotes the nonlinear network function that produces the feature maps at network layer j for an input image. Warped versions of the feature maps from the previous frame are calculated according to $F_{wj} = \text{WARP}(F_{(n-1)j}, flow_j)$ which are then concatenated with F_{nj}, the feature maps of the current frame. Feature map concatenation results in the formation of higher dimensional maps, F_j^m, which are subsequently used to update the motion decoder and obtain a new set of parameters $\theta_{D'_n}$. Intuitively, the intermediate layer outputs from every frame are propagated forward to the next frame in order to train the decoder of MOPN. Note that for the special case of $n = 2$, the baseline decoder network is used for feature map generation, as the shared parameters within the MOPN decoder are initialized by the frozen baseline decoder parameters, θ_D.

Regarding the loss function, the difference between the predicted density map and ground truth is measured by Frobenius Norm. Namely, the loss function is:

$$L(\theta) = \frac{1}{2N} \sum_{n=1}^{N} ||M(f_n, \theta) - M_n^{GT}||_2^2, \tag{1}$$

where, N is the number of training frames, $M(f_n, \theta)$ is the predicted density map and M_n^{GT} is the corresponding ground truth.

For all experiments in the paper, we use the following hyperparameter settings across all the datasets: learning rate = 0.00001, number of epochs = 2000, batch size = 2 (two consecutive frames at a time) with the Adam optimizer [42]. A summary of the training procedure for updating the MOPN decoder is provided in Algorithm 1.

Ground Truth Generation: For crowd density estimation, ground truth generation is very important in order to ensure fair comparison. To remain consistent with previous research, the same approaches described in [6,7,9,11] were used to generate the ground truth density maps in the current paper. For the datasets in which a ROI mask is provided, the ROI was multiplied with each frame to allow density maps to be generated based on the masked input images.

Algorithm 1: MOPN training procedure.

Input: Frame sequence $\{f_n\}_{n=1}^N$ with ground truth density maps $\{M_n^{GT}\}$
Output: Trained parameters $\theta_{D'}$

```
/* θz denotes parameters of the MOPN feature extractor      */
/* θD' denotes parameters of the MOPN decoder               */
/* θP denotes parameters of base network                    */
```

1 Initialize θ_z and $\theta_{D'}$ with θ_P
2 Freeze θ_z

```
/* T denotes the maximum number of epochs.                  */
```

3 **for** $i = 1$ *to* T **do**
4   **for** $n = 2$ *to* N **do**
5   Extract $\{F_{(n-1)j}\}_{j=1}^3$ from $f_{(n-1)}$
6   Extract $\{F_{nj}\}_{j=1}^3$ from f_n

```
          /* {Fnj}³ⱼ₌₁ denotes F as the feature map output for the nᵗʰ
             frame with jᵗʰ scale                              */
```

7   **for** $j = 1$ *to* 3 **do**
8           $flow_j = Optical\_flow(f_{(n-1)j}, f_{nj})$
9           $F_{wj} = WARP(F_{(n-1)j}, flow_j)$
10          $F_j^m = F_{wj} \oplus F_{nj}$

```
          /* From Eq. 1                                        */
```

11       $loss^{best} = argmin[L(\theta)]$
12   Backpropagate and update $\theta_{D'}$

---

4 Experiments

4.1 Evaluation Metric

Following previous works [5–8], Mean Absolute Error (MAE) and Mean Square Error (MSE) are used as evaluation metrics. Let N be the number of test images, $C_{gt}^{(n)}$ the ground truth count, and $C^{(n)}$ be the predicted count for the n-th test image. These two evaluation metrics are defined as follows: $MAE = \frac{1}{N} \sum_{n=1}^N |C^{(n)} - Cgt^{(n)}|$ and $MSE = \sqrt{\frac{1}{N} \sum_{n=1}^N |C^{(n)} - Cgt^{(n)}|^2}$.

4.2 Crowd Counting in Images

UCF_CC_50: The UCF_CC_50 dataset [20] is a benchmark for crowd counting in static images focusing on dense crowds captured from a wide-range of locations around the world. The images in this dataset do not come from a video camera, meaning that it can not be used to test the full, proposed MOPN model; however, the proposed baseline model is evaluated on this dataset. To ensure a fair comparison, 5-fold cross validation was performed, as was done for S-DCNet [22]. As shown in Table 2, the propoed baseline attains the best MAE and second best MSE scores against the alternative approaches. Only DRSAN [43] slightly outperforms our baseline under the MSE mertic (Table 1).

Table 1. Performance comparisons on UCF_CC_50 [20] and UCF-QNRF [44] datasets. For this and subsequent tables throughout the paper, **blue** numbers refer to the best result in each column, while red numbers indicate second best.

Methods	UCF_CC_50		UCF-QNRF	
	MAE	MSE	MAE	MSE
Idrees et al. [3]	468.0	590.3	315	508
Context-Aware Counting [45]	212.2	243.7	107	183
ADCrowdNet [46]	257.1	363.5	–	–
MCNN [8]	–	–	277	426
CMTL [15]	–	–	252	514
Switching-CNN [6]	–	–	228	445
Cross Scene [12]	467.0	498.5	–	–
IG-CNN [47]	291.4	349.4	–	–
D-ConvNet [48]	288.4	404.7	–	–
CSRNet [7]	266.1	397.5	–	–
SANet [49]	258.4	334.9	–	–
DRSAN [43]	219.2	**250.2**	–	–
PGC [23]	244.6	361.2	–	–
TEDnet [50]	249.4	354.5	113	188
MBTTBF-SCFB [51]	233.1	300.9	97.5	165.2
S-DCNet [22]	204.2	301.3	104.4	176.1
Proposed baseline (w/o optical flow)	**181.8**	260.4	**78.65**	**140.63**

UCF-QNRF: UCF-QNRF [44] is a large crowd counting dataset consisting of 1535 high-resolution images and 1.25 million head annotations. This dataset focuses primarily on dense crowds, with an average of roughly 815 persons per image. The training split is comprised of 1201 images, with the remaining left for

Table 2. Comparative performance of the proposed baseline and full model (MOPN) against state-of-the-art alternatives on three standard datasets.

Methods	UCSD		MALL		FDST	
	MAE	MSE	MAE	MSE	MAE	MSE
Switching CNN [6]	1.62	2.10	–	–	–	–
CSRNet [7]	1.16	1.47	–	–	–	–
MCNN [8]	1.07	1.35	–	–	3.77	4.88
Count Forest [52]	1.60	4.40	2.50	10.0	–	–
Weighted VLAD [53]	2.86	13.0	2.41	9.12	–	–
Random Forest [54]	1.90	6.01	3.22	15.5	–	–
LSTN [9]	1.07	1.39	2.03	2.60	3.35	4.45
FCN-rLSTM [10]	1.54	3.02	–	–	–	–
Bidirectional ConvLSTM [11]	1.13	1.43	2.10	7.60	4.48	5.82
Proposed baseline (w/o optical flow)	1.05	1.74	1.79	2.25	3.70	4.80
Full proposed model (MOPN)	**0.97**	**1.22**	**1.78**	**2.25**	**1.76**	**2.25**
% Improvement: MOPN over Baseline	7.6%	29.9%	0.6%	0.0%	52.4%	53.1%

testing. During training, we follow the data augmentation techniques described in [22]. Also, we resized the images to $1/4^{th}$ of their original size.

The results on this dataset from the proposed baseline are impressive, attaining the best result for both MAE and MSE. This result clearly indicates the effectiveness of the proposed baseline network, as it is able to outperform the latest state-of-the-art methods on large-scale datasets with dense crowds.

4.3   Crowd Counting in Videos

UCSD Dataset: The UCSD dataset consists of a single 2,000 frame video taken with a stationary camera overlooking a pedestrian walkway. The video was captured at 10 fps and has a resolution of 238×158. The provided ground truth denotes the centroid of each pedestrian. Following the common evaluation protocol for this dataset (e.g., [18]), Frames 601–1,400 are used for training, while the remaining images are used during testing.

The MAE and MSE results for the baseline (without optical flow) and MOPN are shown in Table 2. The full proposed model, MOPN, attains second-best MAE and MSE, slightly behind while the baseline has second-based MAE results. For MAE, MOPN offers a 9% improvement over the third best result (MCNN [8] and LSTN [9]), while a 10% decrease in MSE is observed compared to the second-best results (of MCNN [8]). Compared to the baseline, the full proposed model provides a 7.6% and 29.9% improvement for MAE and MSE, respectively. This final result demonstrates clearly the benefits of incorporating motion information to complement the appearance cues that are traditionally used for crowd counting.

Mall Dataset: The mall dataset is comprised of a 2,000 frame video sequence captured in a shopping mall via a publicly accessible camera. The video was captured at a resolution of 640×480 and with a framerate of less than 2 fps. As was done in [19], Frames 1–800 were used for training, while the final 1,200 frames were considered for evaluation.

As Table 2 indicates, MOPN and the proposed baseline achieve the best and second best results on this dataset, respectively. Although the MAE with MOPN is better than the baseline, in this case the improvement from motion-related information is marginal. This result is expected, as the frame rate for the Mall Dataset is low. With such a low frame rate, the inter-frame motion of people in the scene can be quite large (e.g., one quarter of the image), meaning that only the scales of the optical flow pyramid corresponding to large displacements are contributing to the full network. The results from the Mall Dataset are encouraging, as they indicate that even in low framerate settings when motion cues are less effective, the full model can rely on the appearance information provided by the baseline network to still achieve state-of-the-art accuracies.

Fudan-ShanghaiTech Dataset: The Fudan-ShanghaiTech (FDST) dataset [9] is currently the most extensive video crowd counting dataset available with a total of 15,000 frames and 394,081 annotated heads. The dataset captures 100 videos from 13 different scenes at resolutions of 1920×1080 and 1280×720.

Following the evaluation protocol defined by the dataset authors, 60 of the videos are used for training while the remaining 40 videos are reserved for testing. Table 2 shows the results for the FDST dataset. Since this dataset is new, only three alternative state-of-the-art approaches have reported results for comparison. MOPN has the lowest MAE and MSE, while the proposed baseline was third-best. MOPN achieves a 47% and 49% improvement over the second-best performer, LSTN [9], for MAE and MSE, respectively. To attain this significant of an accuracy increase on the largest video-based crowd counting dataset illustrates the importance of combining both appearance and motion cues.

4.4   Qualitative Results

To demonstrate the qualitative performance of the proposed system, Fig. 3 shows a zoomed image from the FDST dataset along with superimposed density maps corresponding to ground truth, proposed baseline, and MOPN. The qualitative results show that MOPN produces much more accurate count estimates than the baseline. It can be seen that the baseline model (third column) does not detect three individuals (denoted by red circles); whereas, MOPN (fourth column) is able to detect these individuals (highlighted with green circles).

Fig. 3. Qualitative example of density maps. From left to right, the columns correspond to a cropped input video frame from the FDST dataset [9], ground truth density map, density map from the proposed baseline (without optical flow), and the density map from the full MOPN model. Superimposed red and green circles highlight certain false negatives and true positives, respectively. Best viewed in color and with magnification. (Color figure online)

4.5   Transfer Learning

The goal of this experiment is to consider the performance tradeoffs when only a portion of the network is fine-tuned on a target domain dataset. This scenario can be relevant in situations in which the amount of data in the target domain is limited and therefore it may be more effective to train only a specific portion of the network. The transfer learning experiment is setup as follows. First, the baseline model is trained on a source domain dataset. Once this source domain baseline is in place, the trained model is evaluated on a target domain test dataset.

In the finetuning setting, we simply update the decoder of our baseline model. Table 3 shows the results for this evaluation, where alternative methods that have considered such transfer learning experiments have been included. In addition to several deep learning-based approaches detailed earlier, some methods that do not involve deep learning are also included, as follows: Feature Alignment (FA) [55], Learning Gaussian Process (LGP) [56], Gaussian process (GP) [57], Gaussian Process with Transfer Learning (GPTL) [57]. The proposed fine-tuned baseline model achieves the best MAE compared to the other models on the transfer learning experiment.

Table 3. Results from the transfer learning experiment using the Mall and UCSD datasets. The finetuned baseline model attains best results when completing the transfer learning task from UCSD to MALL, as well as from MALL to UCSD.

Methods	UCSD to MALL	MALL to UCSD
	MAE	MAE
FA [55]	7.47	4.44
LGP [56]	4.36	3.32
GPA [57]	4.18	2.79
GPTL [57]	3.55	2.91
MCNN [8]	24.25	11.26
CSRNet [7]	14.01	13.96
Bidirectional ConvLSTM [11]	2.63	1.82
Proposed baseline (w/o optical flow)	6.18	12.21
Finetuned baseline model	**2.36**	**1.55**

4.6   Ablation Studies

Component Analysis: Table 4 shows a study regarding the performance gains due to the individual extensions of the proposed baseline over CSRNet. The first row from Table 4 corresponds to a network comparable to CSRNet, while the fourth row is the proposed baseline. Rows two and three show the individual contributions of transposed convolution and PReLU, when integrated into the decoder portion of the baseline network. As shown in the table, both modifications contribute evenly to the accuracy gains. Also, the alterations are complementary, leading to further improved results when combined (Row 4).

Multi-scale Pyramid: One of the main parameters of MOPN is the number of layers in the optical flow pyramid for warping the feature maps. Table 5 shows the proposed method's performance on UCSD as a function of the number of levels in the optical flow pyramid. With only a single pyramid level, the warping and feature concatenation can be performed at low, mid, or high resolution, corresponding to specialization in capturing large, medium, and small-scale motions.

Table 4. Individual contributions of network components in the baseline network.

Methods	UCSD
	MAE
ReLU (w/o transposed convolution)	1.26
ReLU (with transposed convolution)	1.18
PReLU (w/o transposed convolution)	1.14
PReLU (with transposed convolution)	**1.05**

The table shows that the multi-scale optical flow pyramid indeed yields best accuracies. When using just a single scale of optical flow, Scale 3 (small inter-frame displacements) performs slightly better than Scale 1 (large inter-frame displacements), but the difference is minimal.

Table 5. The effect of modifying the number of optical flow pyramid levels.

Methods	UCSD	
	MAE	MSE
Proposed with Scale-1	1.07	1.34
Proposed with Scale-3	1.04	1.30
Proposed multi-scale	**0.97**	**1.22**

Effect of Optical Flow Warping: Another ablation study considers providing the full proposed network with two frames of input images without any explicit optical flow. This experiment was performed by concatenating the unwarped feature maps from the previous frame with those of the current frame. For the UCSD dataset, this configuration yielded MAE/MSE = 1.12/1.97 compared to 0.97/1.22 for MOPN (Table 2). Also note that this two-frame configuration is worse than the proposed baseline (1.05/1.74 from Table 2). This finding exemplifies the importance of optical flow to the proposed approach. Without warping, features from previous and current frames are misaligned, which confuses the network, as it is not provided with the necessary motion information to resolve correspondences across the feature maps. With MOPN, optical flow removes this ambiguity, constraining the solution space and yielding less localization error.

5   Conclusion

In this paper, a novel video-based crowd density estimation technique is proposed that combines a pyramid of optical flow features with a convolutional neural network. The proposed video-based approach was evaluated on three challenging, publicly available datasets and universally achieved best MAE and MSE when compared against nine recent and competitive approaches. Accuracy improvements of the full proposed MOPN model were as high as 49% when compared to the second-best performer on the recent and challenging FDST video dataset. These results indicate the importance of using all spatiotemporal information available in a video sequence to achieve highest accuracies rather than employing a frame-by-frame approach. Additionally, results on the UCF_CC_50 and UCF-QNRF datasets, which focus on images of dense crowds, show that the proposed baseline network (without optical flow) achieves state-of-the-art performance for crowd counting in static images.

References

1. Sindagi, V.A., Patel, V.M.: A survey of recent advances in CNN-based single image crowd counting and density estimation. Pattern Recogn. Lett. **107**, 3–16 (2018)
2. Ge, W., Collins, R.T.: Marked point processes for crowd counting. In: Proceedings of the IEEE Conference on Computer Vision and Pattern Recognition, pp. 2913–2920 (2009)
3. Idrees, H., Soomro, K., Shah, M.: Detecting humans in dense crowds using locally-consistent scale prior and global occlusion reasoning. IEEE Trans. Pattern Anal. Mach. Intell. **37**, 1986–1998 (2015)
4. Hu, P., Ramanan, D.: Finding tiny faces. In: Proceedings of the IEEE Conference on Computer Vision and Pattern Recognition, pp. 1522–1530 (2017)
5. Sindagi, V.A., Patel, V.M.: Generating high-quality crowd density maps using contextual pyramid CNNs. In: Proceedings of the IEEE International Conference on Computer Vision, pp. 1861–1870 (2017)
6. Sam, D.B., Surya, S., Babu, R.V.: Switching convolutional neural network for crowd counting. In: IEEE Conference on Computer Vision and Pattern Recognition (CVPR), pp. 4031–4039. IEEE (2017)
7. Li, Y., Zhang, X., Chen, D.: CSRNet: dilated convolutional neural networks for understanding the highly congested scenes. In: Proceedings of the IEEE Conference on Computer Vision and Pattern Recognition, pp. 1091–1100 (2018)
8. Zhang, Y., Zhou, D., Chen, S., Gao, S., Ma, Y.: Single-image crowd counting via multi-column convolutional neural network. In: Proceedings of the IEEE Conference on Computer Vision and Pattern Recognition, pp. 589–597 (2016)
9. Fang, Y., Zhan, B., Cai, W., Gao, S., Hu, B.: Locality-constrained spatial transformer network for video crowd counting. In: 2019 IEEE International Conference on Multimedia and Expo (ICME), pp. 814–819. IEEE (2019)
10. Zhang, S., Wu, G., Costeira, J.P., Moura, J.M.: FCN-rLSTM: deep spatio-temporal neural networks for vehicle counting in city cameras. In: Proceedings of the IEEE International Conference on Computer Vision, pp. 3667–3676 (2017)
11. Xiong, F., Shi, X., Yeung, D.Y.: Spatiotemporal modeling for crowd counting in videos. In: Proceedings of the IEEE International Conference on Computer Vision, pp. 5151–5159 (2017)
12. Zhang, C., Li, H., Wang, X., Yang, X.: Cross-scene crowd counting via deep convolutional neural networks. In: Proceedings of the IEEE Conference on Computer Vision and Pattern Recognition, pp. 833–841 (2015)
13. Oñoro-Rubio, D., López-Sastre, R.J.: Towards perspective-free object counting with deep learning. In: Leibe, B., Matas, J., Sebe, N., Welling, M. (eds.) ECCV 2016. LNCS, vol. 9911, pp. 615–629. Springer, Cham (2016). https://doi.org/10.1007/978-3-319-46478-7_38

14. Boominathan, L., Kruthiventi, S.S., Babu, R.V.: CrowdNet: a deep convolutional network for dense crowd counting. In: Proceedings of the 24th ACM International Conference on Multimedia, pp. 640–644. ACM (2016)
15. Sindagi, V.A., Patel, V.M.: CNN-based cascaded multi-task learning of high-level prior and density estimation for crowd counting. In: 2017 14th IEEE International Conference on Advanced Video and Signal Based Surveillance (AVSS), pp. 1–6. ACM (2016)
16. Horn, B.K.P., Schunck, B.G.: Determining optical flow. Artif. Intell. **17**, 185–203 (1981)
17. Ilg, E., Mayer, N., Saikia, T., Keuper, M., Dosovitskiy, A., Brox, T.: FlowNet 2.0: evolution of optical flow estimation with deep networks. In: Proceedings of the IEEE Conference on Computer Vision and Pattern Recognition, pp. 1647–1655 (2017)
18. Chan, A.B., Liang, Z.S.J., Vasconcelos, N.: Privacy preserving crowd monitoring: counting people without people models or tracking. In: Proceedings of the IEEE Conference on Computer Vision and Pattern Recognition, pp. 1–7 (2008)
19. Chen, K., Loy, C.C., Gong, S., Xiang, T.: Feature mining for localised crowd counting. In: Proceedings of the British Machine Vision Conference, pp. 1–7 (2012)
20. Idrees, H., Saleemi, I., Seibert, C., Shah, M.: Multi-source multi-scale counting in extremely dense crowd images. In: Proceedings of the IEEE Conference on Computer Vision and Pattern Recognition, pp. 2547–2554 (2013)
21. Hossain, M., Hosseinzadeh, M., Chanda, O., Wang, Y.: Crowd counting using scale-aware attention networks. In: 2019 IEEE Winter Conference on Applications of Computer Vision (WACV), pp. 1280–1288. IEEE (2019)
22. Xiong, H., Lu, H., Liu, C., Liu, L., Cao, Z., Shen, C.: From open set to closed set: counting objects by spatial divide-and-conquer. In: The IEEE International Conference on Computer Vision (ICCV) (2019)
23. Yan, Z., et al.: Perspective-guided convolution networks for crowd counting. In: Proceedings of the IEEE International Conference on Computer Vision, pp. 952–961 (2019)
24. Zhao, Z., Li, H., Zhao, R., Wang, X.: Crossing-line crowd counting with two-phase deep neural networks. In: Leibe, B., Matas, J., Sebe, N., Welling, M. (eds.) ECCV 2016. LNCS, vol. 9912, pp. 712–726. Springer, Cham (2016). https://doi.org/10.1007/978-3-319-46484-8_43
25. Ma, Z., Chan, A.B.: Crossing the line: crowd counting by integer programming with local features. In: Proceedings of the IEEE Conference on Computer Vision and Pattern Recognition, pp. 2539–2546 (2013)
26. Ma, Z., Chan, A.B.: Counting people crossing a line using integer programming and local features. IEEE Trans. Circuits Syst. Video Technol. **26**, 1955–1969 (2015)
27. Cong, Y., Gong, H., Zhu, S.C., Tang, Y.: Flow mosaicking: real-time pedestrian counting without scene-specific learning. In: 2009 IEEE Conference on Computer Vision and Pattern Recognition, pp. 1093–1100. IEEE (2009)
28. Cao, L., Zhang, X., Ren, W., Huang, K.: Large scale crowd analysis based on convolutional neural network. Pattern Recogn. **48**, 3016–3024 (2015)
29. Fujisawa, S., Hasegawa, G., Taniguchi, Y., Nakano, H.: Pedestrian counting in video sequences based on optical flow clustering. Int. J. Image Process. **7**, 1–16 (2013)
30. Feichtenhofer, C., Pinz, A., Zisserman, A.: Convolutional two-stream network fusion for video action recognition. In: Proceedings of the IEEE Conference on Computer Vision and Pattern Recognition, pp. 1933–1941 (2016)

31. Carreira, J., Zisserman, A.: Quo vadis, action recognition? A new model and the kinetics dataset. In: Proceedings of the IEEE Conference on Computer Vision and Pattern Recognition, pp. 4724–4733 (2017)
32. Simonyan, K., Zisserman, A.: Two-stream convolutional networks for action recognition in videos. In: Proceedings of the 27th International Conference on Neural Information Processing Systems, pp. 568–576 (2014)
33. Peng, X., Schmid, C.: Multi-region two-stream R-CNN for action detection. In: Leibe, B., Matas, J., Sebe, N., Welling, M. (eds.) ECCV 2016. LNCS, vol. 9908, pp. 744–759. Springer, Cham (2016). https://doi.org/10.1007/978-3-319-46493-0_45
34. Singh, B., Marks, T.K., Jones, M., Tuzel, O., Shao, M.: A multi-stream bidirectional recurrent neural network for fine-grained action detection. In: Proceedings of the 27th International Conference on Neural Information Processing Systems, pp. 1961–1970 (2016)
35. Singh, G., Saha, S., Sapienza, M., Torr, P., Cuzzolin, F.: Online real-time multiple spatiotemporal action localisation and prediction. In: Proceedings of the IEEE International Conference on Computer Vision, pp. 3657–3666 (2017)
36. Zhu, X., Xiong, Y., Dai, J., Yuan, L., Wei, Y.: Deep feature flow for video recognition. In: Proceedings of the IEEE Conference on Computer Vision and Pattern Recognition, pp. 4141–4150 (2017)
37. Li, M., Sun, L., Huo, Q.: Flow-guided feature propagation with occlusion aware detail enhancement for hand segmentation in egocentric videos. Comput. Vis. Image Underst. **187**, 102785 (2019)
38. Gadde, R., Jampani, V., Gehler, P.V.: Semantic video CNNs through representation warping. In: Proceedings of the IEEE International Conference on Computer Vision, pp. 4463–4472 (2017)
39. Simonyan, K., Zisserman, A.: Very deep convolutional networks for large-scale image recognition. arXiv preprint arXiv:1409.1556 (2014)
40. Krizhevsky, A., Sutskever, I., Hinton, G.E.: ImageNet classification with deep convolutional neural networks. In: Advances in Neural Information Processing Systems, pp. 1097–1105 (2012)
41. He, K., Zhang, X., Ren, S., Sun, J.: Delving deep into rectifiers: surpassing human-level performance on imagenet classification. In: Proceedings of the IEEE International Conference on Computer Vision, pp. 1026–1034 (2015)
42. Kingma, D., Ba, J.: Adam: a method for stochastic optimization. In: Proceedings of the International Conference on Learning Representations (2014)
43. Liu, L., Wang, H., Li, G., Ouyang, W., Lin, L.: Crowd counting using deep recurrent spatial-aware network. arXiv preprint arXiv:1807.00601 (2018)
44. Idrees, H., et al.: Composition loss for counting, density map estimation and localization in dense crowds. In: Proceedings of the European Conference on Computer Vision (ECCV), pp. 532–546 (2018)
45. Liu, W., Salzmann, M., Fua, P.: Context-aware crowd counting. In: Proceedings of the IEEE/CVF Conference on Computer Vision and Pattern Recognition (CVPR) (2019)
46. Wan, J., Chan, A.: Adaptive density map generation for crowd counting. In: Proceedings of the IEEE/CVF International Conference on Computer Vision (ICCV) (2019)
47. Babu Sam, D., Sajjan, N.N., Venkatesh Babu, R., Srinivasan, M.: Divide and grow: capturing huge diversity in crowd images with incrementally growing CNN. In: Proceedings of the IEEE Conference on Computer Vision and Pattern Recognition, pp. 3618–3626 (2018)

48. Shi, Z., et al.: Crowd counting with deep negative correlation learning. In: Proceedings of the IEEE Conference on Computer Vision and Pattern Recognition, pp. 5382–5390 (2018)

49. Cao, X., Wang, Z., Zhao, Y., Su, F.: Scale aggregation network for accurate and efficient crowd counting. In: Proceedings of the European Conference on Computer Vision (ECCV), pp. 734–750 (2018)

50. Jiang, X., et al.: Crowd counting and density estimation by trellis encoder-decoder networks. In: Proceedings of the IEEE Conference on Computer Vision and Pattern Recognition, pp. 6133–6142 (2018)

51. Sindagi, V.A., Patel, V.M.: Multi-level bottom-top and top-bottom feature fusion for crowd counting. In: Proceedings of the IEEE/CVF International Conference on Computer Vision (ICCV) (2019)

52. Pham, V.Q., Kozakaya, T., Yamaguchi, O., Okada, R.: Count forest: co-voting uncertain number of targets using random forest for crowd density estimation. In: Proceedings of the IEEE International Conference on Computer Vision, pp. 3253–3261 (2015)

53. Sheng, B., Shen, C., Lin, G., Li, J., Yang, W., Sun, C.: Crowd counting via weighted VLAD on a dense attribute feature map. IEEE Trans. Circuits Syst. Video Technol. **28**, 1788–1797 (2016)

54. Xu, B., Qiu, G.: Crowd density estimation based on rich features and random projection forest. In: 2016 IEEE Winter Conference on Applications of Computer Vision (WACV), pp. 1–8. IEEE (2016)

55. Change Loy, C., Gong, S., Xiang, T.: From semi-supervised to transfer counting of crowds. In: Proceedings of the IEEE International Conference on Computer Vision, pp. 2256–2263 (2013)

56. Yu, K., Tresp, V., Schwaighofer, A.: Learning Gaussian processes from multiple tasks. In: Proceedings of the 22nd International Conference on Machine Learning (ICML 2005), pp. 1012–1019 (2005)

57. Liu, B., Vasconcelos, N.: Bayesian model adaptation for crowd counts. In: Proceedings of the IEEE International Conference on Computer Vision, pp. 4175–4183 (2015)

RealSmileNet: A Deep End-to-End Network for Spontaneous and Posed Smile Recognition

Yan Yang[1]([✉])[iD], Md Zakir Hossain[1,2][iD], Tom Gedeon[1][iD],
and Shafin Rahman[1,3,4][iD]

[1] The Australian National University, Canberra, ACT 0200, Australia
{u6169130,zakir.hossain,tom.gedeon}@anu.edu.au
[2] The University of Canberra, Bruce, ACT 2617, Australia
[3] North South University, Dhaka, Bangladesh
shafin.rahman@northsouth.edu
[4] Data61-CSIRO, Canberra, ACT 0200, Australia

Abstract. Smiles play a vital role in the understanding of social interactions within different communities, and reveal the physical state of mind of people in both real and deceptive ways. Several methods have been proposed to recognize spontaneous and posed smiles. All follow a feature-engineering based pipeline requiring costly pre-processing steps such as manual annotation of face landmarks, tracking, segmentation of smile phases, and hand-crafted features. The resulting computation is expensive, and strongly dependent on pre-processing steps. We investigate an end-to-end deep learning model to address these problems, the first end-to-end model for spontaneous and posed smile recognition. Our fully automated model is fast and learns the feature extraction processes by training a series of convolution and ConvLSTM layer from scratch. Our experiments on four datasets demonstrate the robustness and generalization of the proposed model by achieving state-of-the-art performances.

1 Introduction

Facial expression recognition is a process of identifying human emotion from videos, audios, and even the texts. Understanding facial expressions is essential for various forms of communication, such as the interaction between humans and machines. Also, the development of facial expression recognition contributes to the area of market research, health care, video game testings, and so on [1]. Meanwhile, people tend to hide their natural expression in different environments. Recognising spontaneous and posed facial expressions are necessary for social interaction analysis [2] because it can be deceptive and convey diverse meanings. The *smile* is the most common and easily expressible facial display, but still very hard to recognise. Because of the recurrence and cultural reasons,

H. Ishikawa et al. (Eds.): ACCV 2020, LNCS 12626, pp. 21–37, 2021.
https://doi.org/10.1007/978-3-030-69541-5_2

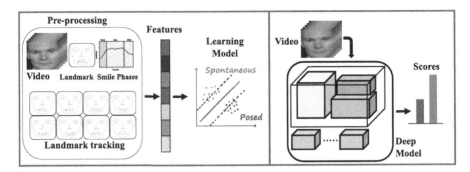

Fig. 1. Overview of different spontaneous smile recognition models. *(left)* Given a video as input, previous approaches [2,4–7,9] perform several manual or semi-automatic prepossessing steps like facial landmark detection [2,4–7], tracking [2,4–7], smile phases segmentation [2,5], and so on. across frames to calculate hand-engineered feature vectors (D-marker [2,4,15], HoG [5,9,16]), then feed the features to a learning model (SVM) for classification. The costly intermediate steps significantly increase the computation and limit the fully automatic process. *(right)* Our proposed end-to-end architecture takes video frames as input and recognizes spontaneous and posed smile by a simple forward pass.

the study of cognitive and computer sciences broadly investigates the recognition of spontaneous (genuine/real/felt) and posed (fake/false/deliberate) smiles [2–14].

Previous efforts on recognizing spontaneous and posed smiles mostly follow a feature-based approach where machine learning (ML) models perform a binary classification based on the extracted visual features from a smile video [2–13,15,16]. We identify several limitations of such approaches. *(a) Manual annotation*: Many methods require manual annotation of facial landmarks for the first frame of a video [2,4–7,15]. It limits the automation of the recognition process. *(b) Landmark tracking*: Methods need to track face landmarks throughout the video [2,4–7,15]. It is a computationally expensive process, and the performance of the recognition broadly depends on it. *(c) Segmentation of temporal phases*: Some methods extract features from temporal stages of a smile (i.e., onset, apex, and offset) separately [2,5]. Automatic segmentation of a smile can be erroneous because, in many smile videos, these phases are not apparent, and methods need to assign zero values in the feature list to satisfy the constant length of the feature set. *(d) Limiting the maximum length of a smile*: Most traditional machine learning methods cannot handle the dynamic length of time series data. Traditional methods need to represent each smile by a fixed length. It decreases the robustness of the system because, in a real application, a smile video may come with variable length. *(e) Hand-engineered features*: Methods depend on hand-crafted features like D-marker [2,4,15], Histogram of Oriented Gradients (HoG) [5,9,16], Local Binary Pattern (LBP) like feature on region of interest [5,16]. The selection of such features sometimes requires extensive research and expert domain-specific knowledge [17]. Because of the issues mentioned above, traditional methods become slow, limits the automation process, and achieves poor generalization ability. Moreover, the overall performance of recognition broadly depends on the availability of many independent pre-processing steps.

Here, we propose an approach that elegantly solves the problems and encapsulates all the broken-up pieces of traditional techniques into a single, unified deep neural network called '*RealSmileNet*'. Our method is end-to-end trainable, fully automated, fast, and promotes real-time recognition. We employ shared convolution neural networks (CNN) layers to learn the feature extraction process automatically, Convolutional Long Short Term Memory network (ConvLSTM) [18] layers to track the discriminative features across frames and a classification sub-network to assign a prediction score. Our model adaptively searches, tracks, and learns both spatial and temporal facial feature representations across the frames in an end-to-end manner. In this way, the spontaneous smile's recognition becomes as simple as a forward pass of the smile video through the network. In Fig. 1, we illustrate the difference between our method and the methods in the literature. Experimenting with four well-known smile datasets, we report state-of-the-art results without compromising the automation process.

Our main contributions are summarized below:

- To the best of our knowledge, we propose the first end-to-end deep network for recognition of spontaneous and posed smiles.
- Our method is fully automated and requires no manual landmark annotation or feature engineering. Unlike traditional methods, the proposed network can handle variable length of smile videos leading to a robust solution.
- As a simple forward pass through the network can perform the recognition process, our approach is fast enough to promote a real-time solution.
- We present extensive experiments on four video smile datasets and achieve state-of-the-art performance.

2   Related Work

Dynamics of the Spontaneous Smile: The smile is the most common facial expression, and usually featured by Action Unit 6 (AU6) and Action Unit 12 (AU12) in the facial action coding system (FACS) [19]. The rise of cheek and pull of lip corners is commonly associated with a smile [19]. In terms of temporal dynamics, the smile can be segmented into the onset, apex, and offset phases. It corresponds to the facial expression variation from neutral to smile and then return to neutral. In physiological research on facial expressions, Duchenne defines the smile as the contraction of both the zygomatic major muscle and the orbicularis oculi muscle, which known as *D-Smile*. A *Non-D-smile* tends to be a polite smile where only the zygomatic muscle is contracted [17]. Recently, Schmidt et al. [15] proposed a quantitative metric called Duchenne Marker (D-Marker) to measure the enjoyment of smiles. Much research uses this (controversial) metric to recognise spontaneous and posed smiles [2,4,6,15]. Our end-to-end network for spontaneous smile recognition does not use the D-Maker feature.

Spontaneous Smile Engineering: The literature of spontaneous smile recognition usually follows a feature-based approach. Those methods extract features from each frame along the time dimension to construct a multi-dimensional signal. A statistical summary of the signal obtained from a smile video, such as duration, amplitude, speed, accelerations, and symmetry, is considered in smile classification. The majority of competitive and notable research on Smile Classification relies on feature extraction by D-marker [2,4,15]. Dibeklioglu *et al.* [2] proposed a linear SVM classifier that uses the movement signal of eyelid, lip, and cheek. Mandal *et al.* [4] proposed a two-stream fusion method based on the movement of eyelid and lip and the dense optical flows with SVM. Pfister *et al.* [9] proposed feature extraction by using appearance-based local spatial-temporal descriptor (CLBP-TOP) for genuine and posed expression classifications. The CLBP-TOP is an extension of LBP, which able to extract the temporal information. Later, Wu *et al.* [5] used CLBP-TOP feature on the region of interests (eyes, lips and cheek) to train SVM for smile classifications. Valstar *et al.* [20] introduced the geometric feature-based smile classifications, using the movement of the shoulder and facial variation. We identify a few drawbacks of features based approaches. First, strongly dependence on accurate localization of the action units. Second, some approaches require manual labeling to track the changes in facial landmarks. Third, spontaneous smile recognition becomes a costly process - requiring laborious feature engineering and careful pre-processing.

End-to-End Solution: In recent decades, the advancement of graphic processing units and deep learning methods allow end-to-end learning of deep neural networks that achieves unprecedented success in object re-identification [21], detection [22,23], segmentation [24] using the image, videos, and 3D point cloud data [25]. An end-to-end network takes the input (image/video/3D point cloud) and produces the output with a single forward pass. This network performs the feature engineering with the convolution layers and reduces the necessity of manual intervention and expert effort on the training process. In this vein, an end-to-end trainable deep learning model to automatically classify the genuine and posed smiles is the next step to solve the problems of feature-based solutions. With this motivation, Mandal *et al.* [16] extract features from pre-trained CNN networks (VGG Face Recognition model [26]) but eventually feed the features to a separate SVM. Instead, we propose the first fully end-to-end solution.

3   Our Approach

In contrast with available methods, an end-to-end deep learning model can provide a convenient solution by ensuring complete automation and saving computational cost after finishing the training. Because of the availability of enormous amounts of data in recent years, such end-to-end learning systems are gradually dominating research in AI. In this section, we describe an end-to-end solution for spontaneous and posed smile recognition.

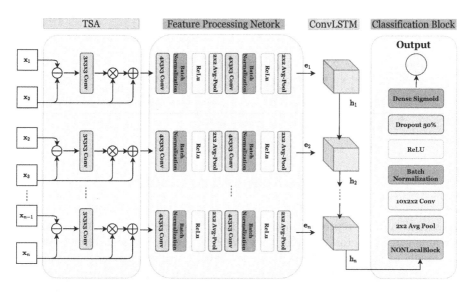

Fig. 2. Our proposed *RealSmileNet* architecture. The TSA layers guide the following feature processing network to extract discriminative facial representations. Then ConvLSTM tracks the face representation across the temporal direction to create a unified length video embedding. Finally, the classification block refines the video embedding and predicts a classification score. The number of kernels is denoted by the first number of Conv block, then the size of the kernel is followed.

3.1   Preliminaries

We consider a binary classification problem assigning labels to a sequence of images or video $\overrightarrow{X}_i = \langle \mathbf{x}_t | 1 \ldots n_i \rangle$ by parameterizable models $\mathcal{F}_\theta$ where, n_i is number of frames associated with $\overrightarrow{X}_i$ and $i \in \mathcal{T}$ and $\mathcal{T}$ is total number of videos in the dataset. The training dataset includes a set of tuples $\{(\overrightarrow{X}_i, y_i) : i \in [0, \mathcal{T}]\}$ where y_i represent the ground-truth label of the ith video. Here, $y_i = 1$ and $y_i = 0$ represent the class label spontaneous / posed smile respectively. Our goal is to train an end-to-end deep network model, $\mathcal{F}_\theta$, that can assign a prediction label, $\hat{y}_j$, to all of $\mathcal{K}$ testing videos, $\{\overrightarrow{V}_j\}_{j=1}^{\mathcal{K}}$. We formulate $\hat{y}_j$ as follows:

$$\hat{y}_j = \begin{cases} 1, & \text{if } \mathcal{F}_\theta(\overrightarrow{V}_j) \geq 0.5 \\ 0, & \text{otherwise} \end{cases} \tag{1}$$

3.2   Architecture

We illustrate our proposed *RealSmileNet* architecture in Fig. 2. It has four components: Temporal based Spatial Attention (TSA), Feature Processing Network (FPN), ConvLSTM, and Classification block. TSA captures the motion of frames using two consecutive frames as input, FPN further processes the motion feature

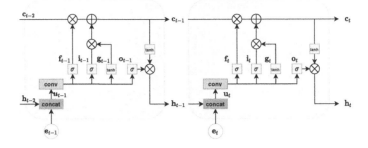

Fig. 3. State transitions of the ConvLSTM.

to generate a frame representation, ConvLSTM processes the temporal variation of frame features across different time frame to produce a video representation, and finally a classification block predicts a label for the input video. We train all components together from scratch as a single and unified deep neural network.

Temporal Based Spatial Attention (TSA): We design the TSA network that learns the variation of pixels i.e. motion of a video by concentrating certain regions using residual attention. Previous research on video classification [27] showed that difference image of adjacent frames provides crude approximation of optical flow images that is helpful in action recognition. With this motivation, this network takes two consecutive frames of a video, applies a 2D convolution on difference map and performs some element-wise operations on the residual (skip) connections from $\mathbf{x}_t$. The overall TSA calculation is defined as:

$$TSA(\mathbf{x}_{t-1}, \mathbf{x}_t) = \Big(\mathcal{C}(\mathbf{x}_t - \mathbf{x}_{t-1}) \otimes \mathbf{x}_t\Big) \oplus \mathbf{x}_t \qquad (2)$$

Where, $\mathcal{C}$ represents a convolution layer that takes the difference between current frame $\mathbf{x}_t$ and previous frame $\mathbf{x}_{t-1}$, $\otimes$ and $\oplus$ are the Hadamard product and element-wise addition respectively. The residual connections augment the output of the convolution and focus on certain area in the context of the current frame.

Feature Processing Network (FPN): We forward the output of the TSA network to the FPN layers to process the TSA features further. We design FPN with two sets of Conv, Batch Normalization, ReLU, and Avg-pooling layers. In FPN block, all the convolution layer and average pooling layer use 3×3 kernel size and 2×2 kernel size respectively. FPN learns a dense spatial feature representation of frames required to model the complex interplay of smile dynamics. During the experiment, we replace this FPN with popular ResNet18 and DenseNet like structure. However, we have achieved the best performance using our proposed implementation of an FPN. Besides, our FPN has less trainable parameters than its alternatives. In our model, TSA and FPN contribute together to get overall spatial information from frames. This representation plays the role of D-marker [2,4,15], HoG [5,9,16], LBP [5,16] of the traditional approach. The main difference is our model learns this representation, unlike conventional methods dependent on handcrafted and computationally intensive features.

ConvLSTM: We employ the ConvLSTM [18] to model the temporal dynamics of the video. We adaptively build up a saliency temporal representation of each video that contributes to the classification processes. Specifically, we concurrently learn the hidden states and input tensors by using convolution layers instead of maintaining different weight matrixes for the hidden state and input. We visualize the state transition in Fig. 3 that performs the following operations: *input vector,* $\mathbf{u}_t = concatenate(\mathbf{e}_t, \mathbf{h}_{t-1})$, *input gate,* $\mathbf{i}_t = \sigma\left(\mathbf{W}_i \circledast \mathbf{u}_t \oplus \mathbf{b}_i\right)$, *forget gate,* $\mathbf{f}_t = \sigma\left(\mathbf{W}_f \circledast \mathbf{u}_t \oplus \mathbf{b}_f\right)$, *output gate,* $\mathbf{o}_t = \sigma\left(\mathbf{W}_o \circledast \mathbf{u}_t \oplus \mathbf{b}_o\right)$, *cell gate,* $\mathbf{g}_t = \tanh\left(\mathbf{W}_g \circledast \mathbf{u}_t \oplus \mathbf{b}_g\right)$, *cell state,* $\mathbf{c}_t = \mathbf{f}_t \otimes \mathbf{c}_{t-1} \oplus \mathbf{i}_t \otimes \mathbf{g}_t$, *hidden state,* $\mathbf{h}_t = \mathbf{o}_t \otimes \tanh\left(\mathbf{c}_t\right)$, where, σ and tanh are the activation function of the sigmoid and hyperbolic tangent. $\circledast$, $\otimes$ and $\oplus$ represent convolution operator, Hadamard product, and element-wise addition. *concatenate* operator stands for concatenating the augments along the channel axis. $[\cdot]_t$ and $\mathbf{W}_{[\cdot]}$ denote the element at time slot t and the corresponding weight matrix respectively. Usually, ConvLSTM updates the input gate, forget gate, cell gate, and output gate by element-wise operations [18]. But, in our case, we learn more complex temporal characteristics by concatenating the input and hidden state as the input of the convolution layer. As nearby pixels of an image are both connected and correlated, using more complex flows within the ConvLSTM cell, the convolution layer can group the local features to generate robust temporal features while preserving more spatial information.

Classification Block: The hidden state of the last frame is passed to the classification block to assign a prediction label. This block is composed of dot product NonLocal block [28], average pooling (2×2 kernel size), convolution layer(with 2×2 kernel size), batch normalization, ReLU, Dropout (with 0.5 probability), and dense layers. The NonLocal block captures the dependency between any two positions [28]. Such reliance is critical because Ekman *et al.* [8] suggested the relative position of facial landmarks (such as symmetry) contributes to the smile classification. Then, we further trim the learned embedding of the video feature through the later layers of the classification block. In this way, the classification space is well-separated for binary classification (see Fig. 5).

Loss Function: Given a video as an input, $\overrightarrow{X}_i$, our proposed network predicts a score, $\mathcal{F}_\theta(\overrightarrow{X}_i)$, which is compared with the ground-truth y_i to calculate the weighted binary cross-entropy loss:

$$\mathcal{L}_{CE} = -\frac{1}{T}\sum_{i=1}^{T}\left[\alpha\, y_i \log\left(\mathcal{F}_\theta(\overrightarrow{X}_i)\right) + \beta\left(1 - y_i\right)\log\left(1 - \mathcal{F}_\theta(\overrightarrow{X}_i)\right)\right], \quad (3)$$

where, α and β are the weights computed as the proportion of spontaneous and posed videos in the training dataset respectively.

Inference: For jth test video, $\overrightarrow{V}_j$, we perform a simple forward pass through the trained network and produce a prediction score, $\mathcal{F}_\theta(\overrightarrow{V}_j)$. Then, we apply Eq. 1 to assign the predicted label, $\hat{y}_j$ for the input.

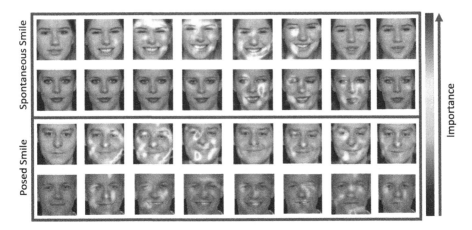

Fig. 4. Visualization of FPN features for spontaneous (top two rows) and posed (bottom two rows) smiles from UVA-NEMO [2] by using score-cam [29, 30]. Keeping equal temporal distance from each other, sample frames are selected for this visualization. The more 'warm' the color, the more important the area becomes during classification.

3.3 Analysis

We analyze and visualize different aspects of our model, which allows us to address many drawbacks of the traditional approaches.

Our model automatically learns discriminative smile features that replace traditional handcrafted features. This learning process does not require manual landmark initialization and their tracking through the video. Our ConvLSTM block enables us to track the learned features automatically until the last frame. The iterative learning process of ConvLSTM does not have any restriction on the maximum length of smile videos, unlike traditional methods requiring maximum fixed video length. Our ConvLSTM block effectively manages the temporal aspect of features in the time dimension, which performs the role of face landmark tracking of other methods. Our classification block, coupled with the ConvLSTM leans to classify time series data. But, using the SVM like classifiers, which are commonly used in the area, are not an excellent fit to classify similar data. Therefore, traditional models perform hand-engineering to make the data fit for SVM. Instead, in our model, every component of traditional methods are embedded in the unified deep network. Thus, once learned, our model handles the intermediate process through a forward pass as a single unit. Such a strategy simplifies the process because that parallel implementation is easy for a deep learning model.

Visualization: In Fig. 4, we visualize the importance of different facial regions across various frames. We extract features (after FPN layers) and blend them on the input frame. This shows that our model extracts features where it finds discriminative information. One can notice that our model puts less emphasis on

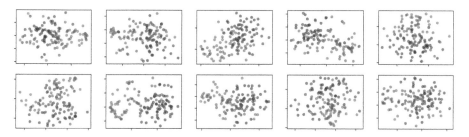

Fig. 5. 2D tSNE [31] visualization of smile video features extracted from the classification block (after ReLU layer) of our proposed model. Blue and Green represent posed and spontaneous smiles respectively. Each plot shows the test fold features from the 10-fold cross-validations data of UvA-NEMO database. Here, spontaneous and posed smiles are reasonably well-separated to recognize using the classification block. (Color figure online)

neutral faces (by assigning cooler color on the heatmap) because those frames have no role in the context of spontaneous or posed smile recognition. Moreover, the starting and ending frames (roughly, onset and offset regions) are promising to be the most discriminative for posed smiles, whereas middle frames (apex regions) are important for spontaneous smiles. To further visualize the feature embedding, we plot learned video features (from the output of ReLU layer of classification block (please see Fig. 2)) of the test fold belonging to the UvA-NEMO dataset in Fig. 5. We notice that spontaneous and posed smile features are properly separated for classification.

4 Experiment

4.1 Setup

Dataset: In this paper, we experiment on four popular smile datasets: Here, we briefly describe the data statistics. **(a) UVA-NEMO Smile Database** [2]: This dataset is recorded in 1920×1080 pixels at a rate of 50 frames per second. It composed of 597 spontaneous and 643 posed smile videos. The length of videos distributed from 1.8 s to 14.2 s. It contains over 400 participants (185 females and 215 males) with ages from 8 years to 76 years. There are 149 young people and 251 adults. **(b) BBC database**[1] [2,5] This dataset contains 20 videos, recorded in 314×286 pixels with 25 frames per second. There are 10 spontaneous and 10 posed smiles. **(c) MMI Facial Expression Database** [32]: They provided spontaneous and posed facial expressions separately including 38 labeled posed smiles. Apart from these posed smiles, we identified 138 spontaneous and 49 posed smile videos from 9 and 25 participants, respectively. The age of participants ranges from 19 to 64. All of the videos contain frontal recordings. The part of the spontaneous smile is in 640×480 pixels at 29 frames per second, and the posed smile part is recorded in 720×576 pixels with 25 frames per second.

---

[1] https://www.bbc.co.uk/science/humanbody/mind/surveys/smiles/.

Table 1. Summary of the smile datasets.

Database	Video spec.		Number of videos		Number of subjects	
	Resolution	FPS	Genuine	Posed	Genuine	Posed
UVA-NEMO	1920 × 1080	50	597	643	357	368
BBC	314 × 286	25	10	10	10	10
MMI	720 × 576	29	138	49	9	25
	640 × 480	25				
SPOS	640 × 480	25	66	14	7	7

(d) SPOS database [9]: It provides both gray and near-infrared sequences of images in 640 × 480 resolution with 25 frames per second. We use gray images in our experiments. The face region of each image has been cropped by the database owners. There are 66 spontaneous smiles, and 14 posed smiles from 7 participants. The age of participants distributed from 22 to 31, while 3 of them are male. Table 1 provides a summary of these datasets.

Train/Test Split: We use the standard train/test split protocol from [2] for UVA-NEMO database. Following the settings from [2,5], we perform 10-fold, 7-fold, and 9-fold cross-validation for BBC, SPOS, and MMI datasets, respectively, while maintains no subject overlap between training and testing folds.

Evaluation Processes: We have evaluated our model with prediction accuracy. The accuracy is the proportion of test data that is correctly predicted by our model. We report the average result of running ten trials.

Implementation Details[2]: We train our model for 60 epoch with the mini-batch size 16. To optimize network parameters, we use Adam optimizer with a learning rate 10^{-3} and decay 0.005. We employ weighted binary cross-entropy loss for training where the weight is the ratio between spontaneous smiles and posed smiles in training data. To prepare the video to be manageable for the network, we sample 5 frames per second, crop the face using DLIB library [33] and resize each frame into the dimension 48 × 48, which are purely automatic processes. We validate the sensitivity of these design choices in experiments. We implement our method using the *PyTorch* library [34].

4.2   Recognition Performance

In this subsection, we will compare our performance with other models, will show an ablation study, will design choice sensitivity, and will analyze the robustness of our approach.

---

[2] Code and evaluation protocols available at: https://github.com/Yan98/Deep-learning-for-genuine-and-posed-smile-classification.

Table 2. Benchmark comparison of methods. '-' means unavailable result.

Method	Process type	UVA-NEMO	MMI	SPOS	BBC
Cohn'04 [7]	Semi-automatic	77.3	81.0	73.0	75.0
Dibeklioglu'10 [6]	Semi-automatic	71.1	74.0	68.0	85.0
Pfister'11[9]	Semi-automatic	73.1	81.0	67.5	70.0
Wu'14 [5]	Semi-automatic	**91.4**	-	79.5	**90.0**
Dibeklioglu'15 [2]	Semi-automatic	89.8	88.1	77.5	**90.0**
Mandal'17 [4]	Semi-automatic	80.4	-	-	-
Mandal'16 [16]	Fully-Automatic	78.1	-	-	-
Ours	Fully-Automatic	82.1	**92.0**	**86.2**	**90.0**

Benchmark Comparisons: In Table 2, we compare our performance of spontaneous and posed smile classification with previously published approaches using four popular datasets. We divide all methods into two categories: semi-automatic and fully-automatic. Semi-automatic methods manually annotate facial landmark locations of the first frame of the video. In contrast, fully-automatic methods require no manual intervention in the complete process. Our model successfully beats all methods in MMI, SPOS, and BBC datasets. For UVA-NEMO, we outperform the automatic method [16]. However, Wu *et al.* reported the best performance on the UVA-NEMO dataset [5]. For all these experiments, the same video and subjects are used during testing. But, being not end-to-end, previous methods apply many pre-processing steps (borrowed from different work) that are not consistent across methods. For example, the performance of [2,6,7,9] are adopted from the work [2] where same landmark initialization tracker [35], face normalization, etc. are used. However, the accuracy of [5] and [4] are reported from the original papers where they employed a different manual initialization and tracker [36,37]. Moreover, the number and position of landmarks used are also different across models. Because of these variations, performance of the semi-automatic methods are difficult to compare in a common framework. The automatic method [16] is our closest competitor because of the lack of requirement of landmark initialization or tracker and their best result can be gained in a fully automatic way. However, their feature extraction and learning model are still separated. Besides, to manage the variable length of video frames, they apply a frame normalization process (using fixed number of coefficients of Discrete Cosine Transform) to create fixed length videos. Our proposed model is fully-automated and end-to-end trainable as a single deep learning model. It requires no landmark detection, tracking, frame normalization to a fixed-length, etc.

Design Choice Sensitivity: In Fig. 6, we report the sensitivity of the design choice of our method for different numbers of frames per second (FPS) and resolutions of the input frames. For all combination of FPS (1, 3, 5 and 7) and resolution ($48 \times 48, 64 \times 64, 96 \times 96$ and 112×112) choices, we find FPS = 5

Table 3. Ablation study. We experiment adding or removing parts of proposed method with reasonable alternatives.

Method	UVA-NEMO	MMI	SPOS	BBC
No TSA	78.5	92.0	81.5	80.0
miniResNet	73.8	84.9	80.5	90.0
miniDenseNet	77.0	71.2	82.2	90.0
No Weighted Loss	80.6	91.7	82.2	90.0
Softmax Function	79.2	71.6	82.2	70.0
Ours	**82.1**	**92.0**	**86.2**	**90.0**

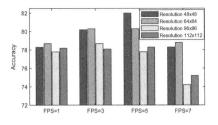

Fig. 6. Varying image size and FPS on UVA-NEMO dataset.

and resolution = 48 × 48 achieves the maximum performance. Note that image resolution is important because it decides the type of visual features extracted by the CNN layers. For example, a low resolution (48 × 48) lets the CNN kernels (of size 3 × 3) extracts coarse features that are the most discriminative for smile classification. Similarly, the choice of FPS also interacts with ConvLSTM layers to track the change of smile features across frames. The FPS = 5 and resolution = 48 × 48 is the trade-off to maximize the performance.

Ablation Studies: In Table 3, we perform ablation studies by replacing part of our proposed network with a suitable alternative. Our observations from the ablation studies are the following. (*1*) We remove the TSA block from our model and directly forward the frame to FPN for feature extraction. In this situation, the network could not get optical flow information and motion from the spatio-temporal region. Smile features based on the difference of consecutive frames extract more discriminative features than a single frame. Thus, without using the TSA block, the performance degrades, especially on UVA-NEMO and SPOS datasets. (*2*) Now, we experiment on the alternative implementation of the FPN network, for example, ResNet12 [38] (composed by 3 layers) or DenseNet [39] (with growth rate 2 and 6,12, 24 and 16 blocks in each layer). We use a relatively small version of that well-known architecture because smile datasets do not contain enough instances (in comparison to large scale ImageNet dataset [40]) to train large networks. Alternative FPNs could not outperform our proposed FPN implementation. One reason could be that the smaller version of those popular architectures is still larger than our proposed FPN, and available smile data overfits the networks. Another reason is that, we could not use pre-trained weights for the alternatives, because of different input resolutions. (*3*) We try without the weighting version of the loss of Eq. 3, i.e, $\alpha = \beta = 1$. This impacts the performance of UVA-NEMO, MMI, and SPOS dataset because of the large imbalance in number of training samples of spontaneous and posed smiles. (*4*) We replace the dense sigmoid at the last layer of the classification block with softmax. In our sigmoid based implementation, we use one neuron at the last layer to predict a score within $[0, 1]$ and apply Eq. 1 for inference. For the softmax case, we add two neurons at the last layer, which increases the number of trainable parameters. We notice that the softmax based network does not perform better than our proposed sigmoid based case. This observation is in line with the recommendation of [41] that Softmax is better for the multi-class problem rather than a binary class case. (*5*) The performance of our final model outperforms all ablation alternatives consistently across datasets.

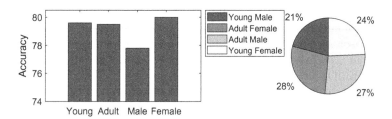

Fig. 7. *(left)* The accuracy of the model trained by individual group. *(right)* The normalized distribution of the total number of wrong predictions among different subject groups.

Effect of Age and Genders: To illustrate our approach's robustness, we analyze the effect of model prediction for the different subject groups concerning age and gender. Firstly, we experiment on whether biologically similar appearance inserts any bias in the prediction. For this, we train and test our proposed model with only male/female/adult/young separately. In Fig. 7(*left*), we show the results on each subgroup: male, female, adult, and young. We notice that the performance is similar to our overall performance reported in Table 2. This shows that our training has no bias on age- and gender-based subgroups. Secondly, in Fig. 7 *(right)*, we visualize the normalized distribution of the total number of wrong predictions among adults/young and males/females. We find that there is no significant bias in misprediction distribution. In other words, as the mispredictions are similar across different groups, our model does not favor any particular group.

Cross-Domain Experiments: We also perform experiments across datasets and subject groups. While training with UVA-NEMO and testing with BBC, MMI, and SPOS dataset, we get 80%, 92.5% & 82.5% accuracy, respectively. Moreover, training with adults and testing with young subjects got 75.9%, and conversely 74.8% accuracy. Again, training on female then testing on male subjects got 74.2% and conversely 75.1% accuracy. These experiments indicate the robustness of our method.

4.3   Discussion

Time Complexity: The processes of facial landmarks tracking/detection followed by handcrafted feature extraction are usually very computationally expensive. As evidence, when we re-implement D-marker feature-based approaches with DLIB library [33] to face normalization and facial landmark detection, it requires more than 28 h for the processes using a single NVIDIA V100 GPU and one Intel Xeon Cascade Lake Platinum 8268 (2.90 GHz) CPU. Although the training is efficient and effective, the pre-processing pipelines are costly. However, for our end-to-end learning models, the whole processing only spends up to eight hours using the same system configuration, which significantly saves time.

Human Response vs. Our Model: Several recent works estimate the ability of the average human to recognize spontaneous smiles [11,12]. In Fig. 8, we show the comparison of our work with human responses using the experiment set-up mentioned in [11]. In an experiment with 26 human and 20 videos selected from the UVA-NEMO dataset, Hossain *et al.* [11] reported a 59% average accuracy of the human. In this set-up, our trained *RealSmileNet* (without using any of those 20 videos and their subjects during training) successfully achieves 95% of accuracy on the same test set. In another experiment with 36 humans and 30 videos from the same UVA-NEMO dataset, Hossain *et al.* [11] reported 70% for humans, whereas our proposed model achieves 90% accuracy. These comparisons show that our end-to-end model is already capable of beating human-level performance.

Limitations: One notable drawback of deep learning-based solutions is the dependence on large-scale balanced data. Being a deep model, our proposed model has also experienced this issue during training with UVA-NEMO dataset, which includes smiles of subjects with a wide range of ages, e.g., child (0–10 years), young (11–18 years), adult (19–69 years), aged people ($\geq$70 years). However, among the 1,240 videos, the distributions are

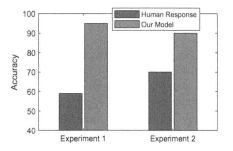

Fig. 8. Human response vs. our model

20.24%, 18.47%, 60.16%, and 1.45% respectively. The imbalanced/skewed distribution usually cannot be well modeled in the deep models [42], and can lead to unexpected bias in the kernel of the convolution layer. Here, our model performs less well than the semi-automatic method of Wu *et al.* [5] (See Table 2). In future, one can collect more data to handle such shortcomings.

5   Conclusion

Traditional approaches for recognizing spontaneous and posed smiles depend on expert feature engineering, manual labeling, and numerous costly pre-processing steps. In this paper, we introduce a deep learning model, *RealSmileNet*, to unify the broken-up pieces of intermediate steps into a single, end-to-end model. Given a smile video as input, our model can generate an output prediction by a simple forward pass through the network. Our proposed model is not only fast but also removes the expert intervention (hand engineering) in the learning process. Experimenting with four large scale smile datasets, we establish state-of-the-art performances on three datasets. Our experiment previews the applicability of *RealSmileNet* to many real-word applications like polygraphy, human-robot interactions, investigation assistance, and so on.

Acknowledgment. This research was supported by the National Computational Infrastructure (NCI), Canberra, Australia.

References

1. Li, S., Deng, W.: Deep facial expression recognition: a survey. IEEE Trans. Affect. Comput. (2020)
2. Dibeklioglu, H., Salah, A., Gevers, T.: Recognition of genuine smiles. IEEE Trans. Multimed. **17**, 279–294 (2015)
3. Frank, M., Ekman, P.: Not all smiles are created equal: the differences between enjoyment and nonenjoyment smiles. Humor-Int. J. Humor Res. - HUMOR **6**, 9–26 (1993)
4. Mandal, B., Ouarti, N.: Spontaneous vs. posed smiles - can we tell the difference? In: International Conference on Computer Vision and Image Processing, vol. 460 (2017)
5. Wu, P., Liu, H., Zhang, X.: Spontaneous versus posed smile recognition using discriminative local spatial-temporal descriptors. In: IEEE International Conference on Acoustics, Speech and Signal Processing, ICASSP 2014, Florence, Italy, 4–9 May 2014, pp. 1240–1244. IEEE (2014)
6. Dibeklioglu, H., Valenti, R., Salah, A.A., Gevers, T.: Eyes do not lie: spontaneous versus posed smiles. In: Bimbo, A.D., Chang, S., Smeulders, A.W.M. (eds.) Proceedings of the 18th International Conference on Multimedia 2010, Firenze, Italy, 25–29 October 2010, pp. 703–706. ACM (2010)
7. Cohn, J.F., Schmidt, K.L.: The timing of facial motion in posed and spontaneous smiles. Int. J. Wavelets Multiresolut. Inf. Process. **02** (2004)
8. Ekman, P., Hager, J., Friesen, W.: The symmetry of emotional and deliberate facial actions. Psychophysiology **18**, 101–106 (1981)
9. Pfister, T., Li, X., Zhao, G., Pietikäinen, M.: Differentiating spontaneous from posed facial expressions within a generic facial expression recognition framework. In: IEEE International Conference on Computer Vision Workshops, ICCV 2011 Workshops, Barcelona, Spain, 6–13 November 2011, pp. 868–875. IEEE Computer Society (2011)
10. Hossain, M.Z., Gedeon, T.D.: An independent approach to training classifiers on physiological data: an example using smiles. In: Cheng, L., Leung, A.C.S., Ozawa, S. (eds.) ICONIP 2018. LNCS, vol. 11302, pp. 603–613. Springer, Cham (2018). https://doi.org/10.1007/978-3-030-04179-3_53
11. Hossain, M.Z., Gedeon, T., Sankaranarayana, R.: Using temporal features of observers' physiological measures to distinguish between genuine and fake smiles. IEEE Trans. Affect. Comput. **11**, 163–173 (2020)
12. Hossain, M.Z., Gedeon, T.: Discriminating real and posed smiles: human and avatar smiles. In: Brereton, M., Soro, A., Vyas, D., Ploderer, B., Morrison, A., Waycott, J. (eds.) Proceedings of the 29th Australian Conference on Computer-Human Interaction, OZCHI 2017, Brisbane, QLD, Australia, 28 November–01 December 2017, pp. 581–586. ACM (2017)
13. Hossain, M.Z., Gedeon, T.: Observers' physiological measures in response to videos can be used to detect genuine smiles. Int. J. Hum. Comput. Stud. **122**, 232–241 (2019)

14. Gao, R., Islam, A., Gedeon, T., Hossain, M.Z.: Identifying real and posed smiles from observers' galvanic skin response and blood volume pulse. In: Yang, H., Pasupa, K., Leung, A.C.-S., Kwok, J.T., Chan, J.H., King, I. (eds.) ICONIP 2020. LNCS, vol. 12532, pp. 375–386. Springer, Cham (2020). https://doi.org/10.1007/978-3-030-63830-6_32

15. Schmidt, K., Bhattacharya, S., Denlinger, R.: Comparison of deliberate and spontaneous facial movement in smiles and eyebrow raises. J. Nonverbal Behav. **33**, 35–45 (2009)

16. Mandal, B., Lee, D., Ouarti, N.: Distinguishing posed and spontaneous smiles by facial dynamics. In: Chen, C.-S., Lu, J., Ma, K.-K. (eds.) ACCV 2016. LNCS, vol. 10116, pp. 552–566. Springer, Cham (2017). https://doi.org/10.1007/978-3-319-54407-6_37

17. Duchenne, B.: The Mechanism of Human Facial Expression. Cambridge University Press, Cambridge (1990)

18. Shi, X., Chen, Z., Wang, H., Yeung, D., Wong, W., Woo, W.: Convolutional LSTM network: a machine learning approach for precipitation nowcasting. In: Cortes, C., Lawrence, N.D., Lee, D.D., Sugiyama, M., Garnett, R. (eds.) Advances in Neural Information Processing Systems 28: Annual Conference on Neural Information Processing Systems 2015, Montreal, Quebec, Canada, 7–12 December 2015, pp. 802–810 (2015)

19. Littlewort, G., Frank, M., Lainscsek, C., Fasel, I., Movellan, J.: Automatic recognition of facial actions in spontaneous expressions. J. Multimed. **1** (2006)

20. Valstar, M.F., Pantic, M., Ambadar, Z., Cohn, J.F.: Spontaneous vs. posed facial behavior: automatic analysis of brow actions. In: Quek, F.K.H., Yang, J., Massaro, D.W., Alwan, A.A., Hazen, T.J. (eds.) Proceedings of the 8th International Conference on Multimodal Interfaces, ICMI 2006, Banff, Alberta, Canada, 2–4 November 2006, pp. 162–170. ACM (2006)

21. Zheng, L., Yang, Y., Hauptmann, A.G.: Person re-identification: past, present and future. CoRR abs/1610.02984 (2016)

22. Rahman, S., Khan, S.H., Porikli, F.: Zero-shot object detection: joint recognition and localization of novel concepts. Int. J. Comput. Vis. **128**, 2979–2999 (2020)

23. Rahman, S., Khan, S., Barnes, N., Khan, F.S.: Any-shot object detection. arXiv preprint arXiv:2003.07003 (2020)

24. Rochan, M., Rahman, S., Bruce, N.D.B., Wang, Y.: Weakly supervised object localization and segmentation in videos. Image Vis. Comput. **56**, 1–12 (2016)

25. Yang, H., Shi, J., Carlone, L.: TEASER: fast and certifiable point cloud registration. CoRR abs/2001.07715 (2020)

26. Parkhi, O.M., Vedaldi, A., Zisserman, A.: Deep face recognition. In: Xie, X., Jones, M.W., Tam, G.K.L. (eds.) Proceedings of the British Machine Vision Conference 2015, BMVC 2015, Swansea, UK, 7–10 September 2015, pp. 41.1–41.12. BMVA Press (2015)

27. Simonyan, K., Zisserman, A.: Two-stream convolutional networks for action recognition in videos. In: Proceedings of the 27th International Conference on Neural Information Processing Systems, NIPS 2014, vol. 1, pp. 568–576. MIT Press, Cambridge (2014)

28. Wang, X., Girshick, R.B., Gupta, A., He, K.: Non-local neural networks. In: 2018 IEEE Conference on Computer Vision and Pattern Recognition, CVPR 2018, Salt Lake City, UT, USA, 18–22 June 2018, pp. 7794–7803. IEEE Computer Society (2018)

29. Wang, H., et al.: Score-cam: score-weighted visual explanations for convolutional neural networks. CoRR (2019)

30. Ozbulak, U.: Pytorch CNN visualizations (2019). https://github.com/utkuozbul ak/pytorch-cnn-visualizations
31. Rauber, P.E., Falcão, A.X., Telea, A.C.: Visualizing time-dependent data using dynamic T-SNE. In: Bertini, E., Elmqvist, N., Wischgoll, T. (eds.) Eurographics Conference on Visualization, EuroVis 2016, Short Papers, Groningen, The Netherlands, 6–10 June 2016, pp. 73–77. Eurographics Association (2016)
32. Valstar, M., Pantic, M.: Induced disgust, happiness and surprise: an addition to the mmi facial expression database. In: Proceedings of the International Conference on Language Resources and Evaluation, Workshop EMOTION, pp. 65–70 (2010)
33. King, D.E.: DLIB-ML: a machine learning toolkit. J. Mach. Learn. Res. **10**, 1755–1758 (2009)
34. Paszke, A., et al.: Pytorch: an imperative style, high-performance deep learning library. In: Wallach, H.M., Larochelle, H., Beygelzimer, A., d'Alché-Buc, F., Fox, E.B., Garnett, R. (eds.) Advances in Neural Information Processing Systems 32: Annual Conference on Neural Information Processing Systems 2019, NeurIPS 2019, Vancouver, BC, Canada, 8–14 December 2019, pp. 8024–8035 (2019)
35. Tao, H., Huang, T.S.: Explanation-based facial motion tracking using a piecewise bézier volume deformation model. In: 1999 Conference on Computer Vision and Pattern Recognition (CVPR 1999), Ft. Collins, CO, USA, 23–25 June 1999, pp. 1611–1617. IEEE Computer Society (1999)
36. Nguyen, T.D., Ranganath, S.: Tracking facial features under occlusions and recognizing facial expressions in sign language. In: 8th IEEE International Conference on Automatic Face and Gesture Recognition (FG 2008), Amsterdam, The Netherlands, 17–19 September 2008, pp. 1–7. IEEE Computer Society (2008)
37. Tomasi, C., Kanade, T.: Detection and tracking of point features. Technical report, Carnegie Mellon University, Technical Report CMU-CS-91-132 (1991)
38. He, K., Zhang, X., Ren, S., Sun, J.: Deep residual learning for image recognition. In: 2016 IEEE Conference on Computer Vision and Pattern Recognition, CVPR 2016, Las Vegas, NV, USA, 27–30 June 2016, pp. 770–778. IEEE Computer Society (2016)
39. Huang, G., Liu, Z., van der Maaten, L., Weinberger, K.Q.: Densely connected convolutional networks. In: 2017 IEEE Conference on Computer Vision and Pattern Recognition, CVPR 2017, Honolulu, HI, USA, 21–26 July 2017, pp. 2261–2269. IEEE Computer Society (2017)
40. Russakovsky, O., et al.: ImageNet large scale visual recognition challenge. Int. J. Comput. Vis. **115**(3), 211–252 (2015). https://doi.org/10.1007/s11263-015-0816-y
41. Nwankpa, C., Ijomah, W., Gachagan, A., Marshall, S.: Activation functions: comparison of trends in practice and research for deep learning. CoRR abs/1811.03378 (2018)
42. Vandal, T., Kodra, E., Dy, J.G., Ganguly, S., Nemani, R.R., Ganguly, A.R.: Quantifying uncertainty in discrete-continuous and skewed data with Bayesian deep learning. In: Guo, Y., Farooq, F. (eds.) Proceedings of the 24th ACM SIGKDD International Conference on Knowledge Discovery & Data Mining, KDD 2018, London, UK, 19–23 August 2018, pp. 2377–2386. ACM (2018)

Decoupled Spatial-Temporal Attention Network for Skeleton-Based Action-Gesture Recognition

Lei Shi[1,2(✉)], Yifan Zhang[1,2], Jian Cheng[1,2,3], and Hanqing Lu[1,2]

[1] NLPR & AIRIA, Institute of Automation, Chinese Academy of Sciences,
Beijing, China
{lei.shi,yfzhang,jcheng,luhq}@nlpr.ia.ac.cn
[2] School of Artificial Intelligence, University of Chinese Academy of Sciences,
Beijing 100049, China
[3] CAS Center for Excellence in Brain Science and Intelligence Technology,
Beijing, China

Abstract. Dynamic skeletal data, represented as the 2D/3D coordinates of human joints, has been widely studied for human action recognition due to its high-level semantic information and environmental robustness. However, previous methods heavily rely on designing hand-crafted traversal rules or graph topologies to draw dependencies between the joints, which are limited in performance and generalizability. In this work, we present a novel decoupled spatial-temporal attention network (DSTA-Net) for skeleton-based action recognition. It involves solely the attention blocks, allowing for modeling spatial-temporal dependencies between joints without the requirement of knowing their positions or mutual connections. Specifically, to meet the specific requirements of the skeletal data, three techniques are proposed for building attention blocks, namely, spatial-temporal attention decoupling, decoupled position encoding and spatial global regularization. Besides, from the data aspect, we introduce a skeletal data decoupling technique to emphasize the specific characteristics of space/time and different motion scales, resulting in a more comprehensive understanding of the human actions. To test the effectiveness of the proposed method, extensive experiments are conducted on four challenging datasets for skeleton-based gesture and action recognition, namely, SHREC, DHG, NTU-60 and NTU-120, where DSTA-Net achieves state-of-the-art performance on all of them.

1 Introduction

Human action recognition has been studied for decades since it can be widely used for many applications such as human-computer interaction and abnormal

Electronic supplementary material The online version of this chapter (https://doi.org/10.1007/978-3-030-69541-5_3) contains supplementary material, which is available to authorized users.

H. Ishikawa et al. (Eds.): ACCV 2020, LNCS 12626, pp. 38–53, 2021.
https://doi.org/10.1007/978-3-030-69541-5_3

behavior monitoring [1–4]. Recently, skeletal data draws increasingly more attention because it contains higher-level semantic information in a small amount of data and has strong adaptability to the dynamic circumstance [5–7].

The raw skeletal data is a sequence of frames each contains a set of points. Each point represents a joint of human body in the form of 2D/3D coordinates. Previous data-driven methods for skeleton-based action recognition rely on manual designs of traversal rules or graph topologies to transform the raw skeletal data into a meaningful form such as a point-sequence, a pseudo-image or a graph, so that they can be fed into the deep networks such as RNNs, CNNs and GCNs for feature extraction [5,8,9]. However, there is no guarantee that the hand-crafted rule is the optimal choice of modeling global dependencies of joints, which limits the performance and generalizability of previous approaches. Recently, transformer [10,11] has achieved big success in the NLP field, whose basic block is the self-attention mechanism. It can learn the global dependencies between the input elements with less computational complexity and better parallelizability. For skeletal data, employing the self-attention mechanism has an additional advantage that there is no requirement of knowing a intrinsic relations between the elements, thus it provides more flexibility for discovering useful patterns. Besides, since the number of joints of the human body is limited, the extra cost of applying self-attention mechanism is also relatively small.

Inspired by above observations, we propose a novel decoupled spatial-temporal attention networks (DSTA-Net) for skeleton-based action recognition. It is based solely on the self-attention mechanism, without using the structure-relevant RNNs, CNNs or GCNs. However, it is not straightforward to apply a pure attention network for skeletal data as shown in following three aspects: (1) The input of original self-attention mechanism is the sequential data, while the skeletal data exists in both the spatial and temporal dimensions. A naive method is simply flattening the spatial-temporal data into a single sequence like [12]. However, it is not reasonable to treat the time and space equivalently because they contain totally different semantics [3]. Besides, simple flattening operation increases the sequence length, which greatly increases the computation cost due to the dot-product operation of the self-attention mechanism. Instead, we propose to decouple the self-attention mechanism into the spatial attention and the temporal attention sequentially. Three strategies are specially designed to balance the independence and the interaction between the space and the time. (2) There are no predefined orders or structures when feeding the skeletal joints into the attention networks. To provide unique markers for every joint, a position encoding technique is introduced. For the same reason as before, it is also decoupled into the spatial encoding and the temporal encoding. (3) It has been verified that adding proper regularization based on prior knowledge can effectively reduce the over-fitting problem and improve the model generalizability. For example, due to the translation-invariant structure of images, CNNs exploit the local-weight-sharing mechanism to force the model to learn more general filters for different regions of images. As for skeletal data, each joint of the skeletons has specific physical/semantic meaning (e.g., head or hand), which is fixed for all the frames and is consistent for all the data samples. Based on this prior knowledge, a spatial global regularization is proposed to force the model to learn more general attentions for different samples. Note the regularization is not suitable for temporal dimension because there is no such semantic alignment property.

Besides, from the data aspect, the most discriminative pattern is distinct for different actions. We claim that two properties should be considered. One property is whether the action is motion relevant or motion irrelevant, which aims to choose the specific characters of space and time. For example, to classify the gestures of "waving up" versus "waving down", the global trajectories of hand is more important than hand shape, but when recognizing the gestures like "point with one finger" versus "point with two finger", the spatial pattern is more important than hand motion. Based on this observation, we propose to decouple the data into the spatial and temporal dimensions, where the spatial stream contains only the motion-irrelevant features and temporal stream contains only the motion-relevant features. By modeling these two streams separately, the model can better focus on spatial/temporal features and identity specific patterns. Finally, by fusing the two streams, it can obtain a more comprehensive understanding of the human actions. Another property is the sensibility of the motion scales. For temporal stream, the classification of some actions may rely on the motion mode of a few consecutive frames while others may rely on the overall movement trend. For example, to classify the gestures of "clapping" versus "put two hands together", the short-term motion detail is essential. But for "waving up" versus "waving down", the long-term motion trend is more important. Thus, inspired by [3], we split the temporal information into a fast stream and a slow stream based on the sampling rate. The low-frame-rate stream can capture more about global motion information and the high-frame-rate stream can focus more on the detailed movements. Similarly, the two streams are fused to improve the recognition performance.

We conduct extensive experiments on four datasets, including two hand gesture recognition datasets, i.e., SHREC and DHG, and two human action recognition datasets, i.e., NTU-60 and NTU-120. Without the need of hand-crafted traversal rules or graph topologies, our method achieves state-of-the-art performance on all these datasets, which demonstrates the effectiveness and generalizability of the proposed method.

Overall, our contributions lie in four aspects: (1) To the best of our knowledge, we are the first to propose a decoupled spatial-temporal attention networks (DSTA-Net) for skeleton-based action recognition, which is built with pure attention modules without manual designs of traversal rules or graph topologies. (2) We propose three effective techniques in building attention networks to meet the specific requirements for skeletal data, namely, spatial-temporal attention decoupling, decoupled position encoding and spatial global regularization. (3) We propose to decouple the data into four streams, namely, spatial-temporal stream, spatial stream, slow-temporal stream and fast-temporal stream, each focuses on a specific aspect of the skeleton sequence. By fusing different types of features, the model can have a more comprehensive understanding for human actions.

(4) On four challenging datasets for action recognition, our method achieves state-of-the-art performance with a significant margin. DSTA-Net outperforms SOTA 2.6%/3.2% and 1.9%/2.9% on 14-class/28-class benchmarks of SHREC and DHG, respectively. It achieves 91.5%/96.4% and 86.6%/89.0% on CS/CV benchmarks of NTU-60 and NTU-120, respectively. The code is released[1].

2   Related Work

Skeleton-based action recognition has been widely studied for decades. The main-stream methods lie in three branches: (1) the RNN-based methods that formulate the skeletal data as a sequential data with a predefined traversal rules, and feed it into the RNN-based models such as the LSTM [9,13–15]; (2) We propose three effective techniques in building attention networks to meet the specific requirements for skeletal data, namely, spatial-temporal attention decoupling, decoupled position encoding and spatial global regularization. (3) the GCN-based methods that encode the skeletal data into a predefined spatial-temporal graph, and model it with the graph convolutional networks [5,6,16]. In this work, instead of formulating the skeletal data into the images or graphs, we directly model the dependencies of joints with pure attention blocks. Our model is more concise and general, without the need of designing hand-crafted transformation rules, and it outperforms the previous methods with a significant margin.

Self-attention mechanism is the basic block of transformer [10,11], which is the mainstream method in the NLP field. Its input consists of a set of queries Q, keys K of dimension C and values V, which are packaged in the matrix form for fast computation. It first computes the dot products of the query with all keys, divides each by $\sqrt{C}$, and applies a softmax function to obtain the weights on the values [10]. In formulation:

$$Attention(Q, K, V) = softmax(\frac{QK^T}{\sqrt{C}}) \tag{1}$$

The similar idea has also been used for many computer vision tasks such as relation modeling [17], detection [18] and semantic segmentation [19]. To the best of our knowledge, we are the fist to apply the pure attention networks for skeletal data and further propose several improvements to meet the specific requirements of skeletons.

3   Methods

3.1   Spatial-Temporal Attention Module

Original transformer is fed with the sequential data, i.e., a matrix $X \in \mathbb{R}^{N \times C}$, where N denotes the number of elements and C denotes the number of channels.

---

[1] https://github.com/lshiwjx/DSTA-Net.

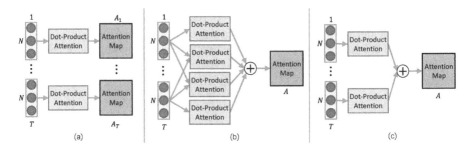

Fig. 1. Illustration of the three decoupling strategies. We use the spatial attention strategy as an example and the temporal attention strategy is an analogy. N and T denote the number of joints and frames, respectively.

For dynamic skeletal data, the input is a 3-order tensor $X \in \mathbb{R}^{N \times T \times C}$, where T denotes the number of frames. It is worth to investigate how to deal with the relationship between the time and the space. Wang et al. [12] propose to ignore the difference between time and space, and regard the inputs as a sequential data $X \in \mathbb{R}^{\hat{N} \times C}$, where $\hat{N} = NT$. However, the temporal dimension and the spatial dimension are totally different as introduced in Sect. 1. It is not reasonable to treat them equivalently. Besides, the computational complexity of calculating the attention map in this strategy is $O(T^2 N^2 C)$ (using the naive matrix multiplication algorithm), which is too large. Instead, we propose to decouple the spatial and temporal dimensions, where the computational complexity is largely reduced and the performance is improved.

We design three strategies for decoupling as shown in Fig. 1. Using the spatial attention as an example, the first strategy (Fig. 1, a) is calculating the attention maps frame by frame, and each frame uses a unique attention map:

$$A^t = softmax(\sigma(X_t)\phi(X_t)') \qquad (2)$$

where $A^t \in \mathbb{R}^{N \times N}$ is the attention map for frame t. $X_t \in \mathbb{R}^{N \times C}$. σ and ϕ are two embedding functions. $'$ denote matrix transpose. This strategy only considers the dependencies of joints in a single frame thus lacks the modeling capacity. The computational complexity of calculating spatial attention of this strategy is $O(TN^2 C)$. For temporal attention, the attention map of joint n is $A^n \in \mathbb{R}^{T \times T}$ and the input data is $X_n \in \mathbb{R}^{T \times C}$. Its calculation is analogical with the spatial attention. Considering both the spatial and temporal attention, the computational complexity of the first strategy for all frames is $O(TN^2 C + NT^2 C)$.

The second strategy (Fig. 1, b) is calculating the relations of two joints between all of the frames, which means both the intra-frame relations and the inter-frame relations of two joints are taken into account simultaneously. The attention map is shared over all frames. In formulation:

$$A^t = softmax(\sum_{t}^{T} \sum_{\tau}^{T} (\sigma(X_t)\phi(X_\tau)')) \qquad (3)$$

The computational complexity of this strategy is $O(T^2N^2C + N^2T^2C)$.

The third strategy (Fig. 1, c) is a compromise, where only the joints in same frame are considered to calculate the attention map, but the obtained attention maps of all frames are averaged and shared. It is equivalent to adding a time consistency restriction for attention computation, which can somewhat reduce the overfitting problem caused by the element-wise relation modeling of the second strategy.

$$A^t = softmax(\sum_t^T (\sigma(X_t)\phi(X_t)'))$$ (4)

By concatenating the frames into an $N \times TC$ matrix, the summation of mat-multiplications can be efficiently implemented with one big mat-multiplication operation. The computational complexity of this strategy is $O(TN^2C + NT^2C)$. as shown in ablation study Sect. 4.3, we finally use the strategy (c) in the model.

3.2 Decoupled Position Encoding

The skeletal joints are organized as a tensor to be fed into the neural networks. Because there are no predefined orders or structures for each element of the tensor to show its identity (e.g., joint index or frame index), we need a position encoding module to provide unique markers for every joint. Following [10], we use the sine and cosine functions with different frequencies as the encoding functions:

$$PE(p, 2i) = sin(p/10000^{2i/C_{in}})$$
$$PE(p, 2i + 1) = cos(p/10000^{2i/C_{in}})$$ (5)

where p denotes the position of element and i denotes the dimension of the position encoding vector. However, different with [10], the input of skeletal data have two dimensions, i.e., space and time. One strategy for position encoding is unifying the spatial and temporal dimensions and encoding them sequentially. For example assuming there are three joints, for the first frame the position of joints is $1, 2, 3$, and for the second frame it is $4, 5, 6$. This strategy cannot well distinguish the same joint in different frames. Another strategy is decoupling the process into spatial position encoding and temporal position encoding. Using the spatial position encoding as an example, the joints in the same frame are encoded sequentially and the same joints in different frames have the same encoding. In above examples, it means for the first frame the position is $1, 2, 3$, and for the second frame it is also $1, 2, 3$. As for the temporal position encoding, it is reversed and analogical, which means the joints in the same frame have the same encoding and the same joints in different frames are encoded sequentially. Finally, the position features are added to the input data as shown in Fig. 2. In this way, each element is aligned with an unique marker to help learning the mutual relations between the joints, and the difference between space and time is also well expressed.

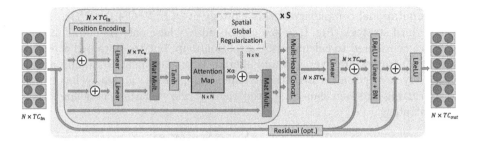

Fig. 2. Illustration of the attention module. We show the spatial attention module as an example. The temporal attention module is an analogy. The purple rounded rectangle box represents a single-head self-attention module. There are totally S self-attention modules, whose output are concatenated and fed into two linear layers to obtain the output. LReLU represents the leaky ReLU [20]. (Color figure online)

3.3 Spatial Global Regularization

As explained in Sect. 1, each joint has a specific meaning. Based on this prior knowledge, we propose to add a spatial global regularization to force the model to learn more general attentions for different samples. In detail, a global attention map ($N \times N$ matrix) is added to the attention map ($N \times N$ matrix) learned by the dot-product attention mechanism introduced in Sect. 3.1. The global attention map is shared for all data samples, which represents a unified intrinsic relationship pattern of the human joints. We set it as the parameter of the network and optimize it together with the model. An α is multiplied to balance the strength of the spatial global regularization. This module is simple and light-weight, but it is effective as shown in the ablation study. Note that the regularization is only added for spatial attention computing because the temporal dimension has no such semantic alignment property. Forcing a global regularization for temporal attention is not reasonable and will harm the performance.

3.4 Complete Attention Module

Because the spatial attention module and the temporal attention module are analogical, we select the spatial module as an example for detailed introduction. The complete attention module is showed in Fig. 2. The procedures inside the purple rounded rectangle box illustrate the process of the single-head attention calculation. The input $X \in \mathbb{R}^{N \times TC_{in}}$ is first added with the spatial position encoding. Then it is embedded with two linear mapping functions to $X \in \mathbb{R}^{N \times TC_e}$. C_e is usually small than C_{out} to remove the feature redundancy and reduce the computations. The attention map is calculated by the strategy (c) of Fig. 1 and added with the spatial global regularization. Note that we found the Tanh is better than SoftMax when computing the attention map. We believe that it is because the output of Tanh is not restricted to positive values thus can generate negative relations and provide more flexibility. Finally the attention map is mat-multiplied with the original input to get the output features.

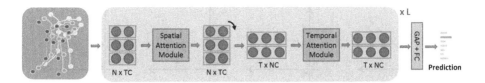

Fig. 3. Illustration of the overall architecture of the DSTA-Net. N, T, C denote the number of joints, frames and channels, respectively. The red rounded rectangle box represents one spatial-temporal attention layer. There are totally L layers. The final output features are global-average-pooled (GAP) and fed into a fully-conected layer (FC) to make the prediction. (Color figure online)

To allow the model jointly attending to information from different representation sub-spaces, there are totally S heads for attention calculations in the module. The results of all heads are concatenated and mapped to the output space $\mathbb{R}^{N \times TC_{out}}$ with a linear layer. Similar with the transformer, a point-wise feed-forward layer is added in the end to obtain the final output. We use the leaky ReLU as the non-linear function. There are two residual connections in the module as shown in the Fig. 2 to stabilize the network training and integrate different features. Finally, all of the procedures inside the green rounded rectangle box represent one whole attention module.

3.5   Overall Architecture

Figure 3 shows the overall architecture of our method. The input is a skeleton sequence with N joints, T frames and C channels. In each layer, we first regard the input as an $N \times TC$ matrix, i.e., N elements with TC channels, and feed it into the spatial attention module (introduced in Fig. 2) to model the spatial relations between the joints. Then, we transpose the output matrix and regard it as T elements each has NC channels, and feed it into the temporal attention module to model the temporal relations between the frames. There are totally L layers stacked to update features. The final output features are global-average-pooled and fed into a fully-connected layers to obtain the classification scores.

3.6   Data Decoupling

The action can be decoupled into two dimensions: the spatial dimension and the temporal dimension as illustrated in Fig. 4 (a, b and c). The spatial information is the difference of two different joints that are in the same frame, which mainly contains the relative position relationship between different joints. To reduce the redundant information, we only calculate the spatial information along the human bones. The temporal information is the difference of the two joints with same spatial meaning in different frames, which mainly describes the motion trajectory of one joint along the temporal dimension. When we recognize the gestures like "Point with one finger" versus "Point with two finger", the spatial information is more important. However, when we recognize the gestures

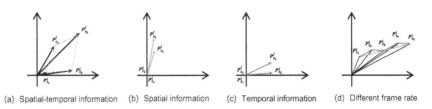

(a) Spatial-temporal information   (b) Spatial information   (c) Temporal information   (d) Different frame rate

Fig. 4. For simplicity, we draw two joins in two consecutive frames in a 2D coordinate system to illustrate the data decoupling. As shown in (a), $P^i_{t_k}$ denotes the joint i in frame k. Assume that joint i and joint j are the two end joints of one bone. (a) denotes the raw data, i.e., the spatial-temporal information. The orange dotted line and blue dotted line denote the decoupled spatial information and temporal information, which are showed as (b) and (c), respectively. (d) illustrates the difference between the fast-temporal information (blue arrow) and the slow-temporal information (orange arrow). (Color figure online)

like "waving up" versus "waving down", the temporal information will be more essential.

Besides, for temporal stream, different actions have different sensibilities of the motion scale. For some actions such as "clapping" versus "put two hands together", the short-term motion detail is essential. But for actions like "waving up" versus "waving down", the long-term movement trend is more important. Inspired by [3], we propose to calculate the temporal motion with both the high frame-rate sampling and the low frame-rate sampling as shown in Fig. 4 (d). The generated two streams are called as the fast-temporal stream and the slow-temporal stream, respectively.

Finally, we have four streams all together, namely, spatial-temporal stream (original data), spatial stream, fast-temporal stream and slow-temporal stream. We separately train four models with the same architecture for each of the streams. The classification scores are averaged to obtain the final result.

4   Experiments

To verify the generalization of the model, we use two datasets for hand gesture recognition (DHG [21] and SHREC [22]) and two datasets for human action recognition (NTU-60 [23] and NTU-120 [24]). We first perform exhaustive ablation studies on SHREC to verify the effectiveness of the proposed model components. Then, we evaluate our model on all four datasets to compare with the state-of-the-art methods.

4.1   Datasets

DHG: DHG [21] dataset contains 2800 video sequences of 14 hand gestures performed 5 times by 20 subjects. They are performed in two ways: using one finger and the whole hand. So it has two benchmarks: 14-gestures for coarse classification and 28-gestures for fine-grained classification. The 3D coordinates of 22 hand joints in real-world space is captured by the Intel Real-sense camera. It uses the leave-one-subject-out cross-validation strategy for evaluation.

SHREC: SHREC [22] dataset contains 2800 gesture sequences performed 1 and 10 times by 28 participants in two ways like the DHG dataset. It splits the sequences into 1960 train sequences and 840 test sequences. The length of sample gestures ranges from 20 to 50 frames. This dataset is used for the competition of SHREC'17 in conjunction with the Euro-graphics 3DOR'2017 Workshop.

NTU-60: NTU-60 [23] is a most widely used in-door-captured action recognition dataset, which contains 56,000 action clips in 60 action classes. The clips are performed by 40 volunteers and is captured by 3 KinectV2 cameras with different views. This dataset provides 25 joints for each subject in the skeleton sequences. It recommends two benchmarks: cross-subject (CS) and cross-view (CV), where the subjects and cameras used in the training/test splits are different, respectively.

NTU-120: NTU-120 [23] is similar with NTU-60 but is larger. It contains 114,480 action clips in 120 action classes. The clips are performed by 106 volunteers in 32 camera setups. It recommends two benchmarks: cross-subject (CS) and cross-setup (CE), where cross-setup means using samples with odd setup IDs for training and others for testing.

4.2 Training Details

To show the generalization of our methods, we use the same configuration for all experiments. The network is stacked using 8 DSTA blocks with 3 heads. The output channels are 64, 64, 128, 128, 256, 256, 256 and 256, respectively. The input video is randomly/uniformly sampled to 150 frames and then randomly/centrally cropped to 128 frames for training/test splits. For fast-temporal features, the sampling interval is 2. When training, the initial learning rate is 0.1 and is divided by 10 in 60 and 90 epochs. The training is ended in 120 epochs. Batch size is 32. Weight decay is 0.0005. We use the stochastic gradient descent (SGD) with Nesterov momentum (0.9) as the optimizer and the cross-entropy as the loss function.

4.3 Ablation Studies

In this section, we investigate the effectiveness of the proposed components of the network and different data modalities. We conduct experiments on SHREC dataset. Except for the explored object, other details are set the same for fair comparison.

Network Architectures. We first investigate the effect of the position embedding. as shown in Table 1, removing the position encoding will seriously harm the performance. Decoupling the spatial and temporal dimension (DPE) is better than not (UPE). This is because the spatial and temporal dimensions actually have different properties and treat them equivalently will confuse the model.

Then we investigate the effect of the proposed spatial global regularization (SGR). By adding the SGR, the performance is improved from 94.3% to 96.3%, but if we meanwhile regularize the temporal dimension, the performance drops. This is reasonable since there are no specific meanings for temporal dimension and forced learning of a unified pattern will cause the gap between the training set an testing set.

Finally, we compare the three strategies introduced in Fig. 1. It shows that the strategy (a) obtains the lowest performance. We conjecture that it dues to the fact that it only considers the intra-frame relations and ignore the inter-frame relations. Modeling the inter-frame relations exhaustively (strategy b) will improve the performance and a compromise (c) obtains the best performance. It may because that the compromise strategy can somewhat reduce the overfitting problem.

Table 1. Ablation studies for architectures of the model on the SHREC dataset. ST-ATT-c denotes the **s**patial **t**emporal **att**ention networks with attention type c introduced in Fig. 1. PE denotes **p**osition **e**ncoding. UPE/DPE denote using **u**nified/**d**ecoupled encoding for spatial and temporal dimensions. STGR denotes **s**patial-**t**emporal **g**lobal **r**egularizations for computing attention maps.

Method	Accuracy
ST-Att-c w/o PE	89.4
ST-Att-c + UPE	93.2
ST-Att-c + DPE	94.5
ST-Att-c + DPE + SGR	**96.3**
ST-Att-c + DPE + STGR	94.6
ST-Att-a + DPE + SGR	94.6
ST-Att-b + DPE + SGR	95.1

We show the learned attention maps of different layers (layer #1 and layer #8) in Fig. 5. Other layers are showed in supplement materials. It shows that the attention maps learned in different layers are not the same because the information contained in different layers has distinct semantics. Besides, it seems the model focuses more on the relations between the tips of the fingers (T4, I4, M4, R4) and wrist, especially in the lower layers. This is intuitive since these joints are more discriminative for human to recognize gestures. On the higher layers, the information are highly aggregated and the difference between each of the joints becomes unapparent, thus the phenomenon also becomes unapparent.

Data Decoupling. To show the necessity of decoupling the raw data into four streams as introduced in Sect. 3.6, we show the results of using four streams

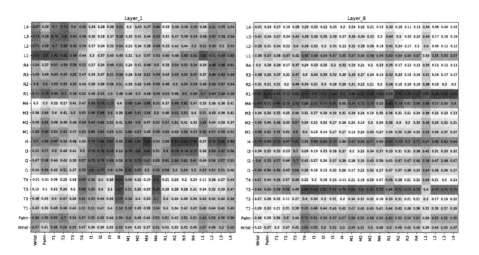

Fig. 5. Examples of the learned attention maps for different layers. T, I, M, R and L denote thumb, index finger, middle finger, ring finger and little finger, respectively. As for articulation, T1 denotes the base of the thumb and T4 denote the tip of the thumb.

separately and the result of fusion in Table 2. It shows that the accuracies of decoupled streams are not as good as the raw data because some of the information is lost. However, since the four streams focus on different aspects and are complementary with each other, when fusing them together, the performance is improved significantly.

Table 2. Ablation studies for feature fusion on the SHREC dataset. Spatial-temporal denotes the raw data, i.e., the joint coordinates. Other types of features are introduced in Sect. 3.6.

Method	Accuracy
Spatial-temporal	96.3
Spatial	95.1
Fast-temporal	94.5
Slow-temporal	93.7
Fusion	**97.0**

As shown in Fig. 6, We plot the per-class accuracies of the four streams to show the complementarity clearly. We also plot the difference of accuracies between different streams, which are represented as the dotted lines. For spatial information versus temporal information, it (orange dotted lines) shows that the network with spatial information obtains higher accuracies mainly in classes that are closely related with the shape changes such as "grab", "expand" and "pinch", and the network with temporal information obtains higher accuracies

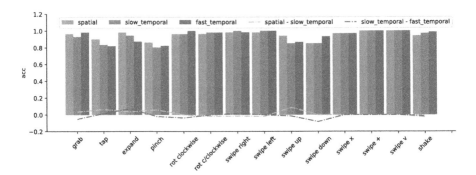

Fig. 6. Per-class accuracies for different modalities on SHREC-14 dataset. The dotted lines shows the difference between two modalities.

mainly in classes that are closely related with the positional changes such as "swipe", "rot" and "shake". As for different frame-rate sampling, it (red dotted lines) shows that the slow-temporal performs better for classes of "expand", "tap", etc, and the fast-temporal performs better for classes of "swipe", "rot", etc. These phenomenons verify the complementarity of the four modalities.

Table 3. Recognition accuracy comparison of our method and state-of-the-art methods on SHREC dataset and DHG dataset.

Method	Year	SHREC		DHG	
		14 gestures	28 gestures	14 gestures	28 gestures
ST-GCN [5]	2018	92.7	87.7	91.2	87.1
STA-Res-TCN [25]	2018	93.6	90.7	89.2	85.0
ST-TS-HGR-NET [26]	2019	94.3	89.4	87.3	83.4
DG-STA. [27]	2019	94.4	90.7	91.9	88.0
DSTA-Net(ours)	-	**97.0**	**93.9**	**93.8**	**90.9**

4.4 Comparison with Previous Methods

We evaluate our model with state-of-the-art methods for skeleton-based action recognition on all four datasets, where our model significantly outperforms the other methods. Due to the space restriction, we only show some representative works, where more comparisons are showed in supplement materials. On SHREC/DHG datasets for skeleton-based hand gestures recognition (Table 3), our model brings 2.6%/1.9% and 3.2%/2.9% improvements for 14-gestures and 28-gestures benchmarks compared with the state-of-the-arts. Note that the state-of-the-art accuracies are already very high (94.4%/91.9% and 90.7%/88.0% for

Table 4. Recognition accuracy comparison of our method and state-of-the-art methods on NTU-60 dataset. CS and CV denote the cross-subject and cross-view benchmarks, respectively.

Methods	Year	CS (%)	CV (%)
ST-GCN [5]	2018	81.5	88.3
SRN+TSL [14]	2018	84.8	92.4
2s-AGCN [6]	2019	88.5	95.1
DGNN [7]	2019	89.9	96.1
NAS [28]	2020	89.4	95.7
DSTA-Net(ours)	-	**91.5**	**96.4**

Table 5. Recognition accuracy comparison of our method and state-of-the-art methods on NTU-120 dataset. CS and CE denote the cross-subject and cross-setup benchmarks, respectively.

Methods	Year	CS (%)	CE (%)
Body Pose Evolution Map [29]	2018	64.6	66.9
SkeletonMotion [30]	2019	67.7	66.9
DSTA-Net(ours)	-	**86.6**	**89.0**

14-gestures and 28-gestures, respectively), but our model still obtains remarkable performance. On NTU-60 dataset (Table 4), our model obtains 1.6% and 0.3% improvements. The performance of CV benchmark is nearly saturated. For both CS and CV benchmarks, we visualize the wrong examples and find that it is even impossible for human to recognize many examples using only the skeletal data. For example, for the two classes of reading and writing, the humans are both in a same posture (standing or sitting) and holding a book. The only difference is whether there is a pen in the hand, which cannot be captured through the skeletal data. On NTU-120 dataset (Table 5), our model also achieves state-of-the-art performance. Since this dataset is released recently, our method can provide a new baseline on it.

5   Conclusion

In this paper, we propose a novel decoupled spatial-temporal attention network (DSTA-Net) for skeleton-based action recognition. It is a unified framework based solely on attention mechanism, with no needs of designing hand-crafted traversal rules or graph topologies. We propose three techniques in building DSTA-Net to meet the specific requirements for skeletal data, including spatial-temporal attention decoupling, decoupled position encoding and spatial global regularization. Besides, we introduce a skeleton-decoupling method to emphasize the spatial/temporal variations and motion scales of the skeletal data, resulting in a more comprehensive understanding for human actions and gestures.

Acknowledgement. This work was supported in part by the National Natural Science Foundation of China under Grant 61872364 and 61876182, in part by the Jiangsu Leading Technology Basic Research Project BK20192004.

References

1. Carreira, J., Zisserman, A.: Quo vadis, action recognition? A new model and the kinetics dataset. In: The IEEE Conference on Computer Vision and Pattern Recognition (CVPR), pp. 6299–6308 (2017)
2. Shi, L., Zhang, Y., Jian, C., Hanqing, L.: Gesture recognition using spatiotemporal deformable convolutional representation. In: IEEE International Conference on Image Processing (ICIP) (2019)
3. Feichtenhofer, C., Fan, H., Malik, J., He, K.: Slowfast networks for video recognition. In: Proceedings of the IEEE International Conference on Computer Vision, pp. 6202–6211 (2019)
4. Shi, L., Zhang, Y., Cheng, J., Lu, H.: Action Recognition via Pose-Based Graph Convolutional Networks with Intermediate Dense Supervision. arXiv:1911.12509 (2019)
5. Yan, S., Xiong, Y., Lin, D.: Spatial temporal graph convolutional networks for skeleton-based action recognition. In: AAAI (2018)
6. Shi, L., Zhang, Y., Cheng, J., Lu, H.: Two-stream adaptive graph convolutional networks for skeleton-based action recognition. In: The IEEE Conference on Computer Vision and Pattern Recognition (CVPR), pp. 12026–12035 (2019)
7. Shi, L., Zhang, Y., Cheng, J., Lu, H.: Skeleton-based action recognition with directed graph neural networks. In: The IEEE Conference on Computer Vision and Pattern Recognition (CVPR), pp. 7912–7921 (2019)
8. Qiu, Z., Yao, T., Mei, T.: Learning spatio-temporal representation with pseudo-3D residual networks. In: The IEEE International Conference on Computer Vision (ICCV), pp. 5533–5541 (2017)
9. Zhang, P., Lan, C., Xing, J., Zeng, W., Xue, J., Zheng, N.: View adaptive recurrent neural networks for high performance human action recognition from skeleton data. In: The IEEE Conference on Computer Vision and Pattern Recognition (CVPR), pp. 2117–2126 (2017)
10. Vaswani, A., et al.: Attention is all you need. In: Guyon, I., Luxburg, U.V., Bengio, S., Wallach, H., Fergus, R., Vishwanathan, S., Garnett, R. (eds.) Advances in Neural Information Processing Systems, pp. 6000–6010 (2017)
11. Dai, Z., et al.: Transformer-XL: attentive language models beyond a fixed-length context. arXiv:1901.02860 (2019)
12. Wang, X., Girshick, R., Gupta, A., He, K.: Non-local neural networks. In: The IEEE Conference on Computer Vision and Pattern Recognition (CVPR) (2018)
13. Li, S., Li, W., Cook, C., Zhu, C., Gao, Y.: Independently recurrent neural network (IndRNN): building a longer and deeper RNN. In: The IEEE Conference on Computer Vision and Pattern Recognition (CVPR), pp. 5457–5466 (2018)
14. Si, C., Jing, Y., Wang, W., Wang, L., Tan, T.: Skeleton-based action recognition with spatial reasoning and temporal stack learning. In: The European Conference on Computer Vision (ECCV), pp. 103–118 (2018)
15. Si, C., Chen, W., Wang, W., Wang, L., Tan, T.: An attention enhanced graph convolutional LSTM network for skeleton-based action recognition. In: The IEEE Conference on Computer Vision and Pattern Recognition (CVPR), pp. 1227–1236 (2019)

16. Tang, Y., Tian, Y., Lu, J., Li, P., Zhou, J.: Deep progressive reinforcement learning for skeleton-based action recognition. In: The IEEE Conference on Computer Vision and Pattern Recognition (CVPR), pp. 5323–5332 (2018)
17. Santoro, A., et al.: A simple neural network module for relational reasoning. In: Guyon, I., et al. (eds.) Advances in Neural Information Processing Systems, pp. 4974–4983 (2017)
18. Hu, H., Gu, J., Zhang, Z., Dai, J., Wei, Y.: Relation networks for object detection. In: The IEEE Conference on Computer Vision and Pattern Recognition (CVPR) (2018)
19. Fu, J., et al.: Dual attention network for scene segmentation. In: Proceedings of the IEEE Conference on Computer Vision and Pattern Recognition, pp. 3146–3154 (2019)
20. Maas, A.L., Hannun, A.Y., Ng, A.Y.: Rectifier nonlinearities improve neural network acoustic models. In: ICML, vol. 30, p. 3 (2013)
21. De Smedt, Q., Wannous, H., Vandeborre, J.P.: Skeleton-based dynamic hand gesture recognition. In: The IEEE Conference on Computer Vision and Pattern Recognition Workshops (CVPRW), pp. 1206–1214 (2016)
22. De Smedt, Q., Wannous, H., Vandeborre, J.P., Guerry, J., Le Saux, B., Filliat, D.: 3D hand gesture recognition using a depth and skeletal dataset: SHREC'17 Track. In: Pratikakis, I., Dupont, F., Ovsjanikov, M. (eds.) Eurographics Workshop on 3D Object Retrieval, pp. 1–6 (2017)
23. Shahroudy, A., Liu, J., Ng, T.T., Wang, G.: NTU RGB+D: a large scale dataset for 3D human activity analysis. In: The IEEE Conference on Computer Vision and Pattern Recognition (CVPR), pp. 1010–1019 (2016)
24. Liu, J., Shahroudy, A., Perez, M., Wang, G., Duan, L.Y., Kot, A.C.: NTU RGB+D 120: a large-scale benchmark for 3D human activity understanding. IEEE Trans. Pattern Anal. Mach. Intell. 1 (2019)
25. Hou, J., Wang, G., Chen, X., Xue, J.-H., Zhu, R., Yang, H.: Spatial-temporal attention res-TCN for skeleton-based dynamic hand gesture recognition. In: Leal-Taixé, L., Roth, S. (eds.) ECCV 2018. LNCS, vol. 11134, pp. 273–286. Springer, Cham (2019). https://doi.org/10.1007/978-3-030-11024-6_18
26. Nguyen, X.S., Brun, L., Lézoray, O., Bougleux, S.: A neural network based on SPD manifold learning for skeleton-based hand gesture recognition. In: The IEEE Conference on Computer Vision and Pattern Recognition (CVPR) (2019)
27. Chen, Y., Zhao, L., Peng, X., Yuan, J., Metaxas, D.N.: Construct dynamic graphs for hand gesture recognition via spatial-temporal attention. In: BMVC (2019)
28. Peng, W., Hong, X., Chen, H., Zhao, G.: Learning graph convolutional network for skeleton-based human action recognition by neural searching. In: AAAI (2020)
29. Liu, M., Yuan, J.: Recognizing human actions as the evolution of pose estimation maps. In: The IEEE Conference on Computer Vision and Pattern Recognition (CVPR), pp. 1159–1168 (2018)
30. Caetano, C., Sena, J., Brémond, F., Dos Santos, J.A., Schwartz, W.R.: SkeleMotion: a new representation of skeleton joint sequences based on motion information for 3D action recognition. In: 2019 16th IEEE International Conference on Advanced Video and Signal Based Surveillance (AVSS), pp. 1–8 (2019)

Unpaired Multimodal Facial Expression Recognition

Bin Xia[1] and Shangfei Wang[1,2]

[1] Key Lab of Computing and Communication Software of Anhui Province,
School of Computer Science and Technology,
University of Science and Technology of China, Hefei, China
xiabin@mail.ustc.edu.cn, sfwang@ustc.edu.cn
[2] Anhui Robot Technology Standard Innovation Base, Hefei, China

Abstract. Current works on multimodal facial expression recognition typically require paired visible and thermal facial images. Although visible cameras are readily available in our daily life, thermal cameras are expensive and less prevalent. It is costly to collect a large quantity of synchronous visible and thermal facial images. To tackle this paired training data bottleneck, we propose an unpaired multimodal facial expression recognition method, which makes full use of the massive number of unpaired visible and thermal images by utilizing thermal images to construct better image representations and classifiers for visible images during training. Specifically, two deep neural networks are trained from visible and thermal images to learn image representations and expression classifiers for two modalities. Then, an adversarial strategy is adopted to force statistical similarity between the learned visible and thermal representations, and to minimize the distribution mismatch between the predictions of the visible and thermal images. Through adversarial learning, the proposed method leverages thermal images to construct better image representations and classifiers for visible images during training, without the requirement of paired data. A decoder network is built upon the visible hidden features in order to preserve some inherent features of the visible view. We also take the variability of the different images' transferability into account via adaptive classification loss. During testing, only visible images are required and the visible network is used. Thus, the proposed method is appropriate for real-world scenarios, since thermal imaging is rare in these instances. Experiments on two benchmark multimodal expression databases and three visible facial expression databases demonstrate the superiority of the proposed method compared to state-of-the-art methods.

1 Introduction

Facial expression is one of the most important emotion communication channels for human-computer interaction. Great progress has recently been made on facial expression recognition due to its wide application in many user-centered fields. Due to their ubiquity, visible images are widely used to build facial expression

© Springer Nature Switzerland AG 2021
H. Ishikawa et al. (Eds.): ACCV 2020, LNCS 12626, pp. 54–69, 2021.
https://doi.org/10.1007/978-3-030-69541-5_4

recognition systems. However, the light-sensitive property of the visible images prevents researchers from constructing better facial expression classifiers. To tackle this problem, researchers turn to thermal images, which record the temperature distribution of the face and are not light sensitive. Therefore, combining visible and thermal images could improve the facial expression recognition task.

The simplest method of multimodal facial expression recognition is feature-level or decision-level fusion [1–4]. However, the unbalanced quantity of visible and thermal images prevents us from applying this method in real-world scenarios. It would be more practical to utilize thermal images as privileged information [5] to assist the learning process of the visible classifier during training. During testing, thermal images are unavailable and only visible images are used to make predictions. Several works apply this learning framework and succeed in the task of visible facial expression recognition [6–8]. One assumption of these works is that the visible and thermal facial images must be paired during training. Since collecting paired visible and thermal facial images is often difficult, requiring paired data during training prevents the usage of the many available unpaired visible and thermal images, and thus may degenerate the learning effect of the visible facial expression classifier.

To address this, we propose an unpaired adversarial facial expression recognition method. We tackle the unbalanced quantity of visible and thermal images by utilizing thermal images as privileged information. We introduce adversarial learning on the feature-level and label-level spaces to cope with unpaired training data. Finally, we add a decoder network to preserve the inherent visible features.

2   Related Work

2.1   Learning with Privileged Information

Privileged information refers to extra information available during training, but not testing. Exploring privileged information can improve the learning process of the original classifier. Many different research fields have made progress by leveraging privileged information. For example, Vapnik *et al.* [5] first introduced privileged information to the support vector machine (SVM) algorithm, and proposed the SVM+ algorithm. Wang *et al.* [9] proposed to utilize privileged information as secondary features or secondary targets to improve classifier performance. Sharmanska *et al.* [10] proposed to close the mismatch between class error distributions in privileged and original data sets to address cross-data-set learning. Niu *et al.* [11] proposed a framework called multi-instance learning with privileged information (MIL-PI) for action and event recognition, which incorporated privileged information to learn from loosely labelled web data. Luo *et al.* [12] proposed a graph distillation framework for action detection, which not only transfers knowledge from the extra modalities to the target modality, but also transfers knowledge from the source domain to the target domain. Garcia *et al.* [13] proposed to learn a hallucination network within a multimodal-stream network architecture by utilizing depth images as privileged information. They introduced an adversarial learning strategy that exploited multiple data modalities at training.

All of the above works demonstrate the benefits of leveraging privileged information. However, all works except for Sharmanska *et al.*'s method [10] require paired privileged and original information during training. This requirement prevents the adoption of large-scale unpaired data to learn better features and classifiers for the original information. Although Sharmanska *et al.*'s method leveraged the unpaired data from the target label by forcing a similarity between the classification errors of the privileged and original information, it didn't explore the feature-level dependencies between privileged and original information. Therefore, we propose to learn visible facial expressions classifier and leverage adversarial learning to force statistical similarity between the visible and thermal views.

2.2   Facial Expression Recognition

Facial expression recognition (FER) has remained as an active research topic during the past decades. The main goal of FER is to learn expression-related features that is discriminative and invariant to variations such as pose, illumination, and identity-related information. Traditionally, previous works have used handcrafted features to study facial expression recognition, including Histograms of Oriented Gradients (HOG) [14], Scale Invariant Feature Transform (SIFT) [15], histograms of Local Binary Patterns (LBP) [16] and histograms of Local Phase Quantization (LPQ) [17].

Recently, deep CNN based methods have been employed to increase the robustness of FER. Identity-Aware CNN (IACNN) [18] was proposed to enhance FER performance by reducing the effect of identity related information with the help of an expression-sensitive contrastive loss and an identity-sensitive contrastive loss. Cai *et al.* [19] transferred facial expressions to a fixed identity to mitigate the effect of identity-related information. De-expression Residue Learning (DeRL) [20] utilized the cGAN to synthesize a neutral facial image of the same identity from any input expressive image, while the person-independent expression information can be extracted from the intermediate layers of the generative model. Although these works mitigate the influence of inter-subject variations, the light-sensitive property of the visible images prevents these works from constructing robust facial expression classifiers under different illumination.

2.3   Multimodal Facial Expression Recognition

Early methods of multimodal facial expression recognition are based on strategies including feature-level and decision-level fusions. For example, Sharma *et al.* [2] concatenated the visible and thermal features and fed them into an SVM to detect the pressure of people. Yoshitomi *et al.* [1] trained three classifiers with voice features, visible images, and thermal images, and adopted decision-level fusion. Wesley *et al.* [3] trained visible and thermal networks and fused the outputs to make predictions for facial expression recognition. Wang *et al.* [4] adopted both feature-level and decision-level fusions to recognize facial expressions. All of the above works ignore the unbalanced quantity of visible and thermal images. In fact, visible cameras are widely used in our daily life, while thermal cameras are only available in laboratory environment. It prevents us from applying the fusion method into real practice.

To address this problem, some researchers view thermal images as privileged information, which is only required during training to help visible images construct a better expression classifier. Unlike fusion methods, which depend on visible and thermal representations containing complementary information, using thermal images as privileged information allows for more robust visible representations. Such visible representations contain unified and view-irrelevant information, rather than complementary information, so only visible data is required during testing. Shi et al. [6] proposed a method of expression recognition from visible images with the help of thermal images as privileged information. They combined canonical correlation analysis (CCA) and SVM. Through CCA, a thermal-augmented visible feature space is obtained. The SVM is used as the classifier on the learned subspace. The shortcoming of this method is that the learned subspace has no direct relation to the target label, since the subspace and the classifier are trained separately. To address this, Wang et al. [7] proposed to train two deep neural networks to extract feature representations from visible and thermal images. Then, two SVMs were trained for classification. Training of the deep networks and SVMs is integrated into a single optimization problem through the use of a similarity constraint on the label space. The main drawback of Wang et al.'s method is that the visible and thermal networks merely interact with each other by means of the similarity constraint, which works on the label space of the two views. There is still great freedom for the feature space below, weakening the correlation between visible and thermal views. Pan et al. [8] improved Wang et al.'s framework by introducing a discriminator to the hidden features of the two-view networks in order to learn view-irrelevant feature representations and enhance the correlation of the visible and thermal networks in the feature representations. Sankaran et al. [21] proposed cross-modality supervised representation learning for facial action unit recognition. They used a latent representation decoder to reconstruct thermal images from visible images. The generated thermal images were applied to construct action unit classifier.

All of the above works require paired visible and thermal images during training. However, it is impractical to collect a great number of paired images in real-life scenarios. Fortunately, recent advances in adversarial learning allow us to deal with multimodal data in terms of distributions rather than pair-wise samples.

Therefore, in this paper we propose a novel unpaired multimodal facial expression recognition method enhanced by thermal images through adversarial learning. Specifically, we first learn two deep neural networks to map the unpaired visible and thermal images to their ground truth labels. Then we introduce two modality discriminators and impose adversarial learning on the feature

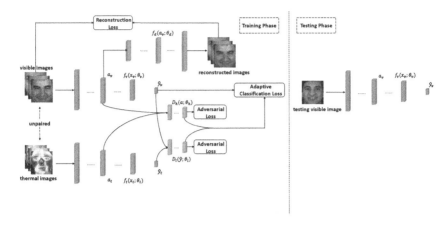

Fig. 1. The framework of the proposed unpaired facial expression recognition method.

and label levels. This forces statistical similarity between the learned visible and thermal representations and minimizes the distribution mismatch between predictions of the visible and thermal images. Because there may be a few unpaired images that are significantly dissimilar across views, forcefully aligning them may have deleterious effects on the visible expression classifier. To remedy this, the variability of the different images' transferability is taken into account via adaptive classification loss. Finally, a decoder network is built upon the visible hidden features in order to preserve some inherent features of the visible view. During training, the two-view neural networks and the two discriminators are optimized alternately, and the visible network is expected to be enhanced by the thermal network with unpaired visible and thermal images. During testing, the prediction of a visible testing image is given by the learned visible neural network.

Compared to related work, our contribution can be summarized as follows: (1) we are the first to tackle the task of facial expression recognition with unpaired visible and thermal images. (2) We propose to close the distributions of the unpaired visible and thermal data through adversarial learning at the feature and label levels. Experimental results demonstrate the effectiveness of our proposed method.

3 Problem Statement

Suppose we have two unpaired data sets $\mathcal{D}_v = \left\{ x_v^{(i)}, y_v^{(i)} \right\}_{i=1}^{N_1}$ and $\mathcal{D}_t = \left\{ x_t^{(i)}, y_t^{(i)} \right\}_{i=1}^{N_2}$. The first is the visible data set containing N_1 training instances and the second is the thermal data set containing N_2 training instances. $x_v \in \mathbb{R}^{d_v}$ and $x_t \in \mathbb{R}^{d_t}$ represent the visible and thermal images respectively, where d_v and d_t represent their dimensions. $y \in \{0, 1, \cdots, K-1\}$ are the ground truth expression labels of images. Our task is to learn a visible expression classifier by utilizing the two unpaired data sets $\mathcal{D}_v$ and $\mathcal{D}_t$ during training phase. When testing a new visible image, the prediction is given by the learned visible expression classifier. No thermal data is involved during the testing phase.

4 Proposed Method

The framework of the proposed unpaired multimodal facial expression recognition method is summarized in Fig. 1. As shown in Fig. 1, there are five networks in the proposed method: the visible network $f_v : \mathbb{R}^{d_v} \rightarrow [0,1]^K$ with parameter θ_v, the thermal network $f_t : \mathbb{R}^{d_t} \rightarrow [0,1]^K$ with parameter θ_t, the discriminator in the image representation layer $D_h : \mathbb{R}^{d_h} \rightarrow [0,1]$ with parameter θ_h, the discriminator in the label layer $D_l : [0,1]^K \rightarrow [0,1]$ with parameter θ_l and the decoder network $f_d : \mathbb{R}^{d_h} \rightarrow \mathbb{R}^{d_v}$ with parameter θ_d.

The visible and thermal networks capture the mapping functions from the visible and thermal facial images to the expression labels. The two discriminators compete with the two-view networks, regularizing them in order to learn the modal-irrelevant image representations and output similar predictions. Since adversarial learning focuses on the statistical similarity of the learned representations and classification errors from two modalities, synchronous visible and thermal imaging is not required. The decoder network ensures the preservation of some inherent features of the visible view.

4.1 Basic Classification Loss for Two Views

We build duplicate neural networks for visible and thermal datasets respectively. The output layers of the visible and thermal networks are K-way softmax layers. The outputs of the visible and thermal networks are denoted as $\hat{y}_v = f_v(x_v)$ and $\hat{y}_t = f_t(x_t)$. Therefore, the supervised classification losses for two views are $L_v(y_v, \hat{y}_v)$ and $L_t(y_t, \hat{y}_t)$ respectively, we use common cross-entropy loss. The visible and thermal networks are first trained with their corresponding datasets. Then we fix the parameters of thermal network, and fine-tuning the visible network by exploiting thermal images as privileged information.

4.2 Adversarial Learning in Feature and Label Levels

After training the visible and thermal networks, the two-view networks are combined and fine-tuned simultaneously. Since the visible and thermal training images are unpaired, we cannot adopt a pair-wise similarity constraint as in Wang et al.'s work [7]. Motivated by He et al.'s work [22], we propose to build discriminators in the feature and label levels in order to make full use of the thermal data as privileged information.

Let a_v and a_t represent the activations of the visible and thermal data in a certain hidden layer. The learning objective of the feature-level discriminator $D_h(a; \theta_h)$ is to classify the source of the activations as accurately as possible.

The visible network serves as a generator which tries to fool the discriminator. We treat the visible view as a positive class and the thermal view as a negative class. The minimax objective can be formulated as follows:

$$\min_{\theta_v} \max_{\theta_h} \mathbb{E}_{a_v \sim P_{a_v}} \log D_h\left(a_v\right) + \mathbb{E}_{a_t \sim P_{a_t}} \log\left(1 - D_h\left(a_t\right)\right) \tag{1}$$

Adversarial learning is introduced in the feature level to reduce the statistical gap between the visible and thermal views and learn view-irrelevant features. At the label level, we also introduce adversarial learning because the tasks of facial expression recognition from visible and thermal views are highly correlated. Therefore, the decision-making behaviour of the two-view networks should be similar. The learning objective is formulated as Eq. 2.

$$\min_{\theta_v} \max_{\theta_l} \mathbb{E}_{\hat{y}_v \sim P_{\hat{y}_v}} \log D_l\left(\hat{y}_v\right) + \mathbb{E}_{\hat{y}_t \sim P_{\hat{y}_t}} \log\left(1 - D_l\left(\hat{y}_t\right)\right) \tag{2}$$

In addition to minimizing the classification errors, the learning objective of the visible network is to fool the two discriminators into making mistakes, so its loss function in the feature and label space can be formulated as Eq. 3 and 4.

$$L_h(\theta_v) = -\log D_h\left(a_t\right) \tag{3}$$

$$L_l(\theta_v) = -\log D_l\left(\hat{y}_t\right) \tag{4}$$

4.3   Visible Reconstruction Loss

Although we introduce a feature-level discriminator in order to learn view-irrelevant feature representations, some inherent features of the original two views may be missing during adversarial learning. We want to preserve some inherent features of the visible view to learn a highly performing visible facial expression classifier. To this end, we set a decoder network f_d upon the visible hidden features a_v and force the visible network f_v to learn some feature representations which can be decoded into the original visible images. The decoder network outputs a reconstructed image $\hat{x}_v = f_d(a_v)$, which has the same size as the original visible image x_v. Then we evaluate the difference between $\hat{x}_v$ and x_v using mean squared error as shown in Eq. 5.[1]

$$L_r(\theta_v) = \|x_v - f_d\left(a_v\right)\|^2 \tag{5}$$

4.4   Adaptive Classification Loss Adjustment

Since there may be a few unpaired visible and thermal images that are significantly dissimilar with each other, and forcefully aligning these images may introduce irrelevant knowledge to the visible network. Therefore, we utilize the feature

---

[1] This term should be written as $L_r(\theta_v, \theta_d)$. In fact, the decoder network can be viewed as a branch of the visible network. We omit the θ_d for convenience.

discriminator's output $p_h = D_h(a_v)$ and label discriminator's output $p_l = D_l(\hat{y}_v)$ to generate attention values to alleviate these effects. In information theory, the entropy function is an uncertainty measure defined as $H(p) = -\sum_j p_j \log p_j$, which we can use to quantify the transferability. We thus utilize the entropy criterion to generate the attention value for each image as:

$$w = 1 + (H(p_h) + H(p_l))/2 \tag{6}$$

Embedding the attention value into the cross entropy loss of visible network $L_v(y_v, \hat{y}_v)$, the adaptive classification loss can be formulated as:

$$L_a(y_v, \hat{y}_v) = wL_v(y_v, \hat{y}_v) \tag{7}$$

4.5 Overall Loss Function

The loss function of the visible networks is defined as Eq. 8.

$$L(\theta_v) = L_a + \lambda_1 L_h + \lambda_2 L_l + \lambda_3 L_r \tag{8}$$

where λ_1, λ_2 and λ_3 are hyper-parameters, controlling the weights of feature-level adversarial loss, label-level adversarial loss and reconstruction loss respectively.

4.6 Optimization

The visible and thermal networks play the role of "generator" in the proposed framework. The optimization procedures of the feature-level and label-level discriminators are mutually independent. Therefore, we can apply alternate optimization steps, as in the original GAN framework [23].

5 Experiment

5.1 Experimental Conditions

We perform our experiments on multimodal databases containing visible and thermal facial images. Currently, available databases include the NVIE database [24], the MAHNOB Laughter database [25], and the MMSE database [26]. The NVIE database is unsuitable for deep learning due to a limited number of training instances. We also perform experiments on facial expression databases containing visible facial images, i.e., CK+ [27], Oulu-CASIA [28] and MMI [29] databases.

The MAHNOB Laughter database consists of audio, visible videos, and thermal videos of spontaneous laughter from 22 subjects captured while the subjects watched funny video clips. Subjects were also asked to produce posed laughter and to speak in their native languages. We cannot conduct expression recognition on this database because it only provides visible and thermal images for laughter. In our experiment, two sub-data sets were used: the laughter versus speech data set (L vs S) which contains 8252 laughter images and 12914 speech images, and the spontaneous laughter versus posed laughter data set (L vs PL) which contains 2124 spontaneous laughter images and 1437 posed laughter images. Following the same experimental conditions as Wang *et al.*'s work [7], a leave-one-subject-out cross validation methodology is adopted. Accuracy and F1-score are used for performance evaluation.

The MMSE database consists of 3D dynamic imaging, 2D visible videos, thermal videos, and physiological records from 140 subjects induced by 10 emotion tasks. We use the same images as Yang *et al.*'s work [20], they semi-automatically select 2468 frames from 72 subjects (45 female and 27 male) on four tasks based on the FACS codes, which contains 676 happiness images, 715 surprise images, 593 pain images and 484 neutral images. A 10-fold cross validation is performed, and the split is subject independent. Accuracy and Macro-F1 are used for performance evaluation.

The CK+ database contains 593 video sequences collected from 123 subjects. Among them, 327 video sequences with 118 subjects are labeled as one of seven expressions, i.e., anger, contempt, disgust, fear, happiness, sadness and surprise. We use the last three frames of each sequence with the provided label, which results in 981 images. A 10-fold cross-validation is performed, and the split is subject independent. Accuracy is used for performance evaluation.

The Oulu-CASIA database contains data captured under three different illumination conditions. During the experiment, only the data captured under strong illumination condition with the VIS camera is used. The Oulu-CASIA VIS has 480 video sequences taken from 80 subjects, and each video sequence is labeled as one of the six basic expressions. The last three frames of each sequence are selected, a 10-fold subject-independent cross validation is performed. Accuracy is used for performance evaluation.

The MMI database consists of 236 image sequences from 31 subjects. Each sequence is labeled as one of the six basic facial expressions. We selected 208 sequences captured in frontal view. We selected three frames in the middle of each sequence as peak frames and associated them with the provided labels. This results a dataset with 624 images. A 10-fold subject-independent cross validation is performed. Accuracy is used for performance evaluation.

On all databases, we crop the facial regions from the visible and thermal images with the help of landmark points and resize the facial regions to 224×224. We use ResNet-34 [30] as the basic architecture for the visible and thermal networks. The last layer of 1000 units in the original ResNet-34 is replaced by fully connected layers with K units. The last layer of the "conv3_x"[2], with a dimension of $28 \times 28 \times 128$, is selected to add feature-level adversarial learning and build the decoder network. The learning rate of the discriminator is 10^{-4}, and the learning rates of the two-view networks start from at 2×10^{-3} and use cosine annealing strategy.

In order to evaluate the influence of each proposed loss function, we conduct a series of ablation experiments to verify our methods when images are unpaired. Firstly, a standard ResNet-34 is trained as baseline using only visible images. Another ResNet-34 is also trained using thermal images and is fixed as

---

[2] See Table 1 in the original ResNet paper [30].

Table 1. Experimental results on the MAHNOB Laughter and MMSE databases.

Scenario	Methods	L vs PL		L vs S		MMSE	
		Acc	F1	Acc	F1	Acc	F1
Single view	Visible neural network [7]	93.98	92.08	83.97	87.01	88.74	89.01
	ResNet	93.93	93.44	85.77	88.96	90.62	90.21
Paired images	SVM2K [7]	91.40	88.52	72.40	77.61	83.01	82.73
	DCCA+SVM [7]	86.42	81.17	65.07	72.29	72.36	71.97
	DCCAE+SVM [7]	86.44	82.21	68.29	74.91	81.30	80.94
	Wang *et al.*'s method [7]	94.14	92.30	85.54	88.38	92.18	91.96
	Pan *et al.*'s method [8]	95.77	94.51	90.23	91.77	93.15	92.88
Unpaired images	L_v+L_h	95.80	94.57	88.60	90.98	92.99	92.78
	L_v+L_l	95.63	94.33	88.35	90.91	92.87	92.75
	$L_v+L_h+L_l$	96.43	95.38	90.08	92.16	93.82	93.78
	$L_a+L_h+L_l$	96.73	95.88	90.72	92.54	94.92	94.79
	Ours:$L_a+L_h+L_l+L_r$	**96.92**	**96.02**	**91.62**	**93.54**	**95.83**	**95.74**

Table 2. Experimental results on the CK+, Oulu-CASIA and MMI databases.

Scenario	Methods	CK+	Oulu-CASIA	MMI
Single view	LBP-TOP [16]	88.99	68.13	59.51
	HOG 3D [14]	91.44	70.63	60.89
	ResNet	94.80	84.58	74.04
	IACNN [18]	95.37	-	71.55
	DeRL [20]	97.30	88.00	73.23
	IF-GAN [19]	95.90	-	74.52
Unpaired images	L_v+L_h	96.64	86.81	77.56
	L_v+L_l	96.33	86.67	77.40
	$L_v+L_h+L_l$	97.15	87.85	78.04
	$L_a+L_h+L_l$	97.86	88.40	78.68
	Ours:$L_a+L_h+L_l+L_r$	**98.37**	**89.11**	**79.33**

guidance later. Secondly, the methods with feature-level adversarial learning L_h, label-level adversarial learning L_l and both of them are trained for comparison. Thirdly, the method with L_h, L_l and adaptive classification loss L_a is trained. Finally, our proposed method which combines L_a, L_h, L_l and L_r is trained.

Note that the visible and thermal training images on the MAHNOB and MMSE databases are all paired. Since we want to conduct unpaired experiment, the most intuitive way is doing cross-dataset experiment. However these two databases have different expression categories, we can't conduct cross-dataset experiment directly. Therefore, in order to simulate the unpaired scenario, we randomly sample visible and thermal training samples $\{x_v^{(i)}, y_v^{(i)}\}_{i=1}^m$ and

$\{x_t^{(i)}, y_t^{(i)}\}_{i=1}^m$ from visible and thermal train set of the same database, and ensure they come from disjoint partitions. On the facial expression databases that only contain visible images, we use the thermal images from MMSE database as privileged information.

5.2   Experimental Results and Analysis

Experimental results are shown in Table 1 and 2. From the tables, we can find the following observations:

Firstly, adopting the introduced losses from the feature and label spaces both lead to a great improvement comparing with the the single-view baseline using ResNet. Specifically, the acc/f1 of L_v+L_h and L_v+L_l are 1.87%/1.13%, 1.70%/0.89% higher than ResNet on the L vs PL data set, 2.83%/2.02%, 2.58%/ 1.95% higher than ResNet on the L vs S data set, 2.37%/2.57%, 2.25%/2.54% higher than ResNet on the MMSE database. The experimental results on the visible facial expression databases, i.e., CK+, Oulu-CASIA and MMI database, show similar trend. Current methods cannot utilize unpaired data, so only one data view can be used. However, our method effectively explores both visible and thermal data to achieve superior results.

Secondly, our method can combine the strengths of adversarial loss from feature and label space to achieve better performance. For example, $L_v+L_h+L_l$ outperforms L_v+L_h and L_v+L_l by 0.83%/1.00% and 0.95%/1.03% of acc/f1 on the MMSE database. Other databases have similar results, which indicate the different privileged informations will not cause the inter-view discrepancy. Guidance in both feature and label spaces can help visible classifier to learn more robust feature representations and make better predictions.

Thirdly, our approach can reduce the irrelevant knowledge impact of some dissimilar visible and thermal images. To be specific, the method of $L_a+L_h+L_l$ is 0.71%, 0.55% and 0.64% better than $L_v+L_h+L_l$ on the CK+, Oulu-CASIA and MMI database. The experimental results demonstrate our introduced adaptive classification loss can highlight transferable images and reduce negative transformation.

Fourthly, our proposed method achieves the best performance by using feature adversarial loss, label adversarial loss, adaptive classification loss and reconstructed loss together. Thermal images are used as privileged information to reduce the statistical gap between the visible and thermal views in both feature and label levels during training. However, adversarial learning focuses on learning view-irrelevant features and may discard the original information of the visible images. Our method adds a decoder network upon the visible feature space, forcing the visible network to preserve inherent features of the visible view. Specifically, the accuracy of our method is 3.57%, 4.53% and 5.29% higher than the baseline using ResNet on the CK+, Oulu-CASIA and MMI database. The experimental results demonstrate that both feature-level and label-level adversarial learning are effective for exploring the dependencies between visible and thermal images, and the decoder network is able to preserve the inherent features of the visible view during adversarial learning.

5.3 Comparison to Related Methods

Comparison to Multimodal FER Methods. As shown in Table 1, our method achieves better performance than three traditional multimodal learning methods, i.e., SVM2K, DCCA+SVM, and DCCAE+SVM. On the L vs S data set, the accuracy of our method is 19.22%, 26.55%, and 23.33% higher than those of SVM2K, DCCA+SVM, and DCCAE+SVM, respectively. SVM2K can be viewed as a shallow version of the ResNet method that includes a similarity constraint. DCCA and DCCAE are learned with an unsupervised objective. Our method is based on the deep convolutional neural network and is learned in an end-to-end manner, resulting in superior accuracy.

Compared to state-of-the-art multimodal FER works, i.e., Wang *et al.*'s method [7] and Pan *et al.*'s method [8], our method achieves better performance by exploiting unpaired images. For example, on the L vs PL data set, the accuracy of our method is 2.78% and 1.15% higher than those of Wang *et al.*'s method and Pan *et al.*'s method, respectively. Wang *et al.*'s method requires paired visible and thermal images during training, and the similarity constraint is imposed on the predictions of the two-view networks in order to make them similar. Our method achieves the same goal without this constraint by learning with unpaired images in an adversarial manner. Pan *et al.*'s method also requires paired images and used adversarial learning in the feature spaces of the visible and thermal views. However, some important information of the visible view may be missing. Our method incorporates a decoder network to ensure the preservation of the original information of the visible view, leading to more robust visible feature representations.

Comparison to Visible FER Methods. As shown in Table 2, our method get better results than the state-of-the-art FER methods which only use visible images. To be specific, our method is 3.00%, 1.07% and 2.47% higher than IACNN [18], DeEL [20] and IF-GAN [19] on the CK+ database, 7.78%, 6.10% and 4.81% higher than these methods on the MMI database. IACNN used expression-sensitive contrastive loss to reduce the effect of identity information, DeEL extracted the information of the expressive component through de-expression procedure, IF-GAN transferred facial expression to a fixed identity to mitigate the effect of identity-related information. Although these works concentrate on extracting the discriminative expressive feature, our method takes full advantage of the thermal images as privileged information to train more robust classifiers.

5.4 Evaluation of Adversarial Learning

To further evaluate the effectiveness of adversarial learning, we visualize the distributions of visible and thermal views. Figure 2 displays the visualization of data from the feature and label spaces with and without adversarial learning on the L vs PL data set. Specifically, we project the hidden feature representations onto a 2D space with t-SNE [31] and plot them on a two-dimensional plane.

Predictions of visible and thermal views are plotted in a histogram. In Fig. 2(a), feature points of visible and thermal views are separate, as feature-level adversarial learning is not used. Introducing adversarial learning on the feature space leads to feature points that are mixed together, as shown in Fig. 2(b). Similarly, when comparing Figs. 2(c) and 2(d), the distributions of visible and thermal predictions become closer in the latter figure, demonstrating the effectiveness of reducing the statistical gap between visible and thermal views via adversarial learning.

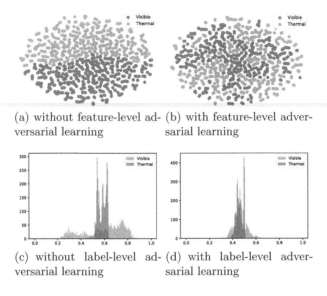

(a) without feature-level adversarial learning

(b) with feature-level adversarial learning

(c) without label-level adversarial learning

(d) with label-level adversarial learning

Fig. 2. Visualization of the visible and thermal distributions on the laughter versus posed laughter data set of the MAHNOB Laughter database.

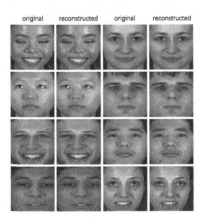

Fig. 3. Comparison between the original facial images and the reconstructed facial images on the MMSE database.

5.5   Visualization of the Decoder Network

As elaborated in Sect. 4.3, a decoder is built upon the visible feature space and the reconstruction loss is included in the overall loss. Thus, we can visualize the outputs of the decoder network, i.e., the reconstructed facial images, to see what the decoder learns. The visualization of the original and reconstructed facial images on the MMSE database is shown in Fig. 3. We can see that the original and reconstructed facial images are nearly identical, indicating that the inherent features of the visible view are preserved during adversarial learning.

6   Conclusions

In this paper, we propose an unpaired facial expression recognition method that utilizes thermal images as privileged information to enhance the visible classifier. Two deep neural networks are first trained with visible and thermal images. Two discriminators are introduced and compete with the two-view networks in the feature and label space to reduce the statistical gap between the learned visible and thermal feature representations and close the distributions between the predictions of the visible and thermal images. Furthermore, a decoder network is built upon the visible hidden features in order to preserve some inherent features of the visible view during adversarial learning. Experimental results on benchmark expression databases demonstrate that our method can achieve state-of-the-art performance on the task of facial expression recognition.

Acknowledgements. This work was supported by the National Natural Science Foundation of China (Grant No. 917418129), and the major project from Anhui Science and Technology Agency (1804a09020038). Thank for Lijun Yin for providing the MMSE database.

References

1. Yoshitomi, Y., Kim, S.I., Kawano, T., Kilazoe, T.: Effect of sensor fusion for recognition of emotional states using voice, face image and thermal image of face. In: Proceedings of the 9th IEEE International Workshop on Robot and Human Interactive Communication, RO-MAN 2000, pp. 178–183. IEEE (2000)
2. Sharma, N., Dhall, A., Gedeon, T., Goecke, R.: Modeling stress using thermal facial patterns: a spatio-temporal approach. In: 2013 Humaine Association Conference on Affective Computing and Intelligent Interaction (ACII), pp. 387–392. IEEE (2013)
3. Wesley, A., Buddharaju, P., Pienta, R., Pavlidis, I.: A comparative analysis of thermal and visual modalities for automated facial expression recognition. In: Bebis, G., et al. (eds.) ISVC 2012. LNCS, vol. 7432, pp. 51–60. Springer, Heidelberg (2012). https://doi.org/10.1007/978-3-642-33191-6_6
4. Wang, S., He, S., Wu, Y., He, M., Ji, Q.: Fusion of visible and thermal images for facial expression recognition. Front. Comput. Sci. **8**(2), 232–242 (2014). https://doi.org/10.1007/s11704-014-2345-1
5. Vapnik, V., Vashist, A.: A new learning paradigm: learning using privileged information. Neural Netw. **22**, 544–557 (2009)

6. Shi, X., Wang, S., Zhu, Y.: Expression recognition from visible images with the help of thermal images. In: Proceedings of the 5th ACM on International Conference on Multimedia Retrieval, pp. 563–566. ACM (2015)

7. Wang, S., Pan, B., Chen, H., Ji, Q.: Thermal augmented expression recognition. IEEE Trans. Cybern. **48**, 2203–2214 (2018)

8. Pan, B., Wang, S.: Facial expression recognition enhanced by thermal images through adversarial learning. In: 2018 ACM Multimedia Conference on Multimedia Conference, pp. 1346–1353. ACM (2018)

9. Wang, Z., Ji, Q.: Classifier learning with hidden information. In: Proceedings of the IEEE Conference on Computer Vision and Pattern Recognition, pp. 4969–4977 (2015)

10. Sharmanska, V., Quadrianto, N.: Learning from the mistakes of others: matching errors in cross-dataset learning. In: Proceedings of the IEEE Conference on Computer Vision and Pattern Recognition, pp. 3967–3975 (2016)

11. Niu, L., Li, W., Xu, D.: Exploiting privileged information from web DT for action and event recognition. Int. J. Comput. Vis. **118**, 130–150 (2016)

12. Luo, Z., Hsieh, J.T., Jiang, L., Niebles, J.C., Fei-Fei, L.: Graph distillation for action detection with privileged modalities. In: Proceedings of the European Conference on Computer Vision (ECCV), pp. 166–183 (2018)

13. Garcia, N.C., Morerio, P., Murino, V.: Learning with privileged information via adversarial discriminative modality distillation. IEEE Trans. Pattern Anal. Mach. Intell. **42**, 2581–2593 (2019)

14. Klaser, A., Marszałek, M., Schmid, C.: A spatio-temporal descriptor based on 3D-gradients. In: 19th British Machine Vision Conference, British Machine Vision Association, BMVC 2008, p. 275-1 (2008)

15. Chu, W., La Torre, F.D., Cohn, J.F.: Selective transfer machine for personalized facial expression analysis. IEEE Trans. Pattern Anal. Mach. Intell. **39**, 529–545 (2017)

16. Zhao, G., Pietikainen, M.: Dynamic texture recognition using local binary patterns with an application to facial expressions. IEEE Trans. Pattern Anal. Mach. Intell. **29**, 915–928 (2007)

17. Jiang, B., Valstar, M.F., Pantic, M.: Action unit detection using sparse appearance descriptors in space-time video volumes. In: Face and Gesture 2011, pp. 314–321. IEEE (2011)

18. Meng, Z., Liu, P., Cai, J., Han, S., Tong, Y.: Identity-aware convolutional neural network for facial expression recognition. In: 2017 12th IEEE International Conference on Automatic Face & Gesture Recognition (FG 2017), pp. 558–565. IEEE (2017)

19. Cai, J., Meng, Z., Khan, A., Li, Z., Oreilly, J., Tong, Y.: Identity-free facial expression recognition using conditional generative adversarial network. arXiv, Computer Vision and Pattern Recognition (2019)

20. Yang, H., Ciftci, U., Yin, L.: Facial expression recognition by de-expression residue learning. In: Proceedings of the IEEE Conference on Computer Vision and Pattern Recognition, pp. 2168–2177 (2018)

21. Sankaran, N., Mohan, D.D., Setlur, S., Govindaraju, V., Fedorishin, D.: Representation learning through cross-modality supervision. In: 2019 14th IEEE International Conference on Automatic Face & Gesture Recognition (FG 2019), pp. 1–8. IEEE (2019)

22. He, L., Xu, X., Lu, H., Yang, Y., Shen, F., Shen, H.T.: Unsupervised cross-modal retrieval through adversarial learning. In: 2017 IEEE International Conference on Multimedia and Expo (ICME), pp. 1153–1158. IEEE (2017)

23. Goodfellow, I., et al.: Generative adversarial nets. In: Advances in Neural Information Processing Systems, pp. 2672–2680 (2014)
24. Wang, S., et al.: A natural visible and infrared facial expression database for expression recognition and emotion inference. IEEE Trans. Multimed. **12**, 682–691 (2010)
25. Petridis, S., Martinez, B., Pantic, M.: The MAHNOB laughter database. Image Vis. Comput. **31**, 186–202 (2013)
26. Zhang, Z., et al.: Multimodal spontaneous emotion corpus for human behavior analysis. In: Proceedings of the IEEE Conference on Computer Vision and Pattern Recognition, pp. 3438–3446 (2016)
27. Lucey, P., Cohn, J.F., Kanade, T., Saragih, J., Ambadar, Z., Matthews, I.: The extended Cohn-Kanade dataset (CK+): a complete dataset for action unit and emotion-specified expression. In: IEEE Computer Society Conference on Computer Vision and Pattern Recognition Workshops, pp. 94–101. IEEE (2010)
28. Zhao, G., Huang, X., Taini, M., Li, S.Z., Pietikainen, M.: Facial expression recognition from near-infrared videos. Image Vis. Comput. **29**, 607–619 (2011)
29. Pantic, M., Valstar, M., Rademaker, R., Maat, L.: Web-based database for facial expression analysis, pp. 317–321 (2005)
30. He, K., Zhang, X., Ren, S., Sun, J.: Deep residual learning for image recognition. In: Proceedings of the IEEE Conference on Computer Vision and Pattern Recognition, pp. 770–778 (2016)
31. van der Maaten, L., Hinton, G.: Visualizing data using T-SNE. J. Mach. Learn. Res. **9**, 2579–2605 (2008)

Gaussian Vector: An Efficient Solution for Facial Landmark Detection

Yilin Xiong[1,2]($\boxtimes$) (iD), Zijian Zhou[2] (iD), Yuhao Dou[2] (iD), and Zhizhong Su[2] (iD)

[1] Central South University, Changsha, Hunan, China
yilin.xiong@csu.edu.cn
[2] Horizon Robotics, Beijing, China
{zijian.zhou,yuhao.dou,zhizhong.su}@horizon.ai

Abstract. Significant progress has been made in facial landmark detection with the development of Convolutional Neural Networks. The widely-used algorithms can be classified into coordinate regression methods and heatmap based methods. However, the former loses spatial information, resulting in poor performance while the latter suffers from large output size or high post-processing complexity. This paper proposes a new solution, Gaussian Vector, to preserve the spatial information as well as reduce the output size and simplify the post-processing. Our method provides novel vector supervision and introduces Band Pooling Module to convert heatmap into a pair of vectors for each landmark. This is a plug-and-play component which is simple and effective. Moreover, Beyond Box Strategy is proposed to handle the landmarks out of the face bounding box. We evaluate our method on 300W, COFW, WFLW and JD-landmark. That the results significantly surpass previous works demonstrates the effectiveness of our approach.

1 Introduction

Facial landmark detection is a critical step for face-related computer vision applications, e.g. face recognition [1–3], face editing [4] and face 3D reconstruction [5–8]. Researchers have achieved great success in this field, especially after using Convolutional Neural Networks (CNNs). The popular algorithms can be divided into coordinate regression methods and heatmap based methods.

Coordinate regression methods use Fully Connected (FC) layers to predict facial landmark coordinates [9,10]. However, the compacted feature maps before the final FC layers cause spatial information loss, leading to performance degradation.

As the advent of Fully Convolution Network [11] and encoder-decoder structure [12], a variety of heatmap based methods [13–18] sprung up to preserve the spatial information. Heatmap based methods predict probability response maps, usually called heatmap, where each pixel predicts the probability that it is the

Electronic supplementary material The online version of this chapter (https://doi.org/10.1007/978-3-030-69541-5_5) contains supplementary material, which is available to authorized users.

H. Ishikawa et al. (Eds.): ACCV 2020, LNCS 12626, pp. 70–87, 2021.
https://doi.org/10.1007/978-3-030-69541-5_5

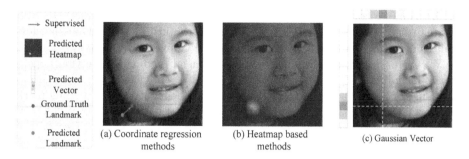

(a) Coordinate regression methods

(b) Heatmap based methods

(c) Gaussian Vector

Fig. 1. Comparison of existing methods and our proposed method. (a) coordinate regression methods and (b) heatmap based methods utilize the scalar coordinates and the heatmap to represent the spatial location of landmarks respectively. (c) Gaussian Vector locates a landmark via a pair of vectors.

landmark location, and find the highest response position by argmax operation. Heatmap based methods boost the performance compared with coordinate regression methods by better utilizing spatial information.

However, heatmap based methods suffer from following problems. **1)** The large output heatmap tensor and complicated post-processing including argmax operation cause heavy burden of data transmission and computation in embedded systems. **2)** The ground truth heatmap consists of a small patch of foreground pixels with positive values and the remaining is full of background pixels with zero values. The background dominates the training process, which causes slow convergence. **3)** Only very few pixels around the highest response position is exploited to locate the landmark. Spatial information is not fully used, causing detection error. **4)** The input of landmark detection model is the face region of interest (RoI) accquried by a face detector. An imperfect face detector causes face bounding box shifting resulting in some of the facial landmarks out of the bounding box. It is difficult for the heatmap based methods to construct a Gaussian surface to locate the landmarks out of the bounding box.

In this case, we are motivated to propose a new facial landmark detection algorithm, which not only maintains the spatial information but also overcome the problems above.

First of all, inspired by the heatmap based methods, we use Gaussian formula to encode landmark coordinates into vectors as supervision. Vector label raises the proportion of foreground pixels in ground truth, which is beneficial to convergence. **Next**, Band Pooling Module (BPM) is proposed to convert the $h \times w$ output heatmap into $h \times 1$ and $1 \times w$ vectors as prediction. On the one hand, vector prediction greatly eases the data transmission burden and simplifies the post-processing. On the other hand, pooling operation helps the network take advantage of more spatial information, which further improves the performance.

Last but not least, we propose Beyond Box Strategy to handle landmarks out of the bounding box. The strategy helps our proposed method to reduce the error caused by bounding box shifting.

We compare our approach with both coordinate regression methods and heatmap based methods in Fig. 1. Considering the utilization of Gaussian formula and vector prediction, we call our method Gaussian Vector (GV).

We evaluate our method on four popular facial landmark detection benchmarks including 300W [19], COFW [20], WFLW [16] and the recent Grand Challenge of 106-p Facial Landmark Localization benchmark [21] (JD-landmark for short). Our approach outperforms state-of-the-art methods in 300W, COFW and WFLW. Without bells and whistles, we achieve the second place in JD-landmark by utilizing a single model.

In summary, our main contributions include:

- We propose an efficient method, Gaussian Vector, for facial landmark detection, which boosts the model performance and reduces the system complexity.
- We introduce novel vector label to encode landmark location for supervision, which alleviates the imbalance of foreground and background in heatmap supervision.
- We design a plug-and-play module, Band Pooling Module (BPM), that effectively converts heatmap into vectors. By this means, the model takes more spatial information into account yet outputs smaller tensor.
- We propose the Beyond Box Strategy, that enables our method to predict landmarks out of the face bounding box.
- Our method achieves state-of-the-art results on 300W, COFW, WFLW and JD-landmark.

2   Related Work

Facial landmark detection, or face alignment, has become a hot topic in computer vision for decades. Early classical methods include Active Appearance Models (AAMs) [22–24], Active Shape Models (ASMs) [25], Constrained Local Models (CLMs) [26], Cascaded Regression Models [20, 27–29] and so on. With the development of deep learning, CNN-based methods have dominated this field. The prevailing approaches fall into two categories.

Coordinate regression methods take the face image as input and output landmark coordinates directly. This kind of methods get better results than the classic without extra post-processing. Sun et al. [9] borrowed the idea of Cascaded Regression and combined serial sub-networks to reduce the location error. TCDCN [10] researched the possibility of improving detection robustness through multi-task learning. MDM [30] employed Recurrent Neural Network (RNN) to replace the cascaded structure in Cascaded Regression. Feng et al. [31] presented a new loss function to pay more attention to small and medium error. Most of the approaches above are proposed with cascaded structure, which largely increases the system complexity.

Heatmap based methods are popular in recent years. Benefit from the encoder-decoder structure, heatmap based methods preserve spatial information by upsampling and significantly improve state-of-the-art performance on all benchmarks. DAN [15] utilized the heatmap information for each stage in the cascaded network and reduced the localization error. Stacked Hourglass [17] introduces repeated bottom-up, top-down architecture for points detection and proposes a shift-based post-processing strategy. HRNet [32,33] presented a novel network architecture for landmark detection, which maintained high-resolution representations through the design of dense fusions on cross-stride layers. LAB [16] proposed a boundary-aware method, which used the stacked hourglass [17] to regress the boundary heatmap for capturing the face geometry structure. Another landmarks regressor fused the sturcture information in multiple stages and got the final results. AWing [14] followed the work of Wing loss [31] and employed the revised version in the heatmap based methods. Also, boundary information and CoordConv [34] are utilized for promoting landmark detection.

However, recovering landmark coordinates from the heatmap still remains to be simplified. Efforts has been devoted to improve the efficiency of this process recently [35–37]. Specifically, Sun *et al.* [35] proposed a differentiable operation to convert heatmap into numerical coordinates for end-to-end training. Yet the calculation of exponent is not computation-efficient in embedded systems.

We believe that brand new supervision is necessary to address problems above. To this end, we encode the location information into vectors for supervision.

3   Our Approach

We first present an overview of our approach in Sect. 3.1. Then Sect. 3.2 introduces the generation of vector label. After that, we illustrate the implementation details of our core component BPM in Sect. 3.3. Finally, we propose a strategy to predict the landmarks out of the face bounding box in Sect. 3.4.

3.1   Overview

An overview of our pipeline is shown in Fig. 2. Similar to heatmap based methods, we use the encoder-decoder structure in our model. The encoder, with fully convolution layers, extracts spatial information on different scales. For the decoder, Feature Pyramid Network (FPN) [38] is adopted. It combines the features of both higher and lower levels through the top-down and botton-up pathways, which improves the pixel-level detection tasks.

The network input is cropped and normalized face image. The network outputs 1/4 resolution heatmap to the original input, where each channel is corresponding to one landmark. A plug-and-play component Band Pooling Module (BPM) compresses heatmap into vectors for end-to-end training.

During training, the predicted vector is supervised by the vector label which is generated from Gaussian formula. More details about vector label can be found in Sect. 3.2. Mean Square Error (MSE) is used as loss function.

During inference, the maximum of predicted vectors indicates the horizontal and vertical location of the landmark respectively. A shift strategy [17], widely

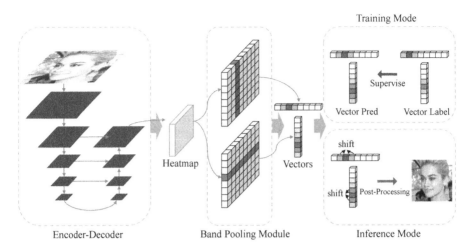

Fig. 2. The overview of the proposed method. Given the face image inputs to the encoder-decoder structure, we can obtain the output heatmap and generate the prediction vectors through Band Pooling Module, match it with vector label for training. Landmark coordinates can be recovered from the vectors by locating the maximum value indexes. Shift strategy [17] is used to reduce quantization error.

used in heatmap based methods, is applied according to its neighbor pixels to reduce location error.

3.2 Vector Label

Vector label $\hat{\mathbf{G}} = (\hat{\mathbf{x}}, \hat{\mathbf{y}})$ for each landmark is generated by the Gaussian formula. Take vector $\hat{\mathbf{x}} \in \mathbb{R}^w$ as an example, where w means the width of the output heatmap. For the landmark coordinate $p(x_0, y_0)$, we first calculate the Euclidean distance between each pixel and x_0 in the vector, getting the distance vector $\mathbf{d} = \{d_x^i\}_{i=0}^{w-1}$, each d_x^i as:

$$d_x^i = \sqrt{(x_i - x_0)^2}, i \in [0, w) \tag{1}$$

Then, we use quasi-Gaussian distribution to transform the distance vector $\mathbf{d}$ to vector label $\hat{\mathbf{x}} = \{\hat{x}^i\}_{i=0}^{w-1}$ with standard deviation σ. The elements are defined as:

$$\hat{x}^i = \begin{cases} e^{-\frac{d_x^i{}^2}{2\sigma^2}}, & \text{if } d_x^i < 3\sigma \text{ and } d_x^i \neq 0 \\ 1 + \theta, & \text{if } d_x^i = 0 \\ 0, & \text{otherwise} \end{cases} \tag{2}$$

We recommend $\sigma = 2$ in most cases. Compared with the normal Gaussian distribution, we reinforce the distribution peak to enhance the supervision by adding a positive constant θ. By this enhancement, we enlarge the value gaps between the horizontal landmark location x_0 and the others to avoid deviation of the highest response position. In the same way, we can get $\hat{\mathbf{y}} \in \mathbb{R}^h$, where h is the heatmap height.

The proposed vector label is beneficial to the model training in two aspects. On the one hand, generating vectors instead of heatmap accelerates the label preparing. On the other hand, extreme foreground background imbalance, as mentioned above, is alleviated in a straightforward way.

3.3   Band Pooling Module

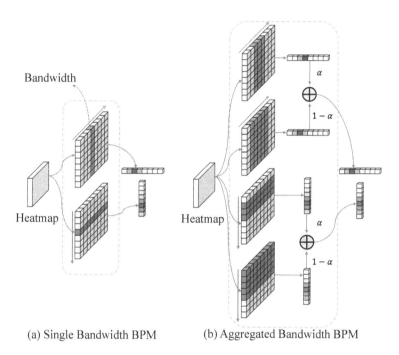

(a) Single Bandwidth BPM   (b) Aggregated Bandwidth BPM

Fig. 3. The illustration of BPM. The vertical band B_v (in *red*) and the horizontal band B_h (in *blue*) slide on the output heatmap. We illustrate the vector generated by single bandwidth (a) and aggregated bandwidth (b). Specifically, the feature vectors of bandwidth $l = 3$ and $l = 5$ are able to aggregated by weighted elementwise sum. (Color figure online)

For end-to-end training, a plug-and-play component Band Pooling Module is presented. The BPM aims to perform the following conversion:

$$\mathbf{H} \rightarrow \mathbf{G} \tag{3}$$

$\mathbf{H}$ is the output feature map and $\mathbf{G} = (\mathbf{x}, \mathbf{y})$ refers to the predicted vectors, matching with vector label $\hat{\mathbf{G}}$ for training.

Band Pooling Module, consisting of horizontal band $B_h \in \mathbb{R}^{l \times w}$ and vertical band $B_v \in \mathbb{R}^{h \times l}$, plays a crucial role in the process of generating predicted vectors. The long side of the band is the same as side length of heatmap (w for B_h and h for B_v). The bandwidth, denoted as l, is a much smaller odd number. The two long and thin bands slide on the output heatmap and average the values of pixels that fall into the band regions, generating predicted vectors $\mathbf{x}$ and $\mathbf{y}$. The pooling operation is shown in Fig. 3(a). It can be described as:

$$\mathbf{x}_l = AvgPooling(\mathbf{H}; B_v, l) \tag{4}$$

The bandwidth l is adjustable, which controls the receptive field size of the vector elements. Undersize bandwidth strictly limits the receptive field, resulting in loss of spatial information, which is essential for the landmark detection. Conversely, overextended receptive field brings in redundant information from the background or nearby landmarks, leading to confusion. In practical, bandwidth l is suggested to be chosen from 1 and 7 and we show the effect of different l in Table 8.

In addition, we extend the basic BPM through fusing the vectors generated by different bandwidths. In general considering the performance and complexity, we aggregate the vectors from only two different bandwidth l_1 and l_2 by weights.

$$\mathbf{x} = \alpha \mathbf{x}_{l_1} + (1 - \alpha)\mathbf{x}_{l_2}, 0 < \alpha < 1 \tag{5}$$

Generally, α is set to be 0.5. Similarly, we can get $\mathbf{y}$. Zero padding is necessary on the edges when $l > 1$. The aggregation is shown in Fig. 3(b).

In this way, the model comprehensively takes spatial information into account via the bigger bandwidth and pay more attention to the adjacent region through the smaller.

By using BPM, we narrow the search regions from 2D maps to 1D vectors when seeking the maximum of the prediction, leading to large reduction on postprocessing complexity (from $O(N^2)$ to $O(N)$).

3.4 Beyond the Box

The face bounding box has a significant impact on facial landmark detection. An oversize bounding box brings in redundant information, especially in the face-crowded image. But a tight box may cause facial landmarks to locate out of the face bounding box. To solve this problem, we propose an effective strategy to predict outer landmarks.

In general, the predicted vectors present smoother quasi-Gaussian distribution than vector label, where the maximum implies the landmark location. When the landmark locates inside, the maximum position is in the middle of the vector. On the contrary, when the landmark falls out of the input, the maximum is close to one of the endpoints and the quasi-Gaussian distribution is cut off. An example of the outside landmark is displayed in Fig. 4. Apparently, the maximum value of $\mathbf{y}$ is much smaller than the normal ones.

 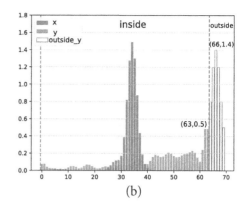

(a)   (b)

Fig. 4. (a) **A visualization of the prediction with the Beyond Box Strategy.** The ground truth and prediction landmarks are shown in *red* and *green*, respectively. The *blue* rectangle refers to the face bounding box. (b) **We use a histogr7am to visualize the predicted vector of landmark in the *yellow circle* of the *left* image.** The *red dashed line* shows the distribution of predicted vector inside, while the outside shows the estimated distribution from Beyond Box Strategy when the maximum locates at the endpoint of vector (e.g. **y**). We calculate the position of ideal distribution peak, i.e. (66, 1.4) in histogram, according to Eq. 6. (Color figure online)

Fortunately, the maximum value tells us whether the landmark goes beyond and how far it goes. If the distribution is cut off and the maximum locate at endpoint (0 or $w-1$ for index s), we assume x^s obeys the distribution:

$$x^s = \tau e^{-\frac{d^2}{2\sigma^2}} \tag{6}$$

where d indicates the distance between s and the distribution peak. τ is a scale parameter and σ is the standard deviation, which control the peak value and smoothness of distribution respectively. The assumption helps the model to estimate the location of the distribution peak, which works only if the vector maximum locates at one of the endpoints, just like the blue vector in Fig. 4(b).

Assume that the maximum locates at the endpoint, we can get the revised landmark location:

$$loc = \begin{cases} -\sqrt{-2\sigma^2 log(\frac{x^0}{\tau})} & \text{if } \underset{i}{argmax}\, x^i = 0 \\ w - 1 + \sqrt{-2\sigma^2 log(\frac{x^{w-1}}{\tau})} & \text{if } \underset{i}{argmax}\, x^i = w - 1 \end{cases} \tag{7}$$

Generally, τ ranges from $0.5 \times (1 + \theta)$ to $0.8 \times (1 + \theta)$ and σ equals to that in Eq. 2.

4   Experiments

To verify the effectiveness of our method, a series of experiments are conducted on public datasets in Sect. 4.4. Ablation study is carried out on 300W in Sect. 4.5

to test the proposed components. In Sect. 4.6, we perform efficiency analysis to validate the points made above. In addition, we give comprehensive analysis of the merits of vector supervision in the supplement material.

4.1 Datasets

300W [19] is a widely-used benchmark for facial landmark detection, which is a compound dataset including HELEN [39], LFPW [40], AFW [41], and IBUG [19] and re-annotated by the 68-point scheme. Same as the previous works [13,16], we utilize 3148 images for training and 689 images for validation. The full test set can be divided into the common subset and the challenge subset.

  COFW [20] is designed to present faces in realistic conditions. Faces in the pictures show large variations in shape and occlusion due to differences in expression, as well as pose. COFW has 1354 images for training and 507 images for testing. Each image is annotated with 29 points consistent with LFPW.

  WFLW [16] is a recently proposed large dataset which consists of 7500 training images and 2500 testing images with 98-point annotation. It is one of the most challenging benchmarks for facial landmark detection because of existing extreme disturbance such as occlusion, large pose, illumination, and blur. In order to evaluate the model in variant conditions, the test dataset is categorized as multiple subsets.

  JD-landmark [21] is introduced for competition in 2019. Each image is manually annotated with 106-point landmarks. It contains three parts of training, validation, and test sets. The training set provides 11393 images with different poses. The validation and test sets come from web open datasets and cover large variations in pose, expression and occlusion, including 2000 images respectively.

4.2 Evaluation Metrics

To facilitate comparison with previous works, we adopt different evaluation metrics for different benchmarks including Normalized Mean Error (NME), Area Under Curve (AUC) based on Cumulative Error Distribution (CED) curve, and Failure Rate (FR).

  NME is widely used in facial landmark detection to evaluate the quality of models. It is calculated by average the Euclidean distance between predicted and ground truth landmarks, then normalized to eliminate the impact caused by the image size inconsistency. NME for each image is defined as:

$$NME = \frac{1}{L} \sum_{k=1}^{L} \frac{\|p_k - \hat{p}_k\|_2}{d} \tag{8}$$

Where L refers to the number of landmarks. p_k and $\hat{p}_k$ refer to the predicted and ground truth coordinates of the k-th landmark respectively. d is the normalization factor, such as the distance of eye centers (inter-pupil normalization, IPN) or the distance of eye corners (inter-ocular normalization, ION). Specially,

For JD-landmark, $d = \sqrt{w_{bbox} \times h_{bbox}}$, where w_{bbox} and h_{bbox} are the width and height of the enclosing rectangle of the ground truth landmarks.

FR is another widely-used metric. It is the percentage of failure samples whose NME is larger than a threshold. As the threshold rises from zero to the target value, we plot the proportion of success (samples with smaller NME than the threshold) as the CED curve. AUC calculates the area under the CED curve.

4.3 Implementation Details

Firstly, for each face bounding box, we extend the short side to the same as the long to avoid *image distortion* since the bounding box is not square in most cases. Then we enlarge the bounding boxes in WFLW and COFW by 25% and 10% respectively, and keep the extended square box size for 300W and JD-landmark. Finally, the images are cropped and resized to 256×256 according to the square boxes from the previous step.

In terms of data augmentation, we use standard methods: 30° max angle of random rotation with the probability of 50%, random scale 75%~125% for all images, random flip horizontally with the probability of 50%. We also try random occlusion in training which improves the performance. We optimize models with Adam [42] for all benchmarks. For bandwdith l, we choose both 3 and 5 for aggregating. For σ in Eq. 2, it is set to 2 on all benchmarks. Our models are trained with MXNet/Gluon 1.5.1 [43] on 4× TITAN X GPUs. During inference our baseline model costs 28ms per face for the entire pipeline (network forward and post-processing) with batch size = 1 and 1× TITAN X.

4.4 Evaluation on Different Benchmarks

We provide two models based on ReNetV2-50 [49] and HRNetV2-W32 [32], represented as GV(ResNet50) and GV(HRNet) respectively, to verify the generality and effectiveness of our approach. Experiments show that our approach achieves state of the art on all benchmarks.[1]

Evaluation on 300W. Our proposed method achieves the best performance on 300W as shown in Table 1. GV(ResNet50) achieves 3.14% for ION (4.41% for IPN), and GV(HRNet) achieves 2.99% for ION (4.19% for IPN). Both models get remarkable results.

Evaluation on COFW. Experiments on COFW is displayed in Table 2. Our baseline model GV(ResNet50) provides a better result than the previously best work AWing [14] with 4.92% for IPN. GV(HRNet) achieves newly state-of-the-art performance with 4.85% and reduces FR from 0.99% to 0.39%.

Evaluation on WFLW. It is one of the most challenging benchmarks. We comprehensively compare the results of NME, FR@0.1, and AUC@0.1 with the previous works on the whole test set as well as all subsets in Table 3. Our method

---

[1] In addition, we analyze the merits of vector supervision in supplemental material.

Table 1. NME (%) on 300W Common, Challenging, Full subset

Method	Common	Challenging	Fullset
Inter-pupil Normalization			
RCPR [20]	6.18	17.26	8.35
LBF [44]	4.95	11.98	6.32
TCDCN [10]	4.80	6.80	5.54
RAR [45]	4.12	8.35	4.94
LAB [16]	4.20	7.41	4.92
DCFE [46]	3.83	7.54	4.55
AWing [14]	3.77	6.52	4.31
GV(ResNet50)	3.78	6.98	4.41
GV(HRNet)	**3.63**	**6.51**	**4.19**
Inter-ocular Normalization			
DAN [15]	3.19	5.24	3.59
DCFE [46]	2.76	5.22	3.24
LAB [16]	2.98	5.19	3.49
HRNetV2 [32]	2.87	5.15	3.32
AWing [14]	2.72	4.52	3.07
GV(ResNet50)	2.73	4.84	3.14
GV(HRNet)	**2.62**	**4.51**	**2.99**

Table 2. NME (%) and FR (%) on COFW testset

Method	NME	$FR_{10\%}$
Inter-pupil Normalization		
Human [20]	5.60	–
RCPR [20]	8.50	20.0
RAR [45]	6.03	4.14
TCDCN [10]	8.05	20.0
DAC-CSR [47]	6.03	4.73
PCD-CNN [48]	5.77	3.73
DCFE [46]	5.27	–
AWing [14]	4.94	0.99
GV(ResNet50)	4.92	0.99
GV(HRNet)	**4.85**	**0.59**
Inter-ocular Normalization		
LAB [47]	3.92	0.39
MobileFAN [13]	3.66	0.59
HRNetV2 [32]	3.45	**0.19**
GV(ResNet50)	3.42	0.59
GV(HRNet)	**3.37**	0.39

achieves evident improvements of NME and AUC in almost all subsets. Notably, ION on the whole test set decreases to 4.33%. We comprehensively compare our method with AWing in the supplement material.

Evaluation on JD-landmark. The results of JD-landmark are exhibited on Table 4. GV(HRNet) achieves comparable results (1.35% for NME with FR 0.10%) to the champion (1.31% for NME with FR 0.10%) with a single model excluding extra competition tricks. It is noteworthy that the champion [21] employed AutoML [53] on architecture search, ensemble model, and a well-designed data augmentation scheme etc. The results further prove the briefness and effectiveness of our method for facial landmark detection.

Table 3. Evaluation on WFLW

Metric	Method	Testset	Pose Subset	Expression Subset	Illumination Subset	Make-up Subset	Occlusion Subset	Blur Subset
NME(%) (Lower is better)	ESR [27]	11.13	25.88	11.47	10.49	11.05	13.75	12.20
	SDM [50]	10.29	24.10	11.45	9.32	9.38	13.03	11.28
	CFSS [51]	9.07	21.36	10.09	8.30	8.74	11.76	9.96
	DVLN [52]	6.08	11.54	6.78	5.73	5.98	7.33	6.88
	LAB [16]	5.27	10.24	5.51	5.23	5.15	6.79	6.32
	Wing [31]	5.11	8.75	5.36	4.93	5.41	6.37	5.81
	AWing [14]	4.36	**7.38**	4.58	4.32	4.27	**5.19**	4.96
	GV(ResNet50)	4.57	7.91	4.85	4.51	4.45	5.50	5.28
	GV(HRNet)	**4.33**	7.41	**4.51**	**4.24**	**4.18**	**5.19**	**4.93**
$FR_{10\%}$(%) (Lower is better)	ESR [27]	35.24	90.18	42.04	30.80	38.84	47.28	41.40
	SDM [50]	29.40	84.36	33.44	26.22	27.67	41.85	35.32
	CFSS [51]	20.56	66.26	23.25	17.34	21.84	32.88	23.67
	DVLN [52]	10.84	46.93	11.15	7.31	11.65	16.30	13.71
	LAB [16]	7.56	28.83	6.37	6.73	7.77	13.72	10.74
	Wing [31]	6.00	22.70	4.78	4.30	7.77	12.50	7.76
	AWing [14]	**2.84**	**13.50**	**2.23**	**2.58**	**2.91**	**5.98**	**3.75**
	GV(ResNet50)	4.44	19.94	3.18	3.72	3.88	8.83	6.47
	GV(HRNet)	3.52	16.26	2.55	3.30	3.40	6.79	5.05
$AUC_{10\%}$ (Higher is better)	ESR [27]	0.2774	0.0177	0.1981	0.2953	0.2485	0.1946	0.2204
	SDM [50]	0.3002	0.0226	0.2293	0.3237	0.3125	0.2060	0.2398
	CFSS [51]	0.3659	0.0632	0.3157	0.3854	0.3691	0.2688	0.3037
	DVLN [52]	0.4551	0.1474	0.3889	0.4743	0.4494	0.3794	0.3973
	LAB [16]	0.5323	0.2345	0.4951	0.5433	0.5394	0.4490	0.4630
	Wing [31]	0.5504	0.3100	0.4959	0.5408	0.5582	0.4885	0.4918
	AWing [14]	0.5719	0.3120	0.5149	0.5777	0.5715	0.5022	0.5120
	GV(ResNet50)	0.5568	0.2769	0.5321	0.5673	0.5640	0.4782	0.4959
	GV(HRNet)	**0.5775**	**0.3166**	**0.5636**	**0.5863**	**0.5881**	**0.5035**	**0.5242**

Table 4. The leadboard of JD-landmark

Ranking	Team	AUC(@0.08)(%)	NME(%)
No.1	Baidu VIS	**84.01**	**1.31**
No.2	USTC-NELSLIP	82.68	1.41
No.3	VIC iron man	82.22	1.42
No.4	CIGIT-ALIBABA	81.53	1.50
No.5	Smiles	81.28	1.50
Baseline	–	73.32	2.16
GV(HRNet)	–	83.34	1.35

Table 5. Ablation study on our method. BBS means Beyond Box Strategy.

Backbone	Original face bounding box		Shrunk face bounding box		
	BPM	NME(%)	BPM	BBS	NME(%)
ResNet50	–	3.42	✓	–	4.57
	✓	**3.14**	✓	✓	**4.10**

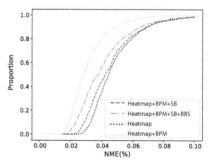

Fig. 5. CED curves of models in Table 5. SB means Shrinking the bounding box by 10%.

4.5 Ablation Study

To demonstrate the effectiveness of Band Pooling Module and Beyond Box strategy, ablation study is implemented on 300W. We choose ResNet50 as the backbone and ION as the test metric.

Effectiveness of BPM. We compare the performance with and without the BPM, that is, our proposed method and the heatmap based method. The result of each model is shown in Table 5, and the BPM greatly improves the model performance from 3.42% to 3.14%. Moreover, we provide CED curves to evaluate the accuracy difference in Fig. 5.

Choice of the Bandwidth. Experiments show that the choice of bandwidth l has a great impact on the performance of the model in Table 8. It is obvious that oversize or undersize bandwidth does harm to the model performance (3.94% when $l = 1$ and 3.38% when $l = 7$). By aggregating different bandwidth, we get better localization results. Specifically, we obtain the best ION 3.14% when fusing the vectors from bandwidth $l = 3$ and $l = 5$.

Choice of θ in Eq. 2. We conduct a series of experiments on 300W with θ range from 0 to 4. Note the backbone is ResNet50. Experiments show that the appropriate θ gets better results in Table 7.

Improvements from the Beyond Box Strategy. In Sect. 3.4, we introduce a strategy to predict the landmarks out of the face bounding box. Now a plain experiments is conducted to illustrate the effectiveness of it. We shrink the ground truth bounding box of 300W fullset by 10% in each dimension to make some points fall out of the image. In this case, the prediction results turn worse (ION raised from 3.14% to 4.57%, shown in Table 5) since the certain parts of face are invisible. We compare different choices for τ and ρ, as illustrated in Table 6. When we pick $\tau = 2.0$ and $\rho = 2.0$, ION decreases from 4.57% to 4.10% (Fig. 6).

Table 6. Different choices for τ and σ in Beyond Box Strategy.

τ	σ				
	1.0	1.5	2.0	2.5	3.0
1.0	4.42	4.35	4.29	4.26	4.24
1.5	4.33	4.23	4.15	4.12	4.14
2.0	4.28	4.17	**4.10**	4.12	4.22
2.5	4.26	4.15	4.13	4.23	4.43

Table 7. Evaluation on different values of θ.

θ	0	1	2	3	4
ION(%)	3.32	3.23	3.21	**3.14**	3.25

Table 8. Comparison among different bandwidth. Diagonal elements indicate that vector generated by single bandwidth BPM, as bandwidth $l = 1$ or $l = 3$. The others attained by aggregating different bandwidth where $\alpha = 0.5$ in Eq. 5.

Bandwidth	$l = 1$	$l = 3$	$l = 5$	$l = 7$
$l = 1$	3.94	3.67	3.61	3.74
$l = 3$	–	3.31	**3.14**	3.22
$l = 5$	–	–	3.21	3.28
$l = 7$	–	–	–	3.38

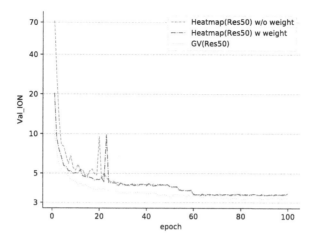

Fig. 6. The training convergence plots of different method. Note the logarithm of the y-axis here.

4.6 Efficiency Analysis

The efficiency of our method is examined in both convergence rate and time cost as follows.

The Comparision of Convergence Rate. We argue that the vector label speeds up model convergence and will experimentally demonstrate that. In addition, a solution for imbalance has been proposed in AWing [14]. By using a weight map, AWing applied different weights on hard examples(1.0) and easy examples(0.1) to alleviate the imbalance of heatmap. Experiments on 300W show the impact of weight map and vector label on convergence. We use the same learning rate and batch size for a fair comparison. The metric is ION. The results show both weight map and vector label facilitate the convergence and our method is better.

Table 9. Comparison of the time cost.

Method	Output tensor size	Net-forward (ms)	Post-processing (ms)	Transmission (ms)
Heatmap	(68, 64, 64)	6.129	2.039	0.311
Gaussian Vector	(68, 64, 2)	6.158	0.062	0.048

Time cost analysis of Heatmap based method and Gaussian Vector. In embedded systems, the network runs on neural net accelerators (e.g. TPU) and post-processing on CPU (e.g. ARM). The former accelerates common ops (Conv/Pool excluding argmax) significantly. So BPM increases little computation complexity and time. However, post-processing is the bottleneck since CPU has to process many other tasks synchronously. For the limitation of the practical system (MT6735 with a NN accelerator), we use MobileNetV3 as the backbone to test the time cost of heatmap based method and ours. As Table 9, our method saves 26% time of the whole process in this case.

5   Conclusion

In this paper, we present a simple yet effective solution for facial landmark detection. We provide novel vector label for supervision, Band Pooling Module to convert output heatmap into vectors, as well as Beyond Box Strategy for predicting landmarks out of the input. By evaluating on different benchmarks, we demonstrate the efficiency of our proposed method. Also, our method and its components are validated via comprehensive ablation study.

References

1. Sun, Y., Wang, X., Tang, X.: Deep learning face representation from predicting 10,000 classes. In: Proceedings of the IEEE Conference on Computer Vision and Pattern Recognition, pp. 1891–1898 (2014)
2. Liu, W., Wen, Y., Yu, Z., Li, M., Raj, B., Song, L.: SphereFace: deep hypersphere embedding for face recognition. In: Proceedings of the IEEE Conference on Computer Vision and Pattern Recognition, pp. 212–220 (2017)
3. Deng, J., Guo, J., Xue, N., Zafeiriou, S.: ArcFace: additive angular margin loss for deep face recognition. In: Proceedings of the IEEE Conference on Computer Vision and Pattern Recognition, pp. 4690–4699 (2019)
4. Thies, J., Zollhofer, M., Stamminger, M., Theobalt, C., Nießner, M.: Face2Face: real-time face capture and reenactment of RGB videos. In: Proceedings of the IEEE Conference on Computer Vision and Pattern Recognition, pp. 2387–2395 (2016)
5. Dou, P., Shah, S.K., Kakadiaris, I.A.: End-to-end 3D face reconstruction with deep neural networks. In: Proceedings of the IEEE Conference on Computer Vision and Pattern Recognition, pp. 5908–5917 (2017)
6. Roth, J., Tong, Y., Liu, X.: Unconstrained 3D face reconstruction. In: Proceedings of the IEEE Conference on Computer Vision and Pattern Recognition, pp. 2606–2615 (2015)
7. Feng, Y., Wu, F., Shao, X., Wang, Y., Zhou, X.: Joint 3D face reconstruction and dense alignment with position map regression network. In: Proceedings of the European Conference on Computer Vision (ECCV), pp. 534–551 (2018)
8. Zhu, X., Liu, X., Lei, Z., Li, S.Z.: Face alignment in full pose range: a 3D total solution. IEEE Trans. Pattern Anal. Mach. Intell. **41**, 78–92 (2017)
9. Sun, Y., Wang, X., Tang, X.: Deep convolutional network cascade for facial point detection. In: Proceedings of the IEEE Conference on Computer Vision and Pattern Recognition, pp. 3476–3483 (2013)
10. Zhang, Z., Luo, P., Loy, C.C., Tang, X.: Facial landmark detection by deep multitask learning. In: Fleet, D., Pajdla, T., Schiele, B., Tuytelaars, T. (eds.) ECCV 2014. LNCS, vol. 8694, pp. 94–108. Springer, Cham (2014). https://doi.org/10.1007/978-3-319-10599-4_7
11. Long, J., Shelhamer, E., Darrell, T.: Fully convolutional networks for semantic segmentation. In: Proceedings of the IEEE Conference on Computer Vision and Pattern Recognition, pp. 3431–3440 (2015)

12. Ronneberger, O., Fischer, P., Brox, T.: U-Net: convolutional networks for biomedical image segmentation. In: Navab, N., Hornegger, J., Wells, W.M., Frangi, A.F. (eds.) MICCAI 2015. LNCS, vol. 9351, pp. 234–241. Springer, Cham (2015). https://doi.org/10.1007/978-3-319-24574-4_28

13. Zhao, Y., Liu, Y., Shen, C., Gao, Y., Xiong, S.: MobileFAN: transferring deep hidden representation for face alignment. Pattern Recogn. **100**, 107114 (2020)

14. Wang, X., Bo, L., Fuxin, L.: Adaptive wing loss for robust face alignment via heatmap regression. In: Proceedings of the IEEE International Conference on Computer Vision, pp. 6971–6981 (2019)

15. Kowalski, M., Naruniec, J., Trzcinski, T.: Deep alignment network: a convolutional neural network for robust face alignment. In: Proceedings of the IEEE Conference on Computer Vision and Pattern Recognition Workshops, pp. 88–97 (2017)

16. Wu, W., Qian, C., Yang, S., Wang, Q., Cai, Y., Zhou, Q.: Look at boundary: a boundary-aware face alignment algorithm. In: Proceedings of the IEEE Conference on Computer Vision and Pattern Recognition, pp. 2129–2138 (2018)

17. Newell, A., Yang, K., Deng, J.: Stacked hourglass networks for human pose estimation. In: Leibe, B., Matas, J., Sebe, N., Welling, M. (eds.) ECCV 2016. LNCS, vol. 9912, pp. 483–499. Springer, Cham (2016). https://doi.org/10.1007/978-3-319-46484-8_29

18. Dong, X., Yu, S.I., Weng, X., Wei, S.E., Yang, Y., Sheikh, Y.: Supervision-by-registration: an unsupervised approach to improve the precision of facial landmark detectors. In: Proceedings of the IEEE Conference on Computer Vision and Pattern Recognition, pp. 360–368 (2018)

19. Sagonas, C., Tzimiropoulos, G., Zafeiriou, S., Pantic, M.: 300 faces in-the-wild challenge: the first facial landmark localization challenge. In: Proceedings of the IEEE International Conference on Computer Vision Workshops, pp. 397–403 (2013)

20. Burgos-Artizzu, X.P., Perona, P., Dollár, P.: Robust face landmark estimation under occlusion. In: Proceedings of the IEEE International Conference on Computer Vision, pp. 1513–1520 (2013)

21. Liu, Y., et al.: Grand challenge of 106-point facial landmark localization. In: 2019 IEEE International Conference on Multimedia & Expo Workshops (ICMEW), pp. 613–616. IEEE (2019)

22. Cootes, T.F., Edwards, G.J., Taylor, C.J.: Active appearance models. IEEE Trans. Pattern Anal. Mach. Intell. **23**, 681–685 (2001)

23. Kahraman, F., Gokmen, M., Darkner, S., Larsen, R.: An active illumination and appearance (AIA) model for face alignment. In: 2007 IEEE Conference on Computer Vision and Pattern Recognition, pp. 1–7. IEEE (2007)

24. Matthews, I., Baker, S.: Active appearance models revisited. Int. J. Comput. Vis. **60**, 135–164 (2004)

25. Milborrow, S., Nicolls, F.: Locating facial features with an extended active shape model. In: Forsyth, D., Torr, P., Zisserman, A. (eds.) ECCV 2008. LNCS, vol. 5305, pp. 504–513. Springer, Heidelberg (2008). https://doi.org/10.1007/978-3-540-88693-8_37

26. Cristinacce, D., Cootes, T.F.: Feature detection and tracking with constrained local models. In: BMVC, vol. 1, p. 3. Citeseer (2006)

27. Cao, X., Wei, Y., Wen, F., Sun, J.: Face alignment by explicit shape regression. Int. J. Comput. Vis. **107**, 177–190 (2014)

28. Chen, D., Ren, S., Wei, Y., Cao, X., Sun, J.: Joint cascade face detection and alignment. In: Fleet, D., Pajdla, T., Schiele, B., Tuytelaars, T. (eds.) ECCV 2014. LNCS, vol. 8694, pp. 109–122. Springer, Cham (2014). https://doi.org/10.1007/978-3-319-10599-4_8

29. Xiong, X., De la Torre, F.: Global supervised descent method. In: Proceedings of the IEEE Conference on Computer Vision and Pattern Recognition, pp. 2664–2673 (2015)
30. Trigeorgis, G., Snape, P., Nicolaou, M.A., Antonakos, E., Zafeiriou, S.: Mnemonic descent method: a recurrent process applied for end-to-end face alignment. In: Proceedings of the IEEE Conference on Computer Vision and Pattern Recognition, pp. 4177–4187 (2016)
31. Feng, Z.H., Kittler, J., Awais, M., Huber, P., Wu, X.J.: Wing loss for robust facial landmark localisation with convolutional neural networks. In: Proceedings of the IEEE Conference on Computer Vision and Pattern Recognition, pp. 2235–2245 (2018)
32. Sun, K., et al.: High-resolution representations for labeling pixels and regions. arXiv preprint arXiv:1904.04514 (2019)
33. Sun, K., Xiao, B., Liu, D., Wang, J.: Deep high-resolution representation learning for human pose estimation. In: Proceedings of the IEEE Conference on Computer Vision and Pattern Recognition, pp. 5693–5703 (2019)
34. Liu, R., et al.: An intriguing failing of convolutional neural networks and the coord-conv solution. In: Advances in Neural Information Processing Systems, pp. 9605–9616 (2018)
35. Sun, X., Xiao, B., Wei, F., Liang, S., Wei, Y.: Integral human pose regression. In: Proceedings of the European Conference on Computer Vision (ECCV), pp. 529–545 (2018)
36. Nibali, A., He, Z., Morgan, S., Prendergast, L.: Numerical coordinate regression with convolutional neural networks. arXiv preprint arXiv:1801.07372 (2018)
37. Levine, S., Finn, C., Darrell, T., Abbeel, P.: End-to-end training of deep visuomotor policies. J. Mach. Learn. Res. **17**, 1334–1373 (2016)
38. Lin, T.Y., Dollár, P., Girshick, R., He, K., Hariharan, B., Belongie, S.: Feature pyramid networks for object detection. In: Proceedings of the IEEE Conference on Computer Vision and Pattern Recognition, pp. 2117–2125 (2017)
39. Le, V., Brandt, J., Lin, Z., Bourdev, L., Huang, T.S.: Interactive facial feature localization. In: Fitzgibbon, A., Lazebnik, S., Perona, P., Sato, Y., Schmid, C. (eds.) ECCV 2012. LNCS, vol. 7574, pp. 679–692. Springer, Heidelberg (2012). https://doi.org/10.1007/978-3-642-33712-3_49
40. Belhumeur, P.N., Jacobs, D.W., Kriegman, D.J., Kumar, N.: Localizing parts of faces using a consensus of exemplars. IEEE Trans. Pattern Anal. Mach. Intell. **35**, 2930–2940 (2013)
41. Zhu, X., Ramanan, D.: Face detection, pose estimation, and landmark localization in the wild. In: IEEE Conference on Computer Vision and Pattern Recognition, pp. 2879–2886. IEEE (2012)
42. Kingma, D.P., Ba, J.L.: Adam: a method for stochastic optimization
43. Chen, T., et al.: MXNet: a flexible and efficient machine learning library for heterogeneous distributed systems. arXiv preprint arXiv:1512.01274 (2015)
44. Ren, S., Cao, X., Wei, Y., Sun, J.: Face alignment at 3000 fps via regressing local binary features. In: Proceedings of the IEEE Conference on Computer Vision and Pattern Recognition, pp. 1685–1692 (2014)
45. Xiao, S., Feng, J., Xing, J., Lai, H., Yan, S., Kassim, A.: Robust facial landmark detection via recurrent attentive-refinement networks. In: Leibe, B., Matas, J., Sebe, N., Welling, M. (eds.) ECCV 2016. LNCS, vol. 9905, pp. 57–72. Springer, Cham (2016). https://doi.org/10.1007/978-3-319-46448-0_4

46. Valle, R., Buenaposada, J.M., Valdes, A., Baumela, L.: A deeply-initialized coarse-to-fine ensemble of regression trees for face alignment. In: Proceedings of the European Conference on Computer Vision (ECCV), pp. 585–601 (2018)
47. Feng, Z.H., Kittler, J., Christmas, W., Huber, P., Wu, X.J.: Dynamic attention-controlled cascaded shape regression exploiting training data augmentation and fuzzy-set sample weighting. In: Proceedings of the IEEE Conference on Computer Vision and Pattern Recognition, pp. 2481–2490 (2017)
48. Kumar, A., Chellappa, R.: Disentangling 3d pose in a dendritic CNN for unconstrained 2D face alignment. In: Proceedings of the IEEE Conference on Computer Vision and Pattern Recognition, pp. 430–439 (2018)
49. He, K., Zhang, X., Ren, S., Sun, J.: Identity mappings in deep residual networks. In: Leibe, B., Matas, J., Sebe, N., Welling, M. (eds.) ECCV 2016. LNCS, vol. 9908, pp. 630–645. Springer, Cham (2016). https://doi.org/10.1007/978-3-319-46493-0_38
50. Xiong, X., De la Torre, F.: Supervised descent method and its applications to face alignment. In: Proceedings of the IEEE Conference on Computer Vision and Pattern Recognition, pp. 532–539 (2013)
51. Zhu, S., Li, C., Change Loy, C., Tang, X.: Face alignment by coarse-to-fine shape searching. In: Proceedings of the IEEE Conference on Computer Vision and Pattern Recognition, pp. 4998–5006 (2015)
52. Wu, W., Yang, S.: Leveraging intra and inter-dataset variations for robust face alignment. In: Proceedings of the IEEE Conference on Computer Vision and Pattern Recognition Workshops, pp. 150–159 (2017)
53. He, Y., Lin, J., Liu, Z., Wang, H., Li, L.J., Han, S.: AMC: AutoML for model compression and acceleration on mobile devices. In: Proceedings of the European Conference on Computer Vision (ECCV), pp. 784–800 (2018)

A Global to Local Double Embedding Method for Multi-person Pose Estimation

Yiming Xu[1], Jiaxin Li[2], Yan Ding[2(✉)], and Hua-Liang Wei[3]

[1] Yingcai Honors College, University of Electronic Science and Technology of China,
Chengdu, China

[2] Key Laboratory of Dynamics and Control of Flight Vehicle, Ministry of Education,
School of Aerospace Engineering, Beijing Institute of Technology,
Beijing 100081, China
dingyan@bit.edu.cn

[3] Department of Automatic Control and Systems Engineering,
University of Sheffield, Sheffield S1 3JD, UK

Abstract. Multi-person pose estimation is a fundamental and challenging problem to many computer vision tasks. Most existing methods can be broadly categorized into two classes: top-down and bottom-up methods. Both of the two types of methods involve two stages, namely, person detection and joints detection. Conventionally, the two stages are implemented separately without considering their interactions between them, and this may inevitably cause some issue intrinsically. In this paper, we present a novel method to simplify the pipeline by implementing person detection and joints detection simultaneously. We propose a Double Embedding (DE) method to complete the multi-person pose estimation task in a global-to-local way. DE consists of Global Embedding (GE) and Local Embedding (LE). GE encodes different person instances and processes information covering the whole image and LE encodes the local limbs information. GE functions for the person detection in top-down strategy while LE connects the rest joints sequentially which functions for joint grouping and information processing in A bottom-up strategy. Based on LE, we design the Mutual Refine Machine (MRM) to reduce the prediction difficulty in complex scenarios. MRM can effectively realize the information communicating between keypoints and further improve the accuracy. We achieve the competitive results on benchmarks MSCOCO, MPII and CrowdPose, demonstrating the effectiveness and generalization ability of our method.

1 Introduction

Human pose estimation aims to localize the human facial and body keypoints (e.g., nose, shoulder, knee, etc.) in the image. It is a fundamental technique for many computer vision tasks such as action recognition [1], human-computer interaction [2,3], person Re-ID [4] and so on.

First two authors equally contributed to this work.

© Springer Nature Switzerland AG 2021
H. Ishikawa et al. (Eds.): ACCV 2020, LNCS 12626, pp. 88–103, 2021.
https://doi.org/10.1007/978-3-030-69541-5_6

Most of the existing methods can be broadly categorized into two classes: top-down methods [5–13] and bottom-up methods [14–18]. As shown in Fig. 1 (a), the top-down strategy first employs a human detector to generate person bounding boxes, and then performs single person pose estimation on each individual person. On the contrary, the bottom-up strategy locates all body joints in the image and then groups joints to corresponding persons. Top-down strategy is less efficient because the need to perform single person pose estimation on each detected instance sequentially. Also, the performance of top-down strategy is highly dependent on the quality of person detections. Compared to top-down strategy, the complexity of bottom-up strategy is independent of the number of people in the image, which makes it more efficient. Though as a faster and more likely to be the real-time technique, the bottom-up methods may suffer from solving an NP-hard graph partition problem [14,15] to group joints to corresponding persons on densely connected graphs covering the whole image.

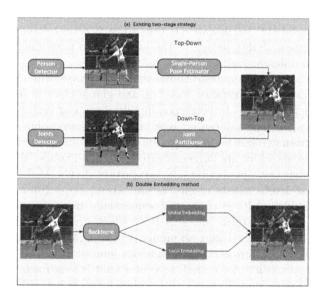

Fig. 1. Comparison between (a) existing two-stage strategy and (b) our Double Embedding method for multi-person pose estimation. The proposed DE model implement the person detection and joints detection parallel, overcoming the intrinsic problems of existing two-stage based top-down and bottom-up strategies.

We analyze and try to bypass the disadvantages of these two conventional strategies. The low efficiency of the top-down strategy comes from the independent single person pose estimation on each person bounding box. For bottom-up strategy, treating all the detected unidentified joints equally causes the high difficulty of joints grouping process. Both top-down and bottom-up strategy are two-stage structure with little interaction between the two stages. They both suffer from the separation of person instance detection and joints detection.

To overcome this intrinsic limitation, we propose to implement person detection and joints detection simultaneously, and realize information communicating between the two procedures to better utilize the structure information of human body. The proposed approach is illustrated in Fig. 1 (b). We observe that the torso joints (shoulders and hips) are more stable than other limbs joints. With much lower degree of freedom than limbs joints, torso joints can represent the identity information to distinguish the different human instances well. We also introduce the center joint of the human body. Center joint is calculated by the average location of annotated joints. Together with the center joint point, torso joints and center points compose the Root Joints Group (RJG). Based on this, we categorize the rest joints on limbs into Adjacency Joints Group (AJG). In this paper, we propose the Double Embedding method to simplify the pipeline and improve the joints localization accuracy. The framework of the DE approach is shown in Fig. 2. Double Embedding consists of Global Embedding (GE) and Local Embedding (LE). GE functions for the person instance separation process through encoding the clustering information of RJG. We follow the associative embedding method [18] to allocate 1D tags to each pixel related to the joints in root joints group. Joints belong to the same person have similar tags while joints belong to different instances have dissimilar tags.

GE encodes global information around the whole image, while LE focuses on local information of each instance based on the global clues from GE. AGJ is connected to identified RJG by corresponding displacement vector field encoded in LE. Basically, we take the center joint as the reference point. However, the displacements from extremities joints (wrists and ankles) to center joint are long-range displacements which are vulnerable to background noises. To optimize the long-range displacement prediction [19], we further divide AGJ into two hierarchies: the first level consists of elbows and knees, the second level consists of wrists and ankles. AJG is connected sequentially from the second level to first level and finally to torso joints in RJG which are identified. Long-range displacements are factorized into accumulative short-range displacements targeting on torso joints (hip joints and shoulder joints). Take the left ankle for example, the displacement from ankle to center joint is long-range displacement which is difficult to predict. To tackle this problem with better utilizing the body structure information, we change the reference joint to left hip, and divide the displacement from left ankle to left hip into shorter displacements: the displacement from left ankle to left knee and the displacement from left knee joint to left hip joint. Thus, AJG (limbs joints) are connected to RJG and identified in sequence. As for facial joints (e.g., Eyes, nose, etc.), we localize them from predicted heatmaps and connect them with the long-range displacements targeting on the center joint.

In addition, we design Mutual Refine Machine (MRM) to further improve the joints localization accuracy and reduce the prediction difficulty in complex scenarios such as pose deformation, cluttered background, occlusion, person overlapping and scale variations. Based on hierarchical displacements and connection information encoded in LE, MRP refines the poor-quality predicted joints by high-quality predicted neighboring joints.

We reduce the person detection task to identifying RJG with associative embedding. This is essential to implement the person detection and joints detection at the same time. This is essential to implement the person detection and the following joints detection and grouping at the same time. Avoiding the independent single person pose estimation on each detected person bounding boxes makes the method more efficient. Compared to directly processing all the unidentified joints around the whole image, LE performs local inference with robust global affinity cues encoded in GE, reducing complexity for joints identifying. Different with the independence of two stages in previous two-stage strategy, GE and LE works mutually to complete the person detection and joints detection parallel.

We implement DE with Convolutional Neural Networks (CNNs) based on the state-of-the-art HigherHRNet [20] architecture. Experiments on benchmarks MSCOCO [21], MPII [22] and CrowdPose [23] demonstrate the effectiveness of our method.

The main contributions of the paper is summarized as follows:

- We attempt to simplify the pipeline for multi-person pose estimation, solving the task in global-to-local way.
- We propose the Double Embedding method to implement person detection and joints detection parallel, overcoming the intrinsic disadvantages caused by two-stage structure.
- Our model achieves competitive performance on multiple benchmarks.

2   Related Works

Top-Down Multi-person Estimation. Top-down methods [5–13] first employ object detection [24–27] to generate person instances within person bounding boxes, and then detect the keypoints of each person by single person pose estimation independently.

Mask R-CNN [9] adopts a branch for keypoints detection based on Faster R-CNN [24]. G-RMI [8] directly divides top-down methods as two stages and employs independent models for person detection and pose estimation. In [28], Gkioxari et al. adopted the Generalized Hough Transform framework for person instance detection, and then classify joint candidates based on the poselets. In [29], Sun et al. proposed a part-based model to jointly detect person instances and generate pose estimation. Recently, both person detection and single person pose estimation benefit a lot from the thriving of deep learning techniques. Iqbal and Gall [16] adopted Faster-RCNN [24] for person detection and convolutional pose machine [30] for joints detection. In [31], Fang et al. used spatial transformer network [32] and Hourglass network [13] for joints detection.

Though these methods have achieved excellent performance, they suffer from high time complexity due to sequential single person pose estimation on each person proposal. Differently, DE performs the person detection and joints detection parallel, which simplifies the pipeline.

Bottom-Up Multi-person Pose Estimation. Bottom-up methods [14–18] detect all the unidentified joints in an image and then group them to corresponding person instances.

Openpose [33] proposes part affinity field to represent the limbs. The method calculates line integral through limbs and connects joints with the largest integral. In [18], Newell et al. proposed associate embedding to assign each joint with a 1D tag and then group joints which have the similar tags. PersonLab [19] groups joints by a 2D vector field in the whole image. In [34], Sven Kreiss et al. proposed Part Intensity Field (PIF) to localize body parts and Part Association Field (PAF) to connect body parts to form full human poses.

Nevertheless, the joints grouping cues of all these methods are covering the whole image, which causes high complexity for joints grouping. Different with the prior methods, global clues from GE reduce the search space for graph partition problem, avoiding high complexity of joint partition in bottom-up strategy.

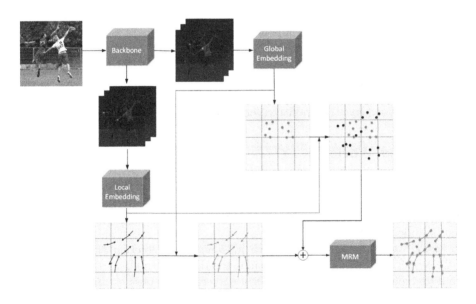

Fig. 2. Overview of the Double Embedding (DE) model. For an image, we generate two kinds of feature maps for Global Embedding (GE) and Local Embedding (LE). GE and LE works parallel with information communicating to support each other. Based on GE and LE, we design Mutual Refine Machine (MRM) to refine the low-quality predicted joints which further improves the accuracy.

3   Double Embedding Method

In this section, we present our proposed Double Embedding method. Figure 2 illustrates the overall architecture of the proposed approach.

Joints Feature Map. For an image I, we generate two kinds of feature maps from backbone network, one for Global Embedding (GE) and one for Local Embedding (LE). We use $J_R = \{J_{R1}, J_{R2}, ..., J_{RU}\}$ to denote Root Joints Group (RJG), J_{Ri} is the i-th kind of joints in RJG for all N persons in image I, and U is the number of joint categories in RJG. Similarly, we use $J_A = \{J_{A1}, J_{A2}, ..., J_{AV}\}$ to denote Adjacency Joints Group (AJG), J_{Ai} is the i-th kind of joints in AJG for all persons in image I, and V is the number of joint categories in RJG. For Global Embedding, let $h_{Gk} \in R^{W \times H}(k = 1, 2, ..., U)$ denote the feature map for the k-th kind of joint in Root Joints Group. For Local Embedding, $h_{Lk} \in R^{W \times H}(k = 1, 2, ..., V)$ denotes the feature map for the k-th kind of joint in AJG. The form and generation method of h_{Gk} and h_{Lk} are the same. To simplify the description, we use h_{fk} to represent both h_{Gk} and h_{Lk}.

It was pointed out that Directly regressing the absolute joint coordinates in an image is difficult [14, 35]. We therefore use heatmap, a confidence map models the joints position as Gaussian peaks. For a position (x, y) in image I, $h_{fk}(x, y)$ is calculated by:

$$h_{fk}(x,y) = \begin{cases} exp(-\frac{\left\| (x,y)-(x_k^i,y_k^i) \right\|_2^2}{\sigma^2}), & (x,y) \in \aleph_k^i \\ 0, & otherwhise \end{cases} \tag{1}$$

In which σ is an empirical constant to control the variance of Gaussian distribution, set as 7 in our experiments. (x_k^i, y_k^i) denotes the i-th groundtruth joint position in h_{fk}. $\aleph_k^i = (x, y)| \left\| (x, y) - (x_k^i, y_k^i) \right\|_2 \leq \tau$ is regressing area for each joint to truncate the Gaussian distribution. Thus, we generate two kinds of feature map for GE and LE. Joints location of RJG and AJG are derived through NMS process.

Global Embedding. Global Embedding functions as a simpler person detection process, reduces person detection problem to identifying the RJG. We use Associate Embedding for this process. The identification information in h_{Gk} is encoded in $1D$ tag space T_k for k-th joint in RJG. Based on the pixel location derived from peak detections in feature map h_{Gk}, corresponding tags are retrieved at the same pixel location in T_k. Joints belonging to one person have similar tags while tags of joints in different persons have obvious difference. Let $p = \{p_1, p_2, ..., p_N\}$ denote the N persons containing in image I. GE can be represented as a function $f_{GE} : h_{Gk} \rightarrow T_k$. f_{GE} learns to densely transform every pixel in h_{Gk} to embedding space T_k. We use $loc_{(p_n, J_{Rk})}(n = 1, 2, ..., N, k = 1, 2, ..., U)$ to denote the ground truth pixel location of the k-th kind of joint in RJG of n-th person.

If U' joints are labeled, the reference embedding for the n-th person is the average of retrieved tags of RJG in this person:

$$\bar{Tag}_n = \frac{1}{U'} \sum_k T_k(loc_{(p_n, J_Rk)}) \tag{2}$$

To pull the tags of joints within an individual together, pull-loss computes the squared distance between the reference embedding and the predicted embedding for each joint.

$$L_{pull} = \frac{1}{NU'} \sum_n \sum_k (\bar{Tag}_n - T_k(loc_{(p_n, J_{Rk})}))^2 \tag{3}$$

To push the tags of joints in different persons, push-loss penalizes the reference embeddings that are close to each other. As the distance between two tags increases, push-loss drops exponentially to zero resembling probability density function of Gaussian distribution:

$$L_{push} = \frac{1}{N^2} \sum_n \sum_{n'} exp\{-\frac{1}{2\sigma^2}(\bar{Tag}_n - \bar{Tag}_{n'})^2\} \tag{4}$$

The loss to train the model as f_{GE} is the sum of L_{pull} and L_{push}:

$$L^G = \frac{1}{NU'} \sum_n \sum_k (\bar{Tag}_n - T_k(loc_{(p_n, J_{Rk})}))^2 + \frac{1}{N^2} \sum_n \sum_{n'} exp\{-\frac{1}{2\sigma^2}(\bar{Tag}_n - \bar{Tag}_{n'})^2\} \tag{5}$$

Local Embedding. Local Embedding performs local inference and builds the connection clues between AJG and identified RJG. Relative position information of h_{Lk} is encoded in displacement space D_k for k-th joint in AJG. For each joint in AJG, we get its corresponding normed displacement to RJG from D_k at the same position in h_{Lk}. We first build the basic displacement to connect to the center joint. Basic displacement for the k-th joint in AJG of the n-th person is represented as the 2D vector:

$$Dis_n^k = (x_n^r, y_n^r) - (x_n^k, y_n^k) \tag{6}$$

In which, (x_n^r, y_n^r) is the location of the center joint in the n-th person. Besides, we design the hierarchical displacement to connect the limbs joints to corresponding torso joints. Compared to basic displacements directly targeting on the center joint, hierarchical displacements are shorter ones which are more robust and easier to predict. Normally, we use hierarchical displacements in inference process. But if some intermediate joints are absent, we directly use the long-range prediction to complete the inference.

The general displacement for joint A to joint B of n-th person is:

$$Dis_n^{A2B} = (x_n^B, y_n^B) - (x_n^A, y_n^A) \tag{7}$$

In some cases, we may use the property $Dis_n^{B2A} = -Dis_n^{A2B}$ to get reverse displacements of paired joints.

Local Embedding $f_{LE} : h_{Lk} \rightarrow D_k$ maps each pixel in feature map h_{Lk} to the embedding space D_k. For learning f_{LE}, we build the target regression map T_n^A for the displacement vector from joint A (the k-th kind of joint in AJG) to joint B of the n-th person as follows:

$$D_k^A(x, y) = \begin{cases} Dis_n^{(x,y)2(x_n^B, y_n^B)}/Z, & if(x, y) \in \aleph_k^A \\ 0, & otherwise \end{cases} \tag{8}$$

where $\aleph_k^A = \{(x,y)|\|(x,y) - (x_n^A, y_n^A)\|_2 \leq \tau\}$. The displacements are created in $\aleph_k^A$ which is the same as regression area in h_{Lk}. $Z = \sqrt{H^2 + W^2}$ is the normalization factor, with H and W denoting the height and width of the image.

The starting point A (x_n^A, y_n^A) is generated from peak detections in feature map h_{Lk}, we get its corresponding displacement to joint B in D_k as $Dis_n^{A2B} = D_k((x_n^A, y_n^A))$. The ending joint is obtained: $(x_n^{End}, y_n^{End}) = (x_n^A, y_n^A) + Z \cdot Dis_n^{A2B}$. Compared with the peak detections in h_{LB} (containing the same category joints as joint B for all persons in the image, including (x_n^B, y_n^B)), it will be confirmed that joint B is the ending joint of joint A. Accordingly, joint A is connected to joints B, meaning they share the same identification. In this way, joints in AJG are connected to RJG and identified.

Mutual Refine Machine. We design the Mutual Refine Machine (MRM) to reduce the prediction difficulty in complex scenes. For a low-quality predicted joint, it can be refined by the neighboring high-quality joints. Based on the displacements and connection information in LE, MRM realizes the information communicating between paired joints. For n-th person, if prediction probability of i-th joint in k-th kind of joints confidence map $h_{fk}((x_n^i, y_n^i))$ is lower than its neighboring paired joints $\{h_{fk'}((x_n^{i'}, y_n^{i'}))\}$(in which $h_{fk'}((x_n^{i'}, y_n^{i'})) > 0.75$), then we refine the location of i-th joint with the weighted fusion of its neighboring joints. Refined location is:

$$\left(x_n^i, y_n^i\right)_{refined} = \frac{h_{fk}((x_n^i, y_n^i))}{Q} * (x_n^i, y_n^i) + \sum_{i'} \frac{h_{fk'}((x_n^{i'}, y_n^{i'}))}{Q} * ((x_n^{i'}, y_n^{i'}) + Dis_n^{i'2i}) \tag{9}$$

$$Q = h_{fk}((x_n^{i'}, y_n^{i'})) + \sum_{i'} h_{fk'}((x_n^{i'}, y_n^{i'})) \tag{10}$$

Training and Inference. To train our model, we adopt L2 loss L^H for joint confidence regression, smooth L1 loss [36] L^D for displacements regression and L^G for GE. The total loss L for each image is the weighted sum of L^H, L^D and L^G:

$$L = \sum_{x=1}^{U+V} L^H(h_{fx}, \hat{h}_{fx}) + \alpha \sum_{y=1}^{V} L^D(D_y, \hat{D}_y) + \beta \sum_{z=1}^{U} L^G \tag{11}$$

where $\hat{h}_{fx}$ and $\hat{D}_y$ denote the predicted joints confidence map and displacements regression map. α and β are constant weight factor to balance three kinds of losses, both set as 0.01. The overall framework of DE is end-to-end trainable via gradient backpropagation.

The overall architecture of DE is illustrated in Fig. 2. For an image, DE generates two kinds of feature maps $\hat{h}_{Gk}$ and $\hat{h}_{Lk}$. through performing NMS and on them, we get predicted joints location of RJG and AJG. GE gives identification tags for RJG and LE provides the connection relation to connect AJG to RGJ. To better present the collaborative work of GE and LE, we add the intermediate illustration. Connected pairs get identification information from GE and joints in GE expand to all joints by connectivity in LE. Based on the displacements and connectivity in LE, MRM refines the low-quality predicted joints. The final result is generated through the combination of refined results from GE and LE.

4 Experiments

4.1 Experiment Setup

Datasets. We evaluate the proposed Double Embedding model on three widely used benchmarks for multi-person pose estimation: MSCOCO [21] dataset, MPII [22] dataset and CrowdPose [23] dataset.

The MSCOCO [21] dataset contains over $200,000$ images and $250,000$ person instances labeled with 17 keypoints. COCO is divided into train/val/test-dev sets with 57k, 5k and 20k images respectively. MPII [22] dataset contains 5,602 images of multiple persons. Each person is annotated with 16 body joints. Images are divided into 3,844 for training and 1,758 for testing. MPII also provides over 28,000 annotated single-person pose samples. The CrowdPose [23] dataset consists of 20,000 images, containing about 80,000 person instances. The training, validation and testing subset are split in proportional to 5:1:4. CrowdPose has more crowded scenes than the COCO and MPII, and therefore is more challenging for multi-person pose estimation.

Data Augmentation. We follow the conventional data augmentation strategies in experiments. For MSCOCO and CrowdPose datasets, we augment training samples with random rotation ($[-30°, 30°]$), random scale $[0.75, 1.5]$, random translation $[\pm 40, 40]$ and random horizontally flip to crop input images to 640×640 with padding. For MPII dataset, random scale is set as ($[0.7, 1.3]$) while other augmentation parameters are set the same as MSCOCO and CrowdPose datasets.

Evaluation Metric. For COCO and CrowdPose datasets, the standard evaluation metric is based on Object Keypoint Similarity (OKS):

$$OKS = \frac{\sum_i exp(-d_i^2/2s^2k_i^2)\delta(v_i > 0)}{\sum_i \delta(v_i > 0)} \tag{12}$$

where d_i is the Euclidean distance between the predicted joints and ground truth, v_i is the visibility flag of the ground truth, s is the object scale, and k_i is a per-keypoint constant that controls falloff. The standard average precision and recall scores are shown as: AP^{50}(AP at OKS = 0.50), AP^{75}, AP (the mean of AP scores at 10 positions, OKS = 0.50, 0.55,..., 0.90, 0.95; AP^M for medium objects, AP^L for large objects, and AR at OKS = 0.50, 0.55,..., 0.90, 0.955.

For MPII dataset, the standard evaluation metric is PCKh (head-normalized probability of correct keypoint) score. A joint is correct if it falls within al pixels of the groundtruth position, where α is a constant and l is the head size that corresponds to 60% of the diagonal length of the ground-truth head bounding box. The PCKh@0.5 ($\alpha = 0.5$) score is reported.

Implementation. For COCO dataset, we use standard validation set for ablation studies while use test-dev set to compare with other state-of-the-art methods. or CrowdPose dataset, we use CrowdPose train and val set to train our model, and use test set for validation. For MPII dataset, following [37], we randomly select 350 groups of multi-person training samples as the validation dataset and use the remaining training samples and all single-person images as train dataset. We use the Adam optimizer [38]. For COCO and CrowdPose datasets, the base learning rate is set to 1e-3, and dropped to 1e-4 and 1e-5 at the 200th and 260th epochs respectively. We train the model for a total of 300 epochs. For MPII dataset, we initialize learning rate by 1e-3. We train the model for 260 epochs and decrease learning rate by a factor of 2 at the 160th, 180th, 210th, 240th epoch. Following [HigherHRNet-30], we adopt flip test for all the experiments.

Table 1. Comparison with state-of-the-arts on COCO2017 test-dev dataset. Top: w/o multi-scale test. Bottom: w/ multi-scale test.

Method	AP	AP^{50}	AP^{75}	AP^M	AP^L
w/o multi-scale test					
CMU-Pose [17]†	61.8	84.9	67.5	57.1	68.2
RMPE [11]	61.8	83.7	69.8	58.6	67.6
Associate Embedding [18]	62.8	84.6	69.2	57.5	70.6
Mask-RCNN [9]†	63.1	87.3	68.7	57.8	71.4
G-RMI [8]†	64.9	85.5	71.3	62.3	70.0
PersonLab [19]	66.5	88.0	72.6	62.4	72.3
PifPaf [34]	66.7	–	–	62.4	72.9
SPM [37]	66.9	88.5	72.9	62.6	73.1
HigherHRNet [39]	68.4	88.2	75.1	64.4	74.2
CPN [12]†	72.1	91.4	80.0	68.7	77.2
DoubleEmbedding(Ours)	69.7	88.4	76.9	65.8	75.1
w/ multi-scale test					
Hourglass [18]	65.5	86.8	72.3	60.6	72.6
Associate Embedding [18]	65.5	86.8	72.3	60.6	72.6
PersonLab [19]	68.7	89.0	75.4	64.1	75.5
HigherHRNet [39]	70.5	89.3	77.2	66.6	75.8
DoubleEmbedding(Ours)	71.6	89.5	78.6	68.8	76.0

† indicates top-down methods

4.2 Results on COCO Dataset

Comparison with State-of-the-Arts. In Table 1, we compare our proposed model with other state-of-the-arts methods on COCO2017 test-dev dataset. We test the run time of single-scale inference, the proposed method realizes the balance on speed and accuracy. We achieve the competitive accuracy which outperforms most existing bottom-up methods. Compared to the typical top-down method CPN [12], we narrow the gap to top-down method in accuracy with less complexity. This demonstrates the effectiveness of DE on multi-person pose estimation.

Ablation Analysis. We conduct ablation analysis on COCO2017 [21] validation dataset without multi-scale test. We evaluate the impact of the introduced hierarchical short-range displacements that factorize the basic displacements. Also, the effect of MRM is studied. MRM is implemented based on the hierarchical displacements, so MRM is non-existent without hierarchical displacements. Results are shown in Table 2 which shows that with basic displacements only, DE achieves 69.3% mAP. By introducing hierarchical displacements, performance improves to 70.7% mAP with 1.3% mAP increasing. Based on the hierarchical displacements, MRM further improve 0.9% mAP. The result shows the effectiveness of hierarchical displacements and MRM.

Table 2. Ablation experiments on COCO validation dataset.

Model settings			Pose estimation				
Basic Dis.	Hierar Dis.	MRM	AP	AP^{50}	AP^{75}	AP^M	AP^L
✓			69.3	87.0	75.9	65.1	76.6
✓	✓		70.7	88.1	76.8	66.5	76.4
✓	✓	✓	71.6	88.3	77.5	66.9	77.8

In addition, we analyze the impact of the hyper-parameter τ which decides the regression area for joints confidence map and displacements in Sect. 3. We observe the performance of proposed model as τ varies from 1 to 20. As shown in Fig. 3, the performance monotonically improves as τ increases from 1 to 7. When $7 < \tau < 10$, performance remains unchanged as τ increases. When $\tau > 10$, performance drops as τ increases. This can be explained by the distribution of positive samples of the dataset. When τ increases in the range between 1 and 7, positive samples increase and larger effective area of joints is counted in joints confidence and displacements regression in training. When τ increases between 7 and 10, effective information and background noise increases with equivalent effect. When $\tau > 10$, more background noise is countered as positive samples, regression area of joints overlaps with each other as τ keeps increasing. Smaller τ means less complexity, thus we set $\tau = 7$ for balancing the accuracy and efficiency.

Qualitative Results. Qualitative results on COCO dataset are shown in the top row of Fig. 4. The proposed model performs well in challenging scenarios, e.g., pose deformation (1st and 2nd examples), person overlapping and self-occlusion (3rd example), crowded scene (4nd example), and scale variation and small-scale prediction (5st example). This presents the effectiveness of our method.

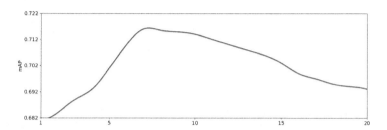

Fig. 3. Studies on hyper-parameter τ, which decides the regression area for joints confidence map and displacements.

Table 3. Comparison with state-of-the-arts on the full testing set of MPII dataset.

Method	Head	Sho	Elb	Wri	Hip	Knee	Ank	Total	Time[s]
Iqbal and Gall [16]	58.4	53.9	44.5	35.0	42.2	36.7	31.1	43.1	10
Insafutdinov et al. [15]	78.4	72.5	60.2	51.0	57.2	52.0	45.4	59.5	485
Levinkov et al. [15]	89.8	85.2	71.8	59.6	71.1	63.0	53.5	70.6	–
Insafutdinov et al. [40]	88.8	87.0	75.9	64.9	74.2	68.8	60.5	74.3	–
Cao et al. [33]	91.2	87.6	77.7	66.8	75.4	68.9	61.7	75.6	0.6
Fang et al. [11]	88.4	86.5	78.6	70.4	74.4	73.0	65.8	76.7	0.4
Newell and Deng [13]	92.1	89.3	78.9	69.8	76.2	71.6	64.7	77.5	0.25
Fieraru et al. [41]	91.8	89.5	80.4	69.6	77.3	71.7	65.5	78.0	–
SPM [37]	89.7	87.4	80.4	72.4	76.7	74.9	68.3	78.5	0.058
DoubleEmbedding (Ours)	91.9	89.7	81.6	74.9	79.8	75.8	71.5	80.7	0.21

Table 4. Ablation experiments on MPII validation dataset.

Model settings			Pose estimation							
Basic Dis.	Hierar Dis.	MRM	Head	Sho	Elb	Wri	Hip	Knee	Ank	Total
✓			92.1	88.4	78.3	68.9	77.5	73.6	63.7	77.5
✓	✓		92.3	89.2	79.8	71.3	78.1	74.8	66.2	78.8
✓	✓	✓	92.3	90.1	81.2	72.6	79.0	75.7	67.1	79.7

4.3   Results on MPII Dataset

Table 3 shows a comparison of the proposed method with state-of-the-arts methods on MPII dataset. The proposed model obtains 80.7% mAP achieving competitive result among other bottom-up methods. In addition, we conduct the ablation study on MPII validation dataset to verify MRM and the hierarchical displacements compared with the basic displacements. As shown in Table 4, DE improves from 77.5% mAP to 78.8% mAP by introducing hierarchical displacements. Moreover, on wrists and ankles are significant from 68.9% to 71.3% mAP and 73.6% to 74.8% mAP, respectively. Indicating the effectiveness of hierarchical displacements to factorize the long-range displacements. MRM further improves 1.1% mAP based on hierarchical displacements.

Qualitative results on MPII are shown in the middle row of Fig. 4, demonstrating the good performance and robustness of our model in complex scenes such as person scale variations (1st example), large pose deformation (2nd and 3rd examples) and small-scale prediction (3rd example).

4.4   Results on CrowdPose Dataset

Table 5. Comparison with state-of-the-arts on CrowdPose test dataset.

Method	AP	AP^{50}	AP^{75}	AP^M	AP^L	AP^H
Openpose [17]	–	–	–	62.7	48.7	32.3
Mask-RCNN† [9]	57.2	83.5	60.3	69.4	57.9	45.8
AlphaPose† [11]	61.0	81.3	66.0	71.2	61.4	51.1
SPPE† [23]	66.0	84.2	71.5	75.5	66.3	57.4
HigherHRNet [39]	67.6	87.4	72.6	75.8	68.1	58.9
HRNet† [42]	71.7	89.8	76.9	79.6	72.7	61.5
DoubleEmbedding (Ours)	68.8	89.7	73.4	76.1	69.5	60.3

† indicates top-down methods

Table 5 shows experimental results on CrowdPose. The proposed model achieves 68.8% AP which outperforms the existing bottom-up methods. but the performance is still lower than the state-of-the-art top-down method, HRNet which has intrinsic advantage in accuracy due to its processing flow. However, it narrows the accuracy gap between other bottom-up methods and top-down methods with less complexity. The performance on CrowdPose dataset indicates the robustness of our method in crowded scene.

Qualitative results on CrowdPose dataset are shown in the bottom row of Fig. 4. The result verifies the effectiveness of our model in complex scenes, e.g., ambiguity pose and small-scale prediction (1st example), self-occluded (2nd example), cluttered background (3rd example) and person overlapping and crowded scene (4th example).

Fig. 4. Qualitative results on MSCOCO dataset (top), MPII dataset (middle) and CrowdPose dataset (bottom).

5   Conclusion

In this paper, we propose the Double Embedding (DE) method for multi-person pose estimation. Through Global Embedding (GE) and Local Embedding (LE), we achieve parallel implementation of person detection and joints detection, overcoming the intrinsic disadvantages of the conventional two-stage strategy on multi-person pose estimation. GE reduces the person instance detection problem to identifying a group of joints and LE connects and identifies the rest joints hierarchically. Based on LE, we design Mutual Refine Machine (MRM) to further enhance the performance for dealing with complex scenarios. We implement DE based on CNNs with end-to-end learning and inference. Experiments on three main benchmarks demonstrate the effectiveness of our model. DE achieves the competitive results among existing bottom-up methods and narrows the gap to the state-of-the-art top-down methods with less complexity.

References

1. Chéron, G., Laptev, I., Schmid, C.: P-CNN: pose-based CNN features for action recognition (2015)
2. Li, Y., et al.: Transferable interactiveness prior for human-object interaction detection. CoRR abs/1811.08264 (2018)
3. Fang, H.-S., Cao, J., Tai, Y.-W., Lu, C.: Pairwise body-part attention for recognizing human-object interactions. In: Ferrari, V., Hebert, M., Sminchisescu, C., Weiss, Y. (eds.) ECCV 2018. LNCS, vol. 11214, pp. 52–68. Springer, Cham (2018). https://doi.org/10.1007/978-3-030-01249-6_4

4. Qian, X., et al.: Pose-normalized image generation for person re-identification. In: Ferrari, V., Hebert, M., Sminchisescu, C., Weiss, Y. (eds.) ECCV 2018. LNCS, vol. 11213, pp. 661–678. Springer, Cham (2018). https://doi.org/10.1007/978-3-030-01240-3_40

5. Xiao, B., Wu, H., Wei, Y.: Simple baselines for human pose estimation and tracking. In: Ferrari, V., Hebert, M., Sminchisescu, C., Weiss, Y. (eds.) ECCV 2018. LNCS, vol. 11210, pp. 472–487. Springer, Cham (2018). https://doi.org/10.1007/978-3-030-01231-1_29

6. Sun, K., Xiao, B., Liu, D., Wang, J.: Deep high-resolution representation learning for human pose estimation (2019)

7. Wang, J., Sun, K., Cheng, T., Jiang, B., Xiao, B.: Deep high-resolution representation learning for visual recognition. IEEE Trans. Pattern Anal. Mach. Intell. **PP**, 1 (2020)

8. Papandreou, G., et al.: Towards accurate multi-person pose estimation in the wild. CoRR abs/1701.01779 (2017)

9. He, K., Georgia, G., Piotr, D., Ross, G.: Mask R-CNN. IEEE Trans. Pattern Anal. Mach. Intell. 1 (2018)

10. Huang, S., Gong, M., Tao, D.: A coarse-fine network for keypoint localization. In: 2017 IEEE International Conference on Computer Vision (ICCV) (2017)

11. Fang, H., Xie, S., Tai, Y., Lu, C.: RMPE: regional multi-person pose estimation (2016)

12. Chen, Y., Wang, Z., Peng, Y., Zhang, Z., Yu, G., Sun, J.: Cascaded pyramid network for multi-person pose estimation (2017)

13. Newell, A., Yang, K., Deng, J.: Stacked hourglass networks for human pose estimation. In: Leibe, B., Matas, J., Sebe, N., Welling, M. (eds.) ECCV 2016. LNCS, vol. 9912, pp. 483–499. Springer, Cham (2016). https://doi.org/10.1007/978-3-319-46484-8_29

14. Pishchulin, L., et al.: DeepCut: joint subset partition and labeling for multi person pose estimation (2016)

15. Insafutdinov, E., Pishchulin, L., Andres, B., Andriluka, M., Schiele, B.: DeeperCut: a deeper, stronger, and faster multi-person pose estimation model. In: Leibe, B., Matas, J., Sebe, N., Welling, M. (eds.) ECCV 2016. LNCS, vol. 9910, pp. 34–50. Springer, Cham (2016). https://doi.org/10.1007/978-3-319-46466-4_3

16. Iqbal, U., Gall, J.: Multi-person pose estimation with local joint-to-person associations. In: Hua, G., Jégou, H. (eds.) ECCV 2016. LNCS, vol. 9914, pp. 627–642. Springer, Cham (2016). https://doi.org/10.1007/978-3-319-48881-3_44

17. Osokin, D.: Real-time 2D multi-person pose estimation on CPU: lightweight openpose. arXiv preprint arXiv:1811.12004 (2018)

18. Newell, A., Deng, J.: Associative embedding: end-to-end learning for joint detection and grouping. CoRR abs/1611.05424 (2016)

19. Papandreou, G., Zhu, T., Chen, L., Gidaris, S., Tompson, J., Murphy, K.: PersonLab: person pose estimation and instance segmentation with a bottom-up, part-based, geometric embedding model. CoRR abs/1803.08225 (2018)

20. Cheng, B., Xiao, B., Wang, J., Shi, H., Zhang, L.: HigherHRNet: scale-aware representation learning for bottom-up human pose estimation. In: 2020 IEEE/CVF Conference on Computer Vision and Pattern Recognition (CVPR) (2020)

21. Lin, T.-Y., et al.: Microsoft COCO: common objects in context. In: Fleet, D., Pajdla, T., Schiele, B., Tuytelaars, T. (eds.) ECCV 2014. LNCS, vol. 8693, pp. 740–755. Springer, Cham (2014). https://doi.org/10.1007/978-3-319-10602-1_48

22. Andriluka, M., Pishchulin, L., Gehler, P., Schiele, B.: Human pose estimation: new benchmark and state of the art analysis. In: Computer Vision and Pattern Recognition (CVPR) (2014)
23. Li, J., Wang, C., Zhu, H., Mao, Y., Fang, H.S., Lu, C.: CrowdPose: efficient crowded scenes pose estimation and a new benchmark (2018)
24. Ren, S., He, K., Girshick, R., Sun, J.: Faster R-CNN: towards real-time object detection with region proposal networks. IEEE Trans. Pattern Anal. Mach. Intell. **39**, 1137–1149 (2015)
25. Lin, T.Y., Dollár, P., Girshick, R., He, K., Hariharan, B., Belongie, S.: Feature pyramid networks for object detection (2016)
26. Cheng, B., Wei, Y., Shi, H., Feris, R.S., Xiong, J., Huang, T.S.: Revisiting RCNN: on awakening the classification power of faster RCNN. CoRR abs/1803.06799 (2018)
27. Cheng, B., Wei, Y., Shi, H., Feris, R., Xiong, J., Huang, T.: Decoupled classification refinement: hard false positive suppression for object detection (2018)
28. Gkioxari, G., Hariharan, B., Girshick, R., Malik, J.: Using k-poselets for detecting people and localizing their keypoints. In: 2014 IEEE Conference on Computer Vision and Pattern Recognition (CVPR) (2014)
29. Min, S., Savarese, S.: Articulated part-based model for joint object detection and pose estimation. In: IEEE International Conference on Computer Vision, ICCV 2011, Barcelona, Spain, 6–13 November 2011 (2011)
30. Wei, S., Ramakrishna, V., Kanade, T., Sheikh, Y.: Convolutional pose machines. In: 2016 IEEE Conference on Computer Vision and Pattern Recognition (CVPR), pp. 4724–4732 (2016)
31. Fang, H.S., Xie, S., Tai, Y.W., Lu, C.: RMPE: regional multi-person pose estimation. In: ICCV (2017)
32. Jaderberg, M., Simonyan, K., Zisserman, A., et al.: Spatial transformer networks. In: Advances in Neural Information Processing Systems, pp. 2017–2025 (2015)
33. Cao, Z., Simon, T., Wei, S., Sheikh, Y.: Realtime multi-person 2D pose estimation using part affinity fields. CoRR abs/1611.08050 (2016)
34. Kreiss, S., Bertoni, L., Alahi, A.: PifPaf: composite fields for human pose estimation. CoRR abs/1903.06593 (2019)
35. Carreira, J., Agrawal, P., Fragkiadaki, K., Malik, J.: Human pose estimation with iterative error feedback. CoRR abs/1507.06550 (2015)
36. Girshick, R.: Fast R-CNN. Computer Science (2015)
37. Nie, X., Zhang, J., Yan, S., Feng, J.: Single-stage multi-person pose machines (2019)
38. Kingma, D., Ba, J.: Adam: a method for stochastic optimization. Computer Science (2014)
39. Cheng, B., Xiao, B., Wang, J., Shi, H., Huang, T.S., Zhang, L.: HigherHRNet: scale-aware representation learning for bottom-up human pose estimation (2019)
40. Insafutdinov, E., et al.: Articulated multi-person tracking in the wild. CoRR abs/1612.01465 (2016)
41. Fieraru, M., Khoreva, A., Pishchulin, L., Schiele, B.: Learning to refine human pose estimation. CoRR abs/1804.07909 (2018)
42. Sun, K., Xiao, B., Liu, D., Wang, J.: Deep high-resolution representation learning for human pose estimation. CoRR abs/1902.09212 (2019)

Semi-supervised Facial Action Unit Intensity Estimation with Contrastive Learning

Enrique Sanchez$^{(\boxtimes)}$, Adrian Bulat, Anestis Zaganidis,
and Georgios Tzimiropoulos

Samsung AI Center, Cambridge, UK
{e.lozano,adrian.bulat,a.zaganidis,georgios.t}@samsung.com

Abstract. This paper tackles the challenging problem of estimating the intensity of Facial Action Units with few labeled images. Contrary to previous works, our method does not require to manually select key frames, and produces state-of-the-art results with as little as 2% of annotated frames, which are *randomly chosen*. To this end, we propose a semi-supervised learning approach where a spatio-temporal model combining a feature extractor and a temporal module are learned in two stages. The first stage uses datasets of unlabeled videos to learn a strong spatio-temporal representation of facial behavior dynamics based on contrastive learning. To our knowledge we are the first to build upon this framework for modeling facial behavior in an unsupervised manner. The second stage uses another dataset of randomly chosen labeled frames to train a regressor on top of our spatio-temporal model for estimating the AU intensity. We show that although backpropagation through time is applied only with respect to the output of the network for extremely sparse and randomly chosen labeled frames, our model can be effectively trained to estimate AU intensity accurately, thanks to the unsupervised pre-training of the first stage. We experimentally validate that our method outperforms existing methods when working with as little as 2% of randomly chosen data for both DISFA and BP4D datasets, without a careful choice of labeled frames, a time-consuming task still required in previous approaches.

Keywords: Semi-supervised learning · Unsupervised representation learning · Facial Action Units

1 Introduction

Facial actions are one of the most important means of non-verbal communication, and thus their automatic analysis plays a crucial role in making machines understand human behavior. The set of facial actions and their role in conveying emotions has been defined by the Facial Action Coding System (FACS [7]). FACS define a set of atomic facial movements, known as Action Units, whose

© Springer Nature Switzerland AG 2021
H. Ishikawa et al. (Eds.): ACCV 2020, LNCS 12626, pp. 104–120, 2021.
https://doi.org/10.1007/978-3-030-69541-5_7

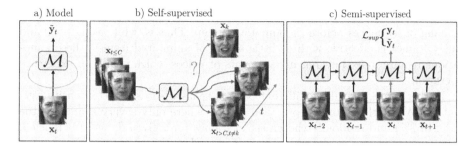

Fig. 1. Overview of our proposed approach. a) We want to learn a temporal model for facial Action Unit intensity estimation that can be learned with a few *randomly chosen* set of annotations. b) We propose to first learn a strong feature representation through *contrastive learning*, by training the model to solve a proxy task, that requires no labeling. The proxy task uses a simple non-linear predictive function, and aims at predicting the feature representation that is similar to that of a specific target frame x_k, and at the same time dissimilar to the rest of the given sequence. c) Once the model is trained to produce rich facial feature representations, we can further train it for facial Action Unit intensity estimation by using sequences in which the labeled frames are in random position in the sequence.

combination can be correlated with both basic and complex emotions. Action Units are categorically modeled according to their intensities, with values that range from 0, indicating the absence of an AU, to 5, indicating the maximum level of expressivity of an AU.

While plenty of works exist for AU detection (i.e. whether an AU occurs or not in an image, regardless of its intensity), the more challenging task of automatically estimating their intensity has received less attention. Recent advances in supervised methods incorporate a variety of techniques including attention [41,51,64], co-occurrence modeling [47,59], or temporal dynamics [4,20]. All these methods however require a large number of training instances to work properly, which entails the time consuming task of dataset labeling. This is even more profound for the problem of AU detection and intensity estimation where labeling is typically performed at a frame-level (i.e. each video frame must be labeled). Our goal in this paper is to devise a method that can effectively estimate AU intensity even when a very small (of the order of 2%) and randomly chosen set of frames is used for model training.

This line of work has been pursued by the research community only recently [30,59–63]. While these works have shown remarkable results, they still have some limitations: 1) They work on a per-frame basis, by learning a strong image-based feature representation that can later be used for AU intensity estimation. While some of these methods impose a temporal smoothing through ranking [60,62], they still aim at learning a per-frame representation. 2) Some of these methods also require having a very specific set of annotations in hand [60–63]. In particular, they work by assuming that annotations are available for "peak" and "valley" frames, i.e. frames corresponding to a local maximum or minimum on the intensity. Identifying these frames requires a qualitative labeling of sequences before the annotation step. That is, while using peak and valley frames is effective with as little as 2% of annotated frames, these annotations require indeed evaluating segments of videos which is also an expensive operation.

In this paper, we take a different path in semi-supervised AU intensity estimation. We firstly assume a practical setting where only a very sparse (of the order of 2%) and randomly chosen set of frames (of a given dataset) is labeled. Our aim is to train a model which, even if trained on this sparse set of annotated frames, it can make dense per-frame predictions of AU intensity for all frames in a given test sequence. To this end, we build a model that combines a feature extraction network (ResNet-18, [17]) with a GRU unit [3], and a regressor head on top of the GRU that can make predictions for each frame and train it using back-propagation through time using only the predictions of the network at the sparsely labeled frames. We found however that training this model from scratch in an end-to-end manner using only a small number of labeled frames is a rather difficult task. Hence, we further propose to firstly train the backbone (i.e. the feature extractor and the GRU unit) in an unsupervised way on different unlabeled datasets, using the recent framework of contrastive learning [1,15,18,36,43,52,54]. The backbone is trained end-to-end with a contrastive loss on unlabeled videos of facial behavior, and used thereafter to train a model for AU intensity estimation using only few labels. An overview of our approach is shown in Fig. 1.

Our **main contributions** can be summarized as follows:

- We are the first to propose a temporal modeling of facial actions that can be learned with a sparse set of discontinuously and randomly chosen annotated facial images. Our practical approach to AU intensity estimation requires as little as 2% of annotated data.
- We are the first to apply the framework of contrastive learning for semi-supervised AU intensity estimation. We propose a two-stage pipeline where a model for obtaining a spatio-temporal facial representation is firstly trained on large unlabeled datasets of facial behavior using a contrastive learning formulation, and, then, the model is effectively trained for the task of AU intensity estimation using a small number of sparsely annotated video frames.
- Our approach achieves state-of-the-art results on both BP4D and DISFA, when using a randomly chosen subset of 2% frames.

2   Related Work

2.1   Action Unit Modeling

The majority of existing works in facial Action Unit intensity estimation work on a fully supervised way, i.e. by assuming that a large amount of labeled data is available[9,31]. Existing supervised methods are often split into methods that exploit the geometric structure of faces, also referred to as patch-based [29,64,

65], methods that exploit the temporal correlation of AUs [4,20], and those that exploit the correlation that exists between different Action Units [10,38–40,47]. Other methods attempt to exploit different types of correlation [5,8,28, 33,49,51,53]. Most recent methods reporting state of the art results on Action Unit intensity estimation build on AutoEncoders [44], or on Heatmap Regression [35,41].

While there is a vast amount of literature in fully supervised methods for Action Unit intensity estimation, few works have focused on the more challenging task of addressing the same goal in a semi-supervised manner. In [30], a twin autoencoder is used to disentangle facial movements from head pose, the learned representation is then used for Action Unit detection. In [63], an ordinal relevance regression method is applied. In [59], the relation between emotions and Action Units is used to generate a knowledge-graph that allows the use of the emotion labels to train the AU detector without labels. In [48] a Restricted Boltzmann Machine and Support Vector Regression approach to model the AUs is proposed. In [60], a knowledge-based approach is proposed, exploiting the temporal variation that exists between peak and valley frames. In [62], the temporal ranking is exploited in a similar way, and a novel ADMM approach is used to enforce different constraints. In [61], a learnable context matrix is used for each AU, which combined with several patch-based feature fusion is capable of learning AU intensity from key frames only. The majority of these methods however impose temporal constraints based on the fact that annotations are available for *peak* and *valley* frames, i.e. frames that correspond to a local maximum and minimum, respectively. Our method bypasses this need by applying a self-supervised pre-learning step, that learns a strong feature representation. Our approach uses as little as 2% of annotated data. However, contrary to these methods, we use a *randomly chosen* set of data.

2.2   Self-supervised Learning in Computer Vision

Self-supervised learning, often referred to as unsupervised learning, is an active research topic in Machine Learning. It involves defining a pretext or proxy task, with a corresponding loss, that leads to strong feature representation. This pretext task does not require the data to be labeled, e.g. it can be predicting relative location of image patches [6], predicting rotation from images [11], sorting frames in a shuffled video [34], denoising [46] or colorization [56], or pseudo-labeling through clustering [2].

More recently, a number of state-of-the-art self-supervised methods based on the so-called contrastive learning formulation have been proposed [1,14,15,18,36, 43,52,54]. The idea is to define a loss for unsupervised learning which maximizes the similarity between the feature representations of two different instances of the same training sample while simultaneously minimizes the similarity with the representations computed from different samples. Among these methods, in this work, we build upon the Contrastive Predictive Coding of [36] which allows for a temporal model to be learned in an unsupervised manner from video data, and hence it is particular suitable for modeling facial behavior dynamics. To our knowledge, we are the first building upon this model for unsupervised modeling of facial behavior. We also show how to apply this model for semi-supervised AU intensity estimation.

3 Method

We are interested in learning a spatio-temporal model for facial Action Unit intensity estimation, that is capable of modeling the temporal dynamics of expressions, as well as their feature representation, and that can be learned with few labels. Thus, we first introduce the problem statement and notation in Sect. 3.1, then we devote Sect. 3.2 to describing the model that will produce a structured output representation, and present our two-stage approach to the model learning in Sect. 3.3 and Sect. 3.4.

3.1 Problem Statement and Notation

We are interested in learning a model capable of predicting the intensity of some Action Units in a given sequence, that at the same time captures the spatial features responsible of displayed expressions and models the temporal correlation between them. We want such a model to be learned in a scenario where only a small set of frames are annotated with Action Unit intensity.

Let $\mathbf{X} = \{\mathbf{x}_t\}_{t=1}^T$ be a sequence of T video frames, where $\mathbf{x}_t \in \mathbb{R}^{3 \times H \times W}$ is an RGB image of size $H \times W$. Our goal is to learn a model $\mathcal{M}$ that produces a structured output $\hat{\mathbf{Y}} = \{\tilde{\mathbf{y}}_t\}_{t=1}^T$, where each $\tilde{\mathbf{y}}_t \in \mathbb{R}^N$ corresponds to the predicted intensity of each of the N Action Units of interest. In a fully supervised setting, we would be given a set of ground-truth labels $\mathbf{y}_t$ for each sequence, and thus the model $\mathcal{M}(\cdot; \theta)$ could be learned through regression and backpropagation through time [50]. However, learning the model $\mathcal{M}$ is a hard task, and requires a vast amount of per-frame labeled sequences. Also, training deep temporal models is often a challenging task, very sensitive to the initialization. We now describe our approach to learning the model efficiently with few labels.

3.2 Network

Our model $\mathcal{M}$ (Fig. 2) is split into a feature extraction block $f(\cdot; \theta_f)$, a temporal module $g(\cdot; \theta_g)$, and a final regressor head $c(\cdot; \theta_c)$, with θ the parameters of each module. The choice for the *feature extractor* $f(\cdot; \theta_f)$ is that of a ResNet-18 [17], without the last fully connected layer. In order to keep a locally-based receptive field for the extracted features, we remove the average pooling layer. To reduce the complexity of the network, the last convolutional block is set to 256 channels rather than the typical 512. This way, for an input resolution of 128×128, the network produces a feature representation of 256 channels, and of a spatial resolution of 8×8, i.e. $f(\cdot; \theta_f) \in \mathbb{R}^{256 \times 8 \times 8}$. This way, each spatial output *attends* a region of 16×16 pixels in the input image.

The form of the *temporal block* $g(\cdot\,;\theta_g)$ is that of a Convolutional Gated Recurrent Unit (GRU [3]), with the latent dimension set to be the same as for the feature representation, i.e. $256 \times 8 \times 8$. The GRU receives, at time t, the input feature representation $f(\mathbf{x}_t;\theta_f) \in \mathbb{R}^{256\times8\times8}$, along with the previous hidden state $\mathbf{h}_{t-1} \in \mathbb{R}^{256\times8\times8}$, and propagates the hidden state at time t as $\mathbf{h}_t = g(f(\mathbf{x}_t;\theta_f), \mathbf{h}_{t-1};\theta_g) \in \mathbb{R}^{256\times8\times8}$. The GRU is modified to receive a tensor rather than a vector, by setting all the internal gates to be convolutional layers, with kernel size 1×1.

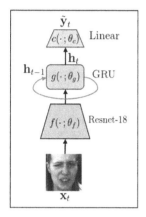

Fig. 2. Network: the model consists of a *feature extractor*, a *temporal block*, and a *regressor head*.

Finally, a *regressor head* $c(\cdot\,;\theta_c)$ is placed on top of the GRU to perform a per-frame Action Unit intensity estimation. This head takes the hidden state at time $\mathbf{h}_t$, and after applying an average pooling operation, forwards the 256-dimensional frame representation to a simple block consisting of a Batch Normalization layer [19], and a linear layer that produces an N-dimensional output, where N is the number of the target AUs.

3.3 Unsupervised Pre-training

It is worth noting that, even when working in a fully supervised manner, training the above model is a rather hard task. For the purposes of semi-supervised learning, we propose to use instead a self-supervised pre-training inspired by the contrastive learning [36], which allows us to make the network produce strong facial feature representations with no labels.

Our learning goal is defined through a proxy *predictive function* $p_k(\cdot\,;\theta_p)$, tasked with predicting the future feature representations $f(\mathbf{x}_{t+k};\theta_f)$, at some time $t + k$ from a given contextual information $g(f(\mathbf{x}_t;\theta_f);\theta_c)$, computed up to time t. The learning goal is to make $p_k\left(g\left(f(\mathbf{x}_t)\right)\right)^1$ similar to $f(\mathbf{x}_{t+k})$, and at the same time different from other feature representations computed at the same time step k for a different image $\mathbf{x}'$, $f(\mathbf{x}'_{t+k})$, at the same image $\mathbf{x}$ but at a different time step k', $f(\mathbf{x}_{t+k'})$, and at a different image $\mathbf{x}'$ and time step k', $f(\mathbf{x}'_{t+k'})$. With p being a simple non-linear function, the learning burden lies on a feature representation capable of predicting the future. While in [36] the time step k is fixed, in [14] the time $t + k$ is added recursively from $t + 1$ to $t + k$.

Put formally, for a sequence $\mathbf{X} = \{\mathbf{x}_t\}_{t=1}^{T}$, the first C frames will represent the *context*, whereas the last $P = T - C$ frames will be used for the *predictive* task. Throughout our experiments, $T = 15$ frames, and C and P are set to 10 and 5 frames, respectively, i.e. from the context estimated for the first 10 frames, the goal is to predict the next 5 feature representations.

---

[1] We drop the dependency on the parameters θ for the sake of clarity.

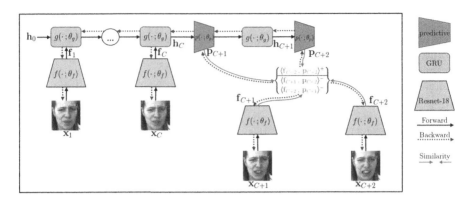

Fig. 3. Self-supervised learning through predictive coding. A predictive function uses the hidden state $\mathbf{h}_C$ of the GRU, at time t_C, to predict the feature representation $\mathbf{p}_{C+1}$ at the next temporal step t_{C+1}. This prediction is also used to obtain the next hidden state $\mathbf{h}_{C+1}$. The feature prediction is then repeated to obtain $\mathbf{p}_{C+2}$. The pair given by $\mathbf{p}_{C+2}$ and $\mathbf{f}_{C+2}$ (in green), is used as a positive sample, whereas all other mixed pairs are used as negatives (orange pairs). For the sake of clarity we illustrate only one positive pair. All other similar correspondences act also as positives during training, see Sect. 3.3. We can then backpropagate (red lines) the similarity scores for the given pairs w.r.t. the contrastive loss defined in Eq. 1, and learn a strong feature representation without labels. (Color figure online)

Let $\mathbf{f}_t^{(i,j)}$ represent the feature representation $f(\mathbf{x}_t)$ at time t, at the spatial location (i,j). Similarly, let $\mathbf{p}_{t+k}^{(i,j)}$ represent the output of the predictive function $p_k(g(f(\mathbf{x}_t)))$, at time $t+k$, at the spatial location (i,j). We use a recursive context generation:

$$\mathbf{p}_{t+1} = p_1(g(f(\mathbf{x}_t)))$$
$$\dots \quad \dots\dots$$
$$\mathbf{p}_{t+k} = p_1(g(\mathbf{p}_{t+k-1}))$$

i.e. we enforce the predictions to be conditioned not only to on previous observations, but also on the previous predictions. Recall that $g(f(\mathbf{x}_t)) = g(f(\mathbf{x}_t), \mathbf{h}_{t-1})$, i.e. all frames before t are summarized in the context at time t.

The learning is accomplished through a Noise Contrastive Estimation [12, 13], where the goal is to classify real from noisy samples. Real samples are in practice formed by pairs $(\mathbf{f}_{t+k}^{(i,j)}, \mathbf{p}_{t+k}^{(i,j)})$, while noisy samples are formed by pairs $(\mathbf{f}_{t+k'}^{(i',j')}, \mathbf{p}_{t+k}^{(i,j)})$. In other words, noisy samples are formed by pairs composed of the feature representation at time t and spatial location (i,j), and all the predictions taken from the same time position at different spatial locations, the predictions taken at different time steps, and even the predictions computed at different images in a given batch. For a given set of P predicted representations with size $H \times W$, the loss is formulated as:

$$\mathcal{L}_{nce} = -\sum_{k,i,j} \left[\log \frac{e^{\langle \mathbf{f}_{t+k}^{(i,j)}, \mathbf{P}_{t+k}^{(i,j)} \rangle}}{\sum_{k',i',j'} e^{\langle \mathbf{f}_{t+k'}^{(i',j')}, \mathbf{P}_{t+k}^{(i,j)} \rangle}} \right] \tag{1}$$

where $\langle \cdot, \cdot \rangle$ denotes the dot product, and is used as a similarity score between the feature representations. In Eq. 1, $k \in \{1 \dots P\}$, and $(i,j) \in \{(1,1) \dots (H,W)\}$. The loss within the brackets represents the typical cross-entropy objective used for classification, where the goal is to classify the positive pair among a set of $P \times H \times W$ classes (i.e. pairwise scores). When the set of negatives is enhanced with other images in the batch, the set of possible classes becomes $B \times P \times H \times W$, with B the batch size. In our setting, $B = 20$, $P = 5$, and $W = H = 8$, as aforementioned, making the number of predictions be 6400. Note that in [36] the number of classes is dozens. This makes our predictive task much harder, making the representations be more locally distinct. The reason behind this approach relies on that we want the representation to be strong for a downstream task based on a *per-frame* classification. Minimizing Eq. 1 leads to learning the weights θ_f and θ_g without requiring labeled videos. This procedure allows us to learn a strong representation with videos collected in-the-wild. A visual description is shown in Fig. 3.

3.4 Learning with Partially Labeled Data

Now, we turn into how to train the network when only a few labeled facial images, randomly and discontinuously sampled, are available. In this paper, we propose a simple approach that consists of choosing random windows around a labeled frame, so that the position of the latter in the sequence varies each time it is queried for updating the network parameters. Using this approach, we apply back-propagation w.r.t. the output at the labeled frame. In other words, if only the frame $\mathbf{x}_t$ is labeled within a sequence $\mathbf{X} = \{\mathbf{x}\}_{t=1}^{T}$, the classifier $c(\cdot; \theta_c)$ is updated only with a given labeled frame, and the feature extractor and temporal units, $f(\cdot; \theta_f)$ and $g(\cdot; \theta_g)$, are updated through back-propagation through time up to the labeled frame t. Denoting with $\mathbf{y}_t$ the label for frame t, the loss is formulated as:

$$\mathcal{L}_{sup} = \|\mathbf{y}_t - c(g(f(\mathbf{x}_t)))\|^2, \tag{2}$$

where it is important to recall the dependency of $c(g(f(\mathbf{x}_t)))$ with all frames up to t. This way, the parameters θ_f and θ_g are updated with all the frames in the sequence up to t, and the parameters θ_c are updated only with the context given by g at time t and the corresponding labeled frame. This approach is illustrated in Fig. 4.

4 Experimental Results

Data Throughout our experiments, we use three different datasets. For the self-supervised pretraining described in Sect. 3.3, we used the raw videos from the **Aff-Wild2** database [22–27,55] (i.e. with no annotations). We use 422 videos

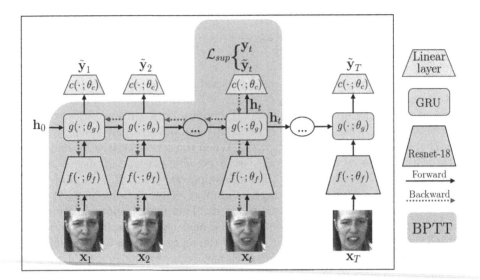

Fig. 4. Learning with partially labeled data: the network produces a structured output $\{\tilde{\mathbf{y}}_t\}_{t=1}^T$, but only one frame $\mathbf{y}_t$ is labeled. We apply Backpropagation through time (BPTT) w.r.t. the labeled frame. While the labeled frames remain the same through the training process, their position in a queried sequence is randomly shifted (i.e. the number of frames before and after the labeled frame are randomly varied).

from Aff-Wild2 with around 1.2 million frames in total. In order to learn the feature representation using the predictive task, we used 351 videos for training, and 71 videos for validation. For the Action Unit intensity estimation, we use the **BP4D** and **DISFA** datasets. The **BP4D** database [58] is the main corpus of the **FERA2015** [45], and consists of videos of 41 subjects performing 8 different tasks, making it a total of 328 videos. For our experiments, we use the official train and validation subject-independent partitions, consisting of 21 and 20 subjects, respectively. The database contains around $140,000$ frames, and is annotated with AU intensity for 5 AUs. In addition to the BP4D, we evaluate our method and perform a thorough ablation study on the **DISFA** database [32], which includes 27 videos, each of a different subject, while performing computer tasks, for an average of $\sim 4\,\mathrm{min}$. It comprises around $130,000$ frames annotated with the intensity of 12 AUs. To compare our method w.r.t. state-of-the-art results, we perform a subject independent three-fold cross-validation, where, for each fold, 18 subjects are used for training and 9 for testing. For our ablation studies, we use only one of the three folds (the same for all studies).

Frame Selection. Following existing works on semi-supervised Action Unit intensity estimation, we consider a labeled set of 2% of frames. However, contrary to existing works, we select the labeled frames *randomly*. To avoid the results of our ablation studies to be different due to the choice of data, we use the same subset of images to train both our models and those used for ablation studies.

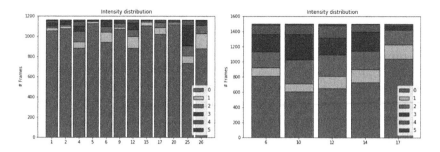

Fig. 5. AU intensity distribution for DISFA (left) and BP4D (right).

The number of training images for BP4D is 1498, whereas the number of images for each fold in DISFA is 1162. Figure 5 shows the AU intensity distribution.

Evaluation Metrics. We use the Intra-Class Correlation (ICC(3,1) [42]), commonly used to rank methods in existing benchmarks. For an AU j with ground-truth labels $\{y_i^j\}_{i=1}^N$, and predictions $\{\tilde{y}_i^j\}_{i=1}^N$, the ICC score is defined as $ICC^j = \frac{W^j - S^j}{W^j + S^j}$, with $W^j = \frac{1}{N} \sum_i \left((y_i^j - \hat{y}^j)^2 + (\tilde{y}_i^j - \hat{y}^j)^2 \right)$, $S^j = \sum_i (y_i^j - \tilde{y}_i^j)^2$, and $\hat{y}^j = \frac{1}{2N} \sum_i (y_i^j + \tilde{y}_i^j)$. In addition, we report the Mean Absolute Error (MAE).

Set Up. We use the PyTorch automatic differentiation package in all our experiments [37]. We use the publicly available S^3FD face detector of [57] to detect a facial bounding box in each video. The images are then tightly cropped around the center and resized to 128×128. Some augmentation is applied to the images for both the self-supervised training and the final stage (see below).

Self-supervised Training. The training is composed of 33509 sequences of 15 frames each, sampled with a stride of 2, and extracted from Aff-Wild2. To avoid discontinuities, sequences where a face is not detected are discarded. The number of valid test sequences to validate the performance of the predictor is 7164. To minimize non-facial content we tightly crop around the center of the bounding box. We apply a set of heavy augmentations during training, including uniform rotation (± 20 deg.), uniform scaling ($\pm 10\%$), random flipping, random jitter, and random hue, contrast, saturation and brightness. The number of context frames is set to 10, and the set of predicted frames is 5. We use the Adam optimizer [21], with an initial learning rate of 10^{-3} and weight decay of 10^{-5}. The model is trained for 300 epochs using 8 GPUs, each having a batch size of 20 sequences. The training takes approximately 1 day to be completed. We evaluate the capacity of the network to pick up the right pair by measuring the Top-n accuracy on the validation set, with $n = 1, 3, 5$. In other words, Top-n shows the percentage of samples in the validation set where the score corresponding to the positive pair was among the highest n scores. The results are shown in the second row of Table 1. As an ablation study, we also used a subset of DISFA to

perform the self-supervised training. See Sect. 4.1 for further details. The Top-n
accuracy for the DISFA is shown in the first row of Table 1.

Semi-supervised Training. To train the
Action Unit intensity regressor, we use learning rate 10^{-5} with weight decay 10^{-5}. We
use Adam with $\beta = (0.5, 0.999)$. For the
model trained from scratch, we use a Kaim-
ing initialization [16]. We observed that the
model is sensitive to the initialization. When
using normally distributed random weights,
the training was unstable, and the performance was very poor.

Table 1. Accuracy on the validation set of DISFA and Aff-Wild2 for
the Contrastive Predictive task. See
Sect. 4.1 for details

Accuracy	Top-1	Top-3	Top-5
DISFA	.165	.467	.695
Aff-Wild2	.303	.651	.781

4.1 Ablation Study

We first perform an ablation study to validate the effectiveness of our proposed
approach w.r.t. different alternatives. To this end, we use the most challenging
fold from DISFA to train and validate each of the models, i.e. we used 18 subjects
to train and 9 to test. The best performing model for each method is chosen.
In particular, we illustrate the results of the following options in Table 2 and
Table 3.

- **R18 - 2%** We train a simple ResNet-18 on the same 2% of the data, by
  minimizing the $\mathcal{L}_2$ loss between the available labels and the predictions on the
  corresponding images. We use the same augmentation as mentioned above.
- **R18 - Sup.** We train the same ResNet-18 on the full dataset (58140 images).
- **R18+GRU-scratch - 2%** We train the whole pipeline without the self-
  supervised training described in Sect. 3.3, i.e. we train the whole model from
  scratch.
- **R18+GRU-scratch Sup.** We also trained the whole pipeline without the
  self-supervised training in a fully supervised manner.
- **R18+GRU-scratch Pseudo-GT** In this setting, we used a different approach to semi-supervised learning, that of pseudo-labeling. In particular, we
  used the R18 - 2% model to generate the labels for the training set, and
  used these labels to train our model. In addition, the weights of the R18-2%
  network are also used to initialize the R18+GRU pipeline.
- **Ours(*DISFA) - 2%** In this setting, we used the same training partition
  to perform the self-supervised training described in Sect. 3.3, i.e. we used the
  18 training videos from DISFA. Then, we initialized our network with the
  generated weights, and trained using only the aforementioned 2% of labels.
- **Ours - 2%** This setting corresponds to using our proposed approach to learn
  the model with 2% of the data.
- **Ours - Sup.** We finally evaluate the performance of the model when the
  whole training set is available. This serves as an upper bound in the performance of the proposed approach.

Table 2. Ablation study on DISFA in a scenario where only 2% of frames are annotated. R18-2% refers to a simple ResNet-18 trained with 2% of the data. R18+GRU-scratch-2% refers to the method described in Sect. 3.4, without the self-supervised learning. Ours(*Disfa) refers to our method, with the self-supervised learning stage being done on the DISFA dataset. Ours(*Affwild2)-2% refers to our method, trained on 2% of the data.[**bold**] indicates best performance

	Dataset	DISFA - Only 2% of frames are annotated												
	AU	1	2	4	5	6	9	12	15	17	20	25	26	Avg.
ICC	R18 2%	[**.144**]	−.014	.375	[**.129**]	.499	[**.366**]	.737	.208	.355	[**.210**]	.901	.458	.364
	R18+GRU-scratch 2%	−.032	−.126	.340	.009	.393	.043	.650	.077	.048	.004	.841	.434	.223
	Ours(*Disfa)-2%	.084	[**.070**]	.489	.033	.481	.225	[**.772**]	[**.337**]	.304	.127	.853	[**.578**]	.363
	Ours (*Affwild2)-2%	−.010	−.022	[**.657**]	.068	[**.566**]	.358	.737	.291	[**.366**]	.109	[**.944**]	.537	[**.383**]
MAE	R18 2%	[**.209**]	[**.228**]	1.022	[**.042**]	.339	.311	.333	[**.137**]	.306	.191	.307	.474	.325
	R18+GRU-scratch 2%	.555	.512	.984	.076	.442	.397	.542	.178	.252	[**.150**]	.546	.436	.423
	Ours(*Disfa)-2%	.238	.236	[**.683**]	.098	.329	.287	[**.326**]	.174	[**.305**]	.217	.428	.389	[**.309**]
	Ours(*Affwild2)-2%	.392	.463	.754	.129	[**.304**]	[**.277**]	.360	.189	.386	.201	[**.260**]	[**.298**]	.334

Discussion. The results of all these models are shown in Table 2 and Table 3. From these results, we can make the following observations:

- *1. Accuracy of self-supervised learning* The results shown in Table 1 indicate that the performance in the predictive task is superior when the network is trained on Aff-Wild2 than when it is trained on DISFA. We attribute this difference to the fact that DISFA has less variability than Aff-Wild2, mainly due to the recording conditions. In addition, the training set for DISFA is composed of barely 18 videos, and hence the number of negative samples are highly likely to include segments that are too similar. In this scenario, the negative samples become almost indistinguishable from the positive ones, making the predictive task harder to learn.

- *2. Importance of pre-text training set* In addition to the lower performance on the predictive task, it is worth noting that the learned representation when using few videos is much weaker than that learned from videos collected in the wild. This is illustrated in the performance that the network yields in the task of facial Action Unit intensity estimation. It is important to remark that collecting videos in-the-wild that *do not* require labeling is nowadays cheaper than annotating all the frames with 12 Action Units even for a small number of videos.

- *3. Influence of self-supervised learning* We observe that, whether on DISFA or on Aff-Wild2, the results on the downstream task are remarkably better than training the network from scratch. We observe this not only for our case of interest where few labels are available, but also when training the network in a fully supervised manner. We also observed that, when trained from scratch, the network is certainly sensitive to the initialization. This has been observed in [16], that indicates that a poor initialization with deep networks can lead to vanishing gradients, making the training process unstable. In our experiments, we observe that training the Resnet-18 in a supervised manner without any temporal modeling yields better results than training the whole pipeline, also

Table 3. Ablation study on DISFA where a fully supervised setting is applied. R18 Sup. corresponds to a Resnet-18 trained in a supervised manner. R18+GRU-scratch-Sup. refers to the supervised training. R18+GRU-scratch-PseudoGT refers to a fully supervised training using the pseudo-labels produced by the R18-2% shown in Table 2. Ours(*Affwild2)-Sup. refers to our method, trained with all the labels. [**bold**] indicates best performance.

Dataset		DISFA - All frames are annotated											
	AU	1	2	4	5	6	9	12	15	17	20	25	26	Avg
ICC	R18 Sup.	.215	.030	.470	[.339]	[.583]	.382	.790	[.387]	.476	.383	.887	.565	.459
	R18+GRU-scratch Sup.	.047	-.056	.366	.097	.455	.145	.775	.089	.313	.126	.812	.501	.306
	R18+GRU-Pseudo-GT	.096	.017	.469	.115	.470	.227	.653	.186	.317	.257	.578	.250	.303
	Ours (*Affwild2)-Sup	[.291]	[.107]	[.495]	.281	.499	[.424]	[.798]	.327	[.513]	[.473]	[.908]	[.648]	[.480]
MAE	R18 Sup.	.216	.222	1.002	.048	[.302]	.302	.314	[.117]	[.200]	.134	.321	[.346]	.294
	R18+GRU-scratch Sup.	.365	.341	1.022	.113	.364	.553	.352	.204	.444	.259	.601	.549	.431
	R18+GRU-Pseudo-GT	.225	.374	.816	.062	.640	.282	.530	.296	.844	.185	1.127	.631	.501
	Ours (*Affwild2)-Sup	[.161]	[.200]	[.815]	[.043]	.334	[.273]	[.292]	.127	.215	[.108]	[.291]	.362	[.268]

in a supervised manner. We can see that our method is effective both when training with few labels and when training in a supervised way.

- *4. Influence of pseudo-labeling* We observe that this technique can be powerful enough, yielding an ICC score similar to that given by training the network from scratch in a fully supervised manner.

4.2   Comparison with State-of-the-Art

We now show the results of our method w.r.t. reported state of the art methods on weakly supervised learning for facial Action Unit intensity estimation. We report our results for both the BP4D case and for the three-fold cross validation performed in DISFA, so as to make our results comparable to existing works. We show the results of our method for BP4D in Table 4, and the results for DISFA in Table 5. We compare our method with the most recent works reporting Action Unit intensity estimation with partially labeled data. In particular, we compare the performance of our method with that of **KBSS** [60], **KJRE** [62], and **CFLF** [61]. Importantly, the three methods require the labeling of key frames, mainly due to the fact that one of the components for weakly supervised learning relies on assuming that intermediate frames between keys follow some monotonic behavior. Also, both the KBSS and CFLF work under the basis of a 1% of labeled frames. However, these methods, reportedly, use a different percentage of frames *per Action Unit*. Different from these methods, our proposed approach works with a randomly chosen subset of data. As shown in both Table 4 and Table 5, our method yields competitive results, and surpasses the three aforementioned methods in terms of average ICC.

Table 4. Intensity estimation results on BP4D. (*) Indicates results taken from reference. [**bold**] indicates best performance.

	Dataset	BP4D					
	AU	6	10	12	14	17	Avg.
ICC	KBSS [60]*	.760	.725	.840	.445	.454	.645
	KJRE [62]* 6%	.710	.610	[**.870**]	.390	.420	.600
	CFLF [61]*	[**.766**]	.703	.827	.411	[**.600**]	.661
	Ours 2%	[**.766**]	[**.749**]	.857	[**.475**]	.553	[**.680**]
MAE	KBSS [60]*	.738	[**.773**]	.694	.990	.895	.818
	KJRE [62]* 6%	.820	.950	[**.640**]	1.080	.850	.870
	CFLF [61]*	[**.624**]	.830	.694	1.000	[**.626**]	[**.741**]
	Ours 2%	.645	.913	.826	[**.979**]	.628	.798

Table 5. Intensity estimation results on DISFA. (*) Indicates results taken from reference. [**bold**] indicates best performance.

	Dataset	DISFA												
	AU	1	2	4	5	6	9	12	15	17	20	25	26	Avg.
ICC	KBSS [60]*	.136	.116	.480	.169	.433	.353	.710	.154	.248	.085	.778	.536	.350
	KJRE [62]* 6%	.270	[**.350**]	.250	.330	.510	.310	.670	.140	.170	.200	.740	.250	.350
	CLFL [61]*	.263	.194	.459	[**.354**]	.516	[**.356**]	.707	[**.183**]	[**.340**]	[**.206**]	.811	.510	.408
	Ours 2%	[**.327**]	.328	[**.645**]	−.024	[**.601**]	.335	[**.783**]	.181	.243	.078	[**.882**]	[**.578**]	[**.413**]
MAE	KBSS [60]*	.532	.489	.818	.237	.389	.375	.434	.321	.497	.355	.613	.440	.458
	KJRE [62]* 6%	1.020	.920	1.860	.700	.790	.870	.770	.600	.800	.720	.960	.940	.910
	CLFL [61]*	[**.326**]	[**.280**]	[**.605**]	[**.126**]	[**.350**]	[**.275**]	[**.425**]	[**.180**]	[**.290**]	[**.164**]	.530	.398	[**.329**]
	Ours 2%	.430	.358	.653	.194	.381	.370	.457	.247	.376	.212	[**.446**]	[**.387**]	.376

5   Conclusion

In this paper, we proposed a novel approach to semi-supervised training of facial Action Unit intensity estimation, that is capable of delivering competing results with as little as 2% of annotated frames. To this end, we proposed a self-supervised learning approach that can capture strong semantic representations of the face, that can later be used to train models in a semi-supervised way. Our approach surpasses existing works on semi-supervised learning of Action Unit intensity estimation. We also demonstrated that our approach, when used in a fully supervised manner, largely outperforms a model trained from scratch, thus demonstrating that our approach is also valid for supervised learning. The experimental evaluation proved the effectiveness of our method, through several ablation studies.

References

1. Bachman, P., Hjelm, R.D., Buchwalter, W.: Learning representations by maximizing mutual information across views. In: NeurIPS (2019)

2. Caron, M., Bojanowski, P., Joulin, A., Douze, M.: Deep clustering for unsupervised learning of visual features. In: Ferrari, V., Hebert, M., Sminchisescu, C., Weiss, Y. (eds.) Computer Vision – ECCV 2018. LNCS, vol. 11218, pp. 139–156. Springer, Cham (2018). https://doi.org/10.1007/978-3-030-01264-9_9

3. Cho, K., et al.: Learning phrase representations using RNN encoder-decoder for statistical machine translation. In: EMNLP (2014)

4. Chu, W., De la Torre, F., Cohn, J.F.: Learning spatial and temporal cues for multi-label facial action unit detection. In: FG (2017)

5. Chu, W.S., la Torre, F.D., Cohn, J.F.: Learning facial action units with spatiotemporal cues and multi-label sampling. Image Vis. Comput. **81**, 1–14 (2019)

6. Doersch, C., Gupta, A., Efros, A.A.: Unsupervised visual representation learning by context prediction. In: ICCV (2015)

7. Ekman, P., Friesen, W., Hager, J.: Facial action coding system. In: A Human Face (2002)

8. Eleftheriadis, S., Rudovic, O., Deisenroth, M.P., Pantic, M.: Variational Gaussian process auto-encoder for ordinal prediction of facial action units. In: Lai, S.-H., Lepetit, V., Nishino, K., Sato, Y. (eds.) ACCV 2016. LNCS, vol. 10112, pp. 154–170. Springer, Cham (2017). https://doi.org/10.1007/978-3-319-54184-6_10

9. Ertugrul, I.O., Cohn, J.F., Jeni, L.A., Zhang, Z., Yin, L., Ji, Q.: Crossing domains for au coding: perspectives, approaches, and measures. IEEE Trans. Biomet. Behav. Identity Sci. **2**(2), 158–171 (2020)

10. Ertugrul, I.O., Jeni, L.A., Cohn, J.F.: PAttNet: patch-attentive deep network for action unit detection. In: BMVC (2019)

11. Gidaris, S., Singh, P., Komodakis, N.: Unsupervised representation learning by predicting image rotations (2018)

12. Gutmann, M., Hyvärinen, A.: Noise-contrastive estimation: a new estimation principle for unnormalized statistical models. In: AISTATS (2010)

13. Hadsell, R., Chopra, S., LeCun, Y.: Dimensionality reduction by learning an invariant mapping. In: CVPR (2006)

14. Han, T., Xie, W., Zisserman, A.: Video representation learning by dense predictive coding. In: CVPR - Workshops (2019)

15. He, K., Fan, H., Wu, Y., Xie, S., Girshick, R.: Momentum contrast for unsupervised visual representation learning. arXiv preprint arXiv:1911.05722 (2019)

16. He, K., Zhang, X., Ren, S., Sun, J.: Delving deep into rectifiers: Surpassing human-level performance on imagenet classification. In: ICCV (2015)

17. He, K., Zhang, X., Ren, S., Sun, J.: Deep residual learning for image recognition. In: CVPR (2016)

18. Hénaff, O.J., Razavi, A., Doersch, C., Eslami, S., van der Oord, A.: Data-efficient image recognition with contrastive predictive coding. arXiv preprint arXiv:1905.09272 (2019)

19. Ioffe, S., Szegedy, C.: Batch normalization: accelerating deep network training by reducing internal covariate shift. In: ICML (2015)

20. Jaiswal, S., Valstar, M.: Deep learning the dynamic appearance and shape of facial action units. In: Winter Conference on Applications of Computer Vision (2016)

21. Kingma, D., Ba, J.: Adam: a method for stochastic optimization. In: International Conference on Learning Representations (2014)

22. Kollias, D., Nicolaou, M.A., Kotsia, I., Zhao, G., Zafeiriou, S.: Recognition of affect in the wild using deep neural networks. In: CVPR - Workshops, pp. 1972–1979. IEEE (2017)

23. Kollias, D., Schulc, A., Hajiyev, E., Zafeiriou, S.: Analysing affective behavior in the first ABAW 2020 competition. arXiv preprint arXiv:2001.11409 (2020)

24. Kollias, D., et al.: Deep affect prediction in-the-wild: aff-wild database and challenge, deep architectures, and beyond. IJCV 1–23 (2019)
25. Kollias, D., Zafeiriou, S.: Aff-wild2: extending the aff-wild database for affect recognition. arXiv preprint arXiv:1811.07770 (2018)
26. Kollias, D., Zafeiriou, S.: A multi-task learning & generation framework: valence-arousal, action units & primary expressions. arXiv preprint arXiv:1811.07771 (2018)
27. Kollias, D., Zafeiriou, S.: Expression, affect, action unit recognition: aff-wild2, multi-task learning and arcface. arXiv preprint arXiv:1910.04855 (2019)
28. Li, W., Abtahi, F., Zhu, Z.: Action unit detection with region adaptation, multi-labeling learning and optimal temporal fusing. In: CVPR (2017)
29. Li, W., Abtahi, F., Zhu, Z., Yin, L.: EAC-Net: a region-based deep enhancing and cropping approach for facial action unit detection. In: FG (2017)
30. Li, Y., Zeng, J., Shan, S., Chen, X.: Self-supervised representation learning from videos for facial action unit detection. In: CVPR (2019)
31. Martinez, B., Valstar, M.F., Jiang, B., Pantic, M.: Automatic analysis of facial actions: a survey. IEEE Trans. Affect. Comput. **10**, 325–347 (2017)
32. Mavadati, S.M., Mahoor, M.H., Bartlett, K., Trinh, P., Cohn, J.F.: DISFA: a spontaneous facial action intensity database. IEEE-TAC **4**, 151–160 (2013)
33. Ming, Z., Bugeau, A., Rouas, J., Shochi, T.: Facial action units intensity estimation by the fusion of features with multi-kernel support vector machine. In: FG (2015)
34. Misra, I., Zitnick, C.L., Hebert, M.: Shuffle and learn: unsupervised learning using temporal order verification. In: Leibe, B., Matas, J., Sebe, N., Welling, M. (eds.) ECCV 2016. LNCS, vol. 9905, pp. 527–544. Springer, Cham (2016). https://doi.org/10.1007/978-3-319-46448-0_32
35. Ntinou, I., Sanchez, E., Bulat, A., Valstar, M., Tzimiropoulos, G.: A transfer learning approach to heatmap regression for action unit intensity estimation. arXiv preprint arXiv:2004.06657 (2020)
36. van den Oord, A., Li, Y., Vinyals, O.: Representation learning with contrastive predictive coding. arXiv preprint arXiv:1807.03748 (2018)
37. Paszke, A., et al.: Automatic differentiation in pytorch. In: Autodiff workshop - NeurIPS (2017)
38. Rudovic, O., Pavlovic, V., Pantic, M.: Automatic pain intensity estimation with heteroscedastic conditional ordinal random fields. In: Bebis, G., et al. (eds.) ISVC 2013. LNCS, vol. 8034, pp. 234–243. Springer, Heidelberg (2013). https://doi.org/10.1007/978-3-642-41939-3_23
39. Rudovic, O., Pavlovic, V., Pantic, M.: Context-sensitive conditional ordinal random fields for facial action intensity estimation. In: ICCV - Workshops (2013)
40. Rudovic, O., Pavlovic, V., Pantic, M.: Context-sensitive dynamic ordinal regression for intensity estimation of facial action units. IEEE-TPAMI **37**, 944–958 (2015)
41. Sanchez, E., Tzimiropoulos, G., Valstar, M.: Joint action unit localisation and intensity estimation through heatmap regression. In: BMVC (2018)
42. Shrout, P., Fleiss, J.: Intraclass correlations: uses in assessing rater reliability. Psychol. Bull. **86**, 420 (1979)
43. Tian, Y., Krishnan, D., Isola, P.: Contrastive multiview coding. arXiv preprint arXiv:1906.05849 (2019)
44. Tran, D.L., Walecki, R., Rudovic, O., Eleftheriadis, S., Schuller, B., Pantic, M.: Deepcoder: semi-parametric variational autoencoders for automatic facial action coding. In: ICCV (2017)
45. Valstar, M.F., et al.: Fera 2015 - second facial expression recognition and analysis challenge. In: FG (2015)

46. Vincent, P., Larochelle, H., Bengio, Y., Manzagol, P.A.: Extracting and composing robust features with denoising autoencoders. In: ICML, pp. 1096–1103 (2008)
47. Walecki, R., Rudovic, O., Pavlovic, V., Schuller, B., Pantic, M.: Deep structured learning for facial action unit intensity estimation. In: CVPR (2017)
48. Wang, S., Peng, G.: Weakly supervised dual learning for facial action unit recognition. IEEE Trans. Multimed. **21**(12) (2019)
49. Wang, S., Pan, B., Wu, S., Ji, Q.: Deep facial action unit recognition and intensity estimation from partially labelled data. IEEE Trans. Affect. Comput. (2019)
50. Werbos, P.J.: Backpropagation through time: what it does and how to do it. Proc. IEEE **78**(10), 1550–1560 (1990)
51. Wu, Y., Ji, Q.: Constrained joint cascade regression framework for simultaneous facial action unit recognition and facial landmark detection. In: CVPR (2016)
52. Wu, Z., Xiong, Y., Yu, S.X., Lin, D.: Unsupervised feature learning via non-parametric instance discrimination. In: CVPR (2018)
53. Yang, L., Ertugrul, I.O., Cohn, J.F., Hammal, Z., Jiang, D., Sahli, H.: FACS3D-Net: 3D convolution based spatiotemporal representation for action unit detection. In: ACII (2019)
54. Ye, M., Zhang, X., Yuen, P.C., Chang, S.F.: Unsupervised embedding learning via invariant and spreading instance feature. In: CVPR (2019)
55. Zafeiriou, S., Kollias, D., Nicolaou, M.A., Papaioannou, A., Zhao, G., Kotsia, I.: Aff-wild: valence and arousal 'in-the-wild' challenge. In: CVPR - Workshops. IEEE (2017)
56. Zhang, R., Isola, P., Efros, A.A.: Colorful image colorization. In: Leibe, B., Matas, J., Sebe, N., Welling, M. (eds.) ECCV 2016. LNCS, vol. 9907, pp. 649–666. Springer, Cham (2016). https://doi.org/10.1007/978-3-319-46487-9_40
57. Zhang, S., Zhu, X., Lei, Z., Shi, H., Wang, X., Li, S.Z.: S3FD: single shot scale-invariant face detector. In: ICCV (2017)
58. Zhang, X., et al.: BP4D-spontaneous: a high-resolution spontaneous 3D dynamic facial expression database. Image Vis. Comput. 32, 692–706 (2014)
59. Zhang, Y., Dong, W., Hu, B.G., Ji, Q.: Classifier learning with prior probabilities for facial action unit recognition. In: CVPR (2018)
60. Zhang, Y., Dong, W., Hu, B.G., Ji, Q.: Weakly-supervised deep convolutional neural network learning for facial action unit intensity estimation. In: CVPR (2018)
61. Zhang, Y., Jiang, H., Wu, B., Fan, Y., Ji, Q.: Context-aware feature and label fusion for facial action unit intensity estimation with partially labeled data. In: ICCV (2019)
62. Zhang, Y., et al.: Joint representation and estimator learning for facial action unit intensity estimation. In: CVPR (2019)
63. Zhang, Y., Zhao, R., Dong, W., Hu, B.G., Ji, Q.: Bilateral ordinal relevance multi-instance regression for facial action unit intensity estimation. In: CVPR (2018)
64. Zhao, K., Chu, W.S., Zhang, H.: Deep region and multi-label learning for facial action unit detection. In: CVPR (2016)
65. Zhao, R., Gan, Q., Wang, S., Ji, Q.: Facial expression intensity estimation using ordinal information. In: CVPR (2016)

MMD Based Discriminative Learning for Face Forgery Detection

Jian Han$^{(\boxtimes)}$ and Theo Gevers

University of Amsterdam, Amsterdam, The Netherlands
{j.han,th.gevers}@uva.nl

Abstract. Face forensic detection is to distinguish manipulated from pristine face images. The main drawback of existing face forensics detection methods is their limited generalization ability due to differences in domains. Furthermore, artifacts such as imaging variations or face attributes do not persistently exist among all generated results for a single generation method. Therefore, in this paper, we propose a novel framework to address the domain gap induced by multiple deep fake datasets. To this end, the maximum mean discrepancy (MMD) loss is incorporated to align the different feature distributions. The center and triplet losses are added to enhance generalization. This addition ensures that the learned features are shared by multiple domains and provides better generalization abilities to unseen deep fake samples. Evaluations on various deep fake benchmarks (DF-TIMIT, UADFV, Celeb-DF and FaceForensics++) show that the proposed method achieves the best overall performance. An ablation study is performed to investigate the effect of the different components and style transfer losses.

1 Introduction

With the rapid development of face manipulation and generation, more and more photo-realistic applications have emerged. These modified images or videos are commonly known as deep fakes [1]. Even human experts find it difficult to make a distinction between pristine and manipulated facial images. Different generative methods exist nowadays to produce manipulated images and videos. In fact, it's easy to generate new types of synthetic face data by simply changing the architectural design or hyper parameters. Attackers don't need to have profound knowledge about the generation process of deep fake (face) attacks [2]. Therefore, it is of crucial importance to develop robust and accurate methods to detect manipulated face images.

Face forensic detection is to distinguish between manipulated and pristine face images. Using the same pair of subjects, different manipulation methods may generate significantly different outcomes (see Fig. 1). If the same modification method is applied on different pairs of data, the results can have quite diverse artifacts due to the variations in pose, lighting, or ethnicity. Because these artifacts do not exist in all samples, simple artifacts-based detection systems are not sufficiently robust to unseen artifacts in the test set. Other methods

© Springer Nature Switzerland AG 2021
H. Ishikawa et al. (Eds.): ACCV 2020, LNCS 12626, pp. 121–136, 2021.
https://doi.org/10.1007/978-3-030-69541-5_8

choose to exploit cues which are specific for the generative network at hand [3,4]. When the dataset is a combination of multiple domains of deep fake data like FaceForensics++, each category of manipulated face images can be a different domain compared to the rest of the data. Performance may be negatively affected by this cross-domain mismatch. In summary, the major challenges of face forensics detection are: 1) The difference among positive and negative samples is much smaller than the difference among positive examples. 2) The artifacts including imaging variations and face attributes do not persist across all generated results for a single generation method.

Our paper focuses on detecting manipulated face images which are produced by generative methods based on neural networks. To distinguish real and fake face images is equivalent to performance evaluations of different generative methods. To this end, the maximum mean discrepancy (MMD) is used to measure different properties and to analyze the performance of different generative adversarial networks [5]. The face manipulation process requires a pair of faces from source and target subjects. This process resembles the neural style transfer operation between content and reference images [6]. The final results are contingent on the source and target images. Inspired by [7], we use a MMD loss to align the extracted features from different distributions. A triplet loss is added to maximize the distance between real and fake samples and to minimize the discrepancies among positive samples. Center loss is further integrated to enhance the generalization ability. In order to fully investigate the performance of the proposed method, we evaluate our method on several deep fake benchmarks: DF-TIMIT [8], UADFV [9], Celeb-DF [10], and FaceForensics++ [1].

Our main contributions are:

- We propose a deep network based on a joint supervision framework to detect manipulated face images.
- We systematically examine the effect of style transfer loss on the performance of face forgery detection.
- The proposed method achieves the overall best performance on different deep fake benchmarks.

2   Related Work

2.1   Face Manipulation Methods

In general, face manipulation methods can be classified into two categories: facial reenactment and identity modification [1]. Deep fake has become the name for all face modification methods. However, it is originally a specific approach based on an auto-encoder architecture. Face swap represents methods that use information of 3D face models to assist the reconstructing process. Face2Face [11] is a facial reenactment framework that transfers the expressions of a source video to a target video while maintaining the identity of the target person. NeuralTextures [12] is a GAN-based rendering approach which is applied to the transformation of facial expressions between faces.

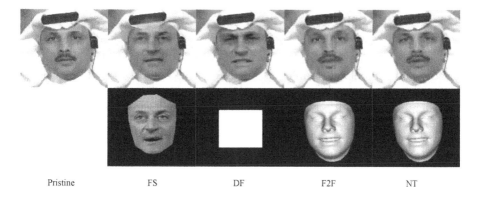

Pristine   FS   DF   F2F   NT

Fig. 1. Visualization of a number of samples from FaceForensics++. The first row shows pristine and generated face images and the second row contains face masks used to add the modifications. "DF": "DeepFakes"; "NT": "Neural Textures"; "FS": "Face Swap"; "F2F": "Face2Face". Although NT and F2F share the same face mask, NT only modifies the region around the mouth.

2.2   Face Forgery Detection

A survey of face forensics detection can be found in [13]. Several methods are proposed to detect manipulated faces [14–17]. While previous literature often relies on hand-crafted features, more and more ConvNet-based methods are proposed. There are two main directions to detect face forgery.

The most straightforward approach is data-driven. Forensic transfer [18] uses the features learned from face forensics to adapt to new domains. [19,20] combine forgery detection and location simultaneously. [21] uses a modified semantic segmentation architecture to detect manipulated regions. Peng et al. [22] provide a two stream network to detect tampered faces. Shruti et al. [2] concentrate on detecting fake videos of celebrities. Ghazal et al. [23] proposes a deep network based image forgery detection framework using full-resolution information. Ekraam et al. [24] propose a recurrent model to include temporal information. Irene et al. [25] propose an optical flow based CNN for deep fake video detection.

Another category of deep network-based methods is to capture features from the generation process. The features include artifacts or cues introduced by the network [26]. The Face Warping Artifacts (FWA) exploit post processing artifacts in generated videos [9]. Falko et al. [27] use visual artifacts around the face region to detect manipulated videos. [28] proposes a capsule network based method to detect a wide range of forged images and videos. Xin et al. [29] propose a fake video detection method based on inconsistencies between head poses. [30,31] exploit the effect of illumination. [3] monitors neuron behavior to detect synthetic face images. [4] uses fingerprints from generative adversarial networks to achieve face forensic detection. And [32] proposes a framework based on detecting noise from blending methods.

2.3 Domain Adaptation

Domain adaptation has been widely used in face-related applications. It aims to transfer features from a source to a target domain. The problem is how to measure and minimize the difference between source and target distributions. Several deep domain generalization methods are proposed [33,34] to improve the generalization ability. Rui et al. [35] propose a multi-adversarial based deep domain generalization with a triplet constraint and depth estimation to handle face anti-spoofing. Maximum mean discrepancy (MMD) [36] is a discrepancy metric to measure the difference in a Reproducing Kernel Hilbert Space. [37] uses MMD-based adversarial learning to align multiple source domains with a prior distribution. [7] considers neural style transfer as a domain adaptation task and theoretically analyzes the effect of the MMD loss.

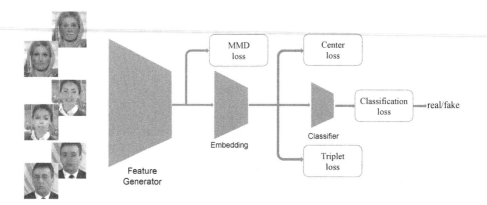

Fig. 2. Overview of the proposed method. Inputs of the network are frames of manipulated face videos. Deep network is used to extract features. Here we use the cross-entropy loss for binary classification. A MMD loss is added to learn a generalized feature space for different domains. Moreover, the triplet and center losses are integrated to provide a discriminative embedding.

3 Method

3.1 Overview

Most current forensic detection approaches fail to address unique issues in face manipulation results. The learned features may not generalize well to unseen deep fake samples. Some approaches choose to extract features from the modification process (e.g., detecting artifacts in manipulated results). Nevertheless, artifacts are dependent on the discrepancy between source and target face images. The discrepancy may originate from differences in head pose, occlusion, illumination, or ethnicity. Therefore, artifacts may differ depending on the discrepancies between source and target face images. Other methods choose to exploit characteristic cues induced by different generative models. However, any minor changes in the architecture or hyper-parameter setting may negatively influence the forgery detection performance. In contrast, our aim is a generic approach to forgery detection.

To this end, we propose a ConvNet-based discriminative learning model to detect forgery faces. A maximum mean discrepancy (MMD) loss is used to penalize the difference between pristine and fake samples. As a result, extracted features are not biased to the characteristics of a single manipulation method or subject. A center loss is introduced to guide the network to focus on more influential regions of manipulated faces. Furthermore, a triplet loss is incorporated to minimize the intra-distances. We consider the task as a binary classification problem for each frame from real or manipulated videos. In Fig. 2, we provide an overview of the proposed framework. Input images are pristine and fake face samples from a deep fake dataset.

3.2   MMD Based Domain Generalization

Maximum mean discrepancy (MMD) measures the difference between two distributions. MMD provides many desirable properties to analyze the performance of GAN [5]. In this paper, we use MMD to measure the performance of forgery detection as follows. Suppose that there are two sets of sample distributions P_s and P_t for a single face manipulation method. The MMD between the two distributions is measured with a finite sample approximation of the expectation. It represents the difference between distribution P_s and P_t based on the fixed kernel function k. A lower MMD means that P_s is closer to P_t. MMD is expressed by

$$MMD^2(P_s, P_t) = \mathbb{E}_{x_s, x_s' \sim P_s, x_t, x_t' \sim P_t} \left[k(x_s, x_s') - 2k(x_s, x_t) + k(x_t, x_t') \right] \quad (1)$$

where $k(a, b) = \langle \phi(a), \phi(b) \rangle$ denotes the kernel function defining a mapping. ϕ is an explicit function. s, t denote the source and target domains respectively. x_s and x_t are data samples from the source and target distributions.

MMD is used to measure the discrepancies among feature embeddings. The MMD loss has been used in neural style transfer tasks [7]. Different kernel functions (Gaussian, linear, or polynomial) can be used for MMD. The MMD loss is defined by:

$$L_{mmd} = \frac{1}{W_k^l} \sum_{i=1}^{M} \sum_{j=1}^{N} \left(k(f_i^l, f_i^l) + k(r_j^l, r_j^l) - 2k(f_i^l, r_j^l) \right) \quad (2)$$

where W_k^l denotes the normalization term based on the kernel function and the feature map l. M and N are numbers of fake and real examples in one batch, respectively. f and r are the features for fake and real examples. The MMD loss can supervise the network to extract more generalized features to distinguish real from fake samples. It can be considered as an alignment mechanism for different distributions.

3.3   Triplet Constraint

For several manipulated videos which are generated from the same video, the background of most samples is the same. Face reenactment methods can manage to keep the identity of the original faces constant. Meanwhile, modifications from generative methods become more and more subtle. This makes the negative examples look more similar than the positives ones for the same subject. As shown in Fig. 1, images which are generated from F2F and NT are nearly the same as the original image. Therefore, intra-distances between positive samples are larger than their inter-distances.

To learn a more generalized feature embedding, a triplet loss is added to architecture. Illustration of the triplet process can be found in Fig. 3. It is introduced in [38,39] and used in various face related applications. We aim to improve the generalization ability by penalizing the triplet relationships among batches. The triplet loss is defined by

$$L_{triplet} = \|g(x_i^a) - g(x_i^p)\|_2^2 - \|g(x_i^a) - g(x_i^n)\|_2^2 + \alpha \tag{3}$$

where α denotes the margin and i represents the batch index. x_i^a, x_i^p and x_i^n are anchor, positive samples, and negative samples respectively. They are selected online in each batch. g is the embedding learned from the network. The triplet loss can force the network to minimize the distance between an anchor and a positive sample and maximize the distance between the anchor and a negative sample. It can also contribute to higher robustness when the input is an unseen facial attribute or identity.

3.4   Center Loss

Different modification methods may select different face regions for manipulation (see Fig. 1). When this region is very small compared to the entire image, the majority of the features may exclude information about the manipulation. Our aim is that the network focuses on influential regions around faces instead of the background. To extract more discriminative embeddings, the center loss is used. It has been applied to face recognition [40], and proven effective in measuring intra-class variations. The center loss is defined by:

$$L_{center} = \sum_{k=1}^{M} \|\theta_k - c_k\|^2, \tag{4}$$

where θ is extracted from feature maps by global average pooling. c denotes the center of feature. Theoretically, the feature center needs to be calculated based on the entire dataset. From [41], a more practical way is used to iteratively update the feature center:

$$c_{k+1} = c_k + \gamma(\theta_k - c_k) \tag{5}$$

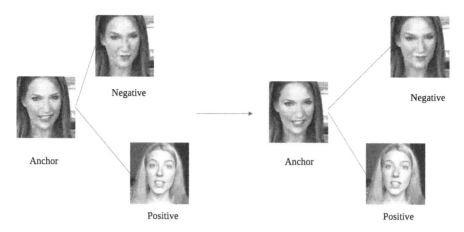

Fig. 3. Visualization of the triplet loss. Images are from FaceForensics++. Normally, the pristine and manipulated images from the same subject look similar. Through the triplet loss, we attempt to minimize the distance between positive examples while maximizing the distance between positive and negative examples.

where γ defines the learning rate of the feature center $c_k \in R^{N \times S}$. k denotes the iteration index, N is the batch size, and S is the dimension of the embedding. This iterative learning process provides a more smooth prediction for the feature center.

Our final loss function is given by:

$$L = L_{cls} + \lambda_1 L_{mmd} + \lambda_2 L_{triplet} + \lambda_3 L_{center}, \qquad (6)$$

where λ_1, λ_2 and λ_3 are balancing factors. L_{cls} is a cross-entropy loss for binary classification.

4   Experiments

4.1   Implementation Details

Our implementation is based on TensorFlow. Adam is used for optimization. We use dlib to detect the face bounding boxes for each frame of the videos. The cropped face image is 300×300. All images contain a single face. For all the experiments, we follow subject-exclusive protocol meaning that each subject exists in one split of the dataset. Inception v4 [42] is used as the backbone architecture. The pre-trained model on Imagenet is used. The batch size is 16. Learning rate is 10^{-5}. The training set has a balanced distribution of real and fake data. λ_1, λ_2, and λ_3 are set to 0.1, 0.05, 10. For the MMD loss, we use a Gaussian kernel function. The kernel bandwidths σ are 1 and 10. Feature maps $Mixed\,3a$, $Mixed\,4a$, $Mixed\,5a$ from the Inception net are used to calculate the MMD loss. For the triplet loss, we use the implementation of [38]. The margin is 2. Triplets are generated online. For every batch, we select hard positive/negative examples. For center loss, γ is 0.095. The dimension for embedding is 1024. The center is randomly initialized. For the experiments on FaceForensics++, our settings are aligned with [1]. As for experiments on Celeb-DF, our settings follow [10].

4.2 Evaluation Results

We evaluate our approach on several deep fake datasets. A summary of the datasets is shown in Table 1. Visualization of the data samples for each dataset are given in Fig. 1 and 4.

Table 1. Main contrasts of several deep fake datasets. "DF": "DeepFakes"; "NT": "Neural Textures"; "FS": "Face Swap"; "F2F": "Face2Face". The "deep fakes" is an overarching name representing a collection of these methods. For each dataset, the manipulation algorithm and process can be different.

Dataset	UADFV [9]	DF-TIMIT [8]	FaceForensics++	Celeb-DF [10]
Number of videos	98	300	5000	6000
Number of frames	34k	68k	2500k	2341k
Method	DF	FS	FS, DF, F2F, NT	DF

DFTIMIT   UADFV   Celeb-DF-v2

Fig. 4. Visualization of data samples from DF-TIMIT (high quality), UADFV and Celeb-DF. For each pair of images, the left one is the real image and the right one is the modified image.

Results on UADFV and DF-TIMIT. Both UADFV [9] and DF-TIMIT [8] are generated by identity swap methods. UADFV has 49 manipulated videos of celebrities obtained from the Internet. DF-TIMIT is created based on Vid-TIMIT [43] under constrained settings. DF-TIMIT has two different settings: low- and high-quality. We choose to evaluate our method on the high-quality subset because it is more challenging. Some pristine videos of the same subjects are selected from VidTIMIT to compose a balanced training dataset. We compare our method with Mesonet [44], XceptionNet [45], Capsule [28], and DSP-FWA [10]. We provide a brief introduction of each method below. Mesonet is based on Inception Net, which is also used in our architecture. XceptionNet is a deep network with separable convolutions and skip connections. Capsule uses a VGG network with capsule structures. DSP-FWA combines a spatial pyramid pooling with FWA [9]. In Table 2, we report all the performances following the same setting as in [10]. Two datasets are relatively small and not very challenging for forensic detection.

Table 2. Evaluation on UADFV [9], DF-TIMIT [8], FF-DF, Celeb-DF [10]. Each datset is evaluated separately. The metric is the Area Under Curve (AUC) score. "FF-DF" is the deep fake subest from FaceForensics++. We follow the same setting of [10].

AUC	UADFV	DF-TIMIT	FF-DF	Celeb-DF
MesoNet [44]	82.1	62.7	83.1	54.8
Xception [45]	83.6	70.5	93.7	65.5
Capsule [28]	61.3	74.4	96.6	57.5
DSP-FWA[10]	97.7	99.7	93.0	64.6
Ours	**98.1**	**99.8**	**97.2**	**88.3**

Results on Celeb-DF. Celeb-DF [10] is one of the largest deep fake video datasets. It is composed of more than 5,000 manipulated videos taken from celebrities. Data is collected from publicly available YouTube videos. The videos include a large range of variations such as face sizes, head poses, backgrounds and illuminants. In addition, subjects show large variations in gender, age, and ethnicity. The generation process of fake faces focuses on reducing the visual artifacts and providing a high-quality synthetic dataset. Table 2 shows that the area under curve (AUC) score of the proposed method on Celeb-DF outperforms all other approaches. The experimental settings remain the same as [10]. Compared to other deep fake datasets, Celeb-DF has fewer artifacts and better quality. The majority of failure cases are false positives. Typical false positives are shown in Fig. 5. Most cases have relatively large poses.

Results on FaceForensics++. FaceForensics++ [1,46] is one of the largest face forgery dataset. It includes pristine and synthetic videos manipulated by Face2Face [11], NeuralTextures [12], Deepfakes and Faceswap. The modified videos are generated from a pair of pristine videos. In Fig. 1, we plot all pristine and manipulated examples from one subject within the same frame. Even though the pair of source and target are the same, different methods lead to different results. The performance on raw and high-quality images from Face-Forensics++ are already good (accuracy exceeding 95%); we therefore focus on the performance on low quality images. For all experiments, we follow the same protocol as in [1] to split the dataset into a fixed training, validation, and test set, consisting of 720, 140, and 140 videos respectively. All the evaluations are based on the test set.

We compare our method with Mesonet [44], XceptionNet [45], and other methods [16,47]. In Table 3, we report the performance while training all the

Fig. 5. Visualization of false negative predictions of Celeb-DF from our method. These cropped images are from frames of deep fake videos.

categories together with our pipeline. The total f1 score is 0.89. In Table 4, we show the performance while training each category separately. In general, a more balanced prediction is obtained among the pristine and generated examples. The overall performance is better than the other methods. As expected, training Face-Forensics++ separately (Table 4) results in a better performance than combined training (Table 3). This is because each generation method is seen as a different domain to the rest. The modified face images contain different types of artifacts and features. When training entirely, manipulated faces from facial reenactment method is extremely similar to real faces. The forgery detector tends to confuse real faces with deep fake data. Our method successfully improves the performance on pristine face without impairing the performance on each deep fake category. When training each category separately, the main challenge becomes the image variations like blur. A number of false negative predictions are shown in Fig. 6. In general, the performance degrades significantly when the face is blurry or the modification region is relatively tiny.

4.3 Analysis

Performance on a single type of deep fake dataset is better than on a dataset containing multiple domains. This is because the extracted features for different manipulated results are diverse. In general, face reenactment may have fewer artifacts than identity modification methods because the transfer of the expressions may require less facial alternations. It results in better performance on detecting identity modification results. We further calculate the prediction accuracy based on each video in the test set of FaceForensics++. On average, the prediction for pristine and fake videos is higher than 80%. Although most of the datasets have many frames, the number of videos is relatively small. In most videos, faces have a limited range of variations like pose, illumination, or occlusion. This can also cause the network to predict negatives when pristine face images are relatively blurry or partially occluded. Also, the number of different subjects for the deep fake dataset is relatively small compared to other face-related datasets. This leads to biased results when testing an unseen identity with unique facial attributes.

Fig. 6. Visualization of false negative predictions of FaceForensics++ for the proposed method. These cropped images are frames taken from the deep fake videos.

Table 3. Evaluation on the test set of FaceForensics++. The training and test set includes all the categories of manipulated dataset. "DF": "DeepFakes", "NT": "Neural Textures", "FS": "Face Swap", "F2F": "Face2Face".

Accuracy	DF	F2F	FS	NT	Real	Total
Rahmouni et al [16]	80.4	62.0	60.0	60.0	56.8	61.2
Bayar and Stamm [47]	86.9	83.7	74.3	74.4	53.9	66.8
MesoNet [44]	80.4	69.1	59.2	44.8	77.6	70.5
XceptionNet [45]	93.4	**88.1**	**87.4**	78.1	75.3	81.0
Ours	**98.8**	78.6	80.8	**97.4**	**89.5**	**89.7**

Table 4. Evaluation on each category of the FaceForensics++ test set. Each category has a balanced distribution between pristine data and fake data.

Accuracy	DF	F2F	FS	NT
Bayar and Stamm [47]	81.0	77.3	76.8	72.4
Rahmouni et al [16]	73.3	62.3	67.1	62.6
MesoNet [44]	89.5	84.4	83.6	75.8
XceptionNet [45]	94.3	**91.6**	93.7	82.1
Ours	**99.2**	89.8	**94.5**	**97.3**

In our framework, we combine several losses to jointly supervise the learning process of the network. MMD loss can be considered as aligning the distributions of different domains. The style of each image can be expressed by feature distributions in different layers of deep network. Network is constrained to learn a more discriminative feature embedding through different domains. Center loss forces network to concentrate on more influential features rather than background noise. Triplet loss can be considered as an additional constraint to reduce the intra-distance effectively among positive examples.

Table 5. Performance comparison with different components of our method. We evaluate our method on test set of FaceForensics++. Metric is f1 score.

Method	Data augmentation	MMD	Center	Triplet	F1
Basic					0.826
Ours	✓				0.846
Ours	✓	✓			0.881
Ours	✓	✓	✓		0.889
Ours	✓	✓		✓	0.887
Ours	✓	✓	✓	✓	0.897

4.4   Ablation Study

To investigate the effect of each component of our method, we evaluate the performance of the proposed method with different components, see Table 5. We start with the baseline architecture and add different components separately.

Table 6. Performance comparison with different style transfer losses. We evaluate our method on test set of FaceForensics++.

Style Loss	GRAM	BN	MMD
F1	0.862	0.887	0.897

Comparison with Other Style Transfer Losses. First, we test our method with other neural style transfer losses for distribution alignment. Here, we choose the GRAM matrix-based style loss and batch normalization (BN) statistics matching [48]. The GRAM-based loss is defined by

$$L_{GRAM} = \frac{1}{W_l} \sum \left(G_R^l - G_F^l \right)^2, \tag{7}$$

where the Gram matrix G^l is the inner product between the vectorized feature maps in layer l. G_R and G_F are GRAM matrix for real and fake samples respectively. W_l is the normalization term.

The BN style loss is described by

$$L_{BN} = \frac{1}{W_l} \sum \left[(\mu_{F_l} - \mu_{R_l})^2 + (\sigma_{F_l} - \sigma_{R_l})^2 \right], \tag{8}$$

where μ and σ is the mean and standard deviation of the vectorized feature maps. μ_{R_l} and σ_{R_l} are corresponding to real face samples. From Table 6, performance of the network with the MMD loss outperforms other types of losses.

Comparison with Different Kernel Functions. A different kernel function k can provide different mapping spaces for the MMD loss. In Table 7, we investigate the effect of different kernel functions. Linear and polynomial kernel functions are defined as $k(a,b) = a^T b + c$, $k(a,b) = (a^T b + c)^d$, respectively. We choose $d = 2$ for polynomial kernel function. The Gaussian kernel outperforms other kernels for the MMD loss.

Table 7. Performance comparison with different kernel functions in the MMD loss. We evaluate our method on the test set of FaceForensics++.

Kernel Function	Polynomial	Linear	Gaussian
F1	0.841	0.876	0.897

Comparison with Different Feature Maps. Different levels of feature maps capture different type of style information. We further examine how different combinations of feature maps influence the face forensic detection performance. In Table 8, we illustrate the performances of using multiple sets of feature maps. Feature maps $Mixed\,3a$, $Mixed\,4a$, $Mixed\,5a$ are slightly better than other options.

Table 8. Performance comparison with different combinations of feature maps from our method. We evaluate our method on the test set of FaceForensics++.

Feature map	F1
$Mixed\,3a$	0.884
$Mixed\,4a$	0.881
$Mixed\,5a$	0.883
$Mixed\,3a, Mixed\,4a$	0.890
$Mixed\,4a, Mixed\,5a$	0.891
$Mixed\,3a, Mixed\,4a, Mixed\,5a$	0.897

5 Conclusions

This work focused on face forgery detection and proposed a deep network based architecture. Maximum mean discrepancy (MMD) loss has been used to learn a more generalized feature space for multiple domains of manipulation results. Furthermore, triplet constraint and center loss have been integrated to reduce the intra-distance and to provide a discriminative embedding for forensics detection.

Our proposed method achieved the best overall performance on UADFV, DF-TIMIT, Celeb-DF and FaceForensics++. Moreover, we provided a detailed analysis of each component in our framework and exploited other distribution alignment methods. Extensive experiments showed that our algorithm has high capacity and accuracy in detecting face forensics.

References

1. Rössler, A., Cozzolino, D., Verdoliva, L., Riess, C., Thies, J., Nießner, M.: Face-Forensics++: learning to detect manipulated facial images. In: International Conference on Computer Vision (ICCV) (2019)
2. Agarwal, S., Farid, H., Gu, Y., He, M., Nagano, K., Li, H.: Protecting world leaders against deep fakes. In: Proceedings of the IEEE Conference on Computer Vision and Pattern Recognition Workshops, pp. 38–45 (2019)
3. Wang, R., Ma, L., Juefei-Xu, F., Xie, X., Wang, J., Liu, Y.: FakeSpotter: a simple baseline for spotting AI-synthesized fake faces. arXiv preprint arXiv:1909.06122 (2019)
4. Yu, N., Davis, L.S., Fritz, M.: Attributing fake images to GANs: learning and analyzing GAN fingerprints. In: Proceedings of the IEEE International Conference on Computer Vision, pp. 7556–7566 (2019)
5. Xu, Q., Huang, G., Yuan, Y., Guo, C., Sun, Y., Wu, F., Weinberger, K.: An empirical study on evaluation metrics of generative adversarial networks. arXiv preprint arXiv:1806.07755 (2018)
6. Gatys, L.A., Ecker, A.S., Bethge, M.: Image style transfer using convolutional neural networks. In: Proceedings of the IEEE Conference on Computer Vision and Pattern Recognition, pp. 2414–2423 (2016)
7. Li, Y., Wang, N., Liu, J., Hou, X.: Demystifying neural style transfer. arXiv preprint arXiv:1701.01036 (2017)
8. Korshunov, P., Marcel, S.: DeepFakes: a new threat to face recognition? Assessment and detection. arXiv preprint arXiv:1812.08685 (2018)
9. Li, Y., Lyu, S.: Exposing deepfake videos by detecting face warping artifacts. arXiv preprint arXiv:1811.00656, 2 (2018)
10. Li, Y., Yang, X., Sun, P., Qi, H., Lyu, S.: Celeb-DF: a new dataset for deepfake forensics. arXiv (2019)
11. Thies, J., Zollhofer, M., Stamminger, M., Theobalt, C., Nießner, M.: Face2Face: real-time face capture and reenactment of RGB videos. In: Proceedings of the IEEE Conference on Computer Vision and Pattern Recognition, pp. 2387–2395 (2016)
12. Thies, J., Zollhöfer, M., Nießner, M.: Deferred neural rendering: image synthesis using neural textures. arXiv preprint arXiv:1904.12356 (2019)
13. Tolosana, R., Vera-Rodriguez, R., Fierrez, J., Morales, A., Ortega-Garcia, J.: Deep-Fakes and beyond: a survey of face manipulation and fake detection. arXiv preprint arXiv:2001.00179 (2020)
14. Dang-Nguyen, D.T., Boato, G., Natale, De, F.G.: Identify computer generated characters by analysing facial expressions variation. In: IEEE International Workshop on Information Forensics and Security (WIFS), pp. 252–257. IEEE (2012)
15. Conotter, V., Bodnari, E., Boato, G., Farid, H.: Physiologically-based detection of computer generated faces in video. In: 2014 IEEE International Conference on Image Processing (ICIP), pp. 248–252. IEEE (2014)
16. Rahmouni, N., Nozick, V., Yamagishi, J., Echizen, I.: Distinguishing computer graphics from natural images using convolution neural networks. In: IEEE Workshop on Information Forensics and Security (WIFS), pp. 1–6. IEEE (2017)
17. Wang, S.Y., Wang, O., Owens, A., Zhang, R., Efros, A.A.: Detecting photoshopped faces by scripting photoshop. In: Proceedings of the IEEE International Conference on Computer Vision, pp. 10072–10081 (2019)
18. Cozzolino, D., Thies, J., Rössler, A., Riess, C., Nießner, M., Verdoliva, L.: Forensictransfer: weakly-supervised domain adaptation for forgery detection. arXiv preprint arXiv:1812.02510 (2018)

19. Nguyen, H.H., Fang, F., Yamagishi, J., Echizen, I.: Multi-task learning for detecting and segmenting manipulated facial images and videos. arXiv preprint arXiv:1906.06876 (2019)
20. Songsri-in, K., Zafeiriou, S.: Complement face forensic detection and localization with faciallandmarks. arXiv preprint arXiv:1910.05455 (2019)
21. Huang, Y., et al.: FakeLocator: robust localization of GAN-based face manipulations via semantic segmentation networks with bells and whistles. arXiv preprint arXiv:2001.09598 (2020)
22. Zhou, P., Han, X., Morariu, V.I., Davis, L.S.: Two-stream neural networks for tampered face detection. In: 2017 IEEE Conference on Computer Vision and Pattern Recognition Workshops (CVPRW), pp. 1831–1839. IEEE (2017)
23. Mazaheri, G., Mithun, N.C., Bappy, J.H., Roy-Chowdhury, A.K.: A skip connection architecture for localization of image manipulations. In: Proceedings of the IEEE Conference on Computer Vision and Pattern Recognition Workshops, pp. 119–129 (2019)
24. Sabir, E., Cheng, J., Jaiswal, A., AbdAlmageed, W., Masi, I., Natarajan, P.: Recurrent convolutional strategies for face manipulation detection in videos. Interfaces (GUI) 3, 1 (2019)
25. Amerini, I., Galteri, L., Caldelli, R., Del Bimbo, A.: DeepFake video detection through optical flow based CNN. In: Proceedings of the IEEE International Conference on Computer Vision Workshops (2019)
26. Kumar, P., Vatsa, M., Singh, R.: Detecting face2face facial reenactment in videos. In: The IEEE Winter Conference on Applications of Computer Vision, pp. 2589–2597 (2020)
27. Matern, F., Riess, C., Stamminger, M.: Exploiting visual artifacts to expose deepfakes and face manipulations. In: IEEE Winter Applications of Computer Vision Workshops (WACVW), pp. 83–92 IEEE (2019)
28. Nguyen, H.H., Yamagishi, J., Echizen, I.: Capsule-forensics: using capsule networks to detect forged images and videos. In: 2019 IEEE International Conference on Acoustics, Speech and Signal Processing (ICASSP), ICASSP 2019, pp. 2307–2311. IEEE (2019)
29. Yang, X., Li, Y., Lyu, S.: Exposing deep fakes using inconsistent head poses. In: 2019 IEEE International Conference on Acoustics, Speech and Signal Processing (ICASSP), ICASSP 2019, pp. 8261–8265. IEEE (2019)
30. De Carvalho, T.J., Riess, C., Angelopoulou, E., Pedrini, H., de Rezende Rocha, A.: Exposing digital image forgeries by illumination color classification. IEEE Trans. Inf. Forensics Secur. 8, 1182–1194 (2013)
31. Carvalho, T., Faria, F.A., Pedrini, H., da Silva Torres, R., Rocha, A.: Illuminant-based transformed spaces for image forensics. IEEE Trans. Inf. Forensics Secur. 11, 720–733 (2015)
32. Li, L., et al.: Face x-ray for more general face forgery detection. arXiv preprint arXiv:1912.13458 (2019)
33. Tzeng, E., Hoffman, J., Saenko, K., Darrell, T.: Adversarial discriminative domain adaptation. In: Proceedings of the IEEE Conference on Computer Vision and Pattern Recognition, pp. 7167–7176 (2017)
34. Li, D., Yang, Y., Song, Y.Z., Hospedales, T.M.: Deeper, broader and artier domain generalization. In: Proceedings of the IEEE International Conference on Computer Vision, pp. 5542–5550 (2017)
35. Shao, R., Lan, X., Li, J., Yuen, P.C.: Multi-adversarial discriminative deep domain generalization for face presentation attack detection. In: Proceedings of the IEEE Conference on Computer Vision and Pattern Recognition, pp. 10023–10031 (2019)

36. Gretton, A., Borgwardt, K.M., Rasch, M.J., Schölkopf, B., Smola, A.: A kernel two-sample test. J. Mach. Learn. Res. **13**, 723–773 (2012)
37. Li, H., Jialin Pan, S., Wang, S., Kot, A.C.: Domain generalization with adversarial feature learning. In: Proceedings of the IEEE Conference on Computer Vision and Pattern Recognition, pp. 5400–5409 (2018)
38. Schroff, F., Kalenichenko, D., Philbin, J.: FaceNet: a unified embedding for face recognition and clustering. In: Proceedings of the IEEE Conference on Computer Vision and Pattern Recognition, pp. 815–823 (2015)
39. Parkhi, O.M., Vedaldi, A., Zisserman, A.: Deep face recognition (2015)
40. Wen, Y., Zhang, K., Li, Z., Qiao, Yu.: A discriminative feature learning approach for deep face recognition. In: Leibe, B., Matas, J., Sebe, N., Welling, M. (eds.) ECCV 2016. LNCS, vol. 9911, pp. 499–515. Springer, Cham (2016). https://doi.org/10.1007/978-3-319-46478-7_31
41. Hu, T., Xu, J., Huang, C., Qi, H., Huang, Q., Lu, Y.: Weakly supervised bilinear attention network for fine-grained visual classification. arXiv preprint arXiv:1808.02152 (2018)
42. Szegedy, C., Ioffe, S., Vanhoucke, V., Alemi, A.A.: Inception-v4, Inception-ResNet and the impact of residual connections on learning. In: Thirty-First AAAI Conference on Artificial Intelligence (2017)
43. Sanderson, C., Lovell, B.C.: Multi-region probabilistic histograms for robust and scalable identity inference. In: Tistarelli, M., Nixon, M.S. (eds.) ICB 2009. LNCS, vol. 5558, pp. 199–208. Springer, Heidelberg (2009). https://doi.org/10.1007/978-3-642-01793-3_21
44. Afchar, D., Nozick, V., Yamagishi, J., Echizen, I.: MesoNet: a compact facial video forgery detection network. In: IEEE International Workshop on Information Forensics and Security (WIFS), pp. 1–7. IEEE (2018)
45. Chollet, F.: Xception: deep learning with depthwise separable convolutions. In: Proceedings of the IEEE Conference on Computer Vision and Pattern Recognition, pp. 1251–1258 (2017)
46. Rössler, A., Cozzolino, D., Verdoliva, L., Riess, C., Thies, J., Nießner, M.: Face-Forensics: a large-scale video dataset for forgery detection in human faces. arXiv (2018)
47. Bayar, B., Stamm, M.C.: A deep learning approach to universal image manipulation detection using a new convolutional layer. In: Proceedings of the 4th ACM Workshop on Information Hiding and Multimedia Security, pp. 5–10 (2016)
48. Li, Y., Wang, N., Shi, J., Liu, J., Hou, X.: Revisiting batch normalization for practical domain adaptation. arXiv preprint arXiv:1603.04779 (2016)

RE-Net: A Relation Embedded Deep Model for AU Occurrence and Intensity Estimation

Huiyuan Yang$^{(\boxtimes)}$ and Lijun Yin

Department of Computer Science,
Binghamton University-State University of New York, Binghamton, NY, USA
hyang51@binghamton.edu, lijun@cs.binghamton.edu

Abstract. Facial action units (AUs) recognition is a multi-label classification problem, where regular spatial and temporal patterns exist in AU labels due to facial anatomy and human's behavior habits. Exploiting AU correlation is beneficial for obtaining robust AU detector or reducing the dependency of a large amount of AU-labeled samples. Several related works have been done to apply AU correlation to model's objective function or the extracted features. However, this may not be optimal as all the AUs still share the same backbone network, requiring to update the model as a whole. In this work, we present a novel AU **R**elation **E**mbedded deep model (**RE-Net**) for AU detection that applies the AU correlation to the model's parameter space. Specifically, we format the multi-label AU detection problem as a domain adaptation task and propose a model that contains both shared and AU specific parameters, where the shared parameters are used by all the AUs, and the AU specific parameters are owned by individual AU. The AU relationship based regularization is applied to the AU specific parameters. Extensive experiments on three public benchmarks demonstrate that our method outperforms the previous work and achieves state-of-the-art performance on both AU detection task and AU intensity estimation task.

1 Introduction

Automatic facial action units (AUs) recognition has attracted increasing attention in recent years due to its wide-ranging applications in affective computing, social signal processing, and behavioral science. Based on the Facial Action Coding System (FACS) [1], action units which refer to the contraction or relaxation of one or more facial muscles, have been used to infer facial behaviors for emotion analysis.

Automatic AU recognition is a challenging task due to many factors, such as image conditions, size of database, and individual differences. Although large-scale training data can facilitate the learning process for AU classification, data

Electronic supplementary material The online version of this chapter (https://doi.org/10.1007/978-3-030-69541-5_9) contains supplementary material, which is available to authorized users.

© Springer Nature Switzerland AG 2021
H. Ishikawa et al. (Eds.): ACCV 2020, LNCS 12626, pp. 137–153, 2021.
https://doi.org/10.1007/978-3-030-69541-5_9

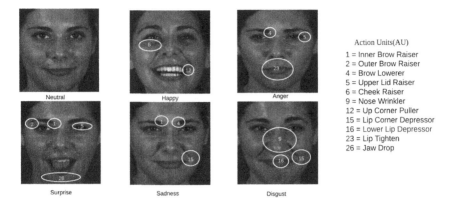

Fig. 1. Coupling effect of multiple AUs caused by a variety of facial expressions.

collection and AU annotation are extremely labor-intensive, thus being a time-consuming and error prone process. Fortunately, behavior research shows that there exist regular spatial and temporal patterns in AU labels due to facial anatomy and human's behavior habits. For example, persons can not *pull lip corner* (AU12) and *depress lip corner* (AU15) at the same time due to the constraint of facial anatomy; *inner brow raiser* (AU1) and *outer brow raiser* (AU2) are both related to the muscle group *Frontalis*, most people cannot make a facial movement of AU1 without AU2, and vice versa. Figure 1 shows the coupling effect of multiple AUs caused by a variety of facial expressions. Such regular spatial and temporal patterns embedded in AU labels could be used as a constraint for AU detection.

Inspired by the above observations, there has been extensive research by exploiting AU relations to facilitate the learning process of AU classifiers. For example, the existing works reported in [2–5] have proposed to apply graphical model to capture the dependencies among AUs through its structure and conditional probabilities. Alternatively, recent works by Benitez-Quiroz et al. [6], Zhang et al. [7] and Peng et al. [8,9] proposed to introduce the dependencies among AUs into the objective function, and Zhao et al. [10,11] exploited the relationship among AUs and active image patches. To further utilize the AU relationships, Corneanu et al. [12], Li et al. [13], and Shao et al. [14] proposed to extract robust features by adding the AU relationship based graph neural networks to the extracted features.

However, the existing AU relationship modeling (at the *objective function level*, *feature level*, and *image patch level*) may not be optimal. First, most of the works that model the AU relationship as a prior rule into the classification predictions are usually not end-to-end trainable; Second, all the AUs still share the same backbone network, which is updated as a whole, thus it may not be the optimal way to utilize the AU relationship. As a matter of fact, the AU relationship can not be effectively used to update the model's parameters because the AU relationship is only involved into the calculation of the loss function. Moreover, in order to apply an AU-relation based graph to the extracted features, existing methods have applied a cropping operation to crop the AU-related region for individual AU feature extraction, which may lead to the information loss due to the neglect of AU correlation. Importantly, all shared parameters of the model may not work equally well for different AUs.

Taking into account the shortcomings, we propose a new end-to-end trainable AU relation embedded deep model (**RE-Net**) that integrates the AU relationship into the model's parameter space. Specifically, instead of sharing the same backbone, different AUs contain both shared and AU-specific model parameters, in which the shared parameters are shared by all the AUs, and the AU-specific parameters are AU dependent. An AU relationship graph is constructed from the AU labels in the training dataset with AU as vertex and relationship as edge, which then used as a regularization of the AU-specific parameters. The benefits of using both shared and AU-specific model parameters with AU relationship are three-fold. First, by splitting the backbone parameters into both shared and AU-specific parts, the deep model is able to get updated both globally (through updating shared parameters for all the AUs) and locally (through updating AU-specific parameters for individual AU). Second, unlike existing methods that may lose information by cropping the facial region for individual feature extraction, our proposed method extracts different features from the input image for individual AU detection (as shown in Fig. 3). Third, optimizing the AU-specific parameters by taking the AU relationship into account, our method is beneficial for recognition of AUs with less occurrence rate, potentially being capable of recognition of new AUs as well (more details in Sect. 4.6).

The contributions of this paper can be summarised as below:

- Built upon the adaptive batch normalization method, we format the multi-label AU detection problem as a domain adaptation problem with AU relation embedded, and propose a framework which contains both shared and AU-specific parameters.
- We conduct extensive experiments on the widely used datasets for both AU recognition and AU intensity estimation, and demonstrate the superiority of the proposed method over the state-of-the-art methods.
- Ablation study shows our model is extendable to recognize new AUs and robust to the scenario of data imbalance.

2 Related Works

AU recognition is a multi-label classification problem, where multiple AUs may be present simultaneously, on the other hand, some AUs just can not happen at the same time. Exploiting AU relations has the potential to facilitate the learning process of AU classifiers.

Generative models are used to model the joint distribution. Li et al. [2] proposed to learn a dynamic Bayesian networks to model the relationships among AUs. Wang et al. [3] used restricted Boltzman Machine to capture both local pair-wise AU dependencies and global relationships among AUs. Tong et al. [4] proposed Bayesian Networks to model the domain knowledge (AU dependencies) through its structure and conditional probabilities, and experimental results demonstrated that the domain knowledge can be used to improve parameter learning accuracy, and also reduced the dependency on the labeled data. Similar idea was also used in [5], which presents a learning algorithm to learn parameters in Bayesian networks under the circumstances that the training data is incomplete or sparse or when multiple hidden nodes exist.

On the other hand, discriminative approaches introduce the dependencies among AUs into the objective function; Zhao et al. [10] proposed a joint-patch and multi-label (JPML) method to exploit dependencies among AUs and facial features, which used the group sparsity and positive and negative AU correlations as the constraints to learn multiple AU classifiers. Zhao et al. [11] proposed a unified Deep Region and Multi-label Learning (DRML) network that simultaneously addresses both the strong statistical evidence of AU correlations and the sparsity of active AUs on facial regions. Peng and Wang [8] utilized the probabilistic dependencies between expressions and AUs as well as dependencies among AUs to train a model from partially AU-labeled and fully expression labeled facial images. Peng and Wang [9] used the dual learning method to model the dependencies between AUs and expressions for AU detection. By leveraging prior expression-independent and expression-dependent probabilities on AUs, Zhang et al. [7] proposed a knowledge-driven method for jointly learning multiple AU classifiers without AU annotations.

Instead of applying AUs dependencies into the objective function, some works also exploit using AU correlation as constraint for feature representation learning. Corneanu et al. [12] proposed a deep structured inference network (DSIN) to deal with patch and multi-label learning for AU recognition, which first extract local and global representations, and then capture AU relations by passing information between predictions using a graphical models. However, the relationship inference is still limited to the label level. Li et al. [13] proposed a AU semantic relationship embedded representation learning framework, which incorporate AU relationships as an extra guidance for the representation learning. A Gated Graph Neural Network (GCNN) is constructed using a knowledge-graph from AU correlation as its structure, and features extracted from facial regions as its nodes. As a result, the learned feature involves both the appearance and the AU relationship. A similar idea is also used in [14] that captures spatial relationships among AUs as well as temporal relations from dynamic AUs.

However, applying AU relationship to the objective function or the extracted features may not be optimal, so we propose to exploit the AU relationship in the model's parameter space.

3   Proposed Method

3.1   Problem Formulation

The primary objective of our methodology is to learn a model with both shared and AU-specific parameters. To this end, our model seeks to learn the AU-specific parameters in order to satisfy the AU correlation, and the shared parameters for AU detection. Formally, Let us consider $\mathcal{C}$ AUs to recognize. A graph $\mathcal{G} = (\mathcal{V}, \mathcal{E})$, where $\mathcal{V} \subset \mathcal{C}$ represents the set of vertices corresponding to AUs and $\mathcal{E} \subseteq \mathcal{V} \times \mathcal{V}$ the set of edges, i.e., relations between AUs. In addition, we define an edge weight $\mathcal{W} : \mathcal{E} \to \mathbb{R}$ that measures the relation between two AUs. The network parameters are represented as $\theta = \{\theta_s, \theta_c\}_{c=1}^{\mathcal{C}}$, where θ_s represents the shared parameters for all AUs, while $\theta_c = (\gamma_c, \beta_c)$ represents the AU specific parameters owned by individual AU. Our goal is to learn a model with parameters of $\{\theta_s, \theta_c\}_{c=1}^{\mathcal{C}}$ by minimizing the supervised loss subject to the graph $\mathcal{G}$ among AU specific parameters $\{\theta_c\}_{c=1}^{\mathcal{C}}$.

3.2   Preliminary: Batch Normalization

A standard Batch Normalization (BN) [15] layer normalizes its input according to:

$$BN(x) = \gamma \cdot \frac{x - \mu}{\sqrt{\sigma^2 + \epsilon}} + \beta \tag{1}$$

where μ, σ^2 are the estimated mean and variance of x; γ, β are learnable scale and bias parameters respectively, and ϵ is a small constant used to avoid numerical instabilitie-s. For simplicity, the channel dimension and spatial location have been omitted.

Recent works [16–19] have shown the effectiveness of extending batch-normalization to address domain adaptation tasks. In particular, these works rewrite each BN to take into account domain-specific statistics. For example, given an AU $c \in \mathcal{C}$, a $\widehat{BN}$ layer differs from the standard BN by including a specific AU information:

$$\widehat{BN}(x, c) = \gamma \cdot \frac{x - \mu_c}{\sqrt{\sigma_c^2 + \epsilon}} + \beta \tag{2}$$

where $\{\mu_c, \sigma_c^2\}$ are the mean and variance statistics estimated from x conditioned on AU c. In other words, for each input x, the normalization is conditioned on which AU we aim to recognize. Since we do not want to share the scale and bias parameters across different AUs, so we include them within the set of private parameters, and rewrite the $\widehat{BN}(x, c)$ as below:

$$\widehat{BN}(x, c) = \gamma_c \cdot \frac{x - \mu_c}{\sqrt{\sigma_c^2 + \epsilon}} + \beta_c \tag{3}$$

here, $\{\gamma_c, \beta_c\}$ are the learnable AU specific parameters.

3.3   AU Relationship Graph

AU relationship graph $\mathcal{G} = (\mathcal{V}, \mathcal{E})$ represents the correlations between each pair of AUs. Each node in graph represents a corresponding AU. Given a dataset with $\mathcal{C}$ AUs, the constructed graph is formed by $|\mathcal{C}|$ nodes.

Figure 2 shows the relation matrix studied on the datasets. Following previous work [13,14], we compute the Pearson correlation coefficient (PCC) between each pair of the j-th and i-th AUs in the dataset, denoted as $\omega_{i,j}$. Unlike [13, 14] that convert the AU correlations to positive or negative relationship based on two thresholds, ignoring the correlations between the two thresholds and also the strength of correlation, we use the original PCC as $\omega_{i,j}$, so both the positive/negative relationship and strength are considered.

3.4   AU Recognition with Graph Constraint

When training the model, $\widehat{BN}(x, c)$ allows to optimize the AU-specific scale γ_c and bia β_c parameters, however, it does not take into account the presence of the relationship between the AUs, as imposed by the AU correlation matrix. As used in [16], one possible way to include the AU correlation matrix within the optimization procedure is to modify Eq. (3) as follows:

$$\widehat{BN}(x, c, \mathcal{G}) = \gamma_c^{\mathcal{G}} \cdot \frac{x - \mu_c}{\sqrt{\sigma_c^2 + \epsilon}} + \beta_c^{\mathcal{G}} \tag{4}$$

where, $\gamma_c^{\mathcal{G}}$ and $\beta_c^{\mathcal{G}}$ are calculated as below:

$$\gamma_c^{\mathcal{G}} = \frac{\sum_{k \in \mathcal{C}} \omega_{c,k} \cdot \gamma_k}{\sum_{k \in \mathcal{C}} \omega_{c,k}}; \qquad \beta_c^{\mathcal{G}} = \frac{\sum_{k \in \mathcal{C}} \omega_{c,k} \cdot \beta_k}{\sum_{k \in \mathcal{C}} \omega_{c,k}}; \tag{5}$$

$\omega_{c,k}$ is set as 1 if $c = k$, otherwise, $\omega_{c,k}$ represents the calculated PCC from training dataset. By doing this, the calculation of any AU-specific scale and bias parameters are influenced by other AUs with graph edge as the weight.

A cross-entropy loss function is used for AU recognitionn:

$$\mathcal{L}_\theta = -\frac{1}{N} \sum_{i=1}^{N} \sum_{c \in \mathcal{C}} -\left[y_{i,c}^T \times log(\bar{y}_{i,c}) + (1 - y_{i,c})^T \times log(1 - \bar{y}_{i,c}) \right] \tag{6}$$

During training, we have two different strategies we can use:

- for each batch, we run the model $|\mathcal{C}|$ times to calculate the loss for each AU, and then update the model's parameters by back-propagating the sum of all the losses;
- for each batch, randomly select a single AU for optimization;

the first training method optimize the shared and all the AU specific parameters together, which may be beneficial for stable training, but the training procedure will be memory-intensive and time consuming. On the other hand, the second training strategy will not add extra burden by optimizing randomly selected single AU for each input batch, so the model can be trained as fast as the baseline model. Through experiments, we find that there is no big difference in performance as using two training strategies, so the second training method is of course preferred.

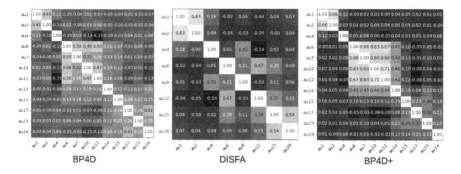

Fig. 2. The relation matrix calculated by PCC on three datasets. $(+, -)$ represents the corresponding positive and negative correlations between AU pairs; the absolute value means the strength of correlations. Zoom in for more details.

4   Experiments

In this section, the proposed method is first evaluated on three benchmark datasets: BP4D [20], DISFA [21] and BP4D+ [22] for AU recognition task, then applied to AU intensity estimation task in both BP4D and DISFA datasets.

4.1   Data

BP4D [20] is a widely used dataset for evaluating AU detection performance. The dataset contains 328 2D and 3D videos collected from 41 subjects (23 females and 18 males) under eight different tasks. As mentioned in the dataset, the most expressive 500 frames (around 20 s) are manually selected and labeled for AU occurrence from each one-minute long sequence, resulting in a dataset of around 140,000 AU-coded frames. For a fair comparison with the state-of-the-art methods, a three-fold subject-exclusive cross validation is performed on 12 AUs.

DISFA [21] is another benchmark dataset for AU detection, which contains videos from left view and right view of 27 subjects (12 females, 15 males). 12 AUs are labeled with AU intensity from 0 to 5, resulting in around 130,000 AU-coded images. Following the experimental setting in [23], 8 of 12 AUs with intensity greater than 0 are used from the left camera. F1-score is reported based on subject-exclusive 3-fold cross-validation.

BP4D+ [22] is a multimodal spontaneous emotion dataset, where high-resolution 3D dynamic model, high-resolution 2D video, thermal (infrared) image and physiological data were acquired from 140 subjects. There are 58 males and 82 females, with ages ranging from 18 to 66 years old. Each subject experienced 10 tasks corresponding to 10 different emotion categories, and the most facially-expressive 20 s from four tasks were AU-coded from all 140 subjects, resulting in a database contains around 192,000 AU-coded frames. Following a similar setting in BP4D dataset, 12 AUs are selected and performance of 3-fold cross-validation is reported.

4.2 Evaluation Metrics

For the AU recognition task, we use the F1-score for comparison study with the state of the arts. F1-score is defined as the harmonic mean of the precision and recall. As the distribution of AU labels are unbalanced, F1-score is a preferable metric for performance evaluation.

For the AU intensity estimation task, we use the Intra-class Correlation ICC(3,1) [24], which is commonly used in behavioral sciences to measure agreement between annotators (in our case, the AU intensity levels between prediction and ground-truth). We also report the Mean Absolute Error (MAE), the absolute differences between target and prediction, commonly used for ordinal prediction tasks.

4.3 Implementation Details

All the face images are aligned and cropped to the size of 256×256 using affine transformation based on the provided facial landmarks, randomly cropped to 224×224 for training, and center-cropping for testing. Random horizontal flip is also applied during training.

To analyze the impact of our proposed method, we use the ResNet-18 [25] architecture as baseline. In particular, the default batch normalization layer is replaced with $\widehat{BN}(x, c, \mathcal{G})$ as described in Eq. (3). To reduce the training complexity, a single AU is randomly selected to optimize for each training batch images, and use all of the AUs for validation and testing. We use an Adam optimizer with learning rate of 0.0001 and mini-batch size 100 with early stopping. We implement our method with the Pytorch [26] framework and perform training and testing on the NVIDIA GeForce 2080Ti GPU.

4.4 AU Detection Results

We compare our method to alternative methods, including Liner SVM (LSVM) [27], Joint Patch and Multi-label (JPML) [10], Deep Region and Multi-label (DRML) [11], Enhancing and Cropping Network (EAC-net) [23], Deep Structure Inference Network (DSIN) [12], Joint AU Detection and Face Alignment (JAA) [28], Optical Flow network (OF-Net) [29], Local relationship learning with Person-specific shape regularization (LP-Net) [30], Semantic Relationships Embedded Representation Learning (SRERL) [13] and ResNet18.

Table 1. F1 scores in terms of 12 AUs are reported for the proposed method and the state-of-the-art methods on the BP4D database. Bold numbers indicate the best performance; bracketed numbers indicate the second best.

Method	AU1	AU2	AU4	AU6	AU7	AU10	AU12	AU14	AU15	AU17	AU23	AU24	*Avg*
LSVM [27]	23.2	22.8	23.1	27.2	47.1	77.2	63.7	64.3	18.4	33.0	19.4	20.7	35.3
JPML [10]	32.6	25.6	37.4	42.3	50.5	72.2	74.1	65.7	38.1	40.0	30.4	42.3	45.9
DRML [11]	36.4	41.8	43.0	55.0	67.0	66.3	65.8	54.1	33.2	48.0	31.7	30.0	48.3
EAC-net [23]	39.0	35.2	48.6	76.1	72.9	81.9	86.2	58.8	37.5	59.1	35.9	35.8	55.9
DSIN [12]	[51.7]	40.4	56.0	76.1	73.5	79.9	85.4	62.7	37.3	[62.9]	38.8	41.6	58.9
JAA [28]	47.2	44.0	54.9	[77.5]	74.6	84.0	86.9	61.9	43.6	60.3	42.7	41.9	60.0
OF-Net [29]	50.8	[45.3]	[56.6]	75.9	75.9	80.9	[88.4]	63.4	41.6	60.6	39.1	37.8	59.7
LP-Net [30]	43.4	38.0	54.2	77.1	76.7	83.8	87.2	63.3	[45.3]	60.5	**48.1**	**54.2**	61.0
SRERL [13]	46.9	[45.3]	55.6	77.1	**78.4**	83.5	87.6	63.9	**52.2**	**63.9**	[47.1]	[53.3]	[62.9]
ResNet18	44.5	45.1	51.1	**81.2**	76.8	[87.6]	86.8	[67.9]	44.2	57.5	42.0	30.8	59.6
Ours	**57.7**	**59.0**	**66.9**	76.3	[77.0]	**88.9**	**89.8**	**70.9**	42.0	62.8	44.8	49.3	**65.5**

Table 1 shows the results of different methods on the BP4D database. It can be seen that our method outperforms all of the SOTA methods. The ResNet18 baseline achieves 59.6% F1-score, and a similar baseline performance is also reported in [31,32]. Compared with the patch or region-based methods: JPML and DRML, our method achieves 19.6% and 17.2% higher performance on BP4D database. Compared with JAA and LP-Net, which used Facial landmarks as a joint task or regularization for AU detection, our method still shows 5.5% and 4.5% improvement in terms of F1-score on the BP4D database. It worth to note that both our method and LP-Net use ResNet as the stem network.

DSIN and SRERL are the closely related methods. Both DSIN and our method are able to predict label for individual AU, while SRERL and our method are similar in concept to learn robust feature for individual AU. The main difference lies in the facts: first, the CNN layers are still shared by all the AUs in both DSIN and SRERL, and the AU correlation is applied to the objective function or the extracted feature; second, DSIN needs incremental training and SRERL uses facial landmarks to crop the AU region for individual feature extraction, which may lead to information loss. Our end-to-end trainable method contains both shared and AU-specific parameters, so features can be extracted for individual AU by AU-relation guided computation of AU-specific parameters. The AU relationship is directly applied to the model's parameter space, and the 6.6% and 2.6% higher F1-scores demonstrate the effectiveness of applying AU relationship into the model's parameter space.

Experimental results on the DISFA database are reported in Table 2. As compared to ResNet18, our method shows 4.6% improvement. Note that, both JAA and LP-Net use facial landmarks as either a joint task or regularization, and SRERL uses AU intensity equal or greater than 2 as positive example, while our method and other methods use AU intensity greater than 0 as positive example, and our method still shows comparable result.

Table 2. F1 scores in terms of 8 AUs are reported for the proposed method and the state-of-the-art methods on DISFA dataset. Bold numbers indicate the best performance; bracketed numbers indicate the second best. [* *means the method used AU intensity greater or equal to 2 as positive example.*]

Method	AU1	AU2	AU4	AU6	AU9	AU12	AU25	AU26	*Avg*
LSVM [27]	10.8	10.0	21.8	15.7	11.5	70.4	12.0	22.1	21.8
DRML [11]	17.3	17.7	37.4	29.0	10.7	37.7	38.5	20.1	26.7
EAC-net [23]	41.5	26.4	66.4	**50.7**	**80.5**	**89.3**	88.9	15.6	48.5
DSIN [12]	42.4	39.0	[68.4]	28.6	46.8	70.8	90.4	42.2	53.6
JAA [28] *	[43.7]	[46.2]	56.0	41.4	44.7	69.6	88.3	58.4	[56.0]*
OF-Net [29]	30.9	34.7	63.9	44.5	31.9	[78.3]	84.7	[60.5]	53.7
LP-Net [30]*	29.9	24.7	**72.7**	46.8	49.6	72.9	[93.8]	**65.0**	**56.9***
SRERL [13] *	**45.7**	**47.8**	59.6	47.1	45.6	73.5	84.3	43.6	55.9*
ResNet18	31.3	33.7	48.7	45.5	33.3	68.6	**94.3**	48.1	50.4
Ours	38.8	31.1	57.2	[50.1]	[50.2]	75.5	86.6	50.6	55.0

Table 3. F1 scores in terms of 12 AUs are reported on the BP4D+ dataset.

Method	AU1	AU2	AU4	AU6	AU7	AU10	AU12	AU14	AU15	AU17	AU23	AU24	*Avg*
ResNet18	34.6	34.6	33.1	84.9	87.0	90.0	88.9	80.4	53.3	38.7	54.7	13.4	57.8
Ours	37.6	33.7	37.1	85.8	89.2	90.7	89.3	80.6	63.0	46.0	55.2	33.5	61.8

Our method is also evaluated on the BP4D+ database, which contains more AU-labeled frames from more subjects, the results are shown in Table 3. Our method achieves 4.0% improvement in F1-score when compared to ResNet18.

4.5 AU Intensity Estimation

Action Units recognition aims to detect the occurrence or absence of AUs; while, AU intensity is used to describe the extent of muscle movement, which presents detailed information of facial behaviours. AU intensity is quantified into six-point ordinal scales in FACS. Compared to AU detection, AU intensity estimation could provide more detailed information for facial behaviour analysis, but it is also a more challenging task, as the subtle difference among neighbor intensities.

Fortunately, a similar relationship also exists among AU intensity. We slightly modify the model for the AU intensity estimation task in both BP4D and DISFA datasets. First, AU intensity relationship is constructed from the AU intensity labels in the training dataset; second, the output of the model is set as six, the number of intensity levels. The results are shown in Table 4 and Table 5. Our method achieves the best average performance on both databases under two evaluation metrics, except ICC(3,1) on the BP4D database, where our method shows comparable result over the state-of-the-art methods.

Table 4. ICC (3,1) and MAE scores in terms of 5 AUs are reported for the proposed method and the state-of-the-art methods on BP4D dataset. Bold numbers indicate the best performance; bracketed numbers indicate the second best.

	Method	AU6	AU10	AU12	AU14	AU17	Avg
ICC	VGP-AE [33]	0.75	0.66	**0.88**	0.47	[0.49]	0.65
	CCNN-IT [34]	0.75	0.69	0.86	0.40	0.45	0.63
	OR-CNN [35]	0.71	0.63	[0.87]	0.41	0.31	0.58
	2DC [36]	[0.76]	0.71	0.85	0.45	**0.53**	[0.66]
	VGG16 [37]	0.63	0.61	0.73	0.25	0.31	0.51
	Joint [38]	**0.79**	[0.80]	0.86	[0.54]	0.43	**0.68**
	Ours	0.54	**0.88**	0.77	**0.70**	0.33	0.64
MAE	VGP-AE [33]	0.82	1.28	0.70	1.43	**0.77**	1.00
	CCNN-IT [34]	1.23	1.69	0.98	2.72	1.17	1.57
	OR-CNN [35]	0.88	1.12	0.68	1.52	0.93	1.02
	2DC [36]	[0.75]	1.02	0.66	[1.44]	0.88	0.95
	VGG16 [37]	0.93	1.04	0.91	1.51	1.10	1.10
	Joint [38]	0.77	[0.92]	[0.65]	1.57	**0.77**	[0.94]
	Ours	**0.48**	**0.47**	**0.64**	**0.67**	0.99	**0.65**

Table 5. ICC(3,1) and MAE scores in terms of 12 AUs are reported for the proposed method and the state-of-the-art methods on DISFA dataset. Bold numbers indicate the best performance; bracketed numbers indicate the second best.

	Method	AU1	AU2	AU4	AU5	AU6	AU9	AU12	AU15	AU17	AU20	AU25	AU26	Avg
ICC	VGP-AE [33]	0.37	0.32	0.43	0.17	0.45	0.52	0.76	0.04	0.21	0.08	0.80	0.51	0.39
	CCNN-IT [34]	0.18	0.15	0.61	0.07	**0.65**	[0.55]	[0.82]	**0.44**	[0.37]	**0.28**	0.77	[0.54]	0.45
	OR-CNN [35]	0.33	0.31	0.32	0.16	0.32	0.28	0.71	[0.33]	**0.44**	[0.27]	0.51	0.36	0.36
	LT-all [39]	0.32	0.37	0.41	0.18	0.46	0.23	0.73	0.07	0.23	0.09	0.80	0.39	0.36
	2DC [36]	**0.70**	[0.55]	[0.69]	0.05	[0.59]	**0.57**	**0.88**	0.32	0.10	0.08	**0.90**	0.50	[0.50]
	BORMIR [40]	0.19	0.24	0.30	0.17	0.38	0.18	0.58	0.15	0.22	0.08	0.70	0.14	0.28
	KJRE [41]	0.27	0.35	0.25	0.33	0.51	0.31	0.67	0.14	0.17	0.20	0.74	0.25	0.35
	CFLF [42]	0.26	0.19	0.45	[0.35]	0.51	0.35	0.70	0.18	0.34	0.20	0.81	0.51	0.40
	Ours	[0.59]	**0.63**	**0.73**	**0.82**	0.49	0.50	0.73	0.29	0.21	0.03	**0.90**	**0.60**	**0.54**
MAE	VGP-AE [33]	1.02	1.13	0.92	0.10	0.67	[0.19]	0.33	0.46	0.58	0.19	0.69	0.65	0.57
	CCNN-IT [34]	0.87	0.63	0.86	0.26	0.73	0.57	0.55	0.38	0.57	0.45	0.81	0.64	0.61
	OR-CNN [35]	0.41	0.44	0.91	0.12	0.42	0.33	0.31	0.42	0.35	0.27	0.71	0.51	0.43
	LT-all [39]	0.44	0.39	0.96	[0.07]	0.41	0.31	0.40	[0.17]	[0.33]	[0.16]	0.61	0.46	0.39
	2DC [36]	[0.32]	0.39	[0.53]	0.26	0.43	0.30	[0.25]	0.27	0.61	0.18	[0.37]	0.55	0.37
	BORMIR [40]	0.87	0.78	1.24	0.58	0.76	0.77	0.75	0.56	0.71	0.62	0.89	0.87	0.78
	KJRE [41]	1.02	0.92	1.86	0.70	0.79	0.87	0.77	0.60	0.80	0.72	0.96	0.94	0.91
	CFLF [42]	[0.32]	[0.28]	0.60	0.12	[0.35]	0.27	0.42	0.18	**0.29**	[0.16]	0.53	**0.39**	[0.32]
	Ours	**0.16**	**0.08**	**0.40**	**0.02**	**0.23**	**0.12**	**0.22**	**0.14**	0.48	**0.12**	0.27	**0.39**	**0.22**

4.6 Ablation Study

Effectiveness of RE-Net: First, we provide evidences to support our claim that applying AU relation to the model's parameters space is more effective than applying to image patches or deep features. JPM [10] and DRML [11] model the AU relation with active image patches, while DSIN [12] and SRERL [13] applied

Table 6. F1 scores in terms of 12 AUs are reported for the proposed method on the BP4D dataset. Colored AU is removed during training, and only used for testing.

AU1	AU2	AU4	AU6	AU7	AU10	AU12	AU14	AU15	AU17	AU23	AU24	*Avg*
44.1	69.0	73.8	80.2	62.2	88.1	89.2	38.5	53.7	60.6	27.6	68.2	62.9
89.9	77.5	53.6	66.9	39.7	70.4	81.5	52.2	86.6	45.7	63.8	37.3	63.6

the AU relation to the extracted deep features. As shown in Table 7, our method applies the AU relation to the parameter space of the model, which achieves the highest F1-score (65.5%), demonstrating the effectiveness of our proposed method.

Second, to show the effectiveness of Eq. (4) and Eq. (5), we set $scale = 1, bias = 0$ in Eq. (4). Since then RE-Net is equivalent to the vanilla Resnet18, by comparing our method and the vanilla Resnet18, we can see a **5.9%** improvement in F1-score, which demonstrates the effectiveness of Eqs. (4 and 5) in improving the performance of AU recognition.

Third, the Pearson correlation coefficient is computed in each dataset and fixed in Eq. (5), which could be biased, as different datasets vary in subjects and tasks. To further investigate this issue, we try to learn the AU relation along with AU detection by setting the AU relation graph $\mathcal{G} = (\mathcal{V}, \mathcal{E})$ as learnable parameters. Specifically, the $\omega_{i,j}$ of AU relation $\mathcal{G}$ is first randomly initialized, and then updated through training by minimizing the loss function in Eq. (6). As indicated by **Ours+learnable** in Table 7, a 63.7% F1-score is achieved. Although the performance is not as good as ours with fixed AU relation, its performance is **4.1%** higher than the Resnet18 baseline, and outperforms the state-of-the-art methods. More importantly, it has the potential to learn a general dataset-independent AU relation.

Table 7. F1-scores of different methods with AU relation are reported on the BP4D dataset. *Learnable indicates the AU relation is learned through training rather than a fixed factor.*

Method	AU relation applied to:	*Avg*
JPML [10]	*image patch*	45.9
DRML [11]	*image patch*	48.3
DSIN [12]	*deep features*	58.9
SRERL [13]	*deep features*	62.9
ResNet18	*none*	59.6
Ours	*model's parameters*	**65.5**
Ours+ *learnable*	*model's parameters*	[63.7]

Imbalance Issue: Most AU databases are imbalanced. Take BP4D as example, the occurrence rate of AU6, AU7, AU10, AU12 and AU14 are almost 2–3 times more than the others. To deal with the imbalanced issue, most works apply a data augmentation method (*i.e.,* duplication) to increase the frames of AUs with less occurrence rate. To evaluate the impact of data augmentation, we duplicate the AUs (AU1, AU2, AU15, AU23 and AU24) one time if a positive label is observed in the training dataset. As we can see in Table 8, ResNet18 achieves 1.3% improvement by using the augmented training dataset; while our method shows only 0.1% difference with/without data augmentation, indicating the effectiveness of our proposed method in handling the data imbalance issue.

Table 8. F1-score of ablation study for 12 AUs on the BP4D database. DA: *data augmentation.*

Method	AU1	AU2	AU4	AU6	AU7	AU10	AU12	AU14	AU15	AU17	AU23	AU24	*Total*
ResNet18 w/o DA	44.5	45.1	51.1	81.2	76.8	87.6	86.8	67.9	44.2	57.5	42.0	30.8	59.6
ResNet18 + DA	49.4	53.0	58.0	79.2	72.7	86.0	89.6	68.1	34.4	65.0	42.3	33.5	60.9
Ours + DA	61.9	50.3	62.3	80.0	73.7	87.3	90.3	70.4	42.0	67.4	47.3	55.5	65.6
Ours w/o DA	57.7	59.0	66.9	76.3	77.0	88.9	89.8	70.9	42.0	62.8	44.8	49.3	65.5

Recognize New AU: Inspired by recent works [16–19] that extend batch-normalization to address domain adaptation tasks, we conduct two initial experiments to verify the ability of recognizing new AU. In Table 6, the label of the colored AU is selected to remove during training. During testing, the AU-specific parameters (γ, β) are calculated by using Eq. (4) and Eq. (5). As we can see in Table 6, transferring the AU-specific parameters to the new AU, our method shows comparable results in recognizing the unseen AU23 and AU24.

Feature Visualization: To provide insight into the feature space for individual AUs, we first extract the features for the testing images on the BP4D dataset using our proposed method and the ResNet18. Figure 3 shows the t-SNE [43] embedding of frames, which are colored in terms of AU4, AU10, AU12 and AU24 (different colors means presence or absence of a specific AU). ResNet18 extracts a single representation for each input image for multiple AUs detection, hence the shapes of t-SNE embedding are all the same. On the contrary, our method extracts different features for individual AU, therefore the shapes of t-SNE embedding are different in AU4, AU10, AU12 and AU24. By comparing the AU related projection, we may find that the features extracted for individual AU by our method are more robust than the features extracted by ResNet18, for example, the green points of AU4 and AU24, which are more challenging to recognize than AU10 and AU12, are more concentrated in our method than ResNet18.

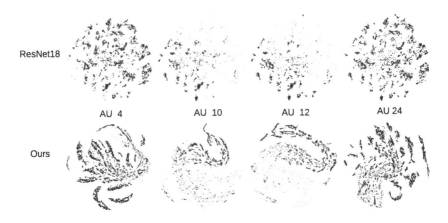

Fig. 3. A visualization of t-SNE embedding using deep features on the BP4D database by coloring each frame from testing images in terms of AU4, AU10, AU12 and AU24 (blue and green means the absent and occurrence of individual AU respectively). Best viewed in color. (Color figure onine)

4.7   Conclusion

In this paper, we format the multi-label AU detection problem as a domain adaptation problem, and propose a new AU relationship embedded deep model (**RE-Net**) for AU detection, which contains both shared and AU-specific parameters. The AU relation is modeled in the model's AU-specific parameters space, therefore, the deep model can be optimized effectively for individual AU. We also apply a new training strategy that will not add extra burden for the model training. Extensive experiments are conducted on the widely used datasets for both AU recognition and AU intensity estimation, demonstrating the superiority of the proposed method over the state-of-the-art methods.

One concern of the proposed method is the running efficiency, as the model needs to be run multiple times for detecting different AUs. We measure the inference time of our method with 12 AUs on the NVIDIA GeForce 2080Ti GPU, which is around 5.4ms/image, equivalent to 183 FPS (frame per second). Although the processing speed is much slower than the ResNet18 baseline, our method has achieved a much higher performance, and the 183 FPS processing speed is more than enough for the real-time processing requirement.

Our future work is to improve the model's efficiency as well as to extend it for detection of new AUs.

Acknowledgment. The material is based on the work supported in part by the NSF under grant CNS-1629898 and the Center of Imaging, Acoustics, and Perception Science (CIAPS) of the Research Foundation of Binghamton University.

References

1. Friesen, E., Ekman, P.: Facial action coding system: a technique for the measurement of facial movement. Palo Alto **3**(2), 5 (1978)
2. Li, Y., Chen, J., Zhao, Y., Ji, Q.: Data-free prior model for facial action unit recognition. IEEE Trans. Affect. Comput. **4**, 127–141 (2013)
3. Wang, Z., Li, Y., Wang, S., Ji, Q.: Capturing global semantic relationships for facial action unit recognition. In: Proceedings of the IEEE International Conference on Computer Vision, pp. 3304–3311 (2013)
4. Tong, Y., Ji, Q.: Learning bayesian networks with qualitative constraints. In: 2008 IEEE Conference on Computer Vision and Pattern Recognition, pp. 1–8. IEEE (2008)
5. Liao, W., Ji, Q.: Learning bayesian network parameters under incomplete data with domain knowledge. Pattern Recognit. **42**, 3046–3056 (2009)
6. Benitez-Quiroz, C.F., Wang, Y., Martinez, A.M.: Recognition of action units in the wild with deep nets and a new global-local loss. In: ICCV, pp. 3990–3999 (2017)
7. Zhang, Y., Dong, W., Hu, B.G., Ji, Q.: Classifier learning with prior probabilities for facial action unit recognition. In: Proceedings of the IEEE Conference on Computer Vision and Pattern Recognition, pp. 5108–5116 (2018)
8. Peng, G., Wang, S.: Weakly supervised facial action unit recognition through adversarial training. In: Proceedings of the IEEE Conference on Computer Vision and Pattern Recognition, pp. 2188–2196 (2018)
9. Peng, G., Wang, S.: Dual semi-supervised learning for facial action unit recognition. In: Proceedings of the AAAI Conference on Artificial Intelligence, vol. 33, pp. 8827–8834 (2019)
10. Zhao, K., Chu, W.S., De la Torre, F., Cohn, J.F., Zhang, H.: Joint patch and multi-label learning for facial action unit detection. In: Proceedings of the IEEE Conference on Computer Vision and Pattern Recognition, pp. 2207–2216 (2015)
11. Zhao, K., Chu, W.S., Zhang, H.: Deep region and multi-label learning for facial action unit detection. In: Proceedings of the IEEE Conference on Computer Vision and Pattern Recognition, pp. 3391–3399 (2016)
12. Corneanu, C., Madadi, M., Escalera, S.: Deep structure inference network for facial action unit recognition. In: Proceedings of the European Conference on Computer Vision (ECCV), pp. 298–313 (2018)
13. Li, G., Zhu, X., Zeng, Y., Wang, Q., Lin, L.: Semantic relationships guided representation learning for facial action unit recognition. In: Proceedings of the AAAI Conference on Artificial Intelligence, vol. 33, pp. 8594–8601 (2019)
14. Shao, Z., Zou, L., Cai, J., Wu, Y., Ma, L.: Spatio-temporal relation and attention learning for facial action unit detection. arXiv preprint arXiv:2001.01168 (2020)
15. Ioffe, S., Szegedy, C.: Batch normalization: accelerating deep network training by reducing internal covariate shift. In: ICML (2015)
16. Mancini, M., Bulo, S.R., Caputo, B., Ricci, E.: Adagraph: unifying predictive and continuous domain adaptation through graphs. In: Proceedings of the IEEE Conference on Computer Vision and Pattern Recognition, pp. 6568–6577 (2019)
17. Sun, Q., Liu, Y., Chua, T.S., Schiele, B.: Meta-transfer learning for few-shot learning. In: Proceedings of the IEEE Conference on Computer Vision and Pattern Recognition, pp. 403–412 (2019)
18. Chang, W.G., You, T., Seo, S., Kwak, S., Han, B.: Domain-specific batch normalization for unsupervised domain adaptation. In: Proceedings of the IEEE Conference on Computer Vision and Pattern Recognition, pp. 7354–7362 (2019)

19. Li, Y., Wang, N., Shi, J., Hou, X., Liu, J.: Adaptive batch normalization for practical domain adaptation. Pattern Recognit. **80**, 109–117 (2018)
20. Zhang, X., et al.: Bp4d-spontaneous: a high-resolution spontaneous 3D dynamic facial expression database. Image Vision Comput. **32**, 692–706 (2014)
21. Mavadati, S.M., Mahoor, M.H., Bartlett, K., Trinh, P., Cohn, J.F.: Disfa: a spontaneous facial action intensity database. IEEE Trans. Affect. Comput. **4**, 151–160 (2013)
22. Zhang, Z., et al.: Multimodal spontaneous emotion corpus for human behavior analysis. In: The IEEE Conference on Computer Vision and Pattern Recognition (CVPR) (2016)
23. Li, W., Abtahi, F., Zhu, Z., Yin, L.: Eac-net: a region-based deep enhancing and cropping approach for facial action unit detection. arXiv preprint arXiv:1702.02925 (2017)
24. Shrout, P.E., Fleiss, J.L.: Intraclass correlations: uses in assessing rater reliability. Psychol. Bull. **86**, 420 (1979)
25. He, K., Zhang, X., Ren, S., Sun, J.: Deep residual learning for image recognition. In: Proceedings of the IEEE Conference on Computer Vision and Pattern Recognition, pp. 770–778 (2016)
26. Paszke, A., et al.: Pytorch: an imperative style, high-performance deep learning library. In: Advances in Neural Information Processing Systems, pp. 8024–8035 (2019)
27. Fan, R.E., Chang, K.W., Hsieh, C.J., Wang, X.R., Lin, C.J.: Liblinear: a library for large linear classification. J. Mach. Learn. Res. **9**, 1871–1874 (2008)
28. Shao, Z., Liu, Z., Cai, J., Ma, L.: Deep adaptive attention for joint facial action unit detection and face alignment. In: Proceedings of the European Conference on Computer Vision (ECCV), pp. 705–720 (2018)
29. Yang, H., Yin, L.: Learning temporal information from a single image for au detection. In: 2019 14th IEEE International Conference on Automatic Face & Gesture Recognition (FG 2019), pp. 1–8. IEEE (2019)
30. Niu, X., Han, H., Yang, S., Huang, Y., Shan, S.: Local relationship learning with person-specific shape regularization for facial action unit detection. In: Proceedings of the IEEE Conference on Computer Vision and Pattern Recognition, pp. 11917–11926 (2019)
31. Mei, C., Jiang, F., Shen, R., Hu, Q.: Region and temporal dependency fusion for multi-label action unit detection. In: 2018 24th International Conference on Pattern Recognition (ICPR), pp. 848–853. IEEE (2018)
32. Ma, C., Chen, L., Yong, J.: Au R-CNN: encoding expert prior knowledge into R-CNN for action unit detection. Neurocomputing **355**, 35–47 (2019)
33. Eleftheriadis, S., Rudovic, O., Deisenroth, M.P., Pantic, M.: Variational Gaussian process auto-encoder for ordinal prediction of facial action units. In: Lai, S.-H., Lepetit, V., Nishino, K., Sato, Y. (eds.) ACCV 2016. LNCS, vol. 10112, pp. 154–170. Springer, Cham (2017). https://doi.org/10.1007/978-3-319-54184-6_10
34. Walecki, R., Pavlovic, V., Schuller, B., Pantic, M., et al.: Deep structured learning for facial action unit intensity estimation. In: Proceedings of the IEEE Conference on Computer Vision and Pattern Recognition, pp. 3405–3414 (2017)
35. Niu, Z., Zhou, M., Wang, L., Gao, X., Hua, G.: Ordinal regression with multiple output CNN for age estimation. In: Proceedings of the IEEE Conference on Computer Vision and Pattern Recognition, pp. 4920–4928 (2016)

36. Linh Tran, D., Walecki, R., Eleftheriadis, S., Schuller, B., Pantic, M., et al.: Deep-coder: semi-parametric variational autoencoders for automatic facial action coding. In: Proceedings of the IEEE International Conference on Computer Vision, pp. 3190–3199 (2017)
37. Simonyan, K., Zisserman, A.: Very deep convolutional networks for large-scale image recognition. arXiv preprint arXiv:1409.1556 (2014)
38. Sánchez-Lozano, E., Tzimiropoulos, G., Valstar, M.: Joint action unit localisation and intensity estimation through heatmap regression. In: BMVC (2018)
39. Kaltwang, S., Todorovic, S., Pantic, M.: Latent trees for estimating intensity of facial action units. In: Proceedings of the IEEE Conference on Computer Vision and Pattern Recognition, pp. 296–304 (2015)
40. Zhang, Y., Zhao, R., Dong, W., Hu, B.G., Ji, Q.: Bilateral ordinal relevance multi-instance regression for facial action unit intensity estimation. In: Proceedings of the IEEE Conference on Computer Vision and Pattern Recognition, pp. 7034–7043 (2018)
41. Zhang, Y., et al.: Joint representation and estimator learning for facial action unit intensity estimation. In: Proceedings of the IEEE Conference on Computer Vision and Pattern Recognition, pp. 3457–3466 (2019)
42. Zhang, Y., Jiang, H., Wu, B., Fan, Y., Ji, Q.: Context-aware feature and label fusion for facial action unit intensity estimation with partially labeled data. In: Proceedings of the IEEE International Conference on Computer Vision, pp. 733–742 (2019)
43. Maaten, L.V.D., Hinton, G.: Visualizing data using T-SNE. J. Mach. Learn. Res. **9**, 2579–2605 (2008)

Learning 3D Face Reconstruction
with a Pose Guidance Network

Pengpeng Liu[1]([✉]), Xintong Han[2], Michael Lyu[1], Irwin King[1], and Jia Xu[2]

[1] The Chinese University of Hong Kong, Hong Kong, China
{ppliu,lyu,king}@cse.cuhk.edu.hk
[2] Huya AI, Guangzhou, China
xintong@umd.edu, xujianjucs@gmail.com

Abstract. We present a self-supervised learning approach to learning monocular 3D face reconstruction with a pose guidance network (PGN). First, we unveil the bottleneck of pose estimation in prior parametric 3D face learning methods, and propose to utilize 3D face landmarks for estimating pose parameters. With our specially designed PGN, our model can learn from both faces with fully labeled 3D landmarks and unlimited unlabeled in-the-wild face images. Our network is further augmented with a self-supervised learning scheme, which exploits face geometry information embedded in multiple frames of the same person, to alleviate the ill-posed nature of regressing 3D face geometry from a single image. These three insights yield a single approach that combines the complementary strengths of parametric model learning and data-driven learning techniques. We conduct a rigorous evaluation on the challenging AFLW2000-3D, Florence and FaceWarehouse datasets, and show that our method outperforms the state-of-the-art for all metrics.

1 Introduction

Monocular 3D face reconstruction with precise geometric details serves as a foundation to a myriad of computer vision and graphics applications, including face recognition [1,2], digital avatars [3,4], face manipulation [5,6], *etc.* However, this problem is extremely challenging due to its ill-posed nature, as well as difficulties to acquire accurate 3D face annotations.

Most successful attempts to tackle this problem are built on parametric face models, which usually contain three sets of parameters: identity, expression, and pose. The most famous one is 3D Morphable Model (3DMM) [7] and its variants [5,8–10]. Recently, CNN-based methods that directly learn to regress the parameters of 3D face models [11–14], achieve state-of-the-art performance.

Are these parameters well disentangled and can they be accurately regressed by CNNs? To answer this question, we conduct a careful study on the AFLW2000-3D dataset [15]. Figure 1(a) illustrates our setting. We first train a neural network that takes an RGB image as input to simultaneously regress

---

P. Liu—Work mainly done during an internship at Huya AI.

© Springer Nature Switzerland AG 2021
H. Ishikawa et al. (Eds.): ACCV 2020, LNCS 12626, pp. 154–169, 2021.
https://doi.org/10.1007/978-3-030-69541-5_10

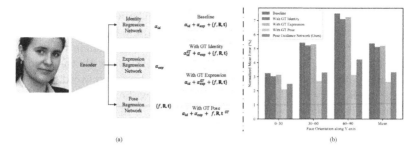

(a)   (b)

Fig. 1. Our CNN baseline takes an RGB image as input, and regresses identity, expression and pose parameters simultaneously. The three sets of parameters are obtained by minimizing the 3D vertex error. We compute the Normalized Mean Error (NME) of this face model and denote it as `Baseline`. Then we replace the predicted identity, expression, pose parameters with their ground truth, and recompute the NME respectively: `With GT Identity, Expression, Pose`. As shown in (b), `With GT Pose` yields the highest performance gain, and the gain is more significant as the face orientation degree increases. Our `Pose Guidance Network` takes advantage of this finding (Sect. 3.2), and greatly reduces the error caused by inaccurate pose parameter regression.

the identity, expression and pose parameters. The `Baseline` 3DMM model is obtained by minimizing the 3D vertex error. Then, we independently replace the predicted identity, expression, and pose parameters with their corresponding ground truth parameters (denoted as `GT Identity`, `GT Expression`, and `GT Pose`), and recompute the 3D face reconstruction error shown in Fig. 1(b).

Surprisingly, we found that `GT Pose` yields almost 5 times more performance gain than its two counterparts. The improvement is even more significant when the face orientation degree increases. We posit that there are two reasons causing this result: (1) These three sets of parameters are heavily correlated, and predicting a bad pose will dominate the identity and expression estimation of the 3D face model; (2) 3D face annotations are scarce especially for those with unusual poses.

To address these issues, we propose a pose guidance network (PNG) to isolate the pose estimation from the original 3DMM parameters regression by estimating a UV position map [16] for 3D face landmark vertices. Utilizing the predicted 3D landmarks help to produce more accurate face poses compared to joint parameters regression (*i.e.*, `Baseline` in Fig. 1), and the predicted 3D landmarks also contain valuable identity and expression information that further refines the estimation of identity and expression. Moreover, this enables us to learn from both accurate but limited 3D annotations, and unlimited in-the-wild images with pseudo 2D landmarks (from off-the-shelf landmark extractor like [17]) to predict more accurate 3D landmarks. Consequently, with our proposed PGN, the performance degradation brought by inaccurate pose parameter regression is significantly mitigated as shown in Fig. 1(b).

To further overcome the scarcity of 3D face annotations, we leverage the readily available in-the-wild videos by introducing a novel set of self-consistency loss functions to boost the performance. Given 3D face shapes in multiple frames of the same subject, we render a new image for each frame by replacing its texture with that of *commonly visible vertices* from other images. Then, by forcing the rendered image to be consistent with the original image in photometric space, optical flow space and semantic space, our network learns to avoid depth ambiguity and predicts better 3D shapes even without explicitly modeling albedo.

We summarize our key contributions as follows:

(1) We propose a PGN to solely predict the 3D landmarks for estimating the pose parameters based on a careful study (Fig. 1). The PGN effectively reduces the error compared to directly regressing the pose parameters and provides informative priors for 3D face reconstruction.
(2) The PGN allows us to utilize both fully annotated 3D landmarks and pseudo 2D landmarks from unlabeled in-the-wild data. This leads to a more accurate landmark estimator and thus helping better 3D face reconstruction.
(3) Built on a visible texture swapping module, our method explores multi-frame shape and texture consistency in a self-supervised manner, while carefully handling the occlusion and illumination change across frames.
(4) Our method shows superior qualitative and quantitative results on ALFW-2000-3D [15], Florence [18] and FaceWarehouse [19] datasets.

2   Related Work

Most recent 3D face shape models are derived from Blanz and Vetter 3D morphable models (3DMM) [7], which represents 3D faces with linear combination of PCA-faces from a collection of 3D face scans. To make 3DMM more representative, Basel Face Model (BFM) [2] improved shape and texture accuracy, and FaceWarehouse [19] constructed a set of individual-specific expression blend-shapes. Our approach is also built on 3DMM—we aim to predict 3DMM parameters to reconstruct 3D faces from monocular frames.

3D Face Landmark Detection and Reconstruction. 3D face landmark detection and 3D face reconstruction are closely related. On the one hand, if the 3DMM parameters can be estimated accurately, face landmark detection can be greatly improved, especially for the occluded landmarks [15]. Therefore, several approaches [15,20,21] aligned 3D face by fitting a 3DMM model. On the other hand, if 3D face landmarks are precisely estimated, it can provide strong guidance for 3D face reconstruction. Our method goes towards the second direction—we first estimates 3D face landmarks by regressing UV position map and then utilizes it to guide 3D face reconstruction.

3D Face Reconstruction from a Single Image. To reconstruct 3D faces from a single image, prior methods [1,5,22] usually conduct iterative optimization methods to fit 3DMM models by leveraging facial landmarks or local features *e.g.*, color or edges. However, the convergence of optimization is very sensitive to the initial parameters. Tremendous progress has been made by CNNs that directly regress 3DMM parameters [15,23,24]. Jackson *et al.* [25] directly regressed the full 3D facial structure via volumetric convolution. Feng *et al.* [16] predicted a UV position map to represent the full 3D shape. MMFace [12] jointly trained a volumetric network and a parameter regression network, where the former one is employed to refine pose parameters with ICP as a post-processing. All these three methods need to be trained in a supervised manner, requiring full 3D face annotations, which are limited at scale [15]. To bypass the limitation of training data, Tewari *et al.* [26] and Genova *et al.* [27] proposed to fit 3DMM models with only unlabeled images. They show that it is possible to achieve great face reconstruction in an unsupervised manner by minimizing photometric consistency or facial identity loss. Later, Chang *et al.* [28] proposed to regress identity, expression and pose parameters with three independent networks. However, due to depth ambiguity, these unsupervised monocular methods fail to capture precise 3D facial structure. In this paper, we propose to mitigate the limitation of datasets by utilizing both labeled and unlabeled datasets, and to learn better facial geometry from multiple frames.

3D Face Reconstruction from Multiple Images. Multiple images of the same person contain rich information for learning better 3D face reconstruction. Piotraschke *et al.* [29] introduced an automated algorithm that selects and combines reconstructions of different facial regions from multiple images into a single 3D face. RingNet [11] considered shape consistency across different images of the same person, while we focus on face reconstruction from videos, where photometric consistency can be well employed. MVF [14] regressed 3DMM parameters from multi-view images. However, MVF assumes that the expressions in different views are the same, therefore its application is restricted to multi-view images. Our method does not have such constraint and can be applied to both single-view and multi-view 3D face reconstruction.

The approach that is closest to ours is FML [30], which learns face reconstruction from monocular videos by ensuring consistent shape and appearance across frames. However, it only adds multi-frame identity consistency constraints, which does not fully utilize geometric constraints among different images. Unlike FML, we do not model albedo to estimate texture parameters, but directly sample textures from images, swap commonly visible texture and project them onto different image planes while enforcing photometric and semantic consistency.

3   Method

We illustrate our framework overview in Fig. 2. First, we utilize a shared encoder to extract semantic feature representations from multiple frames of the same person. Then, an identity regression branch and an expression regression branch are employed to regress 3DMM face identity and expression parameters (Sect. 3.1) with the help of our PGN that predicts 3D face landmarks (Sect. 3.2). Finally, we explore self-consistency (Sect. 3.3) with our newly designed consistency losses (Sect. 3.4).

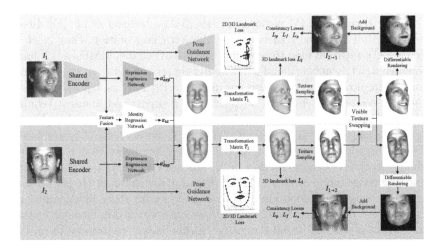

Fig. 2. Framework overview. Our shared encoder extracts semantic feature representation from multiple images of the same person. Then, our identity and expression regression networks regress 3DMM face identity and expression parameters (Sect. 3.1) with accurate guidance of our PGN that predicts 3D face landmarks (Sect. 3.2). Finally, We utilize multiple frames (Sect. 3.3) to train our proposed network with a set of self-consistency loss functions (Sect. 3.4).

3.1 Preliminaries

Let $\mathbf{S} \in \mathbb{R}^{3N}$ be a 3D face with N vertices, $\overline{\mathbf{S}} \in \mathbb{R}^{3N}$ be the mean face geometry, $\mathbf{B}_{id} \in \mathbb{R}^{3N \times 199}$ and $\mathbf{B}_{exp} \in \mathbb{R}^{3N \times 29}$ be PCA basis of identity and expression, $\boldsymbol{\alpha}_{id} \in \mathbb{R}^{199}$ and $\boldsymbol{\alpha}_{exp} \in \mathbb{R}^{29}$ be the identity and expression parameters. The classical 3DMM face model [7] can be defined as follows:

$$\mathbf{S}(\boldsymbol{\alpha}_{id}, \boldsymbol{\alpha}_{exp}) = \overline{\mathbf{S}} + \mathbf{B}_{id}\boldsymbol{\alpha}_{id} + \mathbf{B}_{exp}\boldsymbol{\alpha}_{exp}. \tag{1}$$

Here, we adopt BFM [2] to obtain $\overline{\mathbf{S}}$ and $\mathbf{B}_{id}$, and expression basis $\mathbf{B}_{exp}$ is extracted from FaceWareHouse [19]. Then, we employ a perspective projection model to project a 3D face point $\mathbf{s}$ onto an image plane:

$$\mathbf{v}(\boldsymbol{\alpha}_{id}, \boldsymbol{\alpha}_{exp}) = \begin{bmatrix} 1 & 0 & 0 \\ 0 & 1 & 0 \end{bmatrix} \cdot (f \cdot \mathbf{R} \cdot \mathbf{s} + \mathbf{t}) = \begin{bmatrix} 1 & 0 & 0 \\ 0 & 1 & 0 \end{bmatrix} \cdot \begin{bmatrix} f \cdot \mathbf{R} & \mathbf{t} \end{bmatrix} \cdot \begin{bmatrix} \mathbf{s} \\ 1 \end{bmatrix}, \tag{2}$$

where $\mathbf{v}$ is the projected point on the image plane, f is a scaling factor, $\mathbf{R} \in \mathbb{R}^{3 \times 3}$ indicates a rotation matrix, $\mathbf{t} \in \mathbb{R}^3$ is a translation vector.

However, it is challenging for neural networks to regress identity parameter $\boldsymbol{\alpha}_{id}$, expression parameter $\boldsymbol{\alpha}_{exp}$ and pose parameter $\{f, \mathbf{R}, \mathbf{t}\}$ together, because these parameters cannot be easily disentangled and pose parameters turn to dominate the optimization, making it more difficult to estimate accurate identity and expression (as discussed in Sect. 1 and illustrated in Fig. 1).

To address this issue, we design a robust landmark-based PGN to obtain the transformation matrix $\mathbf{T} = \begin{bmatrix} f \cdot \mathbf{R} & \mathbf{t} \end{bmatrix}$ instead of directly regressing its parameters. Next, we describe our PGN in detail.

3.2   Pose Guidance Network

To decouple the optimization of pose parameter $\{f, \mathbf{R}, \mathbf{t}\}$ with identity parameter $\boldsymbol{\alpha}_{id}$ and expression parameter $\boldsymbol{\alpha}_{exp}$, we design a multi-task architecture with two output branches (shown in Fig. 2). One branch optimizes the traditional 3DMM identity and expression parameters $\boldsymbol{\alpha}_{id}, \boldsymbol{\alpha}_{exp}$. The other branch is trained to estimate a UV position map [16] for 3D face landmarks, which provide key guidance for pose estimation.

Specifically, Let $\mathbf{X}$ be the 3D landmark positions in the face geometry $\mathbf{S}$, and $\mathbf{X}_{UV}$ be the 3D landmarks estimated from our UV position map decoder, we estimate a transformation matrix $\mathbf{T}$ by,

$$\min_{\mathbf{T}} \left\| \mathbf{T} \cdot \begin{bmatrix} \mathbf{X} \\ 1 \end{bmatrix} - \mathbf{X}_{UV} \right\|_2. \tag{3}$$

Here, $\mathbf{T}$ has a closed-form solution:

$$\mathbf{T} = \mathbf{X}_{UV} \cdot \begin{bmatrix} \mathbf{X} \\ 1 \end{bmatrix}^T \cdot \left(\begin{bmatrix} \mathbf{X} \\ 1 \end{bmatrix} \cdot \begin{bmatrix} \mathbf{X} \\ 1 \end{bmatrix}^T \right)^{-1}. \tag{4}$$

As a result, we convert the estimation of $\mathbf{T}$ into the estimation of a UV position map for 3D face landmarks rather than regressing $\mathbf{T}$'s parameters. This disentangles the pose estimation and results in better performance than joint regression of $\boldsymbol{\alpha}_{id}, \boldsymbol{\alpha}_{exp}$ and $\{f, \mathbf{R}, \mathbf{t}\}$. Another merit of this design is enabling us to train our network with two types of images: images with 3D landmark annotations and in-the-wild unlabeled images with 2D facial landmarks extracted by off-the-shelf detectors. During training, we sample one image batch with 3D landmark labels and another image batch from unlabeled datasets. 3D landmark loss and 2D landmark loss are minimized for them, respectively. For 3D landmarks, we calculate the loss across all x, y and z channels of the UV position map, while for 2D landmark loss, only x and y channels are considered. More abundant training data leads to more accurate pose estimation, and hence better face reconstruction.

Note our work is different from PRN [16], which utilizes a CNN to regress dense UV position maps for all 3D face points. PRN requires dense 3D face labels which are extremely difficult to obtain. Our network learns directly from sparse landmark annotations, which are much easier to obtain and more accurate than the synthetic data derived from facial landmarks.

3.3   Learning from Multiple Frames

The PGN combined with identity and expression parameters regression can achieve quite accurate 3D face reconstruction, but the estimated 3D mesh lacks facial details. This is because 3D landmarks can only provide a coarse prediction of identity and expression. To generate meshes with finer details, we leverage multi-frame images from monocular videos as input and explore their inherent complementary information. In contrast to the common perspective that first estimates albedo maps and then enforces photometric consistency [30], we propose a self-consistency framework based on a visible texture swapping scheme.

Every vertex in a 3DMM model has a specific semantic meaning. Given multiple images with the same identity, we can generate one 3D mesh for every image. Every corresponding vertex of different meshes share the same semantic meaning, even though these images are captured with different poses, expressions, lightings, *etc.* If we sample texture from one image and project it onto the second image that has different pose and expression, the rendered image should have the same identity, expression and pose as the second image despite the illumination change. Our multi-image 3D reconstruction is built on this intuition.

More specifically, our method takes multiple frames of the same subject as input, and estimates the same set of identity parameters for all images, and different expressions and poses (obtained from 3D face landmarks output by our PGN) for each image. To generate the same identity parameters, we adopt a similar strategy as [30], which fuses feature representations extracted from the shared encoders of different images via average pooling (Feature Fusion in Fig. 2). In this way, we can achieve both single-image and multi-image face reconstruction.

For simplicity, we assume there are two images of the same person as input (the framework can easily extend to more than two images), denoted as I_1 and I_2 respectively. Then, as illustrated on the left side of Fig. 2, we can generate two 3D meshes with the same identity parameter $\boldsymbol{\alpha}_{id}$, two different expression parameters $\boldsymbol{\alpha}_{exp}^1, \boldsymbol{\alpha}_{exp}^2$, and pose transformation matrices $\mathbf{T}_1, \mathbf{T}_2$ obtained by our PGN. After that, we sample two texture maps C_1, C_2 with Equation 2, and project the first texture C_1 onto the second image I_2 with its expression parameter $\boldsymbol{\alpha}_{exp}^2$ and pose transformation matrix $\mathbf{T}_2$ to obtain rendered image $I_{1 \to 2}$. Similarly, we can project C_2 to I_1 to obtain the rendered image $I_{2 \to 1}$. Ideally, if there is no illumination change, I_2 shall be the same as $I_{1 \to 2}$ over their non-occluded facial regions. However, there exists occlusion and illumination usually changes a lot for different images in real-world scenarios. To this end, we introduce several strategies to overcome these issues.

Occlusion Handling. We adopt a simple strategy to effectively determine if a pixel is occluded or non-occluded based on triangle face normal direction. Given a triangle with three vertices, we can compute its normal $\mathbf{n} = (n_x, n_y, n_z)$. If the normal direction towards outside of the face mesh (*i.e.*, $n_z > 0$), we regard these three vertices as non-occluded; otherwise they are occluded. According to this principle, we can compute two visibility maps M_1 and M_2, where value 1 indicates the vertex is non-occluded and 0 otherwise. A common visibility map M_{12} is then defined as:

$$M_{12} = M_1 \odot M_2, \tag{5}$$

where value 1 means that the vertex is non-occluded for both 3D meshes.

Considering the occlusion, when projecting C_1 onto the second image, we combine C_1 and C_2 by

$$C_{1 \to 2} = C_1 \odot M_{12} + C_2 \odot (1 - M_{12}). \tag{6}$$

That is, we alleviate the influence of the occlusion by only projecting the *commonly visible texture* from I_1 to I_2 to generate $C_{1\to2}$, while *keeping the original pixels for the occluded part*. In this way, the rendered image $I_{1\to2}$ shall have the same identity, pose and expression information as I_2. The projection from I_2 to I_1 can be derived in the same manner.

Illumination Change. The sampled texture is not disentangled to albedo, lighting, etc. Due to lighting and exposure changes, even if we can estimate accurate 3D geometry, the rendered texture $I_{1\to2}$ is usually different from I_2. To cope with these issues, we propose three schemes. First, we adopt the Census Transform [31] from optical flow estimation, which has been shown to be very robust to illumination change when computing photometric difference (Eq. 9). Specifically, we apply a 7×7 census transform and then compute the Hamming distance between the reference image I_2 and the rendered image $I_{1\to2}$. Second, we employ an optical flow estimator [32] to compute the flow between I_2 and the rendered image $I_{1\to2}$. Since optical flow provides a 2D dense correspondence constraint, if the face is perfectly aligned, the optical flow between I_2 and $I_{1\to2}$ should be zeros for all pixels, so we try to minimize difference, *i.e.*, minimize the magnitude of optical flow between them (Eq. 10). Third, even though illumination changes, the identity, expression and pose shall be the same for I_2 and $I_{1\to2}$. Therefore, they must share similar semantic feature representation. Since our shared encoder can extract useful information to predict facial landmarks, identity and expression parameters, we use it as a semantic feature extractor and compare the feature difference between I_2 and $I_{1\to2}$ (Eq. 11).

3.4   Training Loss

To train our network for accurate 3D face reconstruction, we define a set of self-consistency loss functions, and minimize the following combination:

$$L = L_l + L_p + L_f + L_s + L_r. \tag{7}$$

Each loss term is defined in detail as follows. Note that for simplicity, we only describe these loss terms regarding projecting I_1 to I_2 (*i.e.*, $I_{1\to2}$) and the other way around ($I_{2\to1}$) can be defined similarly.

Sparse Landmark Loss. Our landmark loss measures the difference between the landmarks of transformed face geometry $\mathbf{T} \cdot \mathbf{X}$ and the prediction of PGN $\mathbf{X}_{UV}$:

$$L_l = \lambda_l \sum |\mathbf{T} \cdot \mathbf{X} - \mathbf{X}_{UV}| \tag{8}$$

This is the core guidance loss, which is trained with both 3D and 2D landmarks.

Photometric Consistency Loss. Photometric loss measures the difference between the target image and the rendered image over those visible regions. We can obtain the visible mask M^{2d} on the image plane with differentiable mesh render [27]. Note that M^{2d} is different from the vertex visibility map M, where the former denotes whether the pixel is occluded on the image plane, and the latter denotes whether the vertex in 3D mesh is occluded. Besides, considering that most of the face regions have very similar color, we apply a weighted mask W to the loss function, where we emphasize eye, nose, and mouth regions with a larger weight of 5, while the weight is 1 for other face regions [16]. The photometric loss then writes:

$$L_p = \lambda_p \frac{\sum \mathrm{Hamming}|\mathrm{Census}(I_2) - \mathrm{Census}(I_{1\rightarrow2})| \odot M_2^{2d} \odot W}{\sum M_2^{2d} \odot W}, \qquad (9)$$

where $\mathtt{Census}$ represents the census transform, $\mathtt{Hamming}$ denotes Hamming distance, and M_2^{2d} is the corresponding visibility mask.

Flow Consistency Loss. We use optical flow to describe the dense correspondence between the target image and the rendered image, then the magnitude of optical flow is minimized to ensure the visual consistency between two images:

$$L_f = \lambda_f \sum |\mathbf{w}(I_2, I_{1\rightarrow2})| \odot W / \sum W, \qquad (10)$$

where $\mathbf{w}$ is the optical flow computed from [32] and the same weighted mask W is applied as in the photometric consistency loss.

Semantic Consistency Loss. Photometric loss and 2D correspondence loss may break when the illumination between two images changes drastically. However, despite the illumination changes, I_2 and $I_{1\rightarrow2}$ should share the same semantic feature representation, as the target image and the rendered image share the same identity, expression and pose. To this end, we minimize the cosine distance between our semantic feature embeddings:

$$L_s = \lambda_s - \lambda_s < \frac{F(I_2)}{||F(I_2)||_2}, \frac{F(I_{1\rightarrow2})}{||F(I_{1\rightarrow2})||_2} >, \qquad (11)$$

where F denotes our shared feature encoder. Unlike existing approaches (*e.g.*, [27]) which align semantic features in a pre-trained face recognition network, we simply minimize the feature distance from our learned shared encoder. We find that this speeds up our training process and empirically works better.

Regularization Loss. Finally, we add a regularization loss to identity and expression parameters to avoid over-fitting:

$$L_r = \lambda_r \sum_{i=1}^{199} |\frac{\alpha_{id}(i)}{\sigma_{id}(i)}| + \frac{\lambda_r}{2} \sum_{i=1}^{29} |\frac{\alpha_{exp}(i)}{\sigma_{exp}(i)}|, \qquad (12)$$

where σ_{id} and σ_{exp} represent the standard deviation of α_{id} and α_{exp}.

4   Experimental Evaluation

Training Datasets. To train the shared encoder and PGN, we utilize two types of datasets: synthetic dataset with pseudo 3D annotations and in-the-wild

(a) 2D NME on AFLW2000-3D dataset

Method	NME_{2d}^{68}			
	0 to 30	30 to 60	60 to 90	Mean
SDM[33]	3.67	4.94	9.67	6.12
3DDFA [15]	3.78	4.54	7.93	5.42
3DDFA + SDM [15]	3.43	4.24	7.17	4.94
Yu et al. [34]	3.62	6.06	9.56	-
3DSTN[35]	3.15	4.33	5.98	4.49
DeFA[20]	-	-	-	4.50
Face2Face [5]	3.22	8.79	19.7	10.5
3DFAN [17]	2.77	3.48	4.61	3.62
PRN [16]	2.75	3.51	4.61	3.62
ExpNet [13]	4.01	5.46	6.23	5.23
MMFace-PMN [12]	5.05	6.23	7.05	6.11
MMFace-ICP-128 [12]	2.61	3.65	4.43	3.56
Ours (PGN)	**2.49**	**3.30**	4.24	**3.34**
Ours (3DMM)	2.53	3.32	**4.21**	3.36

(b) 3D NME on AFLW2000-3D dataset

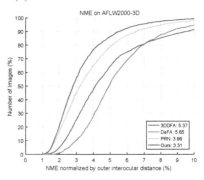

Fig. 3. Performance comparison on AFLW2000-3D. (a) **2D landmarks.** The NME (%) for 68 2D landmarks with different face orientation along the Y-axis are reported. (b) **3D face reconstruction.** X-axis denotes the NME normalized by outer interocular distance, the Y-axis denotes the percentage of images. Following [16], around 45k points are used for evaluation.

datasets. For synthetic dataset, we choose 300W-LP [15], which contains 60k synthetic images with fitted 3DMM parameters. These images are synthesized from around 4k face images with face profiling synthetic method [36]. To enable more robust 3D face landmark detection, we choose a corpus of in-the-wild datasets, including Menpo [37], CelebA [38], 300-VW [39] and Multi-PIE [40] with their 68 2D landmarks automatically extracted by [17].

To train identity and expression regression networks with our proposed self-consistency losses, we utilize 300-VW [39] and Multi-PIE [40], where the former contains monocular videos, and the latter contains faces images of the same identity under different lightings, poses, expressions and scenes.

Evaluation Datasets and Metrics. We evaluate our model on AFLW-2000-3D [15], Florence [18] and FaceWarehouse [19] datasets. AFLW-2000-3D contains the first 2000 images from AFLW [41], which is annotated with fitted 3DMM parameters and 68 3D landmarks in the same way as 300W-LP. We evaluate face landmark detection performance and 3D face reconstruction performance on this dataset, which is measured by Normalized Mean Error (NME). Florence dataset contains 53 subjects with ground truth 3D scans, where each subject contains three corresponding videos: "Indoor-Cooperative", "PTZ-Indoor" and "PIZ-Outdoor". We report Point-to-Plane Distance to evaluate 3D shape reconstruction performance. The Florence dataset only contains 3D scans with the neutral expression, which can only be used to evaluate the performance of shape reconstruction. To evaluate the expression part, we further evaluate our method on the FaceWarehouse dataset. Following previous work [26,30,42,43], we use a subset with 180 meshes (9 identities and 20 expressions each) and report per-vertex error. Florence and FaceWarehouse are also employed to verify the effectiveness of our proposed multi-frame consistency scheme.

Training Details. The face regions are cropped according to either pseudo 3D face landmarks or detected 2D facial landmarks [17]. Then the cropped images are resized to 256×256 as input. The shared encoder and PGN structures are the same as PRN [16]. For PGN, another option is using fully connected layers to regress sparse 3D landmarks, which can reduce a lot of computation with slightly decreased performance. The identity and expression regression networks take the encoder output as input, followed by one convolutional layer, one average pooling layer and three fully-connected layers.

Table 1. Comparison of mean point-to-plane error on the Florence dataset.

Method	Indoor-Cooperative		PTZ-Indoor	
	Mean	Std	Mean	Std
Tran et al. [24]	1.443	0.292	1.471	0.290
Tran et al.+ pool	1.397	0.290	1.381	0.322
Tran et al.+ [29]	1.382	0.272	1.430	0.306
MoFA [26]	1.405	0.306	1.306	0.261
MoFA + pool	1.370	0.321	1.286	0.266
MoFA + [29]	1.363	0.326	1.293	0.276
Genova et al. [27]	1.405	0.339	1.271	0.293
Genova et al.+ pool	1.372	0.353	1.260	0.310
Genova et al.+ [29]	1.360	0.346	1.246	0.302
MVF [14] - pretrain	1.266	0.297	1.252	0.285
MVF [14]	1.220	0.247	1.228	0.236
Ours	**1.122**	**0.219**	**1.161**	**0.224**

Our whole training procedure contains 3 steps: (1) We first train the shared encoder and PGN. We randomly sample one batch images from 300W-LP and another batch from in-the-wild datasets, then employ 3D landmark and 2D landmark supervision respectively. We set batch size to 16 and train the network for 600k iterations. After that, both the shared encoder and PGN parameters are fixed. (2) For identity and expression regression networks, we first pre-train them with only one image for each identity as input using L_l and L_r for 400k iterations. This results in a coarse estimation and speeds up the convergence for training with multiple images. (3) Finally, we sequentially choose 2 and 4 images for each identity as input and train for another 400k iterations by minimizing Eq. (7). The balance weights for loss terms are set to $\lambda_l = 1$, $\lambda_p = 0.2$, $\lambda_f = 0.2$, $\lambda_s = 10$, $\lambda_r = 1$. Due to the memory consumption brought by rendering and optical flow estimation, we reduce the batch size to 4 for multi-image input. All 3 steps are trained using Adam [44] optimizer with an initial learning rate of 10^{-4}. Learning rate decays half after 100k iterations.

3D Face Alignment Results. Figure 3(a) shows the 68 facial landmark detection performance on AFLW2000-3D dataset [15]. By training with a large corpus of unlabeled in-the-wild data, our model greatly improves over previous state-of-the-art 3D face alignment methods (e.g. PRN [16], MMFace [12]) that heavily rely on 3D annotations. Our method achieves the best performance without any post-processing such as the ICP used in MMFace. Moreover, our PGN is robust. We can fix it and directly use its output as ground truth of 3D landmarks to guide the learning of 3D face reconstruction.

Quantitative 3D Face Reconstruction Results. We evaluate 3D face reconstruction performance with NME on AFLW2000-3D, Point-to-Plane error on Florence and Per-vertex error on FaceWarehouse. Thanks to the robustness of our PGN, we can directly fix it and obtain accurate pose estimation without

Table 2. Per-vertex geometric error (measured in mm) on FaceWarehouse dataset. PGN denotes PGN. Our approach obtains the lowest error, outperforming the best prior art [30] by 7.5%.

Method	MoFA [26]	Inversefacenet [45]	Tewari *et al.* [42]	FML [30]	Ours Single-Frame without PGN	Ours Single-Frame with PGN	Ours Multi-Frame without PGN	Ours Multi-Frame with PGN
Error	2.19	2.11	2.03	2.01	2.18	2.09	1.98	**1.86**

further learning. Then, our model can focus more on shape and expression estimation. As shown in Fig. 3(b), we achieve the best results on the AFLW2000-3D dataset, reducing NME_{3d} of previous state-of-the-art from 3.96 to 3.31, with 16.4% relative improvement.

Table 1 shows the results on the Florence dataset. In contrast to MVF that concatenates encoder features as input to estimate a share identity parameter, we employ average pooling for encoder features, enabling us to perform both single-image and multi-image face reconstruction. In the evaluation setting, it does not make much difference using single-frame or multi-frame as input, because we'll finally average all the video frame output. Notably, our method is more general than the previous state-of-the-art MVF that assumes expressions are the same among multiple images (*i.e.*, multi-view images), while our method can directly train on monocular videos.

Table 2 shows the results on FaceWarehouse dataset. For single frame setting, without modeling albedo, we still achieve comparable performance with MoFA [26], Inversefacenet [45] and Tewari *et al.* [42]. For multi-frame settings, we achieve better results than FML [30]. For both single-frame and multi-frame settings, we achieve improved performance with PGN. All these show the effectiveness of PGN and self-consistency losses.

Qualitative 3D Face Reconstruction Results. Figure 4(a) shows the qualitative comparisons with 3DDFA [15], PRNet [16] and the pseudo ground truth. 3DDFA regresses identity, expression and pose parameters together and is only trained with synthetic datasets 300W-LP, leading to performance degradation. The estimated shape and expression of 3DDFA is close to mean face geometry and looks generally similar. PRNet directly regresses all vertices stored in UV position map, which cannot capture the geometric constraints well; thus, it does not look smooth and lacks geometric details, *e.g.*, eye and mouth regions. In contrast, our estimated shape and expression looks visually convincing. Even when compared with the pseudo ground truth generated with traditional matching methods, our estimation is more accurate in many cases. Figure 4(b) shows the comparison on the Florence dataset, which further demonstrates the effectiveness of our method. Compared with FML on FaceWarehouse dataset, our results can generate more accurate expressions with visibly pleasing face reconstruction results (Fig. 4(c)).

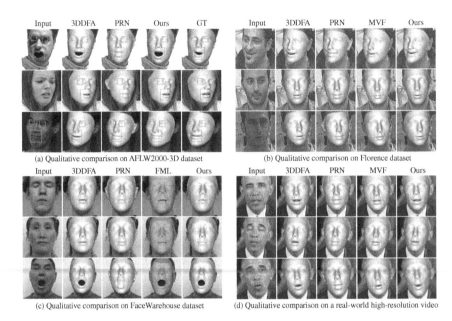

Fig. 4. **Qualitative Comparison on various datasets**. Our model generates more accurate shapes and expressions, especially around the mouth and eye region, as we leverage unlimited 2D face data and cross image consistency. The estimated shape of 3DDFA is close to mean face geometry and the results of PRN lack geometric details. (a) On **AFLW2000-3D**, our results look even more visually convincing than ground truth in many cases. (b) **Florence**. (c) **FaceWarehouse**. Compared with FML, our results are more smooth and visibly pleasing. (d) **Video results**. Our consistency losses work especially well for high resolution images with few steps of fine-tuning. We generate accurate shape and expression, *e.g.*, challenging expression of complete eye-closing. **Zoom in for details.**

Ablation Study. The effectiveness of PGN has been shown in Fig. 3 (a) (for face alignment) and Table 2 (for face reconstruction). To better elaborate the contributions of different components in our self-consistency scheme, we perform detailed ablation study in Fig. 5.

Our baseline model is single-image face reconstruction trained only with L_l and L_r. However, it doesn't lead to accurate shape estimation, because our PGN with sparse landmarks can only provide a coarse shape estimation. To better estimate the shape, we employ multi-frame images as input. As shown in Fig. 5(a), even without census transform, the photometric consistency (L_{p-}) improves the performance. However, photometric loss does not work well when illumination changes among video frames. Therefore, we enhance the photometric loss with census transform to make the model more robust to illumination change. This improves the performance quantitatively (Fig. 5(a)), and qualitatively (Fig. 5(b–f)). Applying semantic consistency (L_s) and flow consistency (L_f) enforces the rendered image and the target image to look semantically similar and generates better face geometry.

(a) **Ablation study on Florence.**

L_{p-}	L_p	L_s	L_f	Indoor-Cooperative Mean	Std	PTZ-Indoor Mean	Std
✗	✗	✗	✗	1.364	0.352	1.379	0.326
✓	✗	✗	✗	1.263	0.312	1.323	0.251
✗	✓	✗	✗	1.219	0.261	1.255	0.256
✗	✓	✗	✓	1.193	0.230	1.221	0.247
✗	✓	✓	✗	1.161	0.268	1.269	0.276
✗	✓	✓	✓	**1.122**	**0.219**	**1.161**	**0.224**

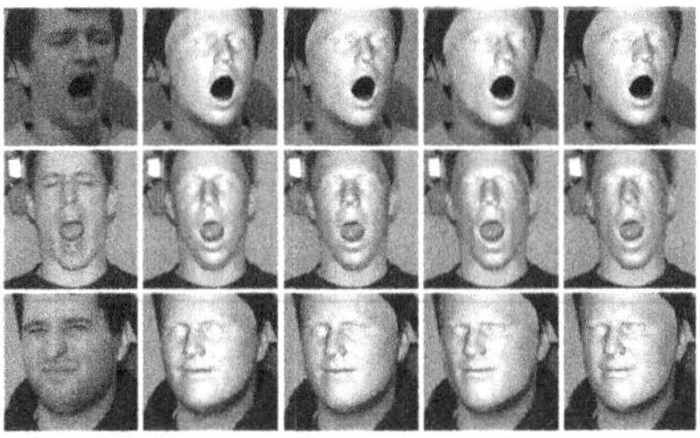

(b) Input (c) Pretrain (d) L_{p-} (e) L_p (f) Full

Fig. 5. (a) **Ablation Study on Florence dataset.** L_{p-} indicates that census transform is not applied when computing photometric differences. We find that census transform is robust for illumination variations. (b–f) **Visual results of our ablations on Multi-PIE dataset:** (b) Input image. (c) Pre-trained model with only landmark loss and regularizer loss. (d) Employ photometric loss. (e) Employ census transform when computing photometric consistency. (f) Full loss. We can find that key components of our model improve the accuracy of shape and expression. **Zoom in for details.**

Video Results. Our proposed multi-image face reconstruction method is based on texture sampling, then it shall obtain better face reconstruction results with higher texture quality (higher video resolution). To verify it, we fine-tune our model on a high-quality video from the Internet, *i.e.*, the fine-tuned model is specialized for the video. No 3D ground truth is used. As shown in Fig. 4(d), our estimated shape and expression look surprisingly accurate after several thousand iterations. Specifically, our model captures the detailed expression (*e.g.*, totally closed eyes) and face shape very well. This can be an interesting application when we need to obtain accurate 3D face reconstruction for one specific person.

5   Conclusion

We have presented a pose guidance network which yields superior performance on 3D face reconstruction from a single image or multiple frames. Our approach effectively makes use of in-the-wild unlabeled images and provides accurate 3D landmarks as an intermediate supervision to help reconstruct 3D faces. Furthermore, we have demonstrated that swapping textures of multiple images and exploring their photometric and semantic consistency greatly improve the final performance. We hope that our work can inspire future research to develop new techniques that leverage informative intermediate representations (*e.g.*, 3D landmarks in this paper) and learn from unlabeled images or videos.

Acknowledgement. This work was partially supported by the RRC of the Hong Kong Special Administrative Region (No. CUHK 14210717 of the General Research Fund) and National Key Research and Development Program of China (No. 2018AAA0100204). We also thank Yao Feng, Feng Liu and Ayush Tewari for kind help.

References

1. Blanz, V., Vetter, T.: Face recognition based on fitting a 3D morphable model. In: TPAMI (2003)
2. Paysan, P., Knothe, R., Amberg, B., Romdhani, S., Vetter, T.: A 3D face model for pose and illumination invariant face recognition. In: AVSS (2009)
3. Nagano, K., et al.: pagan: real-time avatars using dynamic textures. In: SIG-GRAPH Asia (2018)
4. Hu, L., et al.: Avatar digitization from a single image for real-time rendering. TOG **36**(6), 1–14 (2017)
5. Thies, J., Zollhofer, M., Stamminger, M., Theobalt, C., Nießner, M.: Face2face: real-time face capture and reenactment of RGB videos. In: CVPR (2016)
6. Kim, H., et al.: Deep video portraits. TOG **37**(4), 1–14 (2018)
7. Blanz, V., Vetter, T., et al.: A morphable model for the synthesis of 3D faces. In: SIGGRAPH (1999)
8. Saito, S., Li, T., Li, H.: Real-time facial segmentation and performance capture from RGB input. In: ECCV (2016)
9. Cao, C., Hou, Q., Zhou, K.: Displaced dynamic expression regression for real-time facial tracking and animation. TOG **33**(4), 1–10 (2014)
10. Cao, C., Weng, Y., Lin, S., Zhou, K.: 3D shape regression for real-time facial animation. TOG **32**(4), 1–10 (2013)
11. Sanyal, S., Bolkart, T., Feng, H., Black, M.J.: Learning to regress 3D face shape and expression from an image without 3D supervision. In: CVPR (2019)
12. Yi, H., et al.: Mmface: a multi-metric regression network for unconstrained face reconstruction. In: CVPR (2019)
13. Chang, F.J., Tran, A.T., Hassner, T., Masi, I., Nevatia, R., Medioni, G.: Expnet: Landmark-free, deep, 3D facial expressions. In: FG (2018)
14. Wu, F., et al.: MVF-net: multi-view 3D face morphable model regression. In: CVPR (2019)
15. Zhu, X., Lei, Z., Liu, X., Shi, H., Li, S.Z.: Face alignment across large poses: a 3D solution. In: CVPR (2016)
16. Feng, Y., Wu, F., Shao, X., Wang, Y., Zhou, X.: Joint 3D face reconstruction and dense alignment with position map regression network. In: ECCV (2018)
17. Bulat, A., Tzimiropoulos, G.: How far are we from solving the 2D & 3D face alignment problem? (and a dataset of 230,000 3d facial landmarks). In: ICCV (2017)
18. Bagdanov, A.D., Del Bimbo, A., Masi, I.: The florence 2D/3D hybrid face dataset. In: Proceedings of the 2011 Joint ACM Workshop on Human Gesture and Behavior Understanding (2011)
19. Cao, C., Weng, Y., Zhou, S., Tong, Y., Zhou, K.: Facewarehouse: a 3D facial expression database for visual computing. TVCG **20**(3), 413–425 (2013)
20. Liu, Y., Jourabloo, A., Ren, W., Liu, X.: Dense face alignment. In: ICCV (2017)
21. Gou, C., Wu, Y., Wang, F.Y., Ji, Q.: Shape augmented regression for 3D face alignment. In: ECCV (2016)
22. Romdhani, S., Vetter, T.: Estimating 3D shape and texture using pixel intensity, edges, specular highlights, texture constraints and a prior. In: CVPR (2005)
23. Dou, P., Shah, S.K., Kakadiaris, I.A.: End-to-end 3D face reconstruction with deep neural networks. In: CVPR (2017)
24. Tuan Tran, A., Hassner, T., Masi, I., Medioni, G.: Regressing robust and discriminative 3D morphable models with a very deep neural network. In: CVPR (2017)

25. Jackson, A.S., Bulat, A., Argyriou, V., Tzimiropoulos, G.: Large pose 3D face reconstruction from a single image via direct volumetric CNN regression. In: ICCV (2017)
26. Tewari, A., et al.: Mofa: model-based deep convolutional face autoencoder for unsupervised monocular reconstruction. In: ICCV (2017)
27. Genova, K., Cole, F., Maschinot, A., Sarna, A., Vlasic, D., Freeman, W.T.: Unsupervised training for 3D morphable model regression. In: CVPR (2018)
28. Chang, F.-J., Tran, A.T., Hassner, T., Masi, I., Nevatia, R., Medioni, G.: Deep, landmark-free fame: face alignment, modeling, and expression estimation. Int. J. Comput. Vis. **127**(6), 930–956 (2019). https://doi.org/10.1007/s11263-019-01151-x
29. Piotraschke, M., Blanz, V.: Automated 3D face reconstruction from multiple images using quality measures. In: CVPR (2016)
30. Tewari, A., et al.: FML: face model learning from videos. In: CVPR (2019)
31. Hafner, D., Demetz, O., Weickert, J.: Why is the census transform good for robust optic flow computation? In: SSVM (2013)
32. Liu, P., King, I., Lyu, M.R., Xu, J.: Ddflow: learning optical flow with unlabeled data distillation. In: AAAI (2019)
33. Xiong, X., De la Torre, F.: Global supervised descent method. In: CVPR (2015)
34. Yu, R., Saito, S., Li, H., Ceylan, D., Li, H.: Learning dense facial correspondences in unconstrained images. In: ICCV (2017)
35. Bhagavatula, C., Zhu, C., Luu, K., Savvides, M.: Faster than real-time facial alignment: a 3D spatial transformer network approach in unconstrained poses. In: ICCV (2017)
36. Zollhöfer, M., et al.: State of the art on monocular 3D face reconstruction, tracking, and applications. In: Computer Graphics Forum, Wiley Online Library (2018)
37. Deng, J., et al.: The Menpo benchmark for multi-pose 2D and 3D facial landmark localisation and tracking. Int. J. Comput. Vis. **127**(6), 599–624 (2018). https://doi.org/10.1007/s11263-018-1134-y
38. Liu, Z., Luo, P., Wang, X., Tang, X.: Deep learning face attributes in the wild. In: ICCV (2015)
39. Shen, J., Zafeiriou, S., Chrysos, G.G., Kossaifi, J., Tzimiropoulos, G., Pantic, M.: The first facial landmark tracking in-the-wild challenge: benchmark and results. In: ICCVW (2015)
40. Gross, R., Matthews, I., Cohn, J., Kanade, T., Baker, S.: Multi-pie. Image Vis. Comput. **28**(5), 807–813 (2010)
41. Koestinger, M., Wohlhart, P., Roth, P.M., Bischof, H.: Annotated facial landmarks in the wild: a large-scale, real-world database for facial landmark localization. In: ICCVW (2011)
42. Tewari, A., et al.: Self-supervised multi-level face model learning for monocular reconstruction at over 250 HZ. In: CVPR (2018)
43. Tran, L., Liu, X.: Nonlinear 3D face morphable model. In: CVPR (2018)
44. Kingma, D.P., Ba, J.: Adam: a method for stochastic optimization. In: ICLR (2015)
45. Kim, H., Zollhöfer, M., Tewari, A., Thies, J., Richardt, C., Theobalt, C.: Inverse-facenet: deep monocular inverse face rendering. In: CVPR (2018)

Self-supervised Multi-view Synchronization Learning for 3D Pose Estimation

Simon Jenni$^{(\boxtimes)}$ (iD) and Paolo Favaro (iD)

University of Bern, Bern, Switzerland
{simon.jenni,paolo.favaro}@inf.unibe.ch

Abstract. Current state-of-the-art methods cast monocular 3D human pose estimation as a learning problem by training neural networks on large data sets of images and corresponding skeleton poses. In contrast, we propose an approach that can exploit small annotated data sets by fine-tuning networks pre-trained via self-supervised learning on (large) unlabeled data sets. To drive such networks towards supporting 3D pose estimation during the pre-training step, we introduce a novel self-supervised feature learning task designed to focus on the 3D structure in an image. We exploit images extracted from videos captured with a multi-view camera system. The task is to classify whether two images depict two views of the same scene up to a rigid transformation. In a multi-view data set, where objects deform in a non-rigid manner, a rigid transformation occurs only between two views taken at the exact same time, *i.e.*, when they are synchronized. We demonstrate the effectiveness of the synchronization task on the Human3.6M data set and achieve state-of-the-art results in 3D human pose estimation.

1 Introduction

The ability to accurately reconstruct the 3D human pose from a single real image opens a wide variety of applications including computer graphics animation, postural analysis and rehabilitation, human-computer interaction, and image understanding [1]. State-of-the-art methods for monocular 3D human pose estimation employ neural networks and require large training data sets, where each sample is a pair consisting of an image and its corresponding 3D pose annotation [2]. The collection of such data sets is expensive, time-consuming, and, because it requires controlled lab settings, the diversity of motions, viewpoints, subjects, appearance and illumination, is limited (see Fig. 1). Ideally, to maximize diversity, data should be collected in the wild. However, in this case precise 3D annotation is difficult to obtain and might require costly human intervention.

Electronic supplementary material The online version of this chapter (https://doi.org/10.1007/978-3-030-69541-5_11) contains supplementary material, which is available to authorized users.

© Springer Nature Switzerland AG 2021
H. Ishikawa et al. (Eds.): ACCV 2020, LNCS 12626, pp. 170–187, 2021.
https://doi.org/10.1007/978-3-030-69541-5_11

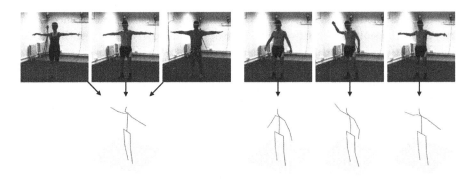

(a) Desired subject invariance.   (b) Desired pose equivariance.

Fig. 1. Monocular 3D human pose estimation. An ideal regressor would be able to generalize across subjects regardless of their appearance, as shown in (a), and be sensitive to small pose variations, such as those shown in (b).

In this paper, we overcome the above limitations via *self-supervised learning* (SSL). SSL is a method to build powerful latent representations by training a neural network to solve a so-called *pretext* task in a supervised manner, but without manual annotation [3]. The pretext task is typically an artificial problem, where a model is asked to output the transformation that was applied to the data. One way to exploit models trained with SSL is to transfer them to some target task on a small labeled data set via *fine-tuning* [3]. The performance of the transferred representations depends on how related the pretext task is to the target task. Thus, to build latent representations relevant to 3D human poses, we propose a pretext task that implicitly learns 3D structures. To collect data suitable to this goal, examples from nature point towards multi-view imaging systems. In fact, the visual system in many animal species hinges on the presence of two or multiple eyes to achieve a 3D perception of the world [4,5]. 3D perception is often exemplified by considering two views of the same scene captured at the same time and by studying the correspondence problem. Thus, we take inspiration from this setting and pose the task of determining if two images have been captured at exactly the same time. In general, the main difference between two views captured at the same time and when they are not, is that the former are always related by a rigid transformation and the latter is potentially not (*e.g.*, in the presence of articulated or deformable motion, or multiple rigid motions). Therefore, we propose as pretext task the detection of *synchronized views*, which translates into a classification of *rigid* versus *non-rigid* motion.

As shown in Fig. 1, we aim to learn a latent representation that can generalize across subjects and that is sensitive to small pose variations. Thus, we train our model with pairs of images, where the subject identity is irrelevant to the pretext task and where the difference between the task categories are small pose variations. To do so, we use two views of the same subject as the synchronized (*i.e.*, rigid motion) pair and two views taken at different (but not too distant) time instants as the unsynchronized (*i.e.*, non-rigid motion) pair.[1] Since these pairs share the same subject (as well as the appearance) in all images, the model cannot use this as a cue to learn the correct classification. Moreover, we believe that the weight decay term that we add to the loss may also help to reduce the effect of parameters that are subject-dependent, since there are no other incentives from the loss to preserve them. Because the pair of unsynchronized images is close in time, the deformation is rather small and forces the model to learn to discriminate small pose variations. Furthermore, to make the representation sensitive to left-right symmetries of the human pose, we also introduce in the pretext task as a second goal the classification of two synchronized views into *horizontally flipped* or not. This formulation of the SSL task allows to potentially train a neural network on data captured in the wild simply by using a synchronized multi-camera system. As we show in our experiments, the learned representation successfully embeds 3D human poses and it further improves if the background can also be removed from the images. We train and evaluate our SSL pre-training on the Human3.6M data set [2], and find that it yields state-of-the-art results when compared to other methods under the same training conditions. We show quantitatively and qualitatively that our trained model can generalize across subjects and is sensitive to small pose variations. Finally, we believe that this approach can also be easily incorporated in other methods to exploit additional available labeling (*e.g.*, 2D poses). Code will be made available on our project page https://sjenni.github.io/multiview-sync-ssl.

Our contributions are: 1) A novel self-supervised learning task for multi-view data to recognize when two views are synchronized and/or flipped; 2) Extensive ablation experiments to demonstrate the importance of avoiding shortcuts via the static background removal and the effect of different feature fusion strategies; 3) State-of-the-art performance on 3D human pose estimation benchmarks.

2   Prior Work

In this section, we briefly review literature in self-supervised learning, human pose estimation, representation learning and synchronization, that is relevant to our approach.

Self-supervised Learning. Self-supervised learning is a type of unsupervised representation learning that has demonstrated impressive performance on image and video benchmarks. These methods exploit pretext tasks that require no human annotation, *i.e.*, the labels can be generated automatically. Some methods are based on predicting part of the data [6–8], some are based on contrastive

---

[1] If the subject does not move between the two chosen time instants, the unsynchronized pair would be also undergoing a rigid motion and thus create ambiguity in the training. However, these cases can be easily spotted as they simply require detecting no motion over time. Besides standing still, the probability that a moving subject performs a rigid motion is extremely low. In practice, we found experimentally that a simple temporal sub-sampling was sufficient to avoid these scenarios.

learning or clustering [9–11], others are based on recognizing absolute or relative transformations [12–14]. Our task is most closely related to the last category since we aim to recognize a transformation in time between two views.

Unsupervised Learning of 3D. Recent progress in unsupervised learning has shown promising results for learning implicit and explicit generative 3D models from natural images [15–17]. The focus in these methods is on modelling 3D and not performance on downstream tasks. Our goal is to learn general purpose 3D features that perform well on downstream tasks such as 3D pose estimation.

Synchronization. Learning the alignment of multiple frames taken from different views is an important component of many vision systems. Classical approaches are based on fitting local descriptors [18–20]. More recently, methods based on metric learning [21] or that exploit audio [22] have been proposed. We provide a simple learning based approach by posing the synchronization problem as a binary classification task. Our aim is not to achieve synchronization for its own sake, but to learn a useful image representation as a byproduct.

Monocular 3D Pose Estimation. State-of-the-art 3D pose estimation methods make use of large annotated in-the-wild 2D pose data sets [23] and data sets with ground truth 3D pose obtained in indoor lab environments. We identify two main categories of methods: 1) Methods that learn the mapping to 3D pose directly from images [24–32] often trained jointly with 2D poses [33–37], and 2) Methods that learn the mapping of images to 3D poses from predicted or ground truth 2D poses [38–46]. To deal with the limited amount of 3D annotations, some methods explored the use of synthetic training data [47–49]. In our transfer learning experiments, we follow the first category and predict 3D poses directly from images. However, we do not use any 2D annotations.

Weakly Supervised Methods. Much prior work has focused on reducing the need for 3D annotations. One approach is weak supervision, where only 2D annotation is used. These methods are typically based on minimizing the re-projection error of a predicted 3D pose [50–56]. To resolve ambiguities and constrain the 3D, some methods require multi-view data [50–52], while others rely on unpaired 3D data used via adversarial training [54,55]. [53] solely relies on 2D annotation and uses an adversarial loss on random projections of the 3D pose. Our aim is not to rely on a weaker form of supervision (*i.e.*, 2D annotations) and instead leverage multi-view data to learn a representation that can be transferred on a few annotated examples to the 3D estimation tasks with a good performance.

Self-supervised Methods for 3D Human Pose Estimation. Here we consider methods that do not make use of any additional supervision, *e.g.*, in the form of 2D pose annotation. These are methods that learn representations on unlabelled data and can be transferred via fine-tuning using a limited amount of 3D annotation. Rhodin *et al.* [57] learn a 3D representation via novel view synthesis, *i.e.*, by reconstructing one view from another. Their method relies on synchronized multi-view data, knowledge of camera extrinsics and background images. Mitra *et al.* [58] use metric learning on multi-view data. The distance in feature space for images with the same pose, but different viewpoint is minimized while the distance to hard negatives sampled from the mini-batch is maximized. By construction, the resulting representation is view invariant (the local camera coordinate system is lost) and the transfer can only be performed in a canonical, rotation-invariant coordinate system. We also exploit multi-view data in our pre-training task. In contrast to [57], our task does not rely on knowledge of camera parameters and unlike [58] we successfully transfer our features to pose prediction in the local camera system.

3   Unsupervised Learning of 3D Pose-Discriminative Features

Our goal is to build image features that allow to discriminate different 3D human poses. We achieve this objective by training a network to detect if two views depict the exact same scene up to a rigid transformation. We consider three different cases: 1) The two views depict the same scene at exactly the same time (rigid transformation); 2) The two views show the same scene, but at a different time (non-rigid transformation is highly likely); 3) The two views show the same scene, but one view is horizontally mirrored (a special case of a non-rigid transformation), which, for simplicity, we refer to as *flipped*.

To train such a network, we assume we have access to synchronized multi-view video data. The data set consists of N examples (in the Human3.6M data set $N = S \times A$, where S is the number of subjects and A the number of actions) $\{x_{\nu,t}^{(i)}\}_{i=1,\dots,N}$, where $\nu \in \mathcal{V}^{(i)} = \{1,\dots,\nu^{(i)}\}$ indicates the different views of the i-th example and $t \in \mathcal{T}^{(i)} = \{1,\dots,t^{(i)}\}$ indicates the time of the frame. Let F denote the neural network trained to solve the self-supervised task. We will now describe the different self-supervision signals.

3.1   Classifying Synchronized and Flipped Views

To train our neural network we define three types image pairs, each corresponding to a different 3D deformation:

Synchronized Pairs. In this case, the scenes in the two views are related by a rigid transformation. This is the case when the two images are captured at the same time instant, *i.e.*, they are synchronized. The input for this category is a sample pair $\mathbf{x}_p = (x_{\nu_1,t}^{(i)}, x_{\nu_2,t}^{(i)})$, where $i \in \{1,\dots,N\}$, $\nu_1 \neq \nu_2 \in \mathcal{V}^{(i)}$, and $t \in \mathcal{T}^{(i)}$, *i.e.*, a pair with different views taken at the same time.

Unsynchronized Pairs. Pairs of images that are captured at different times (*i.e.*, unsynchronized) are likely to undergo a non-rigid deformation (by assuming that objects are non static between these two time instants). To create such image pairs we sample $\mathbf{x}_n = (x_{\nu_1,t_1}^{(i)}, x_{\nu_2,t_2}^{(i)})$, where $i \in \{1,\dots,N\}$, $\nu_1 \neq \nu_2 \in \mathcal{V}^{(i)}$, and $t_1, t_2 \in \mathcal{T}^{(i)}$ such that $d_{min} < |t_2 - t_1| < d_{max}$, where d_{min} and d_{max} define the range in time for sampling unsynchronized pairs. In our experiments, we set $d_{min} = 4$ and $d_{max} = 128$ and sample uniformly within this range.

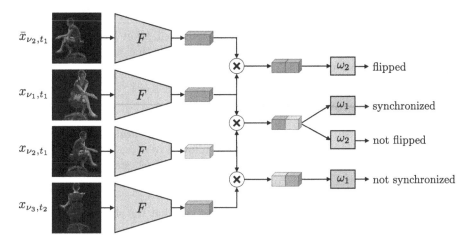

Fig. 2. An overview of the proposed self-supervised task. We train a network F to learn image representations that transfer well to 3D pose estimation by learning to recognize if two views of the same scene are *synchronized* and/or *flipped*. Our model uses a Siamese architecture. The inputs are pairs of frames of the same scene under different views. Frames are denoted by $x_{\nu,t}$, where ν indicates the viewpoint and t the time ($\bar{x}_{\nu,t}$ denotes a flipped frame). Pairs are classified into whether the frames are *synchronized* or *not synchronized*, and whether one of the frames was *flipped* or not.

Flipped Pairs. The last class of image pairs consists of images from two views which are synchronized, but where one of them has been horizontally mirrored. Let $\bar{x}$ denote the image obtained by applying horizontal mirroring to the sample x. Flipped pairs are defined as $\mathbf{x}_f = (x_{\nu_1,t}^{(i)}, \bar{x}_{\nu_2,t}^{(i)})$ or $\mathbf{x}_f = (\bar{x}_{\nu_1,t}^{(i)}, x_{\nu_2,t}^{(i)})$, where $i \in \{1,\ldots,N\}$, $\nu_1 \neq \nu_2 \in \mathcal{V}^{(i)}$ and $t \in \mathcal{T}^{(i)}$. In the case of approximately symmetric objects (such as with human bodies) and in the absence of background cues (since we mirror the entire image) distinguishing this relative transformation between views requires accurate 3D pose discriminative features.

Although both **unsynchronized** and **flipped** pairs exhibit non-rigid deformations, they have distinct characteristics. In the case of flipped pairs, the 3D pose in the second view is heavily constrained by the one in the first view. In contrast, given a non negligible temporal gap between the frames, the 3D pose is much less constrained in the case of unsynchronized views.

We define our self-supervised learning task as a combination of the classification of image pairs into *synchronized vs. unsynchronized* and into *flipped vs. not flipped*. Let $F_1(\mathbf{x})$ denote the predicted probability of synchronization in $\mathbf{x}$ and $F_2(\mathbf{x})$ the predicted probability of no flipping in $\mathbf{x}$ (both implemented via a sigmoid activation). The final loss function is then given by

$$\mathcal{L}_{SSL} = -\sum_j \log F_1\big(\mathbf{x}_p^{(j)}\big) F_2\big(\mathbf{x}_p^{(j)}\big) + \log \Big(1 - F_1\big(\mathbf{x}_n^{(j)}\big)\Big) + \log \Big(1 - F_2\big(\mathbf{x}_f^{(j)}\big)\Big). \quad (1)$$

An illustration of the training is shown in Fig. 2. Note that although $\mathbf{x}_f$ is a synchronized pair, we do not optimize the synchronization head F_1 on these examples. The reason for leaving this term undefined is that we equate synchronization to rigid motion, which does not hold in the case of $\mathbf{x}_f$.

3.2   Static Backgrounds Introduce Shortcuts

A common issue with self-supervised learning is that neural networks exploit low-level cues to solve the pretext task, when allowed to do so. In this case, they often do not learn semantically meaningful features. Such shortcuts have been observed in prior work, where, for instance, chromatic aberration [6] was used as a cue to solve a localization task.

In our self-supervised learning task we observed that the shared image background in the data set can be used as a shortcut. This is most evident in the flipping task: Because the background is shared among all examples in the data set, it is easier to use texture in the background to determine image flipping. As a result, the network focuses on the background (instead of the foreground object of interest) with a decrease in its generalization performance. It is further possible that the network learns to detect and associate the absolute position of the person by focusing on the background as a cue for the synchronization task.

We propose two solutions: One is *background removal* and the other is *background substitution*. Since the data set consists of non-moving cameras, we compute the background as the median image per view. Background removal is then performed via simple per-pixel thresholding. Although the resulting separation is not of high quality, we found it sufficient for our purpose. Similarly, background substitution introduces an additional step where the background from a random view is used to replace the original (removed) one. Both approaches are evaluated in our experiments. More details, qualitative examples, and analysis are provided in the supplementary material. We expect that background removal or substitution would not be necessary for data captured in the wild with synchronized moving cameras or with a large variety of backgrounds.

3.3   Implementation

We implement the network F using a Siamese architecture. As a shared backbone architecture Φ we use standard ResNet architectures [59]. Samples $(x_{\nu_1,t_1}^{(j)}, x_{\nu_2,t_2}^{(j)})$ are hence encoded into features vectors $(\Phi(x_{\nu_1,t_1}^{(j)}), \Phi(x_{\nu_2,t_2}^{(j)}))$. In our experiments we use the output of the global average pooling as the feature representation, *i.e.*, $\Phi(x) \in \mathbb{R}^{2048}$. To fuse the features we choose to use element-wise multiplication followed by a ReLU activation. We found this fusion mechanism to perform better than feature concatenation, which is often used in prior work [6,8,14]. The fused feature is fed as input to linear layers ω_1 and ω_2 to produce the final outputs. To summarize, we define $F_i(\mathbf{x}) = \omega_i(\text{ReLU}(\Phi(x_{\nu_1,t_1}^{(j)}) \odot \Phi(x_{\nu_2,t_2}^{(j)})))$, where $\odot$ denotes the element-wise product.

The training images use the standard image resolution for ResNet architectures of 224×224 pixels. To compare fairly with prior work, we extract crops centered on the subject. As data-augmentation, we add random horizontal flipping applied consistently to both frames in the input pair (this operation is performed before preparing the flipped pairs).

3.4   Transfer to 3D Human Pose Estimation

We transfer the learned image representation to 3D human pose regression via fine-tuning. The training set in this case consists of a set of image[2] and target pairs $\{(x^{(i)}, y^{(i)})\}_{i=1,\dots,N_p}$ with target 3D joint positions $y^{(i)} \in \mathbb{R}^{n_j \times 3}$ represented in the local camera coordinate system. The number of joints is set to $n_j = 17$ in our experiments on Human3.6M. As in prior work [51,57,58], we fix the root joint (at the pelvis) to zero. We effectively only regress the 16 remaining joints and correct for this in evaluation metrics by scaling the per joint errors by $\frac{17}{16}$. We normalize the target poses for training using the per-joint mean and standard deviation computed on the training set as proposed in [32]. During evaluation, we un-normalize the predicted pose accordingly. To predict the 3D pose we simply add a single linear layer ω_p on the feature encoding $\Phi(x^{(i)})$ resulting in our normalized prediction $P(x^{(i)}) = \omega_p(\Phi(x^{(i)}))$. The network P is trained to minimize the mean-squared error on the training set, i.e., $\mathcal{L}_{pose} = \frac{1}{N_p} \sum_{i=1}^{N_p} \|P(x^{(i)}) - y^{(i)}\|_2^2$.

We again extract crops centered on the subject as in prior work [51,57,58]. Since this corresponds to a change of the camera position, we correct for this by rotating the target pose accordingly, i.e., to virtually center the camera on the root joint. As a form of data augmentation, we apply random horizontal flipping jointly to the input images and corresponding target 3D poses.

4   Experiments

Dataset. We perform an extensive experimental evaluation on the Human3.6M data set [2]. The data set consists of 3.6 million 3D human poses with the corresponding images. The data is captured in an indoor setting with 4 synchronized and fixed cameras placed at each corner of the room. Seven subjects perform 17 different actions. As in prior work, we use the five subjects with the naming convention S1, S5, S6, S7, and S8 for training and test on the subjects S9 and S11. We filter the training data set by skipping frames without significant movement. On average, we skip every fourth frame in the training data set. On the test set, we follow prior work and only evaluate our network on one every 64 frames.

Metrics. To evaluate our method on 3D human pose regression we adopt the established metrics. We use the Mean Per Joint Prediction Error (MPJPE) and its variants Normalized MPJPE (NMPJPE) and Procrustes MPJPE (PMPJPE). In NMPJPE the predicted joints are aligned to the ground truth in a least squares

---

[2] We drop the subscripts ν, t indicating viewpoint and time in this notation.

Table 1. Ablation experiments. We investigate the influence of scene background (a)-(d), the influence of the different self-supervision signals (e)-(g), the use of different fusion strategies (h)-(k), and the importance of synchronized multiview data (l) and (m). The experiments were performed on Human3.6M using only subject S1 for transfer learning.

	Ablation	MPJPE	NMPJPE	PMPJPE
(a)	Random with background	167.8	147.1	124.5
(b)	Random without background	165.5	145.4	114.5
(c)	SSL with background	138.4	128.1	100.8
(d)	SSL without background	104.9	91.7	78.4
(e)	Only flip	129.9	117.6	101.1
(f)	Only sync	126.7	115.2	91.8
(g)	Both sync & flip	104.9	91.7	78.4
(h)	Fusion concat	180.0	162.5	130.5
(i)	Fusion add	169.4	158.4	122.8
(j)	Fusion diff	108.2	93.9	80.4
(k)	Fusion mult	104.9	91.7	78.4
(l)	Single-view SSL	158.3	142.0	106.9
(m)	Multi-view SSL	104.9	91.7	78.4

sense with respect to the scale. PMPJE uses Procrustes alignment to align the poses both in terms of scale and rotation.

4.1 Ablations

We perform ablation experiments to validate several design choices for our self-supervised learning task. We illustrate the effect of background removal with respect to the shortcuts in the case of non-varying backgrounds (as is the case for Human3.6M). We also demonstrate the effects of the two self-supervision signals (flipping and synchronization) by themselves and in combination and explore different feature fusion strategies.

The baseline model uses background removal, the combination of both self-supervision signals and element-wise multiplication for feature fusion. The networks are pre-trained for 200K iterations on all training subjects (S1, S5, S6, S7, and S8) using our SSL task and without using annotations. We use a ResNet-18 architecture [59] and initialize with random weights (*i.e.*, we do not rely on ImageNet pre-training). Transfer learning is performed for an additional 200K iterations using only subject S1 for supervision. We freeze the first 3 residual blocks and only finetune the remaining layers. Training of the networks was performed using the AdamW optimizer [60] with default parameters and a weight decay of 10^{-4}. We decayed the learning rate from 10^{-4} to 10^{-7} over the course of training using cosine annealing [61]. The batch size is set to 16.

We perform the following set of ablation experiments and report transfer learning performance on the test set in Table 1:

(a)-(d) **Influence of background removal:** We explore the influence of background removal on the performance of randomly initialized networks and networks initialized with weights from our self-supervised pre-training. We observe that background removal provides only a relatively small gain in the case of training from scratch. The improvement in the case of our self-supervised learning pre-training is much more substantial. This suggests that the static background introduces shortcuts for the pretext task;

(e)-(f) **Combination of self-supervision signals:** We compare networks initialized by pre-training (e) only to detect flipping, (f) only to detect synchronization, and (g) on the combination of both. We observe that the synchronization on its own leads to better features compared to flipping alone. This correlates with the pretext task performance, where we observe that the accuracy on the flipping task is higher than for synchronization. Interestingly, the combination of both signals gives a substantial boost. This suggests that both signals learn complementary features;

(h)-(k) **Fusion of features:** Different designs for the fusion of features in the Siamese architecture are compared. We consider (h) concatenation, (i) addition, (j) subtraction, and (k) element-wise multiplication. We observe that multiplication performs the best. Multiplication allows a simple encoding of similarity or dissimilarity in feature space solely via the sign of each entry. The fused feature is zero (due to the ReLU) if the two input features do not agree on the sign;

(l)-(m) **Necessity of multi-view data:** We want to test how important synchronized multi-view data is for our approach. We compare to a variation of our task, where we do not make use of multi-view data. Instead, we create artificial synchronized views via data augmentation. The images in the input pairs are therefore from the same camera view, but with different augmentations (*i.e.*, random cropping, scaling and rotations). This corresponds to using a 2D equivalent of our self-supervised learning task. We observe drastically decreased feature performance in this case.

4.2 Comparison to Prior Work

We compare our method to prior work by Rhodin *et al.* [51,57] and Mitra *et al.* [58] on Human3.6M. To the best of our knowledge, these are the only methods that use the same training settings as in our approach. Other methods, which we also report, train their networks with additional weak supervision in the form of 2D pose annotation (see Table 2).

We pretrain the networks on our self-supervised learning task for 200K iterations on all training subjects (namely, S1, S5, S6, S7, and S8). Our comparison uses two different protocols: 1) **All**, where transfer learning is performed on all the training subjects and 2) **S1**, where only subject S1 is used for transfer

Table 2. Comparison to prior work. We compare to other prior work. All methods are pre-trained on all the training subjects of Human3.6M. Transfer learning is performed either using all the training subjects or only S1 for supervision. Methods using large amounts of data with 2D pose annotation are *italicized*. * indicates the use of an ImageNet pretrained ResNet-50. [†] indicates a viewpoint invariant representation of the 3D pose.

Supervision	Method	MPJPE	NMPJPE	PMPJPE
All	*Chen et al. [52] **	*80.2*	-	*58.2*
	*Kocabas et al. [50] **	*51.8*	*51.6*	*45.0*
	*Rhodin et al. [51] **	*66.8*	*63.3*	*51.6*
	Rhodin *et al.* [51]*	-	95.4	-
	Rhodin (UNet) *et al.* [57]	-	127.0	-
	Rhodin *et al.* [57]*	-	115.0	-
	Mitra *et al.* [58]*[†]	94.3	92.6	72.5
	Ours	79.5	73.4	59.7
	Ours*	72.6	68.5	54.5
	Ours* (with background)	64.9	62.3	53.5
S1	*Chen et al. [52] **	*91.9*	-	*68.0*
	*Kocabas et al. [50] **	-	*67.0*	*60.2*
	*Rhodin et al. [51] **	-	*78.2*	-
	Rhodin *et al.* [51]*	-	153.3	128.6
	Rhodin (UNet) *et al.* [57]	149.5	135.9	106.4
	Rhodin *et al.* [57]*	131.7	122.6	98.2
	Mitra *et al.* [58]*[†]	121.0	111.9	90.8
	Ours	104.9	91.7	78.4
	Ours*	101.2	89.6	76.9
	Ours* (with background)	101.4	93.7	82.4

learning. We use two different network architectures: 1) A ResNet-18 initialized with random weights, *i.e.*, no ImageNet pre-training, and 2) A ResNet-50 initialized with ImageNet pre-trained weights. Since prior work transfers to images with backgrounds we include results with a ResNet-50 also fine-tuned on images with backgrounds. To reduce the domain gap between pre-training and transfer and to eliminate shortcuts, we pre-train on both images, where backgrounds are removed, and images with substituted backgrounds. We keep the ratio without and with substituted backgrounds to 50:50 during pre-training. During transfer learning we freeze the first 3 residual blocks and fine-tune the remaining layers for 200K iterations using a mini-batch size of 16. Training of the networks was again performed using the AdamW optimizer [60] with default parameters, initial learning rate of 10^{-4} with cosine annealing, and a weight decay of 10^{-4}.

The results and the comparisons to prior work are provided in Table 2. We observe that our fine-tuned network generalizes well and outperforms the rele-

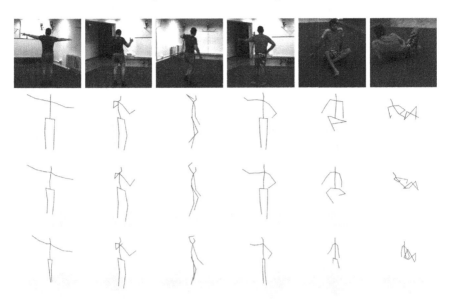

Fig. 3. Examples of predictions. We show predictions on unseen test subjects (S9 and S11) of a model that was pre-trained using our self-supervised learning task and fine-tuned for 3D pose estimation. We show the test images on the first row, the ground truth poses on the second row, the predictions of a model fine-tuned on all training subjects on the third row, and the predictions of a model fine-tuned only on subject S1 on the last row.

vant prior work [51,57,58] by a considerable margin. Note that our ResNet-18 is the only method besides [57] that does not rely on any prior supervision. Interestingly, our model with substituted backgrounds performs better than our model with removed backgrounds in protocol **All** and worse in protocol **S1**. The difference is most severe in the scale sensitive metric MPJPE. We hypothesize that the backgrounds might be useful to learn the correct absolute scale, given a number of different training subjects. We also list methods that make use of large amounts of additional labelled 2D pose data. Using all the training subjects for transfer learning, we even outperform the weakly supervised method [52]. We show some qualitative predictions for the two test subjects in Fig. 3.

4.3   Evaluation of the Synchronization Task

Generalization Across Subjects. We qualitatively evaluate how well our model generalizes to new subjects on the synchronization prediction task. The idea is to look for synchronized frames, where the two frames contain different subjects. A query image $x^{(q)}$ of a previously unseen test subject is chosen. We look for the training image $x^{(a)}$ of each training subject that maximizes the predicted probability of synchronization, $i.e.$, $a = \arg\max_i F_1((x^{(q)}, x^{(i)}))$. Note

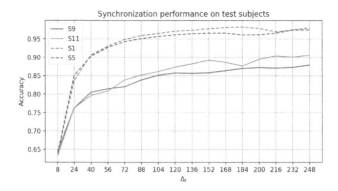

Fig. 4. Synchronization performance on unseen test subjects. We evaluate the pretrained synchronization network on test subjects S9 and S11. Unsynchronized pairs are created with a time difference sampled from the interval $[\Delta_t - 7, \Delta_t + 8]$. We also show the accuracy on two training subjects S1 and S5.

Fig. 5. Synchronization retrievals on test subjects. Query images are shown on the top row and the corresponding predicted synchronized frames are shown in the row below.

that our network was not explicitly trained for this task and that it only received pairs of frames as input containing the same subject during training.

We show example retrievals in Fig. 6. We can observe that the retrieved images often show very similar poses to the query image. The retrieved images also cover different viewpoints. The method generalizes surprisingly well across subjects and manages to associate similar poses across subjects. This indicates a certain degree of invariance to the person appearance. As discussed in the Introduction, such an invariance is welcome in 3D human pose estimation and could explain the good performance in the transfer experiments.

Synchronization performance on test subjects. We evaluate the performance of the synchronization network also on the test subjects. To this end, we sample synchronized and unsynchronized pairs in equal proportion with varying time gaps. We plot the accuracy in Fig. 4. Note that we use all the frames in the test examples in this case. As expected we see an increase in performance with

Fig. 6. Generalization across subjects. We investigate if a network trained on our self-supervised synchronization task generalizes across different subjects. The left-most column shows the query image from test subject S9. The remaining columns shows images of training subjects S1, S5, S6, S7, and S8, respectively, for which our model predicts the highest probability of being synchronized.

a larger temporal gap between the two frames. We also show some qualitative samples of synchronization retrievals in Fig. 5.

5   Conclusions

We propose a novel self-supervised learning method to tackle monocular 3D human pose estimation. Our method delivers a high performance without requiring large manually labeled data sets (*e.g.*, with 2D or 3D poses). To avoid such detailed annotation, we exploit a novel self-supervised task that leads to a representation that supports 3D pose estimation. Our task is to detect when two views have been captured at the same time (and thus the scene is related by a rigid transformation) and when they are horizontally flipped with respect to one another. We show on the well-known Human3.6M data set that these two objectives build features that generalize across subjects and are highly sensitive to small pose variations.

Acknowledgements. This work was supported by grant 169622 of the Swiss National Science Foundation (SNSF).

References

1. Rosenhahn, B., Klette, R., Metaxas, D.: Human Motion: Understanding, Modeling, Capture. Springer, Heidelberg (2008). https://doi.org/10.1007/978-3-540-75703-0
2. Ionescu, C., Papava, D., Olaru, V., Sminchisescu, C.: Human3.6m: large scale datasets and predictive methods for 3D human sensing in natural environments. IEEE Trans. Pattern Anal. Mach. Intell. **36**, 1325–1339 (2014)
3. Doersch, C., Gupta, A., Efros, A.A.: Unsupervised visual representation learning by context prediction. In: Proceedings of the IEEE International Conference on Computer Vision, pp. 1422–1430 (2015)
4. Nityananda, V., Read, J.C.: Stereopsis in animals: evolution, function and mechanisms. J. Exp. Biol. **220**, 2502–2512 (2017)
5. Harland, D.P., Li, D., Jackson, R.R.: How Jumping Spiders See the World. Oxford University Press, New York (2012)
6. Pathak, D., Krahenbuhl, P., Donahue, J., Darrell, T., Efros, A.A.: Context encoders: feature learning by inpainting. In: Proceedings of the IEEE Conference on Computer Vision and Pattern Recognition, pp. 2536–2544 (2016)
7. Zhang, R., Isola, P., Efros, A.A.: Colorful image colorization. In: Leibe, B., Matas, J., Sebe, N., Welling, M. (eds.) ECCV 2016, Part III. LNCS, vol. 9907, pp. 649–666. Springer, Cham (2016). https://doi.org/10.1007/978-3-319-46487-9_40
8. Noroozi, M., Favaro, P.: Unsupervised learning of visual representations by solving jigsaw puzzles. In: Leibe, B., Matas, J., Sebe, N., Welling, M. (eds.) ECCV 2016, Part VI. LNCS, vol. 9910, pp. 69–84. Springer, Cham (2016). https://doi.org/10.1007/978-3-319-46466-4_5
9. Chen, T., Kornblith, S., Norouzi, M., Hinton, G.: A simple framework for contrastive learning of visual representations. arXiv preprint arXiv:2002.05709 (2020)
10. He, K., Fan, H., Wu, Y., Xie, S., Girshick, R.: Momentum contrast for unsupervised visual representation learning. In: Proceedings of the IEEE/CVF Conference on Computer Vision and Pattern Recognition, pp. 9729–9738 (2020)
11. Caron, M., Bojanowski, P., Joulin, A., Douze, M.: Deep clustering for unsupervised learning of visual features. In: Ferrari, V., Hebert, M., Sminchisescu, C., Weiss, Y. (eds.) Computer Vision – ECCV 2018, Part XIV. LNCS, vol. 11218, pp. 139–156. Springer, Cham (2018). https://doi.org/10.1007/978-3-030-01264-9_9
12. Jenni, S., Jin, H., Favaro, P.: Steering self-supervised feature learning beyond local pixel statistics. In: Proceedings of the IEEE/CVF Conference on Computer Vision and Pattern Recognition, pp. 6408–6417 (2020)
13. Gidaris, S., Singh, P., Komodakis, N.: Unsupervised representation learning by predicting image rotations. arXiv preprint arXiv:1803.07728 (2018)
14. Zhang, L., Qi, G.J., Wang, L., Luo, J.: AET vs. AED: unsupervised representation learning by auto-encoding transformations rather than data. In: Proceedings of the IEEE Conference on Computer Vision and Pattern Recognition, pp. 2547–2555 (2019)
15. Wu, S., Rupprecht, C., Vedaldi, A.: Unsupervised learning of probably symmetric deformable 3D objects from images in the wild. In: Proceedings of the IEEE/CVF Conference on Computer Vision and Pattern Recognition, pp. 1–10 (2020)

16. Nguyen-Phuoc, T., Li, C., Theis, L., Richardt, C., Yang, Y.L.: Hologan: unsupervised learning of 3D representations from natural images. In: Proceedings of the IEEE International Conference on Computer Vision, pp. 7588–7597 (2019)
17. Szabó, A., Meishvili, G., Favaro, P.: Unsupervised generative 3D shape learning from natural images. arXiv preprint arXiv:1910.00287 (2019)
18. Agarwala, A., et al.: Panoramic video textures. In: ACM SIGGRAPH 2005 Papers, pp. 821–827 (2005)
19. Sand, P., Teller, S.: Video matching. ACM Trans. Graph. (TOG) **23**, 592–599 (2004)
20. Tuytelaars, T., Van Gool, L.: Synchronizing video sequences. In: Proceedings of the 2004 IEEE Computer Society Conference on Computer Vision and Pattern Recognition, 2004, CVPR 2004, Volume 1, pp. I-I. IEEE (2004)
21. Wieschollek, P., Freeman, I., Lensch, H.P.: Learning robust video synchronization without annotations. In: 2017 16th IEEE International Conference on Machine Learning and Applications (ICMLA), pp. 92–100. IEEE (2017)
22. Liang, J., Huang, P., Chen, J., Hauptmann, A.: Synchronization for multi-perspective videos in the wild. In: 2017 IEEE International Conference on Acoustics, Speech and Signal Processing (ICASSP), pp. 1592–1596. IEEE (2017)
23. Andriluka, M., Pishchulin, L., Gehler, P., Schiele, B.: 2D human pose estimation: new benchmark and state of the art analysis. In: Proceedings of the IEEE Conference on Computer Vision and Pattern Recognition, pp. 3686–3693 (2014)
24. Li, S., Chan, A.B.: 3D human pose estimation from monocular images with deep convolutional neural network. In: Cremers, D., Reid, I., Saito, H., Yang, M.-H. (eds.) ACCV 2014, Part II. LNCS, vol. 9004, pp. 332–347. Springer, Cham (2015). https://doi.org/10.1007/978-3-319-16808-1_23
25. Li, S., Zhang, W., Chan, A.B.: Maximum-margin structured learning with deep networks for 3d human pose estimation. In: Proceedings of the IEEE International Conference on Computer Vision, pp. 2848–2856 (2015)
26. Tekin, B., Katircioglu, I., Salzmann, M., Lepetit, V., Fua, P.: Structured prediction of 3d human pose with deep neural networks. arXiv preprint arXiv:1605.05180 (2016)
27. Zhou, X., Sun, X., Zhang, W., Liang, S., Wei, Y.: Deep kinematic pose regression. In: Hua, G., Jégou, H. (eds.) ECCV 2016, Part III. LNCS, vol. 9915, pp. 186–201. Springer, Cham (2016). https://doi.org/10.1007/978-3-319-49409-8_17
28. Tekin, B., Márquez-Neila, P., Salzmann, M., Fua, P.: Learning to fuse 2D and 3D image cues for monocular body pose estimation. In: Proceedings of the IEEE International Conference on Computer Vision, pp. 3941–3950 (2017)
29. Pavlakos, G., Zhou, X., Derpanis, K.G., Daniilidis, K.: Harvesting multiple views for marker-less 3D human pose annotations. In: Proceedings of the IEEE Conference on Computer Vision and Pattern Recognition, pp. 6988–6997 (2017)
30. Pavlakos, G., Zhou, X., Derpanis, K.G., Daniilidis, K.: Coarse-to-fine volumetric prediction for single-image 3D human pose. In: Proceedings of the IEEE Conference on Computer Vision and Pattern Recognition, pp. 7025–7034 (2017)
31. Mehta, D., et al.: Monocular 3D human pose estimation in the wild using improved CNN supervision. In: 2017 International Conference on 3D Vision (3DV), pp. 506–516. IEEE (2017)
32. Sun, X., Xiao, B., Wei, F., Liang, S., Wei, Y.: Integral human pose regression. In: Ferrari, V., Hebert, M., Sminchisescu, C., Weiss, Y. (eds.) ECCV 2018, Part VI. LNCS, vol. 11210, pp. 536–553. Springer, Cham (2018). https://doi.org/10.1007/978-3-030-01231-1_33

33. Popa, A.I., Zanfir, M., Sminchisescu, C.: Deep multitask architecture for integrated 2D and 3D human sensing. In: Proceedings of the IEEE Conference on Computer Vision and Pattern Recognition, pp. 6289–6298 (2017)
34. Tome, D., Russell, C., Agapito, L.: Lifting from the deep: Convolutional 3D pose estimation from a single image. In: Proceedings of the IEEE Conference on Computer Vision and Pattern Recognition, pp. 2500–2509 (2017)
35. Mehta, D., et al.: VNECT: Real-time 3D human pose estimation with a single RGB camera. ACM Trans. Graph. (TOG) **36**, 1–14 (2017)
36. Rogez, G., Weinzaepfel, P., Schmid, C.: LCR-net: Localization-classification-regression for human pose. In: Proceedings of the IEEE Conference on Computer Vision and Pattern Recognition, pp. 3433–3441 (2017)
37. Dabral, R., Mundhada, A., Kusupati, U., Afaque, S., Sharma, A., Jain, A.: Learning 3D human pose from structure and motion. In: Ferrari, V., Hebert, M., Sminchisescu, C., Weiss, Y. (eds.) ECCV 2018, Part IX. LNCS, vol. 11213, pp. 679–696. Springer, Cham (2018). https://doi.org/10.1007/978-3-030-01240-3_41
38. Martinez, J., Hossain, R., Romero, J., Little, J.J.: A simple yet effective baseline for 3D human pose estimation. In: Proceedings of the IEEE International Conference on Computer Vision, pp. 2640–2649(2017)
39. Zhou, X., Huang, Q., Sun, X., Xue, X., Wei, Y.: Towards 3D human pose estimation in the wild: a weakly-supervised approach. In: Proceedings of the IEEE International Conference on Computer Vision, pp. 398–407 (2017)
40. Moreno-Noguer, F.: 3D human pose estimation from a single image via distance matrix regression. In: Proceedings of the IEEE Conference on Computer Vision and Pattern Recognition, pp. 2823–2832 (2017)
41. Hossain, M.R.I., Little, J.J.: Exploiting temporal information for 3D human pose estimation. In: Ferrari, V., Hebert, M., Sminchisescu, C., Weiss, Y. (eds.) ECCV 2018, Part X. LNCS, vol. 11214, pp. 69–86. Springer, Cham (2018). https://doi.org/10.1007/978-3-030-01249-6_5
42. Fang, H.S., Xu, Y., Wang, W., Liu, X., Zhu, S.C.: Learning pose grammar to encode human body configuration for 3D pose estimation. In: Thirty-Second AAAI Conference on Artificial Intelligence (2018)
43. Chen, C.H., Ramanan, D.: 3D human pose estimation= 2D pose estimation+ matching. In: Proceedings of the IEEE Conference on Computer Vision and Pattern Recognition, pp. 7035–7043 (2017)
44. Zhao, L., Peng, X., Tian, Y., Kapadia, M., Metaxas, D.N.: Semantic graph convolutional networks for 3D human pose regression. In: Proceedings of the IEEE Conference on Computer Vision and Pattern Recognition, pp. 3425–3435 (2019)
45. Sharma, S., Varigonda, P.T., Bindal, P., Sharma, A., Jain, A.: Monocular 3D human pose estimation by generation and ordinal ranking. In: Proceedings of the IEEE International Conference on Computer Vision, pp. 2325–2334 (2019)
46. Wang, K., Lin, L., Jiang, C., Qian, C., Wei, P.: 3D human pose machines with self-supervised learning. IEEE Trans. Pattern Anal. Mach. Intell. **42**, 1069–1082 (2019)
47. Chen, W., et al.: Synthesizing training images for boosting human 3D pose estimation. In: 2016 Fourth International Conference on 3D Vision (3DV), pp. 479–488. IEEE (2016)
48. Rogez, G., Schmid, C.: Mocap-guided data augmentation for 3D pose estimation in the wild. In: Advances in Neural Information Processing Systems, pp. 3108–3116 (2016)
49. Varol, G., et al.: Learning from synthetic humans. In: Proceedings of the IEEE Conference on Computer Vision and Pattern Recognition, pp. 109–117 (2017)

50. Kocabas, M., Karagoz, S., Akbas, E.: Self-supervised learning of 3D human pose using multi-view geometry. In: Proceedings of the IEEE Conference on Computer Vision and Pattern Recognition, pp. 1077–1086 (2019)
51. Rhodin, H., et al.: Learning monocular 3D human pose estimation from multi-view images. In: Proceedings of the IEEE Conference on Computer Vision and Pattern Recognition, pp. 8437–8446 (2018)
52. Chen, X., Lin, K.Y., Liu, W., Qian, C., Lin, L.: Weakly-supervised discovery of geometry-aware representation for 3D human pose estimation. In: Proceedings of the IEEE Conference on Computer Vision and Pattern Recognition, pp. 10895–10904 (2019)
53. Chen, C.H., Tyagi, A., Agrawal, A., Drover, D., Stojanov, S., Rehg, J.M.: Unsupervised 3D pose estimation with geometric self-supervision. In: Proceedings of the IEEE Conference on Computer Vision and Pattern Recognition, pp. 5714–5724 (2019)
54. Kanazawa, A., Black, M.J., Jacobs, D.W., Malik, J.: End-to-end recovery of human shape and pose. In: Proceedings of the IEEE Conference on Computer Vision and Pattern Recognition, pp. 7122–7131 (2018)
55. Wandt, B., Rosenhahn, B.: Repnet: Weakly supervised training of an adversarial reprojection network for 3D human pose estimation. In: Proceedings of the IEEE Conference on Computer Vision and Pattern Recognition, pp. 7782–7791 (2019)
56. Pavllo, D., Feichtenhofer, C., Grangier, D., Auli, M.: 3D human pose estimation in video with temporal convolutions and semi-supervised training. In: Proceedings of the IEEE Conference on Computer Vision and Pattern Recognition, pp. 7753–7762 (2019)
57. Rhodin, H., Salzmann, M., Fua, P.: Unsupervised geometry-aware representation for 3D human pose estimation. In: Ferrari, V., Hebert, M., Sminchisescu, C., Weiss, Y. (eds.) ECCV 2018, Part X. LNCS, vol. 11214, pp. 765–782. Springer, Cham (2018). https://doi.org/10.1007/978-3-030-01249-6_46
58. Mitra, R., Gundavarapu, N.B., Sharma, A., Jain, A.: Multiview-consistent semi-supervised learning for 3D human pose estimation. In: Proceedings of the IEEE/CVF Conference on Computer Vision and Pattern Recognition, pp. 6907–6916 (2020)
59. He, K., Zhang, X., Ren, S., Sun, J.: Deep residual learning for image recognition. In: Proceedings of the IEEE Conference on Computer Vision and Pattern Recognition, pp. 770–778 (2016)
60. Loshchilov, I., Hutter, F.: Fixing weight decay regularization in adam. arXiv preprint arXiv:1711.05101 (2017)
61. Loshchilov, I., Hutter, F.: SGDR: Stochastic gradient descent with warm restarts. arXiv preprint arXiv:1608.03983 (2016)

Faster, Better and More Detailed: 3D Face Reconstruction with Graph Convolutional Networks

Shiyang Cheng[1], Georgios Tzimiropoulos[1,3], Jie Shen[2(✉)], and Maja Pantic[2]

[1] Samsung AI Center, Cambridge, UK
{shiyang.c,georgios.t}@samsung.com
[2] Imperial College London, London, UK
{js1907,m.pantic}@imperial.ac.uk
[3] Queen Mary University of London, London, UK

Abstract. This paper addresses the problem of 3D face reconstruction from a single image. While available solutions for addressing this problem do exist, to our knowledge, we propose the very first approach which is robust, lightweight and detailed i.e. it can reconstruct fine facial details. Our method is extremely simple and consists of 3 key components: (a) a lightweight non-parametric decoder based on Graph Convolutional Networks (GCNs) trained in a supervised manner to reconstruct *coarse* facial geometry from image-based ResNet features. (b) An extremely lightweight (35K parameters) subnetwork – also based on GCNs – which is trained in an unsupervised manner to refine the output of the first network. (c) A novel feature-sampling mechanism and adaptation layer which injects fine details from the ResNet features of the first network into the second one. Overall, our method is the first one (to our knowledge) to reconstruct detailed facial geometry relying solely on GCNs. We exhaustively compare our method with 7 state-of-the-art methods on 3 datasets reporting state-of-the-art results for all of our experiments, both qualitatively and quantitatively, with our approach being, at the same time, significantly faster.

1 Introduction

3D face reconstruction is the problem of recovering the 3D geometry (3D shape in terms of X, Y, Z coordinates) of a face from one or more 2D images. 3D face reconstruction from a single image has recently witnessed great progress thanks to the advent of end-to-end training of deep neural networks for supervised learning. However, it is still considered a difficult open problem in face analysis as existing solutions are far from being perfect.

In particular, a complete solution for 3D face reconstruction must possess at least the following 3 features: (a) Being robust: it should work for arbitrary facial

Electronic supplementary material The online version of this chapter (https://doi.org/10.1007/978-3-030-69541-5_12) contains supplementary material, which is available to authorized users.

poses, illumination conditions, facial expressions, and occlusions. (b) Being efficient: it should reconstruct a large number of 3D vertices without using excessive computational resources. (c) Being detailed: it should capture fine facial details (e.g.. wrinkles). To our knowledge, there is no available solution having all aforementioned features. For example, VRN [1] is robust but it is neither efficient nor detailed. PRNet [2] is both robust and efficient but it is not detailed. CMD [3] is lightweight but not detailed. The seminal work of [4] and the very recent DF^{2}Net [5] produce detailed reconstructions but it is not robust. Our goal in this paper is to make a step forward towards solving all three aforementioned problems.

To address this challenge, we propose a method which effectively combines the favourable properties of many of the methods mentioned above. In particular, our framework – consisting of two connected subnetworks as shown in Fig. 1 – innovates in the following 4 ways:

1. Our first subnetwork is a non-parametric method, like [1], which is trained to perform direct regression of the 3D coordinates in a supervised manner and works robustly for in-the-wild facial images in large poses, expressions and arbitrary illuminations. Contrary to [1] though, we use Graph Convolutional Networks (GCN) to perform regression in a very lightweight manner.
2. Our method also has a second subnetwork, like [4] and [5], which is trained in an unsupervised manner – using a Shape-from-Shading (SfS) loss – to refine the output of the first subnetwork by adding missing facial details. Contrary to [4] and [5] though, we implemented this subnetwork in a extremely lightweight manner using a second GCN, the vertices of which are in full correspondence with the vertices of our first subnetwork.
3. We further improve the ability of our method to reconstruct fine facial details by introducing a novel feature-sampling mechanism and adaptation layer which injects fine details from the mid-level features of the encoder of the first subnetwork into the decoder of the second subnetwork one.
4. We extensively compare our method with 7 state-of-the-art methods on 3 datasets and report better results for all of our experiments, both quantitatively and quantitatively, with our approach being, at the same time, significantly faster than most.

2   Related Work

Dense 3D face reconstruction from a single image is a heavily studied topic in the area of face analysis. In the following section, we will briefly review related works from the Deep Learning era.

Parametric (3DMM) Methods. A large number of methods for 3D reconstruction build upon 3D Morphable Models (3DMMs) [6,7] which was the method of choice for 3D face modelling prior to the advent of Deep Learning.

Early approaches focused on supervised learning for 3DMM parameter estimation using ground truth 3D scans or synthesized data. 3DDFA [8] iteratively applies a CNN to estimate the 3DMM parameters using the 2D image and a 3D representation produced at the previous iteration as input. The authors in [9] fit a 3DMM into a 2D image using a very deep CNN, and describe a method to construct a large dataset with 3D pseudo-groundtruth. A similar 3DMM fitting approach was proposed in [10]. Parameter estimation in 3DMM space is, in general, a difficult optimization problem for CNNs. As a result, these methods (a) fail to produce good results for difficult facial images with large poses, expressions and occlusions while (b) in many cases the reconstructions fail to capture the shape characteristics of the face properly. We avoid both obstacles by using a non-parametric model for our first subnetwork which uses a GCN to learn directly to regress the 3D coordinates of the facial geometry without requiring to perform any 3DMM parameter estimation.

Beyond supervised learning, several methods also attempt to fit or even learn a 3DMM from in-the-wild images in an unsupervised manner (i.e. without 3D ground truth data) via image reconstruction. MOFA [11] combines a CNN encoder with an hand-crafted differentiable model-based decoder that analytically implements image formation which is then used for learning from in-the-wild images. This idea was further extended in [12] which proposed an improved multi-level model that uses a 3DMM for regularization and a learned – in a self-supervised manner – corrective space for out-of-space generalization which goes beyond the predefined low-dimensional 3DMM face prior. A similar idea was also proposed in [13] with a different network and loss design. The authors in [14] propose to learn a non-linear 3DMM, where texture and shape reconstruction is performed with neural network decoders (rather than linear operations as in 3DMM) learned directly from data. This work was extended in [15] which proposes to learn coarse shape and albedo for ameliorating the effect of strong regularisations as well as promoting high-fidelity facial details. The last two methods do not use a linear model for shape and texture however. They are trained in a semi-supervised fashion where 3DMM results for the 300W-LP dataset [8] are used to constrain the learning.

All the aforementioned methods employ at some point a 3DMM (either explicitly or as regularisation), and, as such, inevitably the reconstruction result does not capture well identity-related shape characteristics and is biased towards the mean face. Furthermore, image reconstruction losses provide an indirect way to learn a model which has not been shown effective for completely unconstrained images in arbitrary poses. Our method bypasses these problems by using non-parametric supervised learning to reconstruct coarse facial geometry (notably without a 3DMM) and non-parametric unsupervised learning via image reconstruction to recover the missing facial details.

Non Parametric Methods. There are also a few methods which avoid the use and thus the limitations of parametric models for 3D face reconstruction. By performing direct volumetric regression, VRN [1] is shown to work well for facial images of arbitrary poses. Nonetheless, the method regresses a large volume which is redundant, memory intensive and does not scale well with the number of vertices. Our method avoids these problems by using a GCN to perform direct regression of surface vertices. GCNs for 3D body reconstruction were used in [16].

But this method can capture only coarse geometry and cannot be applied for detailed face reconstruction. Moreover, we used a different GCN formulation based on spiral convolutions. The semi-parametric method of [3] combines GCNs with an unsupervised image reconstruction loss for model training. Owing to the use of GCNs the method is lightweight but not able to capture fine details.

Shape-from-Shading (SfS) Based Methods. Shape-from-Shading (SfS) is a classical technique for decomposing shape, reflectance and illumination from a single image. SfS methods have been demonstrated to be capable of reconstructing facial details beyond the space of 3DMMs [4,5,17–25]. SfS is a highly ill-posed problem and as such SfS methods require regularisation. For example, in Pix2vertex [18], a smoothness constraint was applied on the predicted depth map. The seminal work of [4] was the first one to incorporate an unsupervised image reconstruction loss based on SfS principles for end-to-end detailed 3D face reconstruction. It used a subnetwork trained in a supervised manner to firstly estimate a coarse face (sometimes also called *proxy face*) using a 3DMM and then another subnetwork trained in a unsupervised manner using SfS principles to refine reconstruction. A notable follow-up work is the multi-stage DF^2Net [5] which predicts depth maps in a supervised manner and then refines the result in two more SfS-based stages, where all stages are trained with progressively more detailed datasets. Notably, our method is inspired by [4], but it is based on non-parametric estimation. In addition, ours is based on GCNs, and thus is simpler, faster, and more robust compared to both [4] and [5].

Graph Convolution Networks (GCNs) Based Methods. Graph Convolution Networks (GCNs) are a set of methods that try to define various convolution operations on graphs. They include but are not limited to spectral methods [26–28], local spatial methods [29,30] and soft attention [31–33]. As 3D face mesh is also a graph, applications of GCNs on 3D face modeling [34–37] are emerging. The work of [35] was the first one to build a 3D-to-3D face autoencoder based on spectral convolutions. More recently, the work of [34] employed the spiral convolution network of [29] to build another 3D-to-3D face autoencoder. These works focus on a 3D-to-3D setting. To our knowledge, we are the first to employ spiral convolutions for 3D face reconstruction from a single 2D image. More importantly, we are the first to show how to integrate GCNs with SfS-based losses for recovering facial details in an unsupervised manner.

3 Method

3.1 Overview of Our Framework

The proposed framework is illustrated in Fig. 1, it consists of two connected subnetworks: the first one is an encoder-decoder designed to reconstruct coarse 3D facial geometry. It takes advantage of a simple and light-weight spiral convolution decoder to directly regress the 3D coordinates of a face mesh with arbitrary pose (i.e. in an non-parametric fashion). This mesh will be used to sample and provide features for the second network. Our second network is another GCN that utilises

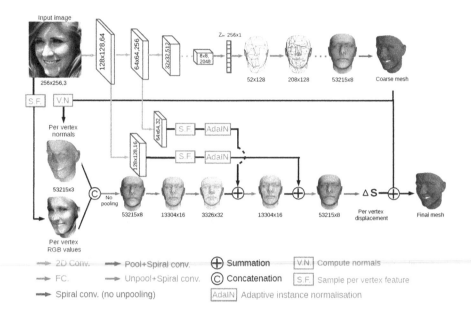

Fig. 1. Overview of our framework. It consists of two connected sub-networks: (1) a coarse 3D facial mesh reconstruction network with a CNN encoder and a GCN decoder; (2) a GCN-based mesh refinement network for recovering the fine facial details. We also device a feature sampling and adaptation layer which injects fine details from the CNN encoder to the refinement network.

the normals of the coarse face and the per vertex RGB values sampled from the input image to estimate per vertex shape displacements (i.e. again in a non-parametric fashion) that are used to synthesise facial geometric details. We then simply superimpose the predicted shape displacement on the coarse mesh to obtain our final 3D face. We also propose a novel feature-sampling mechanism and adaptation layer which injects fine details from the features of the first network into the layers of the second one.

3.2   Coarse 3D Face Reconstruction with GCN

We design an encoder-decoder network trained to reconstruct the coarse 3D facial geometry from a single image in a fully supervised manner. Note that the reconstructed face at this stage is coarse primarily because of the dataset employed to train the network (300W-LP [8]), and not because of some limitation of our decoder. We emphasize that the network is trained to directly regress the 3D coordinates and does not perform any parameter estimation. This is in contrary to many existing non-linear 3DMMs fitting strategies [11, 14, 38–40], where the decoder is trained to regress 3DMMs parameters. To our knowledge, we are the first to leverage a GCN, and in particular, based on spiral convolutions [29] to directly regress a 3D facial mesh from in-the-wild 2D images[1].

As shown in the upper half of Fig. 1, given an input image $\mathbf{I}$, we first employ a CNN encoder (ResNet [41] or MobileNetV2 [42]) to encode this image into a feature vector $\mathbf{z}_{im} = E(\mathbf{I})$. We then employ a mesh decoder D built using the spiral convolution operator of [29] described below. The feature vector $\mathbf{z}_{im}$ is firstly transformed into a mesh-like structure (each node represents a 128-d feature) using a FC layer. Then, it is unpooled and convolved five times until reaching the full resolution of the target mesh. Lastly, another spiral convolution is performed to generate the coarse mesh.

Spiral Convolution and Mesh Pooling. We define the face mesh as a graph $\mathcal{M} = (\mathcal{V}, \mathcal{E})$, in which $\mathcal{V} = \{\mathbf{x}_1, \ldots, \mathbf{x}_n\}$, and $\mathcal{E}$ denote the sets of vertices and edges, respectively. We further denote the vertex feature as $f(\mathbf{x}) \in \mathcal{R}^C$. We built our GCN using the spiral convolution of [29] due to its simplicity: to perform a convolution-like operation over the graph, a local vertex ordering is defined using the spiral operator proposed in [29]. Specifically, for each vertex $\mathbf{x} \in \mathcal{V}$, the operator outputs a spiral S which is an ordered sequence of fixed length of L neighbouring vertices as shown in Fig. 2. Since the order and length is fixed, one can concatenate the features from all vertices in S into a vector $f_S \in \mathcal{R}^{(C \times L) \times 1}$ and define the output of a set of C_{out} filters stored as rows in matrix $\mathcal{W} \in \mathcal{R}^{C_{out} \times (C \times L)}$ as $f_{out} = \mathcal{W} f_S$. This is equivalent to applying a set of filters on a local image window. Furthermore, since the vertices $\mathcal{V}$ of the facial mesh are ordered, this process can be applied sequentially for all $\mathbf{x} \in \mathcal{V}$. This defines a convolution over the graph. Finally, for mesh pooling and unpooling, we follow the practice introduced in [35].

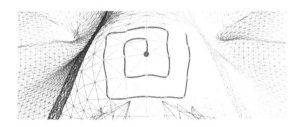

Fig. 2. An example of a spiral neighborhood around a vertex on the facial mesh.

Loss Function. We use the $\mathcal{L}_1$ reconstruction error between the groundtruth 3D mesh $\mathbf{S}_{gt} \in \mathcal{R}^{n \times 3}$ and our predicted mesh $\mathbf{S}_{coarse} = D(E(\mathbf{I}))$:

$$\mathcal{L}_{coarse} = \sum_{i=1}^{N} |D(E(\mathbf{I})) - \mathbf{S}_{gt}|, \tag{1}$$

---

[1] The method of [3] is semi-parametric as it tries to recover 22 parameters for pose and lighting.

where N is the total number of training examples. Note that we do not define any additional scale, pose nor expression parameters in our network. We also observe that the spiral mesh decoder tends to produce smooth results, thus there is no need to define an extra smoothness loss.

3.3   Unsupervised Detailed Reconstruction

Spiral Mesh Refinement Network. As depicted in the lower half of Fig. 1, we devise a mesh refinement network for synthesising fine details over the coarse mesh. Again, our network is fully based on spiral convolution networks. There are two inputs, the first one is the per vertex RGB values sampled from the input image. Specifically, we project the coarse mesh back to the image space and sample the corresponding RGB values using bilinear interpolation. Here, orthographic projection is chosen for simplicity. The second input is the vertex normals of the coarse mesh which provides a strong prior for the detailed 3D shape of the target face. Note that we prefer vertex normals over xyz coordinates because: (1) vertex normals are scale and translation invariant; (2) vertex normals have a fix range of value (*i.e.*, $[-1, 1]$). Both properties lower the training difficulty of our refinement network. These two inputs are concatenated and then convolved and pooled 3 and 2 times respectively until reaching $\sim 1/16$ of the full mesh resolution. Following this, the feature mesh is unpooled and convolved twice. During this process, we adapt and inject intermediate features from the 2D image encoder to the refinement network (we will elaborate this module in the next paragraph). Finally, after another spiral convolution is applied, we obtain the facial details in the form of per vertex shape displacement values $\Delta\mathbf{S}$. We apply the displacement over the coarse mesh to obtain the final reconstruction result, $\mathbf{S}_{final} = \mathbf{S}_{coarse} + \Delta\mathbf{S}$.

Image-Level Feature Sampling and Adaptation Layer. One of the main contributions of our paper is the utilization of fine CNN features from the image encoder into our refinement GCN. More specifically, and as can be seen in Fig. 1, in our framework the coarse and fine networks are bridged by injecting intermediate features from the 2D image encoder into the spiral mesh refinement network. Although this idea is simple, we found it is non-trivial to design an appropriate module for this purpose, because the features from these two networks are coming from different domains (RGB and 3D mesh). We therefore introduce a novel feature-sampling mechanism and adaptation layer to address this problem which we describe here with a concrete example: Given an image feature $\mathbf{f}_{im} \in \mathbb{R}^{128 \times 128 \times 64}$ returned by the first convolution block, we first perform a 1×1 convolution to ensure it has the same number of channels as the target feature $\mathbf{f}_{mesh} \in \mathbb{R}^{13304 \times 16}$ in the refinement network. Next, we sample the feature using the predicted mesh from the coarse reconstruction network. Specifically, we downsample the coarse mesh $\mathbf{S}_{coarse} \in \mathbb{R}^{53215 \times 3}$ to obtain a new mesh $\mathbf{S}_{new} \in \mathbb{R}^{13304 \times 3}$ with identical number of vertices as $\mathbf{f}_{mesh}$, after which, we project (and resize) $\mathbf{S}_{new}$ onto the 128×128 image plane to sample from feature tensor $\mathbf{f}_{im}$ using bilinear interpolation. Nevertheless, the extracted feature $\tilde{\mathbf{f}}_{im} \in \mathbb{R}^{13304 \times 16}$ cannot be used directly, as it comes from another domain, so we design an extra layer to adapt this feature to the target domain. Adpative Instance Normalisation (AdaIN) [43] is chosen for this purpose. Essentially, AdaIN aligns the channel-wise mean and variance of the source features with those of the target feature (this simple approach has been shown effective in the task of style transfer). We normalise the extracted feature $\tilde{\mathbf{f}}_{im}$ as:

$$AdaIN(\tilde{\mathbf{f}}_{im}, \mathbf{f}_{mesh}) = \sigma(\mathbf{f}_{mesh}) \left(\frac{\tilde{\mathbf{f}}_{im} - \mu(\tilde{\mathbf{f}}_{im})}{\sigma(\tilde{\mathbf{f}}_{im})} \right) + \mu(\mathbf{f}_{mesh}), \qquad (2)$$

where $\mu(\cdot)$ and $\sigma(\cdot)$ are the channel-wise mean and variance, respectively. Note that we also tried to replace AdaIN with batch normalization [44], unfortunately, our networks fail to produce sensible results with it. Finally, we add the two features together and feed them into the next spiral convolution layer.

Loss Function. As there does not exist detailed ground truth shape for images in-the-wild, we train the refinement network in an unsupervised manner using Shape-from-Shading (SfS) loss. SfS loss is defined as the $\mathcal{L}_2$ norm of the difference between the original intensity image and the reflected irradiance $\tilde{\mathbf{I}}$. According to [5,45], $\tilde{\mathbf{I}}$ can be computed as:

$$\tilde{\mathbf{I}}(\mathbf{c}^*, \mathbf{N}, \mathbf{A}) = \mathbf{A} \sum_{i=1}^{9} \mathbf{c}_i^* \mathbf{Y}_i(\mathbf{N}), \qquad (3)$$

where $\mathbf{N}$ is the unit normals of the predicted depth image and $\mathbf{A}$ is the albedo map of the target image (estimated using SfSNet [46]), $\mathbf{Y}_i(\mathbf{N})$ are the Spherical Harmonics (SH) basis functions computed from the predicted unit normals $\mathbf{N}$, and $\mathbf{c}^*$ are the second-order SH coefficients that can be precomputed using the original image intensity $\mathbf{I}$ and depth $\mathbf{N}_{gt}$ image:

$$\mathbf{c}^* = \arg \min_{\mathbf{c}} \| \mathbf{A} \sum_{i=1}^{9} \mathbf{c}_i \mathbf{Y}_i(\mathbf{N}_{gt}) - \mathbf{I} \|_2^2. \qquad (4)$$

In practice, we calculate $\mathbf{N}_{gt}$ from the fitted coarse mesh. Different from [5, 18], our model predicts a 3D mesh rather than a depth image, therefore we need to render our final mesh to obtain the unit normals in image space. To achieve this, we first compute the vertex normals of our predicted mesh $\mathbf{S}_{final}$, and then we render the normals to the image using a differentiable renderer [47] to get the normal image $\mathbf{N}$. Our SfS refinement loss function can be written as:

$$\mathcal{L}_{refine} = \| \tilde{\mathbf{I}}(\mathbf{c}^*, \mathbf{N}, \mathbf{A}) - \mathbf{I} \|_2. \qquad (5)$$

Our refinement loss accounts for the difference between the target and reconstructed image using shape-from-shading, and drives the refinement network to reconstruct fine geometric details.

3.4   Network Architecture and Training Details

This section describes the training data and procedure. More details about the network architectures used are provided in the supplementary material.

Training Data and Pre-processing. We train the proposed networks using only 300W-LP database [8] which contains over 60K large-pose facial images synthesized from 300W database [48]. Although the *ground truth* 3D meshes of 300W-LP come from a conventional optimisation-based 3DMM fitting method, they can be used to provide a reliable estimation of the coarse target face, which is then refined by our unsupervised refinement network. Note that we randomly leave out around 10% of the data for validation purposes, and the rest of the data (around 55K images and meshes) are all used for training. For each image, we compute the face bounding box using the ground truth 3D mesh, and then use the bounding box to crop and resize the image to 256×256. During training, we apply several data augmentation techniques that are proven useful in [2]. They include random scaling from 0.85 to 1.15, random in-plane rotation from -45 to 45 degrees, and random 10% translation w.r.t image width and height.

Training Procedure. Because the refinement network requires a reasonable estimation of the coarse mesh, the training of our model consists of two stages. Note that we always use the same training data. The first stage is to train the coarse face reconstruction network only. For this, we use SGD with momentum [49] with an initial learning rate of 0.05 and momentum value of 0.9. We train the coarse network for 120 epochs, and for every two epochs, we decay the learning rate by a ratio of 0.9. The second stage is to jointly train the coarse networks and refinement networks. We do not freeze any layers during this stage, and as our pipeline is fully differentiable, the encoder and the decoder of the coarse network can also adapt and improve with the extra SfS loss. During the second stage training, both $\mathcal{L}_{coarse}$ and $\mathcal{L}_{refine}$ are used to drive the network training. We found that no additional weight balance is needed between them. The second stage is also trained with SGD with momentum equal to 0.9, but the initial learning rate is 0.008. We train the whole network for 100 epochs. Similarly, for every two epochs, we decay the learning rate by a ratio of 0.9. All the models are trained using two 12 GB NVidia GeForce RTX 2080 GPUs with Tensorflow [50].

4   Experiments

4.1   Evaluation Databases

We evaluated the accuracy of our method on the following databases.

Florence. Florence [51] is a widely used database to evaluate face reconstruction quality. It contains 53 high-resolution recordings of different subjects, and the subjects only show neutral expression in the controlled environment recording.

BU3DFE. BU3DFE [52] is the first large scale 3D facial expression database. It contains a neutral face and 6 articulated expressions captured from 100 adults. Since there are 4 different intensities per expression per subject, a total of 2,500 meshes are provided. These 3D faces have been cropped and aligned beforehand.

4DFAB. 4DFAB [53] is the largest dynamic 3D facial expression database. It contains 1.8M 3D meshes captured from 180 individuals. The recordings capture rich posed and spontaneous expressions. We used a subset of 1,482 meshes that display either neutral or spontaneous expressions from different subjects.

AFLW2000-3D. AFLW2000-3D [8] contains 68 3D landmarks of the first 2,000 examples from the AFLW database [54]. We used this database to evaluate our method on the task of sparse 3D face alignment.

4.2 Evaluation Protocol

For each database, we generated test data by rendering ground truth textured mesh with different poses, *i.e.*, $[-20°, 0°, 20°]$ for pitch, and $[-80°, -40°, 0°, 40°, 80°]$ for yaw angles. Orthographic projection was used to project the rotated mesh. Each mesh produced 15 different facial renderings for testing. For each rendering, we also cast arbitrary light from a random direction with a random intensity to make it challenging. We selected the Normalised Mean Error(NME) to measure the accuracy of 3D reconstruction. It is defined as:

$$NME(\mathbf{S}_{pred}, \mathbf{S}_{gt}) = \frac{1}{n} \sum_{i \in \mathcal{S}_{gt}} \frac{\|\mathbf{S}^i_{pred} - \mathbf{S}^i_{gt}\|^2}{d_{occ}}, \tag{6}$$

where $\mathbf{S}_{pred}$ and $\mathbf{S}_{gt}$ are the predicted and ground truth 3D meshes correspondingly, n is the number of vertices, and d_{occ} is the outer interoccular distance. To provide a fair comparison for all the methods, we only use the visible vertices of $\mathbf{S}_{gt}$ to calculate the errors. We denote this set of vertices as $\mathcal{S}_{gt}$. Z-buffering is employed to determine the visibility. Since there is no point-to-point correspondence between $\mathbf{S}_{pred}$ and $\mathbf{S}_{gt}$, we apply Iterative Closest Points (ICP) [55,56] to align $\mathbf{S}_{pred}$ to $\mathbf{S}_{gt}$ to retrieve the correspondence for each visible vertex in $\mathbf{S}_{gt}$. Note that we do not apply the full optimal transform estimated by ICP to the predicted mesh. This is because it is important to test whether each method can correctly predict the target's global pose.

4.3 Ablation Study

For our ablation study, we trained different variants of our method and tested them on the Florence dataset [51]. The results are shown in Fig. 3 in the form of cumulative error curves (CEDs) and NMEs. We start by training a variant of our method that only contains the first GCN for coarse mesh reconstruction. We then train a second variant by adding the second GCN for detailed reconstruction (which we dubbed "SfS" in the figure), and, finally, we add the image-level feature sampling and adaptation layers for additional facial detail injection ("skip" in the figure). The latter represents the full version of our method.

As illustrated in Fig. 3 (left), adding each new component enables the model to achieve higher accuracy. In Fig. 3 (right), we also show examples of the mesh reconstructed by the aforementioned variants and demonstrate that each

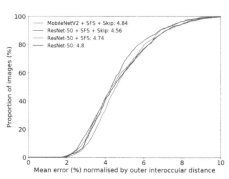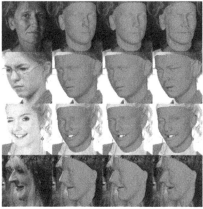

Fig. 3. Ablation study on the reconstruction performance of our proposed method, performed on Florence database [51]. Left shows the CED curves and NMEs of the variants. Right shows some examples they produced. From left to right, we show: the input images and outputs given by the baseline GCN model with ResNet50 image encoder, ResNet50+SfS, and ResNet50+SfS+Skip (the full model), respectively.

component in our method can indeed boost the model's capability in reconstructing fine details (notice the differences in wrinkles). Last but not least, as shown in Fig. 3, switching the image encoder backbone to MobileNet V2 resulted in a small drop in accuracy but it can also drastically decrease the model size and inference time, as shown in Table 2.

4.4 3D Face Alignment Results

Our results on the AFLW2000-3D [8] dataset are shown in Table 1. Our approach, when using ResNet50 as the image encoder, significantly outperformed all other methods. Even after switching to the much lighter MobileNet-v2 as the encoder backbone, our method still achieved very good accuracy which is only slightly worse than that of PRNet [2], the next best-performing method.

Table 1. Face alignment results on the AFLW2000-3D dataset, we reported the average mean error (%) normalised by the face bounding box.

Method	N3DMM [38]	3DDFA [8]	PRNet [2]	CMD [3]	Ours (MobileNetV2)	Ours (ResNet50)
NME	4.12	3.79	3.62	3.98	3.65	**3.39**

4.5 3D Face Reconstruction Results

Our results on Florence [51], BU3DFE [52], and 4DFAB [53] are shown (from left to right) in Fig. 4. On each dataset, we show both the CED curves computed from all test examples (top) and the pose-specific NMEs (bottom). As

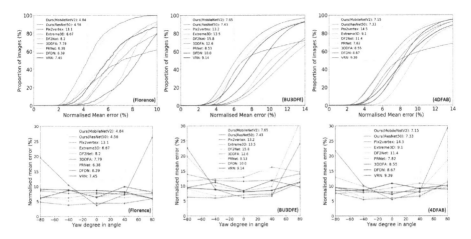

Fig. 4. 3D face reconstruction results on, from left to right Florence [51], BU3DFE [52], and 4DFAB [53] datasets. In each column, the top row shows the CED curves and NMEs of various methods, while the bottom row shows the pose-wise NMEs.

Table 2. Inference speed and model size comparison.

Method	Inference speed (ms per sample)		Total model size (MB)
	Main model (s)	Post-processing	
DF^{2}Net [5]	40.4		222
Extreme3D [23]	230.9	14328.9	503
DFDN [19]	38762.7		1982
3DDFA [8,57]	6.7		45
PRNet [2]	19.4		153
VRN [1]	16.4	220.2	1415
Pix2vertex [18]	40.0	248016.5	1663
CMD [3]	**3.1**		93
Ours (ResNet50)	10.8		209
Ours (MobileNetV2)	6.2		**37**

For CMD [3], we just show the values reported in their paper as the authors did not release their code and model.

the figure shows, our method (with ResNet50) performed the best in all three test datasets. When switching to MobileNet-v2, our method still outperformed all other methods. The NME of our method is also consistently low across all poses, demonstrating the robustness of our approach. This is in contrast to Pix2Vertex [18] and DF^{2}Net [5], which performed relatively well when the face is at a frontal pose but significant worse for large-pose cases. For PRNet [2], 3DDFA [8], and VRN[1], although they achieved decent quantitative results (in terms of CED and NMEs), they lack the ability to reconstruct fine facial details.

200 S. Cheng et al.

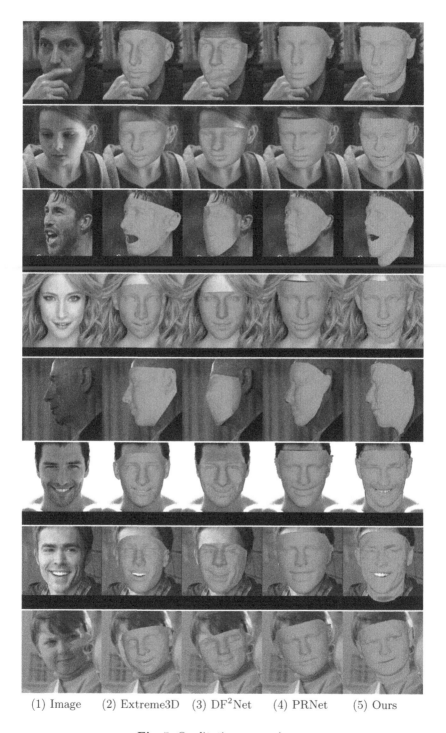

(1) Image   (2) Extreme3D   (3) DF^{2}Net   (4) PRNet   (5) Ours

Fig. 5. Qualitative comparisons.

4.6   Qualitative Evaluation

Figure 5 shows qualitative reconstruction results produced by our method (with a ResNet50 encoder) and other competitive methods. In particular, we compare against Extreme3D, PRNet and DF^{2}Net (comparisons with more methods are provided in the supplementary material). The first two methods are among the best performing in our quantitative evaluations while the latter is one of the best methods for reconstructing fine details. From the figure, we observe that our method is the best being both robust and able to capture fine facial details at the same time.

4.7   Comparisons of Inference Speed and Model Size

We compare the inference speed and model size of our approach to previous methods. The tests were conducted on a machine with an Intel Core i7-7820X CPU @3.6GHz, a GeForce GTX 1080 graphics card, and 96 GB of main memory. For all methods (for CMD [3], no available implementation exists, so we used the result from their paper), we used the implementation provided by the original authors. For more details see supplementary material. As most methods consist of multiple stages involving more than one model, for a fair comparison, we report the *end-to-end* inference time and *total size* of all models (i.e., weights of networks, basis of 3DMMs, etc.) that are needed to estimate the face mesh from an input facial image. As shown in Table 2, our approach is among the fastest, taking only 10.8 ms/6.2 ms (when using ResNet50/MobileNet v2, respectively) to reconstruct a 3D face. Our method also has the smallest model size when using MobileNet-v2 as the image encoder.

5   Conclusions

We presented a robust, lightweight and detailed 3D face reconstruction method. Our framework consists of 3 key components: (a) a lightweight non-parametric GCNs decoder to reconstruct coarse facial geometry from image encoder; (b) a lightweight GCNs model to refine the output of the first network in an unsupervised manner; (c) a novel feature-sampling mechanism and adaptation layer which injects fine details from the image encoder into the refinement network. To our knowledge, we are the first to reconstruct high-fidelity facial geometry relying solely on GCNs. We compared our method with 7 state-of-the-art methods on Florence, BU3DFE and 4DFAB datasets, and reported state-of-the-art results for the experiments, both quantitatively and quantitatively. We also compared the speed and model size of our method against other methods, and showed that it can run faster than real-time, while at the same time, being extremely lightweight (with MobileNet-V2 as backbone, our model size is 37 MB).

References

1. Jackson, A.S., Bulat, A., Argyriou, V., Tzimiropoulos, G.: Large pose 3D face reconstruction from a single image via direct volumetric cnn regression. In: Proceedings of the IEEE International Conference on Computer Vision, pp. 1031–1039 (2017)
2. Feng, Y., Wu, F., Shao, X., Wang, Y., Zhou, X.: Joint 3D face reconstruction and dense alignment with position map regression network. In: Ferrari, V., Hebert, M., Sminchisescu, C., Weiss, Y. (eds.) ECCV 2018, Part XIV. LNCS, vol. 11218, pp. 557–574. Springer, Cham (2018). https://doi.org/10.1007/978-3-030-01264-9_33
3. Zhou, Y., Deng, J., Kotsia, I., Zafeiriou, S.: Dense 3D face decoding over 2500FPS: joint texture & shape convolutional mesh decoders. In: Proceedings of the IEEE Conference on Computer Vision and Pattern Recognition, pp. 1097–1106 (2019)
4. Richardson, E., Sela, M., Or-El, R., Kimmel, R.: Learning detailed face reconstruction from a single image. In: Proceedings of the IEEE Conference on Computer Vision and Pattern Recognition, pp. 1259–1268 (2017)
5. Zeng, X., Peng, X., Qiao, Y.: Df2net: A dense-fine-finer network for detailed 3D face reconstruction. In: Proceedings of the IEEE International Conference on Computer Vision, pp. 2315–2324 (2019)
6. Blanz, V., Vetter, T.: A morphable model for the synthesis of 3D faces. In: Proceedings of the 26th annual conference on Computer graphics and interactive techniques, pp. 187–194 (1999)
7. Paysan, P., Knothe, R., Amberg, B., Romdhani, S., Vetter, T.: A 3D face model for pose and illumination invariant face recognition. In: IEEE AVSS (2009)
8. Zhu, X., Lei, Z., Li, S.Z., et al.: Face alignment in full pose range: a 3D total solution. IEEE Trans. Pattern Anal. Mach. Intell. **41**, 78–92 (2017)
9. Tuan Tran, A., Hassner, T., Masi, I., Medioni, G.: Regressing robust and discriminative 3D morphable models with a very deep neural network. In: Proceedings of the IEEE Conference on Computer Vision and Pattern Recognition, pp. 5163–5172 (2017)
10. Dou, P., Shah, S.K., Kakadiaris, I.A.: End-to-end 3D face reconstruction with deep neural networks. In: Proceedings of the IEEE Conference on Computer Vision and Pattern Recognition, pp. 5908–5917 (2017)
11. Tewari, A., et al.: Mofa: model-based deep convolutional face autoencoder for unsupervised monocular reconstruction. In: Proceedings of the IEEE International Conference on Computer Vision Workshops, pp. 1274–1283 (2017)
12. Tewari, A., et al.: Self-supervised multi-level face model learning for monocular reconstruction at over 250 hz. In: Proceedings of the IEEE Conference on Computer Vision and Pattern Recognition, pp. 2549–2559 (2018)
13. Genova, K., Cole, F., Maschinot, A., Sarna, A., Vlasic, D., Freeman, W.T.: Unsupervised training for 3D morphable model regression. In: Proceedings of the IEEE Conference on Computer Vision and Pattern Recognition, pp. 8377–8386 (2018)
14. Tran, L., Liu, X.: Nonlinear 3D face morphable model. In: Proceedings of the IEEE Conference on Computer Vision and Pattern Recognition, pp. 7346–7355 (2018)
15. Tran, L., Liu, F., Liu, X.: Towards high-fidelity nonlinear 3D face morphable model. In: Proceedings of the IEEE Conference on Computer Vision and Pattern Recognition, pp. 1126–1135 (2019)
16. Kolotouros, N., Pavlakos, G., Daniilidis, K.: Convolutional mesh regression for single-image human shape reconstruction. In: Proceedings of the IEEE Conference on Computer Vision and Pattern Recognition, pp. 4501–4510 (2019)

17. Patel, A., Smith, W.A.: Driving 3D morphable models using shading cues. Pattern Recognit. **45**, 1993–2004 (2012)
18. Sela, M., Richardson, E., Kimmel, R.: Unrestricted facial geometry reconstruction using image-to-image translation. In: Proceedings of the IEEE International Conference on Computer Vision, pp. 1576–1585 (2017)
19. Chen, A., Chen, Z., Zhang, G., Mitchell, K., Yu, J.: Photo-realistic facial details synthesis from single image. In: Proceedings of the IEEE International Conference on Computer Vision, pp. 9429–9439 (2019)
20. Garrido, P., Valgaerts, L., Wu, C., Theobalt, C.: Reconstructing detailed dynamic face geometry from monocular video. ACM Trans. Graph. **32**, 158:1–158:10 (2013)
21. Li, Y., Ma, L., Fan, H., Mitchell, K.: Feature-preserving detailed 3D face reconstruction from a single image. In: Proceedings of the 15th ACM SIGGRAPH European Conference on Visual Media Production, pp. 1–9 (2018)
22. Roth, J., Tong, Y., Liu, X.: Unconstrained 3D face reconstruction. In: Proceedings of the IEEE Conference on Computer Vision and Pattern Recognition, pp. 2606–2615 (2015)
23. Tran, A.T., Hassner, T., Masi, I., Paz, E., Nirkin, Y., Medioni, G.G.: Extreme 3D face reconstruction: seeing through occlusions. In: CVPR, pp. 3935–3944 (2018)
24. Jiang, L., Zhang, J., Deng, B., Li, H., Liu, L.: 3D face reconstruction with geometry details from a single image. IEEE Trans. Image Process. **27**, 4756–4770 (2018)
25. Abrevaya, V.F., Boukhayma, A., Torr, P.H., Boyer, E.: Cross-modal deep face normals with deactivable skip connections. In: Proceedings of the IEEE/CVF Conference on Computer Vision and Pattern Recognition, pp. 4979–4989 (2020)
26. Defferrard, M., Bresson, X., Vandergheynst, P.: Convolutional neural networks on graphs with fast localized spectral filtering. In: NIPS (2016)
27. Kipf, T.N., Welling, M.: Semi-supervised classification with graph convolutional networks. In: ICLR (2017)
28. Klicpera, J., Weißenberger, S., Günnemann, S.: Diffusion improves graph learning. In: Conference on Neural Information Processing Systems (NeurIPS) (2019)
29. Lim, I., Dielen, A., Campen, M., Kobbelt, L.: A simple approach to intrinsic correspondence learning on unstructured 3D meshes. In: Leal-Taixé, L., Roth, S. (eds.) ECCV 2018, Part III. LNCS, vol. 11131, pp. 349–362. Springer, Cham (2019). https://doi.org/10.1007/978-3-030-11015-4_26
30. Fey, M., Lenssen, J.E., Weichert, F., Müller, H.: Splinecnn: Fast geometric deep learning with continuous B-spline kernels. In: CVPR (2018)
31. Veličković, P., Cucurull, G., Casanova, A., Romero, A., Lio, P., Bengio, Y.: Graph attention networks. arXiv preprint arXiv:1710.10903 (2017)
32. Bai, S., Zhang, F., Torr, P.H.: Hypergraph convolution and hypergraph attention. arXiv preprint arXiv:1901.08150 (2019)
33. Verma, N., Boyer, E., Verbeek, J.: Feastnet: feature-steered graph convolutions for 3D shape analysis. In: CVPR (2018)
34. Bouritsas, G., Bokhnyak, S., Ploumpis, S., Bronstein, M., Zafeiriou, S.: Neural 3D morphable models: Spiral convolutional networks for 3D shape representation learning and generation. In: Proceedings of the IEEE International Conference on Computer Vision, pp. 7213–7222 (2019)
35. Ranjan, A., Bolkart, T., Sanyal, S., Black, M.J.: Generating 3D faces using convolutional mesh autoencoders. In: Ferrari, V., Hebert, M., Sminchisescu, C., Weiss, Y. (eds.) ECCV 2018, Part III. LNCS, vol. 11207, pp. 725–741. Springer, Cham (2018). https://doi.org/10.1007/978-3-030-01219-9_43

36. Litany, O., Bronstein, A., Bronstein, M., Makadia, A.: Deformable shape completion with graph convolutional autoencoders. In: Proceedings of the IEEE Conference on Computer Vision and Pattern Recognition, pp. 1886–1895 (2018)
37. Cheng, S., Bronstein, M., Zhou, Y., Kotsia, I., Pantic, M., Zafeiriou, S.: Meshgan: Non-linear 3D morphable models of faces. arXiv preprint arXiv:1903.10384 (2019)
38. Tran, L., Liu, X.: On learning 3D face morphable model from in-the-wild images. IEEE Trans. Pattern Anal. Mach. Intell. **43**, 157–171 (2019)
39. Sanyal, S., Bolkart, T., Feng, H., Black, M.J.: Learning to regress 3D face shape and expression from an image without 3D supervision. In: Proceedings of the IEEE Conference on Computer Vision and Pattern Recognition, pp. 7763–7772 (2019)
40. Tewari, A., et al.: FML: face model learning from videos. In: Proceedings of the IEEE Conference on Computer Vision and Pattern Recognition, pp. 10812–10822 (2019)
41. He, K., Zhang, X., Ren, S., Sun, J.: Deep residual learning for image recognition. In: Proceedings of the IEEE Conference on Computer Vision and Pattern Recognition, pp. 770–778 (2016)
42. Sandler, M., Howard, A., Zhu, M., Zhmoginov, A., Chen, L.C.: Inverted residuals and linear bottlenecks: Mobile networks for classification, detection and segmentation. arXiv preprint arXiv:1801.04381 (2018)
43. Huang, X., Belongie, S.: Arbitrary style transfer in real-time with adaptive instance normalization. In: Proceedings of the IEEE International Conference on Computer Vision, pp. 1501–1510 (2017)
44. Ioffe, S., Szegedy, C.: Batch normalization: Accelerating deep network training by reducing internal covariate shift. arXiv preprint arXiv:1502.03167 (2015)
45. Ramamoorthi, R., Hanrahan, P.: An efficient representation for irradiance environment maps. In: Proceedings of the 28th Annual Conference on Computer Graphics and Interactive Techniques, pp. 497–500 (2001)
46. Sengupta, S., Kanazawa, A., Castillo, C.D., Jacobs, D.W.: Sfsnet: Learning shape, reflectance and illuminance of facesin the wild'. In: Proceedings of the IEEE Conference on Computer Vision and Pattern Recognition, pp. 6296–6305 (2018)
47. Henderson, P., Ferrari, V.: Learning Single-Image 3D Reconstruction by Generative Modelling of Shape, Pose and Shading. Int. J. Comput. Vis. **128**(4), 835–854 (2019). https://doi.org/10.1007/s11263-019-01219-8
48. Sagonas, C., Tzimiropoulos, G., Zafeiriou, S., Pantic, M.: A semi-automatic methodology for facial landmark annotation. In: Proceedings of the IEEE Conference on Computer Vision And Pattern Recognition Workshops, pp. 896–903 (2013)
49. Qian, N.: On the momentum term in gradient descent learning algorithms. Neural Netw. **12**, 145–151 (1999)
50. Abadi, M., et al.: Tensorflow: a system for large-scale machine learning. In: 12th {USENIX} Symposium on Operating Systems Design and Implementation ({OSDI} 16), pp. 265–283 (2016)
51. Bagdanov, A.D., Masi, I., Del Bimbo, A.: The florence 2D/3D hybrid face datset. In: Proc. of ACM Multimedia International Workshop on Multimedia access to 3D Human Objects (MA3HO 2011) (2011)
52. Yin, L., Wei, X., Sun, Y., Wang, J., Rosato, M.J.: A 3D facial expression database for facial behavior research. In: 7th International Conference on Automatic Face and Gesture Recognition (FGR06), pp. 211–216. IEEE (2006)

53. Cheng, S., Kotsia, I., Pantic, M., Zafeiriou, S.: 4DFAB: a large scale 4d database for facial expression analysis and biometric applications. In: Proceedings of the IEEE Conference on Computer Vision and Pattern Recognition, pp. 5117–5126 (2018)
54. Koestinger, M., Wohlhart, P., Roth, P.M., Bischof, H.: Annotated facial landmarks in the wild: A large-scale, real-world database for facial landmark localization. In: 2011 IEEE International Conference on Computer Vision Workshops (ICCV Workshops), pp. 2144–2151. IEEE (2011)
55. Zhang, Z.: Iterative point matching for registration of free-form curves and surfaces. Int. J. Comput. Vis. **13**, 119–152 (1994)
56. Cheng, S., Marras, I., Zafeiriou, S., Pantic, M.: Statistical non-rigid ICP algorithm and its application to 3D face alignment. Image Vis. Comput. **58**, 3–12 (2017)
57. Jianzhu Guo, X.Z., Lei, Z.: 3DDFA (2018). https://github.com/cleardusk/3DDFA

Localin Reshuffle Net: Toward Naturally and Efficiently Facial Image Blending

Chengyao Zheng[1], Siyu Xia[1(✉)] ⓘ, Joseph Robinson[2], Changsheng Lu[3], Wayne Wu[4], Chen Qian[5], and Ming Shao[6]

[1] Southeast University, Nanjing, China
xsy@seu.edu.cn
[2] Northeastern University, Boston, MA, USA
[3] Shanghai Jiao Tong University, Shanghai, China
[4] Tsinghua University, Beijing, China
[5] SenseTime, Beijing, China
[6] University of Massachusetts Dartmouth, Dartmouth, MA, USA

Abstract. The blending of facial images is an effective way to fuse attributes such that the synthesis is robust to the finer details (*e.g.*, periocular-region, nostrils, hairlines). Specifically, facial blending aims to transfer the style of a source image to a target such that violations in the natural appearance are minimized. Despite the many practical applications, facial image blending remains mostly unexplored with the reasons being two-fold: 1) the lack of quality paired data for supervision and 2) facial synthesizers (*i.e.*, the models) are sensitive to small variations in lighting, texture, resolution and age. We address the reasons for the bottleneck by first building Facial Pairs to Blend (FPB) dataset, which was generated through our facial attribute optimization algorithm. Then, we propose an effective normalization scheme to capture local statistical information during blending: namely, Local Instance Normalization (LAN). Lastly, a novel local-reshuffle-layer is designed to map local patches in the feature space, which can be learned in an end-to-end fashion with dedicated loss. This new layer is essential for the proposed Localin Reshuffle Network (LRNet). Extensive experiments, and both quantitative and qualitative results, demonstrate that our approach outperforms existing methods.

1 Introduction

Facial blending is an effective way to synthesize new faces, which has highly practical value in many applications (*e.g.*, face swapping[1,2], rendering facial makeup [3–6], and portrait style transfer [2,7]). Unlike transfer methods tend to transfer global-level statistics from a source to a target domain (*e.g.*, style transfer [8] and color transfer [9]), face blending is a more complex task, as it

Electronic supplementary material The online version of this chapter (https:// doi.org/10.1007/978-3-030-69541-5_13) contains supplementary material, which is available to authorized users.

© Springer Nature Switzerland AG 2021
H. Ishikawa et al. (Eds.): ACCV 2020, LNCS 12626, pp. 206–222, 2021.
https://doi.org/10.1007/978-3-030-69541-5_13

| Target Image | Source Face | *Style Transfer* | *Color Transfer* | *Face Blending* |

Fig. 1. Illustration for different tasks.

aims to mix a source face onto a target in specific local areas (Fig. 1). However, a lack of paired face data prohibits the use modern-day data-driven models (*i.e.*, supervised deep learning), which is one of the challenges posed in the face blending task. Another challenge is the sensitivity to even slight variations in intrinsic image properties (*e.g.*, textures and illuminations). Furthermore, boundary conditions also contribute to the challenge. Specifically, the goal of face blending is to blend a cropped region from source face x_A onto the target x_B. Inherently, there are typically significant conflicts about the boundaries and in textures differences (*e.g.*, skin color, skin texture, and image resolution).

Formally put, a two-stage solutions are most commonly proposed for facial blending: 1) apply a style or color transfer algorithm to x_A, and 2) use Poisson image blending [10] for the final result. More specifically, (1) is an attempt to disentangle content and style (or color). When employed to arbitrary facial images, there exists no style (or color) transfer algorithm that simultaneously handles skin-tone, skin-texture, and lighting conditions robustly. As for (2), it is known for its efficiency and natural results [10]. However, Poisson image blending performs poorly on faces with variations in textures and lighting conditions since texture consistency between background and foreground is ignored.

Recently, one-stage solutions have been proposed. FSGAN [11] combined Poisson optimization with perceptual loss to blend two faces while preserving target skin color, but they did not take some key factors like local texture into consideration. Li *et al.* proposed a blending method that attempts to modify expressions and gestures, which undesirably alters the identity [12].

To overcome shortcomings of our predecessors, we propose a single stage solution called Localin Reshuffle Network (LRNet). Given a pair of face images x_A and x_B, LRNet blends x_A onto x_B, while transferring the local information (*e.g.*, texture and illumination) from x_B to the final output $\tilde{x}$. In support of this work, we introduce the first paired facial image dataset for image blending named Facial Pairs to Blend (FPB). Since the blending of facial images requires pairs of faces of different identities to have similar orientation and shape. Hence, collecting such a large number of real-world samples is a time-consuming challenge. Based on Style-GAN2[13], we design a facial attribute optimization algorithm, to generate images per the requirements.

The contributions of this paper are as follows:

- We introduce the first image dataset for face blending with 12,000 pairs.
- We propose the Local Instance Normalization and Local Reshuffle Layer in our LRNet: the former transfers local statistics and the latter reconstructs texture from a reference to make invariant to intrinsic image properties.
- We clearly demonstrate the improvement over existing methods on high-quality face images using our LRNet to synthesize.

2   Related Works

2.1   Image Blending

As a common image composition task, to blend images is to blend cropped regions of a source image onto a target image at specific locations. For this, one can simply replace the pixels of the target with those cropped from the source. However, it would yield artifacts caused by differences in intensity between foreground and background. Although alpha blending alleviates this issue by blurring the boundary [14], it still suffers from inconsistent coloring and lighting.

Gradient-based methods have been proven an ability to produce a smoother transition, which reduces problems from differences in color and illumination [10, 15–17] - the most popular of these is Poisson image blending [10]. The motivation of gradient-base methods is that humans are sensitive to an abrupt change in intensity change and, thus, these methods attempt to ensure the smoothness of blended images in the gradient domain.

Recently, Gaussian-Poisson Generative Adversarial Network (GP-GAN) [18] explores the capability of a GAN in image blending task, while Zhang *et al.* proposed a Poisson blending loss computed from a neural network [19]. However, these methods do not account for local aspects like texture and illumination. Hence, the proposed Localin Reshuffle Network (LRNet) ensures smoothness of blended images via gradient-domain and transfers the local texture and illumination. In the end, our results are most photo-realistic.

2.2   Neural Style Transfer

In facial image blending, style transfer algorithms tend to reduce the visual difference between the two images. Gatys *et al.* found that feature statistics calculated from the Gram matrix successfully capture the image style [20]. The authors were then inspired to transfer arbitrary styles by matching the feature statistics [21–23]. However, the early methods are time-consuming, since they are based on an iterative optimization framework.

Feed-forward networks to approximate an optimal result were proposed as a means to reduce time costs [24–26]. However, the algorithms are still unable to transfer unseen styles from an arbitrary image. Later developments alleviated the limitation posed from when unseen styles are mishandled [3,8,27]. WCT [3] encodes the style as the feature co-variance matrix to support rich style representation. AdaIN [8] captures arbitrary image style by computing the mean and variance on the feature maps. Adaptive instance normalization is an efficient style transfer method, which is widely used since introduced [8]. MUNIT was proposed with AdaIN adopted as a high-level style expression to do image-to-image translation task [28]. Style-GAN applied AdaIN in generator to control styles at multiple levels [29].

Although better performance were achieved in neural style transfer, developing an algorithm that is all around efficient (*i.e.*, handles textures, semantic-correspondences, and in a realistic manner) is still a challenge to overcome. Nonetheless, the proposed framework is all around efficient.

2.3 Generative Adversarial Networks (GAN)

Generative Adversarial Networks (GAN) have drawn great attention in research [30]. Originally, the GAN was used to generate low-resolution handwritten digit data. Since its début, a lot of literature on improving vanilla GAN, *e.g.*, Laplacian pyramids of adversarial networks [31], deeper neural networks [32], constraints on generator (G) (*e.g.*, cycle consistency), and methods to stabilize training [33].

Other using cases for GAN involve controlling its output. InfoInfogenerative adversarial network (GAN) focuses on learning interpretable latent representations [34]. Conditional GAN (C-GAN) adds a conditional attribute to the latent code and discriminator (D) [35]. Liu *et al.* improves on C-GAN by introducing a flow-based G [36].

Most recently, Style-GAN2 strengthened style controls, along with improved quality in output image [13]. Abda* *et al.* explored a method to embed images into the latent code of the Style-GAN [37]. Specifically, a latent code is randomly initialized for an input, from which an image is generated with a pre-trained Style-GAN. The dissimilarity between the given image (*e.g.*, *real*) and the image generated (*e.g.*, *fake*) is minimized by iterative optimization. In fact, Abda *et al.* inspired our FPB dataset to have minimal dissimilarities in face orientation and shape, and all the while maximizing other face attributes.

3 Facial Pairs to Blend (FPB) Dataset

FPB is proposed as the first image set to support facial blending. For this, our LRNet generated ground-truth (*i.e.*, supervision) for 12,000 pairs (*i.e.*, x_A blended onto x_B, and vice-versa). This allowed for face pairs of different appearance to have the same orientation (*i.e.*, pitch, yaw, and roll) and facial contour. We next explain our data, and then in the proceeding section introduce LRNet.

3.1 Dataset Generation Algorithm

As face blending task requires two faces with similar orientation and shape but different appearance, the collection of such data in the real world could

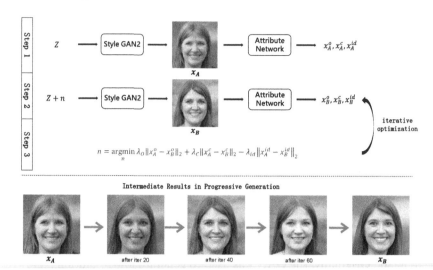

Fig. 2. Our paired-wise facial images generation algorithm. A random latent code Z generates $\mathbf{x_A}$. Then, we add noise to Z to synthesize a completely new image $\tilde{x}_B$. The loss function aims to minimize the difference in the orientation and contour of faces and maximize the identity loss. The bottom row shows the transforming process from $\mathbf{x_A}$ to $\mathbf{x_B}$.

be rather expensive. Inspired by the work of Style-GAN encoder[37], we use Style-GAN2 [13] to generate facial images, and define the loss function as constraints on face attributes (*i.e.*, orientation, facial contour, and appearance). Through minimizing the loss function, paired-wise facial images that meet the requirements can be accessed.

Our paired-wise data generation algorithm is presented in Fig. 2. To illustrate the problem clearly, our method is divided into three steps in the figure.

(1) We randomly generate a latent code Z in Style-GAN2 [13] latent space, Z has a shape of 512×1. Image A is simply achieved by feeding Z to Style-GAN2. A pre-trained facial attribute network [38] gives an estimated result of image A, we denote the facial orientation as $\mathbf{x_A^o}$ (with a size of 3×1), facial contour as $\mathbf{x_A^c}$ (16×2), facial identity vector as $\mathbf{x_A^{id}}$ ($4{,}000 \times 1$).

(2) We add noise n to Z, and treat $Z + n$ in the same way as Z, obtaining $\mathbf{x_B^o}$, $\mathbf{x_B^c}$, and $\mathbf{x_B^{id}}$.

(3) We define a loss to measure the similarity between face images $\mathbf{x_A}$ and $\mathbf{x_B}$. The idea is to ensure two images have similar facial orientation and contour, while they look different in appearance as much as possible. The loss is formulated as Eq. (1). λ_o, λ_c and λ_{id} are the weights to balance different components. To minimize $loss_{AB}$, we take the derivative of $loss_{AB}$ with respect to n, and update the noise, in a similar way of Eq. (2).

$$loss_{AB} = \lambda_o \left\| \mathbf{x_A^o} - \mathbf{x_B^o} \right\|_2 + \lambda_c \left\| \mathbf{x_A^c} - \mathbf{x_B^c} \right\|_2 - \lambda_{id} \left\| \mathbf{x_A^{id}} - \mathbf{x_B^{id}} \right\|_2 \qquad (1)$$

Fig. 3. FPB dataset. Columns show face pairs, with the last two being real images. The similarity in orientation and shape but difference in appearances.

$$n = n - \frac{\partial loss_{AB}}{\partial n} \qquad (2)$$

We noticed that the loss in Eq. (1) usually converged to a minimum after 80 iterations of *Step 2–3* - continued training did not improve results. Then, we adopted the final result as $\mathbf{x_B}$. We also set an early stop strategy to accelerate the generation process.

Even though Style-GAN2 is state-of-the-art (SOTA) in generating photo-realistic images, there still exists a domain gap between the distribution of the *real* and *fake* data. For this, we collect images from the web and manually select 2,000 pairs that have similar orientations and face-shapes. We then use TPS [39] to warp one image per pair so that edges line-up. In total, Facial Pairs to Blend (FPB) consists of 12,000 face pairs (Fig. 3).

3.2 Dataset Implementation Details

Although StyleGAN2 performs well most of the time, artifacts still can be observed in some extreme illumination and pose conditions. After 15,467 pairs of images are generated, we manually select 10,000 pairs of good-quality.

The facial orientation $(\mathbf{x_A^o}, \mathbf{x_B^o})$ is a 3×1 vector (*i.e.*, pitch, yaw, and roll angles, respectively). The facial contour$(\mathbf{x_A^c}, \mathbf{x_B^c})$ is a 16×2 vector made-up of the sixteen facial landmarks along the outside of the face. We normalize these landmarks to $[0, 1]$. The size of facial identity vector$(\mathbf{x_A^{id}}, \mathbf{x_B^{id}})$ is $4,000 \times 1$. To generate the vector, we add a fully connected network(3 layers) after the feature extraction layers of [38], and train the fully connected module for face recognition tasks on CelebA [40]. We apply the output of the third layer in fully connected network as facial identity vector. λ_o, λ_c, λ_{id}, are 0.1, 100, and 0.001 in our experiments.

The generation process would stop if reaching the maximum number of iterations, which is 80 in our paper, or meeting the following three stop criteria:

$$\left\| \mathbf{x_A^o} - \mathbf{x_B^o} \right\|_2 < 10 \ \& \ \left\| \mathbf{x_A^c} - \mathbf{x_B^c} \right\|_2 < 0.01 \ \& \ \left\| \mathbf{x_A^{id}} - \mathbf{x_B^{id}} \right\|_2 > 1000$$

Empirically, if above three conditions are satisfied, the orientation and face shape of image B should be similar to A, while looks like two totally different persons.

4   Localin Reshuffle Network (LRNet)

LRNet, consisting of the our local instance normalization (LocalIN) and *local reshuffle* layer. Specifically, LocalIN is a layer that transfers local statistics and the *local reshuffle* layer reconstructs the new feature maps for $\mathbf{x_A}$ with patches from $\mathbf{x_B}$. Both of the novel layers are essential for a precise transfer of local texture and lighting while blending faces. We discuss all of the parts, the network as a whole, and then the loss functions in the remainder of this section.

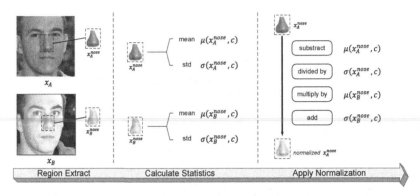

Fig. 4. Example of implementing LocalIN in RGB space about the nose region.

4.1   LocalIN

As mentioned, adaptive instance normalization (AdaIN) has been proved to be an efficient style transfer operation [8]. However, since AdaIN uses global statistics of an image it is insensitive to the local style, which is imperative for objects with finer details (*i.e.*, faces). To achieve style transfer at a semantic level (*e.g.*, nose-to-nose or mouth-to-mouth), we propose LocalIN as a normalization method. It operates in RGB color space (Fig. 4).

More specifically, given two images $\mathbf{x_A}$ and $\mathbf{x_B}$, $\mathbf{x_A}$ will be normalized by $\mathbf{x_B}$. The first step is to divide the image into different semantic regions, normalization will only be implemented in the same region of two images. Take nose as an example, we calculate the mean and standard deviation inside $\mathbf{x_A^{nose}}$ on each channels, respectively. Let $\mu(\mathbf{x_A^{nose}}, c)$ and $\sigma(\mathbf{x_A^{nose}}, c)$ be the mean and standard deviation calculated in $\mathbf{x_A^{nose}}$ on channel c. $\mu(\mathbf{x_B^{nose}}, c)$ and $\sigma(\mathbf{x_B^{nose}}, c)$ are defined in a similar way. Finally, for every pixel inside $\mathbf{x_A^{nose}}$ on each channel, its value $F(\mathbf{x_A^{nose}}, i, c)$ will be calculated as

$$F_n(\mathbf{x_A^{nose}}, i, c) = \frac{F(\mathbf{x_A^{nose}}, i, c) - \mu(\mathbf{x_A^{nose}}, c)}{\sigma(\mathbf{x_A^{nose}}, c)} * \sigma(\mathbf{x_B^{nose}}, c) + \mu(\mathbf{x_B^{nose}}, c). \quad (3)$$

The framework of LocalIN is given in Algorithm 1. The operation is differentiable, and can be executed efficiently. This allows us to easily add the module to a neural network and optimizing with our objective functions. LocalIN transfers high-level style information from $\mathbf{x_B} \rightarrow \mathbf{x_A}$, which includes knowledge of lighting, skin color, and image tone. However, for photo-realistic results we need to handle texture, which is done via the *local reshuffle* layer described next.

4.2 Local Reshuffle

We propose a novel *local reshuffle* for inconsistencies in texture. Specifically, we reconstruct the feature maps of $\mathbf{x_A}$ using patches from the feature maps of $\mathbf{x_B}$. The resulting maps then share the same local texture as $\mathbf{x_A}$, while retaining the structure of $\mathbf{x_B}$. We first demonstrate the proposed *local reshuffle* in RGB space. Then, a more general formula is provided (Algorithm 2).

Given images $\mathbf{x_A}$ and $\mathbf{x_B}$, our goal is to reconstruct a new image $\mathbf{x_A^{reshuffled}}$ made-up of patches from $\mathbf{x_B}$. A patch is defined as a square block with the number of channels equivalent to the feature maps. The patch size is set as $3 \times 3 \times 3$ (height*weight*channel) in RGB space for the reported results. As shown in Fig. 5, patch$(\mathbf{x_A^{nose}}, i)$ represents the i-th patch of $\mathbf{x_A^{nose}}$, while patch$(\mathbf{x_B^{nose}}, j)$ represents the j-th patch in $\mathbf{x_A^{nose}}$. Then, each patch$(\mathbf{x_A^{nose}}, i)$ is matched up with the most similar patch$(\mathbf{x_B^{nose}}, j)$ in $\mathbf{x_B^{nose}}$, which is denoted as $\phi_{\mathbf{x_A} \rightarrow \mathbf{x_B}}(i) = j$. We compute $\phi_{\mathbf{x_A} \rightarrow \mathbf{x_B}}(i)$ by maximizing Eq. (4). After each patch$(\mathbf{x_A^{nose}}, i)$ has been matched with a patch$(\mathbf{x_B^{nose}}, j)$, the new feature maps $F_{re}(\mathbf{x_A^{nose}})$ are reconstructed. By concatenating and feeding all patches in $\mathbf{x_B^{nose}}$ into a convolution kernel, the patch-matches of $\mathbf{x_A^{nose}}$ and $\mathbf{x_B^{nose}}$ can be replaced by a single for-

---

Algorithm 1. Framework of Local Instance Normalization

Input:

The feature maps of $\mathbf{x_A}$ and $\mathbf{x_B}$ in region k (*i.e.*, $F(\mathbf{x_A^k})$ and $F(\mathbf{x_B^k})$, respectively)

Output:

Normalized result: $F_n(\mathbf{x_A^k})$

for each channel c **do**

$$\mu(\mathbf{x_A^k}, c) = \sum_{i}^{i \in \mathbf{x_A^k}} \frac{F(\mathbf{x_A^k}, i, c)}{N}$$

$$\sigma(\mathbf{x_A^k}, c) = \sqrt{\sum_{i}^{i \in \mathbf{x_A^k}} \frac{[F(\mathbf{x_A^k}, i, c) - \mu(\mathbf{x_A^k}, c)]^2}{N}}$$

$$\mu(\mathbf{x_B^k}, c) = \sum_{j}^{j \in \mathbf{x_B^k}} \frac{F(\mathbf{x_B^k}, j, c)}{M}$$

$$\sigma(\mathbf{x_B^k}, c) = \sqrt{\sum_{j}^{j \in \mathbf{x_B^k}} \frac{[F(\mathbf{x_B^k}, j, c) - \mu(\mathbf{x_B^k}, c)]^2}{M}}$$

    for each $i \in \mathbf{x_A^k}$ **do**

$$F_n(\mathbf{x_A^k}, i, c) = \frac{F(\mathbf{x_A^k}, i, c) - \mu(\mathbf{x_A^k}, c)}{\sigma(\mathbf{x_A^k}, c)} * \sigma(\mathbf{x_B^k}, c) + \mu(\mathbf{x_B^k}, c)$$

    end for

end for

return $F_n(\mathbf{x_A^k})$;

---

ward convolution computation. Since an additional *same-region* restriction is included, this was dubbed *local reshuffle*.

$$\phi_{A \to B}(i) = \arg \max_{j} \left\| patch(\mathbf{x_A^{nose}}, i) * patch(\mathbf{x_B^{nose}}, j) \right\|_2 \qquad (4)$$

Algorithm 2 describes the proposed *local reshuffle*. The input feature maps $\mathbf{x_A}$ and $\mathbf{x_B}$ with corresponding channels C are denoted as $F(\mathbf{x_A^k})$ and $F(\mathbf{x_B^k})$. Reshuffling produces the new feature maps $F_n(\mathbf{x_A^k})$. Since patches are $3 \times 3 \times C$, only the center $1 \times 1 \times C$ value is used to reconstruct $F_n(\mathbf{x_A^k})$ via patches in $\mathbf{x_B^k}$.

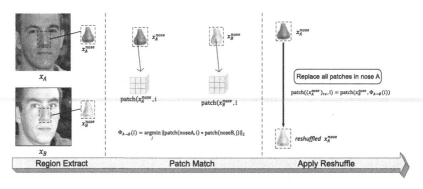

Fig. 5. Example of implementing local reshuffle on RGB space inside nose region.

4.3   Semantic Correspondence Constraint

When blending $\mathbf{x_A}$ into $\mathbf{x_B}$, we expect blended image $\tilde{\mathbf{x}}$ shows similar style(eg: skin color, texture and illumination) inside same semantic region(eg: left eye) with $\mathbf{x_B}$. In this work, we also proposed a novel way to ensure semantic correspondence in *local reshuffle*.

Firstly, we get the 3D facial vertices of $\mathbf{x_A}$ and $\mathbf{x_B}$ via PRNet [38], denoted as P_A and P_B. Then both P_A and P_B are mapped to a sphere whose radius is 1. This process can be seen as fitting the 3D facial mesh onto a sphere. After mapping, the product between two vertices can be used to measure the relative distance. The greater the product, the smaller the distance. The proof process is in the supplementary material. After the conversion, we have an elegant and simple way to measure distance.

The product between 3D vertices can be used as in convolution operations. This allows for the merging of semantic correspondence constraint in the *local reshuffle*. In our experiments, we concatenate 3D vertices with feature maps, which extend the channel C of the feature maps to $C + 3$. Patches within the same semantic region tend to have a greater product that leads to more energy (Eq. (4)). By mapping 3D vertices into feature maps, we achieve the semantic correspondence of *local reshuffle*.

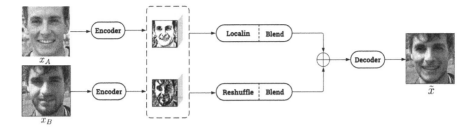

Fig. 6. Overview of Localin-Reshuffle-Net. Concatenation is represented by $\oplus$.

4.4 Network Architecture

LocalIN and local reshuffle are critical component in the network of this work, with the former for high-level style transfer and the latter for local texture transfer. We named the overall architecture LRNet (Fig. 6). As shown, the goal is to blend face $\mathbf{x_A}$ onto $\mathbf{x_B}$. The result yields similar texture and lighting distribution as $\mathbf{x_B}$, while retaining the identity of $\mathbf{x_A}$.

Firstly, LRNet extracts features of $\mathbf{x_A}$ and $\mathbf{x_B}$ with the same encoder– the same encoder used as the feature maps are assumed to share data distribution, which will be used for the dot-product, comparison, and reshuffle. Feature maps $F(\mathbf{x_A})$ and $F(\mathbf{x_B})$ are divided into K semantic regions, and each pair $F(\mathbf{x_A^k})$ and $F(\mathbf{x_B^k})$ will be sent to two branches: Localin and local reshuffle. For each branch, after obtaining $F_{new}(\mathbf{x_A^k})$, we will blend them into $F(\mathbf{x_B})$ through alpha blending [14] to avoid the mutation around the boundary. Next, two blended feature maps are concatenated, and fed to a decoder. Finally, the decoder generates the blended result. Thanks to Localin and local reshuffle, LRNet not only blends $\mathbf{x_A}$ onto $\mathbf{x_B}$, but also transfers the texture and lighting at the same time.

4.5 Loss Functions

Reconstruction Loss. The reconstruction loss of our model is motivated by the following: reconstruction in the *background* should be the same as $\mathbf{x_B}$; the *foreground* should resemble $\mathbf{x_A}$ as much as possible. To that end, we develop a reconstruction loss to penalize induced errors in training. Let $\tilde{\mathbf{x}}$ be the output RGB image. Let $\tilde{\mathbf{x}}(fg)$ and $\tilde{\mathbf{x}}(bg)$ refer to the foreground and background of $\tilde{x}$, respectively. $VGG_{1,2}(\tilde{\mathbf{x}}(fg))$ refers to feeding $\tilde{\mathbf{x}}(fg)$ through a pre-trained VGG19 model [41], and get the feature maps after the $relu1\_1$ and $relu2\_1$ layers. This operation is also known as perceptual loss [26]. Our reconstruction loss can be formulated as Eq. (5). The parameter α is a weighting factor that balances the two, it's 0.2 in this experiment. N and M are the total pixels in the background and foreground, respectively. We chose to use the perceptual loss as penalty from the pixels of the foreground is not as strict as those in the background. This is because difference in detail (e.g., facial texture, illumination), is not only allowed but encouraged.

Algorithm 2. Framework of Local Reshuffle

Input:
  The feature maps of $\mathbf{x_A}$ and $\mathbf{x_B}$ in region k ($i.e.$, $F(\mathbf{x_A^k})$ and $F(\mathbf{x_B^k})$, respectively)
Output:
  Reshuffled result: $F_{re}(\mathbf{x_A^k})$
  for each $i \in \mathbf{x_A^k}$ **do**
    $\phi_{\mathbf{x_A} \to \mathbf{x_B}}(i) = \arg\min_j \|patch(\mathbf{x_A^{nose}}, i) * patch(\mathbf{x_B^{nose}}, j)\|_2$
  end for
  for each $i \in \mathbf{x_A^k}$ **do**
    $patch((\mathbf{x_A^{nose}})_{re}, i) = patch(\mathbf{x_B^{nose}}, \phi_{\mathbf{x_A} \to \mathbf{x_B}}(i))$
  end for
  return $F_{re}(\mathbf{x_A^k})$;

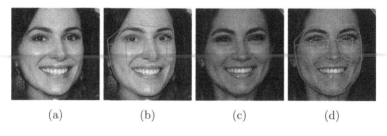

(a)   (b)   (c)   (d)

Fig. 7. A pair of segmentation results in our experiments. There are 10 regions in total. Shown here is $\mathbf{x_A}$ (a), $\mathbf{x_A^{segmented}}$ (b), $\mathbf{x_B}$ (c), and $\mathbf{x_B^{segmented}}$ (d).

$$L_{rec} = \frac{1}{N} \|\mathbf{x_B}(bg) - \tilde{\mathbf{x}}(bg)\|_2 + \frac{\alpha}{M} \|VGG_{1,2}(\mathbf{x_A}(fg)) - VGG_{1,2}(\tilde{\mathbf{x}}(fg))\|_2 \quad (5)$$

Cycle Consistency Loss If we blend $\tilde{\mathbf{x}}$ onto $\mathbf{x_A}$, the most accurate output should look like $\mathbf{x_A}$ itself. $LRNet(\mathbf{x_A} \to \mathbf{x_B})$ means blending $\mathbf{x_A}$ onto $\mathbf{x_B}$. Our cycle consistency loss is defined as

$$L_{cycle} = \frac{1}{N + M} \|\mathbf{x_A} - LRNet(LRNet(\mathbf{x_A} \to \mathbf{x_B}) \to \mathbf{x_A})\|_1. \quad (6)$$

Gradient Consistency Loss. We have discussed in Sect. 2.1 that gradient-based methods plays a key role in producing a seamless blending boundary. We extend this idea to our gradient consistency loss. Let $\nabla A(fg)$ be the gradient of $\mathbf{x_A}$ in background area. The gradient consistency loss can be defined as

$$L_{grad} = \frac{1}{N + M} \|\nabla A(fg) + \nabla B(bg) - \nabla out\|_1. \quad (7)$$

Local Style Loss. In order to ensure the output share a similar texture and lighting with $\mathbf{x_B}$ in local areas, we define a new texture loss based on previous style transfer works [8]. Same as the perceptual loss in Section Reconstruction Loss, we leverage a pre-trained VGG19 model to extract the feature maps for

$\mathbf{x_B}$ and $\tilde{\mathbf{x}}$. Denote $\mu(\mathbf{x_B^k}, c)$ as the mean value of $\mathbf{x_B}$'s feature maps on the c channel, our local style loss is formalized in Eq. (8). Note that feature maps are calculated at the $relu1\_1$ layer, making the loss more sensitive to the low-level style information. The weighting factor β is 2.0 in this work.

$$L_{style} = \frac{1}{KC} \sum_k^K \sum_c^C \left\| \mu(\mathbf{x_B^k}, c) - \mu(\tilde{\mathbf{x}}^k, c) \right\|_2 + \beta \left\| \sigma(\mathbf{x_B^k}, c) - \sigma(\tilde{\mathbf{x}}^k, c) \right\|_2 \quad (8)$$

Total Loss. Integrating aforementioned losses, the total loss function is

$$L_{total} = \lambda_1 L_{rec} + \lambda_2 L_{cycle} + \lambda_3 L_{grad} + \lambda_3 L_{style}, \quad (9)$$

where weighting factors λ_1, λ_2, λ_3, and λ_4 are 3.0, 20, 100, and 0.35, respectively, which are obtained via cross validation experiments.

5   Experiments

5.1   Implementation Details

Network Architecture. The encoder in LRNet accepts a $H \times W \times 3$ ($H > 32$, $W > 32$) RGB image as input, and outputs feature maps with a size of $\frac{H}{2} \times \frac{W}{2} \times 128$. We adopt layers from $conv1 - 1$ to $relu2 - 1$ of VGG19 [41] as the backbone of the encoder, because a too deep network can leads to low efficiency and image details' loss. The decoder in LRNet accepts a $(H/2) \times (W/2) \times 256$ feature maps, and generates a $H \times W \times 3$ RGB image as output. In our experiments, the H and W are set as 256. The decoder uses deconvolution layers to enlarge feature maps and generate RGB images.

Training Details. Facial images are segmented into 10 regions (Fig. 7). Each connected domain is an independent region in the figure. LRNet is trained end-to-end with Adam [42] optimizing with a learning rate of 0.0001 and batch size of 1. 70% pairs in the dataset are used for training, and the rests are for validation. We use stratified sampling to select from both generated and real images.

5.2   Ablation Study

We conduct an ablation study to seeing how each branch in LRNet affects the performance. Let $F_{localin}$ be the feature maps generated by Localin branch, while $F_{reshuffle}$ is the feature maps of the Reshuffle branch. We designed two network structures: (a) remove the reshuffle branch, make a copy of $F_{localin}$, and concatenate $F_{localin}$ with its copy as the input to the following decoder and (b) remove the Localin branch, and process $F_{reshuffle}$ similar to (a).

The convergence processes of 4 losses are shown in Fig. 8. For reconstruction loss, structure(a) converge fastest. But in a face blending task, reducing reconstruction loss to 0 is not our real goal. It's just a constraint to the general structure of the generated image. For style loss, the result shows that both

(a) and (b) have the ability to transfer style. By putting them together, LRNet improves even more. Based on our observations, (a) tends to transfer image statistics, like color and illumination, while (b) is more sensitive to local texture. We also found that the consistency of local texture is critical for face blending, making the reshuffle branch indispensable. For grad loss and cycle loss, (b) performs worse than the others. The reason is that the Localin branch retains many of the details, dropping it makes it harder to recover the original face. Except for convergence processes, we also provide visual results in our supplementary materials.

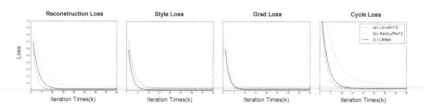

Fig. 8. The ablation study. We graph the convergence processes of loss functions as a function of iteration step k. Note, each loss was scaled by its weight factor.

5.3   Comparison with Baselines

Here, we adopted several methods that are widely adopted in industry and research: *alpha blending*, apply color transfer [9] on $\mathbf{x_A}$ according to $\mathbf{x_B}$, and blend $\mathbf{x_A}$ onto $\mathbf{x_B}$ using alpha blending [14]; *Possion blending*, blend $\mathbf{x_A}$ onto $\mathbf{x_B}$ using Poisson blending [10]; *style blending*, apply style transfer [8] on $\mathbf{x_A}$ according to $\mathbf{x_B}$, and blend $\mathbf{x_A}$ onto $\mathbf{x_B}$ using alpha blending [14]; *deep blending*, a gradient-based blending method using numerical optimization [19] (<50 s to completion).

Qualitative Comparison. We show qualitative comparison results alongside the baselines in Fig. 9. Before blending, we warp [39] the target image to ensure the target face aligns with the face edges of the source. Results show that *Alpha blending* as the simplest way to blend faces, which has the worst performance. It shows significant mutations around the blending boundary. What's worse, it has nothing to do with the inconsistency of texture and illumination at all. *Possion blending*, although successfully produce a smooth transition and reduce the color illumination differences, the problem of texture inconsistency still exists. *Style blending* tends to generate highly stylized images, which doesn't look like a real face. *Deep blending* takes much longer computation time, and sometimes produce artifacts leading to unrealistic faces.

The aforementioned methods inaccurately transfer texture and lighting from the source to the blended results. In face blending, this is critical, and leads to obvious, unwanted artifacts. From this, the improvement of our LRNet is clear. For instance, examine row 5 in Fig. 9: our method is the only to generate results that preserve the highlights and shadows of the source image. At the local-level, LRNet was the only to preserve the facial texture and skin tone of the source. Note that the first two rows are results for real-world images, our method performs as well on real data as it does on generated data.

Quantitative Comparison. First, we performed a user study on 75 volunteers. For this, 200 image pairs were randomly sampled from the validation set. Then, each volunteer was shown the source and target faces, along with the results for the respective pair. Note that the order of results was set randomly each time. Volunteers were asked to score the resulting faces, with a score scale of 0.5-to-4 (increments of 0.5). We ask users to rate according to whether the results look natural, realistic. As illustrated in Table 1, $x \pm y$ represents the mean $\pm$ the variance of all user ratings. In the end, our proposed method was perceived as superior to the others.

We apply "Fréchet Inception Distance" (FID) [43] as another quantitative evaluation criterion. The FID score are also listed in Table 1. Our method out-

Table 1. Quantitative results of different face blending methods.

	Alpha	Possion	Style	Deep	LRNet
User rating	2.43 ± 0.68	2.94 ± 0.47	1.28 ± 0.67	2.19 ± 0.65	$\mathbf{3.54 \pm 0.39}$
Avg. time(s)	**0.12**	0.23	0.19	54.31	0.37
FID score	39.73	31.59	73.41	26.18	**15.47**

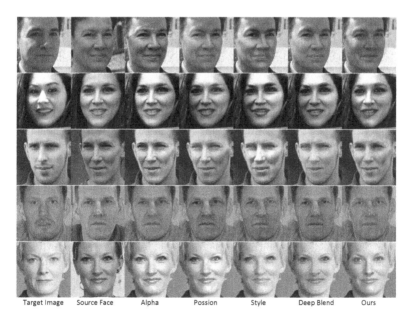

Fig. 9. Qualitative comparisons between LRNet and existing methods. The task is to blend the source faces onto the target.

performs all the baselines under the objective evaluation criterion. Note that the FID score is measured across the validation set, and image size is 256×256.

Table 1 also shows the average computational time of five methods with same configuration - a PC with an Intel i7 4.20 GHz CPU and an NVIDIA GTX 1080Ti GPU. It can be seen that our method is comparable with the fastest face blending method (*i.e.*, Style Blending) in terms of speed.

6   Conclusions

In this paper, we proposed an effective method for facial image blending. Firstly, we introduced a labeled facial image dataset for this task, which contains 12,000 face pairs with the same orientation and facial contour, but different appearance. Secondly, we proposed a normalization method, *i.e.*, LocalIN, to transfer local statistical information. Thirdly, we also introduced a new network, *i.e.*, LRNet, with instances of a new layer-type designed to reshuffle local patches on the forward pass. The extensive experiments demonstrate our approach are very effective compared to existing methods.

References

1. Bitouk, D., Kumar, N., Dhillon, S., Belhumeur, P., Nayar, S.K.: Face swapping: automatically replacing faces in photographs. In: ACM SIGGRAPH 2008 papers, pp. 1–8 (2008)
2. Nirkin, Y., Masi, I., Tuan, A.T., Hassner, T., Medioni, G.: On face segmentation, face swapping, and face perception. In: 2018 13th IEEE International Conference on Automatic Face & Gesture Recognition (FG 2018), pp. 98–105. IEEE (2018)
3. Li, Y., Fang, C., Yang, J., Wang, Z., Lu, X., Yang, M.H.: Universal style transfer via feature transforms. In: Advances in Neural Information Processing Systems, pp. 386–396 (2017)
4. Liu, S., Ou, X., Qian, R., Wang, W., Cao, X.: Makeup like a superstar: deep localized makeup transfer network. arXiv preprint arXiv:1604.07102 (2016)
5. Chang, H., Lu, J., Yu, F., Finkelstein, A.: PairedCycleGAN: asymmetric style transfer for applying and removing makeup. In: Proceedings of the IEEE Conference on Computer Vision and Pattern Recognition, pp. 40–48 (2018)
6. Li, T., et al.: BeautyGAN: instance-level facial makeup transfer with deep generative adversarial network. In: Proceedings of the 26th ACM international conference on Multimedia, pp. 645–653 (2018)
7. Shih, Y., Paris, S., Barnes, C., Freeman, W.T., Durand, F.: Style transfer for headshot portraits. ACM Trans. Graph. (TOG) **33**, 148 (2014)
8. Huang, X., Belongie, S.: Arbitrary style transfer in real-time with adaptive instance normalization. In: Proceedings of the IEEE International Conference on Computer Vision, pp. 1501–1510 (2017)
9. Reinhard, E., Adhikhmin, M., Gooch, B., Shirley, P.: Color transfer between images. IEEE Comput. Graphics Appl. **21**, 34–41 (2001)
10. Pérez, P., Gangnet, M., Blake, A.: Poisson image editing. In: ACM SIGGRAPH 2003 Papers, pp. 313–318 (2003)

11. Nirkin, Y., Keller, Y., Hassner, T.: FSGAN: subject agnostic face swapping and reenactment (2019)
12. Li, L., Bao, J., Yang, H., Chen, D., Wen, F.: FaceShifter: towards high fidelity and occlusion aware face swapping (2019)
13. Karras, T., Laine, S., Aittala, M., Hellsten, J., Lehtinen, J., Aila, T.: Analyzing and improving the image quality of StyleGAN. arXiv preprint arXiv:1912.04958 (2019)
14. Porter, T., Duff, T.: Compositing digital images. In: Proceedings of the 11th Annual Conference on Computer Graphics and Interactive Techniques, pp. 253–259 (1984)
15. Fattal, R., Lischinski, D., Werman, M.: Gradient domain high dynamic range compression. In: Proceedings of the 29th Annual Conference on Computer Graphics and Interactive Techniques, pp. 249–256 (2002)
16. Levin, A., Zomet, A., Peleg, S., Weiss, Y.: Seamless image stitching in the gradient domain. In: Pajdla, T., Matas, J. (eds.) ECCV 2004. LNCS, vol. 3024, pp. 377–389. Springer, Heidelberg (2004). https://doi.org/10.1007/978-3-540-24673-2_31
17. Szeliski, R., Uyttendaele, M., Steedly, D.: Fast poisson blending using multi-splines. In: 2011 IEEE International Conference on Computational Photography (ICCP), pp. 1–8. IEEE (2011)
18. Wu, H., Zheng, S., Zhang, J., Huang, K.: GP-GAN: towards realistic high-resolution image blending. In: Proceedings of the 27th ACM International Conference on Multimedia, pp. 2487–2495 (2019)
19. Zhang, L., Wen, T., Shi, J.: Deep image blending. arXiv preprint arXiv:1910.11495 (2019)
20. Gatys, L.A., Ecker, A.S., Bethge, M.: Image style transfer using convolutional neural networks. In: Proceedings of the IEEE Conference on Computer Vision and Pattern Recognition, pp. 2414–2423 (2016)
21. Li, Y., Wang, N., Liu, J., Hou, X.: Demystifying neural style transfer. arXiv preprint arXiv:1701.01036 (2017)
22. Li, S., Xu, X., Nie, L., Chua, T.S.: Laplacian-steered neural style transfer. In: Proceedings of the 25th ACM International Conference on Multimedia, pp. 1716–1724 (2017)
23. Li, C., Wand, M.: Combining Markov random fields and convolutional neural networks for image synthesis. In: Proceedings of the IEEE Conference on Computer Vision and Pattern Recognition, pp. 2479–2486 (2016)
24. Ulyanov, D., Lebedev, V., Vedaldi, A., Lempitsky, V.S.: Texture networks: feedforward synthesis of textures and stylized images. In: ICML, vol. 1, p. 4 (2016)
25. Chen, D., Yuan, L., Liao, J., Yu, N., Hua, G.: StyleBank: an explicit representation for neural image style transfer. In: Proceedings of the IEEE Conference on Computer Vision and Pattern Recognition, pp. 1897–1906 (2017)
26. Johnson, J., Alahi, A., Fei-Fei, L.: Perceptual losses for real-time style transfer and super-resolution. In: Leibe, B., Matas, J., Sebe, N., Welling, M. (eds.) ECCV 2016. LNCS, vol. 9906, pp. 694–711. Springer, Cham (2016). https://doi.org/10.1007/978-3-319-46475-6_43
27. Li, Y., Liu, M.Y., Li, X., Yang, M.H., Kautz, J.: A closed-form solution to photorealistic image stylization. In: Proceedings of the European Conference on Computer Vision (ECCV), pp. 453–468 (2018)
28. Huang, X., Liu, M.Y., Belongie, S., Kautz, J.: Multimodal unsupervised image-to-image translation. In: Proceedings of the European Conference on Computer Vision (ECCV), pp. 172–189 (2018)

29. Karras, T., Laine, S., Aila, T.: A style-based generator architecture for generative adversarial networks. In: Proceedings of the IEEE Conference on Computer Vision and Pattern Recognition, pp. 4401–4410 (2019)
30. Goodfellow, I., et al.: Generative adversarial nets. In: Advances in Neural Information Processing Systems, pp. 2672–2680 (2014)
31. Denton, E.L., Chintala, S., Fergus, R., et al.: Deep generative image models using a laplacian pyramid of adversarial networks. In: Advances in Neural Information Processing Systems, pp. 1486–1494 (2015)
32. Radford, A., Metz, L., Chintala, S.: Unsupervised representation learning with deep convolutional generative adversarial networks. arXiv preprint arXiv:1511.06434 (2015)
33. Arjovsky, M., Chintala, S., Bottou, L.: Wasserstein GAN. arXiv preprint arXiv:1701.07875 (2017)
34. Chen, X., Duan, Y., Houthooft, R., Schulman, J., Sutskever, I., Abbeel, P.: Info-GAN: interpretable representation learning by information maximizing generative adversarial nets. In: Advances in Neural Information Processing Systems, pp. 2172–2180 (2016)
35. Isola, P., Zhu, J.Y., Zhou, T., Efros, A.A.: Image-to-image translation with conditional adversarial networks. In: Proceedings of the IEEE Conference on Computer Vision and Pattern Recognition, pp. 1125–1134 (2017)
36. Liu, R., Liu, Y., Gong, X., Wang, X., Li, H.: Conditional adversarial generative flow for controllable image synthesis. In: Proceedings of the IEEE Conference on Computer Vision and Pattern Recognition, pp. 7992–8001 (2019)
37. Abdal, R., Qin, Y., Wonka, P.: Image2StyleGAN: how to embed images into the StyleGAN latent space? In: Proceedings of the IEEE International Conference on Computer Vision, pp. 4432–4441 (2019)
38. Feng, Y., Wu, F., Shao, X., Wang, Y., Zhou, X.: Joint 3D face reconstruction and dense alignment with position map regression network. In: Ferrari, V., Hebert, M., Sminchisescu, C., Weiss, Y. (eds.) Computer Vision – ECCV 2018. LNCS, vol. 11218, pp. 557–574. Springer, Cham (2018). https://doi.org/10.1007/978-3-030-01264-9_33
39. Erikson, A.P., Åström, K.: On the bijectivity of thin-plate splines (2012)
40. Liu, Z., Luo, P., Wang, X., Tang, X.: Deep learning face attributes in the wild. In: Proceedings of International Conference on Computer Vision (ICCV) (2015)
41. Simonyan, K., Zisserman, A.: Very deep convolutional networks for large-scale image recognition. arXiv preprint arXiv:1409.1556 (2014)
42. Kingma, D.P., Ba, J.: Adam: a method for stochastic optimization. arXiv preprint arXiv:1412.6980 (2014)
43. Heusel, M., Ramsauer, H., Unterthiner, T., Nessler, B., Hochreiter, S.: GANs trained by a two time-scale update rule converge to a local nash equilibrium. In: Advances in Neural Information Processing Systems, pp. 6626–6637 (2017)

Rotation Axis Focused Attention Network (RAFA-Net) for Estimating Head Pose

Ardhendu Behera$^{(\boxtimes)}$ ⓘ, Zachary Wharton ⓘ, Pradeep Hewage ⓘ, and Swagat Kumar ⓘ

Computer Science, Edge Hill University, Ormskirk Lancashire L39 4QP, UK
{beheraa,zachary.wharton,pradeep.hewage,kumars}@edgehill.ac.uk

Abstract. Head pose is a vital indicator of human attention and behavior. Therefore, automatic estimation of head pose from images is key to many applications. In this paper, we propose a novel approach for head pose estimation from a single RGB image. Many existing approaches often predict head poses by localizing facial landmarks and then solve 2D to 3D correspondence problem with a mean head model. Such approaches rely entirely on the landmark detection accuracy, an ad-hoc alignment step, and the extraneous head model. To address this drawback, we present an end-to-end deep network, which explores rotation axis (yaw, pitch and roll) focused innovative attention mechanism to capture the subtle changes in images. The mechanism uses attentional spatial pooling from a self-attention layer and learns the importance over fine-grained to coarse spatial structures and combine them to capture rich semantic information concerning a given rotation axis. The evaluation of our approach using three benchmark datasets is very competitive to state-of-the-arts, including with and without landmark-based methods. Code can be found at https://github.com/ArdhenduBehera/RAFA-Net.

1 Introduction

Head pose estimation aims to infer the orientation of a person's head relative to the camera view. It is often represented using a 3D vector containing the Euler angles of yaw, pitch and roll. It is a key to many real-world applications such as aiding eye gaze estimation, human attention modeling, driver behavior understanding, human-robot social interactions, face alignments, human-computer interactions and many more. Over the past 20 years, there is a significant advancement in face detection. However, the reliable estimation of head poses from a single RGB image is still challenging, particularly in unconstrained 'in the wild' scenarios. For extreme poses, even face detection is arguably still difficult.

Estimating head pose from an image is essentially solving the mapping problem between 2D and 3D spaces. Traditionally, this is carried out using two steps:

Electronic supplementary material The online version of this chapter (https://doi.org/10.1007/978-3-030-69541-5_14) contains supplementary material, which is available to authorized users.

© Springer Nature Switzerland AG 2021
H. Ishikawa et al. (Eds.): ACCV 2020, LNCS 12626, pp. 223–240, 2021.
https://doi.org/10.1007/978-3-030-69541-5_14

1) detecting 2D facial landmarks in the target face, and 2) establishing the correspondence between landmarks and a head template [1–4]. The recent surge in deep Convolutional Neural Networks (CNNs) has significantly influenced in detecting and localizing facial landmarks [5–8]. This is mainly due to the fact that deep models are often robust to extreme poses and occlusions, encouraging improvements in performance. Most of these models are aimed to estimate head poses and detect facial landmark, jointly. Moreover, the main goal is to improve the accuracy of facial landmark detection with the help of head poses, resulting in head pose estimation itself is not accurate enough.

There is no doubt that the advancement of deep CNNs has significantly improved landmarks detection accuracy. However, there are still possibilities of introducing errors in landmark-based head pose estimation. These are: 1) an insufficient number of detected landmarks, 2) quality of the head models/templates, and 3) their adaptation to each individual is also influenced by the model deformation, which is computationally expensive. To address this, there is a significant interest in estimating head poses directly from image intensities [6,7,9–14]. Existing works also use multimodal information such as RGB+depth images [15–18] and temporal knowledge from videos [19,20] to improve the head pose estimation accuracy. It has significantly helped in improving performance but has its drawbacks. For example, depth cameras to capture depth information can be challenging to use in outdoors, and uncontrolled environments and are not always available. Therefore, there is a need for fast and reliable monocular image-based head pose estimation. On the other hand, temporal information in videos involving detection and tracking of heads could guide the pose estimation. However, modeling temporal information is often achieved with the use of recurrent networks, which are usually computationally expensive.

Our Contribution: We propose a landmark-free end-to-end regression model called RAFA-Net (Rotation Axis Focused Attentional Network) for head pose estimation from monocular images. Head poses in monocular images often exhibit subtle changes. Deep models over the full images with distinctive classes have shown great success, but it raises the question about their performance in recognizing fine-grained changes [21]. Therefore, there is a need for learning meaningful features linking fine-grained changes for performing regression. One way to address this problem by adapting statistical pooling or aggregation approaches [22,23], which learn high-level representative features from the low-level local features. However, such approaches often do not consider the spatial relationships, resulting in them being unable to capture the spatial structure, which is necessary for modeling fine-grained changes. Thus, we propose a novel attentional spatial pooling that *learns to distill* fine-grained to coarse spatial structures and combines them based on their importance to capture rich semantic information for estimating head poses. Moreover, the pooling module is attached to a given rotation axis (yaw, pitch and roll) to capture specific fine-grained changes in the image intensities for accurate head pose estimation.

Our attentional pooling can be interpreted as a more flexible and versatile pooling tool. Conventional pooling uses a pre-defined fixed window size (RoI), strides and types for a given task. Whereas, in our case, we pool features from a set of possible pooling (a combination of types, size and strides) covering smaller area to wider area with a more versatile approach to capture both local and global structures. Our approach is very similar to the recent work of deformable RoI pooling [24,25] for object detection and semantic segmentation. However, to generate new feature maps, we use attentional RoI pooling, which learns to distill the intrinsic consistency between informativeness of pooled features and their usefulness in estimating poses. Moreover, our attention map conveys how much to concentrate a given RoI in focus conditioned on all other RoIs. Whereas, deformable RoI pooling generates feature map via weighted summation of RoIs.

2   Related Work

Facial Landmark-Based Approaches: Detected 2D facial keypoints are used to estimate head poses using 3D techniques such as POSIT [26]. The face alignment is often carried out using regression [1,3,4,27], as well as model-based approaches [28–30]. Lately, CNN models [2,31] for estimating 3D faces have shown superior performance. However, these approaches require manually annotated ground-truth, which is laborious, time-consuming, and often experts cannot accurately assign landmark locations in low-resolution images.

Landmark-Free Approaches: To address the above drawback, recently, there is a significant interest in estimating head poses directly from the image intensities using deep networks [9–14]. Such approaches often encounter problems due to illumination variations or poor illumination during night time. To overcome this, researchers have explored the complementary depth information for higher accuracy [16–18,32]. Similarly, sequential knowledge from videos is explored in [19,20] to benefit from the temporal coherence by using particle filters and recurrent networks to track facial features over time for improved head pose estimation.

Multi-tasking Approaches: Facial modeling and analysis are multi-task learning (e.g. face detection, person identification, landmark detection, recognizing emotions, etc.) and is closely linked to head poses. Therefore, it has been shown that learning-related tasks jointly achieve better performance than individually [4–8]. Most of these methods are based on end-to-end deep learning models.

Attention-Based Approaches: Attention mechanism in machine learning is influenced by the human perception that focuses on selective parts of image/video to acquire salient information at specific locations and times. It has drawn increasing interest in solving machine translation [33,34], image/video captioning [35–37], image/video recognition [38–40] and visual question answering [41] problems. Head pose estimation using attention mechanism is yet to be explored. This could be due to the head pose is a regression model, whereas, most of the existing approaches are applied to the classification of sequence mapping. Recently, Yang et al. [11] use a spatial attention proposal for refining regression

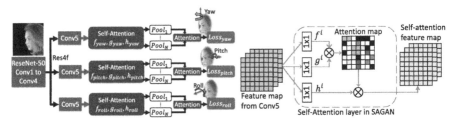

(a) Proposed RAFA-Net based on ResNet   (b) Rotation axis focused self-attention

Fig. 1. RAFA-Net for estimating head poses by introducing rotation axis-specific (yaw, pitch and roll) self-attention and attentional pooling components.

values to estimate head poses. Our method is different from them since we use attentional spatial pooling and *learn to attend* the importance of fine-grained to coarse spatial structures to capture the subtle changes in images. Moreover, our model learns the rotation-axis specific subtle changes for estimating head poses. Our method is simple yet efficient and can be easily applicable to other applications.

We revisit many of the above approaches (especially landmark-free methods, residual networks and attention mechanism) for advancing knowledge and solving the head pose estimation problem. We benefit from the well-known and very efficient ResNet architecture with simple yet efficient network modifications to capture salient information linking fine-grained changes in monocular images for estimating the head poses. We emphasize that our contributions include not only the modification to ResNet architecture but also an empirical study on the role of attentional spatial pooling in improving pose estimation accuracy.

3   Proposed Approach (RAFA-Net)

RAFA-Net is based on the ResNet model [42], which is adapted by introducing rotation axis-specific self-attention and attentional pooling layer to estimate head orientation represented using yaw, pitch and roll (Fig. 1a). In a CNN, initial layers learn more generic features (e.g. edges, corners, color blobs, etc.). As we move towards the output layer, the network gradually moves from generic to task-specific high-level features (e.g. structural/shape information). We explore this by modifying the last convolution (Conv5) layer of the ResNet-50 to learn rotation axis-specific high-level structural information. As a result, we use three parallel Conv5 layers focusing on the respective yaw, pitch and roll axes. The output (width W, height H and C channels) of axis-specific Conv5 is used to compute the respective bandwidth-specific self-attention map $\alpha = \{\alpha^{yaw}, \alpha^{pitch}, \alpha^{roll}\}$ (Fig. 1b) to capture important cues focusing on spatial changes. For each axis, the goal is to explicitly learn the relationships between features (dimension C) spatially located in a given resolution of $W \times H$. It conveys how much to focus the features at a given spatial location when synthesizing feature in another location. To achieve this, we compute the self-attention map $(\alpha^{yaw}, \alpha^{pitch}, \alpha^{roll})$ by adapting the SAGAN concept [43] in which the *query*, the *key*, and the *value* are all the same. For clarity, we describe the process for computing α and is the same for each rotation axis. Let's consider $x \in \mathbb{R}^{W \times H \times C}$ is the output of a Conv5 layer for an image I (Fig. 1a). To compute α, the feature x is first transformed into the concept of *key* $\boldsymbol{f}(x) = \boldsymbol{W_f}x$, *query* $\boldsymbol{g}(x) = \boldsymbol{W_g}x$, and *value* $\boldsymbol{h}(x) = \boldsymbol{W_h}x$. The element $\alpha_{i,j}$ indicates the extent to which the α attends to the jth location while focusing on the ith position in x and is computed using softmax function. It is used to compute the output o_j, which is a column vector of final output $o = (o_1, o_2, \ldots, o_j, \ldots, o_{W \times H}) \in \mathbb{R}^{W \times H \times C}$ and is computed as:

$$o_j = \sum_{i=1}^{W \times H} \alpha_{i,j}\boldsymbol{h}(x_i), \text{where } \alpha_{i,j} = \frac{\exp(s_{i,j})}{\sum_{j=1}^{W \times H} \exp(s_{i,j})}, s_{i,j} = \boldsymbol{f}(x_i)^T \boldsymbol{g}(x_j) \quad (1)$$

$\boldsymbol{W_f}$, $\boldsymbol{W_g}$ and $\boldsymbol{W_h}$ are all 1×1 convolution filters. We compute $o = \{o^k\}$ for each axis $k \in \{yaw, pitch, roll\}$. In addition, we also learn axis-specific scalar β^k and multiply with the output o^k and then add it with the input feature map x^k.

$$\hat{x}^k = \beta^k o^k + x^k, \text{ where } k \in \{yaw, pitch, roll\} \quad (2)$$

β^k is initialized to zero. It allows the network to first rely on the axis-specific local cues and then gradually learns to assign more weight to the global evidence. Afterwards, $\hat{x}^k$ is passed to our novel attentional spatial pooling (Fig. 2a).

3.1 Attentional Spatial Pooling

Spatial pooling is a standard building block of modern CNNs. In terms of the receptive field, there are two types (*local* or *global*) of spatial pooling widely used. Usually, *global* pooling often substitutes for the FC layer in many CNNs [42,44,45] via spatially squeezing the feature map tensor into a vector of channel dimensionality and is fed into the final classification/regression layer. However, global pooling loses the spatial structure and therefore, it might not be able to capture the subtle changes in images containing face orientations. In contrast, *local* pooling in CNNs [45–48] is commonly used to reduce spatial resolution with increasing robustness in variation (e.g. translation) against input images. It deals with only local features in the receptive field [49,50]. To get the best out of both, one needs an appropriate method to combine them.

To address this, we propose a novel trainable *hybrid* spatial pooling, which employs attention mechanism and learns importance over fine-grained (local) to coarse (global) structures and combines them to attain rich semantic information in images. Our approach learns rotation axis specific pooling module (see Fig. 1a) that combines a various combination of pooling parameters (sizes, types and strides) and adaptively tunes it without manually fixing it beforehand. Let's consider our pooling module $\mathcal{P} = \{pool_1, pool_2, \ldots, pool_K\}$ consists of K possible poolings (i.e. combination of types, size and strides). One

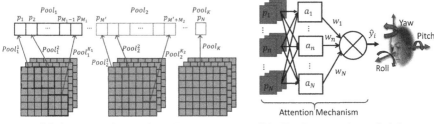

(a) Attentional spatial pooling   (b) Weighting each pooled feature

Fig. 2. Before computing the loss for the respective Euler angle, we use a novel attentional spatial pooling from self-attention layer to capture rich semantic information representing the given rotation axis-specific angle. Afterwards, we combine them with our innovative attention mechanism.

module per axis $i \in \{yaw, pitch, roll\}$ receives input from the respective self-attention map $\hat{x}^i \in \mathbb{R}^{W \times H \times C}$. Each $pool_k$ $(k = 1 \ldots K)$ is a unique combination of pooling size, type and stride resulting in a fixed number of RoI (region-of-interest) per $pool_k$ to be used for pooling (i.e. spatial sliding positions) in the spatial resolution of $W \times H$ (Fig. 2a). As a result, there is K_1 RoIs in $pool_1 = \{pool_1^1, pool_1^2, \ldots, pool_1^{K_1}\}$, K_2 RoIs in $pool_2 = \{pool_2^1, pool_2^2, \ldots, pool_2^{K_2}\}$ and so on, until a single RoI in $pool_K = \{pool_K^1\}$ since $pool_K$ is the *global* pooling considering whole spatial resolution of $W \times H$. We concatenate all RoIs i.e. $\mathcal{P} = (pool_1^1, \ldots, pool_1^{K_1}, pool_2^1, \ldots, pool_2^{K_2}, \ldots, pool_K)$ over K pooling combinations and represent as $\mathcal{P} = (p_1, p_2, \ldots, p_N)$, where N is the total number of RoIs (see Fig. 2a). Each element p_n $(n = 1 \ldots N)$ is a RoI-pooled feature. During decision making, our pooling module $\mathcal{P}$ *learns to focus* on each p_n by its importance. We achieve this by introducing an attention-focused learnable parameter θ_a to compute high-level feature encoding $\mathbf{x} = f_a(p_n, a_n; \theta_a)$, where a_n is the attention-focused representation of RoI-pooled feature p_n and f_a is a mapping function. The element a_n is computed using the weighted summation of all other RoI-pooled features $p_{n'}$ and their similarity (measured in the form of probability) $\tau_{n,n'}$ to a given feature p_n in focus. This novel attention mechanism is implemented using an LSTM (Long Short-Term Memory) cell as follows:

$$a_n = \sum_{n'=1}^{N} \tau_{n,n'} p_{n'}, \text{ where } \tau_{n,n'} = \frac{\exp(\sigma_{n,n'})}{\sum_{n'=1}^{N} \exp(\sigma_{n,n'})},$$

$$\sigma_{n,n'} = W_\sigma \rho_{n,n'} + b_\sigma, \text{ and } \rho_{n,n'} = tanh(W_\rho p_n + W_{\rho'} p_{n'} + b_\rho) \tag{3}$$

W_ρ and $W_{\rho'}$ are weights matrices for the respective RoI pooling combinations n and n'; W_σ is their non-linear fusion. $\tau_{n,n'}$ is computed from $\rho_{n,n'}$ using the sigmoid function; b_ρ and b_σ are the biases. The attention-focused representation a_n conveys how much to *attend the RoI-pooled feature p_n in focus conditioned on all other RoI-pooled features* (Fig. 2b). Finally, high-level feature map $\mathbf{x}$ for a given axis (yaw, pitch and roll) is computed by a weighted summation of all the pooling combinations using the attention importance weight w_n.

$$\mathbf{x} = \sum_{n=1}^{N} a_n w_n, \text{where } w_n = \frac{\exp(\psi_n)}{\sum_{j=1}^{N} \exp(\psi_j)} \text{ and } \psi_n = W_\psi a_n + b_\psi \qquad (4)$$

The weight matrix W_ψ and bias b_ψ are learned. The attention importance score w_n for each a_n is constructed via probability distribution over the pooling representations using the sigmoid function. This approach is similar to the attention-based approach used to solve machine translation problems [51] in which the model automatically searches for parts of a source sentence that are relevant to predicting a target word. The difference is that we do not consider the sequential information. The final feature map $\mathbf{x}$ is used as an input to a final linear regression layer to solve the head pose estimation. Our attentional spatial pooling module consists of learnable parameter $\theta_a = \{W_\rho, W_{\rho'}, W_\sigma, W_\psi, b_\rho, b_\sigma, b_\psi\}$ for each rotation axis (yaw, pitch, and roll) o estimate axis-specific pose angles.

3.2   Learning

RAFA-Net is trained in an end-to-end fashion with the default ResNet input image size of 224×224. The model takes a set of training images $I = \{I^m | m = 1, \ldots, M\}$ and the respective head pose value of yaw (y_{yaw}^m), pitch (y_{pitch}^m) and roll (y_{roll}^m) in Euler angle (radian). The aim is to train the model to predict $\hat{y}_{yaw}^m, \hat{y}_{pitch}^m, \hat{y}_{roll}^m = model(I^m)$ for a given image I^m by minimizing combined regression loss (L_{MSE}), which is computed as a Mean Squared Error.

$$L_{MSE} = \frac{1}{M} \sum_{m=1}^{M} \underbrace{(y_{yaw}^m - \hat{y}_{yaw}^m)^2}_{\text{Yaw MSE Loss}} + \underbrace{(y_{pitch}^m - \hat{y}_{pitch}^m)^2}_{\text{Pitch MSE Loss}} + \underbrace{(y_{roll}^m - \hat{y}_{roll}^m)^2}_{\text{Roll MSE Loss}} \qquad (5)$$

4   Experiments

4.1   Implementation

RAFA-Net is implemented using Keras with TensorFlow as a backend. The convolutional layers (Conv1 to Conv5) are pre-trained layers from the ResNet-50 model [42] trained on the ImageNet [52] dataset. The model is trained with 150 epochs (32 batch size) using RMSProp optimizer [53] with a learning rate of 0.001 and rho of 0.9. The experiments are performed on a Linux PC (Ubuntu OS, Intel Core i9 9820X) with an NVIDIA Titan V GPU (12 GB).

For an input image of size $224 \times 224 \times 3$, the self-attention module's output feature map resolution is $7 \times 7 \times 2048$ (Fig. 1b). For our attentional spatial pooling module $\mathcal{P}$, we experimentally found that *max pooling* is the best possible pooling type for this task. Given the spatial resolution of 7×7, we use pooling sizes of 2, 3, 4, 5 and 7. Similarly, we use the pooling stride of 2 and 3.

(a) 300W-LP   (b) AFLW2000   (c) BIWI

Fig. 3. Example images from three datasets: a) 300W-LP synthetic [31] - the various rendered head poses. b) AFLW2000 [31] - head poses from real-world images with varying background and lighting conditions. c) BIWI [17] - head poses from RGB-D images collected under a controlled environment.

4.2   Datasets and Evaluation Strategies

There are a number of datasets produced so far for head pose estimation [54,55]. Often facial landmarks are used to generate the ground-truth head poses by fitting a mean 3D face with the POSIT algorithm [26] since it is difficult to precisely measure (or manually annotate) them. This approach works well for smaller angle head poses. However, it does not work well for large head poses due to the accuracy of facial landmark detection deteriorates in large poses and is mainly due to occlusion. For our experiments, we have used the three most popular datasets: 1) 300W-LP [31], 2) AFLW2000 [31], and 3) BIWI [17]. A few examples from these datasets are shown in Fig. 3. The 300W-LP [31] dataset is derived from the 300W dataset [55], which is a collection of several datasets for face alignment with 68 facial landmarks. It uses face profiling with 3D image meshing to generate 61,225 images of faces having large poses and further expanded to 122,450 faces with flipping. It is called as the 300W across Large Poses (300W-LP) and is synthetically generated by predicting the depth of each face, and then its profile views are computed with 3D rotation. The AFLW2000 dataset [31] is the subset (first 2000 images) of the AFLW dataset [56], and consists of head pose with large variations, facial expressions, different illumination, and occlusion conditions. It provides ground-truth annotations consisting of 3D faces and the corresponding 68 3D landmarks. The BIWI dataset [17] contains 15,678 frames from 24 RGB-D videos of 20 subjects captured using a Kinect device. These videos are captured in a controlled environment, and the 3D model is fitted to the RGB-D videos to obtain the ground-truth head poses. The head poses angle ranges are $\pm 77^{o}$ for yaw, $\pm 60^{o}$ for pitch, and $\pm 50^{o}$ for the roll.

To compare the performance of the RAFA-Net with state-of-the-arts, we follow the standard evaluation strategies, which are: 1) train on the synthetic 300W-LP large dataset and test on the other two relatively small datasets (AFLW2000 and BIWI). 2) train the model using 70% of videos (16 videos) in the BIWI dataset and evaluate the rest 30% (8 videos). In all three datasets, we use the detected face bounding box provided by Shao et al. [13]. The standard evaluation metric of mean absolute error (MAE) is used. For each pose angle, the average prediction error in degrees over testing images is used for the comparison. We have also compared the average prediction error over three (yaw, pitch and roll) Euler angles to show the overall performance of the proposed approach.

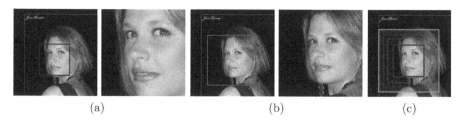

Fig. 4. Data augmentation involving randomization of bounding box margin using a control parameter γ: a) original bounding box from a face detector ($\gamma = 0$) and the corresponding cropped and resized (224×224) image, b) bounding box with $\gamma = 0.3$ and the corresponding cropped and resized image, c) 20 randomly generated bounding boxes (red) between blue and green bounding box, i.e. $0 \leq \gamma \leq 0.5$. Best view in color.

4.3 Data Augmentation

We propose a novel data augmentation approach (Fig. 4) and is inspired by the experiment carried out by Shao et al. [13] to measure the accuracy of their model by selecting a different size of the bounding box (prior to training and evaluation) enclosing a face. Our is different since we randomly generate these bounding boxes during training using a control parameter γ. Let (b_x, b_y) is the provided top-left location of a square bounding box b with size b_s. The corresponding bottom-right corner location will be at $(b_x + b_s, b_y + b_s)$. The aim is to generate different locations of top-left $(b_x - \gamma b_s, b_y - \gamma b_s)$ and bottom-right $(b_x + b_s + \gamma b_s, b_y + b_s + \gamma b_s)$ corners using γ to control bounding box margins. We experimentally found that this randomization gives better generalization resulting in improved performance rather than using standard augmentation techniques such as random scaling, width and/or height sifting and cropping. For all our experiments, we have used $0 \leq \gamma \leq 0.5$.

4.4 Comparison with the State-of-the-Art (SotA) Methods

We first compare the SotA pose estimation methods trained on the 300W-LP [31] and tested on the AFLW2000 [31] and BIWI [17], respectively. The performance comparison is presented in Table 1. In this experiment, the training and testing datasets are very different. For example, 300W-LP is a synthetic one, while the BIWI and AFLW2000 consist of real images. The deep learning-based landmark-free approaches such as Hopenet [10], SSR-Net-MD [12], ResNet-BBM [13], FSA-Net [11] and our RAFA-Net perform better than the landmark-based ones (Dlib [1], 3DDFA [31], FAN [2], KEPLER [5] and Two-stage [3]) tested on both the BIWI and AFLW2000 datasets. This is mainly since the landmark-free approaches can better accommodate the domain discrepancies between training and testing datasets.

Train on 300W-LP and Test on AFLW2000: Our RAFA-Net is significantly outperformed the SotA approaches (Table 1). Among the existing landmark-

Table 1. Comparison with the state-of-the-art approaches, which are trained on 300W-LP [31] dataset and evaluated on the respective AFLW2000 [31] and BIWI [17] datasets. The average error is in Euler angles (degrees).

Method	AFLW2000 dataset [31]				BIWI dataset [17]			
	Yaw	Pitch	Roll	MAE	Yaw	Pitch	Roll	MAE
Dlib (68 landmarks) [1]	23.15	13.63	10.55	15.78	16.76	13.80	6.19	12.25
3DDFA [31]	5.40	8.53	8.25	7.39	36.18	12.25	8:78	19.07
FAN (12 landmarks) [2]	6.36	12.28	8.71	9.12	8.53	7.48	7.63	7.88
KEPLER [5]	–	–	–	–	8.80	17.3	16.2	13.9
Two-stage [3]	11.92	8.25	7.47	9:21	9.49	11:34	6.00	8.94
Ground-truth landmarks [10]	5.92	11.76	8.27	8.65	–	–	–	–
Hopenet ($\alpha = 2$) [10]	6.47	6.56	5.44	6.16	5.17	6.98	3.39	5.18
SSR-Net-MD [12]	5.14	7.09	5.89	6.01	4.49	6.31	3.61	4.65
ResNet-BBM (K = 0.5) [13]	5.07	6.37	4.99	5.48	4.59	7.25	6.15	6.00
FSA-Caps-Fusion [11]	4.50	6.08	4.64	5.07	**4.27**	**4.96**	**2.76**	**4.00**
RAFA-Net(Ours: $\gamma = 0.3$)	**3.60**	**4.92**	**3.88**	**4.13**	5.71	6.28	3.64	5.21
RAFA-Net(Ours: $\gamma = 0.2$)	**3.52**	**4.93**	**3.91**	**4.12**	5.67	6.26	3.60	5.17

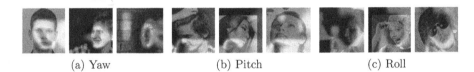

(a) Yaw   (b) Pitch   (c) Roll

Fig. 5. Visualization of the proposed attentional spatial pooling using rotation axis specific class activation map. RAFA-Net is trained on the 300W-LP dataset and tested on AFLW2000. It shows the rotation axis specific representative features are used for angle estimation. Visualization using BIWI images is included in the supplementary document.

free approaches, FSA-Caps-Fusion [11] provides the best performance. It uses the capsule network [23] for feature aggregation and gives equal importance to different fine-grained feature mapping. We found that by providing weighted importance to the fine-grained to coarse spatial structures using our rotation axis-specific attentional spatial pooling produces more robust results. Similarly, KEPLER [5] aims to establish structural relationships between facial landmarks. Our approach is more effective than their iterative method since we learn the importance of fine-grained to coarse spatial structures and combine them by considering their importance to capture the rich semantic information. We have also evaluated the proposed approach by varying the bounding box parameter $0 \leq \gamma \leq 0.5$ during testing. We have found that the overall prediction error (MAE: 4.12) of our approach is the best (lower the better) for $\gamma = 0.2$, but the individual prediction error for pitch and roll is slightly better for $\gamma = 0.3$ (Table 1 and Fig. 6a).

Table 2. Comparison with the state-of-the-art approaches using BIWI dataset [17]. There are three different evaluation methods (RGB only, RGB+Depth, and RGB+Time) by considering different modalities. The training (16 videos) data consists of 70% of the total videos (24) and the rest eight videos being used for testing. The average error is in Euler angles (degrees).

Method	Yaw	Pitch	Roll	MAE
RGB and depth (RGB-D)				
DeepHeadPose [15]	5.32	4.76	–	–
Martin et al. [16]	3.60	2.50	2.60	2.90
3DMM [32]	**2.50**	**1.50**	**2.20**	**2.07**
RGB and time				
VGG16+RNN [19]	3.14	3.48	2.60	3.07
Single RGB frame				
DeepHeadPose [15]	5.67	5.18	–	–
VGG16 [19]	3.91	4.03	3.03	3.66
SSR-Net-MD [12]	4.24	4.35	4.19	4.26
FSA-Caps-Fusion [11]	**2.89**	**4.29**	3.60	3.60
RAFA-Net (ours: $\gamma = 0.2$)	3.08	4.35	**2.85**	**3.43**
RAFA-Net (ours: $\gamma = 0.1$)	3.07	4.30	**2.82**	**3.40**

Train on 300W-LP and Test on BIWI: The overall performance (MAE) of our RAFA-Net is inferior to the FSA-Caps-Fusion [11] and SSR-Net-MD [12] landmark-free approaches (Table 1). However, it is better than the ResNet-BBM [13] and Hopenet [10]. Moreover, the estimated average error in pitch is better (6.26) than the landmark-free approaches except for the FSA-Caps-Fusion [11] (4.96). This could be due to the BIWI dataset is captured in a controlled environment with limited pose variations (yaw: $\pm 77°$, pitch: $\pm 60°$ and roll: $\pm 50°$) and RGB-D videos are used to obtain the ground-truth head poses. Whereas, AFLW2000 consists of head poses with large variations ($\pm 99°$) and is consistent with the training dataset 300W-LP. Nevertheless, our RAFA-Net performs significantly better than the landmark-based ones (Dlib [1], 3DDFA [31], FAN [2], KEPLER [5] and Two-stage [3]) on this dataset.

Train and Test on BIWI: In this experiment, we compare the performance using only the BIWI dataset. We use the same train and test split, as provided in [11]. The dataset consists of RGB-D sequences, including color and depth information. The overall performance (MAE) of our approach is better than all other methods in its peer group (single RGB frame only). For individual yaw and pitch Euler angles, our method is very close to the FSA-Caps-Net [11] (e.g.. Yaw: 2.89 vs 3.07 and Pitch: 4.29 vs 4.30). For roll, our approach is significantly better than the existing approaches. We also report the existing approaches, which combine the different modalities (RGB+Depth and RGB+Time) for improving performance. Our approach does not perform equally well compared to

Table 3. Ablation study involving the performance of individual components. Performance comparison using our novel bounding box (BB) augmentation versus standard spatial augmentation (random scaling, shifting and cropping), as well as rotation axis-specific attentional pooling versus single attentional pooing. The respective model is trained on 300W-LP [31] dataset and evaluated on the respective AFLW2000 [31] and BIWI [17] datasets.

Experiment using	AFLW2000 [31]				BIWI [17]			
	Yaw	Pitch	Roll	MAE	Yaw	Pitch	Roll	MAE
Self-attn. only ($\gamma = 0.3$)	4.19	5.83	4.44	4.82	6.26	9.50	4.36	6.71
Attn. pooling only ($\gamma = 0.3$)	3.34	5.61	3.91	4.29	5.16	9.93	3.56	6.22
No BB augmentation	4.22	5.87	4.53	4.53	7.46	10.31	4.01	7.26
RAFA-Net (single attn)	3.93	5.51	4.13	4.52	6.85	8.45	4.18	6.49
RAFA-Net ($\gamma = 0.2$)	3.52	4.93	3.91	4.12	5.67	6.26	3.60	5.17
	Evaluation using spatial augmentation only							
Self-attn. only	5.83	6.54	5.74	6.04	9.00	7.42	5.67	7.36
Attn. pooling only	4.35	5.89	4.71	4.99	7.32	7.98	4.90	6.73
RAFA-Net	3.63	5.55	3.57	4.25	5.56	6.02	4.54	5.37

Table 4. Ablation study involving the performance of individual components using our novel bounding box (BB) augmentation versus standard spatial augmentation (random scaling, shifting and cropping). RAFA-Net is trained and tested using BIWI [17] datasets.

Experiment BIWI [17]	BB augmentation				Spatial augmentation			
	Yaw	Pitch	Roll	MAE	Yaw	Pitch	Roll	MAE
Self-attn. only ($\gamma = 0.4$)	3.84	5.26	3.91	4.34	4.62	5.99	4.67	5.10
Attn. pooling only ($\gamma = 0.3$)	4.23	6.00	4.11	4.80	4.98	5.54	4.25	4.92
No BB augmentation	4.37	4.74	3.98	4.36	–	–	–	–
RAFA-Net ($\gamma = 0.1$)	3.07	4.30	2.82	3.40	3.50	4.83	3.28	3.87

these methods, which combine multimodal data, but not too far from them. Additionally, our RAFA-Net performs significantly better than the multimodal approaches [15,16,19] in estimating yaw. Similarly, for pitch, our RAFA-Net is better than the DeepHeadPose [15] that uses RGB and depth information.

4.5   Ablation Studies

We have conducted an ablation study to understand the impact of the proposed novel attentional spatial pooling, rotation axis-specific self-attention, and our data augmentation approach involving the randomization of bounding box margin. The results are shown in Table 3 and Table 4. The performance of RAFA-Net trained on 300W-LP and tested on the respective AFLW2000 and BIWI datasets are presented in Table 3. It is observed that the MAE of our attentional spatial pooling is better than the self-attention, as well as our model

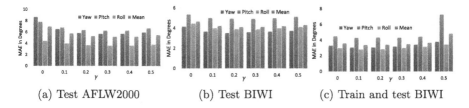

(a) Test AFLW2000   (b) Test BIWI   (c) Train and test BIWI

Fig. 6. Effect of bounding box margin (control with parameter $0 \leq \gamma \leq 0.5$) on pose estimation error. RAFA-Net is trained on 300W-LP and evaluated on the respective a) AFLW2000 and b) BIWI datasets. c) RAFA-Net is trained and tested using BIWI dataset. Mean is the average of yaw, pitch and roll.

without a randomized bounding box. Moreover, for AFLW2000 dataset, the performance of each component in Table 3 is better than the previous best FSA-CAPS-Fusion (MAE: 5.07) [11]. This justifies the benefits of each component. Among the three components, our novel spatial attentional pooling module is the best performer. This proves the significance of the proposed spatial pooling. We have also compared the performance of RAFA-Net using our novel bounding box augmentation versus standard spatial augmentation (random scaling, shifting and cropping). The proposed bounding box augmentation outperforms the standard spatial augmentation (Table 3). A similar trend is also observed when tested on the BIWI dataset. We have also assessed the performance of the above components using the BIWI dataset (train and test like in Table 2). The results are presented in Table 4. The rotation axis-specific attentional spatial pooling is also compared with the single attentional pooling predicting yaw, pitch and roll. The axis-specific attentional pooling is outperformed the single one (Table 3).

We have also carried out the ablation study for understanding the influence of bounding box margin parameter γ while testing. During training, we randomize the value of $0 \leq \gamma \leq 0.5$ while selecting the size of the bounding box enclosing a face (Fig. 4). During testing, we vary the value of γ from 0 to 0.5 with an increment of 0.1 and evaluate the prediction error. The results are reported in Fig. 6. It shows the result of our model trained on 300W-LP [31] and evaluated on the respective AFLW2000 [31] and BIWI [17] datasets. One can observe that as the value of γ increases, the prediction error decreases (less the better) and reaches a minimum at $\gamma = 0.2$ and then increases. A similar trend is observed for $\gamma = 0.1$ when the model is evaluated using BIWI (Fig. 6c). Shao et al. [13] have also studied the effect of bounding box margin on prediction accuracy. However, our approach is different from them since we use the randomization of γ during training and evaluate the prediction accuracy with different γ values during testing. Whereas, they use the same fixed value during training and testing.

We have also studied the impact of bounding box margin parameter γ on different angle ranges (-90:-60, -60:-30, -30:0, 0:30, 30:60, and 60:90) using our RAFA-Net. The model is trained on 300W-LP [31] and tested on AFLW2000 [31] and BIWI [17] datasets. The results are presented in Fig. 7. It is evident that the estimation of the yaw angle is accurate for a wide range of angles, whereas

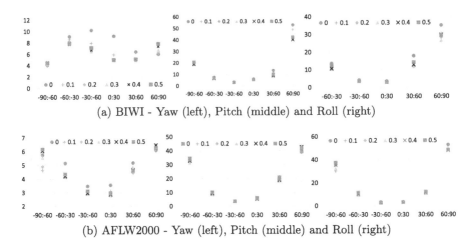

(a) BIWI - Yaw (left), Pitch (middle) and Roll (right)

(b) AFLW2000 - Yaw (left), Pitch (middle) and Roll (right)

Fig. 7. Effect of bounding box margin (control with parameter $0 \leq \gamma \leq 0.5$) on average pose estimation error in degrees (y-axis) on different angle ranges (x-axis) for yaw, pitch, and roll. Our model is trained on 300W-LP and tested on the BIWI and AFLW2000 datasets.

the pitch and roll tend to be inaccurate for larger angles (absolute). This trend is observed in both BIWI and AFLW2000 datasets. It is also observed that the pitch and roll lean to insensitive to the γ values for smaller angles; however, they tend to be sensitive for larger angles. A noticeable observation is that yaw is sensitive to the γ values for a wide range of angles. Therefore, the optimal value of γ has influenced the overall estimation accuracy. We have included the quantitative values in tabular form in the supplementary document.

5 Conclusion

In this paper, we have proposed a simple yet effective way to learn the importance of meaningful salient features in modeling fine-grained changes for head pose estimation using monocular images. By defining *learn to attend* weighting function via exploring attentional pooling mechanism, we are able to learn the importance of fine-grained to coarse spatial structures and combined them based on their importance to capture rich semantic information to solve the problem in hand. The proposed attentional pooling is employed to capture rotation axis specific semantic information, and our experiments have shown that the approach is better than the state-of-the-art methods. The proposed approach has demonstrated to improve the head pose estimation accuracy; however, we believe that this idea can be adapted to other regression and classification problems. Future work will be to apply the proposed technique for multi-task learning linking facial expression analysis, modeling, and recognition.

Acknowledgement. This research was supported in part by the UKIERI-DST (CHARM) under grant DST UKIERI-2018-19-10. The GPU used in this research is generously donated by the NVIDIA Corporation.

References

1. Kazemi, V., Sullivan, J.: One millisecond face alignment with an ensemble of regression trees. In: Proceedings of the IEEE Conference on Computer Vision and Pattern Recognition, pp. 1867–1874 (2014)
2. Bulat, A., Tzimiropoulos, G.: How far are we from solving the 2D & 3D face alignment problem? (and a dataset of 230,000 3D facial landmarks). In: Proceedings of the IEEE International Conference on Computer Vision, pp. 1021–1030 (2017)
3. Lv, J., Shao, X., Xing, J., Cheng, C., Zhou, X.: A deep regression architecture with two-stage re-initialization for high performance facial landmark detection. In: Proceedings of the IEEE Conference on Computer Vision and Pattern Recognition, pp. 3317–3326 (2017)
4. Zhu, X., Ramanan, D.: Face detection, pose estimation, and landmark localization in the wild. In: 2012 IEEE Conference on Computer Vision and Pattern Recognition, pp. 2879–2886. IEEE (2012)
5. Kumar, A., Alavi, A., Chellappa, R.: KEPLER: keypoint and pose estimation of unconstrained faces by learning efficient H-CNN regressors. In: 12th IEEE International Conference on Automatic Face & Gesture Recognition (FG 2017), pp. 258–265. IEEE (2017)
6. Ranjan, R., Sankaranarayanan, S., Castillo, C.D., Chellappa, R.: An all-in-one convolutional neural network for face analysis. In: 2017 12th IEEE International Conference on Automatic Face & Gesture Recognition (FG 2017), pp. 17–24. IEEE (2017)
7. Ranjan, R., Patel, V.M., Chellappa, R.: HyperFace: a deep multi-task learning framework for face detection, landmark localization, pose estimation, and gender recognition. IEEE Trans. Pattern Anal. Mach. Intell. **41**, 121–135 (2017)
8. Zhang, Z., Luo, P., Loy, C.C., Tang, X.: Facial landmark detection by deep multi-task learning. In: Fleet, D., Pajdla, T., Schiele, B., Tuytelaars, T. (eds.) ECCV 2014. LNCS, vol. 8694, pp. 94–108. Springer, Cham (2014). https://doi.org/10.1007/978-3-319-10599-4_7
9. Kuhnke, F., Ostermann, J.: Deep head pose estimation using synthetic images and partial adversarial domain adaption for continuous label spaces. In: Proceedings of the IEEE International Conference on Computer Vision, pp. 10164–10173 (2019)
10. Ruiz, N., Chong, E., Rehg, J.M.: Fine-grained head pose estimation without keypoints. In: Proceedings of the IEEE Conference on Computer Vision and Pattern Recognition Workshops, pp. 2074–2083 (2018)
11. Yang, T.Y., Chen, Y.T., Lin, Y.Y., Chuang, Y.Y.: FSA-net: learning fine-grained structure aggregation for head pose estimation from a single image. In: Proceedings of the IEEE Conference on Computer Vision and Pattern Recognition, pp. 1087–1096 (2019)
12. Yang, T.Y., Huang, Y.H., Lin, Y.Y., Hsiu, P.C., Chuang, Y.Y.: SSR-net: a compact soft stagewise regression network for age estimation. In: IJCAI, no. 6, p. 7 (2018)
13. Shao, M., Sun, Z., Ozay, M., Okatani, T.: Improving head pose estimation with a combined loss and bounding box margin adjustment. In: 14th IEEE International Conference on Automatic Face Gesture Recognition (FG 2019), pp. 1–5 (2019)

14. Chang, F.J., Tuan Tran, A., Hassner, T., Masi, I., Nevatia, R., Medioni, G.: Face-PoseNet: making a case for landmark-free face alignment. In: Proceedings of the IEEE International Conference on Computer Vision Workshops, pp. 1599–1608 (2017)
15. Mukherjee, S.S., Robertson, N.M.: Deep head pose: gaze-direction estimation in multimodal video. IEEE Trans. Multimed. **17**, 2094–2107 (2015)
16. Martin, M., Van De Camp, F., Stiefelhagen, R.: Real time head model creation and head pose estimation on consumer depth cameras. In: 2nd International Conference on 3D Vision, vol. 1, pp. 641–648. IEEE (2014)
17. Fanelli, G., Dantone, M., Gall, J., Fossati, A., Van Gool, L.: Random forests for real time 3D face analysis. Int. J. Comput. Vis. **101**, 437–458 (2013)
18. Meyer, G.P., Gupta, S., Frosio, I., Reddy, D., Kautz, J.: Robust model-based 3d head pose estimation. In: Proceedings of the IEEE International Conference on Computer Vision, pp. 3649–3657 (2015)
19. Gu, J., Yang, X., De Mello, S., Kautz, J.: Dynamic facial analysis: from Bayesian filtering to recurrent neural network. In: Proceedings of the IEEE Conference on Computer Vision and Pattern Recognition, pp. 1548–1557 (2017)
20. Chrysos, G.G., Antonakos, E., Snape, P., Asthana, A., Zafeiriou, S.: A comprehensive performance evaluation of deformable face tracking "in-the-wild". Int. J. Comput. Vis. **126**, 198–232 (2018)
21. Girdhar, R., Ramanan, D.: Attentional pooling for action recognition. In: Advances in NIPS, pp. 33–44 (2017)
22. Arandjelovic, R., Gronat, P., Torii, A., Pajdla, T., Sivic, J.: NetVLAD: CNN architecture for weakly supervised place recognition. In: Proceedings of the IEEE Conference on Computer Vision and Pattern Recognition, pp. 5297–5307 (2016)
23. Sabour, S., Frosst, N., Hinton, G.E.: Dynamic routing between capsules. In: Advances in Neural Information Processing Systems, pp. 3856–3866 (2017)
24. Zhu, X., Hu, H., Lin, S., Dai, J.: Deformable ConvNets V2: more deformable, better results. In: Proceedings of the IEEE Conference on Computer Vision and Pattern Recognition, pp. 9308–9316 (2019)
25. Dai, J., Qi, H., Xiong, Y., Li, Y., Zhang, G., Hu, H., Wei, Y.: Deformable convolutional networks. In: Proceedings of the IEEE International Conference on Computer Vision, pp. 764–773 (2017)
26. Dementhon, D.F., Davis, L.S.: Model-based object pose in 25 lines of code. Int. J. Comput. Vis. **15**, 123–141 (1995)
27. Cao, X., Wei, Y., Wen, F., Sun, J.: Face alignment by explicit shape regression. Int. J. Comput. Vis. **107**, 177–190 (2014)
28. Matthews, I., Baker, S.: Active appearance models revisited. Int. J. Comput. Vis. **60**, 135–164 (2004)
29. Cootes, T.F., Taylor, C.J., Cooper, D.H., Graham, J.: Active shape models-their training and application. Comput. Vis. Image Underst. **61**, 38–59 (1995)
30. Liang, L., Xiao, R., Wen, F., Sun, J.: Face alignment via component-based discriminative search. In: Forsyth, D., Torr, P., Zisserman, A. (eds.) ECCV 2008. LNCS, vol. 5303, pp. 72–85. Springer, Heidelberg (2008). https://doi.org/10.1007/978-3-540-88688-4_6
31. Zhu, X., Lei, Z., Liu, X., Shi, H., Li, S.Z.: Face alignment across large poses: a 3D solution. In: Proceedings of the IEEE Conference on Computer Vision and Pattern Recognition, pp. 146–155 (2016)

32. Yu, Y., Mora, K.A.F., Odobez, J.M.: Robust and accurate 3D head pose estimation through 3DMM and online head model reconstruction. In: 2017 12th IEEE International Conference on Automatic Face & Gesture Recognition (FG 2017), pp.711–718. IEEE (2017)

33. Vaswani, A., et al.: Attention is all you need. In: Advances in Neural Information Processing Systems, pp. 5998–6008 (2017)

34. Cinar, Y.G., Mirisaee, H., Goswami, P., Gaussier, E., Aït-Bachir, A., Strijov, V.: Position-based content attention for time series forecasting with sequence-to-sequence RNNs. In: Liu, D., Xie, S., Li, Y., Zhao, D., El-Alfy, E.-S.M. (eds.) ICONIP 2017. LNCS, vol. 10638, pp. 533–544. Springer, Cham (2017). https://doi.org/10.1007/978-3-319-70139-4_54

35. Huang, L., Wang, W., Chen, J., Wei, X.Y.: Attention on attention for image captioning. In: Proceedings of the IEEE International Conference on Computer Vision, pp. 4634–4643 (2019)

36. Herdade, S., Kappeler, A., Boakye, K., Soares, J.: Image captioning: transforming objects into words. In: Advances in Neural Information Processing Systems, pp. 11137–11147 (2019)

37. Pei, W., Zhang, J., Wang, X., Ke, L., Shen, X., Tai, Y.W.: Memory-attended recurrent network for video captioning. In: Proceedings of the IEEE Conference on Computer Vision and Pattern Recognition, pp. 8347–8356 (2019)

38. Girdhar, R., Carreira, J., Doersch, C., Zisserman, A.: Video action transformer network. In: Proceedings of the IEEE Conference on Computer Vision and Pattern Recognition, pp. 244–253 (2019)

39. Song, S., Lan, C., Xing, J., Zeng, W., Liu, J.: An end-to-end spatio-temporal attention model for human action recognition from skeleton data. In: Thirty-first AAAI Conference on Artificial Intelligence (2017)

40. Sharma, S., Kiros, R., Salakhutdinov, R.: Action recognition using visual attention. arXiv preprint arXiv:1511.04119 (2015)

41. Li, X., et al.: Beyond RNNs: positional self-attention with co-attention for video question answering. In: Proceedings of the AAAI Conference on Artificial Intelligence, vol. 33, pp. 8658–8665 (2019)

42. He, K., Zhang, X., Ren, S., Sun, J.: Deep residual learning for image recognition. In: IEEE CVPR, pp. 770–778 (2016)

43. Zhang, H., Goodfellow, I., Metaxas, D., Odena, A.: Self-attention generative adversarial networks. arXiv preprint arXiv:1805.08318 (2018)

44. Szegedy, C., Ioffe, S., Vanhoucke, V., Alemi, A.A.: Inception-v4, inception-resnet and the impact of residual connections on learning. In: AAAI, pp. 4278–4284 (2017)

45. Szegedy, C., Vanhoucke, V., Ioffe, S., Shlens, J., Wojna, Z.: Rethinking the inception architecture for computer vision. In: IEEE CVPR (2016)

46. Krizhevsky, A., Sutskever, I., Hinton, G.E.: ImageNet classification with deep convolutional neural networks. In: NIPS, pp. 1097–1105 (2012)

47. Zhai, S., et al.: S3Pool: pooling with stochastic spatial sampling. In: Proceedings of the IEEE Conference on Computer Vision and Pattern Recognition, pp. 4970–4978 (2017)

48. Simonyan, K., Zisserman, A.: Very deep convolutional networks for large-scale image recognition. CoRR abs/1409.1556 (2014)

49. Lee, C.Y., Gallagher, P.W., Tu, Z.: Generalizing pooling functions in convolutional neural networks: mixed, gated, and tree. In: Artificial Intelligence and Statistics, pp. 464–472 (2016)

50. Saeedan, F., Weber, N., Goesele, M., Roth, S.: Detail-preserving pooling in deep networks. In: Proceedings of the IEEE Conference on Computer Vision and Pattern Recognition, pp. 9108–9116 (2018)
51. Bahdanau, D., Cho, K., Bengio, Y.: Neural machine translation by jointly learning to align and translate. arXiv preprint arXiv:1409.0473 (2014)
52. Russakovsky, O., et al.: ImageNet large scale visual recognition challenge. IJCV **115**, 211–252 (2015)
53. Bengio, Y., CA, M.: RMSProp and equilibrated adaptive learning rates for non-convex optimization. CORR abs/1502.04390 (2015)
54. Behera, A., Gidney, A.G., Wharton, Z., Robinson, D., Quinn, K.: A CNN model for head pose recognition using wholes and regions. In: IEEE International Conference on Automatic Face & Gesture Recognition (FG) (2019)
55. Sagonas, C., Tzimiropoulos, G., Zafeiriou, S., Pantic, M.: 300 faces in-the-wild challenge: the first facial landmark localization challenge. In: Proceedings of the IEEE International Conference on Computer Vision Workshops, pp. 397–403 (2013)
56. Koestinger, M., Wohlhart, P., Roth, P.M., Bischof, H.: Annotated facial landmarks in the wild: a large-scale, real-world database for facial landmark localization. In: 2011 IEEE International Conference on Computer Vision Workshops (ICCV workshops), pp. 2144–2151. IEEE (2011)

Unified Application of Style Transfer for Face Swapping and Reenactment

Lê Minh Ngô[1,2(✉)] ⓘ, Christian aan de Wiel[1,2] ⓘ, Sezer Karaoğlu[1,2] ⓘ, and Theo Gevers[1,2] ⓘ

[1] 3DUniversum, Amsterdam, The Netherlands
{l.m.ngo,th.gevers}@uva.nl, {m.c.aandewiel,s.karaoglu}@3duniversum.com
[2] Computer Vision Lab, University of Amsterdam, Amsterdam, The Netherlands

Abstract. Face reenactment and face swap have gained a lot of attention due to their broad range of applications in computer vision. Although both tasks share similar objectives (e.g. manipulating expression and pose), existing methods do not explore the benefits of combining these two tasks.

In this paper, we introduce a unified end-to-end pipeline for face swapping and reenactment. We propose a novel approach to isolated disentangled representation learning of specific visual attributes in an unsupervised manner. A combination of the proposed training losses allows us to synthesize results in a one-shot manner. The proposed method does not require subject-specific training.

We compare our method against state-of-the-art methods for multiple public datasets of different complexities. The proposed method outperforms other SOTA methods in terms of realistic-looking face images.

1 Introduction

Generating images or videos by manipulating facial attributes (i.e. face reenactment and swapping) has gained a lot of attention in recent years due to their broad range of computer vision and multimedia applications such as video dubbing [1], gaze correction [2], actor capturing [3,4], and virtual avatar creation [5].

Face reenactment [3,6] aims to manipulate facial attributes such as expression, pose or gaze of a video or a single image, whereas face swap [7,8] tries to seamlessly replace a face from a source image with a target face while maintaining the realism of the facial appearance. To perform such transfer, face swap techniques manipulate face attributes such as expression, pose, and identity. Although the face attribute manipulation for both face reenactment and face swap is similar, they have never been considered in a unified pipeline. To this end, in this paper, we propose a single unified model for both face swapping and

---

L. M. Ngô and C. aan de Wiel—Equal contribution, alphabetical order.

© Springer Nature Switzerland AG 2021
H. Ishikawa et al. (Eds.): ACCV 2020, LNCS 12626, pp. 241–257, 2021.
https://doi.org/10.1007/978-3-030-69541-5_15

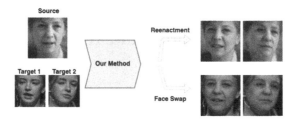

Fig. 1. Our algorithm takes source and target images and produces reenacted and swapped face results using a single unified pipeline.

reenactment tasks allowing the model to produce a more robust face representation and exploiting the constraints from the two tasks to improve the realism of facial appearances.

Before the introduction of deep neural networks, face reenactment and swapping are typically solved by 3D modeling [3,7,9–11]. The 3D face image is transformed into a 3D representation, where latent parameters of the 3D representation are manipulated and projected back in a 2D space. Although those methods produce results with high realism, they are not able to generalize well on unseen data. Hence, for each target face the model parameters have to be tuned.

Current generative models make it feasible to synthesize realistic-looking images [12,13]. Consequently, recent research is focused on improving the quality of the *face image generation* process [12–14] using generative models. Only a few methods explore the direction of using generative models for face reenactment or face swapping. Although these tasks share similarities, previous methods only focus on solving one of the two tasks independently and are supervised [15–17]. Recently methods show that face swap targeted methods can be used for face reenactment and vice versa. Unfortunately, the visual results on the second task are typically inferior to the first one [6,8]. Since those methods are designed for one of the tasks separately, they are not optimal for both. In contrast to existing methods, we integrate both tasks into one combined model. To our knowledge, our method is the first unsupervised method designed to perform both tasks in a unified end-to-end manner.

In this paper, we propose a novel pipeline that unifies face swapping and reenactment (Fig. 1). A combined approach benefits from the similarities of the two tasks. Learning them together allows for robust face representation and enhances the realism of facial appearance. The proposed algorithm learns an isolated disentangled representation for face attributes without any supervision. Hence, our model can manipulate expression/pose, face identity, and style independently in latent space. We achieve this by directly mapping the disentangled latent representation to the latent space of a pre-trained generator. During inference time, the encoders condition the latent space by source and target face images together with their landmarks and generate the reenacted or swapped face using the pre-trained decoder. Prediction is done in a one-shot manner (i.e. only a single image of a person is required). The model's training loss incorporates contextual and identity losses to preserve the face identity, regardless of the source face. As a result, our model obtains visually more appealing results in cross-gender face swapping compared to the baselines.

We evaluate our method on multiple datasets of various complexities: 300VW with videos of talking people [18], and UvA-NEMO with spontaneous and fake smiles in a controlled environment [19]. Experiments demonstrate that our method (on average) performs better on face reenactment and face swapping tasks than existing state-of-the-art methods focusing only on a single task.

To summarize, our contribution is four-fold:

- A novel method is proposed to perform face swapping and reenactment tasks in a joint manner. To our knowledge, our method is the first method to jointly perform the two tasks in a unified end-to-end architecture.
- The proposed method is *subject agnostic*: it does not require subject-specific training.
- A novel approach is proposed to learn an isolated disentangled representation for single visual attributes (i.e. the expression/pose, identity, and style) by using a pre-trained generator with a disentangled latent space. This allows for a full control over the face manipulation process in an unsupervised manner. Hence, our approach does not require ground truth data for expression/pose, identity, and style learning of reenactment outputs.
- A combination of training losses allows us to synthesize results in a one-shot manner and to outperform competitive methods in cross-gender face manipulation.

2 Related Works

2.1 Generative Models

Generative models based on Generative Adversarial Networks (GANs) are advantageous for the task of image synthesis [20,21]. However, until recently, those models can be considered as black boxes with latent representations which are hard to interpret. In addition, the realism of the generated results, in particular for face image synthesis [12,14], is limited (with artifacts in identity preservation).

Recently, StyleGAN [13] introduces a novel way to condition the latent code through an affine transformation, corresponding to a specific style [22], by using Adaptive Instance Normalization (AdaIN) [23]. AdaIN allows the model to generate images with more realistic face appearance compared to previous methods [24]. Furthermore, the aforementioned architecture modifications, combined with a revised training approach [13,22], enable the separation of high-level and stochastic attributes making the latent representation easier to interpret. Hence, the face attributes of a generated image can be changed accordingly by manipulating the latent representation (i.e. disentanglement property). Recent methods integrate StyleGAN into different applications as a pre-trained network for face enhancement and animation [25]. The state-of-the-art StyleGAN2 [22] enhances

L. M. Ngô et al.

the architecture of StyleGAN by redesigning normalization flow and by applying the same network topology for low and high resolution. Image2StyleGAN [26] proposes a method to map an existing image to the latent representation of StyleGAN by iteratively optimizing a latent code to minimize the loss function. Mapping an image to latent space enables a user to change specific image attributes provided by the StyleGAN latent space. However, this method has a drawback in terms of efficiency and generalization: each new image is optimized separately until convergence to obtain a corresponding latent space limiting the applicability of the method for real-time applications. In contrast, our novel isolated disentangled representation learning method solves this problem by introducing encoders that learn to map the desired facial attributes to the corresponding changes in the latent representation. By constraining the mapping by encoders and by using a specific unsupervised training procedure, our approach manipulates the latent space in such a way that it is able to mix disentangled expression/pose, identity and style attributes in a robust manner.

2.2 Face Reenactment

Face reenactment focuses on changing attributes of the face image while keeping the face identity the same. Prior methods focus on different facial attributes like expression [12,14], skin color [12], lighting [27] and pose, or a combination of those [3]. These methods are mostly used in applications such as virtual avatar or puppeteering, targeting high realistic-looking faces but ignoring background preservation [5]. Other approaches focus more on video dubbing and deepfake generation, preserving the realism for both the foreground and background of the scene [3,4,14]. Attribute conditioning is modeled by using different modalities like facial landmarks [28], action units [14] and 3D morphable models [4] for pose and/or expression, and spherical harmonics for lighting [27]. Some methods simplify attribute inference by conditioning directly on the face image. In contrast, our method uses a face image to condition identity and style together with facial landmarks for pose and expression.

Several methods perform face reenactment by manipulating the latent space [26,29,30]. [26] compute the relative difference between two images by calculating the differences in their latent spaces and applied to the source latent code afterwards. [29] propose an approach capable of reenacting faces by using encoders to compute the representations of pose, expression, style and identity in the latent space.

In combination with the use of a pre-trained generator, we aim to condition the generator in a one-shot manner during both training and testing time. Inter-FaceGAN [30] on the other hand, does use a pre-trained generator, but computes latent codes based on attribute scores (e.g. smile, glasses, gender etc.) making it a supervised method. Since our approach does not require ground-truth labels or attribute scores, we have full control over the face manipulation process using only a minimal amount of training data.

Methods that focus on the quality of images and identity/background preservation are typically target-specific [4]. Hence, the model is trained for a particular scene with a single face identity. Other non-target, one-shot methods [12, 14] produce decent results, but they fail in producing consistent face identities between images of the same person (video sequence) [6, 12]. Our method is also a one-shot method. However, in contrast to previous methods, the aim of our method is to produce realistic-looking faces with identity-preservation by exploiting the disentanglement property of the pre-trained model.

2.3   Face Swapping

Face swapping aims to change the facial identity but to keep other face attributes constant. Applications range from face identity obfuscation [31] to recreation [32] and entertainment [7]. Recent methods obtain realistic results by using GANs [8, 15, 17] conditioning identity attributes using either a face image or its facial landmarks. Besides, face segmentation is usually required to position a generated face on the original face [7, 8].

Most face reenactment and swapping approaches rely on the use of generative adversarial networks [12, 14, 26, 29, 33, 34]. A major drawback of the aforementioned methods is their training process, the interpolation quality and lack of disentanglement.

Despite the similarity between face reenactment and face swapping tasks, there are no methods, to the best of our knowledge, which successfully unify these tasks. [6] mainly focuses on the problem of face reenactment, but shows inferior results on the task of face swapping. [8] shows the opposite. This approach is mainly focused on face swapping, but the results on face reenactment lack realistic-looking appearance. Moreover, those methods are complex and multistaged. Thus, [7] proposes four separate GANs for reenactment, segmentation, inpainting and blending. [6] uses a separate motion network to extract dense optical flow and requires an extra segmentation network for face swapping. In contrast, to our knowledge, we are the first method to unify face reenactment and face swap in one single unified pipeline.

3   Proposed Method

An overview of our method is shown in Fig. 2. Our goal is to produce a face image $\hat{x}$ while predicting identity attributes w_i, style attributes w_s and pose/facial expression attributes w_{pe} from a given face image and its landmarks. We propose a novel isolated disentangled representation learning algorithm to separate w_i, w_s and w_{pe}. Using the proposed algorithm, attributes of the source and target images can be manipulated in the latent space via mixing using linear addition, since changing one attribute doesn't influence another due to their isolation. For the `face swapping` task, w_i is taken from the source image, while other attributes are taken from the target image. For the `face reenactment` task, w_{pe} and w_s are taken from the source image, keeping identity w_i from the target.

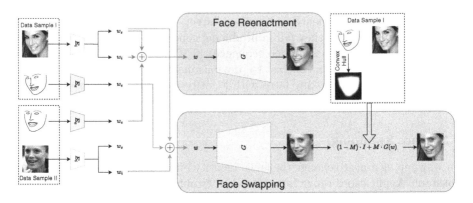

Fig. 2. Our architecture combines face swapping and reenactment into a single unified pipeline with the help of our novel isolated disentangled representation learning algorithm.

3.1 Disentanglement Property and Vector Computations

Our encoders are trained to compute a latent code in the latent space $w \in \mathcal{W}^+$ of a pre-trained generator. Since the latent space is disentangled, face attributes can be manipulated by using vector arithmetics in $\mathcal{W}^+$ [26]. For example, given an image N_A and its latent code w_1 (person A with a neutral expression), N_B and its latent code w_2 (person B with a neutral expression) and another image S_B with a latent code w_3 (person B smiling), it's possible to generate an image of a person A smiling by conditioning the generator G on a latent code $G\big(w_1 + (w_3 - w_2)\big)$.

Our method uses that principle by predicting isolated latent codes for style w_s, identity w_i and pose/expression w_{pe} based on the input image and its corresponding landmarks, assuming those latent codes to be with a disentanglement property. Final latent code can be constructed via linear addition of the three isolated components $w = \mu_G + w_i + w_s + w_{pe}$, where μ_G is the mean of the generator's latent space $\mathcal{W}^+$ with disentanglement property [22,26].

Since w is constructed from the latent codes w_s, w_i, and w_{pe}, full control is obtained for changing the style, identity, pose and expression of the resulting image I, by exploiting the high-quality images produced by the pre-trained generator. Note that our method allows for subject-agnostic face manipulation executed in a one-shot fashion during inference.

3.2 Architecture

The source face and the target face (together with its facial landmarks) are used as inputs to the two separate encoders E_i and E_{pe} respectively. These encoders approximate a latent code for face style w_s, identity w_i and pose/expression w_{pe}. The network latent space is manipulated using encoder outputs to obtain either face swap by swapping the identity latent code or face reenactment by swapping the pose latent code. All latent codes are combined into the final latent code

w. Then, w is fed to a decoder G to produce the final visual result. In the case of face swapping, a face mask M is generated by using the convex hull of the landmarks [35].

Encoders. Our architecture contains two different types of encoders: (1) the identity encoder E_i, and (2) the pose encoder E_{pe}. These encoders predict a latent code $w \in \mathcal{W}^+$ corresponding to either the identity, style, or pose of the input image.

For the design of the architecture, we base our encoders on the encoder of Pix2Pix [36]. To map the input images and landmarks to their corresponding latent codes, we add n separate fully connected blocks to the architecture, where n is the first dimension of the extended latent space. This fully connected blocks consist of 2 fully connected layers. E_i contains 2 of these fully connected block sets, for style (w_s) and identity (w_i) respectively.

Identity encoder $E_i(\mathbf{x})$ takes an input image $\mathbf{x}$ and estimates the identity latent code $w_i \in \mathcal{W}^+$ and style latent code $w_s \in \mathcal{W}^+$. Latent code w_i is trained to contain only pose- and expression-invariant identity features of the person.

Pose encoder $E_{pe}(\mathbf{x}_s)$ uses the facial landmarks of $\mathbf{x}$ denoted by $\mathbf{x}_s$ as an input. $E_{pe}(\mathbf{x}_s)$ predicts a latent code $w_{pe} \in \mathcal{W}^+$ containing both the pose and expression of $\mathbf{x}_s$. The landmarks are represented as *RGB* images of landmark boundaries [34].

$$w_i^{\mathbf{x}}, w_s^{\mathbf{x}} = E_i(\mathbf{x}), \quad w_{pe}^{\mathbf{x}} = E_{pe}(\mathbf{x}_s). \tag{1}$$

Decoder. Generator $G(w)$ is a pre-trained network with fixed weights. It takes a latent code $w \in \mathcal{W}^+$ as an input. Here $\mathcal{W}^+$ is the latent space of $G(w)$. $G(w)$ generates an image $\hat{\mathbf{x}}$ corresponding to latent code w. In this paper, the Style-GANv2 architecture is used. However, other models with similar disentanglement properties and continuous latent spaces can be used instead.

3.3   Face Reenactment and Swapping

The reconstructed original face is defined as a function $G(w)$ over its identity $w_i^{\mathbf{x}}$, style $w_s^{\mathbf{x}}$ and expression/pose $w_{pe}^{\mathbf{x}}$ parameters:

$$\hat{\mathbf{x}} = G(\mu_G + w_i^{\mathbf{x}} + w_s^{\mathbf{x}} + w_{pe}^{\mathbf{x}}). \tag{2}$$

Face Reenactment. Faces are reenacted by changing the expression and pose parameters $w_{pe}^{\mathbf{y}}$ to the pose/expression shown in the target image $\mathbf{y}$ and keeping other parameters identical $w_i^{\mathbf{x}}$ and $w_s^{\mathbf{x}}$. Since $w_i^{\mathbf{x}}$, $w_s^{\mathbf{x}}$ and $w_{pe}^{\mathbf{x}}$ parameters are separated, the resulting image $\dot{\mathbf{x}}$ is defined as a function of their sum:

$$\dot{\mathbf{x}} = G(\mu_G + w_i^{\mathbf{x}} + w_s^{\mathbf{x}} + w_{pe}^{\mathbf{y}}). \tag{3}$$

Face swapping is performed by keeping the $w_s^{\mathbf{x}}$ and $w_l^{\mathbf{x}}$ parameters unchanged and to modify the identity latent code to $w_i^{\mathbf{y}}$:

$$\tilde{\mathbf{x}} = G(\mu_G + w_i^{\mathbf{y}} + w_s^{\mathbf{x}} + w_{pe}^{\mathbf{x}}). \tag{4}$$

To swap faces, a facial mask $\mathbf{M}$ is obtained by computing a convex hull of the landmarks and to add a Gaussian blur [35]. The final swapped face is generated by interpolation $(1 - \mathbf{M}) \cdot \mathbf{x} + \mathbf{M} \cdot \tilde{\mathbf{x}}$.

3.4   Losses

The objective function, to train our unified face swapping/reenactment architecture, consists of 5 terms: reconstruction loss $\mathcal{L}_{MSE}$, perceptual loss $\mathcal{L}_{per}$, landmark loss $\mathcal{L}_L$, identity losses for the aligned reconstructed image $\mathcal{L}_{id}^a$ and for the unaligned identity-swapped/reenacted image $\mathcal{L}_{id}^u$. Those terms are weighted using hyperparameters λ_i, $i \in \{1..5\}$.

$$\mathcal{L} = \lambda_1 \mathcal{L}_{MSE} + \lambda_2 \mathcal{L}_{per} + \lambda_3 \mathcal{L}_L + \lambda_4 \mathcal{L}_{id}^a + \lambda_5 \mathcal{L}_{id}^u. \tag{5}$$

Reconstruction and Perceptual Losses. We compute the mean squared error between input and predicted images as a reconstruction loss for efficient color embedding. $\mathcal{L}_{MSE}$ is calculated for the reconstructed image $\hat{\mathbf{x}}$ and the identity-swapped image $\tilde{\mathbf{x}}$. This loss function mainly helps to isolate w_s ensuring a proper color embedding. To capture finer features, the LPIPS distance is used [22,37,38]. L_{per} is taken as the reconstruction loss and is calculated only for the reconstructed image $\hat{\mathbf{x}}$.

$$\mathcal{L}_{MSE} = \| \hat{\mathbf{x}} - \mathbf{x} \|_2^2 + \| \tilde{\mathbf{x}} - \mathbf{x} \|_2^2, \qquad \mathcal{L}_{per} = \text{LPIPS}(\hat{\mathbf{x}}, \mathbf{x}). \tag{6}$$

Landmark Loss. The landmark loss term is used to isolate pose and expression from identity and style. A pre-trained facial landmark extraction network ψ [39] is taken to extract the landmark heatmaps from an image $\mathbf{x}$. The loss function attempts to minimize the L_2 distance between the extracted heatmaps of the facial landmarks of the source image $\mathbf{x}$ and the target image $\mathbf{y}$, while keeping the latent code for identity and style identical. Landmarks do contain identity (e.g. eye and mouth shape). This means that landmark loss adds an identity bias to the resulting image.

We separate the heatmap sets into two different sets, the expression landmarks ψ_E and the jaw landmarks ψ_J. Parameters γ_1, γ_2 adjust the importance of these landmark sets respectively.

$$\mathcal{L}_L = \gamma_1 \| \psi(\dot{\mathbf{x}})_E - \psi(\mathbf{y})_E \|_2^2 + \gamma_2 \| \psi(\dot{\mathbf{x}})_J - \psi(\mathbf{y})_J \|_2^2. \tag{7}$$

Identity Loss. The identity loss [29,40] isolates identity in a separate latent code w_i. The layer activations are used of a pre-trained identity recognition network Φ [41]. For our purpose, we use activations $l \in L$ of two specific convolution layers and the last two fully connected layers.

The identity loss is applied to the convolution layers by calculating the contextual loss [42] $\mathcal{L}_{id}^a$ over these layers. Note that this will only work for images with the same pose (the reconstructed image), since the convolutions do not capture rotations properly.

$$\mathcal{L}_{id}^a = \sum_{l \in L} \| \, \text{CX}(\Phi(\hat{\mathbf{x}}), \phi(\mathbf{x}) \, \|_2^2 \, . \tag{8}$$

To ensure correct identity in the reenacted frames, a loss function is required to detect the identity of a face independent of the pose. A mean squared error is calculated for the activations of the fully connected layers of Φ. During training, faces are reenacted with random landmarks from the dataset making our approach more robust to landmark biases.

$$\mathcal{L}_{id}^u = \sum_{l \in L} \left(\, \| \, \Phi(\dot{\mathbf{x}}, l) - \Phi(\mathbf{x}, l) \, \|_2^2 + \| \, \Phi(\tilde{\mathbf{x}}, l) - \Phi(\mathbf{y}, l) \, \|_2^2 \, \right) \tag{9}$$

3.5 Training Details

We trained both our method and the pre-trained generator on the subset of 183K images from the CelebA face dataset [43]. Faces are detected using the Dlib [44]. Face bounding boxes are computed based on an expanded by 10% bounding boxes over facial landmarks [39] and resized to 128×128. Parameters of the network were optimized using the Adam optimizer with a learning rate of 10^{-5} for 100 epochs, batch size $= 4$. In our experimental setup, we used $\lambda_1, \lambda_2 = 5$, $\lambda_3 = 1$, $\lambda_4, \lambda_5 = 0.05$, $\gamma_1 = 1$ and $\gamma_2 = 50$, since it yielded the best results.

We use StyleGANv2 in our experiments. For StyleGANv2 latent code manipulation, we use the extended latent space $w \in \mathcal{W}^+$, which predicts a different latent code for every level of a pre-trained generator. Using $\mathcal{W}^+$ allows for a better embedding of an image, but is also possible to cope with images that do not have a latent embedding.

4 Experiments

In this section, we evaluate the qualitative and quantitative performance of our proposed method and compare it to the state-of-the-art. We perform an ablation study to analyze the influence of the loss components in Sect. 4.1. Results on latent space interpolation are discussed in Sect. 4.2. Comparison to state-of-the-art in face swap and reenactment are provided in Sect. 4.3. For all experiments, a cross-dataset evaluation is conducted for our method and baselines.

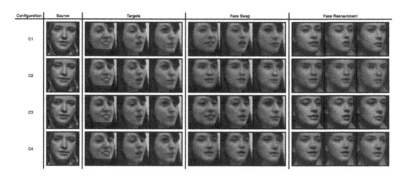

Fig. 3. Ablation study. Face swap and reenactment results of our method trained with different loss configurations. Our full model results are shown in the last row.

Table 1. Quantitative ablation study evaluation on 300VW dataset. Reported metrics are (a) Inception Score, (b) FID source vs generated, (c) KID source vs generated, (d) FID target vs generated and (e) KID target vs generated.

Metric	Face reenactment				Face swap			
	C1	C2	C3	C4	C1	C2	C3	C4
(a)	2.4 ± 0.08	2.02 ± 0.08	1.96 ± 0.1	$\mathbf{2.69 \pm 0.16}$	$\mathbf{2.68 \pm 0.13}$	2.59 ± 0.12	2.63 ± 0.12	2.56 ± 0.14
(b)	1.57	1.57	1.48	**1.46**	1.54	1.50	1.51	**1.48**
(c)	7.12 ± 0.22	7.47 ± 0.21	6.84 ± 0.2	$\mathbf{5.31 \pm 0.23}$	5.44 ± 0.21	5.01 ± 0.21	5.27 ± 0.2	$\mathbf{4.4 \pm 0.21}$
(d)	N/A	N/A	N/A	N/A	**0.42**	0.49	0.52	0.51
(e)	N/A	N/A	N/A	N/A	1.84 ± 0.18	1.78 ± 0.16	2.08 ± 0.16	$\mathbf{1.45 \pm 0.15}$

4.1   Ablation Study

An ablation study is conducted for the loss components to assess their influence on the face swapping and reenactment tasks on the 300VW dataset [18]. This dataset contains 114 high-quality videos of talking people. The dataset is preprocessed by cropping faces based on the given (ground truth) landmark bounding boxes with 10% extension to each direction.

The qualitative results of our method trained with 4 different loss configurations are shown in Fig. 3: [C1] - $\mathcal{L}$ without contextual loss $\mathcal{L}_{id}^{a}$ and identity loss $\mathcal{L}_{id}^{u}$; [C2] - $\mathcal{L}$ without $\mathcal{L}_{id}^{u}$; [C3] - $\mathcal{L}$ without $\mathcal{L}_{id}^{a}$; [C4] - our final model with $\mathcal{L}$. Configurations with other losses being disabled produce significantly degenerated visual results. Consequently, they are crucial for our method.

Contextual loss $\mathcal{L}_{id}^{a}$ supports identity preservation of the source image both in reenactment and face swapping tasks (C2 vs C1). However, it has difficulty with the pose and expression preservation of the target image. Thus, expression and pose are influenced by the content of the source face.

Identity loss $\mathcal{L}_{id}^{u}$ is beneficial for expression/pose isolation and visual sharpness. However, it has difficulties in identity preservation (C3 vs C1). Besides, for the face reenactment task, the reenacted shape of the source person is morphed by target images. It can be seen that the source rounded face becomes oval (C3:

Face Reenactment, columns 1, 2). A trade-off result is obtained by combining $\mathcal{L}_{id}^a$ and $\mathcal{L}_{id}^u$ together (C4 vs C1).

For quantitative evaluation, different metrics are computed which are commonly used in image synthesis evaluation and shown in Table 1. Inception Score [45] uses pre-trained on ImageNet Inception Network to compute the KL divergence between conditional and marginal label distributions over generated data (higher - better). Frechet-Inception distance [46] computes Wasserstein-2 distance between distributions of real and generated samples in the Inception Net feature space (lower - better). Kernel-Inception distance [47] measures dissimilarity between distributions of real and generated samples (lower - better).

Since the generated results of our method are unaligned in term of face attributes, FID and KID metrics are used only as an indicator of how our face identity is similar to the real data distribution. In case of face reenactment, the identity should be as close as possible to source face image. In case of face swap, we want a generated face to capture both properties of source and target image. Consequently, for face swap generated images, the FID and KID metrics are reported both in comparison with the source and target image data distributions. Source and target subjects are randomly selected from the 300VW dataset. Evaluation is performed on a sample of 10K generated images.

In the task of face reenactment, the evaluation metrics support our qualitative experimental results: our method with combined contextual and identity losses generates visual results with identity closer to the source face image distribution (C1 vs C2, 1.57 vs 1.46 FID). In the case of face swap, it can be observed that the distribution of generated images is closer to the distribution of target face images (C4 1.48 vs 0.51 FID). With the introduction of the additional regularization into our model, visual results start to capture more and more properties from the source image (C1 vs C4, 1.54 vs 1.48 FID).

4.2 Latent Space Interpolation

In this section, our method is analyzed to interpolate over different face attribute dimensions. Given a source image, its face attributes are gradually changed where expression/pose, style or identity are modified to become closer to the target face image. Qualitative results on the 300VW dataset are shown in Fig. 4. The 300VW dataset is preprocessed in the same way as described in the Sect. 4.1. The first column shows the source image. Our algorithm changes gradually an attribute dimension to become closer to the target image of the last column.

Given a source w_1 and target attribute w_2, our model generates meaningful face images conditioned on the interpolated latent code $\alpha w_1 + (1 - \alpha)w_2$. Note that in the case of style, a costume of John Oliver gradually starts to appear, while in the case of identity, we can observe the disappearance of beard, an emergence of his glasses and eyebrows. Despite the challenges given by cross-dataset evaluation, our model preserves attributes dimensions on challenging cases with face accessory and occlusion. Image2StyleGAN [26] show the capability to map face attributes into the latent space of StyleGAN. However, the latent space of expression/pose, identity and style are not fully disentangled. For example, it's

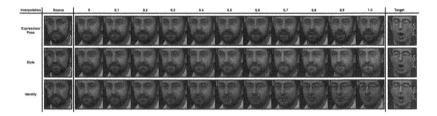

Fig. 4. Interpolation of the latent space. Row 1: expression and pose interpolation. Row 2: style interpolation. Row 3: identity interpolation. The last column represents a target expression/pose, style, or identity respectively. The results show that our novel disentangled representation learning algorithm can robustly isolates face attributes so that we can manipulate each attribute independently.

not possible to manipulate expression/pose property separately without influencing identity or style. In contrast, our mapping to the latent space provides more flexibility.

4.3 Face Swap and Reenactment State-of-the-Art Comparison

Qualitative Evaluation. We evaluate qualitatively our method on the face swapping and face reenactment tasks. We perform cross-dataset evaluation of our method with results produced by FSGAN [8] and First Order Motion Model [6] on the 300VW [18] and UvA-NEMO [19] datasets. These methods are selected because they are state-of-the-art which can do both face swap and reenactment. For our purpose, the available pre-trained model is used provided by authors of FSGAN and First Order Motion. For fairness of comparison, we use models trained on a different dataset from UvA-NEMO and 300VW. The datasets are preprocessed by cropping faces based on landmark bounding boxes with 10% extension to each direction. For 300VW, the provided ground truth landmarks are used. For UvA-NEMO, the landmarks are extracted by using FAN [39].

In the first experiment, we qualitatively compare our method with the state-of-the-art for the face reenactment task. The visual comparison is shown in the Fig. 5. For the First Order Motion model, its pre-trained model is used with *absolute motion* for both face reenactment and face swap experiments, since only the absolute motion mode is capable of computing face swaps. Our method shows comparable quality of reenactment results to First Order Motion and outperforms FSGAN in terms of identity preservation. Besides, since our latent space is constrained by the pre-trained generator, it's less prone to produce artifacts not inherent to a human face (First Order Motion, second row, middle image, eyes). However, this constraint has also a drawback in terms of facial accessories it's capable of modeling (the disappearance of a microphone in the second row). Note that, since First Order Motion is focused on the face reenactment task, it produces better results than the FSGAN model.

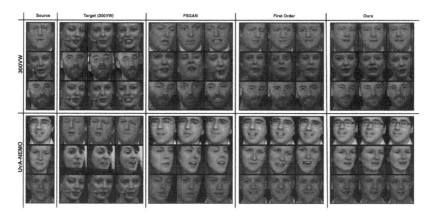

Fig. 5. Qualitative comparison of face reenactment results on 300VW and UvA-NEMO datasets. Pose and expression from target images (second column) are applied on the source image (first column). Faces are produced by the baseline methods, FSGAN and first order motion model, and predictions provided by our novel unified pipeline.

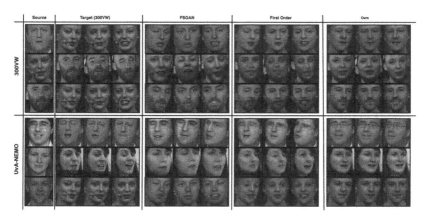

Fig. 6. Qualitative comparison of face swapping results on the 300VW and UvA-NEMO datasets. First column: source image from which identity properties are taken. Second column: target images, on which those properties are applied. Faces produced by the baseline methods, FSGAN [8] and First Order Motion Model [6], and predictions provided by our novel unified pipeline.

In the second experiment, we qualitatively compare our method with state-of-the-art in the context of face swapping. The visual comparison is shown in the Fig. 6. For the face swapping task, GAN based methods may fail in cross-gender face swapping due to the difference between gender appearance and shape. We show that our method produces realistic-looking results both for male-to-female (rows 1, 3, 6) and female-to-male swapping (row 2) compared to competitive methods: First Order Motion keeps the lipstick color of a target face (row 3), FSGAN loses the identity of the source image (rows 1, 3, 6). Note that, since

Table 2. Quantitative evaluation on 300VW.

	Identity ↑			Headpose ↓			Expression ↓		
	First Order	FSGAN	Ours	First order	FSGAN	Ours	First Order	FSGAN	Ours
Reenactment	**0.578**	0.461	0.517	**2.811**	4.268	3.364	4.883	51.56	**3.983**
Swap	0.308	0.317	**0.412**	2.628	2.823	**2.113**	3.902	2.554	**3.072**
Avg	0.443	0.389	**0.464**	**2.719**	3.546	2.739	4.393	27.057	**3.528**

FSGAN is focused on the face swapping task, it produces better results than the First Order Motion model.

Quantitative Evaluation. We provide additional quantitative evaluations on 300VW to verify preservation of identity/expression/pose w.r.t. SOTA and to motivate the benefit of joint learning (Table 2). We compare identity preservation using cosine similarity between latent space of VGGFace2 features [48]. Headpose correctness is compared using absolute distance in degrees of yaw-pitch-roll predicted from a pretrained Hopenet [49]. Expression correctness is compared using mean absolute distance of facial landmarks (in pixels, image resized to 256) using a pretrained FAN detector [39]. Our method outperforms SOTA in the swapping task on 3 benchmarks. On the reenactment task First Order Motion performs better on identity and headpose preservation however, on average, our method outperforms SOTA.

5   Limitations

Despite promising results presented in this paper, our method has several limitations. First, the expressiveness of the generated facial expressions is dependent on its presence in the training dataset and the quality of face landmarks provided by the landmark detector. Second, our model does not explicitly model occlusion and consequently relies on a pre-trained generator to have a capacity of modeling occlusions, such as accessories or makeup. Finally, both landmark plots and source images contain a bias in terms of identity, pose and expression.

6   Conclusion

In this work, we proposed a novel approach to isolated disentangled representation learning combined with an end-to-end method capable of performing both face reenactment and swapping. To our knowledge, our method is the first approach which is designed to solve both objectives in a unified pipeline.

We showed that our method is trained in an unsupervised way to achieve equally good visual results on both tasks. In addition, it's capable of producing results in a one-shot manner during inference time. The qualitative results on multiple public datasets show that the proposed method is outperforming SOTA methods which can perform both face reenactment and swap.

References

1. Suwajanakorn, S., Seitz, S.M., Kemelmacher-Shlizerman, I.: Synthesizing Obama: learning lip sync from audio. ACM Trans. Graph. **36**, 1–13 (2017)
2. Kuster, C., Popa, T., Bazin, J.C., Gotsman, C., Gross, M.: Gaze correction for home video conferencing. ACM Trans. Graph. **31**, 1–6 (2012)
3. Thies, J., Zollhofer, M., Stamminger, M., Theobalt, C., Nießner, M.: Face2Face: real-time face capture and reenactment of RGB videos. In: Proceedings of the IEEE Conference on Computer Vision and Pattern Recognition, pp. 2387–2395 (2016)
4. Kim, H., et al.: Deep video portraits. ACM Trans. Graph. (TOG) **37**, 163 (2018)
5. Nagano, K., et al.: PaGAN: real-time avatars using dynamic textures. ACM Trans. Graph. **37**, 1–12 (2018)
6. Siarohin, A., Lathuilière, S., Tulyakov, S., Ricci, E., Sebe, N.: First order motion model for image animation. In: Conference on Neural Information Processing Systems (NeurIPS) (2019)
7. Nirkin, Y., Masi, I., Tran, A.T., Hassner, T., Medioni, G.: On face segmentation, face swapping, and face perception. In: IEEE Conference on Automatic Face and Gesture Recognition (2018)
8. Nirkin, Y., Keller, Y., Hassner, T.: FSGAN: subject agnostic face swapping and reenactment. In: Proceedings of the IEEE International Conference on Computer Vision, pp. 7184–7193 (2019)
9. Garrido, P., Valgaerts, L., Rehmsen, O., Thormaehlen, T., Perez, P., Theobalt, C.: Automatic face reenactment. In: Proceedings of the 2014 IEEE Conference on Computer Vision and Pattern Recognition, CVPR 2014, USA, pp. 4217–4224. IEEE Computer Society (2014)
10. Dale, K., Sunkavalli, K., Johnson, M.K., Vlasic, D., Matusik, W., Pfister, H.: Video face replacement. ACM Trans. Graph. **30**, 1–130 (2011)
11. Thies, J., Zollhöfer, M., Nießner, M., Valgaerts, L., Stamminger, M., Theobalt, C.: Real-time expression transfer for facial reenactment. ACM Trans. Graph. (TOG) **34**, 183-1 (2015)
12. Choi, Y., Choi, M., Kim, M., Ha, J.W., Kim, S., Choo, J.: StarGAN: unified generative adversarial networks for multi-domain image-to-image translation. In: Proceedings of the IEEE conference on computer vision and pattern recognition, pp. 8789–8797 (2018)
13. Karras, T., Laine, S., Aila, T.: A style-based generator architecture for generative adversarial networks. In: Proceedings of the IEEE Conference on Computer Vision and Pattern Recognition, pp. 4401–4410 (2019)
14. Pumarola, A., Agudo, A., Martinez, A.M., Sanfeliu, A., Moreno-Noguer, F.: GANimation: anatomically-aware facial animation from a single image. In: Proceedings of the European Conference on Computer Vision (ECCV), pp. 818–833 (2018)
15. Korshunova, I., Shi, W., Dambre, J., Theis, L.: Fast face-swap using convolutional neural networks. CoRR abs/1611.09577 (2016)
16. Wu, W., Zhang, Y., Li, C., Qian, C., Loy, C.C.: ReenactGAN: learning to reenact faces via boundary transfer. In: Ferrari, V., Hebert, M., Sminchisescu, C., Weiss, Y. (eds.) ECCV 2018. LNCS, vol. 11205, pp. 622–638. Springer, Cham (2018). https://doi.org/10.1007/978-3-030-01246-5_37
17. Li, L., Bao, J., Yang, H., Chen, D., Wen, F.: FaceShifter: towards high fidelity and occlusion aware face swapping. arXiv preprint arXiv:1912.13457 (2019)

18. Chrysos, G., Antonakos, E., Zafeiriou, S., Snape, P.: Offline deformable face tracking in arbitrary videos. In: Proceedings of IEEE International Conference on Computer Vision Workshops, 300 Videos in the Wild (300-VW): Facial Landmark Tracking in-the-Wild Challenge & Workshop, Santiago, Chile, pp. 1–9. IEEE (2015)
19. Dibeklioğlu, H., Salah, A.A., Gevers, T.: Are you really smiling at me? Spontaneous versus posed enjoyment smiles. In: Fitzgibbon, A., Lazebnik, S., Perona, P., Sato, Y., Schmid, C. (eds.) ECCV 2012. LNCS, vol. 7574, pp. 525–538. Springer, Heidelberg (2012). https://doi.org/10.1007/978-3-642-33712-3_38
20. Radford, A., Metz, L., Chintala, S.: Unsupervised representation learning with deep convolutional generative adversarial networks. CoRR abs/1511.06434 (2015)
21. Nguyen, A., Yosinski, J., Bengio, Y., Dosovitskiy, A., Clune, J.: Plug & play generative networks: conditional iterative generation of images in latent space. CoRR abs/1612.00005 (2016)
22. Karras, T., Laine, S., Aittala, M., Hellsten, J., Lehtinen, J., Aila, T.: Analyzing and improving the image quality of StyleGAN. CoRR abs/1912.04958 (2019)
23. Huang, X., Belongie, S.J.: Arbitrary style transfer in real-time with adaptive instance normalization. CoRR abs/1703.06868 (2017)
24. Karras, T., Aila, T., Laine, S., Lehtinen, J.: Progressive growing of GANs for improved quality, stability, and variation. arXiv preprint arXiv:1710.10196 (2017)
25. Gabbay, A., Hoshen, Y.: Style generator inversion for image enhancement and animation. CoRR abs/1906.11880 (2019)
26. Abdal, R., Qin, Y., Wonka, P.: Image2StyleGAN: how to embed images into the styleGAN latent space? In: Proceedings of the IEEE International Conference on Computer Vision, pp. 4432–4441 (2019)
27. Zhou, H., Hadap, S., Sunkavalli, K., Jacobs, D.W.: Deep single-image portrait relighting. In: The IEEE International Conference on Computer Vision (ICCV) (2019)
28. Sanchez, E., Valstar, M.F.: Triple consistency loss for pairing distributions in GAN-based face synthesis. CoRR abs/1811.03492 (2018)
29. Fu, C., Hu, Y., Wu, X., Wang, G., Zhang, Q., He, R.: High fidelity face manipulation with extreme pose and expression. arXiv preprint arXiv:1903.12003 (2019)
30. Shen, Y., Gu, J., Tang, X., Zhou, B.: Interpreting the latent space of GANs for semantic face editing. In: CVPR (2020)
31. Bitouk, D., Kumar, N., Dhillon, S., Belhumeur, P., Nayar, S.K.: Face swapping: automatically replacing faces in photographs. ACM Trans. Graph. **27**, 1–8 (2008)
32. Kemelmacher-Shlizerman, I.: Transfiguring portraits. ACM Trans. Graph. **35**, 1–8 (2016)
33. Zhu, J.Y., Park, T., Isola, P., Efros, A.A.: Unpaired image-to-image translation using cycle-consistent adversarial networks. In: Proceedings of the IEEE International Conference on Computer Vision, pp.2223–2232 (2017)
34. Zakharov, E., Shysheya, A., Burkov, E., Lempitsky, V.: Few-shot adversarial learning of realistic neural talking head models. In: Proceedings of the IEEE International Conference on Computer Vision, pp. 9459–9468 (2019)
35. Yang, C., Lim, S.N.: Unconstrained facial expression transfer using style-based generator. arXiv preprint arXiv:1912.06253 (2019)
36. Isola, P., Zhu, J.Y., Zhou, T., Efros, A.A.: Image-to-image translation with conditional adversarial networks. CVPR (2017)
37. Banerjee, S., Scheirer, W.J., Bowyer, K.W., Flynn, P.J.: On hallucinating context and background pixels from a face mask using multi-scale GANs. CoRR abs/1811.07104 (2018)

38. Zhang, R., Isola, P., Efros, A.A., Shechtman, E., Wang, O.: The unreasonable effectiveness of deep features as a perceptual metric. In: CVPR (2018)
39. Bulat, A., Tzimiropoulos, G.: How far are we from solving the 2D & 3D face alignment problem? (and a dataset of 230,000 3D facial landmarks). In: International Conference on Computer Vision (2017)
40. Hu, Y., Wu, X., Yu, B., He, R., Sun, Z.: Pose-guided photorealistic face rotation. In: Proceedings of the IEEE Conference on Computer Vision and Pattern Recognition, pp. 8398–8406 (2018)
41. Wu, X., He, R., Sun, Z., Tan, T.: A light CNN for deep face representation with noisy labels. IEEE Trans. Inf. Forensics Secur. **13**, 2884–2896 (2018)
42. Mechrez, R., Talmi, I., Zelnik-Manor, L.: The contextual loss for image transformation with non-aligned data. In: Proceedings of the European Conference on Computer Vision (ECCV), pp. 768–783 (2018)
43. Liu, Z., Luo, P., Wang, X., Tang, X.: Deep learning face attributes in the wild. In: Proceedings of International Conference on Computer Vision (ICCV) (2015)
44. King, D.E.: Dlib-ml: A machine learning toolkit. J. Mach. Learn. Res. **10**, 1755–1758 (2009)
45. Salimans, T., Goodfellow, I.J., Zaremba, W., Cheung, V., Radford, A., Chen, X.: Improved techniques for training GANs. CoRR abs/1606.03498 (2016)
46. Heusel, M., Ramsauer, H., Unterthiner, T., Nessler, B., Klambauer, G., Hochreiter, S.: GANs trained by a two time-scale update rule converge to a nash equilibrium. CoRR abs/1706.08500 (2017)
47. Bińkowski, M., Sutherland, D.J., Arbel, M., Gretton, A.: Demystifying MMD GANs (2018)
48. Cao, Q., Shen, L., Xie, W., Parkhi, O.M., Zisserman, A.: VGGFace2: a dataset for recognising faces across pose and age. In: International Conference on Automatic Face and Gesture Recognition (2018)
49. Ruiz, N., Chong, E., Rehg, J.M.: Fine-grained head pose estimation without keypoints. In: The IEEE Conference on Computer Vision and Pattern Recognition (CVPR) Workshops (2018)

Multiple Exemplars-Based Hallucination for Face Super-Resolution and Editing

Kaili Wang[1,2]([⊠]), Jose Oramas[2], and Tinne Tuytelaars[1]

[1] ESAT-PSI, KU Leuven, Leuven, Belgium
{kaili.wang,tinne.tuytelaars}@esat.kuleuven.be
[2] imec-IDLab, University of Antwerp, Antwerp, Belgium
{kaili.wang,jose.oramas}@uantwerpen.be

Abstract. Given a really low resolution input image of a face (say 16×16 or 8×8 pixels), the goal of this paper is to reconstruct a high-resolution version thereof. This, by itself, is an ill-posed problem, as the high-frequency information is missing in the low-resolution input and needs to be hallucinated, based on prior knowledge about the image content. Rather than relying on a generic face prior, in this paper we explore the use of a set of exemplars, i.e. other high-resolution images of the same person. These guide the neural network as we condition the output on them. Multiple exemplars work better than a single one. To combine the information from multiple exemplars effectively, we introduce a pixel-wise weight generation module. Besides standard face super-resolution, our method allows to perform subtle face editing simply by replacing the exemplars with another set with different facial features. A user study is conducted and shows the super-resolved images can hardly be distinguished from real images on the CelebA dataset. A qualitative comparison indicates our model outperforms methods proposed in the literature on the CelebA and WebFace datasets.

1 Introduction

Super resolution (SR) imaging consists of enhancing, or increasing, the resolution of an image, i.e., going from a coarse low-resolution (LR) input to one with high resolution (HR) depicting more details. Especially challenging is the setting where there is a large scale factor between the resolution of the input and that desired for the output. In that case, there is insufficient information in the LR input. This leads to the need to "hallucinate" what the detailed content of the HR output would look like. As can be seen in Fig. 1 this makes the SR process an ill-defined problem with multiple valid HR solutions for a given LR input.

Using side-information is a promising avenue towards guiding the SR process and addressing the above issue. In particular, we consider using multiple HR

Electronic supplementary material The online version of this chapter (https://doi.org/10.1007/978-3-030-69541-5_16) contains supplementary material, which is available to authorized users.

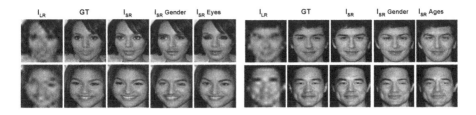

Fig. 1. Super-resolving images with different facial features by using different exemplars. From left to right: input LR image, ground truth HR image, SR image using exemplars of the same person and SR images using two sets of exemplars with different facial features. Please note, the ethnicity of the LR image does not change. For sake of space, please refer to the supplementary material for the exemplars used.

reference images, or *exemplars* as we call them, as a form of side information. Typically, these are HR images of the same person depicted in the LR input. They provide visual cues that are expected to occur in the HR output – think e.g. of the color or shape of the eyes of the person. By guiding the SR process these exemplars help to constrain the output and disambiguate the ill-defined characteristic of the problem. The output becomes conditional on the provided exemplars and a different set of exemplars will lead to a different output.

In this work, we advocate the use of *multiple* exemplars, rather than just one. This gives more flexibility, as it allows the network to pick the visual features that best fit the LR input image, in terms of facial expression, illumination or pose. Our method effectively exploits available information from the exemplars via the proposed Weighted Pixel Average (PWAve) module. This module learns how to select useful regions across the exemplars and produces superior results compared to simply averaging the representations [1].

Rather than just superresolving the LR input, we can also exploit the ambiguity of the problem to our advantage and use different sets of exemplars as a means to inject different visual features in the produced HR image (see again the examples in Fig. 1). This turns the model into a flexible tool for subtle image editing. Since in this manuscript we focus on images depicting faces, we refer to the general SR process as "face/facial hallucination". Similarly, we refer as "face editing" to the task where new features are injected. Investigating these two tasks constitutes the core of this paper.

Taking a broader perspective, the method proposed here to condition a network on a set of exemplars, can be seen as a novel, lightweight and flexible scheme for model personalization, that could have applications well beyond face hallucination or face editing. Indeed, instead of finetuning a model on user-specific data, which requires a large set of labeled data and extra training, or adapting a model using domain adaptation techniques, which requires access to the old training data as well as a large set of unlabeled target data and extra training, the scheme we propose allows to adapt a generic model to a specific user without the need for any retraining. All that is needed is a small set of exemplars and a standard forward pass over the network. This opens new perspectives in terms of on-the-edge applications, where personalization is often a desirable property yet computational resources are limited.

Our contributions are three-fold: i) We propose to use multiple exemplars to guide the model to super-resolve very low resolution (16×16, 8×8) images. ii) Our model does not require any domain-specific features, e.g. facial landmarks, in the training phase. This makes our model general to adapt to other datasets and tasks. Our user study indicates our results are hard to distinguish from real images. Our qualitative analysis suggests that our model outperforms the literature baselines. iii) Besides achieving face super-resolution, our model can also address the face editing task. Unlike traditional conditional generative adversarial networks which can only generate images by modifying pre-defined discrete visual features, our model can dynamically generate HR face images with arbitrary facial features, benefiting from the usage of exemplars.

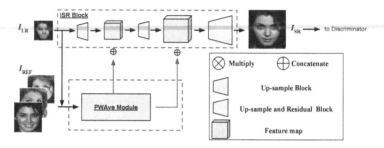

Fig. 2. The proposed model in our paper. For details of the PWAve module, please refer to Sect. 3 and Fig. 3.

2   Related Work

Face Super-Resolution. Using deep neural networks to super-resolve LR images has been applied quite widely. The methods can be gathered into two groups: those using facial priors like landmarks or heatmaps, and those not using any facial priors. [2–5] belong to the first group. Yet to use these facial priors, extra annotations and networks are required. In the other group, [6–11] use a guidance-image or semantic labels (e.g.. facial attributes or face identity) to help the model super-resolve the LR images. [6,7] utilize pre-defined facial attribute labels. Besides super-resolving the LR image, as a conditional adversary model, it allows users to change the feature labels to control the generated SR image. However, to achieve this, they require additional data with annotations for the visual attributes to be added/edited. Furthermore, editing of visual features is also limited to the set of visual attributes pre-defined at design time, and fixed to the possible values that these features may take. Moreover, when new features are desired to be integrated in the editing model, additional data and re-training are required. In addition, [6] manually rotates the input LR image and uses a spatial transformer to cope with this change. Compared with [6,7], our method

can be regarded as conditioned on multiple exemplars, which gives us more flexibility on the subtle editing of facial features. [10] does not use any guiding image,
but uses the facial feature labels to train a channel-wise attention model which
guides the model to recombine the basic features in the super resolution process. Compared with [10], our method uses pixel-level weights generated from
our PWAve module, which provides the user with a more clear visualization on
the usage of exemplars. In addition, the way of using facial features in [10] does
not allow users to control the generation. [11] considers the facial identity label,
where they use a specific person identity loss. [8,9] use one guiding exemplar
while we propose to use multiple guiding images. They warp the guiding exemplar (HR) via a flow field and use a specifically designed network to align with
the input LR image. [8] also uses facial landmarks in the training of the warping network. [12] also considers using multiple exemplars. However, [12] selects
one exemplar from multiple exemplars and only processes the selected exemplar,
while we handle multiple exemplars simultaneously by using our PWave module.

Conditional Image Generation. [13–17] use labels as condition to guide
neural networks to generate images. Therefore, the generated images are limited
to the pre-defined classes. [1,18–20] achieve image translation by using condition
image(s). In the training process, they aim to disentangle the visual features from
both input and condition images and re-combine the features from different
images later. [1] simply averages the features from condition images and uses
adaptive instance normalization to insert them. To achieve the modification of
facial features, our method does not need to re-train the original SR model.
Our SR model is originally trained to restore the LR image with the help of
several exemplars that have similar visual features to the LR image. Besides, our
PWAve module generates the pixel-wise weights among the multiple exemplars.
In addition, the input image in our method is a LR image while conditional
image translation efforts [1,18–20] receive the HR image as part of its input.

3 Methodology

In this section, we describe the architecture of our model and the objective
functions required for its optimization. For each of the LR images to be super-
resolved we assume the availability of a set of high-resolution exemplars. These
exemplars contain a person with the same identity as the person depicted in
the LR image. Specifically, we assume that the exemplars possess detailed facial
features, e.g. eye shape, iris color, gender etc. that are expected to appear in the
SR image. These exemplars are used to provide the network with these facial
features that are invisible in the LR image.

3.1 Architecture

The generator model consists of two parts: the image super resolution block
(ISR) and the Weighted Pixel Average (PWAve) module (see Fig. 2). The ISR

block contains M_1 up-sample blocks and M_2 residual blocks. The ISR block takes the LR image (I_{LR}) as input and integrates at different parts of its feed-forward pass combined feature maps from the exemplars as generated by the PWAve module.

Besides face super-resolution, the combination of feature maps from the input LR image and the exemplars allows the model to dynamically generate HR images with similar facial features to those present in the exemplars.

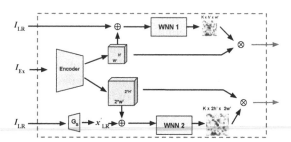

Fig. 3. The proposed PWAve module in our paper. To concatenate with two times higher resolution feature map, we train a small generator to get x'_{LR}. For the whole model, please see Fig. 2.

Weighted Pixel Average (PWAve) Module. The goal of this module is to learn how to perform a good combination of the set of intermediate feature maps computed from the exemplars. The idea is to provide the freedom to the model to learn a different, and perhaps more suitable, combination method rather than the commonly used average method [1]. Our intuition is that the exemplars could depict different features, e.g. facial expression, angle, makeup, etc., that are in the LR image and are expected to appear in the SR image. Therefore, it is meaningful to consider the exemplars when the model generates the HR image so that the model can take into account proper regions of the exemplars.

The PWAve module consists of an encoder E_{Ex} and M pixel weight generation networks (WNN). Here, we set $M = 2$. E_{Ex} encodes the exemplars $I_{Ex} \in \mathbb{R}^{N \times K \times 3 \times h \times w}$, with width w and height h, into feature maps $f_{Ex} \in \mathbb{R}^{N \times K \times C \times h' \times w'}$ of different scales, N and K are the batch size and the number of exemplars, respectively. We use two scales: the same scale with and two times higher than I_{LR}. WNN takes f_{Ex} and I_{LR} of corresponding size and generates the pixel-wise weight matrix W ($W \in \mathbb{R}^{N \times K \times 1 \times h' \times w'}$) across the exemplars. Afterwards, W is L_1-normalized along the second dimension. In order to concatenate with the two times higher resolution feature maps and provide a more precise guidance in WNN-2, we use a small generator G_S to generate I'_{LR} rather than just up-sample I_{LR}. Finally, the combined exemplar feature maps f^c_{Ex} are calculated by applying dot-product between f_{Ex} and W, followed by the summation along the second channel, i.e. $f^c_{Ex} \in \mathbb{R}^{N \times 1 \times C \times h' \times w'}$. Different from [21], we generate pixel-wise weights while taking into account the LR image itself. Taking into account I_{LR} (and I'_{LR}) in the combination process is a more direct way to identify the important region on the exemplars compared with simply relying on loss penalty.

Discriminator (Critic). The architecture of the discriminator (critic) is similar to StyleGAN [22], where it takes either super-resolved images or original images as input and tries to match the distribution between the super-resolved image and real ground-truth HR images.

3.2 Objective Functions

We formulate this task as a supervised learning problem given the simplicity to obtain a low/high resolution image pair from a single high-resolution image.

Content Loss (L_c). We apply a $L1$ loss on the ground truth HR image I_{HR} and the super-resolved image I_{SR}.

$$\mathcal{L}_c = \|I_{SR} - I_{HR}\|_1 \tag{1}$$

We also calculate the content loss for G_S,

$$\mathcal{L}_c^s = \|I_{SR}^s - I_{HR}^d\|_1 \tag{2}$$

where I_{HR}^d and I_{SR}^s are the real image that is downsampled to match the resolution of output of G_S and the output of G_S, respectively.

Perceptual Loss (L_p). This loss aims at preserving the face appearance and identity information of the depicted persons. We use the perceptual similarity model Φ_p [23], which is trained on an external dataset, and the last layer before the classification layer of the face emotion model Φ_{ID} [24] to calculate the perceptual loss.

$$\mathcal{L}_p = \|\Phi_p(I_{SR}) - \Phi_p(I_{HR})\|_2^2 + \|\Phi_{ID}(I_{SR}) - \Phi_{ID}(I_{HR})\|_2^2 \tag{3}$$

where I_{HR} and I_{SR} are the real HR image and corresponding super-resolved HR image, respectively. Similarly, we apply the perceptual loss on I'_{LR} and I_{SR}^d.

$$\mathcal{L}_p^s = \|\Phi_p(I_{SR}^s) - \Phi_p(I_{HR}^d)\|_2^2 + \|\Phi_{ID}(I_{SR}^s) - \Phi_{ID}(I_{HR}^d)\|_2^2 \tag{4}$$

Adversary Loss (L_{adv}). In order to generate a more realistic and sharper image, we use the adversary loss to match data's distribution. Furthermore, here we use Wasserstein GAN with gradient penalty (WGAN-GP) [25] in order to have a more stable training process. The critic loss, used to update the discriminator, is defined as follows:

$$\mathcal{L}_{\text{critic}} = D(I_{SR}) + D(I_{HR}) - \lambda_{gp}\mathcal{L}_{gp} \tag{5}$$

where $D(.)$ is the discriminator (critic) network and λ_{gp} is the coefficient parameter for gradient penalty. The adversary loss for the generator part is $-D(I_{SR})$.

Total loss (L_{total})**.** With the previous terms in place, the total loss is defined as:

$$\mathcal{L}_{\text{total}} = \left[\mathcal{L}_c + \lambda_1 \mathcal{L}_p + \lambda_2 \mathcal{L}_{adv}\right] + \left[\mathcal{L}_c^s + \lambda_3 \mathcal{L}_p^s\right] \qquad (6)$$

where λ_1, λ_2 and λ_3 are the trade-off coefficients of the model. The losses in the first bracket will update the whole model except for G_S, where G_S is updated by the losses in the second bracket.

4   Evaluation

In this section, we start with the introduction of the dataset used in our experiments. This is followed by qualitative and quantitative results obtained by our method. We also conduct a user study on the quality of our super-resolved images. Then, we perform a qualitative comparison of our method w.r.t. methods from the literature. In addition, we conduct an ablation study to show the effectiveness of the number of exemplars and the proposed PWAve module. Finally, we show our method is capable of dynamically introducing features on the generated images via the exemplars.

Dataset. We use two datasets depicting human faces: CelebA [26] and Web-Face [27]. CelebA has 202,599 images with 10,177 identities, each identity has 20 images on average. We follow [6] and crop the images to the size of 128×128 and drop the identities which have less than 5 images. We downsample the original 128×128 image to the size of 16×16 and 8×8. We also follow the training/testing splits in the original CelebA dataset. There is no identity overlapping between these splits. Images from the WebFace dataset have a higher 256×256 resolution. There are 10,575 identities and each of them has several images, ranging from 2 to 804. For each identity, we follow [8] and select the top 10 best quality images. We drop the identities which have less than 10 images. The images of the first 9121 identities are used for training and the rest of them for testing. Unlike [8], for both datasets, we select the LR/HR images and the corresponding exemplars at random. That is, there is no constraint on the facial angle and expression.

Implementation Details. We implement our model in PyTorch [28]. Height and width of I_{LR} is h_{LR} and h_{LR}. For the CelebA dataset with the scaling factor of 8/16, the setting is $M_1 = 3/4$, $M_2 = 1/1$, $h_{LR} = w_{LR} = 16/8$, $N = 8$. For the WebFace dataset with the scaling factor of 8/16, the setting is $M_1 = 3/4$, $M_2 = 1/1$, $h_{LR} = w_{LR} = 32/16$, $N=4$. We use Adam [29] optimizer with $\beta_1 = 0$ and $\beta_2 = 0.99$. The initial learning rate is set to 0.003 for the whole model except for the two WNNs, whose initial learning rate is 0.0001. Please refer to the supplementary material for more details.

4.1 Quality and Quantity Results

Figure 4 and Fig. 5 shows qualitative results from the celebA and WebFace dataset. It is clear that our model can recover most of the details, such as wrinkles, iris color and stubble. In addition, our model is robust to changes in face angle, i.e. not only the front view but side view images can be super-revolved as well. Even when a scaling factor of 16 is used, it is interesting to see that the generated images (the last column of Fig. 4) can also keep the original identity and details for most of the cases. For the fifth example in Fig. 4, the 8×8 LR image has a black region around the eyes due to the downsampling of 16 times, which suggests the model to generate the sunglasses.

For the WebFace dataset with the scaling factor of 16, the task is harder since the original size of the image is larger (256×256), they are not aligned and have much more non-facial regions. However, the super-resolved images are still reasonable good based on the 16×16 input and the corresponding exemplars. Table 1 shows Structural Similarity Index (SSIM) and Peak Signal-to-Noise Ratio (PSNR) scores on the testing set.

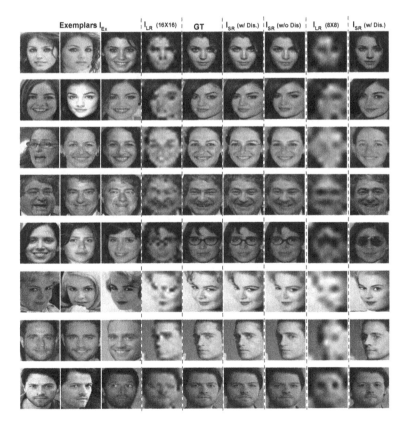

Fig. 4. Qualitative results from the CelebA dataset. We show two scaling factors: ×8 and ×16. The resolution of HR images is 128×128. All the images are from testing set.

Fig. 5. Qualitative results on the WebFace dataset. We show two scaling factors: ×8 and ×16. The resolution of HR images is 256 × 256 All the images are from testing set.

Table 1 shows the scores without discriminators (i.e. no adversary loss), we also remove the perceptual loss on the CelebA dataset (×8), resulting 0.69/22.35 for SSIM/PSNR. This shows that using only the L_1 content loss is not sufficient to produce realistic HR images while preserving identity. To assess how the PWAve module helps the network in the generation process, we visualize the weight matrix W, generated by the PWAve module, using the jet color scale and overlaying it on top of each of the exemplars. Figure 6 shows some examples. The generated heatmaps clearly show that the PWAve module does learn how to select different parts from the exemplars rather than doing a random selection or a uniform average across images. For example, the second row in the left part of this figure, the eyes and mouth parts of the first exemplar image have very low weight. This is reasonable since the face of the target image has a more frontal angle and does not have glasses. If both the exemplar and target images have similar face angle, expression, etc., the PWAve module will generate weights that resemble an average operation. This can be seen in the third row on the right part.

Table 1. SSIM and PSNR scores on CelebA and WebFace dataset.

Method	SSIM (CelebA/WebFace)	PSNR (dB) (CelebA/WebFace)
Bicubic ($\times 8$)	0.61/0.68	20.72/22.04
Ours ($\times 8$, w/o Discriminator)	0.74/0.78	23.45/24.92
Ours ($\times 8$, w/ Discriminator)	0.72/0.76	23.18/24.38
Bicubic ($\times 16$)	0.48/0.57	17.56/19.04
Ours ($\times 16$ w/o Discriminator)	0.62/0.67	19.82/20.55
Ours ($\times 16$ w/ Discriminator)	0.59/0.61	19.13/19.42

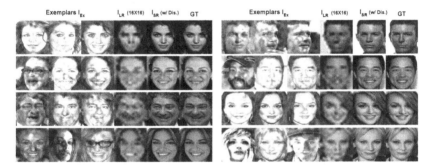

Fig. 6. The visualization of W (Here $W \in R^{1 \times 3 \times 1 \times 16 \times 16}$) generated by the PWAve module. Please note W is normalized along the second channel. The heatmap is in jet color space, the warmer the color, the higher the weight.

4.2   User Study

We conduct an user study in order to quantitatively assess the quality of our super-resolved images as perceived by humans. Our survey was joined by 51 participants from around the world. From these participants, 35 have experience in computer science or informatics. We refer to this group as "CS". The rest of them do not have such experience, we refer to them as "Non-CS".

Table 2. Results from our user study on the celebA dataset.

Error rate (%)	37.70 ± 12.53
TPR (%)	59.79 ± 15.35
TNR (%)	66.80 ± 17.80
FPR (%)	33.34 ± 17.85
FNP (%)	37.29 ± 19.30

The survey was composed by two parts. The first part aims to check whether the participants could distinguish between the super-resolved images from real

GT (HR) images. For each question, we put one HR image (128×128) next to the upsampled version of the corresponding LR image (16×16). Then we ask users to judge whether the shown HR image is the real, i.e. original, one. The HR image is randomly sampled from the ground truth and the images generated by our method. All the generated images shown on the survey are randomly sampled from our testing set. In total, there are 200 questions, half of them with a ground truth HR image. For each survey we randomly sample 25 questions. Before starting the survey, we also "train" the users by showing 12 examples with label (Real or Fake) in order to make them familiar with the task at hand.

The second part is more subjective, it consists on asking the participants to judge which type of the super-resolved images they consider more realistic: the sharp one (with Discriminator) or the smooth one (without Discriminator).

Table 2 shows the results of the first part of the study. The error rate is close to the random guess (50%). The FPR and FNR are quite balanced. In terms of the two user groups, CS group gets $(34.57 \pm 11.22)\%$ error rate while the Non-CS group achieves $(43.62 \pm 13.51)\%$, respectively. As for the second part, although the SSIM and PSNR scores are lower (Table 1), around 60% of the participants think the sharp images look more realistic than the smooth ones. Therefore, we will focus on the sharper qualitative results in the next sections.

4.3   Qualitative Comparison with Respect to the State-of-the-art

Why There is No Quantitative Comparison? We do not provide a quantitative comparison w.r.t. existing methods for the following reasons: i) The SSIM and PSNR scores do not provide a definitive answer: blurry images may have a higher SSIM and PSNR score [30,31] since the optimal solution to minimize reconstruction error in image space is averaging all possible solutions [9,32,33]. This observation was further ratified in our previous experiment. ii) Existing methods are implemented in different frameworks and, currently, there is no unified benchmark for this task. Re-implementation may raise doubt on the quality of the code, and the used data splits and pre-processing. Therefore, we only provide the conducted user-study (Sect. 4.2) and a qualitative comparison.

In this experiment, the presented qualitative results (images) are taken directly from the corresponding papers. These selected images will constitute the point of comparison. Figure 7 shows a qualitative comparison on celebA dataset w.r.t. [6] and on the WebFace dataset w.r.t. [8] and [9]. Generally, our model can generate more detailed results and preserve the person's original identity. [6] uses a manually rotated LR image as input while a few spatial transform networks are utilized to compensate this manual rotation. The results from [6] change the identity and the face shape for some cases. Moreover, some details are missing, e.g.. the moustache is lost during the super resolution process in the first image in the top part of Fig. 7. The images generated by [8] have blurry hair as well as a blurry background. [9] overcomes this problem but also loses some details, e.g. the eyes' shape (i.e. the third row in the bottom left of Fig. 7) and the iris color (i.e. the second row in the bottom right of Fig. 7).

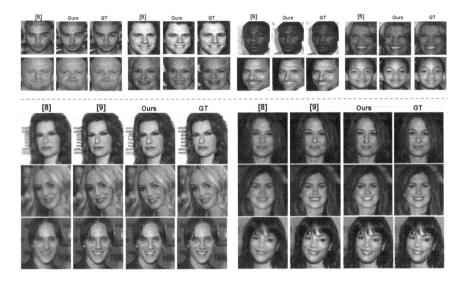

Fig. 7. Top: qualitative comparison w.r.t. state-of-the-art methods on the celebA dataset. The resolution of I_{LR} is 16×16 and the HR image is 128×128. The first column shows the results from [6]. Bottom: qualitatively comparison w.r.t. state-of-the-art baselines on WebFace dataset. The I_{LR} has the resolution of 32 × 32 and HR image is 256 × 256. The first and second column are results from [8] and [9].

4.4 Ablation Study

Our ablation study aims at assessing the effect of i) the number of considered exemplars, and ii) the PWAve module. Towards this goal, we conduct two experiments: gradually increase the number of exemplars K, from 0 (no exemplar) to 5, and replace the PWAve module by simply averaging the feature maps of exemplars. Fig. 8 shows the SSIM and PSNR scores under each setting. The trend is clear - more exemplars bring more benefits. The model with scaling factor of 16 can gain more, it is because the I_{LR} contains less information and the model can gain extra information from the exemplars.

Regarding the PWAve module, the scores are also better than the averaging method. To give a more straightforward comparison on this module, we show some examples in Fig. 9. These examples show that the combination of the feature maps will influence the details in the generated image, such as mouth, eyebrows, etc. With the help of the weights generated by the PWAve module, the model can take into account useful regions from the exemplars and produce a HR image closer to the ground truth.

4.5 Facial Features Editing via Exemplars

Based on the assumption that for most cases, the exemplars possess facial features such as eye shape, iris color, gender etc. that are in the LR image and

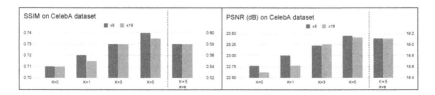

Fig. 8. Ablation study on the number of exemplars and feature map fusion method. The blue bar and the left y-axis are for the experiment with the scaling factor of 8 while the red bar and the right y-axis are for 16. Higher values are better.

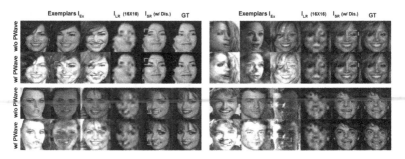

Fig. 9. Examples of ablation study on the PWAve module. For each set, the first row is without PWAve module (standard average). We show the heatmap of W generated by PWAve on each the second row. Please give your attention to the region within the dashed green box highlighting keys aspects of the combination process. (Color figure online)

are expected to appear in the SR image. We have shown that the exemplars do provide useful information to help the model super-resolve the LR image. This observation raises the question, what if we use exemplars with different facial features? Will the super-resolved images still contain the original features from the LR image or adopt the new features from the exemplars? In the CelebA dataset, we still find some cases where the facial features within the same identity are different. We run two experiments considering exemplars with different and the same identity. Please note, in this experiment we just replace the exemplars in the testing phase, no re-training is required.

Figure 10 clearly answers the question above. For both experiments, the super-resolved images adopt the features from exemplars, such as gender, makeup, eyes, mouth etc. More specifically, if the gender of exemplars is different (left part of Fig. 10), the model will change the gender as well as other facial features. We believe changing gender is more difficult since it is a high-level characteristic which is related to other low-level attributes such as eyes, eyebrows, mouth etc. If the gender of the exemplars is the same (right part of Fig. 10), then the identity of the original HR image will be maintained but changes in corresponding facial features occur. Compared with [6], benefiting from using the exemplars, our method can generate face HR image with arbitrary facial

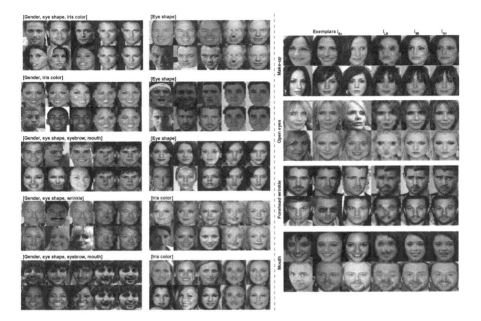

Fig. 10. Examples of editing/modifying facial features via exemplars. The left part shows example using I_{Ex} with different identity. For each set, the first three images are the I_{Ex}, followed by the I_{LR} and I_{SR}. The edited facial features are displayed on the top of each set. On the right part, I_{Ex} has the same identity but different facial features. The edited facial feature is displayed on the left vertically.

features rather than only the pre-defined ones. The experiment shows that our model is capable of dynamically introducing features on the generated images via the exemplars. This suggests that our model can be also applied to subtle image editing tasks without the need of re-retraining or additional modifications on the original model.

5   Conclusion

In this paper, we propose to use multiple exemplars as conditions to guide the model to super-resolve LR images. This is complemented by the proposed PWAve module, a component capable of learning how perform a suitable combination of the set of intermediate feature maps computed from the exemplars. We empirically show the effectiveness of using more than one exemplar and that our method outperforms baselines from the literature. In addition, benefiting from the exemplars, our model can dynamically generate HR face images with arbitrary facial features.

Acknowledgement. This work was partially supported by the KU Leuven AI impuls, FWO G.0A47.20N, and a NVIDIA Academic Hardware Grant. We thank all the people who participated in our user-study.

References

1. Liu, M.Y., et al.: Few-shot unsupervised image-to-image translation. In: IEEE International Conference on Computer Vision (ICCV) (2019)
2. Chen, Y., Tai, Y., Liu, X., Shen, C., Yang, J.: FSRNet: end-to-end learning face super-resolution with facial priors. In: Proceedings of the IEEE Conference on Computer Vision and Pattern Recognition (2018)
3. Bulat, A., Tzimiropoulos, G.: Super-FAN: integrated facial landmark localization and super-resolution of real-world low resolution faces in arbitrary poses with GANs. CVPR abs/1712.02765 (2018)
4. Yu, X., Fernando, B., Ghanem, B., Porikli, F., Hartley, R.: Face super-resolution guided by facial component heatmaps. In: Ferrari, V., Hebert, M., Sminchisescu, C., Weiss, Y. (eds.) ECCV 2018. LNCS, vol. 11213, pp. 219–235. Springer, Cham (2018). https://doi.org/10.1007/978-3-030-01240-3_14
5. Kim, D., Kim, M., Kwon, G., Kim, D. S.: Progressive face super-resolution via attention to facial landmark. In: Proceedings of the 30th British Machine Vision Conference (BMVC) (2019)
6. Yu, X., Fernando, B., Hartley, R., Porikli, F.: Super-resolving very low-resolution face images with supplementary attributes. In: CVPR (2018)
7. Lu, Y., Tai, Y.-W., Tang, C.-K.: Attribute-guided face generation using conditional CycleGAN. In: Ferrari, V., Hebert, M., Sminchisescu, C., Weiss, Y. (eds.) ECCV 2018. LNCS, vol. 11216, pp. 293–308. Springer, Cham (2018). https://doi.org/10.1007/978-3-030-01258-8_18
8. Li, X., Liu, M., Ye, Y., Zuo, W., Lin, L., Yang, R.: Learning warped guidance for blind face restoration. In: Ferrari, V., Hebert, M., Sminchisescu, C., Weiss, Y. (eds.) ECCV 2018. LNCS, vol. 11217, pp. 278–296. Springer, Cham (2018). https://doi.org/10.1007/978-3-030-01261-8_17
9. Dogan, B., Gu, S., Timofte, R.: Exemplar guided face image super-resolution without facial landmarks. In: The IEEE Conference on Computer Vision and Pattern Recognition (CVPR) Workshops (2019)
10. Jingwei, X., Nannan, W., Xinbo, G., Li, J.: Residual attribute attention network for face image super-resolution. In: AAAI (2019)
11. Zhang, K., et al.: Super-identity convolutional neural network for face hallucination (2018)
12. Li, X., Li, W., Ren, D., Zhang, H., Wang, M., Zuo, W.: Enhanced blind face restoration with multi-exemplar images and adaptive spatial feature fusion. In: CVPR (2020)
13. Odena, A., Olah, C., Shlens, J.: Conditional image synthesis with auxiliary classifier GANs. In: Proceedings of the 34th International Conference on Machine Learning, PMLR, pp. 2642–2651 (2017)
14. Mirza, M., Osindero, S.: Conditional generative adversarial nets (2014)
15. Chen, X., Duan, Y., Houthooft, R., Schulman, J., Sutskever, I., Abbeel, P.: Info-GAN: interpretable representation learning by information maximizing generative adversarial nets. In: NIPS (2016)
16. Bao, J., Chen, D., Wen, F., Li, H., Hua, G.: CVAE-GAN: fine-grained image generation through asymmetric training. In: ICCV (2017)
17. Yan, X., Yang, J., Sohn, K., Lee, H.: Attribute2Image: conditional image generation from visual attributes. In: Leibe, B., Matas, J., Sebe, N., Welling, M. (eds.) ECCV 2016. LNCS, vol. 9908, pp. 776–791. Springer, Cham (2016). https://doi.org/10.1007/978-3-319-46493-0_47

18. Esser, P., Sutter, E., Ommer, B.: A variational U-net for conditional appearance and shape generation (2018)
19. Lin, J., Xia, Y., Qin, T., Chen, Z., Liu, T.Y.: Conditional image-to-image translation. In: The IEEE Conference on Computer Vision and Pattern Recognition (CVPR) (2018)
20. Huang, X., Liu, M.-Y., Belongie, S., Kautz, J.: Multimodal unsupervised image-to-image translation. In: Ferrari, V., Hebert, M., Sminchisescu, C., Weiss, Y. (eds.) ECCV 2018. LNCS, vol. 11207, pp. 179–196. Springer, Cham (2018). https://doi.org/10.1007/978-3-030-01219-9_11
21. Liu, Y., Junjie, Y., Ouyang, W.: Quality aware network for set to set recognition. In: IEEE Conference on Computer Vision and Pattern Recognition (2017)
22. Karras, T., Laine, S., Aila, T.: A style-based generator architecture for generative adversarial networks. CVPR abs/1812.04948 (2019)
23. Zhang, R., Isola, P., Efros, A.A., Shechtman, E., Wang, O.: The unreasonable effectiveness of deep features as a perceptual metric. In: CVPR (2018)
24. Albanie, S., Nagrani, A., Vedaldi, A., Zisserman, A.: Emotion recognition in speech using cross-modal transfer in the wild. In: ACM Multimedia (2018)
25. Gulrajani, I., Ahmed, F., Arjovsky, M., Dumoulin, V., Courville, A.C.: Improved training of Wasserstein GANs. In: NIPS (2017)
26. Liu, Z., Luo, P., Wang, X., Tang, X.: Deep learning face attributes in the wild. In: Proceedings of International Conference on Computer Vision (ICCV) (2015)
27. Yi, D., Lei, Z., Liao, S., Li, S.Z.: Learning face representation from scratch (2014)
28. Paszke, A., et al.: Automatic differentiation in PyTorch (2017)
29. Kingma, D.P., Ba, J.: Adam: a method for stochastic optimization (2015)
30. Johnson, J., Alahi, A., Fei-Fei, L.: Perceptual losses for real-time style transfer and super-resolution. In: Leibe, B., Matas, J., Sebe, N., Welling, M. (eds.) ECCV 2016. LNCS, vol. 9906, pp. 694–711. Springer, Cham (2016). https://doi.org/10.1007/978-3-319-46475-6_43
31. Hanhart, P., Korshunov, P., Ebrahimi, T.: Benchmarking of quality metrics on ultra-high definition video sequences. In: 2013 18th International Conference on Digital Signal Processing (DSP), pp. 1–8 (2013)
32. Dosovitskiy, A., Brox, T.: Generating images with perceptual similarity metrics based on deep networks (2016)
33. Ledig, C., et al.: Photo-realistic single image super-resolution using a generative adversarial network. In: 2017 IEEE Conference on Computer Vision and Pattern Recognition (CVPR), pp. 105–114 (2017)

Imbalance Robust Softmax for Deep Embeeding Learning

Hao Zhu[1]([✉]), Yang Yuan[2], Guosheng Hu[2,4], Xiang Wu[3], and Neil Robertson[4]

[1] Australian National University, Canberra, Australia
`Hao.Zhu@anu.edu.au`
[2] Anyvision, Belfast, UK
`bengouawu@gmail.com`
[3] Reconova, Beijing, China
[4] Queens University of Belfast, Belfast, UK

Abstract. Deep embedding learning is expected to learn a metric space in which features have smaller maximal intra-class distance than minimal inter-class distance. In recent years, one research focus is to solve the open-set problem by discriminative deep embedding learning in the field of face recognition (FR) and person re-identification (re-ID). Apart from open-set problem, we find that imbalanced training data is another main factor causing the performance degradation of FR and re-ID, and data imbalance widely exists in the real applications. However, very little research explores why and how data imbalance influences the performance of FR and re-ID with softmax or its variants. In this work, we deeply investigate data imbalance in the perspective of neural network optimisation and feature distribution about softmax. We find one main reason of performance degradation caused by data imbalance is that the weights (from the penultimate fully-connected layer) are far from their class centers in feature space. Based on this investigation, we propose a unified framework, Imbalance-Robust Softmax (IR-Softmax), which can simultaneously solve the open-set problem and reduce the influence of data imbalance. IR-Softmax can generalise to any softmax and its variants (which are discriminative for open-set problem) by directly setting the weights as their class centers, naturally solving the data imbalance problem. In this work, we explicitly re-formulate two discriminative softmax (A-Softmax and AM-Softmax) under the framework of IR-Softmax. We conduct extensive experiments on FR databases (LFW, MegaFace) and re-ID database (Market-1501, Duke), and IR-Softmax outperforms many state-of-the-art methods.

1 Introduction

Recently, convolutional neural networks (CNNs) have significantly boosted the state-of-the-art performance in many computer vision tasks especially in image classification [1–6]. Not surprisingly, CNNs have achieved great success in the

---

H. Zhu and Y. Yuan—Indicates equal contribution.

© Springer Nature Switzerland AG 2021
H. Ishikawa et al. (Eds.): ACCV 2020, LNCS 12626, pp. 274–291, 2021.
https://doi.org/10.1007/978-3-030-69541-5_17

field of biometrics, in particular, face recognition (FR) [7–10] and person re-identification (re-ID) [11–13]. This success is derived from the fact that CNNs are able to encode images into rich, semantic and discriminative representations (features) which can be used to effectively measure the similarity between two identity-related images. These two tasks (FR and re-ID) differ from general image classification in terms of two challenges: open-set setting and data imbalance in the training set.

Open-set setting is much more widely applied than close-set for FR and re-ID. For open-set setting, the identities of test set are disjoint with those of training set. In the real world, FR and re-ID system train the CNN (feature extractor) using images collected from one specific group of people, e.g. celebrities from IMDb in CASIA WebFace [14] database. During test stage, however, the FR and re-ID systems work in places, such as one police station, where the gallery (blacklist) and the probe (people appear in this police station) are mostly likely disjoint with training set (e.g. those celebrities). In contrast, classical image classification (e.g. ImageNet Challenge) uses the close-set setting where training and test sets share the same classes. Traditionally, both open-set and close-set problems adopt the softmax function because of its simplicity and probabilistic interpretation. Together with the cross-entropy loss, they form arguably one of the most commonly-used components in CNN architectures.

Under open-set setting, however, softmax suffers from one drawback: deep learning with softmax loss only learns separable features that are not discriminative enough for 'unseen' classes in testing. It results from the fact that softmax loss does not explicitly optimise the intra- and inter-class distances. To address this, some methods combine the softmax loss with metric learning [9,10,15] to enhance the discrimination power of features. Metric learning based methods commonly suffer from the way of building mini-batches by sampling. Other methods try to add new constraints (e.g. center loss [16], large-margin term [17,18], L2 normalization [19,20]) that make features more compact and thus more discriminative.

Data imbalance is another challenge for FR and re-ID. Unlike those popular datasets MNIST [21], CIFAR-10 [22] and ImageNet [23], FR and re-ID datasets are commonly highly imbalanced. As shown in Fig. 1, only a limited number of identities appear frequently (more than hundreds), while most of the others appear relatively rarely (fewer than ten times) in the popular face database CASIA-Webface [14] and re-ID database Market-1501 [24]. Surprisingly, very little research explores the problem of data imbalance in FR and re-ID. In this paper, we show that deep embedding learning with the most widely used softmax (and its variants such as A-Softmax [18]) encounters difficulty in the presence of imbalanced training data even using either metric learning or other regularizations. Although some softmax variants such as A-Softmax [18] can solve the open-set problem by learning compact features, they do not perform well when the training data is imbalanced. To our knowledge, the only work exploring the data imbalance problem for FR is the range loss [25]. However, range loss does not deeply investigate the reason why this imbalance impacts the deep embedding learning.

In this work, we aim to learn deep embeddings which can achieve two targets: 1) being discriminative for open-set and 2) being robust to data imbalance. As existing works [16–20], target 1) can be achieved by learning compact features (i.e. reduce intra-class variance). To achieve target 2), we have to first investigate why data imbalance influences the performance of softmax-based deep classification. In this work, we explore the reason. *During the back-propagation training with imbalanced data, two strengths, which determine the update of the weights (usually the penultimate fully-connected layer), are imbalanced (see Eq. 2): the one keeping the weights at their class centers is much smaller than that pushing them away. This imbalance causes the weight of the class with minor samples being far away from its class center, leading to degraded classification performance.* Based on this analysis, target 2) can be achieved by making the weight from the class with minor samples close to its class center.

To simultaneously achieve targets 1) and 2), we propose a uniformed framework, Imbalance-Robust Softmax (IR-Softmax). First, IR-Softmax solves the open-set problem by being compatible with the softmax variants (e.g. A-Softmax [18], AM-Softmax [26] which can learn discriminative embeddings. Second, motivated by the aforementioned analysis on data imbalance, IR-Softmax alleviates the influence of data imbalance by setting the weights as their class centers in the feature space instead of updating with back-propagation. In this way, IR-Softmax effectively avoids the shift between the weights and their centers, which is the main reason of performance degradation caused by data imbalance detailed in Sect. 3.1.

Our contributions can be summarised as:

1. We deeply investigate the reason why data imbalance degrades the performance of softmax-based classifications in the perspective of neural network optimisation (Sect. 3.1) and feature distribution (Sect. 3.2).
2. IR-Softmax can learn embeddings which are discriminative under open-set protocol. In particular, IR-Softmax is a unified framework, e.g. it can generalise to softmax and its variants (e.g. A-Softmax [18], AM-Softmax [26]) to achieve discriminative feature learning. More importantly, IR-Softmax can effectively reduce the influence of data imbalance by bridging the gap between weights (the penultimate fully-connected layer) and their class centers in feature space.
3. Our extensive experiments demonstrate the effectiveness and generalisation of the proposed IR-Softmax, and we achieve state-of-the-art performance on challenging FR (LFW [27], MegaFace [28]) and re-ID (Market-1501 [24], DUKE-MTMC [29]) benchmarks. The code will be made publicly available.

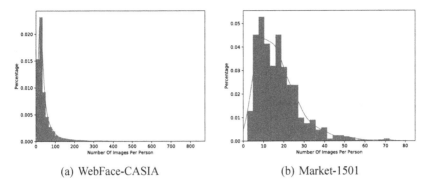

(a) WebFace-CASIA   (b) Market-1501

Fig. 1. Long-tailed distribution on WebFace-CASIA [14] and Market-1501 [24] database. The number of images per person drops drastically, and only a few identities have a large number of images.

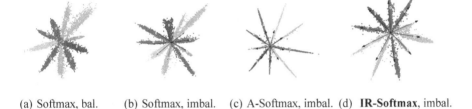

(a) Softmax, bal.   (b) Softmax, imbal.   (c) A-Softmax, imbal. (d) **IR-Softmax**, imbal.

Fig. 2. The distribution of deeply learned features. 'bal.' (balanced) setting contains 10 classes, which all has 6,000 images from MNIST [21]. In contrast, 'imbal.' (imbalanced) setting contains 6000 images for all classes but class '3' with 300 images. A-Softmax in (c) refers to [18]. The label of each class is plotted on its center. In addition, we also plot the weights (from the fully-connected penultimate layer) to each class with an arrow in (b)–(d). Note that our fully-connected layer consists of only 2 neurons to facilitate visualisation.

2   Related Work

In this section, we briefly review the methods of discriminative feature learning in the field of face recognition (FR) and person re-identification (re-ID). Recently, two popular ways of deep embedding learning are: (1) metric learning and (2) discriminative softmax (softmax's variants which are more discriminative for open-set problem). Apart from these two strategies, we discuss the training data imbalanced problem in the field of FR and re-ID.

Metric Learning. Metric learning is widely used for FR and re-ID. In practice, to learn more discriminative features, many works combine softmax loss and deep metric learning loss (contrastive [9,30] loss or triplet loss [10]). Unlike softmax, contrastive and triplet losses accept image pairs or triplets (3 or a multiple of 3) as input respectively. For contrastive loss, if the input pair belongs to the same class, their features are required to be as similar as possible. Otherwise, the contrastive loss would require their distance larger than a particular margin. Similar to contrastive loss, the triplet loss [10] encourages a similar distance constraint. Specifically, the triplet loss minimises the distance between an anchor sample and a positive sample (of the same identity) and maximises the distance between the anchor sample and a negative sample (of different identity). Clearly, the contrastive and triplet losses can encourage intra-class compactness and inter-class separability, making the learned feature more discriminative. However, both contrastive and triplet losses require a carefully-designed pair/triplet selection procedure. For example, using contrastive loss, it is hard to build training pairs from a mini-batch, especially for the training set with many classes. Normally the mini-batch size is not more than 256, while the number of categories is far more than 256 in the application of FR and re-ID. Clearly the online selection only produces a few positive pairs and much more negative ones.

Discriminative Softmax. Apart from metric learning, some softmax variants are proposed, aiming to learn more discriminative features to solve the open-set problem. Wen et al. [16] add a new supervision signal, called center loss, to softmax loss for face recognition. Specifically, the center loss simultaneously learns a feature center for each identity and penalises the distances between the deep features of examples and their corresponding feature centers. With the joint supervision of softmax loss and center loss, this method can easily obtain inter-class dispersion and intra-class compactness. Large-Margin Softmax loss [17] proposes a new perspective to softmax and optimises the angles between weights and features. However, the magnitude of weights are also considered, and thus it is also sensitive to data imbalance just the same as softmax. By contrast, A-Softmax loss [18] controls the magnitude of weights (i.e. $\|w\|_2 = 1$) and thus make the weights optimised in an angular space. Although A-Softmax is theoretically suitable for deep embedding learning, it actually does not work well in the setting of data imbalance detailed in Sect. 3. [26,31,32] relax the margin with more efficient and effective ways. Some works [19,20,32] try to optimise the features on a hyper-sphere to make features more discriminative.

Training Data Imbalance. The aforementioned methods ignore the problem of training data imbalance which widely exist in FR and re-ID. In [33], researchers investigate many factors that influence the performance of fine-tuning for object detection with long-tailed distributions of samples. Their analysis and empirical results indicate that classes with more samples will achieve greater impact on the feature learning, and it is better to make the sample number more uniform across classes. In the field of FR and re-ID, unfortunately, the data imbalance problem is much worse than object detection [33]. Specifically, few identities have more than 1000 images and many identities have fewer than 10 images. Commonly a large-scale face dataset has more than 10,000 identities [14]. However, we still cannot simply discard these identities that only have few images. For face recognition, identities with few images cannot provide enough intra-class information for the model, but provide inter-class information which is more useful to open-set protocol. Many methods [25,34–37] have been proposed to solve the data imbalance in face recognition. However,these works do not deeply investigate the reason why the imbalance impacts softmax based deep embedding learning.

3   Methodology

In this section, we first provide insights into the influence of data imbalance on CNN performance by training a LeNet [21] on an imbalanced MNIST. Based on the conclusion drawn from the experiments, we propose a new loss function, Imbalance Robust Softmax (IR-Softmax), to reduce the influence of data imbalance while perform discriminative feature learning. Last, we discuss the relations between the proposed method and metric learning.

3.1   Motivation

Softmax regression (or multinomial logistic regression) is a generalisation of logistic regression to multi-class problem, therefore, softmax can handle $y_i \in \{1, \ldots, K\}$ (where K is the number of classes). Given a training set $\{(\mathbf{x}_i, y_i), \ldots, (\mathbf{x}_n, y_n)\}$, we learn an embedding/projection $f(\mathbf{x})$, with which the softmax can be written as

$$J = -\frac{1}{n} \left[\sum_{i=1}^{n} \log \frac{\exp\left(f_{y_i}(\mathbf{x}_i)\right)}{\sum_{j=1}^{K} \exp(f_j(\mathbf{x}_i))} \right] \tag{1}$$

where f_j denotes the j-th dimension of the learned function $f(x)$, and n is the number of training samples. In CNNs, f is usually the output of a fully connected layer $\mathbf{W} = [\mathbf{w}_1, \ldots, \mathbf{w}_k]$, so $f_j = \mathbf{w}_j^T \mathbf{x}_i + b_j$ and $f_{y_i} = \mathbf{w}_{y_i}^T \mathbf{x}_i + b_{y_i}$.

To analyse the influence of data imbalance, we come to the neural network optimisation process (we omit the bias term for simplicity):

$$\nabla_{\mathbf{w}_k} J = -\frac{1}{n} \sum_{i=1}^{n} \mathbf{x}_i \left(1\{y_i = k\} - P(k|\mathbf{x}_i)\right)$$

$$= \frac{1}{n} \left(\underbrace{\sum_{i=1}^{n} \mathbf{x}_i (P(k|\mathbf{x}_i) - 1)1\{y_i = k\}}_{term\ 1} + \underbrace{\sum_{i=1}^{n} \mathbf{x}_i P(k|\mathbf{x}_i)1\{y_i \neq k\}}_{term\ 2} \right) \tag{2}$$

where $P(k|\mathbf{x}_i) = \frac{\exp\left(f_k(\mathbf{x}_i)\right)}{\sum_{j=1}^{K} \exp(f_j(\mathbf{x}_i))}$, and $1\{\cdot\}$ is the indicator function: $1\{true\} = 1$, and $1\{false\} = 0$. It can be observed that the gradient of the parameter $\nabla_{\mathbf{w}_k} J$ contains two terms: term 1 (which is activated if $y_i = k$) and term 2 (if $y_i \neq k$). Thus the update of parameter $\mathbf{w}_k$ during optimisation depends on the samples not only from the k-th class but also from the other classes. Term 1 is actually the weighted center of the observed class; Term 2 can be viewed as the weighted centers of all the other classes if n is big enough. The update of $\mathbf{w}_k$ is determined by the balance of two strengths: one leads $\mathbf{w}_k$ to the center of class k (term 1), one 'pushes' w_k away from class k (weighted center of all the other classes). If the training data is imbalanced, the update of $\mathbf{w}_k$ corresponding to class k, which has much fewer samples than other classes, is fully dominated by term 2, making $\mathbf{w}_k$ being far away from center of class k.

To further analyse the influence of data imbalance on optimisation, we take one binary classification with softmax for example. As shown in Fig. 3(a) and (b), there are both five samples for class 1 (blue points) and class 2 (red points) for balance setting; and nine samples for class 1 and one sample for class 2 for imbalance setting. Clearly, both $\mathbf{w}_1$ and $\mathbf{w}_2$ are influenced by all the samples from class 1 and 2. In imbalance setting (Fig. 3(b)), $\mathbf{w}_2$ is determined by term 1 (1 sample from class 2) and term 2 (9 samples of class 1), where term 1 and 2 are detailed in Eq. (2). Clearly, the update of $\mathbf{w}_2$ is dominated by term 2, which pushes $\mathbf{w}_2$ far away from the center of class 2.

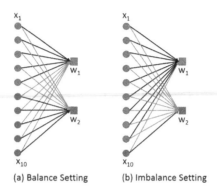

(a) Balance Setting   (b) Imbalance Setting

Fig. 3. One example of binary classification with softmax. (a) balance setting with five samples of class 1 (blue spots) and five samples of class 2 (red spots). (b) imbalance setting with nine samples of class 1 and one sample of class 2. Black and green lines indicate term 1 and term 2 in Eq. (2), influencing the update of $\mathbf{w}_1$ and $\mathbf{w}_2$ respectively. (Color figure online)

To explicitly show the influence of data imbalance on classification performance, we conduct a toy experiment on MNIST [21]. From Fig. 2(b) and 2(c), not surprisingly, the data imbalance degrades the performance of the models trained with softmax and A-Softmax [18]. We can find the main issue caused by data imbalance: centers of relevant feature distributions being away from their weights (from penultimate fully-connected layer). For example, in Fig. 2(b), the feature center of class '3' (minor training data) and centers of '5' and '7' (the neighbours of '3') are all distant from their weights. Thus these biases (feature centers being far from its weights) caused by data imbalance will induce classification error for the corresponding categories. Though A-Softmax can learn discriminative features, it suffers from the same aforementioned bias problem as shown in Fig. 2(c). This observation provides the cue to solve the data imbalance problem and inspires our solution (Fig. 2(d)) detailed in Sect. 3.2.

3.2 Imbalance Robust Softmax (IR-Softmax)

In this work, we aim to learn features which can (i) improve the discriminative power of features in open-set protocol, and (ii) alleviate data imbalance problem.

For (i), the desired open-set criterion is that the maximal intra-class distance is smaller than the minimal inter-class distance. However, softmax only maximises the the distance between weights rather then inter-class distance (Fig. 4(a)). Derived from softmax, A-Softmax [18], however, only focuses on minimising intra-class distance, leading to compact features as shown in Fig. 4(b). For (ii), data imbalance can degrade the performance of deep CNNs. As analysed in Sect. 3.1, in particular Eq. (2), the data imbalance can cause imbalanced gradient updates during optimisation: the strength of making the weights close to feature center (term 1 in Eq. (2)) is much smaller than the strength of pushing away (term 2). This strength imbalance causes the weights being far away from their feature centers as shown in Fig. 4(b), 2(b) and 2(c).

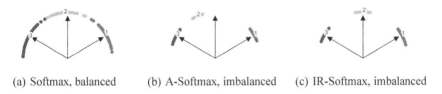

(a) Softmax, balanced   (b) A-Softmax, imbalanced   (c) IR-Softmax, imbalanced

Fig. 4. Feature distributions in angular space: (a) separable features under balanced data, feature center being close to its weight (the black arrow); (b) compact features under imbalanced data, and the feature center being far from its weight; (c) compact features under imbalanced data, the feature center being close to its weight.

Based on the above analysis, to simultaneously solve the open-set and data imbalance problems, two criteria corresponding these two problems are: 1) minimising the intra-class distance by making the feature distribution with the same label more compact; 2) maximising the low bound of inter-class distance by making the center of features of each class being close enough (ideally equal) to its weights (usually the penultimate fully-connect layer). Criterion 1) can be achieved by learning compact features e.g. A-Softmax [18] and AM-Softmax [26]. To our knowledge, we are the first to investigate Criterion 2). To simultaneously achieve these two targets, we propose a novel framework, IR-Softmax[1], which can achieve Criterion 1) by incorporating itself into discriminative softmaxs e.g. A-Softmax [18] and AM-Softmax [26].

Now we detail the way of meeting Criterion 2). As the analysis in Sect. 3.1, we can find that the imbalanced data causes the weights (from penultimate fully-connected layer) being away from their class centers after training as shown in Fig. 2(b), leading to degraded classification performance. Based on Criterion 2), the key idea of IR-Softmax is *setting the weights as their corresponding class centers in the feature space*, naturally avoiding the shift between the weights and their centers.

IR-Softmax is a unified framework which can be incorporated into softmax and its variants, leading to different forms of IR-Softmax. For classical softmax

---

[1] code is available in https://github.com/allenhaozhu/IR-Softmax.

in Eq. (1), $f_j = \mathbf{w}_j^T \mathbf{x}_i + b_j$ is fed into softmax. In our IR-Softmax framework, $f_j' = (\mathbf{c}_j')^T \mathbf{x}_i + b_j$ replaces f_j, where $\mathbf{c}_j'$, the center of features from class j, is defined as:

$$c_j' = \frac{1}{\sum_i^n 1\{y_i = j\}} \sum_i^n \frac{1\{y_i = j\}\mathbf{x}_i}{\|\mathbf{x}_i\|_2} \tag{3}$$

Most importantly, in this work, we formulate two discriminative IR-Softmaxs derived from A-Softmax and AM-Softmax, respectively. To formulate A-Softmax and AM-Softmax which both normalise the weight w_j ($\|\mathbf{w}_j\|_2 = 1$), Eq. (1) can be modified as:

$$J = - \left[\sum_{i=1}^m \log \frac{\exp(\|\mathbf{x}_i\| \psi(\theta_{y_i}))}{\exp(\|\mathbf{x}_i\| \psi(\theta_{\mathbf{y}_i})) + \sum_{j \neq y_i}^K \exp(\|\mathbf{x}_i\| \cos(\theta_j))} \right] \tag{4}$$

From $f_j = \mathbf{w}_j^T \mathbf{x}_i + b_j$ (classical softmax) and $f_j' = (\mathbf{c}_j')^T \mathbf{x}_i + b_j$ (IR-Softmax version), we use $\mathbf{c}_j'$ to replace $\mathbf{w}_j$. Similarly, we use $\mathbf{c}_j^T \mathbf{x}_i$ ($\mathbf{c}_j = \frac{\mathbf{c}_j'}{\|\mathbf{c}_j'\|_2}$) to replace $\|\mathbf{x}_i\| \cos(\theta_j)$ for both A-Softmax and AM-Softmax. Thus, our IR-Softmax version of Eq. (4) is:

$$J = - \left[\sum_{i=1}^m \log \frac{\exp(\|\mathbf{x}_i\| \psi(\theta_{y_i}))}{\exp(\|\mathbf{x}_i\| \psi(\theta_{y_i})) + \sum_{j \neq y_i}^K \exp(\mathbf{c}_j^T \mathbf{x}_i)} \right] \tag{5}$$

For A-Softmax,

$$\psi(\theta_{y_i}) = ((-1)^k \cos(m\theta_{y_i}) - 2k), \theta_{y_i} \in [\frac{k\pi}{m}, \frac{(k+1)\pi}{m}] \tag{6}$$

where $k \in [0, m-1]$ and $m \geq 1$ is an integer that controls the size of angular margin. For original A-Softmax, $\theta_{y_i} (0 \leq \theta_i \leq \pi)$ is the angle between $\mathbf{w}_i$ and $\mathbf{x}_i$. Note that, in our IR-Softmax, θ_{y_i} is *the angle between the* $\mathbf{c}_{y_i}$ *and* $\mathbf{x}_i$, where $\mathbf{c}_{y_i}$ is the center of class i. For AM-Softmax,

$$\psi(\theta_{y_i}) = \cos(\theta_{y_i} + \alpha) \tag{7}$$

$$\psi(\theta_{y_i}) = \cos(m_1 \theta_{y_i} - m_2) - m_3 \tag{8}$$

where $\theta_{y_i} (0 \leq \theta_{y_i} \leq \pi)$ of the original AM-Softmax is the angle between $\mathbf{w}_i$ and $\mathbf{x}_i$. Note that θ_{y_i} of IR-Softmax is *the angle between the* $\mathbf{c}_{y_i}$ *and* $\mathbf{x}_i$.

Now we can summarise the difference between IR-Softmax and softmax (and its variants). First, the weight $\mathbf{w}_i$ of softmax is updated via back-propagation, however, $\mathbf{c}_i$ of IR-Softmax can be computed directly from Eq. (3). Second, the update of $\mathbf{w}_i$ depends on samples of class i and samples from other classes as shown in Eq. (2). In contrast, the update of $\mathbf{c}_i$ of IR-Softmax only depends on the samples from class i, effectively avoiding the influence of data imbalance.

In practice, it is impossible to use all samples to calculate the centers as shown in Eq. (3). We have tried three different updating strategies for feature centres. i. replacing the weight with an instance feature (which makes the proposed method like docFace [34]). ii. memory bank: estimate the centre with last few (in a fixed window) samples in the same class (without BP). iii. a loss function to estimate centres on the unit sphere for different classes. The disadvantage of the first solution is that an additional softmax is necessary in case the convergence is slightly slow and unstable. The second solution relieves the unstable issue but no improvement in performance. The third method is equal to adding a new term $\|\mathbf{c}_i - \frac{\mathbf{x}_i}{\|\mathbf{x}_i\|_2}\|_2^2, s.t.\|\mathbf{c}_i\| = 1$ to Eq. 4 and use the corresponding BP process to update feature centres (weights in Eq. 5) rather than Eq. 4. After that $\ell2$ normalization is used on feature centres to make sure new c_i on the unit sphere. We select the third one in our experiments because it works better than other two approaches.

3.3 Relation to Metric Learning

N-pairs loss [38] enforces softmax cross-entropy loss among the pairwise similarity in the *mini-batch*.

$$E = \frac{-1}{|P|} \sum_{(i,j)\in P} \log \frac{\exp(S_{i,j})}{\exp(S_{i,j}) + \sum_{k:y_k \neq y_j} \exp(S_{i,k})} \qquad (9)$$

where $S_{i,j} = f(\mathbf{x}_i, \mathbf{\Theta})^T f(\mathbf{x}_j, \mathbf{\Theta})$ represents the inner product between two embeddings. and $|P|$ indicates the number of positive pairs (i,j). Comparing Eq. (4) and (9), we can see our method can be viewed as a special form of N-pair loss. However, there are two main differences: (1) Unlike softmax embedded in N-pairs, we employ A-Softmax [18] and AM-Softmax [26] to improve the discriminability of features. (2) The size of *mini-batch* (where N-pair works) limits the number of negative samples. In practice, it is usually difficult to make mini-batch more than 256 due to the memory limitation of GPU. In contrast, our method alleviates the problem by caching historical features. The positive and negative samples are equal to the number of categories.

4 Experiments

In this section, we first describe the experimental settings. We then evaluate our method on two different tasks, face recognition (FR) and person re-identification (re-ID), against four different benchmarks. For FR, we use CASIA-WebFace [14] as training set and evaluate our method on LFW [27] and MegaFace [28]. For re-ID, we evaluate on the Market-1501 [24] and Duke [29] datasets.

4.1 Face Verification

All the faces and their landmarks are detected by MTCNN [39]. We use the detected 5 landmarks (two eyes, nose and two mouth corners) to perform similarity transformation. When the detection fails, we simply discard the image if it is in the training set, but use the provided landmarks if in the test set.

We use the publicly available training dataset CASIA-WebFace [14] (excluding the images of 59 identities appearing in testing sets [26]) to train our CNN models. CASIA-WebFace has 494,414 face images belonging to 10,575 (in fact, 10,516 after removing) different individuals. As shown in Fig. 1, CASIA-WebFace is an imbalance dataset. Some identities have very few images (e.g., only one image), while some have more than 300 images. These face images are horizontally flipped for data augmentation in the training process. Note that the number of samples in training set (0.49M) is relatively small compared to other private datasets used in DeepFace [2] (4M), VGGFace [40] (2M) and FaceNet [10] (200M). In the testing process, we extract the deep features from the output of the FC1 layer and do not employ any pre-processing (such as PCA and flipped features). The cosine distance between two features is applied. A nearest neighbor classifier and thresholding are used for face identification and verification, respectively.

To make fair comparison, we use two widely used CNN architectures for face recognition: 9-layer Light CNN [41] and 20-layer ResNet-20 [18]. Note that the faces are cropped to two different sizes (128×128 and 112×96) to fit the setting in [41] and [18] respectively. In the training process, our IR-Softmax is appended after the feature layer, i.e. the second last inner-product layer. The networks are trained in an end-to-end way.

For simplicity, we denote IR-Softmax (A) as our IR-Softmax instance derived from A-Softmax, and IR-Softmax (AM) from AM-Softmax in the whole experiment section.

LFW. The LFW dataset [27] contains 13,233 images from 5,749 identities, with large variations in pose, expression and illumination. All the images are collected from the internet. We evaluate our methods on two protocols: (1) official protocol [27] and (2) BLUFR protocol [42]. For (1), LFW is divided into 10 predefined splits for cross validation. We follow the standard 'Unrestricted, Labeled Outside Data' protocol. Because the performance of face recognition is almost saturated on this protocol, researchers propose a more challenging BLUFR protocol [42]. For (2), BLUFR utilises all 13,233 images to evaluate the performance in the open-set setting. The Verification Rate (VR) at False Accepted Rate (FAR) 0.1% (VR@FAR = 0.1%) and Detection and Identification rate (DIR) at FAR 1% (DIR@FAR = 1%) are reported under BLUFR. It is noteworthy that not only three identities exist in both CASIA-Webface [14,26] and LFW [27]. We removed them according to [26] during training to build a complete open-set validation.

LFW Official Protocol, Light CNN. As shown in Table 2, the performance is evaluated by six methods. The proposed IR-Softmax(A) and IR-Softmax(AM) greatly outperform their original versions (A-Softmax and AM-Softmax). Compared with the baseline (i.e. Softmax), IR-Softmax (A) improves the verification accuracy from 97.15% to 98.38%, and IR-Softmax (AM) from 97.15% to 98.63%.

LFW Official Protocol, ResNet-20. The evaluation results of ResNet-20 are listed in Table 1. Other state-of-the-art results of A-Softmax and AM-Softmax using ResNet-20 are also presented for comparison. Compared with the baseline (i.e. Softmax), IR-Softmax (A) loss improves the verification accuracy from 97.08% to 99.23% on LFW. From the results, we can see that the proposed methods IR-Softmax(A) and IR-Softmax(AM) can outperform the corresponding original versions.

BLUFR, Light CNN. From Table 2, we can observe that the proposed method significantly outperforms the other methods [17, 18]. Specifically, IR-Softmax(A) beats the softmax baseline (which we finetune our model from), and improves the VR@FAR = 0.1% from 83.32% to 94.61%, while DIR@FAR = 1% from 60.64% to 75.12%. Both versions of IR-Softmax are able to outperform their counterparts. It means that the proposed method can significantly enhance the discriminability of deeply learned features in the open-set protocol, demonstrating the effectiveness of the proposed method.

BLUFR, ResNet-20. Since ResNet-20 models [18, 19] are also widely used for face recognition, we make comparisons based on ResNet-20 in Table 1. IR-Softmax with ResNet-20 keeps the similar superiority compared with other models in the BLUFR protocol of LFW. Note that our approach is better than range loss, which is proposed to solve the problem of data imbalance in face recognition. Though range loss uses a larger training set (MS-celeb [43]) and a deeper network (ResNet-50), our method still outperforms it with VR@FAR = 0.1% from 93.72% to 97.08% (IR-Softmax(A)) or 98.09% (IR-Softmax(AM)) while DIR@FAR = 1% from 71.11% to 81.52% (IR-Softmax(A)) or 85.00% (IR-Softmax(AM)).

MegaFace. One of the most challenging datasets for face recognition is MegaFace [28]. The MegaFace dataset contains a gallery set and a probe set. The gallery set contains more than 1 million images from 690K identities; The probe set consists of two existing datasets: Facescrub [44] and FGNet. MegaFace

Table 1. Performance on ResNet with various loss functions. CenterLoss, NormFace model and sphereface model are provided by authors. NormFace and CenterLoss use ResNet-28 like [16], another two methods use ResNet-20 [18].

Loss function	LFW [27]	BLUFR [42]	BLUFR [42]	MegaFace [28]	MegaFace [28]
	6000 pairs	VR@FAR = 0.1%	DIR@FAR = 1%	rank1@1e−6	VR@FAR = 1e−6
Softmax	97.08%	78.26%	50.85%	45.26%	50.12%
CenterLoss [16]	99.00%	94.50%	65.46%	63.38%	75.68%
NormFace [19]	98.98%	96.16%	75.22%	65.03%	75.88%
A-Softmax [18]	99.08%	96.58%	79.97%	67.41%	78.19%
IR-Softmax (A)	99.23%	97.08%	81.52%	69.48%	80.32%
AM-Softmax [26]	98.98%	97.69%	84.82%	72.47%	84.44%
IR-Softmax (AM)	99.21%	98.09%	85.00%	75.28%	85.67%

Table 2. Performance on lighten CNN with various loss functions. All Results are derived under the same settings used in [41].

Loss function	LFW [27] 6000 pairs	BLUFR [42] VR@FAR = 0.1%	BLUFR [42] DIR@FAR = 1%	MegaFace [28] rank1@1e−6	MegaFace [28] VR@FAR = 1e−6
Softmax	97.15%	83.32%	60.64%	47.31%	54.86%
Large-Margin [17]	98.35%	91.62%	64.76%	59.03%	70.57%
A-Softmax [18]	98.20%	91.16%	66.55%	54.87%	60.75%
IR-Softmax (A)	98.38%	94.61%	75.12%	64.71%	75.94%
AM-Softmax [26]	98.58%	94.67%	72.80%	65.33%	78.76%
IR-Softmax (AM)	98.63%	95.36%	79.92%	66.71%	78.83%

has multiple testing scenarios including identification, verification and pose-invariance under two protocols i.e. large or small training sets. The training set is considered small if it is less than 0.5M. We evaluate our IR-Softmax under the small training set protocol.

Lighten-CNN. Table 2 shows that our IR-Softmax (A) outperforms A-Softmax result by a margin (almost 10% for rank-1 identification rate and 15% for VR at 1e-6 FAR) on the small training dataset protocol while IR-Softmax (AM) outperforms AM-Softmax result by a margin (7% for rank-1 identification rate and 1.4% for VR at 1e-6 FAR). Compared to the softmax baseline, our method performs significantly better: 15% from IR-Softmax (A) and 19% IR-Softmax (AM) for identification, 21% from IR-Softmax (A) and 24% from IR-Softmax (AM) for verification.

ResNet-20. Table 1 shows that our IR-Softmax (A) outperforms A-Softmax result by a margin (almost 2% for rank-1 identification rate and 2% for VR at 1e-6 FAR) on the small training dataset protocol while IR-Softmax (AM) outperforms AM-Softmax result by a margin (almost 3% for rank-1 identification rate and 1.2 % for VR at 1e-6 FAR). Compared to the softmax baseline, our method performs significantly better: 24% from IR-Softmax (A) and 30% from IR-Softmax (AM) for identification, 30% from IR-Softmax (A) and 35% IR-Softmax (AM) for verification.

Note that the performance of any testing methods on Megaface is intimately linked to the quality of face alignment. Thus we do not compared with other methods with different alignments. The results in Table 2 are therefore computed under the same setting of face alignment and are directly comparable. These results demonstrate that our IR-Softmax is well designed for open-set face recognition especially when the training set is imbalanced. One can also see that, smaller intra-class distance is not the only important issue for learning features, but larger and evenly inter-class angular margin can significantly improve face recognition performance.

4.2   Person Re-identification

For the evaluation of re-ID, we focus on two well-known re-ID databases: Market-1501 [24] and DUKE [29] datasets. As shown in Fig. 1, we demonstrate the distribution of market-1501 database. Although there are no identities with more than 100 images like WebFace dataset, the number of images per person ranges from 5 to 80. The DUKE [29] also has the similar imbalance pattern. We use the standard evaluation metrics for both datasets, namely the mean average precision score (mAP) and the cumulative matching curve (CMC) at rank-1. We follow common practice by using random crops and random horizontal flips during training. Specifically, we resize all images to 256×128, of which we take random crops of size 224×112. Many methods for re-ID rely on pre-trained models (e.g. ResNet). Indeed, these models usually lead to impressive results. However, pre-trained models reduce the flexibility to make task-specific changes in a network. For example, some application scenarios need compact models rather than large ones pre-trained on Imagenet. Our method clearly suggests that it is also possible to learn deep models from scratch and achieve state-of-the-art performance. We use a Lighten CNN [41] based on the ResNet Architecture, which is faster than the current ResNet-50 used by many works [45]. Compared with other methods, we do not use the corresponding pretrained models in ImageNet for finetuning. Thus we use the softmax to train a baseline model with the re-ID dataset directly. And other methods (e.g. large-margin and the proposed method) employ the baseline model as the pre-trained model and finetune this model further.

Market-1501. The Market-1501 dataset contains 1,501 identities, 19,732 gallery images and 12,936 training images captured by 6 cameras. All the bounding boxes are generated by the DPM detector [46]. The dataset uses both single and multi-query evaluation, we report the results for both. Table 3 compares our IR-Softmax (A) to other approaches. For Market-1501, the improvements achieved by IR-Softmax are significant: (1) Compared with softmax, the Rank-1 accuracy rises from 81.47% to 91.87%, and the mAP from 57.42% to 76.72% in the setting of single query; (2) In the setting of multi query, the Rank-1 accuracy rises from 86.40% to 94.33%, and the mAP from 65.97% to 82.22%. IR-Softmax (A) significantly outperforms not only the softmax baseline but also other state-of-the-art methods [13].

DukeMTMC-ReID. The DukeMTMC-reID dataset is collected via 8 cameras and used for cross-camera tracking (handover). Table 4 compares our IR-Softmax to other approaches. For DukeMTMC-reID, IR-Softmax(A) works much better than softmax: the Rank-1 accuracy: 76.84% vs 61.98%, and the mAP 57.47% vs 41.17%. Beyond that, the imbalance robust softmax also outperforms other state-of-the-art methods [45].

Table 3. Comparison with the state-of-the-art methods on the Market-1501 dataset. The rank-1 accuracy and mAP on single and multiple query are reported respectively.

Method	Single query		Multi. query	
	rank-1	mAP	rank-1	mAP
BoW + KISSME [24]	44.42	20.76	–	–
MR CNN [47]	45.58	26.11	56.59	32.26
DSN [48]	55.43	29.87	71.56	46.03
Gate Reid [49]	65.88	39.55	76.04	48.45
SOMAnet [50]	73.87	47.89	81.29	56.98
DeepTransfer [30]	83.70	65.50	**89.60**	73.80
Basel+LSRO [13]	**83.97**	**66.07**	88.42	**76.10**
SVDNet [45]	82.30	62.10	–	–
Softmax	81.47	57.42	86.40	65.97
Large-margin [17]	90.08	72.22	92.75	78.79
IR-Softmax (A)	**91.87**	**76.72**	**94.33**	**82.88**

Table 4. Comparison with state-of-the-art methods on DukeMTMC-reID. Rank-1 accuracy and mAP are reported.

Method	Rank-1 (%)	mAP (%)
BoW + KISSME [24]	25.13	12.17
LOMO + XQDA [51]	30.75	17.04
Basel + LSRO [13]	67.68	47.13
ACRN [52]	72.58	51.96
PAN [53]	71.59	51.51
SVDNet [45]	**76.70**	**56.80**
Softmax	61.98	41.17
Large-margin [17]	75.58	56.25
IR-Softmax (A)	**76.84**	**57.47**

5   Conclusion

In this paper, we investigated thoroughly the potential effects of data imbalance on the deep embedding learning and proposed a new framework, Imbalance Robust Softmax (IR-Softmax). IR-Softmax can simultaneously solve the open-set problem and reduce the influence of data imbalance. Extensive experiments on FR and re-ID are conducted, and the results show the effectiveness of IR-Softmax. In Future work, we plan to extend this framework to more softmax based methods and other applications like few-shot learning.

References

1. Krizhevsky, A., Sutskever, I., Hinton, G.E.: ImageNet classification with deep convolutional neural networks. In: NIPS (2012)
2. Sermanet, P., Eigen, D., Zhang, X., Mathieu, M., Fergus, R., LeCun, Y.: OverFeat: integrated recognition, localization and detection using convolutional networks. arXiv preprint arXiv:1312.6229 (2013)
3. Szegedy, C., et al.: Going deeper with convolutions. In: CVPR (2015)
4. He, K., Zhang, X., Ren, S., Sun, J.: Deep residual learning for image recognition. In: CVPR (2016)
5. He, K., Zhang, X., Ren, S., Sun, J.: Delving deep into rectifiers: surpassing human-level performance on ImageNet classification. In: ICCV (2015)
6. Simonyan, K., Zisserman, A.: Very deep convolutional networks for large-scale image recognition. In: ICLR (2015)
7. Taigman, Y., Yang, M., Ranzato, M., Wolf, L.: DeepFace: closing the gap to human-level performance in face verification. In: CVPR (2014)
8. Sun, Y., Wang, X., Tang, X.: Deep learning face representation from predicting 10,000 classes. In: CVPR (2014)
9. Sun, Y., Chen, Y., Wang, X., Tang, X.: Deep learning face representation by joint identification-verification. In: NIPS (2014)
10. Schroff, F., Kalenichenko, D., Philbin, J.: FaceNet: a unified embedding for face recognition and clustering. In: CVPR (2015)
11. Li, W., Zhao, R., Xiao, T., Wang, X.: DeepReID: deep filter pairing neural network for person re-identification. In: Proceedings of the IEEE Conference on Computer Vision and Pattern Recognition, pp. 152–159 (2014)
12. Zheng, L., Zhang, H., Sun, S., Chandraker, M., Tian, Q.: Person re-identification in the wild. CoRR abs/1604.02531 (2016)
13. Zheng, Z., Zheng, L., Yang, Y.: Unlabeled samples generated by gan improve the person re-identification baseline in vitro. In: ICCV (2017)
14. Yi, D., Lei, Z., Liao, S., Li, S.Z.: Learning face representation from scratch. CoRR (2014)
15. Sun, Y., Wang, X., Tang, X.: Deeply learned face representations are sparse, selective, and robust. In: CVPR (2015)
16. Wen, Y., Zhang, K., Li, Z., Qiao, Y.: A discriminative feature learning approach for deep face recognition. In: Leibe, B., Matas, J., Sebe, N., Welling, M. (eds.) ECCV 2016. LNCS, vol. 9911, pp. 499–515. Springer, Cham (2016). https://doi.org/10.1007/978-3-319-46478-7_31
17. Liu, W., Wen, Y., Yu, Z., Yang, M.: Large-margin softmax loss for convolutional neural networks. In: ICML (2016)
18. Liu, W., Wen, Y., Yu, Z., Li, M., Raj, B., Song, L.: SphereFace: deep hypersphere embedding for face recognition (2017)
19. Wang, F., Xiang, X., Cheng, J., Yuille, A.L.: Normface: L_2 hypersphere embedding for face verification. In: ACM MM (2017)
20. Ranjan, R., Castillo, C.D., Chellappa, R.: L2-constrained softmax Loss for discriminative face verification. ArXiv e-prints (2017)
21. LeCun, Y., Cortes, C., Burges, C.J.: The MNIST database of handwritten digits (1998)
22. Krizhevsky, A., Hinton, G.: Learning multiple layers of features from tiny images (2009)

23. Deng, J., Dong, W., Socher, R., Li, L.J., Li, K., Fei-Fei, L.: ImageNet: a large-scale hierarchical image database. In: CVPR (2009)
24. Zheng, L., Shen, L., Tian, L., Wang, S., Wang, J., Tian, Q.: Scalable person re-identification: a benchmark. In: CVPR (2015)
25. Zhang, X., Fang, Z., Wen, Y., Li, Z., Qiao, Y.: Range loss for deep face recognition with long-tail. CoRR abs/1611.08976 (2016)
26. Wang, F., Liu, W., Liu, H., Cheng, J.: Additive margin softmax for face verification. ArXiv e-prints (2018)
27. Huang, G.B., Ramesh, M., Berg, T., Learned-Miller, E.: Labeled faces in the wild: a database for studying face recognition in unconstrained environments. Technical report, Technical Report 07–49, University of Massachusetts, Amherst (2007)
28. Kemelmacher-Shlizerman, I., Seitz, S.M., Miller, D., Brossard, E.: The megaface benchmark: 1 million faces for recognition at scale. In: CVPR (2016)
29. Ristani, E., Solera, F., Zou, R., Cucchiara, R., Tomasi, C.: Performance measures and a data set for multi-target, multi-camera tracking. In: Hua, G., Jégou, H. (eds.) ECCV 2016. LNCS, vol. 9914, pp. 17–35. Springer, Cham (2016). https://doi.org/10.1007/978-3-319-48881-3_2
30. Geng, M., Wang, Y., Xiang, T., Tian, Y.: Deep transfer learning for person re-identification. CoRR abs/1611.05244 (2016)
31. Wang, H., et al.: CosFace: large margin cosine loss for deep face recognition. In: Proceedings of the IEEE Conference on Computer Vision and Pattern Recognition, pp. 5265–5274 (2018)
32. Deng, J., Guo, J., Xue, N., Zafeiriou, S.: ArcFace: additive angular margin loss for deep face recognition. In: Proceedings of the IEEE Conference on Computer Vision and Pattern Recognition, pp. 4690–4699 (2019)
33. Ouyang, W., Wang, X., Zhang, C., Yang, X.: Factors in finetuning deep model for object detection with long-tail distribution. In: CVPR (2016)
34. Shi, Y., Jain, A.K.: DocFace+: ID document to selfie matching. IEEE Trans. Biometr. Behav. Identity Sci. 1, 56–67 (2019)
35. Zhong, Y., et al.: Unequal-training for deep face recognition with long-tailed noisy data. In: Proceedings of the IEEE Conference on Computer Vision and Pattern Recognition, pp. 7812–7821 (2019)
36. Khan, S., Hayat, M., Zamir, S.W., Shen, J., Shao, L.: Striking the right balance with uncertainty. In: Proceedings of the IEEE Conference on Computer Vision and Pattern Recognition, pp. 103–112 (2019)
37. Yin, X., Yu, X., Sohn, K., Liu, X., Chandraker, M.: Feature transfer learning for face recognition with under-represented data. In: Proceedings of the IEEE Conference on Computer Vision and Pattern Recognition, pp. 5704–5713 (2019)
38. Sohn, K.: Improved deep metric learning with multi-class n-pair loss objective. In: NIPS (2016)
39. Zhang, K., Zhang, Z., Li, Z., Qiao, Y.: Joint face detection and alignment using multitask cascaded convolutional networks. SPL 23, 1499–1503 (2016)
40. Parkhi, O.M., Vedaldi, A., Zisserman, A.: Deep face recognition. In: BMVC (2015)
41. Wu, X., He, R., Sun, Z., Tan, T.: A light CNN for deep face representation with noisy labels. CoRR abs/1511.02683 (2015)
42. Liao, S., Lei, Z., Yi, D., Li, S.Z.: A benchmark study of large-scale unconstrained face recognition. In: ICB (2014)
43. Guo, Y., Zhang, L., Hu, Y., He, X., Gao, J.: MS-Celeb-1M: a dataset and benchmark for large-scale face recognition. In: Leibe, B., Matas, J., Sebe, N., Welling, M. (eds.) ECCV 2016. LNCS, vol. 9907, pp. 87–102. Springer, Cham (2016). https://doi.org/10.1007/978-3-319-46487-9_6

44. Ng, H.W., Winkler, S.: A data-driven approach to cleaning large face datasets. In: ICIP (2014)
45. Sun, Y., Zheng, L., Deng, W., Wang, S.: SVDNet for pedestrian retrieval. CoRR abs/1703.05693 (2017)
46. Felzenszwalb, P., McAllester, D., Ramanan, D.: A discriminatively trained, multiscale, deformable part model. In: CVPR (2008)
47. Ustinova, E., Ganin, Y., Lempitsky, V.S.: Multiregion bilinear convolutional neural networks for person re-identification. CoRR abs/1512.05300 (2015)
48. Zhang, L., Xiang, T., Gong, S.: Learning a discriminative null space for person re-identification. In: CVPR (2016)
49. Varior, R.R., Haloi, M., Wang, G.: Gated siamese convolutional neural network architecture for human re-identification. In: Leibe, B., Matas, J., Sebe, N., Welling, M. (eds.) ECCV 2016. LNCS, vol. 9912, pp. 791–808. Springer, Cham (2016). https://doi.org/10.1007/978-3-319-46484-8_48
50. Barbosa, I.B., Cristani, M., Caputo, B., Rognhaugen, A., Theoharis, T.: Looking beyond appearances: synthetic training data for deep CNNs in re-identification. CoRR abs/1701.03153 (2017)
51. Liao, S., Hu, Y., Zhu, X., Li, S.Z.: Person re-identification by local maximal occurrence representation and metric learning. In: CVPR (2015)
52. Schumann, A., Stiefelhagen, R.: Person re-identification by deep learning attribute-complementary information. In: CVPRW (2017)
53. Zheng, Z., Zheng, L., Yang, Y.: Pedestrian alignment network for large-scale person re-identification. CoRR abs/1707.00408 (2017)

Domain Adaptation Gaze Estimation by Embedding with Prediction Consistency

Zidong Guo[1], Zejian Yuan[1(✉)], Chong Zhang[2], Wanchao Chi[2], Yonggen Ling[2], and Shenghao Zhang[2]

[1] Institute of Artificial Intelligence and Robotics, Xi'an Jiaotong University, Xi'an, China
gzd3118311122@stu.xjtu.edu.cn, yuan.ze.jian@xjtu.edu.cn
[2] Tencent Robotics X, Beijing, China
aerentzhang@gmail.com, wanchaochi@tencent.com, ylingaa@connect.ust.hk, popshzhang@pku.edu.cn

Abstract. Gaze is the essential manifestation of human attention. In recent years, a series of work has achieved high accuracy in gaze estimation. However, the inter-personal difference limits the reduction of the subject-independent gaze estimation error. This paper proposes an unsupervised method for domain adaptation gaze estimation to eliminate the impact of inter-personal diversity. In domain adaption, we design an embedding representation with prediction consistency to ensure that linear relationships between gaze directions in different domains remain consistent on gaze space and embedding space. Specifically, we employ source gaze to form a locally linear representation in the gaze space for each target domain prediction. Then the same linear combinations are applied in the embedding space to generate hypothesis embedding for the target domain sample, remaining prediction consistency. The deviation between the target and source domain is reduced by approximating the predicted and hypothesis embedding for the target domain sample. Guided by the proposed strategy, we design Domain Adaptation Gaze Estimation Network(DAGEN), which learns embedding with prediction consistency and achieves state-of-the-art results on both the MPIIGaze and the EYEDIAP datasets.

1 Introduction

Gaze servers as an important visual cue of human attention. Accurate gaze estimation can provide critical support for many applications, such as human-computer interaction [1], virtual reality [2], and driver monitoring systems [3]. Although eye tracker can provide a precise gaze estimation [4], the high price and the demand for specific equipment limit its applications in the real world and more flexible environments. Unconstrained appearance-based gaze estimation methods can predict 2D gaze target position or 3D gaze angles based on patches cropped from RGB images. Thanks to the advancement of convolutional neural

© Springer Nature Switzerland AG 2021
H. Ishikawa et al. (Eds.): ACCV 2020, LNCS 12626, pp. 292–307, 2021.
https://doi.org/10.1007/978-3-030-69541-5_18

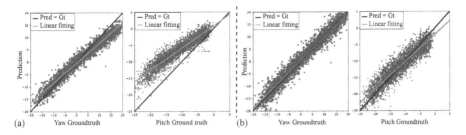

Fig. 1. Scatter plot of the groundtruth (X-axis) and the network gaze estimation (Y-axis) of the yaw and pitch angles in an evaluation set from the MPIIGaze dataset. The results are estimated by (a) Regression from eye region based on CNN and (b) DAGEN (Ours).

networks (CNN) and a large number of publicly available high-quality datasets, the error of gaze estimation has been dramatically decreased in recent years.

Appearance-based gaze estimation can decouple gaze direction from high-dimension images with various noises, but some challenges still restrict the further improvement of estimation precision. Obtaining gaze groundtruth requires specific equipment, a well-defined collection strategy, and highly concentrated attention of participants [5–10]. Under these strict conditions, current datasets violate the identical independent distribution(i.i.d) nature, that is, only tens of persons participating in the collection of thousands of gaze direction data per subject [11]. For gaze estimation that requires open set testing [12], the deviation between the distribution of the training set and the test set is reflected in the prediction as a person-specific bias. As shown in Fig. 1(a), the bias between the network regression and the groundtruth can often be observed, which is also mentioned in [13]. Some methods perform a person-specific gaze estimation through several new subject's labeled data to eliminate the bias [12,13]. However, in practice, even a bit of accurately labeled data is challenging to acquire.

In this work, we propose an unsupervised method for domain adaptation (DA) gaze estimation to eliminate the impact of inter-personal differences and fit new subject's data without groundtruth labels. In domain adaption, we design an embedding representation with prediction consistency to ensure that linear relationships between gaze directions remain consistent on gaze space and embedding space. We then build the Domain Adaptation Gaze Estimation Network (DAGEN) using EPC loss devised to measure this consistency. Moreover, a new training strategy is employed for domain adaptation.

The most crucial element of DAGEN is the embedding with prediction consistency (EPC), which is expected to eliminate the deviation between domains. Following the Locally Linear Embedding (LLE) representation method [14], the hypothesis label predicted on the target domain is linearly interpreted by its neighbor gaze directions from the source domain. Such linear combinations in gaze space would be migrated to embedding space to obtain hypothesis embedding, which ensures locally linear consistency between the embedding and prediction space. For the same gaze directions, we demand the embedding features encoding gaze should also be similar. However, due to the deviation between domains, the embedding also retains some domain-specific features unrelated to gaze direction, which causes a fixed bias in the test. So EPC loss, which weighs the distance between target hypothesis embedding and predicted embedding for each target domain sample, can be used to illustrate the deviation between domains. We optimize the EPC loss to eliminate the deviation between domains, thus achieving domain adaptation. We present our DAGEN estimation results in Fig. 1(b) to exhibit the consequence of domain adaptation.

We evaluate our proposed method on two commonly used gaze datasets and indicate that our DAGEN can effectively improve the accuracy of gaze estimation. On both datasets, our estimation results exceeding the current state-of-the-art method. Specifically, the DAGEN achieves a 9.66% improvement (4.14° to 3.74°) on MPIIGaze, and an 18.9% improvement (5.3° to 4.3°) on EYEDIAP. Note that the input only uses the eye region patch, and the source and target domain are the train and evaluation set, respectively.

The major contributions of our work are summarized as follows:

1) We propose a new representation for the target domain embedding with prediction consistency, as a linear combination of neighbors from the source domain.
2) We design an innovative embedding with prediction consistency (EPC) loss for unsupervised domain adaptation gaze estimation, enabling it to measure the shift between the source and target domain.
3) Our method achieves state-of-the-art performance on MPIIGaze and EYE-DIAP with only eye region as input.

2   Related Work

Gaze estimation methods are typically divided into appearance-based and model-based methods [15]. Model-based methods rely on the biological structure and reflection characteristics of the eyeball, and usually require high-resolution images with homogeneous illumination [16,17]. Appearance-based methods can robustly decouple gaze angles from high-dimensional images with various noises. Recently, due to the application of many large data sets [6,7,10,18] and the development of CNNs, the accuracy of appearance-based gaze estimation methods has been continuously improved. Zhang et al. first use LeNet [19] structure based on CNN and MPIIGaze dataset to process gaze estimation[7]. Subsequently, many works have improved the accuracy of gaze estimation through different methods. For example, multi-modal input was utilized in [18]; the key role of face was proved in [20]; a new convolution paradigm especially for gaze estimation was devised in [21]; timing information was used in [22]; the four models ensemble method was used to increase estimation accuracy in [8]; and a coarse-to-fine estimation strategy was designed in [23].

However, recent work has discovered the fixed deviation in gaze estimation caused by person-specific diversity, as shown in Fig. 1(a). The diversity is reduced by learning gaze differences and applying calibration sets in [12]. Random effects, which actively learns the differences among-subjects during training, was introduced in [11]. And a meta-learning method, performing person-specific calibration for each new subject and generating a person-specific network, is utilized in [13] to eliminate deviations.

Domain adaptation improves prediction performance in the target domain by aligning the distribution from the source domain [24, 25]. Some work attempts to minimize the discrepancy between domains to obtain domain-invariant features directly [26, 27]. Recently, some methods found that aligning targets in both domains could significantly increase prediction performance. For instance, [28] uses the correlation between classes to perform domain adaptation by predicting the target hypothesis label and source groundtruth. For the gaze estimation problem, discriminator is applied to distinguish the source and target domains, thereby aligning the domains [9]. The differences was taken advantage in pairs of gaze directions and performs domain adaptation through gaze redirection and cycle consistency [29].

However, these methods do not address the deviations caused by subject-difference. We propose an unsupervised domain adaptation method to eliminate the inter-personal differences by introducing embedding with prediction consistency.

3 Proposed Method

Domain Adaptation (DA) is applied to solve the inter-personal differences reflected in the domain shift in the data distribution. Our method takes an eye region image I as input, regressing $g = (y, p)$ through a feature extractor and a linear mapping, where y and p means yaw and pitch in gaze direction. Given a source domain $S = \{(I_1^s, g_1^s), \cdots, (I_{N_s}^s, g_{N_s}^s)\}$ with several participants and groundtruth, and a target domain $T = \{I_1^t, \cdots, I_{N_t}^t\}$ using test set data without groundtruth, the proposed network adopts Domain Adaptation (DA) as the training strategy to align the embedding between S and T to increase its estimation performance.

Figure 2 provides an architecture of our Domain Adaptation Gaze Estimation Network (DAGEN). The feature extractor $\phi(\cdot)$ contains an ImageNet [30] pre-trained ResNet-18 [31] followed a multilayer perceptron. The embedding feature $\phi(I)$ will be constrained to keep consistency with predicted gaze direction during DA training. Finally, as the restrained prediction consistency embedding could decouple gaze-related information from the high-dimension image, the gaze direction $\hat{g}$ is calculated through a simple linear mapping operation h.

3.1 Target Domain Gaze Representation

We propose a Locally Linear Representation (LLR) for Target Domain Gaze that employs source domain gaze to represent the target hypothesis label in gaze space $\mathbb{G}$ linearly. For each sample in the target domain, the network prediction is

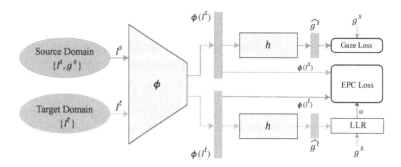

Fig. 2. The architecture of our proposed DAGEN. ResNet-18 and a fully connected layer are employed as feature exactor ϕ. A linear mapping h maps embedding feature $\phi(I)$ to gaze prediction $\hat{g}$. During DA training, LLR is utilized to generate linear weight w by source groundtruth and target prediction. Besides gaze loss for source domain, we apply EPC loss for unsupervised learning embedding features.

considered as a hypothesis label. We linearly combine k source domain samples in its neighborhood in the $\mathbb{G}$ to describe it.

We first define the neighborhood for each target domain prediction in $\mathbb{G}$ to ensure the correct representation. Only when both angles in target hypothesis label $\hat{g}_j^t$ and source gaze direction g_i^s are not much different (less than μ), would g_i^s be set as a neighborhood of $\hat{g}_j^t$. We describe the set of all neighbors of $\hat{g}_j^t$ as $\mathcal{N}_j$, defined as,

$$\mathcal{N}_j = \left\{ g_i^s \mid \max \left(|y_i^s - \hat{y}_j^t|, \; |p_i^s - \hat{p}_j^t| \right) < \mu \right\}. \tag{1}$$

Every target domain prediction $\hat{g}_j^t$ in a mini-batch having over k neighbors would be randomly selected k neighbors to regenerate $\mathcal{N}_j$, which is employed to reconstruct the $\hat{g}_j^t$. We define the weight w_{ij} to summarize the contribution of the ith data in $\mathcal{N}_j$ to the $\hat{g}_j^t$ reconstruction, and the purpose is to find a suitable solution of each w_{ij}.

For 2D gaze direction g, the slightly larger number of neighbors means that it is challenging to find a suitable solution to minimize the reconstruction loss $E(w)$ during training. We consider involving more neighbors in the reconstruction of $\hat{g}_j^t$ and introduce an L2 regularization term to ensure a unique solution. So an L2 regularization term is suitable to solve this problem. The reconstruction loss $E(w)$ is formally expressed as,

$$E(W_j) = \|\hat{g}_j^t - \sum_{i=1}^{k} w_{ji} g_i^s\|_2^2 + \lambda \sum_{i=1}^{k} w_{ji}^2, \quad s.t. \; g_i^s \in \mathcal{N}_j \; and \; \sum_{i=1}^{k} w_{ji} = 1, \tag{2}$$

where $W_j = [w_{j1}, \cdots, w_{jk}]$. The Eq. (2) can be written in matrix form as,

$$E(W_j) = W_j^T (\hat{G}_j^t - G_i^s)^T (\hat{G}_j^t - G_i^s) W_j + \lambda W_j^T W_j,$$
$$= W_j^T (S_j + \lambda I) W_j, \qquad (3)$$

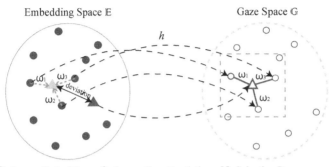

Embedding Space $\mathbb{E}$ Gaze Space $\mathbb{G}$

● Source Embedding   ○ Source Gaze Prediction   ⊡ Selection Range
▲ Target Embedding   △ Target Gaze Prediction   ▲ Target Hypothesis Embedding

Fig. 3. Embedding with prediction consistency. The linear combination relationship in $\mathbb{G}$ is inherited to $\mathbb{E}$ to generate a hypothesis embedding $\hat{\phi}(I^t)$ for each target sample. The distance between $\hat{\phi}(I^t)$ and the target predicted embedding $\phi(I^t)$ measures the deviation between the source and target domain.

where $\hat{G}_j^t = [\hat{g}_j^t, \cdots, \hat{g}_j^t]_{1 \times k}$, $G_i^s = [g_1^s, \cdots, g_k^s]$, and S_j is regarded as a local covariance matrix, defined as,

$$S_j = (\hat{G}_j^t - G_i^s)^T (\hat{G}_j^t - G_i^s). \qquad (4)$$

The solution W_j^* that minimizes $E(W_j)$ obtained by the Lagrange multiplier method is,

$$W_j^* = \frac{(S_j + \lambda I)^{-1} 1_k}{1_k^T (S_j + \lambda I)^{-1} 1_k}. \qquad (5)$$

With the optimized weight $W_j^* = [w_{j1}^*, \cdots, w_{jk}^*]$, LLR is formally described as,

$$\hat{g}_j^t = \sum_{i=1}^{k} w_{ji}^* g_i^s, \quad g_i^s \in \mathcal{N}_j. \qquad (6)$$

3.2 Embedding with Prediction Consistency

Here we propose Embedding with Prediction Consistency (EPC) for domain adaptation. EPC transfers the same linear combination relationship in gaze space

$\mathbb{G}$ to embedding space $\mathbb{E}$ to generate target hypothesis embeddings. For target domain sample I_j^t, the hypothesis embedding is declared as,

$$\hat{\phi}(I_j^t) = \sum_{i=1}^{k} w_{ji}^* \phi(I_i^s), \quad g_i^s \in \mathcal{N}_j. \tag{7}$$

As shown in Fig. 3, the LLR weight in gaze space $\mathbb{G}$ are inherited to the embedding space $\mathbb{E}$. For each target predicted embedding in $\mathbb{E}$, we generate the target hypothesis embedding $\hat{\phi}(I^t)$ by Eq. (7). The linear relationship between target hypothesis embedding and source predicted embedding is the same as that between target and source gaze directions, which is the embedding with prediction consistency.

3.3 Loss Function

With the purpose of domain adaptation between the source and target domain, we propose DA loss consisting of two items, as shown in Eq. (8). Specifically, L_{EPC} measures the deviation between the source and target domain. Meanwhile, L_{gaze} supervises the predicted gaze directions of the source domain to guarantee that the network is always optimized towards reducing gaze estimation error.

$$L_{DA} = \lambda_{EPC} L_{EPC} + \lambda_{gaze} L_{gaze}, \tag{8}$$

where we empirically set $\lambda_{EPC} = 1$ and $\lambda_{gaze} = 1$.

We introduce an embedding with prediction consistency (EPC) loss for domain adaptation gaze estimation, which ensures same gaze directions should have the same embedding features unrelated to any interferences like appearance. Typically this constraint requires pairs of images in totally same gaze directions from different subjects. However, it is nearly unreachable to meet this condition for continuous gaze direction. As mentioned in Sect. 3.1, for each target gaze hypothesis label, we employ LLR of adjacent source gaze to indicate it. The combination relationships in $\mathbb{G}$ are transferred to $\mathbb{E}$ to generate target hypothesis embedding remaining prediction consistency.

Given a batch of B_s source image samples and B_t target image samples during training, we formally compute the L_{EPC} using,

$$L_{EPC} = \frac{1}{B_t} \sum_{j=1}^{B_t} d\left(\phi\left(I_j^t\right), \sum_{i=1}^{k} w_{ji}^* \phi(I_i^s)\right), \quad h(\phi(I_i^s)) \in \mathcal{N}_j, \tag{9}$$

where L1 distance is employed as the function d. L_{EPC} measures the distance between the hypothesis and predicted embedding. Furthermore, since target hypothesis embedding is a linear combination of source predicted embedding, L_{EPC} also evaluates the deviation between the source and target domains. During training, as target hypothesis embedding and predicted embedding get closer and closer, the offset between domains is gradually eliminated.

Algorithm 1. Training Procedure

Input:
   Source Domain: $S = \{(I_1^s, g_1^s), \cdots, (I_{N_s}^s, g_{N_s}^s)\}$
   Target Domain: $T = \{I_1^t, \cdots, I_{N_t}^t\}$
Output:
   Model parameter θ^*

1: **# First Step: Pre-training in the Source Domain**
2: **for** m in $[1, N_s]$ **do**
3:    **for** (I_i^s, g_i^s) in S **do**
4:       Forward I_i^s and obtain prediction $\hat{g_i^s}$.
5:       Back-propagation with Eq.(10) and update network parameters θ.
6:    **end for**
7: **end for**
8: **# Second Step: Joint Optimization**
9: **for** m in $[1, M_t]$ **do**
10:    Sample a mini-batch B_s and B_t from S and T.
11:    Obtain prediction $\hat{g}^s$ and $\hat{g}^t$ with forwarding I^s and I^s.
12:    **for** b in $[1, B_t]$ **do**
13:       Select qualified sample set $\mathcal{N}_b$ from B_s for $\hat{g_t^b}$. (Eq. (1))
14:       **if** $\|\mathcal{N}_b\| < $ k **then**
15:          Continue
16:       **else**
17:          Randomly choosing k samples from $\mathcal{N}_b$.
18:          Obtain LLR representation W^* of $\hat{g}_b$ using k samples (Eq. (5))
19:          Calculate hypothesis embedding $\hat{\phi}(I_b^t)$ by Eq. (7)
20:          Compute L_{EPC} using Eq. (9)
21:       **end if**
22:       Compute L_{gaze} for B_s using Eq. (10)
23:       Back-propagation with Eq. (8) and update network parameters θ.
24:    **end for**
25: **end for**

Besides preserving L_{EPC} for domain adaptation, the source domain with groundtruth should also take part in parameter updating to guide training optimizing. The L_{gaze} is calculated based on cosine similarity as,

$$L_{gaze}\left(\hat{g}^s,\ g^s\right) = \arccos \frac{\hat{g}^s \times g^s}{\|\hat{g}^s\| \cdot \|g^s\|}. \tag{10}$$

3.4 Training

Since the network prediction decides the neighborhood and locally linear gaze representation in L_{EPC}, a well-trained model is necessary to generate credible target hypothesis labels. We pre-train the network using only source domain with groundtruth and the L_{gaze} for N_s epochs at first.

In the joint training procedure, we need to optimize the L_{gaze} and L_{EPC} simultaneously for M_t iterations. We employ an alternative optimization strategy [28] to perform each iteration. Specifically, we first update target hypothesis labels $\hat{g}^t$ with network parameters fixed in each loop and meanwhile estimate the prediction of the source domain. Then given the target label $\hat{g}^t$, we construct $\mathcal{N}_j$ and estimate L_{EPC}. It is worth mentioning that we use the source domain groundtruth for LLR to obtain higher estimation accuracy. Furthermore, network parameters are updated by back-propagation to minimize L_{EPC} and L_{gaze} finally.

Algorithm 1 summarizes the entire optimization precessing of our DAGEN. First step performs the essential pre-training, and Second step shows the joint optimization procedure. We asynchronously update the target label and optimize the network to ensure the effectiveness and efficiency during training. We use SGD with momentum = 0.9 as the optimizer and a base learning rate of 0.001, l2 weight regularization of 5×10^{-4}. B_s and B_t are both set to 64 during training.

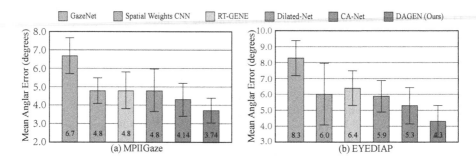

Fig. 4. Performance of gaze estimation on (a)MPIIGaze and (b)EYEDIAP using a leave-one-subject-out strategy. Bars represent the MAE, and the specific value in degrees is on the bottom of each bar; error bars indicate standard deviations.

4   Experiments

4.1   Datasets

We implement the proposed Domain Adaptation Gaze Estimation Network on two current gaze datasets: MPIIGaze [7] and EYEDIAP [6].

MPIIGaze is a very challenging dataset for appearance-based in-the-wild gaze direction estimation, because it has high within-subject variations in facial appearance and environments, for instance, make-up, hair change, illumination intensity and direction. We only use the standard evaluation subset MPI-IFaceGaze provided by MPIIGaze, which contains 37667 images captured from 15 subjects and has facial keypoints label for image pre-processing.

Table 1. Comparison of appearance-based gaze estimation methods.

Methods	Input	Data	GT	MPIIGaze	EYEDIAP
GazeNet [7]	Left eye + head pose	×	×	6.7°	8.3°
SWCNN [20]	Face	×	×	4.8°	6.0°
RT-GENE [8]	Two eyes + face	×	×	4.8°	6.4°
Dilated-Net [21]	Two eyes + face	×	×	4.8°	5.9°
MeNet [11]	Face	×	×	4.9°	—
CA-Net [23]	Two eyes + face	×	×	4.14°	5.3°
FAZE (3-shot) [13]	Eye area	✓	✓	4.1°	—
FAZE (256-shot) [13]	Eye area	✓	✓	3.75°	—
DAGEN (ours)	Eye area	✓	×	**3.74°**	**4.30°**

EYEDIAP contains 94 video sequences of 16 subjects, who were looking at screen targets or physical targets in the collection. Only the videos collected with screen target sessions are used in our training and evaluation set. Note that, since two participants lack the videos in the screen target session, we sample one image every fifteen frames from the other 14 subjects.

4.2 Data Pre-processing

We manipulate the pre-processing procedure similar to [10,20,32] to normalize two datasets, and utilize the Surrey Face Model as the reference 3D face model. In the appearance-based gaze estimation task, the head pose has a significant influence on the accuracy since its six freedoms bring calculational complexity and time-consuming. Consequently, we select four eye corners and two mouth corners described in [10] for PnP-based head pose estimation. Then transfer and rotate the virtual camera according to the head pose to eliminate the impact of position and roll angle.

In our work, considering applying a single image as input cover both eyes, we select the mean of four 3D eye corner landmarks as the gaze origin point to produce groundtruth for source domain. We normalize the camera's intrinsic parameters with a focal length of 960 mm, and a distance of 410 mm from the face to generate image patches of size 256×64 as input for training. In each test period, in order to better verify the effect of domain adaptation, we use the newcomer's entire data without groundtruth as the target domain.

4.3 Comparison with Appearance-Based Methods

We first compare the performance of the proposed method with the state-of-art appearance-based gaze estimation methods. The experiment is carried out in both MPIIGaze and EYEDIAP. For the evaluation protocol, we use leave-one-subject-out strategy on both MPIIGaze and EYEDIAP.

We choose several CNN-based methods proposed from 2015 to 2020 as comparisons, including GazeNet [7], Spatial weights CNN (SWCNN) [20], RT-GENE [8], Dilated-Net [21], MeNet [11], Faze [13] and CA-Net [23].

Although four models ensemble can increase the accuracy of RT-GENE, we do not show the result of that for fairness. Since initializing the model pre-trained on ImageNet can effectively improve accuracy, we apply this strategy for GazeNet, Spatial weights CNN and Dilated-Net refer to [21]. We only present the results in the author's paper for cases where source codes are not provided, or the evaluation protocol is different from us.

Figure 4(a) shows the results of MPIIGaze. The Mean Angular Error (MAE) of most work in recent years has become about 4.8° without any person cali-bration. These methods all have characteristics, such as the use of multi-modal input, the introduction of attention mechanism, the implementation of new train-ing methods, or a new convolution strategy suitable for gaze estimation. CA-Net more cleverly used the coarse-to-fine information from faces to eyes to achieve a breakthrough of about 0.66°. Our method achieves 9.66% to 3.74° comparing to state-of-the-art method CA-Net with only eye area as input.

Figure 4(b) shows the results in EYEDIAP. Due to the lower image resolu-tion, the performance of EYEDIAP is generally worse than that of MPIIGaze. Many innovations in recent years still bring a significant breakthrough in per-formance, and the best accuracy obtained in [23] has reached 5.3°. We get an 18.9% increase with the state-of-the-art method to 4.3°.

Table 1 summarizes some differences and results of recent methods for ref-erence, including that not illustrated in Fig. 4. The header *Data* and *GT* show whether the methods need data or groundtruth for a new subject before evalu-ation. It is noteworthy that some person-specific methods like few-shot (FAZE) have achieved a great improvement for gaze estimation. We show the result of FAZE[13] based on 3-shot and 256-shot within-MPIIGaze leave-one-person-out evaluation. With test images without labels, our method can obtain results close to 256-shot Faze, proving the effectiveness of domain adaptation.

4.4   Ablation Study

We further evaluate our method under different settings to better demonstrate the effectiveness of our various design choices in the DAGEN. For all ablation experiments, the source domain and test set's selection follows the leave-one-subject-out strategy on the MPIIGaze dataset.

Contribution of Domain Adaptation. We first perform an ablation study to demonstrate the effect of domain adaptation. Specifically, we evaluate the conse-quence of adding domain adaptation, the impact of different target domain data, and the influence of domain adaptation objects. Table 2 shows the experimental results and the only change is *DA* is the choice of target domain.

Without DA shows the baseline model supervised by the L_{gaze} during train-ing, having the MAE of 4.84°. In order to better assess the impact of target domain data on accuracy, we compare the estimation accuracy using GazeCap-ture [18] as the target domain. For *GC*, we randomly sample 20 images for each participant in GazeCapture. With a total of 1366 subjects and 27320 images, we

Table 2. Comparison on different DA configurations.

Without DA	DA			
	GCsubset	GC	Pred	Eval
4.84°	4.66°	4.17°	3.99°	**3.74°**

get the MAE of 4.17°. Moreover, we randomly select 100 participants to discuss the influence of diversity in the target domain, named *GCsubset*. *Eval* uses the evaluation set as the target domain. The results show that utilizing diverse and targeted samples as the target domain can effectively improve the estimation performance, which may have reference significance for practical application.

For our proposed method described in Sect. 3, we use the target hypothesis label and the source groundtruth as the domain adaptation targets. *Pred* takes the source predicted value instead of groundtruth as the domain adaptive target, with the MAE of 3.99°. Since in this case, errors in the source domain data would also affect the domain adaptation process. In other words, using groundtruth as the DA target produces more substantial constraints for the updating direction of the parameters.

Effect of Feature Representation. LLR utilizes k source groundtruth to represent a target hypothesis label. We evaluate the different choices of k, shown in Fig. 5(a). Generally, a higher k means more stable and robust LLR. However, because we select the appropriate sample from a mini-batch, a higher k brings a smaller probability of reaching the selection condition. In our experimental protocol, the calculating speed of EPC loss is from 32.17–32.53 ms/iter in one Nvidia 1080Ti for different k, and the training speed is 76.5 ms/iter in training.

Our embedding $\phi(I)$ has the dimension of F_g. Considering $\phi(I)$ perform prediction consistency, different F_g would lead to changes in characterization ability and robustness. We evaluate the accuracy of DAGEN for different dimensions $F_g = \{8, 16, 32, 64\}$ to select the most suitable one. Figure 5(b) shows the result of dimension selection. In our experiments, our method is not sensitive to F_g, indicating that our method is very robust for F_g.

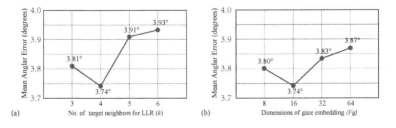

Fig. 5. Impact of different feature representation choice

304   Z. Guo et al.

Table **3.** Impact of pre-trained methods.

ImageNet	Source	MAE
✗	✗	4.63°
✓	✗	4.2°
✗	✓	4.51°
✓	✓	**3.74°**

Table **4.** Impact of selection interval μ.

μ	MAE
0.05	4.04°
0.15	**3.74°**
0.3	3.84°
All	3.86°

Empirically we find $k = 4$ and $F_g = 16$ to be optimal hence select it.

Effect of Pre-trained Model. We use ResNet-18 pre-trained on ImageNet as the backbone. And before the domain adaptation training, the network is first trained for five epochs in the source domain. We evaluated the estimation accuracy of whether the two pre-trainings participate, shown in Table 3, to show the contribution of the two pre-training strategies.

For the model pre-trained on ImageNet, it can effectively avoid the parameters falling into the local optimum, thereby improving the gaze estimation accuracy. In the case of pre-training in the source domain, obtaining a more accurate hypothesis label can significantly improve prediction accuracy. However, while the parameters fall into the local optimum, the quality of the hypothesis label is not improved, so the error is not substantially reduced.

Impact of Selection Range. μ The target hypothesis label needs to be represented by the appropriate source groundtruth. We have defined this selection strategy in Eq. (1), where parameter μ indicates the select interval. We perform the impact of different choices of μ on estimation accuracy, shown in Table 4.

We can see that the estimation accuracy has not changed much when $\mu \geq 0.15$. The results reveal that although we established a locally linear relationship in the gaze space $\mathbb{G}$ and the embedding space $\mathbb{E}$, due to the linear mapping h, the network tends to exhibit a global linear relationship in $\mathbb{G}$ and $\mathbb{E}$. For the case where μ is small, few target samples can participate in DA training. Therefore, the network is straightforward to fall into overfitting, which significantly increases estimation error and even is challenging to converge.

4.5 Visual Results

We display some results in Fig. 6 to show the effectiveness of our method. Fig. 6(a–b) performs the scatter plot and linear fit of the pitch angles, which are predicted by the baseline model and our proposed DAGEN method on the evaluation set. Obviously, the fixed bias between the prediction and the groundtruth is significantly reduced in our method. Furthermore, We randomly pick several samples close to the fitted line (yellow points in Fig. 6(a–b) in the baseline

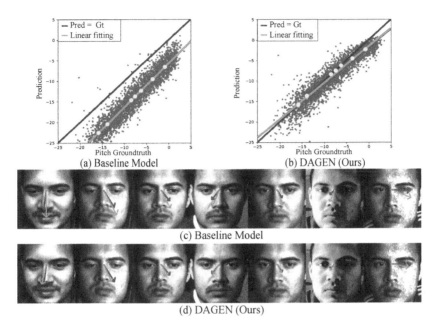

Fig. 6. Visible results of the evaluation set. (a) and (b) show the scatter (red) and linear fit line of pitch angles predicted with the baseline and our DAGEN. Yellow points in (a-b) are samples randomly selected from the linear fit line in (a). The groundtruth (blue) and prediction(green) of the chosen samples are displayed orderly in (c) and (d). (Color figure online)

results and visualize the result of both baseline and DAGEN models in Fig. 6(c–d). We can see that our DAGEN can produce accurate gaze directions with tiny deviations for the evaluated subject in different appearances and illumination.

5   Conclusion

In this paper, we propose an unsupervised method for domain adaptation gaze estimation by embedding with prediction consistency. We utilize source groundtruth to perform a locally linear representation for target gaze estimation. The linear relationships are then inherited from gaze space to embedding space to perform prediction consistency. Moreover, we minimize the distance between the target hypothesis embedding and predicted embedding, which measures the deviation between the source and target domain. We experimentally showed that our approach dramatically reduces the impact of inter-personal differences and achieves state-of-the-art performance in MPIIGaze and EYEDIAP.

Acknowledgement. This work was supported by the National Key R&D Program of China (2016YFB 1001001), the National Natural Science Foundation of China (61976 170, 91648121, 61573280), and Tencent Robotics X Lab Rhino-Bird Joint Research

Program (201902, 201903). (Portions of) the research in this paper used the EYEDIAP dataset made available by the Idiap Research Institute, Martigny, Switzerland.

References

1. Fridman, L., Reimer, B., Mehler, B., Freeman, W.T.: Cognitive load estimation in the wild. In: CHI, p. 652 (2018)
2. Konrad, R., Angelopoulos, A., Wetzstein, G.: Gaze-contingent ocular parallax rendering for virtual reality. ACM Trans. Graph. **39**, 10:1–10:12 (2020)
3. Vicente, F., Huang, Z., Xiong, X., la Torre, F.D., Zhang, W., Levi, D.: Driver gaze tracking and eyes off the road detection system. IEEE Trans. Intell. Transp. Syst. **16**, 2014–2027 (2015)
4. Kassner, M., Patera, W., Bulling, A.: Pupil: an open source platform for pervasive eye tracking and mobile gaze-based interaction. In: UbiComp Adjunct, pp. 1151–1160 (2014)
5. Sugano, Y., Matsushita, Y., Sato, Y.: Learning-by-synthesis for appearance-based 3D gaze estimation. In: CVPR, pp. 1821–1828 (2014)
6. Mora, K.A.F., Monay, F., Odobez, J.: EYEDIAP: a database for the development and evaluation of gaze estimation algorithms from RGB and RGB-D cameras. In: ETRA, pp. 255–258 (2014)
7. Zhang, X., Sugano, Y., Fritz, M., Bulling, A.: Appearance-based gaze estimation in the wild. In: CVPR, pp. 4511–4520 (2015)
8. Fischer, T., Chang, H.J., Demiris, Y.: RT-GENE: real-time eye gaze estimation in natural environments. In: Ferrari, V., Hebert, M., Sminchisescu, C., Weiss, Y. (eds.) ECCV 2018. LNCS, vol. 11214, pp. 339–357. Springer, Cham (2018). https://doi.org/10.1007/978-3-030-01249-6_21
9. Kellnhofer, P., Recasens, A., Stent, S., Matusik, W., Torralba, A.: Gaze360: physically unconstrained gaze estimation in the wild. In: ICCV, pp. 6911–6920 (2019)
10. Zhang, X., Sugano, Y., Fritz, M., Bulling, A.: MPIIGaze: real-world dataset and deep appearance-based gaze estimation. IEEE Trans. Pattern Anal. Mach. Intell. **41**, 162–175 (2019)
11. Xiong, Y., Kim, H.J., Singh, V.: Mixed effects neural networks (MeNets) with applications to gaze estimation. In: CVPR, 7743–7752 (2019)
12. Liu, G., Yu, Y., Mora, K.A.F., Odobez, J.: A differential approach for gaze estimation with calibration. In: BMVC, p. 235 (2018)
13. Park, S., Mello, S.D., Molchanov, P., Iqbal, U., Hilliges, O., Kautz, J.: Few-shot adaptive gaze estimation. In: ICCV, pp. 9367–9376 (2019)
14. Roweis, T.S., Saul, K.L.: Nonlinear dimensionality reduction by locally linear embedding. Science **290**, 2323–2326 (2000)
15. Hansen, D.W., Ji, Q.: In the eye of the beholder: a survey of models for eyes and gaze. IEEE Trans. Pattern Anal. Mach. Intell. **32**, 478–500 (2010)
16. Morimoto, C.H., Amir, A., Flickner, M.: Detecting eye position and gaze from a single camera and 2 light sources. In: ICPR, no. 4, pp. 314–317 (2002)
17. Yoo, D.H., Chung, M.J.: A novel non-intrusive eye gaze estimation using cross-ratio under large head motion. Comput. Vis. Image Underst. **98**, 25–51 (2005)
18. Krafka, K., et al.: Eye tracking for everyone. In: CVPR, pp. 2176–2184 (2016)
19. Lecun, Y., Bottou, L., Bengio, Y., Haffner, P.: Gradient-based learning applied to document recognition. Proc. IEEE **86**, 2278–2324 (1998)
20. Zhang, X., Sugano, Y., Fritz, M., Bulling, A.: It's written all over your face: full-face appearance-based gaze estimation. In: CVPR Workshops, pp. 2299–2308 (2017)

21. Chen, Z., Shi, B.E.: Appearance-based gaze estimation using dilated-convolutions. In: Jawahar, C.V., Li, H., Mori, G., Schindler, K. (eds.) ACCV 2018. LNCS, vol. 11366, pp. 309–324. Springer, Cham (2019). https://doi.org/10.1007/978-3-030-20876-9_20
22. Palmero, C., Selva, J., Bagheri, M.A., Escalera, S.: Recurrent CNN for 3D gaze estimation using appearance and shape cues. In: BMVC, p. 251 (2018)
23. Cheng, Y., Huang, S., Wang, F., Qian, C., Lu, F.: A coarse-to-fine adaptive network for appearance-based gaze estimation. In: AAAI, pp. 10623–10630 (2020)
24. Tzeng, E., Hoffman, J., Saenko, K., Darrell, T.: Adversarial discriminative domain adaptation. In: CVPR, pp. 2962–2971 (2017)
25. Wang, J., Feng, W., Chen, Y., Yu, H., Huang, M., Yu, P.S.: Visual domain adaptation with manifold embedded distribution alignment. In: ACM Multimedia, pp. 402–410 (2018)
26. Long, M., Cao, Y., Wang, J., Jordan, M.I.: Learning transferable features with deep adaptation networks. ICML, vol. 37, pp. 97–105 (2015)
27. Long, M., Zhu, H., Wang, J., Jordan, M.I.: Deep transfer learning with joint adaptation networks. In: ICML, vol. 70, pp. 2208–2217 (2017)
28. Kang, G., Jiang, L., Yang, Y., Hauptmann, A.G.: Contrastive adaptation network for unsupervised domain adaptation. In: CVPR, pp. 4893–4902 (2019)
29. Yu, Y., Liu, G., Odobez, J.: Improving few-shot user-specific gaze adaptation via gaze redirection synthesis. In: CVPR, pp. 11937–11946 (2019)
30. Krizhevsky, A., Sutskever, I., Hinton, G.E.: ImageNet classification with deep convolutional neural networks. In: NIPS, pp. 1106–1114 (2012)
31. He, K., Zhang, X., Ren, S., Sun, J.: Deep residual learning for image recognition. In: CVPR, pp. 770–778 (2016)
32. Zhang, X., Sugano, Y., Bulling, A.: Revisiting data normalization for appearance-based gaze estimation. ETRA, pp. 12:1–12:9 (2018)

Speech2Video Synthesis with 3D Skeleton Regularization and Expressive Body Poses

Miao Liao, Sibo Zhang$^{(\boxtimes)}$, Peng Wang, Hao Zhu, Xinxin Zuo, and Ruigang Yang

Baidu Research, Baidu Inc., Beijing, China
miao.liao@gmail.com, sibozhang1@gmail.com, jerryking234@gmail.com, zhuhaoese@nju.edu.cn, {xinxin.zuo,ryang2}@uky.edu

Abstract. In this paper, we propose a novel approach to convert given speech audio to a photo-realistic speaking video of a specific person, where the output video has synchronized, realistic, and expressive rich body dynamics. We achieve this by first generating 3D skeleton movements from the audio sequence using a recurrent neural network (RNN), and then synthesizing the output video via a conditional generative adversarial network (GAN). To make the skeleton movement realistic and expressive, we embed the knowledge of an articulated 3D human skeleton and a learned dictionary of personal speech iconic gestures into the generation process in both learning and testing pipelines. The former prevents the generation of unreasonable body distortion, while the later helps our model quickly learn meaningful body movement through a few recorded videos. To produce photo-realistic and high-resolution video with motion details, we propose to insert part attention mechanisms in the conditional GAN, where each detailed part, e.g. head and hand, is automatically zoomed in to have their own discriminators. To validate our approach, we collect a dataset with 20 high-quality videos from 1 male and 1 female model reading various documents under different topics. Compared with previous SoTA pipelines handling similar tasks, our approach achieves better results by a user study.

Keywords: Face · Gesture · Body pose · Image and video synthesis · Vision and language · GAN

1 Introduction

Speech2Video is a task of synthesizing a video of human full body movements, including head, mouth, arms etc., from a speech audio input. The produced video

---

Mi. Liao and S. Zhang—Equal contribution.

Electronic supplementary material The online version of this chapter (https://doi.org/10.1007/978-3-030-69541-5_19) contains supplementary material, which is available to authorized users.

© Springer Nature Switzerland AG 2021
H. Ishikawa et al. (Eds.): ACCV 2020, LNCS 12626, pp. 308–323, 2021.
https://doi.org/10.1007/978-3-030-69541-5_19

should be visually natural and consistent with the given speech. Traditional way of *Speech2Video* involves performance capture with dedicated devices and professional operators, and most of the speech and rendering tasks are performed by a team of animators, which is often costly for custom usage. Recently, with the successful application of deep neural networks, data-driven approaches have been proposed for low cost speech video synthesis. For instances, SythesisObama [1] or MouthEditting [2] focus on synthesizing a talking mouth by driving mouth motion with speech using an RNN. Taylor [3] propose to drive a high fidelity graphics model using audio, where not only animates mouth but also other parts on the face are animated to obtain richer speech expressions.

However, mouth movement synthesis is mostly deterministic, given a pronunciation, the movement or shape of the mouth is similar across different persons and context. In our task of *Speech2Video*, a full body gesture movement under the same situation is more generative and has more variations, the gestures are highly dependent on current context and individual person who is doing the speech. Personalized speaking gestures appear at certain moment when delivering important messages. Therefore, useful information is only sparsely present in a video, yielding difficulties for a simple end-to-end learning algorithm [1,3] to capture this diversity from the limited recorded videos.

To the best of our knowledge, LumiereNet [4] is the most related work performing a similar task with ours, which builds an end-to-end network for full upper body synthesis. However, in their experiments, the body motion is less expressive where the major dynamics are still at the talking head. In practice, following a similar method, we build a pipeline for body synthesis, and train it with our collected online speech videos, where three major issue exists. First, as discussed, the generated body movements only have repetitive patterns, while the ground truth video contains emphasis gestures at certain moments. Second, the generated body appearance at detailed parts such as hand and elbow could be unnaturally distorted, which is geometrically infeasible. Last, the generated body and hand appearance are blurry with motions. Therefore, in this work, we propose a novel trainable *Speech2Video* pipeline, which handles all these issues simultaneously. For handling diversity issues, we build a pose dictionary with text for each person from their presentation videos. To guarantee the generated pose are physical plausible, we enforce the 3D skeleton as the intermediate representations, the generated joints should follow the regularity of human body. Finally, to ensure high quality synthesized appearance, we propose an part-aware discriminator to provide additional attention of generated detailed parts like arms and hands.

Finally, in order to better evaluate our system, we create a dataset with recorded speech videos of several target while they are reading some carefully selected articles, using camera with high resolution and frame rate (FPS). In our experiments, we show our approach generates perceptually better human dynamics than other existing pipelines with more gesture variations.

The main contributions of this paper are summarized as follows:

- We proposed a novel 2-stage pipeline of generating an audio-driven virtual speaker with full-body motions including the face, hand, mouth and body. Our 3D driven approach overcomes issues of direct audio-to-video approach where human appearance details are missing. And it also makes it possible to insert key poses in the human motion sequence. It is shown in the result section why we have to decompose this task into a 2-stage generation, instead of direct audio-to-video generation.
- A dictionary of personal key poses is built that adds more dimensions to the generated human poses. Besides, we presented an approach to insert key poses into the existing sequence.
- 3D skeleton constraints are embedded to generate body dynamics, which guarantees the pose is physically plausible.
- We proposed a modified GAN to emphasize on face and hands to recover more details in the final output video.

2   Related Work

Human Body Pose Estimation and Fitting [5] proposed 3d shape and pose estimation specific for hands. [6,7] predicts 3d human motion from video or a single image, but they are limited to fit human model with limb only, not hands or face. While openpose [8] has been so successful at fitting the detailed human model to 2D image with all our demanded parts including face and fingers, their output is 2D landmarks in the image space. Based on openpose, SMPL-X [9] fits a 3D skeleton to those output 2D landmarks through an optimization. It also parameterizes human motion as joint angles, making it much easier to constrain joints under reasonable human articulation.

Audio to Motion [10] drives high fidelity 3D facial model using audio via end-to-end learning, where both poses and emotions are learned. [11] focuses on synthesizing hand motion from music input, rather than speech. Its goal is to animate graphics models of hands and arms with piano or violin music. [12] generates skeleton-based action using Convolutional Sequence Generation Network (CSGN). [13] instead, predict human motion using recurrent neural networks. [14] uses auto-conditioned recurrent networks for extended complex human motion synthesis. They can model more complex motions, including dances or martial arts.

Video Generation from Skeleton pix2pix [15,16] is a milestone in the development of GAN. It outputs an detailed real-life image from an input semantic label image. In our pipeline, the semantic label maps are image frames of the human skeleton. Nevertheless, direct applying pix2pix to an input video without temporal constraints will result in incoherent output videos. Therefore, vid2vid [17] is proposed to enforce temporal coherence between neighboring frames. [18] proposes to render realistic video from skeleton models without

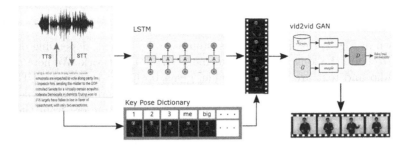

Fig. 1. Pipeline of our system.

building a 3D model, where the second stage of video generation is emphasized. However, it doesn't take care of facial expression and mouth movement, and it doesn't address the problem of how to generate realistic movement of the skeleton body model. [19] proposes a similar pipeline, which generates skeleton pose first and then generate the final video. However, rather than audio, its input is random noise and its skeleton model is very simple only having body limbs. That means its final output video lacks details on the face and fingers.

Character Synthesis [1,2,20] focus on synthesizing a talking head by driving 2D mouth motion with speech. When the mouth sequence is generated via texture mapping, it is pasted onto an existing video after lighting and texture fusion. [21] instead, drives a 3D face model by audio, and render the final video using a technique called neural renderer [22]. [4] attempts to produce videos of an upper-body of a virtual lecturer, but the only moving part is still the mouth. Face2Face [23] transfers expressions from a person to a target subject using a monocular RGB camera. Given a video of a dancing person, [24] transfers the dancing motion to another person, even though the second person does not know how to dance. The second person is only required to record a video of a few poses. While achieving good results, there are still visible distortion and blurriness on the arms, not to mention details of hands. Liquid Warping GAN [25] is a recent work to synthesize human videos of novel poses, viewpoints, and even clothes. They have achieved decent results given that their input is simply a single image. Their work is mainly focused on image/video generation, while our main contribution is simulating human motions. [19] proposed a similar pipeline as ours, which generate skeleton pose first and then generate the final video. However, rather than audio, its input is random noise and its skeleton model is very simple only having body limbs. That means its final output video lacks details on the face and fingers. In contrast, our skeleton model consists of limbs, face, and fingers. [26] learns individual styles of speech gesture via 2 stages as we propose, but its rendering part produces quite a few artifacts in the final generated videos.

3   Methods

As shown in Fig. 1, the input to our system is audio or text, depending on what is used to train the long short-term memory (LSTM) network. We here assume that audio and text are interchangeable, given both text-to-speech (TTS) and speech-to-text (STT) technologies are mature and commercially available. Even though we still get some wrongly recognized words/characters from the state of the art STT engine, our system can tolerate these errors quite successfully, because the main purpose of this LSTM network is to map texts/audios to body shapes. Wrong STT outputs are usually words with similar pronunciations to those of the true ones, meaning they are very likely to have similar spelling too. Therefore, they will eventually map to more or less alike body shapes.

The output of the LSTM is a sequence of human poses, parametrized by SMPL-X [9]. SMPL-X is a joint 3D model of the human body, face, and hands together. This dynamic joint 3D model is visualized as a sequence of 2D colorized skeleton images. These 2D images are further input into a vid2vid generative network [17] to generate final realistic people images.

We found that while successfully synchronize speech and movement, LSTM learns only repetitive human motions most of the time, which results in boring looking videos. In order to make the human motion more expressive and various, we insert certain poses into the output motions of LSTM when some key words are spoken, for example, huge, tiny, high, low, and so on. We manually build a dictionary that maps those key words to their corresponding poses. Please refer to the following sections for details on how we build this dictionary.

Training the LSTM and vid2vid networks requires only some videos of target animation subject reading a script. As shown in Fig. 2, given a video of a talking person, we first fit a human body model to each frame. Together with the extracted audio on the left-hand side, it is fed into the LSTM to train mapping from audio to human poses. On the right-hand side, 2D skeleton images of the human body model and their corresponding true person images are used to train vid2vid generative network. Finally, we manually select some key poses and build a dictionary that maps key words to key poses.

3.1   Speech2Video Dataset

Ideally, our system is capable of synthesizing anyone as long as we can download some of their speech videos from websites such as Youtube. In reality, however, most of those Youtube videos are shot under auto exposure mode, meaning the exposure time could be as long as 33 ms for 30 fps videos. It is impossible to capture clear hand images under such long exposure time when the hands are moving. In fact, most of these frames have motion blur to some extent, which causes big problems when we fit the hand finger model to the images. In addition, our system requires our speaker to be present in a constant viewpoint, but a lot of speech videos keep changing their viewpoint. Though fitting to blurry image itself is a good research topic, we only focus on the video synthesis part and use

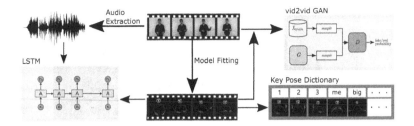

Fig. 2. Overview of our training process.

Fig. 3. Left: our data capture room. Right: 4 frames from captured video.

the existing state-of-the-art approach to fit human model. Therefore, we decided to capture our own data.

We invited two models to capture our training data, one English speaking female and one Chinese speaking male. We capture a total of 3 h of videos for each model when they were reading a variety of scripts, including politics, economy, sports and so on. We set up our own recording studio with a DSLR camera, which captures 1280×720 videos at 60 frames per second. We fix the exposure time at 5 ms so that no motion blur will be present in the frames. In order to reduce data size, we sample every 5 frames from the video and only work on this subset data.

Figure 3 shows our data capture room. Our model stands in front of a camera and screen, and we capture a few videos while he/she reads scripts on the screen. In the end, we ask our model to pose for certain key words, such as huge, tiny, up, down, me, you, and so on.

3.2 Body Model Fitting

Fitting a human body model to images is equivalent to detecting human keypoints. OpenPose [8] has done an excellent work on this. It is a real-time approach to detect the 2D pose of multiple people in an image, including body, foot, hand, and facial keypoints.

We first attempted to take those 2D keypoints as a representation of our human body model, and trained the LSTM network that generates 2D positions

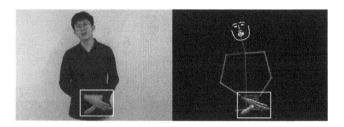

Fig. 4. Failure case with 2d model: elongated fingers.

of these keypoints from audio inputs. The results were not quite satisfactory due to the distortion of output arm and hand (shown in Fig. 4). This because in this simply 2D keypoint human model, there is no relationship between 2 connected keypoints. They can virtually move to anywhere independently without constraints from other keypoint, leading to elongated or shorter arms and fingers. Furthermore, at the stage of inserting key poses into existing body motion, it involves interpolating between 2 poses. Direct interpolation on 2D keypoints usually results in invalid intermediate poses that violate human articulated structure.

Under these observations, we adopt SMPL-X, a true articulated 3D human model. SMPL-X models human body dynamics using a kinematic skeleton model. It has 54 joints including neck, fingers, arms, legs, and feet. It is parameterized by a function $M(\theta, \beta, \psi)$, where $\theta \in R^{3(K+1)}$ is the pose parameter and K is the number of body joints plus an additional global body orientation. $\beta \in R^{|\beta|}$ is the shape parameter which controls the length of each skeleton bone. Finally, the face expression parameter is denoted by $\psi \in R^{|\psi|}$. There are a total of 119 parameters in SMPL-X model, 75 of which come from the global orientation as well as 24 joints excluding hands, each denoted by a 3 DoF axis-angle rotation. The joints on hands are encoded separately by 24 parameters in a lower dimensional PCA space, following approach described in MANO [27]. The shape and face expression both have 10 parameters respectively.

To fit SMPL-X human model to images, in general, we need to find optimal parameters that minimize $E(\theta, \beta, \psi)$, the weighted distance between 2D projection of those 3D joints and 2D detections of the corresponding joints by OpenPose library [8]. The weights are determined by detection confidence scores, so that noisy detection will have less influence on the gradient direction. In our specific scenario, we modified the fitting code to fix body shape parameters β and global orientation during the optimization. Because we are dealing with the same person within a video and the person is standing still during the entire video. We only compute the human body parameter β and human global orientation for the first frame and use them for the remaining frames. So the final objective function for us becomes $E(\theta, \psi)$, where we only look for optimal pose and facial expression parameters. That reduces the total number of parameters to 106.

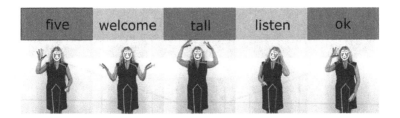

Fig. 5. Key words to key poses dictionary. Note a key pose could be a still single frame pose or a multi-frame motion.

3.3 Dictionary Building and Key Pose Insertion

As shown in Fig. 5, we manually select key poses from the recorded videos and build a word-to-pose lookup dictionary. Again, the pose is represented as 106 SMPL-X parameters. Note that a key pose could be a still single frame pose or a multi-frame motion. We can insert both into an existing human skeleton video by the same approach.

In order to insert a key pose, we first need to know when it's corresponding key word is spoken. For a text-to-speech (TTS) generated audio, the TTS output will include the timestamp of each word in the generated audio. For an audio from a real person, we need to first pass it to a speech-to-text (STT) engine, which generates text script of the speech as well as the timestamp of each individual word. We go over all the words within the speech script and look them up in our word-to-pose dictionary. Once they are found in the dictionary, we decide if we want to insert them into the skeleton video by a certain probability. Since some words like "I", "we", "me" could be spoken a few times in a speech. A real person won't pose every time they speak those words. The probability could vary between different words and should be set when we build the dictionary.

When we insert a pose into a video, we do a smooth interpolation in the 106 parameter space. Illustrated in Fig. 6, a key pose is inserted into a video with a ramp length N frames before and after its insertion time point. The ramp length depends on video frame rate and ramp duration. In all our experiments, the ramp duration is set to be 0.6 s. The key pose is directly copied to its time point within the video and overwrite the original frame. In order to maintain a smooth transition to this pose, we also replace frames from ramp start point all the way to the key pose frame on both sides. The new frames are linear interpolated between ramp start frame and key pose frame, weighted by their distance to those 2 frames.

If our key pose is a single frame still pose, it's inserted exactly as described above, except for one thing. People usually make a pose and keep it for a certain time period. So, instead of showing the key pose in one frame, we also need to keep the key pose for a while. In all our experiments, we keep the pose for 0.3 s by duplicating the key pose frame in place multiple times. If our key pose is a motion (a sequence of frames), then it will be copied to the target video to

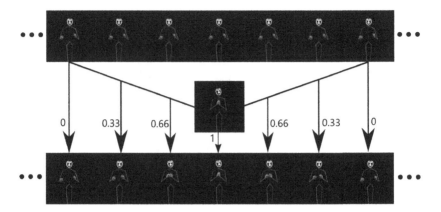

Fig. 6. Inserting a key pose smoothly into an existing video sequence. A key pose is inserted into a video with a ramp length N frames before and after its insertion time point. The ramp length is only 3 here for illustration, but the real ramp length is way longer than this. Those number alongside vertical arrows are interpolation weights of the key pose. The weighted sum of ramp start/end pose and key pose replaces original frames in between.

overwrite a sequence of the same length. The smoothness ramping is done the same way.

3.4 Train LSTM

When we train the LSTM which maps audio sequence to pose sequence, we have to give different weights to different parts of the human body in the loss, because they have different scales. The relative weights we set to body, hands, mouth, and face are 1, 4, 100, 100 respectively. We also enforce a smoothness constraint on the output pose sequence by adding a difference loss between 2 consecutive poses, in order to make sure the output motion is smooth and natural.

Audio to Pose. We extract the audio features using standard MFCC coefficients [28]. The input audio may have various volume level, we first normalize its volume by RMS-based normalization [29]. Then for every 25 ms-length audio clip, we apply discrete Fourier Transform to get its representation in the frequency domain. The audio clip is sampled at 10ms interval. 40 triangular Mel-scale filters are applied to the output of Fourier Transform, followed by a logarithm operator. Next, we reduce the output dimension to 13 by applying a Discrete Cosine Transform. The final feature is a 28D vector, where the first 14D consists of the 13D output of the Discrete Cosine Transform plus the log mean value of volume, and the second 14D is temporal first-order derivatives of the first 14D, a.k.a, the difference to the previous feature vector.

Text to Pose. Voice could be quite different from people to people, even when they are speaking the same words. That could lead to poor performance of the LSTM learning. Alternatively, we can use text, instead of audio to train the LSTM. That requires us to convert to text if the input is audio. Thanks to the development of natural language processing (NLP), there are quite a few prior works [30] that do excellent jobs on this.

For English, we directly use words as the input sequence to LSTM, since word spelling itself incorporates pronunciation information. We pad remaining pausing parts with 0's to form an entire input sequence. On the other hand, for those non-latin languages, for example Chinese, its words/characters don't carry pronunciation information. In this case, we still want to have the same mouth shape and body pose when 2 characters of the same pronunciation are spoken. Therefore, we have to convert characters to representation with phoneme information. For Chinese, we convert each individual character into pinyin, which is composed of 26 English letters. It guarantees 2 characters have the same spelling if they have the same pronunciations.

LSTM Architecture. We opt for a simple 2 layer unidirectional LSTM [31]. Input is vector of audio/text encoding, and output is vector of SMPL-X parameters. Note that a time delay is applied to the output by shifting output parameter forward in timeline as explored in [32]. This gives the network the options to predict human poses by looking in the future of speaking. This is especially true when a speaker tends to pose before he/she starting speaking. The dimension of the cell state is set to 300, and the time delay of output is set to 200 ms. The network is solved by minimizing a L2-loss on the SMPL-X parameters using Adam optimizer [33] implemented under TensorFlow. The network is trained with a batch size of 100 and learning rate of 0.001. The input vector is normalized by its mean and variance, but the output is kept unchanged in order to keep the relative scale of different SMPL-X parameters.

3.5   Train Video Generative Network

We adopt the generative network proposed by vid2vid [17] to convert our skeleton images into real person images. In our applications, the rendering results of human bodies are not equally important. The most important parts are face and hands. To make vid2vid network put more effort on generating details of face and both hands, we modified the network and our input images to achieve this. Specifically, we draw a color circle on both hands on the input skeleton image and also draw face part with white color, which is different from other parts of body (Fig. 7). Within the network, an image is output from the generative network given an input image. Before we pass it to discriminator network, we locate regions of face and both hands by their special colors in the input image. Then we crop those 3 sub images from the generated image, and pass them to the discriminator network along with the entire output image. The loss weights for those sub images are carefully tuned to make sure the discriminator is more picky on the reality of generated face and hands images.

Running Times and Hardware. The most time consuming and memory consuming stage of our system is training the vid2vid network. It takes about a week to finish 20 epochs of training on a cluster of 8 NVIDIA Tesla M40 24G GPUs. The testing stage is much faster. It takes only about 0.5 s to generate one frame on a single GPU.

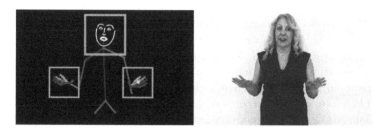

Fig. 7. Sample images pair used to train vid2vid. Both hands are labeled by a special color circle. The color circles are identified within the GAN, in order to crop the sub-images around both hands. Those sub-images are passed to discriminator separately from the whole image to ensure we put more weights on the hand detail generation.

Table 1. Average scores of 248 participants on 4 questions. Q1: Completeness of body. Q2: The face is clear. Q3: The body movement is correlated with audio. Q4: Overall quality.

	Q1	Q2	Q3	Q4
LearningGesture [26]	3.414	3.659	3.914	3.308
LumiereNet [4]	3.585	3.521	3.085	3.265
Neural-voice-puppetry [21]	3.202	3.840	3.180	3.542
EverybodyDance [24]	3.944	3.662	3.680	3.681
Our method	3.894	4.011	3.383	3.762

4   Results

4.1   Evaluation and Analysis

Note it is not straightforward to compare with other methods, because 1) there is no benchmark dataset to evaluate speech to full body videos, 2) people's speech motion is quite subjective and personalized which makes it difficult to define ground truth. As Table 1 showing, we choose to compare our results with 4 SoTA approaches using user study. We get the best overall quality score compared to other 4 SOTA methods.

Inception Score Comparison. Also we evaluate our image generation result using inception scores. The score measures two things simultaneously: The image quality and image diversity.

Table 2. Inception scores for generated videos (IS) and ground truth videos (GT IS) of different methods. The relative incpetion score (Rel. IS) is the ratio of the first to the second.

	SynthesizeObama [1]	EverybodyDance [24]	Ours
IS	1.039	1.690	1.286
GT IS	1.127	1.818	1.351
Rel. IS	0.921	0.929	**0.952**

As shown in Table 2, we compare to SynthesizeObama and EverybodyDance by computing inception scores on all the frames of videos generated by each method. IS is the score for generated videos and GT IS is the score for ground truth videos. For SynthesizeObama [1] the ground truth is the source video of the input audio. For EverybodyDance [24] the ground truth is the source video to transfer motion from. And in our case, the ground truth is the training video. It is expected that dancing videos (EverybodyDance) have higher scores than speech videos (ours), and speech videos (ours) have higher scores than talking head (SynthesizeObama), since dancing has the most motion varieties. Therefore, we use the relative inception scores (inception score of generated videos to ground truth videos) to measure similarity to the ground truth. Our method outperforms the other two methods by this standard, meaning our visual quality is closer to ground truth.

Table 3. Numerical evaluation on mouth motion reconstruction of our system. Number here is average pixel distance.

	Orig	Man1	Man2	Man3	Text
0.5 h	1.769	1.838	1.911	1.992	2.043
1 h	1.730	1.868	1.983	2.012	2.024
2 h	1.733	1.809	1.930	2.047	1.993

Table 4. Average scores of 112 participants on 5 questions. Q1: Completeness of body. Q2: The face is clear. Q3: The human motion looks natural. Q4: The body movement is correlated with audio. Q5: Overall quality.

	Q1	Q2	Q3	Q4	Q5
Synth	4.12	4.21	2.86	3.07	3.42
TTS	4.07	3.81	2.67	2.88	3.28
Real	4.28	4.38	4.45	4.35	4.38

Numerical Evaluation. Since people don't pose exactly the same, even if the same person speaks the same sentence twice. So, it is difficult to tell if our generated body motion is good or not, due to lacking of ground truth. The only part that takes the same shape when speaking the same words is mouth. Thus, we use only mouth to evaluate our motion reconstruction accuracy. Specifically, we record a separate video of our models when they speak totally different sentences than in the training dataset. We extract the audio and input into our pipeline. The output 3D joints of mouth are projected onto the image space and compared to those 2D mouth keypoints detected by OpenPose. The errors are measured by average pixel distance.

As Reported in Table 3, we have done several evaluations on the mouth motion reconstruction and found some interesting facts. We first tried to train our LSTM network using different dataset size to see how it affects the reconstruction accuracy. We used dataset of varying length including 0.5 h, 1 h and 2 h. We use the voice of the same lady (Orig.) as in training data to do the evaluation. In addition, we also lower the pitch of the original voice to simulate a man's voice, in order to see how voice variation affect the results. We simulate voices of a young man (Man1), a middle age man (Man2) and an old man (Man3) by successively lower pitch values of the original audio. Finally, we train and test our LSTM network using text and compare the results to those of audio.

We have 3 observations from Table 3. First, audio has better accuracy than text. Second, longer training dataset doesn't necessarily increase the accuracy for audio but it indeed helps for text. Third, accuracy gets worse when voice is getting more deviated from the original one. The third one is easy to understand, so we expect worse performance if the test voice sounds different from the training voice. For the first and second observations, the explanation is that audio space is smaller than text space, because some words/characters share the same pronunciation, for example, pair vs pear, see vs sea. Therefore, audio training data cover larger parts in its own space than text training data of the same length. In our experiments here, it looks like 0.5-h length audio is enough to cover the entire pronunciation space. Adding more training data doesn't help increase accuracy. On the other hand, 2-h length text is still not enough to cover the entire spelling space, so the error keeps decreasing as we increase the length of training data.

User Study. To evaluate the final output videos, We conducted a human subjective test on Amazon Mechanical Turk (AMT) with 112 participants. We show a total of five videos to the participants. Four of them are our synthesized videos, two of which are generated by real person audios and the other two are generated by TTS audios. The remaining one is a short clip of a real person. Those five videos are ordered randomly and we didn't tell our participants that there is a real video. The participants are required to rate the quality of those videos on a Likert scale from 1 (strongly disagree) to 5 (strongly agree). Those include 1) Completeness of human body (no missing body parts or hand fingers); 2) The face in the video is clear; 3) The human motion (arm, hand, body gesture) in the video looks natural and smooth; 4) The body movement and gesture is correlated with audio; 5) Overall visual quality of the video and it looks real.

As shown in Table 4, our synthesized videos (Synth.) get 3.42 and real video gets 4.38 (out of 5). In particular, our proposed method has the same performance on body completeness, face clarity compared to real video. Another discovery is that TTS generated videos are worse than real-audio generated videos in all aspects. The reason is twofold. First, TTS audios are generally more distant to real audios in MFCC feature space, leading to worse reconstructed motions

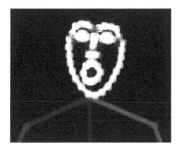   

Fig. 8. One frame generated by TTS audio when people pause speaking. Mouth shape is distorted.

Fig. 9. One frame generated by a skeleton model without hands. It is clear that the hand model is necessary to render hand details in the final image.

and gestures (conclusion from Table 3). Secondly, TTS audio itself sounds fake, which decreases the overall video quality.

4.2   Ablation Study

TTS Noise. When we train our LSTM, the audios are extracted from recorded videos, meaning they contain background noise when people are not speaking. However, TTS generated audios have an absolutely clear background when people pause speaking. That difference causes some problems in the output skeleton motions. As can be seen in Fig. 8, mouth shape is distorted because our network has never seen this absolutely clear signal in the training. To fix this issue, we add some white noise to the TTS generated audios before feeding to LSTM.

Hand Model. As mentioned before, it's necessary to have hands in our skeleton model in order to render hand details in the final output of vid2vid. As in Fig. 9, we have downloaded a video from Youtube and use it as our training data. Due to its motion blur, we can't fit a correct hand model to the video frames. Thus we trained our vid2vid network without hand skeleton, all the way up to 40 epochs. However, it is still impossible to render clear hand images in the final output. This is also evidence of why the end-to-end approach simply doesn't work. A very detailed spatial guidance is necessary for the GAN network to produce high fidelity rendering. An audio input simply can't provide this spatial guidance. Thus, we eventually give up employing the end-to-end method.

Key Pose Insertion. To justify the effectiveness of our key pose insertion approach, we conducted another user study. In this study, we simply present pairs of synthesized videos with and without inserted key poses. The participants just need to choose which one is more expressive. For all participants, videos with key poses get 80.6% of the votes compared to 19.4% for videos without key poses. This demonstrates the necessity of inserting key poses to enrich the expressiveness of speech.

5 Conclusion

We proposed a novel framework to generate realistic speech videos using the 3D driven approach, while avoiding building 3D mesh models. We built a table of personal key gestures inside the framework to handle the problem of data sparsity and diversity. More importantly, we utilized 3D skeleton constraints to generate body dynamics, which guarantees the pose to be physically plausible.

Acknowledgment. This work was supported by the NSFC grant No. 62001213.

References

1. Suwajanakorn, S., Seitz, S.M., Kemelmacher-Shlizerman, I.: Synthesizing Obama: learning lip sync from audio. ACM Trans. Graph. (TOG) **36**, 95 (2017)
2. Fried, O., et al.: Text-based editing of talking-head video. arXiv preprint arXiv:1906.01524 (2019)
3. Taylor, S., et al.: A deep learning approach for generalized speech animation. ACM Trans. Graph. (TOG) **36**, 93 (2017)
4. Kim, B.H., Ganapathi, V.: Lumi\erenet: lecture video synthesis from audio. arXiv preprint arXiv:1907.02253 (2019)
5. Ge, L., et al.: 3D hand shape and pose estimation from a single RGB image. In: Proceedings of the IEEE Conference on Computer Vision and Pattern Recognition, pp. 10833–10842 (2019)
6. Kanazawa, A., Zhang, J.Y., Felsen, P., Malik, J.: Learning 3D human dynamics from video. In: Proceedings of the IEEE Conference on Computer Vision and Pattern Recognition, pp. 5614–5623 (2019)
7. Pavllo, D., Feichtenhofer, C., Grangier, D., Auli, M.: 3D human pose estimation in video with temporal convolutions and semi-supervised training. In: Proceedings of the IEEE Conference on Computer Vision and Pattern Recognition, pp. 7753–7762 (2019)
8. Cao, Z., Hidalgo, G., Simon, T., Wei, S.E., Sheikh, Y.: OpenPose: realtime multi-person 2D pose estimation using part affinity fields. In: arXiv preprint arXiv:1812.08008 (2018)
9. Pavlakos, G., et al.: Expressive body capture: 3D hands, face, and body from a single image. In: Proceedings IEEE Conference on Computer Vision and Pattern Recognition (CVPR) (2019)
10. Karras, T., Aila, T., Laine, S., Herva, A., Lehtinen, J.: Audio-driven facial animation by joint end-to-end learning of pose and emotion. ACM Trans. Graph. (TOG) **36**, 94 (2017)
11. Shlizerman, E., Dery, L., Schoen, H., Kemelmacher-Shlizerman, I.: Audio to body dynamics. In: Proceedings of the IEEE Conference on Computer Vision and Pattern Recognition, pp. 7574–7583 (2018)
12. Yan, S., Li, Z., Xiong, Y., Yan, H., Lin, D.: Convolutional sequence generation for skeleton-based action synthesis. In: Proceedings of the IEEE International Conference on Computer Vision, pp. 4394–4402 (2019)
13. Martinez, J., Black, M.J., Romero, J.: On human motion prediction using recurrent neural networks. In: Proceedings of the IEEE Conference on Computer Vision and Pattern Recognition, pp. 2891–2900 (2017)

14. Li, Z., Zhou, Y., Xiao, S., He, C., Huang, Z., Li, H.: Auto-conditioned recurrent networks for extended complex human motion synthesis. arXiv preprint arXiv:1707.05363 (2017)
15. Isola, P., Zhu, J.Y., Zhou, T., Efros, A.A.: Image-to-image translation with conditional adversarial networks. In: 2017 IEEE Conference on Computer Vision and Pattern Recognition (CVPR) (2017)
16. Wang, T.C., Liu, M.Y., Zhu, J.Y., Tao, A., Kautz, J., Catanzaro, B.: High-resolution image synthesis and semantic manipulation with conditional GANs. In: Proceedings of the IEEE Conference on Computer Vision and Pattern Recognition (2018)
17. Wang, T.C., et al.: Video-to-video synthesis. In: Advances in Neural Information Processing Systems (NeurIPS) (2018)
18. Shysheya, A., et al.: Textured neural avatars. In: Proceedings of the IEEE Conference on Computer Vision and Pattern Recognition, pp. 2387–2397 (2019)
19. Cai, H., Bai, C., Tai, Y.-W., Tang, C.-K.: Deep video generation, prediction and completion of human action sequences. In: Ferrari, V., Hebert, M., Sminchisescu, C., Weiss, Y. (eds.) ECCV 2018. LNCS, vol. 11206, pp. 374–390. Springer, Cham (2018). https://doi.org/10.1007/978-3-030-01216-8_23
20. Mittal, G., Wang, B.: Animating face using disentangled audio representations. In: The IEEE Winter Conference on Applications of Computer Vision, pp. 3290–3298 (2020)
21. Thies, J., Elgharib, M., Tewari, A., Theobalt, C., Nießner, M.: Neural voice puppetry: audio-driven facial reenactment. arXiv preprint arXiv:1912.05566 (2019)
22. Thies, J., Zollhöfer, M., Nießner, M.: Deferred neural rendering: image synthesis using neural textures. ACM Trans. Graph. (TOG) **38**, 1–12 (2019)
23. Thies, J., Zollhofer, M., Stamminger, M., Theobalt, C., Nießner, M.: Face2Face: real-time face capture and reenactment of RGB videos. In: Proceedings of the IEEE Conference on Computer Vision and Pattern Recognition, pp. 2387–2395 (2016)
24. Chan, C., Ginosar, S., Zhou, T., Efros, A.A.: Everybody dance now. In: Proceedings of the IEEE International Conference on Computer Vision, pp. 5933–5942 (2019)
25. Liu, W., Piao, Z., Min, J., Luo, W., Ma, L., Gao, S.: Liquid warping GAN: a unified framework for human motion imitation, appearance transfer and novel view synthesis. In: Proceedings of the IEEE International Conference on Computer Vision, pp. 5904–5913 (2019)
26. Ginosar, S., Bar, A., Kohavi, G., Chan, C., Owens, A., Malik, J.: Learning individual styles of conversational gesture. In: Proceedings of the IEEE Conference on Computer Vision and Pattern Recognition, pp. 3497–3506 (2019)
27. Romero, J., Tzionas, D., Black, M.J.: Embodied hands: modeling and capturing hands and bodies together. ACM Trans. Graph. (ToG) **36**, 245 (2017)
28. Logan, B., et al.: Mel frequency cepstral coefficients for music modeling. In: ISMIR, vol. 270, pp. 1–11 (2000)
29. Katz, B., Katz, R.A.: Mastering Audio: The Art and the Science. Butterworth-Heinemann (2003)
30. Reddy, D.R.: Speech recognition by machine: a review. Proc. IEEE **64**, 501–531 (1976)
31. Hochreiter, S., Schmidhuber, J.: Long short-term memory. Neural Comput. **9**, 1735–1780 (1997)
32. Graves, A., Schmidhuber, J.: Framewise phoneme classification with bidirectional LSTM and other neural network architectures. Neural Netw. **18**, 602–610 (2005)
33. Kingma, D.P., Ba, J.: Adam: a method for stochastic optimization. arXiv preprint arXiv:1412.6980 (2014)

3D Human Motion Estimation via Motion Compression and Refinement

Zhengyi Luo$^{(\boxtimes)}$ (ID), S. Alireza Golestaneh (ID), and Kris M. Kitani (ID)

Carnegie Mellon University, Pittsburgh, PA 15213, USA
{zluo2,sgolesta,kkitani}@cs.cmu.edu

Abstract. We develop a technique for generating smooth and accurate 3D human pose and motion estimates from RGB video sequences. Our method, which we call **M**otion **E**stimation via **V**ariational **A**utoencoder (*MEVA*), decomposes a temporal sequence of human motion into a smooth motion representation using auto-encoder-based motion compression and a residual representation learned through motion refinement. This two-step encoding of human motion captures human motion in two stages: a general human motion estimation step that captures the coarse overall motion, and a residual estimation that adds back person-specific motion details. Experiments show that our method produces both smooth and accurate 3D human pose and motion estimates.

1 Introduction

Estimating the 3D pose sequence of a person from a single video requires a computational model that can extract the underlying kinematics of human motion while also preserving motions that are unique to the person being captured. Since people share a similar body structure (*e.g.,* same number of joints) and similar physical constraints (*e.g..,* joint limitations), it is possible to learn a generalized kinematic model that can be matched against the image to infer the general motion of a person. However, since generalized models of motion can also fail to model person-specific motions, it may also be necessary to 'add back in' or refine the general motion estimates using image evidence. In this work, we present a two-stage 3D motion estimation method that first extracts coarse kinematic sequences of a person in a video and then refines that sequence to produce a more accurate 3D motion estimate. We show that by decomposing the inference process into (1) a general model of motion and (2) a person-specific model of motion, we are able to obtain more accurate and smooth estimates (Fig. 1).

Over the past years, significant progress has been made on improving the accuracy of 3D human pose estimation. Impressive results have been obtained through human mesh recovery from single images [2–5] and videos [1,6–8]. The

Electronic supplementary material The online version of this chapter (https://doi.org/10.1007/978-3-030-69541-5_20) contains supplementary material, which is available to authorized users.

© Springer Nature Switzerland AG 2021
H. Ishikawa et al. (Eds.): ACCV 2020, LNCS 12626, pp. 324–340, 2021.
https://doi.org/10.1007/978-3-030-69541-5_20

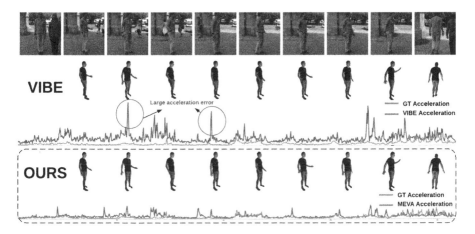

Fig. 1. Given an in-the-wild video, state-of-the-art methods (*e.g.*, VIBE [1]) can achieve high per joint accuracy, but also suffers from high acceleration error. To tackle this, we develop a two-stage motion estimation method, *MEVA*, that is able to produce both accurate and smooth human motion.

main metric used to evaluate these methods is the Mean Per Joint Position Error (MPJPE), which measures the performance in terms of the relative joint positions computed for each frame of a video. However, less emphasis has been given to the temporal smoothness of the estimated motion. Optimizing for this metric, the tendency is to generate pose estimates that 'jitter' near the true pose. This is expected as the MPJPE only penalizes for spatial errors and is not designed to account for temporal consistency. As the methods for 3D pose estimation have improved in recent years, the 'jitter' has become less pronounced, especially when applied to dynamic scenes with vibrant moving backgrounds and camera motion. However, by rendering the estimated 3D pose of state-of-the-art methods on a plain background, the 'jitter' can still be observed, resulting in an overall unnatural motion estimation.

The issue of temporal smoothness is a known problem and has been addressed in part by prior work. Large-scale motion datasets such as Archive of Motion Capture as Surface Shapes (AMAAS) [9]) and adversarial loss have enabled methods to improve both pose accuracy and temporal smoothness [1,6]. Other methods have been developed to enforce temporal smoothness [2] by letting the model predict frame ordering. However, using prior knowledge only in the loss function, it is hard to find the balance between smoothness and accuracy.

In this work, we argue that striking such balance between smoothness and accuracy can be done through an explicit breakdown of coarse and fine motion. First, we learn a coarse motion model by observing a large dataset of human motion–since human motion is typically smooth (*e.g.*, we usually do not shake as we walk), if one were to fit a model to a large set of human motions, most of the data would lie in a sub-space in which motions are smooth. This implies that if we were to compress human motion data, it should learn a latent subspace in which the motions are inherently smooth and coarse. Using this latent space as the regression target, we can directly infer coarse human motion from the input videos. The problem of using such a human motion subspace, of course, is that rare motions (*e.g.*, sudden motions) are removed from the motion data. To retain such motion, we also argue that producing the final 3D motion estimate can be treated as a refinement step to "add back" the fine details to the coarse motion sequence.

To validate our arguments, we propose a two-stage 3D human motion estimation method that first estimates a coarse human pose sequence through data compression using a Variational Autoencoder (VAE), which we call the Variational Motion Estimator (VME). Then we take the output of the VME and refine the pose estimate using the image evidence with a pose regressor, which we call the Motion Refinement Regressor (MRR).

In summary, we propose a video-based 3D human motion estimation method that focuses on producing smooth and accurate human motion sequences. Our main contributions are as follows: (1) we propose a two-stage motion estimation method for ensuring temporal smoothness and accurate pose estimates; (2) we describe a procedure to learn a robust Variational Autoencoder that can serve as a latent human motion subspace for estimating coarse 3D human motion from videos; (3) we demonstrate state-of-the-art pose/motion estimation performance on challenging in-the-wild dataset such as 3DPW [10], reducing acceleration error by 54.3% while achieving state-of-the-art MPJPE results.

2   Related Works

In this section, we will first review the relevant work in human shape and pose recovery from a single image and from videos–human motion recovery can be treated as a subset of human pose estimation, as human motion is a sequence of human poses. Then we will review how existing methods use human motion as a prior and how popular methods map motion sequences to a low-dimensional space.

2.1   Recovering 3D Human Pose and Shape from a Single Image

Here we focus on model-based methods that jointly recover human shape and pose. We choose to use a parametric 3D human body model [11–13] since it can be easily turned into a 3D human mesh that is usable for downstream tasks such as animation. Directly fitting a parametric 3D human body to image input has gained substantial traction over the years, morphing from methods that require silhouette or human input [14–18], to ones that can directly fit model parameters to 2D joint positions [19], and to ones that can directly estimate shape and pose from images [3,7,11,20–23]. Due to the lack of ground truth 3D labels, these methods use a weakly supervised approach to fit the 3D human body to 2D joint positions [7,22,23], body part segmentation [20,24], or dense pixel correspondence [2]. Although these methods achieve amazing results, their extracted motion tends to be unstable due to the lack of temporal information.

2.2   Recovering 3D Human Pose and Shape from Video

Using temporal information to aid 3D human pose estimation is a natural extension to single frame methods. [8, 25–27] focus on "lifting" predicted joint positions from 2D to 3D, and uses LSTM [8], Temporal Convolution [25], and fully connected layers [26] to exploit temporal information. [28, 29], on the other hand, predict 3D joint positions directly from images and use a temporal filter to postprocess the motion sequence. For methods that jointly recover shape and pose. HMMR [6], Sun *et al.* [2] and VIBE [1] are the best performing models that exploit temporal information. HMMR [6] proposes to enforce temporal consistency by letting the model predict future and past frames of motion. Sun *et al.* [2] learns temporal information by predicting the ordering of shuffled frames. VIBE [1] utilizes temporal information by employing a Gated Recurrent Unit (GRU) to convert the input frames of features into a sequence of temporally correlated latent features.

2.3   Human Pose and Motion Prior

Using prerecorded human motion sequences as a prior has also been explored in various tasks related to human motion. Earlier work like [30] tries to quantify unnaturalness in animated human motion by statistically analyzing existing motion capture (MoCap) sequences, and [31, 32] propose to use learned MoCap motions to aid 3D motion tracking. More recently, [6, 7] use an adversarial discriminator at a per-frame level to ensure that the recovered pose is a valid human pose. [11] uses a pretrained pose VAE's latent space for a similar purpose. [1] proposes to use the discriminator at a temporal level, discriminating against a whole motion sequence. All above methods use a pose or motion prior in an adversarial way, utilizing the prior knowledge in the loss function.

2.4   Human Motion Representation

Compressing human motion into a compact latent representation plays an important role in tasks such as human motion generation [33–35], human motion generation across different modalities [36–39], and trajectory forecasting [40–43]. Existing methods leverage different generative models such as VAE [41, 42], generative flow [44], or generative adversarial networks [33] to achieve a compact motion representation in the latent space.

3   Approach

As discussed in Sects. 1 and 2, existing human motion estimation methods often find it difficult to achieve a balance between temporal smoothness and accuracy. To tackle this, we propose *MEVA*, **M**otion **E**stimation via **V**ariational **A**utoencoder, a framework that learns the overall coarse motion first then adds back fine detailed motion as a residual. *MEVA* processes the inputs in three steps: it first extracts correlated temporal features using a spatio-temporal feature extractor (STE), and then captures the overall coarse motion through a variational motion estimator (VME), and finally uses a motion residual regressor (MRR) to add back the fine motion details. Our overall framework can be shown in Fig. 2. In this section, we will first setup the overall problem and then present the details of our framework. Finally, we will discuss the training procedures.

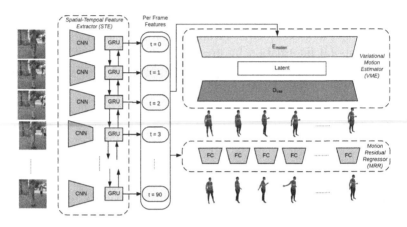

Fig. 2. Overall Architecture. *MEVA* estimates motion from videos by first extracting temporal features using Spatio-Temporal Feature Extractor (STE) and then estimates the overall coarse motion inside the video with Variational Motion Estimator (VME). Finally, a Motion Residual Regressor (MRR) is used to refine the motion estimates.

3.1   Problem Formulation

Given an input video $V_T = \{I_t\}_{t=1}^{T}$, where I_t denotes the tth frame, our task is to recover coherent human motion sequences $M_T = \{\theta_t\}_{t=1}^{T}$ where each θ_t represents the human pose for the tth frame. To represent the human motion, we utilize the SMPL 3D human mesh model [12]. We choose SMPL parametrization over 3D joint positions or other human models due to its versatility: SMPL parameters can be easily converted to 3D joint positions and human mesh. Specifically, a human body is represented by its shape β and pose θ, denoted by $\Theta = \{\beta, \theta\}$. Given θ and β, let S denote the pretrained SMPL function, where $S(\Theta) : \beta, \theta \to R^{6890 \times 3}$ (6890 is the number of vertices of the resulting triangular human mesh). The pose parameter $\theta \in R^{24 \times N}$ stands for the joint angles for the 23 joints plus the root orientation. N is the dimension of the chosen rotation representation ($N = 3$ for axis/euler angle, $N = 4$ for quaternions, $N = 6$ for a 6 degrees-of-freedom rotation representation [45]). The shape parameters $\beta \in R^{10}$ represent the linear coefficient for the principal component of the parametric human shape space. Given a set of β and θ, S can recover the 3D joint positions through a pretrained mesh vertex regressor $P : jp^{3d} = P\{S(\beta, \theta)\} \in R^{N \times 3}$. To project the 3D joint positions back to 2D images, a weak perspective camera $\pi = \{s, t_x, t_y\}$ needs to be estimated: $jp^{2d} = \Pi(P\{S(\beta, \theta)\}) \in R^{N \times 2}$.

Intuitively, recovering human motion from video frames does not require recovering the human shape: one can directly learn a mapping from input video frames to the estimated human motion if sufficient paired ground truth data exist. However, videos paired with ground truth motion annotation (SMPL sequences) require professional capture equipment such as a motion capture (MoCap) rig, which is still rather rare compared to annotated 2D pose datasets. In the absence of 3D data samples, it is critical for our model to learn motion sequences in a semisupervised fashion (*i.e.,* from videos with 3D or 2D labeled joint positions following the approach utilized in [1–3,6,7]).

Overall, our motion estimation objective is to learn a function $\text{MEVA}(V) :$ $V_T \rightarrow M_T$ where $V_T = \{I_t\}_{t=1}^T$ and $M_T = \{\theta_t\}_{t=1}^T$.

3.2 Spatio-Temporal Feature Extractor (STE)

Human motion is inherently temporal and correlated, and past movement can give cues about future motion. Thus, instead of extracting per-frame visual features using a feed-forward convolutional network independently, we can produce temporally correlated features that lead to better motion sequence modeling. Similar to [1], we use a GRU-based temporal feature extractor (STE) that encodes the input video frames $I_1, I_2, I_3, ...I_T$ into a sequence of temporally correlated features $f_1', f_2', f_3', ...f_T'$.

3.3 Variational Motion Estimator (VME)

Human Motion VAE. To learn a human motion subspace that can encapsulate a broad spectrum of human motion, we choose to use a Variational Autoencoder (VAE). VAEs can effectively capture a large number of possible data modes by explicitly mapping each data point to a latent code, and by imposing a Gaussian prior on the learned latent space, similar motions' latent codes will be near each other. Thus, the VAE's latent space allows for more overlap between codes and therefore enforces smoothness in the latent space. Having a smooth latent code is essential in improving the generalizability of the model since the space of possible human motion is highly correlated and limited. Formally, following the previous work on VAEs [42,46,47,47], the objective is to maximize the evidence lower bound of the log-likelihood $p_\lambda(x)$ (λ and ϕ denotes the function parametrization):

$$L_{VAE} = E_{q_\phi}[\log p(x|z)] - \text{KLD}(q_\phi(z|x)||p_\phi(z)), \tag{1}$$

where x is the input and the latent code $z \sim \mathcal{N}(\mathbf{0}, \mathbf{I})$.

In the context of encoding human motion via VAE, the encoder E_{vae} takes in a sequence of W frames of human motion represented in terms of SMPL pose parameters: $x = M_W = [\theta_{w1}, \theta_{w2}, \theta_{w3}, ...] \in R^{W \times 144}$ and outputs the latent code

z. A single frame of SMPL pose is represented in joint rotations, resulting by a $24 \times 6 = 144$ dimensional input (a 6 degrees-of-freedom rotation representation [45] is used for continuity purpose). The decoder D_{vae} takes in the latent code z and reconstructs the motion $\hat{M}_W$. Both the encoder E_{vae} and decoder D_{vae} are implemented as GRUs, and the detailed architectures are given in Fig. 3. Based on the Gaussian parameterization of the VAE, the objective function of Eq. (1) can be written Eq. (2)

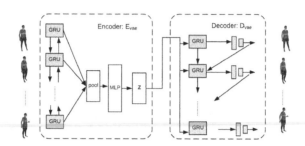

Fig. 3. Motion VAE architecture.

$$\mathcal{L}_{vae}(\mathbf{x}; \theta, \phi) = -\frac{1}{S}\sum_{s=1}^{S}\|\tilde{\mathbf{x}} - \mathbf{x}\|^2 + \beta \cdot \frac{1}{S_z}\sum_{j=1}^{S_z}\left(1 + 2\log\sigma_j - \mu_j^2 - \sigma_j^2\right), \quad (2)$$

where S is the number of samples for the current batch, S_z is the dimension of the current latent variable, and β is the weighing parameter. Once the VAE is trained and converged to a desirable reconstruction accuracy, the decoder D_{vae} is frozen for later use. During inference, given a latent code $z \in R^{1 \times S_z}$, D_{vae} can decode it back into a sequence of human motion: $M_W \in R^{w \times 144}$.

Human Motion Data Augmentation. Our learned VAE should be able to generalize to unseen human motion sequences and achieve high reconstruction accuracy to ensure that the learned latent space can indeed serve as a comprehensive human motion subspace. Using an already large-scale human motion dataset AMASS [9] (13k motion samples with varying length), our trained VAE still has poor generalizability on unseen sequences (for details refer to Sect. 4.3). Thus, we devise an elaborate data augmentation scheme that can augment the existing motion and produce viable yet distinct human motion sequences. While data augmentation has been studied extensively in image processing, to the best of our knowledge, few attempts have been done in augmenting a human motion dataset. When used in trajectory forecasting [42] and human motion generation [33], the generalizability of the VAE latent space has not been discussed extensively since the models only need to generate new motion sequences and do not emphasize on the ability to encode unseen motion sequences.

Given a T frame human motion sequence in SMPL parameters $M_T \in R^{T \times 144}$ with a frame-rate F_{amass}, we employ the following data augmentation scheme:

- **Speeding up and slowing down:** based on F_{amass}, we can uniformly up-sample or downsample the frames and produce novel sequences that are still plausible and natural human motion.
- **Flipping left and right:** The same action, performed using either the left or right hand, will remain a valid human motion. Thus, we can follow the kinematic tree of the SMPL model and mirror the motion across the left and right and generate a new motion sequence.
- **Random root rotation:** We randomly sample a root rotation from a unit sphere to capture different root orientations for possible human motion. Different pose estimators may assume different ground planes and coordinate systems, so SMPL parameters usually come in different root orientations. Sampling random root rotation helps the model cope with different possible coordinate frame choices.

Learning Smooth Motion from Videos. After learning a comprehensive human motion subspace using the VAE, we learn an additional encoder E_{motion} that can directly extract coarse motion sequences from video features, mapping to the same latent space as E_{vae}. Given an input sequence of video features $f_W = \{f_w\}_{w=1}^{W}$, the encoder E_{motion}'s task is to compress the input features into a latent code z that best summarizes the current observation as a coarse human motion sequence. We use the pretrained decoder D_{vae} from the motion VAE to force E_{motion} to sample from our pretrained motion subspace. Constraining the latent space of the E_{motion} to a pretrained human motion subspace provides a strong human motion prior that greatly aids the learning process of E_{motion}. Combining E_{motion} and D_{vae}, we form our Variational Motion Estimator (VME).

3.4   Motion Residual Regressor (MRR)

As noted in the previous section, the learned motion sequences using the VAE's latent space as the target are inherently smooth and coarse, capturing the overall motion signature of the current video frames through information compression. To capture the details, we utilize a SMPL regressor from [7] that can iteratively refine the estimated poses. The regressor takes in an initial pose and shape estimation Θ_t and the visual feature f_t for a single frame to calculate its estimation Θ'_t for k iterations. Notice that though [1,3,6,7] all utilize the same regressor, *MEVA* uses it in a fundamentally different way–in [1,3,6,7], the regressor is initialized with mean SMPL pose Θ_{mean}. At a sequence level, a regressor initialized uniformly with the mean pose Θ_{mean} is trying to capture the overall motion in one pass, while in *MEVA*, the regressor is initialized with the computed poses from VME. Thus, the regressor is only tasked to do small cosmetic changes to the coarse estimation, adding back the fine details of the motion lost during our compression step. Similar to [1], the input visual features f_t to the regressor are encoded using a temporal visual encoder, so even though each frame's estimation is calculated separately at this stage, the visual feature is already temporally correlated. The VME computes the overall coarse motion from videos by using a general model of motion, and the regressor jointly refines motion and human shape estimates, which amounts to adding back the person-specific motion details at a per frame level. We call this regressor the Motion Residual Regressor (MRR). MRR completes the overall framework of our proposed method, as shown in Fig. 2.

3.5 Training and Losses

Our framework is trained in two stages. At first, the motion VAE is pretrained. Then STE, VME, and MRR are trained jointly end-to-end. Using videos with various levels of annotation (2D joint positions, 3D joint positions, SMPL parameters), similar to in [1,3,6], the networks are trained with losses consisting of L_{2D}, L_{3D}, L_{SMPL}, as long as respective data is available. Specifically:

$$L_{meva} = L_{3D} + L_{2D} + L_{SMPL}, \tag{3}$$

$$L_{3D} = \Sigma_{t=1}^{T}||jp_t^{3d} - \hat{jp}_t^{3d}||_2, \tag{4}$$

$$L_{2D} = \Sigma_{t=1}^{T}||jp_t^{2d} - \hat{jp}_t^{2d}||_2, \tag{5}$$

$$L_{SMPL} = ||\beta - \hat{\beta}||_2 + \Sigma_{t=1}^{T}||\theta_t - \hat{\theta}_t||_2. \tag{6}$$

For implementation details, please refer to the supplementary material.

4   Experiments

To demonstrate the effectiveness of our proposed method, we evaluate our method in terms of the overall accuracy and smoothness of the estimated motion on MPI-INF-3DPH [48], 3DPW [10], and human 3.6M [49]. In the following sections, we will first describe the main datasets used to train and evaluate *MEVA*. Then in Sect. 4.2 we provide extensive evaluation results. Finally, in Sect. 4.3, we provide the ablation studies for our proposed method.

4.1   Datasets

For the motion VAE, we use motion sequences from AMASS [9] for training and sequences from 3DPW [10] for evaluation. For training with videos, in addition to the train split of MPI-INF-3DPH [48], 3DPW [10], and human 3.6M [49], which have 3D joint annotation, we also use InstaVariety [6] and PennAction [50] which contain 2D joint annotation.

For training our motion VAE, we use **AMASS** [9]. It is a recent dataset that contains a large sample of human motion sequences in SMPL parameters. These sequences are fitted from MoCap sequences using Mosh++ [9]. There are in total 13k motion sequences with varying length. We use this dataset only for training our motion VAE.

For training with videos, **3DPW** is the only dataset that contains paired SMPL parameters and video sequences (which provide direct supervision to

MEVA). The videos from this dataset are mostly outdoors and in-the-wild. It uses paired IMU sensors and video input to compute the near ground truth SMPL pose and shape parameters. This is a relatively small dataset and we use the official split in [10] for train, validation, and test. There are in total 60 videos with varying length (24 train, 24 test, 12 val). **MPI-INF-3DHP** is a dataset that contains 3D joint position annotation. It is captured using a multiview camera setup, and the 3D joint annotation is calculated through multiview methods [48]. There are 8 subjects and 16 videos per subject, in total 128 videos with varying length. We use the official test and train split. **H3.6M** is a popular pose estimation dataset that contains 3D joint position annotations, captured indoors with MoCap markers. Notice that a number of previous works [1–3,6,7] had access to a near-ground truth SMPL pose and shape parameters calculated by the Mosh [51] method. However, this annotation has since been removed from public access due to legal issues. SMPL parameters provide the best supervision, as noted in [33], so for a fair comparison we retrain some of the state-of-the-art methods without such supervision. There are 840 videos in total across 7 subjects in H3.6M and we use the official train/test subject split ([S1, S5, S6, S7, S8] vs [S9, S11]). During preprocessing, we subsample every 5 frames from the dataset. The **PennAction** dataset contains human annotated ground truth 2D keypoints paired with video sequences. There are in total 2326 videos with varying length. **InstaVariety** dataset contains human annotated pseudo ground truth 2D keypoints paired with video sequences. The 2D keypionts are estimated using openpose [52]. There are in total 28,272 videos with varying length.

4.2   Evaluation Results and Analysis

Metrics. To best capture human motion, we utilize three popular metrics that measure the overall accuracy and smoothness of the motion. Mean per joint position error (MPJPE) and MPJPE after Procrustes Alignment (PA-MPJPE) measure the 3D joint positional discrepancy between the predicted and ground truth 3D joint positions in millimeters (mm), and are calculated after aligning the root position (human pelvis) of the 3D joint positions. Both MPJPE and PA-MPJPE serve as the accuracy indicator of the motion estimator. Acceleration error (ACC-ERR), proposed in [6], measures the difference between the predicted and ground truth 3D acceleration for each keypoint in mm/s^2. ACC-ERR serves as the major smoothness indicator for the estimated motion sequences. Acceleration is calculated using the finite difference between individual frames. It is imperative to view these metrics jointly: a low position error indicates overall correctness in motion capture and a better acceleration error marks a smooth and natural estimation of human motion.

Generalization of Motion VAE. In this section, we study the genealizability of our learned motion VAE. We report the reconstruction error of the VAE on unseen motion sequences from the 3DPW dataset. Table 1 shows VAE motion reconstruction error over the different splits of 3DPW. The Motion VAE model is the best performing model that is trained with all three forms of data augmentation techniques. Detailed analysis about the effects of data augmentation can be found in Sect. 4.3. The result shows that our VAE generalizes well to unseen sequences and the learned subspace can represent the human motion space with reasonable quality.

Table 1. VAE Reconstruction Test Error on 3DPW dataset Here, the VAE is tasked to encode and decode unseen motion sequences from the 3DPW dataset, and we calculate our metrics between the ground truth and reconstructed sequences. Motion sequences from different splits of 3DPW have varying difficulties, but are all unseen by our VAE.

	3DPW train split			3DPW val split			3DPW test split		
	MPJPE ↓	PA-MPJPE ↓	ACC-ERR ↓	MPJPE ↓	PA-MPJPE ↓	ACC-ERR ↓	MPJPE ↓	PA-MPJPE ↓	ACC-ERR ↓
Motion VAE	72.7	52.3	8.9	72.1	52.9	9.3	58.7	43.9	8.2

Quantitative Results. The result in Table 2 shows that our method obtains state-of-the-art results on video motion estimation across all three test datasets. Overall, our method achieves comparable results in terms of position error (MPJPE and PA-MPJPE) while significantly improving the smoothness (acceleration error), signifying a smoother and more natural motion estimation without sacrificing accuracy. Notice that all methods in italics have access to SMPL parameter annotation to the H3.6M dataset, which has since been removed from the web due to legal reasons. The SMPL parameters provide the most direct supervision for the task, so the performance gain is significant especially on the H3.6M test set. For a more direct comparison, we retrain the previous state-of-the-art method, VIBE [1], using the official implementation with the exact same datasets as ours. On 3DPW, under the same training condition, *MEVA* outperforms VIBE on almost all three metrics while reducing the acceleration error by 54.3%, 59.3%, and 41.3 %, respectively. Even compared to VIBE trained with extra data, our model achieves comparable results in accuracy while sporting a great reduction in acceleration error, except for the H3.6M dataset. Note that the H3.6M dataset contains mainly indoor scenes with limited background variation and models trained with direct SMPL supervision tend to perform well on this dataset. Compared to HMMR [6], which is the state-of-the-art on smoothness, our model still achieves a smoother result (23.7% reduction in acceleration error) while improving greatly in MPJPE by 25.4%.

Qualitatively Results. As motions are best seen in videos, please refer to the supplementary video for qualitative results. Overall, our model achieves better acceleration error while preserving high joint position accuracy, resulting in an overall smooth and natural motion.

Table 2. Testing error of state-of-the-art models on 3DPW, MPI-INF-3DHP, and H3.6M. Here we compare with state-of-the-art methods on video pose estimation, and report metrics on positional accuracy (MPJPE and PA-MPJPE) as well as acceleration error. Notice that since an important annotation of H3.6M dataset has since been made unavailable, we put all methods that are trained with such supervision in italics. The most fair comparison is between our method and VIBE [1], the previous best-performing model (trained using the same datasets).

	3DPW			MPI-INF-3DHP			H3.6M		
	MPJPE ↓	PA-MPJPE ↓	ACC-ERR ↓	MPJPE ↓	PA-MPJPE ↓	ACC-ERR ↓	MPJPE ↓	PA-MPJPE ↓	ACC-ERR ↓
HMR (w/ H3.6M SMPL) [7]	*130.0*	*76.7*	*37.4*	*124.2*	*89.8*	*–*	*88*	*56.8*	*–*
HMMR (w/ H3.6M SMPL) [6]	*116.5*	*72.6*	*15.2*	*–*	*–*	*–*	*–*	*56.9*	*–*
SPIN (w/ H3.6M SMPL) [3]	*96.9*	*59.2*	*29.8*	*105.2*	*67.5*	*–*	*–*	*41.1*	*–*
Sun et al. (w/ H3.6M SMPL) [2]	*–*	*69.5*	*–*	*–*	*–*	*–*	*59.1*	*42.4*	*–*
VIBE (w/ H3.6M SMPL) [1]	*82.9*	*51.9*	*23.4*	*96.6*	*64.6*	*31.2*	*65.6*	*41.4*	*27.3*
VIBE (w/o H3.6M SMPL) [1]	91.9	57.6	25.4	103.9	68.9	27.3	78.0	53.3	27.3
MEVA (w/o H3.6M SMPL)	86.9	54.7	**11.6**	96.4	65.4	**11.1**	76.0	53.2	**15.3**

4.3 Ablation Experiments

Effect of Data Augmentation for Training the Motion VAE. As mentioned in Sect. 3.3, data augmentation performed on the AMASS dataset significantly improves the generalizability of our motion VAE. Table 3 demonstrates the VAE reconstruction error on the unseen sequences from the 3DPW dataset (train/test/val), with various levels of data augmentation techniques. Overall, RR (random root) rotation is essential since the motion sequences in AMASS dataset, captured mostly in MoCap studio, have a single fixed initial root rotation. Model trained only on AMASS would suffer greatly when it encounters variation in root rotation. Changing the sampling frame rate (FR) and flip left and right (LR) also provide a significant boost to generalizability. Using all three augmentation techniques results in our best performing motion VAE.

Table 3. Ablation of Data augmentation for VAE. Here we show the effects of data augmentation on the VAE. RR: random root rotation, FR: different sampling framerate, LR: left and right flip

	Train			Val			Test		
	MPJPE ↓	PA-MPJPE ↓	ACC-ERR ↓	MPJPE ↓	PA-MPJPE ↓	ACC-ERR ↓	MPJPE ↓	PA-MPJPE ↓	ACC-ERR ↓
No Aug	200.2	86.0	15.9	181.7	90.5	15.8	172.8	75.2	14.1
RR	146.3	78.0	12.1	133.9	81.2	13.0	115.0	70.4	11.0
FR + LR	291.0	63.03	14.7	308.8	66.1	16.1	261.9	58.9	13.3
FR + LR + RR	**72.7**	**52.3**	**8.9**	**72.1**	**52.9**	**9.3**	**58.7**	**43.9**	**8.2**

Coarse Motion vs Fine Motion Retrieval. *MEVA* benefits from an explicit breakdown of coarse and fine motion retrieval, using a temporal compressive step that captures the overall motion in a given human motion sequence. Just how much coarse/smooth motion information is retrieved in the framework? Table 4 shows the result of *MEVA* if trained only using the VME (capturing only coarse motion). Notice that *MEVA* with only VME achieves result similar to HMMR

[6], the previous state-of-the-art in producing low acceleration error motion estimation. An illustrative visualization of coarse and fine motion decomposition can be found in Fig. 4.

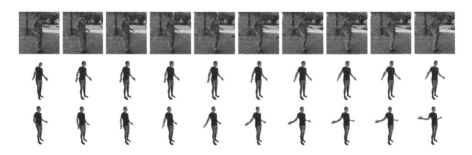

Fig. 4. Breakdown of coarse and fine human motion. The first row of estimated human is the coarse part of the motion (output of VME), while the second row adds back the fine details (output of MRR).

Table 4. Ablation of MEVA. Here we show the *MEVA* model trained with only Variational Motion Estimator (without Motion Residual Regressor) or without using pretrained VAE.

	3DPW		
	MPJPE ↓	PA-MPJPE ↓	ACC-ERR ↓
MEVA-VME only	118.1	73.7	15.4
MEVA-without using pretrained VAE	95.9	59.7	14.1
MEVA	**86.9**	**54.7**	**11.6**

Effects of the Pretrained Motion VAE. *MEVA* benefits from using a pretrained motion VAE's latent space. As argued in Sect. 3.3, using a pretrained VAE provides a human motion subspace that assists in constraining the estimated motion sequences to be natural and plausible human motion. Table 4 shows the result of *MEVA* trained without using a pretrained VAE (not using the pretrained D_{vae}). In this case, the whole framework is trained end-to-end from scratch. Here we observe that the model performed relatively well in both accuracy and smoothness, demonstrating the power of our two-stage estimation framework. However, upon visual inspection, as shown in Fig. 5, a few kinematically invalid human poses are estimated during the sequence, resulting in an overall accurate but flawed estimation.

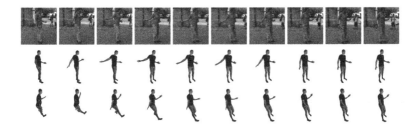

Fig. 5. MEVA results without using pretrained VAE. Here we show an ablative study where we do not use a pretrained VAE. The second row shows **MEVA** result without using a pretrained VAE and the first row shows our full model estimation. Notice that the model estimates unnatural human poses in the first few frames.

5 Conclusion

We have shown that to achieve temporally smooth and accurate 3D human pose estimates, it is important to learn a compressive model that encodes the smoothness of general human motion while also learning an image-based regression model that can capture person-specific motion. We propose a two-stage model that first trains a Variational Autoencoder to model the general statistics of coarse/smooth human motion and then learns a person-specific motion refinement regression module to retain motions not captured by the general motion model. Through comprehensive experiments, we demonstrate that our method produces both smooth and accurate motion.

Acknowledgements. This project was sponsored in part by IARPA (D17PC00340), and JST AIP Acceleration Research Grant (JPMJCR20U1).

References

1. Kocabas, M., Athanasiou, N., Black, M.J.: VIBE: video inference for human body pose and shape estimation. In: Proceedings of the IEEE/CVF Conference on Computer Vision and Pattern Recognition, pp. 5253–5263 (2020)
2. Xu, Y., Zhu, S.C., Tung, T.: DenseRaC: joint 3D pose and shape estimation by dense render-and-compare. In: 2019 IEEE/CVF International Conference on Computer Vision (ICCV), pp. 7759–7769 (2019)
3. Kolotouros, N., Pavlakos, G., Black, M.J., Daniilidis, K.: Learning to reconstruct 3D human pose and shape via model-fitting in the loop. In: 2019 IEEE/CVF International Conference on Computer Vision (ICCV), pp. 2252–2261 (2019)
4. Georgakis, G.V., Li, R., Karanam, S., Chen, T., Kosecka, J., Wu, Z.: Hierarchical kinematic human mesh recovery. ArXiv abs/2003.04232 (2020)
5. Güler, R.A., Neverova, N., Kokkinos, I.: DensePose: dense human pose estimation in the wild. In: 2018 IEEE/CVF Conference on Computer Vision and Pattern Recognition, pp. 7297–7306 (2018)
6. Kanazawa, A., Zhang, J.Y., Felsen, P., Malik, J.: Learning 3D human dynamics from video. In: 2019 IEEE/CVF Conference on Computer Vision and Pattern Recognition (CVPR), pp. 5607–5616 (2019)

7. Kanazawa, A., Black, M.J., Jacobs, D.W., Malik, J.: End-to-end recovery of human shape and pose. In: 2018 IEEE/CVF Conference on Computer Vision and Pattern Recognition, pp. 7122–7131 (2018)
8. Hossain, M.R.I., Little, J.J.: Exploiting temporal information for 3D human pose estimation. In: Ferrari, V., Hebert, M., Sminchisescu, C., Weiss, Y. (eds.) ECCV 2018. LNCS, vol. 11214, pp. 69–86. Springer, Cham (2018). https://doi.org/10.1007/978-3-030-01249-6_5
9. Mahmood, N., Ghorbani, N., Troje, N.F., Pons-Moll, G., Black, M.J.: AMASS: archive of motion capture as surface shapes. In: 2019 IEEE/CVF International Conference on Computer Vision (ICCV), pp. 5441–5450 (2019)
10. von Marcard, T., Henschel, R., Black, M.J., Rosenhahn, B., Pons-Moll, G.: Recovering accurate 3D human pose in the wild using IMUs and a moving camera. In: Ferrari, V., Hebert, M., Sminchisescu, C., Weiss, Y. (eds.) ECCV 2018. LNCS, vol. 11214, pp. 614–631. Springer, Cham (2018). https://doi.org/10.1007/978-3-030-01249-6_37
11. Pavlakos, G., et al.: Expressive body capture: 3D hands, face, and body from a single image. In: 2019 IEEE/CVF Conference on Computer Vision and Pattern Recognition (CVPR), pp. 10967–10977 (2019)
12. Loper, M., Mahmood, N., Romero, J., Pons-Moll, G., Black, M.J.: SMPL: a skinned multi-person linear model. ACM Trans. Graph. 34, 248:1–248:16 (2015)
13. Anguelov, D., Srinivasan, P., Koller, D., Thrun, S., Rodgers, J., Davis, J.: SCAPE: shape completion and animation of people. ACM Trans. Graph. 24, 408–416 (2005)
14. Grauman, K., Shakhnarovich, G., Darrell, T.: Inferring 3D structure with a statistical image-based shape model. In: Proceedings of the IEEE International Conference on Computer Vision, vol. 1, pp. 641–648 (2003)
15. Agarwal, A., Triggs, B.: Recovering 3D human pose from monocular images. IEEE Trans. Pattern Anal. Mach. Intell. 28, 44–58 (2006)
16. Sigal, L., Balan, A., Black, M.J.: Combined discriminative and generative articulated pose and non-rigid shape estimation. In: Advances in Neural Information Processing Systems 20 - Proceedings of the 2007 Conference, pp. 1–8 (2009)
17. Zhou, S., Fu, H., Liu, L., Cohen-Or, D., Han, X.: Parametric reshaping of human bodies in images. In: ACM SIGGRAPH 2010 Papers, SIGGRAPH 2010, vol. 29, pp. 1–10 (2010)
18. Peng Guan, Weiss, A., Bălan, A.O., Black, M.J.: Estimating human shape and pose from a single image. In: 2009 IEEE 12th International Conference on Computer Vision, pp. 1381–1388 (2009)
19. Bogo, F., Kanazawa, A., Lassner, C., Gehler, P., Romero, J., Black, M.J.: Keep it SMPL: automatic estimation of 3D human pose and shape from a single image. In: Leibe, B., Matas, J., Sebe, N., Welling, M. (eds.) ECCV 2016. LNCS, vol. 9909, pp. 561–578. Springer, Cham (2016). https://doi.org/10.1007/978-3-319-46454-1_34
20. Omran, M., Lassner, C., Pons-Moll, G., Gehler, P., Schiele, B.: Neural body fitting: unifying deep learning and model based human pose and shape estimation. In: Proceedings - 2018 International Conference on 3D Vision, 3DV 2018, pp. 484–494 (2018)
21. Guler, R.A., Kokkinos, I.: HoloPose: holistic 3D human reconstruction in-the-wild. In: Proceedings of the IEEE Computer Society Conference on Computer Vision and Pattern Recognition, June 2019, pp. 10876–10886 (2019)
22. Tan, J.K.V., Budvytis, I., Cipolla, R.: Indirect deep structured learning for 3D human body shape and pose prediction. In: British Machine Vision Conference 2017, BMVC 2017, pp. 1–11 (2017)

23. Tung, H.Y.F., Tung, H.W., Yumer, E., Fragkiadaki, K.: Self-supervised learning of motion capture. In: Advances in Neural Information Processing Systems, December 2017, pp. 5237–5247 (2017)
24. Pavlakos, G., Zhu, L., Zhou, X., Daniilidis, K.: Learning to estimate 3D human pose and shape from a single color image. In: Proceedings of the IEEE Computer Society Conference on Computer Vision and Pattern Recognition, pp. 459–468 (2018)
25. Pavllo, D., Feichtenhofer, C., Grangier, D., Auli, M.: 3D human pose estimation in video with temporal convolutions and semi-supervised training. In: Proceedings of the IEEE Computer Society Conference on Computer Vision and Pattern Recognition, June 2019, pp. 7745–7754 (2019)
26. Dabral, R., Mundhada, A., Kusupati, U., Afaque, S., Sharma, A., Jain, A.: Learning 3D human pose from structure and motion. In: Ferrari, V., Hebert, M., Sminchisescu, C., Weiss, Y. (eds.) ECCV 2018. LNCS, vol. 11213, pp. 679–696. Springer, Cham (2018). https://doi.org/10.1007/978-3-030-01240-3_41
27. Xu, J., Yu, Z., Ni, B., Yang, J., Yang, X., Zhang, W.: Deep kinematics analysis for monocular 3D human pose estimation. In: Proceedings of the IEEE/CVF Conference on Computer Vision and Pattern Recognition (CVPR) (2020)
28. Mehta, D., et al.: VNect real-time 3D human pose estimation with a single RGB camera. ACM Trans. Graph. **36**, 1–13 (2017)
29. Mehta, D., et al.: Xnect: real-time multi-person 3D motion capture with a single RGB camera. In: SIGGRAPH 2020 (2020)
30. Ren, L., Patrick, A., Efros, A.A., Hodgins, J.K., Rehg, J.M.: A data-driven approach to quantifying natural human motion. In: SIGGRAPH 2005 (2005)
31. Urtasun, R., Fleet, D.J., Fua, P.: 3D people tracking with Gaussian process dynamical models. In: Proceedings of the IEEE Computer Society Conference on Computer Vision and Pattern Recognition, vol. 1, pp. 238–245 (2006)
32. Ormoneit, D., Sidenbladh, H., Black, M.J., Hastie, T.: Learning and tracking cyclic human motion. In: Advances in Neural Information Processing Systems (2001)
33. Wang, Z., et al.: Learning diverse stochastic human-action generators by learning smooth latent transitions. ArXiv abs/1912.10150 (2020)
34. Cai, H., Bai, C., Tai, Y.-W., Tang, C.-K.: Deep video generation, prediction and completion of human action sequences. In: Ferrari, V., Hebert, M., Sminchisescu, C., Weiss, Y. (eds.) ECCV 2018. LNCS, vol. 11206, pp. 374–390. Springer, Cham (2018). https://doi.org/10.1007/978-3-030-01216-8_23
35. Walker, J., Marino, K., Gupta, A., Hebert, M.: The pose knows: video forecasting by generating pose futures. In: The IEEE International Conference on Computer Vision (ICCV) (2017)
36. Plappert, M., Mandery, C., Asfour, T.: Learning a bidirectional mapping between human whole-body motion and natural language using deep recurrent neural networks. Robot. Auton. Syst. **109**, 13–26 (2018)
37. Ahuja, C., Morency, L.P.: Language2pose: Natural language grounded pose forecasting. In: 2019 International Conference on 3D Vision (3DV), pp. 719–728 (2019)
38. Yamada, T., Matsunaga, H., Ogata, T.: Paired recurrent autoencoders for bidirectional translation between robot actions and linguistic descriptions. IEEE Robot. Autom. Lett. **3**, 3441–3448 (2018)
39. Lee, H.Y., et al.: Dancing to music. In: NeurIPS (2019)
40. Fragkiadaki, K., Levine, S., Felsen, P., Malik, J.: Recurrent network models for human dynamics. In: Proceedings of the IEEE International Conference on Computer Vision 2015 Inter, pp. 4346–4354 (2015)

41. Yan, X., et al.: MT-VAE: learning motion transformations to generate multimodal human dynamics. In: Ferrari, V., Hebert, M., Sminchisescu, C., Weiss, Y. (eds.) ECCV 2018. LNCS, vol. 11209, pp. 276–293. Springer, Cham (2018). https://doi.org/10.1007/978-3-030-01228-1_17

42. Yuan, Y., Kitani, K.: Diverse trajectory forecasting with determinantal point processes. In: International Conference on Learning Representations (2020)

43. Butepage, J., Black, M.J., Kragic, D., Kjellstrom, H.: Deep representation learning for human motion prediction and classification. In: The IEEE Conference on Computer Vision and Pattern Recognition (CVPR) (2017)

44. Yuan, Y., Kitani, K.: DLow: diversifying latent flows for diverse human motion prediction. In: Vedaldi, A., Bischof, H., Brox, T., Frahm, J.-M. (eds.) ECCV 2020. LNCS, vol. 12354, pp. 346–364. Springer, Cham (2020). https://doi.org/10.1007/978-3-030-58545-7_20

45. Zhou, Y., Barnes, C., Lu, J., Yang, J., Li, H.: On the continuity of rotation representations in neural networks. In: 2019 IEEE/CVF Conference on Computer Vision and Pattern Recognition (CVPR), pp. 5738–5746 (2019)

46. Kingma, D.P., Welling, M.: Auto-encoding variational bayes. In: 2nd International Conference on Learning Representations, ICLR 2014 - Conference Track Proceedings, pp. 1–14 (2014)

47. Walker, J., Marino, K., Gupta, A., Hebert, M.: The pose knows: video forecasting by generating pose futures. In: Proceedings of the IEEE International Conference on Computer Vision, October 2017, pp. 3352–3361 (2017)

48. Mehta, D., et al.: Monocular 3D human pose estimation in the wild using improved CNN supervision. In: 2017 International Conference on 3D Vision (3DV), pp. 506–516 (2017)

49. Ionescu, C., Papava, D., Olaru, V., Sminchisescu, C.: Human3.6M: large scale datasets and predictive methods for 3D human sensing in natural environments. IEEE Trans. Pattern Anal. Mach. Intell. **36**, 1325–1339 (2014)

50. Zhang, W., Zhu, M., Derpanis, K.G.: From actemes to action: a strongly-supervised representation for detailed action understanding. In: Proceedings of the IEEE International Conference on Computer Vision, pp. 2248–2255 (2013)

51. Loper, M., Mahmoody, N., Blackz, M.J.: MoSh: motion and shape capture from sparse markers. ACM Trans. Graph. **33**, 1–13 (2014)

52. Cao, Z., Simon, T., Wei, S.E., Sheikh, Y.: Realtime multi-person 2D pose estimation using part affinity fields. In: CVPR (2017)

Spatial Temporal Attention Graph Convolutional Networks with Mechanics-Stream for Skeleton-Based Action Recognition

Katsutoshi Shiraki[✉], Tsubasa Hirakawa, Takayoshi Yamashita, and Hironobu Fujiyoshi

Chubu University, 1200 Matsumotocho, Kasugai-shi, Aichi, Japan
{siraki,hirakawa}@mprg.cs.chubu.ac.jp,
{yamashita,fujiyoshi}@isc.chubu.ac.jp

Abstract. The static relationship between joints and the dynamic importance of joints leads to high accuracy in skeletal action recognition. Nevertheless, existing methods define the graph structure beforehand by skeletal patterns, so they cannot capture features considering the relationship between joints specific to actions. Moreover, the importance of joints is expected to be different for each action. We propose spatial-temporal attention graph convolutional networks (STA-GCN). It acquires an attention edge that represents a static relationship between joints for each action and an attention node that represents the dynamic importance of joints for each time. STA-GCN is the first method to consider joint importance and relationship at the same time. The proposed method consists of multiple networks, that reflect the difference of spatial (coordinates) and temporal (velocity and acceleration) characteristics as mechanics-stream. We aggregate these network predictions as final result. We show the potential that the attention edge and node can be easily applied to existing methods and improve the performance. Experimental results with NTU-RGB+D and NTU-RGB+D120 demonstrate that it is possible to obtain a attention edge and node specific to the action that can explain behavior and achieves state-of-the-art performances.

1 Introduction

Human action recognition has been actively proposed and widely applied to surveillance systems and sports analysis. The skeleton based method is robust to environmental and viewpoint changes. These methods convert the skeletal data into a grid structure or sequence and extract features using a convolutional neural network (CNN) or a recurrent neural network (RNN) [1–13]. Grid structures or sequences cannot represent human skeletons completely. Meanwhile, graph structure can represent the skeleton naturally.

A graph convolutional network (GCN) have been used for skeletal action recognition that inputs skeletons as a graph structure [14–20]. A GCN applies

© Springer Nature Switzerland AG 2021
H. Ishikawa et al. (Eds.): ACCV 2020, LNCS 12626, pp. 341–357, 2021.
https://doi.org/10.1007/978-3-030-69541-5_21

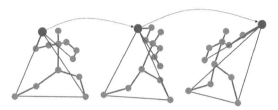

Fig. 1. Important relationships between joints and important joints in throwing.

convolutions to a graph structure and extract features. By using a GCN, features can be acquired that consider relationships between joints, so that complex actions can be recognized. A typical GCN-based method is spatial-temporal GCN (ST-GCN) [14]. ST-GCN achieves high performance by representing skeletons using two graph structures: spatial and temporal graphs. The graph connection in ST-GCN is fixed by human skeleton patterns. However, the important relationships between joints are expected to change depending on each action. For example, when we throw an object with the right arm while using the left leg as an axis foot, the relationship between the left leg and the right arm is important (Fig. 1). Therefore, fixing connection patterns in advance cannot acquire features considering joint relationships specific to action.

To solve this problem, there are methods to automatically obtain graph connection patterns from feature maps [17,18]. These methods acquires the connection pattern from the feature map representing the optimal relationship between joints for each action. However, these methods focus only on the relationships between joints. The important joints differ for each action, and the importance may change over the action frames. Considering the importance of different joints for each action and each frame could improve the recognition performance.

In this paper, we propose spatial-temporal attention graph convolutional networks (STA-GCN) that consider the important joint relationships and the importance of joints that differ for each action. An *attention edge* represents important relationship between joints statically. By convolving the feature map with the attention edge, features considering the important relationships between joints can be acquired. An *attention node* represents the dynamic importance of joints for each frame as a two-dimensional map. The attention edge and node are acquired during forward propagation. The attention node emphasizes important joints in a feature map by attention mechanism. Consequently, our method emphasizes the spatial and temporal features at the same time. We call the combined graph as a *spatial-temporal attention graph* (attention graph). The attention graph enables a network to learn the important joints and relationships between joints. Attention edge and node can be acquired by adding a module called *attetntion branch* to the network. Therefore, it can be applied into existing skeleton-based methods.

In addition, we introduce a multi-modal learning. We use six modals: coordinates, velocity, and acceleration for joint and bone. Existing methods have revealed multi-modal learning is effective [18,20]. However, few methods have examined the effects of modal combinations. Coordinates indicate spatial position, and velocity and acceleration indicate the amount of temporal movement, so the characteristics of each modal are different. Also, since the scales of the coordinates, velocity, and acceleration are different, training on the same network may be difficult. Therefore, we propose a *mechanics-stream structure* based on the spatial-temporal mechanical characteristics and value scale of each modal. Experimental results show the effect of modal combinations on accuracy.

2 Related Work

Skeleton-Based Action Recognition. Skeleton-based action recognition can be divided into two methods: handcrafted feature based and deep learning based. The handcrafted-feature based methods use features designed on the basis of human knowledge [21–23]. The deep-learning based methods can acquire features automatically, many methods using CNNs and RNNs have been proposed due to the recent advances in deep learning [1–13]. The CNN-based methods [1–6] manually convert skeletons into a grid structure and use it as an input. The RNN-based methods [7–13] input skeletons as a sequence and extract features representing temporal relationship between consecutive frames. CNN- and RNN-based methods achieve high recognition accuracy. However, since CNN and RNN represent the input data as a grid structure or sequence, they cannot completely represent human skeletons. To solve this problem, methods representing skeletons as a graph structure have been proposed and have achieved higher accuracy [14–20]. When the skeletons are represented as a graph structure, nodes correspond to joint coordinates, and edges correspond to relationships between joints. The efficient representation between joints can recognize complex actions.

Graph Convolutional Networks. GCN is a CNN that inputs a graph structure [24–26]. Kipf and Welling [26] performed graph convolution in the frequency domain using the graph Fourier transform. GCN are used in many fields because the graph structure can effectively represent various data [27–34]. In [27] and [28], the molecular structure was represented as a graph, and a GCN was applied to molecular classification. In [31] and [32], a GCN was applied to video summarization by connecting objects with high spatial and temporal correlation in the video with edges.

Visual Explanation for Deep Learning. Research into understanding the basis of cognitive judgment in deep learning is being actively pursued and visual explanation using attention maps are widely investigated [35–38]. Visual explanation methods can be divided into two types: bottom-up and top-down. In the bottom-up methods [37,38], an attention map is obtained by using gradient, noise, and class information. Therefore, backpropagation must be performed to obtain the attention map. Since it can be applied to various networks, it is widely

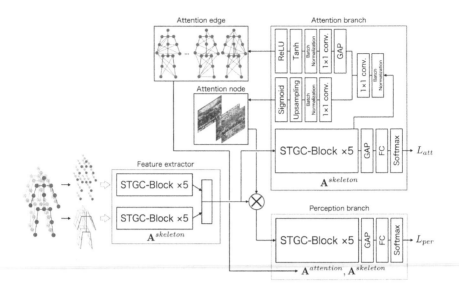

Fig. 2. Spatial-temporal attention graph convolutional networks.

used as a visual explanation method for deep learning. The top-down methods have been studied more actively because they can acquire the attention map during forward propagation [35,36]. ABN [35] is a top-down method that acquires an attention map during forward propagation and applies it to the attention mechanism. ABN has an advantage that the network can be learned while gazing at important areas in image recognition, and realized high recognition performance and analysis of the network decision simultaneously.

3   Proposed Method

We propose a spatial-temporal attention graph convolutional networks (STA-GCN) that considers the static relationships between joints and the dynamic importance of joints. Figure 2 shows the proposed network structure. STA-GCN consists of three modules: feature extractor, attention branch, and perception branch. The feature extractor extracts features of two input modals separately using multiple graph convolutional layers and then connects the feature maps. The attention branch generates an attention edge indicating the static relationship between joints and an attention node indicating a dynamic importance of joints for each frame. The perception branch outputs the final class probabilities by using the feature map obtained from the feature extractor, the attention node, a skeleton pattern, and attention edge.

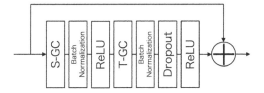

Fig. 3. Spatial-temporal graph convolutional block (STGC-Block).

3.1 Spatial-Temporal Graph Convolutional Block

The Spatial-Temporal Graph Convolutional Block (STGC-Block) shown in Fig. 2. Spatial Graph Convolution (S-GC) and Temporal Graph Convolution (T-GC) are graph convolutions for spatial and temporal graphs, respectively. A spatial graph connects joints in the same frame, and a temporal graph connects the same joints in adjacent frames. After each graph convolution layer, a batch normalization layer and a ReLU are arranged. A dropout is applied after T-GC, and each STGC-Block has a skip connection (Fig. 3).

Here, let $\mathbf{X}_{in} \in \mathbb{R}^{V \times C}$ be a feature input to a graph convolution with node V and dimension C and $\mathbf{A}^{skel} \in \mathbb{R}^{V \times V}$ be a skeleton pattern adjacency matrix, respectively. By using weight matrix $\mathbf{W}^{skel} \in \mathbb{R}^{V \times F}$ with the output dimension F, the graph convolution of $\mathbf{X}_{in}$ is defined by

$$\mathbf{X}_{out}^{skel} = \sum_q^Q \mathbf{M}_q^{skel} \circ \hat{\mathbf{A}}_q^{skel} \mathbf{X}_{in} \mathbf{W}_q^{skel}, \tag{1}$$

where $\mathbf{M}^{skel} \in \mathbb{R}^{V \times V}$ is a learning weight matrix for capturing the importance of edges. Q is an optional parameter that indicates the number of hops in the graph structure and can be connected to joints that are hops away. In the case of 1-hop, the graph structure becomes a human skeletal pattern because it connects joints that are one distance away. By increasing the number of hops, we can capture more global features. $\mathbf{M}^{skel}$, $\hat{\mathbf{A}}^{skel}$, and $\mathbf{W}^{skel}$ are defined separately for each Q. $\mathbf{A}_q^{skel} = \mathbf{A}_q + \mathbf{I}$ is calculated by the sum of $\mathbf{A}_q \in \mathbb{R}^{V \times V}$, which indicates the connection relationship with the adjacent node, and the identity matrix $\mathbf{I} \in \mathbb{R}^{V \times V}$, which indicates the loop structure. When graph convolution is performed, the normalized adjacency matrix of $\hat{\mathbf{A}}_q^{skel} = \Lambda_q^{-\frac{1}{2}} \mathbf{A}_q^{skel} \Lambda_q^{-\frac{1}{2}}$ is used, where $\Lambda \in \mathbb{R}^{V \times V}$ is a diagonal matrix with the eigenvalues of graph Laplacian as diagonal components, and the diagonal components are obtained by $\Lambda_{ii} = \sum_j (A_{ij}^{skel} + I_{ij})$. The output of the S-GC $\mathbf{X}_{out}^{skel}$ can be represented by a three-dimensional tensor $(F \times T \times V)$, where T indicates a frame. Therefore, T-GC can be implemented by general convolution with arbitrary kernel size $1 \times \Gamma$, as in ST-GCN [14].

3.2   Attention Branch

The attention branch generates the attention edge and node. In the attention branch, the feature map obtained from the feature extractor is input to five STGC-Blocks. The feature map from the five STGC-Blocks passes through global average pooling (GAP), fully connected layers, and the softmax layer to obtain class probabilities. In addition, the attention edge and attention node are generated using the feature map from the last STGC-Block. The output of the last STGC-Block is a three-dimensional tensor $(C \times T \times V)$. To generate attention edges and nodes, the number of dimensions is reduced by using a batch normalization layer and a general convolution layer with a kernel size of 1×1. Then, an attention edge and an attention node are generated by individual processing.

Attention Edge. The attention edge is an adjacency matrix that represents the optimal joint relationship for each action. Attention edges can be expressed as $(K \times V \times V)$ by using the number K of attention edges generated for each action and the node V. K is an optional parameter. The feature map $(C \times T \times V)$ obtained by 1×1 general convolutional layers becomes $(C \times 1 \times V)$ due to the GAP layer. Next, the feature map is extended to $(KV \times 1 \times V)$ by 1×1 convolutional layers. The feature map is converted into $(K \times V \times V)$ and passes through the batch normalization. By passing through the Tanh function, low-value (i.e., insignificant) elements in the feature map are converted to negative values. Finally, by passing through the ReLU, negative elements in the feature map become zero. In short, there is no connection. Therefore, an attention edge with only important connections is generated. The generated attention edge is passed to the perception branch, and the graph is convolved with two graph structures (the skeleton pattern and the attention edge) in the perception branch.

Attention Node. The attention node represents the dynamic importance of joints that differ depending on each action and each frame. The attention node for each action can be expressed as $(T' \times V)$, where T' is frame. The feature map $(C \times T \times V)$ obtained by 1×1 general convolutional layers is reduced to $(1 \times T \times V)$ by the second 1×1 convolutional layer and passes through the batch normalization. At the T-GC layer in attention branch, the number of frames is reduced with one half compared to the feature map obtained from the feature extractor. Therefore, the feature map is extended to $(1 \times T' \times V)$. Then, the upsampling layer interpolates feature map by nearest neighbor. Finally, an attention node is generated by applying the sigmoid function to the feature map $(1 \times T' \times V)$.

The generated attention node is applied to the attention mechanism. The feature map that emphasizes important joints is obtained by reflecting the attention node on the feature map of the feature extractor. Reflecting the attention node is defined by

$$\mathbf{X}'_{out} = M(\mathbf{X}^{FE}_{out}) \cdot \mathbf{X}^{FE}_{out}, \tag{2}$$

where $\mathbf{X}_{out}^{FE}$ is a feature map from the feature extractor, and $M(\mathbf{X}_{out}^{FE})$ indicates an attention node. The feature map $\mathbf{X}'_{out}$ in which important joints are emphasized is used as input for the perception branch.

3.3   Perception Branch

The perception branch inputs a feature map in which important joints are emphasized and performs graph convolution with two graph structures: a human skeleton pattern and an attention edge. Let $\mathbf{A}^{att} \in \mathbb{R}^{K \times V \times V}$ be the attention edge and $\mathbf{X}_{in} \in \mathbb{R}^{V \times C}$ be the input feature map. By using the weight matrix $\mathbf{W}^{att} \in \mathbb{R}^{K \times V \times F}$ with output dimension F, the graph convolution with $\mathbf{A}^{att}$ and $\mathbf{X}_{in}$ is defined as follows:

$$\mathbf{X}_{out}^{att} = \sum_{k=1}^{K} \hat{\mathbf{A}}_k^{att} \mathbf{X}_{in} \mathbf{W}_k^{att}, \tag{3}$$

where K is the number of attention graphs generated for each action. $\hat{\mathbf{A}}^{att}$ is a normalized adjacency matrix, which performs normalization in the same way as Eq. (1). Attention edge emphasizes the relationship of joints for each action, but human actions essentially depend on the skeletal pattern. Therefore in the perception branch, graph convolutions are performed for the both attention edge and the human skeleton pattern. We denote outputs of graph convolution for attention edge and skeleton pattern as $\mathbf{X}_{out}^{att}$ and $\mathbf{X}_{out}^{skel}$, respectively. $\mathbf{X}_{out}^{skel}$ is calculated in the same way as Eq. (1). The output $\mathbf{X}_{out}$ can be obtained by

$$\mathbf{X}_{out} = \mathbf{X}_{out}^{skel} + \mathbf{X}_{out}^{att}. \tag{4}$$

By using multiple STGC-Blocks, a feature map is obtained that considers important relationships between joints and important joints. The acquired feature map passes through the GAP layer and the fully connected layer and is sent to the softmax to obtain the class probability. We use the output from the perception branch as the final class probability of the network.

3.4   Learning Method

The network of the proposed method has two branches (attention and perception), and class probabilities are obtained from each branch. The learning error L of the proposed method is calculated by $L = L_{att} + L_{per}$, where L_{att} and L_{per} are the learning errors of the attention and perception branches, respectively. The learning error of each branch is calculated using the cross entropy error.

3.5   Mechanics-Stream

From the joint coordinates of the skeletons, the joint velocity, joint acceleration, bones, bone velocity, and bone acceleration are calculated and input to the network. The joint coordinates and bones contain spatial position information,

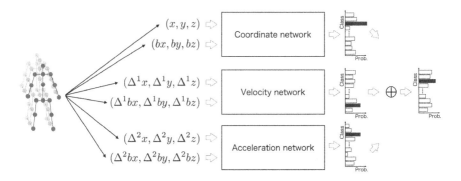

Fig. 4. Mechanics-stream structure.

while the velocity and acceleration contain information on temporal movement. Therefore, the characteristics of coordinates, velocity, and acceleration are different. In addition, it is considered that learning is difficult even if those are input to the same network because the scales of their values are different. We propose a mechanics-stream structure to solve the problems of different spatial-temporal characteristics and different value scales of each modal.

Figure 4 shows the mechanics-stream structure, which prepares three networks for six modals. Two types of modals are input to one network. The mechanics-stream structure consists of a coordinate network that inputs joint coordinates and bones, a velocity network that inputs joint and bone velocities, and an acceleration network that inputs joint and bone accelerations. The three networks are trained separately. The class probabilities obtained from each network are summed for each class to obtain the final class probability.

Multi-modal. Joint velocity, joint acceleration, bones, bone velocity, and bone acceleration are calculated on the basis of joint coordinates. The joint velocity $\Delta^1 v_A^t = (\Delta^1 x, \Delta^1 y, \Delta^1 z)$ of a joint $v_A = (x, y, z)$ in the t frame indicates the amount of movement of each joint frame, which is calculated by

$$\Delta^1 v_A^t = v_A^{t-1} - v_A^t. \tag{5}$$

In addition, the joint acceleration $\Delta^2 v_A^t = (\Delta^2 x, \Delta^2 y, \Delta^2 z)$ of the joint v_A in the t frame can be obtained by using the formula of linear action with uniform acceleration as follows:

$$\Delta^2 v_A^t = \frac{(\Delta^1 v_A^t)^2 - (\Delta^1 v_A^{t-1})^2}{2}. \tag{6}$$

A bone is the distance in the x, y, and z directions between each joint in the skeletal pattern. Therefore, the direction of the joint can be expressed. The bone $b_{AB}^t = (bx, by, bz)$ at the adjacent joint v_A^t, v_B^t in the skeletal pattern is determined by $b_{AB}^t = v_A^t - v_B^t$. The bone velocity is the amount of movement of the bone in one frame and expresses the angular velocity in the direction of the joint. The bone velocity $\Delta^1 b^t_{AB} = (\Delta^1 bx, \Delta^1 by, \Delta^1 bz)$ of the bone b^t_{AB} in the t frame can be calculated by the same calculation as Eq. (5) with the bone b^{t-1}_{AB} one frame before. The bone acceleration $\Delta^2 b^t_{AB} = (\Delta^2 bx, \Delta^2 by, \Delta^2 bz)$ can also be obtained by the same calculation as Eq. (6) with the bone velocity $\Delta^1 b^t_{AB}$ and $\Delta^1 b^{t-1}_{AB}$.

4   Experiment

We first evaluate the accuracy when applying the attention graph to a conventional method. In addition, we show the effectiveness of the mechanics-stream structure by changing the combination of modals input to the network. After that, we compare the proposed method with the conventional methods by using two datasets for action recognition.

4.1   Datasets

NTU-RGB+D. NTU-RGB+D [8] is a dataset for action recognition that with 60 different action classes such as daily and exercise action. The skeletons was captured by Microsoft Kinect v2, and the number of joints is 25, the skeleton consists of three-dimensional coordinates (X, Y, Z). This dataset has two evaluation methods: cross-subject and cross-view. Cross-subject divides the data of 40 subjects into training and validation. In cross-view, data taken from the left and right 45 degrees is used for training, and data taken from the front is used for validation. The subjects for training and validation is determined in advance.

NTU-RGB+D120. NTU-RGB+D120 [39] contains 120 action classes by adding 60 new action classes to NTU-RGB+D. As with NTU-RGB+D, the number of joints is 25, which consists of three-dimensional coordinates (X, Y, Z). While keeping the same shooting direction, the camera height and the distance to a subject are given. This is a large dataset for action recognition with skeletons. There are two evaluation methods: cross-subject and cross-setup. Cross-subject uses the data of the specified subjects for training and the data of the remaining subjects for validation. Cross-setup splits data for training and validation by IDs assigned on the basis of camera height and distance.

4.2   Implementation Details

The output dimensions of the STGC-Block in the feature extractor were 32 dimensions for the first three blocks and 64 dimensions for the remaining two blocks. Feature maps obtained from the different modals are concatenated to form a 128-dimensional feature map. The attention branch passes through two blocks with 128 output dimensions and three blocks with 256 output dimensions. The perception branch sets the same output dimension as the attention branch. In the skeletal pattern, hop Q is set to 3. The number of attention edges generated

Table 1. Accuracy of applying attention edge and attention node to conventional method. Evaluation was performed with cross-subject of NTU-RGB+D.

Attention edge	Attention node	ST-GCN [14]	AS-GCN [17]	2s-AGCN [18]
×	×	81.5	86.8	88.5
✓	×	84.1	86.9	89.2
×	✓	82.8	86.8	89.1
✓	✓	**84.8**	**87.0**	**89.3**

Table 2. Accuracy of an Independent network (Ind.net) and stream structure (X-stream). Evaluation was performed with cross-subject of NTU-RGB+D.

Input data	w/o attention		w/ attention	
	Ind. net	X-stream	Ind. net	X-stream
Joint (coordinate, velocity)	86.0	87.1	86.2	87.2
Bone (coordinate, velocity)	86.1		86.3	
Joint (coordinate, velocity, acceleration)	86.7	87.8	85.7	86.7
Bone (coordinate, velocity, acceleration)	86.7		85.8	
Coordinate (joint, bone)	87.5	89.3	88.6	**90.1**
Velocity (joint, bone)	85.6		87.0	
Coordinate (joint, bone)	87.5	89.1	88.6	89.4
Velocity (joint, bone)	85.6		87.0	
Acceleration (joint, bone)	74.6		77.2	

K for each action is set to 4. The kernel size Γ in temporal graph convolution is 9. The number of input frames is 300. In addition, we used the process implemented by Maosen *et al.* [17] to interpolate the inactive frame in the input frame with the active frame.

4.3   Adaptation of Attention Graph to Conventional Method

We show the effectiveness of the attention graph by applying the attention graph to the conventional methods [14,17,18]. The conventional method used for the experiment is a skeleton-based action recognition method whose code is published by the authors. The adapted method generates an attention graph by adding an attention branch to the hidden layer. The acquired attention graph is adapted to the attention mechanism and graph convolution as in the proposed method.

Table 1 shows the accuracy of applying the attention graph to the conventional methods. The accuracy was improved in most cases where only the attention edge or node was applied to the conventional method. In all conventional methods, the accuracy is highest when both the attention edge and node are applied. These results show that the attention edge and node contribute to improve recognition accuracy, and it is the most effective to apply both simultaneously.

Table 3. Comparison of accuracy on NTU-RGB+D.

Methods	Cross-subject (%)	Cross-view (%)
Lie group [22]	50.1	52.8
Deep LSTM [8]	60.7	67.3
TCN [1]	74.3	83.1
ST-GCN [14]	81.5	88.3
AS-GCN [17]	86.8	94.2
2s-AGCN [18]	88.5	95.1
AGC-LSTM [19]	89.2	95.0
DGNN [20]	89.9	**96.1**
STA-GCN	**90.1**	95.6

Table 4. Comparison of accuracy on NTU-RGB+D120.

Method	Cross-subject (%)	Cross-setup (%)
Soft RNN [40]	36.3	44.9
Dynamic skeleton [41]	50.8	54.7
Spatio-temporal LSTM [9]	55.7	57.9
GCA-LSTM [12]	58.3	59.2
Multi-task learning network [3]	58.4	57.9
FSNet [4]	59.9	62.4
Skeleton visualization [2]	60.3	63.2
Two-stream attention LSTM [13]	61.2	63.3
Multi-task CNN with RotClips [5]	62.2	61.8
Body pose evolution map [42]	64.6	66.9
SkeleMotion [6]	67.7	66.9
TSRJI [43]	67.9	62.8
ST-GCN [14]	72.8	75.4
STA-GCN	**83.9**	**86.5**

4.4 Accuracy with Multi-modal Learning

Table 2 shows the accuracy of an independent network (Ind.net) that inputs multiple modals and the accuracy of stream structure (X-stream). The structure in which the coordinates and velocity are trained in another network has higher accuracy than the structure in which the coordinates and velocity are trained in the same network. These results demonstrate the validity of the mechanics-stream structure. However, when acceleration was added as an input, the accuracy decreased even in the mechanics-stream structure. Acceleration is composed of very small values and does not have enough features for action recognition. Therefore, a model using acceleration achieved poorer result.

4.5   Comparison with State-of-the-Arts

Table 3 shows comparison results in NTU-RGB+D. Compared with the best conventional method (DGNN), STA-GCN improved the cross-subject by 0.2 points, and achieved comparable accuracy in cross-view.

Table 4 shows comparison results in NTU-RGB+D120. STA-GCN significant improbed both cross-subject and cross-setup compared with the best conventional methods. NTU-RGB+D120 contains similar action classes that are difficult to recognize due to the increase the number of classes. The proposed method, which can emphasize specific features by using an attention graph for each action, acquired different features even for similar action classes and contributed to accuracy improvement.

4.6   Visualization of Attention Graph

Figure 5 shows the attention graph obtained by the proposed method. We visualized the top 30 attention edges having the highest edge weight as red lines. The color of each joint indicates the value of the attention node: red joints is the most important and blue joints is the least important.

As for the throwing (Fig. 5(a)), the edge is concentrated on the right arm. The attention node shows that the importance of the right hand increases while right hand extends upward and decreases after the throw is completed. In addition, the importance of the left foot gradually increases during the throwing. This is due to the weight shifting to the left foot during the throw.

The attention edge of the kicking (Fig. 5(b)) was concentrated on the le.g. The edges of upper results are concentrated on the right leg and the edges of lower results are concentrated on the left leg because the kick was with right and left legs, respectively. This shows that the proposed method can obtain a connection pattern specific to the action.

The Attention edge of the jumping (Fig. 5(c)) is almost symmetrical. In the attention node, the legs have higher importance just before jumping. The importance of the center of the body increases during the jump. Since there are symmetrica attention edges and body center is high importance, jumping is an action using the whole body conceivably.

The attention edge of the drinking (Fig. 5(d)) is concentrated on the right arm because the right hand holds the drink. Although there was no concentration of edges on the face, the importance of the face as well as the right arm tended to be higher in the attention node. Drinking is similar to throwing, where the right arm is an important joint. Although, when throwing, there are important joints on the left leg, when drinking, few important joints appear on the lower body. This shows that the attention node can also express important joints specific to an action.

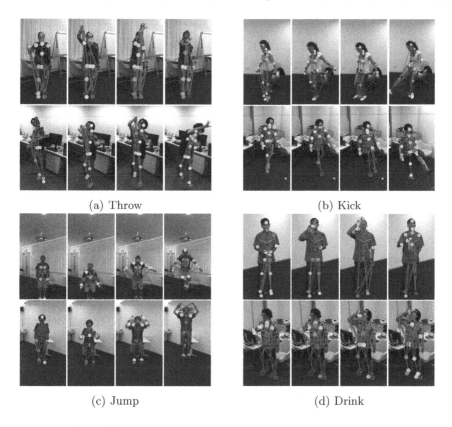

(a) Throw   (b) Kick

(c) Jump   (d) Drink

Fig. 5. Visualization of attention graph. (Color figure online)

4.7   Ablation Study

Effect of Each Modal on Attention Graph. To evaluate the effect of each modal on the attention graph, Fig. 6 shows the attention graph of the throwing when one modal is input. Although some attention edges concentrate to joints other than the arms, one attention edge concentrates to the arms for every modal inputs. Therefore, the arm can be regarded as important regardless of the modal input.

The attention node shows the right arm is the most important joint for joint coordinate and bone inputs. However, when the velocity was input, the results showed that the elbow and head had higher importance than the hand. When the joint acceleration is input, only the importance of the arm increases. With bone acceleration, the importance of the whole body increases. From these results, it is considered that the attention node when velocity and acceleration are input tends to strengthen joints with small values. Since the velocity is the amount of movement for one frame, the value of the moved joint (i.e., hands and toes) increases, while the values of body center, elbows, and knees decrease. The attention node played a role in increasing the value of the elbows and knees

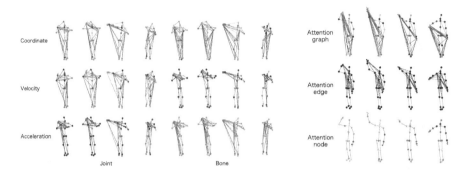

Fig. 6. Attention graph when one modal is input.   **Fig. 7.** Interaction of attention edge and node.

around large and important joints. Acceleration has a smaller value scale than coordinates and velocity. For joint acceleration, the value of the toe is very low and is difficult to increase even with the attention node. Therefore, only the joints around the arm that have slight values tended to be emphasized. Bone acceleration has the smallest value scale among all modals. It was difficult to determine which joints were important, resulting in increased whole body values.

Interaction of Attention Edge and Attention Node. To investigate the interaction between the attention edge and the attention node, Fig. 7 shows the attention of the throwing when acquiring only the attention edge, only the attention node, and both. When only the attention edge, the edge concentrate on the right arm, but there is no connection with the foot. The attention edge connects the highly correlated joints, so many edges connect to the relatively moving right and left hands. The relationship between the hand and the foot is also important, but in the upright throwing, the foot does not change relative to the hand movement. In addition, when only the attention node is acquired, a specific joint cannot be emphasized. If the attention node places a strong constraint on a specific joint, the joints are convoluted only by the skeletal pattern, making it difficult to transmit information between joints. In the case of acquiring both an attention edge and node, the importance of the right arm is increasing. Even if a particular joint is regarded as important, there is a connection with various joints by the attention edge and it is easy to transmit information to other joints. Similarly, the hand and foot edges were obtained not only for the highly correlated joints, but also to capture the relationships with important joints obtained from the attention node. Therefore, both important relationships between joints and the importance of joints need to be simultaneously acquired.

5   Conclusions

We proposed a STA-GCN that considers the static relationships between joints for each action and the dynamic importance of joints for each frame. The attention edge expresses the important connection for each action, and the attention node expresses the importance of the joint that differs for each frame. STA-GCN simultaneously generates an attention edge and node, and the attention node is adapted to the feature map by using the attention mechanism. The feature map that emphasizes important joints is graph convolved by using an attention edge. Therefore, our method recognized actions while taking into account important joints and important relationships between joints. In addition, we propose the mechanics-stream structure that considers the mechanical characteristics and scale differences of each modal. The mechanics-stream structure separately inputs coordinates, velocities, and accelerations of joint and bone into the different networks. In the evaluation experiments, we demonstrated our method outperforms conventional methods using two datasets: NTU-RGB+D and NTU-RGB+D120.

Acknowledgement. This paper is based on results obtained from a project, JPNP20006, commissioned by the New Energy and Industrial Technology Development Organization (NEDO).

References

1. Soo Kim, T., Reiter, A.: Interpretable 3D human action analysis with temporal convolutional networks. In: Computer Vision and Pattern Recognition Workshop (CVPRW) (2017)
2. Mengyuan, L., Hong, L., Chen, C.: Enhanced skeleton visualization for view invariant human action recognition. Pattern Recogn. **68**, 346–362 (2017)
3. Ke, Q., Bennamoun, M., An, S., Sohel, F., Boussaid, F.: A new representation of skeleton sequences for 3D action recognition. In: Computer Vision and Pattern Recognition (CVPR) (2017)
4. Jun, L., Amir, S., Gang, W., Ling-Yu, D., Alex, K.: Skeleton-based online action prediction using scale selection network. Trans. Pattern Anal. Mach. Intell. (TPAMI) **42**, 1453–1467 (2019)
5. Qiuhong, K., Mohammed, B., Senjian, A., Ferdous, S., Boussaid, F.: Learning clip representations for skeleton-based 3D action recognition. Trans. Image Process. (TIP) **27**, 2842–2855 (2018)
6. Caetano, C., Sena, J., Brémond, F., dos Santos, J.A., Schwartz, W.R.: SkeleMotion: a new representation of skeleton joint sequences based on motion information for 3D action recognition. In: Advanced Video and Signal-based Surveillance (AVSS) (2019)
7. Yong, D., Wei, W., Liang, W.: Hierarchical recurrent neural network for skeleton based action recognition. In: Computer Vision and Pattern Recognition (CVPR) (2015)
8. Amir, S., Jun, L., Tian-Tsong, N., Gang, W.: NTU RGB+D: a large scale dataset for 3D human activity analysis. In: Computer Vision and Pattern Recognition (CVPR) (2016)
9. Liu, J., Shahroudy, A., Xu, D., Wang, G.: Spatio-temporal LSTM with trust gates for 3D human action recognition. In: Leibe, B., Matas, J., Sebe, N., Welling, M. (eds.) ECCV 2016. LNCS, vol. 9907, pp. 816–833. Springer, Cham (2016). https://doi.org/10.1007/978-3-319-46487-9_50

10. Song, S., Lan, C., Xing, J., Zeng, W., Liu, J.: An end-to-end spatio-temporal attention model for human action recognition from skeleton data. In: Association for the Advancement of Artificial Intelligence (AAAI) (2017)

11. Jun, L., Amir, S., Dong, X., Alex, K., Gang, W.: Skeleton-based action recognition using spatio-temporal LSTM network with trust gates. Trans. Pattern Anal. Mach. Intell. (TPAMI) **40**, 3007–3021 (2018)

12. Liu, J., Wang, G., Hu, P., Duan, L.Y., Kot, A.C.: Global context-aware attention LSTM networks for 3D action recognition. In: Computer Vision and Pattern Recognition (CVPR) (2017)

13. Jun, L., Gang, W., Duan, L.-Y., Abdiyeva, K., Kot, A.C.: Skeleton-based human action recognition with global context-aware attention LSTM networks. Trans. Image Process. (TIP) **27**, 1586–1599 (2018)

14. Yan, S., Xiong, Y., Lin, D.: Spatial temporal graph convolutional networks for skeleton-based action recognition. In: Association for the Advancement of Artificial Intelligence (AAAI) (2018)

15. Si, C., Jing, Y., Wang, W., Wang, L., Tan, T.: Skeleton-based action recognition with spatial reasoning and temporal stack learning. In: Ferrari, V., Hebert, M., Sminchisescu, C., Weiss, Y. (eds.) ECCV 2018. LNCS, vol. 11205, pp. 106–121. Springer, Cham (2018). https://doi.org/10.1007/978-3-030-01246-5_7

16. Thakkar, K., Narayanan, P.J.: Part-based graph convolutional network for action recognition. In: The British Machine Vision Conference (BMVC) (2018)

17. Maosen, L., Siheng, C., Xu, C., Ya, Z., Yanfeng, W., Tian, Q.: Actional-structural graph convolutional networks for skeleton-based action recognition. In: Computer Vision and Pattern Recognition (CVPR) (2019)

18. Shi, L., Zhang, Y., Cheng, J., Lu, H.: Two-stream adaptive graph convolutional networks for skeleton-based action recognition. In: Computer Vision and Pattern Recognition (CVPR) (2019)

19. Si, C., Chen, W., Wang, W., Wang, L., Tan, T.: An attention enhanced graph convolutional LSTM network for skeleton-based action recognition. In: Computer Vision and Pattern Recognition (CVPR) (2019)

20. Lei, S., Yifan, Z., Jian, C., Hanqing, L.: Skeleton-based action recognition with directed graph neural networks. In: Computer Vision and Pattern Recognition (CVPR) (2019)

21. Hussein, M.E., Torki, M., Gowayyed, M.A., El-Saban, M.: Human action recognition using a temporal hierarchy of covariance descriptors on 3D joint locations. In: International Joint Conference on Artificial Intelligence (IJCAI) (2013)

22. Raviteja, V., Felipe, A., Rama, C.: Human action recognition by representing 3D skeletons as points in a lie group. In: Computer Vision and Pattern Recognition (CVPR) (2014)

23. Basura, F., Gavves, E., Oramas, M.J., Amir, G., Tinne, T.: Modeling video evolution for action recognition. In: Computer Vision and Pattern Recognition (CVPR) (2015)

24. Joan, B., Wojciech, Z., Arthur, S., Yann, L.: Spectral networks and locally connected networks on graphs. In: International Conference on Learning Representations (ICLR) (2014)

25. Michaël, D., Xavier, B., Pierre, V.: Convolutional neural networks on graphs with fast localized spectral filtering. In: Advances in Neural Information Processing Systems (NIPS) (2016)

26. Kipf, T.N., Welling, M.: Semi-supervised classification with graph convolutional networks. In: International Conference on Learning Representations (ICLR) (2017)

27. Duvenaud, D., et al.: Convolutional networks on graphs for learning molecular fingerprints. In: Advances in Neural Information Processing Systems (NIPS) (2015)
28. Gilmer, J., Schoenholz, S.S., Riley, P.F., Vinyals, O., Dahl, G.E.: Neural message passing for quantum chemistry. In: International Conference on Machine Learning (ICML) (2017)
29. Yao, L., Mao, C., Luo, Y.: Graph convolutional networks for text classification. In: Association for the Advancement of Artificial Intelligence (AAAI) (2019)
30. Xiang, Z., Junbo, Z., Yann, L.: Character-level convolutional networks for text classification. In: Advances in Neural Information Processing Systems (NIPS) (2015)
31. Wang, X., Gupta, A.: Videos as space-time region graphs. In: Ferrari, V., Hebert, M., Sminchisescu, C., Weiss, Y. (eds.) ECCV 2018. LNCS, vol. 11209, pp. 413–431. Springer, Cham (2018). https://doi.org/10.1007/978-3-030-01228-1_25
32. Qi, S., Wang, W., Jia, B., Shen, J., Zhu, S.-C.: Learning human-object interactions by graph parsing neural networks. In: Ferrari, V., Hebert, M., Sminchisescu, C., Weiss, Y. (eds.) ECCV 2018. LNCS, vol. 11213, pp. 407–423. Springer, Cham (2018). https://doi.org/10.1007/978-3-030-01240-3_25
33. Yao, T., Pan, Y., Li, Y., Mei, T.: Exploring visual relationship for image captioning. In: Ferrari, V., Hebert, M., Sminchisescu, C., Weiss, Y. (eds.) Computer Vision – ECCV 2018. LNCS, vol. 11218, pp. 711–727. Springer, Cham (2018). https://doi.org/10.1007/978-3-030-01264-9_42
34. Yang, X., Tang, K., Zhang, H., Cai, J.: Auto-encoding scene graphs for image captioning. In: Computer Vision and Pattern Recognition (CVPR) (2019)
35. Hiroshi, F., Tsubasa, H., Takayoshi, Y., Hironobu, F.: Attention branch network: learning of attention mechanism for visual explanation. In: Computer Vision and Pattern Recognition (CVPR) (2019)
36. Zhou, B., Khosla, A., Lapedriza, A., Oliva, A., Torralba, A.: Learning deep features for discriminative localization. In: Computer Vision and Pattern Recognition (CVPR) (2016)
37. R., S.R., Michael, C., Abhishek, D., Ramakrishna, V., Devi, P., Batra, D.: Grad-CAM: visual explanations from deep networks via gradient-based localization. In: International Conference on Computer Vision (ICCV) (2017)
38. Chattopadhyay, A., Sarkar, A., Howlader, P., Balasubramanian, V.N.: Grad-CAM++: generalized gradient-based visual explanations for deep convolutional networks. In: Winter Conference on Applications of Computer Vision (WACV) (2017)
39. Jun, L., Amir, S., Mauricio, P., Gang, W., Duan, L.Y., Kot, A.C.: NTU RGB+D 120: a large-scale benchmark for 3D human activity understanding. Trans. Pattern Anal. Mach. Intell. (TPAMI) **42**, 1–18 (2019)
40. Hu, J.F., Zheng, W.S., Ma, L., Wang, G., Lai, J., Zhang, J.: Early action prediction by soft regression. Trans. Pattern Anal. Mach. Intell. (TPAMI) **41**, 2568–2583 (2019)
41. Jianfang, H., Wei-Shi, Z., Jian-Huang, L., Jianguo, Z.: Jointly learning heterogeneous features for RGB-D activity recognition. In: Computer Vision and Pattern Recognition (CVPR) (2015)
42. Liu, M., Yuan, J.: Recognizing human actions as the evolution of pose estimation maps. In: Computer Vision and Pattern Recognition (CVPR) (2018)
43. Caetano, C., Brémond, F., Schwartz, W.R.: Skeleton image representation for 3D action recognition based on tree structure and reference joints. In: Conference on Graphics, Patterns and Images (SIBGRAPI) (2019)

DiscFace: Minimum Discrepancy Learning for Deep Face Recognition

Insoo Kim[1(✉)], Seungju Han[1], Seong-Jin Park[1], Ji-won Baek[1], Jinwoo Shin[2], Jae-Joon Han[1], and Changkyu Choi[1]

[1] Samsung Advanced Institute of Technology (SAIT), Suwon-si, South Korea
{insool.kim,sj75.han,sj210.park,jw0328.baek,jae-joon.han,
changkyu_choi}@samsung.com
[2] Korea Advanced Institute of Science and Technology (KAIST),
Daejeon, South Korea
jinwoos@kaist.ac.kr

Abstract. Softmax-based learning methods have shown state-of-the-art performances on large-scale face recognition tasks. In this paper, we discover an important issue of softmax-based approaches: the sample features around the corresponding class weight are similarly penalized in the training phase even though their directions are different from each other. This directional discrepancy, i.e., process discrepancy leads to performance degradation at the evaluation phase. To mitigate the issue, we propose a novel training scheme, called minimum discrepancy learning that enforces directions of intra-class sample features to be aligned toward an optimal direction by using a single learnable basis. Furthermore, the single learnable basis facilitates disentangling the so-called class-invariant vectors from sample features, such that they are effective to train under class-imbalanced datasets.

1 Introduction

Recently, deep learning models have been utilized to extract robust and accurate features with state-of-the-art performance for various computer vision tasks. In particular, a multitude of efforts has been devoted to developing a face recognition model that could handle unconstrained variations in large-scale datasets, e.g., variations in pose, illumination, occlusion, facial expression, blur, and low resolution. Convolutional neural networks (CNNs) have shown remarkable face recognition performances by extracting discriminative features. Such breakthroughs were achieved by adopting different effective loss functions tailored for variation-robust face recognition [1–10].

In this paper, we are particularly interested in training on extreme class-imbalanced datasets; the training set consists of an enormous number of classes, with an extremely small number of data per class. In earlier years, deep metric learning methods achieved promising results under the class-imbalanced datasets, by learning face embeddings through local relationships in distances between pairs (or triplets) of samples [1–3,11]. Deep metric learning has the

© Springer Nature Switzerland AG 2021
H. Ishikawa et al. (Eds.): ACCV 2020, LNCS 12626, pp. 358–374, 2021.
https://doi.org/10.1007/978-3-030-69541-5_22

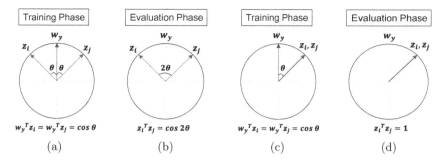

Fig. 1. Conceptual visualization of process discrepancy. Geometric view of a scenario having *process discrepancy* between (a) training phase and (b) evaluation phase. Geometric view of a scenario having *no process discrepancy* between (c) training phase and (d) evaluation phase. Here, z_i and z_j are the normalized intra-class feature vectors, and w_y denotes the corresponding class weight. (a) and (c) incur the same score ($cos\theta$) during the training, but (b) and (d) produce the different scores ($cos2\theta \neq 1$) at the evaluation phase.

ability to directly capture more discriminative power by utilizing certain metric losses. However, their performance highly depends on sampling and mining strategies [12]. Metric learning models typically require time-consuming back-and-forth procedures to train.

In recent years, softmax-based deep learning methods have been more widely used in face recognition tasks. They are easy to train and have achieved state-of-the-art performances in large-scale face recognition tasks. Softmax-based methods consider a classification loss in the training so that the learned features are separable. In contrast to the classification task, learning large-margin discriminative features is essential for face recognition tasks, particularly under the open-set protocol, which is a more realistic yet challenging face recognition protocol [6]. Many works have attempted to revise the softmax loss to obtain effective large-margin discriminative features [5–8,13]. Such variants are able to directly optimize the angles between features and the corresponding class weights in the hypersphere manifold.

Nevertheless, our observation is that their evaluation performance can suffer from discrepancy between training and evaluation processes under the open-set protocol: the matching scores between sample features and a softmax class weight are used during the training, while the matching scores are calculated between different sample features (without the class weight) at the evaluation phase. This difference leads to a directional discrepancy between sample features, as shown in Fig. 1. We refer to this issue as "process discrepancy".

In this paper, we investigate the fundamental issue of process discrepancy in softmax-based learning methods for face recognition tasks. In particular, we first define displacement vectors which represent feature variations originated from the corresponding class weights in order to address the directional discrepancy between sample features. Then, we propose a new training scheme, called *minimum discrepancy learning* that encourages the directional discrepancy to be minimized by fitting all displacement vectors even with different classes to a single learnable representative vector as described in Fig. 2. This single representative vector (e.g., basis) facilitates not only aligning directions of intra-class sample features toward an optimal direction but also disentangling class-invariant displacement vectors from their sample features, such that they are effective to train under the extreme class-imbalanced datasets.

In summary, the proposed scheme is specialized to mitigate process discrepancy between the training and evaluation phase for providing better performance at the evaluation phase. To the best of our knowledge, this is the first softmax-based learning method for face recognition tasks addressing process discrepancy issue, while previous methods focus on discriminative learning only. We demonstrate the superiority of our method under various benchmarks that include a large amount of hard positive examples, such as CPLFW [14], IJB-B [15], IJB-C [16] and QMUL-SurvFace dataset [17]: our regularization method consistently improves previous softmax-based training schemes such as Softmax, CosFace [7] and ArcFace [8].

2 Related Works

Metric-Based Learning. Metric-based learning methods [1–3] directly learn discriminative features from the relationship between samples. The contrastive loss [1] uses positive and negative pairs of samples to learn the relationship between the two samples. The triplet loss [3] learns that the distance between an anchor and a positive sample is smaller than the distance between an anchor and a negative sample. Even though the metric-based learning is an intuitive way to solve the verification problem, the main drawback of metric-based learning resides on the difficulty of data sampling. It is hard to train all possible pairs or triplets, and the performance highly depends on the mining strategies.

Softmax-Based Learning. Many approaches have been studied for softmax-based discriminative feature learning in various applications [18–25]. In face recognition task, several approaches have discussed to make more discriminative features based on softmax loss. Center loss [4] proposed a method to minimize intra-class variance. This method computes the centroid of samples for each class and minimizes the intra-class distances between feature vectors and their corresponding centroids. Crystal loss [26] introduced a constraint to enforce the norms of feature vectors to be a certain value. Ring loss [27] makes the norms to be a trainable parameter and encourages the norm of feature vectors to be optimally trained. NormFace [5] is a scheme to learn features on the hypersphere manifold such that the discrimination between classes can be done by angles. Sphereface [6] introduced a multiplicative angular margin loss to make features more discriminative. In a similar way, the effectiveness of the angular margin was demonstrated from CosFace [7] and ArcFace [8]. They used the angular margin in different ways.

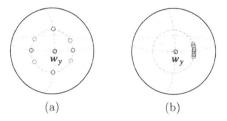

(a)   (b)

Fig. 2. A geometric view of process discrepancy. Note that all features around the class weight w_y belong to the same class. (a) All features produce the same cosine similarity with the corresponding class weight w_y, while they are separately placed. (b) All features are in similar positions with the same cosine similarity around w_y, which are forced by the proposed scheme.

3 Minimum Discrepancy Learning

We explain process discrepancy issue of softmax-based learning schemes for face recognition tasks in more detail in Sect. 3.1. In Sect. 3.2, we present the proposed training scheme designed to minimize process discrepancy.

3.1 Discrepancy in Face Recognition Schemes

Consider a dataset $\mathcal{D} = \{(x, y)\}$, which contains a sample (e.g., image) x and its corresponding label (or class) $y \in \mathcal{C} = \{1, 2, \ldots, C\}$. We are interested in finding a learnable model parameterized by $\{\theta, w\}$ that outputs a learned feature $\varphi_\theta(x)$ and a classification score $w_k^T \varphi_\theta(x)$ for each class k. This can be done by minimizing the following softmax loss with respect to $\{\theta, w\}$:

$$L_{\texttt{softmax}}(\theta, w; \mathcal{D}) = -\frac{1}{|\mathcal{D}|} \sum_{(x,y) \in \mathcal{D}} \log \frac{e^{w_y^T \varphi_\theta(x)}}{\sum_{k \in \mathcal{C}} e^{w_k^T \varphi_\theta(x)}}, \quad (1)$$

where $|\mathcal{D}|$ is the number of samples. Note that the class weights not only contribute to inter-class variations by the denominator term $w_k^T \varphi_\theta(x)$ of (1), but intra-class variations by the numerator term $w_y^T \varphi_\theta(x)$ of (1). Once the model is trained, the evaluation phase in face recognition takes two input images x_i and x_j whose corresponding classes may not be in $\mathcal{C}$. Then, the cosine similarity between normalized feature vectors, i.e., $z_i = \frac{\varphi_\theta(x_i)}{\|\varphi_\theta(x_i)\|_2}, z_j = \frac{\varphi_\theta(x_j)}{\|\varphi_\theta(x_j)\|_2}$, is measured to identify whether they are in the same class or not.

As described in Fig. 2(a), the features around the corresponding class weight w_y lie on a hypersphere manifold. In the training phase, these features are able to produce the same scores by $w_y^T \varphi_\theta(x)$ of the softmax function (1) even though their directions are different from each other. On the other hand, this directional discrepancy is attributed to different displacement vectors $(\varphi_\theta(x) - w_y)$ and leads to an undesirable effect at the evaluation stage. Namely, the directional relationship between features are important in the evaluation phase, but it is not directly considered during the training. We call this issue, *process discrepancy*

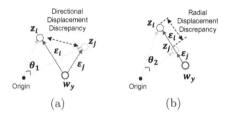

Fig. 3. Intra-class variations when considering two types of discrepancies: (a) Directional displacement discrepancy and (b) Radial displacement discrepancy. Note that the directional and radial displacement discrepancies cause the angle difference between features.

that might not appear in deep metric-based learning because the underlying functions in both the training and evaluation process are identical. However, as aforementioned in Sect. 1, deep metric-based learning is not widely used due to the performance sensitivity to sampling and mining methods. In fact, process discrepancy comes from the different underlying functions in both the training and evaluation process. Furthermore, process discrepancy directly influences the evaluation performance, as described in Fig. 1. This means that even a well-trained model under the softmax loss could not ensure the high performance in the evaluation phase (see Sect. 4.3 for more details).

3.2   Learning Discrepancy-Free Representations

Discrepancy Loss. The main idea for minimizing process discrepancy is to enforce the directions of intra-class features to be aligned in a single direction from the perspective of their class weights as illustrated in Fig. 2(b). In essence, process discrepancy occurs because $w_y^T z_i \approx w_y^T z_j$ for the training phase does not guarantee $z_i^T z_j \approx 1$ for the evaluation phase. The proposed idea of directional alignment can minimize the angle between z_i and z_j. To handle the variation of each feature $\varphi_\theta(x)$, we first define the displacement vector ε as follows:

$$\varepsilon(x, y) = \frac{\varphi_\theta(x)}{\|\varphi_\theta(x)\|_2} - \frac{w_y}{\|w_y\|_2}, \tag{2}$$

i.e., it is the difference vector between a feature $\varphi_\theta(x)$ and its class weight w_y as shown in Fig. 3. Note that the feature vector $\varphi_\theta(x)$ is normalized in (2) because the evaluation phase calculates the angle difference between features by using normalized features. As mentioned in Sect. 3.1, the directional discrepancy between features (i.e., process discrepancy) is due to different intra-class displacement vectors of their features, as shown in Fig. 2(a). Inspired by this observation, we introduce an additional learnable representative vector ξ that fits all displacement vectors, which is named here, *deep displacement basis*, in order to minimize the discrepancy between displacement vectors of their features. The discrepancy-free features and model parameters θ, w, ξ are jointly learned by minimizing the following loss with the softmax loss (1):

$$L_{\mathtt{discrepancy}}(\theta, w, \xi; \mathcal{D}) = \frac{1}{|\mathcal{D}|} \sum_{(x,y) \in \mathcal{D}} \| \varepsilon(x,y) - \xi \|_2. \tag{3}$$

The above loss minimizes the directional intra-class discrepancy, such that the training/evaluation process discrepancy can be mitigated. An additional advantage of optimizing (3) is that the class information in the displacement vectors is implicitly forced to be eliminated by fitting all of them to a single displacement basis (regardless of their classes). In other words, it learns to disentangle class-free variations (e.g., displacement vectors) from their features. Hence, manipulating displacement vectors has a negligible effect on inter-class separability, while it helps to minimize process discrepancy.

In summary, we suggest to minimize the following loss:

$$L_{\mathtt{total}}(\theta, w, \xi; \mathcal{D}) = L_{\mathtt{softmax}}(\theta, w; \mathcal{D}) + \lambda L_{\mathtt{discrepancy}}(\theta, w, \xi; \mathcal{D}), \tag{4}$$

where $\lambda > 0$ is a hyper-parameter to balance both loss terms. In the above, one can use $L_{\mathtt{softmax}}$ as any softmax-based loss for face recognition tasks, e.g.., angular-margin losses [6–8,13] for improving the performance further.

Directional vs. Radial Displacement Discrepancy. We further remark that process discrepancy can be decomposed into two types as described in Fig. 3: *directional displacement discrepancy* and *radial displacement discrepancy*. The directional displacement discrepancy is the angle difference between displacement vectors and is defined by $\frac{\varepsilon(x_i,y_i)}{\|\varepsilon(x_i,y_i)\|_2}^T \frac{\varepsilon(x_j,y_j)}{\|\varepsilon(x_j,y_j)\|_2}$. Also, the radial displacement discrepancy is the norm difference between displacement vectors and is defined by $|\|\varepsilon(x_i,y_i)\|_2 - \|\varepsilon(x_j,y_j)\|_2|$. As shown in Fig. 3(a) and (b), the directional displacement discrepancy causes the angle difference (θ_1) between features, while the radial displacement discrepancy leads to another angle difference (θ_2) between features as well. Namely, both discrepancies in the displacement domain result in directional discrepancies (θ_1 and θ_2) between features, and should simultaneously be suppressed. Since the discrepancy loss (3) is defined by using a non-normalized version of displacement vector $\varepsilon(x,y)$ and basis ξ, it can penalize both directional and radial displacement discrepancies.

Comparison to Other Methods. As mentioned in Sect. 3.1, most softmax-based approaches may generate process discrepancy due to their limited ability in softmax-based loss. Although softmax loss is able to maximize $w_y^T \varphi_\theta(x)$, in practice, some hard features are placed around their class weights as in Fig. 2(a) and it causes process discrepancy. On the other hand, our method at least helps place these features directionally close to each other as in Fig. 2(b), which is not explicitly done by previous works. For example, center loss [4] attempts to minimize intra-class variations by introducing centroids, but process discrepancy is not considered. This means that $w_y^T z_i \approx w_y^T z_j$ for the training phase does not guarantee $z_i^T z_j \approx 1$ for the evaluation phase. Since intra-class features are concentrated only on their centroids (not their class weights), this effect may lead to diminishing inter-class separability as in Fig. 4(b). In contrast, the proposed method introduces the class-free concept of the displacement vector, which enables to minimize directional intra-class variations without hurting

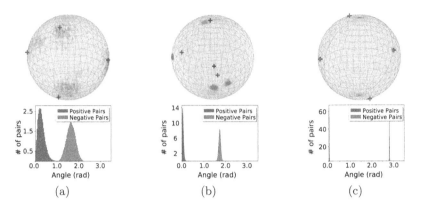

Fig. 4. Toy examples on VGGFace2 dataset [28] for 4 classes: (a) CosFace [8], (b) Center Loss [4], (c) Cos-DiscFace (ours). We use ResNet-18 [29] as a baseline network architecture to learn 3 dimensional features. We replace the global average pooling of ResNet-18 by a fully-connected layer. The colored point is a feature vector and the color of points indicates the corresponding class. In figures, "+" indicates a class weight. The first row visualizes the hypersphere manifold with 4 classes. The second row shows the angle distribution of positive and negative pairs. We select 2 classes to generate their angle distributions.

inter-class separability as in Fig. 4(c). Alternatively, adding metric losses such as triplet loss [3] and contrastive loss [1] is one of ways to mitigate process discrepancy. However, the performance may depend on sampling strategy. On the other hand, our method is the one that minimizes process discrepancy without any sampling method. As a result, our method overcomes the fundamental limitation of softmax-based methods by suppressing process discrepancy and provides performance improvement at the evaluation phase.

4   Analytical Study

4.1   Feature Visualization

We demonstrate a toy example to visualize the feature distributions on methods. To observe intra-class compactness effectively, we choose VGGFace2 dataset [28] which contains an average of 362.6 samples per class. The baselines such as CosFace and Center Loss are performed and their results are illustrated in Fig. 4(a) and (b), respectively. As shown in Fig. 4(c) and (d), our method is conducted to visualize the feature distribution when it uses a single basis and two bases, respectively. The center loss minimizes intra-class variations as depicted in Fig. 4 (b), which needs to be more compact. More importantly, Fig. 4(a) shows that ArcFace causes many directions of variations. On the other hand, we observe that the directions of variations are aligned in a single direction by our method. As shown in Fig. 4(c), the position of the feature distribution per class is located to the left side of the corresponding class weight. Moreover, we indeed observe that

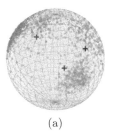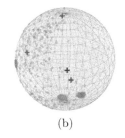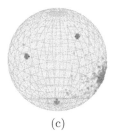

(a)   (b)   (c)

Fig. 5. Visualization results under the extreme class-imbalanced dataset. (a) Cos-Face [8] (b) Center Loss [4] (c) Cos-DiscFace (ours). Samples from three classes are fed to every mini-batch while only a single sample for the remaining class is fed to a mini-batch every two epochs. In figures, "+" indicates a class weight and the green points are of the class with insufficient samples during the training. (Color figure online)

the proposed method minimizes intra-class variations under preserving inter-class separability, as the angle distributions are shown in the second row of Fig. 4.

4.2 A Recognition Task Under Extreme Class-Imbalanced Dataset

The enormous number of classes, and extreme scarcity of samples per class, i.e., extreme class-imbalanced dataset, makes it difficult to learn features robust to unconstrained variations. Namely, samples for a certain class may appear quite rarely in a mini-batch during the training phase. The proposed method enables us to use all mini-batch samples (even the ones that belong to different classes) as if they were intra-class samples due to class-invariant attributes of displacement vectors. To prove this, we use the following trick to visualize intra-class compactness under the extreme class-imbalanced dataset: a certain class appears in a mini-batch only one (i.e., a single sample) every two epochs. By doing so, the class samples become insufficient to produce intra-class compactness. The remaining experimental setup follows that of the toy example described in Fig. 4. In this configuration, we run three methods: CosFace [8], Center Loss [4] and Cos-DiscFace (ours).

The results are presented in Fig. 5. Center loss produces intra-class compactness only in three classes, while our method results in intra-class compactness even in the class that appears rarely during the training. Further experiments are conducted to demonstrate the effectiveness of our method under the extreme class-imbalanced datasets as reported in Table 4.

4.3 Effects on Process Discrepancy

We also analyze process discrepancy via investigating the relationship between classification and verification performance. Once process discrepancy is minimized, the performance improvement in both classification and verification tasks should be consistent. To show this, we use 90% of the CASIA-WebFace [30] as

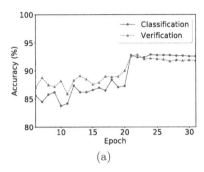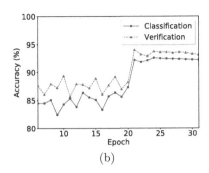

(a)   (b)

Fig. 6. Accuracy (%) on both classification and verification tasks. (a) CosFace [7], and (b) Cos-DiscFace (Ours). This experiment aims to show the effect of process discrepancy, by demonstrating the inconsistency of performance between classification and verification tasks.

training samples, while 10% of the CASIA-WebFace are used for classification evaluation. For verification evaluation, CFP-FP [31] is chosen. This experiment follows the setup of CASIA-WebFace as described in Sect. 5.1. CosFace [7] is chosen as a baseline in this analysis.

In particular, we investigate the trends of the relationship between classification and verification performance along training goes. When the classification performance is increased, our method consistently produces the improved verification performance as shown in Fig. 6(b). In the case of the previous method, relatively smaller improvement for verification performance is revealed, compared with classification performance, as shown in Fig. 6(a). As aforementioned in Sect. 3.1, higher classification performance does not guarantee higher verification performance when process discrepancy occurs, as in Fig. 6(a). The experimental results confirm that the proposed method (i.e., the discrepancy loss) serves as making verification performance consistent with classification performance.

5   Experiments on Various Benchmark Datasets

5.1   Experimental Setup

Training Datasets. To verify the robustness of the proposed method, training the models is performed using both small-scale and large-scale datasets. As a small-scale training dataset, CASIA-WebFace dataset [30] is selected. The CASIA-WebFace contains 0.49M face images collected from 10K subjects. For a fair comparison with the state-of-the-art methods on a large-scale dataset, MS1MV2 dataset is utilized. The MS1MV2 is a refined version of MS-Celeb-1M dataset [8], and it comprises over 5.8M face images from 85K different identities. For low-resolution surveillance face recognition task, we use QMUL-SurvFace dataset [17]. The face images for QMUL-SurvFace are re-scaled to 112 × 112 by using bicubic interpolation while the other training datasets are cropped to 112 × 112 by MTCNN [32].

Algorithm 1. The Pseudo-code of DiscFace on Pytorch

Require: Feature x, Class weight w, Displacement basis b, Label t

$x = $ F.normalize(x)

$w = $ F.normalize(w)

$w_{\texttt{batch}} = w[\texttt{t},:]$

$d = x - w_{\texttt{batch}}$

$b_{\texttt{norm}} = b$.norm(p=2, dim=1)

$b_{\texttt{norm}} = $ torch.clamp$(b_{\texttt{norm}}$, min=0, max=0.05)

$y = $ F.linear(x,w)

$L_{\texttt{softmax}} = $ F.cross_entropy(y,t)

$L_{\texttt{discrepancy}} = (d - $ F.normalize$(b)*b_{\texttt{norm}})$.norm(p=2, dim=1).mean()

$L_{\texttt{total}} = L_{\texttt{softmax}} + \lambda L_{\texttt{discrepancy}}$

Implementation Details. As our network architectures, we use ResNet-34 [29] for QMUL-SurvFace, LResNet50E-IR [8] for CASIA-WebFace and LResNet100E-IR [8] for MS1MV2. The learning rate is initially set to 0.1 for all experiments. It is then divided by 10 at the 100K, 160K and 220K iterations for the MS1MV2, the 20K and 28K iterations for the CASIA-WebFace, and the 10K and 15K iterations for the QMUL-SurvFace. The training is complete at the 360K-th iteration for MS1MV2, the 32K-th iteration for the CASIA-WebFace, and 26K-th iteration for QMUL-SurvFace. The batch size is set to 512 for the CASIA-WebFace and MS1MV2, and 128 for the QMUL-SurvFace. The training is performed on 2 GPUs and the network architectures are optimized by using stochastic gradient decent (SGD) algorithm.

Evaluation Datasets and Protocols. Our method is evaluated on several benchmarks. As small-scale datasets, LFW [33], CPLFW [14], CALFW [34], CFP-FP [31], and AgeDB-30 [35] are employed. CPLFW and CFP-FP contain different pose variations. CALFW and AgeDB-30 include different age variations. To evaluate the proposed method on large-scale test datasets, IJB-B [15], IJB-C [16] and MegaFace dataset [36] with FaceScrub dataset [37] are utilized for open-set face verification. To further verify that the proposed method is robust to hard positive examples, we employ QMUL-SurvFace dataset [17]. All face images are cropped or bicubic-interpolated to 112×112 to make them consistent with the images from the training datasets. Cosine similarity between probe and gallery features is used to measure whether the given features belong to the same identity or not. Performance is assessed by calculating *Accuracy* and *True Acceptance Rate* (TAR) with a fixed *False Acceptance Rate* (FAR).

Methods. As mentioned in Sect. 3.2, the proposed method could be combined with any softmax-based method. Our method is applied to the standard softmax loss (1), which is referred to as Soft-DiscFace. We also apply our method to the angular-margin softmax schemes, such as ArcFace [8] and CosFace [7]. We refer to these models as Arc-DiscFace and Cos-DiscFace, respectively. Similarly, the other losses such as center loss [4], contrastive loss [1] and triplet loss [3] are combined with ArcFace, which are referred to as Arc-CenterLoss,

Table 1. Face Verification (%) on QMUL-SurvFace dataset. The hyperparameter ($\lambda = 1$) of our method are used in the experiments. Note that "*" indicates our implementations and the best results are indicated in bold.

Methods	TAR(%)@FAR			Accuracy (%)
	10%	1%	0.1%	
DeepID2 [38]	60.0	28.2	13.4	76.1
FaceNet [3]	79.9	40.3	12.7	85.3
SphereFace [6]	63.6	34.1	15.6	77.5
Center Loss [4]	86.0	53.3	26.8	88.0
CosFace*	72.0	44.0	14.7	81.3
Cos-DiscFace (Ours)*	74.4	44.7	23.0	82.3
Softmax*	83.3	52.4	17.8	86.5
Soft-DiscFace (Ours)*	**86.8**	**62.9**	**35.9**	**88.6**

Arc-ContrastiveLoss and Arc-TripletLoss. The hyperparameter of CosFace ($m = 30, s = 0.25$), ArcFace ($m = 64, s = 0.5$), Center Loss ($\lambda = 0.003, \alpha = 0.5$), Contrastive Loss, Triplet Loss ($\lambda = 0.1, m = 0.3$) and ours ($\lambda = 0.2$) are used unless specified. To avoid the dependency on the initial setting of the displacement basis, its norm value is constrained (or clipped) by a certain upper bound (set by 0.05). To implement our method, we provide the pytorch pseudo-code as described in Algorithm 1.

5.2 QMUL-SurvFace Dataset

QMUL-SurvFace dataset [17] has been recently released to verify the robustness of low-resolution surveillance facial images. This dataset is drawn from real surveillance videos, not synthesized by artificial down-sampling of high-resolution images. The dataset is suitable to evaluate realistic performance since it contains the wild environment characteristics such as low-resolution, motion blur, unconstrained poses, poor illumination and background clutters. The QMUL-SurvFace consists of 463,507 facial images with 15,573 unique identities. The positive and negative pairs in the evaluation set are 5,319 pairs, respectively.

According to [17], it is reported that the center loss produces the best performance for the QMUL-SurvFace. Since the standard softmax loss is adopted to the center loss, the standard softmax and CosFace [7] are chosen as baselines. The experimental results are summarized in Table 1. The proposed method achieves the best performance among all tested methods. Since the proposed method is designed to effectively reduce process discrepancy (i.e., directional intra-class variations), its effect can be significant on datasets mainly consisting of hard positive pairs. In the sense, the results from the QMUL-SurvFace are the best demonstration of the effectiveness of the proposed method, where Soft-DiscFace improves TAR for FAR 10^{-3}, from 17.8% to 35.9%, compared with softmax loss only. Interestingly, we found that the standard softmax loss outperforms

Table 2. Face verification (%) on the LFW, CFP-FP, Age30-DB, CALFW, and CPLFW. Note that "*" indicates our implementations and the best results are indicated in bold. CosFace and ArcFace are selected as baselines in these implementations since they show the best performance on CASIA-WebFace and MS1M training datasets, respectively.

Methods	Dataset	LFW	CFP-FP	AgeDB-30	CALFW	CPLFW
FaceNet [3]	200M	99.65	–	–	–	–
OE-CNNs [39]	1.7M	99.47	–	–	–	–
Center loss [4]	0.7M	99.28	–	–	–	–
NormFace [5]	CASIA	99.19	–	–	–	–
SphereFace [6]		99.42	–	–	–	–
RegularFace [9]		99.33	–	–	–	–
AMSoftmax [13]		99.28	94.77	–	–	–
PFE-AMSoftmax [40]		99.55	95.92	–	–	–
CosFace*		99.42	96.29	93.33	92.62	89.28
Cos-DiscFace (Ours)*		**99.62**	**96.54**	**93.63**	**93.30**	**89.73**
Ring Loss [27]	MS1M	99.52	–	–	–	–
AdaptiveFace [41]		99.62	–	–	–	–
CosFace [7]		99.73	–	–	–	–
ArcFace [8]		99.82	98.37	98.15	95.45	92.08
Arc-DiscFace (Ours)*		**99.83**	**98.54**	**98.35**	**96.15**	**93.37**

the angular-margin based softmax loss in the experiments. We conjecture that the margin penalty during the training show an undesirable effect on hard positive examples such as low-resolution, motion blur and so on. The intra-class compactness methods such as center loss and our method show a positive effect on performance, compared with the result of the softmax loss. Moreover, our method shows better performance, compared to center loss, since it exclusively considers process discrepancy.

5.3   Comparison Results

Results on LFW, CFP-FP, Age30-DB, CALFW and CPLFW Benchmarks. In this experiment, we compare our method with state-of-the art methods. LFW [33] contains 13,233 face images collected from 5,749 different identities, forming 6,000 pairs of face images. Other face benchmarks such as AgeDB-30 [35], CPLFW [14], CFP-FP [31] and CALFW [34] are also chosen to compare with state-of-the-art methods. CPLFW contains 6,000 pairs in the profile-profile configuration. CFP-FP contains 7,000 pairs in the frontal-profile configuration. Note that CALFW and AgeDB-30 include age variations and generate 6,000 positive and negative pairs of face images. The experimental results trained on MS1MV2 [42] are reported in Table 2. One can observe that the proposed methods (Cos-DiscFace and Arc-DiscFace) provide improved performance over the previous methods. Specifically, Arc-DiscFace improves the accuracy from 92.08% to 93.37% on CPLFW and 95.45% to 96.15% on CALFW (trained on

Table 3. Comparison results (%) on CPLFW, IJB-B, IJB-C and MegaFace. IJB-B and IJB-C results are based on 1:1 verification for TAR at FAR 10^{-5}. MF Id. and MF Ver. indicate results on MegaFace Challenge 1 using FaceScrub as the probe set. MF Id. refers to the rank-1 face identification accuracy with 1M distractors, and MF Ver. refers to the face verification for TAR at FAR 10^{-6}. Note that "*" indicates our implementations and the best results are indicated in bold.

Methods	Dataset	CPLFW	IJB-B	IJB-C	MF Id.	MF Ver.
ArcFace*	MS1M	92.70	86.05	92.46	80.77	96.88
Arc-Center Loss*		92.77	86.36	92.34	80.38	96.98
Arc-Contrastive Loss*		92.92	88.16	93.52	80.44	96.98
Arc-Triplet Loss*		92.95	87.25	93.03	**81.25**	97.05
Arc-DiscFace (Ours)*		**93.37**	**88.83**	**93.71**	81.23	**97.44**

Table 4. Comparison results (%) on IJB-C under the class-imbalanced dataset. IJB-C results are based on 1:1 verification. We train with long-tailed MS1M (MS1M-LT [43]) that has 11.9 mean images per ID. Note that "*" indicates our implementations and the best results are indicated in bold.

Method	Dataset	TAR (%) @ FAR on IJB-C				
		10^{-1}	10^{-2}	10^{-3}	10^{-4}	10^{-5}
ArcFace*	MS1M-LT	98.81	97.59	95.84	93.78	90.48
Arc-Center Loss*		98.87	97.62	96.07	93.79	90.68
Arc-DiscFace (Ours)*		**98.89**	**97.87**	**96.57**	**94.82**	**92.42**

MS1M). Meanwhile, Cos-DiscFace improves the accuracy from 92.62% to 93.30% on CALFW (trained on CASIA). These results indicate that further improvement is achieved when the proposed method is combined with any softmax-based losses such as CosFace and ArcFace. Moreover, our method provides the consistency of performance improvement under various training datasets.

Results on Challenging Benchmarks. The goal of this experiment is to verify the robustness on more challenging benchmarks. MegaFace dataset [36] contains 1M images collected from 690K identities, which is mainly used as a gallery set. The FaceScrub dataset [37] consists of 106,863 images collected from 530 individuals, as a probe set. The IJB-B dataset [15] contains 1,845 subjects with 21.8K still images and 55K frames from 7,011 videos. The IJB-C dataset [16] is an extension of IJB-B, which contains 3,531 subjects with 31.3K still images and 117.5K frames from 11,779 videos. We choose CPLFW as a hard small-scale benchmark. We train LResNet100E-IR [8] on a large-scale training dataset (MS1MV2). For contrastive and triplet loss, anchor, positive and negative images are randomly sampled. The performance result is reported in Table 3. Our method consistently improves the verification performance from 86.05% to 88.83% on IJB-B for TAR at FAR 10^{-5}, 92.46% to 93.71% on IJB-C for TAR at FAR 10^{-5}, and 96.98% to 97.44% on MegaFace for TAR at FAR 10^{-6}. We remark that discrepancy-free methods such as Arc-ContrastiveLoss,

Table 5. Ablation study (%) on λ for Cos-DiscFace trained with CASIA-WebFace dataset. Note that Cos-DiscFace with $\lambda = 0.0$ indicates CosFace. Our method is less sensitive to the performance with respect to λ. The best results are indicated in bold.

Benchmarks	$\lambda = 0.0$	$\lambda = 0.2$	$\lambda = 0.4$	$\lambda = 0.6$	$\lambda = 0.8$	$\lambda = 1.0$
LFW	99.23	**99.62**	99.30	99.33	99.38	99.35
AGEDB-30	93.15	93.63	93.65	**93.92**	93.58	93.65
CFP-FP	96.44	96.54	**96.71**	**96.71**	96.59	96.50
CPLFW	89.10	89.73	**90.32**	89.82	89.78	89.23
CALFW	92.63	93.30	92.90	**93.47**	93.02	92.97

Arc-TripletLoss produce performance improvement compared with their counterparts (ArcFace) whereas Arc-CenterLoss seems not apparently to improve performance probably due to process discrepancy. Although the discrepancy-free methods improve performance on some benchmarks, there is still a performance gap between our method and the discrepancy-free methods. To further improve performance for them, the elaborated sampling strategy should be investigated. On the other hand, our method does not require such a back-and-forth procedure while it provides better performance.

Results on Class-Imbalanced Dataset. As discussed in Sect. 3.2, all displacement vectors are imposed to be the displacement basis. This means that the feature variation of minor class ideally becomes identical to that of major class. Namely, the relative lack of variations for minor classes is alleviated by forcing all variations to a single variation. To confirm the efficacy, we train on MS1M long-tailed version (i.e., MS1M-LT [43]) and evaluate the performance on IJB-C. The results are shown in Table 4. The results show the effectiveness of our method on the class-imbalanced dataset, resulting in 90.48%@ArcFace, 90.68%@Arc-CenterLoss and 92.42%@Arc-DiscFace for TAR at FAR 10^{-5}. This explains the superiority of the proposed method under the extreme class-imbalanced datasets.

5.4   Ablation Study on λ

We explore the hyperparameter λ in order to investigate performance sensitivity across λ. We train Cos-DiscFace on CASIA-WebFace datasets with λ varying from 0.0 to 1.0 with step 0.2. The results are presented in Table 5. Note that Cos-DiscFace with $\lambda = 0.0$ indicates CosFace. One can observe that our method is less sensitive across the range of the hyperparameter λ. In particular, the higher performance improvement is achieved at $\lambda = 0.4$ and 0.6. In contrast, the greater impact ($\lambda = 1.0$) of discrepancy loss may hinder softmax loss minimization, such that the performance degradation is observed as shown in Table 5.

6   Conclusion

In this paper, we propose a new training loss to address the fundamental issue of process discrepancy in softmax-based learning methods for face recognition tasks. The proposed method is particularly effective for minimizing the intra-class variations under the extreme class-imbalanced dataset. We demonstrate its superiority on various benchmarks when it combines with existing softmax-based losses. We think it would be interesting to apply our idea to other related tasks such as speaker verification [44] and imbalanced classification [45].

References

1. Ghahramani, Z., Welling, M., Cortes, C., Lawrence, N.D., Weinberger, K.Q.: Deep learning face representation by joint identification-verification. Advances in Neural Information Processing Systems (NIPS), pp. 1988–1996 (2014)
2. Hu, J., Lu, J., Tan, Y.P.: Discriminative deep metric learning for face verification in the wild. In: The IEEE Conference on Computer Vision and Pattern Recognition (CVPR), pp. 1875–1882 (2014)
3. Schroff, F., Kalenichenko, D., Philbin, J.: FaceNet: a unified embedding for face recognition and clustering. In: The IEEE Conference on Computer Vision and Pattern Recognition (CVPR) (2015)
4. Wen, Y., Zhang, K., Li, Z., Qiao, Yu.: A discriminative feature learning approach for deep face recognition. In: Leibe, B., Matas, J., Sebe, N., Welling, M. (eds.) ECCV 2016. LNCS, vol. 9911, pp. 499–515. Springer, Cham (2016). https://doi.org/10.1007/978-3-319-46478-7_31
5. Wang, F., Xiang, X., Cheng, J., Yuille, A.L.: NormFace: L2 hypersphere embedding for face verification. In: Proceedings of the 25th ACM International Conference on Multimedia, pp. 1041–1049 (2017)
6. Liu, W., Wen, Y., Yu, Z., Li, M., Raj, B., Song, L.: SphereFace: deep hypersphere embedding for face recognition. In: The IEEE Conference on Computer Vision and Pattern Recognition (CVPR) (2017)
7. Wang, H., et al.: CosFace: large margin cosine loss for deep face recognition. In: The IEEE Conference on Computer Vision and Pattern Recognition (CVPR) (2018)
8. Deng, J., Guo, J., Xue, N., Zafeiriou, S.: ArcFace: additive angular margin loss for deep face recognition. In: The IEEE Conference on Computer Vision and Pattern Recognition (CVPR) (2019)
9. Zhao, K., Xu, J., Cheng, M.M.: RegularFace: deep face recognition via exclusive regularization. In: The IEEE Conference on Computer Vision and Pattern Recognition (CVPR) (2019)
10. Yin, X., Yu, X., Sohn, K., Liu, X., Chandraker, M.: Feature transfer learning for face recognition with under-represented data. In: The IEEE Conference on Computer Vision and Pattern Recognition (CVPR) (2019)
11. Han, C., Shan, S., Kan, M., Wu, S., Chen, X.: Face recognition with contrastive convolution. In: Ferrari, V., Hebert, M., Sminchisescu, C., Weiss, Y. (eds.) ECCV 2018. LNCS, vol. 11213, pp. 120–135. Springer, Cham (2018). https://doi.org/10.1007/978-3-030-01240-3_8
12. Wang, M., Deng, W.: Deep face recognition: a survey. arXiv preprint arXiv:1804.06655 (2018)
13. Wang, F., Cheng, J., Liu, W., Liu, H.: Additive margin softmax for face verification. IEEE Signal Process. Lett. **25**, 926–930 (2018)
14. Zheng, T., Deng, W.: Cross-pose LFW: a database for studying crosspose face recognition in unconstrained environments. Technical report (2018)

15. Whitelam, C., et al.: IARPA janus benchmark-b face dataset. In: IEEE Conference on Computer Vision and Pattern Recognition Workshops (CVPRW), pp. 592–600 (2017)
16. Maze, B., et al.: IARPA janus benchmark-C: face dataset and protocol. In: International Conference on Biometrics (ICB), pp. 158–165 (2018)
17. Cheng, Z., Zhu, X., Gong, S.: Surveillance face recognition challenge. arXiv preprint arXiv:1804.09691 (2018)
18. Chen, B., Deng, W., Shen, H.: Virtual class enhanced discriminative embedding learning. In: Advances in Neural Information Processing Systems (NIPS), pp. 1942–1952 (2018)
19. Zhang, H., Cisse, M., Dauphin, Y.N., Lopez-Paz, D.: Mixup: beyond empirical risk minimization. In: International Conference on Learning Representations (ICLR), pp. 6438–6447 (2018)
20. Verma, V., et al.: Manifold mixup: better representations by interpolating hidden states. In: The International Conference on Machine Learning (ICML), pp. 6438–6447 (2019)
21. Kim, I., Kim, K., Kim, J., Choi, C.: Deep speaker representation using orthogonal decomposition and recombination for speaker verification. In: ICASSP 2019 - 2019 IEEE International Conference on Acoustics, Speech and Signal Processing (ICASSP), pp. 6129–6130 (2019). https://doi.org/10.1109/ICASSP.2019.8683332
22. Jang, E., Gu, S., Poole, B.: Categorical reparametrization with gumble-softmax. In: International Conference on Learning Representations (ICLR) (2017)
23. Guo, C., Pleiss, G., Sun, Y., Weinberger, K.Q.: On calibration of modern neural networks. In: International Conference on Machine Learning (ICML), pp. 1321–1330 (2017)
24. Maddison, C.J., Mnih, A., Teh, Y.W.: The concrete distribution: a continuous relaxation of discrete random variables. In: International Conference on Learning Representations (ICLR) (2017)
25. Hinton, G., Vinyals, O., Dean, J.: Distilling the knowledge in a neural network. arXiv preprint arXiv:1503.02531 (2015)
26. Ranjan, R., et al: Crystal loss and quality pooling for unconstrained face verification and recognition. arXiv preprint arXiv:1804.01159 (2018)
27. Zheng, Y., Pal, D.K., Savvides, M.: Ring loss: convex feature normalization for face recognition. In: The IEEE Conference on Computer Vision and Pattern Recognition (CVPR) (2018)
28. Cao, Q., Shen, L., Xie, W., Parkhi, O.M., Zisserman, A.: VGGFace2: a dataset for recognising faces across pose and age. In: The IEEE Conference on Automatic Face & Gesture Recognition (FG 2018), pp. 67–74 (2018)
29. He, K., Zhang, X., Ren, S., Sun, J.: Deep residual learning for image recognition. In: The IEEE Conference on Computer Vision and Pattern Recognition (CVPR) (2016)
30. Dong, Y., Zhen Lei, S.L., Li, S.Z.: Learning face representation from scratch. arXiv preprint arXiv:1411.7923 (2014)
31. Sengupta, S., Chen, J.C., Castillo, C., Patel, V.M., Chellappa, R., Jacobs, D.W.: Frontal to profile face verification in the wild. In: The IEEE Winter Conference on Applications of Computer Vision (WACV) (2016)
32. Zhang, K., Zhang, Z., Li, Z., Qiao, Y.: Joint face detection and alignment using multitask cascaded convolutional networks. IEEE Signal Process. Lett. 23, 1499–1503 (2016)

33. Huang, G.B., Mattar, M., Berg, T., Learned-Miller, E.: Labeled faces in the wild: a database for studying face recognition in unconstrained environments. Technical Report 07–49, University of Massachusetts, Amhertst (2007)
34. Zheng, T., Deng, W., Hu, J.: Cross-age LFW: a database for studying cross-age face recognition in unconstrained environments. arXiv:1708.08197 (2017)
35. Moschoglou, S., Papaioannou, A., Sagonas, C., Deng, J., Kotsia, I., Zafeiriou, S.: AgeDB: the first manually collected, in-the-wild age database. In: The IEEE Conference on Computer Vision and Pattern Recognition Workshops (CVPRW), pp. 51–59 (2017)
36. Kemelmacher-Shlizerman, I., Seitz, S.M., Miller, D., Brossard, E.: The megaface benchmark: 1 million faces for recognition at scale. In: The IEEE Conference on Computer Vision and Pattern Recognition (CVPR), pp. 4873–4882 (2016)
37. Ng, H.W., Winkler, S.: A data-driven approach to cleaning large face datasets. In: IEEE International Conference on Image Processing (ICIP), pp. 343–347 (2014)
38. Sun, Y., Wang, X., Tang, X.: Deeply learned face representations are sparse, selective, and robust. In: The IEEE Conference on Computer Vision and Pattern Recognition (CVPR), pp. 2892–2900 (2015)
39. Wang, Y., et al.: Orthogonal deep features decomposition for age-invariant face recognition. In: Ferrari, V., Hebert, M., Sminchisescu, C., Weiss, Y. (eds.) ECCV 2018. LNCS, vol. 11219, pp. 764–779. Springer, Cham (2018). https://doi.org/10.1007/978-3-030-01267-0_45
40. Shi, Y., Jain, A.K.: Probabilistic face embeddings. In: The IEEE International Conference on Computer Vision (ICCV) (2019)
41. Liu, H., Zhu, X., Lei, Z., Li, S.Z.: AdaptiveFace: adaptive margin and sampling for face recognition. In: The IEEE Conference on Computer Vision and Pattern Recognition (CVPR) (2019)
42. Guo, Y., Zhang, L., Hu, Y., He, X., Gao, J.: MS-Celeb-1M: a dataset and benchmark for large-scale face recognition. In: Leibe, B., Matas, J., Sebe, N., Welling, M. (eds.) ECCV 2016. LNCS, vol. 9907, pp. 87–102. Springer, Cham (2016). https://doi.org/10.1007/978-3-319-46487-9_6
43. Liu, Z., Miao, Z., Zhan, X., Wang, J., Gong, B., Yu, S.X.: Large-scale long-tailed recognition in an open world. In: The IEEE Conference on Computer Vision and Pattern Recognition (CVPR) (2019)
44. Reynolds, D.A., Quatieri, T.F., Dunn, R.B.: Speaker verification using adapted Gaussian mixture models. Digit. Signal Proc. **10**, 19–41 (2000)
45. Chawla, N.V., Bowyer, K.W., Hall, L.O., Kegelmeyer, W.P.: SMOTE: synthetic minority over-sampling technique. J. Artif. Intell. Res. **16**, 321–357 (2002)

Uncertainty Estimation and Sample Selection for Crowd Counting

Viresh Ranjan[1(✉)], Boyu Wang[1], Mubarak Shah[2], and Minh Hoai[1]

[1] Department of Computer Science, Stony Brook University,
Stony Brook, NY 11790, USA
viresh.ranjan@stonybrook.edu, {boywang,minhhoai}@cs.stonybrook.edu
[2] University of Central Florida, Orlando, FL 32816, USA
shah@crcv.ucf.edu

Abstract. We present a method for image-based crowd counting, one that can predict a crowd density map together with the uncertainty values pertaining to the predicted density map. To obtain prediction uncertainty, we model the crowd density values using Gaussian distributions and develop a convolutional neural network architecture to predict these distributions. A key advantage of our method over existing crowd counting methods is its ability to quantify the uncertainty of its predictions. We illustrate the benefits of knowing the prediction uncertainty by developing a method to reduce the human annotation effort needed to adapt counting networks to a new domain. We present sample selection strategies which make use of the density and uncertainty of predictions from the networks trained on one domain to select the informative images from a target domain of interest to acquire human annotation. We show that our sample selection strategy drastically reduces the amount of labeled data from the target domain needed to adapt a counting network trained on a source domain to the target domain. Empirically, the networks trained on the UCF-QNRF dataset can be adapted to surpass the performance of the previous state-of-the-art results on NWPU dataset and Shanghaitech dataset using only 17% of the labeled training samples from the target domain.
Code: https://github.com/cvlab-stonybrook/UncertaintyCrowdCounting.

1 Introduction

Crowd counting from unconstrained images is a challenging task due to the large variation in occlusion, crowd density, and camera perspective. Most recent methods [26,31,32,34,39,40,43,50] learn a Convolutional Neural Network (CNN) to map an input image to the corresponding crowd density map, from which the total count can be computed by summing all the predicted density values at all

Electronic supplementary material The online version of this chapter (https://doi.org/10.1007/978-3-030-69541-5_23) contains supplementary material, which is available to authorized users.

© Springer Nature Switzerland AG 2021
H. Ishikawa et al. (Eds.): ACCV 2020, LNCS 12626, pp. 375–391, 2021.
https://doi.org/10.1007/978-3-030-69541-5_23

pixels. Although the performance of the crowd counting methods have improved significantly in the recent years, their performance on the challenging datasets such as [9,10,50] is far below the human-level performance. One factor affecting the performance of the existing crowd counting systems is the limited amount of annotated training data. The largest crowd counting dataset [44] consist of 5,109 images. Annotating dense crowd images, which involves placing a dot over the head of each person in the crowd, is time consuming. This makes it harder to create large-scale crowd counting datasets.

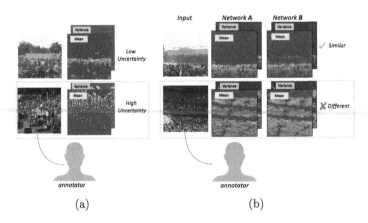

(a)   (b)

Fig. 1. Different sample selection strategies based on uncertainty estimation. (a) uncertainty based sample selection: Images with higher average uncertainty values are selected for annotation. (b) Ensemble disagreement based sample selection: Given networks A and B trained on a source domain, and a set of unlabeled images from a target domain, we obtain the crowd density map and uncertainty values from both networks for all images in the target domain. Based on the prediction, we compute the disagreement between the two networks. Images with large disagreement are picked for human annotation.

In this paper, we present an approach to tackle the prohibitively large costs involved in annotating crowd images. Our approach draws inspiration from Active Learning, which is based on the hypothesis that a learning algorithm can perform well with less training data if it is allowed to select *informative samples* [15,35]. Given a pool of labeled crowd images from the source domain and a large pool of unlabeled crowd images, we are interested in identifying a subset of informative samples from the unlabeled pool, and instead of annotating the whole pool, we obtain the annotation for these selected samples. To find most informative samples from the unlabeled pool, we train networks on the labeled pool first. Next, we select those samples from the unlabeled pool for which the networks are uncertain about their predictions. However, most existing crowd counting methods do not provide any measure of uncertainty for their predictions. We develop a fully convolutional network architecture for estimating the crowd density and the corresponding uncertainty of prediction. For uncertainty estimation, we follow the approach of Nix and Weigand [28] who used a Multi-Layer Perceptron (MLP) to estimate the uncertainty of prediction. This approach assumes that observed output values are drawn from a Gaussian distribution, and the MLP predicts the mean and variance of the Gaussian distribution. The network is trained by maximizing the log likelihood of the data. The variance serves as a measure of uncertainty of the prediction.

Inspired by Nix and Weigand [28], we develop a fully convolutional architecture with a shared trunk for feature extraction and two prediction heads for predicting the crowd density map and the corresponding variance. This network is trained on the source domain by maximizing the log likelihood of the data. We use the predictions from this network, and present two sampling strategies for selecting informative samples from the target domain for human annotation. We present the overview of our sampling strategy in Fig. 1. Our sampling strategy can be used for selecting images from a large pool of unlabeled images, and it can also be used to pick informative crops from an image. Depending on the annotation budget, it might be useful to get partial annotations for an image by picking informative crops from an image and getting human annotations for the informative crops rather than annotating the entire image. We present experiments on image level sample selection[1] and empirically show that the networks trained on UCF-QNRF dataset can be adapted to surpass the performance of the previous state-of-the-art results on NWPU dataset using less than 17% of the labeled training samples. We also show that the UCF-QNRF pretrained networks can be adapted to perform well on the Shanghaitech dataset as well, with only a third of annotated examples from Shanghaitech dataset. Our results clearly show the usefulness of using our sampling strategy in saving human annotation cost, and it can help reduce human annotation cost involved with annotating large scale crowd datasets. Our sampling strategy isn't specific to crowd counting, and it can be applied to any other pixel level prediction task such as optical flow estimation, semantic segmentation as well. We decide to focus on Crowd Counting in this paper since human annotation is particularly expensive for Crowd Counting.

The main contributions of our work are: (**1**) We propose a novel network architecture for crowd density prediction and corresponding uncertainty estimation that uses both local features and self-attention based non-local features for prediction. (**2**) We show that modeling prediction uncertainty leads to a more robust loss function, which outperforms the commonly used mean squared loss, obtaining state of the art results on multiple crowd counting datasets. (**3**) We present a novel uncertainty guided sample selection strategy that enables using networks trained on one domain to select informative samples from another domain for human annotation. To the best of our knowledge, ours is the first work focusing on using predictive uncertainty for sample selection pertaining to any pixel level prediction task in Computer Vision. We show empirically that using the proposed sampling strategy, it is possible to adapt a network trained on a source domain to perform well on the target domain using significantly less annotated data from the target domain.

---

[1] Experiments on crop sample selection are presented in the supplementary materials.

2 Related Work

Crowd counting is an active area of research with two general approaches: detection approach and density estimation approach. Despite lots of related works, none of them use non-local features to reduce the ambiguity of the estimation, nor use the uncertainty estimates for sample selection.

Detection and Regression Based Approaches. Crowd counting has been studied for a long time. Initial crowd counting approaches [16, 19] were based on detection, which used a classifier such as SVMs trained on top of hand crafted feature representation. These approaches performed well on simpler crowd counting datasets, but their performance was severely affected by occlusion, which is quite common in dense crowd datasets. Some of the later approaches [4, 5] tried to tackle the occlusion problem by avoiding the detection problem, and directly learning a regression function to predict the count.

Density Estimation Based Approaches. The precursor to the current density estimation based approaches was the work of Lempitsky and Zisserman [14], who presented one of the earliest works on density estimation based crowd counting. In the recent deep learning era, density estimation has become the de facto strategy for most of the recent crowd counting approaches [3, 6, 10, 12, 17, 18, 20–26, 30, 31, 34, 37, 42, 43, 45, 46, 49–51].

Starting with Zhang et al. [50], many approaches [2, 31, 40] used multiple parallel feature convolutional columns to extract features at different resolution. Zhang et al. [50] used a multi-column architecture comprising of three columns to address the large variation in crowd size and density. The different columns had kernels of varying sizes. The column with larger kernels could extract features for less dense crowd, while the column with finer kernels is for denser crowd. Sam et al. [34] proposed to decouple different columns, and train them separately. Each column was specialized towards a certain density type. This made the task of each regressor easier, since it had to handle similar density images. They also trained a switch classifier which routed an image patch to the appropriate regressor. However, unlike [50], the training procedure comprised of multiple stages. Sindagi and Patel [40] presented an approach which utilized local and global context information for crowd counting. They trained a classifier for classifying an image into multiple density categories, and the classifier score was used to create context feature maps. Ranjan et al. [31] used a two stage coarse to fine approach to predict crowd density map. In the first stage, a low resolution density map was predicted, which was later utilized as a feature map while predicting the final high resolution density map.

Uncertainty Estimation. For Computer Vision tasks, we typically consider two types of uncertainty: *aleatoric* and *epistemic* [13]. Aleatoric uncertainty captures the uncertainty inherent in the data, and can be modeled by predicting the parameters of a Gaussian distribution and maximizing the log likelihood [13, 28] of the observed data. Epsitemic uncertainty, also called model uncertainty, is related to the uncertainty in the model parameters, and can be explained away given a large enough dataset. Epistemic uncertainity can be captured by Bayesian Neural Networks [27]. Although performing inference with earlier Bayesian Neural Networks was inefficient, recent techniques like Monte Carlo Dropout [7] can be used to capture epistemic uncertainty even with large neural networks. Some of the earlier works have focused on uncertainty prediction for tasks such as optical flow estimation [11] and crowd counting [29]. However, none of these earlier works have focused on using uncertainty estimates for sample selection.

3   Uncertainty Estimation for Crowd Counting

We take motivation from earlier work Kendall and Gal [13] which shows the usefulness of both Aleatoric and Epistemic Uncertainty estimates for various Computer Vision tasks, and present architectures which can be used for obtaining the two types of uncertainties. In Sect. 3.1, we present our proposed network architecture for estimating the aleatoric uncertainty[2], followed by training objective in Sect. 3.2.

3.1   Crowd Transformer Network

In this section, we describe our Crowd Transformer Network (CTN) architecture, which predicts the crowd density map along with the corresponding uncertainty values. CTN models the predictive uncertainty, i.e., the uncertainty inherent in the input image which might arise from sensor noise, or from the ambiguity in the image itself.

The block diagram of CTN is presented in Fig. 2. CTN uses both local and non-local features for estimating the crowd density map. Let X be a crowd image of size $H \times W$ and Y the corresponding ground truth density map of the same size. We assume that each value in Y is generated by a Gaussian distribution, and CTN predicts the mean and the variance of the Gaussian distribution. The proposed CTN takes input X and predicts mean and variance maps as:

$$X \to \mu(X, \theta), \sigma^2(X, \theta) \tag{1}$$

where $\mu(X, \theta)$ is the crowd density map and $\sigma^2(X, \theta)$ the uncertainty map. We use uncertainty and variance interchangeably in the rest of the paper. Both $\mu(X, \theta)$ and $\sigma^2(X, \theta)$ have the same size as the input image X as well as the crowd density map Y. The key components of CTN architecture are: 1) a *local feature block*, 2) a *non-local feature block*, 3) a *density prediction branch*, and 4) a *uncertainty prediction branch*. These components are described below.

Local Feature Block. Given an input image X of size $H \times W$, we pass it through a local feature block to obtain the convolutional feature maps. The local

---

[2] See supplementary materials for the architecture for estimating epistemic uncertainty.

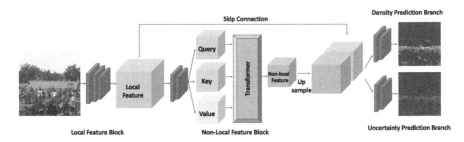

Fig. 2. CTN architecture predicts both crowd density map and corresponding uncertainty values. It combines local and non-local features. The local features are computed by the convolution layers in the local feature block. The resulting feature map is passed to the non-local feature block. Both density prediction branch and uncertainty prediction branch utilize local and non-local features.

feature block consists of five convolution layers with kernels of size 3×3, and the number of filters in the convolution layers are 64, 64, 128, 128, and 256. We use the VGG16 network [38] pretrained on ImageNet to initialize the convolution layers in the local feature block. The local feature block has two max pooling layers, after the second and fourth convolution layers. The resulting feature map is a tensor of size $\frac{H}{4} \times \frac{W}{4} \times 256$. The feature map is passed to the non-local block as well as the density prediction branch and uncertainty branch.

Non-local Feature Block. For computing the non-local features, we use the Transformer architecture [41] which was proposed as an alternative to recurrent neural network [33] for solving various sequence analysis tasks. It uses an attention mechanism to encode non-local features. The architecture consists of an encoder and a decoder, where the encoder maps the input sequence into an intermediate representation, which in turn is mapped by the decoder into the output sequence. The transformer uses three types of attention layers: *encoder self-attention, encoder-decoder attention,* and *decoder self-attention.* For the proposed crowd counting approach in this paper, only the first one is relevant which we describe briefly next. Henceforth, we will use self-attention to refer to the self-attention of the encoder.

Encoder Self-attention. Given a query sequence along with a key-and-value sequence, the self-attention layer outputs a sequence where the i-th element in the output sequence is obtained as a weighted average of the value sequence, and the weights are decided based on the similarity between the i-th query element and the key sequence. Let $X \in R^{n \times d}$ be a matrix representation for a sequence consisting of n vectors of d dimensions. The self-attention layer first transforms X into query X_Q, key X_K, and value X_V matrices by multiplying X with matrices W_Q, W_K, and W_V, respectively:

$$X_Q = XW_Q, X_K = XW_K, X_V = XW_V. \tag{2}$$

The output sequence Z is computed efficiently with matrix multiplications:

$$Z = softmax(X_Q X_K^T) X_V. \tag{3}$$

The encoder consists of multiple self-attention layers, arranged in a sequential order so that the output of one layer is fed as input to the next layer.

Architecture Details. The non-local feature block takes as input the feature map from the local feature block, and passes it through three convolution layers of kernel size 3×3 and a max pooling layer, which results in a feature map of size $\frac{H}{8} \times \frac{W}{8} \times 512$. We reduce the depth of the feature map by passing it through a 1×1 convolution layer, which yields a feature map of size $\frac{H}{8} \times \frac{W}{8} \times 240$. The resulting feature map is flattened into a matrix of size $M \times 240$, where $M = \frac{H}{8} \times \frac{W}{8}$. Each row in this matrix corresponds to some location in the convolution feature map. The flattened matrix is passed through three self-attention layers. The output from final transformer layer is reshaped back into a tensor of size $\frac{H}{8} \times \frac{W}{8} \times 240$.

Density Prediction Branch. Both local and non-local features are important for estimating an accurate crowd density map. Hence, the Density Prediction Branch uses a skip connection to obtain the convolutional features from the local feature block, and combines it with the features from the non-local feature block. The non-local features are upsampled to the same spatial size as local features, which results in a tensor of size $\frac{H}{4} \times \frac{W}{4} \times 240$. The local and non-local features are concatenated and passed through four convolution layers (with 196, 128, 48, and 1 filters), where the last layer is a 1×1 convolution layer. We add a ReLU non-linearity after the 1×1 convolution layer to prevent the network from predicting negative density values. We use two bilinear interpolation layers, after the second and third convolution layers in the prediction head. Each interpolation layer upsamples its input by the factor of two. The input to the final 1×1 convolution layer is a feature map of size $H \times W \times 48$, which is transformed into a 2D map by the last convolution layer.

Predictive Uncertainty Estimation Branch. The *Predictive Uncertainty Estimation Branch* outputs the variance map $\sigma^2(X, \theta)$. Similar to the density prediction branch, the uncertainty branch also uses both the local and non-local features for prediction. The uncertainty prediction branch has the same architecture as the density prediction branch, with one major difference being that we use point-wise softplus nonlinearity instead of ReLU nonlinearity after the last 1×1 convolution layer. Softplus nonlinearity can be expressed as: $softplus(x) = \frac{1}{\beta} \log(1 + \exp(\beta x))$. For brevity, we will refer to this type of uncertainty estimation as Predictive Uncertainty.

3.2   Training Objective

The network is trained by minimizing the negative conditional log likelihood of the observed ground truth density values Y, conditioned on the input image X:

$$\mathcal{L}(Y|X,\theta) = -\sum_{i=1}^{HW} \log(\mathbb{P}(Y_i|\mu_i(X,\theta),\sigma_i^2(X,\theta))), \tag{4}$$

where $\mathbb{P}(y|\mu,\sigma^2) = \frac{1}{\sqrt{2\pi\sigma^2}} \exp(-\frac{(y-\mu)^2}{2\sigma^2})$, a univariate Gaussian distribution. The negative conditional log likelihood is proportional to:

$$\mathcal{L}(Y|X,\theta) \propto \sum_{i=1}^{HW} \left(\log \sigma_i(X,\theta) + \frac{(Y_i - \mu_i(X,\theta))^2}{2\sigma_i^2(X,\theta)} \right).$$

The above objective can be seen as a weighted sum of the squared differences, where the weights depend on the estimated uncertainty of the input X. This objective can be seen as a robust regression objective, where higher importance is given to pixels with lower ambiguity [28].

4   Uncertainty Guided Sample Selection

Given a labeled dataset $\{(X_A, Y_A)\}$ from domain A, and an unlabeled dataset $\{X_B\}$ from domain B, we are interested in finding a small subset of informative samples from domain B. Each instance X_B of domain B can be sent to an oracle (human) to obtain the label Y_B. Our motivation behind selecting a small subset from domain B is to reduce the human annotation cost without sacrificing the performance on domain B. Next, we propose different strategies for selecting informative samples. In Sect. sec:aleatoricSampling, we propose to use the aleatoric uncertainty predicted by CTN to select informative samples. In Sect. sec:EnsembleSampling, we draw inspiration from Query-by-committee [35] sampling strategies in Active Learning, and present a sampling strategy that uses the disagreement between the members of an ensemble of CTN networks for selecting informative samples. We present two strategies for computing the disagreement, the first one uses both the density and the uncertainty predictions while the other uses just the density prediction.

4.1   Aleatoric Uncertainty Based Sample Selection

When picking samples from the target domain, we want to select those samples for which the network makes erroneous prediction. Previous works and our own experiments show that aleatoric uncertainty is correlated to the prediction error (see supplementary materials and Fig. 3). Hence, we propose to use the aleatoric uncertainty for selecting informative samples. We use the CTN network trained on the source domain to compute the aleatoric uncertainty (averaged across the image) for all the images in the target domain, and select those samples from the target domain for labeling that have a high average aleatoric uncertainty.

4.2 Ensemble Disagreement Based Sample Selection

Inspired by the Query-By-Committee [36] sampling algorithm in Active Learning, we present another sampling strategy which uses the predictions from our CTN network trained on a source domain to select informative samples from a target domain. The Query-By-Committee algorithm keeps a committee of students, and picks the sample with maximal disagreement between the committee members to acquire annotation. In this work, the committee is a set of two CTN networks as described in the previous section. These networks are trained on different subsets of labeled data from domain A, and the disagreement between the two networks are used as a measure of informativeness. Let the two networks be represented by their parameters θ_1 and θ_2 and the outputs of the networks are the mean and variance maps:

$$\left[\mu(X, \theta_1), \sigma^2(X, \theta_1)\right] \text{ and } \left[\mu(X, \theta_2), \sigma^2(X, \theta_2)\right]. \tag{5}$$

The values $\mu_i(X, \theta_1)$ and $\sigma_i^2(X, \theta_1)$ are the mean and variance of a Gaussian distribution for the density value at pixel i. Similarly, the values $\mu_i(X, \theta_2)$ and $\sigma_i^2(X, \theta_2)$ correspond to another Gaussian distribution. We use the KL divergence between these two distributions as a measure of disagreement between the two density estimation networks. We denote the KL divergence at location i of image X as $KL(X_i)$, which can be computed in close form as:

$$KL(X_i) = \frac{\sigma_i^2(X, \theta_1) + (\mu_i(X, \theta_1) - \mu_i(X, \theta_2))^2}{2\sigma_i^2(X, \theta_2)} + \log\left(\frac{\sigma_i(X, \theta_2)}{\sigma_i(X, \theta_1)}\right) - \frac{1}{2}. \tag{6}$$

The overall informativeness of an image is obtained by computing the average KL divergence over all pixels. We sort all the images in domain B according to their informativeness, and select the most informative samples for annotation. Note that this approach can be easily extended for more than two networks.

We present another strategy called *Density-difference based Ensemble disagreement* to compute the disagreement between the members of an ensemble. This disagreement is computed by averaging the pixel wise squared difference between the the density maps predicted by the members of the ensemble as

$$Diff(X_i) = (\mu_i(X, \theta_1) - \mu_i(X, \theta_2))^2. \tag{7}$$

The informativeness score is obtained by averaging $Diff(X_i)$ over the entire prediction map. The score can be generalized to work with an ensemble of multiple networks.

5 Experiments

We validate the proposed approach by conducting experiments on four publicly available datasets: UCF-QNRF [10], UCF CC [9], Shanghaitech [50] and NWPU [44]. In Sect. 5.1, we discuss the crowd counting results on all datasets. Note that we use the entire training set from each dataset for this experiment.

In Sect. 5.2, we show the effectiveness of the proposed sample selection strategies. Following previous works, we report Mean Absolute Error (MAE) and Root Mean Squared Error (RMSE) metrics:

$$MAE = \frac{1}{n} \sum_{i=1}^{n} |C_i - \hat{C}_i|; RMSE = \sqrt{\frac{1}{n} \sum_{i=1}^{n} (C_i - \hat{C}_i)^2},$$

where C_i is the ground truth count, $\hat{C}_i$ is the predicted count, and the summation is computed over all test images.

5.1   Crowd Density Prediction

Experiments on UCF-QNRF Dataset. The UCF-QNRF dataset [10] consists of 1201 training and 334 test images of variable sizes, with 1.2 million dot annotations. For our experiments, we rescale those images for which the larger side is greater than 2048 pixels to 2048. For training, we take random crops of size 512×512 from each image. Keeping the variance prediction branch fixed, we first train the other blocks of the proposed network for 20 epochs using the mean squared error loss. Next, we train only the uncertainty variance prediction head by minimizing the negative log likelihood objective for five epochs. Finally, we train the entire network by minimizing the negative log likelihood for 10 more epochs, and report the best results. We use a learning rate of 10^{-4}, and a batch size of three for training.

Comparison with Existing Approaches. Table 1 shows the performance of various approaches on the UCF-QNRF dataset. Bayesian Loss [26] is a novel loss function for training crowd counting networks. It outperforms mean squared error, and it has the current state-of-the-art performance. This loss function is complimentary to what we propose here, and it can be used together with CTN. In fact, the method CTN* displayed in Table 1 is the combination of CTN and Bayesian Loss. CTN* improves the performance of Bayesian Loss [26] and advances the state-of-the-art result on this dataset.

Ablation Study. The proposed CTN consists of three main components: Local Feature Block, Non-Local Feature Block, and Predictive Uncertainty Estimation Branch. To further understand the contribution of each component, we perform an ablation study, and the results are shown in Table 2. As can be seen, all constituent components of CTN are important for maintaining its good performance on the UCF-QNRF dataset.

Experiments on NWPU-Crowd Dataset. NWPU [44] is the largest crowd counting dataset comprising of 5,109 crowd images taken from the web and video sequences, and over 2.1 million annotated instances. The ground truth for test images are not available, here we present the results on the validation set of NWPU in Table 1. For this experiment, we use the pretrained CTN model from UCF-QNRF dataset and adapt the network on the NWPU dataset. Our proposed approach outperforms the previous methods.

Table 1. Performance of various methods on the UCF-QNRF test dataset and NWPU validation dataset. Bayesian Loss is a recently proposed novel loss function for training a crowd counting network. CTN* is the method that combines CTN and Bayesian Loss, advancing the state-of-the-art performance in both MAE and RMSE metrics. Following [26], we use the first four blocks from Vgg-19 as the backbone for local feature extraction.

	UCF-QNRF		NWPU	
	MAE	RMSE	MAE	RMSE
Idrees *et al.* [9]	315	508	–	–
MCNN [50]	277	426	219	701
CMTL [39]	252	514	–	–
Switch CNN [2]	228	445	–	–
Composition Loss-CNN [10]	132	191	–	–
CSR net [17]	–	–	105	433
CAN [23]	107	183	94	490
SFCN [43]	102	171	–	–
ANF [47]	110	174	–	–
Bayesian Loss [26]	89	155	93	470
SCAR [8]	–	–	82	**398**
CTN* (Proposed)	**86**	**146**	**78**	448

Table 2. Ablation study on UCF-QNRF. CTN is the proposed counting network that consists of: Local Feature Block, Non-local Feature Block, and Uncertainty Prediction Branch. All three components are important for maintaining the good performance of CTN on this dataset. Note that ablation study is done using the Vgg-16 backbone.

Components	Combinations			
Local features	✓	✓	✓	
Non-local features	✓	✓		✓
Predictive uncertainty	✓			
MAE	93	106	120	123
RMSE	166	185	218	206

Experiments on UCF-CC Dataset. The UCF-CC dataset [9] consists of 50 images collected form the web, and the count across the dataset varies between 94 and 4545. We use random crops of size $\frac{H}{3} \times \frac{W}{3}$ for training. Following previous works, we perform 5-fold cross validation and report the average result in Table 3. The proposed CTN with the Predictive Uncertainty (CTN) is comparable to other state-of-the-art approaches in both MAE and RMSE metrics. For all the approaches, the error on UCF CC dataset is higher compared to the other datasets since it has a small number of training samples.

Table 3. Count errors of different methods on the UCF-CC dataset and Shanghaitech dataset. This dataset has two parts: Part A was collected from the web, and Part B was collected from the streets of Shanghai. The average ground truth crowd count for Part A is larger than that for Part B. We report both MAE and RMSE metrics.

	UCF-CC		Shtech Part A		Shtech Part B	
	MAE	RMSE	MAE	RMSE	MAE	RMSE
Crowd CNN [48]	–	–	181.8	277.7	32.0	49.8
MCNN [50]	377.6	509.1	110.2	173.2	26.4	41.3
Switching CNN [34]	–	–	90.4	135.0	21.6	33.4
CP-CNN [40]	295.8	320.9	73.6	106.4	20.1	30.1
IG-CNN [1]	291.4	349.4	72.5	118.2	13.6	21.1
ic-CNN [31]	260.9	365.5	68.5	116.2	10.7	16.0
SANet [3]	258.4	334.9	67.0	104.5	8.4	13.6
CSR Net [17]	266.1	397.5	68.2	115.0	10.6	16.0
PACNN [37]	241.7	320.7	62.4	102.0	7.6	**11.8**
SFCN [43]	214.2	318.2	64.8	107.5	7.6	13.0
ANF [47]	250.2	340.0	63.9	**99.4**	8.3	13.2
Bayesian loss [26]	229.3	308.2	62.8	101.8	7.7	12.7
CTN (proposed)	**210.0**	**305.4**	**61.5**	103.4	**7.5**	11.9

Experiments on Shanghaitech Dataset. The Shanghaitech dataset [50] consists of two parts. Part A contains 482 images collected from the web, and Part B contains 716 images collected on the streets of Shanghai. The average ground truth crowd counts for Part A and Part B are 501 and 124, respectively. For training, we use random crops of size $\frac{H}{3} \times \frac{W}{3}$. Results are shown in Table 3. The proposed approach outperforms all existing approaches in terms of MAE. Part A is more challenging with denser crowds than Part B. As a result, the average error of all the approaches on Part A is larger than those on Part B. Note that the CTN network in Table 3 is first trained on UCF-QNRF and later finetuned on Shanghitech dataset. This may not be a fair comparison for those approaches in Table 3 where the networks are trained from scratch on Shanghaitech dataset. Hence, for a more fair comparison, we train the current state of the art model [26] on UCF-QNRF dataset first, and finetune it on Shanghaitech Part A dataset. We use the official implementation by the authors and use the hyper parameters reported by the authors [26]. This results in MAE/RMSE of 63.4/107.9 on the test set of ShanghaiTech Part A. Our CTN outperforms [26] in this experiment, with MAE/RMSE of 61.5/103.4 reported in Table 3. This is a fair comparison since both methods are pretrained on UCF-QNRF, and later finetuned on Shanghaitech Part A.

Table 4. Comparing different strategies for selecting images for annotation.
We train the network on the UCF-QNRF dataset, and use it to select images from
the NWPU and Shanghaitech train data for acquiring annotation. We compare the
random selection baseline with the proposed uncertainty-guided selection strategy. For
NWPU dataset, using just 500 training samples selected using our sampling strategy,
we achieve state-of-the-art results compared to the previous state-of-art [8] trained on
entire training set in terms of MSE. For Shanghaitech Part A, using just 50 labeled
training samples, selected using our density based ensemble disagreement sampling
strategy, we perform comparably to the state-of-the-art networks trained on the entire
training set.

Selection approach	Shtech Part A			NWPU		
	#Train	MAE	RMSE	#Train	MAE	RMSE
None (pretrained)	NA	69.2	113.5	NA	118.4	632.3
Random	50	68.7	117.1	100	117.4	640.7
Count	50	67.3	107.4	100	107.9	458.8
Aleatoric uncertainty	50	62.9	108.1	100	104.9	522.1
Density based ensemble disagr.	**50**	**61.4**	**105.5**	100	112.8	526.8
KL-ensemble disagreement	50	65.5	118.4	100	105.8	481.9
Random	100	65.5	125.5	500	96.7	539.4
Count	100	63.3	109.8	500	95.9	442.5
Aleatoric uncertainty	100	64.7	107.8	**500**	**81.5**	**313.7**
Density based Ensemble Disagreement	100	62.2	109.6	500	90.0	438.6
KL-ensemble disagreement	100	62.1	103.3	500	95.6	511.3
Full dataset (previous best methods)	300	62.8	99.4	3109	82	398
Full dataset (CTN)	300	61.5	103.4	3109	78.1	448.2

5.2   Uncertainty Guided Image Annotation

In this section, we evaluate the effectiveness of the proposed selective annotation strategy. We train the network on the UCF-QNRF dataset and use it to
select the informative samples from the Shanghaitech Part A dataset and NWPU
dataset for acquiring annotation (results on Shanghaitech Part B are presented
in the Supplementary). We use the labels of the selected samples, keep the variance prediction branch frozen, and finetune CTN using the selected subset. We
compare our sampling approach with two baseline sampling approaches: 1) *random sampling approach*: images are randomly sampled from the unlabeled pool
in the target domain, and 2) *Count based sampling*: we select those samples
from the target domain for which the pretrained network predicts a high count.
We report the results in Table 4. Note that the entire training sets of Shanghaitech Part A and NWPU have 300 and 3109 images respectively. Our sampling
approaches outperform the random baseline by a large margin. We also outperform the Count based sampling baseline. For NWPU dataset, using just 500
training samples, we achieve state-of-the-art results compared to the previous
state-of-art [8] trained on the entire training set in terms of MSE. For Shanghaitech Part A, using just 50 labeled training samples, selected using our density
based ensemble disagreement sampling strategy, we perform comparably to the

Image	Ground truth	Mean	Variance	Error

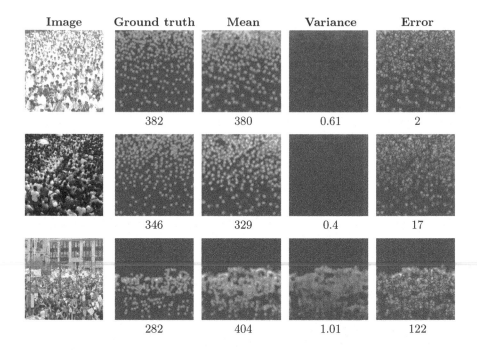

Fig. 3. **Qualitative Results.** This figure shows Image, Ground truth, Predicted Mean, Predicted Variance, and Error map. We specify the sum of the map below the corresponding map. The first two examples are success cases for density estimation, while the last is a failure cases. The variance maps correlate with the error maps.

state-of-the-art networks trained on the entire training set. Our results clearly show the usefulness of our informative sample selection strategy for transferring counting networks from one domain to another.

5.3   Qualitative Results

Figure 3 displays some qualitative585 results from UCF-QNRF dataset. Error is correlated with the variance which suggests the appropriateness of using the variance maps for estimating the uncertainty of the density prediction.

6   Conclusions

To tackle large human annotation costs involved with annotating large scale crowd datasets, we have presented uncertainty based and ensemble disagreement based sampling strategies. These strategies were shown to be useful for the task of transferring a crowd network trained on one domain to a different target domain. Using just 17% of the training samples obtained using our sampling strategy, we obtained state-of-the-art results on two challenging crowd counting datasets. We also showed that our proposed architecture, when trained on the full dataset, achieved state-of-the-art results on all the datasets in terms of mean absolute error.

Acknowledgements. This project is partially supported by MedPod and the SUNY2020 Infrastructure Transportation Security Center.

References

1. Babu, D., Sajjan, N., Babu, V.R., Srinivasan, M.: Divide and grow: capturing huge diversity in crowd images with incrementally growing CNN. In Proceedings of the IEEE Conference on Computer Vision and Pattern Recognition (2018)
2. Sam, D.B., Surya, S., Babu, R.V.: Switching convolutional neural network for crowd counting. In: Proceedings of the IEEE Conference on Computer Vision and Pattern Recognition (2017)
3. Cao, X., Wang, Z., Zhao, Y., Su, F.: Scale aggregation network for accurate and efficient crowd counting. In: Ferrari, V., Hebert, M., Sminchisescu, C., Weiss, Y. (eds.) ECCV 2018. LNCS, vol. 11209, pp. 757–773. Springer, Cham (2018). https://doi.org/10.1007/978-3-030-01228-1_45
4. Chan, A.B., Vasconcelos, N.: Bayesian poisson regression for crowd counting. In: Proceedings of the International Conference on Computer Vision (2009)
5. Chen, K., Loy, C.C., Gong, S., Xiang, T.: Feature mining for localised crowd counting. In: Proceedings of the British Machine Vision Conference (2012)
6. Cheng, Z.-Q., Li, J.-X., Dai, Q., Wu, X., Hauptmann, A.G.: Learning spatial awareness to improve crowd counting. In: Proceedings of the International Conference on Computer Vision (2019)
7. Gal, Y., Ghahramani, Z.: Bayesian convolutional neural networks with bernoulli approximate variational inference. arXiv preprint arXiv:1506.02158 (2015)
8. Gao, J., Wang, Q., Yuan, Y.: SCAR: spatial-/channel-wise attention regression networks for crowd counting. Neurocomputing **363**, 1–8 (2019)
9. Idrees, H., Saleemi, I., Seibert, C., Shah, M.: Multi-source multi-scale counting in extremely dense crowd images. In: Proceedings of the IEEE Conference on Computer Vision and Pattern Recognition (2013)
10. Idrees, H., et al.: Composition loss for counting, density map estimation and localization in dense crowds. In: Proceedings of the European Conference on Computer Vision (2018)
11. Ilg, E., et al.: Uncertainty estimates and multi-hypotheses networks for optical flow. In: Ferrari, V., Hebert, M., Sminchisescu, C., Weiss, Y. (eds.) ECCV 2018. LNCS, vol. 11211, pp. 677–693. Springer, Cham (2018). https://doi.org/10.1007/978-3-030-01234-2_40
12. Jiang, X. et al.: Crowd counting and density estimation by trellis encoder-decoder networks. In: Proceedings of the IEEE Conference on Computer Vision and Pattern Recognition (2019)
13. Kendall, A., Gal, Y.: What uncertainties do we need in Bayesian deep learning for computer vision? In: Advances in Neural Information Processing Systems (2017)
14. Lempitsky, V., Zisserman, A.: Learning to count objects in images. In: Advances in Neural Information Processing Systems (2010)
15. Lewis, D.D., Gale, W.A.: A sequential algorithm for training text classifiers. In: Croft, B.W., van Rijsbergen, C.J. (eds.) SIGIR 1994, pp. 3–12. Springer, London (1994). https://doi.org/10.1007/978-1-4471-2099-5_1

16. Li, M., Zhang, Z., Huang, K., Tan, T.: Estimating the number of people in crowded scenes by mid based foreground segmentation and head-shoulder detection. In: Proceedings of the International Conference on Pattern Recognition (2008)

17. Li, Y., Zhang, X., Chen, D.: CSRNet: dilated convolutional neural networks for understanding the highly congested scenes. In: Proceedings of the IEEE Conference on Computer Vision and Pattern Recognition (2018)

18. Lian, D., Li, J., Zheng, J., Luo, W., Gao, S.: Density map regression guided detection network for RGB-D crowd counting and localization. In: Proceedings of the IEEE Conference on Computer Vision and Pattern Recognition (2019)

19. Lin, S.-F., Chen, J.-Y., Chao, H.-X.: Estimation of number of people in crowded scenes using perspective transformation. IEEE Trans. Syst. Man Cybern.-Part A: Syst. Hum. **31**(6), 645–654 (2001)

20. Liu, C., Weng, X., Mu, Y.: Recurrent attentive zooming for joint crowd counting and precise localization. In: Proceedings of the IEEE Conference on Computer Vision and Pattern Recognition (2019)

21. Liu, L., Qiu, Z., Li, G., Liu, S., Ouyang, W., Lin, L.: Crowd counting with deep structured scale integration network. In: Proceedings of the International Conference on Computer Vision (2019)

22. Liu, N., Long, Y., Zou, C., Niu, Q., Pan, L., Wu, H.: ADCrowdNet: an attention-injective deformable convolutional network for crowd understanding. In: Proceedings of the IEEE Conference on Computer Vision and Pattern Recognition (2019)

23. Liu, W., Salzmann, M., Fua, P.: Context-aware crowd counting. In: Proceedings of the IEEE Conference on Computer Vision and Pattern Recognition (2019)

24. Liu, Y., Shi, M., Zhao, Q., Wang, X.: Point in, box out: beyond counting persons in crowds. In: Proceedings of the IEEE Conference on Computer Vision and Pattern Recognition (2019)

25. Lu, E., Xie, W., Zisserman, A.: Class-agnostic counting. arXiv:1811.00472 (2018)

26. Ma, Z., Wei, X., Hong, X., Gong, Y.: Bayesian loss for crowd count estimation with point supervision. In: Proceedings of the International Conference on Computer Vision (2019)

27. Neal, R.M.: Bayesian Learning for Neural Networks, vol. 118. Springer, Heidelberg (2012)

28. Nix, D.A., Weigend, A.S.: Estimating the mean and variance of the target probability distribution. In: Proceedings of IEEE International Conference on Neural Networks (1994)

29. Oh, M., Olsen, P.A., Ramamurthy, K.N.: Crowd counting with decomposed uncertainty. arXiv preprint arXiv:1903.07427 (2019)

30. Oñoro-Rubio, D., López-Sastre, R.J.: Towards perspective-free object counting with deep learning. In: Leibe, B., Matas, J., Sebe, N., Welling, M. (eds.) ECCV 2016. LNCS, vol. 9911, pp. 615–629. Springer, Cham (2016). https://doi.org/10.1007/978-3-319-46478-7_38

31. Ranjan, V., Le, H., Hoai, M.: Iterative crowd counting. In: Ferrari, V., Hebert, M., Sminchisescu, C., Weiss, Y. (eds.) ECCV 2018. LNCS, vol. 11211, pp. 278–293. Springer, Cham (2018). https://doi.org/10.1007/978-3-030-01234-2_17

32. Ranjan, V., Shah, M., Hoai, M.: Crowd transformer network (2019)

33. Rumelhart, D., Hinton, G., Williams, R.: Learning internal representations by error propagation. In: Parallel Distributed Processing, vol. 1, chap. 8, pp. 318–362. MIT Press, Cambridge (1986)

34. Sam, D.B., Surya, S., Babu, R.V.: Switching convolutional neural network for crowd counting. In: Proceedings of the IEEE Conference on Computer Vision and Pattern Recognition (2017)

35. Settles, B.: Active learning literature survey. Technical report, University of Wisconsin-Madison Department of Computer Sciences (2009)
36. Seung, H.S. Opper, M., Sompolinsky, H.: Query by committee. In: Proceedings of the Fifth Annual Workshop on Computational Learning Theory (1992)
37. Shi, M., Yang, Z., Xu, C., Chen, Q.: Revisiting perspective information for efficient crowd counting. In: Proceedings of the IEEE Conference on Computer Vision and Pattern Recognition (2019)
38. Simonyan, K., Zisserman, A.: Very deep convolutional networks for large-scale image recognition. arXiv:1409.1556 (2014)
39. Sindagi, V.A., Patel, V.M.: CNN-based cascaded multi-task learning of high-level prior and density estimation for crowd counting. In: IEEE International Conference on Advanced Video and Signal Based Surveillance (2017)
40. Sindagi, V.A., Patel, V.M.: Generating high-quality crowd density maps using contextual pyramid CNNs. In Proceedings of the International Conference on Computer Vision (2017)
41. Vaswani, A., et al.: Attention is all you need. In: Advances in Neural Information Processing Systems (2017)
42. Wan, J., Luo, W., Wu, B., Chan, A.B., Liu, W.: Residual regression with semantic prior for crowd counting. In: Proceedings of the IEEE Conference on Computer Vision and Pattern Recognition (2019)
43. Wang, Q., Gao, J., Lin, W., Yuan, Y.: Learning from synthetic data for crowd counting in the wild. In: Proceedings of the IEEE Conference on Computer Vision and Pattern Recognition (2019)
44. Wang, Q., Gao, J., Lin, W., Li, X.: NWPU-crowd: a large-scale benchmark for crowd counting. arXiv preprint arXiv:2001.03360 (2020)
45. Xu, C., Qiu, K., Fu, J., Bai, S., Xu, Y., Bai, X.: Learn to scale: generating multipolar normalized density maps for crowd counting. In: Proceedings of the International Conference on Computer Vision (2019)
46. Yan, Z., et al.: Perspective-guided convolution networks for crowd counting. In: Proceedings of the International Conference on Computer Vision (2019)
47. Zhang, A., et al.: Attentional neural fields for crowd counting. In: Proceedings of the International Conference on Computer Vision (2019)
48. Zhang, C., Li, H., Wang, X., Yang, X.: Cross-scene crowd counting via deep convolutional neural networks. In: Proceedings of the IEEE Conference on Computer Vision and Pattern Recognition (2015)
49. Zhang, Q., Chan, A.B.: Wide-area crowd counting via ground-plane density maps and multi-view fusion CNNs. In: Proceedings of the IEEE Conference on Computer Vision and Pattern Recognition (2019)
50. Zhang, Y. Zhou, D., Chen, S., Gao, S., Ma, Y.: Single-image crowd counting via multi-column convolutional neural network. In: Proceedings of the IEEE Conference on Computer Vision and Pattern Recognition (2016)
51. Zhao, M. Zhang, J., Zhang, C., Zhang, W.: Leveraging heterogeneous auxiliary tasks to assist crowd counting. In: Proceedings of the IEEE Conference on Computer Vision and Pattern Recognition (2019)

Multi-task Learning for Simultaneous Video Generation and Remote Photoplethysmography Estimation

Yun-Yun Tsou, Yi-An Lee, and Chiou-Ting Hsu[✉]

National Tsing Hua University, Hsinchu, Taiwan
tsou0320@gmail.com, andy75527552andy@gmail.com, cthsu@cs.nthu.edu.tw

Abstract. Remote photoplethysmography (rPPG) is a contactless method for estimating physiological signals from facial videos. Without large supervised datasets, learning a robust rPPG estimation model is extremely challenging. Instead of merely focusing on model learning, we believe data augmentation may be of greater importance for this task. In this paper, we propose a novel multi-task learning framework to simultaneously augment training data while learning the rPPG estimation model. We design three networks: rPPG estimation network, Image-to-Video network, and Video-to-Video network, to estimate rPPG signals from face videos, to generate synthetic videos from a source image and a specified rPPG signal, and to generate synthetic videos from a source video and a specified rPPG signal, respectively. Experimental results on three benchmark datasets, COHFACE, UBFC, and PURE, show that our method successfully generates photo-realistic videos and significantly outperforms existing methods with a large margin. (The code is publicly available at https://github.com/YiAnLee/Multi-Task-Learning-for-Simultaneous-VideoGeneration-and-Remote-Photoplethysmography-Estimation).

1 Introduction

Heart rate (HR) is a major health indicator of human body and has been widely used to aid diagnosis of heart diseases, such as detection of atrial fibrillation [1,2]. Existing methods usually rely on specific contact devices to detect Electrocardiography (ECG) or Photoplethysmography (PPG) signals for monitoring the heart rate. Although these contact devices provide accurate readings, they require professional attention to collect the signals and can hardly be used to monitor a large group of subjects at the same time.

Y.-Y. Tsou and Y.-A. Lee—The first two authors contributed equally.

Electronic supplementary material The online version of this chapter (https://doi.org/10.1007/978-3-030-69541-5_24) contains supplementary material, which is available to authorized users.

© Springer Nature Switzerland AG 2021
H. Ishikawa et al. (Eds.): ACCV 2020, LNCS 12626, pp. 392–407, 2021.
https://doi.org/10.1007/978-3-030-69541-5_24

A number of contactless video-based methods have been developed [3–5] to support remote estimation of physiological signals. Especially, remote photo-plethysmography (rPPG), which aims to analyze the blood volume changes in optical information, has been shown to be able to capture heart rate information [3,6], to aid detection of atrial fibrillation [1,2], and can even be extended to applications such as face anti-spoofing [7–10]. However, because visual appearance is more vulnerable to environmental interference (e.g.., illumination) and subjects' motion (e.g., body and muscular movement during the recording stage), many efforts have been devoted to robust estimation of rPPG signals through learning-based methods [2–4,11].

Nevertheless, success of learning-based methods heavily relies on large and good supervised datasets; there are unfortunately few datasets available for training robust rPPG or HR estimation. Unlike other video analysis tasks, collection of face videos and their ground truth for rPPG estimation is extremely complex. Voluntary subjects are required to wear specific devices to obtain the ground truth PPG labels. Moreover, if the subjects are hospital patients, not only the data collection takes enormous time, but also the usage of their face videos is highly restricted. Therefore, only a few datasets of face videos with ground-truth PPG signals are publicly available, and these datasets are small-scaled with very limited number of subjects. For example, UBFC-RPPG [12] dataset contains 42 videos from 42 subjects, and PURE dataset [13] contains 60 videos from only 10 subjects. Although in [1] a larger dataset OBF was collected with 200 videos from 100 healthy adults, this dataset cannot be publicly released because of privacy concern. Consequently, performance of existing methods remains unsatisfactory. To tackle the problem of insufficient data, in [14], the authors proposed to pre-train their model on large-scaled data of synthetic rhythm signals. Because these synthetic rhythm signals need to be converted to a spatial-temporal representation before estimating heart rates, its practicability in real-world scenarios is doubtful. Moreover, any pre-processing step may diminish the subtle chrominance changes in face videos and yield inaccurate estimates. For example, previous multi-stage methods usually involve spatial/temporal sampling, and/or conversion from video frames to spatial-temporal maps. The conversion step heavily relies on an accurate and stable ROI selection algorithm (so as to align the same location into the spatial dimension of the map) and also incurs information loss while collapsing the two spatial dimensions into one dimension in the map. There is indeed a dearth of research on resolving this dilemma.

To resolve the aforementioned problems, in this paper, we propose to generate augmented data by synthesizing videos containing specific rPPG signals and to learn the rPPG estimator from both the source videos and the synthetic videos. We formulate two tasks, that is, data augmentation and rPPG estimation, in a multi-task learning framework. Figure 1 illustrates the proposed idea of generating synthetic videos by embedding a target rPPG signal into either a still image or a video sequence. A more detailed framework is given in Fig. 2, where the three networks: rPPG network, Image-to-Video network, and Video-to-Video

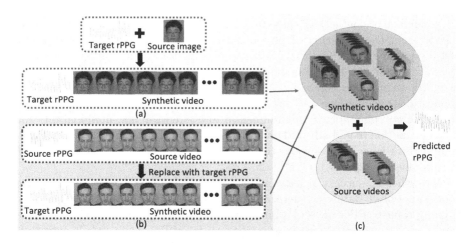

Fig. 1. Illustration of the proposed idea. (a) Generation of a synthetic video from a given source image and a target rPPG signal, (b) generation of a synthetic video from a given source video and a target rPPG signal, and (c) learning the robust rPPG estimator from both the source videos and the synthetic videos.

network, are successively trained. We first pre-train the rPPG network using source videos of the benchmark dataset. Next, we train the two video generation networks (i.e., Image-to-Video and Video-to-Video networks) by concatenating them with the pre-trained rPPG network but without updating the parameters of rPPG network. Finally, we fine-tune the pre-trained rPPG network using synthetic videos obtained from the two video generation networks. As mentioned before, the performance of rPPG network highly depends on the quantity and quality of the training data. In this paper, we aim to create a win-win situation and to reinforce these tasks to mutually support each other. Specifically, because the data augmentation task (i.e., Image-to-Video network and Video-to-Video network) needs to refer to the rPPG network to verify whether the synthesized videos capture the target rPPG signals or not, a robust estimation naturally leads to a better generation performance. On the other hand, with the increased number of synthetics videos, the estimation task is able to learn from various combinations of face videos (e.g., different skin colors, environmental illuminations, and motions) and rPPG signals (e.g., healthy subjects or patients with heart disease) to increase its robustness. Our experimental results on three benchmark datasets: COHFACE [15], PURE [13] and UBFC-RPPG [12], show that we successfully generate photo-realistic videos with different rPPG signals and that the learned rPPG estimator achieves state-of-the-art performance.

Our contributions are summarized below:

– To the best of our knowledge, this is the first work focusing on generating synthetic videos with specific rPPG signals. The augmented dataset will benefit the future study on remote monitoring of human physiological signals.

- We propose a multi-task learning framework to simultaneously learn the data augmentation and the rPPG estimation tasks. These tasks, modeled with three networks, are thus enforced to improve each other to boost the overall performance.
- The proposed method successfully learns rich augmented data and yields robust rPPG estimation. Experimental results show that our method achieves state-of-the-art results.

2   Related Work

Remote Photoplethysmography Estimation has attracted enormous research interests for heart rate estimation [6,12,16–21]. Earlier methods focus on designing either feature descriptors or color filters to capture the strongest PPG information from facial videos. For example, in [6], the authors proposed a chrominance-based approach to project RGB channels into a subspace for extracting the rPPG signals. In [21], the authors estimated a spatial subspace of skin-pixels and measured its temporal rotation for rPPG estimation. However, because these methods are developed based on assumed domain knowledge, they may not generalize well to other data not complying with the assumption.

Many learning-based methods [2–5,11,22,23] have been recently introduced for rPPG or HR estimation. In [2], a 3D CNN-based spatio-temporal network was proposed to measure rPPG signal. In [23], the authors focused on compression artifacts and proposed a two-stage method to recover rPPG signals from highly compressed videos. The other methods [3–5,11,22] mostly focused on improving the estimation accuracy but hardly address the lack of large-scale data issue. Although a larger OBF dataset was introduced in [1], it was not publicly available for experimental comparison. The problem of insufficient training data is still far from being resolved.

Data Augmentation has been widely utilized to overcome the burden of collecting large supervised datasets for training deep neural networks. In addition to traditional augmentation strategies (e.g. horizontal flipping, rotating, cropping), learning to automate the data generation process has been shown to significantly improve object detection and image classification tasks. In [24], the authors proposed a context-based data augmentation for object detection by automatically placing new objects in suitable locations of images. In [25], a data augmentation method was proposed to generates synthetic medical images using Generative Adversarial Networks (GANs) for liver lesion classification.

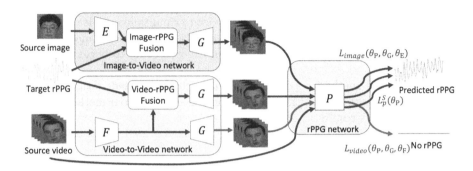

Fig. 2. The proposed multi-task learning framework, which contains three networks: rPPG network, Image-to-Video network, and Video-to-Video network.

3 Proposed Method

3.1 Overview

The goal of this paper is two-fold: to augment the training data by synthesizing photo-realistic face videos containing specific rPPG signals, and to leverage the rPPG estimation accuracy by learning from the augmented data. As shown in Fig. 2, we propose a multi-task learning framework containing three networks: rPPG network, Image-to-Video network, and Video-to-Video network, to simultaneously fulfill the two tasks.

1. **rPPG network** aims to estimate rPPG signals directly from input face videos.
2. **Image-to-Video network** aims to generate a face video $v_{image} \in \mathbb{R}^{H \times W \times C \times T}$ from a single face image $x_{source} \in \mathbb{R}^{H \times W \times C}$ and a target rPPG signal $y_{target} \in \mathbb{R}^T$, where H, W, C denote the height, width, and the number of channels of the source image, and T is the length of the target rPPG signal.
3. **Video-to-Video network** aims to replace the original rPPG signal of a source video $v_{source} \in \mathbb{R}^{H \times W \times C \times T}$ with a target rPPG signal y_{target}. The synthesized video $v_{video} \in \mathbb{R}^{H \times W \times C \times T}$ is expected to look similar to the source video v_{source} but should capture the target rPPG signal y_{target}.

Note that, although it is possible to design and train the three networks independently, their capability will be severely limited by the scale and quality of their individual training data. Below we will detail each network and describe how we formulate these highly correlated problems in a multi-tasking learning framework to strongly reinforce the capability of each network.

3.2 RPPG Network

To estimate rPPG signals from face videos, previous methods [3,14,26] usually require image pre-processing steps, such as detection of regions-of-interest (RoIs), conversion of video frames to spatial-temporal maps, etc. However, because any pre-processing step will unavoidably diminish the subtle chromi-nance changes in face videos, we propose to directly estimate the rPPG sig-nals from face videos in an end-to-end manner without any pre-processing. We develop the rPPG network P in terms of 3D CNN and summarize its network architecture in the supplementary file.

Given a ground truth PPG signal $y' \in \mathbb{R}^T$, our goal is to train the rPPG network P to estimate the signal $y \in \mathbb{R}^T$ to have the same periodic pattern of wave crests and troughs as y'. An eligible criterion is to measure the linear correlation through Pearson correlation:

$$\rho(y, y') = \frac{(y - \overline{y})^t (y' - \overline{y'})}{\sqrt{(y - \overline{y})^t (y - \overline{y})} \sqrt{(y' - \overline{y'})^t (y' - \overline{y'})}}, \tag{1}$$

where $\overline{y}$ and $\overline{y'}$ are the means of the predicted rPPG signal y and the ground truth PPG signal y', respectively. Hence, we define the loss function of P in terms of Negative Pearson by

$$L_p^S(\theta_P) = 1 - \rho(y_{source}, y'_{source}), \tag{2}$$

where

$$y_{source} = P(v_{source}; \theta_P). \tag{3}$$

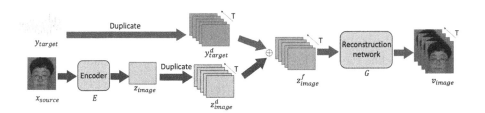

Fig. 3. Image-to-Video network

3.3 Image-to-Video Network

Figure 3 illustrates the proposed Image-to-Video network. Given a source image x_{source}, we first introduce an encoder E to obtain the feature representation of the source image by:

$$z_{image} = E(x_{source}; \theta_E), \tag{4}$$

where $z_{image} \in \mathbb{R}^{H_I \times W_I \times C_I}$; H_I, W_I, and C_I denote the height, width and the number of channels of the image feature, respectively.

Next, we design a fusion method to incorporate the target rPPG signal $y_{target} \in \mathbb{R}^T$ into the feature map z_{image}. Because the dimensions of z_{image} and y_{target} are inconsistent, we cannot directly combine the two signals. We thus pix-elwisely duplicate the rPPG signal y_{target} into $y^d_{target} \in \mathbb{R}^{H_I \times W_I \times C_I \times T}$, and tem-porally duplicate the feature map z_{image} into $z^d_{image} \in \mathbb{R}^{H_I \times W_I \times C_I \times T}$. The resul-tant y^d_{target} and z^d_{image} are of the same dimension and are then fused through the element-wise addition to obtain the fused feature map $z_{image}^{f} \in \mathbb{R}^{H_I \times W_I \times C_I \times T}$ by:

$$z_{image}^{f} = z_{image}^{d} + y_{target}^{d}. \tag{5}$$

With this fusion step, we guarantee that all the spatial elements in z_{image}^{f} reflect the same rPPG characteristics. Then, we design a reconstruction network G to generate synthetic face video $v_{image} \in \mathbb{R}^{H \times W \times C \times T}$:

$$v_{image} = G(z_{image}^{f}; \theta_G). \tag{6}$$

To ensure the synthetic video v_{image} carries the target rPPG signal, we include the learning of rPPG network P together with the learning of Image-to-Video Network to formulate the loss term. We impose two constraints to define the loss function for Image-to-Video Network. First, we let the rPPG network P guide the encoder E and the reconstruction network G to generate a video v_{image} containing the rPPG signal which is highly correlated with y_{target}:

$$L_p^I(\theta_P, \theta_G, \theta_E) = 1 - \rho(P(G((E(x_{source}; \theta_E)^d + y_{target}^d); \theta_G); \theta_P), y_{target}). \tag{7}$$

Second, as the synthetic video v_{image} should also capture the visual appearance of the input image x_{source}, we define a reconstruction loss in terms of absolute difference by:

$$L_r^I(\theta_G, \theta_E) = \frac{1}{T} \sum_{t=1}^{T} |G((E(x_{source}; \theta_E)^d + y_{target}^d); \theta_G)(t) - x_{source}|. \tag{8}$$

Finally, we define the total loss of Image-to-Video Network as follows,

$$L_{image}(\theta_P, \theta_G, \theta_E) = L_p^I(\theta_P, \theta_G, \theta_E) + \lambda_1 L_r^I(\theta_G, \theta_E), \tag{9}$$

where λ_1 is a hyper-parameter and is empirically set as 0.01 in all our experiments.

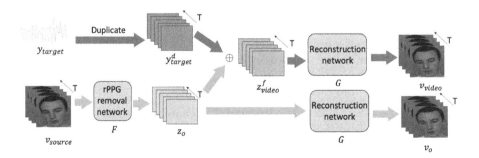

Fig. 4. Video-to-Video network

3.4   Video-to-Video Network

Given a source video v_{source} and a target rPPG signal y_{target}, the Video-to-Video network aims to synthesize a target video v_{video} which should be visually similar to the source video but capture the target rPPG signal. Unlike the case in Sect. 3.3, the source video itself inherently captures its own rPPG signal; thus, we need to erase this rPPG signal before embedding the target signal y_{target}. As shown in Fig. 4, we replace the encoder E in the Image-to-Video network with an rPPG removal network F:

$$z_o = F(v_{source}; \theta_F), \qquad (10)$$

where $z_o \in \mathbb{R}^{H_V \times W_V \times C_V \times T}$ is the video feature representation that should contain no rPPG signal; H_V, W_V, and C_V are the height, width and the number of channels, respectively.

Next, we use the same reconstruction network G to generate synthetic video but with additional constraints. Firstly, the reconstructed appearance $v_o \in \mathbb{R}^{H \times W \times C \times T}$ from z_o:

$$v_o = G(z_o; \theta_G), \qquad (11)$$

is expected to be visually indistinguishable from the source video v_{source} but should contain no rPPG periodic characteristics. We therefore formulate a reconstruction loss term and a No-rPPG loss term by:

$$L_r^O(\theta_G, \theta_F) = \frac{1}{T}\sum_{t=1}^{T} |G(F(v_{source}; \theta_F); \theta_G)(t) - v_{source}(t)|, \qquad (12)$$

and

$$L^O(\theta_P, \theta_G, \theta_F) = Var(P(G(F(v_{source}; \theta_F); \theta_G); \theta_P)), \qquad (13)$$

where $Var(\cdot)$ measures the signal variance. Note that, a constant (or zero frequency) signal will have zero variance. Thus, we use $Var(\cdot)$ to quantify the periodicity of the estimated rPPG signal.

Secondly, to embed the target signal y_{target}, we adopt the same duplication and fusing steps of Image-to-Video network by:

$$v_{video} = G(z_{video}^f; \theta_G), \qquad (14)$$

where

$$z_{video}^f = z_o + y_{target}^d. \qquad (15)$$

Then, we again impose two constraints on the synthetic video v_{video} to ensure that it carries the target rPPG signal y_{target} and also preserves its original visual appearance by:

$$L_p^V(\theta_P, \theta_G, \theta_F) = 1 - \rho(P(G((F(v_{source}; \theta_F) + y_{target}^d); \theta_G); \theta_P), y_{target}), \qquad (16)$$

and

$$L_r^V(\theta_G, \theta_F) = \frac{1}{T}\sum_{t=1}^{T} |G((F(v_{source}; \theta_F) + y_{target}^d); \theta_G)(t) - v_{source}(t)|. \qquad (17)$$

Finally, we define the total loss of Video-to-Video Network by:

$$
\begin{aligned}
L_{video}(\theta_P, \theta_G, \theta_F) = {} & L^O(\theta_P, \theta_G, \theta_F) + L^V_p(\theta_P, \theta_G, \theta_F) \\
& + \lambda_2 L^O_r(\theta_G, \theta_F) + \lambda_3 L^V_r(\theta_G, \theta_F),
\end{aligned}
\tag{18}
$$

where λ_2 and λ_3 are hyper-parameters and both are empirically set as 0.01 in our experiments.

3.5 Overall Framework

To sum up, the three networks are designed to mutually support each other. With the rPPG network P, the Image-to-Video network and Video-to-Video network are able to generate synthetic videos containing the target rPPG signals. The reconstruction network G, which is included in both the Image-to-Video and Video-to-Video networks, is constrained to generate photo-realistic synthetic videos. In addition, because the synthetic videos are considered as augmented data, the rPPG network is able to learn from videos with more diversity and with different rPPG characteristics. Our total loss term for the multi-task learning framework is defined by:

$$
Loss(\theta_P, \theta_G, \theta_E, \theta_F) = L^S_p(\theta_P) + \alpha L_{image}(\theta_P, \theta_G, \theta_E) + \beta L_{video}(\theta_P, \theta_G, \theta_F),
\tag{19}
$$

where α and β are coefficients to balance different loss terms and both are set as 0.5 in the experiments.

4   Experiments

4.1   Datasets

We conduct a series of experiments on three benchmark datasets.

COHFACE dataset [15] comprises 160 one-minute-long RGB video sequences of 40 subjects. Each subject contributes four videos: two of them are filmed in well-lighted environment and the other two are filmed under natural light. All the videos are filmed by Logitech HD C525 webcam; the resolution is set to 640×480 and the frame rate is 20 fps. A contact PPG sensor is attached to the subjects to obtain the blood volume pulse signal. The dataset is split into a training set of 24 subjects and a testing set of 16 subjects.

UBFC-RPPG dataset [12] comprises 42 face videos, each belongs to different individuals. The training set consists of 28 subjects and the testing set consists of 14 subjects. All the videos are recorded by Logitech C920 HD Pro, with resolution of 640×480 pixels in uncompressed 8-bit format, and the frame rate is set to 30 fps. CMS50E transmissive pulse oximeter was used to monitor the PPG data and PPG heart rates.

PURE dataset [13] consists of 60 one-minute-long videos from 10 subjects, and each subject was asked to performs six different movements during recording. The six setups are: (1) sitting still and looking directly at the camera, (2)

Table 1. Ablation study on COHFACE dataset.

Method	MAE	RMSE
Source-150	1.86	3.77
Image-150	1.51	3.29
Video-150	1.54	3.32
All-150	1.33	2.71
Source-200	1.10	2.22
Image-200	1.02	2.12
Video-200	0.98	2.02
All-200	0.93	2.01
Source-256	0.91	2.16
Image-256	0.82	1.81
w/o L_r^O, L^O-256	0.85	1.93
Video-256	0.84	1.76
All-256	0.68	1.65

Table 2. Comparison on COHFACE dataset.

Method	R	MAE	RMSE
2SR [21]	−0.32	20.98	25.84
CHROME [6]	0.26	7.80	12.45
LiCVPR [18]	−0.44	19.98	25.59
HR-CNN [11]	0.29	8.10	10.78
Two stream [5]	0.40	8.09	9.96
Ours-Source	0.68	0.91	2.16
Ours-Image	0.64	0.82	1.81
Ours-Video	0.66	0.84	1.76
Ours-All	0.72	0.68	1.65

talking but avoiding head movements, (3) slowly moving the head parallel to the camera, (4) moving the head quickly, (5) rotating the head with 20° angle, and (6) rotating the head with 35° angle. The training set contains 7 subjects and the testing set contains the rest 3 subjects. The videos are recorded using eco274CVGE camera with resolution of 640 × 480 pixels, and the frame rate is set to 30 fps. Pulox CMS50E finger clip pulse oximeter is adopted to capture PPG data with sampling rate 60 Hz.

4.2 Implementation Setting

The architectures of the rPPG network P, the encoder E, the reconstruction network G, and the rPPG removal network F in the Video-to-Video Networks are given in the supplementary file. We train the network with Nvidia GTX 2080 for 280 epochs with batch size 4, using Adam optimizer and set the learning rate 0.001. For comparison, experiments using traditional visual data augmentations are also conducted in UBFC and PURE dataset.

4.3 Evaluation Metrics

Because existing methods evaluate the performance on the estimated heart rate instead of on the rPPG signals, to have a fair comparison, we follow [22] to derive the heart rate from the estimated rPPG signals and evaluate the results in terms of the following metrics: (1) Pearson correlation coefficient (R), (2) Mean absolute error (MAE), (3) Root mean square error (RMSE), and (4) Precision at 2.5 and 5 bpm (beats per minute), (5) Peak signal-to-noise ratio (PSNR) and (6) Structural similarity (SSIM).

4.4   Ablation Study

To show the effectiveness of our proposed method, we design several ablative settings on the COHFACE dataset and summarize the results in Table 1. "Source-", "Image-", "Video-", "w/o L_r^O, L^O-", "All-" refer to different combinations of the tasks described in Fig. 2, that is, (1) the single task P trained from the source data, (2) training of Image-to-Video network and P, (3) training of Video-to-Video network and P, (4) the proposed multi-tasking framework but without loss terms L_r^O, L^O, (5) the proposed multi-task framework, respectively. "-150", "-200" and "-256" refer to different lengths of T in terms of frame numbers.

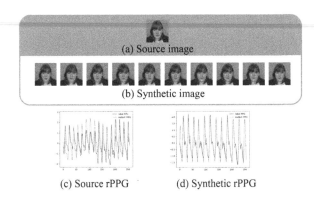

Fig. 5. A visualized example of Image-to-Video network. (a) A source image from the UBFC-RPPG dataset; (b) The synthetic video with target rPPG; (c) The source rPPG label (blue) and the predicted rPPG (orange); (d) The target rPPG (blue) and the predicted rPPG (orange). (Color figure online)

As shown in Table 1, all the settings yield better performance with increased T. These results suggest that observing a longer duration of video frames is essential to derive stable rPPG periodicity and robust HR estimation. In addition, for each setting of T, "Image-", "Video-" and "All-" all have improved performance over "Source-". These results verify that the data augmentation and rPPG estimation tasks indeed promote each other and substantially boost the overall performance.

Figures 5 and 6 give two examples synthesized by Image-to-Video network and Video-to-Video network, respectively. In both cases, the generated videos in Figs. 5(b) and 6(b) are visually indistinguishable from the source data, and the estimated rPPG signals in Figs. 5(c) and 6(d) are very accurately aligned with the ground truth. In addition, Fig. 6(e), where the estimated rPPG signal from the rPPG-removed video becomes a flat signal (with the average variance

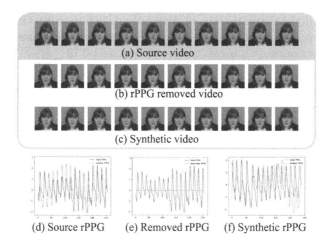

Fig. 6. A visualized example of Video-to-Video network. (a) Source video from the UBFC-RPPG dataset; (b) rPPG removed video after F; (c) The synthesized videos; (d) The source PPG label (blue) and the predicted rPPG (orange); (e) The source PPG label (blue) and the estimated rPPG from rPPG-removed video (orange); (f) The target rPPG (blue) and the predicted rPPG (orange). (Color figure online)

of 3.6×10^{-4}), demonstrates that the proposed removal network F successfully erases the rPPG information from the source video. The target rPPG signals and their estimated results in Figs. 5(d) and 6(f) also demonstrate that the proposed framework successfully embeds the target signals into the synthesized videos.

We also evaluate the visual quality of synthetic videos in terms of PSNR and SSIM on COHFACE dataset. As shown in Table 3, both the Image-to-Video network and the Video-to-Video network generate synthetic videos with high PSNR and SSIM and show that our method successfully generates photo-realistic videos visually indistinguishable from source data.

4.5 Results and Comparison

Table 2 shows the comparison with existing methods on the COHFACE dataset. The first three methods, i.e., 2SR [21], CHROME [6], and LiCVPR [18] are not learning-based methods; thus, there is a performance gap between them and the other two learning-based methods HR-CNN [11] and Two stream [5]. As to the proposed method "Ours-", we use the same settings "-source", "-image", "-video" and "-all" as mentioned in Table 1 with $T = 256$. The result of "Ours-Source" shows that, even without data augmentation, the proposed rPPG network P alone has already outperformed all these existing methods with a large margin. We believe there are two main reasons. First, P is an end-to-end network which directly processes the input video without any pre-processing step; hence, there involves no information loss in comparison with other multi-stage methods. Second, the 3D CNN architecture in P effectively captures the temporally periodic characteristics of rPPG signals in face video. Once we further include the data augmentation task, the proposed method "Ours-all" achieves the best performance with correlation coefficient (R) 0.72.

Table 3. Quality evaluation of synthetic videos on COHFACE dataset.

	PSNR	SSIM
Image-to-Video	33.38	0.993
Video-to-Video	34.07	0.994
rPPG removed video	37.71	0.996

Table 4 shows the results on the original PURE dataset containing lossless PNG files. Because the uncompressed PNG files have better visual quality, most of the methods achieve a high correlation coefficient (R) larger than 0.9. Once we follow the settings in [11] to compress the PURE dataset into MPEG-4 and experiment on the compressed videos, the results in Table 5 show that our method is least sensitive to compression artifacts and significantly outperforms previous methods.

Moreover, in order to show that the proposed video generation largely enriches the training data than the simple data augmentation, we also conduct the experiments "Ours-Trad.Aug" using traditional augmentation, including random rotation, brightness, and saturation, for comparison. In Table 4 and Table 5, "Ours-Trad.Aug" shows no improvement over "Ours-Source" in both cases. Note that, because the training and testing videos are recorded in similar lighting environments with the same device, traditional data augmentation provides little information than the original training set. Instead, the proposed video generation method is able to generate videos with a variety of rPPG signals and is particularly advantageous for creating new benchmark datasets for rPPG estimation task.

Table 6 shows the results and comparison on the UBFC-RPPG dataset. The setting "Ours-Source" again outperforms the other methods. The precision 1.0 at 2.5 bpm indicates that there is no subjects' MAE larger than 2.5 bpm and verifies the robustness of the proposed method. As to the traditional augmentation, although "Ours-Trad.Aug." shows little improvement by decreasing the MAE and RMSE to 0.63 and 2.08, the proposed method "Ours-All" further decreases MAE and RMSE to 0.47 and 2.09, respectively. These results again show that our augmentation method effectively enriches the variety of dataset and largely improves the robustness of model training.

In addition, we conduct cross-dataset experiments to evaluate the generalization of the proposed method. As shown in Table 7, we show the results when training the network on PURE dataset but directly testing the model on UBFC-RPPG dataset and vice versa. Note that, this cross-dataset HR estimation inevitably leads to degraded performance, especially when the training dataset is of smaller-scale and less diversity than the testing dataset. Therefore,

Table 4. Comparison on PURE dataset.

Method	R	MAE	RMSE
2SR [21]	0.98	2.44	3.06
CHROME [6]	0.99	2.07	2.50
LiCVPR [18]	−0.38	28.22	30.96
HR-CNN [11]	0.98	1.84	2.37
Ours-Source	0.88	0.44	1.16
Ours-Trad.Aug.	0.79	1.06	2.12
Ours-All	0.92	0.40	1.07

Table 5. Comparison on PURE dataset (MPEG-4 visual).

Method	R	MAE	RMSE
2SR [21]	0.43	5.78	12.81
CHROME [6]	0.55	6.29	11.36
LiCVPR [18]	−0.42	28.39	31.10
HR-CNN [11]	0.7	8.72	11.00
Two stream [5]	0.42	9.81	11.81
Ours-Source	0.86	0.79	1.76
Ours-Trad.Aug.	0.70	1.19	2.61
Ours-All	0.87	0.75	1.69

Table 6. Comparison on UBFC-RPPG dataset.

Method	MAE	RMSE	2.5 bpm	5 bpm
PVM [20]	4.47	–	0.71	0.81
MODEL [17]	3.99	5.55	0.75	0.87
SKIN-TISSUE [12]	–	2.39	0.89	0.83
MAICA [19]	3.34	–	0.72	0.88
BIC [16]	1.21	2.41	0.951	0.975
Ours-Source	0.73	2.38	1.0	1.0
Ours-Trad.Aug.	0.63	2.08	1.0	1.0
Ours-All	0.47	2.09	1.0	1.0

Table 7. Comparison of cross-dataset estimation.

Training-Testing	MAE	RMSE
PURE-PURE	0.40	1.07
UBFC-PURE	4.24	6.44
UBFC-UBFC	0.47	2.09
PURE-UBFC	1.06	2.70

we have increased MAE from 0.40 to 4.24 and RMSE from 1.07 to 6.44 when testing on PURE dataset but training on UBFC-RPPG dataset. The main cause of this performance degradation comes from that PURE dataset contains different head movements whereas UBFC-RPPG dataset has none; therefore, the model trained on UBFC-RPPG is unable to adapt to different poses and head movements of PURE testing data. On the other hand, when testing on UBFC-RPPG dataset, we only have a slight increase in MAE and RMSE, and our result (i.e., MAE 1.06) still outperforms existing methods and shows good generalization of the proposed model.

5   Conclusions

To the best of our knowledge, this is the first work targeting generating synthetic face videos with specific rPPG signals. We study the impact of data augmentation and propose a novel multi-task learning method to simultaneously accomplish the data augmentation and the rPPG estimation tasks. By generating photo-realistic videos, we successfully augment the existing small-scale datasets with enriched characteristics and yield robust rPPG estimation. Our experimental results verify the effectiveness of the proposed method and show its great potential for promoting contactless estimation of human physiological signals.

References

1. Li, X., et al.: The OBF database: a large face video database for remote physiological signal measurement and atrial fibrillation detection. In: 2018 13th IEEE International Conference on Automatic Face Gesture Recognition (FG 2018), pp. 242–249 (2018)
2. Yu, Z., Li, X., Zhao, G.: Recovering remote photoplethysmograph signal from facial videos using spatio-temporal convolutional networks. CoRR abs/1905.02419 (2019)
3. Chen, W., McDuff, D.: DeepPhys: video-based physiological measurement using convolutional attention networks. In: Ferrari, V., Hebert, M., Sminchisescu, C., Weiss, Y. (eds.) ECCV 2018. LNCS, vol. 11206, pp. 356–373. Springer, Cham (2018). https://doi.org/10.1007/978-3-030-01216-8_22
4. Chen, W., McDuff, D.J.: DeepMag: source specific motion magnification using gradient ascent. CoRR abs/1808.03338 (2018)
5. Wang, Z.K., Kao, Y., Hsu, C.T.: Vision-based heart rate estimation via a two-stream CNN. In: 2019 IEEE International Conference on Image Processing (ICIP), pp. 3327–3331 (2019)
6. de Haan, G., Jeanne, V.: Robust pulse rate from chrominance-based rPPG. IEEE Trans. Biomed. Eng. **60**, 2878–2886 (2013)
7. Hernandez-Ortega, J., Fierrez, J., Morales, A., Tome, P.: Time analysis of pulse-based face anti-spoofing in visible and NIR. In: Proceedings of IEEE Conference on Computer Vision and Pattern Recognition (2018)
8. Liu, Y., Jourabloo, A., Liu, X.: Learning deep models for face anti-spoofing: binary or auxiliary supervision. In: Proceedings of IEEE Conference on Computer Vision and Pattern Recognition, pp. 389–398 (2018)
9. Liu, S., Lan, X., Yuen, P.C.: Remote photoplethysmography correspondence feature for 3D mask face presentation attack detection (2018)
10. Liu, S., Yuen, P.C., Zhang, S., Zhao, G.: 3D mask face anti-spoofing with remote photoplethysmography. In: Leibe, B., Matas, J., Sebe, N., Welling, M. (eds.) ECCV 2016. LNCS, vol. 9911, pp. 85–100. Springer, Cham (2016). https://doi.org/10.1007/978-3-319-46478-7_6
11. Špetlík, R., Franc, V., Čech, J., Matas, J.: Visual heart rate estimation with convolutional neural network. In: Proceedings of British Machine Vision Conference (2018)
12. Bobbia, S., Macwan, R., Benezeth, Y., Mansouri, A., Dubois, J.: Unsupervised skin tissue segmentation for remote photoplethysmography. Pattern Recogn. Lett. **124**, 82–90 (2017)
13. Stricker, R., Müller, S., Gross, H.M.: Non-contact video-based pulse rate measurement on a mobile service robot, vol. 2014, pp. 1056–1062 (2014)
14. Niu, X., Han, H., Shan, S., Chen, X.: SynRhythm: learning a deep heart rate estimator from general to specific. In: 2018 24th International Conference on Pattern Recognition (ICPR), pp. 3580–3585 (2018)

15. Heusch, G., Anjos, A., Marcel, S.: A reproducible study on remote heart rate measurement. CoRR abs/1709.00962 (2017)
16. Benezeth, Y., Bobbia, S., Nakamura, K., Gomez, R., Dubois, J.: Probabilistic signal quality metric for reduced complexity unsupervised remote photoplethysmography, pp. 1–5 (2019)
17. Li, P., Yannick Benezeth, K.N., Gomez, R., Yang, F.: Model-based region of interest segmentation for remote photoplethysmography. In: 14th International Conference on Computer Vision Theory and Applications, pp. 383–388 (2019)
18. Li, X., Chen, J., Zhao, G., Pietikäinen, M.: Remote heart rate measurement from face videos under realistic situations. In: 2014 IEEE Conference on Computer Vision and Pattern Recognition, pp. 4264–4271 (2014)
19. Macwan, R., Benezeth, Y., Mansouri, A.: Heart rate estimation using remote photoplethysmography with multi-objective optimization. Biomed. Signal Process. Control 49, 24–33 (2019)
20. Macwan, R., Bobbia, S., Benezeth, Y., Dubois, J., Mansouri, A.: Periodic variance maximization using generalized eigenvalue decomposition applied to remote photoplethysmography estimation. In: 2018 IEEE/CVF Conference on Computer Vision and Pattern Recognition Workshops (CVPRW), pp. 1413–14138 (2018)
21. Wang, W., Stuijk, S., de Haan, G.: A novel algorithm for remote photoplethysmography: spatial subspace rotation. IEEE Trans. Biomed. Eng. 63, 1974–1984 (2016)
22. Tsou, Y.Y., Lee, Y.A., Hsu, C.T., Chang, S.H.: Siamese-rPPG network: remote photoplethysmography signal estimation from face video. In: The 35th ACM/SIGAPP Symposium on Applied Computing (SAC 2020) (2020)
23. Yu, Z., Peng, W., Li, X., Hong, X., Zhao, G.: Remote heart rate measurement from highly compressed facial videos: an end-to-end deep learning solution with video enhancement. In: International Conference on Computer Vision (ICCV) (2019)
24. Dvornik, N., Mairal, J., Schmid, C.: Modeling visual context is key to augmenting object detection datasets. In: Ferrari, V., Hebert, M., Sminchisescu, C., Weiss, Y. (eds.) ECCV 2018. LNCS, vol. 11216, pp. 375–391. Springer, Cham (2018). https://doi.org/10.1007/978-3-030-01258-8_23
25. Frid-Adar, M., Klang, E., Amitai, M., Goldberger, J., Greenspan, H.: Synthetic data augmentation using GAN for improved liver lesion classification, pp. 289–293 (2018)
26. Qiu, Y., Liu, Y., Arteaga-Falconi, J., Dong, H., Saddik, A.E.: EVM-CNN: real-time contactless heart rate estimation from facial video. IEEE Trans. Multimed. 21, 1778–1787 (2019)

Video Analysis and Event Recognition

Interpreting Video Features:
A Comparison of 3D Convolutional Networks and Convolutional LSTM Networks

Joonatan Mänttäri(ⓘ), Sofia Broomé(✉)(ⓘ), John Folkesson(ⓘ),
and Hedvig Kjellström(ⓘ)

Robotics, Perception and Learning, KTH Royal Institute of Technology,
Stockholm, Sweden
{manttari,sbroome,johnf,hedvig}@kth.se

Abstract. A number of techniques for interpretability have been presented for deep learning in computer vision, typically with the goal of understanding what the networks have based their classification on. However, interpretability for deep video architectures is still in its infancy and we do not yet have a clear concept of how to decode spatiotemporal features. In this paper, we present a study comparing how 3D convolutional networks and convolutional LSTM networks learn features across temporally dependent frames. This is the first comparison of two video models that both convolve to learn spatial features but have principally different methods of modeling time. Additionally, we extend the concept of meaningful perturbation introduced by [1] to the temporal dimension, to identify the temporal part of a sequence most meaningful to the network for a classification decision. Our findings indicate that the 3D convolutional model concentrates on shorter events in the input sequence, and places its spatial focus on fewer, contiguous areas.

1 Introduction

Two standard approaches to deep learning for sequential image data are 3D convolutional neural networks (3D CNNs), e.g., the I3D model [2], and recurrent neural networks (RNNs). Among the RNNs, the convolutional long short-term memory network (hereon, C-LSTM) [3] is especially suited for sequences of images, since it learns both spatial and temporal dependencies simultaneously. Although both methods can capture aspects of the semantics pertaining to the temporal dependencies in a video clip, there is a fundamental difference in how 3D CNNs treat time compared to C-LSTMs. In 3D CNNs, the time axis is treated just like a third spatial axis, whereas C-LSTMs only allow for information flow in the direction of increasing time, complying with the second law of thermodynamics. More concretely, C-LSTMs maintain a hidden state that is continuously updated when forward-traversing the input video sequence,

---

J. Mänttäri and S. Broomé—Equal contribution.

© Springer Nature Switzerland AG 2021
H. Ishikawa et al. (Eds.): ACCV 2020, LNCS 12626, pp. 411–426, 2021.
https://doi.org/10.1007/978-3-030-69541-5_25

and are able to model non-linear transitions in time. 3D CNNs, on the other hand, convolve (i.e., take weighted averages) over both the temporal and spatial dimensions of the sequence.

The question investigated in this paper is whether this difference has consequences for how the two models compute spatiotemporal features. We present a study of how 3D CNNs and C-LSTMs respectively compute video features: what do they learn, and how do they differ from one another?

As outlined in Sect. 2, there is a large body of work on evaluating video architectures on spatial and temporal correlations, but significantly fewer investigations of what parts of the data the networks have used and what semantics relating to the temporal dependencies they have extracted from them. Deep neural networks are known to be large computational models, whose inner workings are difficult to overview for a human. For video models, the number of parameters is typically significantly higher due to the added dimension, which makes their interpretability all the more pressing.

We will evaluate these two types of models (3D CNN and C-LSTM) on tasks where temporal order is crucial. The 20BN-Something-something-V2 dataset [4] (hereon, Something-something) will be central to our investigations; it contains time-critical classes, agnostic to object appearance, such as *move something from left to right* or *move something from right to left*. We additionally evaluate the models on the smaller KTH actions dataset [5].

Our contributions are listed as follows.

- We present the first comparison of 3D CNNs and C-LSTMs in terms of temporal modeling abilities. We point to essential differences between their assumptions concerning temporal dependencies in the data through qualitative and quantitative experiments.
- We extend the concept of meaningful perturbation introduced by [1] to the temporal dimension, to search for the most critical part of a sequence used by the networks for classification.

2 Related Work

The field of interpretability in deep learning is still young but has made considerable progress for single-image networks, owing to works such as [6–9]. One can distinguish between data centric and network centric methods for interpretability. *Activity maximization*, first coined by [10], is network centric in the sense that specific units of the network are studied. By maximizing the activation of a given unit by gradient ascent with reference to the input, one can compute its optimal input. In data centric methods, the focus is instead on the input to the network in order to reveal which patterns of the data the network has discerned.

Grad-CAM [11] and the meaningful perturbations explored in the work by [1] (Sect. 3), which form the basis for our experiments, belong to the data centric category. Layer-wise relevance propagation [9] (LRP) and Excitation backprop [12] are two other examples of data centric backpropagation techniques designed for interpretability, where Excitation backprop follows from a simpler parameter setting of LRP. In Excitation backprop, saliency maps are produced without the use of gradients. Instead, products of forward weights and activations are normalized in order to be used as conditional probabilities, which are back-propagated. Building on Excitation backprop, [13] produce saliency maps for video RNNs. In our experiments, we produce spatial saliency maps using Grad-CAM, since it is efficient, easy to implement, widely used, and one of the saliency methods in [14] that passes the article's sanity checks.

Few works have been published with their focus on interpretability for video models [13,15–18]. Other works have treated it, but with less extensive experimentation [19], while mainly presenting a new spatiotemporal architecture [20,21]. We build on the work by [18], where the aim is to measure a network's ability to model *video time* directly, and not via the proxy task of action classification, which is most commonly seen. Three defining properties of video time are defined in the paper: temporal symmetry, temporal continuity and temporal causality, each accompanied by a measurable task. The third property is measured using the classification accuracy on Something-something. An important contribution of ours is that we compare 3D CNNs and C-LSTMs, whereas [18] compare 3D CNNs to standard LSTMs. Their comparison can be argued as slightly unfair, as standard LSTM layers only take 1D input, and thus need to vectorize each frame, which removes some spatial dependencies in the pixel grid. [20,22,23] all use variants of convolutional RNNs, but train them on CNN features. To the best of our knowledge, there has been no published convolutional RNNs trained on raw image data. This is crucial since information is lost when downsampling an image into CNN features, and we want to study networks having sufficient degrees of freedom to learn temporal patterns from scratch.

Similar to our work, [20] investigate the temporal modeling capabilities of convolutional gated recurrent units (ConvGRUs) trained on Something-something. The authors find that recurrent models perform well for the task, and present a qualitative analysis of the trained model's learned hidden states. For each class of the dataset, they obtain the hidden states of the network corresponding to the frames of one clip and display its nearest neighbors from other clips' per-frame hidden state representations. These hidden states had encoded information about the relevant frame ordering for the classes. [16] examine video architectures and datasets on a number of qualitative attributes. [17] investigate how much the motion contributes to the classification performance of a video architecture. To measure this, they vary the number of sub-sampled frames per clip and examine how much the accuracy changes as a result.

In a search-based precursor to our temporal mask experiments, [24] crop sequences temporally to obtain the most discriminative sub-sequence for a certain class. The crop corresponding to the highest classification confidence is selected as the most discriminative sub-sequence. This selection is done using an exhaustive search for crops across all frames, which increases in complexity with the sequence length according to $\frac{|f|^2}{2}$, where $|f|$ is the number of frames. Our proposed method, however, is gradient-descent based and has a fixed number of iterations regardless of sequence length. Furthermore, our approach can identify more than one temporal sub-region in the sequence, in contrast to [24].

[15] present the first network centric interpretability work for video models. The authors investigate spatiotemporal features using activity maximization. [21] introduce the Temporal Relational Network (TRN), which learns temporal dependencies between frames through sampling the semantically relevant frames for a particular action class. The TRN module is put on top of a convolutional layer and consists of a fully connected network between the sampled frame features and the output. Similar to [20], they perform temporal alignment of clips from the same class, using the frames considered most representative for the clip by the network. They verify the conclusion previously made by [25], that temporal order is crucial on Something-something and also investigate for which classes it is most important.

3   Approach

3.1   Temporal Masks

The proposed temporal mask method aims to extend the interpretability of deep networks into the temporal dimension, utilizing meaningful perturbation of the input, as shown effective in the spatial dimension by [1]. When adopting this approach, it is necessary to define what constitutes a *meaningful* perturbation. In the mentioned paper, a mask that blurs the input as little as possible is learned for a single image, while still maximizing the decrease in class score. Our proposed method applies this concept of a learned mask to the temporal dimension. The perturbation, in this setting, is a noise mask approximating either a 'freeze' operation, which removes motion data through time, or a 'reverse' operation that inverses the sequential order of the frames. This way, we aim to identify which frames are most critical for the network's classification decision.

The temporal mask is defined as a vector of real numbers on the interval [0,1] with the same length as the input sequence. For the 'freeze' type mask, a value of 1 for a frame at index t duplicates the value from the previous frame at $t-1$ onto the input sequence at t. The pseudo-code for this procedure is given below.

```
for i in maskIndicesExceptFirst do
  originalComponent := (1-mask[i])*originalInput[i]
  perturbedComponent := mask[i]*perturbedInput[i-1]
  perturbedInput[i] := originalComponent + perturbedComponent
end for
```

For the 'reverse' mask type, all indices of the mask **m** that are activated are first identified (threshold 0.1). These indices are then looped through to find all contiguous sections, which are treated as sub-masks, m_i. For each sub-mask, the frames at the active indices in the sub-mask are reversed. For example (binary for clarity), an input indexed as $t_{1:16}$ perturbed with a mask with the value $[0,0,0,1,1,1,1,1,0,0,0,0,0,1,1,0]$ results in the sequence with frame indices $[1,2,3,8,7,6,5,4,9,10,11,12,13,15,14,16]$.

In order to learn the mask, we define a loss function (Eq. 1) to be minimized using gradient descent, similar to the approach in [1].

$$\mathcal{L} = \lambda_1 \|\mathbf{m}\|_1^1 + \lambda_2 \|\mathbf{m}\|_\beta^\beta + F_c, \tag{1}$$

where $\mathbf{m}$ is the mask expressed as a vector $m \in [0,1]^t$, $\|\cdot\|_1^1$ is the L^1 norm, $\|\cdot\|_\beta^\beta$ is the Total Variation (TV) norm, $\lambda_{1,2}$ are weighting factors, and F_c is the class score given by the model for the perturbed input. The L^1 norm punishes long masks, in order to identify only the most important frames in the sequence. The TV norm penalizes masks that are not contiguous. This approach allows our method to automatically learn masks that identify one or several contiguous sequences in the input. The mask is initialized centered in the middle of the sequence. To keep the perturbed input class score differentiable with respect to the mask, the optimizer operates on a real-valued mask vector. A sigmoid function is applied to the mask before using it for the perturbing operation in order to keep its values in the [0,1] range. The ADAM optimizer is then used to learn the mask through 300 iterations of gradient descent. After the mask has converged, its sigmoidal representation is thresholded for visualisation purposes.

3.2   Grad-CAM

Grad-CAM [11] is a method for producing visual explanations in the form of class-specific saliency maps for CNNs. One saliency map, L_t^c, is produced for each image input based on the activations from k filters, A_{ij}^k, at the final convolutional layer. In order to adapt the method to sequences of images, the activations for all timesteps t in the sequences are considered (Eq. 2).

$$L_{ijt}^c = \sum_k w_{kt}^c A_{ijt}^k; \qquad w_{kt}^c = \frac{1}{Z} \sum_{ij} \frac{\partial F^c}{\partial A_{ijt}^k}, \tag{2}$$

where Z is a normalizing constant and F^c is the network output for the class c. By up-sampling these saliency maps to the resolution of the original input image, the aim is to examine what spatial data in specific frames contributed most to the predicted class.

4   Experiments

4.1   Datasets

Something-something [4] contains over 220,000 sequences from 174 classes with a duration of more than 200 h. The videos are recorded against varying backgrounds from different perspectives. The classes are action-oriented and object-agnostic. Each class is defined as performing some action with one or several arbitrary objects, such as *closing something* or *folding something*. This encourages the classifier to learn the action templates, since object recognition does not give enough information for the classifying task. We train and validate according to the provided split, and use a frame resolution of 224×224.

The KTH Actions dataset [5] consists of 25 subjects performing six actions (*boxing, waving, clapping, walking, jogging, running*) in four different settings, resulting in 2391 sequences, and a duration of almost three hours (160×120 pixels at 25 fps). They are filmed against a homogeneous background with the different settings exhibiting varying lighting, distance to the subject and clothing of the participants. For this dataset, we train on subjects 1–16 and evaluate on 17–25.

Both datasets have sequences varying from one to almost ten seconds. As 3D CNNs require input of fixed sequence length, all input sequences from both datasets are sub-sampled to cover the entire sequence in 16 frames (Something-something) and 32 frames (KTH Actions). The same set of sub-sampled frames is then used as input for both architectures.

4.2   Architecture Details

Both models were trained from scratch on each dataset, to ensure that the learned models were specific to the relevant task. Pre-training on Kinetics can increase performance, but for our experiments, the models should be trained on the temporal tasks presented by the Something-something dataset specifically. It can be noted that our I3D model reached comparable performance to another I3D trained from scratch on Something-something presented in the work of [25]. Hyperparameters are listed on the project webpage. Any remaining settings can be found in the public code repository.

I3D consists of three 3D convolutional layers, nine Inception modules and four max pooling layers (Fig. 1). In the original setting, the temporal dimension of the input is down-sampled to $L/8$ frames by the final Inception module, where L is the original sequence length. In order to achieve a higher temporal resolution in the produced Grad-CAM images, the strides of the first convolutional layer and the second max pooling layer are reduced to $1 \times 2 \times 2$ in our code, producing $L/2$ activations in the temporal dimension. The Grad-CAM images are produced from the gradients of the class scores with respect to the final Inception module.

We have not found any published C-LSTMs trained on raw pixels, and thus conducted our own hyperparameter search for this model. The model was selected solely based on classification performance; all feature investigations were conducted after this selection. The C-LSTM used for Something-something consists of three C-LSTM layers (two for KTH) with 32 filters, each followed by batch normalization and max pooling layers. The convolutional kernels used for each layer had size 5×5 and stride 2×2. The C-LSTM layers return the entire transformed sequence as input to the next layer. When calculating the Grad-CAM maps for the C-LSTM, the final C-LSTM layer was used.

There is a substantial difference in the number of parameters for each model, with $12, 465, 614$ for I3D and $1, 324, 014$ for the three-layer C-LSTM. Other variants of the C-LSTM with a larger number of parameters (up to five layers) were evaluated as well, but no significant increase in performance was observed. Also, due to the computational complexity of back-propagation through time (BPTT), the C-LSTM variants were significantly more time demanding to train than their I3D counterparts.

4.3 Comparison Method

To study the differences in the learned spatiotemporal features of the two models, we first compute spatial saliency maps using Grad-CAM and temporal masks using the proposed method. Once these are obtained for each model and dataset, we both examine them qualitatively and compute the quantitative metrics listed below. A 'blob' is defined as a contiguous patch within the Grad-CAM saliency map for one frame. The blobs were computed using the blob detection tool from OpenCV [26]. OS, FS and RS are the softmax scores for one class resulting from the original input, and from the freeze and reverse perturbed input, respectively.

- **Blob count:** The average number of blobs (salient spatial areas, as produced by the Grad-CAM method), per frame.
- **Blob size:** The average size of one salient spatial area (blob), in pixels, computed across all detected blobs.
- **Center distance:** The average distance in pixels to the center of the frame for one blob, computed across all detected blobs.
- **Mask length:** The average number of salient frames per sequence, as produced by the temporal mask method.
- **Drop ratio:** The average ratio between the drop in classification score using the freeze and reverse perturbations, defined as $\frac{OS-FS}{OS-RS}$, across all sequences.
- **Drop difference:** The average difference between the drop in classification score using the freeze and reverse perturbations, defined as $(OS-FS)-(OS-RS)$ (and equivalent to $RS-FS$), across all sequences.

We consider the difference and ratio between the freeze and reverse drops as the most relevant measures of how sensitive one model was for the reverse perturbation. FS and RS should not be compared in absolute numbers, since they depend on OS which might have been different for the two models. Moreover, using the same number of iterations for the optimization of the temporal mask, the two models typically reached different final losses (generally lower for I3D).

5 Results

For reference, the global validation F1-scores for both architectures and datasets are shown in Table 1. To emphasize the importance of temporal direction between the datasets, we first conduct a test where all the input validation sequences are entirely reversed. On Something-something, both C-LSTM and I3D were affected drastically, while on KTH, both performed well. Likely, this is because KTH's classes have distinct spatial features. As expected, Something-something is more time-critical than KTH. Overall, this shows that both models are indeed globally sensitive to temporal direction, when they need to be. In Sects. 5.1–5.2, we examine in detail which spatiotemporal features are learned by the two models, and how they differ from one another.

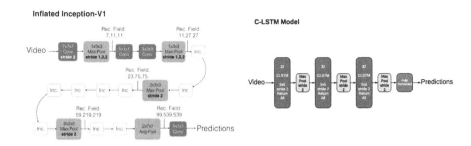

Fig. 1. I3D network (figure from [2]) and C-LSTM network (*right*).

Table 1. Validation F1-score per model on the two datasets. 'Rev.' indicates that the validation sequences were reversed at test time.

Model	KTH Actions (Top-1)	Smth-Smth (Top-1)	Smth-Smth (Top-5)
C-LSTM	0.84	0.23	0.48
C-LSTM (rev.)	0.78	0.05	0.17
I3D	0.86	0.43	0.73
I3D (rev.)	0.80	0.09	0.27

5.1 Interpretability Results on Something-Something

The less widely used C-LSTM architecture could not reach the same global performance as the state-of-the-art I3D (Table 1), which also has an order of magnitude more parameters. The models were only compared on sequences from classes for which they had similar performance (Table 2). We include a variety of per-class F1-scores, ranging from approximately 0.1 to 0.9. All are, however, well above the random chance performance of $1/174 \approx 0.006$. The reason to include a variety of performance levels when studying the extracted features is to control for the general competence of the model. A well performing model might extract different features than a poor one.

In this section, we present an analysis of the Grad-CAM saliency maps and temporal masks generated for each architecture on the eleven classes. We evaluated the models on all validation sequences from these classes (1575 sequences in total). Quantitative results from the feature analysis are shown in Tables 3 and 4 and in Fig. 4. We display eight sample sequences in Figs. 2 and 3, but more on the project webpage.

Trends Regarding the Spatial Focus of the Two Models. We observe that the I3D generally focuses on contiguous, centered blobs, while the C-LSTM attempts to find relevant spatial features in multiple smaller areas (Table 3). Figures 2a and c show examples of this, where I3D focuses on a single region covering both objects, while the C-LSTM has separate activations for the two objects, hands and the surface affected by the movement.

Table 2. F1-score per class and model on the Something-something dataset.

Class	I3D	C-LSTM
Burying something in something	0.1	0.06
Moving something and something away from each other	0.76	0.58
Moving something and something closer to each other	0.77	0.57
Moving something and something so they collide with each other	0.16	0.03
Moving something and something so they pass each other	0.37	0.31
Moving something up	0.43	0.40
Pretending to take something from somewhere	0.10	0.07
Turning the camera downwards while filming something	0.67	0.56
Turning the camera left while filming something	0.94	0.79
Turning the camera right while filming something	0.91	0.8
Turning the camera upwards while filming something	0.81	0.73

Table 3. Statistics for the Grad-CAM maps for each model on eleven classes from the validation set of Something-something (1575 sequences, 16 frames per sequence) and the whole test set of the KTH dataset (863 sequences, 32 frames per sequence). The 'blobs', i.e., the contiguous patches within each Grad-CAM map, were computed per frame, using the blob detection tool from OpenCV [26].

Model (Dataset)	Blob count	Blob size	Center distance
I3D (Smth-smth)	1.6 ± 0.97	33.7 ± 19.6	54.4 ± 33.6
C-LSTM (Smth-smth)	3.6 ± 1.9	26.7 ± 24.5	96.8 ± 34.9
I3D (KTH)	1.1 ± 0.5	44.0 ± 18.7	44.6 ± 19.4
C-LSTM (KTH)	32.6 ± 15.1	5.8 ± 7.0	49.9 ± 22.4

We further find that the I3D has a bias of starting its focus around the middle of the frame (Figs. 2 and 3), often even before the motion starts. This trend persists throughout the sequence, as the average distance to the center of the image for each blob in each frame is shorter for I3D (Table 3). The typical behavior for the C-LSTM is instead to remain agnostic until the action actually starts (e.g., Fig. 3a). In Fig. 3a, the I3D maintains its foveal focus even after the green, round object is out of frame. In Fig. 3b, the focus splits midway to cover both the moped and some features on the wall, while the C-LSTM focuses mainly on numerous features along the wall, as it usually does in classes where the camera turns. The C-LSTM also seems to pay more attention to hands appearing in the clips, rather than objects (Figs. 2a and c–e). Figure 4 shows the normalized histograms of these spatial features. The distributions for the two models differ significantly for all three measures.

Table 4. Statistics for the temporal masks of both models for both datasets (1575 sequences for Something-something and 863 sequences for KTH).

Model (Dataset)	Mask length	Drop ratio	Drop diff.
I3D (Smth-smth)	6.2 ± 3.3	8.4 ± 47	0.2 ± 0.3
C-LSTM (Smth-smth)	9.9 ± 4.1	2.6 ± 6.9	0.08 ± 0.2
I3D (KTH)	10.6 ± 8.5	81.4 ± 174	0.57 ± 0.34
C-LSTM (KTH)	15.2 ± 5.7	17.4 ± 45.2	0.22 ± 0.18

Trends of the Temporal Masks of the Two Models. The quantitative results from the temporal mask experiments are shown in Table 4[1]. We first note that the average temporal mask is shorter for the I3D. This suggests that it has learned to react to short, specific events in the sequences. As an example, its temporal mask in Fig. 2c is active only on the frames where the objects first pass each other, and in Fig. 2b, it is active on the frames leading to the objects touching (further discussed in Sect. 5.3). Second, we note that the drop ratio and drop difference are generally higher for the I3D compared to C-LSTM (Table 4), suggesting that I3D is less sensitive to the reverse perturbation.

The normalized histograms of the three measures are shown in Fig. 4. The mask length distributions clearly have different means. For drop ratio and drop difference, the distributions have more overlap. A t-test conducted in Scipy [27] of the difference in mean between the two models assuming unequal variance gives a p-value $< 10^{-6}$ for both measures. We conclude that there is a significant difference in mean between the two models for drop ratio and drop difference.

Class Ambiguity of the Something-Something Dataset. The Something-something classes can be ambiguous (one class may contain another class) and, arguably, for some samples, incorrectly labeled. Examining the spatiotemporal features may give insight as to how the models handle these ambiguities. Figure 2e shows a case of understandable confusion, where I3D answers *taking one of many similar things on the table*. The surface seen in the image is a tiled floor, and the object is a transparent ruler. Once the temporal mask activates during the lifting motion in the last four frames, the Grad-CAM images show the model also focusing on two lines on the floor. These could be considered similar to the outline of the ruler, which could explain the incorrect classification. An example of ambiguous labeling can be seen for example in Fig. 2b, where I3D's classification is *moving something and something so they collide with each other* and the C-LSTM predicts *pushing something with something*. Although the two objects in the sequence do move closer to each other, they also touch at the end, making both predictions technically correct.

---

[1] For the drop ratio, if the denominator OS-RS ≤ 0.001, the sample was filtered out since its ratio would explode. The OS-FS ≤ 0.001 were also excluded for balance. When using 10^{-9} as threshold instead, the drop ratio results for Something-something were 215 ± 6346 (I3D) and 4.9 ± 47.6 (C-LSTM).

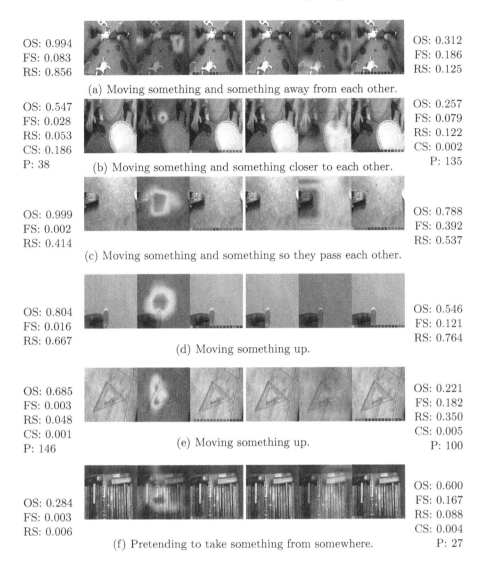

OS: 0.994
FS: 0.083
RS: 0.856

OS: 0.312
FS: 0.186
RS: 0.125

(a) Moving something and something away from each other.

OS: 0.547
FS: 0.028
RS: 0.053
CS: 0.186
P: 38

OS: 0.257
FS: 0.079
RS: 0.122
CS: 0.002
P: 135

(b) Moving something and something closer to each other.

OS: 0.999
FS: 0.002
RS: 0.414

OS: 0.788
FS: 0.392
RS: 0.537

(c) Moving something and something so they pass each other.

OS: 0.804
FS: 0.016
RS: 0.667

OS: 0.546
FS: 0.121
RS: 0.764

(d) Moving something up.

OS: 0.685
FS: 0.003
RS: 0.048
CS: 0.001
P: 146

OS: 0.221
FS: 0.182
RS: 0.350
CS: 0.005
P: 100

(e) Moving something up.

OS: 0.284
FS: 0.003
RS: 0.006

OS: 0.600
FS: 0.167
RS: 0.088
CS: 0.004
P: 27

(f) Pretending to take something from somewhere.

Fig. 2. Best displayed in Adobe Reader where the figures can be played as videos, or on **the project webpage**. I3D (*left*) and C-LSTM (*right*) results for validation sequences from Something-something. The three columns show, from left to right, the original input, the Grad-CAM result, and the input as perturbed by the temporal freeze mask. The third column also visualizes when the mask is on (*red*) or off (*green*), with the current frame highlighted. *OS*: original score (softmax output) for the guessed class, *FS*: freeze score, *RS*: reverse score, *CS*: score for the ground truth class when there was a misclassification and *P*: predicted label, if different from ground truth. (Color figure online)

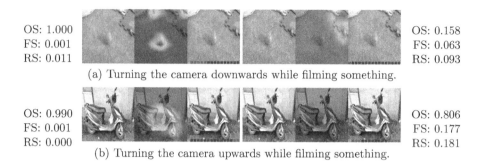

OS: 1.000   OS: 0.158
FS: 0.001   FS: 0.063
RS: 0.011   RS: 0.093

(a) Turning the camera downwards while filming something.

OS: 0.990   OS: 0.806
FS: 0.001   FS: 0.177
RS: 0.000   RS: 0.181

(b) Turning the camera upwards while filming something.

Fig. 3. Best displayed in Adobe Reader where the figures can be played as videos. Same structure as Fig. 2.

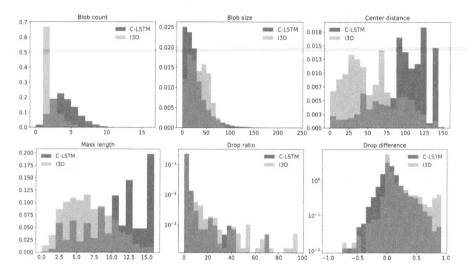

Fig. 4. Normalized histogram results for the Grad-CAM and temporal mask analysis for the I3D (*orange*) and C-LSTM (*blue*) networks. The histograms correspond to the results in Tables 3-4. (Color figure online)

5.2 Interpretability Results on the KTH Actions Dataset

For the KTH dataset, we make similar observations regarding temporal and spatial features. In Fig. 5a, we observe results for the class 'handclapping'. Interestingly, the mask of each model covers at least one entire cycle of the action. The reverse perturbation affects both models very little since one action cycle is symmetrical in time. For the 'running' class (Fig. 5b), we see that the temporal mask identifies the frames in which the subject is in-frame as the most salient for both models, with I3D placing more focus on the subject's legs.

OS: 0.999
FS: 0.026
RS: 0.999

OS: 0.996
FS: 0.997
RS: 0.996

(a) Handclapping, subject 18.

OS: 0.993
FS: 0.208
RS: 0.999

OS: 0.669
FS: 0.339
RS: 0.605

(b) Running, subject 25.

Fig. 5. The figures can be displayed as videos in Adobe Reader. Same structure as Fig. 2.

5.3 Discussion

As stated in Sect. 1, 3D CNNs and C-LSTMs have fundamentally different ways of modeling time. In the following, we discuss two related observations: the shorter temporal masks of I3D and the fact that the classification scores after the freeze and reverse perturbations often are lower for I3D than for the C-LSTM.

For the I3D, all dimensions including the temporal axis of the input are progressively compressed through either convolutional strides or max pooling. The general understanding of CNNs are that later layers encode higher level features. In the deep video network examined in the work by [15], it is shown that the later layer units activate maximally for higher level actions. The representation that is input to the prediction layer in a 3D CNN has compressed high level motions or spatial relations through time to a shorter representation. The classification is then dependent on the presence or absence of these high level features in this representation. If perturbing the input would alter these critical high level features, the resulting prediction might be drastically affected.

For the C-LSTM, however, hidden states resulting from the entire input sequence are sent to the prediction layer. Ultimately, this means that it has a more temporally fine-grained feature space than its 3D CNN counterpart. We hypothesize that this is related to the two observed results. Due to this fine-grained and enveloping temporal feature space, the perturbation must remove larger sub-sequences from the data to obscure enough information through time to cause a large change in prediction score, possibly accounting for the longer temporal masks observed for C-LSTM. Furthermore, as we penalize the length of the mask during optimization, the resulting converged mask is often too short to fully bring down the classification score of the C-LSTM method. Examples of where the freeze score is brought close to, or below, 0.1 are when the mask is nearly or fully active, as seen in Figs. 2b, d and 3a.

6   Conclusions and Future Work

We have presented the first comparison of the spatiotemporal information used by 3D CNN and C-LSTM based models in action recognition. We have presented

424   J. Mänttäri et al.

indications that the difference in temporal modeling has consequences for what features the two models learn. Using the proposed temporal mask method, we presented empirical evidence that I3D on average focuses on shorter and more specific sequences than the C-LSTM. On average, our experiments showed that I3D also tends to focus on fewer or a single contiguous spatial patch closer to the center of the image, instead of smaller areas on several objects like the C-LSTM. Also, when comparing the effect of reversing the most salient frames or removing motion through 'freezing' them, the C-LSTM experiences a relatively larger decrease in prediction confidence than I3D upon reversal. We have also seen that the temporal mask is capable of identifying salient frames in sequences, such as one cycle of a repeated motion.

There is still much to explore in the patterns lying in temporal dependencies. It would be of interest to extend the study to other datasets where temporal information is important, e.g., Charades [28]. Other possible future work includes evaluating the effect of other noise types beyond 'freeze' and 'reverse'. We hope that this empirical study can guide future development and understanding of deep video models.

It is desirable that a model can be trained with as little data as possible. 3D CNNs do not represent video (time) in a physically sound way, treating it as a third spatial dimension. In our view, this is often made up for using large amounts of data and brute-force learning of its correlations, as most state-of-the-art video CNNs are from industry, trained on hundreds of GPUs, e.g., SlowFast [29]. For efficiency, it is important that the representation learned by the model should correspond to the world, and that variables that are uncorrelated in the world remain so in the model. With our evaluation framework it will be possible to gain further insight into what state-of-the-art video models have actually learned.

References

1. Fong, R.C., Vedaldi, A.: Interpretable explanations of black boxes by meaningful perturbation. In: The IEEE International Conference on Computer Vision (ICCV) (2017)
2. Carreira, J., Zisserman, A.: Quo Vadis, action recognition? A new model and the kinetics dataset. In: The IEEE Conference on Computer Vision and Pattern Recognition (CVPR) (2017)
3. Shi, X., Chen, Z., Wang, H.: Convolutional LSTM network : a machine learning approach for precipitation nowcasting arXiv:1506.04214v1 [cs. CV], 13 June 2015, pp. 1–11 (2015)
4. Mahdisoltani, F., Berger, G., Gharbieh, W., Fleet, D.J., Memisevic, R.: Fine-grained video classification and captioning. CoRR abs/1804.09235 (2018)
5. Schuldt, C., Laptev, I., Caputo, B.: Recognizing human actions: a local SVM approach. In: Proceedings of the 17th International Conference on Pattern Recognition, ICPR 2004, vol. 3, pp. 32–36 IEEE (2004)
6. Zeiler, M.D., Fergus, R.: Visualizing and understanding convolutional networks. In: Fleet, D., Pajdla, T., Schiele, B., Tuytelaars, T. (eds.) ECCV 2014. LNCS, vol. 8689, pp. 818–833. Springer, Cham (2014). https://doi.org/10.1007/978-3-319-10590-1_53

7. Simonyan, K., Vedaldi, A., Zisserman, A.: Deep inside convolutional networks: visualising image classification models and saliency maps, pp. 1–8 (2014)
8. Kim, B., et al: Interpretability beyond feature attribution: quantitative testing with concept activation vectors (TCAV). In: ICML (2018)
9. Montavon, G., Samek, W., Müller, K.R.: Methods for interpreting and understanding deep neural networks. Digit. Signal Process.: Rev. J. **73**, 1–15 (2018)
10. Erhan, D., Bengio, Y., Courville, A., Vincent, P.: Visualizing higher-layer features of a deep network. Bernoulli, pp. 1–13 (2009)
11. Selvaraju, R.R., Cogswell, M., Das, A., Vedantam, R., Parikh, D., Batra, D.: Grad-CAM: visual explanations from deep networks via gradient-based localization. In: Proceedings of the IEEE International Conference on Computer Vision 2017-October, pp. 618–626 (2017)
12. Zhang, J., Lin, Z., Brandt, J., Shen, X., Sclaroff, S.: Top-down neural attention by excitation backprop. CoRR abs/1608.00507 (2016)
13. Adel Bargal, S., Zunino, A., Kim, D., Zhang, J., Murino, V., Sclaroff, S.: Excitation backprop for RNNs. In: The IEEE Conference on Computer Vision and Pattern Recognition (CVPR) (2018)
14. Adebayo, J., Gilmer, J., Muelly, M., Goodfellow, I.J., Hardt, M., Kim, B.: Sanity checks for saliency maps. CoRR abs/1810.03292 (2018)
15. Feichtenhofer, C., Pinz, A., Wildes, R.P., Zisserman, A.: What have we learned from deep representations for action recognition? pp. 1–64 (2018)
16. Sigurdsson, G.A., Russakovsky, O., Gupta, A.: What actions are needed for understanding human actions in videos? (2017)
17. Huang, D.A., et al.: What makes a video a video: analyzing temporal information in video understanding models and datasets. In: The IEEE Conference on Computer Vision and Pattern Recognition (CVPR) (2018)
18. Ghodrati, A., Gavves, E., Snoek, C.G.M.: Video time: properties, encoders and evaluation. In: British Machine Vision Conference (2018)
19. Chattopadhyay, A., Sarkar, A., Howlader, P., Balasubramanian, V.N.: Grad-CAM++: generalized gradient-based visual explanations for deep convolutional networks (2017)
20. Dwibedi, D., Sermanet, P., Tompson, J.: Temporal reasoning in videos using convolutional gated recurrent units. In: The IEEE Conference on Computer Vision and Pattern Recognition (CVPR) Workshops (2018)
21. Zhou, B., Andonian, A., Oliva, A., Torralba, A.: Temporal relational reasoning in videos. In: Ferrari, V., Hebert, M., Sminchisescu, C., Weiss, Y. (eds.) ECCV 2018. LNCS, vol. 11205, pp. 831–846. Springer, Cham (2018). https://doi.org/10.1007/978-3-030-01246-5_49
22. Ballas, N., Yao, L., Pal, C., Courville, A.C.: Delving deeper into convolutional networks for learning video representations. In: The International Conference on Learning Representations (2016)
23. Li, Z., Gavrilyuk, K., Gavves, E., Jain, M., Snoek, C.G.: VideoLSTM convolves, attends and flows for action recognition. Comput. Vis. Image Underst. **166**, 41–50 (2018)
24. Satkin, S., Hebert, M.: Modeling the temporal extent of actions. In: Daniilidis, K., Maragos, P., Paragios, N. (eds.) ECCV 2010. LNCS, vol. 6311, pp. 536–548. Springer, Heidelberg (2010). https://doi.org/10.1007/978-3-642-15549-9_39
25. Xie, S., Sun, C., Huang, J., Tu, Z., Murphy, K.: Rethinking spatiotemporal feature learning for video understanding. CoRR abs/1712.04851 (2017)
26. Bradski, G.: The OpenCV library. Dr. Dobb's J. Softw. Tools (2000)

27. Virtanen, P., et al.: SciPy 1.0: fundamental algorithms for scientific computing in python. Nat. Methods **17**, 261–272 (2020)
28. Sigurdsson, G.A., Varol, G., Wang, X., Farhadi, A., Laptev, I., Gupta, A.: Hollywood in homes: crowdsourcing data collection for activity understanding. In: Leibe, B., Matas, J., Sebe, N., Welling, M. (eds.) ECCV 2016. LNCS, vol. 9905, pp. 510–526. Springer, Cham (2016). https://doi.org/10.1007/978-3-319-46448-0_31
29. Feichtenhofer, C., Fan, H., Malik, J., He, K.: SlowFast networks for video recognition. In: The IEEE International Conference on Computer Vision (ICCV) (2019)

Encode the Unseen: Predictive Video Hashing for Scalable Mid-stream Retrieval

Tong Yu[(✉)] and Nicolas Padoy

ICube, University of Strasbourg, CNRS, IHU Strasbourg, Strasbourg, France
tyu@unistra.fr

Abstract. This paper tackles a new problem in computer vision: mid-stream video-to-video retrieval. This task, which consists in searching a database for content similar to a video right as it is playing, e.g. from a live stream, exhibits challenging characteristics. Only the beginning part of the video is available as query and new frames are constantly added as the video plays out. To perform retrieval in this demanding situation, we propose an approach based on a binary encoder that is both **predictive** and **incremental** in order to (1) account for the missing video content at query time and (2) keep up with repeated, continuously evolving queries throughout the streaming. In particular, we present the first hashing framework that infers the unseen future content of a currently playing video. Experiments on FCVID and ActivityNet demonstrate the feasibility of this task. Our approach also yields a significant mAP@20 performance increase compared to a baseline adapted from the literature for this task, for instance 7.4% (2.6%) increase at 20% (50%) of elapsed runtime on FCVID using bitcodes of size 192 bits.

1 Introduction

Video-to-video retrieval is an emerging problem in computer vision due to the growth of large-scale video databases such as Youtube (720K h uploaded daily) or Instagram. Current search modalities for those databases rely on keywords, which are effective to some degree for an adequately tagged set of videos but inevitably fail to capture the rich visual information contained in video data.

Solutions for visual search are already widely in use for static images, with publicly available services such as TinEye or Google Image Search. These tools take an image supplied by the user and return a list of visually similar pictures, allowing the user to search for content that would otherwise be difficult to find via a text-based search engine. Video, on the other hand, has not received nearly the same amount of attention when it comes to retrieval tasks. Furthermore, the few existing works on video retrieval treat the problem as a pure

Electronic supplementary material The online version of this chapter (https://doi.org/10.1007/978-3-030-69541-5_26) contains supplementary material, which is available to authorized users.

H. Ishikawa et al. (Eds.): ACCV 2020, LNCS 12626, pp. 427–442, 2021.
https://doi.org/10.1007/978-3-030-69541-5_26

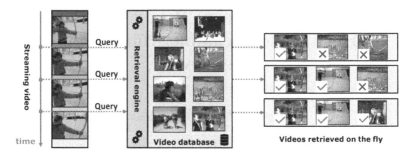

Fig. 1. Our hashing technique enables incremental video retrieval from incomplete queries, as needed for real-time retrieval in live video streams. A streamed video of archery is used for querying. On the last query all 3 returned videos are relevant.

postprocessing task by only considering prerecorded videos as inputs. There is, however, huge potential for retrieving content directly from non-prerecorded **live video sources**, in order to provide **dynamic search results**. Recent advances in text-based search engines, which can now refresh results while the user is typing, prove how useful this innovation would be. This work therefore introduces a framework for **unsupervised real-time-stream-to-video retrieval** (Fig. 1) and proposes, to our best knowledge, the first solution to this problem. Popular livestreaming platforms such as Twitch or Youtube Live would highly benefit from such a method, which dynamically searches for content from the live stream. This would enable on-the-fly content suggestion, a powerful feature with a wide variety of potential applications:

- **advertising**: commercials, content curation relevant to a live stream
- **sports & entertainment**: highlights during live events, enhanced by replays of similar past content
- **education**: live tutoring. A person films themselves cooking or performing repairs, while an algorithm follows and assists their process in real time with retrieved instructional clips
- **surveillance & security**: anomaly detection from a live security feed. An algorithm continuously searches a database of security events to provide reference for monitoring the feed in real time
- **healthcare**: relevant surgical actions shown to a surgeon simultaneously to real-time events in the intervention

This task presents two main challenges that make it particularly difficult:

A. The search protocol needs to be **fast** enough for real-time use. This is a brutal constraint, considering the typical size of a large-scale video database, as well as the size of video data itself compared to static image data.
B. The real-time streaming setting implies that the video is **incomplete**; at the beginning of a video, most of the visual information is missing.

An efficient solution for technical challenge A is **hashing** [1–6]. Hashing employs a hashing function ϕ that maps high dimensional data entries - in our case videos - to compact binary codes, or **bitcodes**. A good choice of ϕ should respect visual similarity: two videos with similar visual content should yield bitcodes differing only by a small number of bits. Once ϕ is determined, the video database to search from is mapped to a set of bitcodes referred to as the **codebook** (also called *gallery* in certain papers). Search can then be performed in the following manner: the query video is mapped to its bitcode, the **hamming distance** between the query's bitcode and each bitcode in the codebook is computed, and finally the top K closest entries are returned. This search protocol can be extremely fast: distance computation has linear complexity w.r.t. the number codebook entries, and each distance computation can be performed as a bitwise XOR operation. For mid-stream retrieval however, an additional highly desirable feature is **incrementality**: new information added by the currently playing video should be incorporated into the bitcode without reprocessing the entire video from its beginning. This keeps time and space requirements to a minimum, which is crucial for scalability when considering extremely large video databases, as well as large numbers of simultaneous queries to process.

Our first contribution is therefore to propose **the first incremental video hashing method**. It relies on a self-supervised binary video encoder consisting of a 3D CNN combined with a RNN. RNNs are naturally suitable for incremental tasks; their output at each timestep only depends on the corresponding new input and the value of their internal memory, which accounts for all previous timesteps on its own. Existing video hashing approaches, which did not consider the case of partial videos, either use pooling [4], or employ RNNs with sampling schemes that render them non-incremental [1–3,5,6]. The expected use case for those methods is a single retrieval from a full video taken from beginning to end, while our method generates bitcodes throughout the video's duration, making it capable of supporting repeated mid-stream queries.

In order to deal with the incomplete videos, our approach needs to learn to anticipate the future video content. We therefore introduce our second contribution, which is **the first predictive hashing method**. Instead of generating bitcodes according to what is actually seen, which is the paradigm followed by all image [7–10] and video [1–3,5,6] hashing methods up to this point, we generate them according to what is *expected*. To achieve this, we introduce two unsupervised knowledge distillation methods where the binary encoder, by learning to anticipate future content from incomplete videos, generates bitcodes that account for the unseen part of the video in addition to the part it has already seen. This form of distillation relies on *binary* embeddings, and is radically different from other methods considering future frames [11–13], as these have employed *real-valued* embeddings and targeted tasks completely different from retrieval. The enriched bitcodes formed by our method produce better matches with relevant content in the database and significantly improve retrieval results when incomplete queries are used.

2   Related Work

2.1   Video Activity Understanding

Due to the high dimensionality of the data involved, deep neural networks have become the go-to approach in video activity understanding methods. Videos may be considered as sets of static frames with each frame processed individually - for instance with a 2D CNN. However, a video-specific deep architecture should account for temporal dependencies in video data. A wide range of methods were designed for this purpose; we mention a few below that are relevant to this work.

The LRCN architecture [14] is an early example of temporal and spatial model combination. A CNN maps video frames to low-dimensional visual feature vectors. Those features are then fed to an LSTM [15], responsible for learning the video's temporal dynamics in order to perform tasks such as video captioning. Similarly, [16] runs an LSTM autoencoder on VGG features. Trained in an unsupervised manner, this model learns compact and discriminative representations of videos that can be repurposed for action recognition tasks. Two-stream networks [17–19] approach the problem from a different angle, by combining two 2D CNNs: one for color data and one for optical flow. Instead of accounting for the spatial aspect and the temporal aspect of the problem in two separate components, the TSM [20] and 3D CNN approaches [21–25] combine them into a single architecture. The C3D model[21], and later on the I3D model [22] employ 3D convolutions (one temporal and two spatial dimensions) in order to directly process video inputs. I3D is the architecture we use for visual feature extraction.

2.2   Early Activity Recognition

In early activity recognition (EAR) tasks, a model attempts to classify an action depicted in a video by only observing its beginning. The potentially large amount of missing visual information introduces a level of difficulty that is not found in general activity recognition tasks, but which we also encounter in our problem.

Methods such as [26] and [27] rely on elapsed time or progress. [26] trains an LSTM model with a temporally weighted loss enhancing the importance of predictions made early on in the video. [27] proposes a method for early recognition based on soft labels at different levels of video progress. A different type of approach for early recognition tasks is to synthesize the content in the video's future: [28] attempts to guess future frame embeddings in videos with a multi-layer fully connected network. [13] employs video representations fed to generator models trained to synthesize embeddings future frame embeddings. Finally, teacher-student distillation methods train a student model that has not seen future frames to replicate representations learnt by a teacher model that has. [12] employs a distillation method that trains an LSTM to predict the state of another LSTM at a further point in the input video. A different distillation method, as introduced in [11], trains a forward-directional LSTM to match at each timestep the hidden states of a trained bidirectional LSTM.

Although EAR and mid-stream video retrieval operate on similar inputs, which are the early parts of videos, EAR is entirely different from our problem in the very same sense that recognition is different from retrieval. Retrieval involves comparisons to all items in a database to retrieve those that are similar. Similarity in this context can consist of much more than simply having identical class labels, although the evaluation protocol relies on class labels to provide quantitative results. EAR, on the other hand, is entirely label-dependent. The output of EAR is a class, while the output of our approach consists of a large selection of items from an entire video database.

2.3 Video Hashing

For static image data, a large number of hashing methods exist in the literature [7–10]. Video data is substantially more challenging. First, video data requires capturing **rich temporal dependencies**. Second, **the sequence length is variable**: reducing a video to a fixed-length representation is not straightforward. Third, **data dimensionality is considerably higher**: a minute of video at 30 fps contains 1800 times the amount of data contained in any of its frames. Capturing enough visual information from it in a single vector of a few hundreds, if not tens of bits is a tough challenge. Finally, large-scale video databases require considerably larger amounts of time than images to annotate; **unsupervised learning** is therefore heavily favored.

Six unsupervised video hashing methods have addressed the first challenge in a significant manner by incorporating some degree of temporal modeling: SSTH [1] uses an encoder-decoder pair of RNNs with a binary state for the encoder in order to learn rich, discriminative bitcodes. SSVH [2] improves over this architecture by aggregating information at different time scales in the video with stacked RNNs. JTAE [5] also follows the encoder-decoder type of approach with separate encoders for appearance and temporal dynamics. NPH [6] uses an encoder-decoder similarly to the previous approaches, but trained with losses that attempt to preserve neighborhood structures from the embeddings it receives. UDVH-LSTM [3] applies geometric transformations to embeddings obtained from temporally pooled features from a CNN-LSTM, before binarizing those embeddings. UDVH-TSN [4] employs a similar approach, replacing the CNN-LSTM with a modified Temporal Segment Network [29].

All those methods deal with the issue of variable sequence length by resorting to fixed-rate sampling schemes, rendering them non-incremental. Those schemes select a set number of evenly-spaced frames in all input videos and discard the rest. This results in a fixed-length but variable-rate and sparse representation that would be unsuitable in a live setting, as explained in Sect. 3.2. All methods other than SSTH also exhibit additional characteristics that are unsuitable for incremental use in real-time: feature pooling from the beginning to the end of a video [3–5], hierarchical aggregation of timesteps [2], video anchor fetching at query time [6]. For this reason, we build our baseline approach on SSTH. **None of the aforementioned approaches have examined the mid-stream, incomplete video case.**

3   Methods

3.1   Overview

The problem can be formally stated as follows: given a **level of observation** $\alpha \in (0, 1]$, a video $\mathcal{Q}$ with duration $T(\mathcal{Q})$, a query $\mathcal{Q}_\alpha$ consisting of $\mathcal{Q}$ truncated mid-stream at time $\alpha T(\mathcal{Q})$, and a database of videos $\mathcal{B} = \{V_0...V_N\}$, use only $\mathcal{Q}_\alpha$ to find the K videos from $\mathcal{B}$ most similar to $\mathcal{Q}$.

Since hashing is the method employed here, $\mathcal{B}$ and $\mathcal{Q}$ are represented by binary codes during search operations. The overall protocol is therefore composed of the following steps: video-level feature extraction, self-supervised hash function training, codebook mapping and finally query operations.

3.2   Sampling and Feature Extraction

As mentioned in the related work section, previous approaches have chosen sparse, fixed-length video-level representations which can result in the loss of large amounts of visual information in long videos. More importantly, such sampling and feature extraction schemes are inadequate for real-time usage: the sampling rate in that case is dependent on the length of the full video, which would be unknown mid-stream. An early retrieval algorithm should be capable of delivering search results at a fast and steady pace.

To solve this issue, we have chosen a dense, fixed-rate sampling and feature extraction scheme that leverages a 3D CNN to aggregate visual information over short time windows. The chosen architecture is I3D [22], pretrained on the Kinetics [30] dataset for action recognition. Input frames from the videos are center-cropped to 224×224. Clip input length is 64 frames (roughly 2 s at 30 fps). This yields a feature tensor with dimensions $8 \times 7 \times 7 \times 1024$, which we average pool into a feature vector of size $N_f = 1 \times 2 \times 2 \times 1024 = 4096$. The entire video is processed in consecutive clips, resulting in a $30/64 = 0.47$ Hz constant feature output rate.

3.3   Binary RNN Encoder

An RNN (Fig. 2) takes the feature vectors $f_0, f_1, ..., f_t, ..., f_{T(V)}$ from I3D in chronological order and maps each one to a bitcode of size N_{bits}. This RNN is built on two stacked LSTMs, with a binary LSTM as introduced in [1]. The hidden state circulating from one RNN timestep t to the next is the above mentioned bitcode noted $b(V, t)$ for a video V. Batch normalization is applied to the cell state as done in [1]. This RNN is trained as the encoder part of an autoencoder model. The final hidden state of the decoder - the video's bitcode - is passed to two decoder RNNs tasked with reconstructing the sequence of input feature vectors in opposite orders. This training process encourages the encoder to incorporate rich, discriminative information into the bitcodes.

Formally, the autoencoder is trained to minimize the following **unsupervised** loss function: $\mathcal{L}_{decoder}(V) = \sum_{j=0}^{T(V)} \|f_j - \overleftarrow{f}_j\|_2 + \|f_j - \overrightarrow{f}_j\|_2$ with $\overleftarrow{f}, \overrightarrow{f}$ being the reverse and forward reconstructed sequences, respectively.

Backpropagation relies on the gradient substitution method shown in [1]. Trained as such with full videos, we call this configuration **SSTH-RT** (Fig. 3, top left) for real-time, as each new increment of the video playing in real-time is incorporated into the bitcode. This is, in the form presented here, our first baseline approach.

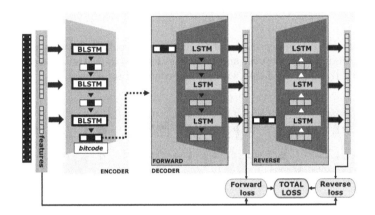

Fig. 2. Illustration of the self-supervised binary video autoencoder [1].

3.4   Data-Augmentated Encoder via Truncated Training Duplicates

Since the training process for the baseline setting always involves complete videos, a straightforward data augmentation method for training the autoencoder is to simply give the autoencoder videos truncated at various levels of observation to reconstruct (Fig. 4, left). This approach provides some training exposure to videos that are incomplete. This is referred to as **SSTH-RT$^+$** in the later sections.

3.5   Augmented Codebook with Truncated Database Duplicates

Another idea to improve early retrieval results is to incorporate trimmed videos, both during training - as in SSTH-RT$^+$ - and codebook construction (Fig. 4, center). We refer to this later on as **SSTH-RT^{++}**. While this idea might seem appealing at a first glance, it causes the search protocol to slow down due to the insertion of bitcodes from trimmed duplicates. This requires inserting as many duplicates per video as levels of observation employed - in our case: 10 from 0.1 to 1.0 - which is also a source of scalability issues. Assuming N_α levels of observation are employed, search time and storage space requirements both get multiplied by N_α. Duplicates in the search results, namely, videos truncated at

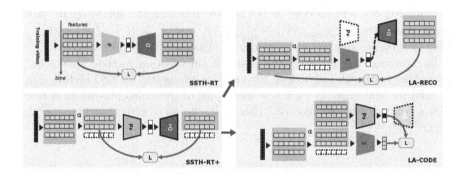

Fig. 3. Overview of training setups for all models. P stands for primary encoder, S for secondary encoder, D for decoder and L for loss. The (+) indicates the use of truncated videos during training. Elements with dashed contours are unused.

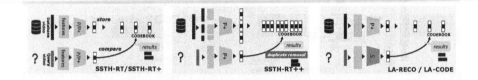

Fig. 4. Overview of retrieval setups for all models, depicting the generation of the codebooks, their size, as well as the trained encoders used.

different levels of observations from the same original video, would also need to be purged, the cost of which has $N_{cb} \times N_\alpha$ complexity, N_{cb} being the size of the codebook without duplicates. Correctly retrieved results that are duplicates may improve retrieval metrics, but do not suit general application cases: a search operation returning truncated versions of the same video would be unhelpful to the user. The approaches proposed in the next section are faster as they employ codebooks with the exact same population size as the original video database.

3.6   Look-Ahead Distillation for Encoders

We propose two forms of distillation in order to train **predictive encoders** that can anticipate the future content when presented with incomplete videos, and therefore generate richer, more discriminative bitcodes that are more likely to yield better search results.

Indirect Distillation: Look-Ahead Reconstruction (LA-RECO) Loss. An encoder, which will from now on be referred to as the primary encoder (P in Fig. 3), is trained following the same process as SSTH-RT$^+$ jointly with a decoder. Once this training is done, the main encoder is set aside and a secondary encoder (S in Fig. 3, top right) is introduced. Only incomplete videos are fed into it - i.e. videos truncated to $\alpha T(V)$ with randomized *alpha* for each training step. The resulting bitcode is passed to the trained decoder with frozen parameters. The output of the decoder is compared to the full sequence in the loss, not just the truncated part fed to the secondary. This forces the secondary encoder to guess a representation accounting for future video frames.

Direct Distillation: Look-Ahead Bitcode (LA-CODE) Loss. A secondary encoder is introduced as in the previous section, however this time the primary is put to use and the decoder is set aside (Fig. 3, bottom right). During training, the primary encoder, which has its parameters frozen, receives the entire video while the secondary encoder is only fed the αT first frames, again with randomized *alpha*. From the secondary, we extract the real-valued input β to the *sgn* function that leads to the last bitcode - we refer to this as the *prebitcode* - and compare that to the bitcode b given by the primary using an L2 loss function:

$$\mathcal{L}_{LA-CODE} = \|\beta(V, \alpha T) - b(V)\|_2. \tag{1}$$

This conditions the encoder, despite being only fed part of a video, to mimic the full video's bitcode.

3.7 Experimental Setup

Datasets. For our experiments we employed two datasets. The first is FCVID [31], a public video dataset used for research on video retrieval and activity understanding depicting various activities, objects, sports and events. 234 video classes are present. The average video duration is $134 \pm 92\,$s. Data was split as follows: 45K for training, 45K for testing. Within the test videos, 42.5K constitute the database while the remaining 2.5k (about 10 videos per class on average) are used for querying. The second dataset we employed is ActivityNet [32]. We used the 18 K videos available for download. 200 activity classes are featured. A number of videos had their labels concealed by the organizers of the ActivityNet challenge; those videos were put in the training set. The average duration is $117 \pm 67\,$s. Data was split as follows: 9K for training, 9K for testing, and within the testing 8 K for the codebook, 1K (about 5 per class on average) for the query. In both datasets, the videos are untrimmed, which implies that the content reflecting a given video's class may not be shown for its entire duration. All videos have been resampled at 30 fps and a few excessively long videos have been cropped to 4 min 30 s.

Training. Video-level features are extracted separately by I3D and reloaded from binary files. Training is done in batches; to achieve batching with variable sequence lengths we grouped videos of similar length into buckets and randomly pick batches from a single bucket at a time during training. Batches are then trimmed to the shortest duration present in each of them. Encoder/decoder pairs are trained for 60 epochs with a learning rate of 5.10^{-3} and a batch size of 40. With N_{bits} being the size of the bitcode, the encoder is a 2-layer RNN with $2 \cdot N_{bits}$ in the first layer and N_{bits} units in the second. The decoder also has two layers, with N_{bits} in the first layer and $2 \cdot N_{bits}$ units in the second. Secondary encoders in LA-RECO or LA-CODE are trained for 15 epochs with a learning rate of 5.10^{-4}. Their weights are initialized from the values of the trained primary encoder's weights (Fig. 6).

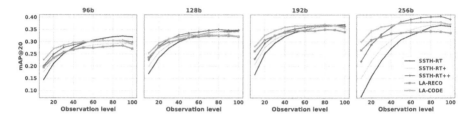

Fig. 5. Overall results, **FCVID**: mAP@20 for all models and 4 different bitcode sizes at 10 different observation levels (%).

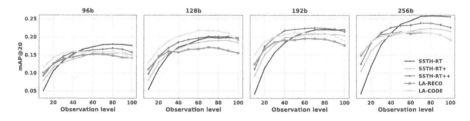

Fig. 6. Overall results, **ActivityNet**: mAP@20 for all models and 4 different bitcode sizes at 10 different observation levels (%).

Evaluation. Evaluation is performed as in classical video retrieval by performing queries and comparing them to the search results based on their class labels. This way of assessing visual similarity is limited but also the only available option for quantitative evaluation; qualitative results (Sect. 4.1) show that information much richer than the classes is captured during retrieval. Once the primary and secondary encoders are trained, we use the primary to generate the codebook from the corresponding videos picked from the test set, as shown in Fig. 4. The remainder of the test set forms the query set. The query encoder generates a bitcode for each query video, truncated at αT frames. The code is compared to codebook entries, which are then ranked by Hamming distance to the query bitcode starting from the nearest. Query videos are truncated using 10 different values for α ranging from 0.1 to 1.0, representing different stages of elapsed video.

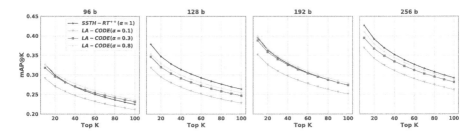

Fig. 7. Detailed results, **FCVID**: mAP@K for LA-CODE and 4 different bitcode sizes at 3 different observation levels (%).

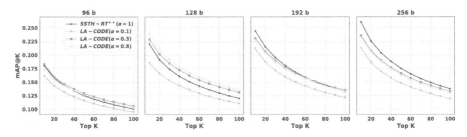

Fig. 8. Detailed results, **ActivityNet**: mAP@K for LA-CODE and 4 different bitcode sizes at 3 different observation levels (%).

Average precision at K for a single video, as employed in [1], is given by $AP@K = \frac{1}{K}\sum_{j=0}^{K}\frac{N_{correct}(j)}{j}$, where $N_{correct}(j)$ is the number of matching results among the top j. The mean over all query videos is the Mean Average Precision at K - or mAP@K. We report this metric by level of observation for all methods and all bitcode sizes for K = 20. Lower values of K are more relevant in a real-time use case, where one can only handle a small number of search results; nonetheless we provide mAP@K curves for K up to 100 for our best model. We also provide qualitative retrieval results for two cases. All experiments are repeated for four different bitcode sizes: 96, 128, 192, 256 bits. The compared approaches are (Fig. 7):

- **SSTH-RT**: binary autoencoder trained to reconstruct full sequences from full sequences. **This provides a point of comparison against the literature, since it is SSTH** [1] **implemented with a different feature extraction scheme to cope with fixed-rate sampling** (see Sect. 3.2)
- **SSTH-RT$^+$**: binary autoencoder trained to reconstruct full sequences from full sequences, as well as partial sequences from partial sequences
- **SSTH-RT^{++}**: same encoder as SSTH-RT$^+$, with truncated duplicates hashed into the codebook
- **LA-RECO**: SSTH-RT$^+$ as primary encoder, with secondary trained to reconstruct full sequences from partial sequences
- **LA-CODE**: SSTH-RT$^+$ as primary encoder, with secondary trained to predict the primary's full sequence bitcodes from partial sequences

Implementation Details and Performance Considerations. We timed the search protocol in a separate experiment combining all its steps from beginning to end. This includes the I3D forward pass, the encoding, the xor computation with the codebook and the ranking. Results on FCVID show that one search operation using 256b bitcodes and a codebook of 42.5k videos takes 2.7 s with a 1080Ti GPU. This enables a query rate of 22 queries per minute, which is sufficient for an end user.

4 Results

The mAP@20 results are compared by level of observation for each method in Fig. 5 with separate graphs for each size of bitcode. SSTH-RT serves as the reference baseline and point of comparison against the literature. SSTH-RT$^+$ is a much more competitive model to compare to, SSTH-RT^{++} even more so, but at the cost of 10 times the space requirements and search time.

Table 1. Results breakdown by α range. For each bitcode size: left column shows very early results (VE, average mAP@20 for α from 0.1 to 0.2); Middle column shows early results (E, average for α from 0.1 to 0.5); Right column shows overall results (O, average over all α).

	96 bits			128 bits			192 bits			256 bits		
FCVID	VE	E	O	VE	E	O	VE	E	O	VE	E	O
SSTH-RT	17.8	23.5	27.6	20.2	25.9	29.9	20.9	27.4	31.8	11.5	20.6	27.9
SSTH-RT$^+$	20.3	24.2	26.6	22.9	27.6	30.6	24.2	29.4	32.6	18.5	25.6	31.0
SSTH-RT^{++}	22.5	26.2	28.2	25.5	29.7	32.1	26.2	30.9	33.6	25.4	31.6	35.6
LA-RECO	21.5	24.6	26.2	25.7	28.8	30.5	28.4	31.5	33.0	28.6	31.2	32.6
LA-CODE	**24.8**	**27.5**	**28.8**	**27.4**	**30.2**	**31.4**	**30.3**	**33.5**	**35.0**	**32.0**	**34.9**	**36.3**
ActivityNet	VE	E	O	VE	E	O	VE	E	O	VE	E	O
SSTH-RT	7.8	12.2	14.9	8.3	13.4	16.5	7.8	14.0	17.9	8.0	15.7	20.6
SSTH-RT$^+$	9.7	12.1	13.7	10.4	14.2	16.5	12.1	16.4	18.5	13.3	17.3	19.6
SSTH-RT^{++}	10.9	13.6	**15.0**	12.2	15.8	17.8	14.2	18.4	**20.3**	15.4	**19.5**	21.4
LA-RECO	11.3	13.2	14.0	12.7	14.8	15.6	14.5	17.2	18.1	16.8	19.3	19.9
LA-CODE	**12.9**	**14.6**	**15.0**	**14.7**	**17.9**	**19.4**	**16.8**	**19.1**	19.8	**17.0**	19.2	19.9

We start with a general overview of the results. The general tendency observed is that **retrieval degrades as the observed portion of video decreases**. With 128 bits and complete videos ($\alpha = 1$), mAP@20 for SSTH-RT on FCVID reaches 34% but drops to 30 % when only the first 40% of the video are available, down to 17% with 10% observation. The trend on ActivityNet is similar with 20%, 17% and 5% mAP@20 respectively.

When considering different bitcode sizes, the tendency observed in Fig. 5 is that retrieval performance generally increases with size, as more bits enable richer encodings. Looking at one method, bottom mAP@20 for LA-CODE on FCVID starts at 22.5% for 96 bits, then moves up to 25.3% for 128 bits, 28.0% for 192 bits and 29.8% for 256 bits. In similar fashion, bottom mAP@20 for LA-CODE on ActivityNet respectively reaches 11.4%, 12.8%, 15.0% and 15.4%.

When considering the different methods, results for non-predictive approaches (SSTH-RT, SSTH-RT$^+$ and SSTH-RT^{++}) tend to be heavily imbalanced with much higher mAP@20 at high α values. In comparison, results for predictive methods are more even across the α range. An example of this can be seen for 256 bits on ActivityNet, where LA-CODE starts at 30% and ends at 36% while SSTH-RT starts at 7% and ends at 36%.

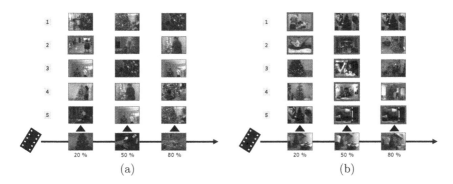

Fig. 9. Retrieval over time with LA-CODE, illustrating a successful live retrieval (a) and a less successful one (b) on two videos depicting the action *decorating a christmas tree*. Red borders indicate a mismatch.(Color figure online)

To allow for clearer comparison, we break down our results into ranges of observation levels. We consider the average of mAP@20 over very early observations (VE, α from 0.1 to 0.2), early (E, α from 0.1 to 0.5) and overall (O, α from 0.1 to 1.0) in Table 1.

We first consider all levels of observation together, (O) in Table 1. On ActivityNet for 96, 192 and 256 bits SSTH-RT^{++} ranks best overall. This comes, however, at the cost of a codebook 10 times larger and 10 times longer search time, which puts it at a severe disadvantage compared to LA-CODE. For all bitcode sizes on FCVID, for 96 and 128 bits on ActivityNet, LA-CODE is however the top ranking approach.

Although sustaining good performance at higher levels of observation is valuable due to the current level of observation being potentially unknown during streaming in a real use case, **the focus of this work is on lower levels of observation** (under 50%). In this range, the main novel challenge specific to our problem, namely missing visual information, is the most manifest.

The performance increase in the very low α range is generally accentuated compared to the whole range of α. This makes sense since the losses employed emphasize anticipation. For 192 bits on FCVID, LA-RECO surpasses SSTH-RT$^+$ by 2.1% for early observations, and 4.2% for very early observations. Similar results are obtained with LA-CODE, which even beats SSTH-RT^{++} by a 2.6% margin for low α and 4.1% for very low α. It surpasses SSTH-RT$^+$ by 4.1% in the early α range and 6.1% in the very early α range. Finally, it solidly outperforms SSTH-RT by 6.1% and 9.4% for early and very early observations, respectively.

We display mAP@K for LA-CODE for increasing observation levels, compared with SSTH-RT^{++}'s evaluated on *complete* queries (SSTH-RT$^{++}_{\alpha=1}$) in Fig. 7. With 10% of video observed at 192 bits, LA-RECO loses to SSTH-RT$^{++}_{\alpha=1}$ by 5%, which is expected since it has access to far less information. However LA-RECO catches up with 30% of video observed. At 80% of video observed LA-RECO even surpasses SSTH-RT$^{++}_{\alpha=1}$ by a small margin. MAP@K plots for other bitcode sizes and methods are provided in the supplementary material.

4.1 Qualitative Results

We selected two FCVID queries from the query set on which LA-RECO returned successful results at the end of the video, i.e. the top 10 results are correct. We followed the evolution of the top 5 search results at different points in time. Both query videos depict the action *"decorating a christmas tree"*. Retrieval might be subpar early on in the video, but the model should ideally adapt and return more relevant database entries as the video plays.

Figure 9a shows an example of a successful case. A mistake is made early on at 20%, but the top 5 search results improve to a perfect 5/5 after 50% of the video is seen. On the other hand, in Fig. 9b the model starts with 3/5 correct results, then drops to 1/5 in the middle. Retrieval eventually improves towards the end with 4/5 correct results at 81% progression. The video supplementary material (https://youtu.be/Eq-lIUipd4E) shows examples of **label-agnostic** similarity in the retrieved videos. For instance at 2:25 a video of a person operating a lawnmower is the query. **Certain results have mismatched labels such as cello or archery, while retaining the same fine-grained motion semantics, in these examples the arm movement.**

5   Conclusion

In this paper, we present an unsupervised video hashing approach designed for incremental retrieval performed mid-stream using incomplete video queries. To tackle this challenging new problem, we propose a predictive encoder that learns to generate enhanced bitcode representations of incomplete queries by acquiring knowledge distilled from another encoder trained on complete videos. Our approach yields a large performance improvement over the baseline. It also outperforms a naive approach that inflates the codebook by adding codes generated from truncated copies of the videos in the database, while being at the same time much faster and more scalable for live hashing and retrieval on video streams.

Acknowledgements. This work was supported by French state funds managed by the ANR under reference ANR-16-CE33-0009 (DeepSurg) and by BPI France (project CONDOR). The authors would also like to acknowledge the support of NVIDIA with the donation of a GPU used in this research.

References

1. Zhang, H., Wang, M., Hong, R., Chua, T.: Play and rewind: optimizing binary representations of videos by self-supervised temporal hashing. In: Proceedings of the 24th ACM International Conference on Multimedia (MM), pp. 781–790 (2016)
2. Song, J., Zhang, H., Li, X., Gao, L., Wang, M., Hong, R.: Self-supervised video hashing with hierarchical binary auto-encoder. IEEE Trans. Image Process. **27**, 3210–3221 (2018)
3. Wu, G., et al.: Unsupervised deep video hashing with balanced rotation. In: International Joint Conference on Artificial Intelligence (IJCAI), pp. 3076–3082 (2017)
4. Wu, G., et al.: Unsupervised deep video hashing via balanced code for large-scale video retrieval. IEEE Trans. Image Process. **28**, 1993–2007 (2019)
5. Li, C., Yang, Y., Cao, J., Huang, Z.: Jointly modeling static visual appearance and temporal pattern for unsupervised video hashing. In: Proceedings of the 2017 ACM on Conference on Information and Knowledge Management, pp. 9–17 (2017)
6. Li, S., Chen, Z., Lu, J., Li, X., Zhou, J.: Neighborhood preserving hashing for scalable video retrieval. In: The IEEE International Conference on Computer Vision (ICCV), pp. 8211–8220 (2019)
7. Gong, Y., Lazebnik, S., Gordo, A., Perronnin, F.: Iterative quantization: a procrustean approach to learning binary codes for large-scale image retrieval. IEEE Trans. Pattern Anal. Mach. Intell. **35**, 2916–2929 (2013)
8. Heo, J., Lee, Y., He, J., Chang, S., Yoon, S.: Spherical hashing. In: 2012 IEEE Conference on Computer Vision and Pattern Recognition (CVPR), pp. 2957–2964 (2012)
9. Yang, E., Liu, T., Deng, C., Liu, W., Tao, D.: Distillhash: unsupervised deep hashing by distilling data pairs. In: IEEE Conference on Computer Vision and Pattern Recognition (CVPR), pp. 2946–2955 (2019)
10. He, X., Wang, P., Cheng, J.: K-nearest neighbors hashing. In: IEEE Conference on Computer Vision and Pattern Recognition (CVPR), pp. 2839–2848 (2019)
11. Wang, X., Hu, J.F., Lai, J.H., Zhang, J., Zheng, W.S.: Progressive teacher-student learning for early action prediction. In: IEEE Conference on Computer Vision and Pattern Recognition (CVPR), pp. 3556–3565 (2019)
12. Kannan, S., Yengera, G., Mutter, D., Marescaux, J., Padoy, N.: Future-state predicting LSTM for early surgery type recognition. IEEE Trans. Med. Imaging **39**, 556–566 (2019)
13. Gammulle, H., Denman, S., Sridharan, S., Fookes, C.: Predicting the future: a jointly learnt model for action anticipation. In: The IEEE International Conference on Computer Vision (ICCV) (2019)
14. Donahue, J., et al.: Long-term recurrent convolutional networks for visual recognition and description. In: IEEE Conference on Computer Vision and Pattern Recognition, CVPR, pp. 2625–2634 (2015)
15. Hochreiter, S., Schmidhuber, J.: Long short-term memory. Neural Comput. **9**, 1735–1780 (1997)

16. Srivastava, N., Mansimov, E., Salakhutdinov, R.: Unsupervised learning of video representations using LSTMs. In: Proceedings of the 32nd International Conference on Machine Learning (ICML), pp. 843–852 (2015)
17. Simonyan, K., Zisserman, A.: Two-stream convolutional networks for action recognition in videos. In: Advances in Neural Information Processing Systems 27: Annual Conference on Neural Information Processing Systems 2014, Montreal, Quebec, Canada, 8–13 December 2014, pp. 568–576 (2014)
18. Feichtenhofer, C., Pinz, A., Zisserman, A.: Convolutional two-stream network fusion for video action recognition. In: 2016 IEEE Conference on Computer Vision and Pattern Recognition, pp. 1933–1941 (2016)
19. Zhu, Y., Lan, Z., Newsam, S., Hauptmann, A.: Hidden two-stream convolutional networks for action recognition. In: Jawahar, C.V., Li, H., Mori, G., Schindler, K. (eds.) ACCV 2018. LNCS, vol. 11363, pp. 363–378. Springer, Cham (2019). https://doi.org/10.1007/978-3-030-20893-6_23
20. Lin, J., Gan, C., Han, S.: TSM: temporal shift module for efficient video understanding. In: 2019 IEEE/CVF International Conference on Computer Vision, ICCV 2019, Seoul, Korea (South), 27 October–2 November 2019, pp. 7082–7092. IEEE (2019)
21. Tran, D., Bourdev, L., Fergus, R., Torresani, L., Paluri, M.: Learning spatiotemporal features with 3D convolutional networks. In: IEEE International Conference on Computer Vision (ICCV), pp. 4489–4497 (2015)
22. Carreira, J., Zisserman, A.: Quo vadis, action recognition? A new model and the kinetics dataset. In: IEEE Conference on Computer Vision and Pattern Recognition (CVPR), pp. 4724–4733 (2017)
23. Hara, K., Kataoka, H., Satoh, Y.: Learning spatio-temporal features with 3D residual networks for action recognition. In: 2017 IEEE International Conference on Computer Vision Workshops, pp. 3154–3160 (2017)
24. Hara, K., Kataoka, H., Satoh, Y.: Can spatiotemporal 3D CNNS retrace the history of 2D CNNS and imagenet? In: IEEE Conference on Computer Vision and Pattern Recognition, pp. 6546–6555 (2018)
25. Feichtenhofer, C., Fan, H., Malik, J., He, K.: SlowFast networks for video recognition. In: Proceedings of the IEEE/CVF International Conference on Computer Vision (ICCV) (2019)
26. Akbarian, M.S.A., Saleh, F., Salzmann, M., Fernando, B., Petersson, L., Andersson, L.: Encouraging LSTMS to anticipate actions very early. In: IEEE International Conference on Computer Vision (ICCV), pp. 280–289 (2017)
27. Hu, J., Zheng, W., Ma, L., Wang, G., Lai, J., Zhang, J.: Early action prediction by soft regression. IEEE Trans. Pattern Anal. Mach. Intell. **41**, 2568–2583 (2019)
28. Kong, Y., Tao, Z., Fu, Y.: Deep sequential context networks for action prediction. In: 2017 IEEE Conference on Computer Vision and Pattern Recognition, pp. 3662–3670 (2017)
29. Wang, L., et al.: Temporal segment networks for action recognition in videos. IEEE Trans. Pattern Anal. Mach. Intell. **41**, 2740–2755 (2019)
30. Kay, W., et al.: The kinetics human action video dataset (2017)
31. Jiang, Y.G., Wu, Z., Wang, J., Xue, X., Chang, S.F.: Exploiting feature and class relationships in video categorization with regularized deep neural networks. IEEE Trans. Pattern Anal. Mach. Intell. **40**, 352–364 (2018)
32. Heilbron, F.C., Escorcia, V., Ghanem, B., Niebles, J.C.: Activitynet: a large-scale video benchmark for human activity understanding. In: IEEE Conference on Computer Vision and Pattern Recognition, CVPR, pp. 961–970 (2015)

Active Learning for Video Description with Cluster-Regularized Ensemble Ranking

David M. Chan[1(✉)], Sudheendra Vijayanarasimhan[2], David A. Ross[2], and John F. Canny[1,2]

[1] University of California, Berkeley, Berkeley, USA
{davidchan,canny}@berkeley.edu
[2] Google Research, Cambridge, USA
{svnaras,dross}@google.com

Abstract. Automatic video captioning aims to train models to generate text descriptions for all segments in a video, however, the most effective approaches require large amounts of manual annotation which is slow and expensive. Active learning is a promising way to efficiently build a training set for video captioning tasks while reducing the need to manually label uninformative examples. In this work we both explore various active learning approaches for automatic video captioning and show that a cluster-regularized ensemble strategy provides the best active learning approach to efficiently gather training sets for video captioning. We evaluate our approaches on the MSR-VTT and LSMDC datasets using both transformer and LSTM based captioning models and show that our novel strategy can achieve high performance while using up to 60% fewer training data than the strong state of the art baselines.

Keywords: Active learning · Video captioning

1 Introduction

Automatic video captioning is an emerging area in computer vision research that aims to generate textual descriptions of the visual components of a video. This has various applications including improving video accessibility for the blind and visually impaired [1], summarizing video [2], searching and indexing. Unfortunately, training models to do video captioning requires manual descriptions of every second of the video from a large corpus of representative videos. One of the largest current single-clip video captioning datasets, MSR-VTT, has only tens of thousands of unique uncorrelated videos whereas solving video captioning will likely require several orders of magnitude more to express the wide diversity of subjects, situations, and relationships possible in video data.

Electronic supplementary material The online version of this chapter (https://doi.org/10.1007/978-3-030-69541-5_27) contains supplementary material, which is available to authorized users.

Active learning is a valuable approach in domains where unlabeled and partially labeled examples are readily available but obtaining manual annotations is expensive, such as is the case with automatic video captioning. However, while there has been significant investigation of active learning for computer vision tasks such as object recognition [3], object detection [4], video classification [5] and video segmentation [6], video captioning has received comparatively little attention. The reason for this is likely rooted in the complexity of the label space. Video captioning requires both sequential input and output, dramatically increasing the complexity of traditional active learning frameworks. To our knowledge, this is one of the first works to define active learning strategies for efficiently collecting training sets for automatic video captioning.

In this paper we explore several active learning strategies for sequence to sequence active learning in video captioning, including uncertainty sampling based on label confidence, sequence entropy and query by committee methods. There are several unique challenges to active learning for deep sequence to sequence models: While traditional active learning methods [7] select one example at a time to label, retraining the model in its entirety after each new example selection, this strategy is impractical for training models such as transformer networks and LSTMs [8,9], due to increased training time (hours vs. minutes) and increased inference time (seconds vs. milliseconds). Thus, it is far more efficient to select a large batch of examples at a time to label when using a crowd-sourced collection process [10,11]. Traditional batch-active learning often uses ranking functions which are intractable in deep sequence to sequence learning [12–14], making active learning for video description a challenging problem, with no tractable solutions for deep neural networks.

In this work we conduct a thorough empirical analysis of various active learning strategies on two recent and standard video captioning datasets, MSR-VTT and LSMDC, using both transformer based and LSTM based captioning models, and describe a novel cluster-regularized method which is both tractable to compute, and provides strong performance in our test scenario. Our key contributions are:

1. Demonstrating that traditional uncertainty sampling techniques do not significantly outperform random sampling, likely because of the difficulty of estimating the sequence entropy.
2. A novel ensemble based ranking method (Cluster-Regularized Ensemble Divergence Active Learning, Sect. 3.1) specifically designed for video description active learning which outperform random sampling by a significant margin.
3. A clustering-based active learning regularization method which can help to increase sample diversity, and when combined with our query-by-committee methods can save as much as 60% of the manual annotation effort while maintaining high performance (Sect. 3.2).

2   Related Work

In order to reduce human effort when constructing training sets, various active learning strategies have been proposed for computer vision tasks such as object recognition [3,15], detection [4], video classification [5] and video segmentation [6]. These methods typically select the next example to query for a label based on uncertainty sampling, entropy, or predicting reductions in risk to the underlying model (see [7] for a comprehensive review). However, active learning for sequence labeling tasks such as automatic video captioning has received little attention.

In the natural language processing literature, active learning methods have been proposed for actively selecting examples based on uncertainty sampling [16,17] or query by committee approaches [18]. In [19], the authors provide a thorough analysis of various active learning methods for sequence labeling tasks using conditional random field (CRF) models. Current state-of-the-art video captioning models, however, typically utilize neural network based architectures such as transformer networks [8] or LSTMs [9] and very little research exists on how to successfully apply active learning for complex models — Transformer networks and LSTMs are expensive to train, taking hours to days to converge, compared to shallow linear models or CRFs employed in previous active learning studies (taking only minutes). Therefore querying a single example at a time is inefficient. It is far more efficient to select a large batch of examples at a time to label when using a crowd-sourced collection process as is typically the case [4].

Batch-mode active learning methods have been proposed for vision and other tasks in [12–14]. Batch selection requires more than selecting the N-best queries at a given iteration because such a strategy does not account for possible overlap in information. Therefore, the selection functions typically try to balance informativeness with a diversity term to avoid querying overlapping examples [13]. In this work, we take cues from [13], and develop a batch active-learning method for sequence learning, that is regularized using a measure of information diversity (an idea from [13]), but is tuned to be computed efficiently over sequence learning tasks, such as those in [7].

In addition to moving to batch sampling, automated video description is unique in that it has multiple possible correct sequence labels. Recent methods are usually based on expected gradient updates [20] or the entropy of a sample distribution [19], and are unable to account for scenarios where there are multiple correct labels, or there is dynamic underlying label entropy. In addition, these methods often require computing an estimate of expected model updates over the space of possible labels. This estimate can be extremely expensive for sequence learning (which has exponential label space growth), and there's no clear way of sampling from caption spaces without learning a complex language model.

Among recent methods, Coreset active learning [21], uses an integer linear program (or a greedy optimization) to find a lambda-cover over the feature set. By operating at a feature level, Coreset takes advantage of the semantic compression of the model to find sets of unlabeled samples that are useful to the model's prediction. We discuss our method compared to Coreset in Sect. 3.3.

Some recent methods including VAAL [22] and ALISE [23] have approached active learning from an adversarial perspective. These methods train a discriminator which attempts to determine which samples are labeled and unlabeled, then select the likely unlabeled samples for training. However, they typically require large number of samples to reliably train the discriminator which is unavailable in the beginning of the active learning process. Nonetheless, it would be an interesting future direction to explore adversarial models for active learning on complex latent spaces. Deep Bayesian active learning [24] shows some promise, however strong Bayesian networks for multi-modal vision and language problems are still out out of reach for large scale complex datasets.

3   Methods

In this work we introduce a new method for sequence active learning for video description, and compare against several baseline algorithms (Those listed below, along with Coreset [21] active learning and ALISE [23]). Throughout this section, we refer to a video v_i, and its associated set of descriptions $\mathcal{D} = \{c_1(v_i) \dots c_n(v_i)\}$. A set of descriptions generated by a model m_j is referred to by $\{c_{m_j,1}(v_i) \dots c_{m_j,n}(v_i)\}$. Videos may have multiple descriptions either through multiple-sampling of the model generative distribution, or through multiple ground-truth labels of the same video. The probability distribution $P_{m_j}(c_i)$ is the likelihood of a description c_i under the model m_j, and the distribution $\mathcal{P}^{cond}(m_j, c_i^k) = P_{m_j}(c_i^k(v_i)|c_i^{k-1}(v_i), \dots, c_i^0(v_i))$ is the conditional distribution of the next word k under the model given the previous words in the description.

3.1   Active Learning Methods

Random Selection Baseline: Our baseline method is to sample new data points from the training set uniformly at random. Random selection is a strong baseline. It directly models the data distribution through sampling, placing emphasis on representative data, but not "novel" data. Trying to sample outside the random distribution is more likely to cause over-sampling of parts of the data (demonstrated in Figs. 3), leading to poorer overall validation performance.

Maximum Entropy Active Learning: Traditional methods for active learning [7] are often entropy based. As a second strong baseline, we present a maximum entropy active learning method in which we rank samples based on a sample of the entropy of the dataset. Unfortunately, given the exponential number of computations that have to be made in the sequence length, the entropy of the entire output distribution is intractable to compute directly. Thus, to approximate the entropy of the description distribution we compute the mean entropy of the word output distributions at each new word along the generation process of a new description of a sample using our current model. Thus, using a candidate model m, we sample K candidate sentences for each video, and we select samples which maximize the ranking function:

$$R(v_i) = \frac{1}{K} \sum_{k=1}^{K} \sum_{w=1}^{|c_{m,k}(v_i)|} -P_m(c_{m,k}^w(i)) \log P_m(c_{m,k}^w(v_i)) \tag{1}$$

where $R(v_i)$ is our approximate estimate of the entropy of any given sample's distribution.

Minimum Likelihood Active Learning: In the minimum likelihood active learning scenario, we select samples where the descriptions that the model generates have the lowest log likelihood under the model distribution. Thus, using a candidate model m, we sample K candidate sentences for each video, and then choose samples which minimize the ranking function:

$$R(v_i) = \frac{1}{K} \sum_{k=1}^{K} \sum_{w=1}^{|c_{m,k}(v_i)|} \log P_m(c_{m,k}^w(v_i) | c_{m,k}^{w-1}(v_i) \dots c_{m,k}^0(v_i)) \tag{2}$$

Empirically, we find that the minimum likelihood active learning method is a stronger method than the entropy for use in video captioning (See Fig. 2), however this measure of uncertainty suffers from the fact that the model may be very confident about its wrong answers, and will be unable to learn effectively when this is the case. Because these very confident wrong answers are never sampled (or are sampled later in the training process), the model is unable to correct for the initially introduced bias.

Query By Committee Ensemble Agreement Active Learning: To help alleviate the issues with single model uncertainty, we introduce the notion of an ensemble agreement active learning ranking based on query by committee methods for traditional active learning [18]. With this method, we sample a set of likely captions from each member of an ensemble of models (using beam search), and compute the mean pairwise likelihood. For an ensemble of L models $\{m_1, \dots, m_L\}$, from each model m_l we sample captions $\{c_{m_i,1} \dots c_{m_i,K}\}$ for each available unlabeled video. Our ranking criterion is then to minimize:

$$R(v_i) = \frac{1}{L(L-1)} \sum_{\substack{p=1}}^{L} \sum_{\substack{q=1 \\ q \neq p}}^{L} \sum_{k=1}^{K} \sum_{w=1}^{|c_{m_p,k}(v_i)|} \frac{\log \mathcal{P}^{cond}(m_q, c_{m_p,k}^w(i))}{K |c_{m_p,k}(v_i)|} \tag{3}$$

The idea here is to select samples for labeling which have low agreement, as these are the samples have higher uncertainty under our model/training process. In this scenario, we alleviate many of the concerns with models having high confidence in wrong answers, as this phenomenon tends to be local to particular models, and these highly incorrect answers will have low likelihood under the learned distributions of the other members of the ensemble.

Query By Committee Ensemble Divergence Active Learning (Proposed Method): While entropy/perplexity measures for active learning have been well explored in the literature [7], it is unclear if these measures are correct for the captioning task. Even if the caption distribution for a video has high entropy, meaning there are many possible likely captions (or even many possible correct captions), this high entropy does not mean that the model is unsure of the outcome. Samples that have many possible captions will thus be over-sampled, since any of the generated captions will have fundamentally lower likelihood than a sample with fewer possible captions. In order to avoid this, we present a method, which computes the KL-divergence between the conditional distributions of the ensemble members. Thus, if the models would choose similar words, given similar inputs - we consider the models to be in agreement. Similarly to the above, for an ensemble of L models $\{m_1...m_L\}$, from each model m_l we sample captions $\{c_{m_i,1}...c_{m_i,K}\}$ for each available unlabeled video. We then choose samples which maximize:

$$R(v_i) = \frac{1}{L(L-1)zhou} \sum_{p=1}^{L} \sum_{\substack{q=1 \\ q \neq p}}^{L} \sum_{k=1}^{K} \frac{D_{KL}\left(P_{m_p}(c_{m_p,k}(v_i)) || P_{m_q}(c_{m_p,k}(v_i))\right)}{K} \quad (4)$$

Unfortunately, computing the full joint distribution is prohibitively expensive. Thus, instead we restrict the computation of the divergence to the sum of per-word divergences:

$$R(v_i) = \frac{1}{L(L-1)} \sum_{p=1}^{L} \sum_{\substack{q=1 \\ q \neq p}}^{L} \sum_{k=1}^{K} \frac{D(m_p, m_q, c_{m_p,k}(v_i))}{K} \quad (5)$$

where

$$D(m_p, m_q, c_{m_p,k}(v_i)) =$$
$$\frac{\sum_{w=1}^{|c_{m_p,k}(i)|} D_{KL}\left(\mathcal{P}^{cond}(m_p, c_{m_p,k}^{w}(v_i)) || \mathcal{P}^{cond}(m_q, c_{m_p,k}^{w}(v_i))\right)}{|c_{m_p,k}(v_i)|}$$
$$(6)$$

is the per-word KL-divergence along the generation of the description $c_{m_p,k}(v_i)$ in each of the models. Compared to the likelihood method, this model gives a better estimate of the divergence of the distributions learned by the models of the ensemble. This measure is also independent of the sample length, and distribution perplexity, confounding factors when looking only at the likelihood of the samples.

3.2   Improving Diversity with Clustering

During the training of the initial active learning models, we noticed through a qualitative investigation that models seemed to be over-sampling parts of the training feature space. This was confirmed by running the experiments shown in Fig. 3. To help combat this, we enforced a clustering-based diversity criterion.

We first performed a k-means clustering of the training data using the mean (across the temporal dimension) of our visual features. We chose $K = N/20$ clusters, where N is the number of training samples in the dataset. See Sect. 4 for a justification for this number of clusters. We then force the active learning algorithm to select at most ϕ samples from each cluster, which notably increases diversity. For the experiments in this paper, we found $\phi = 3$ to be the best hyper-parameter value, out of $\phi = 1, 2, 3, \ldots 10$.

3.3   Comparison with Coreset Active Learning

While our method shares some significant similarities at a glance to Coreset [21] (i.e. we both use delta-covers of a space to regularize the sampling), they have some notable differences. The Coreset method uses the distribution of the feature space, combined with k-centers over the unlabeled data to select a set of samples which should be annotated. This is equivalent to finding a delta cover over the distribution of the data in the unlabeled space. Our proposed method (Ensemble Divergence + Cluster Regularization) uses the uncertainty of the underlying model to compute a score, and then attempts to regularize this score across the data space by enforcing that no two samples are too close together. Our method not only achieves better performance on our sequence learning tasks, but also runs notably quicker than Coreset, which can fail to solve the Integer Linear Program efficiently. It is interesting future work, however outside the scope of this exploratory paper, to explore selecting among Coresets using our uncertainty metric. Figure 1 directly compares Coreset and Greedy Coreset with our proposed model on the video description problem.

3.4   Models

The goal of this paper is to explore active learning methods across multiple different model structures. In our experiments we use both a transformer-based model based on Zhou *et al.* [25], and the popular S2VT RNN architecture [9] (See supplementary materials for details). Our models are able to achieve performance comparable to state-of-the-art models using vision-only features and without using policy gradients to optimize a downstream metric [9, 26]. By adding multi-modal features, and direct REINFORCE optimization, you can gain 7–10 CIDEr points over our implementations [26]. However, while there are more complex model pipelines, we chose two very simple architectures to demonstrate the efficacy of active learning, improve iteration time, and decrease the chance of confounding visual effects. We expect the presented methods to transfer to more complex optimization schemes, and powerful architectures given the flexibility of the formulation and our ablation results.

3.5   Datasets

We demonstrate the performance of our model on two common video description datasets, MSR-VTT [10] and the LSMDC [27]. While these methods may apply to video datasets generated using Automated Speech Recognition (HowTo-100M [28]) or dense captioning tasks (ActivityNet Captions [29]), we focus on pre-clipped videos with high quality descriptive annotations. We refer the reader to the supplementary materials for a description of the datasets in use.

3.6 Experimental Setup

Feature Extraction and Pre-processing: To avoid conflating the visual representations of the data with the performance of the captioning model, we follow video-captioning convention and pre-extract features from the videos using a Distill-3D (D3D) [30] model pre-trained on the Kinetics-600 dataset for activity recognition. The videos are resized on the short-edge to 256px, then center-cropped to 256×256. They are down-sampled to 64 frames at 3 frames per second (with cyclic repetition for videos that are too short), and then passed through the D3D model to generate a 7×1024 representational tensor for the video which is used in the captioning process. The text data is tokenized using a sub-word encoding [31] with a vocabulary size of 8192.

Training: Each model is trained in PyTorch [32] with a batch-size of 512 for 80 epochs. We use the ADAM [33] optimizer with a warm-up learning rate schedule with 1000 steps of warm-up, ranging from $1e^{-6}$ to $1e^{-3}$, then decaying over 250,000 steps to 0. We run our experiments using 8 Tesla T4 accelerators on Google Cloud Platform, making use of NVIDIA Apex[1] for mixed-precision fp-16 training.

3.7 Evaluation

In all active learning methods, we begin by seeding the method with 5% of the data, chosen randomly. For a fair comparison, this random slice is shared across each of the active learning methods. We then train an initial classifier for use with our active learning method. When the classifier has converged (achieved minimum loss on a validation dataset, or trained for 80 epochs, whichever comes first), we use the classifier, and the proposed ranking methods (Using a cluster-limit $\phi = 3$, and a set of 8 sampled captions) to select an additional 5% of the training data. This happens 19 additional times (20 total evaluation points), until all of the training data has been selected. At each step, we run an evaluation of the model to determine the performance. Exploring the active learning process when using larger and smaller batches is interesting future work—when selecting very few examples, there is more potential benefit, but more computation required, selecting more samples requires less computation, but can be a more difficult task. Exploring ideas in continual learning, where the classifiers are re-initialized with weights from the previous active learning step is also interesting future work, however we found in practice that this does not heavily influence the training process.

---

[1] https://github.com/NVIDIA/apex.

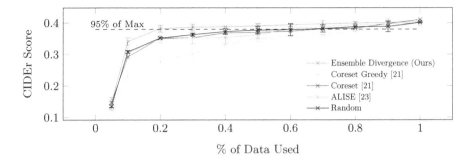

Fig. 1. Validation performance of active learning methods on the MSR-VTT dataset using the CIDEr metric [35]. Each run represents the mean of a bootstrap sample of ten runs. Our proposed method significantly outperforms all other methods, achieving 95% of the max performance while using only 25% of the data. This figure is measured 10 intervals instead of 20, due to the cost of Coreset's ILP solver.

During evaluation, we sample 8 candidate sentences with a temperature of 0.8, which are then evaluated using the COCO Captions Evaluation Tools [34]. For tuning, we use a validation dataset sub-sampled from the training dataset, and we report the results on the official validation dataset (unseen during training/tuning) below. For ensemble-based metrics, we use the mean performance of the ensemble members. For non-ensemble based metrics, we perform multiple runs of active learning, and report the error as a 95% bootstrapped confidence interval. While the 95% is somewhat arbitrary, we present the full trajectories, for readers to explore.

4   Results and Discussion

Our key results using the transformer architecture on the MSR-VTT dataset are presented in Fig. 1. Clearly, we can see that the clustered-divergence outperforms the benchmark models by a wide margin, using about 25% of the data to achieve a CIDEr score of 0.38 (95% of max). A full set of results is shown in Fig. 2 for the methods from Sect. 3.1. Some additional qualitative results are presented in the supplementary materials.

Our method is highly prone to over-sampling parts of the distribution. To demonstrate over-sampling by examining the performance of our models across multiple clusters. Figure 3 shows that enforcing diversity is key to our approach: If we use no clustering, we actually fail to outperform random performance while adding a few clusters allows us to mitigate this effect and adding sufficient clustering allows for significant performance benefits. We can also see the effect of clustering by examining the mean distance to the validation set over the active learning iterations. We can also see from Fig. 3 that the agreement method alone is unable to efficiently distribute across the validation set, however random

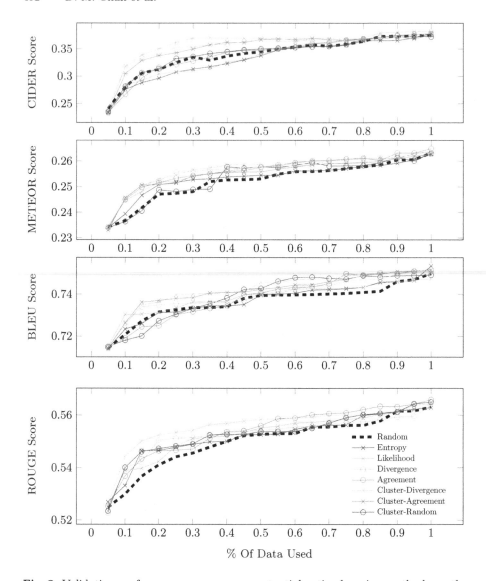

Fig. 2. Validation performance across many potential active learning methods on the MSR-VTT dataset using the transformer model structure with respect to CIDEr Score [35], METEOR Score [36], BLEU Score [37] and ROUGE-L Score [38]. The curves presented are the means of 3 individual experiments using each method. Error bars are omitted for clarity. ALISE and Coreset are omitted due to computation time costs (However see Fig. 1 for a comparison on CIDEr).

and clustered methods achieve similar distribution effects. It's interesting to note, however, that even without the cluster enforcement the agreement metrics select from more visual diversity than the entropy/likelihood methods - leading

Table 1. Average number of clusters selected per iteration. The random and cluster-normalized methods select from a wider visual variety of samples, while the non-normalized samples select very few clusters on average.

Method	Mean number of clusters selected/iteration
Random selection	195.47 ± 21.2
Cluster-regularized divergence	212.5 ± 14.4
Cluster-regularized agreement	202.3 ± 17.6
Cluster-regularized entropy	215.7 ± 12.8
Agreement only	181.00 ± 16.9
Entropy	160.31 ± 16.4
Likelihood	169.25 ± 13.7

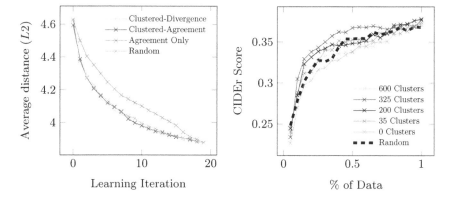

Fig. 3. (Left) Average distance of validation samples to the nearest training sample over the active learning process. Models with improved diversity improve the distance to the training set more rapidly. We suspect this diversity is why random methods work well vs. non-diversity enforced methods as random methods contain a built-in coverage of the dataset. (Right) Performance of the cluster-divergence active learning method across different numbers of clusters. Performance is greater with greater numbers of clusters, until saturation, where performance regresses to random.

to better performance (Table 1). The results for a cluster-regularized random selection method are given in Fig. 2, however it is not significantly different from random alone, since the random method already samples uniformly from the set of input samples. Figure 4 shows that as we increase the number of ensemble members, the performance increased, however there are diminishing returns, as the models begin to capture the same data.

We can also see from Fig. 2 that the ordering of methods can be dependent on the metrics chosen. While our proposed method outperforms all of the baseline methods, it is most helpful under the CIDEr and ROUGE metrics which prefer higher-level descriptions of the scenes. The method helps less for improving metrics that depend on lower-level semantics, such as BLEU and METEOR.

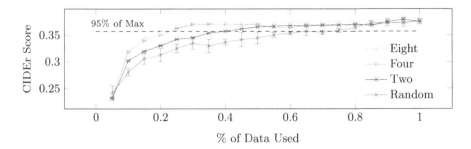

Fig. 4. Validation performance with differing numbers of ensemble members on the MSR-VTT dataset. We see increasing the number of ensemble members leads to increased performance. We speculate that the diminishing returns are caused by independent models capturing similar information.

Fig. 5. Visualization of four clusters of videos from the training dataset. Highlighted elements were selected by the cluster-divergence learning method (red), or the random method (yellow) in the first two iterations. In clusters with low visual diversity active learning selects fewer samples (top-left, bottom-left, bottom-right), while selecting more samples in clusters with high visual diversity (top-right), suggesting that the active method is choosing more informative samples. (Color figure online)

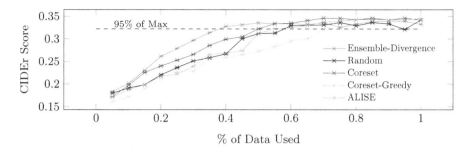

Fig. 6. Performance using the LSTM model. While overall performance is lower, the clustered-divergence learning method can save more than 20% percent of the data.

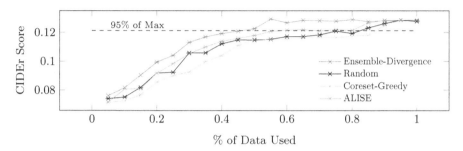

Fig. 7. Validation performance for the LSMDC dataset. We achieve strong performance using almost 35% less data. We do not include Coreset, as it took >24 h per active-learning step to compute.

We suspect that this is due to the influence of the active learning method on sampling a diverse set of samples - as increasing the sample diversity can help to improve high-level understanding of a scene, while perhaps having detrimental impacts on the language modeling process.

While we have made the case that a strong diversity of samples is required, it is also interesting to look at exactly which samples were selected. Figure 5 demonstrates some of the diversity of samples selected by our methods in comparison to the samples selected by the random method. We can see that the active learning method is sampling from a diverse set of elements from each cluster, while the random method is sampling a representative sample, but not necessarily the most relevant or useful videos.

One important thing to note is that because we are sampling from data that is in the initial training data for the two datasets, the results presented in this paper may be an optimistic upper bound for the performance of an active learning tool. There is a significant amount of cleaning and curating that goes into these datasets which may or may not impact the final results of the classification, and the effort may be higher when annotating video in the wild. Future techniques may need to be developed for efficiently cleaning data, or curating samples that are relevant to captioning as a whole.

One downside to our experimental method is that our models do not achieve optimal performance in each training step, as the optimal hyper-parameters of the model change as more data is added. To ease this issue we use an adaptive training scheme which trains for more iterations than necessary with early stopping, however it is an interesting direction of future work to explore auto-tuning during the learning process to improve performance.

Our proposed method is not limited to the dataset or model. Figure 7 demonstrates the performance of our best method, clustered divergence, on the LSMDC dataset. We can see here that we achieve a CIDEr score of 0.121 (95% of max) with only 50% of data required by random sampling. Thus, we can see that the performance of the active learning method is not just limited to the MSR-VTT dataset. In addition, Fig. 6 demonstrates that the performance is not limited only to our transformer based model. The S2VT model also improves, achieving a CIDEr score of 0.3219 with only 60% of data required by random selection.

In addition to requiring fewer data, our method can be significantly more efficient than the current state of the art methods. On our test-bench machine, we saw the following ranking times using the MSR-VTT dataset (Samples/Sec): Random: 2012.04, Entropy: 12.41, Cluster-Regularized Ensemble Ranking: 11.08, ALISE: 6.89, Coreset-Optimal: 0.11, and Coreset-Greedy: 11.89.

5 Conclusion and Future Work

In this paper, we have presented an initial set of methods aiming to tackle the active learning problem for video description, a challenging task requiring complex modeling where due to the complexity of the output distribution, many active learning methods are unable to function efficiently, or at all. We have shown that we can achieve 95% of the full performance of a trained model with between 25% and 60% of the training data (and thus, manual labeling effort), across varying models and datasets.

While pairwise measures among ensemble members may be a good model of uncertainty, there are many such measures. Expected gradient variance methods such as [19,20] are good candidates for future exploration. While such methods now do not account for the complexity of multiple correct labels, and dynamic entropy distributions, we may be able to compute high quality estimates. Such gradient methods may work in scenarios where the KL divergence between the final distributions of the models may be relatively low, but the evaluated sample has useful second-order gradient information.

It is also interesting, and likely fruitful, future work to explore different methods for clustering the elements of the training dataset. In many cases, we would like to enforce a subject-level diversity among the different inputs (as show by Fig. 5), however visual similarity may not necessarily be the best metric to use for clustering. Using additional features to rank the diversity of the samples may provide better results, by increasing the individual diversity of each cohort more than k-means clustering in the visual space.

By exploring the applications of our work in practice, we can build robust active learning methods and collect large and effective datasets for video description. We hope these datasets will be used to improve the performance of downstream description tools in this complex and challenging labeling domain.

Acknowledgements. This work is supported in part by Berkeley Deep Drive, the BAIR commons project, and Google Cloud Platform. The authors would like to thank Trevor Darrell, Forrest Huang, Roshan Rao, and Philippe Laban for their insightful conversations and assistance.

References

1. Yoon, I., Mathur, U., Gibson, B., Fazli, T.P., Miele, J.: Video accessibility for the visually impaired. In: International Conference on Machine Learning AI for Social Good Workshop (2019)
2. Zhang, K., Chao, W.-L., Sha, F., Grauman, K.: Video summarization with long short-term memory. In: Leibe, B., Matas, J., Sebe, N., Welling, M. (eds.) ECCV 2016. LNCS, vol. 9911, pp. 766–782. Springer, Cham (2016). https://doi.org/10.1007/978-3-319-46478-7_47
3. Collins, B., Deng, J., Li, K., Fei-Fei, L.: Towards scalable dataset construction: an active learning approach. In: Forsyth, D., Torr, P., Zisserman, A. (eds.) ECCV 2008. LNCS, vol. 5302, pp. 86–98. Springer, Heidelberg (2008). https://doi.org/10.1007/978-3-540-88682-2_8
4. Vijayanarasimhan, S., Grauman, K.: Large-scale live active learning: training object detectors with crawled data and crowds. Int. J. Comput. Vis. **108**, 97–114 (2014). https://doi.org/10.1007/s11263-014-0721-9
5. Yan, R., Yang, J., Hauptmann, A.: Automatically labeling video data using multiclass active learning. In: Proceedings of the Ninth IEEE International Conference on Computer Vision, ICCV 2003, USA, vol. 2, p. 516. IEEE Computer Society (2003)
6. Vijayanarasimhan, S., Grauman, K.: Active frame selection for label propagation in videos. In: Fitzgibbon, A., Lazebnik, S., Perona, P., Sato, Y., Schmid, C. (eds.) ECCV 2012. LNCS, vol. 7576, pp. 496–509. Springer, Heidelberg (2012). https://doi.org/10.1007/978-3-642-33715-4_36
7. Settles, B.: Active learning literature survey. Computer Sciences Technical Report 1648, University of Wisconsin-Madison (2009)
8. Zhou, L., Zhou, Y., Corso, J., Socher, R., Xiong, C.: End-to-end dense video captioning with masked transformer (2018)
9. Venugopalan, S., Rohrbach, M., Donahue, J., Mooney, R., Darrell, T., Saenko, K.: Sequence to sequence - video to text. In: Proceedings of the IEEE International Conference on Computer Vision (ICCV) (2015)
10. Xu, J., Mei, T., Yao, T., Rui, Y.: MSR-VTT: a large video description dataset for bridging video and language. In: Proceedings of the IEEE Conference on Computer Vision and Pattern Recognition, pp. 5288–5296 (2016)
11. Deng, J., Dong, W., Socher, R., Li, L.J., Li, K., Fei-Fei, L.: ImageNet: a large-scale hierarchical image database. In: 2009 IEEE Conference on Computer Vision and Pattern Recognition, pp. 248–255. IEEE (2009)
12. Hoi, S.C.H., Jin, R., Zhu, J., Lyu, M.R.: Semisupervised SVM batch mode active learning with applications to image retrieval. ACM Trans. Inf. Syst. **27**, 1–29 (2009)

13. Brinker, K.: Incorporating diversity in active learning with support vector machines. In: Proceedings of the Twentieth International Conference on International Conference on Machine Learning, ICML 2003, pp. 59–66. AAAI Press (2003)

14. Vijayanarasimhan, S., Jain, P., Grauman, K.: Far-sighted active learning on a budget for image and video recognition. In: IEEE Conference on Computer Vision and Pattern Recognition (CVPR) (2010)

15. Vijayanarasimhan, S., Grauman, K.: What's it going to cost you?: Predicting effort vs. informativeness for multi-label image annotations. In: IEEE Conference on Computer Vision and Pattern Recognition (CVPR) (2009)

16. Culotta, A., McCallum, A.: Reducing labeling effort for structured prediction tasks. In: Proceedings of the 20th National Conference on Artificial Intelligence, AAAI 2005, vol. 2, pp. 746–751. AAAI Press (2005)

17. Scheffer, T., Decomain, C., Wrobel, S.: Active hidden Markov models for information extraction. In: Hoffmann, F., Hand, D.J., Adams, N., Fisher, D., Guimaraes, G. (eds.) IDA 2001. LNCS, vol. 2189, pp. 309–318. Springer, Heidelberg (2001). https://doi.org/10.1007/3-540-44816-0_31

18. Dagan, I., Engelson, S.P.: Committee-based sampling for training probabilistic classifiers. In: Proceedings of the Twelfth International Conference on International Conference on Machine Learning, ICML 1995, San Francisco, CA, USA, pp. 150–157. Morgan Kaufmann Publishers Inc. (1995)

19. Settles, B., Craven, M.: An analysis of active learning strategies for sequence labeling tasks. In: Proceedings of the 2008 Conference on Empirical Methods in Natural Language Processing, Honolulu, Hawaii, pp. 1070–1079. Association for Computational Linguistics (2008)

20. Huang, J., Child, R., Rao, V., Liu, H., Satheesh, S., Coates, A.: Active learning for speech recognition: the power of gradients. arXiv preprint arXiv:1612.03226 (2016)

21. Sener, O., Savarese, S.: Active learning for convolutional neural networks: a core-set approach. arXiv preprint arXiv:1708.00489 (2017)

22. Sinha, S., Ebrahimi, S., Darrell, T.: Variational adversarial active learning. In: Proceedings of the IEEE International Conference on Computer Vision, pp. 5972–5981 (2019)

23. Deng, Y., Chen, K., Shen, Y., Jin, H.: Adversarial active learning for sequences labeling and generation. In: IJCAI, pp. 4012–4018 (2018)

24. Gal, Y., Islam, R., Ghahramani, Z.: Deep Bayesian active learning with image data. In: Proceedings of the 34th International Conference on Machine Learning, vol. 70, pp. 1183–1192. JMLR. org (2017)

25. Zhou, L., Zhou, Y., Corso, J.J., Socher, R., Xiong, C.: End-to-end dense video captioning with masked transformer. In: Proceedings of the IEEE Conference on Computer Vision and Pattern Recognition, pp. 8739–8748 (2018)

26. Aafaq, N., Mian, A., Liu, W., Gilani, S.Z., Shah, M.: Video description: a survey of methods, datasets, and evaluation metrics. ACM Comput. Surv. (CSUR) **52**, 1–37 (2019)

27. Rohrbach, A., et al.: Movie description. Int. J. Comput. Vis. **123**, 94–120 (2017). https://doi.org/10.1007/s11263-016-0987-1

28. Miech, A., Zhukov, D., Alayrac, J.B., Tapaswi, M., Laptev, I., Sivic, J.: HowTo100M: learning a text-video embedding by watching hundred million narrated video clips. In: Proceedings of the IEEE International Conference on Computer Vision, pp. 2630–2640 (2019)

29. Krishna, R., Hata, K., Ren, F., Fei-Fei, L., Carlos Niebles, J.: Dense-captioning events in videos. In: Proceedings of the IEEE International Conference on Computer Vision, pp. 706–715 (2017)
30. Stroud, J., Ross, D., Sun, C., Deng, J., Sukthankar, R.: D3D: distilled 3D networks for video action recognition. In: The IEEE Winter Conference on Applications of Computer Vision, pp. 625–634 (2020)
31. Kudo, T., Richardson, J.: SentencePiece: a simple and language independent subword tokenizer and detokenizer for neural text processing. arXiv preprint arXiv:1808.06226 (2018)
32. Paszke, A., et al.: Automatic differentiation in pytorch (2017)
33. Kingma, D.P., Ba, J.: Adam: a method for stochastic optimization. arXiv preprint arXiv:1412.6980 (2014)
34. Chen, X., et al.: Microsoft coco captions: data collection and evaluation server. arXiv preprint arXiv:1504.00325 (2015)
35. Vedantam, R., Lawrence Zitnick, C., Parikh, D.: Cider: consensus-based image description evaluation. In: Proceedings of the IEEE Conference on Computer Vision and Pattern Recognition, pp. 4566–4575 (2015)
36. Agarwal, A., Lavie, A.: Meteor, M-BLEU and M-TER: evaluation metrics for high-correlation with human rankings of machine translation output. In: Proceedings of the Third Workshop on Statistical Machine Translation, pp. 115–118 (2008)
37. Papineni, K., Roukos, S., Ward, T., Zhu, W.J.: Bleu: a method for automatic evaluation of machine translation. In: Proceedings of the 40th Annual Meeting on Association for Computational Linguistics, pp. 311–318. Association for Computational Linguistics (2002)
38. Lin, C.Y., Hovy, E.: Manual and automatic evaluation of summaries. In: Proceedings of the ACL-02 Workshop on Automatic Summarization, vol. 4, pp. 45–51. Association for Computational Linguistics (2002)

Condensed Movies: Story Based Retrieval with Contextual Embeddings

Max Bain[(⊠)], Arsha Nagrani, Andrew Brown, and Andrew Zisserman

Visual Geometry Group, Department of Engineering Science, University of Oxford, Oxford, UK
{maxbain,arsha,abrown,az}@robots.ox.ac.uk

Abstract. Our objective in this work is long range understanding of the narrative structure of movies. Instead of considering the entire movie, we propose to learn from the 'key scenes' of the movie, providing a **condensed** look at the full storyline. To this end, we make the following three contributions: (i) We create the **Condensed Movies Dataset** (CMD) consisting of the key scenes from over 3 K movies: each key scene is accompanied by a high level semantic description of the scene, character face-tracks, and metadata about the movie. The dataset is scalable, obtained automatically from YouTube, and is freely available for anybody to download and use. It is also an order of magnitude larger than existing movie datasets in the number of movies; (ii) We provide a deep network baseline for text-to-video retrieval on our dataset, combining character, speech and visual cues into a single video embedding; and finally (iii) We demonstrate how the addition of context from other video clips improves retrieval performance.

1 Introduction

Imagine you are watching the movie *'Trading Places'*, and you want to instantly fast forward to a scene, one where 'Billy reveals the truth to Louis about the Duke's bet, a bet which changed both their lives'. In order to solve this task automatically, an intelligent system would need to watch the movie up to this point, have knowledge of Billy, Louis and the Duke's identities, understand that the Duke made a bet, and know the outcome of this bet (Fig. 1). This high level understanding of the movie narrative requires knowledge of the characters' identities, their relationships, motivations and conversations, and ultimately their behaviour. Since movies and TV shows can provide an ideal source of data to test this level of story understanding, there have been a number of movie related datasets and tasks proposed by the computer vision community [1–5].

However, despite the recent proliferation of movie-related datasets, high level semantic understanding of human narratives still remains a challenging task.

Electronic supplementary material The online version of this chapter (https://doi.org/10.1007/978-3-030-69541-5_28) contains supplementary material, which is available to authorized users.

© Springer Nature Switzerland AG 2021
H. Ishikawa et al. (Eds.): ACCV 2020, LNCS 12626, pp. 460–479, 2021.
https://doi.org/10.1007/978-3-030-69541-5_28

time

   ...

Billy gets busted by the cops for pan-handling in disguise as a blind, crippled Vietnam War veteran.

Billy discovers the true nature of Mortimer and Randolph Duke's bet.

Billy reveals the truth to Louis about the Duke's bet which changed both their lives.

Fig. 1. Condensed Movies: The dataset consists of the key scenes in a movie (ordered by time), together with high level semantic descriptions. Note how the caption of a scene (far right) is based on the knowledge of past scenes in the movie – one where the Dukes exchange money to settle their bet (highlighted in yellow), and another scene showing their lives before the bet, homeless and pan-handling (highlighted in green). (Color figure online)

There are a number of reasons for this lack of progress: (i) semantic annotation is expensive and challenging to obtain, inherently restricting the size of current movie datasets to only hundreds of movies, and often, only part of the movie is annotated in detail [1–3]; (ii) movies are very long (roughly 2 h) and video architectures struggle to learn over such large timescales; (iii) there are legal and copyright issues surrounding a majority of these datasets [1, 3], which hinder their widespread availability and adoption in the community; and finally (iv) the subjective nature of the task makes it difficult to define objectives and metrics [6].

A number of different works have recently creatively identified that certain domains of videos, such as narrated instructional videos [7–9] and lifestyle vlogs [10, 11] are available in large numbers on YouTube and are a good source of supervision for video-text models as the speech describes the video content. In a similar spirit, videos from the MovieClips channel on YouTube[1], which contains the key scenes or clips from numerous movies, are also accompanied by a semantic text description describing the content of each clip.

Our first objective in this paper is to curate a dataset, suitable for learning and evaluating long range narrative structure understanding, from the available video clips and associated annotations of the MovieClips channel. To this end, we curate a dataset of 'condensed' movies, called the Condensed Movie Dataset (CMD) which provides a *condensed* snapshot into the entire storyline of a movie. In addition to just the video, we also download and clean the high level semantic descriptions accompanying each key scene that describes characters, their motivations, actions, scenes, objects, interactions and relationships. We also provide labelled face-tracks of the principal actors (generated automatically), as well as the metadata associated with the movie (such as cast lists, synopsis, year, genre). Essentially, all the information required to (sparsely) generate a MovieGraph [4]. The dataset consists of over 3000 movies.

---

[1] https://www.youtube.com/user/movieclips.

Previous work on video retrieval and video understanding has largely treated video clips as independent entities, divorced from their context [2,12,13]. But this is not how movies are understood: the meaning and significance of a scene depends on its relationship to previous scenes. This is true also of TV series, where one episode depends on those leading up to it (the season arc); and even an online tutorial/lesson can refer to previous tutorials. These contextual videos are beneficial and sometimes even necessary for complete video understanding.

Our second objective is to explore the role of context in enabling video retrieval. We define a text-to-video retrieval task on the CMD, and extend the popular Mixture of Embedding Experts model [14], that can learn from the subtitles, faces, objects, actions and scenes, by adding a *Contextual Boost Module* that introduces information from past and future clips. Unlike other movie related tasks – e.g. text-to-video retrieval on the LSMDC dataset [2] or graph retrieval on the MovieQA [15] dataset that ignore identities, we also introduce a character embedding module which allows the model to reason about the identities of characters present in each clip and description. Applications of this kind of story-based retrieval include semantic search and indexing of movies as well as intelligent fast forwards. The CMD dataset can also be used for semantic video summarization and automatic description of videos for the visually impaired (Descriptive Video Services (DVS) are currently available at a huge manual cost).

Finally, we also show preliminary results for aligning the semantic captions to the plot summaries of each movie, which places each video clip in the larger context of the movie as a whole. Data, code, models and features can be found at https://www.robots.ox.ac.uk/~vgg/research/condensed-movies/.

2   Related Work

Video Understanding from Movies: There is an increasing effort to develop video understanding techniques that go beyond action classification from cropped, short temporal snippets [16–18], to learning from longer, more complicated videos that promise a higher level of abstraction [7,19–21]. Movies and TV shows provide an ideal test bed for learning long-term stories, leading to a number of recent datasets focusing exclusively on this domain [1–3,15]. Early works, however, focused on using film and TV to learn human identity [22–27] or human actions [28–32] from the scripts or captions accompanying movies. Valuable recent works have proposed story-based tasks such as the visualization and grouping of scenes which belong to the same story threads [33,34], the visualization of TV episodes as a chart of character interactions [1], and more recently, the creation of more complicated movie graphs (MovieGraphs [4] is the most exhaustively annotated movie dataset to date). Such graphs have enabled explicit learning of interactions and relationships [35] between characters. This requires understanding multiple factors such as human communication, emotions, motivation, scenes and other factors that affect behavior. There has also been a recent interest in evaluating story understanding through visual question

Table 1. Comparison to other movie and TV show datasets. For completeness, we also compare to datasets that *only* have character ID or action annotation. 'Free' is defined here as accessible online at no cost at the time of writing. *Refers to number of TV shows.

	#Movies	#Hours	Free	Annotation type
Sherlock [37]	1*	4		Character IDs
TVQA[38]	6*	460		VQA
AVA [17]	430	107.5	✓	Actions only
MovieGraphs [4]	51	93.9		Descriptions, graphs
MovieQA (video) [15]	140	381		VQA
MovieScenes [34]	150	250		Scene segmentations
LSMDC [2]	202	158		Captions
MSA [3]	327	516		Plots
MovieNet [5]	1,100	2,000		Plots, action tags, character IDs
CMD (Ours)	**3,605**	**1,270**	✓	Descriptions, metadata, character IDs, plots

answering [15] and movie scene segmentation [34]. In contrast, we propose to evaluate story understanding through the task of text-to-video retrieval, from a set of key scenes in a movie that condense most of the salient parts of the storyline. Unlike retrieval through a complex graph [4], retrieval via text queries can be a more intuitive way for a human to interact with an intelligent system, and might help avoid some of the biases present inherently in VQA datasets [36].

Comparison to Other Movie Datasets: Existing movie datasets often consist of short clips spanning entire, full length movies (which are subject to copyright and difficult for public release to the community). All such datasets also depend on exhaustive annotation, which limit their scale to hundreds of movies. Our dataset, in contrast, consists of only the key scenes from movies matched with high quality, high level semantic descriptions, allowing for a condensed look at the entire storyline. A comparison of our dataset to other datasets can be seen in Table 1.

Text-to-Video Retrieval: A common approach for learning visual embeddings from natural language supervision is to learn a joint embedding space where visual and textual cues are adjacent if they are semantically similar [14,39]. Most of these works rely on manually annotated datasets in which descriptive captions are collected for short, isolated video clips, with descriptions usually focusing on low-level visual content provided by annotators [2,12,13]. For example LSMDC [2], which is created from DVS, contains mostly low-level descriptions of the visual content in the scene, e.g. 'Abby gets in the basket', unlike the descriptions in our dataset. Most similar to our work is [40], which obtains story level descriptions for shots in full movies, by aligning plot sentences to shots, and then attempting video retrieval. This, however, is challenging because often there is no shot that matches a plot sentence perfectly, and shots cover very small timescales. Unlike this work our semantic descriptions are more true to the clips themselves.

Temporal Context: The idea of exploiting surrounding context has been explored by [41], for the task of video captioning, and by [42] for video understanding. Krishna *et al.* [41] introduces a new captioning module that uses contextual information from past and future events to jointly describe all events, however this work focuses on short term context (few seconds before and after a particular clip). Wu *et al.* [42] go further, and introduce a feature bank architecture that can use contextual information over several minutes, demonstrating the performance improvements that results. Our dataset provides the opportunity to extend such feature banks (sparsely) over an entire movie.

3   Condensed Movie Dataset

We construct a dataset to facilitate machine understanding of narratives in long movies. Our dataset has the following key properties:

(1) Condensed Storylines: The video data consists of over 33,000 clips from 3,600 movies (see Table 2). For each movie there is a set of ordered clips (typically 10 or so) covering the salient parts of the film (examples can be seen in Fig. 2, top row). Each around two minutes in length, the clips contain the same rich and complex story as full-length films but an order of magnitude shorter. The distribution of video lengths in our dataset can be seen in Fig. 2 – with just the key scenes, each movie has been condensed into roughly 20 min each. Each clip is also accompanied by a high level description focusing on intent, emotion, relationships between characters and high level semantics (Figs. 2 and 3). Compared to other video-text datasets, our descriptions are longer, and have a higher lexical diversity [43] (Table 2). We also provide face-tracks and identity labels for the main characters in each clip (Fig. 2, bottom row).

(2) Online Longevity and Scalability: All the videos are obtained from the licensed, freely available YouTube channel: MovieClips[2]. We note that a common problem plaguing YouTube datasets today [16,17,44,45] is the fast shrinkage of datasets as user uploaded videos are taken down by users (over 15% of Kinetics-400 [16] is no longer available on YouTube at the time of writing, including videos from the eval sets). We believe our dataset has longevity due to the fact that the movie clips on the licensed channel are rarely taken down from YouTube. Also, this is an actively growing YouTube channel as new movies are released and added. Hence there is a potential to continually increase the size of the dataset. We note that from the period of 1st Jan 2020, to 1st September 2020, only 0.3% of videos have been removed from the YouTube channel, while an additional 2,000 videos have been uploaded, resulting in a dataset growth of 5.8% over the course of 9 months.

---

[2]   https://www.youtube.com/user/movieclips/. Screenshots of the channel are provided in supplementary material of the ArXiV version.

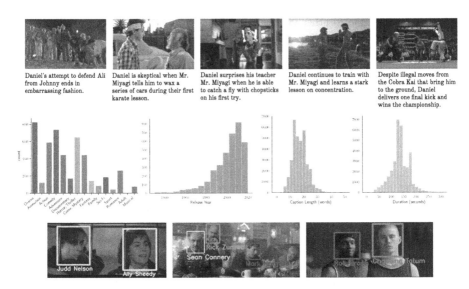

Fig. 2. The Condensed Movie Dataset (CMD). *Top:* Samples of clips and their corresponding captions from *The Karate Kid (1984)* film. In movies, as in real life, situations follow from other situations and the combination of video and text tell a concise story. Note: Every time a character is mentioned in the description, the name of the actor is present in brackets. We remove these from the figure in the interest of space. *Middle, from left to right:* Histogram of movie genres, movie release years, description length and duration of video clips. Best viewed online and zoomed in. *Bottom:* Example facetracks labelled with the actor's name in the clips. These labels are obtained from cast lists and assigned to facetracks using our automatic labelling pipeline.

3.1 Dataset Collection Pipeline

In this section we describe the dataset collection pipeline.

Videos and Descriptions: Raw videos are downloaded from YouTube. Each video is accompanied by an outro at the end of the clip which contains some advertising and links to other movies. This is automatically removed by using the observation that each outro has a consistent length of either 10 s (if the clip is uploaded before May 2017) or 30 s if uploaded after. Approximately 1,000 videos from the channel were manually excluded from the dataset because they contained low quality descriptions or did not contain scenes from a movie. For each video, we also download the YouTube closed captions, these are a mix of high quality, human generated subtitles and automatic captions. Closed captions are missing for 36.7% of the videos. The MovieClips channel also provides a rich and high level description with each video, which we extract, clean (removing the movie title, links and advertising) and verify manually. We note that the videos also contain a watermark, usually at the bottom left of the frame. These can be easily cropped from the videos.

Table 2. Comparison to other video text retrieval datasets. MTLD is the Measure of Textual Lexical Diversity [43] for all of the descriptions in the dataset.

Dataset	#Videos/#Clips	Median caption len. (words)	MTLD	Median clip len. (secs)
MSVRTT [12]	7,180/10,000	7	26.9	15
DiDemo [13]	10,464/26,892	7	39.9	28
LSMDC [2]	200/118,114	8	61.6	5
CMD (Ours)	3,605/33,976	**18**	**89.1**	**132**

INTENT   RELATIONSHIP   EMOTION   PAST CONTEXT   FUTURE CONTEXT

Sean wants to sulk alone in the snow but is interrupted by Paul. | Adam meets his therapist Katherine, who is much younger than he expected. | Barbara Jean succumbs to her stress and anxiety on stage. | Ronny tries to get his camera back from Zip who is still angry about their previous altercation. | Frankie reveals his master plan to steal $10,000 from charity, and how the group of kids will be used to help him

Fig. 3. Semantic descriptions: Examples of high level semantic descriptions accompanying each video clip in our dataset (note: actor names are removed to preserve space). Our semantic descriptions cover a number of high level concepts, including intent/motivation, relationships, emotions and attributes, and context from surrounding clips in the storyline.

Metadata: For each clip, we identify its source movie by parsing the movie title from the video description and, if available, the release year (since many movies have non-unique titles). The title and release year are queried in the IMDb search engine to obtain the movie's IMDb ID, cast list and genre. IMDb identification enables correspondence to other popular movie datasets [2,15]. Plot synposes were gathered by querying the movie title and release year in the Wikipedia search engine and extracting text within the 'Plot' section of the top ranked entry. For each movie we include: (i) the movie description (short, 3–5 sentences), accompanying the video clips on the MovieClips YouTube channel; (ii) Wikipedia plot summaries (medium, 30 sentences); and (iii) IMDB plot synposes (long, 50+ sentences).

Face-tracks and Character IDs: We note that often character identities are the focal point of any storyline, and many of the descriptions reference key characters. In a similar manner to [37], we use face images downloaded from search engines to label detected and tracked faces in our dataset. Our technique involves the creation of a character embedding bank (CEB) which contains a list of characters (obtained from cast lists), and a corresponding embedding vector obtained by passing search engine image results through a deep CNN model pretrained on human faces [46]. Character IDs are then assigned to face-tracks in the video dataset when the similarity between the embeddings from the face tracks and the embeddings in the CEB (using cosine similarity) is above a certain threshold. This pipeline is described in detail in the supplementary material of the ArXiV version. We note that this is an automatic method and so does not yield perfect results, but a random manual inspection shows that it is accurate 96% of the time. Ultimately, we are able to recognize 8,375 different characters in 25,760 of the video clips.

3.2 Story Coverage

To quantitatively measure the amount of the story covered by movie clips in our dataset, we randomly sample 100 movies and manually aligned the movie clips (using the descriptions as well as the videos) to Wikipedia plot summaries (the median length of which is 32 sentences). We found that while the clips totalled only **15%** of the full-length movie in time duration, they cover **44%** of the full plot sentences, suggesting that the clips can indeed be described as key scenes. In addition, we find that the movie clips span a median range of **85.2%** of the plot, with the mean midpoint of the span being **53%**. We further show the distribution of clip samplingw in the supplementary material of the ArXiV version, and find that in general there is an almost uniform coverage of the movie. While we focus on a baseline task of video-text retrieval, we also believe that the longitudinal nature of our dataset will encourage other tasks in long range movie understanding.

4 Text-to-Video Retrieval

In this section we provide a baseline task for our dataset – the task of text-to-video retrieval. The goal here is to retrieve the correct 'key scene' over all movies in the dataset, given just the high level description. Henceforth, we use the term 'video clip' to refer to one key scene, and 'description' to refer to the high level semantic text accompanying each video clip. In order to achieve this task, we learn a common embedding space for each video and the description accompanying it. More formally, if V is the video and T is the description, we learn embedding functions f and g such that the similarity $s = \langle f(V), g(T) \rangle$ is high only if T is the correct semantic description for the video V. Inspired by previous works that achieve state-of-the-art results on video retrieval tasks [14, 39], we encode each video as a combination of different streams of descriptors. Each descriptor is a semantic representation of the video learnt by individual experts (that encode concepts such as scenes, faces, actions, objects and the content of conversational speech from subtitles).

Inspired by [14], we base our network architecture on a mixture of 'expert' embeddings model, wherein a separate model is learnt for each expert, which are then combined in an end-to-end trainable fashion using weights that depend on the input caption. This allows the model to learn to increase the relative weight of motion descriptors for input captions concerning human actions, or increase the relative weight of face descriptors for input captions that require detailed face understanding. We also note, however, that often the text query not only provides clues as to which expert is more valuable, but also whether it is useful to pay attention to a previous clip in the movie, by referring to something that happened previously, eg. 'Zip is *still* angry about their *previous altercation*'. Hence we introduce a Contextual Boost module (CBM), which allows the model to learn to increase the relative weight of a past video feature as well. A visual overview of the retrieval system with the CBM can be seen in Fig. 4. In regular movie datasets, the space of possible previous clips can be prohibitively large [40], however this becomes feasible with our *Condensed Movies* dataset.

Besides doing just *cross-movie* retrieval, we also adapt our model to perform *within-movie* retrieval. We note that characters are integral to a storyline, and hence for the case of within-movie retrieval, we introduce a character module, which computes a weighted one-hot vector for the characters present in the description query and another for each video clip in the dataset. We note that for cross-movie retrieval, the retrieval task becomes trivial given the knowledge of the characters in each movie, and hence to make the task more challenging (and force the network to focus on other aspects of the story), we remove the character module for this case.

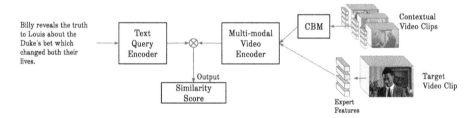

Fig. 4. Model architecture: An overview of text-to-video retrieval with our Contextual Boost module (CBM) that computes a similarity score between a query sentence T and a target video. CBM receives contextual video features (which are previous clips from the same movie) to improve the multimodal encoding of the target video clip. The expert features are extracted using pre-trained models for speech, motion, faces, scenes and objects.

4.1 Model Architecture

Expert Features. Stories in movies are communicated through many modalities including (but not limited to) speech, body language, facial expressions and actions. Hence we represent each input video V with K different expert streams (in our case, $K = 5$ – face, subtitles, objects, motion and scene, but our framework can be extended to more experts as required).

Each input stream is denoted as I_i, where $i = 1, ..., K$. Adopting the approach proposed by [14], we first aggregate the descriptors of each input stream over time, using a temporal aggregation module (see Sect. 5 for details), and the resulting time-aggregated descriptor is embedded using a gated embedding module (for the precise details of the gated embedding module, please see [14]). We then finally project each embedding to a common dimension D using a fully connected layer, giving us one expert embedding E_{V_i} for each input stream i. Hence the final output is of dimensions $K \times D$.

Text Query Encoder. The query description input is a sequence of BERT word embeddings [47] for each input sentence. These individual word embedding vectors are then aggregated into a single vector $h(T)$ representing the entire sentence using a NetVLAD [48] aggregation module. This vector $h(T)$, is used to predict the mixture weights (described in the next section). We project $h(T)$ to the same dimensions as the video expert features using the same gated embedding module followed by a fully connected layer as for the video experts (described above), once for each input source i, giving us expert embeddings E_{T_i}. Hence the final output is also of dimensions $K \times D$.

Contextual Boost Module. In both [14] and [39], the resulting expert embeddings E_{V_i} are then weighted using normalized weights $w_i(T)$ estimated from the text description T. The final similarity score s is obtained by a weighted combination of the similarity scores $s_i(E_{T_i}, E_{V_i})$ between the embeddings E_{T_i} of the query sentence T and the expert embeddings E_{V_i} (obtained from the input video descriptors I_i). More formally, this is calculated as:

$$s(T, V) = \sum_{i=1}^{K} w_i(T) s_i(E_{T_i}, E_{V_i}), \qquad \text{where} \qquad w_i(T) = \frac{e^{h(T)^\intercal a_i}}{\sum_{j=1}^{K} e^{h(T)^\intercal a_j}} \qquad (1)$$

where s_i is the scalar product, $h(T)$ is the aggregated text query representation described above and a_i, $i = 1, .., .K$ are learnt parameters used to obtained the mixture weights.

In this work, however, we extend this formulation in order to incorporate past context into the retrieval model. We would like the model to be able to predict weights for combining experts from previous clips – note we treat each expert separately in this formulation. For example, the model might want to heavily weight the subtitles from a past clip, but downweight the scene representation which is not informative for a particular query. More formally, given the total number of clips we are encoding to be N, we modify the equation above as:

$$s(T, V) = \sum_{n=1}^{N} \sum_{i=1}^{K} w_{i,n}(T) s_{i,n}(E_{T_i}, E_{V_{i,n}}), \qquad (2)$$

$$w_{i,n}(T) = \frac{e^{h(T)^\intercal a_{i,n}}}{\sum_{m=1}^{N} \sum_{j=1}^{K} e^{h(T)^\intercal a_{j,m}}}. \qquad (3)$$

Hence instead of learning K scalar weights a_i, $i = 1, ..., K$ as done in [14] and [39], we learn $K \times N$ scalar weights $a_{i,n}$, $i = 1, ..., K$, $n = 1, ..., N$ to allow combination of experts from additional clips.

Dealing with Missing Streams. We note that these experts might be missing for certain videos, e.g. subtitles are not available for all videos and some videos do not have any detected faces. When expert features are missing, we zero-pad the missing experts and compute the similarity score. This is the standard procedure followed by existing retrieval methods using Mixture of Embedding Experts models [14,39]. The similarity score is calculated only from the available experts by re-normalizing the mixture weights to sum to one, allowing backpropagation of gradients only to the expert branches that had an input feature. We apply this same principle when dealing with missing video clips in the past, for example if we are training our model with $N = 1$ past clips, for a video clip which is right at the start of the movie (has no past), we treat all the experts from the previous clip as missing so that the weights are normalized to focus only on the current clip.

Character Module. The character module computes the similarity between a vector representation of the character IDs mentioned in the query y and a vector representation of the face identities recognised in the clip x. The vector representations are computed as follows: For the query, we search for actor names in the text from the cast list (supplied by the dataset) and create a one-hot vector y the same length as the cast list, where $y_i = 1$ if actor i is identified in any face track in the video and $y_i = 0$ otherwise. For the face identities acquired in the face recognition pipeline (described earlier), we compare the following three methods: first, we encode a one-hot vector x in a manner similar to the query character encoding. While this can match the presence and absence of characters, it doesn't allow any weighting of characters based on their importance in a clip. Hence inspired by [49], we also propose a second method ("track-frequency normalised"), where x_i is the number of face tracks for identity i. Lastly, in "track length normalised", our vector encodes the total amount of time a character appears in a clip i.e. x_i is the sum of all track lengths for actor i, divided by the total sum of all track lengths in the clip. The performances of the three approaches are displayed and discussed in Table 5 and Sect. 5 respectively. The character similarity score $s_C = \langle y, x \rangle$ is then modulated by its own scalar mixture weight $w_C(T)$ predicted from $h(T)$ (as is done for the other experts in the model). This similarity score is then added to the similarity score obtained from the other experts to obtain the final similarity score, i.e. $s(T, V) = \sum_{i=1}^{K} w_i(T) s_i(E_{T_i}, E_{V_i}) + w_C(T) s_C(T, V)$.

Training Loss. As is commonly done for video-text retrieval tasks, we minimise the Bidirectional Max-margin Ranking Loss [50].

5   Experiments

5.1   Experimental Set-Up

We train our model for the task of cross-movie and within-movie retrieval. The dataset is split into disjoint training, validation and test sets by movie, so that

Table 3. Training splits for cross-movie retrieval (left) and within-movie retrieval (right). For within-movie retrieval, we restrict the dataset to movies which have at least 5 video clips in total.

	Cross-Movie				Within-Movie			
	TRAIN	VAL	TEST	TOTAL	TRAIN	VAL	TEST	TOTAL
#Movies	2,551	358	696	3,605	2,469	341	671	3,481
#Video clips	24,047	3,348	6,581	33,976	23,963	3,315	6,581	33,859

there are no overlapping movies between the sets. The dataset splits can be seen in Table 3. We report our results on the *test set* using standard retrieval metrics including median rank (lower is better), mean rank (lower is better) and R@K (recall at rank K—higher is better).

Cross-movie Retrieval: For the case of cross-movie retrieval, the metrics are reported over the entire test set of videos, i.e. given a text query, there is a 'gallery' set of 6,581 possible matching videos (Table 3). We report R@1, R@5, R@10, mean and median rank.

Within-Movie Retrieval: In order to evaluate the task of within-movie retrieval, we remove all movies that contain less than 5 video clips from the dataset. For each query text, the possible gallery set consists only of the videos in the same movie as the query. In this setting the retrieval metrics are calculated separately for each movie and then averaged over all movies. We report R@1, mean and median rank.

5.2   Baselines

The **E2EWS** (End-to-end Weakly Supervised) is a cross-modal retrieval model trained by [51] using weak supervision from a large-scale corpus of (100 million) instructional videos (using speech content as the supervisory signal). We use the video and text encoders without any form of fine-tuning on Condensed Movies, to demonstrate the widely different domain of our dataset.

The **MoEE** (Mixture of Embedded Experts) model proposed by [14] comprises a multi-modal video model in combination with a system of context gates that learn to fuse together different pretrained experts.

The **CE** model [39] similarly learns a cross-modal embedding by fusing together a collection of pretrained experts to form a video encoder, albeit with pairwise relation network sub-architectures. It represents the state-of-the-art on several retrieval benchmarks.

Context Boosting Module: Finally, we report results with the addition of our Context Boosting module to both MoEE and CE. We use the fact that the video clips in our dataset are ordered by the time they appear in the movie, and encode previous and future 'key scenes' in the movie along with every video clip using the CBM. An ablation on the number of clips encoded for context can be found in the supplementary material.

We finally show the results of an ablation study demonstrating the importance of different experts for this task on the task of cross-movie retrieval.

In the next sections, we first describe the implementation details of our models and then discuss quantitative and qualitative results.

5.3   Implementation Details

Expert Features: In order to capture the rich content of a video, we draw on existing powerful representations for a number of different semantic tasks. These are first extracted at a frame-level, then aggregated by taking the mean to produce a single feature vector per modality per video.

RGB object frame-level embeddings of the visual data are generated with an SENet-154 model [52] pretrained on ImageNet for the task of image classification. Frames are extracted at 25 fps, where each frame is resized to 224×224 pixels. Features collected have a dimensionality of 2048.

Motion embeddings are generated using the I3D inception model [53] trained on Kinetics [16], following the procedure described by [53].

Face embeddings for each face track are extracted in three stages: (1) Each frame is passed through a dual shot face detector [54] (trained on the Wider Face dataset [55]) to extract bounding boxes. (2) Each box is then passed through an SENet50 [56] trained on the VGGFace2 dataset [46] for the task of face verification, to extract a facial feature embedding, which is L2 normalised. (3) A simple tracker is used to connect the bounding boxes temporally within shots into face tracks. Finally the embeddings for each bounding box within a track are average pooled into a single embedding per face track, which is again L2 normalised. The tracker uses a weighted combination of intersection over union and feature similarity (cosine similarity) to link bounding boxes in consecutive frames.

Subtitles are encoded using BERT embeddings [47] averaged across all words.

Scene features of 2208 dimensions are encoded using a DenseNet161 model [57] pretrained on the Places365 dataset [58], applied to 224×224 pixel centre crops of frames extracted at 1fps.

Descriptions are encoded using BERT embeddings, providing contextual word-level features of dimensions $W \times 1024$ where W is the number of tokens. These are concatenated and fed to a NetVLAD layer to produce a feature vector of length of 1024 times the number of NetVLAD clusters for variable length word tokens.

Training Details and Hyperparameters: All baselines and CBM are implemented with PyTorch [59]. Optimization is performed with Adam [60], using a learning rate of 0.001, and a batch size of 32. The margin hyperparameter m

for the bidirectional ranking loss is set to a value of 0.121, the common projection dimension D to 512, and the description NetVLAD clusters to 10. For CBM, we select the number of past and future context videos to be $N = 3$, ablations for hyperparameters and using different amounts of context are given in the supplementary material. Training is stopped when the validation loss stops decreasing.

Table 4. Cross-movie text-video retrieval results on the CMD *test* set of 6,581 video clips, with varying levels of context. Random weights refers to the MoEE model architecture with random initialization. We report Recall@k (higher is better), Median rank and Mean rank (lower is better).

Method	Recall@1	Recall@5	Recall@10	Median rank	Mean rank
Random weights	0.0	0.1	0.2	3209	3243.5
E2EWS [51]	0.7	2.2	3.7	1130	1705.5
CE [39]	2.3	7.4	11.8	190	570.0
MoEE [14]	4.7	14.9	22.1	65	285.3
CE + CBM (ours)	3.6	12.0	18.2	103	474.6
MoEE + CBM (ours)	**5.6**	**17.6**	**26.1**	**50**	**243.9**

Table 5. Within-Movie Retrieval results on the CMD test set. All movies with less than 5 video clips are removed. Metrics are computed individually for each movie and then averaged (m-MdR and m-MnR refers to the mean of the median and mean rank obtained for each movie respectively). R@1 denotes recall@1. We show the results of 3 different variations of embeddings obtained from the character module.

Method	m-R@1	m-MdR	m-MnR
Random weights	11.1	5.32	5.32
MoEE	38.9	2.20	2.82
MoEE + Character Module [one-hot]	45.5	1.91	2.60
MoEE + Character Module [track-len norm]	46.2	1.88	2.53
MoEE + Character Module [**track-freq norm**]	**47.2**	**1.85**	**2.49**

Table 6. Expert ablations. The value of different experts in combination with a baseline for text-video retrieval (left) and (right) their cumulative effect (here Prev. denotes the experts used in the previous row). R@k: recall@k, MedR: median rank, MeanR: mean rank

Experts	R@1	R@5	R@10	MedR	MeanR	Experts	R@1	R@5	R@10	MedR	MeanR
Scene	0.8	3.2	5.9	329	776.3	Scene	0.8	3.2	5.9	329	776
Scene+Face	3.7	12.7	19.7	100	443.1	Prev.+Face	3.7	12.7	19.7	100	443.1
Scene+Obj	1.0	4.6	8.0	237	607.8	Prev.+ Obj	3.9	13.1	20.5	79	245.5
Scene+Action	1.9	6.4	10.5	193	575.0	Prev.+ Action	4.0	14.0	20.4	78	233.3
Scene+Speech	2.3	8.3	12.4	165	534.7	Prev.+Speech	5.6	17.7	25.7	50	243.9

Out on a date with Michael, Lelaina gets uncomfortable when he gives her a compliment and asks about her friends.

Bill puts Bobby on the stand, and uses a hockey metaphor to draw out the truth.

Chucky chases Tyler into a haunted house ride at a nearby carnival. Right as he captures Tyler, he gets half his face cut off by an automated scythe.

Fig. 5. Qualitative results of the MoEE+CBM model for cross-movie retrieval. On the left, we provide the input query, and on the right, we show the top 4 video clips retrieved by our model on the CMD *test set*. A single frame for each video clip is shown. The matching clip is highlighted with a green border, while the rest are highlighted in red (best viewed in colour). Note how our model is able to retrieve semantic matches for situations (row 1: male/female on a date), high level abstract concepts (row 2: the words 'stand' and 'truth' are mentioned in the caption and the retrieved samples show a courtroom, men delivering speeches and a policeman's office) and also notions of violence and objects (row 3: scythe). (Color figure online)

5.4   Results

Results for cross-movie retrieval can be seen in Table 4. E2EWS performs poorly, illustrating the domain gap between CMD and generic YouTube videos from HowTo100M. Both the CE and MoEE baselines perform much better than random, demonstrating that story-based retrieval is achievable on this dataset. We show that the Contextual Boost module can be effectively used in conjunction with existing video retrieval architectures, improving performance for both CE and MoEE, with the latter being the best performing model. Results for within-movie retrieval can be seen in Table 5. We show that adding in the character module provides a significant boost (almost a 10% increase in Recall@1 compared to the MoEE without the character module), with the best results obtained from normalizing the character embeddings by the track frequency. The value of different experts is assessed in Table 6. Since experts such as subtitles and face are missing for many video clips, we show the performance of individual experts combined with the 'scene' expert features, the expert with the lowest performance that is consistently available for all clips (as done by [39]). In Table 6, right, we show the cumulative effect of adding in the different experts. The highest boosts are obtained from the face features and the speech features, as expected, since we hypothesize that these are crucial for following human-centric storylines. We show qualitative results for our best cross-movie retrieval model (MoEE + CBM) in Fig. 5.

6   Plot Alignment

A unique aspect of the Condensed Movies Dataset is the story-level captions accompanying the ordered key scenes in the movie. Unlike existing datasets [2] that contain low level visual descriptions of the visual content, our semantic captions capture key plot elements. To illustrate the new kinds of capabilities afforded by this aspect, we align the video descriptions to Wikipedia plot summary sentences using Jumping Dynamic Time Warping [61] of BERT sentence embeddings. This alignment allows us to place each video clip in the global context of the larger plot of the movie. A qualitative example is shown in Fig. 6. Future work will incorporate this global context from movie plots to further improve retrieval performance.

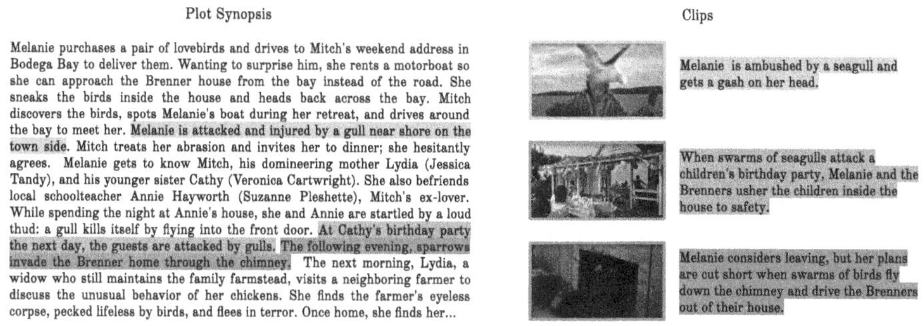

Plot Synopsis

Melanie purchases a pair of lovebirds and drives to Mitch's weekend address in Bodega Bay to deliver them. Wanting to surprise him, she rents a motorboat so she can approach the Brenner house from the bay instead of the road. She sneaks the birds inside the house and heads back across the bay. Mitch discovers the birds, spots Melanie's boat during her retreat, and drives around the bay to meet her. Melanie is attacked and injured by a gull near shore on the town side. Mitch treats her abrasion and invites her to dinner; she hesitantly agrees. Melanie gets to know Mitch, his domineering mother Lydia (Jessica Tandy), and his younger sister Cathy (Veronica Cartwright). She also befriends local schoolteacher Annie Hayworth (Suzanne Pleshette), Mitch's ex-lover. While spending the night at Annie's house, she and Annie are startled by a loud thud: a gull kills itself by flying into the front door. At Cathy's birthday party the next day, the guests are attacked by gulls. The following evening, sparrows invade the Brenner home through the chimney. The next morning, Lydia, a widow who still maintains the family farmstead, visits a neighboring farmer to discuss the unusual behavior of her chickens. She finds the farmer's eyeless corpse, pecked lifeless by birds, and flees in terror. Once home, she finds her...

Clips

Melanie is ambushed by a seagull and gets a gash on her head.

When swarms of seagulls attack a children's birthday party, Melanie and the Brenners usher the children inside the house to safety.

Melanie considers leaving, but her plans are cut short when swarms of birds fly down the chimney and drive the Brenners out of their house.

Fig. 6. A sample Wikipedia movie plot summary (left) aligned with an ordered sample of clips and their descriptions (right). The alignment was achieved using Jumping Dynamic Time Warping [61] of sentence-level BERT embeddings, note how the alignment is able to skip a number of peripheral plot sentences.

7   Conclusion

In this work, we introduce a new and challenging *Condensed Movies Dataset* (CMD), containing captioned video clips following succinct and clear storylines in movies. Our dataset consists of long video clips with high level semantic captions, annotated face-tracks, and other movie metadata, and is freely available to the research community. We investigate the task of story-based text retrieval of these clips, and show that modelling past and previous context improves performance. Beside improving retrieval, developing richer models to model longer term temporal context will also allow us to follow the evolution of relationships [35] and higher level semantics in movies, exciting avenues for future work.

Acknowledgements. This work is supported by a Google PhD Fellowship, an EPSRC DTA Studentship, and the EPSRC programme grant Seebibyte EP/M013774/1. We are grateful to Samuel Albanie for his help with feature extraction.

References

1. Tapaswi, M., Bauml, M., Stiefelhagen, R.: StoryGraphs: visualizing character interactions as a timeline. In: Proceedings of the IEEE Conference on Computer Vision and Pattern Recognition, pp. 827–834 (2014)
2. Rohrbach, A., et al.: Movie description. Int. J. Comput. Vis. **123**, 94–120 (2017). https://doi.org/10.1007/s11263-016-0987-1
3. Xiong, Y., Huang, Q., Guo, L., Zhou, H., Zhou, B., Lin, D.: A graph-based framework to bridge movies and synopses. In: The IEEE International Conference on Computer Vision (ICCV) (2019)
4. Vicol, P., Tapaswi, M., Castrejon, L., Fidler, S.: MovieGraphs: towards understanding human-centric situations from videos. In: IEEE Conference on Computer Vision and Pattern Recognition (CVPR) (2018)
5. Huang, Q., Xiong, Yu., Rao, A., Wang, J., Lin, D.: MovieNet: a holistic dataset for movie understanding. In: Vedaldi, A., Bischof, H., Brox, T., Frahm, J.-M. (eds.) ECCV 2020. LNCS, vol. 12349, pp. 709–727. Springer, Cham (2020). https://doi.org/10.1007/978-3-030-58548-8_41
6. Jolly, S., Pezzelle, S., Klein, T., Dengel, A., Nabi, M.: The wisdom of masses: majority, subjectivity, and semantic similarity in the evaluation of VQA. CoRR abs/1809.04344 (2018)
7. Miech, A., Zhukov, D., Alayrac, J.B., Tapaswi, M., Laptev, I., Sivic, J.: HowTo100M: learning a text-video embedding by watching hundred million narrated video clips. arXiv preprint arXiv:1906.03327 (2019)
8. Tang, Y., et al.: Coin: a large-scale dataset for comprehensive instructional video analysis. In: Proceedings of the IEEE Conference on Computer Vision and Pattern Recognition, pp. 1207–1216 (2019)
9. Zhou, L., Xu, C., Corso, J.J.: Towards automatic learning of procedures from web instructional videos. In: Thirty-Second AAAI Conference on Artificial Intelligence (2018)
10. Ignat, O., Burdick, L., Deng, J., Mihalcea, R.: Identifying visible actions in lifestyle vlogs. arXiv preprint arXiv:1906.04236 (2019)
11. Fouhey, D.F., Kuo, W.C., Efros, A.A., Malik, J.: From lifestyle vlogs to everyday interactions. In: Proceedings of the IEEE Conference on Computer Vision and Pattern Recognition, pp. 4991–5000 (2018)
12. Xu, J., Mei, T., Yao, T., Rui, Y.: MSR-VTT: a large video description dataset for bridging video and language. In: Proceedings of the IEEE Conference on Computer Vision and Pattern Recognition, pp. 5288–5296 (2016)
13. Hendricks, L.A., Wang, O., Shechtman, E., Sivic, J., Darrell, T., Russell, B.: Localizing moments in video with natural language. In: Proceedings of the IEEE International Conference on Computer Vision, pp. 5803–5812 (2017)
14. Miech, A., Laptev, I., Sivic, J.: Learning a Text-Video Embedding from Imcomplete and Heterogeneous Data. In: arXiv (2018)
15. Tapaswi, M., Zhu, Y., Stiefelhagen, R., Torralba, A., Urtasun, R., Fidler, S.: MovieQA: understanding stories in movies through question-answering. In: IEEE Conference on Computer Vision and Pattern Recognition (CVPR) (2016)
16. Kay, W., et al.: The kinetics human action video dataset. CoRR abs/1705.06950 (2017)
17. Gu, C., et al.: AVA: a video dataset of spatio-temporally localized atomic visual actions. In: Proceedings of the IEEE Conference on Computer Vision and Pattern Recognition, pp. 6047–6056 (2018)

18. Monfort, M., et al.: Moments in time dataset: one million videos for event understanding. IEEE Trans. Pattern Anal. Mach. Intell. **42**, 502–508 (2019)

19. Sener, O., Zamir, A.R., Savarese, S., Saxena, A.: Unsupervised semantic parsing of video collections. In: Proceedings of the IEEE International Conference on Computer Vision, pp. 4480–4488 (2015)

20. Alayrac, J.B., Bojanowski, P., Agrawal, N., Sivic, J., Laptev, I., Lacoste-Julien, S.: Unsupervised learning from narrated instruction videos. In: Proceedings of the IEEE Conference on Computer Vision and Pattern Recognition, pp. 4575–4583 (2016)

21. Sun, C., Myers, A., Vondrick, C., Murphy, K., Schmid, C.: VideoBERT: a joint model for video and language representation learning. arXiv preprint arXiv:1904.01766 (2019)

22. Everingham, M., Sivic, J., Zisserman, A.: "Hello! My name is... Buffy" - automatic naming of characters in TV video. In: Proceedings of BMVC (2006)

23. Naim, I., Al Mamun, A., Song, Y.C., Luo, J., Kautz, H., Gildea, D.: Aligning movies with scripts by exploiting temporal ordering constraints. In: 2016 23rd International Conference on Pattern Recognition (ICPR), pp. 1786–1791. IEEE (2016)

24. Cour, T., Sapp, B., Jordan, C., Taskar, B.: Learning from ambiguously labeled images. In: 2009 IEEE Conference on Computer Vision and Pattern Recognition, pp. 919–926. IEEE (2009)

25. Sivic, J., Everingham, M., Zisserman, A.: "Who are you?" - learning person specific classifiers from video. In: Proceedings of CVPR (2009)

26. Tapaswi, M., Bäuml, M., Stiefelhagen, R.: "Knock! Knock! Who is it?" probabilistic person identification in TV-series. In: 2012 IEEE Conference on Computer Vision and Pattern Recognition, pp. 2658–2665. IEEE (2012)

27. Huang, Q., Yang, L., Huang, H., Wu, T., Lin, D.: Caption-supervised face recognition: training a state-of-the-art face model without manual annotation. In: Vedaldi, A., Bischof, H., Brox, T., Frahm, J.-M. (eds.) ECCV 2020. LNCS, vol. 12362, pp. 139–155. Springer, Cham (2020). https://doi.org/10.1007/978-3-030-58520-4_9

28. Bojanowski, P., Bach, F., Laptev, I., Ponce, J., Schmid, C., Sivic, J.: Finding actors and actions in movies. In: Proceedings of the IEEE International Conference on Computer Vision, pp. 2280–2287 (2013)

29. Duchenne, O., Laptev, I., Sivic, J., Bach, F., Ponce, J.: Automatic annotation of human actions in video. In: 2009 IEEE 12th International Conference on Computer Vision, pp. 1491–1498. IEEE (2009)

30. Laptev, I., Marszałek, M., Schmid, C., Rozenfeld, B.: Learning realistic human actions from movies (2008)

31. Marszałek, M., Laptev, I., Schmid, C.: Actions in context. In: CVPR 2009-IEEE Conference on Computer Vision & Pattern Recognition, pp. 2929–2936. IEEE Computer Society (2009)

32. Nagrani, A., Sun, C., Ross, D., Sukthankar, R., Schmid, C., Zisserman, A.: Speech2Action: cross-modal supervision for action recognition. In: The IEEE/CVF Conference on Computer Vision and Pattern Recognition (CVPR) (2020)

33. Ercolessi, P., Bredin, H., Sénac, C.: StoViz: story visualization of TV series. In: Proceedings of the 20th ACM International Conference on Multimedia, pp. 1329–1330 (2012)

34. Rao, A., et al.: A local-to-global approach to multi-modal movie scene segmentation. In: Proceedings of the IEEE/CVF Conference on Computer Vision and Pattern Recognition, pp. 10146–10155 (2020)

35. Kukleva, A., Tapaswi, M., Laptev, I.: Learning interactions and relationships between movie characters. In: IEEE Conference on Computer Vision and Pattern Recognition (CVPR 2020) (2020)

36. Jasani, B., Girdhar, R., Ramanan, D.: Are we asking the right questions in MovieQA? In: ICCVW (2019)

37. Nagrani, A., Zisserman, A.: From benedict cumberbatch to sherlock holmes: character identification in tv series without a script. In: Proceedings of BMVC (2017)

38. Lei, J., Yu, L., Berg, T.L., Bansal, M.: TVQA+: spatio-temporal grounding for video question answering. Technical Report, arXiv (2019)

39. Liu, Y., Albanie, S., Nagrani, A., Zisserman, A.: Use what you have: video retrieval using representations from collaborative experts. In: Proceedings of BMVC (2019)

40. Tapaswi, M., Bäuml, M., Stiefelhagen, R.: Aligning plot synopses to videos for story-based retrieval. Int. J. Multimed. Inf. Retrieval **4**, 3–16 (2015). https://doi.org/10.1007/s13735-014-0065-9

41. Krishna, R., Hata, K., Ren, F., Fei-Fei, L., Carlos Niebles, J.: Dense-captioning events in videos. In: Proceedings of the IEEE International Conference on Computer Vision, pp. 706–715 (2017)

42. Wu, C.Y., Feichtenhofer, C., Fan, H., He, K., Krahenbuhl, P., Girshick, R.: Long-term feature banks for detailed video understanding. In: The IEEE Conference on Computer Vision and Pattern Recognition (CVPR) (2019)

43. McCarthy, P.M., Jarvis, S.: MTLD, vocd-D, and HD-D: a validation study of sophisticated approaches to lexical diversity assessment. Behav. Res. Methods **42**, 381–392 (2010). https://doi.org/10.3758/BRM.42.2.381

44. Caba Heilbron, F., Escorcia, V., Ghanem, B., Carlos Niebles, J.: ActivityNet: a large-scale video benchmark for human activity understanding. In: Proceedings of the IEEE Conference on Computer Vision and Pattern Recognition, pp. 961–970 (2015)

45. Nagrani, A., Chung, J.S., Xie, W., Zisserman, A.: Voxceleb: large-scale speaker verification in the wild. Comput. Speech Lang. **60**, 101027 (2019)

46. Cao, Q., Shen, L., Xie, W., Parkhi, O.M., Zisserman, A.: VGGFace2: a dataset for recognising faces across pose and age. In: Proceedings of International Conference Automatic Face and Gesture Recognition (2018)

47. Devlin, J., Chang, M.W., Lee, K., Toutanova, K.: Bert: pre-training of deep bidirectional transformers for language understanding. arXiv preprint arXiv:1810.04805 (2018)

48. Arandjelovic, R., Gronat, P., Torii, A., Pajdla, T., Sivic, J.: NetVLAD: CNN architecture for weakly supervised place recognition. In: Proceedings of the IEEE Conference on Computer Vision and Pattern Recognition, pp. 5297–5307 (2016)

49. Tapaswi, M., Bäuml, M., Stiefelhagen, R.: Book2Movie: aligning Video scenes with Book chapters. In: IEEE Conference on Computer Vision and Pattern Recognition (CVPR) (2015)

50. Socher, R., Karpathy, A., Le, Q.V., Manning, C.D., Ng, A.Y.: Grounded compositional semantics for finding and describing images with sentences. Trans. Assoc. Comput. Linguist. **2**, 207–218 (2014)

51. Miech, A., Alayrac, J.B., Smaira, L., Laptev, I., Sivic, J., Zisserman, A.: End-to-end learning of visual representations from uncurated instructional videos. In: The IEEE/CVF Conference on Computer Vision and Pattern Recognition (CVPR) (2020)

52. Hu, J., Shen, L., Albanie, S., Sun, G., Wu, E.: Squeeze-and-excitation networks. IEEE Trans. Pattern Anal. Mach. Intell. (2019)

53. Carreira, J., Zisserman, A.: Quo vadis, action recognition? A new model and the Kinetics dataset. In: Proceedings of the IEEE Conference on Computer Vision and Pattern Recognition, pp. 6299–6308 (2017)

54. Li, J., et al.: DSFD: dual shot face detector. In: Proceedings of the IEEE Conference on Computer Vision and Pattern Recognition, pp. 5060–5069 (2019)

55. Yang, S., Luo, P., Loy, C.C., Tang, X.: WIDER FACE: a face detection benchmark. In: IEEE Conference on Computer Vision and Pattern Recognition (CVPR) (2016)

56. Hu, J., Shen, L., Sun, G.: Squeeze-and-excitation networks. In: Proceedings of CVPR (2018)

57. Iandola, F., Moskewicz, M., Karayev, S., Girshick, R., Darrell, T., Keutzer, K.: Densenet: implementing efficient convnet descriptor pyramids. arXiv preprint arXiv:1404.1869 (2014)

58. Zhou, B., Lapedriza, A., Khosla, A., Oliva, A., Torralba, A.: Places: a 10 million image database for scene recognition. IEEE Trans. Pattern Anal. Mach. Intell. **40**, 1452–1464 (2017)

59. Paszke, A., et al.: Automatic differentiation in pytorch (2017)

60. Kingma, D.P., Ba, J.: Adam: a method for stochastic optimization. CoRR abs/1412.6980 (2014)

61. Feng, L., Zhao, X., Liu, Y., Yao, Y., Jin, B.: A similarity measure of jumping dynamic time warping. In: 2010 Seventh International Conference on Fuzzy Systems and Knowledge Discovery, vol. 4, pp. 1677–1681 (2010)

Play Fair: Frame Attributions in Video Models

Will Price[(✉)] and Dima Damen

University of Bristol, Bristol, UK
{will.price,dima.damen}@bristol.ac.uk

Abstract. In this paper, we introduce an attribution method for explaining action recognition models. Such models fuse information from multiple frames within a video, through score aggregation or relational reasoning. We break down a model's class score into the sum of contributions from each frame, *fairly*. Our method adapts an axiomatic solution to fair reward distribution in cooperative games, known as the Shapley value, for elements in a variable-length sequence, which we call the Element Shapley Value (ESV). Critically, we propose a tractable approximation of ESV that scales linearly with the number of frames in the sequence.

We employ ESV to explain two action recognition models (TRN and TSN) on the fine-grained dataset Something-Something. We offer detailed analysis of supporting/distracting frames, and the relationships of ESVs to the frame's position, class prediction, and sequence length. We compare ESV to naive baselines and two commonly used feature attribution methods: Grad-CAM and Integrated-Gradients.

1 Introduction

Progress in Action Recognition has seen remarkable gains in recent years thanks to architectural advances [1–7] and large-scale datasets [8–13]. The task of action recognition is to classify the action depicted in a video, from a sequence of frames. We address a question previously unexplored in action recognition: given a video and a trained model, *how much did each frame contribute to the model's output?*

Determining the contribution of each frame is similar to feature attribution, which assigns a value to each input feature, representing its weight to a scalar output in the model's response. Note that this is distinct from feature selection which computes the value of the feature globally across a dataset, and not for a specific example. Previous works in feature attribution [14–18] have taken inspiration from cooperative game theory The Shapley value [19] was proposed as an axiomatic solution to *fairly* distributing a reward amongst the players in a cooperative game based on each player's contribution. We offer the first attempt

Electronic supplementary material The online version of this chapter (https://doi.org/10.1007/978-3-030-69541-5_29) contains supplementary material, which is available to authorized users.

H. Ishikawa et al. (Eds.): ACCV 2020, LNCS 12626, pp. 480–497, 2021.
https://doi.org/10.1007/978-3-030-69541-5_29

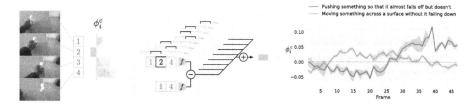

Fig. 1. We assign ϕ_i^c, the Element Shapley Value, to each frame i in a video *fairly*, given a model f and a specific class c. We calculate differences in the class score for subsequences with and without the specified frame—e.g. $(1, \mathbf{2}, 4)$ vs $(1, 4)$, and combine these for all subsequences (tiled boxes) to produce the element's attribution (e.g. for frame 2). Class-specific ϕ_i^c are shown for two classes (right), the ground-truth class (in blue) and another class (in orange), highlighting positive/negative frame attributions. (Color figure online)

to integrate the Shapley axioms of fairness for video understanding—hence our paper's title 'Play Fair'.

In contrast to general feature attribution, and similar approaches applied to images [20–25], our focus is on attributing elements (frames) in a time-varying sequence (video). We depict our approach, *Element Shapley Value* (ESV), in Fig. 1. ESV assigns an attribution to each frame representing its contribution to the model output. This attribution is computed from the change in the model output as the frame is added to different subsequences of the input video. We compute *class-specific* attributions (Fig. 1 right). Additionally, as attributions produced by ESV can be combined, we introduce *class-contrastive* attributions to determine which frames contribute more to one class than another.

Our contributions can be summarised as follows:

1. We introduce Element Shapley Value (ESV) to determine the contribution of each element in a variable-length sequence to a model's output[1].
2. We propose and evaluate a tractable approximation to computing ESVs that linearly scales with the number of elements in the sequence.
3. We calculate class-specific and class-contrastive ESVs for two action recognition models on the fine-grained dataset Something-Something.
4. We demonstrate that some frames have a negative impact on the model's output. This deviates from the common misconception that utilising all frames in a sequence always improves performance.

We next explain our approach to determining the contribution of each element in a sequence to a model's response, which we term *element attribution*. Related work is deferred until the end of the paper, to offer the best insight into how our work relates to feature attribution and approaches in video explanation.

---

[1] We focus on individual frames, but our approach naturally extends to determining attributions of video clips fed to a 3D CNN (e.g. [26]). As these models average clip scores, ESV can explain how much did each *clip* contribute to the model's output.

2   Element Attribution in Sequences

In this section, we introduce the Shapley value as an axiomatic solution to attribution. We discuss the limitations of feature attribution methods, showcasing how these can be overcome when attributing elements in sequences. We then introduce our approach to tractably computing ESVs for variable-length sequences.

2.1   Element Attribution and the Shapley Value

To answer our motivational question, *how much did each frame contribute to the model's output?*, we introduce *element attribution* as the task of determining the contribution ϕ_i of an element x_i in a sequence $X = (x_i)_{i=1}^n$ to the output of the model $f(X)$. For a classification model, where the output is a vector of class scores $f(X) \in \mathbb{R}^C$, we obtain the contribution ϕ_i^c for each element x_i to the score $f_c(X)$ of any class c.

Element attribution can be viewed as special case of grouped-feature attribution, where an element is represented by a group of features and elements are ordered by their observation time. Of the previously-proposed feature attribution methods, *additive* ones [16] have a desirable trait where the sum of attributions equals the model output, up to a constant additive bias b_c specific to f:

$$f_c(X) = b_c + \sum_{x_i \in X} \phi_i^c. \tag{1}$$

Dividing the model's output should be done *fairly*, reflecting the element's actual contribution to the model's output. A natural way of measuring the contribution of an element x_i, is to consider the change in the model's response when it is added[2] to a subsequence $X' \subset X$, where X' does not contain x_i:

$$\Delta_i^c(X') = f_c(X' \cup \{x_i\}) - f_c(X'), \tag{2}$$

this is known as the *marginal contribution* of x_i on X'. Note when $\Delta_i^c(X')$ is positive, the addition of x_i increases the response of the model for class c and when negative, decreases it. However, $\Delta_i^c(X')$ will differ depending on the subsequence X'. As such, it is necessary to consider the marginal contribution of x_i on all subsequences it can join to calculate element attributions. This has the benefit of capturing the effects of resampling the sequence at all possible rates.

Lloyd Shapley (1953) defined a set of axioms that ϕ_i^c should satisfy if it is to be considered *fair* [19] (later refined by Young [27] in 1985), we explain these in the context of element attribution:

A1: Efficiency. The sum of element attributions should equal the output of the model on the input X, minus the output of the model on the empty sequence $\emptyset$:

$$\sum_{x_i \in X} \phi_i^c = f_c(X) - f_c(\emptyset). \tag{3}$$

---

[2] We adapt set notation to sequences using subset ($\subset$) and union ($\cup$) operations to form new subsequences. Elements preserve the same ordering as in the full sequence.

We call this difference, $f'_c(X) = f_c(X) - f_c(\emptyset)$, the *evidential score* of X w.r.t to class c, as it is the difference in class score when X is observed over observing nothing. We use the empirical class distribution of the training set as $f_c(\emptyset)$.

A2: Symmetry. Any pair of elements x_i and x_j should be assigned equal contributions, $\phi_i^c = \phi_j^c$, if $f_c(X' \cup \{x_i\}) = f_c(X' \cup \{x_j\})$ for all $X' \subseteq X \setminus \{x_i, x_j\}$.

A3: Monotonicty. For any pair of classes c_1, c_2, if $\Delta_i^{c_1}(X') \geq \Delta_i^{c_2}(X')$ for all subsequences $X' \subseteq X \setminus \{x_i\}$ then $\phi_i^{c_1} \geq \phi_i^{c_2}$.

There is a unique formulation of ϕ_i^c satisfying the above axioms, known as the Shapley value, which consequently assigns attributions *fairly*. The Shapley value [19] was originally proposed as a solution to the problem of fairly distributing a reward amongst players in a cooperative game. A cooperative game is one where a group of players known as a *coalition* collaborate to earn some reward. Players are treated as sets, as opposed to sequences. By analogy, each element in the sequence acts as a player and subsequences act as ordered coalitions. Accordingly, we refer to our element attribution method, that satisfies the Shapley axioms, as the Element Shapley Value (ESV). This is the weighted average of the marginal contributions of x_i to all subsequences $X' \subseteq X \setminus \{x_i\}$ it can join:

$$\phi_i^c = \sum_{X' \subseteq X \setminus \{x_i\}} w(X') \Delta_i^c(X') \qquad w(X') = \frac{(|X| - |X'| - 1)! |X'|!}{|X|!}. \qquad (4)$$

where $w(X')$ can be interpreted as the probability of drawing a subsequence X' from $X \setminus \{x_i\}$, considering each way of forming X by adding an element at a time starting from $\emptyset$, going via X' and $X' \cup \{x_i\}$, as equally likely. Consequently, ϕ_i^c can be rewritten as the expectation over a random variable X' with sample space $2^{X \setminus \{x_i\}}$ and probability mass function $w(X')$ (proof in Appendix B.1):

$$\phi_i^c = \mathbb{E}_{X'} \left[\Delta_i^c(X') \right], \qquad (5)$$

which can be reformulated again in terms of the expected model response on the sequences before and after x_i is added to X':

$$\phi_i^c = \mathbb{E}_{X'} \left[f_c(X' \cup \{x_i\}) \right] - \mathbb{E}_{X'} \left[f_c(X') \right]. \qquad (6)$$

This is an easier form to compute, as we don't have to measure the marginal contributions of each element on each subsequence, but instead measure the expected model score on subsequences containing x_i and those not containing x_i. We take one final step towards the form that we will actually use to compute element attributions, expanding Eq. (6) via the law of total expectation to

$$\phi_i^c = \mathbb{E}_s \left[\mathbb{E}_{X'|s} \left[f_c(X' \cup \{x_i\}) \right] - \mathbb{E}_{X'|s} \left[f_c(X') \right] \right], \qquad (7)$$

where the subsequence length s ranges from 0 to $|X| - 1$ with equal probability, and the random variable X' conditioned on s takes on values from $\{X' \subseteq X \setminus$

$\{x_i\} : |X'| = s\}$ with equal probability (proof in Appendix B.1). This allows us to compute ϕ_i^c by first considering the expected marginal contributions at each scale s and then combining these across scales.

2.2 Element Attribution in Variable-Length Sequences

As shown in Eq. (4), computing element attributions requires evaluating the model on different subsequences. We first consider approaches used to evaluate a model on feature subsets, then the options we have in element attribution.

Feature Ablation. Evaluating a model on feature subsets is challenging as models rarely support the notion of a 'missing feature'. Two approaches exist: re-training the model on all combinations of features [28] or substituting missing features with those from a reference [14, 16, 22, 24, 25, 29, 30], but both approaches have limitations. Retraining is computationally infeasible for more than a handful of features, and the choice of reference in feature substitution has a significant impact on the resulting attribution values [18, 31].

Element Ablation. Training an exponential number of models for each subsequence is infeasible for large models and thus ruled out. We could substitute frames by a *reference*, e.g. the mean element from the training set, or the nearest element still present, amongst other reasonable alternatives. However, similar to feature substitution [31], the choice of reference will have a large impact on the resulting attribution values. Feeding sequences that are out-of-distribution (such as one created by duplicating frames) to an action recognition model can result in uncharacteristic model responses [32]. We instead propose a more attractive option: utilising models that support variable-length input sequences.

Supporting Variable Length Inputs. When the model to be explained does not support variable-length inputs, we take inspiration from multi-scale models (e.g. TRN [1]) to build a model f^{ms} capable of operating over variable-length sequences. Let $f^s(X)$ be a fixed-scale model which takes a sequence of length s as input. We construct a set of models operating at different scales $\{f^s\}_{s=1}^{n_{\max}}$, up to a maximum subsequence length $n_{\max}$. We then combine these, such that each scale contributes equally to the overall output:

$$f^{\mathrm{ms}}(X) = \mathbb{E}_s \left[\mathbb{E}_{X'|s} \left[f^s(X') \right] \right], \qquad (8)$$

where s is a random variable over subsequence lengths $\{1 .. \min(|X|, n_{\max})\}$, all equally likely, and X' is a random variable over subsequences of size s. This has similarities to the retraining approach [28], however we can leverage the homogeneity of our input to reduce the number of models from $\mathcal{O}(2^{|X|})$ (one for each possible subsequence) to $\mathcal{O}(n_{\max})$. Another contrast is that the same models are used in inference and element attribution, unlike the work in [28].

2.3   Tractable Approach to Element Shapley Values

We have now defined the Element Shapley Value (ESV), as well as how these can be calculated using models supporting variable-length inputs. We next show how we can tractability compute the ESVs for *all elements in a variable-length sequence in parallel* culminating in Algorithm 1.

Bottom-Up Computation. We compute the model's output for each subsequence once by deriving a recurrence relation between $f^{\mathrm{ms}}(X')$ and $f^{\mathrm{ms}}(X)$, where $X' \subset X$, $|X| = n$, and $|X'| = n - 1$ (proof in Appendix B.2),

$$f^{\mathrm{ms}}(X) = \begin{cases} f^1(X) & n = 1 \\ \frac{1}{n}\left[f^n(X) + (n-1)\,\mathbb{E}_{X'|s=n-1}\left[f^{\mathrm{ms}}(X')\right]\right] & n \le n_{\max} \\ \mathbb{E}_{X'|s=n-1}\left[f^{\mathrm{ms}}(X')\right], & n > n_{\max} \end{cases} \tag{9}$$

To compute $f^{\mathrm{ms}}(X)$, we start with subsequences of one element, moving up one scale at a time by combining results according to Eq. (9), obtaining $f^{\mathrm{ms}}(X')$ for all $X' \subseteq X$ in the process. To compute ESVs simultaneously, we compute the expected model scores on subsequences with/without each element at each scale. We then combine these to obtain all elements' ESVs as in Eq. (7).

Sampling Subsequences. The bottom-up computation improves the efficiency, but doesn't deal with the exponential number of subsequences. We apply a sampling approximation to the expectations over subsequences in the definition of f^{ms} (Eq. (9)) and the ESV (Eq. (7)). This is similar to the Monte-Carlo approach used in prior applications of the Shapley value [14,15] but is more sample efficient. Our sampling approach aims to maximise the number of subsequence relationships across scales to best approximate f^{ms}. Given a sample of subsequences $\mathcal{X}^s$ at scale s, we grow subsequences by one element to obtain subsequences at the next scale, We then form a pool of all possible candidate subsequences of length $s + 1$:

$$\mathcal{C}^{s+1} = \bigcup_{\mathcal{X}_j^s \in \mathcal{X}^s} \{\mathcal{X}_j^s \cup \{x\} : x \in X \setminus \mathcal{X}_j^s\}, \tag{10}$$

from which we sample at most m subsequences to construct $\mathcal{X}^{s+1}$. We start our sampling approach with all single element subsequences: $\mathcal{X}^1 = \{(x_i)\}_{i=1}^n$.

Tying it All Together. Combining the above techniques, we present our approach in Algorithm 1 for computing ESVs. When the number of sampled subsequences, m, is chosen to be $\max_k \binom{|X|}{k}$, it computes the *exact* ESVs ϕ_i^c for $f^{\mathrm{ms}}(X)$. When m is less than this, the algorithm computes the approximate ESVs $\hat{\phi}_i^c$. We repeat the inner loop that computes the marginal contributions across all scales a number of iterations to improve the accuracy of the approximation.

Additional Definitions. Elements whose $\phi_i^c > 0$ are termed *supporting* elements for class c, otherwise, if $\phi_i^c \le 0$, they are termed *distracting* elements.

A common question when diagnosing a model is to understand why it classified a sequence incorrectly. We utilise the linear property of ESVs to compute a class-contrastive ESV δ_i. This is the ESV for the class-contrastive (cc) model $f_{cc}(X) = f_{gt}(X) - f_{pt}(X)$, where gt is the ground-truth class and pt is the incorrectly predicted class. The class-constrastive ESV can thus be computed as: $\delta_i = \phi_i^{gt-pt} = \phi_i^{gt} - \phi_i^{pt}$. When $\delta_i > 0$, the element contributes more to the ground-truth class than the predicted class.

Limitations. We foresee two limitations to our current implementation of ESVs: (i) when the model's output for a given class is too small ϵ, frame-level ESVs are uninformative; (ii) when frame-level features are similar for multiple frames in the input sequence, our implementation calculates ESV for each independently, and does not benefit from feature similarities.

3 Experiments

We have now explained how ESVs can be computed in a tractable manner for all elements in a variable-length sequence. While our approach is applicable to sequences of any type of data, in this paper we focus on frames in video sequences. We compare ESV against baselines and two other commonly used feature attribution methods in a frame ablation experiment. We show that the

---

Algorithm 1. Element Shapley Value (ESV) computation using f^{ms}

Input: A sequence $X = (x_i)_{i=1}^n : \mathbb{R}^{n \times D}$, Single-scale models $\{f^s : \mathbb{R}^{s \times D} \to \mathbb{R}^C\}_{s=1}^{n_{max}}$ comprising f^{ms}, and a class c to explain.
Output: Element Shapley Values ϕ_i^c for all $x_i \in X$
Intermediates:
$\mathcal{X}_j^s$: A subsequence of X of length s.
$\mathcal{S}_i^s, \bar{\mathcal{S}}_i^s$: Sum of scores over sequences that contain/don't contain element x_i at scale s.
$\mathcal{N}_i^s, \bar{\mathcal{N}}_i^s$: Number of sequences that contain/don't contain element x_i at scale s.
$\mathcal{F}_j^s$: Results of f_c^{ms} on the subsequence $\mathcal{X}_j^s$.

1: $\bar{\mathcal{S}}_i^0 \leftarrow f_c(\emptyset),\ \bar{\mathcal{N}}_i^0 \leftarrow 1,\ \mathcal{X}^0 \leftarrow \{\{\}\}$
2: **for** iteration from 0 to max iterations **do**
3:      **for** scale s from 1 to n **do**
4:          $\mathcal{C}^s$: Form extended subsequence candidate pool according to Eq. (10).
5:          $\mathcal{X}^s \leftarrow$ Randomly select $\min(m, |\mathcal{C}^s|)$ subsequences from $\mathcal{C}^s$.
6:          $Z_j \leftarrow \sum_k \mathbb{1}[\mathcal{X}_k^{s-1} \subset \mathcal{X}_j^s]$
7:          **if** $s = 1$ **then**
8:              $\mathcal{F}_j^1 \leftarrow f_c^1(\mathcal{X}_j^s)$
9:          **else if** $s \leq n_{max}$ **then**
10:             $\mathcal{F}_j^s \leftarrow \frac{1}{s}\left(f_c^s(\mathcal{X}_j^s) + (s-1)\frac{1}{Z_j}\sum_k \mathbb{1}[\mathcal{X}_k^{s-1} \subset \mathcal{X}_j^s]\mathcal{F}_k^{s-1}\right)$
11:         **else**
12:             $\mathcal{F}_j^s \leftarrow \frac{s-1}{s}\frac{1}{Z_j}\sum_k \mathbb{1}[\mathcal{X}_k^{s-1} \subset \mathcal{X}_j^s]\mathcal{F}_k^{s-1}$
13:         $\mathcal{S}_i^s \leftarrow \mathcal{S}_i^s + \sum_j \mathbb{1}[x_i \in \mathcal{X}_j^s]\mathcal{F}_j^s,\quad \bar{\mathcal{S}}_i^s \leftarrow \bar{\mathcal{S}}_i^s + \sum_j \mathbb{1}[x_i \notin \mathcal{X}_j^s]\mathcal{F}_j^s$
14:         $\mathcal{N}_i^s \leftarrow \mathcal{N}_i^s + \sum_j \mathbb{1}[x_i \in \mathcal{X}_j^s],\quad \bar{\mathcal{N}}_i^s \leftarrow \bar{\mathcal{N}}_i^s + \sum_j \mathbb{1}[x_i \notin \mathcal{X}_j^s]$
15: $\phi_i^c \leftarrow \frac{1}{|X|}\sum_{s=1}^{|X|} \mathcal{S}_i^s/\mathcal{N}_i^s - \bar{\mathcal{S}}_i^{s-1}/\bar{\mathcal{N}}_i^{s-1}$

---

choice of attribution method can have a big impact on the frames' attribution values. We then analyse exact ESVs across a range of facets demonstrating how they can be used to understand models' behaviour. Finally, we evaluate our proposed approximation showing that we can scale up our method to compute ESVs for all frames in variable-length videos.

Experimental Setup. Our experiments are conducted on the validation set of the large-scale Something-Something v2 dataset [10], frequently used to probe video models [1,29,33] due to its fine-grained nature, large number of classes (174), and the temporal characteristics of most of its classes e.g. "Pulling [...] from behind of [...]". Unless otherwise stated, ϕ_i^c is calculated for the ground-truth class of the example video. We implement f^{ms} using single hidden-layer MLPs atop of extracted features with $n_{max} = 8$.

ESV is best applied to models where frame level features are extracted and combined through a temporal module. In this case, only the temporal module is evaluated to compute the ESVs. We primarily explain one commonly used action recognition model: Temporal Relational Network (TRN) [1]. However, we also use ESVs to explain Temporal Segment Network (TSN) [34], and provide open-source code for explaining other models[3]. Further implementation and training details can be found in Appendix C in addition to how we compute ESVs for TSN.

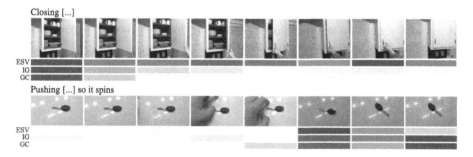

Fig. 2. Element attributions for two example sequences comparing our method (ESV) to Integrated Gradients (IG), and Grad-CAM (GC). ▇ 0 ⊞

3.1 Analysing Element Shapley Values

Our analysis is provided by answering questions that give new insights into how individual frames contribute to the model's output.

How do ESVs Differ from Other Attribution Methods? We compare ESV against Integrated Gradients (IG) [17] and Grad-CAM[4] (GC) [20]. These methods produce attributions for each feature, so to obtain element attributions, we

---

[3] https://github.com/willprice/play-fair/.

[4] We remove the ReLU from the formulation to produce signed attributions.

marginalise the spatial and channel dimensions by averaging. We chose GC as the most-commonly used approach in explaining networks for video-understanding (e.g. [35–38]) and IG as an axiomatic approach based on Aumann-Shapley values [39], an extension of the Shapley value to infinite player games. IG computes the integral of gradients along a path from a reference to the input being explained (we use the mean frame feature as our reference). We use the public implementation of these approaches from Captum [40].

We first present a qualitative comparison on two sequences in Fig. 2 demonstrating disagreement amongst the methods in their element attributions. The top example ("Closing [...]") shows that our method (ESV) highlights the first frame showing the open cupboard as well as the frame where the cupboard door has just been closed as the most important. Both IG and GC only highlight the first frame, missing the action completion, with GC considering the completion as marginally distracting. In the bottom example, ESV assigns the first three frames negative attributions, with positive attributions restricted to frames after the hand appears. ESV considers the frame with the visibly spinning key as most important while IG and SG highlight the last frame instead.

We compute the Pearson correlation between the attribution values produced by each pair of methods on the validation set. For ESV×IG, ESV×GC and IG×GC we get 0.60, 0.56 and 0.81 respectively for TRN compared to 0.85, 0.89 and 0.82 for TSN. We note that agreement differs per model. IG is more similar to GC when analysing TRN, but more similar to ESV when analysing TSN model attributions. Critically, we believe our fairness axioms and avoidance of out-of-distribution inputs make ESV a more founded technique for element attribution as we will demonstrate next.

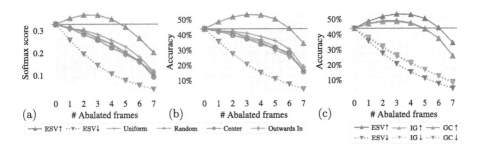

Fig. 3. TRN class score and accuracy after iteratively discarding frames in order of their attribution rank (ascending ▲ vs descending ▼). We compare our method (ESV) to baselines (a, b) and two alternate attribution methods (c): GradCam (GC) and Integrated Gradients (IG). We keep figures (b) and (c) separate for readability. Removing frames with the highest ESV first causes the quickest degradation, whilst removing frames with the lowest ESV improves performance by avoiding distractor frames.

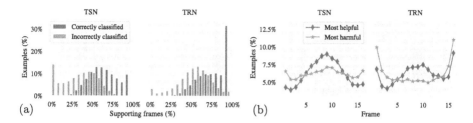

Fig. 4. (a) The percentage of supporting frames for correctly/incorrectly classified examples, comparing TSN to TRN. (b) % of examples where the frame is the most supporting/distracting show that TSN/TRN make use of frames in different positions.

How Does Performance Change When We Discard Frames According to their? For TRN, we iteratively discard frames from the input sequence in descending/ascending order of their attributions. We compare this approach to four baselines: discarding frames from the center frame outwards, from the edges of the sequence inwards, uniformly, and randomly. Figures 3a and 3b report results of this investigation on the full validation set uniformly sampling 8 frames from each video. Whilst a boost in performance is expected when removing frames with the lowest attribution value, since this approach has privileged knowledge of the ground-truth class, these figures show that (i) on average, 4 frames in an 8-frame sequence negatively influence the class score, and (ii) it is possible to maintain the model's accuracy whilst discarding the majority (6/8) of the frames.

We perform the same test, discarding frames by attribution rank for ESV, IG and GC in Fig. 3c. When discarding 4 frames by their decreasing rank, the model's accuracy increases by 20% for ESV compared to 8% for GC and 7% for IG. These results demonsrate that ESV's attribution values are more representative of how the model values frames compared to the other attribution methods.

What Can We Learn from *Supporting* and *Distracting* Frames? We analyse the proportion of supporting frames across correctly and incorrectly classified examples in Fig. 4a, comparing TRN to TSN. Correctly classified examples are more likely to have a larger proportion of supporting frames, however a number of correctly classified videos contain *distracting* frames. There are more supporting frames for TRN compared to TSN for correctly classified examples.

Is There a Correlation Between a Frame's Position in the Sequence and Its ESV? We consider the proportion of videos where each frame, by its position in the sequence, is the most helpful or harmful in Fig. 4b. The first/last frames are often the most impactful for TRN, as the model learns temporal relationships.

We further analyse TRN, reporting the percentage of videos for which $\phi_i^c > \phi_j^c$ for all combinations of frame positions i and j across the validation set as well as per-class. Figure 5 shows that (i) frames residing in the middle of the

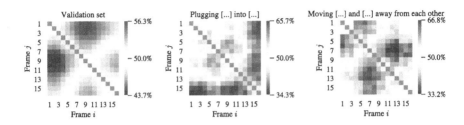

Fig. 5. Comparing the percentage of videos where $\phi_i^c > \phi_j^c$ for TRN. This shows that, across the dataset, some frames are on average more informative than others, and for certain classes this can be quite different to the overall trend.

sequence have higher attributions on average than those at the edges; (ii) class trends can deviate from this distinctly. The later frames for the class "Plugging [...] into [...]" are most important, as these are the ones that discriminate it from the similar action "Plugging [...] into [...] but pulling it right out"; (iii) Early frames from "Moving [...] and [...] away from each other" contribute most, as the objects move further from one another as the video progresses.

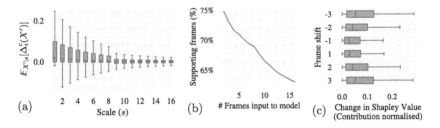

Fig. 6. TRN: (a) Box-plot of marginal contributions at each scale. (b) Increasing the number of frames fed to the model decreases the percentage of supporting frames. (c) Change in ESV when compared to neighbouring frames.

How Do Subsequences of Various Lengths Contribute to the ESV?
Since ESV is the average of the marginal contributions of subsequences at each scale, we analyse the per-scale average marginal contributions to probe the contribution of subsequences of a certain length s (Fig. 6a). The average marginal contributions steadily decreases as longer subsequences are considered, indicating that the majority of the frame's attribution is already extracted from shorter subsequences. We then consider whether there is a relationship between the number of frames fed to the model and the proportion of supporting frames in Fig. 6b. The longer the subsequence, the more likely it is some frames become redundant and potentially distracting. This is an interesting finding—it showcases that utilising all frames in the sequence could harm model performance in the presence of distracting frames.

Are ESVs Temporally Smooth? We modify 16-frame sequences by replacing one frame in the uniformly sampled sequence with the frame 1, 2, or 3 places to the left/right. We compute the normalised difference in ESV[5] for the original and replaced frame. We plot the distribution of changes in Fig. 6c. The figure shows a general trend of temporal smoothness, symmetric for both left/right shifts; the further the shift in either direction, the greater the change in ESV.

What About Class-Contrastive ESVs? Up to this point we have focused on ESVs for one class, the ground truth class of a video. We present qualitative examples of class-contrastive ESVs in Fig. 7. These show which frames contribute more to the ground-truth class than the predicted class. In the top sequence, the first frames confuse the model contributing more to "Pulling [...] from left to right". Frames when the battery is rolling contribute highly to the ground truth class. The second sequence shows that plugging the cable into the laptop contributes to both the predicted and ground truth class, but there is insufficient support from the frame where the cable is unplugged to make the correct classification.

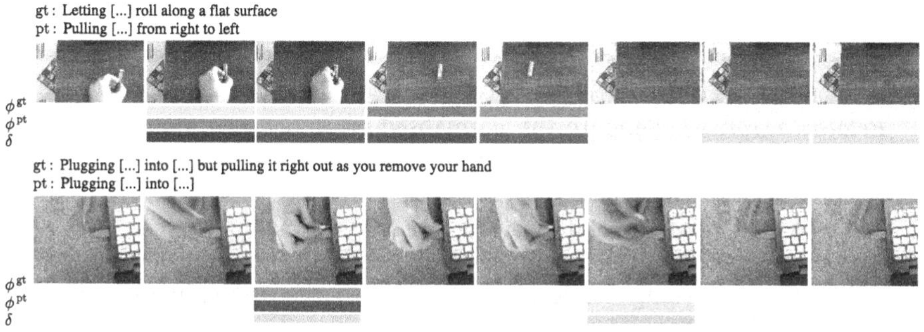

Fig. 7. Class-contrastive ESVs comparing the ground truth class (gt) to the predicted class (pt). − 0 +

3.2 ESV Approximation Evaluation

We now evaluate our ability to approximate Shapley values through our tractable approach proposed in Sect. 2.3. We first compare approximate to exact ESVs on 16 frame sequences (longer sequences limited by GPU memory). We then scale up our analysis to compute ESVs for all frames in variable-length videos and show approximate ESVs are consistent with those computed exactly for shorter sequences.

In Algorithm 1, we sample m subsequences per scale every iteration. We compare the approximate ESV $\hat{\phi}_i^c$ produced by subsequence sampling against exact

[5] As the contributions vary between sequences, we first normalise the ESVs so that the mass of contributions sum to one before comparing them, i.e. $\sum |\phi_i^c| = 1$.

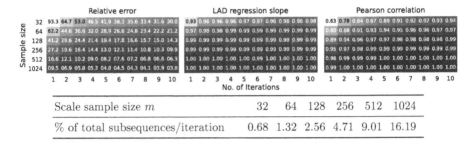

Fig. 8. Comparing approximate vs. exact ESVs for 16-frame videos, as we vary m, the maximum number of subsequences at each scale, (y-axis) and the number of iterations (x-axis). For relative error, lower is better, and for LAD regression slope and Pearson correlation, closer to one is better. The table shows % of subsequences sampled per iteration as m varies.

ESV ϕ_i^c, to assess the error introduced by approximation. For this assessment, we randomly sample 1,000 videos where $f'_c(X) \geq 0.05$ so the ESVs aren't so small as to compromise the approximation evaluation. We then uniformly sample 16 frames from each video. We consider three evaluation metrics to assess the effect of sampling:

1. *Relative error*, we compute the normalised error between approximate and exact ESVs per element $|(\hat{\phi}_i^c - \phi_i^c)|/A$ where $A = \frac{1}{|X|}\sum_j |\phi_j^c|$ is the video-level mean of the unsigned ESVs.
2. *Bias*, we fit a Least Absolute Deviance (LAD) regression between ϕ_i^c and $\hat{\phi}_i^c$. A regression slope < 1 shows an over-estimate.
3. *Correlation*, we compute Pearson's r between the approximate and exact ESVs computed for each video.

These metrics are computed per video and averaged across all videos. We present the results in Fig. 8 and demonstrate the efficiency of the sampling by reporting the percentage of subsequences sampled per iteration, for various m values in the table underneath. For instance, at $m = 256$ over 4 iterations, we would have considered less than 19% of all subsequences, but would achieve $r = 0.99$ and no bias in the approximation. Increasing the sample size m and/or number of iterations improves all metrics. Similar to Fig. 1, in Fig. 9 we plot ESVs computed for all 49 frames in a video. Without approximation we would require 10^{14} evaluations of f^{ms}, but with our approximation requires only 49k evaluations.

4   Related Work

Feature Attribution. These techniques can be categorised into backprop [17, 20,23,23,35,41–44] or perturbation based [16,22,24,43,45] methods. Backprop methods either use standard or modified backpropagation rules to work out a

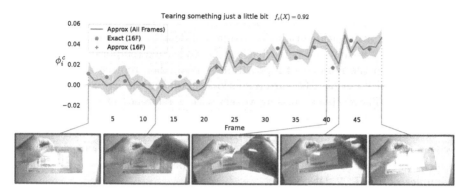

Fig. 9. ESVs for all frames computed using our approximation method (we plot the mean ESVs over 10 runs of our algorithm and shade $\mu \pm \sigma$, $m = 1024$ with 4 iterations). We also plot the approximate and exact ESVs for 16 uniformly sampled frames demonstrating these are representative of the ESVs for longer sequences.

feature's contribution to an output neuron. These are more attractive computationally, as they don't require multiple model evaluations, but often don't satisfy expected principles of an attribution method such as implementation invariance, sensitivity to the input or the model parameters [17,46]. Grad-CAM [20] is most popular, but a variety of others exist [21,23,35,42–44].

In contrast, perturbation-based methods evaluate the model on perturbed inputs. Occlusion [43] was first utilised, sliding an occluding patch over the image and evaluating the change in the model's output. Štrumbelj and Kononenko [14] proposed the use of Shapley values as a model explanation, initially retraining a model on every possible subset of features, but later [15] using feature substitution. SHAP [16] unified various attribution methods [23,25,44] by showing how each could compute or approximate Shapley values under certain assumptions (e.g. feature independence, model linearity).

Recent hybrid approaches combine perturbation with backprop [17,22,24]. Integrated gradients (IG) [17] uses Aumann-Shapley values [39] to compute feature attributions for differentiable models, however the method requires a reference and evaluates the model on out-of-distribution examples generated by linearly interpolating between the input and the reference. Meaningful perturbations [24] learn a mask to retain the most important pixels in an input image to a class neuron. They add regularisers to encourage sparsity and contiguous region formation. Extremal perturbations [22] address some of the shortcomings of [24] such as the non-uniqueness of masks. Both works [22,24] produce binary masks, rather than pixel attributions.

Explaining Video Models. Most works [29,35–38,41] in attribution for video understanding use backprop methods originally designed for images, such as Grad-CAM [20] or EBP [21]. A few recent works propose video-specific attribution methods. EBP-RNN [41] extends EBP [21] to CNN+RNN to explain video models. Saliency tubes[47] use a Grad-CAM like formulation to provide spatio-temporal attributions of the last convolutional layer. They extend the approach in [48] by backpropagating gradients to different depths in the network. Mänttäri et al. [29] apply meaningful perturbations [24] to learn a temporal mask over the input. To keep the number of input frames fixed, they replace missing frames by duplication. Li et al. [30] learn a spatio-temporal mask via extremal perturbations [22]. They replace missing voxels with a reference of a blurred voxel, analysing R(2+1)D [49] and a CNN+LSTM model.

In contrast to these works, we offer the first perturbation method for video explanation that is based on the Shapley axioms of fairness. Our method obeys principled criteria (Sect. 2.1) and does not feed models with out-of-distribution examples as in [17, 22, 24].

Alternate efforts in explaining video models take a network-centric approach. Feichtenhofer et al. [50] use activation maximisation [42] to explain a variety of two-stream architectures [34, 51, 52], synthesizing inputs that maximally activate a chosen class neuron. Huang et al. [32] explain the temporal signal in video by training a temporal generative model to produce within-distribution videos of shorter or re-ordered frames. They explain C3D [53] on a fixed-length sequence, analysing the model's performance drop. These approaches offer a complimentary viewpoint to model explanations, and do not attempt frame attributions.

5   Conclusion

In this paper, we introduced the notion of element attribution for determining the contribution of each frame to the output of an action recognition model. We adopted the Shapley axioms as a way of determining these contributions in a fair and principled manner in our proposed Element Shapley Value (ESV). We side-step the issues present in feature-attribution by reformulating the Shapley value and utilise multi-scale models to determine the marginal contributions of frames without having to substitute them. We used ESV to analyse frame-based action recognition models on the Something-something dataset, showing insights into how trained models make classification decisions.

Acknowledgement. Research supported by EPSRC UMPIRE (EP/T004991/1) and EPSRC Doctoral Training Partnershipts (DTP).

References

1. Zhou, B., Andonian, A., Oliva, A., Torralba, A.: Temporal relational reasoning in videos. In: Proceedings of the European Conference on Computer Vision (ECCV), pp. 803–818 (2018)
2. Tran, D., Wang, H., Torresani, L., Ray, J., LeCun, Y., Paluri, M.: A closer look at spatiotemporal convolutions for action recognition. In: Proceedings of the IEEE Conference on Computer Vision and Pattern Recognition (CVPR), pp. 6450–6459 (2018)
3. Hussein, N., Gavves, E., Smeulders, A.W.M.: Timeception for complex action recognition. In: Proceedings of the IEEE Conference on Computer Vision and Pattern Recognition (CVPR), pp. 254–263 (2019)

4. Girdhar, R., Carreira, J., Doersch, C., Zisserman, A.: Video action transformer network. In: Proceedings of the IEEE Conference on Computer Vision and Pattern Recognition (CVPR), pp. pp. 244–253 (2019)
5. Chen, Y., Kalantidis, Y., Li, J., Yan, S., Feng, J.: Multi-fiber networks for video recognition. In: Ferrari, V., Hebert, M., Sminchisescu, C., Weiss, Y. (eds.) ECCV 2018. LNCS, vol. 11205, pp. 364–380. Springer, Cham (2018). https://doi.org/10.1007/978-3-030-01246-5_22
6. Lin, J., Gan, C., Han, S.: TSM: temporal shift module for efficient video understanding. In: Proceedings of the IEEE Conference on Computer Vision and Pattern Recognition (CVPR), pp. 7083–7093 (2019)
7. Feichtenhofer, C., Fan, H., Malik, J., He, K.: SlowFast networks for video recognition. In: Proceedings of the IEEE Conference on Computer Vision and Pattern Recognition (CVPR), pp. 6202–6211 (2019)
8. Abu-El-Haija, S., et al.: YouTube-8M: a large-scale video classification benchmark. ArXiv160908675 Cs (2016)
9. Kay, W., et al.: The kinetics human action video dataset. ArXiv170506950 Cs (2017)
10. Goyal, R., et al.: The "Something something" video database for learning and evaluating visual common sense. In: Proceedings of the IEEE International Conference on Computer Vision (ICCV) (2017)
11. Diba, A., et al.: Large scale holistic video understanding. In: Vedaldi, A., Bischof, H., Brox, T., Frahm, J.-M. (eds.) ECCV 2020. LNCS, vol. 12350, pp. 593–610. Springer, Cham (2020). https://doi.org/10.1007/978-3-030-58558-7_35
12. Gu, C., et al: AVA: a video dataset of spatio-temporally localized atomic visual actions. In: Proceedings of the IEEE Conference on Computer Vision and Pattern Recognition (CVPR), pp. 6047–6056 (2018)
13. Damen, D., et al.: Scaling Egocentric vision: the EPIC-KITCHENS dataset. In: Proceedings of the European Conference on Computer Vision (ECCV), pp. 720–736 (2018)
14. Štrumbelj, E., Kononenko, I.: An efficient explanation of individual classifications using game theory. J. Mach. Learn. Res. **11**, 1–18 (2010)
15. Štrumbelj, E., Kononenko, I.: Explaining prediction models and individual predictions with feature contributions. Knowl. Inf. Syst. **41**, 647–665 (2014)
16. Lundberg, S.M., Lee, S.I.:A unified approach to interpreting model predictions. In: Guyon, I., et al. (eds.) Advances in Neural Information Processing Systems (NeurIPS), vol. 30, pp. 4765–4774. Curran Associates, Inc. (2017)
17. Sundararajan, M., Taly, A., Yan, Q.: axiomatic attribution for deep networks. In: Proceedings of the 34th International Conference on Machine Learning (ICML), ICML 2017, Sydney, NSW, Australia, pp. 3319–3328. JMLR.org (2017)
18. Sundararajan, M., Najmi, A.: The many shapley values for model explanation. In: Proceedings of the 37th International Conference on Machine Learning (ICML), ICML 2020 (2020)
19. Shapley, L.S.: A value for n-person games. In: Contributions to the Theory of Games (AM-28), vol. II. Princeton University Press, Princeton (1953)
20. Selvaraju, R.R., Cogswell, M., Das, A., Vedantam, R., Parikh, D., Batra, D.: Grad-CAM: visual explanations from deep networks via gradient-based localization. In: Proceedings of the IEEE International Conference on Computer Vision (ICCV), pp. 618–626 (2017)
21. Zhang, J., Bargal, S.A., Lin, Z., Brandt, J., Shen, X., Sclaroff, S.: Top-down neural attention by excitation Backprop. Int. J. Comput. Vis. **126**, 1084–1102 (2018)

22. Fong, R., Patrick, M., Vedaldi, A.: Understanding deep networks via extremal perturbations and smooth masks. In: Proceedings of the IEEE International Conference on Computer Vision (ICCV), pp. 2950–2958 (2019)
23. Bach, S., Binder, A., Montavon, G., Klauschen, F., Müller, K.R., Samek, W.: On pixel-wise explanations for non-linear classifier decisions by layer-wise relevance propagation. PLoS One **10**, e0130140 (2015)
24. Fong, R.C., Vedaldi, A.: Interpretable explanations of black boxes by meaningful perturbation. In: Proceedings of the IEEE International Conference on Computer Vision (ICCV), pp. 3429–3437 (2017)
25. Ribeiro, M.T., Singh, S., Guestrin, C.: "Why should i trust you?": explaining the predictions of any classifier. In: Proceedings of the 22nd ACM International Conference on Knowledge Discovery and Data Mining (SIGKDD), KDD 2016, San Francisco, California, USA, pp. 1135–1144. Association for Computing Machinery (2016)
26. Carreira, J., Zisserman, A.: Quo vadis, action recognition? A new model and the kinetics dataset. In: Proceedings of the IEEE Conference on Computer Vision and Pattern Recognition (CVPR), pp. 6299–6308 (2017)
27. Young, H.P.: Monotonic solutions of cooperative games. Int. J. Game Theory **14**, 65–72 (1985)
28. Štrumbelj, E., Kononenko, I., Robnik Šikonja, M.: Explaining instance classifications with interactions of subsets of feature values. Data Knowl. Eng. **68**, 886–904 (2009)
29. Mänttäri, J., Broomé, S., Folkesson, J., Kjellström, H.: Interpreting video features: a comparison of 3D convolutional networks and convolutional LSTM networks. ArXiv200200367 Cs (2020)
30. Li, Z., Wang, W., Li, Z., Huang, Y., Sato, Y.: A comprehensive study on visual explanations for spatio-temporal networks. ArXiv200500375 Cs (2020)
31. Sturmfels, P., Lundberg, S., Lee, S.I.: Visualizing the impact of feature attribution baselines. Distill **5**, e22 (2020)
32. Huang, D.A., et al.: What makes a video a video: analyzing temporal information in video understanding models and datasets. In: Proceedings of the IEEE Conference on Computer Vision and Pattern Recognition (CVPR), pp. 7366–7375 (2018)
33. Dwibedi, D., Sermanet, P., Tompson, J.: Temporal reasoning in videos using convolutional gated recurrent units. In: Proceedings of the IEEE Conference on Computer Vision and Pattern Recognition Workshops (CVPRW), pp. 1111–1116 (2018)
34. Wang, L., et al.: Temporal segment networks: towards good practices for deep action recognition. In: Leibe, B., Matas, J., Sebe, N., Welling, M. (eds.) ECCV 2016. LNCS, vol. 9912, pp. 20–36. Springer, Cham (2016). https://doi.org/10.1007/978-3-319-46484-8_2
35. Chattopadhay, A., Sarkar, A., Howlader, P., Balasubramanian, V.N.: Grad-CAM++: generalized gradient-based visual explanations for deep convolutional networks. In: 2018 IEEE Winter Conference on Applications of Computer Vision (WACV), pp. 839–847 (2018)
36. Doughty, H., Damen, D., Mayol-Cuevas, W.: Who's better? Who's best? Pairwise deep ranking for skill determination. In: Proceedings of the IEEE Conference on Computer Vision and Pattern Recognition (CVPR), pp. 6057–6066 (2018)
37. Goyal, R., Mahdisoltani, F., Berger, G., Gharbieh, W., Bax, I., Memisevic, R.: Evaluating visual "common sense" using fine-grained classification and captioning tasks. In: 6th International Conference on Learning Representations, Workshop Track Proceedings (ICLRW) (2018)

38. Srinivasan, V., Lapuschkin, S., Hellge, C., Müller, K.R., Samek, W.: Interpretable human action recognition in compressed domain. In: 2017 IEEE International Conference on Acoustics, Speech and Signal Processing (ICASSP), pp. 1692–1696 (2017)
39. Aumann, R.J., Shapley, L.S.: Values of Non-Atomic Games. Princeton University Press, Princeton (1974)
40. Kokhlikyan, N., et al.: PyTorch captum. GitHub Repos (2019)
41. Adel Bargal, S., Zunino, A., Kim, D., Zhang, J., Murino, V., Sclaroff, S.: Excitation backprop for RNNs. In: Proceedings of the IEEE Conference on Computer Vision and Pattern Recognition (CVPR), pp. 1440–1449 (2018)
42. Simonyan, K., Vedaldi, A., Zisserman, A.: Deep inside convolutional networks: visualising image classification models and saliency maps. In: Bengio, Y., LeCun, Y. (eds.) 2nd International Conference on Learning Representations (ICLR) (2014)
43. Zeiler, M.D., Fergus, R.: Visualizing and understanding convolutional networks. In: Fleet, D., Pajdla, T., Schiele, B., Tuytelaars, T. (eds.) ECCV 2014. LNCS, vol. 8689, pp. 818–833. Springer, Cham (2014). https://doi.org/10.1007/978-3-319-10590-1_53
44. Shrikumar, A., Greenside, P., Kundaje, A.: Learning important features through propagating activation differences. ArXiv170402685 Cs (2019)
45. Petsiuk, V., Das, A., Saenko, K.: RISE: randomized input sampling for explanation of black-box models. In: British Machine Vision Conference 2018 (BMVC), p. 151. BMVA Press (2018)
46. Adebayo, J., Gilmer, J., Muelly, M., Goodfellow, I., Hardt, M., Kim, B.: Sanity checks for saliency maps. In: Bengio, S., Wallach, H., Larochelle, H., Grauman, K., Cesa-Bianchi, N., Garnett, R. (eds.) Advances in Neural Information Processing Systems (NeurIPS), vol. 31, pp. 9505–9515. Curran Associates, Inc. (2018)
47. Stergiou, A., Kapidis, G., Kalliatakis, G., Chrysoulas, C., Veltkamp, R., Poppe, R.: Saliency tubes: visual explanations for spatio-temporal convolutions. In: 2019 IEEE International Conference on Image Processing (ICIP), pp. 1830–1834 (2019)
48. Stergiou, A., Kapidis, G., Kalliatakis, G., Chrysoulas, C., Poppe, R., Veltkamp, R.: Class Feature Pyramids for Video Explanation. In: Proceedings of the IEEE/CVF International Conference on Computer Vision Workshops (ICCVW), pp. 4255–4264 (2019)
49. Xie, S., Sun, C., Huang, J., Tu, Z., Murphy, K.: Rethinking spatiotemporal feature learning: speed-accuracy trade-offs in video classification. In: Proceedings of the European Conference on Computer Vision (ECCV), pp. 305–321 (2018)
50. Feichtenhofer, C., Pinz, A., Wildes, R.P., Zisserman, A.: Deep insights into convolutional networks for video recognition. Int. J. Comput. Vis. **128**, 420–437 (2020)
51. Feichtenhofer, C., Pinz, A., Wildes, R.: Spatiotemporal residual networks for video action recognition. In: Lee, D.D., Sugiyama, M., Luxburg, U.V., Guyon, I., Garnett, R. (eds.) Advances in Neural Information Processing Systems (NeurIPS), vol. 29. Curran Associates, Inc. (2016) 3468–3476
52. Feichtenhofer, C., Pinz, A., Zisserman, A.: Convolutional two-stream network fusion for video action recognition. In: Proceedings of the IEEE Conference on Computer Vision and Pattern Recognition (CVPR), pp. 1933–1941 (2016)
53. Tran, D., Bourdev, L., Fergus, R., Torresani, L., Paluri, M.: Learning spatiotemporal features with 3D convolutional networks. In: Proceedings of the 2015 IEEE International Conference on Computer Vision (ICCV), ICCV 2015, Washington, DC, USA, pp. 4489–4497. IEEE Computer Society (2015)

Transforming Multi-concept Attention into Video Summarization

Yen-Ting Liu[1]([✉]), Yu-Jhe Li[2]([✉]), and Yu-Chiang Frank Wang[1]([✉])

[1] National Taiwan University, Taipei, Taiwan
{r06942114,ycwang}@ntu.edu.tw
[2] Carnegie Mellon University, Pittsburgh, PA, USA
yujheli@cs.cmu.edu

Abstract. Video summarization is among the challenging tasks in computer vision, which aims at identifying highlight frames or shots over a lengthy video input. In this paper, we propose a novel attention-based framework for video summarization with complex video data. Unlike previous works which only apply attention mechanism on the correspondence between frames, our *multi-concept video self-attention (MC-VSA)* model is presented to identify informative regions across temporal and concept video features, which jointly exploit context diversity over time and space for summarization purposes. Together with consistency between video and summary enforced in our framework, our model can be applied to both labeled and unlabeled data, making our method preferable to real-world applications. Extensive and complete experiments on two benchmarks demonstrate the effectiveness of our model both quantitatively and qualitatively, and confirms its superiority over the state-of-the-arts.

1   Introduction

Video summarization [1–4] aims at identifying highlighted video frames or shots, which is among the challenging tasks in computer vision and machine learning. Real-world applications such as video surveillance, video understanding and retrieval would benefit from successful video summarization outputs. To address this challenging task, several deep learning-based models [5–9] employing long short-term memory (LSTM) cells [10] have been recently proposed. However, the use of such recurrent neural network (RNN) based techniques might fail if the length of the input video is long [11]. Therefore, even the training video data are with ground-truth labels, there is no guarantee that RNN-based models would achieve satisfactory results using the last output state. To address the aforementioned issue, several approaches (also based on deep learning) are proposed [12–14]. For example, [12,13] advances hierarchical structure LSTMs to capture longer video, which is shown to be able to handle video with longer

Electronic supplementary material The online version of this chapter (https://doi.org/10.1007/978-3-030-69541-5_30) contains supplementary material, which is available to authorized users.

ⓒ Springer Nature Switzerland AG 2021
H. Ishikawa et al. (Eds.): ACCV 2020, LNCS 12626, pp. 498–513, 2021.
https://doi.org/10.1007/978-3-030-69541-5_30

lengths. [14] proposes SUM-FCN which considers a CNN-based semantic segmentation model to deal with videos while alleviating the above concern. Yet, these existing techniques might not exhibit capabilities in modeling the relationship between video frames, since they generally treat each frame equally important. Thus, their summarization performance might be limited.

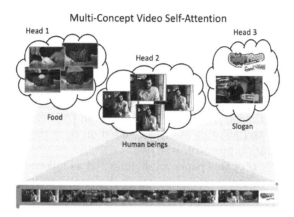

Fig. 1. Illustration of advancing self-attention while preserving visual diversity for video summarization. Noted that Head 1 to 3 denote attention performed in a subspace, which describes proper visual concept information across frames. We proposed a multi-concept video self-attention (MC-VSA) framework for solving this task.

To advance the attention mechanism for video summarization, a number of methods are recently proposed [15–17]. With the ability of learning importance weights across all video frames, attention-based models are expected to be more robust while it is still able to tackle lengthy video as well as the video semantic meanings. For example, [16] firstly proposes an attentive video summarization model (AVS) for improved attention on summarization tasks. [17] also employs attention models for properly identifying video shot boundaries. Nevertheless, these attention-based methods might not generalize to general videos with complex content information, since they typically perform attention on pre-selected feature representations or latent spaces. To make a summarization model more robust to real-world video, one needs to better observe and relate the temporal-concept information within and across video frames, rather than exclusively attend correlation between frames in the video.

In this paper, we propose a novel attention-based deep learning framework for video summarization. With the goal to attend temporally and concept informative features for summarization in the sense, we present a *multi-concept video self-attention (MC-VSA)* model in a discriminative learning mechanism. Based on the idea of [18], we add the multi-head attention mechanism in our model to transform input video frames features into different subspaces. Different from the previous attention model [15–17], this allows us to exploit a variety of visual appearances during the attention process, and thus identify visual concept informative regions across frames for both *summarization* and *video semantic consistency* purposes, which we call multi-concept attention cross whole video time step (temporal and concept attention).

Take an example as illustrated in Fig. 1, it would be desirable to be able to extract different visual concepts corresponding to different semantics or objects with the highlight guidance, so that the joint attention across these concepts would allow satisfactory video summarization outputs. More importantly, our learning framework can be generalized well in a semi-supervised setting, i.e., only a number of training data are with ground-truth labels. More details of our proposed framework will be presented in Sect. 3. In addition, we found that the current evaluation protocol using pre-defined procedure has some problems [3,19] (e.p., random summaries outperform even the human-generated summaries in leave-one-out experiments), which are mentioned in [20]. Therefore, our quantitative experiment and ablation study are based on both the current [3,19] and the new [20] evaluation protocol.

The contributions of this paper are highlighted as follows:

- We present a multi-concept video self-attention model (MC-VSA) that aims at attending temporally and concept informative features via transforming input video frames in different subspaces, which is beneficial to video summarization purposes.
- We are among the first to propose the attention-based framework that observes semantic consistency between input videos and learned summarization outputs, which allows the video summarization model can be generalized in semi-supervised settings.
- Experimental results on benchmark datasets confirm that our proposed method achieves favorable performances against the state-of-the-art approaches in two evaluation protocols.

2 Related Work

Video Summarization. Video summarization is among the active research topics in computer vision. Several deep methods [5–9] developed for video summarization choose to employ long short-term memory (LSTM) cells [10]. For instance, [5] consider video summarization as a key-frame/shot selection task, and propose an LSTM-based model for addressing this task. Since most of the videos contain hundreds even thousands of frames, it might not be easy for LSTMs to handle such long-term temporal dependency of videos. Hence, some existing approaches [12–14] are further developed to deal with long videos. [12,13] propose a hierarchical structure of RNN to exploit intra and inter-shot temporal dependency via two LSTM layers, respectively. Such a hierarchical structure is considered to be more preferable for handling video data with hundreds of frames. On the other hand, [14] develop fully convolutional networks for video summarization which requires less training time due to the use of parallel computation techniques. Nevertheless, solving video summarization problems typically requires one to consider the importance across video frames. Existing models generally view the contributions of each frame are equally important during their training stage, which might limit the summarization performance.

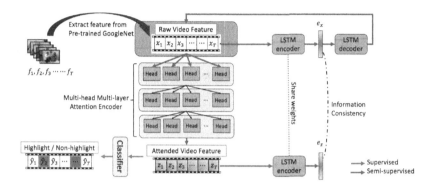

Fig. 2. Overview of our Multi-Concept Video Self-Attention (MC-VSA) for video summarization. Our MC-VSA is composed of three modules: the multi-head multi-layer attention encoder, classifier, and the LSTM-based auto-encoder module. Note that the attention encoder takes input videos $X = \{x_i\}_{i=1}^{T}$ and transforms them into attended features $Z = \{z_i\}_{i=1}^{T}$, followed by the classifier to output the associated highlight scores $\hat{y}_i$. The LSTM-based auto-encoder module preserves data representation ability while enforcing visual concept similarity, allowing guidance of self-attention for summarization purposes.

Attention Based Summarization. Attention-based models [15–17,21] have been proposed to video summarization tasks to alleviate the aforementioned problems. For example, [17] introduces an attention mechanism for detecting the shot boundaries, aiming at improving the summarization performances. An attentive encoder-decoder framework is presented in [16], with the models AVS to video summarization via matrix addition and multiplication techniques. [15] utilizes adversarial learning for visual attention with models of [22], which aims at learning a discriminator to detect highlighted fragments as a summary in the input video. Yet, these attention-based methods typically require ground-truth highlighted supervision, and thus it might not be easy to extend to the cases when such labels are not available.

Semi-supervised and Unsupervised Summarization. In order to overcome the above concerns, unsupervised [7,21] and semi-supervised [8] method have been proposed. [7] is the first unsupervised deep learning paper for video summarization, which uses GAN_{dpp} [7] with different LSTM modules to select keyframes from the input video via adversarial learning. Similarly, [21] uses transformer [18] in conditional GAN and achieve improved performance in unsupervised setting. On the other hand, [8] uses an encoder-decoder mechanism aim at enforcing similarity between the input and the summarized outputs. Nevertheless, the above models [7,8] take two different LSTM module to maintain the information consistency between raw video and the summary, which cannot ensure the video information is in the embedding from the LSTM module. Also, even though [21] improves the unsupervised model using an additional attentive module with GAN, there is still a large gap compared with SOTAs in a supervised setting, and their model lacks discussion for the attentive module. To overcome the above limitations, our MC-VSA model uses a share-weighted LSTM module to encode the video feature and attended feature (resulting in the summary later) enforcing the embedding from the LSTM encoder represents the semantic meaning of the video, and focus on the benefit the attention module brings.

3   Proposed Method

3.1   Problem Formulation and Notation

Given an input video with a total of T frames, our goal is to select the most important key-frames, about 15% of the whole video, as the summarization output. We now define the notations to be used in this paper. Assume that we have frame set $F = \{f_i\}_{f=1}^T$ with the associated label set $Y = \{y_i\}_{i=1}^T$, where $f_i \in \mathbb{R}^{H \times W \times 3}$ and $y_i \in \mathbb{R}$ represent the ith frame in the target video. To extract the visual features from the frame set F, we apply a CNN (pre-trained on ImageNet) and obtain the video feature set $X = \{x_i\}_{i=1}^T$, where $x_i \in \mathbb{R}^d$ (d denotes the dimension of the visual feature).

3.2   Overview of MC-VSA

As shown in Fig. 2, we propose a Multi-Concept Video Self-Attention model (MC-VSA) to identify the most representative frames for summarization purposes. Our Multi-Concept Video Self-Attention model is composed of three modules: the multi-head multi-layer attention encoder, classifier, and the LSTM auto encoder decoder module. First, the model takes $X = \{x_i\}_{i=1}^T$ with T sequential features as input of its attention encoder. Our attention encoder then transforms input features x_i in X into different subspaces where attention can be performed accordingly. As stated earlier, the attention encoder allows one to exploit various visual appearances during the attention process, and thus identify concept informative regions across frames.

We note that, while the learning of MC-VSA can be simply trained using unlabeled data, we further introduce the visual concept loss, which would guide the MC-VSA if the input video data is with ground-truth highlighted labels. To be more precise, we encourage the learned attention weighted features $Z = \{x_i\}_{i=1}^T$ to preserve the same video information as the original one ($X = \{x_i\}_{i=1}^T$). To achieve this, the shared LSTM encoder in our framework is designed to match latent vectors e_z and e_x from the same video, thus implying visual concept similarity. If ground-truth highlighted labels are available, the final classifier thus takes the attended features $Z = \{z_i\}_{i=1}^T$ to produce the final highlighted scores $\hat{y}_i$ for each z_i. With label supervision available, we encourage the output labels $\hat{Y} = \{\hat{y}_i\}_{i=1}^{T}$ to match the corresponding ground truths $Y = \{y_i\}_{i=1}^{T}$. More details about our MC-VSA model are elaborated in the following.

As for testing, we take the input video with T' frames and produce the final summarization outputs from $\hat{Y} = \{\hat{y}_i\}_{i=1}^{T}$. We note that our MC-VSA is able to handle a different number of frames in a video as input. The experimental results will be presented in the next section.

3.3 Video Self-attention for Summarization

The multi-head multi-layer attention encoder in our MC-VSA is inspired by the Transformer [18]. To perform concept-temporal attention from the input video, we project the "temporal" video features across video frames onto different subspaces. Each sub-space aims at observing distinct visual concepts as verified later. To be more specific, this attention encoder module is developed to transform input video frames into N subspaces by the introduced N self-attention heads, with the goal of observing and distilling potentially representative information across video frames. It then aggregates the attended results from each subspace and produces the final attended features, which can be seen as jointly incorporating the temporal and concept information. In addition, we also perform such multi-head attention across image layers to exhibit robustness in identifying representative visual concepts.

Standard Self-attention. For the sake of completeness, we briefly review the self-attention module [23]. Typical self-attention mechanisms transform the input features into three inputs: query Q, key K, and value V by matrix multiplication with transforming matrix. The softmax layer will take the result of the multiplication of Q and K, and produce the attention weights. Hence, the target attention result is produced from the result of the final matrix multiplication of softmax and the V.

Multi-concept Visual Self-attention for Video Summarization. To observe both temporal and concept information from the input video frames $F = \{f_i\}_{i=1}^{T}$, we advance the idea of multi-head multi-layer self-attention as described below. As depicted in Fig. 3, we have the attention encoder comprise of N self-attention modules (i.e., the head number equals N), and each of them is developed to derive the attended feature each of N subspaces. We firstly transform the input X into N subspace by the N projection layers P_n ($\mathbb{R}^{d^n} \leftarrow \mathbb{R}^d$) where n denotes the projection layer number ($n = 1 \sim N$) and d^n denotes the subspace dimension.

To produce the finalized attended results from all of the N subspaces, we introduce the linear projection layer M^R to derive the final attended features $R = \{r_i\}_{i=1}^{T}$, where $r_i \in \mathbb{R}^d$ (same dimention as X_i), for the original input features $X = \{x_i\}_{i=1}^{T}$, which can be formulated as:

$$R = M^R \cdot \text{concat}(O_{1:N}), \tag{1}$$

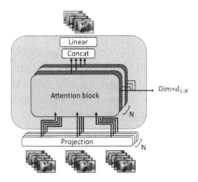

Fig. 3. Illustration of multi-head multi-layer self-attention module of our attention encoder (note that only a single layer is shown for simplicity). With N different single-head attention blocks (each with a projection matrix layer), self-attention can be performed in different subspaces (dimension d_n for each) for capturing diverse visual concepts. We concatenate the outputs $O_{1:N}$ from all attention blocks and obtain the joint attention result R at the output of the final linear transform layer.

where concat means we concatenate the outputs $O_{1:N}$ from all of the N self-attention blocks in the subspace.

To extract rich information from video, we employ L layers in the attention encoder as shown in Fig. 2. Namely, the output of R' at the first layer will be passed to the second one to produce the fine-grained output R''. Hence, the finalized attention features $Z = \{z_i\}_{i=1}^{T}$ is denoted as $Z = R^{(L)}$.

Later in our experiments, we will present example visual self-attention results produced by different heads e.g., Fig. 4 confirming that the attention encoder exhibits sufficient capability in exploiting visual appearance variations across video frames for attention.

3.4 Self-learning of Video Semantic Consistency for Video Summarization

The aforementioned attention mechanism can be viewed as a self-summarization process, but lack the ability to ensure that the attended outputs produced by the attention modules would preserve the information in the input video.

To alleviate this limitation, we apply a Siamese network based on a shared LSTM encoder and a single decoder as illustrated in Fig. 2. This shared LSTM encoder aims at deriving the compressed latent vectors e_z and e_x for the attended feature set Z and the original feature set X, while the LSTM decoder is to recover the encoded representation for reconstruction purposes. Thus, we have the reconstruction loss $\mathcal{L}_{rec}$ observe the output of this auto-encoder module:

$$\mathcal{L}_{rec} = \sum_{i=1}^{T} \|\hat{x}_i - x_i\|^2, \tag{2}$$

where $\hat{X} = \{\hat{x}_i\}_{i=1}^{T}$ denotes the reconstructed feature set and $\hat{x}_i$ indicates the ith recovered video frame feature.

More importantly, to preserve visual concept consistency, we require the encoded vectors e_z and e_x to be close if they are from the same video input. As a result, we enforce the visual concept consistency loss $\mathcal{L}_{con}$ as follows:

$$\mathcal{L}_{con} = \|e_x - e_z\|^2. \tag{3}$$

It is worth noting that, our reconstruction loss $\mathcal{L}_{rec}$ and consistency loss $\mathcal{L}_{con}$ are both computed without observing any ground-truth label. That is, the introduction of this module allows training using unlabeled video. Together with the labeled ones, our proposed framework can be learned in a semi-supervised fashion. As later verified in our experiments, this would result in promising video summarization performances when comparing against the state of the arts.

3.5 Full Objectives

As depicted in Fig. 2, our proposed framework can be learned with fully labeled video. That is, the classification layer takes the resulted attended feature set $Z = \{z_i\}_{i=1}^{T}$ to produce the final highlight potential score $\hat{y}_i$ for each attended feature z_i. More precisely, we encourage the output highlight labels $\hat{Y} = \{\hat{y}_i\}_{i=1}^{T}$ produced by our method can be closed to the ground truth $Y = \{y_i\}_{i=1}^{T}$ and the binary cross-entropy classification loss $\mathcal{L}_{cls}$ is formulated as below:

$$\mathcal{L}_{cls} = -\frac{1}{T}\sum_{t=1}^{T} y_t \, \log(\hat{y}_t) + (1 - y_t) \, \log(1 - \hat{y}_t). \tag{4}$$

Thus, the total loss $\mathcal{L}$ is summarized as:

$$\mathcal{L} = \mathcal{L}_{cls} + \mathcal{L}_{rec} + \mathcal{L}_{con}, \tag{5}$$

where $\mathcal{L}_{cls}$ is calculated by labeled data, while the $\mathcal{L}_{rec}$ and $\mathcal{L}_{con}$ are derived by both the labeled and unlabeled ones.

We note that, if there is no labeled video data is available during training, $\mathcal{L}_{cls}$ in (5) cannot be computed. Following [9,14], we train our MC-VSA in such *unsupervised* setting and introduce a diversity loss $\mathcal{L}_{div}$ (6) to (5). This modification would encourage MC-VSA to select informative yet distinct frames with representative information in an unsupervised learning scenario.

$$\mathcal{L}_{div} = \sum_{s=1}^{S} \sum_{x^s \in c^s} \sum_{\substack{x^{s\prime} \in c^s \\ x^s \neq x^{s\prime}}} d(x^s, x^{s\prime}). \tag{6}$$

4 Experiment

In this section, we first describe the datasets in Sect. 4.1, followed by the experimental protocols and implementation details in Sect. 4.2. For evaluating our MC-VSA, we present quantitative results in Sect. 4.3 and Sect. 4.4. We also provide ablation studies in Sect. 4.6. Finally, we provide qualitative results and visual analysis in Sect. 4.5.

Table 1. Comparisons with existing supervised summarization methods on SumMe and TvSum in different experimental settings. The numbers in bold and under line indicate the best and the second result.

Method	SumMe			TvSum		
	C	A	T	C	A	T
Bi-LSTM [5]	37.6	41.6	40.7	54.2	57.9	56.9
DPP-LSTM [5]	38.6	42.9	41.8	54.7	59.6	58.7
GAN_{sup} [7]	41.7	43.6	–	56.3	61.2	–
$DR-DSN_{sup}$ [9]	42.1	43.9	42.6	58.1	59.8	58.9
SUM-FCN [14]	47.5	51.1	44.1	56.8	59.2	58.2
re-SEQ2SEQ [8]	44.9	–	–	**63.9**	–	–
UnpairedVSN [24]	47.5	–	41.6	55.6	–	55.7
H-RNN [12]	44.3	–	–	62.1	–	–
HSA-RNN [13]	44.1	–	–	59.8	–	–
M-AVS [16]	44.4	46.1	–	61.0	61.8	–
VASNet [17]	49.7	51.1	–	61.4	62.4	–
MC-VSA (Ours)	**51.6**	**53.0**	**48.1**	<u>63.7</u>	**64.0**	**59.5**

Table 2. Comparisons with recent unsupervised approaches for video summarization using SumMe and TvSum. Note that * indicates the non deep-learning based methods. The number in bold indicates the best performance.

DATASET	[19]*	[7]	[14]	[9]	[24]	MC-VSA (Ours)
SumMe	26.6	39.1	41.5	41.4	**47.5**	<u>44.6</u>
TvSum	50.0	51.7	52.7	57.6	55.6	**58.0**

4.1   Datasets

We evaluate our method on two public benchmark datasets SumMe [2] and TvSum [19], and use the additional dataset: OVP and YouTube [9] in the Augmented and Transfer settings:

SumMe. SumMe consists of 25 videos with several different topics such as holidays and sports. Each video ranges from 1 to 6 min and annotated by 15 to 18 persons. Thus, there are multiple ground truth summaries for each video.

TvSum. TvSum is a larger dataset with 50 videos and includes topics like news and documentaries. The duration of each video is from 2 to 10 min. Same as SumMe, TvSum dataset has 20 annotators providing frame-level importance scores. Following [5] and [9], we convert important scores to shot-based summaries for evaluation.

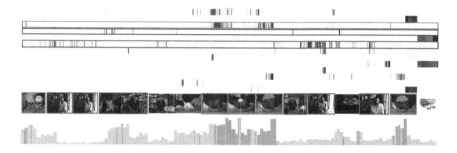

Fig. 4. Visualization example of our MC-VSA for video summarization on TvSum. We visualize selected attention maps generated by the second layer in the attention encoder, with ground truth (grey) and predicted outputs (orange) summarization shown below. Note that the attention outputs bounded in different colors (blue, red and purple) correspond to different multi visual concepts (e.g., burger, commentator, and chef) in this video. (Color figure online)

OVP and YouTube. Followed by [5] and [9], we consider two additional challenging datasets released by [9]: OVP and YouTube, which contain 50 videos and 39 videos in the augmented and transfer settings.

4.2 Protocols and Implementation Details

Evaluation Protocols. We follow the three settings adopted in [5,9,14] to evaluate our methods:

- Canonical: we use the standard supervised learning on the dataset, i.e., 80% for training and the rest for testing following previous work [5,7,9,14,16].
- Augmented: we use the standard supervised training as the canonical setting but augment the training data with OVP and YouTube datasets.
- Transfer: We use three datasets as the training data and a target dataset (e.g. SumMe or TvSum) as the testing data to evaluate the transfer ability of our model.

For a fair comparison, we follow the commonly adopted metric in previous works [5,9,14], and computed F-score to assess the similarity between automatic and ground-truth summaries. As for the training/testing data, we apply the same standard supervised learning setting as [5,7,9,14,16] where the training and testing are from the disjoint part of the same dataset. We report the results at F-score in all of the settings. To avoid the shortage with F-score, which is mentioned by [20], we additionally conduct the experiments using new protocols [20] and make comparisons with state-of-the-arts as well in Table 3.

Table 3. Ablation studies and performance comparisons on TvSum dataset. We take dppLSTM [5] and [9] for comparisons in Kendall's τ, and Spearman's ρ evaluation protocol. The number in bold denotes the best performance.

Method	w/ knapsack algo.	w/o knapsack algo.	
	F1 score	Kendall's τ	Spearman's ρ
dppLSTM	60.0	0.042	0.055
DR-DSN$_{dpp}$	58.0	0.020	0.026
[26]	58.4	0.078	0.116
VASNet	61.4	–	–
Ours (w/o attention)	59.7	0.005	0.006
Ours (1layer-1head)	60.1	0.065	0.079
Ours (3layers-24heads)	**63.7**	**0.116**	**0.142**

Implementation Details. We downsample the video data into frame sequences in 2 fps as previous work [5,9]. For fair comparisons with [5,9,14,16], we also employ GoogleNet [25] pre-trained on ImageNet as backbone as our CNN for extracting the video features while the output dimension d is 1024 (output of pool5 layer of the GoogleNet). All of the attention modules are composed of linear projection matrices as mentioned in Sect. 3. We set the number of heads N as 24 while the dimension d_n of each subspace features are set as $\{64 \,|n = 1 \sim 12\}$ and $\{128 \,|n = 13 \sim 24\}$. Our MC-VSA comprises of 3 multi-head attention layer, i.e., we set L as 3. The classifier is composed of a fully connected layer followed by a sigmoid activation. The LSTM encoder and decoder in our model contain 512 units. Besides, we set the learning rate as $1e^{-4}$ for all of our components. We use Adam optimizer to train the MC-VSA by optimizing the objective loss. We produce the summary outputs by KNAPSACK algorithm following [5,14].

4.3   Comparison with Supervised Approaches

We compare our proposed MC-VSA with state-of-the-art methods on two benchmark datasets and summarize the results in Table 1. In canonical setting, we see that our MC-VSA performed favorably against recent LSTM based approaches (e.g., Bi-LSTM [5], DPP-LSTM [5], GAN$_s up$ [7], and DR-DSN$_s up$ [9]), and the CNN-based model (SUM-FCN [14]). Our model also achieves the improvement over LSTM module Bi-LSTM [5], DPP-LSTM [5], GAN$_s up$ [7], and DR-DSN$_s up$ [9]) by a large margin. For both augment and transfer settings, we also observe similar trends and achieve improved performances against state-of-the-art methods. It is worth noting that, though our model exhibit inferior to re-SEQ2SEQ [8] by 0.2% at F-score on the TvSum dataset, our approach and several competitors outperform [8] by a large margin on the SumMe dataset.

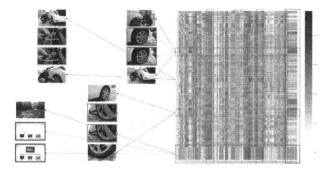

Fig. 5. Visualization for multi-head self-attention at the first layer of MC-VSA. We show that this low-level attention layer not only implies shot-level attention, visual concepts associated with similar objects are properly attended across video frames (e.g., attention outputs bounded in difference colors). (Color figure online)

4.4 Comparisons with Unsupervised Approaches

We report our unsupervised learning results and comparisons in Table 2. With training strategies presented in Sect. 3, we evaluate the effectiveness of our MC-VAS in the unsupervised setting by comparing it with five existing unsupervised summarization methods [6,7,9,14]. As shown in Table 2, our MC-VAS was able to achieve comparable results with the state-of-the-art did on both SumMe and TvSum. Thus, even without any supervision, we can confirm that our model takes advantage of multi-concept video self-attention with visual concept consistency for video recovery and summarization.

4.5 Qualitative Results

To analyze the effectiveness of the self-attention module in MC-VSA, we present visualization results in Fig. 4, in which the attention outputs were observed from the second (high-level) layer in our model. In Fig. 4, the upper half part illustrates frame-level attention weights for the selected 13 heads in our model. Note that each row in the upper part of this figure represents a single head, in which the darkness of the color indicates the importance of the associated frame. From this example result, we see that the attention weights for different heads are quite different, which confirms that our multi-head self-attention mechanism leads to visual concept diversity. For example, by comparing the learned attention weights and the corresponding frames (i.e., upper vs. lower parts of Fig. 4), we see that one head in the blue rectangular box exhibits the semantic meaning of hamburger, while the red one indicates the appearance of the food critic. And, as confirmed by earlier quantitative experiments, these resulting attention weights across different heads are indeed correlated with the summarization outputs.

On the other hand, Fig. 5 illustrates the attention observed in the first layer of our MC-VSA, which can be viewed as a low-level self-attention of multiple heads from the input video. Take the entry of the ith column at the jth row, its

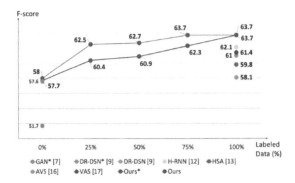

Fig. 6. Performance analysis of our model in semi-supervised settings on TvSum. The x/y-axis indicate the percentage of labels in the training set and the F-score, respectively. Results of recent supervised and unsupervised approaches are depicted for comparison purposes. Note that Ours* denotes our MC-VSA excluding the LSTM auto-encoder module while Ours represents the full model.

value reflects the attention for the corresponding frame pair. From this figure, we see that the attention boundaries were visible and generally matched the shot boundaries. In addition, we see that visual concepts with similar visual appearances (e.g., wheel, car, etc.) were properly identified in particular video segments, which reflect the concept-specific video shot information of this input video. Guided by the classification and data recovery losses, this explains why our proposed model is able to capture multiple representative visual information, achieving satisfactory summarization outputs.

4.6   Ablation Studies

Semi-supervised Settings. We first conduct a semi-supervised learning analysis of our proposed MC-VSA on the TvSum dataset. As illustrated in Fig. 6, the vertical axis indicates the F-score, and the horizontal axis represents the percentage of the labeled data observed during training. For the completeness of analysis, we compare our approach with 5 supervised or unsupervised summarization methods in the same figure. From the results presented in the figure, we see that our MC-VSA achieved improved performances over others. Moreover, we see that our method was able to perform favorably against existing supervised approaches by a large margin, even when only 25% labels were observed by our model during training. Furthermore, Fig. 6 compares our model with its variants in semi-supervised settings. Note that Ours* denotes our model excluding both reconstruction loss and visual concept consistency loss. Refer to the semi-supervised analysis, the performance drop between Ours and Ours* confirms that such two loss terms are crucial when observing unlabeled data. We note that in Fig. 6 for cases 100%, the performances achieved by ours and ours* respectively are the same. This is because when we use the entire label set in

100%, the LSTM module only serves to train our model more stable instead of achieving improved performance.

Network Architecture Design. We now further discuss the design of our model architecture. In Fig. 7, we show the performance of our multi-head multi-layer attention model with varying numbers of layers and heads (x-axis). From this figure, we see that while such hyperparameters need to be determined in advance, the results were not sensitive to their choices. In other words, with a sufficient number of heads and layers, multiple visual concepts can be extracted for summarization purposes as shown in our supplementary video. As shown in Table 3, we

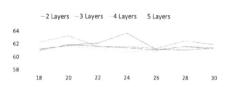

Fig. 7. Performance of our attention model with varyingnumbers of layers (L) and heads (N) (i.e., x-axis). We fix L= 3 and N = 24 for our model in all experiments.

apply three evaluation protocols, including F1, Kendall's τ, and Spearman's ρ, to evaluate our MC-VSA model. Kendall's τ, and Spearman's ρ are proposed by [20] for impartial comparison. We compare our full model (3layers-24heads) with other baseline models. To be more specific, we take the VASNet [17] as the naive self-attention model baseline. Ours (w/o attention) represents the MC-VSA model consisting of the only classifier while ours (1layer-1head) indicates a only single layer and head in the attention encoder. The performance drop is observed when comparing ours with the above-mentioned baseline models. We additionally report the performance provided by [5] and [9] in [20] in Kendall's τ and Spearman's ρ evaluation protocol for benchmark comparison.

5 Conclusion

We presented a novel deep learning framework *multi-concept video self-attention (MC-VSA)* and consistency constraint between the input video and the output summary for video summarization. The core technical novelty lies in the unique design of multi-concept visual self-attention model, which jointly exploits concept and temporal attention diversity in the input videos, while enforcing the summarized outputs to have consistency with original video. Our proposed framework not only generalized in supervised, semi-supervised and unsupervised settings but also in both evaluation protocols. Also, our experiments and qualitative results confirmed the effectiveness of our proposed model and its ability to identify certain informative visual concepts.

References

1. Chao, W.L., Gong, B., Grauman, K., Sha, F.: Large-margin determinantal point processes. In: UAI, pp. 191–200 (2015)

2. Gygli, M., Grabner, H., Riemenschneider, H., Van Gool, L.: Creating summaries from user videos. In: Fleet, D., Pajdla, T., Schiele, B., Tuytelaars, T. (eds.) ECCV 2014. LNCS, vol. 8695, pp. 505–520. Springer, Cham (2014). https://doi.org/10.1007/978-3-319-10584-0_33
3. Gygli, M., Grabner, H., Van Gool, L.: Video summarization by learning submodular mixtures of objectives. In: Proceedings of the IEEE Conference on Computer Vision and Pattern Recognition, pp. 3090–3098 (2015)
4. Zhang, K., Chao, W.L., Sha, F., Grauman, K.: Summary transfer: exemplar-based subset selection for video summarization. In: Proceedings of the IEEE Conference on Computer Vision and Pattern Recognition, pp. 1059–1067 (2016)
5. Zhang, K., Chao, W.-L., Sha, F., Grauman, K.: Video summarization with long short-term memory. In: Leibe, B., Matas, J., Sebe, N., Welling, M. (eds.) ECCV 2016. LNCS, vol. 9911, pp. 766–782. Springer, Cham (2016). https://doi.org/10.1007/978-3-319-46478-7_47
6. Jung, Y., Cho, D., Kim, D., Woo, S., Kweon, I.S.: Discriminative feature learning for unsupervised video summarization. In: Proceedings of the AAAI Conference on Artificial Intelligence (AAAI) (2018)
7. Mahasseni, B., Lam, M., Todorovic, S.: Unsupervised video summarization with adversarial LSTM networks. In: Proceedings of the IEEE Conference on Computer Vision and Pattern Recognition (CVPR) (2017)
8. Zhang, K., Grauman, K., Sha, F.: Retrospective encoders for video summarization. In: Ferrari, V., Hebert, M., Sminchisescu, C., Weiss, Y. (eds.) ECCV 2018. LNCS, vol. 11212, pp. 391–408. Springer, Cham (2018). https://doi.org/10.1007/978-3-030-01237-3_24
9. Zhou, K., Qiao, Y., Xiang, T.: Deep reinforcement learning for unsupervised video summarization with diversity-representativeness reward. In: Proceedings of the AAAI Conference on Artificial Intelligence (AAAI) (2018)
10. Hochreiter, S., Schmidhuber, J.: Long short-term memory. Neural Comput. **9**, 1735–1780 (1997)
11. Yue-Hei Ng, J., Hausknecht, M., Vijayanarasimhan, S., Vinyals, O., Monga, R., Toderici, G.: Beyond short snippets: deep networks for video classification. In: Proceedings of the IEEE Conference on Computer Vision and Pattern Recognition, pp. 4694–4702 (2015)
12. Zhao, B., Li, X., Lu, X.: Hierarchical recurrent neural network for video summarization. In: Proceedings of the 25th ACM International Conference on Multimedia, pp. 863–871. ACM (2017)
13. Zhao, B., Li, X., Lu, X.: HSA-RNN: hierarchical structure-adaptive RNN for video summarization. In: Proceedings of the IEEE Conference on Computer Vision and Pattern Recognition, pp. 7405–7414 (2018)
14. Rochan, M., Ye, L., Wang, Y.: Video summarization using fully convolutional sequence networks. In: Ferrari, V., Hebert, M., Sminchisescu, C., Weiss, Y. (eds.) ECCV 2018. LNCS, vol. 11216, pp. 358–374. Springer, Cham (2018). https://doi.org/10.1007/978-3-030-01258-8_22
15. Fu, T.J., Tai, S.H., Chen, H.T.: Attentive and adversarial learning for video summarization. In: 2019 IEEE Winter Conference on Applications of Computer Vision (WACV), pp. 1579–1587. IEEE (2019)
16. Ji, Z., Xiong, K., Pang, Y., Li, X.: Video summarization with attention-based encoder-decoder networks. arXiv preprint arXiv:1708.09545 (2017)
17. Ji, Z., Hajar Sadeghi, S., Vasileios, A., Dorothy, M., Paolo, R.: Summarizing videos with attention. In: Proceedings of the AAAI Conference on Artificial Intelligence Workshops (AAAI Workshops) (2018)

18. Vaswani, A., et al.: Attention is all you need. In: Advances in Neural Information Processing Systems, pp. 5998–6008 (2017)
19. Song, Y., Vallmitjana, J., Stent, A., Jaimes, A.: TVSum: summarizing web videos using titles. In: Proceedings of the IEEE Conference on Computer Vision and Pattern Recognition, pp. 5179–5187 (2015)
20. Otani, M., Nakashima, Y., Rahtu, E., Heikkila, J.: Rethinking the evaluation of video summaries. In: Proceedings of the IEEE Conference on Computer Vision and Pattern Recognition, pp. 7596–7604 (2019)
21. He, X., et al.: Unsupervised video summarization with attentive conditional generative adversarial networks. In: Proceedings of the ACM Conference on Multimedia (MM) (2019)
22. Vinyals, O., Fortunato, M., Jaitly, N.: Pointer networks. In: Advances in Neural Information Processing Systems, pp. 2692–2700 (2015)
23. Xu, K., Ba, J., Kiros, R., Cho, K., Courville, A., Salakhudinov, R., Zemel, R., Bengio, Y.: Show, attend and tell: Neural image caption generation with visual attention. In: International Conference on Machine Learning, pp. 2048–2057 (2015)
24. Rochan, M., Wang, Y.: Video summarization by learning from unpaired data. In: Proceedings of the IEEE Conference on Computer Vision and Pattern Recognition, pp. 7902–7911 (2019)
25. Szegedy, C., et al.: Going deeper with convolutions. In: The IEEE Conference on Computer Vision and Pattern Recognition, pp. 1–9 (2015)
26. Chen, Y., Tao, L., Wang, X., Yamasaki, T.: Weakly supervised video summarization by hierarchical reinforcement learning. In: Proceedings of the ACM Multimedia Asia, pp. 1–6 (2019)

Learning to Adapt to Unseen Abnormal Activities Under Weak Supervision

Jaeyoo Park, Junha Kim, and Bohyung Han$^{(\boxtimes)}$

ECE & ASRI, Seoul National University, Seoul, Korea
{bellos1203,junha.kim,bhhan}@snu.ac.kr

Abstract. We present a meta-learning framework for weakly supervised anomaly detection in videos, where the detector learns to adapt to unseen types of abnormal activities effectively when only video-level annotations of binary labels are available. Our work is motivated by the fact that existing methods suffer from poor generalization to diverse unseen examples. We claim that an anomaly detector equipped with a meta-learning scheme alleviates the limitation by leading the model to an initialization point for better optimization. We evaluate the performance of our framework on two challenging datasets, UCF-Crime and ShanghaiTech. The experimental results demonstrate that our algorithm boosts the capability to localize unseen abnormal events in a weakly supervised setting. Besides the technical contributions, we perform the annotation of missing labels in the UCF-Crime dataset and make our task evaluated effectively.

Keywords: Anomaly detection · Meta-learning · Weakly supervised learning

1 Introduction

Humans easily identify unusual events from a video by generalizing prior knowledge spontaneously despite the ill-defined nature of anomaly detection. On the contrary, computer vision algorithms rely on an extensive learning process based on a large number of annotated training examples to obtain a model for abnormal event detection. There exist various approaches proposed for anomaly detection in videos. The methods based on generative models [1,2] claim the capability to reconstruct normal patterns while [3,4] propose discriminative techniques based on binary classifiers. Despite the significant advance in anomaly detection on videos [1–5], existing methods in both categories may suffer from critical drawbacks. A recent study [3] presents that generative approaches are not suitable for the recognition problems on videos with substantial scene variations since

---

J. Park and J. Kim—These authors contributed equally.

Electronic supplementary material The online version of this chapter (https://doi.org/10.1007/978-3-030-69541-5_31) contains supplementary material, which is available to authorized users.

© Springer Nature Switzerland AG 2021
H. Ishikawa et al. (Eds.): ACCV 2020, LNCS 12626, pp. 514–529, 2021.
https://doi.org/10.1007/978-3-030-69541-5_31

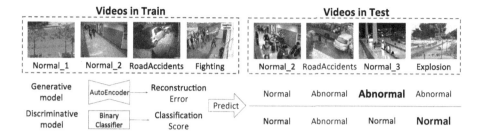

Fig. 1. Limitation of the existing abnormal event detection approaches in videos. The generative models (*e.g.*, auto-encoder) attempt to learn normal patterns in training data; they successfully reconstruct the normal videos seen during training (Normal_2) while they fail to reconstruct the videos captured from new viewpoints (Normal_3). Meanwhile, the discriminative approaches (*e.g.*, binary classifier) focus on classifying each frame into two classes, abnormal and normal, by learning abnormal patterns from the given data. Therefore, the discriminative classifiers detect the abnormal events that have been seen during training (RoadAccidents) while they fail to recognize unseen types of abnormal events (Explosion) at test time. The bold-faced letters in red correspond to the wrong predictions of individual approaches. (Color figure online)

they are prone to predict unseen normal patterns as abnormal. Also, the generated videos often have limited diversity, especially having the same viewpoint as the cameras used to construct training examples. On the other hand, the discriminative classifiers may not be robust to unseen types of normal or abnormal activities. In particular, they can detect the predefined types of abnormal events only and tend to overfit to training data. Figure 1 illustrates the limitations of the existing methods mentioned above.

Since it is infeasible to collect the videos containing all kinds of normal and abnormal activity patterns, the detector should be able to spot the eccentricity even with limited prior information. Here, one crucial question arises. When we learn a model to detect unseen patterns in videos, how can we take advantage of prior knowledge? The simplest solution would be pretraining a model using the data of seen patterns followed by fine-tuning it with the examples of unseen types. To address this problem in spite of a practical limitation—weak diversity of training examples, we formulate anomaly detection as learning to adapt to various unseen abnormalities rather than learning the universal representation. To this end, we harness the meta-learning concept [6,7], which claims that the model parameters of a deep neural network can be located at a desirable initial point for better optimization, not necessarily fast convergence, by simulating the learning process for adaptation to new data distribution. By constructing learning episodes containing diverse abnormal events, where the variance across individual examples is large, the model learns to reach the appropriate initialization point, which leads the model to adapt well to novel abnormal events.

Moreover, we explore whether detecting unseen abnormal events can be effectively performed under weak supervision in the meta-learning framework. Since it is expensive to obtain precise annotations of temporal locations of individual abnormal events in videos, we prefer constructing base-learner models using the examples with video-level binary labels, normal vs. abnormal. Note that we aim to localize abnormal activities in the temporal domain via learning a model based on binary annotations of abnormality in video level.

We validate the proposed training scheme on two challenging datasets, UCF-Crime [3] and ShanghaiTech [8]. Since the UCF-Crime dataset provides temporal annotations of abnormal events only for a small portion of videos, we annotated the examples without ground-truths for our experiments. The experimental results show that the proposed algorithm outperforms the baseline in detecting novel abnormal events. The source codes and new annotations are available at our project page[1].

The main contributions of the proposed approach are summarized below:

- We formulate anomaly detection in videos as a learning-to-adapt task to unseen abnormal activities to address the limitations of existing approaches.
- We propose a novel meta-learning approach under weak supervision, where the base-learner utilizes video-level binary labels only for training, while the final model estimates the localization information of unseen abnormal events.
- We labeled the missing ground-truths for temporal locations of abnormal events in the UCF-Crime dataset.
- The experiment on UCF-Crime with label augmentations and ShanghaiTech shows that our method is effective in learning novel types of abnormal events.

The rest of the paper is organized as follows. We first discuss related work in Sect. 2. The overall procedure and the experimental results with their analysis are described in Sect. 3 and 4, respectively. Section 5 concludes this paper.

2   Related Work

2.1   Anomaly Detection

Many researchers have been interested in anomaly detection in the video [1–5, 9–11]. Given a video, the detector localizes unexpected incidents that are rarely observed. The task is challenging due to its ill-defined nature, its innate complexity, and the diversity of examples.

The advances in generative modeling techniques based on deep neural networks allow us to construct the anomaly detector in a generative manner [2, 12–14]. They attempt to find the general pattern of in-distribution data points with the generative models such as auto-encoder [1, 2, 15] and generative adversarial network [16]. Based on the assumption that abnormal events are rare, the generative models learn how to reconstruct normal and usual patterns. These models consider the examples that have large reconstruction errors as the out-of-distribution samples. However, they assume that all the videos have the same

---

[1] https://cv.snu.ac.kr/research/Learning-to-Adapt-to-Unseen-Abnormal-Activities/.

viewpoint. As a result, the models are prone to overfit to training data and predict unaccustomed normal patterns as abnormal.

A recent study [3] claims that the classic generative approaches are unable to generalize normal patterns captured by the camera from a novel viewpoint. It also introduces a novel dataset for anomaly detection, UCF-Crime, which consists of more complex and diverse events than existing ones. Based on the dataset, [3, 4] suggest predicting abnormality scores in a discriminative manner. They treat the anomaly detection task as a binary classification problem under weak supervision, where the model classifies whether the video contains abnormal or normal events based only on video-level labels. Specifically, [3] proposes a binary classifier based on multiple instance learning, and [4] employs a label noise cleaner using a graph convolutional neural network. Nevertheless, those methods still suffer from a lack of generalizability, especially when they face unseen types of abnormality. This fact raises the need for a reasonable initial model that handles unseen abnormality effectively. Hence, we propose a meta-learning framework to obtain basic information from prior knowledge.

2.2 Meta-learning

The objective of meta-learning is to realize the learn-to-learn capability, where the meta-learner supervises the learning process of the base-learner [6,17,18]. The common approaches to address this problem include 1) metric learning-based methods, where the meta-learner focuses on the similarity metric within the task [19–21], 2) memory augmented methods, where the meta-learner stores training examples or class embedding features [22–25], and optimization-based methods, where the meta-learner is directly parameterized by the information from the base-learner (e.g., gradients, etc,.) [6,26–28]. Our work employs a popular optimization-based framework, Model-Agnostic Meta-Learning (MAML) [6]. Further description of MAML will be provided in Sect. 3.3. Following the recent works in other applications that take advantage of meta-learning schemes [29–34], we facilitate anomaly detection in videos using the meta-learning framework. Our work is distinct from existing models because we construct the meta-learning model upon base-learner under weak supervision, *i.e.,* when only video-level labels are available. There is a prior study that focuses on the generalization capability of meta-learning in domain generalization task [35]. Recently, [36] addresses an anomaly detection problem based on meta-learning. However, its direction is different from ours in the sense that it attempts to learn the normality of scenes using generative models, while our approach aims adapt to novel anomaly via discriminative models.

3   Method

3.1   Overview

Our goal is to learn an anomaly detection model that adapts to novel types of abnormal events effectively using weakly labeled examples. Since it is infeasible to capture common abnormal patterns generally acceptable in the videos with huge diversity, we formulate anomaly detection as learning to adapt to various abnormal events rather than learning universal representations.

We assume that there exists a video dataset $\mathcal{D}_{base}$ with two different types of annotations per video—binary label whether a video contains abnormal events or not, and c_{base} abnormal event categories (subclasses) for the positive videos. We learn to identify the initial model parameters optimized for adapting to novel abnormal events in the videos that belong to $\mathcal{D}_{novel}$ with c_{novel} subclasses. Note that the subclasses in $\mathcal{D}_{base}$ and $\mathcal{D}_{novel}$ are disjoint although we do not use the subclass information in the training procedure of the proposed framework. Another assumption is that, given a video $v = \{v_i\}_{i=1}^N \in \mathcal{D}$ ($= \mathcal{D}_{base} \cup \mathcal{D}_{novel}$) with N segments, we only have the video-level label $y \in \{0, 1\}$, where 1 indicates that the video has at least one abnormal segment, 0 otherwise. Note that our weakly-supervised detector should predict per-segment label, $\hat{y} = \{\hat{y}_i\}_{i=1}^N$, without segment-level or localization ground-truths.

We propose to harness meta-learning to boost the localization accuracy of unseen abnormal events based on weak supervision. We claim that simple knowledge transfer from pretrained models may not work well in our scenario since the variations of abnormality is significant and the prior knowledge obtained from seen abnormal events is difficult to be generalized to unseen ones. Hence, by exploiting meta-learning based on the episodes with large variations, we alleviate the limitation of transfer learning and facilitate to learn models for unseen anomaly detection via meta-testing. Specifically, we construct an episode by sampling a small subset of videos from $\mathcal{D}_{base}$, and perform an iteration of meta-training using the episode. In the meta-testing phase, we fine-tune the model using the videos sampled from $\mathcal{D}_{novel}$ to obtain the final model. Note that the entire training procedure relies only on video-level binary class labels.

The rest of this section describes the details about the individual components of our framework, which include 1) the base anomaly detector relying on weak labels, and 2) the meta-learning algorithm to obtain better generalizable models.

3.2   Weakly Supervised Anomaly Detector

We adopt the anomaly detection method proposed in [3] as our base detector. The detector learns to score how abnormal each video segment is under weak supervision. The score of each segment is given by a binary classifier distinguishing between abnormal and normal events. To train a segment-wise anomaly detector based only on video-level annotations, we employ Multiple Instance Learning (MIL) with a ranking loss.

MIL. The concept of MIL is employed in our problem to learn the rank between normal and abnormal bags. We divide a video into N segments, each of which is denoted by v_i ($i = 1, \ldots, N$). A video $v = \{v_i\}_{i=1}^N$ with N segments is regarded as a positive bag $\mathcal{B}_a$ if at least one of the segments is abnormal, i.e., $\exists i, y_i = 1$. Otherwise, the video is normal and its segments construct a negative bag $\mathcal{B}_n$.

The segments in $\mathcal{B}_a$ and $\mathcal{B}_n$ pass through a scoring function $f(\cdot)$, which consists of three fully-connected layers with ReLUs and sigmoid functions, to predict abnormality scores.

Ranking Loss. We employ a ranking loss for MIL as in [3], which produces higher scores for abnormal segments than normal ones. Since segment-level labels are not available in our setting, the loss for a pair of a positive bag and a negative one is defined by the segments with the maximum scores in both bags as

$$\mathcal{L}(\theta; \{\mathcal{B}_a, \mathcal{B}_n\}) = \max(0, m - \max_{v_i \in \mathcal{B}_a} f(v_i; \theta) + \max_{v_i \in \mathcal{B}_n} f(v_i; \theta)), \tag{1}$$

where θ denotes model parameters, v_i means the i-th segment in a bag, and m indicates the score margin between the two bags. In addition, the loss function has two regularization terms—a temporal smoothness loss and a sparsity loss. The former encourages temporally adjacent segments to have similar scores, while the latter enforces only a small subset of segments in a video to have high scores upon the assumption that abnormal activities rarely happen in videos. By combining all the loss terms, the final loss function is given by

$$\mathcal{L}(\theta; \{\mathcal{B}_a, \mathcal{B}_n\}) = \max(0, m - \max_{v_i \in \mathcal{B}_a} f(v_i; \theta) + \max_{v_i \in \mathcal{B}_n} f(v_i; \theta))$$
$$+ \lambda_1 \sum_{v_i \in \mathcal{B}_a} (f(v_i; \theta) - f(v_{i+1}; \theta))^2 + \lambda_2 \sum_{v_i \in \mathcal{B}_a} f(v_i; \theta), \tag{2}$$

where λ_1 and λ_2 are the hyperparmaters to control the impact of individual terms. Following [3], we set $m = 1$ and $\lambda_1 = \lambda_2 = 8 \times 10^{-5}$ throughout our training procedure. Note that, since $f(v_i; \theta)$ is the output of a sigmoid function and always positive, the last term in Eq. (2) is equivalent to ℓ_1 norm of a segment-wise score vector.

Training Base Detector. We train the anomaly detector based on the objective function in Eq. (2) using $\mathcal{D}_{base}$. To train the detector, we split a video into multiple segments, where each segment consists of 16 consecutive frames, and extract 3D convolutional features from I3D networks [37] pretrained on the Kinetics dataset. We represent each variable-length video using 32 non-overlapping transformed features as described in [3] and feed them to our base detector model for training.

3.3 Meta-Training

In the meta-training phase, our goal is to make the model learn to adapt to novel types of abnormal examples by repeatedly simulating the learning procedure using the data sampled from the distribution with large intra-class variations. To achieve this goal, we adopt a meta-learning approach based on MAML [6]. Our meta-learning scheme aims to find an optimal set of initial model parameters, which is suitable for adapting to unseen types of data. Since there is no external meta-learner in MAML, the model parameters are solely updated by the gradient descent method.

(a) Conventional episodes   (b) Our episodes

Fig. 2. Comparison of the methods to construct episodes between the conventional N-way K-shot classification and our anomaly detection. (a) The tasks are different across episodes and the intra-class variation is relatively small. The images are sampled from *miniImageNet* [38] dataset. (b) Every episode is for binary classification between abnormal and normal classes. The abnormal class consists of the subclasses in $\mathcal{D}_{base}$, so the intra-class variation is large.

Episode in Anomaly Detection. We first describe how to construct episodes for anomaly detection. Most of the few-shot classification studies formulate an episode as a classification task, where a model for each episode is optimized for a unique set of classes, and have the target tasks for meta-testing separate from the ones for meta-training. We refer to this kind of strategy as the conventional meta-learning in the rest of this section.

In contrast, all the tasks in anomaly detection are identical: binary classification between *normal* and *abnormal*. We sample both normal and abnormal videos from $\mathcal{D}_{base}$ with c_{base} subclasses to construct a task $\mathcal{T}$. Note that the sampled abnormal videos belong to any subclass but the subclasses for meta-training and meta-testing should be disjoint. The major difference between the conventional and our meta-learning lies in the source of diversity. The intra-class variation in anomaly detection is much larger than that of the conventional meta-learning. While the existing few-shot learning studies attempt to generalize models over the task distribution, our approach focuses on the generalization of the model over the data distribution within the individual classes, abnormal and normal, during meta-training. The difference between the conventional meta-learning and our approach is illustrated in Fig. 2.

Training Method. We construct each task $\mathcal{T}_i$, which is divided into training and testing denoted respectively by $\mathcal{T}_i^{trn}$ and $\mathcal{T}_i^{tst}$, by sampling abnormal and normal videos from $\mathcal{D}_{base}$. Using the training and testing splits, meta-training is performed by the bi-level optimization on the base detector.

We first, as in a typical training scenario, adapt the base detector to $\mathcal{T}_i^{trn}$ based on the objective function in Eq. (2). This adaptation step is referred to as the *inner loop*. For the i-th task $\mathcal{T}_i$, the model parameters of the base detector, denoted by θ, are then updated to $\tilde{\theta}_{\mathcal{T}_i}$ by the gradient descent method using the loss function $\mathcal{L}_{\mathcal{T}}(\theta; \mathcal{T}_i^{trn})$, which is expressed as

$$\tilde{\theta}_{\mathcal{T}_i} = \theta - \alpha \nabla_\theta \mathcal{L}_{\mathcal{T}_i}(\theta; \mathcal{T}_i^{trn}), \tag{3}$$

where α is the learning rate for the base detector.

Next, the adapted base detector is evaluated by $\mathcal{T}_i^{tst}$, and the meta-learner is optimized using the resulting error. Since the meta-optimization contains the adaptation step, it is also referred to as the *outer loop*. The meta-learner is optimized by $\mathcal{L}_{\mathcal{T}}(\tilde{\theta}_{\mathcal{T}}; \mathcal{T}^{tst})$. In MAML-based approaches, the meta-update is performed by updating the model parameters, denoted by θ, of the base detector before the adaptation step using the meta-objective function, which is given by

$$\min_\theta \sum_{\mathcal{T}_i \sim p(\mathcal{T})} \mathcal{L}_{\mathcal{T}_i}(\tilde{\theta}_{\mathcal{T}_i}; \mathcal{T}_i^{tst}) = \sum_{\mathcal{T}_i \sim p(\mathcal{T})} \mathcal{L}_{\mathcal{T}_i}(\theta - \alpha \nabla_\theta \mathcal{L}_{\mathcal{T}_i}(\theta; \mathcal{T}_i^{trn}); \mathcal{T}_i^{tst}). \tag{4}$$

Therefore, the model parameters are meta-updated as

$$\theta = \theta - \beta \nabla_\theta \sum_{\mathcal{T}_i \sim p(\mathcal{T})} \mathcal{L}_{\mathcal{T}_i}(\tilde{\theta}_{\mathcal{T}_i}; \mathcal{T}_i^{tst}), \tag{5}$$

where β is the meta-learning rate.

3.4 Meta-testing

In the meta-testing stage, we evaluate whether the model adapts to the novel types of abnormal events well. To this end, we fine-tune the model for the abnormal events in c_{novel} subclasses, which are disjoint from c_{base} normal subclasses, by constructing episodes for meta-testing using sampled examples from $\mathcal{D}_{novel}$. Since we do not have a validation set $\mathcal{D}_{novel}^{val}$ due to the small size of the datasets, we perform 10-fold cross-validation by exploiting $\mathcal{D}_{novel}^{trn}$ to decide the number of iterations for fine-tuning.

4   Experiments

4.1   Datasets

We conduct the experiments on two benchmark datasets, UCF-Crime [3] with our label augmentation and ShanghaiTech [8].

UCF-Crime. This large-scale dataset consists of real-world surveillance videos captured in various circumstances. It contains 13 subclasses of abnormal events including *Abuse, Arrest, Arson, Assault, Burglary, Explosion, Fighting, RoadAccidents, Robbery, Shooting, Shoplifting, Stealing,* and *Vandalism*. The dataset has 1,900 untrimmed videos, including 950 abnormal videos and 950 normal ones.

Table 1. Over-estimated performance issue in the existing evaluation method. The AUC score of our base detector is approximately 84% when evaluating the entire test videos using the anomaly split in [3]. The value is slightly higher than the one reported in [3] because we employ two-stream features from I3D network [37] for video representations. However, when we exclude the normal videos from the test set, the performance drops to about 68%.

Class	AUC (%)	# of test samples
Abnormal	68.35	140
Abnormal+Normal	84.39	290

There exist a couple of critical limitations in this dataset that hamper direct compatibility with our task. First, the subclass distribution in the original training and testing splits given by [3] for anomaly detection is severely imbalanced. Hence, we conduct our experiments using the action recognition split provided by [3]. In the action recognition split, every subclass has 38 videos for training and 12 videos for testing. Second, [3] provides the temporal durations of abnormal events for the test videos in its anomaly detection split while some videos in the test set of the action recognition split do not have such annotations. To make the dataset complete for performance evaluation, we annotate the ground-truth intervals of abnormal events for some videos in the dataset.

ShanghaiTech. This is a medium-scale dataset composed of 437 videos from 13 different scenes. Since all training videos are normal, we use a new split proposed by [4]. In addition, we employ this dataset only for meta-test since there are not a sufficient number of videos containing abnormal events for meta-training. We believe that the experiment in this dataset shows the cross-dataset generalization performance of the proposed method.

4.2   Evaluation Metric and Protocol

Following the previous works [2–4], we draw the frame-wise receiver operation characteristic (ROC) curve and compute its area under curve (AUC) score. However, our evaluation method is different from the existing ones in the following two parts.

First, we only evaluate the AUC performance on the abnormal videos. Since there is a significantly larger number of normal frames than abnormal ones, especially if we count both abnormal and normal videos, performance evaluation using the videos in both classes leads to a biased result towards accuracy overestimation as illustrated in Table 1. Therefore, we exclude normal videos for the computation of the AUC scores in our experiments. Note that we use the original splits and annotations instead of the revised ones to obtain the statistics.

Second, we evaluate the average frame-wise AUC score for each video while existing methods estimate the scores using all frames collected from all videos in their test datasets. This is because the overall performance is often dominated by a small subset of extremely long videos, which are as long as 10^5 frames and substantially longer than the average length, about 4×10^3 frames.

4.3 Experimental Settings and Implementation Details

To validate our claim that meta-learning provides a proper initialization point, we compare the following three scenarios, which are given by fine-tuning the detector on $\mathcal{D}_{novel}$ starting from 1) the randomly initialized model, 2) the pretrained model on $\mathcal{D}_{base}$, and 3) the meta-trained model on $\mathcal{D}_{base}$.

For the experiments, we re-implemented the detector proposed in [3] and use it as the base learner. Our implementation is identical to [3] except the following three parts. First, we utilized the pretrained two-stream I3D features [37] trained on the Kinetics dataset instead of C3D features [39] employed in [3]; the optical flows are computed by the TVL1 algorithm [40] and the fusion of two modalities—RGB and optical flow—is given by the concatenation of their features. Second, we removed the dropout layers [41] since training the MAML model [6] was unstable. Finally, we used the Adam optimizer instead of Adagrad.

For pretraining, we sampled 30 videos from both the abnormal and normal classes to form a mini-batch. After splitting $\mathcal{D}_{base}$ into train and validation videos following the action recognition split, we trained the model with a learning rate 10^{-3} until the validation AUC score arrives at the peak.

For meta-training, we construct each episode using 10 samples for training and 30 for testing from both categories, abnormal and normal classes. The learning rate of the inner loop is set to 10^{-3} while the learning rate for the outer loop, which is a meta-learning rate, is set to 10^{-5}. We trained the model for 3,000 outer iterations with meta-batch size 15, and used an SGD optimizer for inner loop optimization.

Fine-tuning is performed on $\mathcal{D}_{novel}$ regardless of the initialization methods with the learning rate 10^{-3}. We fine-tuned the model for 300 iterations at maximum and performed 10-fold cross-validation to choose the best model.

4.4 Quantitative Results

UCF-Crime. We conduct our experiments on two action recognition data splits in the UCF-Crime dataset. Even though UCF-Crime is the largest dataset for anomaly detection in videos, it is still too small to conduct meta-learning experiments. We generated 13 subtasks for the experiment, where each subtask has a different novel subclass while the rest of 12 subclasses are employed to construct $\mathcal{D}_{base}$.

Table 2 reports the AUC scores for all 13 subtasks, where we compare the results from the three scenarios described in Sect. 4.3. Since the statistics of each subclass are different from each other, it is not straightforward to identify

Table 2. AUC score (%) comparisons among three different scenarios on each target subclass. The fine-tuning process of all the compared methods is identical while the initial point of fine-tuning is different. In the algorithm denoted by S, the model is fine-tuned from a random scratch model. In the scenario P, the model is pretrained with $\mathcal{D}_{base}$ before fine-tuning. Two versions of the meta-learning approach, denoted by M_S and M_G, which performs meta-training with $\mathcal{D}_{base}$ to obtain the initial model, correspond to two different model selection strategies, "sampling" and "global". Details of "sampling" and "global" are described in Sect. 4.4. The bold-faced numbers correspond to the best accuracy for each subclass.

Split	Algo.	Abus	Arre	Arso	Assa	Burg	Expl	Figh	Road	Robb	Shoo	Shop	Stea	Vand	Avg
1	S	62.99	67.91	56.93	80.05	72.02	63.62	70.94	73.19	77.86	75.81	57.70	66.77	72.86	69.13
	P	69.71	67.57	60.22	81.18	77.51	71.85	70.65	**77.11**	80.48	82.69	52.37	65.41	74.61	71.64
	M_S	**70.93**	**72.05**	61.26	**82.67**	81.08	**73.32**	71.35	76.72	**82.56**	**82.85**	59.19	**70.75**	77.30	**74.00**
	M_G	69.89	71.30	59.97	82.19	78.75	**73.32**	69.96	74.85	**82.56**	**82.85**	56.20	66.37	75.33	72.58
2	S	79.64	61.08	77.57	77.86	74.10	**77.31**	79.24	74.96	**80.02**	79.60	**67.29**	65.63	75.26	74.58
	P	73.60	73.91	83.81	79.62	75.22	73.62	83.21	74.27	71.32	80.13	64.96	72.56	78.56	75.75
	M_S	79.01	**76.36**	82.34	**79.75**	**77.20**	73.32	84.39	74.14	76.16	**81.58**	67.27	**77.41**	**79.26**	**77.55**
	M_G	76.01	72.22	**83.82**	79.08	76.83	68.34	**84.62**	**75.07**	73.92	80.92	65.97	77.02	79.25	76.39

the optimal model for a fair comparison. Hence, we choose the following two different models for the evaluation of each subtask. First, we sample 10 models for each subtask from the uniformly sampled meta-iterations, and select the best model for each subclass. We call this model selection strategy "sampling". Second, to make the evaluation more strict, we choose a global model from the same meta-iteration to handle all subclasses, which is called "global". For both splits, a meta-trained model shows better average performance than the others; the proposed model improves accuracy in most of the subclasses while we observe accuracy drops by pretraining and meta-training in a few cases including *Explosion* and *Shoplifting* in the second split. This is probably because their data distributions of these two subclasses are substantially different from the others and the prior knowledge is not helpful. However, in the case of *Stealing*, our approach outperforms the pretraining method by about 5% margin, which indicates the proposed technique is effective even for the scenario that pretraining does not help.

ShanghaiTech. To validate the generalization capability of our model, we conduct an additional experiment on the ShanghaiTech dataset [8]. As mentioned in Sect. 4.1, it is not feasible to perform meta-training on this dataset due to its small size. Since the examples in ShanghaiTech belong to abnormal events in campus life, which are unique compared to UCF-Crime, we consider the ShanghaiTech dataset as $\mathcal{D}_{novel}$ and use UCF-Crime as $\mathcal{D}_{base}$ to learn the prior knowledge. All hyperparameters of the experiments for ShanghaiTech are identical to those for UCF-Crime.

Table 3 presents the results of the three training scenarios. The proposed strategy also outperforms the other training methods, which implies that the

Table 3. Quantitative results on the ShanghaiTech dataset. For P and M_S, UCF-Crime dataset is employed to train the model. Then, each model is fine-tuned with a train split of ShanghaiTech, and the final evaluation is conducted on the test split of ShanghaiTech. The results show that the meta-initialized model adapts better to novel anomaly than the others, S and P.

Algorithm	AUC (%)
S	79.53
P	79.34
M_S	**84.70**

knowledge from one dataset learned by our meta-learning approach is transferable to other datasets; the proposed framework provides a promising initial model for localizing abnormalities in diverse situations.

4.5 Qualitative Results

Figure 3 demonstrates the qualitative results from three training scenarios on two test videos in (a) the UCF-Crime and (b) ShanghaiTech datasets. The shaded regions in the graphs correspond to the ground-truth intervals of abnormal events. The area under the ROC curve (AUROC or AUC) for each video and model is also reported in the graph. Since the AUC metric is computed by the rank of scores, the performance of all the three methods looks comparable. However, the scores given by the meta-trained model are more discriminative than the other two methods. In other words, the models trained from scratch or pretrained models are prone to suffer from mis-detections and/or false alarms. This observation implies that the proposed approach would be more robust than the others in more challenging examples. We will enclose more sample results of anomaly detection with scores in the supplementary document.

4.6 Further Analysis

To analyze whether the meta-learning scheme has a real impact on adapting to novel abnormalities, we plot performance curves during fine-tuning at the meta-testing stage with the UCF-Crime and ShanghaiTech datasets and present the results in Fig. 4. The followings are the lessons from the observation of the fine-tuning curves.

First, the anomaly detection benefits from prior knowledge. In most cases, both of the pretrained model and the meta-trained model demonstrate better performance at the initial epoch than the scratch case. From this observation, we conclude that the model has the utility to detect the novel types of abnormal events even without their direct prior knowledge. Second, the performance of a model is sometimes degraded during the fine-tuning procedure. Figure 4(b), and (d) illustrates that the learning curves go downward with iterations. For

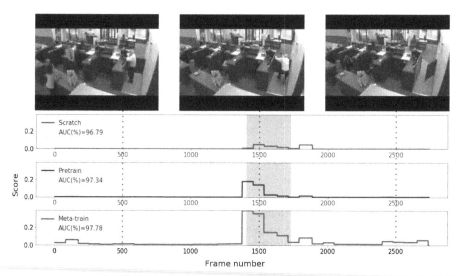

(a) Shooting048 sequence in UCF-Crime dataset

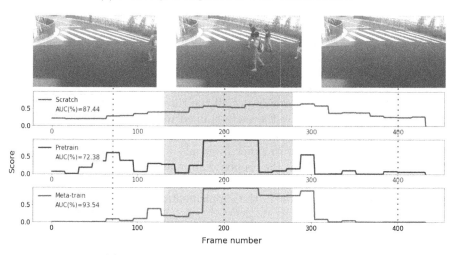

(b) 03 0059 sequence in ShanghaiTech dataset

Fig. 3. Qualitative results from (a) the UCF-Crime and (b) the ShanghaiTech datasets. The scores of three different methods are presented together with the ground-truths represented by the shaded regions.

these cases, we conclude that there are data samples with significant noise or large intra-class variations; it is challenging for a model to detect anomalies with weak supervision only. This stems from the inherent weakness of the detector trained based only on weak supervision. Due to space limitations, the learning curves for the rest of the subclasses are included in the supplementary document.

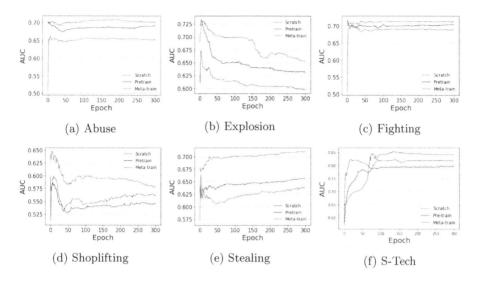

Fig. 4. Fine-tuning curves of individual subclasses for three training scenarios

5   Conclusion

We presented a weakly supervised learning-to-adapt formulation of anomaly detection in videos, which alleviates the limitation of existing methods in the generalization to diverse unseen data samples. To this end, we proposed a learning strategy to adapt to unseen types of abnormal events effectively by taking advantage of meta-learning. We meta-train the model by constructing episodes that are well-aligned with anomaly detection. Our experimental results from challenging UCF-Crime and ShanghaiTech demonstrate that the models given by the proposed technique learn to adapt to new types of abnormal videos successfully and verify the efficacy of meta-learning in adaptation quality compared to the pretrained models. In addition, we pointed out the limitation of UCF-Crime dataset in terms of annotation completeness and data imbalance, and supplement temporal annotations of abnormal activities for the videos which do not have such ground-truths.

Acknowledgments. This work was partly supported by Vision AI Product Center of Excellence in T3K of SK telecom and Institute for Information & Communications Technology Promotion (IITP) grant funded by the Korea government (MSIT) [2017-0-01779, 2017-0-01780].

References

1. Gong, D., et al.: Memorizing normality to detect anomaly: memory-augmented deep autoencoder for unsupervised anomaly detection. In: ICCV (2019)
2. Hasan, M., Choi, J., Neumann, J., Roy-Chowdhury, A.K., Davis, L.S.: Learning temporal regularity in video sequences. In: CVPR (2016)

3. Sultani, W., Chen, C., Shah, M.: Real-world anomaly detection in surveillance videos. In: CVPR (2018)
4. Zhong, J.X., Li, N., Kong, W., Liu, S., Li, T.H., Li, G.: Graph convolutional label noise cleaner: train a plug-and-play action classifier for anomaly detection. In: CVPR (2019)
5. Antić, B., Ommer, B.: Video parsing for abnormality detection. In: ICCV (2011)
6. Finn, C., Abbeel, P., Levine, S.: Model-agnostic meta-learning for fast adaptation of deep networks. In: ICML (2017)
7. Raghu, A., Raghu, M., Bengio, S., Vinyals, O.: Rapid learning or feature reuse? Towards understanding the effectiveness of MAML. arXiv preprint arXiv:1909.09157 (2019)
8. Liu, W., W. Luo, D.L., Gao, S.: Future frame prediction for anomaly detection - a new baseline. In: CVPR (2018)
9. Kratz, L., Nishino, K.: Anomaly detection in extremely crowded scenes using spatio-temporal motion pattern models. In: CVPR (2009)
10. Wu, S., Moore, B.E., Shah, M.: Chaotic invariants of Lagrangian particle trajectories for anomaly detection in crowded scenes. In: CVPR (2010)
11. Zhao, B., Fei-Fei, L., Xing, E.P.: Online detection of unusual events in videos via dynamic sparse coding. In: CVPR (2011)
12. Lu, C., Shi, J., Jia, J.: Abnormal event detection at 150 FPS in MATLAB. In: ICCV (2013)
13. Xu, D., Ricci, E., Yan, Y., Song, J., Sebe, N.: Learning deep representations of appearance and motion for anomalous event detection. In: BMVC (2015)
14. Zhao, Y., Deng, B., Shen, C., Liu, Y., Lu, H., Hua, X.S.: Spatio-temporal autoencoder for video anomaly detection. In: Proceedings of the 25th ACM international conference on Multimedia (2017)
15. Nguyen, T.N., Meunier, J.: Anomaly detection in video sequence with appearance-motion correspondence. In: ICCV (2019)
16. Vu, H., Nguyen, T.D., Le, T., Luo, W., Phung, D.: Robust anomaly detection in videos using multilevel representations. In: AAAI (2019)
17. Lake, B.M., Ullman, T.D., Tenenbaum, J.B., Gershman, S.J.: Building machines that learn and think like people. Behav. Brain Sci. **40** (2017)
18. Thrun, S., Pratt, L.: Learning to learn: Introduction and overview. In: Thrun, S., Pratt, L. (eds.) Learning to Learn, pp. 3–17. Springer, Boston (1998). https://doi.org/10.1007/978-1-4615-5529-2_1
19. Snell, J., Swersky, K., Zemel, R.: Prototypical networks for few-shot learning. In: NIPS (2017)
20. Sung, F., Yang, Y., Zhang, L., Xiang, T., Torr, P.H., Hospedales, T.M.: Learning to compare: Relation network for few-shot learning. In: CVPR (2018)
21. Vinyals, O., Blundell, C., Lillicrap, T., Wierstra, D., et al.: Matching networks for one shot learning. In: NIPS (2016)
22. Mishra, N., Rohaninejad, M., Chen, X., Abbeel, P.: A simple neural attentive meta-learner. In: ICLR (2018)
23. Munkhdalai, T., Yu, H.: Meta networks. In: ICML (2017)
24. Oreshkin, B., López, P.R., Lacoste, A.: Tadam: task dependent adaptive metric for improved few-shot learning. In: NeurIPS (2018)
25. Santoro, A., Bartunov, S., Botvinick, M., Wierstra, D., Lillicrap, T.: Meta-learning with memory-augmented neural networks. In: ICML (2016)
26. Andrychowicz, M., et al.: Learning to learn by gradient descent by gradient descent. In: NIPS (2016)

27. Antoniou, A., Edwards, H., Storkey, A.: How to train your MAML. In: ICLR (2019)
28. Rusu, A.A., et al.: Meta-learning with latent embedding optimization. In: ICLR (2019)
29. Choi, J., Kwon, J., Lee, K.M.: Deep meta learning for real-time target-aware visual tracking. In: ICCV (2019)
30. Gui, L.-Y., Wang, Y.-X., Ramanan, D., Moura, J.M.F.: Few-shot human motion prediction via meta-learning. In: Ferrari, V., Hebert, M., Sminchisescu, C., Weiss, Y. (eds.) ECCV 2018. LNCS, vol. 11212, pp. 441–459. Springer, Cham (2018). https://doi.org/10.1007/978-3-030-01237-3_27
31. Park, E., Berg, A.C.: Meta-tracker: fast and robust online adaptation for visual object trackers. In: Ferrari, V., Hebert, M., Sminchisescu, C., Weiss, Y. (eds.) ECCV 2018. LNCS, vol. 11207, pp. 587–604. Springer, Cham (2018). https://doi.org/10.1007/978-3-030-01219-9_35
32. Shaban, A., Bansal, S., Liu, Z., Essa, I., Boots, B.: One-shot learning for semantic segmentation. In: BMVC (2017)
33. Wang, K., Liew, J.H., Zou, Y., Zhou, D., Feng, J.: PANet: few-shot image semantic segmentation with prototype alignment. In: ICCV (2019)
34. Yan, X., Chen, Z., Xu, A., Wang, X., Liang, X., Lin, L.: Meta R-CNN: towards general solver for instance-level low-shot learning. In: ICCV (2019)
35. Li, D., Yang, Y., Song, Y.Z., Hospedales, T.M.: Learning to generalize: meta-learning for domain generalization. In: AAAI (2018)
36. Lu, Y., Yu, F., Reddy, M.K.K., Wang, Y.: Few-shot scene-adaptive anomaly detection. In: Vedaldi, A., Bischof, H., Brox, T., Frahm, J.-M. (eds.) ECCV 2020. LNCS, vol. 12350, pp. 125–141. Springer, Cham (2020). https://doi.org/10.1007/978-3-030-58558-7_8
37. Carreira, J., Zisserman, A.: Quo vadis, action recognition? A new model and the kinetics dataset. In: CVPR (2017)
38. Ravi, S., Larochelle, H.: Optimization as a model for few-shot learning. In: ICLR (2017)
39. Tran, D., Bourdev, L., Fergus, R., Torresani, L., Paluri, M.: Learning spatiotemporal features with 3D convolutional networks. In: ICCV (2015)
40. Zach, C., Pock, T., Bischof, H.: A duality based approach for realtime TV-L^1 optical flow. In: Hamprecht, F.A., Schnörr, C., Jähne, B. (eds.) DAGM 2007. LNCS, vol. 4713, pp. 214–223. Springer, Heidelberg (2007). https://doi.org/10.1007/978-3-540-74936-3_22
41. Srivastava, N., Hinton, G., Krizhevsky, A., Sutskever, I., Salakhutdinov, R.: Dropout: a simple way to prevent neural networks from overfitting. JMLR **15**, 1929–1958 (2014)

TSI: Temporal Scale Invariant Network for Action Proposal Generation

Shuming Liu[1], Xu Zhao[1(✉)], Haisheng Su[1], and Zhilan Hu[2]

[1] Department of Automation, Shanghai Jiao Tong University, Shanghai, China
{shumingliu,zhaoxu}@sjtu.edu.cn
[2] The Central Media Technology Institute of Huawei Co., Ltd., Shenzhen, China

Abstract. Despite the great progress in temporal action proposal generation, most state-of-the-art methods ignore the impact of action scales and the performance of short actions is still far from satisfaction. In this paper, we first analyze the sample imbalance issue in action proposal generation, and correspondingly devise a novel scale-invariant loss function to alleviate the insufficient learning of short actions. To further achieve proposal generation task, we adopt the pipeline of boundary evaluation and proposal completeness regression, and propose the **Temporal Scale Invariant network**. To better leverage the temporal context, boundary evaluation module generates action boundaries with high-precision-assured global branch and high-recall-assured local branch. Simultaneously, the proposal evaluation module is supervised with introduced scale-invariant loss, predicting accurate proposal completeness for different scales of actions. Comprehensive experiments are conducted on ActivityNet-1.3 and THUMOS14 benchmarks, where TSI achieves state-of-the-art performance. Especially, AUC performance of short actions is boosted from 36.53% to 39.63% compared with baseline.

1 Introduction

As an important and fundamental video understanding task, temporal action detection has attracted extensive attention recently. Akin to object detection, detecting action clips in a given untrimmed video can be divided into two stages: temporal action proposal generation and proposal classification. For action proposal generation task, the start and end time of real action instances in the video need to be temporally localized. Action proposal generation is extremely useful for many advanced video understanding tasks, such as action recognition, video captioning, spatio-temporal action localization, and so forth.

Previous proposal generation methods can be mainly categorized as three frameworks. The first one follows the **top-down** pathway. By utilizing sliding window or anchor mechanism, a large number of default proposals are generated

This work has been supported in part by the funding from NSFC (61673269, 61273285), Huawei cooperative project and the project funding of the Institute of Medical Robotics at Shanghai Jiao Tong University.

H. Ishikawa et al. (Eds.): ACCV 2020, LNCS 12626, pp. 530–546, 2021.
https://doi.org/10.1007/978-3-030-69541-5_32

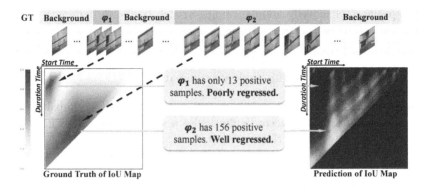

Fig. 1. What's the impact of action's temporal scale in proposal generation? For an untrimmed video with two actions φ_1 and φ_2, current proposal confidence prediction module would regress a promising score for long action φ_2 yet miss the short action φ_1. This problem is caused by the imbalance of positive samples for different actions.

densely, which are designed to cover different duration ground truth. Then these redundant proposals are revised by offset prediction and confidence regression, such as [1–6]. The second framework takes ***bottom-up*** methodology, where the temporal feature sequence is firstly used for boundary detection and actionness evaluation, and the proposals are explicitly formed by pairing the start and end points. Then, proposals are also refined by confidence regression, such as BSN [7] and TSA [8]. In the third framework, to combine the advantage of both bottom-up and top-down methods, boundary detection and dense confidence regression are performed simultaneously by using ROI align. This complementary framework obtains impressive results in BMN [9] and DBG [10].

Despite the remarkable progress achieved in action proposal generation, there are still many issues remain unsolved. Among them, how to deal with the ***scale*** change in temporal dimension is a long-standing problem. As shown in Fig. 1, in an untrimmed video with two ground truth actions, the shorter action is prone to be missed in completeness prediction, which is reflected as the extreme low recall compared to long actions in Table 5. We delve deep into this phenomenon, and conclude that the ignorance of short actions can be caused by the unbalanced positive sample distribution. Another bottleneck that limits performance gains is the module of boundary detection. Current methods mainly focus on local information and low-level features, however the critical global context is missed when determining the action boundaries. Local-global combination is an intuitive and promising direction to widen this bottleneck.

To address the aforementioned issues, we first analyze the sample-imbalance problem in action proposal generation, and correspondingly propose a general scale-invariant loss function for confidence regression, which can evidently enhance the detection ability for short actions. Furthermore, in order to achieve complete action proposal generation, we combine the bottom-up and top-down pathways, and introduce our **Temporal Scale Invariant network (TSI)**.

To be specific, TSI novelly adopts a multi-branch temporal boundary detector to capture action boundaries with both high recall and high precision. Simultaneously, IoU map regressor, supervised by the proposed scale-invariant loss function, is able to regress accurate confidence score especially for short actions. The main contributions of this work are summarized as:

1. Centered on the temporal scale issue, we analyze the sample-imbalance phenomena behind it, and accordingly devise a scale-invariant loss function to improve the detection performance on short actions.
2. To achieve the complete action proposal generation, besides handling the scale issue, TSI also takes advantage of temporal context for boundary detection with local-global-complementary structure to enhance the performance.
3. Comprehensive experiments are conducted on THUMOS14 and ActivityNet benchmarks. Results show that TSI outperforms other state-of-the-art action proposal generation methods and achieves AUC of 68.35% on ActivityNet.

2 Related Work

Temporal action detection can be grouped into two types of methods: the first type is "one-stage" method that intends to localize the actions and predict its category simultaneously. The other type is "two-stage" method, which follows the pipeline of "detection by classifying proposals".

Temporal Action Detection. The advantage of one-stage method is to naturally avoid sub-optimization for action localization and classification. For example, akin to SSD in object detection, SSAD [3] defines multi-scale anchors and uses temporal convolution to extract corresponding contextual features for offset regression and category prediction. What's more, GTAN [11] uses Gaussian kernels to model the temporal structure, which can dynamically optimize the temporal scale of each proposal. Besides, P-GCN [12] and G-TAD [13] exploits proposal-proposal relations and temporal-temporal relations by graph convolution networks and achieves significant performance gains.

Temporal Action Proposal Generation. The motivation of two-stage method is the success of video classification task for a given trimmed video [14–18]. Therefore, how to localize possible action instance with precise boundary and high overlap in long untrimmed video becomes the key issue in action detection. The mainstream of top-down action proposal generation methods would first initiate a default proposal set, which is often predefined by clustering ground truth actions, and then revise them with confidence regression [5,10,19–24]. For example, RapNet [6] introduces a relation-aware module to exploit long-range temporal relations and follows a two-stage adjustment scheme to refine the proposal boundaries and measure their confidence. As for bottom-up methods [8], TAG [2] designs temporal watershed algorithm to generate proposals, yet missing the regression for proposal confidence. Considering the boundary information, BSN [7] firstly utilizes temporal evaluation module to predict the starting and ending probabilities, and uses proposal evaluation module to regress the confidence score. To take advantage of both bottom-up and top-down method, MGG [25] first attempts to embed position information and generate proposals from different granularities. Improved from BSN, BMN [9] develops boundary matching mechanism to regress the confidence of all potential proposals. To further regress densely distributed proposals, DBG [10] propose an unified framework to achieve boundary classification and action completeness regression.

Although the great progress in action detection, the long-standing problem of temporal scale variation still has not been pertinently studied, which is the main motivation of this paper.

3   Our Approach

3.1   Problem Definition and Video Representation

Given an untrimmed video X, the temporal proposal annotation is denoted as $\Psi_g = \{\varphi_i = [t_{s,i}, t_{e,i}]\}_{i=1}^{N_g}$, where N_g is the number of ground truth, and $[t_{s,i}, t_{e,i}]$ is the start and end time of action instance φ_i. The aim of temporal action proposal generation is to predict candidate proposal set $\Psi_p = \{\varphi_i = [t_{s,i}, t_{e,i}, s_i]\}_{i=1}^{N_p}$ to cover Ψ_g with high recall and high overlap, where s_i is the confidence score of predicted φ_i and will be used for proposal ranking.

Following previous work [7,9,22,26], we adopt two-stream network [14] to encode the raw RGB frames and optical flow of video X into representative video feature sequence $F_0 \in \mathbb{R}^{C \times T}$, where C is the fixed feature channel and T is the video feature length. Then we rescale the feature sequence to length D by linear interpolation and eventually obtain the feature $F \in \mathbb{R}^{C \times D}$, as the input of action proposal generation network.

It is worth noticing that, in BMN, DBG and other methods, a proposal is considered as the composition of a start point and an end point, which are both selected from D quantified time index. Therefore, the upper limit number of candidate proposals can be calculated as $N = \binom{D}{2} = \frac{D(D-1)}{2}$, meaning the algorithm need to retrieve real actions from these N candidates.

3.2   Scale-Imbalance Analysis in Proposal Generation

As introduced before, short actions are prone to be missed in confidence regression. By contrast, AUC can decrease significantly from 94.48% of long actions to 36.53% of short actions in state-of-the-art baseline BMN (see Table 5). In fact, the inferior detection ability of short actions can be interpreted as many folds, such as the insufficient feature representation with limited granularity, the stringent boundary overlap requirements due to the IoU evaluation metrics. In addition to above reasons, **the unbalanced training** also leads to the overwhelming learning of large actions but severe weak learning for short actions.

To discuss this issue, we need to clarify the definition of action scale first. The scale of an action s is regarded as *the ratio of action length to video length*, thus,

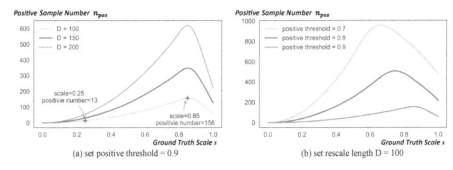

Fig. 2. The distribution of positive sample numbers with action scale. Take D equals to 100 in (a) for example, a long action with $s = 0.85$ will have 156 positive samples while a short action with $s = 0.25$ has only 13 positive samples. This sample imbalance causes severe weak learning for short actions but excessive learning for long actions.

s should belong to $(0, 1)$. Now we inspect a video with two ground truth actions. By computing the IoU between GT actions with aforementioned N proposals, the IoU map is obtained as shown in Fig. 1 left. In this map, point(i, j) represents the maximum IoU between GTs with proposal(i, j) (following the definition in BMN, proposal(i, j) indicates a proposal with duration time i and start time j). Therefore IoU values around GT are closer to 1 and should be considered as *high quality proposals*. However, as visualized in Fig. 1, the area of high quality proposals of long action φ_2 is much larger than short action φ_1, which reminds us: **Is the short action overlooked in such dense regression mechanism?**

The answer is Yes. No matter what loss function we choose in IoU regression, for example binary logistic loss used in BMN and L2 loss in DBG, positive samples and negative samples need to be defined first. Normally, a proposal with its $IoU > \varepsilon$ is regarded as positive, where ε is a predefined threshold. Thus, we can use sampling or reweight methods to balance the positive/negative samples. However, inside the positive samples, with the change of action scale s, the number of positive samples n_{pos} of each ground truth would vary significantly, as shown in Fig. 2. Take Fig. 2(a) for instance, when $D = 100$, an action with scale 0.85 has 10x positive samples than the action with scale 0.25. Consequently, the short action with less positive samples can not be learned adequately.

To address above problem, the loss function of confidence regression must satisfy two conditions (1) the contribution of each ground truth should be equal considering the n_{pos} (2) the positive/negative samples should be balanced appropriately. To this end, we propose the **scale-invariant loss** (SI-Loss) as Eq. 1.

$$L_{SI} = \sum_{i,j} b_{i,j} w_{i,j} \log (p_{i,j}) + (1 - b_{i,j}) w_{i,j} \log (1 - p_{i,j}) \tag{1}$$

$$w_{i,j} = \begin{cases} (1 - \alpha)/n_{pos,c} & \text{if } b_{i,j} = 1 \\ \alpha/(N - \sum_c n_{pos,c}) & \text{if } b_{i,j} = 0 \end{cases} \tag{2}$$

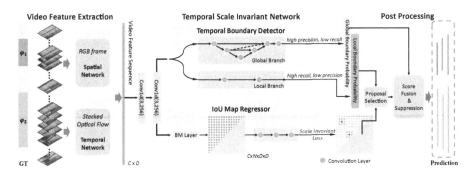

Fig. 3. The framework of our method. TSI contains two modules: temporal boundary detector (TBD) and IoU map regressor (IMR). In TBD, local branch focuses on local information and generates high-recall-assured boundaries, while U-shaped global branch distills contextual features and provides high precision-assured boundaries. Meanwhile, IMR densely regresses the completeness of potential proposals supervised with scale-invariant loss, which can greatly improve the detection ability for short actions.

SI-Loss essentially is a scale-weighted binary logistic loss. In Eq. 1, $w_{i,j}$ is the weight coefficient for proposal(i, j). $b_{i,j}$ stands for the positive mask whether proposal(i, j) is a positive sample given threshold ε. To balance the change of n_{pos} in loss contribution, we define $w_{i,j}$ as following: if a proposal(i, j) is a positive sample and it belongs to annotation φ_c, we divide its loss with φ_c's total positive sample number $n_{pos,c}$, which can guarantee the aggregate positive loss of each GT the same. In this way, taking positive sample number distribution into consideration, each action in a video can be learned equally in the training loss, which achieves the scale-invariant purpose. What's more, to control the balance of positive and negative samples, hyper-parameter α is adopted in SI-Loss.

When video only contains one annotation and α takes 0.5, scale-invariant loss would degenerate into normal binary logistic loss. What's more, when α is bigger than 0.5, SI-Loss would have a higher weight on negative samples, which can reduce the false positive response. Supervised with SI-Loss, in proposal completeness regression module, the ability to retrieve small targets is greatly enhanced and its effectiveness has been proved as shown in Table 5.

3.3 Temporal Scale Invariant Network

With the scale-invariant loss, to achieve the complete action proposal generation process, we combine the bottom-up and top-down pathways and propose Temporal Scale Invariant Network. The framework of TSI can be demonstrated as Fig. 3, which contains two modules: **Temporal Boundary Detector (TBD)** and **IoU Map Regressor (IMR)**.

Temporal Boundary Detector. It is acknowledged that one of the necessary conditions for a well-performed action proposal generation method is the precise

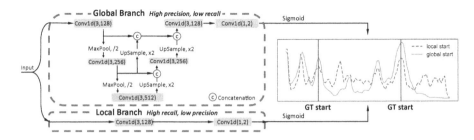

Fig. 4. TBD architecture. TBD contains local branch and global branch to detect boundaries with high precision and high recall. c stands for the concatenation operation.

prediction for action boundary. Conventional approaches [7,9] hold that boundary is a local information which does not require much attention on temporal context or deep semantic features, thus they both share a limited receptive field.

Such viewpoints, however, are biased as revealed in [6,8]. Actions with different scales should require corresponding receptive field, thus the boundary detection module need to be able to leverage local apparent information and global contextual semantic information in a unified framework. Taking into account of such requirements, we design a local-global complementary network named TBD to detect accurate temporal boundaries, as shown in Fig. 4.

In TBD, the local branch observes a small receptive field with only two temporal convolution layers. Therefore this branch focuses on the local abrupt change and generates a rough boundary with high recall to cover all actual start/end points, yet bringing extreme low precision. To make up this shortcoming, global branch enlarges the receptive field and presents boundaries with contextual U-shaped network, which is inspired by UNet [27]. The global branch uses multiple temporal convolution layers followed by down-sampling steps to distill semantic information of different granularity. To restore the resolution of temporal feature sequence, several up-sampling operations are repeated and features in the same resolutions are concatenated.

In Fig. 4, *conv1d(3,128)* represents the temporal convolution layer with kernel size 3 and output channel 128. If not stated specifically, ReLU is used for activation function. At last, 1×1 convolution with 2 channels and sigmoid function is used to generate starting and ending boundaries for both branches. To sum up, this combination of local and global structure will best leverage the low-level fine-grained features with contextual features and extract accurate boundaries with high recall and high precision.

IoU Map Regressor. Besides the bottom-up pathway of boundary evaluation, proposal confidence regression is also vital for action proposal generation. To densely regress potential proposal confidence, we adopt the Boundary-Matching mechanism in BMN [9], which can transfer temporal feature sequence $F \in \mathbb{R}^{C \times D}$ to proposal feature matrix $M_F \in \mathbb{R}^{C \times M \times D \times D}$ through BM layer.

Boundary-Matching mechanism essentially is a ROI align layer implemented in matrix product. By using such module, the completeness of all proposals can be regressed simultaneously.

For fair comparison, we follow the exact network structure of proposal evaluation module in BMN. After IoU Map Regressor, each proposal will be predicted with two confidence score, which is supervised with IoU classification loss and IoU regression loss. However, the classification loss in BMN ignores the impact of action scales that leads to the low recall of short actions. Therefore, we use the aforementioned scale-invariant loss as the IoU classification loss to enforce the network to focus on different scale actions equally.

4   Training and Inference

4.1   Training of TSI

Label Assignment. For a ground truth action $\varphi_g = [t_s, t_e]$, action starting region is defined as $r_s = [t_s - d/10, t_s + d/10]$, where $d = t_e - t_s$. Then by computing the maximum overlap ratio of each temporal interval with r_s, we can obtain $G_s = \{g_i^s\}$ as the starting label of TBD. The same label assignment process is adopted for ending label G_e. As for IMR, the label of IoU map is denoted as $G_{iou} = \{g_{i,j}\}$, which follows the definition in BMN.

Loss of TBD. The output of TBD are the starting and ending probability sequence from local and global branch, denoted as $P_{s,l}$, $P_{e,l}$, $P_{s,g}$, and $P_{e,g}$ respectively. We follow [7] to adopt binary logistic loss L_{bl} to supervise the boundary prediction with G_s, G_e, denoted as

$$L_{TBD} = \frac{1}{2} \left(L_{bl} \left(P_{s,l}, G_s \right) + L_{bl} \left(P_{e,l}, G_e \right) + L_{bl} \left(P_{s,g}, G_s \right) + L_{bl} \left(P_{e,g}, G_e \right) \right) \quad (3)$$

Loss of IMR. The output of IMR is a probability map P_{iou} with two channels. Following BMN, we construct the classification loss and regression loss as the IMR loss, where we use proposed SI-Loss as classification loss L_C and L2 loss as regression loss L_R. Especially, positive threshold ε is set as 0.9 in SI-Loss.

$$L_{IMR} = L_C(P_{iou,c}, G_{iou}) + L_R(P_{iou,r}, G_{iou}) \quad (4)$$

The training objective of TSI is the multi-task learning in the unified framework. The overall loss function contains TBD loss, IMR loss, and L2 regularization term, where λ is the weight term set to 10^{-4}:

$$L = L_{TBD} + L_{IMR} + \lambda \cdot L_2 (\Theta) \quad (5)$$

4.2   Inference of TSI

Proposal Selection. To ensure the diversity of proposals and guarantee a high recall, only local branch of TBD is used for proposal selection. Following [7,9], all temporal locations satisfying (1) local peak in boundary probabilities and (2) probabilities higher than $0.5 \cdot max(P)$ are regarded as the starting and ending locations. Then we match all starting and ending locations to generate redundant candidate proposals, denoted as Ψ_p.

Score Fusion and Proposal Suppression. For each proposal(i, j) in Ψ_p, whose duration time is i, start time is j and end time is $i+j$, its IoU completeness is denoted as fusion of classification score and regression score $p_{iou} = p_{i,j,c} \cdot p_{i,j,r}$. Its starting probability is denoted as $p_{start} = \sqrt{p_{s,l}(i) \cdot p_{s,g}(i)}$, which is the same as p_{end} for ending probability. Therefore the proposal confidence score is defined as $p_f = p_{start} \cdot p_{end} \cdot p_{iou}$. Then we adopt Soft-NMS [28] to remove redundant proposals to retrieve final high quality proposals.

5   Experiments

5.1   Datasets and Settings

ActivityNet-1.3 [29] is a large-scale video understanding dataset, consisting of 19,994 videos annotated for action proposal task. The dataset is divided into training, validation and testing set with the ratio of 2:1:1.

THUMOS14 dataset contains 200 annotated untrimmed videos in validation set and 213 annotated untrimmed videos in testing set. We use the validation set to train TSI and evaluate our model on testing set.

Implementation Details. On ActivityNet dataset, rescaling length D is set to 100. On THUMOS dataset, we slide the temporal window with length 128 and overlap ratio 0.5 by following [7]. On both datasets, we use batch size of 16 and Adam optimizer to train TSI. The learning rate is set to 10^{-3} and decay it to 10^{-4} after 7 epochs. Besides, α is set to 0.8 as experimented on ablation study.

5.2   Temporal Action Proposal Generation

For action proposal generation task, Average Recall (AR) under Average Number of proposals (AN) with different IoU thresholds is the widely used evaluation metrics. Besides, the area under AR vs AN curve (AUC) is also used for comparison on ActivityNet-1.3 in our experiments.

Comparison with State-of-the-Art Methods. Table 1 illustrates the performance of our proposal generation method compared with other state-of-the-art methods on ActivityNet-1.3 dataset. The result shows that TSI outperform other methods and improves the AUC from 67.10% to 68.35% on validation set.

Table 1. Comparison between TSI and other state-of-the-art temporal action proposal generation methods on ActivityNet-1.3 in terms of AR@100 and AUC.

Method	CTAP [5]	BSN [7]	MGG [25]	BMN [9]	DBG [10]	**TSI**
AR@100(val)	73.17	74.16	74.56	75.01	**76.65**	76.31
AUC(val)	65.72	66.17	66.54	67.10	68.23	**68.35**
AUC(test)	–	66.26	66.47	67.19	68.57	**68.85**

Table 2. Comparison between TSI and other state-of-the-art temporal action proposal generation methods on test set of THUMOS14 dataset in terms of AR@AN.

Method	Feature	@50	@100	@200	@500	Feature	@50	@100	@200	@500
TURN [22]	C3D	19.63	27.96	38.34	53.52	Flow	21.86	31.89	43.02	57.63
MGG [25]	C3D	29.11	36.31	44.32	54.95	2Stream	39.93	47.75	54.65	61.36
BSN [7]	C3D	29.58	37.38	45.55	54.67	2Stream	37.46	46.06	53.21	60.64
BMN [9]	C3D	32.73	40.68	47.86	56.42	2Stream	39.36	47.72	54.70	62.07
DBG [10]	C3D	32.55	41.07	48.83	57.58	2Stream	40.89	49.24	55.76	62.21
TSI	C3D	**33.46**	**41.64**	**49.97**	**57.73**	2Stream	**42.30**	**50.51**	**57.24**	**63.43**

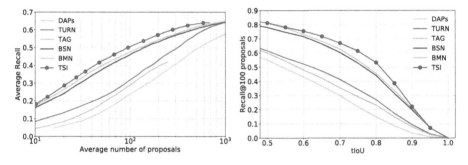

Fig. 5. Comparison between TSI and other state-of-the-art methods on test set of THUMOS14 in terms of **(left)** AR@AN **(right)** Recall@100 with different tIoU.

Especially, the AR@100 is improved from 75.01% to 76.31%, suggesting TSI can generate rich and accurate proposals.

We also implement our method on THUMOS14, as shown in Table 2. C3D feature [15] and two stream feature [14] used in BMN are adopted for fair comparison. Experiment shows that TSI outperforms other methods in all AN sets and achieves state-of-the-art performance. Figure 5 further illustrates that TSI can guarantee higher recall with fewer proposals and in terms of different tIoU.

Ablation Study. To fully confirm the effectiveness of TSI, we conduct extensive ablation experiments on our proposed method.

Table 3. Ablation study of different boundary detection modules on ActivityNet-1.3.

	BSN-TEM	BMN-TEM	TSI-TBD
AUC(val)	64.80	65.17	**66.31**
AR@100	73.57	73.72	**74.13**

Table 4. Ablation study of hyper parameter α in Scale-Invariant loss.

α	0.5	0.6	0.7	0.8	0.9
AUC(val)	67.98	68.08	68.13	**68.35**	68.33

Table 5. Ablation study of Scale-Invariant Loss with AUC performance of different action scales on ActivityNet-1.3 validation set. s stands for the scale of ground truth

Method	AUC	$0.0 \leq s < 0.06$	$0.06 \leq s < 0.65$	$0.65 \leq s \leq 1.0$
BMN	67.10	36.53	70.43	94.48
BMN+SI-Loss	**67.98**	40.24	70.32	94.41
DBG	67.90	39.07	72.18	93.08
DBG+SI-Loss	**68.23**	40.57	70.25	94.73
TSI(TBD)	66.31	36.65	68.55	94.59
TSI(TBD+IMR)	67.47	36.87	71.11	**95.20**
TSI(TBD+IMR+SI-loss)	**68.35**	**39.63**	**71.40**	94.79

Effectiveness of Temporal Boundary Detector. First, we evaluate our temporal boundary detector with other boundary-based methods. As shown in Table 3, we only use TBD without IMR to generate action proposals, which can already achieve higher AUC and recall of 66.31%, compared with other temporal evaluation module in BSN and BMN. This result proves that TBD with local-global branches can better leverage the temporal context to detect precise boundaries and well balance the recall and precision of retrieved boundary location. Note that in all comparisons, Soft-NMS is used for redundant proposal suppression.

Ablation Study of α In Scale-Invariant Loss. The hyper parameter α is the coefficient to balance the positive/negative samples. As shown in Table 4, with the increase of α, AUC is correspondingly boosted from 67.98% to 68.35%, indicating (1) network supervised with scale-invariant loss can achieve high AUC regardless of α (2) the larger α would reduce the false positive response of IoU prediction, which can improve the detection ability.

Effectiveness of Scale-Invariant Loss. To further verify the effectiveness proposed scale-invariant loss function, we conducted several ablation experiments, which is shown in Table 5. (Note: we use the same video feature of BMN on DBG and TSI, thus the result of DBG is lower than reported in their paper.)

Table 6. Generalization ability of TSI on validation set of ActivityNet-1.3 in terms of AR@100 and AUC.

BMN/TSI	Seen		Unseen	
	AR@100	AUC	AR@100	AUC
Training with *Seen+Unseen*	72.96/74.69	65.02/66.54	72.68/74.31	65.06/66.14
Training with *Seen*	72.47/73.59	64.37/65.60	72.46/**73.07**	64.47/**65.05**

First, to verify the detection ability on short actions, we compare the AUC performance on different scales of actions on ActivityNet-1.3 validation set. According to the value of s from small to large, we artificially divide the dataset into three groups: small scale actions that $0 \leq s < 0.06$, middle scale actions that $0.06 \leq s < 0.65$, and large scale actions $0.65 \leq s \leq 1.0$. Each subset has almost the same amount of ground truth, which guarantees the fairness of comparison. Then we evaluate methods on each sub dataset.

What's more, we transfer our scale-invariant loss to our methods to prove its generality. The results demonstrate:

1. Both BMN, DBG and TSI behave worse on the subset of short actions compared with long actions. This phenomenon is intuitive because small actions naturally don't have sufficient feature representation against the background, and the IoU evaluation metrics are sensitive especially on small action length, not surprisingly, bringing the extreme low recall.
2. Without bells and whistles, we transfer the scale-invariant loss into BMN and DBG, and achieve steady improvements. In BMN, AUC of short actions has been boosted from 36.53% to 40.24%. Specifically, because the imbalance issue in DBG is not severer as BMN, AUC gains for DBG is not as much as BMN, which is acceptable.
3. Except for the significant improvement on short actions, to middle actions and long actions, TSI also provide performance gains than baseline BMN.
4. If we only adopt boundary detection module in TSI, AUC can achieve 66.31%. When we integrate TBD with IMR, performance is already better than the BMN baseline. Overall, our TSI achieves the 68.35% in validation set and 68.85% on test set of ActivityNet-1.3.

Generalization Ability. To evaluate the generalization ability of action proposal methods for unseen videos, following [9], we choose two un-overlapped subsets "Sports, Exercise, and Recreation" and "Socialing, Relaxing, and Leisure" classes of ActivityNet-1.3, as seen and unseen subset respectively. C3D [15] pretrained on Sports-1M dataset [30] is adopted for feature extraction. We train TSI with seen and seen+unseen videos separately and evaluate on both sub-datasets. As shown in Table 6, TSI can localize the actions of unseen data with high AUC. Compared with BMN, TSI also achieves better generalization ability.

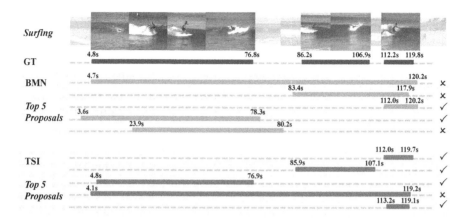

Fig. 6. Qualitative results of top-5 proposals generated by BMN and TSI on ActivityNet-1.3.

Visualization of Qualitative Results. As illustrated in Fig. 6, we visualize the top-5 proposal prediction of BMN and TSI on ActivityNet dataset. The demonstrated surfing video has three ground truth actions. However, due to the excessive learning for long actions, BMN may regard two individual actions as only one and predict more proposals with long duration. Besides, the temporal boundary of BMN is also not accurate enough. Compared with BMN, our proposed method can retrieve three actions independently with higher overlap and more accurate boundaries, because of the introduced modules.

5.3   Temporal Action Proposal Detection

With retrieved high quality action proposals, many video understanding tasks will be benefited, such as temporal action detection. In the detection task, Mean Average Precision (mAP) is used as the evaluation metrics. For a fair comparison, we combine our TSI proposals with state-of-the-art action classifier to achieve "detection by classifying proposals" framework.

On THUMOS14, we select top-200 TSI proposals with UntrimmedNet classifier [17] following [9]. The results on THUMOS14 datasets are shown in Table 7. Experiments prove that our generated proposals can satisfy the demand for detection task and outperform other state-of-the-art methods on THUMOS14 benchmarks, indicating that TSI can retrieve high quality action proposals.

On ActivityNet-1.3, we adopt top-100 TSI proposals with top-2 video level classification results provided by CUHK [31] as detection results. More specific, to enhance the detection performance on ActivityNet, we first adopt the proposal selection introduced in Sect. 4.2. Then, instead of using $p_{start} \cdot p_{end} \cdot p_{iou}$ as proposal confidence, we directly use the p_{iou} as final proposal confidence and utilize NMS with threshold 0.5 to reduce the redundant proposals, which is the same setting in BMN for fair comparison. The results are reported in Table 8.

Table 7. Action detection results on testing set of THUMOS14, where video-level classifier UntrimmedNet [17] is combined with our proposals.

Method	0.7	0.6	0.5	0.4	0.3
TURN [22]	6.3	14.1	25.6	35.3	46.3
BSN [7]	20.0	28.4	36.9	45.0	53.5
MGG [25]	21.3	29.5	37.4	46.8	53.9
BMN [9]	20.5	29.7	38.8	47.4	56.0
DBG [10]	21.7	30.2	39.8	49.4	57.8
G-TAD [13]	**23.4**	30.8	40.2	47.6	54.5
TSI	22.4	**33.2**	**42.6**	**52.1**	**61.0**

Table 8. Action detection results on validation set of ActivityNet-1.3, where video-level classification results generated by [31] are combined with our proposals.

Method	Validation			
	0.5	0.75	0.95	Average
SSN [2]	39.12	23.48	5.49	23.98
BSN [7]	46.45	29.96	8.02	30.03
DBG [10]	42.59	26.24	6.56	29.72
BMN [9]	50.07	34.78	8.29	33.85
G-TAD [13]	50.36	34.60	**9.02**	34.09
TSI	50.86	33.89	7.28	33.71
TSI(reweight)	**51.18**	**35.02**	6.59	**34.15**

To further improve the detection performance, we reweight the iou classification score and iou regression score, which can achieve the mAP of 34.15%.

It is worth discussing the differences and connections between temporal action proposal generation task and temporal action detection task. Although the proposal generation results with proposal classification results can be combined for the detection task, however, the proposal confidence used for ranking must be carefully designed. For example, DBG has achieved state-of-the-art action proposal generation performance with AUC of 68.23%, while the detection performance is unexpected low with only 29.72% mAP, which is far below current baseline methods. The reason of this phenomenon is the different evaluation metrics of each task. The action proposal generation focuses on the diversity of retrieved proposals and judges the performance by the recall of top N proposals. However, the action detection task focuses on the precision of top proposals, such as top-5. Therefore, some action proposal generation method, such as DBG, may retrieve the actions with well diversity, yet sacrificing the precision of top 1 proposal. In fact, the top-1 precision of DBG is much lower than TSI, leading to the low detection performance. This insight also reminds us that one possible trick for improving detection performance, which is, using two-stage methods to learn the proposal confidence again with proposal generation results, and re-rank proposals with proposal-relation-aware model, such as P-GCN.

6   Conclusion

In this paper, we introduced the Temporal Scale Invariant Network (TSI) for action proposal generation, which can predict precise action boundaries with temporal contextual information and regress accurate proposal confidence. Especially, we analyze the positive sample imbalance problem in temporal action proposal generation and correspondingly devise a scale-invariant loss function to make up the insufficient learning of short actions and reduce the impact of the action scale change. Extensive experiments prove the effectiveness of proposed TSI and the state-of-the-art performance on ActivityNet-1.3 and THUMOS14 benchmarks is reported.

References

1. Buch, S., Escorcia, V., Shen, C., Ghanem, B., Carlos Niebles, J.: SST: single-stream temporal action proposals. In: Proceedings of the IEEE Conference on Computer Vision and Pattern Recognition, pp. 2911–2920 (2017)
2. Zhao, Y., Xiong, Y., Wang, L., Wu, Z., Tang, X., Lin, D.: Temporal action detection with structured segment networks. In: Proceedings of the IEEE International Conference on Computer Vision, pp. 2914–2923 (2017)
3. Lin, T., Zhao, X., Shou, Z.: Single shot temporal action detection. In: Proceedings of the 25th ACM international conference on Multimedia, pp. 988–996. ACM (2017)
4. Chao, Y.W., Vijayanarasimhan, S., Seybold, B., Ross, D.A., Deng, J., Sukthankar, R.: Rethinking the faster R-CNN architecture for temporal action localization. In: Proceedings of the IEEE Conference on Computer Vision and Pattern Recognition, pp. 1130–1139 (2018)
5. Gao, J., Chen, K., Nevatia, R.: CTAP: complementary temporal action proposal generation. In: Ferrari, V., Hebert, M., Sminchisescu, C., Weiss, Y. (eds.) ECCV 2018. LNCS, vol. 11206, pp. 70–85. Springer, Cham (2018). https://doi.org/10.1007/978-3-030-01216-8_5
6. Gao, J., et al.: Accurate temporal action proposal generation with relation-aware pyramid network. In: AAAI Conference on Artificial Intelligence, pp. 10810–10817 (2020)
7. Lin, T., Zhao, X., Su, H., Wang, C., Yang, M.: BSN: boundary sensitive network for temporal action proposal generation. In: Ferrari, V., Hebert, M., Sminchisescu, C., Weiss, Y. (eds.) ECCV 2018. LNCS, vol. 11208, pp. 3–21. Springer, Cham (2018). https://doi.org/10.1007/978-3-030-01225-0_1
8. Gong, G., Zheng, L., Mu, Y.: Scale matters: temporal scale aggregation network for precise action localization in untrimmed videos. In: IEEE International Conference on Multimedia and Expo, pp. 1–6 (2020)
9. Lin, T., Liu, X., Li, X., Ding, E., Wen, S.: BMN: boundary-matching network for temporal action proposal generation. In: Proceedings of the IEEE International Conference on Computer Vision, pp. 3889–3898 (2019)

10. Lin, C., et al.: Fast learning of temporal action proposal via dense boundary generator. In: AAAI Conference on Artificial Intelligence, pp. 11499–11506 (2020)
11. Long, F., Yao, T., Qiu, Z., Tian, X., Luo, J., Mei, T.: Gaussian temporal awareness networks for action localization. In: Proceedings of the IEEE Conference on Computer Vision and Pattern Recognition, pp. 344–353 (2019)
12. Zeng, R., et al.: Graph convolutional networks for temporal action localization. In: Proceedings of the IEEE International Conference on Computer Vision, pp. 7094–7103 (2019)
13. Xu, M., Zhao, C., Rojas, D.S., Thabet, A., Ghanem, B.: G-TAD: sub-graph localization for temporal action detection. In: Proceedings of the IEEE Conference on Computer Vision and Pattern Recognition, pp. 10156–10165 (2020)
14. Simonyan, K., Zisserman, A.: Two-stream convolutional networks for action recognition in videos. In: Advances in Neural Information Processing Systems, pp. 568–576 (2014)
15. Tran, D., Bourdev, L., Fergus, R., Torresani, L., Paluri, M.: Learning spatiotemporal features with 3D convolutional networks. In: Proceedings of the IEEE International Conference on Computer Vision, pp. 4489–4497 (2015)
16. Qiu, Z., Yao, T., Mei, T.: Learning spatio-temporal representation with pseudo-3D residual networks. In: Proceedings of the IEEE International Conference on Computer Vision, pp. 5533–5541 (2017)
17. Wang, L., Xiong, Y., Lin, D., Van Gool, L.: UntrimmedNets for weakly supervised action recognition and detection. In: Proceedings of the IEEE Conference on Computer Vision and Pattern Recognition, pp. 4325–4334 (2017)
18. Carreira, J., Zisserman, A.: Quo vadis, action recognition? A new model and the kinetics dataset. In: Proceedings of the IEEE Conference on Computer Vision and Pattern Recognition, pp. 6299–6308 (2017)
19. Caba Heilbron, F., Carlos Niebles, J., Ghanem, B.: Fast temporal activity proposals for efficient detection of human actions in untrimmed videos. In: Proceedings of the IEEE Conference on Computer Vision and Pattern Recognition, pp. 1914–1923 (2016)
20. Shou, Z., Chan, J., Zareian, A., Miyazawa, K., Chang, S.F.: CDC: convolutional-de-convolutional networks for precise temporal action localization in untrimmed videos. In: Proceedings of the IEEE Conference on Computer Vision and Pattern Recognition, pp. 5734–5743 (2017)
21. Buch, S., Escorcia, V., Ghanem, B., Fei-Fei, L., Niebles, J.C.: End-to-end, single-stream temporal action detection in untrimmed videos. In: British Machine Vision Conference, vol. 2, p. 7 (2017)
22. Gao, J., Yang, Z., Chen, K., Sun, C., Nevatia, R.: Turn tap: temporal unit regression network for temporal action proposals. In: Proceedings of the IEEE International Conference on Computer Vision, pp. 3628–3636 (2017)
23. Ji, J., Cao, K., Niebles, J.C.: Learning temporal action proposals with fewer labels. In: Proceedings of the IEEE International Conference on Computer Vision, pp. 7073–7082 (2019)
24. Schlosser, P., Munch, D., Arens, M.: Investigation on combining 3d convolution of image data and optical flow to generate temporal action proposals. In: IEEE Conference on Computer Vision and Pattern Recognition Workshops (2019)
25. Liu, Y., Ma, L., Zhang, Y., Liu, W., Chang, S.F.: Multi-granularity generator for temporal action proposal. In: Proceedings of the IEEE Conference on Computer Vision and Pattern Recognition, pp. 3604–3613 (2019)

26. Escorcia, V., Caba Heilbron, F., Niebles, J.C., Ghanem, B.: DAPs: deep action proposals for action understanding. In: Leibe, B., Matas, J., Sebe, N., Welling, M. (eds.) ECCV 2016. LNCS, vol. 9907, pp. 768–784. Springer, Cham (2016). https://doi.org/10.1007/978-3-319-46487-9_47

27. Ronneberger, O., Fischer, P., Brox, T.: U-Net: convolutional networks for biomedical image segmentation. In: Navab, N., Hornegger, J., Wells, W.M., Frangi, A.F. (eds.) MICCAI 2015. LNCS, vol. 9351, pp. 234–241. Springer, Cham (2015). https://doi.org/10.1007/978-3-319-24574-4_28

28. Bodla, N., Singh, B., Chellappa, R., Davis, L.S.: Soft-NMS-improving object detection with one line of code. In: Proceedings of the IEEE International Conference on Computer Vision, pp. 5561–5569 (2017)

29. Caba Heilbron, F., Escorcia, V., Ghanem, B., Carlos Niebles, J.: ActivityNet: a large-scale video benchmark for human activity understanding. In: Proceedings of the IEEE Conference on Computer Vision and Pattern Recognition, pp. 961–970 (2015)

30. Karpathy, A., Toderici, G., Shetty, S., Leung, T., Sukthankar, R., Fei-Fei, L.: Large-scale video classification with convolutional neural networks. In: Proceedings of the IEEE Conference on Computer Vision and Pattern Recognition, pp. 1725–1732 (2014)

31. Zhao, Y., et al.: CUHK & ETHZ & SIAT submission to ActivityNet challenge 2017. In: CVPR ActivityNet Workshop (2017)

Discovering Multi-label Actor-Action Association in a Weakly Supervised Setting

Sovan Biswas$^{(\boxtimes)}$ and Juergen Gall

University of Bonn, 53115 Bonn, Germany
{biswas,gall}@iai.uni-bonn.de

Abstract. Since collecting and annotating data for spatio-temporal action detection is very expensive, there is a need to learn approaches with less supervision. Weakly supervised approaches do not require any bounding box annotations and can be trained only from labels that indicate whether an action occurs in a video clip. Current approaches, however, cannot handle the case when there are multiple persons in a video that perform multiple actions at the same time. In this work, we address this very challenging task for the first time. We propose a baseline based on multi-instance and multi-label learning. Furthermore, we propose a novel approach that uses sets of actions as representation instead of modeling individual action classes. Since computing the probabilities for the full power set becomes intractable as the number of action classes increases, we assign an action set to each detected person under the constraint that the assignment is consistent with the annotation of the video clip. We evaluate the proposed approach on the challenging AVA dataset where the proposed approach outperforms the MIML baseline and is competitive to fully supervised approaches.

1 Introduction

In recent years, we have seen a major progress for spatially and temporally detecting actions in videos [1–10]. For this task, the bounding box of each person and their corresponding action labels need to be estimated for each frame as shown in Fig. 1. Such approaches, however, require the same type of dense annotations for training. Thus, collecting and annotating datasets for spatio-temporal action detection becomes very expensive.

To alleviate this problem, weakly supervised approaches have been proposed [11–13] where the bounding boxes are not given, but only the action that occurs in a video clip. Despite the promising results of the weakly supervised approaches for spatio-temporal action detection, current approaches are limited to video clips that predominantly contain a single actor performing a single

Electronic supplementary material The online version of this chapter (https:// doi.org/10.1007/978-3-030-69541-5_33) contains supplementary material, which is available to authorized users.

H. Ishikawa et al. (Eds.): ACCV 2020, LNCS 12626, pp. 547–561, 2021.
https://doi.org/10.1007/978-3-030-69541-5_33

Fig. 1. The image shows a scene where two persons are talking. In this case there are two person that perform multiple actions at the same time. **Person A** indicated by the blue bounding box performs the actions *Stand*, *Listen to*, and *Watch*. **Person B** indicated by the orange bounding box performs the actions *Stand*, *Talk to*, and *Watch*. While in the supervised setting this information is also given for training, we study for the first time a weakly supervised setting where the video clip is only annotated by the actions *Stand*, *Listen to*, *Talk to*, and *Watch* without any bounding boxes or associations to the present persons. (Color figure online)

action as in the datasets UCF 101 [14] and JHMDB [15]. However, most real world videos are more complex and contain multiple actors performing multiple actions simultaneously. In this paper, we move a step forward and introduce the task of weakly supervised multi-label spatio-temporal action detection with multiple actors in a video. The goal is to infer a list of multiple actions for each actor in a given video clip as in the fully supervised case [5–10]. However, in the weakly supervised setting only actions occurring in each training video are known. Any spatio-temporal information about the persons performing these actions is not provided. This is illustrated in Fig. 1 that shows two people standing and chatting. The video clip is only annotated by the four occurring actions *Stand*, *Listen to*, *Talk to*, and *Watch*. Additional information like bounding boxes or the number of present persons is not provided. In contrast to previous experimental settings for weakly supervised learning, the proposed task is much more challenging since a video clip can contain multiple persons, each person can perform multiple actions at the same time, and multiple persons can perform the same action. For instance, both persons in Fig. 1 perform the actions *Stand* and *Watch* at the same time.

In order to address multi-label spatio-temporal action detection in the proposed weakly supervised setup, we first introduce a baseline that uses multi-instance and multi-label (MIML) learning [16–18]. Second, we introduce a novel approach that is better suited for the multi-label setting. Instead of modeling the class probabilities for each action class, we build the power set of all possible action combinations and model the probability for each subset of actions. Using a set representation has the advantage that we model directly the combination of multiple occurring actions instead of the probabilities of single actions. Since computing the probabilities for the full power set becomes intractable as the number of action classes increases, we assign an action set to each detected person under the constraint that the assignment is consistent with the annotation of the video clip. This is done by linear programming, which maximizes the overall gain across all plausible actors and action subset combinations. We evaluate the proposed approach on the challenging AVA 2.2 dataset [19], which is currently the only dataset that can be used for evaluating this task. In our experiments, we show that the proposed approach outperforms the MIML baseline by a large margin and that the proposed approach achieves 83% of the mAP compared to a model trained with full supervision.

In summary, the contribution of this paper is three-fold:

– We introduce the novel task of weakly supervised multi-label spatio-temporal action detection with multiple actors.
– We introduce a first baseline for this task based on multi-instance and multi-label learning.
– We propose a novel approach based on an action set representation.

2 Related Work

Spatio-Temporal Action Detection. A popular approach for fully supervised spatio-temporal action detection comprises the joint detection and linking of bounding boxes [1,3,4,20]. These linked bounding boxes form tubelets which are subsequently classified. Recently, many methods [9,10,21,22] use standard person detectors for actor localization and focus on learning implicitly or explicitly spatio-temporal interactions. All these approaches, however, require that each frame is annotated with person locations and corresponding action labels. Since such dense annotations are expensive to obtain on a large scale, recent approaches [8,19,23] deal with temporally sparse annotations. Here, the action labels and locations are annotated only for a subset of frames. Even though there is a reduction in annotation, these methods still require person specific bounding boxes and their actions. Very few methods such as [11,13] explore the possibility of weakly supervised learning. Most of these methods such as [24,25] use multiple instance learning to recognize distinct action characteristics. These works, however, consider the case where a single person performs not more than one action.

Actor-Action Associations. Actor-action associations have been key to identify actions both in a fully supervised and weakly supervised settings. [26] performs soft actor-action association using tags as pre-training on a very large dataset for fully supervised action recognition. With respect to weak supervision, a few approaches use movie subtitles [27,28] or transcripts [29,30] to temporally align actions to frames. In terms of actor-action associations for multiple persons, [31,32] associate a single action to various persons. To the best of our knowledge, our work is the first to perform multi-person and multi-label associations.

Multi-instance and Multi-label Learning. In the past, many MIML algorithms [33,34] have been proposed. For example, [17] propose the MIMLBoost and MIMLSVM algorithms based on boosting or SVMs. [35] optimize a regularized rank-loss objective. MIML has been also used for different computer vision applications such as scene classification [16], multi-object recognition [18], and image tagging [36]. Recently, MIML based approaches have been used for action recognition [32,37].

3   Multi-label Action Detection and Recognition

Given a video clip with multiple actors where each actor can perform multiple actions at the same time as shown in Fig. 1, the goal is to localize these actors and predict for each actor the corresponding actions. In contrast to fully supervised learning, where bounding boxes with multiple action labels are given for training, we address for the first time a weakly supervised setting where only a list of actions is provided for each video clip during training. This is a very challenging task as we do not know how many actors are present and each actor can perform multiple actions at the same time. This is in contrast to weakly supervised spatio-temporal action localization where it is assumed that only one person is in the video and that the person does not perform more than one action at a given point in time.

In order to address this problem, we first discuss a baseline, which uses multi-instance and multi-label (MIML) learning [16–18], in Sect. 4. In Sect. 5, we will then propose a novel method which uses a set representation instead of a representation of individual actions. This means that we build from the annotation of a video clip the power set of all possible action combinations. For example, the power set Ω for the three action labels *Listen*, *Talk*, and *Watch* is given by $\{\varnothing, \{Listen\}, \{Talk\}, \{Watch\}, \{Listen, Talk\}, \{Listen, Watch\}, \{Talk, Watch\}, \{Listen, Talk, Watch\}\}$. We then assign one set $\omega_i \in \Omega \setminus \varnothing$ to each actor a_i under the constraint that each action c occurs at least once, i.e., $c \in \bigcup_i \omega_i$. Using a set representation has the advantage that we model directly the combination of multiple occurring actions instead of the probabilities of single actions.

4   Multi-instance and Multi-label (MIML) Learning

One way to address the weakly supervised learning problem is to use multiple-instance learning. Since we have a multi-label problem, i.e., an actor can perform multiple actions at the same time, we use the concept of multi-instance and multi-label (MIML) learning [16–18]. We first use a person detector [38] to spatially localize the actors in a frame t and use a 3D-CNN such as I3D [39] or Slowfast [10] for predicting the action probabilities similar to fully supervised methods [8,9]. However, we use the MIML loss to train the networks.

We denote by $A_t = \{a_1^t, a_2^t, \ldots, a_{n_t}^t\}$ the detected bounding boxes and by $f(a_i^t)$ the class probabilities that are predicted by the 3D-CNN. Let Y be the vector which contains the annotations of the video clip, i.e., $Y(c) = 1$ if the

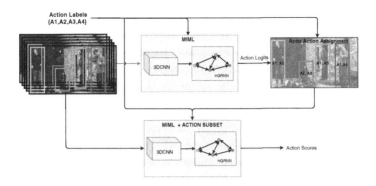

Fig. 2. Overview of the proposed approach. Given a training video clip with action labels {A1, A2, A3, A4}, we first detect persons in the video. We then train a 3D CNN with a graph RNN that models the spatio-temporal relations between the detected persons using the MIML loss to obtain initial estimates of the action logits. During actor-action association, subsets of the action labels are assigned to each detected person. The training of the network is continued using the MIML loss and the actor-action associations.

action class c occurs in the video clip and $Y(c) = 0$ otherwise. In other words, the bag A_t is labeled by $Y(c) = 1$ if at least one actor performs the action c and by $Y(c) = 0$ if none of the actors performs the action. The MIML loss is then given by

$$\mathcal{L}_{MIML} = \mathcal{L}\left(Y, \max_i(f(a_i^t))\right) \tag{1}$$

where $\mathcal{L}$ is the binary cross entropy. This means that the class probability should be close to one for at least one bounding box if the action is present and it should be close to zero for all bounding boxes if the action class is not present.

5   Actor-Action Association

While multi-instance and multi-label learning discussed in Sect. 4 already provides a good baseline for the new task of weakly supervised multi-label action detection, we propose in this section a novel method that outperforms the baseline by a large margin. As discussed in Sect. 3, the main idea is to change the representation from individual action labels to sets of actions. This means that we have one probability for a subset of actions $\omega \in \Omega$ instead of C probabilities where C is the number of action labels. We discuss how the probability of a set actions is estimated in Sect. 5.1. Due to the weakly supervised setting not all combinations of subsets are possible for each video clip. We therefore assign an action set $\omega \in \Omega$ to each actor a under the constraint that the assignment is consistent with the annotation of the video clip, i.e., each annotated action c needs to occur at least once and actions that are not annotated should not occur. The assignment is discussed in Sect. 5.2.

Figure 2 illustrates the complete approach. As described in Sect. 4, we use a 3D CNN such as I3D [39] or Slowfast [10]. Since the actors in a frame often interact with each other, we use a graph to model the relations between the actors. The graph connects all actors and we use a graph RNN to infer the action probabilities for each actor based on the spatial and temporal context. In our approach, we use the hierarchical Graph RNN (HGRNN) [7] where the features per node are obtained by ROI pooling over the 3D CNN feature maps. The HGRNN and 3D CNN are learned using the MIML loss (1). From the action class probabilities, we infer the action set probabilities as described in Sect. 5.1 and we infer the action set for each actor as described in Sect. 5.2. Finally, we train the HGRNN and the 3D CNN based on the assignments. This will be discussed in Sect. 5.3.

5.1   Power Set of Actions

In principle, we could modify our network to predict the probability for each subset of all action classes instead of the probabilities for all action classes. However, this is infeasible since the power set of all actions is very large. If C is the number of actions in a dataset, the power set for all actions consists of 2^C subsets. Already with 50 action classes, we would need to predict the probabilities for over one quadrillion subsets. Instead, we use an idea that was proposed for HEX graphs [40] where the probabilities of a hierarchy are computed from the probabilities of the leave nodes. While we do not use a hierarchy, we can compute the probability of a subset of actions from the predictions of a network for individual actions.

Let $s_c \in (-\infty, \infty)$ denote the logit that is predicted by the network for the action class c. The probability of a subset of actions ω can then be computed by

$$p_\omega = \frac{\exp\left(\sum_{c \in \omega} s_c\right)}{\sum_{\omega'} \exp\left(\sum_{c \in \omega'} s_c\right)}. \tag{2}$$

The normalization term, however, is still infeasible to compute since we still need to sum over all possible subsets (ω') for the dataset.

Since our goal is the assignment of a subset of actions ω to each actor, we do not need to compute the full probability (2). Instead of using the power set of all actions, we build the power set only for the actions that are provided as weak labels for each training video clip. This means that the power set will differ for each video clip. For the example shown in Fig. 1, we build the power set Ω for the actions *Stand*, *Listen*, *Talk*, and *Watch*. In this example, $|\Omega| = 16$. We exclude $\varnothing$ since in the used dataset each actor is annotated with at least one action. Furthermore, we multiply p_ω with the confidence d of the person detector. The scoring function $p_{\omega,i}$ that we use for the assignment of a subset $\omega \in \Omega \setminus \varnothing$ to a detected actor a_i is therefore given by

$$p_{\omega,i} = \frac{\exp\left(\sum_{c \in \omega} s_{c,i}\right) d_i}{\sum_{\omega' \in \Omega \setminus \varnothing} \exp\left(\sum_{c \in \omega'} s_{c,i}\right)} \tag{3}$$

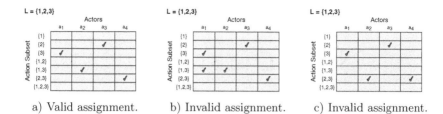

Fig. 3. For the annotated actions $L = \{1, 2, 3\}$ and the actors $A = \{a_1, a_2, a_3, a_4\}$, the figures demonstrate various actor-action assignments. While the assignment a) satisfies all constraints, b) violates (5) since two subsets are assigned to actor a_1 and c) violates (6) since the action 1 is not part of any assigned subset.

where $s_{c,i}$ is the predicted logit for action c and person a_i. Taking the detection confidence d_i of person a_i into account is necessary to reduce the impact of false positives that usually have a low detection confidence.

5.2 Actor-Action Association

While the scoring function (3) indicates how likely a given subset of actions $\omega \in \Omega \setminus \varnothing$ fits to an actor a_i, it does not take all information that is available for each video clip into account. For instance, we know that each annotated action is performed by at least one actor. In order to exploit this additional knowledge, we find the optimal assignment of action subsets to actors based on the constraints that each actor performs at least one action and that each action c occurs at least once, i.e., $c \in \bigcup_i \omega_i$. Since we build the power set only from the actions that occur in a video clip, which we denote by L, the power set $\Omega(L)$ varies for each training video clip.

The association of subsets $\omega \in \Omega(L) \setminus \varnothing$ to actors $A = \{a_1, a_2, \dots, a_n\}$ can be formulated as a binary linear program where the binary variables $x_{\omega,i}$ are one if the subset ω is assigned to actor a_i and it is zero otherwise. The optimal assignment is defined by the assignment with the highest score (4). While the first constraint (5) enforces that exactly one subset ω is assigned to each actor a_i, the second constraint (6) enforces that $c \in \bigcup_{\omega : x_{\omega,i}=1} \omega$ for all $c \in L$, where $\{\omega : x_{\omega,i} = 1\}$ is the set of all subsets that have been assigned. Note that (6) rephrases this constraint such that it can be used for optimization where the indicator function $\mathbb{1}_\omega(c)$ is one if $c \in \omega$ and it is zero otherwise. The left hand side of the inequality therefore counts the number of assigned subsets that contain the action class c. Since this number must be larger than zero, it ensures that each action $c \in L$ is assigned to at least one actor. The complete binary linear program is thus given by:

$$\underset{x_{\omega,i}}{\operatorname{argmax}} \sum_{i=1}^{n} \sum_{\omega \in \Omega(L) \setminus \varnothing} p_{\omega,i} x_{\omega,i} \tag{4}$$

$$\text{subject to} \sum_{\omega \in \Omega(L) \setminus \varnothing} x_{\omega,i} = 1 \qquad\qquad \forall i = 1, ..., n \qquad (5)$$

$$\sum_{i=1}^{n} \sum_{\omega \in \Omega(L) \setminus \varnothing} \mathbb{1}_{\omega}(c) x_{\omega,i} \geq 1 \qquad\qquad \forall c \in L \qquad (6)$$

$$x_{\omega,i} \in \{0,1\} \qquad\qquad \forall \omega \in \Omega(L) \setminus \varnothing; \ \forall i = 1, ..., n.$$

Figure 3 illustrates the constraints.

5.3 Training

We train first the network using the MIML loss (1) to obtain initial estimates of the logits $s_{c,i}$. We then assign subsets of actions to the detected persons using the scoring function (3). Finally, we train our network using the loss

$$\mathcal{L} = \mathcal{L}_{MIML} + \alpha \sum_{i=1}^{n_t} \mathcal{L}\left(\hat{Y}_{\omega_i^t}, f(a_i^t)\right) \qquad (7)$$

where ω_i^t denotes the action subset that has been assigned to actor a_i^t in frame t and $\hat{Y}_{\omega_i^t}$ is a vector with $\hat{Y}_{\omega_i^t}(c) = 1$ if $c \in \omega_i^t$ and $\hat{Y}_{\omega_i^t}(c) = 0$ otherwise. $\mathcal{L}$ is the binary cross entropy. Since $\mathcal{L}_{MIML}$ is computed once per frame but $\mathcal{L}(\hat{Y}_{\omega_i^t}, f(a_i^t))$ is computed for each detected person, we use $\alpha = 0.3$ to compensate for this difference.

6   Experiments

6.1   Dataset and Implementation Details

We use the AVA 2.2 dataset [19] for evaluation. The dataset contains 235 videos for training, 64 videos for validation, and 131 videos for testing. The dataset contains 60 action classes. The persons perform often multiple actions at the same time and the videos contain multiple persons. For each annotated person a bounding box is provided. An example is given in Fig. 1. Only one frame per second is annotated. The accuracy is measured by mean average precision (mAP) over all actions with an IoU threshold for bounding boxes of 0.5 as described in [19]. In the weakly supervised setting, we use only the present actions for training, but not the bounding boxes.

To detect persons, we use Faster RCNN [41] with ResNext-101 [38] as backbone. The detector was pre-trained on ImageNet and fine-tuned on the COCO dataset. In our experiments, we report results for two 3D CNNs, namely I3D [39] and Slowfast [10]. I3D is pre-trained on Kinetics-400. For Slowfast, we use the ResNet-101 + NL (8 × 8) version that is pre-trained on Kinetics 600. The temporal scope was set to 64 frames with a stride of 2. For HGRNN we use a temporal window of 11 frames. For training, we use the SGD optimizer until the validation error saturated. The learning rate with linear warmup was set to

0.04 and 0.025 for I3D and Slowfast, respectively. The batch size was set to 16. We used cropping as data augmentation where we crop images of size 224×224 pixels from the frames that have 256×256 image resolution.[1]

6.2   Experimental Results

Comparison of MIML with Proposed Method. Table 1 shows the comparison of the proposed approach with the multi-instance and multi-label (MIML) baseline on the validation set. When I3D is used as 3D CNN, the proposed approach improves the MIML baseline by +3.2%. When Slowfast is used, the accuracy of all methods is higher but the improvement of the proposed approach over the MIML approach remains nearly the same with +3.3%. We also report the result when HGRNN is trained only with the MIML loss. In this case, the actor-action association is not used and we denote this setting by MIML+HGRNN.

Table 1. Comparison of MIML with proposed method. The proposed approach outperforms MIML in case of I3D and Slowfast.

Method	3D CNN	Val-mAP
MIML	I3D	14.1
MIML + HGRNN	I3D	15.2
Proposed Approach	I3D	17.3
MIML	Slowfast	21.8
MIML + HGRNN	Slowfast	23.1
Proposed Approach	Slowfast	25.1

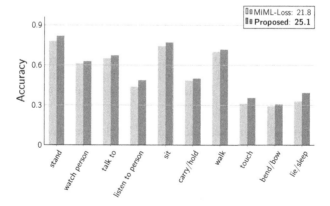

Fig. 4. Comparison of MIML with proposed method. The plot shows the per class mAP for the 10 most frequently occurring classes in the training set. The actions are sorted by the number of occurrences in an decreasing order from left to right. A plot with all 60 action classes is part of the supplementary material.

[1] Code: https://github.com/sovan-biswas/MultiLabelActorActionAssignment.

Table 2. Results of various actor-action assignment approaches using HGRNN over different 3D CNNs. The Frequent-5 column and the Least-10 column show the average mAP over the 5 most frequently and 10 least occurring classes in the training set.

Actor-action association	Backbone	Val-mAP	Frequent-5	Least-10
MIML+HGRNN	I3D	15.2	51.5	2.0
Proposed Approach w/o LP	I3D	16.4	52.8	2.1
Proposed Approach	I3D	**17.3**	**53.7**	**3.4**
MIML+HGRNN	Slowfast	23.1	65.7	7.3
Proposed Approach w/o LP	Slowfast	22.9	65.9	6.8
Proposed Approach	Slowfast	**25.1**	**67.5**	**7.6**

Table 3. Performance with ground-truth bounding boxes for evaluation. The results show the improvement in mAP on the validation set when ground-truth bounding boxes (GT bb) instead of detected bounding boxes (Detected bb) are used for evaluation. Furthermore, the results are reported when the model is trained with full supervision.

Method	3D CNN	Detected bb	GT bb
MIML	I3D	14.1	21.2
Proposed Approach	I3D	17.3	24.3
Full Supervision	I3D	20.7	25.4
MIML	Slowfast	21.8	30.6
Proposed Approach	Slowfast	25.1	32.3
Full Supervision	Slowfast	30.1	35.7

While HGRNN improves the results since it models the spatio-temporal relations between persons better than a 3D CNN alone, the proposed actor-action assignment improves the mAP compared to MIML+HGRNN by +2.1% and +2.0% for I3D and Slowfast, respectively. Figure 4 shows the improvement of the proposed approach over the MIML baseline for the 10 action classes that occur most frequently in the training set. A few qualitative results are show in Fig. 5.

Impact of Actor-Action Association. In Table 1, we have observed that the actor-action association improves the accuracy. In Table 2, we analyze the impact of the actor-action association more in detail. We use HGRNN using both I3D and Slowfast as 3D CNN backbone. In case of MIML+HGRNN, the actor-action association is not used. We also report the result if we perform the association directly by the confidences without solving a binary linear program. We denote this setting by Proposed Approach w/o LP. In this case, we associate an action to an actor if the class probability is greater than 0.5. For I3D, the association without LP improves the results mainly for the most frequent classes with almost no improvement on least frequent classes. For Slowfast, the performance even

Table 4. Comparison to fully supervised approaches. We also report the result of our approach if it is trained with full supervision. Note that we do not use multi-scale and horizontal flipping augmentation as in Slowfast++.

Weakly Supervised Approaches		
Methods	Val-mAP	Test-mAP
MIML	21.8	–
Proposed Approach	**25.1**	**23.5**
Fully Supervised Approaches		
Methods	Val-mAP	Test-mAP
ARCN [5]	17.4	–
RAF [6]	20.4	–
HGRNN [7]	20.9	–
ATN [8]	25.0	24.9
LFB [9]	27.7	27.2
Slowfast [10]	29.0	–
Slowfast++ [10]	30.7	34.3
Proposed Approach	30.1	–

decreases in comparison to MIML+HGRNN without LP. Instead, solving the linear program results in better associations for both I3D and Slowfast.

Impact of the Object Detector. We use the Faster RCNN with ResNext [38] person detector which achieves 90.10% mAP for person detection on the AVA training set and 90.45% on the AVA validation set. Irrespective of the high detection performance, we analyze how much the accuracy improves if the detected bounding boxes are replaced with the ground-truth bounding boxes during evaluation. Note that the ground-truth bounding boxes are not used for training, but only for evaluation. The results are shown in Table 3. We observe that the performance improves by +7.0% and +7.2% mAP on the validation set for I3D and Slowfast, respectively. We also report the results if the approach is trained using full supervision. In this case, the network is trained on the ground-truth bounding boxes and the ground-truth action labels per bounding box. Compared to the fully supervised approach, our weakly supervised approach achieves around 83% of the mAP for both 3D CNNs (17.3% vs. 20.7% for I3D and 25.1% vs. 30.1% for Slowfast) if detected bounding boxes are used for evaluation. The gap gets even smaller when ground-truth bounding boxes are used for evaluation. In this case, the relative performance is 95.7% for I3D and 90.5% for Slowfast. This demonstrates that the proposed approach learns the actions very well despite of the weak supervision.

Comparison to Fully Supervised Methods. Since this is the first approach that addresses weakly supervised learning for multi-label and multi-person action

Ground-Truth   MIML   Proposed

Fig. 5. Qualitative results. The left column shows the ground-truth annotations. The middle column shows the results of the MIML baseline. The right column shows the results of the proposed method. The colors distinguish only different persons, but they are otherwise irrelevant. The predicted action classes with confidence scores are on top of the estimated bounding boxes. The proposed approach recognizes more action classes per bounding box correctly compared to MIML. Both methods also detect genuine actions that are not annotated in the dataset as seen from the missing persons in the second and fourth row. The bias of the proposed method towards the background is visible in last row, where the "swim" action is associated to both persons. Best viewed using the zoom function of the PDF viewer.

detection, we cannot compare to other weakly supervised approaches. However, we compare our approach with the state-of-the-art for fully supervised action detection in Table 4. Our approach is competitive to fully supervised approaches [5–8]. When we train our approach with full supervision, we improve over Slow-Fast [10] by +1.1% mAP on the validation set. While the Slowfast++ network performs slightly better, it uses additional data augmentation and a different network configuration. We expect that these changes would improve our approach as well.

7   Conclusion

In this paper, we introduced the challenging task of weakly supervised multi-label spatio-temporal action detection with multiple actors. We first introduced a baseline based on multi-instance and multi-label learning. We furthermore presented a novel approach where the multi-label problem is represented by the power set of the action classes. In this context, we assign an element of the power set to each detected person using linear programming. We evaluated our approach on the challenging AVA dataset where the proposed method outperforms the MIML approach. Despite of the weak supervision, the proposed approach is competitive to fully supervised approaches.

Acknowledgment. The work has been financially supported by the ERC Starting Grant ARCA (677650).

References

1. Gkioxari, G., Malik, J.: Finding action tubes. In: CVPR, pp. 759–768 (2015)
2. Hou, R., Chen, C., Shah, M.: Tube convolutional neural network (T-CNN) for action detection in videos. In: ICCV, pp. 5822–5831 (2017)
3. Kalogeiton, V., Weinzaepfel, P., Ferrari, V., Schmid, C.: Action tubelet detector for spatio-temporal action localization. In: ICCV, pp. 4415–4423 (2017)
4. Singh, G., Saha, S., Sapienza, M., Torr, P., Cuzzolin, F.: Online real-time multiple spatiotemporal action localisation and prediction. In: ICCV, pp. 3657–3666 (2017)
5. Sun, C., Shrivastava, A., Vondrick, C., Murphy, K., Sukthankar, R., Schmid, C.: Actor-centric relation network. In: Ferrari, V., Hebert, M., Sminchisescu, C., Weiss, Y. (eds.) ECCV 2018. LNCS, vol. 11215, pp. 335–351. Springer, Cham (2018). https://doi.org/10.1007/978-3-030-01252-6_20
6. Sun, C., Shrivastava, A., Vondrick, C., Sukthankar, R., Murphy, K., Schmid, C.: Relational action forecasting. In: CVPR (2019)
7. Biswas, S., Souri, Y., Gall, J.: Hierarchical graph-RNNs for action detection of multiple activities. In: ICIP (2019)
8. Girdhar, R., Carreira, J., Doersch, C., Zisserman, A.: Video action transformer network. In: CVPR, pp. 244–253 (2019)
9. Wu, C.Y., Feichtenhofer, C., Fan, H., He, K., Krahenbuhl, P., Girshick, R.: Long-term feature banks for detailed video understanding. In: CVPR, pp. 284–293 (2019)
10. Feichtenhofer, C., Fan, H., Malik, J., He, K.: SlowFast networks for video recognition. In: ICCV, pp. 6202–6211 (2019)

11. Mettes, P., Snoek, C.G., Chang, S.F.: Localizing actions from video labels and pseudo-annotations. In: BMVC (2017)
12. Soomro, K., Shah, M.: Unsupervised action discovery and localization in videos. In: ICCV, pp. 696–705 (2017)
13. Chéron, G., Alayrac, J.B., Laptev, I., Schmid, C.: A flexible model for training action localization with varying levels of supervision. In: NIPS, pp. 942–953 (2018)
14. Soomro, K., Zamir, A.R., Shah, M.: UCF101: a dataset of 101 human actions classes from videos in the wild (2012)
15. Jhuang, H., Gall, J., Zuffi, S., Schmid, C., Black, M.J.: Towards understanding action recognition. In: ICCV, pp. 3192–3199 (2013)
16. Zhou, Z.H., Zhang, M.L.: Multi-instance multi-label learning with application to scene classification. In: NIPS, pp. 1609–1616 (2006)
17. Zhou, Z.H., Zhang, M.L., Huang, S.J., Li, Y.F.: Multi-instance multi-label learning. Artif. Intell. **176**, 2291–2320 (2012)
18. Yang, H., Tianyi Zhou, J., Cai, J., Soon Ong, Y.: MIML-FCN+: multi-instance multi-label learning via fully convolutional networks with privileged information. In: CVPR, pp. 1577–1585 (2017)
19. Gu, C., et al.: AVA: a video dataset of spatio-temporally localized atomic visual actions. In: CVPR, pp. 6047–6056 (2018)
20. Song, L., Zhang, S., Yu, G., Sun, H.: TACNet: transition-aware context network for spatio-temporal action detection. In: CVPR, pp. 11987–11995 (2019)
21. Feichtenhofer, C.: X3D: expanding architectures for efficient video recognition. In: CVPR (2020)
22. Ji, J., Krishna, R., Fei-Fei, L., Niebles, J.C.: Action genome: actions as compositions of spatio-temporal scene graphs. In: CVPR (2020)
23. Weinzaepfel, P., Martin, X., Schmid, C.: Towards weakly-supervised action localization. arXiv preprint arXiv:1605.05197 (2016)
24. Siva, P., Xiang, T.: Weakly supervised action detection. In: BMVC, p. 6 (2011)
25. Mettes, P., Snoek, C.G.: Spatio-temporal instance learning: action tubes from class supervision. arXiv preprint arXiv:1807.02800 (2018)
26. Ghadiyaram, D., Tran, D., Mahajan, D.: Large-scale weakly-supervised pre-training for video action recognition. In: CVPR (2019)
27. Bojanowski, P., Bach, F., Laptev, I., Ponce, J., Schmid, C., Sivic, J.: Finding actors and actions in movies. In: ICCV, pp. 2280–2287 (2013)
28. Laptev, I., Marszalek, M., Schmid, C., Rozenfeld, B.: Learning realistic human actions from movies. In: CVPR, pp. 1–8 (2008)
29. Kuehne, H., Richard, A., Gall, J.: A hybrid RNN-HMM approach for weakly supervised temporal action segmentation. PAMI **42**, 765–779 (2018)
30. Richard, A., Kuehne, H., Gall, J.: Action sets: weakly supervised action segmentation without ordering constraints. In: CVPR, pp. 5987–5996 (2018)
31. Ramanathan, V., Huang, J., Abu-El-Haija, S., Gorban, A., Murphy, K., Fei-Fei, L.: Detecting events and key actors in multi-person videos. In: CVPR, pp. 3043–3053 (2016)
32. Li, J., Liu, J., Yongkang, W., Nishimura, S., Kankanhalli, M.: Weakly-supervised multi-person action recognition in 360° videos. In: WACV (2020)
33. Nguyen, C.T., Zhan, D.C., Zhou, Z.H.: Multi-modal image annotation with multi-instance multi-label LDA. In: IJCAI (2013)
34. Nguyen, N.: A new SVM approach to multi-instance multi-label learning. In: ICDM, pp. 384–392 (2010)
35. Briggs, F., Fern, X.Z., Raich, R.: Rank-loss support instance machines for MIML instance annotation. In: SIGKDD, pp. 534–542 (2012)

36. Zha, Z.J., Hua, X.S., Mei, T., Wang, J., Qi, G.J., Wang, Z.: Joint multi-label multi-instance learning for image classification. In: CVPR, pp. 1–8 (2008)
37. Zhang, X.Y., Shi, H., Li, C., Li, P.: Multi-instance multi-label action recognition and localization based on spatio-temporal pre-trimming for untrimmed videos. In: AAAI, pp. 12886–12893 (2020)
38. Xie, S., Girshick, R., Dollár, P., Tu, Z., He, K.: Aggregated residual transformations for deep neural networks. In: CVPR (2017)
39. Carreira, J., Zisserman, A.: Quo Vadis, action recognition? A new model and the kinetics dataset. In: CVPR, pp. 4724–4733 (2017)
40. Deng, J., et al.: Large-scale object classification using label relation graphs. In: Fleet, D., Pajdla, T., Schiele, B., Tuytelaars, T. (eds.) ECCV 2014. LNCS, vol. 8689, pp. 48–64. Springer, Cham (2014). https://doi.org/10.1007/978-3-319-10590-1_4
41. Ren, S., He, K., Girshick, R., Sun, J.: Faster R-CNN: towards real-time object detection with region proposal networks. In: NIPS, pp. 91–99 (2015)

Reweighted Non-convex Non-smooth Rank Minimization Based Spectral Clustering on Grassmann Manifold

Xinglin Piao[1,2,4], Yongli Hu[3(✉)], Junbin Gao[5], Yanfeng Sun[3], Xin Yang[4], and Baocai Yin[1,3]

[1] Peng Cheng Laboratory, Shenzhen 518055, China
piaoxl@pcl.ac.cn
[2] Peking University Shenzhen Graduate School, Shenzhen 518055, China
[3] Beijing Key Laboratory of Multimedia and Intelligent Software Technology,
Beijing Artificial Intelligence Institute, Faculty of Information Technology,
Beijing University of Technology, Beijing 100124, China
{huyongli,yfsun,ybc}@bjut.edu.cn
[4] Faculty of Electronic Information and Electrical Engineering,
Dalian University of Technology, Dalian 116024, China
xinyang@dlut.edu.cn
[5] Business Analytics Discipline, The University of Sydney Business School,
Camperdown, NSW 2006, Australia
junbin.gao@sydney.edu.au

Abstract. Low Rank Representation (LRR) based unsupervised clustering methods have achieved great success since these methods could explore low-dimensional subspace structure embedded in original data effectively. The conventional LRR methods generally treat the data as the points in Euclidean space. However, it is no longer suitable for high-dimension data (such as video or imageset). That is because high-dimension data are always considered as non-linear manifold data such as Grassmann manifold. Besides, the typical LRR methods always adopt the traditional single nuclear norm based low rank constraint which can not fully reveal the low rank property of the data representation and often leads to suboptimal solution. In this paper, a new LRR based clustering model is constructed on Grassmann manifold for high-dimension data. In the proposed method, each high-dimension data is formed as a sample on Grassmann manifold with non-linear metric. Meanwhile, a non-convex low rank representation is adopt to reveal the intrinsic property of these high-dimension data and reweighted rank minimization constraint is introduced. The experimental results on several public datasets show that the proposed method outperforms the state-of-the-art clustering methods.

1 Introduction

Unsupervised clustering is a fundamental topic in machine learning, artificial intelligence and data mining areas [1,2], which attempts to group data into dif-

© Springer Nature Switzerland AG 2021
H. Ishikawa et al. (Eds.): ACCV 2020, LNCS 12626, pp. 562–577, 2021.
https://doi.org/10.1007/978-3-030-69541-5_34

ferent clusters according to their own intrinsic pattern. In past decades, a large number of clustering methods have been proposed and achieved great success in many applications [3,4]. The representative ones are the statistical methods [5], the conventional iterative methods [6], the factorization-based algebraic methods [7], and the spectral clustering methods [8]. Among them, the spectral clustering methods are considered having promising performance. In this kind of methods, an affinity matrix is usually learned, and then Normalized Cuts (NCut) [9] or other standard clustering algorithms are then used to obtain the final clustering results. Inspired by Sparse and Low Rank representation method, a series of classical methods have been proposed. Elhamifar and Vidal adopted ℓ_1 norm to explore the sparse relationship within data and proposed Sparse Subspace Clustering (SSC) [10] for data clustering. Liu et al. used nuclear norm to construct a low-rank representation matrix for data and proposed Low-Rank Representation (LRR) clustering method [11]. Later, Liu et al. proposed Latent Low-Rank Representation (LatLRR) method [12] for clustering. Zhang et al. proposed Robust Latent Low Rank Representation (RobustLatLRR) clustering method [13]. To get better representation matrix, some researchers adopt the kernel trick and proposed some kernel based clustering methods, such as the kernel SSC clustering method [14] and the kernel LRR clustering method [15].

In the aforementioned methods, vector feature and Euclidean distance are combined for building the affinity matrix by self-expression approach for sample data. However, this conventional linear approach would be no longer suitable for complex or high-dimension data, such as imagesets or video clips data. That is because high-dimension data are always treated as a sample point on non-linear manifold space with non-linear metric. For example, an imageset or a video clip is can be modeled as a data sample on Grassmann manifold [16,17]. Therefore, to address the high-dimension data clustering task, researchers try to extend the traditional methods and proposed a series of effective clustering approaches for these complex data. Turaga et al. proposed a statistical computations based manifold representation method (SCGSM) [18]. Shirazi et al. proposed a kernel embedding clustering method on Grassmann manifold (K-GM) [19]. Inspired by low rank and sparse theory, Wang et al. first proposed low rank based clustering method on Grassmann manifold (G-LRR) [20]. Liu et al. adopted kernel method and proposed kernel sparse representation based clustering method [21]. Wang et al. proposed Cascaded Low Rank and Sparse Representation on Grassmann manifold method (G-CLRSR) [22]. Later, Wang et al. proposed Partial Sum Minimization of Singular Values Representation on Grassmann manifold method (G-PSSVR) [23], in which partial sum minimization of singular values norm was adopted for better low rank representation. Piao et al. proposed Double Nuclear norm based Low Rank Representation clustering method on Grassmann manifold (G-DNLR) [24]. Further, combined with the Laplacian regularizer, researchers proposed Laplacian Low-Rank Representation on Grassmann manifold method (G-LLRR) [25], Laplacian Partial Sum Minimization of Singular Values Representation on Grassmann manifold method (G-LPSSVR) [23] and Laplacian Double Nuclear norm based Low Rank Rep-

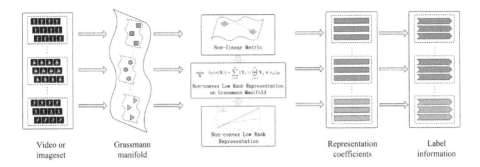

| Video or imageset | Grassmann manifold | | Representation coefficients | Label information |

Fig. 1. The pipeline of our paper.

resentation clustering method on Grassmann manifold [24], in which authors constructed the affinity matrix by original Grassmann manifold data samples.

Although these current low rank representation and their extension based methods on Grassmann manifold show good performance in clustering task, they generally adopt traditional nuclear norm based low rank constraint for the data representation. This traditional norm treats all singular values equally and prefers to punish the larger singular values than the small ones, which would deviate the optimal solution and lead to suboptimal solution [26,27]. Recently, to overcome the limitation of convex and smooth nuclear norm, non-convex or non-smooth low rank approximation (such as logarithmic function and Schatten-p norm for $0 < p < 1$) [28] are adopted to replace the traditional nuclear norm for low rank based problems, which could recover a more accurate low rank matrix than the traditional nuclear norm [29]. Especially, these non-convex and non-smooth low rank based methods could increase the punishment on smaller values and decrease the punishment on larger values simultaneously [30]. Inspired from these methods, we propose a novel low rank based clustering model on Grassmann manifold. In the proposed model, the high-dimension data samples are firstly represented as Grassmann points, then a Reweighted Non-convex and Non-smooth Rank Minimization based model on Grassmann manifold (G-RNNRM) is built, where the data representation matrix is constrained by non-convex and non-smooth low rank constraint. The NCut method [9] is used to obtain the final clustering results. Figure 1 shows the pipeline of our paper and the contributions of this paper are following:

– Proposing a novel non-convex and non-smooth low rank representation model on Grassmann for high-dimension data clustering;
– Reweighted approach is introduced in the proposed non-convex and non-smooth low rank approximation norm to reveal low-rank property more exactly. To our best knowledge, this the first reweighted low rank based method on Grassmann manifold;
– An effective algorithm is proposed to solve the complicated optimization problems of the proposed model.

The paper is organized as follows. We introduce the notation and definition of Grassmann manifold in Sect. 2. Section 3 review the related works. We will introduce the formulation and optimization of the propose G-RNNRM model in Sect. 4. Section 5 assesses the proposed method on several datasets. Finally, conclusions are discussed in Sect. 6.

2   Notation and Definition of Grasssmann Manifold

2.1   Notation

We use bold lowercase letters for vectors, e.g. $\mathbf{x}, \mathbf{y}, \mathbf{a}$, bold uppercase for matrices, e.g. $\mathbf{X}, \mathbf{Y}, \mathbf{A}$, calligraphy letters for tensors e.g. $\mathcal{X}, \mathcal{Y}, \mathcal{A}$, lowercase letters for scalars such as dimension and class numbers, e.g. m, n, c. $\mathbf{x}_i$ represents the i-th column of matrix $\mathbf{X}$. x_{ij} represents the i-th element in j-th column from matrix $\mathbf{X}$. $\mathbb{R}$ represents the space of real numbers.

2.2   Definition of Grassmann Manifold

According to [31], a Grassmann manifold is always denoted as $\mathcal{G}(p, m)$, which consists of all linear p-dimension subspaces in m-dimension Euclidean space $\mathbb{R}^m (0 \leq p \leq m)$. It also could be represented by the quotient space of all the $m \times p$ matrices with p orthogonal columns under the p-order orthogonal group. Thus, we could construct a Grassmann manifold as below:

$$\mathcal{G}(p, m) = \{\mathbf{Y} \in \mathbb{R}^{m \times p} : \mathbf{Y}^T \mathbf{Y} = \mathbf{I}_p\}/\mathcal{O}(p), \tag{1}$$

where $\mathcal{O}(p)$ represents the p-order orthogonal group. For two Grassmann manifold data samples $\mathbf{Y}_1$ and $\mathbf{Y}_2$, there are two metric approaches: one is to define a consistent metrics in tangent spaces for Grassmann manifold data [32], the other one is to embed Grassmann manifold data into the symmetric matrix space [33]. The later one is easier and the Euclidean distance could be applied, which could be defined as below:

$$\mathrm{dist}_g(\mathbf{Y}_1, \mathbf{Y}_2) = \frac{1}{2}\|\Pi(\mathbf{Y}_1) - \Pi(\mathbf{Y}_2)\|_F, \tag{2}$$

where $\|\mathbf{X}\|_F = \sqrt{\sum_{i=1,j=1}^n x_{ij}^2}$ represents the Frobenius norm, $\Pi(\cdot)$ is a mapping function defined as below:

$$\Pi : \mathcal{G}(p, m) \longrightarrow Sym(m), \Pi(\mathbf{Y}) = \mathbf{Y}\mathbf{Y}^T, \tag{3}$$

where $Sym(m)$ represents the m-dimension symmetric matrix space. With the function $\Pi(\cdot)$, Grassmann manifold could be embedded into the symmetric matrices. Each sample data on Grassmann manifold could be regarded as an equivalent class of all the $m \times p$ orthogonal matrices, any one of which can be converted to the other by a $p \times p$ orthogonal matrix. Thus, Grassmann manifolds is naturally regarded as a good representation for video clips/image sets, thus can be used to tackle the problem of videos matching.

3   Related Works

We first introduce related clustering methods on the Euclidean Space. Given a set of sample vectors $\mathbf{Y} = [\mathbf{y}_1, \mathbf{y}_2, ..., \mathbf{y}_n] \in \mathbb{R}^{m \times n}$ drawn from a union of c subspaces $\{\mathcal{S}_i\}_{i=1}^c$, where m denotes the dimension of each sample $\mathbf{y}_i$ and n represents the number of samples $\mathbf{Y}$. Let $\mathbf{Y}_i \subset \mathbf{Y}$ come from the subspace $\mathcal{S}_i$. The task of subspace clustering is to segment the sample set $\mathbf{Y}$ according to the underlying subspaces. Researchers have proposed a large number of methods to solve this problems. As we mentioned in Sect. 1, the spectral clustering methods are considered as the state-of-the-art ones, in which the data could be self-represented by introducing a representation matrix $\mathbf{X} \in \mathbb{R}^{n \times n}$ with linear combination as $\mathbf{Y} = \mathbf{YX}$. To avoid the trivial solution, some matrix constraints are adopted on $\mathbf{X}$ such as Frobenius norm [34]:

$$\min_{\mathbf{X}} \quad \lambda \|\mathbf{X}\|_F^2 + \|\mathbf{Y} - \mathbf{YX}\|_F^2. \tag{4}$$

In the past decade, sparse and low rank theories have been applied to subspace clustering successfully. Elhamifar and Vidal [10] proposed Sparse Subspace Clustering (SSC) method, which aimed to find the sparsest representation matrix $\mathbf{X}$ by using ℓ_1 norm $\|\cdot\|_1$. The SSC model is formulated as follows,

$$\min_{\mathbf{X}} \quad \lambda \|\mathbf{X}\|_1 + \|\mathbf{Y} - \mathbf{YX}\|_F^2, \tag{5}$$

where λ is balance parameter and $\|\mathbf{X}\|_1 = \sum_{i=1, j=1}^n |x_{ij}|$. Instead of adopting the sparse constraint, Liu *et al.* [11] proposed Low Rank Representation (LRR) method for clustering by using nuclear norm $\|\cdot\|_*$ for the representation matrix $\mathbf{X}$, which is formulated as follows,

$$\min_{\mathbf{X}} \quad \lambda \|\mathbf{X}\|_* + \|\mathbf{Y} - \mathbf{YX}\|_F^2, \tag{6}$$

where $\|\mathbf{X}\|_* = \sum_i^r \sigma_i(\mathbf{X})$ and $\sigma_i(\mathbf{X})$ represents the i-th singular value of $\mathbf{X}$, $\sigma_1 > \sigma_2 > ... > \sigma_r$, r represents the rank of $\mathbf{X}$.

All above related works all construct the representation matrix of data samples by employing Euclidean distance. However, the high-dimension datum are always assumed as Grassmann manifold samples and the Euclidean distance is no longer suitable. Therefore, researchers proposed a series of clustering methods for Grassmann manifold based on the non-distance defined in (2). For a set of Grassmann samples $\mathcal{Y} = \{\mathbf{Y}_1, \mathbf{Y}_2, ..., \mathbf{Y}_n\}$ where $\mathbf{Y}_i \in \mathcal{G}(p, m)$, Wang *et al.* [20] proposed a Low Rank model with non-linear metric for Grassmann (G-LRR) by generating the (6) on Grassmann:

$$\min_{\mathbf{X}} \quad \lambda \|\mathbf{X}\|_* + \sum_{i=1}^n \left\| \mathbf{Y}_i \ominus \biguplus_{j=1}^n \mathbf{Y}_j \circledast x_{ji} \right\|_{\mathcal{G}}, \tag{7}$$

where $\left\| \mathbf{Y}_i \ominus \biguplus_{j=1}^n \mathbf{Y}_j \circledast x_{ji} \right\|_{\mathcal{G}}$ represents the reconstruction error of the sample $\mathbf{Y}_i$ on Grassmann manifold, $\biguplus_{j=1}^n \mathbf{Y}_j \circledast x_{ji}$ denotes the "combination" of $\{\mathbf{Y}_j\}_{j=1}^n$

with the coefficients $\{x_{ji}\}_{i=1,j=1}^{n}$, the symbol $\ominus, \uplus, \circledast$ are abstract symbols which are used to simulated the "linear" operations on Grassmann manifold. They also proposed a cascaded Low Rank and Sparse model on Grassmann manifold (G-CLRSR) model:

$$\min_{\mathbf{X},\mathbf{Z}} \quad \lambda\|\mathbf{X}\|_* + \alpha\|\mathbf{Z}\|_1 + \beta\|\mathbf{X} - \mathbf{X}\mathbf{Z}\|_F^2$$
$$+ \sum_{i=1}^{n} \left\| \mathbf{Y}_i \ominus \biguplus_{j=1}^{n} \mathbf{Y}_j \circledast x_{ji} \right\|_{\mathcal{G}}. \tag{8}$$

Further, to achieve a better low rank representation matrix for clustering, Wang *et al.* [23] adopted Partial Sum Minimization of Singular Values (PSSV) norm to instead the nuclear norm for formulating PSSV Low Rank model on Grassmann manifold (G-PSSVLR) model:

$$\min_{\mathbf{X}} \quad \lambda\|\mathbf{X}\|_{>r} + \sum_{i=1}^{n} \left\| \mathbf{Y}_i \ominus \biguplus_{j=1}^{n} \mathbf{Y}_j \circledast x_{ji} \right\|_{\mathcal{G}}, \tag{9}$$

where r represents the expected rank of $\mathbf{X}$ and $\|\cdot\|_{>r}$ represents the PSSV norm defined as below [35]:

$$\|\mathbf{X}\|_{>r} = \sum_{i=r+1}^{n} \sigma_i(\mathbf{X}), \tag{10}$$

Although the above methods achieve great performance in Grassmann manifold clustering problem, the traditional convex nuclear based norm is adopted, which would reduce the ability to represent the correlation among data.

4   Reweighted Non-convex and Non-smooth Rank Minimization Model on Grassmann Manifold

In this section, we will introduce the formulation and optimization of the proposed G-RNNRM model in detail.

4.1   Model Formulation

For a set of Grassmann samples $\mathcal{Y} = \{\mathbf{Y}_1, \mathbf{Y}_2, ..., \mathbf{Y}_n\}$ where $\mathbf{Y}_i \in \mathcal{G}(p, m), i = 1, 2, ..., n$, we could formulate a self-expression clustering model as below:

$$\min_{\mathbf{X}} \quad \lambda f(\mathbf{X}) + g(\mathbf{X}, \mathbf{Y}), \tag{11}$$

where $f(\mathbf{X})$ represents a function satisfying some specific conditions for matrix $\mathbf{X}$, $g(\mathbf{X}, \mathbf{Y})$ represents a function of self-representation of samples $\{\mathbf{Y}_i\}_{i=1}^{n}$ with representation matrix $\mathbf{X}$. According to the preliminary knowledge in Sect. 2, $\{\mathbf{Y}_i\}_{i=1}^{n}$ could be self-represented by $\mathbf{X}$ with non-linear metric. Therefore, (11) could be rewritten as below:

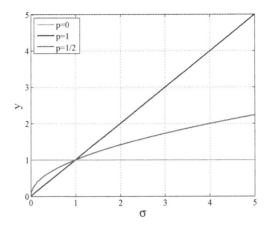

Fig. 2. The illustration of three terms on one dimensional data.

$$\min_{\mathbf{X}} \quad \lambda f(\mathbf{X}) + \sum_{i=1}^{n} \left\| \mathbf{Y}_i \ominus \biguplus_{j=1}^{n} \mathbf{Y}_j \circledast x_{ji} \right\|_{\mathcal{G}}. \tag{12}$$

As we discussed in Sect. 1, to obtain a better low-rank representation matrix, we intend to replace the traditional nuclear norm by Schatten-p norm $(0 < p < 1)$ which is a non-convex low rank norm. Then the (12) could be rewritten as below:

$$\min_{\mathbf{X}} \quad \lambda \sum_{i=1}^{r} \rho(\sigma_i(\mathbf{X})) + \sum_{i=1}^{n} \left\| \mathbf{Y}_i \ominus \biguplus_{j=1}^{n} \mathbf{Y}_j \circledast x_{ji} \right\|_{\mathcal{G}}, \tag{13}$$

where r represents the rank of matrix $\mathbf{X}$, $\rho(\cdot) : \mathbb{R}^+ \rightarrow \mathbb{R}^+$ is a proper and lower semicontinuous on $[0, +\infty)$. In this paper, we choose the Schatten-p norm $(0 < p < 1)$ as the low rank constraint. Figure 2 is an illustration of three terms on one dimensional data. The function of Schatten-p norm $(p = \frac{1}{2})$ is a neutralization between rank norm $(p = 0)$ and nuclear norm $(p = 1)$, which could increase the punishment on smaller values and decrease the punishment on larger ones simultaneously. Then, to further reduce the influence of smaller singular values to the matrix $\mathbf{X}$, we introduce the reweighted approach inspired by [36] and (13) could be rewritten as below:

$$\min_{\mathbf{X}, \mathbf{w}} \quad \lambda \sum_{i=1}^{r} w_i \rho(\sigma_i(\mathbf{X})) + \sum_{i=1}^{n} \left\| \mathbf{Y}_i \ominus \biguplus_{j=1}^{n} \mathbf{Y}_j \circledast x_{ji} \right\|_{\mathcal{G}}, \tag{14}$$

where $\mathbf{w} = (w_1, w_2, ..., w_r)$ represents the weighting vector with $w_1 < w_2 < ... < w_r$, which could be regarded as the adaptive weights for the singular values of $\mathbf{X}$. Therefore, the first term in (14) could be regarded as a reweighted Non-convex and Non-smooth Rank Minimization based low rank norm, and we call this the reweighted Non-convex and Non-smooth Rank Minimization based clustering model on Grassmann manifold (G-RNNRM).

The objective function in (14) is hard to solve directly owing to the non-linear metric on Grassmann manifold. According to the property and definition in Sect. 2, we could use the embedding distance defined in (2) to replace the construction error in (14) as below:

$$\left\| \mathbf{Y}_i \ominus \biguplus_{j=1}^{n} \mathbf{Y}_j \circledast x_{ji} \right\|_{\mathcal{G}} = \text{dist}_g^2 \left(\mathbf{Y}_i, \biguplus_{j=1}^{n} \mathbf{Y}_j \circledast x_{ji} \right)$$

$$= \left\| \mathbf{Y}_i \mathbf{Y}_i^T - \sum_{j=1}^{n} x_{ji} \mathbf{Y}_j \mathbf{Y}_j^T \right\|_F^2. \tag{15}$$

With this measurement, the function in (14) could be rewritten as below:

$$\min_{\mathbf{X},\mathbf{w}} \ \lambda \sum_{i=1}^{r} w_i \rho(\sigma_i(\mathbf{X})) + \sum_{i=1}^{n} \left\| \mathbf{Y}_i \mathbf{Y}_i^T - \sum_{j=1}^{n} x_{ji} \mathbf{Y}_j \mathbf{Y}_j^T \right\|_F^2. \tag{16}$$

Denoting $g_{ij} = \text{tr}((\mathbf{Y}_j^T \mathbf{Y}_i)(\mathbf{Y}_i^T \mathbf{Y}_j))$ according to [20], we could rewrite (16) as below:

$$\min_{\mathbf{X},\mathbf{w}} \ \lambda \sum_{i=1}^{r} w_i \rho(\sigma_i(\mathbf{X})) + \text{tr}(\mathbf{X}^T \mathbf{G}\mathbf{X}) - 2\text{tr}(\mathbf{G}\mathbf{X}), \tag{17}$$

where matrix $\mathbf{G} = \{g_{ij}\}_{n \times n} \in \mathbb{R}^{n \times n}$ is a symmetric matrix, tr represents the inner product of matrices. With these transformation, the original non-linear self-representation function in (14) could be converted into a linear one, which could be solved by standard optimization.

4.2 Optimization of G-RNNRM

The proposed G-RNNRM model is a complicated optimization problem which is difficult to solve directly. According to [36], we have the following proposition:

Proposition 1: Let $\rho(\cdot) : \mathbb{R}^+ \to \mathbb{R}^+$ be a function such that the proximal operator denoted by $\text{Prox}_\rho()$ is monotone. For $\lambda > 0$, let $\mathbf{Z} = \mathbf{U}_\mathbf{Z} \mathbf{S}_\mathbf{Z} \mathbf{V}_\mathbf{Z}^T$, where $\mathbf{S}_\mathbf{Z} = \text{diag}(\sigma_1(\mathbf{Z}), \sigma_2(\mathbf{Z}), ..., \sigma_r(\mathbf{Z}))$ and all weighting values satisfy $0 \leq w_1 \leq w_2 \leq ... \leq w_r$. Then, the optimal solution to $\mathbf{X}$ could be written as below:

$$\sigma_i(\mathbf{X}) \in \text{Prox}_\rho(\sigma_i(\mathbf{Z}))$$

$$= \arg \min_{\sigma_i(\mathbf{X}) \geq 0} \lambda w_i \rho(\sigma_i(\mathbf{X})) + \frac{1}{2}(\sigma_i(\mathbf{X}) - \sigma_i(\mathbf{Z}))^2. \tag{18}$$

According to Proposition 1, we could obtain the optimal solution to (17). First, let $h(\mathbf{X}) = \text{tr}(\mathbf{X}^T \mathbf{G}\mathbf{X}) - 2\text{tr}(\mathbf{G}\mathbf{X})$. Then we linearize $h(\mathbf{X})$ at $\mathbf{X}^{(t)}$ and add a proximal term as below:

$$h(\mathbf{X}) \approx h(\mathbf{X}^{(t)}) + \langle \nabla h(\mathbf{X}^{(t)}), \mathbf{X} - \mathbf{X}^{(t)} \rangle + \frac{\mu}{2} \|\mathbf{X} - \mathbf{X}^{(t)}\|_F^2, \tag{19}$$

where μ is larger than the Lipschitz constant L_h, $\nabla h(\mathbf{X}^{(t)})$ represents the first derivative of $h(\mathbf{X})$ at $\mathbf{X}^{(t)}$. In our paper, $\mu = 2\|\mathbf{G}\|_2$ and $\nabla h(\mathbf{X}^{(t)}) = 2\mathbf{G}\mathbf{X}^{(t)} - 2\mathbf{G}$. Therefore, we could obtain the update function of $\mathbf{X}$ in (17) as below:

$$
\begin{aligned}
\mathbf{X}^{(t+1)} = \arg\min_{\mathbf{X}} \quad & \lambda \sum_{i=1}^{r} w_i \rho(\sigma_i(\mathbf{X})) + h(\mathbf{X}^{(t)}) \\
& + \langle \nabla h(\mathbf{X}^{(t)}), \mathbf{X} - \mathbf{X}^{(t)} \rangle \\
& + \frac{\mu}{2}\|\mathbf{X} - \mathbf{X}^{(t)}\|_F^2.
\end{aligned}
\tag{20}
$$

(20) could be rewritten as below:

$$
\mathbf{X}^{(t+1)} = \arg\min_{\mathbf{X}} \quad \lambda \sum_{i=1}^{r} w_i^{(t)} \rho(\sigma_i(\mathbf{X})) + \frac{\mu}{2}\|\mathbf{X} - \mathbf{Z}^{(t)}\|_F^2,
\tag{21}
$$

where $\mathbf{Z}^{(t)} = \mathbf{X}^{(t)} - \frac{\nabla h(\mathbf{X}^{(t)})}{\mu}$. According to (18), we could obtain the solution to (21) by solving the optimal singular values and we select $p = \frac{1}{2}$ for examples. The closed-form of singular values is as below [27,37]:

- if $\sigma_i(\mathbf{Z}^{(t)}) > \varphi(\lambda w_i^{(t)})$:

$$
\sigma_i(\mathbf{X}^{(t+1)}) = \frac{2}{3}\sigma_i(\mathbf{Z}^{(t)})(1 + \cos(\frac{2}{3}(\pi - \phi(\sigma_i(\mathbf{Z}^{(t)}))))),
\tag{22}
$$

- otherwise:

$$
\sigma_i(\mathbf{X}^{(t+1)}) = 0,
\tag{23}
$$

where $\phi(\sigma_i(\mathbf{Z}^{(t)})) = \arg\cos(\frac{\lambda w_i^{(t)}}{4}(\frac{\sigma_i(\mathbf{Z}^{(t)})}{3})^{-\frac{3}{2}})$, and $\varphi(\lambda w_i^{(t)}) = \frac{3\sqrt[3]{2}}{4}(2\lambda w_i^{(t)})^{\frac{2}{3}}$. After updating $\mathbf{X}^{(t+1)}$, we could update the weighting vector $\mathbf{w}$ as below:

$$
w_i^{(t+1)} \in \partial\rho(\rho(\sigma_i(\mathbf{X}^{(t+1)}))), i = 1, 2, ..., r.
\tag{24}
$$

In our algorithm, the stopping criterion is measured by the following condition:

$$
\|\mathbf{X}^{(t+1)} - \mathbf{X}^{(t)}\| \le \varepsilon.
\tag{25}
$$

We summarized all update steps in Algorithm 1 for the proposed G-RNNRM.

4.3   Converge and Complexity Analysis

For the proposed G-RNNRM, we first transform the original complex objective function (14) into the standard function (21). Therefore, the algorithm convergence analysis in [36] could be applied to Algorithm 1. Besides, these algorithms always converge in our experiments.

Further, we discuss the complexity of the proposed model. In each iteration step, the complexity of updating $\mathbf{X}$ is $\mathcal{O}(nr^2)$. The complexity of updating $\mathbf{w}$ is $\mathcal{O}(r)$. Therefore, the total complexity of G-RNNRM is $\mathcal{O}(nr^2 + r)$. We also

---

Algorithm 1. The solution to G-RNNRM

Require: The Grassmann sample set $\mathcal{Y} = \{\mathbf{Y}_1, \mathbf{Y}_2, ..., \mathbf{Y}_n\}$, the parameters λ.
1: **Initialize :** $\mathbf{X}^{(0)} \in \mathbb{R}^{n \times n}$ and $\mathbf{w}^{(0)} \in \mathbb{R}^r$, $\varepsilon = 10^{-4}$, the number of maximum iteration $MaxIter = 1000$.
2: Calculate matrix $\mathbf{G}$ by $g_{ij} = \text{tr}((\mathbf{Y}_j^T \mathbf{Y}_i)(\mathbf{Y}_i^T \mathbf{Y}_j))$;
3: $t = 0$;
4: **while** not converged and $t \leq MaxIter$ **do**
5:    Update $\mathbf{X}$ by (18) to (23);
6:    Update $\mathbf{w}$ by (24);
7:    Check the convergence condition defined as (25);
8:    $t = t + 1$.
9: **end while**
Ensure:
   The matrices $\mathbf{X}$ and weighting vector $\mathbf{w}$.

---

list the complexities of other methods in Table 1. Meanwhile, we test all the methods on Extended Yale B dataset as an example. The running time is also shown in Table 1. It demonstrates that the proposed G-RNNRM have acceptable executive time. All methods are coded in Matlab R2014a and implemented on an Intel(R) Xeon(R) Gold 5115 CPU @ 3.60 GHz CPU machine with 8 G RAM.

Table 1. The complexity and running time (second) on Extended Yale B dataset of various methods.

Method	Complexity	Running time
SSC	$\mathcal{O}(tn^2(1 + n))$	2.78
LRR	$\mathcal{O}(2tn^3)$	27.67
LS3C	$\mathcal{O}(tn^2(sn^2 + 1))$	39.02
SCGSM	$\mathcal{O}(m^3 p^3 d^2 t(n + d))$	2198.84
G-KM	$\mathcal{O}(3n^3)$	1.43
G-CLRSR	$\mathcal{O}(tn^2(3n + 1))$	108.32
G-LRR	$\mathcal{O}(2tn^3)$	25.42
G-PSSVLR	$\mathcal{O}(2tn^3)$	29.94
G-RNNRM	$\mathcal{O}(t(nr^2 + r))$	32.74

5   Experimental Results

We test the proposed method for facial imageset and action video clip clustering tasks, and the whole experiments are evaluated on four datasets, including the Extended Yale B face dataset [38], CMU-PIE face dataset [39], Ballet action dataset [40] and SKIG gesture dataset [41]. Facial images are usually corrupted by rich expression, different pose, various illustration intensities and directions, which affect the performance of facial clustering task. Action clustering task is also difficult since human actions are always captured by large range of scenes and viewpoints. Besides, small movement, the illumination and background would change great. These problems would make the clustering task challenging.

The performance of the proposed method is compared with some state-of-the-art clustering algorithms, such as SSC [10], LRR [11], LS3C [42], SCGSM [18], G-KM [19], G-LRR [20], G-PSSVLR [23] and G-CLRSR [22]. In our method, after learning the representation $\mathbf{X}$, we use the NCut method [9] to obtain the final clustering results. The clustering results are measured by the clustering Accuracy (ACC), Normalized Mutual Information (NMI), Rand Index(RI) and Purity (PUR). The details of data setting and results analysis are given below.

5.1 Data Setting

In our experiments, we first transform each image into a m-dimension vector. For vector based LRR, SSC and LS3C methods, we stack all image vectors from the same imageset as a long vector and adopt PCA to reduce the dimension which equals to the dimension of PCA components retaining 95% of its variance energy. For other Grassmann manifold based methods, we form all image vectors from the same imageset as a matrix. Then SVD is applied on the matrix and we pick up the first p columns of the left singular matrix as a sample data on Grassmann manifold $\mathcal{G}(p,m)$. The detailed data setting for Grassmann manifold based methods is as below:

Extended Yale B Face Dataset. Extended Yale B face dataset contains 2,414 frontal face images of $c = 38$ subjects under different light directions and illumination conditions, and each subject has about 64 images. In our experiments, we resize images into 20 × 20. To construct Grassmannian data, we randomly choose 8 images from the same subject to construct an image-set for clustering. We set the subspace dimension of Grassmann manifolds as $p = 4$.

CMU-PIE Face Dataset. The CMU-PIE face dataset is composed of 68 subjects with 1632 front face images. Each subject has 42 images under different lighting conditions. In our experiments, each grey image is down-sampled as a fixed size of 32 × 32. Every 4 images from the same subject are selected to form an imageset sample. The image-sets are also represented as Grassmannian points $\mathcal{G}(4, 1024)$.

Ballet Action Dataset. This dataset comprises of 8 basic ballet actions performed by 3 persons. The 8 ballet actions are *left-to-right hand opening, right-to-left hand opening, standing hand opening, leg swinging, jumping, turning, hopping* and *standing still*. In our experiments, we resize each image into 30 × 30 and divide each video clip into sections of 12 images to form the imagesets. We set the dimension of Grassmann manifolds as $p = 6$, then we construct a Grassmann manifolds $\mathcal{G}(6, 900)$ for clustering.

SKIG Gesture Dataset. The SKIG dataset consists of 1080 RGB-D videos collected from 6 subjects captured by a Kinect sensor. In this dataset, there are 10 gesture types: *circle, triangle, up-down, rightleft, wave, Z, cross, comehere, turn-around,* and *pat.* All the gestures are performed by fist, finger, and elbow, respectively, under three backgrounds (wooden board, white plain paper, and paper with characters) and two illuminations (strong light and poor light). In our experiments, each image is resized as 24 × 32 and each clip is regarded as an imageset.

5.2   Parameters Setting

To obtain the suitable parameter for the proposed model, the influence of λ on the clustering accuracy is learned by some pre-experiments. λ is tuned within $[10^{-10}, 10^8]$ and Fig. 3 shows the influence of λ on Extended Yale B dataset, CMU-PIE face dataset, Ballet action dataset and SKIG gesture dataset respectively. The parameter for each dataset is set as: $\lambda = 0.1$ for Extended Yale B dataset; $\lambda = 0.15$ for CMU-PIE dataset; $\lambda = 20$ for Ballet dataset; $\lambda = 2.5$ for SKIG dataset.

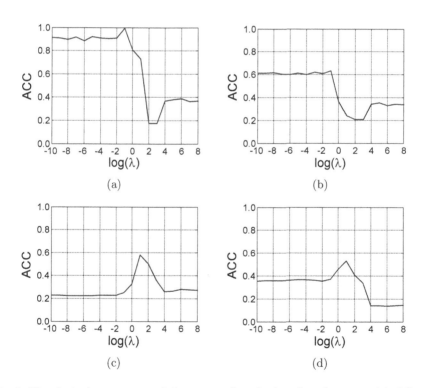

Fig. 3. The clustering accuracy of the proposed method on four datasets with different λ: (a) Extended Yale B dataset; (b) CMU-PIE face dataset; (c) Ballet action dataset; (d) SKIG gesture dataset.

Table 2. The clustering results of various methods on four datasets: (a) Accuracy (ACC), (b) Normalized Mutual Information (NMI), (c) Rand Index (RI) and (d) Purity (PUR).

(a)

Method	SSC	LRR	LS3C	SCGSM	G-KM	G-CLRSR	G-LRR	G-PSSVLR	G-RNNRM
Extended Yale B	0.4032	0.4659	0.2461	0.7946	0.8365	0.8194	0.8135	<u>0.9035</u>	**0.9872**
CMU-PIE	0.5231	0.4034	0.2761	0.5732	0.6025	<u>0.6289</u>	0.6153	0.6213	**0.6418**
Ballet	0.2962	0.2923	0.4262	0.5613	0.5699	0.5931	0.5912	<u>0.6013</u>	**0.6143**
SKIG	0.3892	0.2537	0.2941	0.3716	0.5308	0.5083	0.5022	<u>0.5502</u>	**0.5949**
avg.	0.4029	0.3538	0.3106	0.5733	0.6349	0.6374	0.6306	<u>0.6691</u>	**0.7127**

(b)

Method	SSC	LRR	LS3C	SCGSM	G-KM	G-CLRSR	G-LRR	G-PSSVLR	G-RNNRM
Extended Yale B	0.6231	0.6813	0.4992	0.9326	<u>0.9341</u>	0.9103	0.8903	0.9262	**0.9921**
CMU-PIE	0.7865	0.7321	0.6313	0.5736	0.5976	<u>0.8132</u>	0.8103	0.7926	**0.8341**
Ballet	0.2813	0.2910	0.4370	0.5646	0.5779	<u>0.5862</u>	0.5762	0.5837	**0.6405**
SKIG	0.4762	0.3343	0.3421	0.5367	0.5671	0.5679	0.5450	<u>0.5692</u>	**0.6342**
avg.	0.5418	0.5097	0.4774	0.6519	0.6692	<u>0.7194</u>	0.7055	0.7179	**0.7752**

(c)

Method	SSC	LRR	LS3C	SCGSM	G-KM	G-CLRSR	G-LRR	G-PSSVLR	G-RNNRM
Extended Yale B	0.9503	0.9581	0.9525	0.9537	0.9647	0.9772	0.9793	<u>0.9812</u>	**0.9868**
CMU-PIE	0.9727	0.9752	0.9737	0.9235	0.9482	0.9721	<u>0.9811</u>	0.9727	**0.9878**
Ballet	0.8135	0.8273	0.8202	0.8301	0.8319	0.8321	0.8377	<u>0.8382</u>	**0.8496**
SKIG	0.8595	0.7223	0.8160	0.8135	0.8392	0.8577	0.8782	<u>0.8763</u>	**0.8910**
avg.	0.8990	0.8707	0.8906	0.8802	0.8960	0.9098	<u>0.9191</u>	0.9171	**0.9288**

(d)

Method	SSC	LRR	LS3C	SCGSM	G-KM	G-CLRSR	G-LRR	G-PSSVLR	G-RNNRM
Extended Yale B	0.4347	0.4932	0.2375	0.8104	0.8582	0.8375	0.8275	<u>0.9017</u>	**0.9937**
CMU-PIE	0.5371	0.4415	0.2695	0.5637	0.5976	0.6559	0.6429	<u>0.6711</u>	**0.6941**
Ballet	0.4175	0.4302	0.4581	0.5854	0.5867	0.6281	0.6298	<u>0.6376</u>	**0.6578**
SKIG	0.4352	0.3577	0.3102	0.3502	0.6097	0.5819	0.5322	<u>0.6268</u>	**0.6630**
avg.	0.4311	0.4307	0.3188	0.5774	0.6631	0.6759	0.6581	<u>0.7093</u>	**0.7522**

5.3 Results Analysis

We show clustering results in Tables 2. Each clustering experiment is repeated 20 times and the average results are reported. The best results are bold, the second ones are underlined. From the results, Grassmann manifold representation based methods always have better performances than the vectors based ones (SSC, LRR, LS3C), which explains that the manifold representation have the advantage of revealing the complicated relationship within the imageset or video data effectively. In all the methods, the low rank representation based ones always obtain the top results, which shows the benefit of low rank representation. From the results, our proposed G-RNNRM always obtains the best results. Especially, G-RNNRM outperform the second ones with about 4 to 5% points gap in terms of ACC, NMI and PUR on avenges respectively. The significant improvement of our method is analyzed and own to the superiority that the proposed method not only adopts the Non-convex Non-smooth Rank Minimization but also constructs reweighted approach.

6 Conclusion

In this paper, we propose a new low rank model on Grassmann manifold for high-dimension data clustering task. Instead of the traditional convex nuclear norm, we adopt non-convex and non-smooth rank minimization approach to formulate a novel clustering model on Grassmann manifold with non-linear metric. Further, reweighting approach has been introduced to obtain a better low-rank representation matrix. In addition, an effective alternative algorithm is proposed as solution. The proposed model has been evaluated on four public datasets. The experimental results show that our proposed model outperforms state-of-the-art ones.

Acknowledgements. The research project is supported by National Natural Science Foundation of China under Grant No. 61902053, 61672071, U1811463, U19B2039, 61632006, 61972067, 91748104.

References

1. Biswas, A., Jacobs, D.: Active image clustering: seeking constraints from humans to complement algorithms. In: Proceedings of IEEE Conference on Computer Vision and Pattern Recognition, pp. 2152–2159 (2012)
2. Krinidis, S., Chatzis, V.: A robust fuzzy local information C-means clustering algorithm. IEEE Trans. Image Process. **19**, 1328–1337 (2010)
3. You, C., Robinson, D., Vidal, R.: Scalable sparse subspace clustering by orthogonal matching pursuit. In: Proceedings of IEEE Conference on Computer Vision and Pattern Recognition, pp. 3918–3927 (2016)
4. Liu, H., Shao, M., Li, S., Fu, Y.: Infinite ensemble for image clustering. In: Proceedings of ACM SIGKDD International Conference on Knowledge Discovery and Data Mining, pp. 1745–1754 (2016)
5. Gruber, A., Weiss, Y.: Multibody factorization with uncertainty and missing data using the EM algorithm. In: Proceedings of IEEE Conference on Computer Vision and Pattern Recognition, pp. 707–714 (2004)
6. Ho, J., Yang, M.H., Lim, J., Lee, K.C., Kriegman, D.: Clustering appearances of objects under varying illumination conditions. In: Proceedings of IEEE Conference on Computer Vision and Pattern Recognition, pp. 11–18 (2003)
7. Ma, Y., Yang, A.Y., Derksen, H., Fossum, R.: Estimation of subspace arrangements with applications in modeling and segmenting mixed data. SIAM Rev. **50**, 413–458 (2008)
8. Elhamifar, E., Vidal, R.: Sparse subspace clustering. In: Proceedings of IEEE Conference on Computer Vision and Pattern Recognition, pp. 1–8 (2009)
9. Shi, J., Malik, J.: Normalized cuts and image segmentation. IEEE Trans. Pattern Anal. Mach. Intell. **22**, 888–905 (2010)
10. Elhamifar, E., Vidal, R.: Sparse subspace clustering: algorithm, theory, and applications. IEEE Trans. Pattern Anal. Mach. Intell. **35**, 2765–2781 (2013)
11. Liu, G., Lin, Z., Yu, Y.: Robust subspace segmentation by low-rank representation. In: Proceedings of International Conference on Machine Learning, pp. 663–670 (2010)

12. Liu, G., Yan, S.: Latent low-rank representation for subspace segmentation and feature extraction. In: Proceedings of International Conference on Computer Vision, pp. 1615–1622 (2011)
13. Zhang, H., Lin, Z., Zhang, C., Gao, J.: Robust latent low rank representation for subspace clustering. Neurocomputing **145**, 2765–2781 (2014)
14. Patel, V.M., Vidal, R.: Kernel sparse subspace clustering. In: Proceedings of IEEE International Conference on Image Processing, pp. 2849–2853 (2014)
15. Xiao, S., Tan, M., Xu, D., Dong, Z.Y.: Robust kernel low-rank representation. IEEE Trans. Neural Netw. Learn. Syst. **27**, 2268–2281 (2015)
16. Wu, T., Bajwa, W.U.: Learning the nonlinear geometry of high-dimensional data: Models and algorithms. IEEE Trans. Sig. Process. **63**, 6229–6244 (2015)
17. Wang, B., Hu, Y., Gao, J., Sun, Y., Yin, B.: Laplacian LRR on product Grassmann manifolds for human activity clustering in multicamera video surveillance. IEEE Trans. Circuits Syst. Video Technol. **27**, 554–566 (2017)
18. Turaga, P., Veeraraghavan, A., Srivastava, A., Chellappa, R.: Statistical computations on Grassmann and Stiefel manifolds for image and video-based recognition. IEEE Trans. Pattern Anal. Mach. Intell. **33**, 2273–2286 (2011)
19. Shirazi, S., Harandi, M.T., Sanderson, C., Alavi, A., Lovell, B.C.: Clustering on Grassmann manifolds via kernel embedding with application to action analysis. In: Proceedings of IEEE International Conference on Image Processing, pp. 781–784 (2012)
20. Wang, B., Hu, Y., Gao, J., Sun, Y., Yin, B.: Low rank representation on Grassmann manifolds. In: Proceedings of Asian Conference on Computer Vision, pp. 81–96 (2014)
21. Liu, T., Shi, Z., Liu, Y.: Visual clustering based on kernel sparse representation on Grassmann manifolds. In: Proceedings of IEEE 7th Annual International Conference on CYBER Technology in Automation, Control, and Intelligent Systems, pp. 920–925 (2017)
22. Wang, B., Hu, Y., Gao, J., Sun, Y., Yin, B.: Cascaded low rank and sparse representation on Grassmann manifolds. In: Proceedings of International Joint Conference on Artificial Intelligence, pp. 2755–2761 (2018)
23. Wang, B., Hu, Y., Gao, J., Sun, Y., Yin, B.: Partial sum minimization of singular values representation on Grassmann manifolds. ACM Trans. Knowl. Discov. Data **12**, 1–22 (2018). Article 13
24. Piao, X., Hu, Y., Gao, J., Sun, Y., Yin, B.: Double nuclear norm based low rank representation on Grassmann manifolds for clustering. In: Proceedings of IEEE Conference on Computer Vision and Pattern Recognition, pp. 12075–12084 (2019)
25. Wang, B., Hu, Y., Gao, J., Sun, Y., Yin, B.: Localized LRR on Grassmann manifold: an extrinsic view. IEEE Trans. Circuits Syst. Video Technol. **28**, 2524–2536 (2018)
26. Candès, E.J., Wakin, M.B., Boyd, S.P.: Enhancing sparsity by reweighted ℓ_1 minimization. J. Fourier Anal. Appl. **14**, 877–905 (2008)
27. Zhang, H., Yang, J., Shang, F., Gong, C., Zhang, Z.: LRR for subspace segmentation via tractable Schatten-p norm minimization and factorization. IEEE Trans. Cybern. **49**, 172–1734 (2019)
28. Nie, F., Hu, Z., Li, X.: Matrix completion based on non-convex low rank approximation. IEEE Trans. Image Process. **28**, 2378–2388 (2019)
29. Malek-Mohammadi, M., Babaie-Zadeh, M., Skoglund, M.: Performance guarantees for Schatten-p quasi-norm minimization in recovery of low-rank matrices. Sig. Process. **114**, 225–230 (2015)

30. Lu, C., Tang, J., Yan, S., Lin, Z.: Nonconvex nonsmooth low rank minimization via iteratively reweighted nuclear norm. IEEE Trans. Image Process. **25**, 829–839 (2016)
31. Absil, P.A., Mahony, R.E., Sepulchre, R.: Optimization Algorithms on Matrix Manifolds. Princeton University Press, Princeton (2009)
32. Goh, A., Vidal, R.: Clustering and dimensionality reduction on Riemannian manifolds. In: Proceedings of IEEE Conference on Computer Vision and Pattern Recognition, pp. 1–7 (2008)
33. Harandi, M., Sanderson, C., Shen, C., Lovell, B.C.: Dictionary learning and sparse coding on Grassmann manifolds: an extrinsic solution. In: Proceedings of International Conference on Computer Vision, pp. 3120–3127 (2013)
34. Lu, C.-Y., Min, H., Zhao, Z.-Q., Zhu, L., Huang, D.-S., Yan, S.: Robust and efficient subspace segmentation via least squares regression. In: Fitzgibbon, A., Lazebnik, S., Perona, P., Sato, Y., Schmid, C. (eds.) ECCV 2012. LNCS, vol. 7578, pp. 347–360. Springer, Heidelberg (2012). https://doi.org/10.1007/978-3-642-33786-4_26
35. Oh, T.H., Tai, Y.W., Bazin, J.C., Kim, H., Kweon, I.S.: Partial sum minimization of singular values in robust PCA: algorithm and applications. IEEE Trans. Pattern Anal. Mach. Intell. **38**, 744–758 (2015)
36. Zhang, H., Gong, C., Qian, J., Zhang, B., Xu, C., Yang, J.: Efficient recovery of low-rank matrix via double nonconvex nonsmooth rank minimization. IEEE Trans. Neural Netw. Learn. Syst. **30**, 2916–2925 (2019)
37. Cao, W., Sun, J., Xu, Z.: Fast image deconvolution using closed-form thresholding formulas of $l_q(q = 1/2, 2/3)$ regularization. J. Vis. Commun. Image Represent. **24**, 31–41 (2013)
38. Lee, K.C., Ho, J., Kriegman, D.J.: Acquiring linear subspaces for face recognition under variable lighting. IEEE Trans. Pattern Anal. Mach. Intell. **27**, 684–698 (2005)
39. Sim, T., Baker, S., Bsat, M.: The CMU pose, illumination, and expression database. IEEE Trans. Pattern Anal. Mach. Intell. **25**, 1615–1618 (2003)
40. Fathi, A., Mori, G.: Action recognition by learning mid-level motion features. In: Proceedings of IEEE Conference on Computer Vision and Pattern Recognition, pp. 1–8 (2008)
41. Liu, L., Shao, L.: Learning discriminative representations from RGB-D video data. In: Proceedings of International Joint Conference on Artificial Intelligence, pp. 1493–1500 (2013)
42. Patel, V.M., Nguyen, H.V., Vidal, R.: Latent space sparse subspace clustering. In: Proceedings of IEEE International Conference on Computer Vision, pp. 225–232 (2013)

Biomedical Image Analysis

Descriptor-Free Multi-view Region Matching for Instance-Wise 3D Reconstruction

Takuma Doi[1], Fumio Okura[1,2]([✉]) [iD], Toshiki Nagahara[1],
Yasuyuki Matsushita[1] [iD], and Yasushi Yagi[1]

[1] Graduate School of Information Science and Technology,
Osaka University, Osaka, Japan
{doi,t-nagahara,yagi}@am.sanken.osaka-u.ac.jp,
{okura,yasumat}@ist.osaka-u.ac.jp
[2] Japan Science and Technology Agency, Saitama, Japan

Abstract. This paper proposes a multi-view extension of instance segmentation without relying on texture or shape descriptor matching. Multi-view instance segmentation becomes challenging for scenes with repetitive textures and shapes, *e.g.*, plant leaves, due to the difficulty of multi-view matching using texture or shape descriptors. To this end, we propose a multi-view region matching method based on epipolar geometry, which does not rely on any feature descriptors. We further show that the epipolar region matching can be easily integrated into instance segmentation and effective for instance-wise 3D reconstruction. Experiments demonstrate the improved accuracy of multi-view instance matching and the 3D reconstruction compared to the baseline methods.

1 Introduction

One of the important applications of computer vision is to analyze the shape and structure of natural objects, *i.e.*, quantifying the size, number, and shape of plant leaves. In such applications, *instance segmentation* plays an important role because of the need for accurately determining individual object instances. A single-view instance segmentation has gained attention, and there have been a series of previous works [1–3] to address the problem. However, for scenes suffering from severe occlusions, it is needed to perform instance segmentation in a *multi-view* setting as shown in Fig. 1. We call it a *multi-view instance segmentation (MVIS)* problem.

An extension of single-view instance segmentation to the multi-view setting is a challenging task, especially when the individual instances are look-alike, for example, plant leaves. Although external markers or background objects,

---

Electronic supplementary material The online version of this chapter (https:// doi.org/10.1007/978-3-030-69541-5_35) contains supplementary material, which is available to authorized users.

© Springer Nature Switzerland AG 2021
H. Ishikawa et al. (Eds.): ACCV 2020, LNCS 12626, pp. 581–599, 2021.
https://doi.org/10.1007/978-3-030-69541-5_35

582   T. Doi et al.

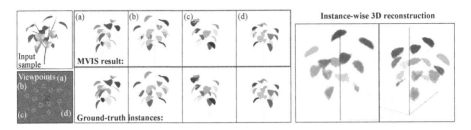

Fig. 1. An example of MVIS and instance-wise 3D reconstruction. The same color indicates the corresponding instances across different views. We propose a multi-view instance matching without relying on texture or shape descriptors. (Color figure online)

e.g., plant pots, can be a guide for obtaining sparse correspondences to determine camera poses, we cannot expect dense point correspondences on similar instances, *e.g.*, leaves, across views. This setting makes it difficult to directly use existing approaches, such as 3D instance segmentation [4] and multi-view semantic segmentation [5–7], which heavily rely on 3D shape information.

To overcome the problem, we propose an MVIS method based on region matching that does not rely on dense correspondences, which can be used for matching objects across views without distinctive textures or shape but with similar appearances. The key idea of our method is to use the epipolar constraint to determine the multi-view region correspondences of segmented instances that are computed at each view. By treating each instance in each view as a node in a graph, and by assigning edge weights based on the degree of intersection of epipolar lines and instance regions, we cast the problem of multi-view instance segmentation to a graph clustering problem. We call the approach the *epipolar region matching*. We show that it enables reliably establishing correspondences of view-wise segmented instances across multiple views. Further, our epipolar region matching can be easily integrated in modern instance segmentation methods [1,3,8]. Our method can be combined with any region segmentation methods; while given a set of regions, our region matching method does not rely on any descriptors. The estimated instances with multi-view correspondences can be used for the *instance-wise 3D reconstruction* via existing 3D reconstruction methods, yielding superior reconstruction results.

Experimental results show that the proposed method yields accurate multi-view instance correspondence compared to an instance matching method based on a traditional multi-view stereo (MVS) and a point-based matching. We also demonstrate the effectiveness of MVIS for instance-wise 3D reconstruction.

Contributions. We propose a multi-view region matching method without using texture and shape descriptors, as a key technical component of MVIS for texture/shape-repetitive scenes. The matching method can be put together in instance segmentation and 3D reconstruction methods for instance-wise 3D reconstruction.

2   Related Works

Our work is closely related to multi-view correspondence matching, as well as the multi-view or 3D extensions of semantic/instance segmentation. This section discusses the related works in these subject areas.

Multi-view Correspondence Matching. Multi-view correspondence matching is a fundamental problem in multi-view image analysis, such as structure from motion (SfM) [9] and multi-view stereo (MVS) [10]. As a veteran but still frequently used approach, keypoint detection and matching (*e.g.*, [11–13]) is used to obtain sparse correspondences; while dense correspondence matching often involves a patch [14] and plane-based [15] matching.

For target scenes containing partly texture-less objects, various approaches have been studied, such as a belief propagation [16,17] for MVS. More recently, deep-learning-based approaches to correspondence matching for partially texture-less scenes, which often assume the smoothness of the target scene, have been studied [18,19]. Correspondence matching for objects in which surface is fully texture-less, or with repetitive textures is notably challenging because it becomes difficult to find dense correspondences. For string-like objects (*e.g.*, hairs), which have the matching ambiguity along the strings or lines, an MVS method using line-shaped patches has been proposed [20]. Regarding the sparse point matching, Dellaert *et al.* [21] presented a method for the SfM problem without using texture features, which calculates the camera pose and sparse point correspondences based only on the geometric relationship of keypoints.

Shape-based matching [22–24] such as using the Fourier shape descriptors [25] or shape contexts [22], is another line of the region matching. These approaches encode the region shape information, *e.g.*, instance shape, into descriptors. In our cases, since the target scene is composed of objects with similar 3D shapes (*e.g.*, plant leaves), it is not realistic to use shape-based matching. Although it is different from the context of instance segmentation, region-based information [26], such as the statistics of textures, is a useful cue for the correspondence matching. For example, superpixel stereo [27,28] or segment-based stereo [29] were developed to increase the robustness of correspondence matching. Segmentation of the same object among multiple views can be categorized in multi-view co-segmentation [5–7], which also uses the texture features.

Unlike the previous methods, we achieve the descriptor-free multi-view region matching using the epipolar constraint. The epipolar matching is a traditional yet important problem. As far as we are aware, *searching regions without (texture or shape) descriptor matching* remains unsolved.

Instance Segmentation and Its Multi-view Extension. While various implementations of instance segmentation including one-stage methods [30] are developed, two-stage frameworks that combine object detection and mask generation are often used due to the advantage of performance and simplicity. A major implementation of two-stage instance segmentation is Mask R-CNN [1] based on Faster R-CNN [31], which computes the region proposals of the target objects followed by the mask generation for selected proposals.

Video instance segmentation is a multi-image extension of instance segmentation. These approaches perform the instance tracking, as well as the segmentation [32–35]. An early attempt of this approach [36] used superpixels for instance tracking. A recent study configures the problem as multi-object tracking and segmentation (MOTS), and provides a Mask-R-CNN-based implementation [8]. PanopticFusion [37] aggregates multi-view instances in a 3D volumetric space, while it inputs a video sequence that enables the instance tracking. Video instance tracking is applied for plant image analysis, such as the 3D reconstruction of grape clusters [38]. This batch of approaches assumes the time-series image sequences, which allows the object tracking with smaller displacement between the consequent frames. We rather focus on the multi-view setting, where the images are captured with wider baselines between the viewpoints.

3D Semantic/Instance Segmentation. Somewhat related to MVIS, 3D semantic/instance segmentation is studied. Approaches for 3D segmentation often input 3D shapes of target objects, such as point cloud [39,40], volumetric space [41], and RGB-D images [4,42]. Semantic segmentation on multi-view RGB images can be used for 3D reconstruction via the aggregation on a 3D space, which are called semantic 3D reconstruction [43–45]. These methods do not distinguish the objects in a same category in principle.

Nassar *et al.* [46] proposes an instance warping for multi-view instance correspondence matching using the 3D shape of target scenes. Instance segmentation on 3D point clouds are also studied [47–49], which needs the input of high-quality 3D point clouds. Unlike these approaches, we focus on the instance matching of objects where the 3D reconstruction is challenging; *e.g.*, plants due to thin shape, repetitive textures, and heavy occlusions. As an application-specific study, a plant modeling method proposed by Quan *et al.* [50] uses the combination of 2D segmentation and 3D point cloud clustering for 3D leaf modeling. Because their method assumes a good-quality 3D point cloud as input, it is difficult for the reconstruction of plants with texture-less leaves.

3   Multi-view Instance Segmentation (MVIS)

Our goal is to find multi-view instance correspondences from the multi-view images of the target. We assume that the camera poses and intrinsics are known, *e.g.*, by an SfM [9] using the sparse correspondences obtained from the scene background. We here assume that instance segmentation in each view is available for now, while the instance correspondence *across views* is unknown.

3.1   Epipolar Region Matching

Given a set of instances in each image and camera pose information, we establish instance correspondences across multi-view images. We approach this problem by epipolar geometry; namely, finding the correspondences via epipolar lines drawn on other views. Since multiple instances appear on the same epipolar line (see Fig. 2), we cast the matching problem to a *graph clustering* problem.

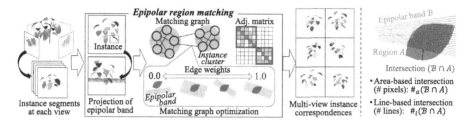

Fig. 2. Overview of epipolar region matching which does not rely on the feature descriptors. The proposed method creates a matching graph based on the epipolar constraint, where the edge weights are defined as the degree of intersection between the instances and epipolar bands (*i.e.*, projections of instances in other views). Instance correspondences are extracted by a graph clustering method.

We create an undirected edge-weighted graph $G = (V, E, w)$, where V is the node set that consists of instances appeared in all views, $E \subseteq V \times V$ is the edge set, and $w : E \to \mathbb{R}_+$ is the weight function defining the edge weights. The number of nodes $|V|$ corresponds to the total number of instances that appear in all the images.

To define the edge weights, we compute a set of epipolar lines from densely-sampled points on each instance. Here we define the i-th view image as I_i, m-th instance segment in the i-th image as $v_{i,m} \in V$ and its region (set of pixels) in the image coordinates as $\mathcal{A}_{i,m} \subset \mathbb{R}^2$. Let $\mathbf{F}_{ij}$ be a fundamental matrix between i-th and j-th views. Then an image point $\mathbf{p}$ in instance segment $\mathcal{A}_{i,m}$, *i.e.*, $\mathbf{p} \in \mathcal{A}_{i,m}$, forms an epipolar line $\mathbf{l}_j(\mathbf{p})$ in the j-th view image as

$$\mathbf{l}_j(\mathbf{p}) = \mathbf{F}_{ij}\tilde{\mathbf{p}}, \tag{1}$$

where $\tilde{\mathbf{p}}$ is the homogeneous representation of $\mathbf{p}$. From all points in region $\mathcal{A}_{i,m}$, we have a set of epipolar lines forming a pencil of epipolar lines passing through the epipole. In what follows, we call the pencil an *epipolar band* $\mathcal{B}$ in this paper. The epipolar band $\mathcal{B}$ of region $\mathcal{A}_{i,m}$ on the j-th image is thus defined as

$$\mathcal{B}(\mathcal{A}_{i,m}, I_j) = \{\mathbf{F}_{ij}\tilde{\mathbf{p}}\}, \quad \mathbf{p} \in \mathcal{A}_{i,m}. \tag{2}$$

We define the edge weights w in the graph G as the degree of intersection of an epipolar band $\mathcal{B}$ and instance regions $\mathcal{A}$ in analogous to the intersection-over-union (IoU) computation. While original IoU is defined between two areas, the extension to a similarity measure between the epipolar band and a region is not straightforward. To evaluate the degree of intersection between the epipolar band and instance region, we use two measures: The area of intersection and the number of epipolar lines in the epipolar band passing through the instance region, as illustrated in the right side of Fig. 2. In this manner, the edge weight w between nodes $v_{i,m}$ and $v_{j,n}$ can be obtained as

$$w(v_{i,m}, v_{j,n}) = \frac{\#_a(\mathcal{B}(\mathcal{A}_{i,m}, I_j) \cap \mathcal{A}_{j,n})}{\#_a \mathcal{A}_{j,n}} \cdot \frac{\#_l(\mathcal{B}(\mathcal{A}_{i,m}, I_j) \cap \mathcal{A}_{j,n})}{\#_l \mathcal{B}(\mathcal{A}_{i,m}, I_j)}, \tag{3}$$

where the function $\#_a$ counts the number of pixels belonging to the region, while $\#_l$ counts the number of epipolar lines passing through the area. During the computation of $\#_a(\mathcal{B}(\mathcal{A}_{i,m}, I_j) \cap \mathcal{A}_{j,n})$, we draw epipolar lines with the same thickness (two pixels was used in our experiment). As with many other similarity measures, $w(v_{i,m}, v_{j,n})$ takes the range $[0, 1]$, where it becomes one if all epipolar lines in the epipolar band passes through the instance area and a whole part of the area is filled with epipolar lines (see Fig. 2).

Once the edge weights $\{w\}$ are defined, we form an adjacency matrix $\mathbf{W}$ of $|V| \times |V|$ elements from the graph G and perform a graph clustering using symmetric non-negative matrix factorization (SymNMF) [51], as $\mathbf{W} \approx \mathbf{H}\mathbf{H}^T$. After the factorization, the largest element in each row of $\mathbf{H}$ indicates the *cluster ID*, where each cluster forms a set of corresponding instances across multi-view. Hereafter, we call the cluster an *instance cluster*.

3.2 Application: Epipolar Region Matching for Region Proposals

As an application of the proposed method, we here describe the integration of multi-view region matching method with modern instance segmentation. While our region matching method can be used with any instance segmentation methods, we can optionally utilize the correspondences across multi-view *region proposals* to retain partly occluded instances. Most instance segmentation methods [1,3,8] rely on region proposals [31], which performs region unification by the non-maximum suppression (NMS) [52] to merge overlapping region proposals. As a result, region proposals for partially occluded instances are often suppressed. To this end, we implemented an NMS process considering the multi-view region correspondences. We found our implementation recovered partially occluded instances, while it did not significantly affect the overall instance segmentation accuracy (see the supplementary material for detailed discussions).

Our method starts from the initial segmentation result, *e.g.*, by Mask R-CNN, and their tentative multi-view correspondence computed by the epipolar region matching. The NMS and region matching processes can be performed alternately to update the set of detected instances and their multi-view correspondences as illustrated in Fig. 3. We assign the instance cluster IDs for each region proposal by the region matching method, and avoid to unify the proposals with different cluster IDs by the NMS process.

To update the cluster ID of each region proposals, sets of corresponding instances (*i.e.*, instance clusters estimated in the previous iteration) are projected to the view using the same manner as the epipolar band projection described in Sect. 3.1. Let the k-th instance cluster in the previous iteration be $\{\mathcal{A}_k\} \subset \{\mathcal{A}\}$,

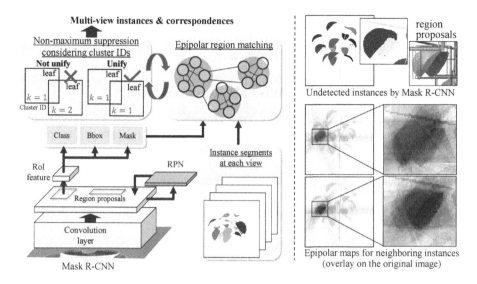

Fig. 3. Epipolar region matching integrated in a two-stage instance segmentation network. It updates the instance detection and multi-view correspondence via an iterative process. The projections of epipolar bands are used to distinguish the undetected region proposal from neighboring instances.

which is denoted as a set of instances. The projection onto the i-th image, $\mathcal{M}_{i,k}$, is calculated based on the sum of epipolar bands by the instances (we call $\mathcal{M}_{i,k}$ an *epipolar map* hereafter).

$$\mathcal{M}_{i,k} = \frac{\sum_{\{\mathcal{A}_k\}} \mathcal{B}(\mathcal{A} \in \{\mathcal{A}_k\}, I_i)}{\#_c\{\mathcal{A}_k\}}, \tag{4}$$

where $\#_c\{\mathcal{A}_k\}$ counts the number of instances in the cluster $\{\mathcal{A}_k\}$. The right side of Fig. 3 shows an example of the epipolar map.

An updated cluster ID for each region proposal is calculated based on the highest degree of intersection between the epipolar map and the region proposal. Letting the instance mask of r-th region proposal in i-th image as $\mathcal{A}'_{i,r}$, the similarity of the two maps, $\mathcal{M}_{i,m}$ and $\mathcal{A}'_{i,r}$, is obtained by the similar manner to the IoU computation. Since the epipolar map does not take the value of $\{0, 1\}$, we use an extension of the IoU, which is called Ruzicka similarity [53].

$$s(\mathcal{M}_{i,k}, \mathcal{A}'_{i,r}) = \frac{Sigma_{\mathbf{x}} \min(\mathcal{M}_{i,k}(\mathbf{x}), \mathcal{A}'_{i,r}(\mathbf{x}))}{Sigma_{\mathbf{x}} \max(\mathcal{M}_{i,k}(\mathbf{x}), \mathcal{A}'_{i,r}(\mathbf{x}))}, \tag{5}$$

where $\mathbf{x}$ denotes the pixel location. In the equation, we deal with each instance mask $\mathcal{A}'_{i,r}$ as a map taking $\{0, 1\}$ values, where the value takes one if the pixel is inside the mask. The updated cluster ID for the region proposal $\mathcal{A}'_{i,r}$ is selected as k with the largest similarity $s(\mathcal{M}_{i,k}, \mathcal{A}'_{i,r})$. The update process of cluster ID is followed by the NMS that does not unify the region proposals with different cluster IDs to retain the partly occluded instances. Our implementation allows to iterate the region matching and NMS processes while updating the set of instances and multi-view correspondences.

3.3 Application: Instance-Wise 3D Reconstruction

Multi-view correspondences of instance segments can be used for the *instance-wise* 3D reconstruction, by independently applying a 3D reconstruction method for each of instance clusters. We implemented a simple volumetric reconstruction method based on a back-projection used in a traditional computed tomography [54], which is analogous to the visual hull method [55].

Let a set of k-th instance cluster $\{\mathcal{A}_k\}$ and the set of projection functions $\{\theta\}$ from 3D to 2D image coordinates, $\theta : \mathbb{R}^3 \rightarrow \mathbb{R}^2$. The aggregated value $\mathcal{I}_k$ at voxel $\mathbf{x}_{3D} \in \mathbb{R}^3$ can be computed as:

$$\mathcal{I}_k(\mathbf{x}_{3D}) = \frac{\sum_{\mathcal{A}_k \in \{\mathcal{A}_k\}} \mathcal{L}_{\mathcal{A}_k}(\theta_k(\mathbf{x}_{3D}))}{\#_c\{\mathcal{A}_k\}}, \tag{6}$$

in which θ_k represents a projection from the voxel to the image coordinates corresponding to the instance $\mathcal{A}_k$. Here, $\mathcal{L}_{\mathcal{A}_k}$ denotes a mask representation of $\mathcal{A}_k$, which returns 1 if the pixel is inside the instance region $\mathcal{A}_k$. The resultant voxel space $\mathcal{I}_k$ represents the ratio of voted instances; while we simply yielded the binarized version of the voxel space for the evaluation of the reconstruction accuracy, using the threshold of $\mathcal{I}_k(\mathbf{x}_{3D}) = 0.5$.

3.4 Implementation Details

Region Matching. During the epipolar band projection, we randomly sampled 200 points in each instance to draw the epipolar lines. The graph clustering is based on a Python implementation of SymNMF [51]. Since the clustering algorithm requires the number of instance clusters $|k|$ as an input, we implemented a framework to search the optimal number of clusters. Assuming the instances are evenly occluded and are projected onto the similar number of views, we selected the optimal $|k|_{opt}$ with the minimum standard deviation of the number of instances contained in the clusters.

$$|k|_{opt} = \operatorname*{argmin}_{|k|} \sqrt{\sum_{\mathcal{A}_k} (\#_c\{\mathcal{A}_k\}_{mean} - \#_c\{\mathcal{A}_k\})^2}, \tag{7}$$

where $\#_c\{\mathcal{A}_k\}_{mean}$ denotes the mean number of instances in instance clusters. In the supplementary material, we provide a detailed analysis when the number of instance clusters $|k|$ is given (*i.e.*, using the ground-truth number of objects).

MVIS Application. For the integration of the region matching for region proposals, we used a Keras implementation[1] of Mask R-CNN. We implemented

---

[1] https://github.com/matterport/Mask_RCNN.

an NMS using **numpy** and **nms** package outside the computation graph of Mask R-CNN. To obtain the initial instances, we used the original Mask R-CNN with NMS by a large RoI threshold (0.7 in our experiment) and obtained excessive numbers of object RoIs with their instance masks. During the iterations, our NMS is performed for each instance ID independently with a smaller threshold (0.3 was used in the experiment). With our unoptimized implementation, the whole process took up to several hours on a CPU (2.1 GHz, 8 threads); the projection of epipolar bands spent most of the time, which should be greatly optimized through a better implementation.

Fig. 4. Datasets used in the experiment.

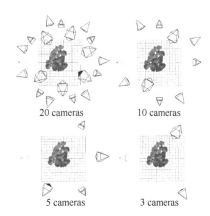

Fig. 5. Camera setting for simulated plant dataset.

4 Experiments

We conducted experiments to assess the quality of the multi-view matching and instance-wise 3D reconstruction, which are core part of our framework. The supplementary material provides the detailed analysis and discussions, including the effect on the instance detection by our implementation.

4.1 Dataset

We used the following datasets for the experiment (samples are shown in Fig. 4).

Simulated Plant Dataset. We used simulated plant models, which were modified from a dataset used in a plant modeling study [56]. This dataset contains the ground truth instance masks and their multi-view correspondences, as well as the 3D shape information. For training of Mask R-CNN, we prepared 14 simulated plant models rendered from $32,760$ viewpoints ($458,640$ images in total).

For evaluation, we used four plant models with a different number of leaves (4, 8, 16, and 32), not used for the training. To assess the effect of the varying number of views, we rendered the plants from different number of viewpoints (3, 5, 10, and 20) illustrated in Fig. 5, where we used the ground truth camera parameters.

Real-World Dataset. We prepared the real-world scenes for experiment, in which the ground truth instance masks and multi-view correspondences were manually created. The camera poses for these scenes were estimated via SfM [9].

Real plant (soybeans) scene is a set of multi-view images of a soybean plant captured by a multi-view capturing system [57], which was originally created for plant science studies. We used 28 views for instance matching. The number of distinctive leaves in the plant was 28. COCO-trained Mask R-CNN was fine-tuned using the images of eight soybeans plants captured by the same system, which were not used during the evaluation.

Multi-view balloon scene contains a scene with 27 balloons captured from 18 views. Mask R-CNN, pre-trained with the COCO dataset, was fine-tuned using 61 balloon images in the balloon dataset[2].

Tree ornament scene contains an artificial tree with 33 decorations captured from 21 views. Because the ornaments have spherical shapes, we fine-tuned the balloon-trained Mask R-CNN using a small number of (*i.e.*, 25) training images with tree ornaments, which were not used in the evaluation.

4.2   Multi-view Matching Results

We evaluated the accuracy of multi-view region matching using the dataset.

Baselines. Because of no established baseline methods for descriptor-free region matching, we compared the proposed approach with straightforward implementations of instance matching 1) using MVS-based point cloud as guidance, 2) using the center point of regions, and 3) using sparse correspondences.

MVS-Based Matching. 3D model by traditional MVS should be a guide for multi-view matching. We implemented a baseline matching method using dense 3D point clouds, called *MVS-based matching* hereafter. In this implementation, we used dense 3D point clouds reconstructed by COLMAP [10]. For $\mathcal{A}_{i,m}$, the m-th instance in the i-th view, we selected a 3D position $\mathbf{p}_{\mathcal{A}_{i,m}}$ that represents the region of $\mathcal{A}_{i,m}$. An straightforward way to select $\mathbf{p}_{\mathcal{A}_{i,m}}$ that is closest to the camera from among the points projected in the region of $\mathcal{A}_{i,m}$. To increase the robustness to the outliers, we designated $\mathbf{p}_{\mathcal{A}_{i,m}}$ as the centroid of the set of top 10% closest points among those projected in the region.

---

[2] https://github.com/matterport/Mask_RCNN/tree/master/samples/balloon.

We then project $\mathbf{p}_{\mathcal{A}_{i,m}}$ to the other views; for example, if $\mathbf{p}_{\mathcal{A}_{i,m}}$ is projected on the n-th instance in the j-th view, $\mathcal{A}_{j,n}$, we deemed $\mathcal{A}_{i,m}$ and $\mathcal{A}_{j,n}$ are corresponding instances. In the same manner to our proposed method, we constructed a matching graph with $|V|$ nodes, where the edge weights record the correspondences; *e.g.*, the edge between $\mathcal{A}_{i,m}$ and $\mathcal{A}_{j,n}$ are weighted by one. We solved the graph clustering using SymNMF [51]. This baseline method expects that a good-quality 3D model is given, which is under the same assumption as the methods using point clouds as an input (*e.g.*, [50]).

Point-Based Matching. Another baseline of the proposed approach is to match the centroid of instance regions instead of using the region matching. This method is analogous to the traditional *point-based* epipolar matching, *i.e.*, methods using epipolar *lines* instead of *bands*. In our implementation, an epipolar line is drawn for the centroid of each instance region. The correspondences between instances in different views can be yielded as the nearest epipolar lines in 3D space. Similar to the MVS-based method, we constructed a matching graph, where the edge weights between the corresponding instances are weighted by one, and solved the graph clustering by SymNMF.

Matching Based on Sparse Feature Correspondences. We also assessed a multi-view region matching method using sparse correspondences, which is a typical example of feature descriptors. We used AKAZE keypoints and descriptors [12]. For each instance region, a corresponding instance for each different view is searched based on the number of corresponding points within the regions. We solved the graph matching similarly with the other baseline methods. This method is expected to work well when the scene is observed from similar viewing angles, which is a similar assumption to the video instance tracking.

Evaluation Metric. The matching accuracy s_{match} was calculated by the number of correctly classified instances over the number of all instances $|V|$. Because we solve the multi-view matching as a clustering problem, we need to associate estimated instance clusters and the ground-truth clusters. We determined the ground-truth cluster ID k_{gt} corresponding to the ID of an estimated cluster k_{est}, by searching the mode of k_{gt} among instances belonging to k_{est}.

$$s_{match} = \frac{\sum_{k_{est}} \max_{k_{gt} \in \{k_{gt}\}} |\mathrm{id}(\mathcal{A}_{k_{est}}) \cap k_{gt}|}{|V|}, \tag{8}$$

where $\mathrm{id}(\mathcal{A}_{k_{est}})$ denotes the estimated ID of the instance $\mathcal{A}_{k_{est}}$, while $\{k_{gt}\}$ is the set of ground-truth instance cluster ID. Therefore, $|\mathrm{id}(\mathcal{A}_{k_{est}}) \cap k_{gt}|$ returns 1 if the two instance IDs are same. The number of *correct* matches is divided by $|V|$, the total number of instances among multi-view images. As an evaluation of clustering problems, s_{match} is equivalent to the *purity* metric, which is a common measure for evaluating the success of clustering.

We also evaluated the accuracy of the estimated number of clusters $|k|_{opt}$ by computing the mean absolute error (MAE) $e_{|k|}$ of the estimated number of clusters via Eq. (7).

Result. Table 1 shows the matching accuracy s_{match} and the MAE of cluster numbers $e_{|k|}$ for the simulated plant dataset. The table compares the accuracy and error averaged over different number of cameras and leaves. The proposed MVIS implementation yielded a better accuracy for most cases and achieved the average matching accuracy of 88.3%, which outperforms the accuracy by the baseline methods. Also, the result shows MVIS accurately estimates the number of clusters (*i.e.*, the number of objects in the scene). MVS-based matching yielded better accuracy when using a larger number of cameras (*i.e.*, 20) because the smaller differences in the viewing angles enable it to find the dense texture-based correspondences. In the cases using a smaller number of views, the MVS-based method notably drops the performance, although the proposed approach still achieved the matching accuracy of over 85% when the number of views is 3.

Table 2 shows the matching performance for the real-world scenes. The proposed approach also achieved a reasonable accuracy for both multi-view matching and cluster number estimation. For the tree ornament scenes, the matching accuracy was comparable among the methods. Ornaments were small spheres, and well approximated as a point. Proposed MVIS has an advantage for the scenes with difficulties of dense 3D reconstruction (*e.g.*, real plant scene) or with relatively large objects (*e.g.*, balloon scene).

Table 1. Multi-view matching accuracy s_{match} and MAE of the number of clusters $e_{|k|}$ for CG plant dataset. The values are averaged over the number of cameras and leaves. (Bold: the best accuracy among the methods.)

	Method	# cameras				# leaves				Average
		20	10	5	3	32	16	8	4	
$s_{match}\uparrow$	MVS-based	**0.935**	0.735	0.211	0.215	0.337	0.584	0.543	0.631	0.524
	Point-based	0.715	0.697	0.521	0.463	0.477	0.497	0.612	0.810	0.599
	Sparse	0.392	0.488	0.562	0.509	0.376	0.455	0.500	0.620	0.488
	MVIS	0.905	**0.910**	**0.860**	**0.856**	**0.655**	**0.895**	**0.987**	**0.994**	**0.883**
$e_{|k|}\downarrow$	MVS-based	**1.50**	7.25	13.25	9.25	17.00	10.00	3.25	1.00	7.81
	Point-based	19.50	25.75	4.00	8.50	11.75	16.75	20.25	9.00	14.44
	Sparse	31.00	26.00	21.50	9.25	15.25	25.75	22.25	24.50	21.94
	MVIS	2.00	**2.25**	**3.00**	**2.50**	**9.00**	**0.75**	**0.00**	**0.00**	**2.44**

Table 2. Multi-view matching accuracy s_{match} and MAE of number of clusters $e_{|k|}$ for real-world dataset. (Bold: the best accuracy among the methods.)

Method	Real plant		Balloon		Ornament		Average	
	$s_{match}\uparrow$	$e_{|k|}\downarrow$	$s_{match}\uparrow$	$e_{|k|}\downarrow$	$s_{match}\uparrow$	$e_{|k|}\downarrow$	$s_{match}\uparrow$	$e_{|k|}\downarrow$
MVS-based	0.220	36	0.081	25	0.680	**1**	0.327	20.7
Point-based	0.239	34	0.545	40	**0.683**	34	0.489	36.0
Sparse	0.237	41	0.270	36	0.679	33	0.395	36.7
MVIS	**0.562**	**26**	**0.751**	**3**	0.676	**1**	**0.663**	**10.0**

4.3   Instance-Wise 3D Reconstruction Results

We here describe the quantitative result of 3D reconstruction using simulated plant models, which we have the ground-truth shape of the leaves.

Baselines. We used two baselines for the evaluation of 3D reconstruction accuracy, although these methods do not provide the instance-wise 3D reconstruction. Since we used back-projection-based 3D reconstruction described in Sect. 3.3, we implemented a simple method using the back projection. Without relying on the instance correspondence, we unified the silhouettes of all leaves and inputted to the back projection. This mimics the *semantic segmentation* of leaves as the silhouette source, instead of using multi-view instances. As another baseline, we simply used the *MVS-based point clouds* reconstructed by COLMAP [10].

Evaluation Metric. We evaluated the geometric error between the dense point clouds of the reconstructed and the ground truth leaf shapes. For the evaluation, we first unify all 3D shapes of reconstructed leaf instances and convert the 3D voxel representation to a dense point cloud, where a 3D point is located if the voxel is inside leaves. The ground-truth leaf shape was originally modeled using

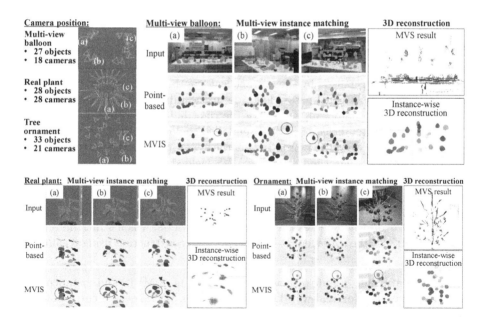

Fig. 6. Visual results for real-world examples. We show multi-view instances via the proposed MVIS and the point-based matching, which yielded a better matching accuracy than the other baselines. Although some instances are undetected or misclassified, MVIS yields convincing correspondences (*e.g.*, the circled objects) and 3D reconstructions.

Table 3. 3D reconstruction error $d(\mathcal{I}, \mathcal{T})$ normalized by the mean leaf length. N/A denotes the failure of the reconstruction (*i.e.*, no point cloud was generated).

Method	# cameras (averaged)				# leaves (10 cameras)			
	20	10	5	3	32	16	8	4
MVS (COLMAP)	**0.027**	0.125	N/A	N/A	0.311	0.111	**0.046**	**0.030**
Semantic segmentation	1.593	1.707	2.556	2.068	1.306	2.269	1.396	1.858
MVIS (proposed)	0.077	**0.082**	**0.185**	**0.129**	**0.183**	**0.057**	**0.046**	0.042

polygons, we oversampled the vertices by Catmull–Clark subdivision [58] to yield the dense point clouds.

Let $\mathbf{i} \in \mathcal{I}$ and $\mathbf{t} \in \mathcal{T}$ be estimated and the ground-truth 3D points, respectively. The geometric error is defined as a bidirectional Euclidean distance [59] between the two point sets written as

$$d(\mathcal{I}, \mathcal{T}) = \frac{1}{2} \left(\frac{\sum_{\mathcal{I}} \|\mathbf{i} - N_{\mathcal{T}}(\mathbf{i})\|}{|\mathcal{I}|} + \frac{\sum_{\mathcal{T}} \|\mathbf{t} - N_{\mathcal{I}}(\mathbf{t})\|}{|\mathcal{T}|} \right),$$

where $N_{\mathcal{I}}(\mathbf{x})$ and $N_{\mathcal{T}}(\mathbf{x})$ are functions to acquire the nearest neighbor point to $\mathbf{x}$ from point sets $\mathcal{I}$ and $\mathcal{T}$, respectively, and $|\mathcal{I}|$ and $|\mathcal{T}|$ denote the numbers of points in $\mathcal{I}$ and $\mathcal{T}$.

Results. Table 3 shows the 3D reconstruction error $d(\mathcal{I}, \mathcal{T})$. Since the geometric error is defined only up to scale like most multi-view 3D reconstruction methods, the errors were normalized by the average leaf length. For the comparison across the different number of cameras (left side of the table), we averaged the error over the different number of leaves. For the right half of the table, results using 10 cameras are listed because MVS often failed the dense reconstruction for the smaller number of views. The proposed method (MVIS) achieved better accuracy in most cases. Although the traditional MVS yielded an accurate reconstruction when using a larger number of (*i.e.*, 20) cameras or smaller number of leaves, the reconstruction was inaccurate or failed due to the difficulties of finding dense correspondences. The average reconstruction error by the proposed MVIS did not notably drop when decreasing the number of views, which still achieved the error of 12.9% of the average leaf length via the reconstruction using 3 cameras.

Visual Examples. Figure 6 shows example results of MVIS and instance-wise 3D reconstruction for real-world datasets. In the MVIS result, corresponding instances are visualized with the same color. The proposed method yields the multi-view correspondences and instance-wise 3D shapes convincingly, although we do not have access to the ground-truth 3D shapes for real-world datasets.

Failure Cases. Because the proposed method relies on the region segmentation, the failure in segmentation due to *e.g.*, contact/occlusions of objects, affects the matching accuracy. Our experiment includes such cases when increasing the number of objects (*e.g.*, Fig. 7). The low quality of instance masks is the dominant cause of the mismatching, which is a limitation of the proposed method.

Fig. 7. Failure case.

5 Discussion

We introduced a multi-view matching method of object instances, which does not rely on the texture or shape descriptors instead of using geometric (*i.e.*, epipolar) constraint and a graph clustering. Experiments with simulated plant models demonstrated the proposed method yielded the average accuracy of the multi-view instance matching over 85%, which outperforms the performances of baseline methods based on descriptor-based approaches such as MVS. Our method also showed the potential to be used for instance-wise 3D reconstruction via the integration with 3D reconstruction methods such as the back projection.

Beyond the computer vision study, potential applications of the proposed method include the growth analysis of plants, as our experiments used a dataset from plant science and agricultural research field.

Acknowledgements. This work was supported in part by JST PRESTO Grant Number JPMJPR17O3.

References

1. He, K., Gkioxari, G., Dollár, P., Girshick, R.: Mask R-CNN. In: Proceedings of International Conference on Computer Vision (ICCV) (2017)
2. Ren, M., Zemel, R.S.: End-to-end instance segmentation with recurrent attention. In: Proceedings of IEEE Conference on Computer Vision and Pattern Recognition (CVPR), pp. 6656–6664 (2017)
3. Xiong, Y., et al.: UPSNet: a unified panoptic segmentation network. In: Proceedings of IEEE Conference on Computer Vision and Pattern Recognition (CVPR), pp. 8818–8826 (2019)
4. Hou, J., Dai, A., Nießner, M.: 3D-SIS: 3D semantic instance segmentation of RGB-D scans. In: Proceedings of IEEE Conference on Computer Vision and Pattern Recognition (CVPR), pp. 4421–4430 (2019)
5. Kowdle, A., Sinha, S.N., Szeliski, R.: Multiple view object cosegmentation using appearance and stereo cues. In: Fitzgibbon, A., Lazebnik, S., Perona, P., Sato, Y., Schmid, C. (eds.) ECCV 2012. LNCS, vol. 7576, pp. 789–803. Springer, Heidelberg (2012). https://doi.org/10.1007/978-3-642-33715-4_57
6. Djelouah, A., Franco, J.S., Boyer, E., Le Clerc, F., Pérez, P.: Multi-view object segmentation in space and time. In: Proceedings of International Conference on Computer Vision (ICCV), pp. 2640–2647 (2013)

7. Mustafa, A., Hilton, A.: Semantically coherent co-segmentation and reconstruction of dynamic scenes. In: Proceedings of IEEE Conference on Computer Vision and Pattern Recognition (CVPR), pp. 422–431 (2017)

8. Voigtlaender, P., et al.: MOTS: multi-object tracking and segmentation. In: Proceedings of IEEE Conference on Computer Vision and Pattern Recognition (CVPR), pp. 7942–7951 (2019)

9. Schönberger, J.L., Frahm, J.M.: Structure-from-motion revisited. In: Proceedings of IEEE Conference on Computer Vision and Pattern Recognition (CVPR) (2016)

10. Schönberger, J.L., Zheng, E., Frahm, J.-M., Pollefeys, M.: Pixelwise view selection for unstructured multi-view stereo. In: Leibe, B., Matas, J., Sebe, N., Welling, M. (eds.) ECCV 2016. LNCS, vol. 9907, pp. 501–518. Springer, Cham (2016). https://doi.org/10.1007/978-3-319-46487-9_31

11. Lowe, D.G.: Distinctive image features from scale-invariant keypoints. Int. J. Comput. Vis. (IJCV) **60**, 91–110 (2004). https://doi.org/10.1023/B:VISI.0000029664.99615.94

12. Alcantarilla, P.F., Nuevo, J., Bartoli, A.: Fast explicit diffusion for accelerated features in nonlinear scale spaces. In: Proceedings of British Machine Vision Conference (BMVC) (2013)

13. Rublee, E., Rabaud, V., Konolige, K., Bradski, G.R.: ORB: an efficient alternative to SIFT or SURF. In: Proceedings of International Conference on Computer Vision (ICCV) (2011)

14. Bleyer, M., Rhemann, C., Rother, C.: PatchMatch Stereo - stereo matching with slanted support windows. In: Proceedings of British Machine Vision Conference (BMVC) (2011)

15. Gallup, D., Frahm, J.M., Mordohai, P., Yang, Q., Pollefeys, M.: Real-time plane-sweeping stereo with multiple sweeping directions. In: Proceedings of IEEE Conference on Computer Vision and Pattern Recognition (CVPR) (2007)

16. Sun, J., Zheng, N.N., Shum, H.Y.: Stereo matching using belief propagation. IEEE Trans. Pattern Anal. Mach. Intell. (PAMI) **25**, 787–800 (2003)

17. Furukawa, Y., Sethi, A., Ponce, J., Kriegman, D.: Structure and motion from images of smooth textureless objects. In: Pajdla, T., Matas, J. (eds.) ECCV 2004. LNCS, vol. 3022, pp. 287–298. Springer, Heidelberg (2004). https://doi.org/10.1007/978-3-540-24671-8_23

18. Zhang, J., et al.: Learning two-view correspondences and geometry using order-aware network. In: Proceedings of International Conference on Computer Vision (ICCV) (2019)

19. Romanoni, A., Matteucci, M.: TAPA-MVS: textureless-aware patchmatch multi-view stereo. In: Proceedings of International Conference on Computer Vision (ICCV) (2019)

20. Nam, G., Wu, C., Kim, M.H., Sheikh, Y.: Strand-accurate multi-view hair capture. In: Proceedings of IEEE Conference on Computer Vision and Pattern Recognition (CVPR), pp. 155–164 (2019)

21. Dellaert, F., Seitz, S.M., Thorpe, C.E., Thrun, S.: Structure from motion without correspondence. In: Proceedings of IEEE Conference on Computer Vision and Pattern Recognition (CVPR), vol. 2, pp. 557–564 (2000)

22. Belongie, S., Malik, J., Puzicha, J.: Shape matching and object recognition using shape contexts. IEEE Trans. Pattern Anal. Mach. Intell. (PAMI) **24**, 509–522 (2002)

23. Berg, A.C., Berg, T.L., Malik, J.: Shape matching and object recognition using low distortion correspondences. In: Proceedings of IEEE Conference on Computer Vision and Pattern Recognition (CVPR), vol. 1, pp. 26–33 (2005)

24. Mikolajczyk, K., et al.: A comparison of affine region detectors. Int. J. Comput. Vis. (IJCV) **65**, 43–72 (2005)
25. Bartolini, I., Ciaccia, P., Patella, M.: WARP: accurate retrieval of shapes using phase of Fourier descriptors and time warping distance. IEEE Trans. Pattern Anal. Mach. Intell. (PAMI) **27**, 142–147 (2005)
26. Matas, J., Chum, O., Urban, M., Pajdla, T.: Robust wide-baseline stereo from maximally stable extremal regions. Image Vis. Comput. **22**, 761–767 (2004)
27. Li, L., Zhang, S., Yu, X., Zhang, L.: PMSC: PatchMatch-based superpixel cut for accurate stereo matching. IEEE Trans. Circuits Syst. Video Technol. **28**, 679–692 (2016)
28. Mičušík, B., Košecká, J.: Multi-view superpixel stereo in urban environments. Int. J. Comput. Vis. (IJCV) **89**, 106–119 (2010)
29. Klaus, A., Sormann, M., Karner, K.: Segment-based stereo matching using belief propagation and a self-adapting dissimilarity measure. In: Proceedings of International Conference on Pattern Recognition (ICPR), vol. 3, pp. 15–18 (2006)
30. Kulikov, V., Lempitsky, V.: Instance segmentation of biological images using harmonic embeddings. In: Proceedings of IEEE Conference on Computer Vision and Pattern Recognition (CVPR), pp. 3843–3851 (2020)
31. Ren, S., He, K., Girshick, R., Sun, J.: Faster R-CNN: towards real-time object detection with region proposal networks. In: Proceedings of Conference on Neural Information Processing Systems (NeurIPS), pp. 91–99 (2015)
32. Milan, A., Leal-Taixé, L., Schindler, K., Reid, I.: Joint tracking and segmentation of multiple targets. In: Proceedings of IEEE Conference on Computer Vision and Pattern Recognition (CVPR), pp. 5397–5406 (2015)
33. Jun Koh, Y., Kim, C.S.: CDTS: collaborative detection, tracking, and segmentation for online multiple object segmentation in videos. In: Proceedings of International Conference on Computer Vision (ICCV), pp. 3601–3609 (2017)
34. Ošep, A., Mehner, W., Voigtlaender, P., Leibe, B.: Track, then decide: category-agnostic vision-based multi-object tracking. In: Proceedings of International Conference on Robotics and Automation (ICRA) (2018)
35. Sharma, S., Ansari, J.A., Murthy, J.K., Krishna, K.M.: Beyond pixels: leveraging geometry and shape cues for online multi-object tracking. In: Proceedings of International Conference on Robotics and Automation (ICRA), pp. 3508–3515 (2018)
36. Seguin, G., Bojanowski, P., Lajugie, R., Laptev, I.: Instance-level video segmentation from object tracks. In: Proceedings of IEEE Conference on Computer Vision and Pattern Recognition (CVPR), pp. 3678–3687 (2016)
37. Narita, G., Seno, T., Ishikawa, T., Kaji, Y.: PanopticFusion: online volumetric semantic mapping at the level of stuff and things. In: Proceedings of IEEE/RSJ International Conference on Intelligent Robots and Systems (IROS) (2019)
38. Schöler, F., Steinhage, V.: Automated 3D reconstruction of grape cluster architecture from sensor data for efficient phenotyping. Comput. Electron. Agric. **114**, 163–177 (2015)
39. Qi, C.R., Su, H., Mo, K., Guibas, L.J.: PointNet: deep learning on point sets for 3D classification and segmentation. In: Proceedings of IEEE Conference on Computer Vision and Pattern Recognition (CVPR), pp. 652–660 (2017)
40. Wang, L., et al.: Multi-view fusion-based 3D object detection for robot indoor scene perception. Sensors **19**, 4092 (2019)

41. Lahoud, J., Ghanem, B., Pollefeys, M., Oswald, M.R.: 3D instance segmentation via multi-task metric learning. In: Proceedings of International Conference on Computer Vision (ICCV) (2019)
42. Dai, A., Nießner, M.: 3DMV: joint 3D-multi-view prediction for 3D semantic scene segmentation. In: Ferrari, V., Hebert, M., Sminchisescu, C., Weiss, Y. (eds.) ECCV 2018. LNCS, vol. 11214, pp. 458–474. Springer, Cham (2018). https://doi.org/10.1007/978-3-030-01249-6_28
43. Hane, C., Zach, C., Cohen, A., Angst, R., Pollefeys, M.: Joint 3D scene reconstruction and class segmentation. In: Proceedings of IEEE Conference on Computer Vision and Pattern Recognition (CVPR), pp. 97–104 (2013)
44. Savinov, N., Ladicky, L., Hane, C., Pollefeys, M.: Discrete optimization of ray potentials for semantic 3D reconstruction. In: Proceedings of IEEE Conference on Computer Vision and Pattern Recognition (CVPR), pp. 5511–5518 (2015)
45. Savinov, N., Hane, C., Ladicky, L., Pollefeys, M.: Semantic 3D reconstruction with continuous regularization and ray potentials using a visibility consistency constraint. In: Proceedings of IEEE Conference on Computer Vision and Pattern Recognition (CVPR), pp. 5460–5469 (2016)
46. Nassar, A.S., Lefèvre, S., Wegner, J.D.: Simultaneous multi-view instance detection with learned geometric soft-constraints. In: Proceedings of International Conference on Computer Vision (ICCV) (2019)
47. Wang, W., Yu, R., Huang, Q., Neumann, U.: SGPN: similarity group proposal network for 3D point cloud instance segmentation. In: Proceedings of IEEE Conference on Computer Vision and Pattern Recognition (CVPR), pp. 2569–2578 (2018)
48. Yi, L., Zhao, W., Wang, H., Sung, M., Guibas, L.J.: GSPN: generative shape proposal network for 3D instance segmentation in point cloud. In: Proceedings of IEEE Conference on Computer Vision and Pattern Recognition (CVPR), pp. 3947–3956 (2019)
49. Engelmann, F., Bokeloh, M., Fathi, A., Leibe, B., Nießner, M.: 3D-MPA: multi-proposal aggregation for 3D semantic instance segmentation. In: Proceedings of IEEE Conference on Computer Vision and Pattern Recognition (CVPR), pp. 9031–9040 (2020)
50. Quan, L., Tan, P., Zeng, G., Yuan, L., Wang, J., Kang, S.B.: Image-based plant modeling. ACM Trans. Graph. **25**, 599–604 (2006)
51. Kuang, D., Ding, C., Park, H.: Symmetric nonnegative matrix factorization for graph clustering. In: Proceedings of SIAM International Conference on Data Mining (SDM), pp. 106–117 (2012)
52. Girshick, R., Iandola, F., Darrell, T., Malik, J.: Deformable part models are convolutional neural networks. In: Proceedings of IEEE Conference on Computer Vision and Pattern Recognition (CVPR), pp. 437–446 (2015)
53. Deza, M.M., Deza, E.: Encyclopedia of Distances. Springer, Heidelberg (2009). https://doi.org/10.1007/978-3-642-00234-2
54. Brooks, R.A., Di Chiro, G.: Theory of image reconstruction in computed tomography. Radiology **117**, 561–572 (1975)
55. Laurentini, A.: The visual hull concept for silhouette-based image understanding. IEEE Trans. Pattern Anal. Mach. Intell. (PAMI) **16**, 150–162 (1994)
56. Isokane, T., Okura, F., Ide, A., Matsushita, Y., Yagi, Y.: Probabilistic plant modeling via multi-view image-to-image translation. In: Proceedings of IEEE Conference on Computer Vision and Pattern Recognition (CVPR) (2018)

57. Tanabata, T., Hayashi, A., Kochi, N., Isobe, S.: Development of a semi-automatic 3D modeling system for phenotyping morphological traits in plants. In: Proceedings of Annual Conference of IEEE Industrial Electronics Society (IECON), pp. 5439–5444 (2018)
58. Catmull, E., Clark, J.: Recursively generated B-spline surfaces on arbitrary topological meshes. Comput.-Aided Des. **10**, 350–355 (1978)
59. Zhu, J., Du, S., Yuan, Z., Liu, Y., Ma, L.: Robust affine iterative closest point algorithm with bidirectional distance. IET Comput. Vis. **6**, 252–261 (2012)

Hierarchical X-Ray Report Generation via Pathology Tags and Multi Head Attention

Preethi Srinivasan$^{(\boxtimes)}$, Daksh Thapar, Arnav Bhavsar, and Aditya Nigam

Indian Institute of Technology Mandi, Mandi, India
{s18001,d18033}@students.iitmandi.ac.in, {arnav,aditya}@iitmandi.ac.in

Abstract. Examining radiology images, such as X-Ray images as accurately as possible, forms a crucial step in providing the best healthcare facilities. However, this requires high expertise and clinical experience. Even for experienced radiologists, this is a time-consuming task. Hence, the automated generation of accurate radiology reports from chest X-Ray images is gaining popularity. Compared to other image captioning tasks where coherence is the key criterion, medical image captioning requires high accuracy in detecting anomalies and extracting information along with coherence. That is, the report must be easy to read and convey medical facts accurately. We propose a deep neural network to achieve this. Given a set of Chest X-Ray images of the patient, the proposed network predicts the medical tags and generates a readable radiology report. For generating the report and tags, the proposed network learns to extract salient features of the image from a deep CNN and generates tag embeddings for each patient's X-Ray images. We use transformers for learning self and cross attention. We encode the image and tag features with self-attention to get a finer representation. Use both the above features in cross attention with the input sequence to generate the report's Findings. Then, cross attention is applied between the generated Findings and the input sequence to generate the report's Impressions. We use a publicly available dataset to evaluate the proposed network. The performance indicates that we can generate a readable radiology report, with a relatively higher BLEU score over SOTA. The code and trained models are available at https://medicalcaption.github.io.

1 Introduction

Understanding radiology images such as X-Rays is essential for diagnosis and treatment of many diseases. Given the amount of skill required for accurately reading such images [1], it is challenging for less-experienced radiologists to write medical reports. Hence in healthcare, writing medical reports from X-Ray images becomes a bottleneck for clinical patient care. To aid radiologists, many researchers are investigating the generation of automatic reports from X-Ray

---

P. Srinivasan and D. Thapar—Equal Contribution.

© Springer Nature Switzerland AG 2021
H. Ishikawa et al. (Eds.): ACCV 2020, LNCS 12626, pp. 600–616, 2021.
https://doi.org/10.1007/978-3-030-69541-5_36

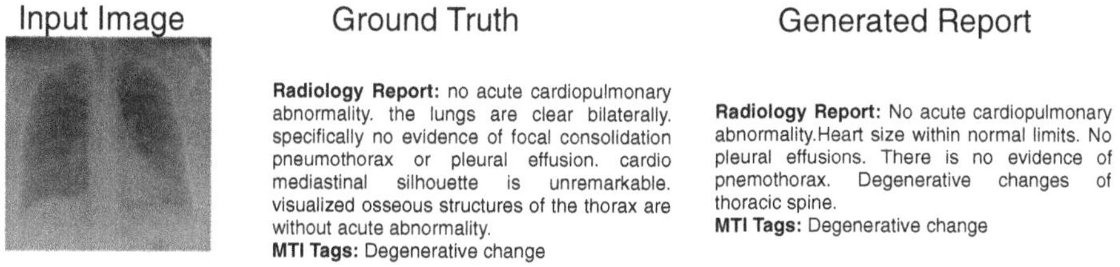

Input Image   Ground Truth   Generated Report

Radiology Report: no acute cardiopulmonary abnormality. the lungs are clear bilaterally. specifically no evidence of focal consolidation pneumothorax or pleural effusion. cardio mediastinal silhouette is unremarkable. visualized osseous structures of the thorax are without acute abnormality.
MTI Tags: Degenerative change

Radiology Report: No acute cardiopulmonary abnormality.Heart size within normal limits. No pleural effusions. There is no evidence of pnemothorax. Degenerative changes of thoracic spine.
MTI Tags: Degenerative change

Fig. 1. Shows the actual medical report with MTI tags corresponding to an X-Ray image with the report and tags generated from the proposed network. MTI tags are automatically generated. They are the critical components of the report which capture the essence of the diagnosis.

images [2,3] by formulating the problem as image captioning [4]. Although Xray report generation task looks similar to a generic image captioning task, there are fundamental differences and challenges to report generation. The Xray images contain complex spatial information and the abnormalities present in it are difficult to find requiring subject matter expertise. Beyond everything, reports need to be accurate. Hence, we focus on generating clinically accurate reports with reasonably good readability in this work. Figure 1 shows one example of the medical report and tags present in the IU dataset [5] with the generated report and tags from our proposed system. Every aspect of the proposed methodology is designed to tackle the challenges present in automatic report generation.

The IU X-ray dataset [5] is used to perform our experiment. Each report in the dataset corresponds to one patient. There is a variable number (N) of X-Ray images of each patient. In the rest of the paper, Pid_{img} refers to a set of N X-Ray images corresponding to a single patient id. Automatically generated tags from the report represent most of the critical components of the report. Findings and Impressions together constitute a report. Tags are identified for each patient, and its embeddings are used in the report generation along with image features. The two parts of the report are generated sequentially. The significant contributions of this paper are as follows:

1. Since in any consortium of diagnostic data a large number of normal patient data exists compared to abnormal patient data, we propose a 2 stage divide-and-conquer approach. First, abnormal patients are identified from normal patients, and their tag embeddings are generated. Conditional learning is done based on the status of the patient's data.
2. For predicting the report, we propose to use a novel architecture involving transformers with 2 Encoders and 2 Decoders instead of traditionally used recurrent neural networks.
3. Tag embeddings and Image features are encoded separately using two Encoders. Findings and Impressions are different and can be learned by two stacked Decoders, helping the former to improve the generation of later.

2   Related Work

An automatic understanding of Radiology images, especially X-ray images, is a well-studied problem. To facilitate that, Wang et al. [6] proposed a large scale dataset for detection and localization of thoracic diseases from X-ray images. They also provided various benchmarks. Yao et al. [7] and Rajpurkar et al. [8] proposed using deep learning-based algorithms for efficient detection of various diseases from chest X-ray images. Later works extended the problem by attributing 'texts' like tags and templates to the x-ray images. Kisilev et al. [9] build a pipeline to predict the attributes of medical images. Shin et al. [10] adopts a CNN-RNN based framework to predict tags (e.g., locations, severities) of chest x-ray images. Zang et al. [11] aimed at generating semi-structured pathology reports, whose contents are restricted to 5 predefined topics.

However, the first work that successfully created an automatic medical report from X-ray images was proposed by Jing et al. [2]. They proposed to use a hierarchical LSTM based recurrent model, exploiting the attention between tags and the image features, opening the field of medical image captioning. Many other works like Wang et al. [3], Li et al. [12], and Xiong et al. [13] enhanced the performance achieved in medical image captioning by proposing various techniques like feature level attention, reinforcement learning, and spatial attention over the localized image regions.

The success in medical image captioning has been possible due to the latest advances in deep learning. DenseNet [14], being a densely connected convolutional network, enabled us to learn high order dependencies by using a large number of layers with a minimal number of parameters, enabling the architectures to understand complex images like X-ray images without overfitting. Xception [15] proposed depth-wise separable convolutional operation, which in-turn extracts efficient image features with a decreased number of parameters in the model. Different training strategies like triplet loss function [16] and ranking based loss functions [17–19] also enhanced the performance of deep learning based systems for application problems. Moreover, the latest enhances in image captioning problems also played a vital role in developing radiology reports. Karpathy et al. [20] achieved image captioning using deep learning by providing the image features to the initial state of RNN. The RNN then uses the state information to predict the caption of the image. Though RNN's capture temporal dependencies, they have substantial computational overhead. Transformers [21], on the other hand, can efficiently capture long and short term dependencies with minimal computation. Hence, this work tries to utilize the latest deep learning based techniques to generate accurate medical reports of radiology images.

3   Proposed Methodology

This work aims to propose a technique that can generate accurate medical reports using X-ray images of variable sizes (N). Some of the images may cover the neck and abdomen portions too. To avoid the network from getting confused, first, a Single shot multibox object detector (SSD) [22] is used to detect

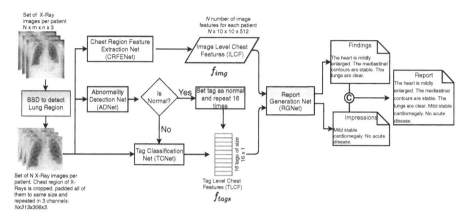

Fig. 2. Shows the overall pipeline of the proposed system. The system's input is a set of X-Rays taken of a patient, and output is the generated medical report containing Findings and Impressions.

and crop the lung region from the given X-ray images. The images are then padded to a consistent size of 313 × 306. For the viability of using pretrained models for extracting image features, we repeat the images in 3 channels of RGB, forming a 313 × 306 × 3 image. Figure 2 shows the overall pipeline that is proposed for generating medical reports from a patient's X-ray images. It consists of 4 modules, namely (i) Chest Region Feature Extraction Net (CRFENet), (ii) Abnormality Detection Net (ADNet), (iii) Tag Classification Net (TCNet), and (iv) Report Generation Net (RGNet). The CRFENet takes the input X-Ray image (I) of size 313 × 306 × 3 and provides a feature of size 10 × 10 × 512. This module is intended to provide contextual information of the image. ADNet also takes an input X-Ray image (I) and does a binary classification to identify any abnormality present. Since there is data imbalance with more data from healthy patients, a hierarchical classification technique is chosen to classify the samples between healthy and unhealthy classes, allowing conditional learning. Only the abnormal samples are put through the TCNet, which ranks the tags to their relevance to the report. The top 16 tags are chosen for each patient. We take only the top 16 tags because the maximum number of tags associated with any patient is 16. In the case of a normal patient, we manually set all the 16 tags to normal. Then, the RGNet takes image features and tags to generate Findings. Then in step 2, it takes Findings to generate Impressions. Finally, Findings and Impressions are concatenated to form the full report. For efficient training and hyper-parameterization, we employ modular training and modular hyper-parameterization. This section discusses each module, the training procedure, and the hyper-parameterization strategy in detail.

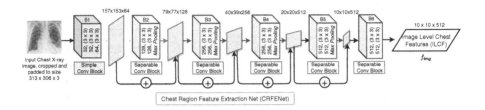

Fig. 3. Shows the architecture of the proposed Chest Region feature extractor. The module contains residual blocks of depth-separable convolutions to decrease the number of overall parameters and computations. It helps to eliminate the over-fitting issues with medical datasets in which the available data is scarce.

3.1 Chest Region Feature Extractor Net (CRFENet)

The first task in generating automatic radiology reports is to identify the salient features present in X-Ray images that lead to the diagnosis. However, the challenge is that these features are complex to recognize and prone to subjectivity; they are highly non-linear. Hence, for extracting such features, we need to learn a complex non-linear function that maps an input image (I) to its feature ($fimg$)) as shown in Fig. 3. We have designed a deep convolutional neural network (CNN) for extracting such sophisticated non-linear features. However, using deep CNNs have other disadvantages, such as large number of parameters and vanishing gradient problems. Since medical datasets are scarce (this dataset has only around 3999 patient records), learning deep networks is difficult. We chose to ease the job by incorporating the following two ideas in CRFENet - (i) Use Depth wise separable convolutions [15] over simple convolutions to reduce the number of parameters. (ii) Use residual connections to solve the vanishing gradient problem of deep networks. CRFENet contains one block of simple convolutional layers and four blocks of depth-wise separable convolutional layers, as shown in Fig. 3. Batch-normalization and Relu non-linearity are used after each conv layer.

Separable Convs: In convolution operation, the kernel aggregates the input feature map's depth information to produce a single output. Hence, to generate an output having depth d, d such kernels are applied, giving us a vast amount of parameters that need to be optimized. Whereas in depth-wise separable convolution operation, one kernel is applied without aggregating depth-wise information. Instead, apply d pointwise convolution kernels to provide us with the final feature with depth d. Using this technique, we can efficiently create a deep model with few parameters avoiding the overfitting problem.

Training: Learning a highly complex non-linear function to map image to its features is a difficult job, especially when the data is scarce. For the CRFENet to understand the X-Ray images, we trained it for chest disease classification on NIH Dataset [6]. The image features of IU Dataset extracted from CRFENet for final report generation are found to be better than the features extracted from deep CNNs like Dense121 [14], VGG [23], and ResNet [24].

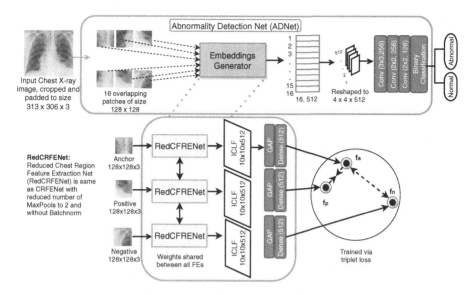

Fig. 4. Shows the architecture of the Abnormality Detection Net (ADNet). It identifies the presence or absence of abnormality in an X-Ray image using the triplet loss function.

3.2 Abnormality Detection Net (ADNet)

As indicated earlier, before we generate medical reports, we need to find whether a patient has any abnormality required to be included in the generated report. To detect abnormal cases, we have proposed a binary classification module called ADNet. ADNet classifies X-ray images into normal and abnormal classes. The patients who do not have any MTI tag associated with them are defined as normal patients. Figure 4 shows the detailed architecture of the proposed ADNet. As the abnormalities present in X-ray images are usually localized, it processes the images in patches. Each input image I is divided into 16 overlapping patches of size $128 \times 128 \times 3$. These patches are passed through a sub-network called Embeddings Generator (EG), which produces embedding of size (512×1) for each patch. EG is trained to produce embeddings such that normal patches and abnormal patches are as far as possible from each other in feature space. The 16 embeddings corresponding to a single I are concatenated to form a feature vector of size (16×512). It is further reshaped to $(4 \times 4 \times 512)$ to preserve the spatial relationship present between these patches. Upon applying 2 Convolutional layers and a fully connected layer of 1 neuron to $(4 \times 4 \times 512)$ feature vector, ADNet gives a probability of abnormality. Since every patient's dataset contains a variable number (N) of X-Ray images, we take the average probability and threshold it at 0.5 to classify the patient as normal or abnormal.

Embeddings Generator (EG): As discussed above, EG's task is to extract a 512-D feature from a patch $(128 \times 128 \times 3)$ of the X-ray image. EG is trained via

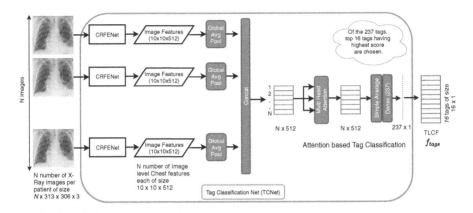

Fig. 5. Shows the architecture of the proposed Tag Classification Net (TCNet). It generates the top 16 relevant tags about a set of X-Ray images of an abnormal patient.

triplet loss function [16] to discriminate between normal and abnormal patches. Each patch of size $128 \times 128 \times 3$ is passed through rCRFENet, a reduced version of CRFENet, to produce the output of the same size $10 \times 10 \times 512$ feature for a $128 \times 128 \times 3$ patch. rCRFENet only contains two maxpool layers as compared to 4 in CRFENet. rCRFENet is pretrained on NIH data [6] because it contains the localization information of abnormality in X-Ray images, through an ROI. Patches of $128 \times 128 \times 3$ are chosen around the ROI for training. Given two patches i and j, the EG must produce an embedding Θ, such that if both i and j lie in the same class (normal or abnormal), then $L_2(\Theta^i, \Theta^j)$ should tend to 0, otherwise, $L_2(\Theta^i, \Theta^j) \geq \beta$, where β is the margin. The loss has been defined over 3 embeddings:

1. Θ^i: embedding of an anchor patch,
2. Θ^{i^+}: embedding of another patch from the same category, and
3. Θ^{i^-}: embedding of a patch from other categories.

Formally:

$$\mathcal{L}(i, i^+, i^-) = \max(0, (\Theta^i - \Theta^{i^+})^2 - (\Theta^i - \Theta^{i^-})^2 + \beta) \tag{1}$$

We sum the loss for all possible triples (i, i^+, i^-) to form the cost function J which is minimized during training of EG:

$$J = \frac{1}{N} \sum_{i=1}^{N} \mathcal{L}(i, i^+, i^-) \tag{2}$$

For efficiently training the EG network, we apply online semi-hard negative mining and dynamic adaptive margin as proposed by [25].

3.3   Tag Classification Net (TCNet)

As the second step of hierarchy, TCNet predicts the tags associated with each Pid_{img}. MTI tags play a crucial role in generating the report. As shown in Fig. 5, N images in (Pid_{img}) are passed through CRFENet one after another to obtain image features ($10 \times 10 \times 512$). Upon applying Global Average Pooling to each of the image features, we get (1×512) feature vector, concatenated to get an (Nx512) feature vector. This Nx512 feature vector passed through a Multi-Head Attention module (MHA) to get the same dimensional output. MHA checks the information in all the N images and produces a result. Over that, a simple averaging and Dense layer of 237 neurons is applied. TCNet is trained using log sum exponential pairwise loss function [19]. It assigns a value to each tag relative to other tags by learning to rank via pairwise comparisons. Then, the values are sorted, and the top 16 tags are picked to produce an output of size (16×1).

Multi Head Attention (MHA): The basic building block of multi-head attention [21] is the scaled dot product mechanism. The scaled dot product mechanism is a sequence to sequence operation: given a sequence of values vectors v_1, v_2, ..., v_n, it learns to provide an output sequence vectors y_1, y_2, ..., y_n, based on a query sequence q_1, q_2, ..., q_n, and key sequence k_1, k_2, ..., k_n. where each vector in the sequence is d-dimensional. First we learn three weight matrices of size $d \times d$ to transform each of the three sequences: $Q_i = W_q q_i$ $K_i = W_k k_i$ $V_i = W_v v_i$. Each y_i is computed as weighted average over the all transformed value vector V: $y_i = \sum_j w_{ij} V_j$, where j iterates over the whole sequence. Here w_{ij} is derived from dot product of query and key sequences: $w'_{ij} = \frac{Q_i^T K_j}{\sqrt{d}}$, $w_{ij} = softmax(w'_{ij})$. Alternatively, in the scaled dot product mechanism, to compute one particular output y_i, the corresponding vector of query Q_i is compared (via. dot product) to the whole sequence of key vectors K_1, K_2, ..., K_n to provide the attention weights for each of the value vectors V_1, V_2, ..., V_n. We use the scaled dot product mechanism to form the multi-head attention mechanism. For a given set of value, query, and key vectors of $n \times d$, where n is the sequence length, and d is the dimensionality of each vector; we break each vector into r subparts of $n \times \frac{d}{r}$. We apply r different scaled dot product mechanisms, each having independent weight matrices of $\frac{d}{r} \times \frac{d}{r}$ giving us r outputs of $n \times \frac{d}{r}$. We concatenate these outputs to get the final output of shape $n \times d$. Here the total number of parameters is only $\frac{3d^2}{r}$ (3 weight matrices for each of r parts of the input sequence).

3.4   Report Generation Net (RGNet)

This is based on transformer architecture inspired from [21]. RGNet consists of 2 Encoders called Data Encoder (E_D) and Tag Encoder (E_T), and 2 Decoders called Findings Decoder (D_{fin}) and Impressions Decoder (D_{imp}). The network architecture is shown in Fig. 6.

Data Encoder (E_D): It takes N images of (Pid_{img}), passes each of them through CRFENet to get ($10 \times 10 \times 512$) for each image. N features are

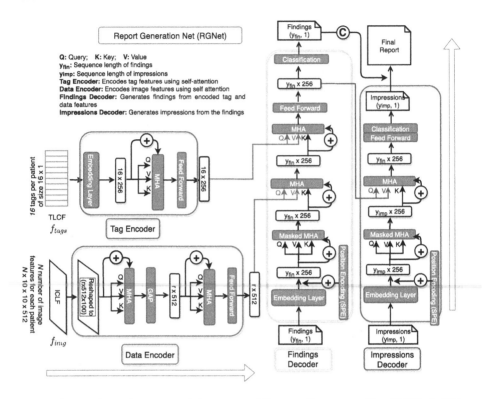

Fig. 6. Shows the architecture of the proposed Report Generation Net (RGNet). This module generates the report using a blend of information from image feature and tag embeddings. Also, sequentially uses the report's Findings to generate the report's Impressions.

concatenated to form a feature of size $(N \times 10 \times 10 \times 512)$ and reshaped to $(N \times 512 \times 100)$. Since neither all the N images are equally important nor every 512 features, we try to enhance the appropriate features and images using 2 MHA modules. The first one learns self-attention over each of N images' features providing us with $(N \times 512)$ feature map. The second MHA learns self-attention to combine the features across N images forming feature embeddings efficiently.

Tag Encoder (E_T)**:** It takes the (16×1) tags extracted from TCNet and creates an embedding for each of the tags. Later an MHA is used to learn self-attention over the tag embeddings providing us with relevant tags only.

Findings Decoder (D_{fin})**:** The task of (D_{fin}) is, given a sequence of words corresponding to the Findings, tag embeddings, and image features; it has to generate the next word of the Findings. The next word will depend upon previous words as well as both tag embeddings and image features. We use a transformer block to learn the attention required on previous words of the report over the tags embeddings and image features. Firstly, we learn self-attention on the previous words of the report. It consumes all the previous information to generate the next word. A multi-head attention mechanism is used to learn the self-attention, where the report is given as the key, query, and value. Secondly, we learn cross-attention between the output of the first self-attention block and image features. We again use the multi-head attention mechanism, but for learning cross-attention over tag embeddings. In both cases, the embeddings are given as value and key, where the previous attention block's output is given as query to multi-head attention block. Self-attention gives us the next word's dependence on previous words, whereas the cross-attention provides us with the dependence of the next word on the image features and tag embeddings. Both Self and Cross attention matrices update their parameters based on the loss generated for next word prediction. A feed-forward layer is applied after the cross attention forming the transformer block. An embedding layer is used to convert the words into embeddings of 256 dimensions, and sinusoidal positional encoding (SPE) [21] is applied over the embeddings before inputting them into the transformer block. Finally, a linear layer followed by softmax cross-entropy loss gives us the probability for each word in the dictionary to be the next word in the Findings.

Impressions Decoder (D_{imp}): Given a sequence of words corresponding to the Impressions and output feature from D_{fin}), (D_{imp}) generates the next word of the Impressions. It first learns the dependence of the next word on previous words by learning self-attention using MHA. Later cross-attention is learned between previous words of Impressions and the generated Findings from D_{fin}) using MHA, enabling the network to produce Impressions depending upon the previously produced Findings. Finally, the Findings and Impressions are concatenated to form the final report.

3.5 Modular Training and Hyper-parameterization

For training and searching for the optimal hyper-parameters of the proposed methodology, we use modular training. We follow the below sequence of steps, and each model is hyper-parameterized for efficiently performing its pretraining task: (i) Pre-train the CRFENet and rCRFENet for chest disease classification on NIH Dataset [6]. (ii) Then we train the EG using the triplet loss function over patches extracted from the NIH dataset. (iii) Then ADNet is trained over IU-dataset for normal vs. abnormal classification. (iv) The pretrained CRFENet is used to finetune the TCNet using the ranking loss function. (v) Finally, we train the RGNet for report generation using the image features extracted from CRFENet and tags from TCNet.

4 Experimental Analysis

In this section, we provide the details of the experimental analysis performed to validate the proposed methodology. We have performed a thorough ablation study for experimentally validating every contribution proposed in this work. Later, we show that our proposed model can produce accurate reports using qualitative and quantitative comparative analysis.

Table 1. Parametric comparison and modular ablation analysis. Acc: Accuracy, wBCE: weighted Binary Cross Entropy, M: Million. Bold represents the proposed systems.

Task	Model	# layers	# parameters	Performance
Feature Extractor	DenseNet	100	27.2 M	0.175 Loss
	CRFENet	**17**	**12.3 M**	**0.19 Loss**
Abnormality Detection	DenseNet	100	27.2 M	70.5% Acc
	ADNet	**18**	**13.1 M**	**74% Acc**
Tag Classification	TCNet with wBCE	19	12.6 M	0.44 Loss
	TCNet	**19**	**12.6 M**	**0.26 Loss**
Report Generation	**RGNet**	**12**	**0.7 M**	**0.464 Bleu-1**

4.1 Dataset Used and Evaluation Metric

For validating the proposed methodology, we use a publicly available IU X-ray dataset [5]. It contains the medical data of 3999 patients. Each data contains findings, impressions, MTI tags, and a set of N number of X-ray images taken for each patient. Findings and impressions are combined to make the medical report of the patient. Medical text indexer (MTI) is used to extract keywords from the report forming the MTI tags (referred to as tags in this work). Since each patient has had multiple X-rays, there are a total of 7470 x-ray images. We tokenize each word of the report and remove nonalphabetic tokens. Moreover, we computed the frequency percentile of all the unique words in all the reports and picked only the top 99 percentile of words, which amounts to 1000. The dataset contains 573 unique tags. We take only those tags that appeared in at least three reports. Hence we are left with 283 tags for the tag prediction task. We discarded those patients' data, which did not contain either findings or impressions or X-ray images. For testing the performance of our proposed network, as suggested by Li et al. [12], we randomly split patients for training/validation/testing in the ratio of 7/2/1. For evaluating the report generated against the original report, we use standard image captioning evaluation metric BLEU score (Papineni et al. [26]). BLEU score measures the quality of the text generated and assigns a metric between 0 and 1. It analyses the statistics of overlapping words with the reference sequence. The original report is taken as a reference to run the string matching algorithm. A value of 0 means there is no overlap with the original report, and 1 means there perfect overlap with the original report.

4.2 Ablation Study

For validating the contributions of the proposed network, we have performed an extensive ablation study, as shown in Table 2 and Table 1. It is important to note, though the system is broken into multiple modules, the complexity of the overall system (38.7 M parameters and 66 layers) is comparable or lesser than state-of-the-art systems. Table 1 shows the parametric comparison and performance of each of the individual modules concerning corresponding state-of-the-art systems. In the first row of the Table 2, we have shown our proposed methodology,

Table 2. Ablation study of the proposed methodology validating our contributions.

Model	Bleu-1	Bleu-2	Bleu-3	Bleu-4
Proposed Methodology	0.464	0.301	0.212	0.158
Model A (without CRFENet)	0.414	0.287	0.198	0.143
Model B (without ADNet)	0.320	0.218	0.156	0.116
Model C (without ranking loss)	0.295	0.192	0.104	0.092
Model D (without 2 decoder RGNet)	0.423	0.292	0.204	0.148

which contains four modules named CRFENet, ADNet, TCNet, and RGNet, as described in Sect. 3. We performed an ablation study with alternatives for every network mentioned above to testify each of the proposed networks' contributions. Firstly, we have tested the system by replacing the proposed CRFENet with pre-trained state-of-the-art CNN architectures (Model A). Among such architectures, Densenet provides us with the best performance, as shown in the table's second row. Since CRFENet is only a six-block module with separable convs, fewer parameters prevent overfitting than DenseNet and other CNN modules. Secondly, instead of ADNet, we used a simple VGG network for abnormality detection (Model B). Since most of the X-rays' abnormalities are localized, patch-based siamese abnormality detection (ADNet) provides us better results than standard-sized image-based classifiers like VGG. Thirdly, we trained the TCNet with weighted binary cross-entropy loss rather than ranking loss (Model C). Since most of the tags are only associated with very few reports, the ranking loss is better able to capture the association of tags with particular X-Ray images. Finally, we train a single decoder RGNet, rather than the proposed two decoder RGNet (Model D). The sequentially stacked decoders' training, one for Findings and Impressions, will learn better to optimize their respective models. It will force the network to generate accurate Findings so that better Impressions can get generated and vice-versa. It is evident from Table 2 that each of the ablated models performs inferior to the proposed network, which concretely validates every contribution proposed in this work. We can also notice the magnitude of the gain obtained from each of these changes. Usage of ranking loss and hierarchical tag classification techniques gave the relatively biggest deltas in the report generation's quality.

4.3 Comparative Analysis

Table 3 shows the comparative analysis of the proposed system with state-of-the-art networks. It can be seen from the table that our proposed methodology achieves state-of-the-art for report generation task. Key components of our proposed methodology like hierarchical tag classification, ranking based loss, attention-based feature extraction, and transformer architecture could be the leading cause for our model's performance to be better than the rest.

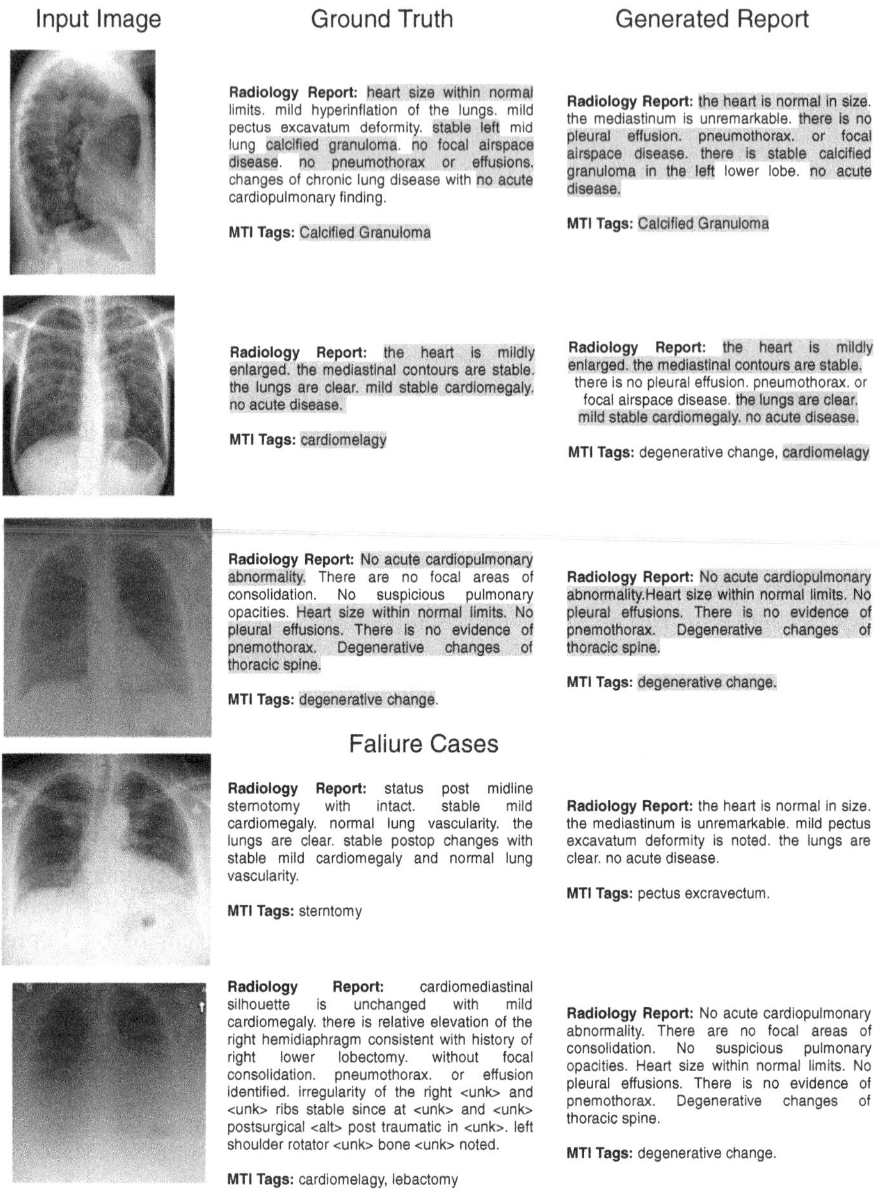

Input Image	Ground Truth	Generated Report

Radiology Report: heart size within normal limits. mild hyperinflation of the lungs. mild pectus excavatum deformity. stable left mid lung calcified granuloma. no focal airspace disease. no pneumothorax or effusions. changes of chronic lung disease with no acute cardiopulmonary finding.

MTI Tags: Calcified Granuloma

Radiology Report: the heart is normal in size. the mediastinum is unremarkable. there is no pleural effusion. pneumothorax. or focal airspace disease. there is stable calcified granuloma in the left lower lobe. no acute disease.

MTI Tags: Calcified Granuloma

Radiology Report: the heart is mildly enlarged. the mediastinal contours are stable. the lungs are clear. mild stable cardiomegaly. no acute disease.

MTI Tags: cardiomelagy

Radiology Report: the heart is mildly enlarged. the mediastinal contours are stable. there is no pleural effusion. pneumothorax. or focal airspace disease. the lungs are clear. mild stable cardiomegaly. no acute disease.

MTI Tags: degenerative change, cardiomelagy

Radiology Report: No acute cardiopulmonary abnormality. There are no focal areas of consolidation. No suspicious pulmonary opacities. Heart size within normal limits. No pleural effusions. There is no evidence of pnemothorax. Degenerative changes of thoracic spine.

MTI Tags: degenerative change.

Radiology Report: No acute cardiopulmonary abnormality.Heart size within normal limits. No pleural effusions. There is no evidence of pnemothorax. Degenerative changes of thoracic spine.

MTI Tags: degenerative change.

Faliure Cases

Radiology Report: status post midline sternotomy with intact. stable mild cardiomegaly. normal lung vascularity. the lungs are clear. stable postop changes with stable mild cardiomegaly and normal lung vascularity.

MTI Tags: sterntomy

Radiology Report: the heart is normal in size. the mediastinum is unremarkable. mild pectus excavatum deformity is noted. the lungs are clear. no acute disease.

MTI Tags: pectus excravectum.

Radiology Report: cardiomediastinal silhouette is unchanged with mild cardiomegaly. there is relative elevation of the right hemidiaphragm consistent with history of right lower lobectomy. without focal consolidation. pneumothorax. or effusion identified. irregularity of the right <unk> and <unk> ribs stable since at <unk> and <unk> postsurgical <alt> post traumatic in <unk>. left shoulder rotator <unk> bone <unk> noted.

MTI Tags: cardiomelagy, lebactomy

Radiology Report: No acute cardiopulmonary abnormality. There are no focal areas of consolidation. No suspicious pulmonary opacities. Heart size within normal limits. No pleural effusions. There is no evidence of pnemothorax. Degenerative changes of thoracic spine.

MTI Tags: degenerative change.

Fig. 7. Shows the qualitative results of report generated from our proposed network. The first 3 rows depict examples from high accuracy outputs. The correctly predicted vocabularies are highlighted. The last 2 rows contain failure cases.

Table 3. Comparative analysis of the proposed system with state-of-the-art.

Model	Bleu-1	Bleu-2	Bleu-3	Bleu-4
S&T [27]	0.265	0.157	0.105	0.073
SA&T [28]	0.328	0.195	0.123	0.080
TieNet [3]	0.330	0.194	0.124	0.081
Lie et al. [29]	0.359	0.237	0.164	0.113
CNN-RNN [10]	0.216	0.124	0.087	0.066
LRCN [30]	0.223	0.128	0.089	0.067
AdaAtt [31]	0.220	0.127	0.089	0.068
Att2in [32]	0.224	0.129	0.089	0.068
RTMIC [13]	0.350	0.234	0.143	0.096
Li et al. [12]	0.438	0.298	0.208	0.151
CoAtt [2]	0.455	0.288	0.205	0.154
Proposed Methodology	**0.464**	**0.301**	**0.212**	**0.158**

4.4 Qualitative Analysis

Figure 7 shows the qualitative results of the report generated from our proposed network. The first three rows depict examples from high accuracy outputs, whereas the last two rows contain the failure cases. In the first row, the proposed system can correctly identify calcified granulomas and generate a technically sound report. In the second row, the proposed system identifies cardiomelagy. Moreover, for cases where there were only degenerative changes, our method performed well. We can also understand from the highlighted portion that most of the report's predicted characteristics match the original report. We did find two significant cases of failures; one example of both is depicted in the figure. The first case being those abnormalities that only come ones or twice in the dataset. In such cases, the proposed system was not able to learn about them. The second case of failure is where the images were blurry or hazy. In such cases, the network predicted the patient to have no disease at all.

5 Conclusion

Captioning medical images is a complex task because, unlike the natural images, the salient features are not apparent. Here, we proposed a technique to blend the image and tag features and use it in a unique way to generate a medical report from a patient's set of X-Ray images. Traditional use of recurrent neural networks (RNNs) to solve such sequential data has a massive computational overload. On the other hand, transformer architecture, which also captures the sequential data, uses far fewer parameters. Furthermore, it applies attention between and across features obtained from images, tags, and reports. While significant improvements have been achieved over the SOTA, there is still scope for improvement in generating useful quality reports, especially in hazy X-Rays or cases where different X-Rays are acquired under different exposures.

References

1. Delrue, L., Gosselin, R., Ilsen, B., Van Landeghem, A., de Mey, J., Duyck, P.: Difficulties in the interpretation of chest radiography. In: Coche, E., Ghaye, B., de Mey, J., Duyck, P. (eds.) Comparative Interpretation of CT and Standard Radiography of the Chest. MEDRAD, pp. 27–49. Springer, Heidelberg (2011). https://doi.org/10.1007/978-3-540-79942-9_2
2. Jing, B., Xie, P., Xing, E.: On the automatic generation of medical imaging reports. ACL (2018)
3. Wang, X., Peng, Y., Lu, L., Lu, Z., Summers, R.M.: TieNet: text-image embedding network for common thorax disease classification and reporting in chest x-rays. In: Proceedings of the IEEE Conference on Computer Vision and Pattern Recognition, pp. 9049–9058 (2018)
4. Johnson, J., Karpathy, A., Fei-Fei, L.: DenseCap: fully convolutional localization networks for dense captioning. In: Proceedings of the IEEE Conference on Computer Vision and Pattern Recognition, pp. 4565–4574 (2016)
5. Demner-Fushman, D., et al.: Preparing a collection of radiology examinations for distribution and retrieval. J. Am. Med. Inform. Assoc. **23**, 304–310 (2016)
6. Wang, X., Peng, Y., Lu, L., Lu, Z., Bagheri, M., Summers, R.: Hospital-scale chest x-ray database and benchmarks on weakly-supervised classification and localization of common thorax diseases. In: IEEE CVPR (2017)
7. Yao, L., Poblenz, E., Dagunts, D., Covington, B., Bernard, D., Lyman, K.: Learning to diagnose from scratch by exploiting dependencies among labels. arXiv preprint arXiv:1710.10501 (2017)
8. Rajpurkar, P., et al.: CheXNet: radiologist-level pneumonia detection on chest x-rays with deep learning. arXiv preprint arXiv:1711.05225 (2017)
9. Kisilev, P., Walach, E., Barkan, E., Ophir, B., Alpert, S., Hashoul, S.Y.: From medical image to automatic medical report generation. IBM J. Res. Dev. **59**, 2:1–2:7 (2015)
10. Shin, H.C., Roberts, K., Lu, L., Demner-Fushman, D., Yao, J., Summers, R.M.: Learning to read chest X-rays: recurrent neural cascade model for automated image annotation. In: Proceedings of the IEEE conference on computer vision and pattern recognition, pp. 2497–2506 (2016)
11. Zhang, Z., Xie, Y., Xing, F., McGough, M., Yang, L.: MDNet: a semantically and visually interpretable medical image diagnosis network. In: Proceedings of the IEEE Conference on Computer Vision and Pattern Recognition, pp. 6428–6436 (2017)
12. Li, Y., Liang, X., Hu, Z., Xing, E.P.: Hybrid retrieval-generation reinforced agent for medical image report generation. In: Advances in Neural Information Processing Systems, pp. 1530–1540 (2018)
13. Xiong, Y., Du, B., Yan, P.: Reinforced transformer for medical image captioning. In: Suk, H.-I., Liu, M., Yan, P., Lian, C. (eds.) MLMI 2019. LNCS, vol. 11861, pp. 673–680. Springer, Cham (2019). https://doi.org/10.1007/978-3-030-32692-0_77

14. Huang, G., Liu, Z., Van Der Maaten, L., Weinberger, K.Q.: Densely connected convolutional networks. In: Proceedings of the IEEE Conference on Computer Vision and Pattern Recognition, pp. 4700–4708 (2017)
15. Chollet, F.: Xception: deep learning with depthwise separable convolutions. In: Proceedings of the IEEE Conference on Computer Vision and Pattern Recognition, pp. 1251–1258 (2017)
16. Schroff, F., Kalenichenko, D., Philbin, J.: FaceNet: a unified embedding for face recognition and clustering. In: Proceedings of the IEEE Conference on Computer Vision and Pattern Recognition, pp. 815–823 (2015)
17. Weston, J., Bengio, S., Usunier, N.: WSABIE: scaling up to large vocabulary image annotation. In: Twenty-Second International Joint Conference on Artificial Intelligence (2011)
18. Zhang, M.L., Zhou, Z.H.: Multilabel neural networks with applications to functional genomics and text categorization. IEEE Trans. Knowl. Data Eng. **18**, 1338–1351 (2006)
19. Li, Y., Song, Y., Luo, J.: Improving pairwise ranking for multi-label image classification. In: Proceedings of the IEEE Conference on Computer Vision and Pattern Recognition, pp. 3617–3625 (2017)
20. Karpathy, A., Fei-Fei, L.: Deep visual-semantic alignments for generating image descriptions. In: Proceedings of the IEEE Conference on Computer Vision and Pattern Recognition, pp. 3128–3137 (2015)
21. Vaswani, A., et al.: Attention is all you need. In: Advances in Neural Information Processing Systems, pp. 5998–6008 (2017)
22. Liu, W., et al.: SSD: single shot multibox detector. In: Leibe, B., Matas, J., Sebe, N., Welling, M. (eds.) ECCV 2016. LNCS, vol. 9905, pp. 21–37. Springer, Cham (2016). https://doi.org/10.1007/978-3-319-46448-0_2
23. Simonyan, K., Zisserman, A.: Very deep convolutional networks for large-scale image recognition. arXiv preprint arXiv:1409.1556 (2014)
24. He, K., Zhang, X., Ren, S., Sun, J.: Deep residual learning for image recognition. In: Proceedings of the IEEE Conference on Computer Vision and Pattern Recognition, pp. 770–778 (2016)
25. Thapar, D., Jaswal, G., Nigam, A., Arora, C.: Gait metric learning Siamese network exploiting dual of spatio-temporal 3D-CNN intra and LSTM based inter gait-cycle-segment features. Pattern Recogn. Lett. **125**, 646–653 (2019)
26. Papineni, K., Roukos, S., Ward, T., Zhu, W.J.: BLEU: a method for automatic evaluation of machine translation. In: Proceedings of the 40th Annual Meeting on Association for Computational Linguistics, pp. 311–318. Association for Computational Linguistics (2002)
27. Vinyals, O., Toshev, A., Bengio, S., Erhan, D.: Show and tell: a neural image caption generator. In: Proceedings of the IEEE Conference on Computer Vision and Pattern Recognition, pp. 3156–3164 (2015)
28. Xu, K., et al.: Show, attend and tell: neural image caption generation with visual attention. In: International conference on machine learning, pp. 2048–2057 (2015)
29. Liu, G., Hsu, T.M.H., McDermott, M., Boag, W., Weng, W.H., Szolovits, P., Ghassemi, M.: Clinically accurate chest x-ray report generation. arXiv preprint arXiv:1904.02633 (2019)
30. Donahue, J., et al.: Long-term recurrent convolutional networks for visual recognition and description. In: Proceedings of the IEEE Conference on Computer Vision and Pattern Recognition, pp. 2625–2634 (2015)

31. Lu, J., Xiong, C., Parikh, D., Socher, R.: Knowing when to look: adaptive attention via a visual sentinel for image captioning. In: Proceedings of the IEEE Conference on Computer Vision and Pattern Recognition, pp. 375–383 (2017)
32. Rennie, S.J., Marcheret, E., Mroueh, Y., Ross, J., Goel, V.: Self-critical sequence training for image captioning. In: Proceedings of the IEEE Conference on Computer Vision and Pattern Recognition, pp. 7008–7024 (2017)

Self-guided Multiple Instance Learning for Weakly Supervised Disease Classification and Localization in Chest Radiographs

Constantin Seibold[1,3]($\boxtimes$) (iD), Jens Kleesiek[2]($\boxtimes$) (iD), Heinz-Peter Schlemmer[2]($\boxtimes$) (iD), and Rainer Stiefelhagen[1]($\boxtimes$) (iD)

[1] Karlsruhe Institute of Technology, Karlsruhe, Germany
{constantin.seibold,rainer.stiefelhagen}@kit.edu
[2] German Cancer Research Center Heidelberg, Heidelberg, Germany
{j.kleesiek,h.schlemmer}@dkfz-heidelberg.de
[3] HIDSS4Health - Helmholtz Information and Data Science School for Health, Karlsruhe/Heidelberg, Germany

Abstract. The lack of fine-grained annotations hinders the deployment of automated diagnosis systems, which require human-interpretable justification for their decision process. In this paper, we address the problem of weakly supervised identification and localization of abnormalities in chest radiographs. To that end, we introduce a novel loss function for training convolutional neural networks increasing the *localization confidence* and assisting the overall *disease identification*. The loss leverages both image- and patch-level predictions to generate auxiliary supervision. Rather than forming strictly binary from the predictions as done in previous loss formulations, we create targets in a more customized manner, which allows the loss to account for possible misclassification. We show that the supervision provided within the proposed learning scheme leads to better performance and more precise predictions on prevalent datasets for multiple-instance learning as well as on the NIH ChestX-Ray14 benchmark for disease recognition than previously used losses.

1 Introduction

With millions of annually captured images, chest radiographs (*CXR*) are one of the most common tools assisting radiologists in the diagnosing process [1]. The emergence of sizeable CXR datasets such as Open-I or ChestX-ray14 [2–6], allowed deep Convolutional Neural Networks (*CNN*) to aid the analysis for the detection of pulmonary anomalies [6–24]. Despite the success of deep learning, inferring the correct abnormality location from the network's decision remains challenging. While for supervised tasks, this is achieved through algorithms such as Faster R-CNN [25–27], the necessary amount of fine-grained annotation for CXR images to train these models is vastly missing and expensive to obtain. Instead, models are trained using image-level labels parsed from medical reports,

© Springer Nature Switzerland AG 2021
H. Ishikawa et al. (Eds.): ACCV 2020, LNCS 12626, pp. 617–634, 2021.
https://doi.org/10.1007/978-3-030-69541-5_37

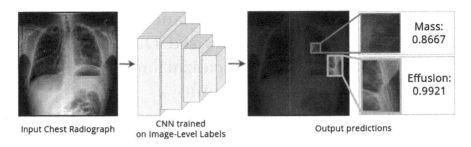

Input Chest Radiograph   CNN trained on Image-Level Labels   Output predictions

Mass: 0.8667

Effusion: 0.9921

Fig. 1. In our framework, the network reads chest X-ray images and produces overall image-level pathology prediction scores and their corresponding locations.

which might be inaccurate [5]. As such, the problem of pulmonary pathology identification and localization is at best weakly supervised (Fig. 1).

Existing work for weakly-supervised pathology localization in CXR builds either upon network saliency or Multiple-Instance Learning (*MIL*). Saliency-based methods [6–13] focus primarily on the multi-class recognition task and predict locations implicitly through saliency visualization methods such as CAM, GradCAM, or excitation backpropagation [28–30]. These methods employ global average pooling to merge spatial features during the classification process. However, through this process the CNN makes less indicative decisions, as healthy regions are heavily outweighing the few regions of interest containing the abnormality. The other direction combines Fully Convolutional Networks (*FCN*) with MIL to implicitly learn patch-level predictions used for localization [20–23]. In MIL-based methods, the input data is regarded as a bag of instances where the label is only available on bag-level. The bag will be assigned a positive label if and only if there exists at least one positive instance. This problem formulation fits for diagnosis in medical images as small regions might define the existence of a pathology within the overall image.

In this paper, we focus on MIL-based approaches to diagnose and localize pulmonary abnormalities in CXRs. Much MIL-related work investigated the use of different pooling functions resembling a max-function to aggregate either predictions or embeddings [6,31–37]. By balancing all given outputs, networks learn implicitly from the bag label. We argue that this approach overlooks the explicit use of instance-level predictions into training. We present a novel loss formulation split into two stages. While the first stage leads through conventional bag-level classification, the second stage leads to more definitive predictions by generating auxiliary supervision from instance-level predictions. By segregating the prediction maps into foreground, background, and ambiguous regions, the network can provide itself instance-wise targets with differing levels of certainty.

The main contributions of our study can be summarized as follows: We provide a novel loss function that applies prediction maps for self-guidance to achieve better classification and localization performance without the necessity to expand a given fully convolutional network architecture. We present the effect of this loss on MIL-specific datasets as well as the ChestX-Ray14 benchmark. The experiments demonstrate competitive results with the current state-of-the-art for weakly supervised pathology classification and localization in CXRs.

2   Related Work

Automated Chest Radiograph Diagnosis. With the release of large-scale CXR datasets [2–6] the development of deep learning-based automated diagnosis methods made noticeable progress in both abnormality identification [6–24,38–40] and the subsequent step of report generation [17,19,41]. However, despite CNNs, at times, surpassing the accuracy of radiologists in detecting pulmonary diseases [11,14], inferring the correct pathology location remains a challenge due to the lack of concretely annotated data. Initial work such as done by Wang *et al.* [6] or Rajpurkar *et al.* [11] uses CAM [28] to obtain pathology locations. Due to the effectiveness and ease of use, saliency-based methods like CAM became a go-to method for showcasing predicted disease regions [6,11–14,37]. As such, there exists work to improve CAM visualizations through the use of auxiliary modules or iterative training [42–44].

Alternatively, Li *et al.* [21] propose a slightly modified FCN trained in MIL-fashion to address the problem. Here, each image patch is assigned a likelihood of belonging to a specific pathology. These likelihood-scores are aggregated using a noisy-OR pooling for the means of computing the loss. This approach is extended by Yao *et al.* [39] and Liu *et al.* [22] who while using different architecture or preprocessing methods stick with the same MIL-based training regime. Similarly, Rozenberg *et al.* [23] expand Li *et al.*'s approach through the usage of further postprocessing steps such as the integration of CRFs.

All of these methods approach this task through image-level supervision and try to gain improved localization through changes in architecture, iterative training or postprocessing. In contrast, rather than modifying a given architecture, we leverage network predictions within the same training step to achieve more confident localization.

Multiple Instance Learning. MIL has become a widely adopted category within weakly supervised learning. It was first proposed for drug activity prediction [45] and has since found a use for applications such as sound [34,35,46] and video event tagging [33] as well as weakly supervised object detection [47–49]. While max- and mean- pooling have been common choices for deep MIL networks, recent work investigates the use of the pooling function to combine instance embeddings or predictions to deliver a bag-level prediction [32–36,39]. The choice of pooling function will often resemble the max-operator or an approximation of such to stay in line with common MIL-assumptions. Static functions such as Noisy-OR, Log-Sum-Exp or Softmax [6,21,34] along with learnable ones like adaptive generalized mean, auto-pooling or attention have been proposed [32–34]. While the choice of pooling function is a vital part of the overall inference and loss computation in training step in MIL, it in itself does not provide sufficient information as the optimization will still occur only based on the bag-level prediction. In order to accurately impact the training, instance-level predictions are necessary to influence the loss. There exist few methods that leverage the use of artificial supervision within a MIL setting to train the network additionally through instance-level losses [33,50–52]. One direction is to introduce artificial instance-labels for prediction scores above a specified threshold [33,51,52]. The loss function splits into a bag-level loss acting in standard MIL fashion by aggregating the predictions and an instance-level prediction where the network gains pixel-wise supervision based on a set prediction threshold [33]. While this approach provides supervision for each instance, it is heavily depending on the initialization potentially introducing a negative bias. On the other side, Morfi et al. [50] introduce the MMM loss for audio event detection. This loss provides direct supervision for the extreme values of the bag, whereas the overall bag accumulated using a mean pooling for a bag-level prediction. Despite all instances influencing the optimization, the supervision of this method is limited as it disregards the association for probable positive/negative instances.

In an ideal scenario, each positive instance should have a near maximal prediction whereas negative ones should be minimal. However, often, the case presents where the amount of positive bags will sway a classifier towards a biased prediction due to class imbalance. This might lead to all instances within a bag for a certain class to get either high or low prediction scores making strict thresholding difficult to apply. Furthermore, as long as the prediction value distribution within a bag is not separable but rather clumped or uniform existing methods cannot account for a fitting expansion of the decision boundary. In contrast, we adopt instance-level supervision in an adapting way, where the distinctness of the prediction directly defines the influence of the loss.

3   Methodology

We start this section by defining multiple-instance learning. We, then, introduce our proposed Self-Guiding Loss (SGL) and how it differs from existing losses. Lastly, we address the use of SGL for classification and weakly supervised localization of CXR pathologies in a MIL setting.

3.1   Preliminaries of Multiple-Instance Learning

Assume, we are given a set of bag-of-instances of size N with the associated labels $\mathcal{B} = \{(B_1, y_1), \ldots, (B_N, y_N)\}$. Let $B_i, i = \{1, \ldots, N\}$ be the i-th bag-of-instances and $B_{i,j} \in B_i, j \in \{1, \ldots, N_i\}$ be the j-th instance with N_i being the number of instances of the i-th bag. The associated labels $y_i \in \{0,1\}^C$ describe the presence or absence of classes, which can occur independently of each other. Let $c \in \{1, \ldots, C\}$ describe a certain class out of C classes in total. The label of a bag and an instance for a specific class c is thus shown by $y_i^c \in \{0,1\}$ and $y_{i,j}^c \in \{0,1\}$, respectively. We refer to a target of 1 as positive and 0 as negative. The MIL-assumption requires that $y_i^c = 1$ if and only if there exists at least a single positive instance, hence we can define

$$y_i^c = \max_j y_{i,j}^c. \tag{1}$$

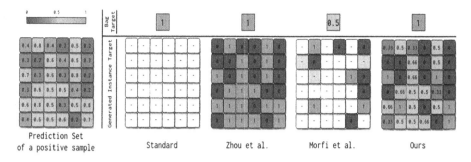

Fig. 2. Illustration of supervision for different loss function concepts for MIL. Strict bag-level supervision (left) provided, Zhou *et al.*'s BIL [33] (center left), Morfi *et al.*'s MMM [50] (center right) and on the right our proposed SGL.

Note that while the bag-level annotation y_i^c is available within the training data, the instance-level annotation $y_{i,j}^c$ is unknown.

We aim at learning a classifier to predict the likelihood of each instance in regard to each class within a bag-of-instances. In several works for deep MIL, this classifier might consist of a convolutional backbone Ψ linked with a pooling layer Φ to combine predictions or features. The class-wise likelihood of a single instance is denoted by $p_{i,j}^c(B_{i,j}) \in [0,1]$ with

$$\mathbf{p}_i^c(B_i) = \{p_{i,1}^c(B_{i,1}), p_{i,2}^c(B_{i,2}), \dots, p_{i,N_i}^c(B_{i,N_i})\} = \Psi_c(B_i) \tag{2}$$

being the set of all instance-level predictions for class c of the i-th bag. These instance-level predictions are aggregated using a pooling layer to obtain bag-level predictions

$$p_i^c(B_i) = \Phi_c(\mathbf{p}_i^c(B_i)) \tag{3}$$

with $p_i^c(B_i) \in [0,1]$. For brevity, we omit the arguments of the presented functions from this point on.

3.2   Self-guiding Loss

The SGL is designed to address the MIL-setting. Here, one faces an inherent lack of knowledge of the correct instance labels joined with an imbalance between positive and negative instances. Commonly used MIL approaches merge instance predictions and train entirely by optimizing any loss function using the bag's label y and the bag prediction $\mathbf{p}$. This level of supervision is illustrated on the left in Fig. 2. The bag label is presented in the top row, while the types of instance supervision are displayed in the bottom. Numbers designate the target label whereas "-" denotes no existing supervision for that particular instance. While this level of supervision will lead the network to accurate bag-level predictions, inferring the determining instance is not ensured.

Rather than just utilizing the bag, our loss formulation is split in two parts. The first part defines the bag-level loss, while the second part describes how the network's predictions induce artificial supervision to train the network.

Bag-Level Loss. The bag-level loss behaves as in classic MIL approaches. A bag-level prediction is generated by aggregating the network's instance-level predictions. We calculate the loss of this stage using common loss functions $\mathcal{L}$ such as the binary cross-entropy by passing the prediction and target for all classes and bags as follows:

$$\mathcal{L}_{Bag}(\mathcal{B}, y) = \frac{1}{C \cdot N} \sum_c \sum_i \mathcal{L}(p_i^c, y_i) \tag{4}$$

with $i \in \{1, \ldots, N\}$ and $c \in \{1, \ldots, C\}$. This loss is, hereby, depending on the choice of the pooling function Φ and provides leeway for the instance-level loss to step in.

Instance-Level Loss. To outline the instance-level loss, we start with the assumption that a network trained just from bag labels will inevitably assign some positive instances a noticeably higher prediction score than most negative instances. From this, we derive three types of instance predictions. Instances with a high score are likely to be considered positive, whereas instances with a low score as negative. Instances with scores close to the decision boundary are rather ambiguous as they may easily be swayed in the course of training and as such do not pose an as concrete implication about the actual class of the instance. Pursuing this line of thought we establish three types of supervision based on the certainty level of each prediction within a bag.

Our first step is to normalize the prediction set using the common min-max feature scaling. We apply this to avoid cases of biases stemming from either algorithmic decisions such the choice of the pooling function or general data imbalance. We denote the resulting rescaled bag of predictions θ by

$$\theta_{ij}^c = \frac{p_{ij}^c - \min(\mathbf{p}_i^c)}{\max(\mathbf{p}_i^c) - \min(\mathbf{p}_i^c)} \tag{5}$$

with min and max being functions returning the minimal and maximal values within a set respectively. The normalized predictions are then used within a ternary mask M depicting targets stemming from the previously named cases similar to Hou *et al.* [53] and Zhang *et al.* [42]. For this, we define a higher and lower threshold to partition the prediction set, δ_h and δ_l respectively with $\delta_h + \delta_l = 1$ and $\delta_h \geq \delta_l \geq 0$. Everything larger than the upper threshold δ_h will be regarded as a positive instance and all instances with scores lower than δ_l as negative. The target mask M is then defined for each instance j in the bag i for class c by

$$M_{i,j}^c = \begin{cases} 0 & , \text{ if } \theta_{i,j}^c < \delta_l \text{ or } y_i^c = 0 \\ \theta_{i,j}^c & , \text{ if } \delta_l \leq \theta_{i,j}^c \leq \delta_h \\ 1 & , \text{ if } \delta_h < \theta_{i,j}^c \end{cases} \tag{6}$$

For distinctly positive and negative predictions, we obtain instance-wise supervision with a target value of 1 and 0 respectively. We can also presume based on Eq. 4. that each instance within negative bags is also negative. Thus, we can set all values of their masks to 0. The remaining uncertain regions, however, do not allow for as explicit label assignment. While we want to enforce the networks decision process, we also have to account for possible misassignment. Thus, rather than setting a fixed target value, we set the target to be θ. This process shows some similarity to the popular label smoothing procedure [54]. Rather than using maximal valued targets, the maps adjusted value is inserted into the loss function as target value. This slightly pushes the loss into the direction of the most extreme predictions within the uncertain instance set. By doing so we steadily increase the amount distinctly positive and negative predictions over the course of training.

We can construct the loss using a fundamental loss function $\mathcal{L}$ like binary cross entropy by utilizing M as target. The instance-level loss is then defined as

$$\mathcal{L}_{Inst}(\mathcal{B}, M) = \sum_i \sum_c \sum_j 2^{\alpha_i^c - 1} \cdot \mathcal{L}(p_{i,j}^c, M_{i,j}^c), \tag{7}$$

where each part is being normalized by the number of pixels with the respective supervision types. This way, we strengthen the networks decision process for its more certain instances. We, further, consider a weighing factor α to influence the bag's impact based on the overall certainty of its prediction. We define α by

$$\alpha_i^c = \max(\max(\mathbf{p}_i^c) - \text{median}(\mathbf{p}_i^c)), 1 - y_i) \tag{8}$$

Since a positive bag in a common MIL setting should have a low valued median due to a limited amount of positive instances, it is weighted highly if the network is able to clearly separate positive from negative predictions. Thus, for positive bags, $\alpha = 0$ if all predictions result in the same value and $\alpha = 1$ if the network is able to clearly separate positive from negative instances under the assumption that the number of positive instances is vastly smaller than the number of negative ones. For negative bags, $\alpha = 1$ holds due to the given supervision.

The complete loss is then defined by

$$\mathcal{L}_{SGL}(p_i, y_i) = \mathcal{L}_{Bag} + \lambda \cdot \mathcal{L}_{Inst}, \tag{9}$$

with λ denoting the weighing hyperparameter of the instance-level loss.

An example of the final supervision for our loss is displayed in Fig. 2. The standard approach on the left uses no instance-level supervision. In the center left, Zhou et al.'s BIL provides a positive label for each instance above the 0.5 threshold and a negative else, while maintaining the bag supervision. The MMM loss by Morfi et al. , in the center right, considers positive labels for the maximum instances and negative ones for minimal instances. It further uses the target of 0.5 for a mean pooled prediction. Opposed to this, our loss adapts its assumed supervision to the produced predictions. Rather than just using the maximum or applying set thresholding, we threshold on a rescaled set of predictions, thus avoiding a common problem occurring with imbalanced data. Our formulation incorporates all instance predictions while providing a margin of error based on the networks certainty over the smoothed targets θ and the weighing factor α.

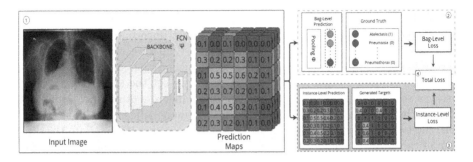

Fig. 3. Overview of considered framework for thoracic disease identification and localization. A chest X-ray is passed through an FCN and produces a prediction map. The prediction map is used to compute the instance- and bag-level losses.

3.3   MIL for Chest Radiograph Diagnosis

We consider a MIL scenario for CXR diagnosis. We build upon the assumption that singular patches (instances) of an image (bag-of-instances) can infer the occurrence of such a pathology (class). An example of this is the class "nodules", which can take up minimal space within the image. We are given just image-level labels for pathologies, while more detailed information such as bounding box or pixel-level supervision remains hidden. The bag is associated with a class if and only if there exists at least one instance causing such implication. The goal is to learn a model that when given a bag of instances can predict the bag's label based on the instance information. By classifying the bag's instances the model provides insight regarding which regions are affected by a pathology.

Overview. In Fig. 3, we illustrate an overview of the considered scheme for CXR diagnosis. Firstly, an FCN processes CXR-images, which results in patch-wise classification scores for each abnormality. The number of patches stems from their perceptual field, which is a result of backbone architecture. Each patch is independently processed via a 1×1 convolutional classification layer. In this work, we do not add specific modules to our backbone network. These patch predictions are aggregated in the second part using a pooling layer, which produces a bag-level prediction for our bag-level loss. The third part applies an instance-level loss function based on the patch-wise predictions. In the fourth part, both the instance and bag-level losses join for optimization. Here, we further penalize the occurrence of non-zero elements in M using an L_2-Norm.

Choice of Pooling Function. The choice of the correct pooling function is vital for any MIL-setting to produce accurate bag-level predictions. Methods like max and mean pooling will lead to imprecise decisions. In the context of MIL in CXR diagnosis, Noisy-OR found use, but this function suffers from the numerical instability stemming from the product of a multitude of instances. Rather than letting singular instances influence the decision process, we choose to employ the Softmax-pooling, which has found success in audio event detection [34,35]. It provides a meaningful balance between instance-level predictions to let each instance influence the bag level loss based on its intensity.

4   Experiments

4.1   Datasets

MNIST-Bags. In a similar fashion to Ilse *et al.* [32], we use the MNIST-bags [32,55] dataset to evaluate our method for a MIL-setting. A bag is created grayscale MNIST-images of size 28×28, which are resized to 32×32. A bag is considered positive if it contains the label "9". The number of images in a bag is Gaussian-distributed based on a fixed bag size. We investigate different average bag sizes and amounts of training bags. During evaluation 1000 bags created from the MNIST test set of the same bag size as used in training. We average the results of ten training procedures.[1]

CIFAR10-Bags. We build CIFAR10-bags from CIFAR10 [56] in a similar fashion to MNIST-bags. We choose to create 2500 and 5000 training and test bags respectively with fixed bag sizes. A bag here is considered positive if it contains the label "dog". We investigate in these experiments the influence of a varying number of positive instances per bag. We average five training runs.

NIH ChestX-ray14. To present the effect of our loss for medical diagnosis, we conduct experiments on the NIH ChestX-ray14 dataset [6]. It contains 112,120 frontal-view chest X-rays taken from 30,805 patients with 14 disease labels. Unless further specified, we resize the original image size of 1024×1024 to 512×512. We use the official split between train/val and test, as such we get a 70%/10%/20% split. Also, 880 images with a total of 984 images with bounding boxes for 8 of the 14 pathologies from the test set.

4.2   Implementation Details

For all MNIST-Bags-experiments, we use a LeNet5 model [55] as Ilse *et al.* [32]. We apply max-pooling, $\delta_l = 0.3$ and $\lambda = 1$ for our method unless further specified. We train BIL [33] using mean-pooling as we found it unable to train with max-pooling.

For all CIFAR10-bags-experiments, we train a ResNet-18 [57] with the same optimizer hyperparameters and batchsize of 64 for 50 epochs. We apply max-pooling, $\delta_l = 0.3$ and $\lambda = 1$ for our method.

For the experiments on NIH ChestX-ray14, each network is initialized using an Image-Net pretraining. We use the same base model as Wang *et al.* [6] by employing a ResNet-50 [57]. We replace the final fully connected and pooling layers with a convolutional layer of kernel size 1×1, resulting in the same number of parameters as Wang *et al.* We follow standard image normalization [58]. For training, we randomly crop the images to size 7/8-th of the input image size, whereas we use the full image size during test time. We train the network for 20 epochs using the maximum batch-size for our GPU using Adam [59] with a learning rate, weight decay, β_1 and β_2 of $10^{-4}, 10^{-4}, 0.9$ and 0.999 respectively.

---

[1] www.github.com/ConstantinSeibold/SGL.

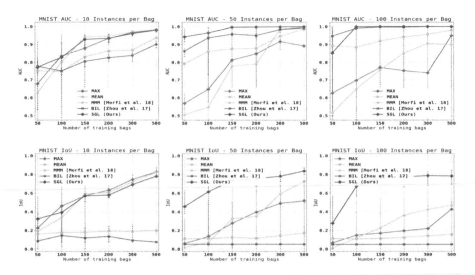

Fig. 4. Test AUC and IoU for MNIST-Bags for differing avg. instances per bag.

We decay the learning rate by 0.1 every 10 epochs. We set $\delta = 0.3$ and $\lambda = 20$. We increase λ to keep the two losses on similar magnitudes. The model is implemented using Pytorch [60].

4.3   Evaluation Metrics

We evaluate the classification ability of our network via the area under the ROC-curve (AUC). To evaluate the localization ability we apply average intersection-over-union (IoU) to calculate the class-wise localization accuracy similar to Russakovsky *et al.* [58]. To compute the localization scores, we threshold the probability map at the scalar value T_p to get the predicted area and compute the intersection between predicted and ground truth area to compute the IoU. In the case of MNIST- and CIFAR10-bags IoU is computed as the intersection between predicted positive instances and ground truth positive instances at $T_p = 0.5$. The localization accuracy is calculated by $\frac{\#hit}{\#hit + \#miss}$, where an image has the correct predicted localization (hit) iff it has the correct class prediction and a higher overlap than a predefined threshold T_{IoU}.

4.4   Results

MNIST-Bags. The AUC and IoU results for the mean bag sizes of 10, 50, and 100 with a varying number of given training bags are displayed from left to right in the top and bottom row of Fig. 4. We present the average of the runs as well as the best and worst runs for each method. For small bags, our method performs similarly to the simple max-pooling in both AUC and IoU. We attribute this average performance to the small number of instances in a bag, which does not allow to make proper use of our ternary training approach. As

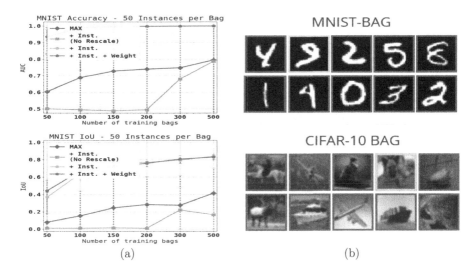

Fig. 5. Ablation study of SGL in Figure (a). Figure (b) displays exemplary positive bags of size 10 for MNIST-bags (top) and CIFAR10-bags (bottom). Positive instances denoted in   , negative ones in red. (Color figure online)

we increase the bag size to 50 and 100 our proposed loss performs better than the max-pooling baseline but also than the other methods for both metrics. We can see the difference notably in the IoU, where our loss achieves nearly double the performance of the next best method for almost all amounts of training bags. We notice that our approach does not pose a trade-off between confident predictions and overall AUC but manages to facilitate a training environment which improves both metrics. It is also worth mentioning that while increasing the amount of training bags improves the method for any bag size our loss achieves exceptional performance for both AUC and IoU with a relatively small number training examples for larger bag sizes. We can reason that the further use of self-guidance can potentially improve a method regardless of dataset size.

In Fig. 5 (a), we present ablation studies involving different constellations of the loss. When considering the loss components, we start with just max-pooling baseline and successively add parts of SGL. Max-pooling alone struggles with the identification of positive/negative bags, however, improves slowly in terms of IoU and AUC with increasing numbers of training bags. When adding the proposed loss without the rescaling mentioned in Eq. 3.2 and weighting component (shown by *Inst.(No Rescale)*) the method becomes incapable to learn as even random initializations might skew the network towards incorrect conclusions. When adding the rescaling component (shown by *Inst.*) the model drastically outperforms prior parts in both metrics. Doing so achieves higher maximums than with the applied weighting factor α displayed by *Inst.+Weight*. However, the addition of the weighting factor provides a more stable training, specifically for smaller amounts of training data.

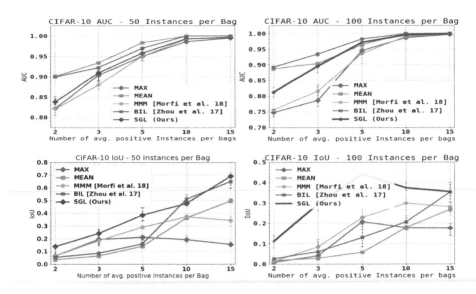

Fig. 6. Test AUC and IoU for CIFAR10-Bags for differing number of average positive instances per bag with a bag size of 50 and 100.

CIFAR10-Bags. The AUC and IoU results for the mean bag sizes of 50 and 100 with a varying number of positive instances per bag are in the top and bottom row of Fig. 6. For smaller bag sizes, we observe that straight forward mean-pooling achieves the best AUC scores for CIFAR10-Bags. Overall SGL improves over straight forward max-pooling for any number of instances. In regards to IoU, our method manages to outperform other methods for nearly any number of positive instances per bag. For larger bag sizes SGL achieves roughly the same performance as BIL which trained using mean-pooling in terms of AUC while outperforming it in IoU for all amounts of positive instances per bag. The addition of self-guidance manages to bridge shortcomings of max-pooling, boosting its classification accuracy for any bag size or number of positive instances.

NIH ChestX-Ray 14: Multi-Label Pathology Classification. Table 1 shows the AUC scores for all the disease classes. We compare the results of our loss function with a common classification approach by Wang *et al.* [6], the

Table 1. Comparison of classification performance for CXR pathologies on the NIH ChestX-Ray14 dataset. Here, 70% of all images were used for training with no bounding box annotations available. Evaluations were performed on the official test split containing 20% of all images. "*" denotes usage of additional bounding box supervision.

Method	Pathologies													
	At.	Card.	Cons.	Ed.	Eff.	Emph.	Fib.	Hernia.	Inf.	Mass.	Nod.	Pl. Th.	Pn.	Pt.	Mean
Wang *et al.*	0.70	0.81	0.70	0.81	0.76	0.83	0.79	0.87	0.66	0.69	0.67	0.68	0.66	0.80	0.75
Li *et al.* *	**0.80**	0.87	**0.80**	0.88	0.87	0.91	0.78	0.70	0.70	0.83	0.75	0.79	0.67	0.87	0.81
Liu *et al.* *	0.79	0.87	0.79	**0.91**	**0.88**	0.93	0.80	0.92	0.69	0.81	0.73	0.80	**0.75**	0.89	**0.83**
ResNet-50+SGL	0.78	**0.88**	0.75	0.86	0.84	**0.95**	**0.85**	**0.94**	**0.71**	**0.84**	**0.81**	**0.81**	0.74	**0.90**	**0.83**

Table 2. Disease localization accuracy are evaluated with a classification threshold of 0.5. "*" denotes additional bounding box supervision.

T_{IoU}	Model	Atelectasis	Cardiomegaly	Effusion	Infiltration	Mass	Nodule	Pneumonia	Pneumothorax	Mean
0.1	Wang et al. [6]	0.69	0.94	0.66	0.71	0.40	0.14	0.63	0.38	0.57
	Li et al. [21]*	**0.71**	**0.98**	**0.87**	**0.92**	**0.71**	0.40	0.60	**0.63**	**0.73**
	Liu et al. [22]	0.39	0.90	0.65	0.85	0.69	0.38	0.30	0.39	0.60
	SGL (Ours)	0.67	0.94	0.67	0.81	**0.71**	**0.41**	**0.66**	0.43	0.66
0.3	Wang et al. [6]	0.24	0.46	0.30	0.28	0.15	0.04	0.17	0.13	0.22
	Li et al. [21]*	**0.36**	**0.94**	**0.56**	**0.66**	0.45	**0.17**	**0.39**	**0.44**	**0.50**
	Liu et al. [22]	0.34	0.71	0.39	0.65	**0.48**	0.09	0.16	0.20	0.38
	SGL (Ours)	0.31	0.76	0.30	0.43	0.34	0.13	**0.39**	0.18	0.36
0.5	Wang et al. [6]	0.05	0.18	0.11	0.07	0.01	0.01	0.01	0.03	0.06
	Li et al. [21]*	0.14	**0.84**	**0.22**	0.30	0.22	0.07	**0.17**	**0.19**	**0.27**
	Liu et al. [22]	**0.19**	0.53	0.19	**0.47**	**0.33**	0.03	0.08	0.11	0.24
	SGL (Ours)	0.07	0.32	0.08	0.19	0.18	**0.10**	0.12	0.04	0.13
0.7	Wang et al. [6]	0.01	0.03	0.02	0.00	0.00	0.00	0.01	0.02	0.01
	Li et al. [21]*	0.04	**0.52**	0.07	0.09	0.11	**0.01**	**0.05**	0.05	0.12
	Liu et al. [22]	**0.08**	0.30	**0.09**	**0.25**	**0.19**	**0.01**	0.04	**0.07**	**0.13**
	SGL (Ours)	0.02	0.01	0.1	0.00	0.04	0.00	0.03	0.01	0.01

MIL-based methods proposed by Li et al. [21] and Liu et al. [22]. The latter two employ noteworthy architectural adaptations and train using bounding box supervision. All of the named methods utilize a ResNet-50 as backbone network. We outperform the baseline ResNet-50 of Wang et al. in all categories. We observe that our loss formulation achieves better classification performance than all other methods in **9** of **14** classes in total. We also reach a better mean performance than other methods, which use further bounding box annotations and architectural modifications such employing additional networks [22] or further convolutional layer [21,22].

NIH ChestX-Ray 14: Pathology Localization. We evaluate the localization ability of the prior named methods through the accuracy over an IoU threshold. For our method, we upsample each prediction map using Nearest-Neighbor-Interpolation. We construct bounding boxes around the connected component of the maximum prediction after applying common morphological operations. The results are displayed in Table 2 for the IoU thresholds $T_{IoU} \in \{0.1, 0.3, 0.5, 0.7\}$. We, further, display qualitative examples for each pathology in Fig. 7. For the visualization, we use no morphological postprocessing. We compare our method against a baseline version of our model trained only using the bag-level loss with a mean-pooling function. The expert annotation is displayed by a green bounding box, while the predicted one is orange.

Our method achieves favourable performance across all pathologies on a threshold of $T_{IoU} = 0.1$. It generally outperforms the baseline of Wang et al. [6]. For higher thresholds, our model falls behind the more specified approaches of Li et al. [21] and Liu et al. [22]. We ascribe the suboptimal quantitative performance to the factors of low spatial output resolution, which can hinder passing the IoU threshold especially for naturally small classes such as *Nodules*, and the overall coarse annotation as can be seen in Fig. 7 e.g. the pathology *Infiltrate*. Here, an infiltrate affects the lung area, which the model correctly marks,

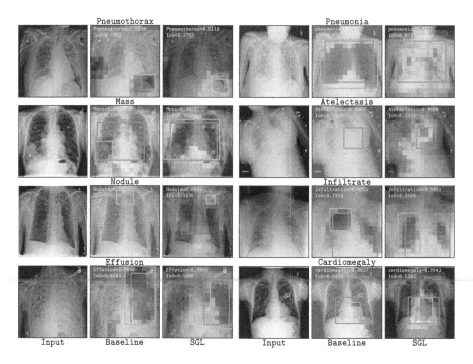

Fig. 7. We compare the patch-wise predictions between a mean-pooling trained baseline to our proposed method for different diseases. The value ranges from 0 (blue) to 1 (red). We show prediction boxes (orange) around the connected component of the maximum prediction and Ground-Truth bounding boxes (green). (Color figure online)

yet the bounding box naturally includes the cardiac area, thus diminishing the IoU.

In Fig. 7, we see that our proposed method can generally make more precise predictions compared to the baseline model. Furthermore, the model can more distinctly separate between healthy and abnormal tissue. These results indicate the ability of our loss to lead itself towards more refined predictions.

5   Conclusion

In this paper, we propose a novel loss formulation in which one gathers auxiliary supervision from the network's predictions to provide instance-level supervision. In comparison to existing MIL-based loss functions, we do not rely on initialization and still provide pixel-wise supervision driving the network. Due to the design of this loss, it can support any MIL-setting such as patch-based pathology diagnosis. We demonstrate our method on two MIL-based datasets as well as the challenging NIH ChestX-Ray14 dataset. We display promising classification and localization performance qualitatively and quantitatively.

Acknowledgements. The present contribution is supported by the Helmholtz Association under the joint research school "HIDSS4Health – Helmholtz Information and Data Science School for Health".

References

1. NHS England: Diagnostic imaging dataset statistical release (2020). https://www.england.nhs.uk/
2. Kohli M.D., R.M.: Open-i: Indiana university chest x-ray collection. https://openi.nlm.nih.gov (2013)
3. Bustos, A., Pertusa, A., Salinas, J.M., de la Iglesia-Vayá, M.: PadChest: a large chest x-ray image dataset with multi-label annotated reports. arXiv preprint arXiv:1901.07441 (2019)
4. Johnson, A.E., et al.: MIMIC-CXR: a large publicly available database of labeled chest radiographs. arXiv preprint arXiv:1901.07042 (2019)
5. Irvin, J., et al.: CheXpert: a large chest radiograph dataset with uncertainty labels and expert comparison. Proceedings of the AAAI Conference on Artificial Intelligence, vol. 33, pp. 590–597 (2019)
6. Wang, X., Peng, Y., Lu, L., Lu, Z., Bagheri, M., Summers, R.M.: ChestX-ray8: hospital-scale chest x-ray database and benchmarks on weakly-supervised classification and localization of common thorax diseases. In: Proceedings of the IEEE Conference on Computer Vision and Pattern Recognition, pp. 2097–2106 (2017)
7. Cai, J., Lu, L., Harrison, A.P., Shi, X., Chen, P., Yang, L.: Iterative attention mining for weakly supervised thoracic disease pattern localization in chest x-rays. In: Frangi, A.F., Schnabel, J.A., Davatzikos, C., Alberola-López, C., Fichtinger, G. (eds.) MICCAI 2018. LNCS, vol. 11071, pp. 589–598. Springer, Cham (2018). https://doi.org/10.1007/978-3-030-00934-2_66
8. Shen, Y., Gao, M.: Dynamic routing on deep neural network for thoracic disease classification and sensitive area localization. In: Shi, Y., Suk, H.-I., Liu, M. (eds.) MLMI 2018. LNCS, vol. 11046, pp. 389–397. Springer, Cham (2018). https://doi.org/10.1007/978-3-030-00919-9_45
9. Tang, Y., Wang, X., Harrison, A.P., Lu, L., Xiao, J., Summers, R.M.: Attention-guided curriculum learning for weakly supervised classification and localization of thoracic diseases on chest radiographs. In: Shi, Y., Suk, H.-I., Liu, M. (eds.) MLMI 2018. LNCS, vol. 11046, pp. 249–258. Springer, Cham (2018). https://doi.org/10.1007/978-3-030-00919-9_29
10. Baltruschat, I.M., Nickisch, H., Grass, M., Knopp, T., Saalbach, A.: Comparison of deep learning approaches for multi-label chest x-ray classification. Sci. Rep. **9**, 1–10 (2019)
11. Rajpurkar, P., et al.: ChexNet: radiologist-level pneumonia detection on chest x-rays with deep learning. arXiv preprint arXiv:1711.05225 (2017)
12. Wang, H., Xia, Y.: ChestNet: a deep neural network for classification of thoracic diseases on chest radiography. arXiv preprint arXiv:1807.03058 (2018)
13. Park, B., et al.: A curriculum learning strategy to enhance the accuracy of classification of various lesions in chest-pa x-ray screening for pulmonary abnormalities. Sci. Rep. **9**, 1–9 (2019)
14. Rajpurkar, P., et al.: Deep learning for chest radiograph diagnosis: a retrospective comparison of the CheXNeXt algorithm to practicing radiologists. PLoS Med. **15**, e1002686 (2018)

15. Wang, Q., et al.: Low-shot multi-label incremental learning for thoracic diseases diagnosis. In: Cheng, L., Leung, A.C.S., Ozawa, S. (eds.) ICONIP 2018. LNCS, vol. 11307, pp. 420–432. Springer, Cham (2018). https://doi.org/10.1007/978-3-030-04239-4_38

16. Li, C.Y., Liang, X., Hu, Z., Xing, E.P.: Knowledge-driven encode, retrieve, paraphrase for medical image report generation. In: Proceedings of the AAAI Conference on Artificial Intelligence, vol. 33, pp. 6666–6673 (2019)

17. Li, X., Cao, R., Zhu, D.: Vispi: automatic visual perception and interpretation of chest x-rays. arXiv preprint arXiv:1906.05190 (2019)

18. Li, Y., Pang, Y., Shen, J., Cao, J., Shao, L.: NETNet: neighbor erasing and transferring network for better single shot object detection. arXiv preprint arXiv:2001.06690 (2020)

19. Wang, X., Peng, Y., Lu, L., Lu, Z., Summers, R.M.: TieNet: text-image embedding network for common thorax disease classification and reporting in chest x-rays. In: Proceedings of the IEEE Conference on Computer Vision and Pattern Recognition, pp. 9049–9058 (2018)

20. Yan, C., Yao, J., Li, R., Xu, Z., Huang, J.: Weakly supervised deep learning for thoracic disease classification and localization on chest x-rays. In: Proceedings of the 2018 ACM International Conference on Bioinformatics, Computational Biology, and Health Informatics, pp. 103–110 (2018)

21. Li, Z., et al.: Thoracic disease identification and localization with limited supervision. In: Proceedings of the IEEE Conference on Computer Vision and Pattern Recognition, pp. 8290–8299 (2018)

22. Liu, J., Zhao, G., Fei, Y., Zhang, M., Wang, Y., Yu, Y.: Align, attend and locate: chest x-ray diagnosis via contrast induced attention network with limited supervision. In: Proceedings of the IEEE International Conference on Computer Vision, pp. 10632–10641 (2019)

23. Rozenberg, E., Freedman, D., Bronstein, A.: Localization with limited annotation for chest x-rays (2019)

24. Guan, Q., Huang, Y.: Multi-label chest x-ray image classification via category-wise residual attention learning. Pattern Recogn. Lett. **130**, 259–266 (2018)

25. Ren, S., He, K., Girshick, R., Sun, J.: Faster R-CNN: towards real-time object detection with region proposal networks. In: Advances in Neural Information Processing Systems, pp. 91–99 (2015)

26. Liu, W., et al.: SSD: single shot multibox detector. In: Leibe, B., Matas, J., Sebe, N., Welling, M. (eds.) ECCV 2016. LNCS, vol. 9905, pp. 21–37. Springer, Cham (2016). https://doi.org/10.1007/978-3-319-46448-0_2

27. Redmon, J., Farhadi, A.: YOLOv3: an incremental improvement. arXiv preprint arXiv:1804.02767 (2018)

28. Zhou, B., Khosla, A., Lapedriza, A., Oliva, A., Torralba, A.: Learning deep features for discriminative localization. In: Proceedings of the IEEE Conference on Computer Vision and Pattern Recognition, pp. 2921–2929 (2016)

29. Selvaraju, R.R., Cogswell, M., Das, A., Vedantam, R., Parikh, D., Batra, D.: Grad-CAM: visual explanations from deep networks via gradient-based localization. In: Proceedings of the IEEE International Conference on Computer Vision, pp. 618–626 (2017)

30. Zhang, J., Bargal, S.A., Lin, Z., Brandt, J., Shen, X., Sclaroff, S.: Top-down neural attention by excitation backprop. Int. J. Comput. Vis. **126**, 1084–1102 (2018). https://doi.org/10.1007/s11263-017-1059-x

31. Yao, L., Poblenz, E., Dagunts, D., Covington, B., Bernard, D., Lyman, K.: Learning to diagnose from scratch by exploiting dependencies among labels. arXiv preprint arXiv:1710.10501 (2017)
32. Ilse, M., Tomczak, J.M., Welling, M.: Attention-based deep multiple instance learning. arXiv preprint arXiv:1802.04712 (2018)
33. Zhou, Y., Sun, X., Liu, D., Zha, Z., Zeng, W.: Adaptive pooling in multi-instance learning for web video annotation. In: Proceedings of the IEEE International Conference on Computer Vision Workshops, pp. 318–327 (2017)
34. McFee, B., Salamon, J., Bello, J.P.: Adaptive pooling operators for weakly labeled sound event detection. IEEE/ACM Trans. Audio Speech Lang. Process. **26**, 2180–2193 (2018)
35. Wang, Y., Li, J., Metze, F.: A comparison of five multiple instance learning pooling functions for sound event detection with weak labeling. In: ICASSP 2019–2019 IEEE International Conference on Acoustics, Speech and Signal Processing (ICASSP), pp. 31–35. IEEE (2019)
36. Liao, F., Liang, M., Li, Z., Hu, X., Song, S.: Evaluate the malignancy of pulmonary nodules using the 3-D deep leaky noisy-or network. IEEE Trans. Neural Netw. Learn. Syst. **30**, 3484–3495 (2019)
37. Yan, Y., Wang, X., Guo, X., Fang, J., Liu, W., Huang, J.: Deep multi-instance learning with dynamic pooling. In: Asian Conference on Machine Learning, pp. 662–677 (2018)
38. Chen, H., Miao, S., Xu, D., Hager, G.D., Harrison, A.P.: Deep hierarchical multi-label classification of chest x-ray images. Proc. Mach. Learn. Res. **1**, 13 (2019)
39. Yao, L., Prosky, J., Poblenz, E., Covington, B., Lyman, K.: Weakly supervised medical diagnosis and localization from multiple resolutions. arXiv preprint arXiv:1803.07703 (2018)
40. Guendel, S., et al.: Multi-task learning for chest x-ray abnormality classification on noisy labels. arXiv preprint arXiv:1905.06362 (2019)
41. Liu, G., et al.: Clinically accurate chest x-ray report generation. arXiv preprint arXiv:1904.02633 (2019)
42. Zhang, X., Wei, Y., Kang, G., Yang, Y., Huang, T.: Self-produced guidance for weakly-supervised object localization. In: Ferrari, V., Hebert, M., Sminchisescu, C., Weiss, Y. (eds.) ECCV 2018. LNCS, vol. 11216, pp. 610–625. Springer, Cham (2018). https://doi.org/10.1007/978-3-030-01258-8_37
43. Zhang, X., Wei, Y., Feng, J., Yang, Y., Huang, T.S.: Adversarial complementary learning for weakly supervised object localization. In: Proceedings of the IEEE Conference on Computer Vision and Pattern Recognition, pp. 1325–1334 (2018)
44. Wei, Y., Feng, J., Liang, X., Cheng, M.M., Zhao, Y., Yan, S.: Object region mining with adversarial erasing: a simple classification to semantic segmentation approach. In: Proceedings of the IEEE Conference on Computer Vision and Pattern Recognition, pp. 1568–1576 (2017)
45. Dietterich, T.G., Lathrop, R.H., Lozano-Pérez, T.: Solving the multiple instance problem with axis-parallel rectangles. Artif. Intell. **89**, 31–71 (1997)
46. Kong, Q., Xu, Y., Sobieraj, I., Wang, W., Plumbley, M.D.: Sound event detection and time-frequency segmentation from weakly labelled data. IEEE/ACM Trans. Audio Speech Lang. Process. **27**, 777–787 (2019)
47. Tang, P., Wang, X., Bai, X., Liu, W.: Multiple instance detection network with online instance classifier refinement. In: Proceedings of the IEEE Conference on Computer Vision and Pattern Recognition, pp. 2843–2851 (2017)

48. Cinbis, R.G., Verbeek, J., Schmid, C.: Weakly supervised object localization with multi-fold multiple instance learning. IEEE Trans. Pattern Anal. Mach. Intell. **39**, 189–203 (2016)
49. Felipe Zeni, L., Jung, C.R.: Distilling knowledge from refinement in multiple instance detection networks. In: Proceedings of the IEEE/CVF Conference on Computer Vision and Pattern Recognition Workshops, pp. 768–769 (2020)
50. Morfi, V., Stowell, D.: Data-efficient weakly supervised learning for low-resource audio event detection using deep learning. arXiv preprint arXiv:1807.06972 (2018)
51. Wang, X., Zhu, Z., Yao, C., Bai, X.: Relaxed multiple-instance SVM with application to object discovery. In: Proceedings of the IEEE International Conference on Computer Vision, pp. 1224–1232 (2015)
52. Shamsolmoali, P., Zareapoor, M., Zhou, H., Yang, J.: AMIL: adversarial multi-instance learning for human pose estimation. ACM Trans. Multimed. Comput. Commun. Appl. (TOMM) **16**, 1–23 (2020)
53. Hou, Q., Jiang, P., Wei, Y., Cheng, M.M.: Self-erasing network for integral object attention. In: Advances in Neural Information Processing Systems, pp. 549–559 (2018)
54. Szegedy, C., Vanhoucke, V., Ioffe, S., Shlens, J., Wojna, Z.: Rethinking the inception architecture for computer vision. In: Proceedings of the IEEE Conference on Computer Vision and Pattern Recognition, pp. 2818–2826 (2016)
55. LeCun, Y., Bottou, L., Bengio, Y., Haffner, P.: Gradient-based learning applied to document recognition. Proc. IEEE **86**, 2278–2324 (1998)
56. Krizhevsky, A., Hinton, G., et al.: Learning multiple layers of features from tiny images (2009)
57. He, K., Zhang, X., Ren, S., Sun, J.: Deep residual learning for image recognition. In: Proceedings of the IEEE Conference on Computer Vision and Pattern Recognition, pp. 770–778 (2016)
58. Russakovsky, O., et al.: ImageNet large scale visual recognition challenge. Int. J. Comput. Vis. **115**, 211–252 (2015). https://doi.org/10.1007/s11263-015-0816-y
59. Kingma, D.P., Ba, J.: Adam: a method for stochastic optimization. arXiv preprint arXiv:1412.6980 (2014)
60. Paszke, A., et al.: Automatic differentiation in PyTorch. In: NIPS-W (2017)

MBNet: A Multi-task Deep Neural Network for Semantic Segmentation and Lumbar Vertebra Inspection on X-Ray Images

Van Luan Tran[1]($\boxtimes$) , Huei-Yung Lin[1] , and Hsiao-Wei Liu[2]

[1] Department of Electrical Engineering, National Chung Cheng University,
Chiayi 621, Taiwan
`tranvanluan07118@gmail.com`, `lin@ee.ccu.edu.tw`
[2] Biomedical Technology and Device Research Laboratories, Industrial Technology
Research Institute, Hsinchu 310, Taiwan
`rachel_liu@itri.org.tw`

Abstract. Deep learning methods, especially multi-task learning with CNNs, have achieved good results in many fields of computer vision. Semantic segmentation and shape detection of lumbar vertebrae, sacrum, and femoral heads from clinical X-ray images are important and challenging tasks. In this paper, we propose a multi-task deep neural network, MBNet. It is developed based on our new multi-path convolutional neural network, BiLuNet, for semantic segmentation on X-ray images. Our MBNet has two branches, one is for semantic segmentation of lumbar vertebrae, sacrum, and femoral heads. It shares the main features with the second branch to learn and classify by supervised learning. The output of the second branch is to predict the inspected values for lumbar vertebra inspection. These networks are capable of performing the two tasks with very limited training data. We collected our dataset and annotated it by doctors for model training and performance evaluation. Compared to the state-of-the-art methods, our BiLuNet model provides better mIoUs with the same training data. The experimental results have demonstrated the feasibility of our MBNet for semantic segmentation of lumbar vertebrae, as well as the parameter prediction for the doctors to perform clinical diagnosis of low back pains. Code is available at: https://github.com/LuanTran07/BiLUnet-Lumbar-Spine.

1 Introduction

Semantic segmentation and shape detection are fundamental to the object identification and location computation in medical images [1,2]. While the X-ray inspection is of great clinical necessity, the automatic understanding of X-ray

Electronic supplementary material The online version of this chapter (https://doi.org/10.1007/978-3-030-69541-5_38) contains supplementary material, which is available to authorized users.

H. Ishikawa et al. (Eds.): ACCV 2020, LNCS 12626, pp. 635–651, 2021.
https://doi.org/10.1007/978-3-030-69541-5_38

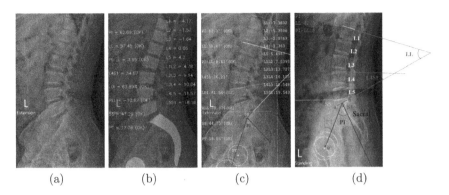

(a)   (b)   (c)   (d)

Fig. 1. An overview of the lumbar vertebra inspection on X-ray images by our multi-task deep neural network for semantic segmentation and inspection. (a) the input X-ray image. (b) our MBNet generates the semantic segmentation result and inspected values. The vertebrae, sacrum, and femoral heads are segmented with red, green, blue, and cyan color respectively. (c) annotation reference is provided by doctors. (d) defined for the parameters used for lumbar vertebra inspection, S1 is defined by the line segment *ab* constructed between the posterior superior corner of the sacrum and the anterior tip of the S1 endplate. The hip axis (*o*) is the midpoint of the line segment connecting the centers of femoral heads. The pelvic radius is drawn from the hip axis to the center of S1. (Color figure online)

images is still a very challenging task. It is primarily due to the projective nature of X-ray imaging, which causes large overlaps among the object shapes, blurred boundaries, and complicated composition patterns [3]. For specific medical applications such as the treatment for low back pain, the images of spine bones are acquired by X-ray [4], computed tomography [5], or magnetic resonance imaging [6,7], to facilitate the assessment of the causes by doctors. Consequently, the automatic detection and segmentation of vertebrae in medical images is an important step for the analysis of the disease severity and recovery from the treatment.

The recent state-of-the-art techniques for vertebra detection, segmentation, and localization from images usually adopt two main strategies: the approaches using traditional computer vision and image processing algorithms and the methods based on deep neural networks. The former utilizes image enhancement, feature extraction, clustering, and classification for local region segmentation [8–10], and the latter adopts convolutional neural networks with the models trained using the datasets labeled by the experts in the field [11,12]. Due to the overlapping shadows of chest organs, including lungs, bowels, and other bony structures such as ribs, the automatic detection, and segmentation of vertebrae using traditional methods are more difficult for X-ray images than for CT or MRI images [3,13,14]. Nevertheless, the use of X-ray imaging techniques is popular because of the least amount of radiation.

With the traditional approach, Ebrahimi *et al.* proposed a technique for posterior corner detection in X-ray images of the lumbar spine [9]. They first enhanced the image region of the lumbar area and performed Canny edge detection. The corner points were then selected via Haar-filtering to automatically extract the positions of lumbar (L) vertebrae posterior corners for L1 to L5. The results provided a localization accuracy at about 0.6~1.4 mm, which was comparable to the manual expert variability. In [15], Larhmam *et al.* presented a method for vertebra detection on X-ray images using the generalized Hough transform (GHT). They adopted contrast-limited adaptive histogram equalization (CLAHE) to enhance the image for edge detection. A GHT accumulator construction was then used to determine the position of the center points of vertebrae in the X-ray image with the information stored in the table created based on the vertebra model. Their detection results demonstrated an 89% global accuracy from 200 investigated vertebrae.

In the past few years, the progress of deep learning with convolutional neural networks (CNNs) has shown a remarkable performance on biomedical image segmentation. However, the existing literature for CNN based lumbar vertebra segmentation is mostly related to the techniques which take MRI images as inputs and is very limited for the processing of X-ray images [16]. Fully automatic segmentation on X-ray images for the lumbar vertebrae still has many challenges. In [12], Arif *et al.* proposed a novel shape predictor network for vertebra segmentation with X-ray images. They modified the U-Net [17] architecture to generate a signed distance function (SDF) from the input image. The predicted SDF was then converted to the parameters represented in a shape space for loss computation. After the shape was transferred to the corresponding symbolic distance function, a principal component analysis (PCA) was performed. However, their results were still very limited since it was not easy to derive the shape information for complicated cases.

As machine learning techniques become more powerful, multi-task deep neural networks also gain considerable attention [10,18–21]. Multi-task learning (MTL) performs model training for several tasks simultaneously to share information in the network and solve multiple tasks at the same time. In [22], Liu *et al.* proposed a multi-task deep learning model for automated lung nodule analysis. They built a bi-branch model used for the classification and attribute score regression tasks. This method makes the neural network more reliable in detecting marginal lung nodules. In [23], Xiao *et al.* proposed a new regularized multi-task learning model to jointly select a small set of standard features across multiple tasks. The experimental results demonstrated that the model achieved high performance compared with other methods.

In this paper, we present a multi-task network for the semantic segmentation of lumbar vertebrae as well as the parameter prediction for inspection and diagnosis. It is designed based on our effective semantic segmentation network, BiLuNet, for the robust detection of unclear overlapping shadow regions in the images. For comparison, BiLuNet is trained independently to determine the location of five lumbar (L1 to L5), S1 on the sacrum and the hip axis. The parameters for the diagnosis of lumbar vertebrae are then derived. In the experiments, the training data are labeled at the pixel level manually and annotated by doctors. The datasets are used to train our MBNet and BiLuNet, as well as other networks for performance comparison. Experimental results have demonstrated the effectiveness and feasibility of our proposed MBNet for both the semantic segmentation and lumbar vertebra inspection on X-ray images with very high accuracy.

1.1 Background

The inspection of the lumbar vertebrae includes object segmentation, target localization, and analysis of several inclination angles in the X-ray images. Figure 1(d) depicts the surgical measurements of interest in this work for identification and future examination. Pelvic incidence (PI) is defined as the angle between the line perpendicular to the sacral plate at its midpoint (c) and the line connecting this point to the axis of femoral heads [24]. PI is an important pelvic anatomic parameter which determines the pelvic orientation. It is a specific constant for each individual and remains relatively stable during childhood. Afterward, it increases significantly during youth until reaching its maximum, and does not change after adolescence [25].

Pelvic tilt (PT) is defined as the angle between the anterior pelvic plane (APP) and a vertical line in the standing position. To be more specific, it is the angle given by the line passing through the hip axis o and the line segment $\overline{oc}$ in the X-ray image (see Fig. 1(d)). Sacral slope (SS) is defined as the angle between the sacral endplate S1 and the horizontal axis passing through its endpoint (b). PT and SS are position-dependent angles in the spatial orientation of the pelvis [26]. PI, SS, and PT are particularly useful since it can be shown that PI is the arithmetic sum of SS and PT, and these two position-dependent variables can determine the pelvic orientation in the sagittal plane [27].

Lumbar lordosis (LL) is the inward curve of the lumbar spine, and defined as the angle between the lines drawn along the superior endplate of L1 and the superior endplate of S1 [28]. The angle L4S1 is measured by the intersection of the lines drawn along the superior endplate of L4 and the superior endplate of S1. Most bodyweight and movement are carried by the two lowest segments in the lumbar spine, L5/S1, and L4/L5, which makes the area prone to injury. In 95% of disc herniated cases, L4/L5 or L5/S1 levels are involved. Low back pain with degenerative disc disease is when normal changes take place in the discs of the spine, mostly at the sites L4/L5 lumbar vertebrae and S1 sacrum [29,30]. The surgery for patients with unbalanced lumbar spondylolisthesis is helpful to correct the spine-pelvic sagittal parameters (PI, PT, SS, L4S1, and LL) closer to the normal range [31].

PI-LL is the value of PI minus LL. Given a PI value, it offers an estimate of the lordosis and quantifies the mismatch between pelvic morphology and the lumbar curve. Lordosis distribution index (LDI) defines the magnitude of the arc lordosis (L4S1) in proportion to the arc of the lumbar lordosis (LL). Relative lumbar lordosis (RLL) quantifies the magnitude of lumbar lordosis relative to the ideal lordosis as defined by the magnitude of PI. RLL and LDI are used to describe the state where the lumbar lordosis is rehabilitated to the ideal magnitude and distribution. The evaluation of RLL and PI-LL provides the prediction of postoperative complications and the correlation with health-related quality of life (HRQOL) scores [32].

2   Multi-Task Deep Neural Network (MBNet)

In this section, we describe our MBNet architecture, where M represents the multi-task network structure and B denotes the BiLuNet backbone model. Our MBNet automatically learns appropriate representation sharing through end-to-end training, and makes full use of the correlations among different tasks. The MBNet with supervised learning is applied for two tasks, semantic segmentation and parameter inspection for the diagnosis of lumbar vertebrae as presented in Fig. 3.

2.1   Semantic Segmentation Branch

For semantic segmentation, this work is specifically concerned with an accurate segmentation method to extract the object mask. It is used to detect the locations of lumbar vertebrae, sacrum, and femoral heads. In this regard, U-Net is one of the well-known fully convolutional networks (FCNs) utilized in medical image understanding [17]. It has many variants in the literature, and most of them consist of an encoder-decoder structure. However, U-Net can hardly segment well for challenging cases or the image with a complex background. To deal with these issues, we propose a new multi-path convolutional neural network, BiLuNet, where Lu represents the shape of the network structure and Bi denotes the bilateral segmentation network. As shown in Fig. 2, our network has two main paths, a spatial path to recover the spatial information and a downsampling path to extract the features.

In BiLuNet, Spatial Path is to preserve the spatial information and generate high-resolution features [33]. It contains three layers, and each convolutional layer has $stride = 2$, followed by batch normalization and Rectified Linear Unit (ReLU). Thus, this path extracts the output feature maps at 1/8 of the original image size. It encodes the rich spatial information from the large spatial size of the feature maps. The spatial path and downsampling path are crucial to the prediction of the detailed output to cover large objects, which leads to a rich discriminative ability.

The spatial information acquired by Spatial Path encodes most rich and detailed messages in the low levels, while the robust features extracted from the downsampling path are in the high levels. These two feature paths with different levels are fused by a Feature Fusion Module (FFM) [33]. Given the features from different levels, we first concatenate the outputs of the spatial path and the downsampling path. The batch normalization is then utilized to balance the scales of the features. Next, a global pool is used for the concatenated features

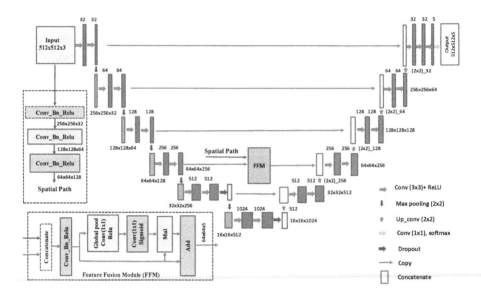

Fig. 2. The end-to-end BiLuNet architecture for object semantic segmentation. White boxes present the concatenation results of a copied feature map and an *up_conv*, an upsampled and convolutional layer. Purple boxes indicate the results of the node dropped out between two convolutional layers. BiLuNet takes a three-channel input image at the resolution of 512×512, and the output contains five channels, the classes with background, vertebra, sacrum, femoral head1, and femoral head2.

to form a feature tensor, and the weight is computed by a sigmoid function. This weight tensor can re-weight the features by multiplying the concatenated features and adding to the feature selection. The details of this FFM function is shown in Fig. 2. The dimension of the output space is 5, which corresponds to the 5 classes of the segmentation requirement (background, vertebra, sacrum, femoral head1, and femoral head2).

Similar to U-Net, the proposed BiLuNet operates with both the downsampling and upsampling paths and adds a spatial path to recover the spatial information lost in the pooling layers of the contracting path. The downsampling path decreases the feature size while increasing the number of feature maps, whereas the upsampling path increases the feature size while decreasing the number of feature maps. The latter eventually leads to a pixel-wise mask. For the upsampling operation, we modify the existing architecture to reconstruct high-resolution feature maps. The detailed network structure with the parameter settings is illustrated in Fig. 2.

To maintain the same number of channels in the encoder and decoder, skip connections are added between the corresponding blocks in the downsampling and upsampling paths. The skip connections are also used to explicitly copy features from the earlier layers to the subsequent layers. This prevents the neural network from having to learn the identity functions. Further functions are solely tasked with building on the representation. Through the skip connections, the nodes from a shallow layer are concatenated to the nodes in a deeper layer. The deeper layer is then treated as a wider layer and connected to the next layer. We use a dropout layer between these two convolutional layers to prevent overfitting and co-adaptation of the features. In the implementation, 50% of the nodes are dropped out during the forward and backward passes. The network totally has 29 convolutional layers. In the final layer, a 1×1 convolution, 5 dimensional space, and a sigmoid activation function are used to output the probability map of the semantic segmentation, which has the same size as the original 512×512 input.[1]

2.2   Inspected Values Branch

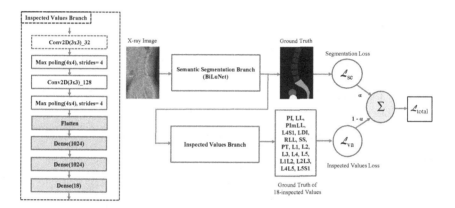

Fig. 3. MBNet architecture. It consists of two branches. The semantic segmentation branch is trained to produce a semantic segmentation of the lumbar vertebrae, sacrum, and femoral heads. The inspected values branch generates the inspected values for the related parameters for the diagnosis of the lumbar vertebrae.

Besides generating the sematic segmentation map, our network also has other functions, which can estimate the physical quantities. It is automatically estimated to provide accurate parameters for the doctors to perform clinical diagnosis of low back pains. Here, the classification task is considered as an auxiliary task. While the semantic segmentation task provides the local supervision for the segmentation of lumbar vertebrae, sacrum, and femoral heads from clinical X-ray images. The regression values level classification task provides global supervision about how inspected values. The integrated classification part can drive our model more robust to the inspected values variation and boost performance. Via the dataset, the segmentation mask, and the inspected values ground

---

[1] The full training and testing code is open source at https://github.com/LuanTran07/BiLUnet-Lumbar-Spine.

truth, we train our network to predict the parameters used for lumbar vertebra inspection.

As presented in Fig. 3, the input of the inspected values branch is shared from the final layer of the semantic segmentation branch. The inspected values branch designed to extracted from the shared feature maps. This network branch consisting of two 3×3 convolutional layers, two 4×4 max-pooling layers, and three fully connected (FC) layers were constructed as an inspected values classifier. The first and second FC layer consists of 1024 neurons with the rectified linear unit activation function. The output FC layer consists of 18 neurons followed by a linear activation function, indicating the probabilities of the 18-inspected values. To train the inspected values classifier supervised learning, the mean squared error regression loss is used, which can be calculated by Eq. 3.

2.3   Multiple Loss Function

Our loss function is a weighted sum of a semantic segmentation loss (L_{se}) and a inspected values loss (L_{va}):

$$L_{total} = \alpha \cdot L_{se} + (1 - \alpha) \cdot L_{va} \tag{1}$$

where $\alpha \in [0, 1]$ is loss weights. It adjusts the relative importance of L_{se} and L_{va}. The loss weights (α) is set to 0.9 in our method.

We use categorical cross-entropy loss function for the semantic segmentation loss. The categorical cross-entropy is given by

$$L_{se} = -\frac{1}{N} \sum_{i=1}^{N} \sum_{c=1}^{C} y_c \cdot \log(\hat{y}_c) + (1 - y_c) \cdot \log(1 - \hat{y}_c) \tag{2}$$

where y_j and $\hat{y}_j$ denote the predicted and ground-truth values of the object in the image, respectively. C is the number of categories, and N is the number of training samples. The categorical cross-entropy cost function works in tandem with a softmax activation function. It computes the loss between network predictions and target values for multi-class classification.

The inspected values loss is defined by mean squared error regression loss. It is the most commonly used regression loss function. The mean squared error (MSE) is the sum of squared distances between our target variable and predicted values. The inspected values loss is given by

$$L_{va} = \frac{\sum_{i=1}^{n} (y_i - \hat{y}_i)^2}{n} \tag{3}$$

where y_i and $\hat{y}_i$ denote the predicted and ground-truth values of the inspected values in the X-ray image, respectively. n is the number of training samples.

3   Experiments

In this work, we collect our own image data for the experiments. The dataset consists of 650 images (with a half before surgery and half after surgery) for network training, and additional 100 images for testing (also with a half before surgery and half after surgery). The training images are labeled with four categories (vertebra, sacrum, femoral head1, and femoral head2), ground-truth of 18-inspected values are annotated by doctors. For the CPU configuration, the computer is with an Intel i7-7700 CPU at 3.6 GHz and 32 GB RAM. The GPU is an NVIDIA TITAN RTX with 24 GB RAM. For training parameters, the number of epochs is set to 200, and the batch size is set to 4. Our initial learning rate is set to $3e-4$ for Adam.

3.1   Semantic Segmentation Evaluation

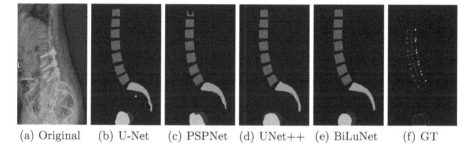

(a) Original   (b) U-Net   (c) PSPNet   (d) UNet++   (e) BiLuNet   (f) GT

Fig. 4. An example of lumbar vertebra segmentation output on a challenging X-ray image. Our result shows a significant improvement compared to those derived from U-Net, UNet++, and PSPNet.

The testing dataset is also used to evaluate other methods for performance comparison with the same training parameters and data. Figure 5 illustrates the mIoU (mean intersection over union) of U-Net, UNet++, PSPNet, and our BiLuNet. In 100 testing images, the proposed network has 84.10%, 83.67%, 80.35%, 78.67% and 98.48% mIoUs for vertebrae, sacrum, femoral head1, femoral head2 and background, respectively. The proposed BiLuNet outperforms state-of-the-art methods in all categories. Figure 4 also shows the higher accuracy semantic segmentation results compared to others. Our model can cover the most region of input X-ray images by the feature fusion between the spatial path and the downsampling path. The spatial path designed in our network preserves the spatial information from the original X-ray image. As shown in the figure, very precise results of lumbar vertebrae, sacrum, and femoral heads are obtained. More specifically, we are able to derive the accurate shapes of femoral head1 and femoral head2, which are failed by all other methods.

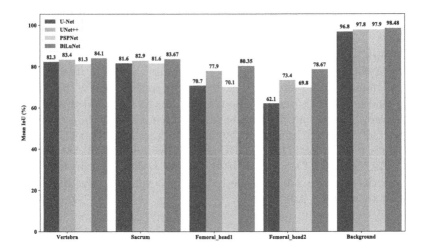

Fig. 5. The performance comparison on our dataset for different algorithms, U-Net [17], UNet++ [34], and PSPNet [35], and our BiLuNet. It shows the IoU (intersection over union) and mean IoU for the evaluation between the semantic segmentation testing results and ground-truth labels.

Table 1. Ablation study on different cases

Methods	Vertebrae	Sacrum	Femoral head1	Femoral head2	Background	Average mIoU
Case 1	82.98%	81.95%	72.89%	60.91%	95.90%	78.93%
Case 2	83.15%	82.71%	77.26%	69.42%	97.96%	80.64%
BiLuNet	84.10%	83.67%	80.35%	78.67%	98.48%	85.05%

We conduct several experiments to demonstrate the effectiveness of different modules in our framework. The ablation study is carried out with three cases. In the first case, the network is implemented without Spatial Path and Feature Fusion Module. The network in the second case does not include FFM, but use a concatenation function to combine Spatial Path and the downsampling path. The third case denotes the full BiLuNet. Table 1 reports the mIoUs (mean intersection over union) of the three cases using 100 images for evaluation. The average mIoUs are 78.93%, 82.10% and 85.05%, respectively. It demonstrates that the spatial path designed in our network does improve the segmentation results by preserving the spatial information from the X-ray image input. The ablation analysis also shows that our network can effectively combine two feature paths fused by Feature Fusion Module.

3.2 Lumbar Vertebra Inspection Results

The results of our MBNet tested on the images acquired before and after the operations are shown in Figs. 6(a)–(c) and (e)–(g), respectively. Two sample test

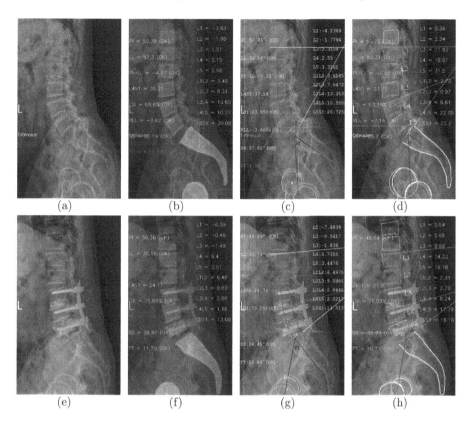

Fig. 6. The lumbar vertebra inspection with our MBNet and BiLuNet on X-ray images. (a), (e) the input X-ray images before and after surgery, respectively, (b), (f) Our MBNet results with the inspection results and the semantic segmentation of vertebrae, sacrum, left and right hip joints, in red, green, blue, and cyan, respectively, (c), (g) the reference annotation by a doctor, (d), (h) Our BiLuNet results with deriving the parameters from the segmentation and the identified shape and location of these objects (L1, L2, L3, L4, L5, S1, hip axis). (Color figure online)

X-ray images with the resolution of 2035×3408 captured before and after surgery are shown in Figs. 6(a) and (e), respectively. The semantic segmentation is carried out with four target classes (vertebra, sacrum, femoral head1, and femoral head2) represented by red, green, blue and cyan, respectively (see Figs. 6(b) and (f)). As shown in Figs. 6(b) and (f), the inspection results of our MBNet are very close to the annotation provided by doctors (Figs. 6(c) and (g)). To the best of our knowledge, no related studies are published for comparison. Thus, BiLuNet is trained with the same parameters and data for semantic segmentation of vertebrae, sacrum, and femoral heads. The post-processing is then carried out to identify the shape and location of the objects (L1, L2, L3, L4, L5, S1, hip axis). The locations of five vertebrae (L1 to L5), sacrum (S1) and hip axis (o) are used

Table 2. The standard range for our lumbar vertebra inspection.

Parameter	PI	LL	PImLL	LDI	RLL	SS	PT
Standard range	34°∼84°	31°∼79°	−10°∼10°	50%∼80%	−14°∼11°	−20°∼65°	5°∼30°

Table 3. The accuracy evaluation for the testing image shown in Fig. 6 (before surgery) for our MBNet and BiLuNet. Acc is the accuracy of our inspection results with respect to the annotation by doctors (GT).

Names	MBNet	BiLuNet	Ground-truth	Acc MBNet (%)	Acc BiLuNet (%)
PI°	50.38	50.73	52.84	95.08	95.78
LL°	57.30	53.31	58.16	98.21	89.90
PImLL°	−4.67	−2.58	−5.32	96.75	86.30
LDI%	68.60	63.38	63.85	84.17	98.43
RLL°	−3.62	−7.14	−3.60	99.92	85.84
SS°	56.19	53.70	57.82	98.08	95.15
PT°	4.82	−2.96	4.98	99.36	68.24

to derive the parameters for lumbar vertebra inspection as shown in Figs. 6(d) and (h).

Table 2 shows the standard ranges of common interests, PI, LL, PImLL, LDI, RLL, SS and PT [36] . The angles PI and PT are determined by the center of S1 and the hip axis, so they are affected by the locations of femoral heads and S1. More specifically, the derivation of most parameters depends on the accuracy of S1. PImLL (PI – LL) presents an appreciation of the lordosis required for a given PI value and quantifies the mismatch between pelvic morphology and the lumbar curve [32]. The value LDI and the angle RLL are defined by

$$LDI = (L4S1/LL) \tag{4}$$
$$RLL = LL - (0.62 \cdot PI + 29) \tag{5}$$

In the experiments, the inspection result is marked as OK if the value is in the standard range.

To evaluate our parameter estimation with respect to the annotated values (ground-truth), we define the accuracy as

$$Acc = 1 - \frac{|v_e - v_a|}{r_s} \tag{6}$$

where v_e and v_a are the parameter estimates of our inspection and the value annotated by doctors, respectively, and r_s is the standard range shown in Table 2. The accuracy evaluation of lumbar vertebra inspection is shown in Table 3 and 4. Comparative accuracy levels are obtained for both the preoperative and postoperative images.

This testing set consists of 100 X-ray images, with a half before and a half after surgeries. The testing images are selected randomly based on the femoral

Table 4. The accuracy evaluation for the testing image shown in Fig. 6 (after surgery) for our MBNet and BiLuNet. Acc is the accuracy of our inspection results with respect to the annotation by doctors (GT).

Names	MBNet	BiLuNet	Ground-truth	Acc MBNet(%)	Acc BiLuNet (%)
PI°	50.36	46.64	49.29	97.86	95.08
LL°	35.16	30.39	33.79	97.15	98.21
PImLL°	16.53	16.25	15.50	94.85	96.75
LDI%	75.68	71.09	73.15	91.57	84.17
RLL°	−24.71	−27.53	−25.77	95.76	99.92
SS°	38.57	35.93	38.45	99.86	98.08
PT°	11.79	10.71	10.84	96.2	99.36

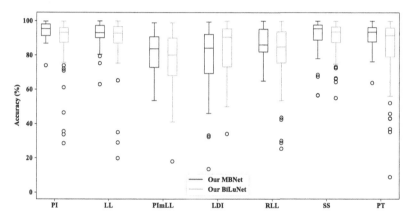

Fig. 7. The accuracy evaluation for Our MBNet and BiLuNet using 100 X-ray images (with a half before surgery and half after surgery). They are calculated based on the comparison with the inspection result annotated by doctors.

head locations. Figure 7 shows the evaluation results of 100 images with our MBNet and BiLuNet. MBNet is able to achieve the high average accuracy of PI, LL, PImLL, LDI, RLL, SS, and PT with 94.48%, 92.10%, 81.09%, 78.55%, 86.63%, 91.29%, and 91.15%, respectively. The mean accuracy of LDI is lower than other cases due to the limited training data for a large variation range. BiLuNet is able to achieve the average accuracy of PI, LL, PImLL, LDI, RLL, SS, and PT with 88.30%, 89.24%, 78.14%, 83.90%, 81.36%, 90.10%, and 83.77%, respectively. The parameter inspection of PT, PI, PImLL, and RLL is affected by the femoral head locations and less accurate as expected. The X-ray images with femoral heads unclear or missing are considered as challenging cases. One typical example is shown in Fig. 8, where the second femoral head is not available for segmentation.

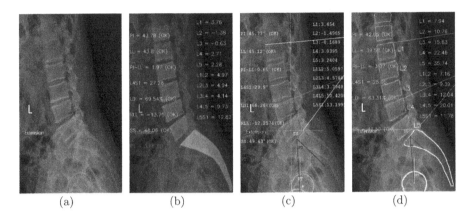

(a)   (b)   (c)   (d)

Fig. 8. Our MBNet and BiLuNet results with the challenging case of the second femoral head. (a) the input X-ray images before surgery, (b) Our MBNet results with the inspection results and the semantic segmentation of vertebrae, sacrum, left and right hip joints, in red, green, blue and cyan, respectively, (c) is the reference annotation by a doctor, (d) Our BiLuNet results with deriving the parameters from the segmentation and the identified shape and location of these objects (L1, L2, L3, L4, L5, S1, hip axis). (Color figure online)

4   Conclusion

In this paper, we propose a multi-task deep neural network for the semantic segmentation of lumbar vertebrae as well as the parameter prediction for inspection and diagnosis. A multi-path convolutional neural network, BiLuNet, is presented for semantic segmentation on X-ray images. It is able to achieve high accuracy for the automated segmentation of lumbar vertebrae, sacrum, and femoral heads. In performance evaluation, our BiLuNet model with global pooling and spatial path outperforms other state-of-the-art semantic segmentation methods. Our MBNet is able to provide accurate parameters to the doctors for clinical diagnosis of low back pains. The experimental results have demonstrated that our approach is able to achieve high accuracy on lumbar vertebra inspection.

Acknowledgment. The authors would like to thank the support of this work in part by the Ministry of Science and Technology of Taiwan under Grant MOST 106-2221-E-194-004 is gratefully acknowledged.

References

1. Sekuboyina, A., et al.: Btrfly Net: vertebrae labelling with energy-based adversarial learning of local spine prior. In: Frangi, A.F., Schnabel, J.A., Davatzikos, C., Alberola-López, C., Fichtinger, G. (eds.) MICCAI 2018, Part IV. LNCS, vol. 11073, pp. 649–657. Springer, Cham (2018). https://doi.org/10.1007/978-3-030-00937-3_74

2. Han, Z., Wei, B., Leung, S., Chung, J., Li, S.: Towards automatic report generation in spine radiology using weakly supervised framework. In: Frangi, A.F., Schnabel, J.A., Davatzikos, C., Alberola-López, C., Fichtinger, G. (eds.) MICCAI 2018, Part IV. LNCS, vol. 11073, pp. 185–193. Springer, Cham (2018). https://doi.org/10.1007/978-3-030-00937-3_22

3. Zhang, Y., Miao, S., Mansi, T., Liao, R.: Task driven generative modeling for unsupervised domain adaptation: application to X-ray image segmentation. In: Frangi, A.F., Schnabel, J.A., Davatzikos, C., Alberola-López, C., Fichtinger, G. (eds.) MICCAI 2018, Part II. LNCS, vol. 11071, pp. 599–607. Springer, Cham (2018). https://doi.org/10.1007/978-3-030-00934-2_67

4. Horng, M., Kuok, C., Fu, M., Lin, C., Sun, Y.: Cobb angle measurement of spine from X-ray images using convolutional neural network. Comp. Math. Methods Med. **2019**, 6357171:1–6357171:18 (2019)

5. Kalichman, L., Kim, D.H., Li, L., Guermazi, A., Hunter, D.J.: Computed tomography-evaluated features of spinal degeneration: prevalence, intercorrelation, and association with self-reported low back pain. Spine J. Off. J. North Am. Spine Soc. **10**(3), 200–208 (2010)

6. Jamaludin, A., et al.: Automation of reading of radiological features from magnetic resonance images (MRIs) of the lumbar spine without human intervention is comparable with an expert radiologist. Eur. Spine J. **26**, 1374–1383 (2017)

7. Fu, M., et al.: Inter-rater and intra-rater agreement of magnetic resonance imaging findings in the lumbar spine: significant variability across degenerative conditions. Spine J. **14**, 2442–2448 (2014)

8. Tang, M., Valipour, S., Zhang, Z., Cobzas, D., Jagersand, M.: A deep level set method for image segmentation. In: Cardoso, M.J., et al. (eds.) DLMIA/ML-CDS -2017. LNCS, vol. 10553, pp. 126–134. Springer, Cham (2017). https://doi.org/10.1007/978-3-319-67558-9_15

9. Ebrahimi, S., Angelini, E., Gajny, L., Skalli, W.: Lumbar spine posterior corner detection in X-rays using haar-based features. In: 2016 IEEE 13th International Symposium on Biomedical Imaging (ISBI), pp. 180–183 (2016)

10. Moeskops, P., et al.: Deep learning for multi-task medical image segmentation in multiple modalities. CoRR abs/1704.03379 (2017)

11. Ebner, M., et al.: An automated localization, segmentation and reconstruction framework for fetal brain MRI. In: Frangi, A.F., Schnabel, J.A., Davatzikos, C., Alberola-López, C., Fichtinger, G. (eds.) MICCAI 2018, Part I. LNCS, vol. 11070, pp. 313–320. Springer, Cham (2018). https://doi.org/10.1007/978-3-030-00928-1_36

12. Al Arif, S.M.M.R., Knapp, K., Slabaugh, G.: SPNet: shape prediction using a fully convolutional neural network. In: Frangi, A.F., Schnabel, J.A., Davatzikos, C., Alberola-López, C., Fichtinger, G. (eds.) MICCAI 2018, Part I. LNCS, vol. 11070, pp. 430–439. Springer, Cham (2018). https://doi.org/10.1007/978-3-030-00928-1_49

13. Li, X., et al.: 3D multi-scale FCN with random modality voxel dropout learning for intervertebral disc localization and segmentation from multi-modality MR images. Med. Image Anal. **45**, 41–54 (2018)

14. Liu, C., Zhao, L.: Intervertebral disc segmentation and localization from multi-modality MR images with 2.5D multi-scale fully convolutional network and geometric constraint post-processing. In: Zheng, G., Belavy, D., Cai, Y., Li, S. (eds.) CSI 2018. LNCS, vol. 11397, pp. 144–153. Springer, Cham (2019). https://doi.org/10.1007/978-3-030-13736-6_12

15. Larhmam, M.A., Mahmoudi, S., Benjelloun, M.: Semi-automatic detection of cervical vertebrae in X-ray images using generalized hough transform. In: 2012 3rd International Conference on Image Processing Theory, Tools and Applications (IPTA), pp. 396–401 (2012)

16. Nie, D., Gao, Y., Wang, L., Shen, D.: ASDNet: attention based semi-supervised deep networks for medical image segmentation. In: Frangi, A.F., Schnabel, J.A., Davatzikos, C., Alberola-López, C., Fichtinger, G. (eds.) MICCAI 2018, Part IV. LNCS, vol. 11073, pp. 370–378. Springer, Cham (2018). https://doi.org/10.1007/978-3-030-00937-3_43

17. Ronneberger, O., Fischer, P., Brox, T.: U-Net: convolutional networks for biomedical image segmentation. In: Navab, N., Hornegger, J., Wells, W.M., Frangi, A.F. (eds.) MICCAI 2015, Part III. LNCS, vol. 9351, pp. 234–241. Springer, Cham (2015). https://doi.org/10.1007/978-3-319-24574-4_28

18. Girard, N., Charpiat, G., Tarabalka, Y.: Aligning and updating cadaster maps with aerial images by multi-task, multi-resolution deep learning. In: Jawahar, C.V., Li, H., Mori, G., Schindler, K. (eds.) ACCV 2018, Part V. LNCS, vol. 11365, pp. 675–690. Springer, Cham (2019). https://doi.org/10.1007/978-3-030-20873-8_43

19. Khalel, A., Tasar, O., Charpiat, G., Tarabalka, Y.: Multi-task deep learning for satellite image pansharpening and segmentation, pp. 4869–4872 (2019)

20. Chen, Q., et al.: A multi-task deep learning model for the classification of age-related macular degeneration. CoRR abs/1812.00422 (2018)

21. Li, X., Hu, X., Yu, L., Zhu, L., Fu, C.W., Heng, P.A.: Canet: Cross-disease attention network for joint diabetic retinopathy and diabetic macular edema grading (2019)

22. Liu, L., Dou, Q., Chen, H., Olatunji, I.E., Qin, J., Heng, P.-A.: MTMR-Net: multi-task deep learning with margin ranking loss for lung nodule analysis. In: Stoyanov, D., et al. (eds.) DLMIA/ML-CDS -2018. LNCS, vol. 11045, pp. 74–82. Springer, Cham (2018). https://doi.org/10.1007/978-3-030-00889-5_9

23. Xiao, L., Stephen, J.M., Wilson, T.W., Calhoun, V.D., Wang, Y.: A manifold regularized multi-task learning model for IQ prediction from two fMRI paradigms. IEEE Trans. Biomed. Eng. **67**, 796–806 (2020)

24. Sohn, S., et al.: Sagittal spinal alignment in asymptomatic patients over 30 years old in the Korean population. Acta Neurochir. **159**(6), 1119–1128 (2017). https://doi.org/10.1007/s00701-017-3100-9

25. Labelle, H., Roussouly, P., Berthonnaud, E., Dimnet, J., O'Brien, M.: The importance of spino-pelvic balance in l5–s1 developmental spondylolisthesis. Spine **30**, S27–34 (2005)

26. Janssen, M., Kouwenhoven, J.W., Castelein, R.: The role of posteriorly directed shear loads acting on a pre-rotated growing spine: a hypothesis on the pathogenesis of idiopathic scoliosis. Stud. Health Technol. Inf. **158**, 112–7 (2010)

27. Weinberg, D., Morris, W., Gebhart, J., Liu, R.: Pelvic incidence: an anatomic investigation of 880 cadaveric specimens. Eur. Spine J. **25**, 3589–3595 (2015)

28. Singh, R., Yadav, S., Sood, S., Yadav, R., Rohilla, R.: Spino-pelvic radiological parameters in normal Indian population. SICOT-J **4**, 14 (2018)

29. Natarajan, R., Andersson, G.: Lumbar disc degeneration is an equally important risk factor as lumbar fusion for causing adjacent segment disc disease: Fusion, degeneration adjacent disc disease. J. Orthop. Res. **35**, 123–130 (2016)

30. Legaye, J. In: Analysis of the Dynamic Sagittal Balance of the Lumbo-Pelvi-Femoral Complex (2011)

31. Kim, M., Lee, S.H., Kim, E.S., Eoh, W., Chung, S.S., Lee, C.S.: The impact of sagittal balance on clinical results after posterior interbody fusion for patients with degenerative spondylolisthesis: A pilot study. BMC Musculoskelet. Disor **12**, 69 (2011). https://doi.org/10.1186/1471-2474-12-69

32. Yilgor, C., et al.: Relative lumbar lordosis and lordosis distribution index: individualized pelvic incidence-based proportional parameters that quantify lumbar lordosis more precisely than the concept of pelvic incidence minus lumbar lordosis. Neurosurg. Focus **43**, E5 (2017)

33. Yu, C., Wang, J., Peng, C., Gao, C., Yu, G., Sang, N.: Bisenet: Bilateral segmentation network for real-time semantic segmentation. CoRR abs/1808.00897 (2018)

34. Zhou, Z., Siddiquee, M.M.R., Tajbakhsh, N., Liang, J.: Unet++: A nested u-net architecture for medical image segmentation. CoRR abs/1807.10165 (2018)

35. Zhao, H., Shi, J., Qi, X., Wang, X., Jia, J.: Pyramid scene parsing network. In: 2017 IEEE Conference on Computer Vision and Pattern Recognition, CVPR 2017, Honolulu, HI, USA, 21–26 July 2017, pp. 6230–6239 (2017)

36. Zheng, G.Q., et al.: Relationship between postoperative lordosis distribution index and adjacent segment disease following L4–S1 posterior lumbar interbody fusion. J. Orthop. Surg. Res. **15**, 129 (2020). https://doi.org/10.1186/s13018-020-01630-9

Attention-Based Fine-Grained Classification of Bone Marrow Cells

Weining Wang[1], Peirong Guo[1], Lemin Li[1], Yan Tan[2], Hongxia Shi[2], Yan Wei[2], and Xiangmin Xu[1,3(✉)]

[1] South China University of Technology, Guangzhou, China
[2] Peking University People's Hospital, Beijing, China
[3] Institute of Modern Industrial Technology of SCUT in Zhongshan, Zhongshan, China
xmxu@scut.edu.cn

Abstract. Computer aided fine-grained classification of bone marrow cells is a significant task because manual morphological examination is time-consuming and highly dependent on the expert knowledge. Limited methods are proposed for the fine-grained classification of bone marrow cells. This can be partially attributed to challenges of insufficient data, high intra-class and low inter-class variances.

In this work, we design a novel framework Attention-based Suppression and Attention-based Enhancement Net (ASAE-Net) to better distinguish different classes. Concretely, inspired by recent advances of weakly supervised learning, we develop an Attention-based Suppression and Attention-based Enhancement (ASAE) layer to capture subtle differences between cells. In ASAE layer, two parallel modules with no training parameters improve the discrimination in two different ways. Furthermore, we propose a Gradient-boosting Maximum-Minimum Cross Entropy (GMMCE) loss to reduce the confusion between subclasses. In order to decrease the intra-class variance, we adjust the hue in a simple way. In addition, we adopt a balanced sampler aiming to alleviate the issue of the data imbalance.

Extensive experiments prove the effectiveness of our method. Our approach achieves favorable performance against other methods on our dataset.

Keywords: Fine-grained classification · Bone marrow cell · Attention · Weakly supervised learning

1 Introduction

Morphological examination of bone marrow cells is the most commonly used diagnostic method for acute leukemia. The manual classification method, which is time-consuming and repetitive, highly depends on the knowledge of experts and is prone to variances among observers. Automatic classification based on computers is conducive to diagnosing acute leukemia efficiently. The computer-aided classification can quickly obtain objective results [1,2], effectively process

© Springer Nature Switzerland AG 2021
H. Ishikawa et al. (Eds.): ACCV 2020, LNCS 12626, pp. 652–668, 2021.
https://doi.org/10.1007/978-3-030-69541-5_39

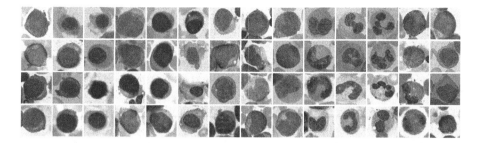

Fig. 1. Some instances in our bone marrow cell dateset. Bone marrow cells are classified into 14 categories for fine-grained classification in our dataset and one column represents one category. Four cell images in each category are randomly selected and shown in a single column.

a large amount of data [3] and greatly reduce the workload of doctors. It has attracted the attention of many scholars. We conduct a survey on the bone marrow cell classification in bone marrow smears and a similar task done on blood cells in peripheral blood smears.

In the past 40 years, most of the methods for these two similar tasks are based on traditional image processing methods like [4–10], consisting of three steps including image segmentation, feature extraction and image classification. With the development of deep learning, many researchers [11–19] consider to adopt it to these tasks.

To be specific, bone marrow cell classification can be divided into two categories including coarse-grained and fine-grained classification. Coarse-grained classification only considers meta-categories like lymphocytes and monocytes, which does not meet the requirements in the clinical practice. Fine-grained classification aims to distinguish similar sub-categories in different maturity stages.

Challenges come from three aspects: (1) High intra-class variances. Cells belonging to the same class may be variant in the saturation, hue and brightness due to the light, dyeing duration and dose. In addition, crowding degree and background complexity vary especially in bone marrow smears. (2) Low inter-class variances. Bone marrow cells in adjacent maturity stages can be easily confused and hard to be distinguished even by experts. (3) Limited and imbalanced datasets. It takes a large amount of time for experts to label them with fine-grained annotations. Currently, there are few studies on the fine-grained classification of bone marrow cells to tackle the aforementioned challenges. As shown in Fig. 1, we find the above challenges in our dataset.

Fine-grained classification has made great progress in some other areas, such as birds [20], flowers [21] and cars [22]. Common methods imitate the process of experts to locate discriminative regions and extract the features. The existing methods can be divided into two categories according to whether leveraging extra annotations or not. Methods relying on extra annotations like [20] meet the demands on the knowledge of experts so they do not suit for medical images analysis because of its high cost. Some other methods like [23–33] with only image-level annotations locate key parts of an object based on the weakly supervised learning, which improves the availability and scalability. Motivated by it, we aim to design a flexible and efficient architecture for the task of classification on bone marrow cells with the help of weakly supervised learning.

Based on our observation, the existing weakly supervised methods have one or more limitations as follows: (1) Some models like [26] can locate object parts or mine discriminative regions with a limited quantity, which cannot be easily modified. (2) Some models can cover only a part of discriminative region because the loss focuses mainly on the most discriminative region and ignores the others. (3) Currently, some methods like Attention-based Dropout Layer [23] and Diversification Block [33] force the model to learn from other regions by discarding some discriminative regions while they have some disadvantages. ADL may discard excessive information. (4) Some models like [25,29] have disadvantages of repeated training, extra classification branches and multiple forward computations. Our model overcomes the disadvantages mentioned above.

The contributions of this paper are as follows:

1. We propose a two-branch framework called Attention-based Suppression and Attention-based Enhancement Net (ASAE-Net) well designed for the fine-grained classification of bone marrow cells. ASAE-Net achieves the superiority without increasing training parameters compared with the backbone.
2. Our model can flexibly locate multiple discriminative regions with an unlimited quantity. Our Attention-based Suppression (AS) branch adopts a suppression approach with two restrictions leading to a good performance.
3. Our Gradient-boosting Maximum-Minimum Cross Entropy (GMMCE) loss alleviates the problem of the category confusion and improves the classification performance.
4. We adopt a balanced sampler and the hue adjustment aiming to alleviate the problem of data imbalance and the high intra-class variance.
5. Our method outperforms the existing fine-grained classification methods for bone marrow cells and some other methods based on attention mechanism.

The rest of the paper is organized as follows. We first review the related work of bone marrow cell classification and Gradient-boosting Cross Entropy loss in Sect. 2. Then we illustrate our proposed ASAE-Net, GMMCE loss and improved strategies on dataset in Sect. 3. In Sect. 4, adequate experiments and results are presented and analyzed. We conclude our work in Sect. 5.

2   Related Work

2.1   Bone Marrow Cell Classification

As we know, convolutional neural network (CNN) is a strong tool for image processing. In the last few years, CNNs are widely adopted in many medical applications [18,34–36]. In the coarse-grained classification on bone marrow cells and blood cells, many methods have gained great performance. However, there are few studies for the fine-grained classification on them.

In [11], Chandradevan et al. propose a two-stage method to detect and classify bone marrow cells in the fine-grained field. In the classification phase, they adopt ensembled models to improve the performance. Proposed by Qin et al., Cell3Net [17] is a residual model to classify cells into 40 categories. The model consists of seven convolutional layers, three pooling layers, three residual layers, two fully-connected layers and an output layer, gaining an accuracy of 76.84%. Similarly, Jiang et al. [14] design a 33-layers network called WBCNet referring to AlexNet [37], and improve its accuracy by modifying the residual layers and the activation function. Based on our observation, the model ensemble is effective but complicated. Cell3Net and WBCNet are simple but lack of pertinence for the fine-grained classification and the distribution of categories.

Compared with them, our model is well-designed, showing its effectiveness on the fine-grained classification task of bone marrow cells.

2.2 Gradient-Boosting Cross Entropy Loss

Cross entropy loss is one of the most widely used loss functions in the classification task. $\mathbf{s}$ and l are respectively the confidence scores and the true label. J is the set of all categories. The loss can be defined as:

$$CE(\mathbf{s}, l) = -log \frac{exp(s_l)}{\sum_{i \in J} exp(s_i)} \tag{1}$$

According to the definition, CE loss treats all negative categories equally. However, in our task, some negative classes are confusable and obtain relatively high confidence scores from the model. To ease this problem, Gradient-boosting Cross Entropy (GCE) loss presented in [33] focuses on the true category and some of the negative categories according to different confidence scores. Concretely, it only considers negative classes with top-k highest scores. $J_>^{'}$ is the set of negative classes with top-k highest scores. GCE can be defined as:

$$GCE(\mathbf{s}, l) = -log \frac{exp(s_l)}{exp(s_l) + \sum_{i \in J_>^{'}} exp(s_i)} \tag{2}$$

Our Gradient-boosting Maximum-Minimum Cross Entropy (GMMCE) loss enhances GCE loss by considering negative classes with bottom-k lowest scores.

3 Proposed Method

In this section, we present our attention-based framework ASAE-Net for the fine-grained classification of bone marrow cells, as shown in Fig. 2. This is a two-branch framework containing an attention-based suppression branch and an attention-based enhancement branch. Furthermore, we make a comparison between the proposed ASAE layer and other similar works. Then we introduce our proposed GMMCE loss, a preprocessing strategy and a sampling strategy for specific problems.

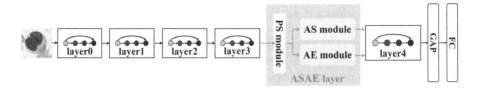

Fig. 2. The network structure of ASAE-Net. It contains the backbone (divided into five layers) and an ASAE layer. The ASAE layer consists of PS module, AS module and AE module.

3.1 Framework

ASAE-Net is designed aiming to capture more discriminative regions to improve the ability of distinguishing cells with subtle differences. Our ASAE-Net is formed by a common backbone and a novel ASAE layer, which is plug-and-play to capture more discriminative regions precisely without training parameters.

To build our ASAE-Net, we adopt ResNet-50 [38] as our backbone and divide it into five layers (layer0, layer1, layer2, layer3, layer4) based on the output feature size. As we know, shallow layers prefer to learn fundamental features like the texture and the shape. As pointed out by Choe et al. in [23], masks in the deep layers discard discriminative regions more precisely. Hence, we decide to insert our ASAE layer, which includes Attention-based Suppression branch and Attention-based Enhancement branch, in a deep layer (layer3 or layer4). Subsequently, we conduct experiments on the effect of the inserted position of our Attention-based Suppression branch.

We divide our framework into two parts by the inserted position. In the training phase, the front part takes an image as input, and feeds its own output, $F_{mid} \in R^{C \times H \times W}$, to two parameter-shared branches. Then, an attention-based suppression mask M_{sup} and an attention-based enhancement map M_{enh} are generated respectively. Next, they are applied to F_{mid} by spatial-wise multiplication. Two new features are sent to the latter part to gain two probability distributions. We average them to gain the final probability. While in the testing phase, the input image skips our ASAE layer.

Our framework has two characteristics: (1) It is an end-to-end model without extra training parameters than the backbone. (2) It consists of two branches sharing parameters and promoting each other.

3.2 ASAE Layer

In this part, we introduce our proposed ASAE layer shown in Fig. 3. It contains three key modules including: (1) Peak Stimulation (PS) module. (2) Attention-based Suppression (AS) module. (3) Attention-based Enhancement (AE) module.

Peak Stimulation Module. It is proved in [39] that the local peak value of the class response map is corresponding to strong visual cues. Actually, when it comes to the feature maps in the hidden layer, we have the similar result. Hence, to obtain strong visual cues, we design a peak stimulation module to generate the peak distribution of feature maps.

Given the feature map $F \in R^{C \times H \times W}$, where C denotes the channel number and $H \times W$ denotes the shape of maps, the peak is defined as the maximum in a local region of $r \times r$. The positions of peaks are represented as $P = \{(i_1, j_1), (i_2, j_2), \cdots, (i_N, j_N)\}$, where N is the total number of local peaks, which may be different in different feature maps.

Our peak stimulation module consists of two pooling layers as shown in Fig. 3. The first one is an average pooling layer to squeeze the channel information to form a self-attention map $M_{att} \in R^{H \times W}$. The higher value in the map represents the more discriminative ability. The second one is a max pooling layer of size r to obtain the peak distribution including values and positions in the self-attention map. In this way, we can effectively approximate the spatial distribution of components.

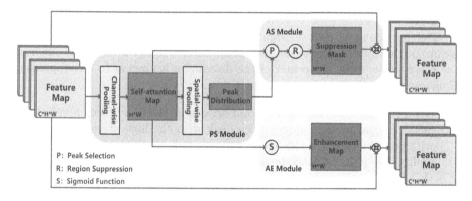

Fig. 3. Attention-based Suppression and Attention-based Enhancement (ASAE) layer. The self-attention map and peak distribution are generated by Peak Stimulation (PS) Module with two pooling layers. Attention-based Suppression (AS) Module generates a suppression mask by adopting two strategies. Attention-based Enhancement (AE) Module transfers the self-attention map into an enhancement map by using Sigmoid Function. Two new feature maps are generated by using spatial-wise multiplication.

The peak stimulation module can effectively capture multiple local peaks with an unlimited quantity but without extra training parameters. In this module, we generate a self-attention map for the following two modules and the peak distribution for the following AS module.

Attention-Based Suppression Module. Based on the self-attention map and the peak distribution from the peak stimulation module, our proposed AS module hides one discriminative region in the training phase aiming to force the model to locate and learn from other discriminative regions.

As illustrated above, local peak values are corresponding to strong visual cues within images. Hence, we define a peak and its local region as a discriminative region. Higher values represent higher discrimination. It has advantages as follows: (1) No manual part annotations required. (2) No extra training parameters. (3) Flexibility on the number of discriminative regions. (4) Flexibility to be applied in different layers.

A keypoint of AS module is how to suppress the discriminative regions. To design a better method, we firstly explore some similar approaches. Dropout [40], Spatial Dropout [41], MaxDrop [42], Dropblock [43] are some popular methods of suppression. We find these methods unsuitable for our task. When discarding the max values, it encounters the high-correlation problem and when randomly discarding regions, it may not discard a discriminative one. Also, without restrictions on areas and values, the model may discard more than one discriminative region, which is bad for the latter learning.

To avoid the above disadvantages, we restrict the suppression size and the value threshold when discarding a region. Also, we ensure our model to discard only one discriminative region effectively. We present our strategies in the following.

The first one is *the peak selection strategy*. After the peak stimulation module, we obtain multiple local peaks in each image. Our strategy is to choose one from the top-k peaks to be the center of the discriminative region to be suppressed. Concretely, our strategy is as follows:

(1) Set the number of candidates k and arrange peaks in a descending order.
(2) Select a local peak randomly. The peak with the highest value is selected with probability p_{top1}, which means the most discriminative one. With probability $1 - p_{top1}$, a local peak is randomly selected from top-2 to top-k ($k \geq 2$).

In the fine-grained classification, different classes of cells often have subtle differences. With our strategy of peak selection, we choose randomly a discriminative region to suppress. In this way, we decrease the risk of mis-classification when cells suffer from lack of salient characteristics like cytoplasmic particles.

The second one is *the region suppression strategy* with two restrictions. We define the suppressed region as the one centered on the selected local peak. We leverage an area threshold and a value threshold to restrict the local region. The concrete operations are as follows:

(1) Set a suppression ratio γ and an area threshold β.
(2) Define the value threshold α as the product of peak value $Peak$ and γ:

$$\alpha = Peak * \gamma \tag{3}$$

(3) Define the original suppression region R_{sup} in M_{att} to be a square with a local peak at the center and the length of side $\sqrt{\beta}$.

(4) Define a suppression mask M_{sup} with the same shape of M_{att}.

(5) Set the value v_{ij}^{sup} in M_{sup} to be 0, if v_{ij}^{att} in M_{att} is higher than α and the pixel (i, j) is in R_{sup} at the same time. Otherwise set it to be 1.

$$v_{ij}^{sup} = \begin{cases} 0, & (i, j) \ in \ R_{sup} \cap v_{ij}^{att} \geq \alpha \\ 1, & otherwise \end{cases} \tag{4}$$

After obtaining M_{sup}, we apply it to the input feature map by spatial-wise multiplication to obtain F_{sup} with a discriminative region suppressed. The same region is suppressed in different channels.

The superiors of our AS module lie in: (1) It hides only one discriminative region in a single iteration. (2) It randomly discards different discriminative regions to encourage the model to learn from other regions. (3) It adopts useful strategies to avoid the model from discarding excessive information by two restrictions. (4) It has no training parameters.

Attention-Based Enhancement Module. The AE module aims to strengthen the most discriminative region to improve the performance. In this module, we adopt the same method as ADL [23] to generate an enhancement map $M_{enh} \in R^{H \times W}$. It is yielded by using sigmoid function on the self-attention map. In M_{enh}, the pixel is discriminative if the value is close to 1. Similar to the AS module, M_{enh} is applied to the feature map by spatial-wise multiplication to obtain F_{enh}. Similarly, the AE module has no training parameters.

3.3   Comparison with Similar Methods

Comparison with Attention-Based Dropout Layer (ADL) [23]. From the motivation, we both aim to hide the discriminative regions and encourage the model to learn from others.

From the architecture, we both generate a suppression mask and an enhancement map but we differ from each other when generating the suppression mask. ADL discards all pixels whose values are higher than the value threshold. Without restricting the area or the continuity, it may easily discard the most discriminative and several sub-discriminative regions at the same time. Thus the feature maps lose excessive information. However, our ASAE layer adopts the suppression ratio and the area threshold to restrict the discriminative region with a local peak in the center, in which way it avoids discarding too many continuous discriminative regions. At the same time, our AS module can sometimes discard a sub-discriminative region instead of the most discriminative one, which alleviates the problem of subtle differences.

From the combination of two branches, ADL randomly selects one branch in one time while ASAE-Net uses two branches at the same time by averaging the two probability distributions, which is better for the information learning.

Comparison with Diversification Block (DB) [33]. From the motivation, we both aim to erase discriminative regions to enhance the ability of feature learning.

From the input size, the channel of the input is limited to be the class number in DB while our ASAE layer does not restrict the size of the input or the channel number, which is more flexible to be inserted into the backbone.

From the suppression mask, DB discards different regions in different channels while our layer discards the same regions in all input channels, which is more close to the human behavior and increases the robustness.

3.4   GMMCE Loss

In multiple-instance learning, it is proved that the regions with max and min scores are both important [44] though they can bring in different kinds of information. Motivated by it and GCE loss introduced in Sect. 2.2, we design an enhanced loss called GMMCE loss to focus on both high and low confidence scores.

Following the setting and denotations of GCE loss, J is the set of all categories and J' is the set of negative categories. s_i is the confidence score of category i. $J'_>$ and $J'_<$ can be defined as:

$$J'_> = \left\{ i : i \in J' \cap s_i \geqslant t_{k+} \right\} \tag{5}$$

$$J'_< = \left\{ i : i \in J' \cap s_i \leqslant t_{k-} \right\} \tag{6}$$

where t_{k+} and t_{k-} denote the k^+th highest and k^-th lowest confidence scores in J'. We denote l as the true label. It is easy to find the relationship:

$$J'_> + \{l\} \subset J'_> + J'_< + \{l\} \subset J' + \{l\} = J \tag{7}$$

Our GMMCE loss and its gradient can be defined as:

$$GMMCE(\mathbf{s}, l) = -\log \frac{exp(s_l)}{exp(s_l) + \sum_{i \in J'_>} exp(s_i) + \sum_{i \in J'_<} exp(s_i)} \tag{8}$$

$$\frac{\partial GMMCE(\mathbf{s}, l)}{\partial s_c} = \begin{cases} \frac{exp(s_l)}{exp(s_l) + \sum_{i \in J'_<} exp(s_i) + \sum_{i \in J'_>} exp(s_i)}, & c \in \left\{ J'_> + J'_< \right\} \\ \frac{exp(s_l)}{exp(s_l) + \sum_{i \in J'_<} exp(s_i) + \sum_{i \in J'_>} exp(s_i)} - 1, & c = l \end{cases} \tag{9}$$

Compared with CE and GCE [33], we can obtain the relationship:

$$\frac{\partial GCE(\mathbf{s}, l)}{\partial s_c} > \frac{\partial GMMCE(\mathbf{s}, l)}{\partial s_c} > \frac{\partial CE(\mathbf{s}, l)}{\partial s_c} \tag{10}$$

For the ground truth label and the confusing negative classes, the gradient of GMMCE falls in between GCE and CE, which implies a moderate update rate. GMMCE focuses on negative classes with high scores and low scores. The negative classes with low scores can be regarded as a regularization method like label smoothing, which can avoid the model from over-fitting.

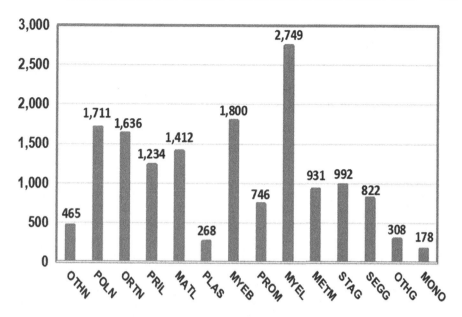

Fig. 4. The category distribution of our dataset.

3.5 Preprocessing and Sampling Strategies

As illustrated above, bone marrow cell datasets generally suffer from severe imbalance and high intra-class variances. In this part, we introduce our approaches to adjust the hue and sample data during training.

Hue Adjustment. Generally, images of bone marrow cells have variant saturation, hue and brightness due to the dyeing duration, dyeing dose and light, even in the same class. The uniform hue improves the classification accuracy by decreasing the intra-class variance. Based on the consideration, we adopt a linear transformation in H channel of images to adjust the hue of images. Steps are as follows:

(1) Convert an RGB image into an HSV image.
(2) Conduct a linear transformation in the H channel of images as:

$$h_{out} = \frac{Max - Min}{max - min}(h_{in} - min) + Min \tag{11}$$

where h_{in} and h_{out} denote the values of H channel before and after the transformation. Max and Min denote the highest and lowest target values of the output while max and min denote the highest and lowest values of the input.

Balanced Sampler. Based on our observation, bone marrow cell datasets generally face the challenge of severe imbalance due to the distribution of cells in bone marrow smears. Classes with few training samples may have a low true positive rate without balancing strategies. Because of it, we adopt a balanced sampler to alleviate the imbalance without augmenting data offline.

Concretely, in a single iteration, we sample the same number of images in different classes from the train set. Hence, the balanced sampler can make the model learn from all classes in an equal probability.

4   Experiments

4.1   Dataset

Our dataset contains 15,252 images of 27 classes of bone marrow cells. Cells are cropped by 10 medical students and annotated by 3 medical experts. Some classes contain few images so we combine them into 14 classes according to the expert advice. The 14 classes are named respectively Other Normoblast (OTHN), Poly-chromatic Normoblast (POLN), Orthochromatic Normoblast (ORTN), Primitive Lymphocyte (PRIL), Mature Lymphocyte (MATL), Plasma Cell (PLAS), Myeloblast (MYEB), Promyelocyte (PROM), Myelocyte (MYEL), Metamyelocyte (METM), Neutrophilic Stab Granulocyte (STAG), Neutrophilic Segmented Granulocyte (SEGG), Other Granulocyte (OTHG), Monocyte (MONO). Some instances in our dataset are shown in Fig. 1. The 14 columns from the left to the right follow the order listed above. The distribution of classes is shown in Fig. 4.

4.2   Implementation Details

We adopt the stratified sampling to divide our dataset into the train set and the test set in a ratio of 8:2. Concretely, the train set includes 12,201 images and the test set includes 3,051 images. We conduct the same method of data augmentation as [38]. Especially, we random crop the input images into the size of 224×224. Besides, we add random vertical flip, rotation and color jitter to our train set, while an offline augmentation is excluded.

In this work, we choose ResNet-50 [38] as our backbone. We use SGD with a batch size of 84. The weight decay is set as $1e-4$ and the momentum is set as 0.9. The initial learning rate is set to be $1e-3$ and decreases to 85% every 2 epochs.

The kernel size in PS module is set as 5. We set p_{top1} as 0.7 and k as 5 for peak selection. γ and β in AS module are 0.8 and 36. k^+ and k^- for GMMCE loss are both 3. Our experiments are implemented with PyTorch.

4.3   Ablation Study

To fully evaluate our method, progressive experiments are conducted to verify the effectiveness of the hue adjustment and the balanced sampler, our ASAE layer and GMMCE loss. Further, we compare our method with other works on bone marrow cells.

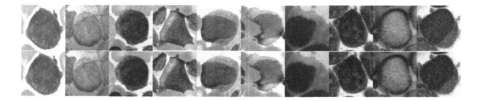

Fig. 5. Effect of the hue adjustment. The upper row shows some cells in our dataset before the hue adjustment. The below row shows the corresponding cells after the hue adjustment.

Table 1. Ablation experiments on the hue adjustment and the balanced sampler

Hue adjustment	Balanced sampler	Accuracy(%)
		72.61
✓		73.02
✓	✓	**73.53**

Hue Adjustment and Balanced Sampler. As illustrated in Sect. 3.5, the variance of hue increases the intra-class variance. In our dataset, we adjust the hue of images to be close to the purple hue. Hence, we set Max as 155 and Min as 125. Some examples before and after the adjustment are seen in Fig. 5. As shown in Table 1, applying the hue adjustment to our dataset increases our accuracy from 72.61% to 73.02%. It indicates that the uniform hue makes sense to increase the accuracy of our model.

As shown in Fig. 4, the problem of the class imbalance is severe in our dataset. Without the balanced sampler, we find the number of monocytes to be 0 or 1 in many batches. We randomly sample 6 images in each class to form a single batch in an iteration and the balanced sampler effectively avoids the absence of some classes of cells in a batch. With the balanced sampler, the accuracy increases from 73.02% to 73.53%. It indicates the effectiveness of a balanced sampler.

ASAE Layer. We propose an AS branch to hide a discriminative region in order to force the model to learn better from the others. Also, we propose a novel ASAE-Net based on ResNet-50 with two branches sharing parameters. We conduct experiments to verify the effectiveness of our ASAE-Net and explore which layer to insert our AS branch. To better verify the effectiveness of our proposed ASAE layer, we also conduct experiments on different backbones including VGG-16 [45] and ResNet-18 [38].

Based on the results in Table 2, ResNet-50 benefits from our AS branch. With AS branch inserted after layer3, our model gains 1.26% improvement from 73.53% to 74.79% and with AS branch inserted after layer4, our model gains 0.50% improvement from 73.53% to 74.03%. It demonstrates AS branch is more effective when inserted after layer3.

Table 2. Ablation experiments on ASAE layer

Network	Accuracy(%)
ResNet-50	73.53
ResNet-50 + AS branch (after layer4)	74.03
ResNet-50 + AS branch (after layer3)	74.79
ResNet-50 + ASAE layer (after layer3)	**75.11**

Table 3. Experiments on different backbones

Network	Accuracy(%)
VGG-16	71.21
VGG-16 + ASAE layer	**72.03**
ResNet-18	72.13
ResNet-18 + ASAE layer	**73.36**
ResNet-50	73.53
ResNet-50 + ASAE layer	**75.11**

Based on our analysis, with AS branch after layer3, suppressed feature maps are sent to layer4 and then modeled in a non-linear way. The non-linear model exploits the information of suppressed feature maps. However, when AS branch is inserted after layer4, suppressed feature maps are sent to the classifier directly, which cannot maximize its effect.

Also, when we insert our AE branch into ResNet-50, we gain 0.57% improvement. When we combine AS branch and AE branch together with sharing parameters, our model gains 0.32% improvement than using a single AS branch. It shows that the two branches promote each other. Also, it verifies that our ASAE-Net with ASAE layer after layer3 is effective without increasing training parameters.

Based on the results in Table 3, three different backbones gain different degrees of improvement when an ASAE layer is inserted after the penultimate layer. VGG-16 gains 0.82% improvement from 71.21% to 72.03% and ResNet-18 gains 1.23% from 72.13% to 73.36%. Also, ResNet-50 gains 1.58% improvement from 73.53% to 75.11%. The results amply prove the effectiveness of our ASAE layer.

GMMCE Loss. We propose a GMMCE loss to alleviate the problem of category confusion. To verify the effectiveness of it, we train the model with different losses including CE loss, GCE loss and GMMCE loss. Based on Table 4, training with our GMMCE loss outperforms the others. When trained with our proposed GMMCE loss, the model gains 2.52% and 1.21% improvement than CE and GCE loss respectively. The results prove that considering negative classes unequally is an effect strategy. Also, it verifies that taking negative classes with low confidence scores into consideration is effective when compared with GCE loss. As we illustrate, it can be regarded as a regularization method like label smoothing.

Table 4. Ablation experiments on the training loss

Training loss	Accuracy(%)
CE	75.11
GCE	76.42
GMMCE	**77.63**

4.4 Comparison with Other Methods

There are some related studies including WBCNet [14] and Cell3Net [17] in the fine-grained classification task of bone marrow cells. Also, there are several methods based on attention mechanism including Non-local Neural Network (NLNet) [46], Squeeze-and-Excitation Net (SENet) [47] and ADL [23]. We conduct experiments on different methods on our dataset. Among them, NLNet, SENet and ADL are based on the backbone ResNet-50 [38]. We discover our method outperforms all the others. It indicates our well-designed method for the fine-grained bone marrow cells classification is effective (Table 5).

Table 5. Comparison with other methods

Method	Accuracy(%)
WBCNet [14]	69.63
Cell3Net [17]	70.21
ResNet-50 [38]	72.61
NLNet [46]	73.12
SENet [47]	73.29
ADL [23]	73.84
Proposed method	**77.63**

5 Conclusion

In the paper, we proposed a two-branch framework called ASAE-Net based on attention mechanism and weakly supervised learning for the fine-grained classification of bone marrow cells. It can locate several discriminative regions with an unlimited quantity to capture subtle differences between subclasses. The inserted layer is plug-and-play without training parameters. Besides, we put forward a novel suppression approach to encourage the model to learn better. In addition, a

GMMCE loss is designed to alleviate the confusion. Due to the problems of data, we adopted a hue adjustment strategy and a balanced sampler. The experiments have shown the superiors of our method.

Acknowledgements. This work is supported in part by the National Natural Science Foundation of China under Grant U1801262, the Guangzhou Key Laboratory of Body Data Science under Grant 201605030011, the Science and Technology Project of Zhongshan under Grant 2019AG024 and the Guangzhou City Science and Technology Plan Project under Grant 202002020019.

References

1. Labati, R.D., Piuri, V., Scotti, F.: ALL-IDB: the acute lymphoblastic leukemia image database for image processing. In: International Conference on Image Processing (ICIP), pp. 2045–2048 (2011)
2. Pan, C., Park, D.S., Yang, Y., Yoo, H.M.: Leukocyte image segmentation by visual attention and extreme learning machine. Neural Comput. Appl. **21**, 1217–1227 (2012). https://doi.org/10.1007/s00521-011-0522-9
3. Razzak, M.I., Naz, S.: Microscopic blood smear segmentation and classification using deep contour aware CNN and extreme machine learning. In: Computer Vision and Pattern Recognition Workshops (CVPRW), pp. 801–807 (2017)
4. Hegde, R.B., Prasad, K., Hebbar, H., Singh, B.M.K.: Development of a robust algorithm for detection of nuclei and classification of white blood cells in peripheral blood smear images. J. Med. Syst. **42**, 110 (2018). https://doi.org/10.1007/s10916-018-0962-1
5. Madhloom, H.T., Kareem, S.A., Ariffin, H.: A robust feature extraction and selection method for the recognition of lymphocytes versus acute lymphoblastic leukemia. In: Advanced Computer Science Applications and Technologies (ACSAT), pp. 330–335 (2012)
6. Rajendran, S., Arof, H., Mokhtar, N., Mubin, M., Yegappan, S., Ibrahim, F.: Dual modality search and retrieval technique analysis for leukemic information system. Sci. Res. Essays **6**, 247–255 (2011)
7. Ramesh, N., Dangott, B., Salama, M.E., Tasdizen, T.: Isolation and two-step classification of normal white blood cells in peripheral blood smears. J. Pathol. Inform. **3**, 13 (2012)
8. Sinha, N., Ramakrishnan, A.G.: Automation of differential blood count. In: Conference on Convergent Technologies for Asia-Pacific Region, vol. 2, pp. 547–551 (2003)
9. Theera-Umpon, N., Dhompongsa, S.: Morphological granulometric features of nucleus in automatic bone marrow white blood cell classification. IEEE Trans. Inf. Technol. Biomed. **11**, 353–359 (2007)
10. Vincent, I., Kwon, K., Lee, S., Moon, K.: Acute lymphoid leukemia classification using two-step neural network classifier. In: Frontiers of Computer Vision (FCV), pp. 1–4 (2015)
11. Chandradevan, R., et al.: Machine-based detection and classification for bone marrow aspirate differential counts: initial development focusing on nonneoplastic cells. Lab. Invest. **100**, 98–109 (2020)
12. Choi, J.W., et al.: White blood cell differential count of maturation stages in bone marrow smear using dual-stage convolutional neural networks. PLoS One **12**, e0189259 (2017)

13. Hegde, R.B., Prasad, K., Hebbar, H., Singh, B.M.K.: Comparison of traditional image processing and deep learning approaches for classification of white blood cells in peripheral blood smear images. Biocybern. Biomed. Eng. **39**, 382–392 (2019)
14. Jiang, M., Cheng, L., Qin, F., Du, L., Zhang, M.: White blood cells classification with deep convolutional neural networks. Int. J. Pattern Recognit. Artif. Intell. **32**, 1857006 (2018)
15. Liang, G., Hong, H., Xie, W., Zheng, L.: Combining convolutional neural network with recursive neural network for blood cell image classification. IEEE Access **6**, 36188–36197 (2018)
16. Matek, C., Schwarz, S., Spiekermann, K., Marr, C.: Human-level recognition of blast cells in acute myeloid leukemia with convolutional neural networks. bioRxiv (2019)
17. Qin, F., Gao, N., Peng, Y., Wu, Z., Shen, S., Grudtsin, A.: Fine-grained leukocyte classification with deep residual learning for microscopic images. Comput. Meth. Programs Biomed. **162**, 243–252 (2018)
18. Shahin, A.I., Guo, Y., Amin, K.M., Sharawi, A.A.: White blood cells identification system based on convolutional deep neural learning networks. Comput. Meth. Programs Biomed. **168**, 69–80 (2017)
19. Tiwari, P., et al.: Detection of subtype blood cells using deep learning. Cogn. Syst. Res. **52**, 1036–1044 (2018)
20. Zhang, N., Donahue, J., Girshick, R., Darrell, T.: Part-based R-CNNs for fine-grained category detection. In: Fleet, D., Pajdla, T., Schiele, B., Tuytelaars, T. (eds.) ECCV 2014, Part I. LNCS, vol. 8689, pp. 834–849. Springer, Cham (2014). https://doi.org/10.1007/978-3-319-10590-1_54
21. Angelova, A., Zhu, S., Lin, Y.: Image segmentation for large-scale subcategory flower recognition. In: Workshop on Applications of Computer Vision (WACV), pp. 39–45 (2013)
22. Yang, Z., Luo, T., Wang, D., Hu, Z., Gao, J., Wang, L.: Learning to navigate for fine-grained classification. In: Ferrari, V., Hebert, M., Sminchisescu, C., Weiss, Y. (eds.) ECCV 2018, Part XIV. LNCS, vol. 11218, pp. 438–454. Springer, Cham (2018). https://doi.org/10.1007/978-3-030-01264-9_26
23. Choe, J., Lee, S., Shim, H.: Attention-based dropout layer for weakly supervised single object localization and semantic segmentation. IEEE Trans. Pattern Anal. Mach. Intell. **1**, (2020). https://doi.org/10.1109/TPAMI.2020.2999099
24. Fu, J., Zheng, H., Mei, T.: Look closer to see better: recurrent attention convolutional neural network for fine-grained image recognition. In: Computer Vision and Pattern Recognition (CVPR), pp.4476–4484 (2017)
25. Hu, T., Qi, H.: See better before looking closer: Weakly supervised data augmentation network for fine-grained visual classification. arXiv:1901.09891 (2019)
26. Sun, M., Yuan, Y., Zhou, F., Ding, E.: Multi-attention multi-class constraint for fine-grained image recognition. In: Ferrari, V., Hebert, M., Sminchisescu, C., Weiss, Y. (eds.) ECCV 2018, Part XVI. LNCS, vol. 11220, pp. 834–850. Springer, Cham (2018). https://doi.org/10.1007/978-3-030-01270-0_49
27. Tianjun Xiao, Yichong Xu, Kuiyuan Yang, Jiaxing Zhang, Yuxin Peng, Zhang, Z.: The application of two-level attention models in deep convolutional neural network for fine-grained image classification. In: Computer Vision and Pattern Recognition (CVPR), pp. 842–850 (2015)
28. Wang, D., Shen, Z., Shao, J., Zhang, W., Xue, X., Zhang, Z.: Multiple granularity descriptors for fine-grained categorization. In: International Conference on Computer Vision (ICCV), pp. 2399–2406 (2015)

29. Wei, Y., Feng, J., Liang, X., Cheng, M., Zhao, Y., Yan, S.: Object region mining with adversarial erasing: a simple classification to semantic segmentation approach. In: Computer Vision and Pattern Recognition (CVPR), pp. 6488–6496 (2017)
30. Zhang, X., Xiong, H., Zhou, W., Lin, W., Tian, Q.: Picking deep filter responses for fine-grained image recognition. In: Computer Vision and Pattern Recognition (CVPR), pp.1134–1142 (2016)
31. Zhao, B., Wu, X., Feng, J., Peng, Q., Yan, S.: Diversified visual attention networks for fine-grained object classification. IEEE Trans. Multimed. **19**, 1245–1256 (2017)
32. Zheng, H., Fu, J., Mei, T., Luo, J.: Learning multi-attention convolutional neural network for fine-grained image recognition. In: International Conference on Computer Vision (ICCV), pp. 5219–5227 (2017)
33. Sun, G., Cholakkal, H., Khan, S., Khan, F.S., Shao, L.: Fine-grained recognition: Accounting for subtle differences between similar classes. arXiv:1912.06842 (2019)
34. Gao, X., Li, W., Loomes, M., Wang, L.: A fused deep learning architecture for viewpoint classification of echocardiography. Inf. Fusion **36**, 103–113 (2017)
35. Zhang, J., et al.: Computerized detection of leukocytes in microscopic leukorrhea images. Med. Phys. **44**, 4620–4629 (2017)
36. Zhao, J., Zhang, M., Zhou, Z., Chu, J., Cao, F.: Automatic detection and classification of leukocytes using convolutional neural networks. Med. Biol. Eng. Comput. **55**(8), 1287–1301 (2016). https://doi.org/10.1007/s11517-016-1590-x
37. Krizhevsky, A., Sutskever, I., Hinton, G.E.: Imagenet classification with deep convolutional neural networks. In: Neural Information Processing Systems (NIPS), pp. 1097–1105 (2012)
38. He, K., Zhang, X., Ren, S., Sun, J.: Deep residual learning for image recognition. In: Computer Vision and Pattern Recognition (CVPR), pp. 770–778 (2016)
39. Zhou, Y., Zhu, Y., Ye, Q., Qiu, Q., Jiao, J.: Weakly supervised instance segmentation using class peak response. In: Computer Vision and Pattern Recognition (CVPR), pp. 3791–3800 (2018)
40. Srivastava, N., Hinton, G.E., Krizhevsky, A., Sutskever, I., Salakhutdinov, R.: Dropout: a simple way to prevent neural networks from overfitting. J. Mach. Learn. Res. **15**, 1929–1958 (2014)
41. Tompson, J., Goroshin, R., Jain, A., Lecun, Y., Bregler, C.: Efficient object localization using convolutional networks. In: Computer Vision and Pattern Recognition (CVPR), pp. 648–656 (2015)
42. Park, S., Kwak, N.: Analysis on the dropout effect in convolutional neural networks. In: Lai, S.-H., Lepetit, V., Nishino, K., Sato, Y. (eds.) ACCV 2016, Part II. LNCS, vol. 10112, pp. 189–204. Springer, Cham (2017). https://doi.org/10.1007/978-3-319-54184-6_12
43. Ghiasi, G., Lin, T., Le, Q.V.: Dropblock: a regularization method for convolutional networks. In: Neural Information Processing Systems (NIPS), pp. 10727–10737 (2018)
44. Durand, T., Thome, N., Cord, M.: Mantra: minimum maximum latent structural SVM for image classification and ranking. In: International Conference on Computer Vision (ICCV), pp. 2713–2721 (2015)
45. Simonyan, K., Zisserman, A.: Very deep convolutional networks for large-scale image recognition. In: International Conference on Learning Representations (ICLR),(2015)
46. Wang, X., Girshick, R., Gupta, A., He, K.: Non-local neural networks. In: Computer Vision and Pattern Recognition (CVPR) (2018)
47. Hu, J., Shen, L., Albanie, S., Sun, G., Wu, E.: Squeeze-and-excitation networks. IEEE Trans. Pattern Anal. Mach. Intell. **42**, 2011–2023 (2020)

Learning Multi-instance Sub-pixel Point Localization

Julien Schroeter[1]([✉]), Tinne Tuytelaars[2], Kirill Sidorov[1], and David Marshall[1]

[1] School of Computer Science and Informatics, Cardiff University, Cardiff, UK
{SchroeterJ1,SidorovK,MarshallAD}@cardiff.ac.uk
[2] ESAT-PSI, Leuven.ai, KU Leuven, Leuven, Belgium
Tinne.Tuytelaars@esat.kuleuven.be

Abstract. In this work, we propose a novel approach that allows for the end-to-end learning of multi-instance point detection with inherent sub-pixel precision capabilities. To infer unambiguous localization estimates, our model relies on three components: the continuous prediction capabilities of offset-regression-based models, the finer-grained spatial learning ability of a novel continuous heatmap matching loss function introduced to that effect, and the prediction sparsity ability of count-based regularization. We demonstrate strong sub-pixel localization accuracy on single molecule localization microscopy and checkerboard corner detection, and improved sub-frame event detection performance in sport videos.

1 Introduction

Sub-pixel point localization (i.e., estimating the coordinates of point objects with a precision beyond pixel accuracy) is a challenging task that is characterized by the discrepancy between the precision required of the point predictions and the granularity of the input image. In this context, the standard paradigm [1–5] of operating directly on the discrete space defined by pixel locations (e.g., discrete heatmap matching), and thus coupling the precision of the detections to the input resolution, is clearly not sufficient. Several methods have thus emerged to extend the classical discrete setup to allow for sub-pixel capabilities [6–14]. The majority of these approaches however work on the assumption that there is *exactly one* instance per object class. By restricting the setup to single instance localization, the point location can be inferred, for instance, through continuous spatial density estimation [7], weighted integration [8,9,12], or displacement field estimation [6]. These approaches find direct application in human pose estimation [1–4] and facial landmark detection [5,15], where the single instance assumption is fulfilled through image cropping and assigning each landmark to a different prediction class. However, the uniqueness assumption they rely on is often too constraining in other scenarios, especially in multi-instance sub-pixel localization (Table 1).

Electronic supplementary material The online version of this chapter (https://doi.org/10.1007/978-3-030-69541-5_40) contains supplementary material, which is available to authorized users.

© Springer Nature Switzerland AG 2021
H. Ishikawa et al. (Eds.): ACCV 2020, LNCS 12626, pp. 669–686, 2021.
https://doi.org/10.1007/978-3-030-69541-5_40

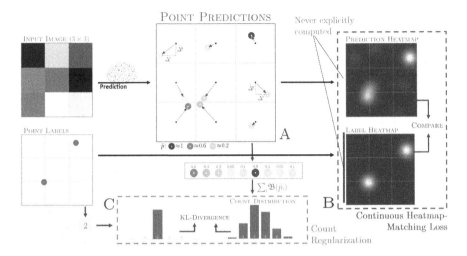

Fig. 1. Model overview. A) The model infers numerous point predictions through dense offset regression. B) The point estimates are compared to the label locations through *continuous* heatmap-matching. C) The predicted count is compared against the number of labelled objects (count-regularization). As the heatmaps are never explicitly determined, the loss is computed with infinite spatial resolution.

In practice, multi-instance sub-pixel point localization is relevant to various fields. For instance, in single molecule localization microscopy [16,17], a precise and useful account of molecule locations requires sub-pixel localization capabilities, as the resolution of the input image is limited by inherent sensor properties (e.g., diffraction-limited images). Additionally, as hundreds of molecules can emit light at the same time, successful models have to be able to detect multiple instances in dense settings (i.e., potentially more than one instance per pixel). In camera calibration, an accurate estimation of the camera parameters requires an extremely precise detection of the multiple checkerboard corners [18,19]. Thus, the ability to infer multi-instance sub-pixel corner locations is especially relevant to the effective calibration of low-resolution cameras. In these two examples, the instance uniqueness assumption does not hold, and thus calls for the development of models that are able to detect and disentangle with precision the location of multiple objects (of a same class), which might even lie within a same pixel.

In this work, we introduce a novel model that learns—in an end-to-end fashion—to directly output one single clear-cut and spatially precise *point* estimate in $\mathbb{R}^2$ per point label. More precisely, the model infers point localizations through dense offset regression (comparable to [6,7]) and is trained using a novel loss function based on a *continuous* generalization of heatmap matching, which allows to bypass any issue induced by space discretization (see Sect. 3.2). We further ensure that the model learns to output a unique high probability point estimate per point label through sparsity regularization (see Sect. 3.3). (See Fig. 1 for an overview of the model.) Overall, by obviating the need for post-processing operations such as non-maximum suppression (NMS) [6] or maxima

Table 1. Related work. No prior work allows for an end-to-end learning of point localization in dense multi-instance settings without the use of spatial upsampling.

	Sub-pixel	Multi-Instance	Dense Settings	No post-processing	No Explicit Upsampling
DISCRETE HEATMAP MATCHING		✓			✓
+ REFINEMENT [11,14,15,20]	✓	✓	(✓)		✓
CHARUCONET [19]	✓	✓		✓	
DEEP-STORM [17]	✓	✓	(✓)	✓	
Tiny People Pose [7]	✓			✓	✓
Fractional Heatmap Reg. [13]	✓			✓	✓
GLOBAL REGRESSION [21,22]	✓	(✓)		✓	✓
OFFSET REGRESSION [10,23]	✓	✓	(✓)		✓
G-RMI [6]	✓	✓			✓
INTEGRAL POSE REG. [8,9,12]	✓			✓	✓
OURS	✓	✓	✓	✓	✓

refinement [11] which are set to deteriorate the accuracy of the predictions (see Sect. 3.3) and by inferring spatially unambiguous point predictions, the approach offers an effective solution to the challenging problem of multi-instance sub-pixel localization.

Contributions. This work: a) proposes a novel loss function for the end-to-end learning of multi-instance sub-pixel point localization, b) shows the effectiveness of instance counting as an additional means of supervision to achieve prediction sparsity, c) evaluates the model on single molecule localization microscopy and checkerboard corner detection against standard benchmarks, and d) demonstrates the versatility of the approach on temporal sub-frame event detection in videos.

2 Related Work

Methods for *sub-pixel* point detection can be classified into three categories: upsampling-based, refinement-based, and regression-based approaches.

Upsampling. The standard paradigm of first transforming the point detection problem into a heatmap prediction problem (e.g., [1,5]), before estimating point locations from the maxima of the discrete prediction heatmap [24,25], is not well-suited for sub-pixel applications. Indeed, the precision of these models is inherently limited to pixel accuracy. Several works achieve sub-pixel accuracy in this setting by simply inferring finer-grained discrete heatmaps through explicit *upsampling*. This artificial increase in resolution can be implemented in several ways ranging from a naïve upsampling of the input image [17] to a sophisticated upsampling of the prediction map itself with a trained refinement network [19]. While this process enables sub-pixel predictions with respect to the original image resolution, it suffers from two drawbacks: first, the estimates are still constrained to pixel locations in the upsampled space, and thus the precision of the predictions is directly bounded by the amount of upsampling performed; secondly, the explicit upsampling of the visual representations significantly increases the memory requirement. In addition, as these approaches lack the ability to precisely detect multiple instances per pixel, they need to resort to large upsampling factors to deal with dense multi-instance applications such as molecule localization microscope—exacerbating the issue of computational complexity.

Refinement-Based. Instead of resorting to upsampling to obtain finer-grained discrete grids, other works propose first inferring heatmaps on coarser resolutions, before *refining* the estimates of the maxima locations to obtain predictions in $\mathbb{R}^2$ [11,14,15,20]. For instance, Graving et al. [11] use Fourier-based convolutions to align a 2D continuous Gaussian filter with the discrete predicted heatmap, while Zhang et al. [14] estimate the maxima (in $\mathbb{R}^2$) through log-likelihood optimization. However, while they can be deployed on top of any state-of-the-art discrete models, refinement-based methods introduce a clear disparity between the optimization objective (heatmap estimation) and the overall goal of the pipeline (sub-pixel localization). Consequently, as the refinement operation is not part of the optimization loop, the learning of sub-pixel localization is not achieved in an end-to-end fashion which leads to suboptimal results.

Regression-Based. In contrast to heatmap matching, regression models can infer continuous locations without resorting to intermediate discretized representations. The most trivial approach consists in directly regressing the coordinates of the points of interest [21,22]. However, this simple method suffers from several drawbacks (e.g., no translational invariance to the detriment of generalization capabilities and the number of points to detect has to be rigidly set in the model architecture). In contrast, offset regression models [26,27] first subdivide the input space into a grid of smaller sub-regions, before inferring relative object coordinates and class probabilities within each region via regression. While originally proposed for object detection, this approach has also seen applications in point detection [10,23,28], with the specificity that classification probabilities are commonly assigned through heatmap matching. However, despite their ability to infer predictions in the continuous space and to leverage local features more efficiently than their global counterparts, these models often rely on loss functions that are highly discontinuous at the edges of the grid cells ([28] is a noticeable exception). Thus, in order to alleviate the discontinuity issues, large grid cells often have to be considered which is reminiscent of global coordinates regression models and their inherent drawbacks. More importantly, these methods often have to rely heavily on NMS to obtain sparse predictions, thus breaking the end-to-end learning of point localization. Both of these features are detrimental to the overall precision of the point estimates, and by extension, to the sub-pixel localization capabilities of these models, especially in multi-instance settings.

In this work, we leverage *both* the continuous prediction ability of offset regression and the finer-grained spatial learning capabilities of heatmap matching-based learning to achieve precise multi-instance sub-pixel point localization.

3   Model

We propose to tackle multi-instance sub-resolution point localization through dense offset prediction, continuous heatmap matching-based learning and instance counting regularization. An overview of the model is given in Fig. 1.

3.1   Dense Offset Prediction

As in standard offset regression [26,27], we propose to train a model to infer, for each pixel of the final representation, n tuples $(\hat{\Delta}^x, \hat{\Delta}^y, \hat{\mathbf{p}})$ with coordinate offsets $\hat{\Delta}^x, \hat{\Delta}^y \in [-\frac{1}{2}, \frac{1}{2}]$ and class probabilities $\mathbf{p} \in [0,1]^d$, where d is the number of classes. In contrast to standard approaches, the loss introduced in this work (see Eq. 3) does not present any discontinuity at the sub-regions borders and, thus, does not explicitly require the resolution of the input image to be down-sampled. As a result, a one-to-one correspondence between the pixels in the final representation and the pixels in the input image can be exploited, which makes it possible to infer a set of n point tuples $(\hat{\Delta}^x, \hat{\Delta}^y, \hat{\mathbf{p}})$ for each pixel in the input image—even smaller granularity can be considered. More specifically, the model $\hat{f}_\theta$ maps any given input image $\mathbf{X}$ of size $(w \times h)$ to a *dense* ensemble of $N := n \cdot w \cdot h$ points $(\hat{x}, \hat{y}, \hat{\mathbf{p}})$, where the point coordinates $\hat{x}$ and $\hat{y}$ are equal to the sum of the continuous offsets predictions $\hat{\Delta}^x, \hat{\Delta}^y$ and the respective pixel center locations $(\bar{x}, \bar{y})$, namely

$$
\begin{aligned}
\hat{f}_\theta(\mathbf{X}) &= \left\{ (\hat{x}, \hat{y}, \hat{\mathbf{p}})_{(i)} \mid i \leq N \right\} \\
&= \left\{ \left(\bar{x}_{(j,k)} + \hat{\Delta}^x_{(j,k,l)}, \ \bar{y}_{(j,k)} + \hat{\Delta}^y_{(j,k,l)}, \ \hat{\mathbf{p}}_{(j,k,l)} \right) \mid j \leq w, k \leq h, l \leq n \right\} =: \mathcal{P}_\theta.
\end{aligned}
\tag{1}
$$

Overall, this mapping offers a full and fine-grained coverage of the original image space and, thus, makes the precise prediction of multiple point locations in $\mathbb{R}^2$ possible, thereby unlocking multi-instance sub-pixel capabilities. Indeed, the object locations $(\hat{x}, \hat{y})$ can lie anywhere in $\mathbb{R}^2$, in contrast to standard point detection models [1,2,15,29,30] where point locations are limited to the discrete grid defined by the input pixels. Similarly, the true point labels are not discretized, i.e., $\mathcal{L} := \{(x,y)_j \in \mathbb{R}^2 \mid j \leq M\}$, with M the number of labels in an image. Since such dense oversampling of point predictions is not suitable for classical offset regression loss functions [31], a novel flexible loss function has to be introduced.

Remark. The points $(\hat{x}, \hat{y}, \hat{\mathbf{p}}) \in \mathcal{P}_\theta$ outputted by the model correspond to the final point localization estimates (see Sect. 3.3 for details on how the model converges almost all instance probabilities to zero, thus turning the dense set of predictions into a sparse one) and not to intermediate representations that span a density—or a heatmap—[1,7,15,29,30] or that require extensive post-processing [6].

3.2 Continuous Heatmap Matching

In order to estimate the model parameters θ through backpropagation, the model predictions $\mathcal{P}_\theta$ and the ground-truth labels $\mathcal{L}$ have to be compared using a sensible and differentiable measure. To that end, we propose a novel *continuous* generalization of the standard discrete heatmap matching paradigm [1,15,29] that effectively solves the problems inherent to classical offset regression loss functions while retaining their continuous localization learning ability. First, the point predictions $\mathcal{P}_\theta$ and point labels $\mathcal{L}$ are mapped to continuous heatmaps using a Gaussian kernel K with smoothing parameter λ (similar to Gaussian mixture). Thus, the value of the continuous prediction heatmap (induced by $\mathcal{P}_\theta$) at any given point $(x_0, y_0) \in \mathbb{R}^2$ is equal—up to a normalization factor—to: (to simplify notation, we consider a single class, i.e. $d = 1$; generalization for $d > 1$ is trivial)

$$\hat{\mathcal{H}}(x_0, y_0 \mid \mathcal{P}_\theta) = \sum_i^N \hat{p}_i K(\hat{x}_i, \hat{y}_i, x_o, y_o) = \sum_i \hat{p}_i \exp\left(-\frac{(\hat{x}_i - x_0)^2}{\lambda^2} - \frac{(\hat{y}_i - y_0)^2}{\lambda^2}\right). \quad (2)$$

Classical models explicitly compute and compare (e.g., through an $L2$-loss) the *discrete* label heatmap obtained through the smoothing of the point labels and the *discrete* prediction heatmap inferred by the model. As a result, the heatmap comparison becomes gradually more approximate as lower-resolution inputs are considered, which inevitably has a detrimental effect on the sub-pixel learning capability. In contrast, we propose to directly compute *analytically* the difference between the *continuous* label and prediction heatmaps induced by the point labels and predictions. More precisely, we propose the integrated local squared distance between the two planes as loss function for the learning of point localization:

$$\mathcal{L}_{\mathrm{HM}}(\mathcal{P}_\theta, \mathcal{L}) = \iint_{\mathbb{R}^2} \left[\mathcal{H}(x_0, y_0 \mid \mathcal{L}) - \hat{\mathcal{H}}(x_0, y_0 \mid \mathcal{P}_\theta)\right]^2 dx_0 dy_0$$

$$= \iint_{\mathbb{R}^2} \left[\sum_j \exp\left(-\frac{(x_j - x_0)^2}{\lambda^2} - \frac{(y_j - y_0)^2}{\lambda^2}\right) \right. \quad (3)$$

$$\left. - \sum_i \hat{p}_i \exp\left(-\frac{(\hat{x}_i - x_0)^2}{\lambda^2} - \frac{(\hat{y}_i - y_0)^2}{\lambda^2}\right)\right]^2 dx_0 dy_0.$$

Performing integration over the entire $\mathbb{R}^2$ space, rather than over the image domain only, helps to avoid special treatment of points at image boundaries.

Overall, since the heatmaps are never explicitly computed, their comparison is performed with infinite spatial resolution thus alleviating the issues arising from space discretization. Moreover, as the computation of the heatmap comparison is exact regardless of the resolution of the input image, the smoothing bandwidth λ can be selected as tight as needed without any loss of information. This allows among others for a more precise learning of localization and, thus, increased sub-pixel detection capabilities.

Closed-Form Loss Computation. A closed-form solution of the loss function (Eq. 3) can be derived (see Appendix A) by successively using the distributivity property, Fubini's theorem, and the limits of the Gaussian error function:

$$
\begin{aligned}
\mathscr{L}_{\mathrm{HM}}(\mathcal{P}, \mathcal{L}) = &\sum_i \sum_j \frac{\pi\lambda^2}{2} \exp\left(-\frac{(x_i - x_j)^2 + (y_i - y_j)^2}{2\lambda^2}\right) \\
&+ \sum_i \sum_j \hat{p}_i \hat{p}_j \frac{\pi\lambda^2}{2} \exp\left(-\frac{(\hat{x}_i - \hat{x}_j)^2 + (\hat{y}_i - \hat{y}_j)^2}{2\lambda^2}\right) \\
&- 2\sum_i \sum_j \hat{p}_i \frac{\pi\lambda^2}{2} \exp\left(-\frac{(\hat{x}_i - x_j)^2 + (\hat{y}_i - y_j)^2}{2\lambda^2}\right).
\end{aligned}
\tag{4}
$$

This equation allows for an efficient computation of the partial derivatives of the loss function with respect to the class probability predictions and the location estimates used for backpropagation, see Appendix A for formulas and derivations.

Remark. While the use of dense offset regression in conjunction with Gaussian mixtures is reminiscent of [6,7], our model significantly differs in the nature of the predictions it infers. Indeed, previous works have as underlying objective the explicit estimation of prediction heatmaps. For instance, the dense point predictions in [7] are used to estimate a continuous density, which in turn is used to infer the final point locations. Thus, similar to classical heatmap matching approaches, the density—or heatmap—is the target of the learning and not the localization itself. In contrast, the points outputted by our model directly correspond to the final point predictions; the heatmaps are not a goal in themselves, but are rather used as building blocks of our loss function to assess the quality of the predictions. Consequently, in our framework, the final point predictions are an integral part of the optimization loop which allows for an end-to-end learning of multi-instance sub-pixel point localization.

3.3   Detection Sparsity Through Counting Regularization

Detection sparsity (i.e., obtaining one clear-cut non-ambiguous point estimate per label) is a critical issue in dense multi-instance sub-pixel localization applications. Indeed, relying on post-processing operations such as NMS to map a set of ambiguous estimates to clear-cut predictions is not suitable in this setting: for instance, in dense setups, two predictions made within the same pixel may correspond to two distinct ground-truth point locations, and thus should not necessarily be merged into a single prediction. Additionally, systematically combining several low-probability predictions into a single high-probability point estimate is not advisable as it will inevitably have a negative impact on the spatial precision of the predictions and, by extension, the model sub-pixel capability.

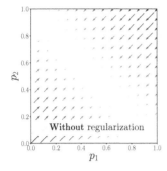 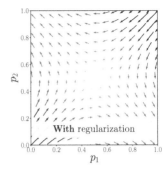

Fig. 2. Prediction sparsity through counting regularization. Gradients of the loss function with respect to instance probabilities p_1, p_2 for situations described in the example of Sect. 3.3. *(See also convergence video in supplemental material)*

The continuous heatmap-matching loss function $\mathscr{L}_{\mathrm{HM}}$ does not guarantee detection sparsity on its own; indeed, splitting a point prediction $(\hat{x}, \hat{y}, \hat{p})$ into two point predictions with half probability each $(\hat{x}, \hat{y}, \hat{p}/2)$ has no effect on the loss. To remedy this issue without resorting to ineffective post-processing operations, we propose adding a sparsity regularizer to the training objective; in this way, clear-cut and precise predictions can be learned and inferred in an end-to-end fashion.

Counting Regularization. To that effect, we propose leveraging instance counting as an additional means of supervision. In fact, the number of non-zero instances for each training sample is implicitly given by the labels (i.e., $c := |\mathcal{L}|$), and thus can easily be compared to the predicted number of instances ($\hat{c}$). Unfortunately, traditional counting models based on a naïve formulation of count (i.e., $\hat{c} = \sum_i \hat{p}_i$) [32–34] have no particular impact on the sparsity of the instance probabilities $\hat{p}_i$. An alternative is offered by Poisson-Binomial counting: counts modelled as sums of independent Bernoulli (i.e., $\hat{c} = \sum_i \mathfrak{B}(\hat{p}_i)$). In this setting, comparing the estimates count distribution with the label count through Kullback-Leibler divergence [35] has actually a unique prediction sparsity-inducing effect [36]. More precisely, a key feature of the resulting loss function is that it rewards prediction sparsity by implicitly converging the individual probabilities $\hat{p}_i$ towards either 1 or 0, as the model learns to count instances (see [36] for full proof of this convergence property). Hence, in this work, we propose leveraging the Kullback-Leibler divergence between the number of labelled objects ($c = |\mathcal{L}|$) and the Poisson-Binomial predicted count distribution implied by the class probability estimates ($\hat{c} = \sum_i \mathfrak{B}(\hat{p}_i)$) as a regularizer to our novel heatmap-matching loss:

$$\mathcal{L}_{\text{Count}}(\theta) = -\log\Big(\sum_{A\in F}\prod_{i\in A}\hat{p}_i\prod_{j\in A^c}(1-\hat{p}_j)\Big), \tag{5}$$

where F is the set of all subsets of $\{1,...,|\hat{\mathbf{p}}|\}$ of size $c = |\mathcal{L}|$. Thus, while the heatmap matching loss $\mathcal{L}_{\text{HM}}$ does not ensure prediction sparsity (e.g., it does not penalize the splitting of predictions into several lower-likelihood ones), this regularizer does. For instance—recalling the example from earlier—a unique high-likelihood prediction $(\hat{x},\hat{y},\hat{p}{=}1)$ yields $\mathcal{L}_{\text{Count}}{=}0$, whereas two lower-likelihood predictions $(\hat{x},\hat{y},\hat{p}{=}1/2)$ produce a higher value of $\mathcal{L}_{\text{Count}}{=}0.3$. Figure 2, which displays the gradient of our loss in this two-points scenario, clearly illustrates the benefit of the counting-based regularization as a means to obtain probabilities that converge towards the 0,1 extremes. A full discussion including additional advantages of this regularizer can be found in Appendix B.

4 Experiments

The code for all experiments is publicly available[1].

4.1 Single Molecule Localization Microscopy

In this section, we replicate the experiment on molecule localization microscopy proposed by Nehme et al. [17]. The task consists in determining the localization of multiple blinking molecules on diffraction-limited images of fluorescent simulated microtubules. The overall setting is particularly challenging as multiple instances can fall within the same pixel of the input image, thus requiring precise multi-instance sub-pixel localization capabilities.

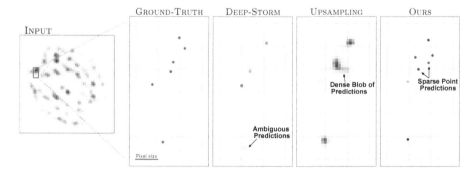

Fig. 3. Model predictions for multi-instance sub-pixel molecule localization. No non-maximum suppression was performed on our predictions, our model learns to *directly* infer sparse point predictions as a result of counting regularization.

---

[1] https://github.com/SchroeterJulien/ACCV-2020-Subpixel-Point-Localization.

Model and Benchmarks. The model in [17] achieves sub-pixel localization by explicitly increasing the resolution of the input image by a factor 8 before inferring a single localization probability for each pixel of the upsampled input (DEEP-STORM). By keeping the architecture as suggested and replacing the loss with a classical discrete heatmap-matching approach, we obtain a benchmark reminiscent of upsampling-based heatmap-matching (UPSAMPLING). As the input image is subject to high levels of upsampling, the model architecture relies on a series of downsampling layers followed by a series of upsampling layers to obtain a wide enough receptive field. In contrast, since our approach decouples the resolution of the input image from the resolution of the predictions and thereby obviates the need for upsampling, these layers are not needed to learn meaningful representations; our method can directly operate on the original images instead and infer $n=2$ points (i.e., n tuples of offsets and probabilities) for each pixel.

Evaluation and Results. All models are trained with the data provided by [17] and tested on the fluorescent simulated microtubules from [16]. The Jaccard index—a standard metric of set similarity—is computed with the tool provided by [16] using various tolerances τ. Table 2 reveals that our approach not only displays the best overall performance on this experiment, but also achieves fast inference as it can perform precise multi-instance sub-pixel localization using the original input resolution without the need for any explicit upsampling. This outperformance can partially be attributed to our approach's ability to infer sparse clear-cut point estimates without requiring any additional post-processing, see Fig. 3. The overall rendering of the test microtubules is presented in Fig. 4, see [17] for details.

STACKED INPUT

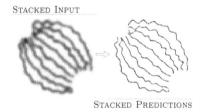

STACKED PREDICTIONS

Fig. 4. Test microtubules rendering.

Table 2. Single molecule localization microscopy results. Comparison of various methods on the sub-pixel single molecule localization experiment proposed in [17]. The Jaccard index [and F_1 score] are computed with the software from [16].

METHOD	JACCARD INDEX [F_1]		INFERENCE SPEED
	$\tau = 25$nm	$\tau = 50$nm	time/image
DEEP-STORM [17]	0.153 [0.266]	0.416 [0.588]	17.44 ms
UPSAMPLING	0.171 [0.292]	0.448 [0.618]	17.44 ms
REFINEMENT	0.195 [0.326]	0.448 [0.619]	0.76 ms
OURS	**0.234** [0.379]	**0.517** [0.681]	0.76 ms

Ablation Study. We replicate the same experiment with various forms of sparsity regularization to assess the impact of the count supervision on the performance of our model. Table 3 shows that the theoretical benefits of count-based regularization directly translate to improved sub-pixel molecule localization capabilities in practice.

Table 3. Regularization ablation study.

	JACCARD	
REGULARIZATION	$\tau = 25$nm	50nm
NONE	0.211	0.456
l_1 (as in [17])	0.208	0.454
COUNTING ($\mathscr{L}_{\text{Count}}$)	**0.234**	**0.517**

4.2 Checkerboard Corner Detection

The precise detection of corners in checkerboards is a key component of camera calibration. This challenging task requires the predictions to lie within a fraction of a pixel of the ground-truth in order to be of practical use. In this section, we compare the sub-pixel localization capabilities of our method and other learning-based approaches with state-of-the-art classical local feature-based methods that are specifically tailored to the sub-pixel detection of such corners [18,37,38].

Training Data. To train the various learning-based models, we generate a *synthetic* dataset composed of 20k checkerboard images. This not only allows us to automatically simulate numerous transformations (lens distortions, lighting variations, perspective transformations, noise) in a controllable environment, but most importantly gives us an exact account of the ground-truth corner locations, as opposed to human-annotated datasets that are inherently prone to inaccuracies. More details about the dataset generation process are included in Appendix D.

Model Architecture. In line with previous checkerboard corner detection methods [20,39], a "shallow" architecture comprised of only three convolutional layers—with 32, 32 and 64 filters respectively—is considered for all learning-based models, including ours. For faster training, two downsampling convolutional layers, with stride 2, are added to our model, after both the first and second convolutional layers. This modification merely enables our model to assign probabilities and offsets to bigger regions of 4×4 pixels rather than to each pixel of the original input. In contrast, no downsampling could be performed on all other learning-based benchmarks, as it would only deteriorate the precision of their predictions.

Baselines. The following classical baselines are considered: OCamCalib [40], ROCHADE [18], OpenCV [41], and MATLAB [42]. We also include three learning-based benchmarks which use the model architecture described above and are trained on our synthetic dataset: standard discrete heatmap-matching with naïve argmax maximum picking (similar to [20,39]), heatmap-matching

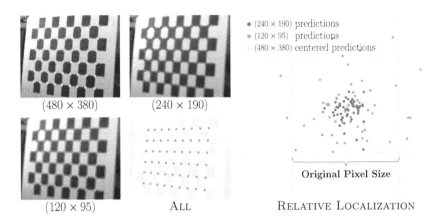

Fig. 5. Corner detection across different resolutions. The low-resolution location estimates stay well within half a pixel of the original predictions, which corresponds to 1/8 of a pixel in the lowest resolution.

with local refinement through Gaussian distribution fitting (comparable to standard refinement-based approaches [11]), and higher resolution heatmap-matching where the input images are explicitly upsampled with a factor 8 (similar to [17]).

Evaluation and Results. We evaluate the methods on the standard uEye and GoPro datasets [18]. Since these real-world test datasets do not contain any ground-truth corner positions, we assess the sub-pixel localization capabilities of the different approaches both through prediction consistency across resolutions and through corner reprojection errors. Note that, in these experiments, the upsampling approach yields representations that are far too large to be supported by standard GPUs, especially on the GoPro dataset, which illustrates its limits.

First, we measure prediction consistency by comparing the corner localizations obtained on the original high-resolution images with those obtained on the lower-resolution inputs downsampled by a factor δ. This experiment thus posits that a direct correlation exists between a model's ability to infer consistent sub-pixel locations and its capacity to output consistent predictions across various resolutions. The mean absolute displacement and the 90th quantile reported in Table 4 show that our approach yields very consistent corner location estimates (see also Fig. 5). Among others, this performance demonstrates that our model is capable of inferring point locations well beyond pixel accuracy. Second, we compute the reprojection errors—a standard metric in camera calibration— of the predicted checkerboard corners in low-resolution settings (i.e., input downsampled with factor δ) after performing camera calibration with the standard OpenCV implementation [41]. Overall, the excellent performance of our approach on this task (see Table 5), much higher than most classical state-of-the-art approaches, reveals once again the high sub-pixel capabilities of our model.

Table 4. Corner localization performance in low-resolution settings on the uEye and GoPro datasets [18]. **Consistency:** mean-absolute displacement (and 90th quantile) between predictions on high and low-resolution images downsampled by δ. **Reprojection Error:** corresponding errors in corner reprojection [and number of fully detected boards]. In units of original pixel size.

	METHODS	CONSISTENCY		REPROJECTION ERROR	
		uEye ($\delta=4$)	GoPro ($\delta=6$)	uEye ($\delta=4$)	GoPro ($\delta=6$)
CLASSIC	OCamCalib [40]	1.447 (2.92)	1.989 (3.61)	0.197 [114]	—— [18]
	Rochade [18]	0.587 (1.05)	1.125 (2.07)	0.107 [197]	1.716 [71]
	OpenCV [41]	0.889 (2.66)	0.336 (0.50)	—— [0]	0.994 [73]
	MATLAB [42]	**0.174** (0.29)	**0.314** (0.50)	**0.059** [204]	**0.325** [100]
LEARN.	DL-Heatmap (sim. [20,39])	1.666 (2.24)	2.395 (3.61)	0.230 [175]	0.797 [77]
	+ Refinement (sim. [11])	0.562 (1.20)	0.428 (0.76)	0.086 [162]	0.531 [100]
	OURS	**0.348** (0.64)	**0.378** (0.66)	**0.073** [187]	**0.417** [100]

(Additional results are included in Appendix D.) These results are all the more remarkable when considering that the learning-based models are trained solely on synthetic images and that the classical benchmarks are specifically designed for this task *only*—they are not portable to other applications in contrast to our approach.

4.3 Sub-frame Temporal Event Detection in Videos

The precise *temporal* localization of *point* events in sequential data (i.e., answering when do instantaneous events occur?) is a widespread task with applications in numerous fields from accurate audio-to-score music transcription, to detection of sport events in videos. In this section, we show that the loss function introduced in Sect. 3.2 can be leveraged not only for spatial applications, but also for sequential data to achieve *sub-frame* temporal detection. Indeed, by inferring event occurrence times directly in $\mathbb{R}$ rather than on a discrete timeline [43–45], our approach decouples the precision of the predictions from the resolution of the input sequence, and can thus output accurate predictions without the need for high temporal resolution inputs.

Experiment Specifications. In this section, we replicate the experiment introduced by McNally et al. [45] on golf swing events detection in videos. In order to evaluate the sub-frame capability of our model and its ability to infer precise localization in low-resolution settings, we downsample the training and testing videos with a temporal decimation rate δ. A wide spectrum of downsampling rates are considered, ranging from the original experiment ($\delta=1$) to highly downsampled settings where only 1 out of 16 frames of the video samples are kept ($\delta=16$). Since the tolerance within which a prediction is considered correct

Table 5. Golf swing event detection accuracy (within a ± 1 frame tolerance) as a function of the downsampling factor δ. Averages and standard deviations (in brackets) are reported over 4 folds. The model architecture is from [45].

LOSS	$\delta = 1$ frame	2 frames	4 frames	8 frames	16 frames
NAÏVE UPSAMPLING	67.6 (0.8)	68.5 (0.7)	59.8 (1.3)	44.7 (1.0)	23.9 (0.5)
FRAME INTERPOLATION [46]	— " —	67.4 (0.6)	67.1 (0.6)	60.5 (1.3)	41.6 (1.9)
PREDICTION UPSAMPLING	— " —	69.6 (0.6)	69.9 (0.6)	66.3 (1.1)	57.8 (1.2)
OURS	**70.9** (1.4)	**70.4** (1.2)	**70.7** (1.3)	**69.8** (1.4)	**60.6** (1.6)

(i.e., ± 1 frame of the original resolution) is kept unchanged across all experiments, the task becomes progressively more challenging as the downsampling rate δ increases. Indeed, even though the downsampled sequences retain less and less information, predictions are expected to remain as precise as in higher resolution settings. (The code from [45] was used as is, without any fine-tuning in all experiments.)

Our Approach. The continuous heatmap-matching loss function can be adapted for 1-dimensional applications by dropping all dependence on y. Thus, the model is trained to infer, for each timestep in the sequence, temporal offsets $\Delta^x \in [0,1]$ and event occurrence probabilities $\mathbf{p} \in [0,1]^d$. Since our loss is agnostic to the underlying model, it can be directly applied in conjunction with the architecture proposed in the original paper [45]. Once again, we leverage the properties of the counting-based regularization to achieve prediction sparsity (see Sect. 3.3).

Benchmarks. McNally et al. [45] leverage the widely used (e.g., [43,44]) standard average stepwise cross-entropy as loss function. As this loss function requires the predictions to be set on a discrete grid, we consider two different video temporal upsampling regimes to augment the original model with subframe detection capabilities. The first one consists in duplicating each frame of the input δ times in order to match the original ($\delta = 1$) sequence resolution (*Naïve upsampling*), while the second leverages the state-of-the-art frame interpolation method proposed by [46] to estimate the $\delta - 1$ missing frames (*Frame interpolation*). We also consider an additional benchmark that operates on the downsampled resolution without any explicit input upsampling: instead of inferring only one event probability per timestep, the model infers δ probabilities, one for the current timestep and $\delta - 1$ for the missing time steps in an effort to match the original resolution of the predictions (*Prediction upsampling*). This final benchmark is reminiscent of the upsampling-based approach used in [17,19].

Results. Table 5 shows that our approach outperforms the traditional ones for all downsampling factors δ; the performance gap becomes even more apparent

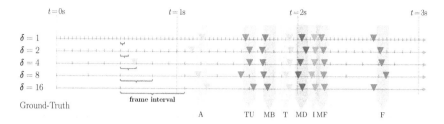

Fig. 6. Consistency of our temporal point predictions across all resolutions.

as the downsampling rate is increased. For instance, our loss function allows for the training of a very competitive golf event detector using only 1 out of 8 frames of the original video (i.e., $\delta = 8$). This prediction consistency across the various downsampling rates for a given test sequence is depicted in Fig. 6.

These results overall demonstrate that our proposed approach does not only achieve precise multi-instance sub-pixel detection accuracy in spatial applications, but can also be effective for sub-frame temporal event detection. (Note that additional results with detailed per event class metrics can be found in Appendix E.) Additionally, by being able to operate on lower resolution inputs without any significant performance deterioration, our approach allows for both a more efficient training and a faster inference, which is key for low-resource and real-time applications, especially on mobile and embedded devices.

5 Conclusion

In this work, we leveraged dense offset regression, continuous heatmap matching-based learning, and instance counting regularization to improve multi-instance sub-pixel localization accuracy. The novel loss function—which allows for an end-to-end learning of point localization—is derived as a continuous generalization of standard heatmap matching approaches. We further showed the utility of counting-based regularization to improve convergence and prediction sparsity. The model demonstrates strong performance on molecule localization microscopy, checkerboard corner detection, and sub-frame temporal video event detection.

Acknowledgement. We are extremely thankful for the support of the Collaborative Research Fund between KU Leuven and Cardiff University who made this collaboration possible. We also gratefully acknowledge the support of NVIDIA Corporation with the donation of a GPU used for this research.

References

1. Tompson, J., Goroshin, R., Jain, A., LeCun, Y., Bregler, C.: Efficient object localization using convolutional networks. In: Proceedings of Conference on Computer Vision and Pattern Recognition (CVPR), pp. 648–656 (2015)

2. Newell, A., Yang, K., Deng, J.: Stacked Hourglass networks for human pose estimation. In: Leibe, B., Matas, J., Sebe, N., Welling, M. (eds.) ECCV 2016, Part VIII. LNCS, vol. 9912, pp. 483–499. Springer, Cham (2016). https://doi.org/10.1007/978-3-319-46484-8_29

3. Wei, S.E., Ramakrishna, V., Kanade, T., Sheikh, Y.: Convolutional pose machines. In: Proceedings of Conference on Computer Vision and Pattern Recognition (CVPR), pp. 4724–4732 (2016)

4. Xiao, B., Wu, H., Wei, Y.: Simple baselines for human pose estimation and tracking. In: Ferrari, V., Hebert, M., Sminchisescu, C., Weiss, Y. (eds.) ECCV 2018, Part VI. LNCS, vol. 11210, pp. 472–487. Springer, Cham (2018). https://doi.org/10.1007/978-3-030-01231-1_29

5. Merget, D., Rock, M., Rigoll, G.: Robust facial landmark detection via a fully-convolutional local-global context network. In: Proceedings of Conference on Computer Vision and Pattern Recognition (CVPR), pp. 781–790 (2018)

6. Papandreou, G., et al.: Towards accurate multi-person pose estimation in the wild. In: Proceedings of Conference on Computer Vision and Pattern Recognition (CVPR), pp. 4903–4911 (2017)

7. Neumann, L., Vedaldi, A.: Tiny people pose. In: Jawahar, C.V., Li, H., Mori, G., Schindler, K. (eds.) ACCV 2018, Part III. LNCS, vol. 11363, pp. 558–574. Springer, Cham (2019). https://doi.org/10.1007/978-3-030-20893-6_35

8. Nibali, A., He, Z., Morgan, S., Prendergast, L.: Numerical coordinate regression with convolutional neural networks. arXiv preprint arXiv:1801.07372 (2018)

9. Sun, X., Xiao, B., Wei, F., Liang, S., Wei, Y.: Integral human pose regression. In: Ferrari, V., Hebert, M., Sminchisescu, C., Weiss, Y. (eds.) ECCV 2018, Part VI. LNCS, vol. 11210, pp. 536–553. Springer, Cham (2018). https://doi.org/10.1007/978-3-030-01231-1_33

10. Fieraru, M., Khoreva, A., Pishchulin, L., Schiele, B.: Learning to refine human pose estimation. In: Proceedings of the IEEE Conference on Computer Vision and Pattern Recognition Workshops, pp. 205–214 (2018)

11. Graving, J.M., et al.: DeepPoseKit, a software toolkit for fast and robust animal pose estimation using deep learning. eLife **8**, e47994 (2019)

12. Luvizon, D.C., Tabia, H., Picard, D.: Human pose regression by combining indirect part detection and contextual information. Comput. Graph. **85**, 15–22 (2019)

13. Tai, Y., Liang, Y., Liu, X., Duan, L., Li, J., Wang, C., Huang, F., Chen, Y.: Towards highly accurate and stable face alignment for high-resolution videos. Proceedings of the AAAI Conference on Artificial Intelligence, vol. 33, pp. 8893–8900 (2019)

14. Zhang, F., Zhu, X., Dai, H., Ye, M., Zhu, C.: Distribution-aware coordinate representation for human pose estimation. In: Proceedings of Conference on Computer Vision and Pattern Recognition (CVPR), pp. 7093–7102 (2020)

15. Yang, J., Liu, Q., Zhang, K.: Stacked hourglass network for robust facial landmark localisation. In: Proceedings of the IEEE Conference on Computer Vision and Pattern Recognition Workshops, pp. 79–87 (2017)

16. Sage, D., Kirshner, H., Pengo, T., Stuurman, N., Min, J., Manley, S., Unser, M.: Quantitative evaluation of software packages for single-molecule localization microscopy. Nat. Methods **12**, 717–724 (2015)

17. Nehme, E., Weiss, L.E., Michaeli, T., Shechtman, Y.: Deep-STORM: super-resolution single-molecule microscopy by deep learning. Optica **5**, 458–464 (2018)

18. Placht, S., Fürsattel, P., Mengue, E.A., Hofmann, H., Schaller, C., Balda, M., Angelopoulou, E.: ROCHADE: robust checkerboard advanced detection for camera calibration. In: Fleet, D., Pajdla, T., Schiele, B., Tuytelaars, T. (eds.) ECCV 2014, Part IV. LNCS, vol. 8692, pp. 766–779. Springer, Cham (2014). https://doi.org/10.1007/978-3-319-10593-2_50

19. Hu, D., DeTone, D., Malisiewicz, T.: Deep ChArUco: dark ChArUco marker pose estimation. In: Proceedings of Conference on Computer Vision and Pattern Recognition (CVPR), pp. 8436–8444 (2019)

20. Donné, S., De Vylder, J., Goossens, B., Philips, W.: MATE: machine learning for adaptive calibration template detection. Sensors 16, 1858 (2016)

21. Toshev, A., Szegedy, C.: DeepPose: Human pose estimation via deep neural networks. In: Proceedings of Conference on Computer Vision and Pattern Recognition (CVPR), pp.1653–1660 (2014)

22. Carreira, J., Agrawal, P., Fragkiadaki, K., Malik, J.: Human pose estimation with iterative error feedback. In: Proceedings of Conference on Computer Vision and Pattern Recognition (CVPR), pp. 4733–4742 (2016)

23. Zhou, X., Wang, D., Krähenbühl, P.: Objects as points. arXiv preprint arXiv:1904.07850 (2019)

24. Li, J., Su, W., Wang, Z.: Simple pose: Rethinking and improving a bottom-up approach for multi-person pose estimation. In: Thirty-Fourth AAAI Conference on Artificial Intelligence (2020)

25. Tompson, J.J., Jain, A., LeCun, Y., Bregler, C.: Joint training of a convolutional network and a graphical model for human pose estimation. In: Advances in Neural Information Processing Systems (NIPS), pp. 1799–1807 (2014)

26. Liu, W., et al.: SSD: single shot MultiBox detector. In: Leibe, B., Matas, J., Sebe, N., Welling, M. (eds.) ECCV 2016, Part I. LNCS, vol. 9905, pp. 21–37. Springer, Cham (2016). https://doi.org/10.1007/978-3-319-46448-0_2

27. Redmon, J., Divvala, S., Girshick, R., Farhadi, A.: You only look once: Unified, real-time object detection. In: Proceedings of Conference on Computer Vision and Pattern Recognition (CVPR), pp. 779–788 (2016)

28. Vahdat, A.: Toward robustness against label noise in training deep discriminative neural networks. In: Advances in Neural Information Processing Systems (NIPS), pp. 5596–5605 (2017)

29. Bulat, A., Tzimiropoulos, G.: Human pose estimation via convolutional part heatmap regression. In: Leibe, B., Matas, J., Sebe, N., Welling, M. (eds.) ECCV 2016, Part VII. LNCS, vol. 9911, pp. 717–732. Springer, Cham (2016). https://doi.org/10.1007/978-3-319-46478-7_44

30. Pfister, T., Charles, J., Zisserman, A.: Flowing convnets for human pose estimation in videos. In: Proceedings of International Conference on Computer Vision (ICCV), pp. 1913–1921 (2015)

31. Redmon, J., Farhadi, A.: YOLOv3: An incremental improvement. arXiv preprint arXiv:1804.02767 (2018)

32. Zhang, C., Li, H., Wang, X., Yang, X.: Cross-scene crowd counting via deep convolutional neural networks. In: The IEEE Conference on Computer Vision and Pattern Recognition (CVPR) (2015)

33. Trott, A., Xiong, C., Socher, R.: Interpretable counting for visual question answering. In: Proceedings of International Conference on Learning Representations (ICLR) (2018)

34. Idrees, H., et al.: Composition loss for counting, density map estimation and local-ization in dense crowds. In: Ferrari, V., Hebert, M., Sminchisescu, C., Weiss, Y. (eds.) ECCV 2018, Part II. LNCS, vol. 11206, pp. 544–559. Springer, Cham (2018). https://doi.org/10.1007/978-3-030-01216-8_33
35. Kullback, S., Leibler, R.A.: On information and sufficiency. Ann. Math. Stat. **22**, 79–86 (1951)
36. Schroeter, J., Sidorov, K., Marshall, D.: Weakly-supervised temporal localization via occurrence count learning. In: Proceedings of International Conference on Machine Learning (ICML), pp. 5649–5659 (2019)
37. Duda, A., Frese, U.: Accurate detection and localization of checkerboard corners for calibration. In: British Machine Vision Conference (BMVC) (2018)
38. Sinzinger, E.D.: A model-based approach to junction detection using radial energy. Pattern Recognit. **41**, 494–505 (2008)
39. Chen, B., Xiong, C., Zhang, Q.: CCDN: checkerboard corner detection network for robust camera calibration. In: Chen, Z., Mendes, A., Yan, Y., Chen, S. (eds.) ICIRA 2018, Part II. LNCS (LNAI), vol. 10985, pp. 324–334. Springer, Cham (2018). https://doi.org/10.1007/978-3-319-97589-4_27
40. Scaramuzza, D., Martinelli, A., Siegwart, R.: A toolbox for easily calibrating omni-directional cameras. In: 2006 IEEE/RSJ International Conference on Intelligent Robots and Systems, pp. 5695–5701. IEEE (2006)
41. Bradski, G.: The OpenCV library. Dr. Dobb's J. Soft. Tools **120**, 122–125 (2000)
42. Geiger, A., Moosmann, F., Car, Ö., Schuster, B.: Automatic camera and range sensor calibration using a single shot. In: 2012 IEEE International Conference on Robotics and Automation, pp. 3936–3943. IEEE (2012)
43. Hawthorne, C., et al.: Enabling factorized piano music modeling and generation with the MAESTRO dataset. In: Proceedings of International Conference on Learning Representations (ICLR) (2019)
44. Wu, C.W., et al.: A review of automatic drum transcription. IEEE/ACM Trans. Audio Speech Lang. Process. **26**, 1457–1483 (2018)
45. McNally, W., Vats, K., Pinto, T., Dulhanty, C., McPhee, J., Wong, A.: GolfDB: a video database for golf swing sequencing. In: Proceedings of the IEEE Conference on Computer Vision and Pattern Recognition Workshops (2019)
46. Bao, W., Lai, W.S., Ma, C., Zhang, X., Gao, Z., Yang, M.H.: Depth-aware video frame interpolation. In: Proceedings of Conference on Computer Vision and Pattern Recognition (CVPR), pp. 3703–3712 (2019)

Utilizing Transfer Learning and a Customized Loss Function for Optic Disc Segmentation from Retinal Images

Abdullah Sarhan[1]([✉]), Ali Al-Khaz'Aly[1], Adam Gorner[2], Andrew Swift[2], Jon Rokne[1], Reda Alhajj[1,3], and Andrew Crichton[4]

[1] Department of Computer Science, University of Calgary, Calgary, AB, Canada
asarhan@ucalgary.ca
[2] Cumming School of Medicine, University of Calgary, Calgary, Canada
[3] Department of Computer Engineering, Istanbul Medipol University,
Istanbul, Turkey
[4] Department of Ophthalmology and Visual Sciences, University of Calgary,
Calgary, Canada

Abstract. Accurate segmentation of the optic disc from a retinal image is vital to extracting retinal features that may be highly correlated with retinal conditions such as glaucoma. In this paper, we propose a deep-learning based approach capable of segmenting the optic disc given a high-precision retinal fundus image. Our approach utilizes a UNET-based model with a VGG16 encoder trained on the ImageNet dataset. This study can be distinguished from other studies in the customization made for the VGG16 model, the diversity of the datasets adopted, the duration of disc segmentation, the loss function utilized, and the number of parameters required to train our model. Our approach was tested on seven publicly available datasets augmented by a dataset from a private clinic that was annotated by two Doctors of Optometry through a web portal built for this purpose. We achieved an accuracy of 99.78% and a Dice coefficient of 94.73% for a disc segmentation from a retinal image in 0.03 s. The results obtained from comprehensive experiments demonstrate the robustness of our approach to disc segmentation of retinal images obtained from different sources.

1 Introduction

Sight is one of the most important senses for humans, allowing us to visualize and explore our surroundings. Over the years, several degenerative ocular conditions affecting sight have been identified such as glaucoma and diabetic retinopathy. These conditions can threaten our precious sense of sight by causing irreversible visual-field loss [1]. Glaucoma is the world's second most prominent cause of

Electronic supplementary material The online version of this chapter (https:// doi.org/10.1007/978-3-030-69541-5_41) contains supplementary material, which is available to authorized users.

H. Ishikawa et al. (Eds.): ACCV 2020, LNCS 12626, pp. 687–703, 2021.
https://doi.org/10.1007/978-3-030-69541-5_41

irreversible vision loss after cataracts, accounting for 12% of annual cases of blindness worldwide [2]. According to one estimate, around 80 million people are currently affected by glaucoma, and around 112 million will be affected by 2024. Approximately 80% of patients do not know they have glaucoma until advanced vision loss occurs [1,3].

The optic disc is one of the main anatomical structures in the eye which must be monitored and evaluated for progression when glaucoma is suspected [1]. Changes within the optic disc, such as the displacement of vessels or enlargement of the optic cup to optic disc ratio can be used to help determine if glaucoma is present and if there is progression of the disease [4]. These changes occur because of an irreversible decrease in the number of nerve fibres, glial cells and blood vessels.

Several methods have been proposed for disc segmentation. These can be categorized as follows: morphological approaches [5], template based matching approaches [4,6], adaptive-thresholding based approaches [7], and pixel-classification based approaches [8]. Approaches related to the first three categories mainly fail in the presence of bright objects similar to the ones shown in Fig. 1 [9]. The red arrows in Fig. 1 indicate some bright regions that can be encountered in retinal images that may affect disc segmentation.

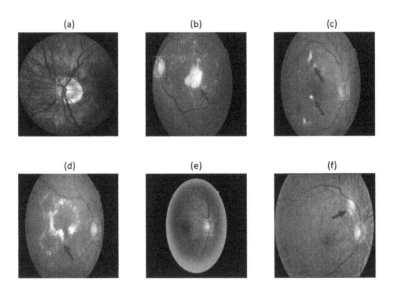

Fig. 1. Images showing various bright regions that can be observed in retinal images. The green box shows the location of the disc and the red arrows indicate other bright regions that may mislead some approaches when segmenting the disc. (Color figure online)

With the rise of deep learning comes the potential for achieving high performance when segmenting a retinal image. Researchers have been working to develop models that place each pixel of a retinal image into a specific class during semantic segmentation. However, the performances of these approaches tend to decrease when new datasets emerge with different disc appearances or images with different resolutions. For instance, the deep-learning model M-Net, proposed by [10] performs well on the ORIGA dataset [11], but not on other datasets (e.g. the DRISHTI-GS dataset) [12] as reported by [13]. One cause might be related to improper handling of the variance between classes when training. This is because the optic disc class may comprise between 2%–10% of an image depending on the angle and resolution of the captured image, whilst the background class would take up the rest of the image. This causes some models to converge toward the background and miss key details related to the disc.

In this paper, we propose a deep-learning approach to disc segmentation from retinal images using the UNET architecture to build the model and the VGG16 convolutional model as our encoder. Given the challenges related to having insufficient annotated disc datasets for deep learning, we adopted the idea of using transfer learning (TL) and image augmentation (IA). Instead of using random weights to initialize our model, we use weights trained on millions of images for semantic segmentation from the Imagenet dataset, which we then fine-tune to match the object we wanted to segment. To handle the issue of imbalanced classes, we use a customized loss function that allows the loss function to penalize more when the wrong classification is made for a pixel related to a disc than that of background. To prove the robustness of our proposed approach in segmenting the disc with various sizes, angles, and orientations, we tested the approach on seven publicly available datasets and one private dataset that we formed.

Our contributions can be listed as follows:

1. We proposed a UNET based deep learning model for disc segmentation that uses VGG16 as the encoder.
2. We demonstrated the effectiveness of using TL and IA for limited data.
3. We handled the issue of imbalanced image classes which may lead to inaccurate results by adopting a weighted loss function.
4. We contributed a new retinal image dataset for disc segmentation (ORDS).
5. We developed an online portal that can be used for annotating disc by multiple contributors.

2   Related Work

Two types of approaches have been developed for disc segmentation: those that locate the optic-disc center but do not segment the disc and those that both locate the disc region and then segment the disc. In this section, we cover approaches that aim to segment the disc rather than just locating it.

Earlier work entails the development of hand-crafted features that rely mainly on the shape of the disc and the intensity of pixels [4,6,14]. However, the performance of these hand-crafted approaches is easily affected by the presence of pathological regions and images with different resolutions (Fig. 1). Recently, advancements made in the field of deep learning have opened the door to using deep learning based models in the field of medical-image analysis. Such approaches exhibit superior performance over the hand-crafted ones [1,15].

Several approaches have been developed for segmenting the optic disc with deep learning: e.g., using an edge-attention guidance network to perform proper edge detection when segmenting the disc [16], using disc-region localization and then disc segmentation via a pyramidal multi-label network [17], using entropy-driven adversarial-learning models [18], using residual UNet based models [19], and using generative adversarial networks combined with VGG16 and transfer learning [20].

In [8], researchers used an ensemble-learning based convolutional neural-network model to segment the optic disc by first localizing the disc region. Entropy was used to select informative points; then the graph-cut algorithm was used to obtain the final segmentation of the disc. The researchers tested their approach only on the Drishti-GS [12], and RimOnev3 [21], datasets. However, they used only 50 images from the Drishti-GS dataset with 40 for training and 10 for testing, even though the Drishti-GS dataset contains 101 images with 50 for training and 51 for testing.

The use of transfer learning when working with deep learning to analyze medical images has been adopted by various studies [22–24]. In the study performed by [20] researchers adopted transfer learning to train their encoder for segmenting the disc when given the whole image without the need for cropping. They used the PASC AL VOC 2012 pretrained weights [25]. They used only the Drishti-GS dataset in both training and testing their model. Moreover, the number of training parameters used by their model, $30.85 * 10^6$, is double that of our approach. In [13] transfer learning for disc segmentation was also used. They started by cropping the disc region using the UNET model developed in [26] initializing their encoder using the weights of the MobileNetV2 [27] trained on the ImageNet dataset [28].

The majority of the developed approaches tend to first locate the disc region and then feed this region into their model to avoid bright regions like the one shown in Fig. 1. For proper segmentation, such approaches are highly dependent on successful localization of this disc region. Moreover, these approaches tend to handle the issue of imbalanced classes, which makes their approach perform differently when new images with different resolutions emerge. In this paper, we show a model with an encoder that uses transfer learning, proper data augmentation, and a customized loss function can segment the optic disc with high precision, giving results comparable to the above-mentioned approaches. In this study, we do not localize the disc prior to performing the segmentation and instead feed the whole image to our model, rather than a specific region of the image.

3   Proposed Method

Our goal is to segment the optic disc given a retinal image. To achieve this, we propose a deep learning model with the same architecture as the UNET model

[26]. A pixel matrix I is associated with each retinal image indicating the pixels either belong to the disc and the background. If I_{xy} represents a pixel at location (x, y) in the retinal image, this pixel will have a value of 1 if it belongs to the disc and 0 if it is a background pixel. The model will use these labeled images and the actual retinal image to produce a new image with the same dimensions, where each pixel has a probability between 0 and 1 inclusive, thus indicating whether this pixel belongs to the disc or not. The closer the value is to 1, the higher the model's confidence is that it belongs to a disc. In this section, we describe the model adopted in this study[1].

3.1   Network Architecture

Instead of creating a new architecture, we adopted the U-Net architecture which consists of an encoder and a decoder. The encoder is responsible for down-sampling the image, and the decoder is responsible for up-sampling the image to provide the final output. In our case, we used the VGG16 [29] model as the encoder and built the decoder by using a series of skip connections, convolutional, up-sampling, and activation layers, as shown in Fig. 2.

The original VGG16 model with a down-sampling factor of 32 is customized so that it could be used for semantic segmentation. It contains five down-sampling layers followed by two densely connected layers and a softmax layer for prediction. We removed the two densely connected layers at the end of the original model and replaced them with a single convolutional layer found in the center of our model, as shown in Fig. 2. Doing so reduced the number of parameters used to train the model from 134,327,060 to 16,882,452. Fixing this bottleneck significantly cut down the time and computational power required to train the model without causing any observable changes to the model's predictions.

We also removed the softmax layer and added all of the upsampling and convolutional layers seen on the right half of the model as is needed in image segmentation to regenerate the original image shape, finally our last layer is a sigmoid activation layer which predicts on the feature matrix. The 5 upsampling layers achieve an upsampling factor of 32, allowing the output images to have the same shape as input images, counteracting the data reshaping effects caused by down-sampling layers. The feature map for each convolutional layer is the ReLU [30] activation method, which applies Eq. 1 to each parameter coming out of the layer, thereby removing all negative pixel values.

$$f(x) = max(0, x) \tag{1}$$

Throughout the architecture, there are several instances where we use skip connections. In Fig. 2, the first and second maxpooling layers utilize a skip connection to convolutional layers further down in the pipeline of the model. Whilst the third and fourth maxpooling layers are connected directly to a convolutional layer which attaches either directly or indirectly to the later layers. This was

---

[1] source code: https://github.com/AbdullahSarhan/ACCVDiscSegmentation.

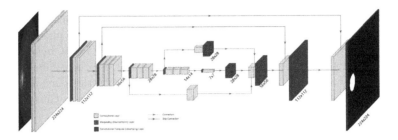

Fig. 2. Architecture of the Customized VGG-16 model Adopted in this Study.

used to shorten the distance between the earlier and later layers. Short connections from early to later layers are useful in preserving high-level information about the positioning of the disc. This is opposed to the low-level pixel-based information which is transferred across the long pipeline of the architecture in a combination of convolutional and maxpooling/upsampling layers. High-level information tends to be lost as the image gets down-sampled and the shape and structure of the image is changed. Therefore, we maintain this information by using connections to earlier layers in the model. Better results were observed when using instead of not using these connections.

3.2   Transfer Learning

To handle the challenge faced in the field of medical imaging of not having enough datasets to train a deep-learning model, we used an approach referred to as transfer learning. As discussed in Sect. 2, such approaches can alleviate the issues caused by insufficient training data by using weights generated by training on millions of images [23]. In our study, we adopted the weights generated when training the VGG16 model on the ImageNet dataset [28] which contains around 14 million labeled images. We thus provided a diverse set of images that the model had been exposed to.

By using transfer learning, we could reduce the problem of over-fitting caused when training on limited images and improve the overall performance of the model. Using the ImageNet weights, we initialized the weights of the encoder network component, and other layers were randomly initialized using a Gaussian distribution. We then trained our model using a mini-batch gradient to tune the weights of the whole network. When training, we realized when using transfer learning that the model converged faster than without transfer learning.

In addition to transfer learning, we applied random augmentation to each image by randomly applying any of the following: horizontal shifting, vertical shifting, rotation within a range of 360°, horizontal flipping, vertical flipping, or any combination of the above. We tested the evaluation effectiveness of data augmentation with and without transfer learning.

3.3   Loss Function

During the training of the network, we decided whether a model had improved on the value returned from the loss function by running it on validation data. Initially, we adopted the binary cross-entropy function (BCE), as shown in Eq. 2 where N is the number of all pixels, y_i is the label of that pixel (0 for background and 1 for the disc), $p(y_i)$ is the predicted probability that the pixel belongs to the disc and $p(y_i)$ is the predicted probability of being a background pixel. Note that the BCE can penalize both false positives and false negatives when working with foreground and background classification.

$$BCE = -\frac{1}{N}\sum_{i=1}^{N} y_i.\log(p(y_i)) + (1 - y_i).\log(1 - (p(y_i))) \tag{2}$$

For any given retinal image, the disc will be only occupy a small region of the image (usually 2–10%), with the large majority of the image being background, i.e. 90% or more. Using this loss function alone would therefore not be sufficient for a precise disc segmentation output. This is because the BCE will be biased toward the background and hence, the disc will not be properly segmented. Thus, it may give an accuracy of 90%, which may be misleading. To bypass this issue, we decided also to use the Jaccard distance. The Jaccard distance measures how dissimilar two sets of data are. The Jaccard loss function is defined as:

$$L_j = 1 - \frac{|Y_d \cap \hat{Y}_d|}{|Y_d \cup \hat{Y}_d|} = 1 - \frac{\sum_{d \in Y_d}(1 \wedge \hat{y}_d)}{|Y_d| + \sum_{b \in Y_b}(0 \vee \hat{y}_b)} \tag{3}$$

where Y_d and Y_b represent the ground truth of the disc and background respectively. $\hat{Y}_d$ and $\hat{Y}_b$ represent the predicted disc and background pixels. $|Y_d|$ $|\hat{Y}_b|$ represents the cardinality of the disc Y_d and background $\hat{Y}_b$ respectively with $\hat{y}_d \in \hat{Y}_d$ and $\hat{y}_b \in \hat{Y}_b$. Since $\hat{Y}_d$ and $\hat{Y}_b$ are both probabilities, and their value will always be between 0 and 1, we can approximate this loss function as shown in Eq. 4 and the model will then be updated by Eq. 5 where j represents the the the jth pixel of the input image and $\hat{y}_j$ represents the predicted value for that pixel.

$$\tilde{L}_j = 1 - \frac{\sum_{d \in Y_d} min(1, \hat{y}_d)}{|Y_d| + \sum_{b \in Y_b} max(0, \hat{y}_b)} = 1 - \frac{\sum_{d \in Y_d} \hat{y}_d}{|Y_d| + \sum_{b \in Y_b} \hat{y}_b} \tag{4}$$

$$L_j y_i \begin{cases} -\frac{1}{|Y_d| + \sum_{b \in Y_b} \hat{y}_b} & for \quad i \in Y_d \\ \\ -\frac{\sum_{d \in Y_d} \hat{y}_d}{|Y_d| + \sum_{b \in Y_b} \hat{y}_b} & for \quad i \in Y_b \end{cases} \tag{5}$$

Given the Jaccard loss function, we are able to balance the emphasis the model gives to each of the classes: namely, the disc class and background class. In this, we combine BCE with Jaccard to optimize the results. We realize that, when both are combined, the model can converge faster than it can when using only the Jaccard while still achieving better results than BCE or Jaccard alone. Hence, our final loss function is:

$$Loss = BCE + L_j \tag{6}$$

694   A. Sarhan et al.

3.4   Implementation Details

To implement this model we used a windows machine with a NVIDIA GeForce 2060 RTX with 6 GB dedicated GDDR6 memory and 8 GB of shared random access memory which the GPU is free to use as necessary. We used the Python language to implement the proposed approach using Keras with TensorFlow back-end.

Training was performed using the NAdam optimizer [31] function with learning rate set to 0.0001, $\beta_1 = 0.9$, $\beta_2 = 0.999$, $\epsilon = 10^{-8}$, and batch size of 4 images. During training, three callbacks were used. First, the model checkpoints would save the model whenever a smaller value was returned on validation data from the custom loss function when comparing to the value at the last checkpoint. Secondly, the learning rate was reduced by a factor of 0.5 whenever 25 epochs passed without any improvement in the validation loss values. Finally, the training was stopped if 100 epochs passed without any improvement.

4   ORDS Dataset

Datasets obtained from different resources had to be used in order to evaluate the reliability and applicability of the proposed method. One of the issues faced when working with disc segmentation is the lack of diverse datasets. To augment the available data sets we decided to contribute a new dataset obtained from a private clinic, annotated by two experts in this field. In this section, we discuss the new data collected.

The ORDS dataset, our new dataset[2], was obtained from a private clinic in Calgary, and the disc was annotated by two Doctors of Optometry. We built a customized web portal to help optometrists trace the disc[3]. Each optometrist was assigned a username and password to log into the portal and view the assigned images. Upon successful login, a user can navigate to the tracing page and start tracing, as shown in Fig. 3. Both optometrists traced the same set of images; and hence each image received two annotations for the disc. In total, 135 images were annotated. On the tracing page, a list of images is presented; the user can click on any image, and a pop-up dialogue will appear. Once the pop-up model appears, the user can start tracing; an erase option is presented should the user wish to erase any of the tracing. Once the tracing is done, the user can click on the submit button, which will allow the storage of tracing information on a dedicated server. Users have the option either to trace the whole disc at once or in steps. Upon successful submission of the tracing, the traced image will be eliminated from the list of images on the tracing page.

5   Experimental Results

We evaluated our methods on eight different datasets which allows us to evaluate our approach when discs with different sizes, orientations, and resolutions are

---

[2] https://github.com/AbdullahSarhan/ACCVDiscSegmentation.
[3] Link and login credentials can be provided upon request.

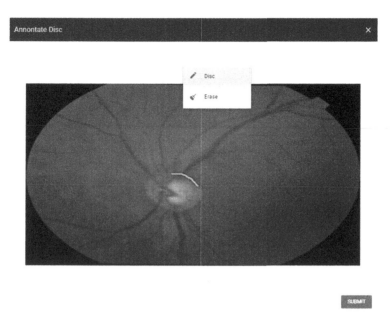

Fig. 3. Web portal showing images assigned to the Optometrists along with the tracing form utilized for disc tracing.

fed to our model. In this section, we discuss the datasets adopted, experiments conducted, and compare the performance of our model with other approaches.

5.1 Datasets

To verify the robustness of our method, we tested our approach on seven publicly available datasets and our dataset. Table 1 provides an overview of these datasets along with the machines used to capture these images, including our new dataset. These datasets contain information regarding multiple retinal conditions: namely, glaucoma and diabetic retinopathy. Moreover, retinal images that belong to these datasets were acquired at different angles and resolutions, as can be seen in Fig. 4. For datasets that contained multiple annotations, including our new dataset which had two expert tracings, we used the average of the tracings when training and evaluating our model, which is the common technique used in such scenarios [12,21]. In total 1,442 images were used for training and 705 were used for testing. To test our model, we had to have the data split into training and testing portions. The model could only see the training images, and we checked the performance by evaluating the model's predictions on the test images and comparing it to labels. Doing so makes it fair to compare our model with other approaches, as they would test their approach on the same test images we are using. However, not all datasets are split in this manner. For some datasets, we had to do the splitting with 75% of the dataset used for training and 25% for testing, selection done randomly. We did this split for the Messidor,

Table 1. Dataset properties and machines used to capture their images.

Dataset	Images		Dimensions	Machine
	Train	Test		
Drishti-GS [12]	50	51	2049 * 1757	-
Refuge [32]	400	400	2124 * 2056	Zeiss Visucam 500
IDRID [33]	54	27	4288 * 2848	Kowa VX-10 alpha
Rim_r3 [21]	128	31	1072 * 712	Nidek AFC-210
BinRushed [34]	147	35	2376 * 1584	Canon CR2 non-mydriatic
Magrebia [34]	52	11	2743 * 1936	Topcon TRC 50DX mydriatic
Messidor [34]	365	92	2240 * 1488	Topcon TRC NW6 non-mydriatic
ORDS	110	25	1444 * 1444	Zeiss, Visucam 200

ORDS, BinRushed, Magrebia, and RimOneV3 datasets. Note that the annotation used for Messidor is different from that used by other approaches,(e.g. [35]) as the annotation used by such studies is not available anymore. We used the one provided by [34]. The testing images for all datasets are provided with our code so that other researchers can make fair comparisons to ours, and thereby standardize the images these comparisons are made on. Figure 4 shows the performance of our model on a test image from each dataset, each dataset being different in terms of angle and resolution.

Doing this allows other researchers to compare their approaches by standardizing the set of test images without using the leave-one-out strategy, [36], which would be time-consuming due to the number of training experiments that must be conducted for each dataset. For instance, if we have a dataset with 200 images then we need to train our model 200 times each time using 199 images and test on the excluded image; we would have to train 200 models and average the test results of them. Images found across different datasets and even within a single

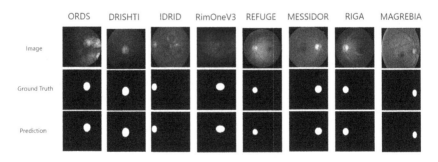

Fig. 4. A sample image from each dataset used in our study. The first row shows the actual retinal image while the second and third shows the related ground truth and prediction made by our model respectively. The name of the dataset to which each image belongs is written at the top of its column.

dataset can be extremely inconsistent in shape, size of optic disc region, and pixel values. Therefore, a general rule is applied to preprocess all images before they are passed to the model. They are first resized to 224 * 224 pixels, normalized so that all pixel values are within the range (0,1), and finally, undergo binary thresholding for disc ground-truth images.

5.2 Evaluation Methods

We used four evaluation methods to evaluate and compare our approach: namely, accuracy (Acc): $\frac{TP+TN}{TP+FP+TN+FN}$, dice coefficient (DC): $2 * \frac{Area(A \cap B)}{Area(A)+Area(B)}$, sensitivity (Sen): $\frac{TP}{TP+FN}$, and intersection over union (IoU): $\frac{Area(A \cap B)}{Area(A) \cup Area(B)}$. Moreover, we also show the time required by our approach to segment the disc and compare it with information obtained by other approaches (when applicable).

5.3 Effectiveness of TL and IA

To test the impact of using transfer learning (TL) and image augmentation (IA) when training our model we conducted a series of experiments and then evaluated the model obtained using the test images for all datasets. In this section we show the overall performance without showing performance on each dataset. Note that in all these experiments we used the loss function defined in Eq. 6.

We first checked the performance of the model without transfer learning by randomly initializing weights using Gaussian distribution, which needed 128 epochs to finish training. Then we did an experiment using data augmentation also without transfer learning and this needed 141 epochs. The third and fourth experiment using TL but with and without IA and they needed 184 and 207 epochs to finish training respectively. The evaluation results for each of these experiments are shown in Table 2. The results obtained show that using TL and IA together achieve the best results especially for DC and IoU values, which really reflect how precisely the disc is segmented along with it being slightly faster than the other models.

Table 2. Performance comparison of proposed method with and without using transfer learning (TL) and/or image augmentation (IA).

Experiment	Acc	DC	Sen	IoU	Time (s)
No TL and No IA	99.68	92.41	97.01	86.41	0.0317
IA with no TL	99.74	93.80	96.18	88.59	0.0366
TL with No IA	99.72	93.41	97.13	87.94	0.0308
TL with IA	99.78	94.73	96.26	90.13	0.0306

5.4   Effectiveness of Loss Functions

A well known loss function for binary classification is the binary cross entropy loss function. This loss function works great when the classes in the image are balanced. However in our case, the object we are trying to segment represents 10% or less of the total image area of the image. Hence, we decided to use the Jaccard distance approach as noted earlier.

We conducted three experiments to test which configuration would achieve the best results. First, we trained our model using the BCE loss function alone, which is a built-in loss function in the keras library, second, we trained using only the Jaccard loss function and finally, we trained using a combination of both loss functions. The results obtained are shown in Table 3. We realized there is slight improvement in performance when we combine both loss functions compared to using either one of them alone. We also realized that using Jaccard alone achieved better results than BCE but it took 516 epochs to finish training compared to 210 epochs when using BCE alone and 374 epochs when combining both. Note that in all these experiments we used TL and IA.

Table 3. Performance of the model across different loss functions.

Loss function	Acc	DC	Sen	IoU	Time (s)
BCE	99.75	94.01	94.89	88.82	0.0358
Jaccard Distance	99.76	94.03	95.72	88.85	0.0329
Jaccard Distance+BCE	99.78	94.73	96.26	90.13	0.0306

5.5   Comparing with Other Approaches

To evaluate our proposed method we compared with approaches which were tested on some of the same datasets we used, as shown in Table 4. Unfortunately, these approaches did not evaluate using all available datasets and hence when comparing we split our results per dataset to be able to do a fair comparison. We achieved an overall average accuracy of 99.78%, DC of 94.73%, Sensitivity of 96.26% and IoU of 90.13%. Our approach outperformed other approaches tested on some of the online publicly available datasets as shown in Table 4 except two approaches for some of the dataset they used. Further, we achieved a prediction time that is the best among the current state of the art approaches with average segmentation time is 0.03 s.

For the Refuge dataset we achieved better results than the ones reported by [17] and [16] yet we achieved slightly lower than the values reported by [13] whom reported achieving 96% where we achieved 94.09%. However, we achieved better than them in the RimOneV3 dataset and Drishti-GS. Note that they first localize a region of interest and then segment the disc whereas in our case we directly segment the disc from the whole retinal image without first localizing the region the disc is located in.

Table 4. Performance comparison of proposed method on optic disc segmentation.

Method	Dataset	Performance metrics				Time (s)
		Acc	DC	Sen	IoU	
Wang et al. [18]	RimOnev3	-	89.80	-	-	-
	Drishti-GS	-	96.40	-	-	-
PM-Net [17]	Refuge	97.90	-	-	-	-
ET-Net [16]	Refuge	-	92.29	-	86.70	-
	Drishti-GS	-	93.14	-	87.90	-
Thakur et al. [35]	RimOneV3	94.84	93.00	-	-	38.66
	Drishti-GS	93.23	92.00	-	-	-
GAN-VGG16 [20]	Drishti-GS	-	**97.10**	-	-	1
ResUNet [19]	IDRID	-	86.50	-	-	-
pOSAL [13]	Refuge	-	**96.00**	-	-	-
	Drishti-GS	-	96.50	-	-	-
	RimOneV3	-	86.50	-	-	-
Proposed approach	Drishti-GS	**99.79**	96.50	**97.54**	**93.18**	**0.03**
	IDRID	**99.80**	**95.39**	**96.94**	**91.30**	**0.12**
	RimOneV3	**99.50**	**94.91**	**96.11**	**90.44**	**0.03**
	Refuge	**99.80**	94.09	**95.77**	**89.00**	**0.02**
	BinRushed	**99.82**	**95.57**	**96.97**	**91.53**	**0.03**
	Magrebia	**99.80**	**96.18**	**95.58**	**92.68**	**0.04**
	Messidor	**99.83**	**96.16**	**97.18**	**92.62**	**0.03**
	ORDS	**99.50**	**93.58**	**96.83**	**88.25**	**0.03**

For the Drishti-GS dataset our model performed better than [16,18,35], the same as [13], and slightly lower than [20]. However, in [20] they only trained and tested their approach one the Refuge dataset, which is not enough to show how well their system work on images from multiple sources. Moreover, their model requires $30.85 * 10^6$ parameters which is almost double what our model requires.

Our model achieved better results than the approaches mentioned above for the IDRID and RimOneV3 datasets. For the dataset provided by [34] they are still a new dataset and up to our knowledge there is no study with published testing images that we can use to compare the performance of our model with. To ensure continuity of this research and allow researchers to be able to perform fair comparison we will publish all test images used to evaluate our model in our supporting material. We also publish both the training history log and our model which was tested on in Table 4. In general our model demonstrated high performance segmenting the disc for images obtained from different resources with different angles of the disc and resolutions, including challenging ones as shown in Fig. 1 (check supplementary material for more images).

5.6 Leave One Out Experiment

Clinics may capture images with different resolutions and angles. To verify the
robustness of our model on images that it was not trained on, that may have
different characteristics than what it was trained on, we conducted 8 experiments
where a model was trained on all datasets except for one which was used for
evaluation. The results obtained for each dataset are showing in Table 5. This
table shows that for instance, when the model is trained on all datasets except
for Refuge, it will achieve a DC value of 92.51% which is slightly less than when
using the cross training which is 94.09%. The results seem consistent in that our
model can effectively segment the disc, except for the RimOneV3 dataset. This
is likely because this dataset only provides the images of the area surrounding
the disc.

Table 5. Performance of the model when being trained on all datasets except for the
one being evaluated on.

Dataset	Acc	DC	Sen	IoU	Time (s)
Drishti-GS	99.76	95.94	96.82	92.25	0.07
IDRID	99.66	92.47	97.83	86.11	0.03
RimOneV3	98.23	80.00	89.49	70.00	0.03
Refuge	99.75	92.51	96.34	86.42	0.02
BinRushed	99.74	95.01	92.67	90.54	0.03
Magrebia	99.76	95.68	93.77	91.74	0.04
Messidor	99.66	94.11	97.83	90.00	0.03
ORDS	99.29	89.29	86.00	81.51	0.03

6 Conclusion and Future Work

In this paper, we proposed a deep learning based approach for disc segmentation where we proved the effectiveness of transfer learning, image augmentation,
and a customized loss function. Our approach achieved state of the art performance on disc segmentation when compared to other modern approaches.
We also contribute a new dataset the can be used by researchers for improving
disc segmentation. This will help researchers testing their approaches on images
obtained from various sources with diverse data. Our new dataset was annotated
by two doctors of optometry using an online portal we built for the annotation
task.

As for future work, we would like to expand our approach to include glaucoma
detection by analyzing the disc region. Using the cup/disc alone is not always an
indicator for glaucoma and hence we need to analyze the disc region and make
an assessment. Moreover, we would like also to expand our portal to be used
for educational and research purposes where people can share and annotate the

datasets. Further, we would like to improve our dataset to include annotation for other anatomical objects in the retina such as peripapillary atrophy and exudates.

References

1. Sarhan, A., Rokne, J., Alhajj, R.: Glaucoma detection using image processing techniques: A literature review. Comput. Med. Imaging Graph. **78**, 101657 (2019)
2. Fu, H., et al.: Segmentation and quantification for angle-closure glaucoma assessment in anterior segment OCT. IEEE Trans. Med. Imaging **36**, 1930–1938 (2017)
3. Tham, Y.C., Li, X., Wong, T.Y., Quigley, H.A., Aung, T., Cheng, C.Y.: Global prevalence of glaucoma and projections of glaucoma burden through 2040: a systematic review and meta-analysis. Ophthalmology **121**, 2081–2090 (2014)
4. Issac, A., Sarathi, M.P., Dutta, M.K.: An adaptive threshold based image processing technique for improved glaucoma detection and classification. Comput. Methods Programs Biomed. **122**, 229–244 (2015)
5. Panda, R., Puhan, N., Panda, G.: Robust and accurate optic disk localization using vessel symmetry line measure in fundus images. Biocybern. Biomed. Eng. **37**, 466–476 (2017)
6. Sun, J., Luan, F., Wu, H.: Optic disc segmentation by balloon snake with texture from color fundus image. Int. J. Biomed. Imaging **2015**, (2015)
7. De La Fuente-Arriaga, J.A., Felipe-Riverón, E.M., Garduño-Calderón, E.: Application of vascular bundle displacement in the optic disc for glaucoma detection using fundus images. Comput. Biol. Med. **47**, 27–35 (2014)
8. Zilly, J., Buhmann, J.M., Mahapatra, D.: Glaucoma detection using entropy sampling and ensemble learning for automatic optic cup and disc segmentation. Comput. Med. Imaging Graph. **55**, 28–41 (2017)
9. Sarhan, A., Rokne, J., Alhajj, R.: Approaches for early detection of glaucoma using retinal images: a performance analysis. In: Alhajj, R., Moshirpour, M., Far, B. (eds.) Data Management and Analysis. SBD, vol. 65, pp. 213–238. Springer, Cham (2020). https://doi.org/10.1007/978-3-030-32587-9_13
10. Fu, H., Cheng, J., Xu, Y., Wong, D.W.K., Liu, J., Cao, X.: Joint optic disc and cup segmentation based on multi-label deep network and polar transformation. IEEE Trans. Med. Imaging **37**, 1597–1605 (2018)
11. Zhang, Z., et al.: Origa-light: an online retinal fundus image database for glaucoma analysis and research. In: 2010 Annual International Conference of the IEEE Engineering in Medicine and Biology, pp. 3065–3068. IEEE (2010)
12. Sivaswamy, J., Krishnadas, S., Joshi, G.D., Jain, M., Tabish, A.U.S.: Drishti-GS: Retinal image dataset for optic nerve head (ONH) segmentation. In: International Symposium on Biomedical Imaging (ISBI), pp. 53–56. IEEE (2014)
13. Wang, S., Yu, L., Yang, X., Fu, C.W., Heng, P.A.: Patch-based output space adversarial learning for joint optic disc and cup segmentation. IEEE Trans. Med. Imaging **38**, 2485–2495 (2019)
14. Mohamed, N.A., Zulkifley, M.A., Zaki, W.M.D.W., Hussain, A.: An automated glaucoma screening system using cup-to-disc ratio via simple linear iterative clustering superpixel approach. Biomed. Signal Process. Control **53**, 101454 (2019)
15. Shen, D., Wu, G., Suk, H.I.: Deep learning in medical image analysis. Ann. Rev. Biomed. Eng. **19**, 221–248 (2017)

16. Zhang, Z., Fu, H., Dai, H., Shen, J., Pang, Y., Shao, L., et al.: ET-Net: a generic edge-attention guidance network for medical image segmentation. In: Shen, D., et al. (eds.) MICCAI 2019, Part I. LNCS, vol. 11764, pp. 442–450. Springer, Cham (2019). https://doi.org/10.1007/978-3-030-32239-7_49

17. Yin, P., et al.: PM-Net: pyramid multi-label network for joint optic disc and cup segmentation. In: Shen, D., et al. (eds.) MICCAI 2019, Part I. LNCS, vol. 11764, pp. 129–137. Springer, Cham (2019). https://doi.org/10.1007/978-3-030-32239-7_15

18. Wang, S., Yu, L., Li, K., Yang, X., Fu, C.-W., Heng, P.-A.: Boundary and entropy-driven adversarial learning for fundus image segmentation. In: Shen, D., et al. (eds.) MICCAI 2019, Part I. LNCS, vol. 11764, pp. 102–110. Springer, Cham (2019). https://doi.org/10.1007/978-3-030-32239-7_12

19. Baid, U., Baheti, B., Dutande, P., Talbar, S.: Detection of pathological myopia and optic disc segmentation with deep convolutional neural networks. In: TENCON 2019 - 2019 IEEE Region 10 Conference (TENCON), pp. 1345–1350. IEEE (2019)

20. Jiang, Y., Tan, N., Peng, T.: Optic disc and cup segmentation based on deep convolutional generative adversarial networks. IEEE Access **7**, 64483–64493 (2019)

21. Pena-Betancor, C., et al.: Estimation of the relative amount of hemoglobin in the cup and neuroretinal rim using stereoscopic color fundus images. Invest. Ophthalmol. Visual Sci. **56**, 1562–1568 (2015)

22. Shin, H.C., et al.: Deep convolutional neural networks for computer-aided detection: Cnn architectures, dataset characteristics and transfer learning. IEEE Trans. Med. Imaging **35**, 1285–1298 (2016)

23. Pan, S.J., Yang, Q.: A survey on transfer learning. IEEE Trans. Knowl. Data Eng. **22**, 1345–1359 (2009)

24. Karri, S.P.K., Chakraborty, D., Chatterjee, J.: Transfer learning based classification of optical coherence tomography images with diabetic macular edema and dry age-related macular degeneration. Biomed. Opt. Express **8**, 579–592 (2017)

25. Everingham, M., Van Gool, L., Williams, C.K., Winn, J., Zisserman, A.: The pascal visual object classes (VOC) challenge. Int. J. Comput. Vis. **88**, 303–338 (2010). https://doi.org/10.1007/s11263-009-0275-4

26. Ronneberger, O., Fischer, P., Brox, T.: U-Net: convolutional networks for biomedical image segmentation. In: Navab, N., Hornegger, J., Wells, W.M., Frangi, A.F. (eds.) MICCAI 2015, Part III. LNCS, vol. 9351, pp. 234–241. Springer, Cham (2015). https://doi.org/10.1007/978-3-319-24574-4_28

27. Sandler, M., Howard, A., Zhu, M., Zhmoginov, A., Chen, L.C.: Mobilenetv 2: inverted residuals and linear bottlenecks. In: Proceedings of the IEEE Conference on Computer Vision and Pattern Recognition (CVPR), pp. 4510–4520 (2018)

28. Russakovsky, O., et al.: Imagenet large scale visual recognition challenge. Int. J. Comput. Vis. **115**, 211–252 (2015). https://doi.org/10.1007/s11263-015-0816-y

29. Simonyan, K., Zisserman, A.: Very deep convolutional networks for large-scale image recognition. arXiv preprint arXiv:1409.1556 (2014)

30. Kingma, D.P., Ba, J.: Adam: A method for stochastic optimization. arXiv preprint arXiv:1412.6980 (2014)

31. Dozat, T.: Incorporating nesterov momentum into adam (2016)

32. Orlando, J.I., et al.: Refuge challenge: a unified framework for evaluating automated methods for glaucoma assessment from fundus photographs. Med. Image Anal. **59**, 101570 (2020)

33. Porwal, P., et al.: IDRID: diabetic retinopathy-segmentation and grading challenge. Med. Image Anal. **59**, 101561 (2020)

34. Almazroa, A., et al.: Retinal fundus images for glaucoma analysis: the RiGA dataset. In: Medical Imaging 2018: imaging Informatics for Healthcare, Research, and Applications, vol. 10579, pp. 105790B. International Society for Optics and Photonics (2018)
35. Thakur, N., Juneja, M.: Optic disc and optic cup segmentation from retinal images using hybrid approach. Expert Syst. Appl. **127**, 308–322 (2019)
36. Wang, X., Jiang, X., Ren, J.: Blood vessel segmentation from fundus image by a cascade classification framework. Pattern Recognit. **88**, 331–341 (2019)

Author Index

Printed in the United States
By Bookmasters